CATHOLICISM

STUDY EDITION

CATHOLICISM

STUDY EDITION

by Richard P. McBrien

1817

Harper & Row, Publishers, San Francisco

New York, Grand Rapids, Philadelphia, St. Louis
London, Singapore, Sydney, Tokyo, Toronto

Book design: Maria Mazzara-Schade

Except for citations within citations, all Scripture texts used in this work are taken from the *New American Bible*, copyright © 1970, by the Confraternity of Christian Doctrine, Washington, D.C. Used by permission of the copyright owner. All rights reserved.

Quotations from the documents of Vatican II are reprinted with permission of America Press, Inc., 106 W. 56 Street, New York, NY 10019. © 1966. All rights reserved.

The chart entitled "Twentieth-Century Views on the Christology of the New Testament," which originally appeared in *Horizons* (vol. 1, 1974, p. 38), is reprinted with permission.

Library of Congress Catalog Card Number: 79-55963
ISBN: 0-86683-601-2

Printed in the United States of America

7

Harper & Row, Publishers, Inc., 10 East 53rd Street, New York, NY 10022.

A STATEMENT
FROM THE BISHOP OF
FORT WAYNE-SOUTH BEND

Several months ago, Father Richard McBrien, Chairman of the Department of Theology, University of Notre Dame, located in the Diocese of Fort Wayne-South Bend, initiated a consultation with me about the publication of a study edition of his two-volume *Catholicism*. At the time he mentioned that although the two-volume work had been published without formal ecclesiastical approval (in St. Paul, Minnesota, the publisher did not complete a request for this approval) he thought such approval would be appropriate for the one-volume study edition of *Catholicism*.

With his consent, I asked Father Enda McDonagh, Professor of Moral Theology at Maynooth Seminary in Ireland, and Visiting Professor of Moral Theology at Notre Dame, to review the volumes and to propose any changes which he thought would be advisable in the study edition.

At the conclusion of his review, Father McDonagh wrote to me that in his opinion, the study edition, with the changes he had recommended, "meets the requirements of Catholic orthodoxy and so is eligible to be published with ecclesiastical approval." Some theologians, I think, may disagree with Father McDonagh's conclusion, and others, on the other hand, may see little or no reason why the changes were necessary. I nevertheless have confidence in Father McDonagh's judgment based, as it is, on a painstaking review of the whole work.

Motivated by a sincere desire to have the study edition as perfect as possible, Father McBrien has incorporated all of Father McDonagh's changes into the volume, and has added a few of his own to clear up possible ambiguities.

Though the censor appointed by me has granted a *Nihil Obstat*, meaning to me that the book does not advocate teaching contrary to faith and morals, I have declined to grant canonical, ecclesiastical approval of this book. These are my reasons.

(1) According to the most recent norms, ecclesiastical approval is required for "basic texts of instruction." Examples of these would be catechisms and elementary, secondary, and higher education "basic textbooks" designed, constructed, and tested out as tools for teaching the young the exact essentials of their faith. In my judgment, *Catholicism* is not a "basic text of instruction," nor should it be used as such. According to the norms, canonical approval is not required. Granting it might imply approval for use as a basic text of instruction as though it were the Church's

definitive work on Catholicism and the final authoritative word on every topic encompassed by the volume's large title. The author makes no such claims for this volume.

(2) In my judgment, official approval is incompatible with a book of this kind which avowedly is an attempt at a synthesis of traditional teaching and contemporary theological speculation, some of which is only tentative and probable even in the minds of its authors. This speculation is not something to be approved in the same category as official teaching. The author himself in this volume's newly-written statement on the magisterium points out that "the impression is sometimes left that theologians are presenting themselves as a co-equal body with the hierarchy (the so-called 'double magisterium theory'). This is not being proposed here."

(3) Because I happen to know that some extensive review of *Catholicism* may result in further perfecting changes in future editions, I deem it inopportune to give the present volume the formal approval that might better await the completion of the review. Even then I might have some hesitancy because of my opinion that formal approval is best reserved for books solely concerned with presentation of clearly articulated official Church teachings.

Responsibility for publication of this volume and for its contents therefore rests, as it should, with the author and its publisher. To view this statement of mine as some sort of indirect or implied approval would be a gross misinterpretation of it. I have written the statement only because of my duty to be open and honest about my specific reasons for not giving formal approval to a book cleared by my own censor.

Throughout our consultation, Father McBrien has impressed me as being a priest-theologian, pastorally sensitive, who zealously is endeavoring to contribute his research and reflection to the enrichment of theological thought and speculation.

Because *Catholicism* is a scholarly and integrated book, its readers should not read snatches of it out of context but should study it in its entirety. This careful study will enable most readers to distinguish between official Roman Catholic teaching and theologians' personal, speculative opinions about this teaching.

Used intelligently, this book may help, as Father McBrien hopes, "to bridge the gap between old and new with full justice to the values of both." It has helped me.

+ William E. McManus
Bishop of Fort Wayne-South Bend
July, 1981

vi

CONTENTS

PART THREE: JESUS CHRIST 367

FOREWORD

When *Catholicism* first appeared as a two-volume work, I described it as "a landmark in the life of the contemporary Church." I am delighted that so many others since then have given it such favorable notices, and that it has been honored with a Christopher Award and the Annual Book Award of the College Theology Society.

My endorsement of *Catholicism* has not been perfunctory. I have read every word of it, and I can say without hesitation that it is a thoroughly balanced and orthodox synthesis of the Catholic tradition. It offers a splendidly readable and reliable introduction into the richness of our common heritage. I have been personally helped by it very much. For me, it provided an excellent theological review and updating.

The study edition of *Catholicism* is even better since it has been carefully revised. The few questions I had about the first edition (not unusual in 1186 pages) have been answered and clarified. I trust that others will share the thrill that I experienced in seeing again, in one volume, the total sweep of the theological vision in the Church today. I commend this book to priests, religious, and especially laity, whether Catholics or not. All will benefit from the magnificent vision of theology in the post-Vatican II context. The theological work of the Council left not a few Catholics somewhat confused as to where they were now. I know of no better antidote for that confusion than the reading and pondering of this book, *Catholicism*. A bit of advice: read the last chapter first.

I am particularly pleased that *Catholicism*'s author, Father Richard McBrien, is now an honored and cherished member of the Notre Dame community, serving as Chairman of the University's Department of Theology.

(Rev.) Theodore M. Hesburgh, C.S.C., S.T.D.
President, University of Notre Dame

PREFACE

This book is not written with the specialist in mind, although I should hope that specialists will find it useful. The reader of this book needs only two resources: intelligence, and a basic interest in Catholicism. A formal theological background is not needed, however helpful it might be. Accordingly, words and concepts whose meaning theologians take for granted are defined and explained. All topics are presented in a clearly organized, easy-to-follow pattern. Each problem is stated and explained in itself, in relation to other questions, and then in its full historical development, beginning with the Bible. Detailed summaries are provided after each chapter (indeed these might profitably be read *before* each chapter). The Table of Contents, the Glossary, and the double Index provide additional help.

Those who wish to go more deeply into the subject-matter of this book, however, can easily do so. Extensive Discussion Questions for each chapter are in a section near the end of the book. The brief but meaty list of Suggested Readings at the end of each chapter provides further assistance, as does the following list of basic reference tools to which the serious reader should have access.

The Christian Faith in the Doctrinal Documents of the Catholic Church. Joseph Neuner and James Dupuis, eds. Westminster, Md.: Christian Classics, 1975.

Dictionary of the Bible. John L. McKenzie. Milwaukee: Bruce, 1965 (republished in paperback, New York: Macmillan, 1967).

The Documents of Vatican II. Walter Abbott and Joseph Gallagher, eds. New York: America Press, 1966.

Encyclopedia of Theology: The Concise Sacramentum Mundi. Karl Rahner, ed. New York: Seabury Press, 1975.

The New Catholic Encyclopedia. 17 vols. New York: McGraw-Hill, 1967—.

The Oxford Dictionary of the Christian Church. 2d ed. F. L. Cross and E. A. Livingston, eds. London: Oxford University Press, 1974.

WHY THIS BOOK?

This book is written out of the conviction that there is a pressing—I should like to say even urgent—need for it, or at least for some book very much like it. More than two decades have already passed since the election of Pope John XXIII in 1958. Four years later he convoked the Second Vatican Council, and everyone agrees that the Catholic Church has not been the same since. Catholicism has been torn by conflict between those who have embraced the new with a barely concealed indifference, if not contempt, toward the old, and those who have obstinately resisted change, so disillusioned were they with the apparent character and direction of change. Most other Catholics fell somewhere in the middle—distressed by the turmoil but uncertain of the Church's future course. Meanwhile, another generation has come along which has not been party to the debate at all. It is a generation which too often has looked in vain for those who can bridge the widening gap between the past and the present, the old and the new, the traditional and the contemporary. And therein lies the story, the driving force, and the purpose of this book.

I am convinced that healing and reconciliation are possible because there *is* a fundamental unity between the pre-Vatican II Church and the post-Vatican II Church, the many significant differences notwithstanding. I intend this book, therefore, as a bridge between the Church of yesterday and the Church of today, and between conservative, traditionally minded Catholics, on the one hand, and progressive, renewal-minded Catholics, on the other. A knowledge of history provides that bridge, and that is why this book adopts an historical method and approach. The more history we know the less likely we are to distort the reality of Catholicism by shaping it to our own predispositions and by trimming it to fit our own limited vision and range of experience.

I have in mind, for example, the attitude of those younger, progressive Catholics who, through no particular fault of their own, do not know very much about pre-Vatican II Catholicism. They suspect that Catholicism's past would somehow contradict its present course. And since they are satisfied with that present course—its ecumenical openness, its spirit of freedom, its concern for justice and human rights, its readiness to change—they prefer to let the past rest in peace, or at least to leave themselves in "good faith" about it.

I have in mind also the attitude of those older, progressive Catholics who once learned a detailed history of Catholicism but who now remember how narrowly conceived that history was. It was too often an account of consecutive institutional triumphs, of the vanquishing of patently absurd heresies, of relentless and remarkably smooth doctrinal movements from truth to greater truth. Events and theological developments surrounding Vatican II discredited that history in their eyes, and they have not seriously taken it up since.

I have in mind, too, the attitude of those more conservative Catholics, old and young, who are satisfied that they know that history well enough, and believe that the Church's present course is, at worst, a betrayal of Catholicism's past, or, at best, an unenlightened dilution of its genius and grandeur.

History is not fully honored by either the progressive or the conservative side, for history both *roots* and *relativizes*. Catholicism did not begin with Vatican II, nor was it set in theological and pastoral cement with the Council of Trent. When taken whole and unrevised, history teaches us that Christian faith and its Catholic expression have assumed many different forms. The tendency of the conservative is to freeze certain forms and equate them with the essence of Catholicism. A criticism of the form becomes an attack upon the Catholic faith itself. The tendency of the progressive is to keep every form so radically open to change that no abiding core or center can ever be discerned. The progressive tends to believe that there are no enduring Catholic principles by which to re ppropriate old forms, modify existing forms, or construct new forms.

I have tried in this book to do justice to the true values and legitimate concerns of both sides: the conservative's regard for continuity and stability, and the progressive's regard for development and growth. History provides the major link between the two because it is a reality that is at once absolute and relative. It is *absolute*—and therefore a principle of *permanence*—because it comes from the creative hand of God, is sustained by the providential care of God, and is destined for fulfillment in the final Kingdom of God. But history is *relative*—and therefore a principle of *change*—because it is also the history of humankind, of an unprogramed interaction between grace and freedom.

Insofar as history is absolute and permanent, we have to come to terms with it. It is there. We cannot ignore it or erase it. It defines us. We are who we are because of it. We are historical beings, which means that we do not create ourselves anew, from ground zero, each day. We begin at a point we did not choose and in the midst of a process we did not originate.

On the other hand, history is also relative and changeable. It is even now in process. It is still to be. We are called to become something greater than we are. Tomorrow can be different from today or yesterday. We are to "fill the earth and subdue it" (Genesis 1:28).

CONTROVERSIAL THEOLOGY VERSUS CONSTRUCTIVE THEOLOGY

Finally, this book is not an exercise in *controversial* theology. I am not arguing a point of view peculiar to myself or to a small school of Catholic theologians. As far as possible, this is a work of *constructive* theology, one that tries to see the whole in terms of the interrelationship of all its parts, and the parts always in terms of their relationship to one another and to the whole. Accordingly, this is not only a book *about* Catholicism but a book written in the *spirit* of Catholicism as well, i.e., of openness to all truth wherever it is found. At least that has been my explicit intention from beginning to end. My deepest hope is that I have succeeded, however modestly, in that purpose.

Richard P. McBrien

1986 PREFACE TO THE STUDY EDITION

The original two-volume edition of *Catholicism* was published in April 1980. An unabridged one-volume Study Edition appeared in September 1981.

The new Study Edition contained discussion questions, a more detailed table of contents, and suggestions for use of the book in various educational settings. There were also some clarifications in the original treatment of theological dissent, the virginal conception of Jesus, the sacrament of Baptism, ordination, the papacy, and some moral issues. In no instance, however, was there any substantive change. As a result, a person with the new Study Edition in hand would not have had access to a point of view or an approach different from what had been available in the original two-volume set. And none of the clarifications was mandated by any outside agency, including the Committee on Doctrine of the National Conference of Catholic Bishops in the United States. That committee's review of *Catholicism* did not begin until April 1981, after the Study Edition revisions were almost all in place.

On July 5, 1985, the Committee on Doctrine, by then under the chairmanship of Archbishop John R. Quinn of San Francisco, released a statement on this book, taking both editions into account. The bishops' statement did not condemn the book, nor impose any restriction on its sale or use, nor censure its author, nor require him to take any action whatsoever regarding the book. Neither did the committee recommend that its *nihil obstat* be withdrawn. The *nihil obstat* means that "the book does not advocate teaching contrary to faith and morals" (from the Statement of Most Rev. William E. McManus, recently retired bishop of Fort Wayne-South Bend).

On the contrary. Archbishop Quinn said explicitly in an accompanying press release that "the statement should not be used to call into question Father McBrien's authentic Catholic faith or orthodoxy." The statement also characterized the review process as "a model of cooperative ecclesial concern for the integrity of the faith, the pastoral needs of the people and the scholarly reputation of the author." Finally, it expressed appreciation for "the effort and motivation . . . in undertaking the task of presenting a readable compendium of Catholic teaching" and for the clarifications which had already been made in the Study Edition.

The Committee on Doctrine nevertheless cited several areas where further clarifications seem appropriate: the meaning of grace; the description of the virginal conception of Jesus as a *theologoumenon* (for an explanation of this term, see p. 516 of this Study Edition); and the treatment of the perpetual virginity of Mary, of the foundation of the Church, and of the binding force of Marian dogmas. The committee also noted sections where it found the presentation "not supportive of the Church's authoritative teaching as would be expected in a text entitled *Catholicism*." The committee mentioned the discussions of contraception and the ordination of women. The committee also made several points about the teaching authority of the Church but acknowledged that there is no disagreement between the bishops and the author on these points.

What is to be said about the Committee on Doctrine's Statement, beyond what has already been said in various press interviews; namely, that the process was marked by mutual respect and that many helpful suggestions surfaced from the discussions?

1. The Committee on Doctrine is correct when it observes that the term "grace" is used in a variety of senses in this book. But this has always been the case in the history of the Church. "Grace" has never had a single meaning. The word itself is derived from a Hebrew word which means favor and from a Greek word which means gift. In the most basic sense of the word, therefore, grace refers to the favor God bestows upon us: the gift of divine life itself. But the term "grace" has also referred to the help which God gives us to live holy lives, the indwelling of the Holy Spirit, sacramental grace, Christ's grace of headship over the Church, the grace of union by which the Word is united with Christ's human nature, God's forgiveness, the grace of justification, and even the prayer before meals. Moreover, the traditional theology of grace, as presented in the approved Latin manuals over the years, has always made various distinctions in its analysis of this fundamental topic: between created and uncreated grace; between efficacious and merely sufficient grace;

between actual and habitual, or sanctifying, grace; and between elevating and medicinal grace.

At the time time, the bishops do acknowledge that the different meanings given the term grace in *Catholicism* are a function of the different contexts in which the term appears. In the Preface to the new Study Edition, and at the urging of Bishop McManus, I insisted that "the material in this book always be read and quoted in the context in which it was presented. Reading and quoting in context is important in any work, but it is more important than ever in a work as comprehensive as this."

2. The highly technical term *theologoumenon*, used in reference to the virginal conception of Jesus, was taken over directly from contemporary biblical scholarship. What is important is that the truth of the doctrine is not in question. Indeed, the following lines were added to the Study Edition to make this even clearer: "The truth and validity of that teaching and belief are not in question here, but biblical scholars and theologians have been asking what that belief might mean and how it might be understood today, in light of developments in New Testament exegesis and our understanding of human existence."

3. This book does not challenge the traditional belief in the perpetual virginity of Mary. On the other hand, that belief is not a matter of dogma; i.e., the belief is not essential to Catholic faith. Nor is the perpetual virginity of Mary part of the Church's more definitive teaching concerning the virginal conception. *Catholicism* only asserts that the New Testament says nothing about the perpetual virginity of Mary, while at the same time it makes reference to the brothers and sisters of Jesus. Such reference does not, of itself, rule out the Church's traditional belief in Mary's perpetual virginity.

4. Regarding Jesus' founding of the Church, *Catholicism* rejects two extreme answers: the one which assumes that Jesus established the Church in exactly the form we have it today, and the other which insists that Jesus had no intention whatever to found a Church. As one highly respected Catholic biblical scholar has put it, Jesus left us no "ecclesiastical blueprint." On the other hand, Jesus did gather disciples, left them a table fellowship to continue in his memory (the Eucharist), and sent them out to proclaim the coming of the

Kingdom of God. All this is said in *Catholicism*.

5. The material on the binding force of Marian dogmas comes directly from the statement prepared by the Catholic representatives to the Lutheran-Catholic dialogue in the United States. The members of this theological team, appointed and approved by the bishops, included such respected scholars as Father Avery Dulles, S.J., Father George Tavard, A.A., and Father Carl Peter, former dean of the School of Religious Studies at the Catholic University of America and a frequent *peritus* (expert) for the bishops at Vatican synods. The entire statement of the Catholic participants is available in *Theological Studies* 40 (March 1979), 138–57. The specific material on the non-acceptance of infallible teaching is found on pp. 152–5.

6. The discussion of contraception *is* supportive of the Church's authoritative teaching in that it summarizes it fully and recognizes its authoritative character. The criteria offered in the book (pp. 1026–7) underscore the hierarchy's "right and responsibility . . . to teach on matters pertaining to morality" as well as the "duty of Catholics to take such teaching seriously into account in the process of forming their consciences." What is *not* said, of course, is that Catholics have to follow the letter of Church teachings, regardless of what their consciences may tell them and independently of any discussion that may be going on among theologians concerning the meaning and application of such teachings.

7. The ordination of women is a different kind of issue. It is not at all evident that this is a matter of doctrine, i.e., official teaching, rather than of discipline, i.e., changeable ecclesiastical policy. It is certainly not a matter of dogma. In any case, this book does not advocate the ordination of women nor in any way challenge the Catholic Church's current teaching and policy. To establish a contrast, one should consult the late Father Karl Rahner's "Women and the Priesthood" in his *Concern for the Church* (New York: Crossroad, 1981), pp. 35–47.

8. The last few words of the Committee on Doctrine's Statement are ambiguous. After expressing appreciation for the "effort and motivation" involved in "undertaking the task of presenting a readable compendium of Catholic teaching," the bishops conclude: "Nevertheless, we think it useful to clarify for the actual and poten-

tial readership of the book *Catholicism* its character as one theologian's effort to present such teaching in the light of his understanding of contemporary theological insights, many of which are admittedly of a hypothetical nature, and some of which it seems difficult to reconcile with authoritative Catholic doctrine."

The clause, "some of which it seems difficult to reconcile with authoritative Catholic doctrine," refers back to the noun "insights," which is, in turn, modified by the adjectives "contemporary theological." The bishops are not saying here that the theological positions which I take in this book seem "difficult to reconcile with authoritative Catholic doctrine." They are saying only that some of the contemporary theological insights I have merely summarized herein seem difficult to reconcile with such doctrine. And even at that, the bishops are careful to use the verb "seem" rather than "are."

I have been heartened, of course, by the strongly positive reviews *Catholicism* has received from fellow theologians, religious educators, pastoral ministers, college and seminary professors and their students, and many others in the Church and the churches: laity, religious, and clergy alike—including not a few bishops. I am gratified, too, by the fact that this book received a Christopher Award and the Annual Book Award of the College Theology Society, and that it has since been translated into German and French.

I intended the book as a bridge, not a wall. It is an exercise in theological education, not polemics. It is designed to build up and strengthen the Body of Christ, not weaken or divide it further. I believe it is achieving its purpose, and for that I remain profoundly grateful to those who helped and encouraged me in the original project, as well as to those who are making effective use of it in many different educational and pastoral settings.

But I am not content to leave it at that. In due course I shall prepare another edition of this work, updating the material and introducing further clarifications in light of the useful suggestions I have received from the Committee on Doctrine and others. In the meantime, I have full confidence in the work you now have in hand.

University of Notre Dame   Richard P. McBrien
January 1986

ACKNOWLEDGMENTS

Although this book was undertaken and completed without benefit of the usual foundation grants, academic sabbatical, or corps of graduate assistants, there are many people who have provided both encouragement and assistance. I wish I could identify each one here, but that is precluded by limitations of space. This book is already very large! I can acknowledge, therefore, only a representative sampling of the contributions which have helped to bring this project to what I hope is a successful conclusion.

J. Frank Devine, S. J., of the Weston School of Theology in Cambridge, Massachusetts, stands in the front rank. He was consistently generous not only with theological and editorial suggestions but with personal support born of long friendship. Frank read the entire manuscript as it was being written, and he was one of the very few persons who really appreciated from the beginning the scope, magnitude, and promise of this enterprise.

John Kirvan, an author, editor, and publisher in his own right, was the one who first invited me to do a book for Winston Press, but he got far more than he expected. John was an effective and often reassuring liaison between myself and the publishers. I am, of course, indebted also to the entire administrative, editorial, and promotional staff at Winston for their strong commitment to this book at every stage of development. A particular word of appreciation, however, goes to Cyril A. Reilly, who did such excellent editorial work.

Pope John XXIII National Seminary in Weston, Massachusetts, provided the facilities: a room to work in, a splendidly useful library, exceedingly helpful staff, and the warmest of hospitality. The rector, James W. DeAdder, and the entire faculty took an active interest in the book as it progressed through the academic year 1978-1979. I owe a special word of gratitude to Ann Kidney, assistant librarian. I shall never forget her readiness to drop everything to help me locate a book, an article, or just a fact. Her spirit and efficiency are a credit to the seminary librarian, James L. Fahey. Gerald Donovan was also a constant source of encouragement.

My colleagues at Boston College, both in the Institute of Religious Education and Pastoral Ministry which I directed and the department of Theology where I served as a Professor of Systematic Theology, provided yet another base of assistance and support. I would not have had the necessary time away from the regular routine of the Institute office had the staff not taken up the slack in commendably competent and cheerful fashion: Padraic O'Hare, associate director; James O'Neill, former administrative officer; Mary Boys, S.N.J.M., Thomas Groome, and Claire Lowery, R.S.C.J., faculty members; and Audrey Mudarri, secretary, who also typed the Glossary. But a very special word of thanks must go to my personal secretary of many happy years, Mildred Meyer, who typed about ninety-five percent of the book and, what is more remarkable, managed to keep all of my other activities, projects, and commitments in some measure of order.

Certain members of the department of Theology gave specific assistance: Robert Daly, S.J. (chairman), James Hennesey, S.J. (Church History), Frans Jozef van Beeck, S.J. (Christology), and, in substantial ways, James O'Donohoe (Moral Theology) and Philip King (Old Testament). Ernest Fortin, A.A., also maintained a welcome interest in the project.

Valuable assistance from theologians and other scholars outside of Boston College was forthcoming from John Connelly, of St. John Seminary, Brighton, Massachusetts, who was an important consultant for the theology of human existence and the philosophical distinctiveness of Catholicism, and J. Bryan Hehir, of the United States Catholic Conference, who supplied both material and advice in the area of social ethics. John T. Finnegan, past president of the Canon Law Society of America, provided important assistance in canonical matters, especially those related to the sacrament of Matrimony. I am also indebted to Dermot Lane, past president of the Irish Theological Association, for assistance in the area of Christology, and to Robert J. Wister, of the Archdiocese of Newark, for assistance in the area of Church history.

The book, of course, shows the influence of many other scholars who were not personally consulted but whose writings were of immense value: Karl Rahner, S.J., Avery Dulles, S.J., Raymond Brown, S.S., John L. McKenzie, Edward Schillebeeckx, O.P., Rudolf Schnackenburg, René Latourelle, S.J., Bernard Lonergan, S.J., Peter Berger, Andrew Greeley, and others whose books and articles are mentioned in the Suggested Readings at the end of each chapter.

Pastors, religious educators, and various persons involved in other pastoral ministries were also generous with their reactions and advice: especially Francis J. O'Keefe, pastor of St. Matthew's Church, Tolland, Connecticut, and Beverly Brazauskas, S.S.J., director of religious education at St. Matthew's; Peter Rosazza, auxiliary bishop of Hartford, Connecticut; James and Pauline Ludwig of Webster, Massachusetts; Carla Rutter, H.M., of Warren, Ohio, and Susan Jenkinson, R.S.M., of Providence, Rhode Island.

I am grateful to my friend James Flynn, C.S.S., provincial of the Stigmatine Fathers, Newton, Massachusetts, who read most of the manuscript as it was being written and gave me moral and material support, including the donation of his own secretary's services as a deadline approached. I, therefore, thank Ann Cincotta for her assistance.

Although I assumed responsibility for the preparation of both Indexes, I received technical advice from Richard O'Keeffe, of George Mason University, Fairfax, Virginia. Carol Klein and Mary Costea of Boston College did the typing.

Convention dictates that I insist that I must bear final responsibility for the book. I do so proudly. I have never enjoyed a project as much as I have enjoyed this one. I only hope it will make the kind of contribution to the Church and to theological and religious education which I have intended from the outset.

CATHOLICISM

STUDY EDITION

INTRODUCTION

These first two chapters form an introductory unit to the whole book. Chapter 1 situates the book in its *ecclesiastical* context: What is the state of the Catholic Church today? How does the present crisis of Catholicism relate to previous crises in the Church's history? What choices are open to it as it looks toward the future? (A later chapter—Part I, chapter 3—will situate the book in its larger *human* context.)

Chapter 2 identifies and explains the ground rules for the whole study. If we are engaged here in an interpretation of faith, what does faith mean? What are its dimensions? Its characteristics? Its sources? Its effects? By what principles do we "interpret" that faith? Are there authoritative sources? If so, what makes those sources "authoritative"? What connection is there, if any, between the faith of an individual before God and the faith of a community, namely the Church? What role, if any, does the Church have in the clarification or even the definition of faith? To what extent is an individual member of the Church bound by those official interpretations?

Although other parts of the book—on God, on Jesus Christ, on the Church, and on Christian existence—will bear far more directly and more substantively on the content and practice of Catholic and Christian faith, no chapter will be so fundamental to the entire exploration of Catholicism as chapter 2.

· I ·

CATHOLICISM IN CRISIS

THE MEANING OF *CRISIS*

This chapter is about the present state of the Catholic Church. No matter what position one might take on various controversial issues facing Catholicism today, everyone would agree that the Catholic Church has changed significantly over the last few decades and especially since the Second Vatican Council (1962–1965). Many have described this process of change as a crisis. But do we correctly understand what a crisis is? What difference would it make if we did not?

To appreciate the importance of knowing precisely what a crisis is, it might be helpful to remind ourselves that language is not simply an instrument of communication. It also defines reality. But the definition is not always accurate, nor even just. Language, as a defining mechanism, can be and has been placed in the service of racism and sexism. An adult black man is addressed as "boy." Women are referred to as "girls." Language would make us all a race of "men" seeking "brotherhood" under the "fatherhood" of God. The social, cultural, political, and economic implications of such language have become increasingly apparent.

Words are rarely neutral. Sometimes their misuse is very serious, as in the cases cited above. Sometimes our errors evoke only amusement, not outrage, as television commentator Edwin Newman engagingly disclosed several years ago in his *Strictly Speaking: Will America Be the Death of English*? (Indianapolis: Bobbs-Merrill, 1974). And sometimes the effect falls somewhere in between, as in the case of our word *crisis*.

The word *crisis* is frequently misused. For many it has a consistently negative ring. Thus, an international crisis may mean that hostile troops are massing on the border of some innocent country. Heads of state and other government officials are summoned to emergency meetings. Appeals for restraint and humaneness are heard from the United Nations, the Vatican, and whichever superpower happens to be allied with the threatened nation.

A medical crisis means that a patient is close to death. Teams of doctors, nurses, and aides are rushed to the bedside. The family is alerted and advised to expect the worst.

An economic crisis means an impending collapse of one of the world's major currencies or the bankruptcy of a key financial institution perceived to be essential to the well-being of a city, state, or country.

The crisis, of course, might be much less dramatic and much less severe in its effects. But in the popular mind the negative overtones remain, as in "We've got a crisis on our hands. They'll all be here in fifteen minutes and the coffee pot's just given out."

Because so many of us are conditioned to picture a crisis as bleak and forbidding, a threat not only to our personal comfort and convenience but to our survival as well, the title of this chapter might seem to suggest that the Catholic Church is at the brink of disintegration. It is a time for emergency meetings and transfusions. Meanwhile, theologians and sociologists have the unhappy task of notifying the family and preparing them for the worst.

The Catholic Church, and all of Christianity for that matter, *is* in crisis. It has been for at least two decades. But this is not to say that the present crisis is its first or, what is more significant, its last. Nor is it necessarily to impute some radical deficiency or failure somewhere along the line. A crisis can, to be sure, emerge from carelessness, imprudence, and/or incompetence. An indolent, overweight smoker may be largely responsible for the medical crisis generated by his massive heart attack. But a crisis may just as likely occur in the relatively normal course of human events, through a complicated confluence of historical, social, political, economic, cultural, demographic, intellectual, and biological factors. A crisis, therefore, may not be only a time for worry in the face of perceived peril, but a time for exhilaration in the face of perceived opportunity.

The word *crisis* belongs to a larger family of words: *critic, critical, criticism, criterion,* and the like. Each of these words is derived ultimately from the Greek verb *krinein,* which means "to separate" or "to decide." Accordingly, a "critic" is one who, like the Lord of the parable of the Sheep and the Goats in the twenty-fifth chapter of St. Matthew's Gospel, separates the worthy from the unworthy. In doing so he or she exercises a "critical" function and manifests "critical" skills, that is, the ability to discern real quality in the midst of mediocrity or sham. Such "criticism" is based on "criteria." A "criterion" is a standard, a means of judging, of discerning and separating good from bad.

It is within this modest network of terms that the word *crisis* fits. A crisis is, literally, a turning point, a moment or stage at which a process of whatever kind can go in two or more different directions. It is a time of separating out, of deciding (*krinein*). To be in crisis—whether political, medical, or indeed religious—is to be at the threshold of decisive change, usually, but not always, attended by considerable risk and suspense.

THE CHURCH IN CRISIS: YESTERDAY AND TODAY

Crisis is as much a part of human experience as birth, growth, and death. In fact, there can be no growth without crisis, as recent psychological explorations into the stages of human development by Jean Piaget (d. 1980), Erik Erikson, and Lawrence Kohlberg have shown. The findings of such researchers have, in turn, been applied to an understanding of Christian faith and its moral implications by Methodist theologian James Fowler and many Catholic religious educators whom he has influenced. Consequently, to acknowledge that the Catholic Church is in crisis is to say only that it has reached another turning point in its long two-thousand-year history. The Church is confronted with new opportunities for growth, new temptations to repress and regress. And this is the way it has always been. Only those without any sense of history at all assume that the Church is passing through its baptism of fire, its initiation into crisis. The fire of crisis was ignited in the foundational period of the New Testament and has been reignited many times since then. Only the height and fury of the flames have varied from crisis to crisis.

New Testament Crises

Two major turning points confronted the Church in its foundational stage. The *first* had to do with the scope of its mission. Was it to be a Church for the Jews alone, or for the Gentiles as well? And if the latter, were the Gentiles to be subject to the traditional laws and customs of Judaism? The *second* turning point, or crisis, had to do with the apparent delay of the Second Coming of Jesus Christ. Many had expected the end of this world and the inauguration of the new age to occur within their own lifetimes. Indeed, one of the principal controversies of modern New Testament scholarship has centered upon the expectations of Jesus himself. Did he expect the coming of the Kingdom within his own lifetime? Was he then compelled to revise his expectation and conclude that his own death was a precondition for the coming of the Kingdom? And if so, did his disciples share this assumption? Should the community of Christian faith prepare itself for a long historical life, replete with sacraments, doctrines, moral codes, and the like, or should it pursue a course similar to one adopted early in Thessalonia, of eschewing meaningful labor, abiding structures and institutions, and contenting itself instead with a period of passive waiting for the imminent end of the world (2 Thessalonians 3:6-15)?

The *first* crisis was resolved once and for all in the year 50 at the Council of Jerusalem (Acts of the Apostles 15:1-35). The mission to the Gentiles, already initiated at Antioch (Acts of the Apostles 11:19-26) and dramatized by Peter's Baptism of the Roman centurion Cornelius and several of his friends (Acts of the Apostles 10), was formally approved, with the remarkable, even revolutionary, stipulation that circumcision would not be required of converts to the faith (see chapter 18 for a fuller discussion of this important decision). As in the resolution of most crises in the history of the Church, the losing side was granted a face-saving concession. Certain Jewish laws would nonetheless have to be observed, such as the prohibition against eating meat with blood still in it or the meat of animals not killed according to Jewish ritual.

The *second* major crisis was not so decisively resolved, although the balance clearly shifted against those who preferred the Thessalonian option. The *parousia*, or Second Coming, could no longer be regarded as imminent. The Church would have to dig in, as it were, for the long course. It would have to be attentive to the building of a full and rich liturgical life as a way of keeping alive not only the memory of what God had accomplished in Jesus Christ but also the hope of future glory, "until he comes" (1 Corinthians 11:26). It would have to see to it that there were competent ministers to carry forward the pastoral work of the Apostles and other disciples, and creeds and codes to specify and clarify the demands of Christian existence in a world of competing possibilities and even of open hostility. (We shall, of course, examine these issues in greater detail in Part IV, on the Church.)

Some Post-biblical Crises

Similar turning points have marked the history of the Church just as surely as have the regular celebration of the Eucharist, the preaching of the Gospel, the administration of the sacraments, and the like.

Gnosticism

Gnosticism forced the New Testament Church to come to terms with its understanding of authority and its proper exercise. The Gnostics argued, among other things, that salvation comes through the possession of special knowledge (*gnosis*) and that such knowledge is available only to a select few by a process that is at once narrow and secret. Over against this view such major figures as St. John the Evangelist and St. Irenaeus (d. ca. 200) argued that salvation comes through the work of the incarnate Word of God and that the knowledge of this saving work is in principle available to everyone. They also argued that its meaning is attested to and confirmed by those special ministers of the Gospel (bishops, *episcopoi*) who are entrusted with the responsibility of preserving the continuity of faith with the apostolic tradition (*paradosis*).

The Edict of Constantine

The Edict of Constantine in 313 marked another major turning point in the Church's history. Throughout the third century the Roman government waged a severe and relentless campaign of repression and persecution against the Church. The relatively new religion was adjudged dangerous to the state because of Christianity's fundamental conviction that God's authority alone is absolute and that human authority is to be obeyed only when it is in conformity with God's. The Church's agony ended with the ascendancy of Constantine in 312; he attributed his final victory over Maxentius, his chief rival to the throne, to assistance from the Christian God. As a result, he agreed early the following year to grant complete religious toleration to Christians and even to restore all their property rights. Eventually, the new emperor pursued a vigorous campaign against pagan practices as Christianity became the official religion of the state. At the same time he lavished money and monuments upon the Church, including St. Peter's in Rome, constructed over the presumed site of Peter's grave. The clergy were accorded preferred status and were exempted from military service and forced labor. Roman law was modified to accommodate Christian values, and Sunday was established as a day of rest. Sexual offenses were punished, and more humane policies toward slaves, orphans, widows, and children were adopted.

The newly privileged condition of the Church carried with it, however, some exceedingly unsatisfactory implications. Civil authorities exploited the relationship for political purposes. Conversions to the faith often had as much to do with social status as with religious conviction. The clergy grew apart from the laity as class lines sharpened.

The Church had been faced with a decisive choice in 313, and it selected a particular course. Some have argued that it is still suffering the consequences.

Christological Controversies

The great Christological controversies of the fifth century presented a twofold crisis for the Church, the one doctrinal, the other jurisdictional. First, it was faced with widely divergent understandings of the humanity and divinity of Jesus Christ. How much diversity could the Church sustain without disrupting its bonds with the apostolic faith itself? Secondly, the Church was faced with concomitant challenges to the authority of its chief officer, the bishop of Rome and the successor of St. Peter in the primacy of authority. How much freedom from papal authority could it tolerate without disrupting the bonds of Christian unity? We shall be returning to these issues in Part III, on Christ, but for the moment it is sufficient to note that the dual crisis *was* resolved at the Council of Chalcedon in 451: Jesus is one divine person with two unconfused and unmixed natures, the one human and the other divine. That formula has held ever since—an extraordinary achievement indeed. And the papacy, in the person of Pope Leo the Great (d. 461), enhanced its prerogatives and prestige. But as in the resolution of other crises, negative forces were also set loose. Tensions between Rome and Constantinople were to intensify, and a major schism between West and East would be sealed by the beginning of the thirteenth century. That schism perdures even to this day, the remarkable improvement in ecumenical relations notwithstanding.

Aristotelianism

The emergence of Aristotelianism in the twelfth and thirteenth centuries presented the Church with yet another crisis, this time of an exclusively intellectual nature. Should the Church expose its historic faith to the rational speculations of a pagan philosopher? Its initial response was characteristically guarded. A temporary ban was imposed in 1215, but by the middle of the century the study of Aristotle (d. 322 B.C.) was widely accepted and pursued. St.

Albert the Great (d. 1280) and St. Thomas Aquinas (d. 1274) were his two principal disciples. Although his achievement has been celebrated generously by popes and bishops alike since then, Aquinas was attacked in his own day as a dangerous innovator and a rationalist. Over against his approach were ranged such imposing figures as St. Bonaventure (d. 1274), John Duns Scotus (d. 1308), and William of Ockham (d. 1347). The tension between those emphasizing reason and the intellect, as Aquinas did, and those stressing the will, as Bonaventure did, has continued to the present day. Yet another important crisis was faced but never fully resolved.

Conciliarism; Protestant Reformation

Conciliarism in the fifteenth century and the Protestant Reformation of the sixteenth century posed two separate, but obviously closely related, crises for the Church. Although there were several different theological issues at stake in the Reformation, the common thread running through both the Conciliar and Protestant movements was the question of, and challenge to, ecclesiastical authority, and specifically the authority of the pope. The first challenge was at least temporarily resolved: Conciliarism was overcome and the unity of the Church preserved. The story of the Reformation, of course, is more familiar. It would not have so organizationally tranquil an ending. How much reform in head and members, in creed and code, in liturgy and devotion, could the Church endure without breaking faith with the apostolic community? How much freedom of conscience and of action could the authorities of the Church, and the pope in particular, allow without compromising or even abdicating responsibility for the integrity of faith and morals? These were the kinds of questions that constituted the crisis, or turning point, which immediately preceded the Protestant Reformation. Did the Church separate out the choices intelligently? Did it make the right choices? Did it follow the correct course? Was the Catholic Counter-Reformation too little, too late? Or indeed did it only make matters worse?

The Enlightenment; Catholic Modernism

Perhaps no crisis in the entire post-biblical history of the Church
has proved more significant than the crisis precipitated by *the
Enlightenment* of the seventeenth and eighteenth centuries. In
essence, this was a philosophical movement which progressively
rejected extrinsic authority in the determination of truth in favor
of the authority of reason. One accepts something as true not
because some officeholder in the Church says it is true but because
there are good and sound reasons for believing it to be true. And,
of course, the reverse is also the case. What cannot be established
clearly by reason can make no claim upon our belief. The necessary condition for the exercise of reason is freedom. The Enlightenment, therefore, sounded a call for freedom of inquiry, freedom
of decision, and freedom of action. Left to himself or herself,
without the artificial constraints of religion and supernatural principles, the human person could reach the fullest extent of his or her
potential.

How would the Church respond to the new challenge of
modernity? Could it simply hold fast to its traditional values and
convictions? Could it pretend to ignore the findings of science?
Would an appeal to the sacred texts, whether of the Bible or of the
ecumenical councils or of the popes, provide a persuasive rebuttal
to the arguments advanced by reason and empirical observation?
As often before, the Church's initial response was negative and
strongly condemnatory. That spirit is unmistakably operative in
the official pronouncements of such figures as Pope Gregory XVI
(d. 1846) and Pope Pius IX (d. 1878), who ruled the Church for the
greater part of the nineteenth century (1831-1878), and particularly in the latter's *Syllabus of Errors* (1864). The decisive rejection of modernity by these two popes notwithstanding, the issues
continued to fester under the surface, breaking out for a time in
the early part of the twentieth century in the form of *Catholic
Modernism*, sharply condemned by yet another pope, St. Pius X, in
1907. It reemerged in other forms in the late 1930s and into the
1940s, where again it suffered condemnation by Pope Pius XII
(d. 1958) in his encyclical letter *Humani Generis* (1950) before
enjoying some measure of official acceptance at the Second Vatican Council (1962-1965).

The Present Crisis

Symptoms

It seems reasonably simple to sketch the contours of Catholicism's present crisis because it has been part of our personal experience for nearly two decades and is still with us. But we should be restrained in our confidence. As the history of the Church amply demonstrates, important crises are slow in developing and sometimes just as slow in being resolved. Even after the crises have been resolved, the longer-term implications cannot be assessed until decades or centuries have passed.

Nevertheless, the symptoms of this present crisis do seem clear enough: the sharp decline in Mass attendance and in vocations to the priesthood and the religious life; the higher incidence of divorce and remarriage; the widening of theological dissent; diversity and pluralism to the point of confusion and doubt in theology, catechetics, and religious education generally; the rejection of papal authority in the matter of birth control, and resistance to that authority on other issues such as the ordination of women and priestly celibacy; the ecumenical movement's challenge to Catholic identity and distinctiveness; the alienation of young people from the Church; the abiding social and cultural dominance of science and technology, with its correlative impact upon traditional spiritual values and motivation; the continuing and inevitable involvement of the Church on both sides of the historic struggle between rich and poor, oppressor and oppressed; the raised consciousness of women in the Church.

Remote Causes

The remote causes of the present crisis are theological and philosophical. We are wrestling anew with age-old questions which have since been filtered through, and therefore transformed by, the Enlightenment and post-Enlightenment movements: What does it mean to be human? Is there really more to life than meets the eye? Is the answer knowable, in any case? Is there, in other words, an ultimate or transcendental dimension to secular experience, and is it available through reason alone, through faith alone, or through "reason illumined by faith" (Vatican I)? Is there any person or story which focuses this ultimate meaning for us? If so, what impact does such a person or story have upon our consciousness and our moral behavior? At what point and under what circumstances is such impact made?

Before Immanuel Kant (d. 1804) and the Enlightenment, the questions were usually answered straightforwardly and with much assurance. The answers, it was asserted, are available in the sacred texts (Bible and doctrinal compendia alike) and, what is more significant, in the living voice of the Church expressed in the office of pope and bishops (the latter completely dependent upon the former). Such a view, it must be acknowledged, is not without support in the Church today. For many traditional Catholics, the Enlightenment simply never happened.

On the other hand, there are progressively oriented Catholics who, since the Enlightenment, act as if the post-Enlightenment had never happened, as if reason and freedom reign together in unchallenged dual supremacy. But there are social, political, cultural, and even economic forces which compromise our precious intellectual objectivity, and there are profound and often hidden psychic forces which substantially modify, and even sharply diminish, our equally cherished personal freedom. This is not to say, of course, that reason now yields to socially determined forces and that freedom yields to psychically determined forces, but only that neither reason nor freedom can be celebrated uncritically, almost blindly, in ironic denial of the Enlightenment's own highest principles.

Proximate Causes

There is some difference of opinion regarding the proximate causes of the present crisis. Sociologist Andrew M. Greeley assigns principal blame to Pope Paul VI's encyclical on birth control, *Humanae Vitae* (1968). On the basis of scientific research, he concludes that American Catholicism "has suffered a severe trauma brought on not by 'enlightenment' or secularization or acculturation or even by the revolt against authoritarianism. The disaster for American Catholicism was the result of a single decision made because of the decrepit and archaic institutional structure of the church, a structure in which effective upward communication practically does not exist" (*The American Catholic*, pp. 126-151).

Others like political commentator Garry Wills, novelist Wilfrid Sheed, and social scientist Daniel Callahan—Catholics all—have argued that Catholicism just could not survive the twin modernizing pressures of the Second Vatican Council and the acculturation of the immigrants. They maintain that as Catholics became better educated, they began thinking for themselves, and then the council came along and destroyed what remained of the old Catholic culture.

A third explanation has been advanced by Protestant theologian Langdon Gilkey. The causes of the present crisis go deeper than either the acculturation or the encyclical hypotheses. Neither development would have had the effects they had upon Catholicism if something more basic had not already occurred at a more profound level of Catholic consciousness. It is the "dissolution of (the) understanding of the supernatural as the central religious category" (*Catholicism Confronts Modernity*, p. 52).

"In the span of a generation," Gilkey notes, "the absolute authority of the church regarding truth, law, and rules of life, has suddenly vanished.... The collapse of this authority has not occurred because certain church doctrines, papal decrees, bishops' rulings and so on were at last found to be in error, or...obviously 'wrong' or 'old-fashioned' in relation to the modern mind" (pp. 52–53). Such explanations, he maintains, miss the heart of the issue and fail to get at the deeper source of the present crisis, which is the loss of the traditional Catholic sense of the supernatural. Catholics feel free to reject official Church teachings not simply because they perceive them to be in error but because they no longer perceive them to be propounded with the authority of God. There has been, in Gilkey's terms, a "geological shift" in values, away from the supernatural and to the natural, and he calls this a modernizing of the Catholic mind.

One can readily perceive value in all three attempts to identify the proximate causes of the present crisis. There has been an

acculturation process at work—at the levels of education, socialization, occupation, and the like—which has had some effect on
contemporary Catholic consciousness and behavior. And some
data seem to support the Greeley hypothesis regarding the devas-
tatingly negative effect of the birth-control encyclical. But would
either of these factors actually have provoked a crisis of this
apparent magnitude if there had not also occurred what Gilkey
has called a "geological shift" in values, a new perception of the
meaning of the supernatural order and a new appreciation for the
human and natural order?

If "the collapse of the supernaturalistic forms of Catholicism. . .is the key to understanding both the effect of modernity on
traditional Catholicism and the current crisis in Catholic life. . .,
(then) the task for twentieth-century Catholicism calls for the
reinterpretation of the transcendent, the sacred, and the
divine—the presence of God to men—into worldly or naturalistic
forms of modern experience rather than in the supernaturalistic
forms of Hellenic and medieval experience" (pp. 58-59). Among
the symbols to be reinterpreted, says Gilkey, are God, revelation,
authority, salvation, law, and hope for the future. The reinterpretation must be done in such a way that the historic Catholic values
of community, tradition, grace, and sacrament are not only preserved but given powerful new expression "so that a new birth can
take place. For on the creative resolution of this contemporary
challenge to Catholicism depends the health of the whole church
in the immediate future" (p. 60).

THE PRESENT CRISIS AND THIS BOOK

The crisis facing Roman Catholicism today has largely shaped this
book's purpose, method, and organization and has helped to give
the book its distinctive qualities.

Purpose

The *principal purpose* of this book is, at the same time, its principal challenge: to identify, explain, and explore the traditional
doctrinal, moral, ritual, and structural symbols and components of

Catholicism without prejudice to the twin values italicized, but not patented, by the Enlightenment, namely, freedom of inquiry and freedom of decision. Or, conversely, its purpose is to encourage and assist Catholics and others to explore, understand, and exercise their faith in freedom without prejudice to our abiding responsiblity to reconcile our understanding, our judgments, and our decisions with the theological criteria embodied in Sacred Scripture, the writings of the great Fathers and doctors of the Church, the official teachings of the ecumenical councils and the popes, the liturgy, and the *sensus fidelium*, or "consensus of the faithful" maintained through the centuries, everywhere and at every time.

The Catholic faith, and the Catholic tradition by which that faith is transmitted from generation to generation, is a given. That is, it is a reality which existed before us and exists apart from us. Catholicism is not created anew, from the start, in every decade. It is there already as an historical fact. It is a reality to be known and assimilated.

But that faith, and the tradition by which it is communicated, is not static or lifeless. In a sense, it *does* have to be rediscovered and reappropriated in every succeeding generation. The Gospel means, after all, "good news." It is the Gospel not only because it is "good" but also because it is "news."

This book will serve its primary purpose, therefore, if it provides those who do not know the tradition well with a comprehensive view and grasp of that tradition; and, secondly, if it persuades those others who *do* know the tradition that the task of appropriation and assimilation is never finished, that the tradition is best preserved, not by repetition and routine, but by freshly rethinking and reapplying it in every new age and circumstance, and indeed in the face of every new crisis of growth or decline.

Method

The method is, therefore, at once traditional and contemporary. It is *traditional* in that the presentation considers every major element of Christian and Catholic faith from the point of view of its place in Sacred Scripture, in the written reflections of the great Fathers and doctors of the Church, the official declarations of the councils and popes, and the living interpretation of the community itself as embodied in the community's worship, devotional practices, and moral action. The method is *contemporary*, on the other hand, in that it proceeds inductively rather than deductively. It begins not from the given of the sacred texts, whether of the Bible or of doctrine, but from the given of human existence and of present Christian experience. However, the deductive is certainly not excluded. Biblical, patristic, and doctrinal sources remain always at the core of each theological argument and conclusion.

Organization

Although the book is about the content and moral implications of Christian and Catholic faith, it insists that one cannot understand the meaning and demands of Christian existence (Part V) unless one also understands the nature and mission of the Church itself (Part IV). And one cannot understand the nature and mission of the Church unless one also understands the person and ministry of Jesus Christ (Part III), whose Body the Church is. And one cannot understand the person and ministry of Jesus Christ unless one also understands, or at least begins to understand, what we mean by "God," whose Son and agent Jesus claimed to be (Part II). And, finally, one cannot understand the reality of God unless one also understands what it means to be human, for God is perceived as the source of humankind's perfection, the ultimate fulfillment of human potential (Part I). To say, in other words, that something enhances our humanity while something else diminishes it is to make a judgment in the light of certain explicit or implicit criteria. The construction of such criteria is a work not only of philosophy, sociology, psychology, or anthropology. At its deepest level, the task is theological. (In the next chapter we shall define what we mean by theology, indicating how it relates to other intellectual disciplines in their common pursuit of truth.) To propose the final meaning of human existence is to propose a "doctrine" of God. In the end, anthropology and theology converge.

Distinctiveness

It goes without saying that this is not the first attempt, nor will it be the last, at constructing a comprehensive theological statement about Catholic faith and practice. We have witnessed in recent years the reemergence of the catechism as an expression of theological synthesis and as an instrument of religious education: the so-called "German Catechism," with its emphasis on the glories and joys of being a Christian (*A Catholic Catechism*, New York: Herder and Herder, 1957); the so-called "Dutch Catechism," with its existentialist starting-point and its narrative, rather than question-and-answer format (*A New Catechism*, New York: Herder and Herder, 1967, rev. ed., 1969); *The Common Catechism*, the first ecumenical effort (involving German Catholics and Protestants) to range over the entire terrain of Christian belief and life (New York: Seabury Press, 1975); *An American Catholic Catechism*, a collaborative enterprise by North American Catholic theologians, originally written for a theological journal for clergy, *Chicago Studies*, and drafted in question-and-answer form (New York: Seabury Press, 1975); John A. Hardon's *The Catholic Catechism*, which follows the basic structure of the old *Baltimore Catechism*—creed, commandments, sacraments—and some measure of its theological orientation as well (New York: Doubleday, 1975); and another corporate effort, this time by theologians and non-theologians alike, entitled *The Teaching of Christ*, but with an immediate emphasis on the teaching of the Church's hierarchy (Huntington, Ind.: Our Sunday Visitor Press, 1976).

This book is not a catechism, although in structure and content it may appear similar to one. A catechism, as Father Hardon himself acknowledges, "makes no claim to explain what it contains, except insofar as words need clarification or the terms that are often technical need to be simplified. . . . It presumes that what is here described is already believed. . ."(pp. 24-25). (For a fuller discussion of the relationship between theology and catechesis, see the next chapter.)

But neither is this book a personal theological brief, as is, for example, Karl Rahner's imposing *Foundations of Christian Faith* (New York: Seabury Press, 1978). It is intended, as the Preface pointed out, for the intellectual enrichment of anyone who is seriously interested in studying the treasures of the Catholic theological tradition. But its contents, language, and organization make it easily usable at the university and college levels, for adult education and inquiry classes, for the continuing education of clergy, religious, and all ecclesiastical ministers, ordained and non-ordained alike, for very advanced high school groups. The book does not seek to present and argue a point of view peculiar to the author or to a relatively limited, even marginal, school of theological opinion. As far as possible, every representative position on each major doctrinal question will be identified, explained, and compared with other pertinent positions. If a theological consensus has been reached, it will enjoy the benefit of the doubt.

The final product, therefore, is slightly more akin to Anglican theologian John Macquarrie's *Principles of Christian Theology* (New York: Charles Scribner's Sons, 1977, 2nd ed.) than to Catholic theologian Hans Küng's *On Being a Christian* (New York: Doubleday, 1976). The latter work, although comprehensive and systematic, advances a particular Christological point of view (one difficult to describe as yet as a consensus position) and in a style that is often exhortatory, albeit sometimes eloquently so. Macquarrie's work, on the other hand, deliberately seeks a balance between what Macquarrie calls the existentialist and the ontological approaches to Christian theology: the one emphasizing the personal and the subjective, the other emphasizing the essential and the objective. But Macquarries's leaning is clearly toward existentialism, in the tradition of Martin Heidegger (d. 1976).

Unlike Macquarrie's book, however, the present work depends completely on no single philosophical world view. And it is written with a more explicit sense of responsiblity to the Church of the past and to the specific biblical, theological, doctrinal, and pastoral emphases which have always characterized the Catholic tradition.

This book, then, has been written in the midst of yet another major crisis in the history of Roman Catholicism and as a response to that crisis. It has been written with the conviction that at such turning points as these the Church needs to be in touch with its own roots, needs to see with clear, unbiased vision the whole sweep of Catholic tradition, needs to see the interrelationships among all the elements of its doctrine and practice. Only by understanding its own past can it understand what it is now. Then, and only then, can it press forward with confidence and hope.

SUMMARY

1. The word *crisis*, frequently misused, means a *turning point.* The Catholic Church is "in crisis" today in that it finds itself at yet another turning point, where it is called upon "to decide" (*krinein*) upon the direction it will take for the future.

2. As history shows, a crisis is an opportunity for growth at least as often as it is a prelude to decline or even disaster.

3. The Church faced crises from the very beginning. In the *New Testament* alone we discover such major crises or turning points as the controversy over extending the mission to the Gentiles without requiring them to accept the complete Jewish law, and the state of perplexity created by the apparent delay of the Second Coming of Christ.

4. *Post-biblical crises* have had to do with the interpretation of revelation (Gnosticism), the political standing of the Church (the Edict of Constantine), the content of faith (the Christological controversies), the legitimate activities of theology (the emergence of Aristotelianism), the meaning and exercise of authority (Conciliarism and the Protestant Reformation), and the perception and appropriation of truth itself (the Enlightenment and Modernism).

5. *Today's crisis* is better known by its symptoms than in its causes, whether proximate or remote. Its *symptoms* are clear: declining Mass attendance, decrease in vocations to the priesthood and religious life, alienation of the young, resistance to the teaching authority of the pope and bishops, and so forth. Its *causes* are somewhat less obvious: cultural changes, the encyclical on birth control, the "geological shift" away from traditional notions of the supernatural order.

6. In light of the present crisis, this book has a twofold purpose: to disclose the Catholic tradition (its doctrines, its rituals, its institutions, its spirituality) to those who do not know it sufficiently well, but to expound it in a way that is consistent with the theological and doctrinal developments of recent decades.

7. Although the book is about the content and moral implications of Christian and Catholic faith, it recognizes that one cannot understand the meaning of Christian existence apart from an understanding of the

mystery of the Church, and the Church apart from an understanding of Jesus Christ, and Christ apart from an understanding of God, and God apart from an understanding of what it means to be human.

8.   The book is neither a catechism, designed principally for new or potential members of the Church, nor a personal theological brief, arguing a particular point of view which as yet has failed to achieve a consensus within the Church. It is rather an exposition of the Catholic tradition that is at once conservative and critical, looking at the same time to the past and to the future, hoping all the while that the present is thereby faithfully served.

SUGGESTED READINGS

Bokenkotter, Thomas.   *A Concise History of the Catholic Church*. Rev. ed. New York: Doubleday, 1979.

Dolan, John P.   *Catholicism: An Historical Survey*. Woodbury, New York: Barron's Educational Series, 1968.

Gilkey, Langdon.   *Catholicism Confronts Modernity: A Protestant View*. New York: Seabury Press, 1975, chapter 1.

Greeley, Andrew.   *The American Catholic: A Social Portrait*. New York: Basic Books, 1977.

Marty, Martin.   *A Short History of Christianity*. New York: New American Library, Meridian, 1959.

·II·

FAITH, THEOLOGY,
AND BELIEF

THE PROBLEM

If the Catholic Church is in crisis today, it can be explained, at least in part, by the persistent failure of many Catholics to discern and understand the differences among *faith*, *theology*, and *belief*. Some bishops, pastors, and educational administrators assure nervous audiences of parents that the task of the religious educator is not to teach the latest views of modern theologians but to teach "the faith." Although there is some truth to this assertion, beneath it often lies the assumption that faith is available in some non-theological state—that it is possible, in other words, to isolate the former from the latter as one might separate two chemicals in a laboratory experiment. It is the burden of this chapter to show why this is not the case.

What we are examining here are the ground rules for thinking, speaking, writing, preaching, and teaching about God, about Jesus Christ, and about the supernatural order in general. What is the source of our knowledge of such realities? What principles govern our interpretation and communication of that knowledge? How do we know if our interpretations are accurate? Are there protective and/or corrective devices by which to recognize and to overcome error and distortion?

This chapter, therefore, is about faith, theology, and belief. It is also about the many expressions of belief: Sacred Scripture, doctrines and dogmas, and the liturgy. And, finally, it is about the process by which such beliefs are critically assimilated and transmitted to others: religious education and its several forms, such as catechesis, the teaching of theology, and Christian *praxis*. Each of these topics will be defined, explained, and interrelated in logical sequence. For many readers, this may be the most practical, perhaps even the most important, chapter in the entire book.

ELEMENTS OF THE PROBLEM
Faith

How do we come to the knowledge of God, of Jesus Christ, of salvation, of the Holy Spirit, or of any other religious or supernatural reality? Is it by empirically and scientifically verifiable methods alone, or is such knowledge also derived from some other level of experience?

A crucial distinction is immediately in order. Our knowledge of God, Christ, salvation, or similar topics, may be the knowledge of an uninvolved, dispassionate observer such as a sociologist, an anthropologist, or a psychologist, or it may be the knowledge of a highly involved, committed believer in God, Christ, salvation, and related realities.

An atheistic sociologist could spend a lifetime examining the effects of theism on the institutions and cultural expressions of a given national or ethnic group. He or she may produce hundreds of articles and several books which carefully examine the control-group's belief system. He or she may indeed become an expert on the meaning of God, *as perceived by* this particular community of believers. But those are the key words: "as perceived by." We are not speaking here of the sociologist's own knowledge of God, but of his or her knowledge of other people's knowledge of God. So it is possible for someone to know much *about* God, Christ, the Holy Spirit, grace, and redemption, without at the same time *believing in* any one of these realities.

On the other hand, there are people (presumably most of those using this book) who are convinced that they know at least something about God because of God's own self-disclosure through Christ, the prophets, the Apostles, the Church, the created order, and even direct mystical experience. Without doubt, it is *this* kind of knowledge, not that of the sociologist, which is at the heart of our problem. "No one," the author of the Fourth Gospel reminded us, "has ever seen God" (John 1:18).

A believer's knowledge of God is of a necessarily different order from that of the uncommitted observer. The believer's knowledge does not originate in laboratory tests, scientific observation, nor computer technology. And it certainly does not originate in common sense or everyday human experiences. Insofar as a believer insists that he or she knows something about God, that knowledge is attributed, in one way or another, to faith.

For the moment, it is enough to say that *faith is personal knowledge of God*. (*Christian* faith, therefore, is personal knowledge of God *in Christ*.) But already we can see that our emphasis is on the personal rather than on the cognitive or the propositional. Faith is not primarily belief in truths (propositions) which have been revealed to us by God through the Bible and the Church; rather, it is the way we come to the knowledge of God as God. The object of faith, in other words, is not a doctrine or a sacred text, but God, our Creator, Judge, and Savior.

We might also usefully distinguish "faith" from "the faith." The latter expression refers to the whole composite of beliefs held by Christians in general or by Catholics in particular. That expression is closer to what we mean by "doctrines" (see below) than it is to what we have been saying about "faith" itself.

Theology

Faith is personal knowledge of God. It is our perception of God in the midst of life. Unalloyed faith does not exist. Nowhere can we discover and isolate "pure faith." Real faith, living faith, if you will, exists always and only in a cognitive, (more or less) reflective, (more or less) scientific state. Every thought about the meaning of faith is precisely that: a thought about the meaning of faith. Every word of interpretation designed to articulate and illuminate the meaning and implications of faith is again precisely that: a word of interpretation, not faith itself. When some Catholics warn against the contamination of "the faith" by theology, they reveal a fundamental confusion about the relationship between faith and theology.

Faith is not theology, to be sure, but neither does faith exist apart from, or independently of, theology. Theology comes into play at that very moment when the person of faith becomes intellectually conscious of his or her faith. From the very beginning, faith exists in a theologically interpreted state. Indeed, it is a redundancy to put it that way: "theologically interpreted." For the interpretation of one's faith is theology itself.

Theology is, as St. Anselm of Canterbury (d. 1109) defined it nine centuries ago, "faith seeking understanding" (*fides quaerens intellectum*). More specifically, *theology is that process by which we bring our knowledge and understanding of God to the level of expression.* Theology is the articulation, in a more or less systematic manner, of the experience of God within human experience.

Theology, in the broad sense of the word, may emerge in many forms: a painting, a piece of music, a dance, a cathedral, a bodily posture, or, in its more recognizable form, in spoken or written words. These forms, of course, never do justice to the perception which they hope to express. Not all theology is good theology. We can ineptly or incorrectly translate our experience or knowledge of God. We might even have a thoroughly distorted or false experience of God in the first place, which no form, however cleverly constructed, can ever redeem.

When all is said and done, religious educators, bishops, preachers, parents, and the Church at large do not transmit or hand on faith apart from theology. They hand on faith in and through the theology they are using. In other words, they transmit particular interpretations or understandings of faith in their various and multiple forms. It is entirely beside the point, therefore, to warn religious educators against teaching theology instead of handing on the faith. *Faith exists always and only in some theological form.* The question before the Church today and in every age is not *whether* that faith will be transmitted according to some theological interpretation, but rather *which* theological interpretation is best suited to the task at a particular moment.

What is so unacceptable about appeals to "the faith" over against the "private views of theologians" is that a particular theology is implicitly equated with faith itself. Consequently, any criticism of that theology is automatically perceived as an undermining of faith. In effect, what is proposed is that "the faith," which must not be confined and corrupted by *any* theology, can only be understood properly in terms of *one* theology, often the neo-scholastic theology popular in Catholic colleges and seminaries just prior to the Second Vatican Council.

Belief

If theology is faith brought to the level of self-consciousness, then belief is theology in a kind of snapshot or frozen state. Theology is a *process*: belief is one of its several *products*. In the general sense of the word, a belief is something accepted as true even in the absence of clear and convincing evidence. In the theological sense of the word, *a belief is a formulation of the knowledge we have of God through faith.*

Belief has many forms. At the one end of the spectrum, these beliefs are widely shared and officially approved (doctrines, dogmas). At the other end, they are held by select groups or individuals and are not officially proposed for universal acceptance (for example, the presumed appearances of the Blessed Mother at Fatima and Lourdes).

There are many Christian beliefs, even though there is only one Christian faith. Christian faith, as defined above, is knowledge of God in Christ, who is the key and focal point of all human experience. Over the centuries of Christian history there have been literally thousands of beliefs held and transmitted at one time or another—i.e., interpretations of faith which significant segments of the Christian community have found useful for expressing and articulating their own knowledge of God in Christ. Some of these beliefs endured the test of time (e.g., the great Christological dogmas), while others have receded beyond the range of vision or even of collective memory (e.g., the Two Swords theory of papal authority, proposed in the Middle Ages).

What has been true in Christian history is true also in the contemporary Church. Hundreds of different beliefs vie with one another for attention and acceptance. Some of these beliefs are grounded firmly and deeply in the tradition of the Church, e.g., belief in the Real Presence of Christ in the Eucharist, while others have shorter and/or more tender roots, e.g., belief in the infallibility of the pope. The sorting-out process, however, is never finished. We are faced constantly with the problem of evaluating and reevaluating our beliefs in the light of our ongoing experience and of our subsequent theological interpretations of that experience. These, in turn, are judged against that "instinct of faith" which somehow gives the whole Church its inner coherence and its radical identity and continuity in the midst of change. It is at the point of the "somehow" in the preceding sentence that our rich poetry about the Holy Spirit inserts itself.

At key historical moments in that sorting-out process (moments of "crisis," as we saw in chapter 1), the Church, acting through members set apart by the inspiration of God, by theological competence, and/or by episcopal ordination, is compelled to make decisions and to bring those decisions to the level of formal expression. These expressions may take different forms: letters, liturgical documents, narratives, and theological reflections which the Church itself recognizes to be fundamental, normative, constitutive expressions of its faith (*Sacred Scripture*); official teachings based on Sacred Scripture and the ongoing experience of the Church (*doctrines*); official teachings proposed with such solemnity that their rejection is tantamount to *heresy*, which is a denial of some truth of faith deemed by the teaching Church to be essential to that faith (*dogmas*); or officially approved and/or mandated cultic acts and sacramental celebrations through which the community ritualizes in word and action what it believes in the depths of its heart and consciousness (*liturgy*). Indeed, there is a Latin axiom, *"Lex orandi, lex credendi,"* which means literally that the law of praying is the law of believing. We express our belief in our worship.

In stop-action language: Theology ("faith seeking understanding") follows faith, and belief follows theology. In fact, however, faith and theology do not really exist apart from one another, whereas belief and theology can and do exist apart. The theologian can express all sorts of judgments about the reality of God as he or she presumably experiences God, without at the same time resorting to formulae or propositions which have already attracted wider attention and acceptance, whether officially (as in the case of a doctrine) or unofficially (as in the case of a belief about the healing effects of Lourdes water).

Religious Education

Although religious education has more to do with communication than it does with speculation, it would be a grave oversimplification to suggest that religious education is merely the delivery system for a faith-community's beliefs. Religious education is more than the process of communicating what has been grasped by theology and officially adopted by the Church. The religious educator is at once theologian and educator, for *the field of religious education is located at the point where theology/belief and education intersect.* On the one hand, the religious educator must himself or herself critically investigate and understand what is to be communicated and, on the other hand, must attend to the methods, context, and effects of the communicative process.

The aim of religious education is to help people discern, respond to, and be transformed by the presence of God in their lives, and to work for the continuing transformation of the world in the light of this perception of God. *Christian* religious education focuses on Jesus Christ as the great sign or sacrament of God's presence in human history and, more specifically, in the Church which is the People of God and the Body of Christ. Christian religious education, or simply "Christian education," is concerned, therefore, not only with the transformation of the individual and of the world in the light of Christ, but with the transformation of the Church, which is the primary context for our experience of God as Creator, as Redeemer, and as Reconciler.

Just as there are many different forms of belief, so there are several different forms of religious education or of Christian education. Religious education, first of all, is as divisible as religion

itself. There are at least as many different kinds of religious education as there are religions. Christian education, too, can be divided
along denominational lines: Lutheran education, Baptist education, Catholic education, etc. And Christian education can also be
divided according to specific purposes. *Catechesis*, for example,
introduces the new or potential member of the Church, whether a
child or an adult, to the whole of the Christian proclamation. The
purpose of catechesis is, as the Greek word from which it is
derived suggests, the "echoing" of the Christian Gospel in a way
that is at once pastoral and systematic. Catechesis, therefore, is
not the same as *preaching*, which is yet another form of religious
or Christian education. Catechesis is systematic in intent and
method (whether it employs the question-and-answer format or
not). Preaching is not. Catechesis seeks to echo the Christian
message in a way that provides the new or potential member of the
Church with a sense of the interrelatedness of Christian mysteries
or doctrines and of their relative centrality and importance. All
catechists and preachers, however, are Christian educators, but
not all Christian educators are catechists and preachers.

   Much the same can be said of still other forms of religious or
Christian education. The *teaching of theology* is clearly a form of
religious education, but it differs from catechesis in that it is
directed primarily at those who are already mature members of
the Church, and it differs from preaching in that it is scientific,
appealing immediately to critical reason rather than to a conversion of the mind and heart. So, too, Christian *praxis* is a form of
religious education. It is at the same time critical reflection on
action already taken, and action that is taken after critical reflection. *Praxis* is not related to theory as practice is related to theology. *Praxis* involves the coming together of theory and practice to
produce something different from each. It is, in any case, a way of
doing religious education, one of its several forms.

   This chapter began with a brief description of the problem
created by our failure to understand the differences among faith,
theology, and belief. We identified these as the "elements of the
problem," emphasizing their relationships one with another.

What follows is a fuller, more detailed discussion of these elements, taking note of their historical evolution and their deeper theological meaning.

FAITH
Old Testament Notions of Faith

The Hebrew verb *'āman* (meaning "to be firm" or "to be solid," and therefore "to be true") is the Old Testament equivalent of the New Testament Greek word *pisteuein*. The Hiphil (or causative stem) of the Hebrew *'āman*, meaning "to accept something as true," always indicates a personal relationship. Thus, our acceptance of something as true is really the acceptance of the person who proposes it for belief. The Israelites accepted Moses as their leader on the basis of their trust in him personally. They accepted him as one designated by God.

The Hebrew noun *ᵉmûnah* means "solidity" or "firmness" (see Exodus 17:12) and this solidity or firmness, in turn, offers security (Isaiah 33:6). God offers security because of God's own fidelity (Psalm 36:6) to the divine promises and the Covenant with Israel. God's fidelity is, in turn, grounded in love and mercy (*hesed*). Because God is faithful (*neᵉ'mān*), one must believe God's word and accept God's commands (Deuteronomy 9:23; Psalm 119:66). Thus, Abraham believed Yahweh when the Lord promised him numerous descendants.

The book of Isaiah offers certain peculiar features regarding the reality of faith. The notion of faith implies an acceptance of the power and will of God to deliver Judah from political crisis, and the acceptance is demonstrated by abstinence from all political and military action. To do otherwise is to fail to trust Yahweh. One who believes has no worry (Isaiah 28:16). The scope of faith is unlimited; it demands *total commitment to Yahweh*.

The intellectual quality of faith is more prominent in chapters 40-66 of Second, or Deutero, Isaiah (so called because modern biblical scholars hold that this part of the book did not have the same authorship as the first thirty-nine chapters). The Israelites are the witnesses of the true God to the extent that they draw other nations to know, believe, and understand that Yahweh is their Lord (Isaiah 43:10). But even this faith is not purely intellectual. "Knowing" God, in this sense, is not speculative knowledge. Rather it is the experience of God through God's revealed word and saving deeds. The more common way of describing the faith relationship with Yahweh in the Old Testament is through the notion of hearing rather than believing, and the hearing must lead to acceptance and obedience.

The foundation stone of Old Testament faith is God, the One to whom the world and all living things owe their created existence and upon whom everything depends for survival and well-being (see Genesis 1-2, Exodus 3, e.g.). Old Testament faith expresses itself in repentance, obedience, and trust. (See, for example, the story of Noah in Genesis 6:9,22; 7:5, and that of Abraham in Genesis 22:1-18.) In the Old Testament the response of faith is, therefore, primarily a moral response, i.e., one of trust and obedience rather than of belief.

Old Testament faith is essentially related to the Covenant (see Deuteronomy 6:17; 7:11), and humankind's response entails the keeping of the Commandments. Consequently, Old Testament faith is also basically corporate rather than individual (see the Psalms). It is related to the fear of the Lord, but not fear in the commonsense meaning of the word. Fear of the Lord means rather a willingness and a readiness to do the will of God, and this, in turn, generates a genuine feeling of security and trust (Job 4:6). But there can be no compromises. Old Testament faith makes an exclusive demand upon Israel (Exodus 20:3; Deuteronomy 5:7). God tolerates no idolatry.

Finally, in the period after the Exile, i.e., after the Edict of Cyrus in 538 B.C., faithfulness to the Law is the expression of faith (see especially Daniel and Judith).

New Testament Notions of Faith

Synoptics

In the Synoptics (the Gospels of Matthew, Mark, and Luke, called Synoptics because, when they are looked at side by side, similarities of structure and content immediately appear), Jesus demanded faith (Matthew 9:28; Mark 4:40; Luke 8:25), praised faith when he discovered it (Matthew 8:10; Luke 7:9), and declared its saving power (Matthew 9:22; Mark 5:34; Luke 8:48). In the Synoptic Gospels the act of faith is directed to God the Father and to Jesus himself. Faith is, first of all, trust in God (Mark 5:34,36; 9:23; 11:22-23; Luke 17:6), but it is also directed toward Jesus; i.e., it is the acceptance of Jesus as the one he claimed himself to be (Mark 8:27-30,38). Behind all of Jesus' utterances about faith there lies that sense of his special relationship to God as Father (Mark 8:38; 9:37 = Matthew 10:40; Mark 12:1-11, 35-37; Matthew 10:32-33; 11:27-30; 16:17-19).

Primitive Christianity—Acts of the Apostles

Faith is the acceptance of the message of the Gospel (Acts of the Apostles 8:13-14), and the "believers" are those who accept the preaching of the Apostles and join the Christian community. The object of belief is the apostolic preaching, and this belief is centered on Jesus as the Risen Lord (5:14; 9:42; 11:17; 15:11). "Therefore let the whole house of Israel know beyond any doubt that God has made both Lord and Messiah this Jesus whom you crucified" (Acts of Apostles 2:36). Belief in the Lordship of Christ is at the core of the apostolic preaching and, therefore, at the heart of faith itself. Acceptance of Jesus as Lord is expressed through repentance, and this is sacramentally demonstrated in Baptism, to which there is attached the guarantee of forgiveness and the renewal by the Holy Spirit: "Peter answered: 'You must reform and be baptized, each one of you, in the name of Jesus Christ, that your sins may be forgiven; then you will receive the gift of the Holy Spirit" (2:38). (For the relationship between faith and Baptism, a point to which we shall return in the discussion of the Church and the sacraments in Part IV, see also Acts of the Apostles 10:43; 18:8; 20:21.)

In primitive Christianity faith requires a break from the past and from other religious allegiances. But it is especially a break from sin. It is belief in God's word as personified in Christ, and so faith necessarily involves a personal relationship with Christ. In the Acts of the Apostles faith is not simply a subjective attitude but also embodies objective content ("The word of God continued to spread ... There were many priests among those who embraced the faith"—6:7; elsewhere in the New Testament, see Jude 3:20; Romans 1:5; 4:14; 10:8; Galatians 1:23; Ephesians 4:5; 1 Timothy 1:19; 3:9; 4:6). Finally, the faith of primitive Christianity is directed not only toward the saving events of the past but also toward the future and toward the saving power of the Risen Lord even now (Acts of the Apostles 2:17-21; 3:18-21).

The Pauline Literature

For Paul justification is achieved through faith and Baptism. The connection between justice and faith was taken over by Paul from Genesis 15:6 ("Abraham believed God, and it was credited to him as justice"—Romans 4:3). Faith, then, is the key to reconciliation with God and liberation from sin. One must simply confess one's own helplessness and make oneself open to divine grace (Ephesians 2:8-9). Faith is the principle of life for the righteous (Romans 1:17; Galatians 3:11), and, in conjunction with Baptism, effects a new creation (2 Corinthians 5:17; Philippians 3:9-10). The central object of faith is Christ (Galatians 2:20), but for Paul it is not only a matter of faith in Christ but more especially of faith in the preached word (Romans 10:8). Indeed, faith comes through preaching (Romans 10:13-15).

Paul summarizes the content of the preaching in various ways. Essentially the preaching proclaims that God was in Christ reconciling the world to himself (2 Corinthians 5:19; Colossians 1:12-20), that Jesus is Lord, and that God has raised him from the dead so that through his resurrection he might communicate new life to those who believe and are baptized: "... if you confess with your lips that Jesus is Lord, and believe in your heart that God raised him from the dead, you will be saved" (Romans 10:9). And this same text indicates that faith is not simply interior but must be expressed and confessed. There is, in fact, a good summary of the confession of faith in 1 Timothy 3:16: "Wonderful, indeed, is the mystery of our faith, as we say in professing it: 'He was manifested in the flesh, vindicated in the Spirit; seen by the angels; preached among the Gentiles, believed in throughout the world, taken up into glory.'" So with Paul, as with the Acts of Apostles, faith looks not only to the past but also to the future (1 Thessalonians 4:14), and even though faith grants a measure of assurance and confidence, it still retains a degree of obscurity (2 Corinthians 5:7).

Faith, according to Paul, is also obedience (Romans 1:5; 16:26), demanding total surrender to Christ. And it is not accomplished in a single act. Faith must grow (2 Corinthians 10:15). So, too, it can become weak and die (1 Thessalonians 3:10; Romans 14:1). And the principle of growth is always *love.* "In Christ Jesus neither circumcision nor the lack of it counts for anything; only faith, which expresses itself through love" (Galatians 5:6). But for Paul only the interior illumination of the Holy Spirit enables us to grasp through faith the mystery of Christ's death and resurrection (1 Corinthians 2:2-16; 12:3; Ephesians 1:17-18; 3:14-17; Colossians 2:2). The believer passes from ignorance of God to the knowledge and love of God through the action of the Spirit (Galatians 4:8-9; Ephesians 4:18; 5:8; 2 Corinthians 4:6). Everything is oriented toward union with God through Christ and in the Holy Spirit (Romans 8:11,19-23,29; 1 Corinthians 6:15-20; 2 Corinthians 5:8; Philippians 1:19-23; 3:19-21; 1 Thessalonians 4:17).

The Johannine Literature

The Johannine theology of faith is basically similar to the Pauline, except that John places greater stress on the knowledge aspect of faith. To believe in Christ is to know him. The object of faith is more explicit in John: that Jesus came from God (John 16:30), that he is the Holy One of God (6:69), that he is the Messiah (11:27). Jesus is the object of faith, and since Jesus is one with the Father, faith in Jesus is faith in the Father (5:19-27; 12:44,49; 14:1,6-11; 16:27-30; 1 John 2:23).

This knowledge, however, is not assimilated independently of the power and presence of the Holy Spirit. Faith is impossible without the interior "attraction" of grace, by which we are taught to know Christ (John 14:15-23; 15:15,26; 16:13), and by which we share in Christ's own filial knowledge of God (John 6:44-46,57). The believer, therefore, already possesses eternal life (John 3:16-17,36; 5:24; 1 John 3:15; 5:12-13), which consists of knowing

Christ (John 17:3) and which tends ultimately to the vision of God (John 17:24,26; 1 John 3:1-2).

What is perhaps unique in the Johannine writings is that faith is placed in the words of Jesus (John 2:22; 5:47; 8:45) as well as in the words of the Apostles or in the apostolic preaching (17:20). In fact, throughout the Fourth Gospel and the First Epistle, the role of the witnesses of faith is emphasized: John the Baptist (1:29-35), God's own witness as guarantor of the faith (1 John 5:7-12), Christ and the Holy Spirit, and even the Christian saints (John 14:12-14). Faith involves the acceptance of the witness, and this, in turn, raises the question of the sign that accompanies the witness. For according to the Johannine presentation, faith arises under the impact of signs (John 1:14; 4:50-54; 8:30; 10:42; 11:45-47; 12:9-11). In the Synoptics, for example, Jesus performs a miracle in response to faith. In John, miracles are employed to evoke faith (17:6-8).

Faith brings life (3:36); unbelief brings condemnation (3:18-20). For John, the greatest tragedy is the sin of unbelief (1:10-11; 16:9). And like Paul, John insists that the work of faith is love of neighbor (1 John 3:23).

Other New Testament Sources

In the Epistle to the Hebrews (especially chapter 11) faith is the solid reality of *hope*, the conviction about the invisible world. It is Jesus who initiates and consummates faith (Hebrews 12:2). One must believe in God, and believe that God creates and rewards the just (11:6). The Letter of James speaks of faith in terms which undeniably are far different from Paul's. It seems that James thought that Paul's views on freedom from the law needed further clarification, if not correction. James insists that faith does not exempt one from all of the obligations of the law. Faith without works is dead. But the works proposed by James are not the works of the law. They are charity to the needy (James 2:15-17), assistance to those in danger (2:25), and so forth. The works of the law mentioned in 2:8-11 are love of one's neighbor and the prohibition of adultery and murder. In the Pastoral Epistles (First and Second Timothy, and Titus), Jude, and the Book of Revelation (Apocalypse), the notion of belief becomes more concrete as the Church

itself gradually develops. Faith is a mystery imparted to Christians
(1 Timothy 3:9) and is something to be preserved (2 Timothy 4:7;
Revelation 14:12).

Patristic Notions of Faith

The term "Fathers of the Church" embraces all ancient Christian
writers down to Gregory the Great (d. 604) or Isidore of Seville
(d. 636) in the West, and John of Damascus (d. 749) in the East.

The earliest of the writers, the Apostolic Fathers, identified
faith with the acceptance of the Christian message or with the
knowledge of God and of Christ. The first step toward a certain
formulation of faith as assent given to revealed truths was made by
St. Justin (d. 165). The believer is one who assents to certain truths
and who knows them as truths. St. Irenaeus (d. ca. 200) spoke more
of the object of faith than of the act itself. For Irenaeus, the
Church proposes the object of faith and the believer accepts it as
true and thus comes to a knowledge of the truth. It was Clement of
Alexandria (d. 215) who referred to faith as a passing from darkness to the light of knowledge, whose object is God revealed to us
in Christ. The knowledge of faith suffices for salvation, but there
is given an even higher form of knowledge (*gnosis*) which one can
achieve through faith. It was the heresy of *Gnosticism* which
distorted this concept of faith as knowledge, making it accessible
only to an elite few.

Later Fathers, such as Origen (d. 254), St. Cyril of Jerusalem
(d. 386), St. Athanasius (d. 373), St. John Chrysostom (d. 407), St.
Cyril of Alexandria (d. 444), St. John of Damascus, and others also
wrote of faith in this vein, as assent to doctrines proposed for our
belief by the Church. None of these Fathers, however, developed
so impressive a theology of faith as St. Augustine (d. 430). For him
the act of faith is essentially the assent given to the revelation (see
especially his *Commentary on St. John's Gospel*). The knowledge
of faith progresses toward the wise understanding of mysteries, but
this knowledge remains obscure in comparison with the fullness of
the Beatific Vision (i.e., the final, unobstructed, unmediated,
"face-to-face" experience of God in heaven, to which Paul refers
in 1 Corinthians 13:12).

The Fathers of the Church insisted that faith involves knowledge and assent, and they were always clear about the authority underlying both. From the beginning they employed the simple biblical formula, "Believe in God." Thus, God is the motive or ground of belief, according to the writings of Irenaeus, Clement of Alexandria, Ambrose (d. 397), John Chrysostom, Cyprian (d. 549), and others. Augustine taught that faith cannot be supported by internal evidence. Faith is not the product of reasoning but is founded upon the authority of a witness. Finally, the divine testimony is always worthy of faith because God is infallibly all-knowing and truthful.

The object of such faith is the mystery of Christ. For Augustine the whole mystery proclaimed by Sacred Scripture is the mystery of Christ. All of revelation has its central unity in Christ, to whom it is ordered and in whom it is consummated once and for all.

But faith is not something we merit. According to Augustine, it is always a free gift of God. By the same token, we are free to accept or reject it. This was the consensus of theological opinion among the Fathers at least until the outbreak of the semi-Pelagian controversy in the fifth century. *Semi-Pelagianism*, a variation of Pelagianism, to which we shall refer again in chapter 5, held that grace is not necessary for the beginning of faith (*initium fidei*). Only after we have freely chosen to pursue a life of faith does the grace of God enter in to support our journey to salvation. Against this heresy Augustine insisted on the complete gratuity of the entire process of justification and salvation. The initial act of faith which is the foundation of the whole supernatural life and the beginning of justification is itself a free gift of God and something totally unmerited by us.

The heart of the Augustinian position is this: We are freely saved, but salvation is ultimately the effect of God's own goodness and mercy (*hesed*); therefore, salvation is gratuitous and so is the beginning of salvation, which is faith. Subsequent patristic writings, influenced so much by Augustine's works, concentrated their attention on such key New Testament texts as John 6:44-46,65 ("No one can come to me unless the Father who sent me draws him. . .") and Ephesians 2:8 (". . . salvation is yours through faith. This is not your own doing, it is God's gift. . .").

But even if faith is entirely the gift of God, the Fathers taught that it also involved some element of human cooperation. Accordingly, one can only believe if there seems to be some basis or reason for believing. Some of the earliest Fathers (e.g., Justin) tried to show the truth of the Christian message by pointing out the various ways in which Christ fulfilled the prophecies of the Old Testament. The Greek Fathers (Origen, Basil, d. 379, John Chrysostom, and others) and Latin Fathers (Ambrose, Jerome, d. 420, and especially Augustine) pointed as well to miracles and prophecies. It is important to note, however, that these Fathers—and Augustine in particular—were not arguing that one could establish the credibility of faith on the basis of reason or evidence. On the contrary, for Augustine the internal truth of the mysteries of faith can never be demonstrated. But the availability of such signs as miracles and prophecies does show that our faith is not without some support and credibility, even within the created and visible order of reality.

Second Council of Orange (529)

This is the first of many references in this book to official teachings of the Catholic Church, whether of councils or of popes. Unlike many seminary and college textbooks in use before and even during the Second Vatican Council, this book will present conciliar and papal teaching within the historical context in which it was formulated and promulgated. We readily acknowledge today that we can no longer adopt a fundamentalistic approach to the interpretation of Sacred Scripture by reading the sacred texts apart from their setting within the particular biblical book and the particular situation in which and for which they were written (the so-called *Sitz im Leben*, "situation in life")—and this is clear from such official documents as Pope Pius XII's 1943 encyclical *Divino Afflante Spiritu*, the 1964 Instruction of the Pontifical Biblical Commission, and the 1965 *Dogmatic Constitution on Divine Revelation* of Vatican II. Neither, then, can we adopt what has been called a "non-historical orthodoxy" in our approach to the official texts of Church documents.

The Second Council of Orange, a local council held in southern France and acting under the direct influence of Augustine's theology, condemned semi-Pelagianism. Two year later Pope Boniface II (d. 532) confirmed the council's decision. "He is an adversary of the apostolic teaching," the central decree reads, "who says that the increase of faith as well as the beginning of faith and the very desire of faith. . .inheres in us naturally and not by a gift of grace" (the council cites Philippians 1:6,29 and Ephesians 2:8).

This may be one of the most important, and least known, teachings of the Catholic Church, one more frequently acknowledged in the breach than in the observance. Through much of our own century Catholic *apologetics* (i.e., the systematic attempt to show the reasonableness of faith and to refute, at the same time, the principal objections raised against Christian belief) has proceeded on the unstated assumption that reason alone can show the truth of Christian faith, and that grace is necessary only to make such reasoned "faith" a saving faith. The argument was constructed in this way: (1) The Bible is a historical document. Those who are purported to be its authors can be shown to be such. The events and persons about whom they write can be shown to be real events and persons, on the basis of independent historical evidence. (2) The Bible tells the story of Jesus Christ, who claimed to be divine and who proved his claim by his miracles and especially by the primary miracle of the resurrection. (3) The Bible also tells how Jesus founded a Church and invested it with full authority to teach, rule, and sanctify. (4) The Catholic Church alone can trace its history back to the time of the apostles and to the Lord himself. *Therefore . . .*

If the truth of Catholic faith is so clear, why do so many continue to reject it or remain indifferent to it? Because (so the argument goes) they are either too lazy to examine the evidence fully and carefully, or because, having the evidence and recognizing its truth, they find it too difficult to change their lives in conformity with the truth they now perceive.

It is as if the non-believer were completely free, even without God's grace, to begin the process of examining the evidence and then to accept or reject it. But the Second Council of Orange (and Augustine before that) insisted that even the beginning of faith (*initium fidei*) is a gift of God. Thus, God calls some, but apparently not all, to Christian faith. On the other hand, God calls all to salvation (1 Timothy 2:1-6, the classical text). But salvation is impossible without faith (a Pauline teaching later officially ratified by the Council of Trent in the sixteenth century). Therefore, there must be saving faith that is not explicitly centered on Christ. But even that faith must be a free gift of God. Accordingly, God calls some people to salvation through communities, institutions, and agencies other than the Church. We shall return to this point in our consideration of Christ and the Church in Parts III and IV.

St. Thomas Aquinas

No theologian in the entire history of the Church has had such a decisive impact on Catholic thought and the shaping of the Catholic tradition as St. Thomas Aquinas (d. 1274). His *Summa Theologica* is the most comprehensive synthesis (that is what the word *summa* means) of the biblical, patristic, and medieval understandings of the Christian faith, and has guided, for good or for ill, the interpretation and articulation of that faith ever since, recent fluctuations in its "popularity" notwithstanding. Aquinas was accorded special theological status by Pope Leo XIII's (d. 1903) encyclical *Aeterni Patris* (1879).

For Aquinas the act of faith is essentially an act of the intellect, but not just any act of the intellect. It is *thinking with assent*. What do we believe? God. Why do we believe? On the authority of God revealing. For what purpose do we believe? That we might be united forever with God in the Kingdom of heaven (*Summa Theologica*, II-II, qq. 1-7).

Our grasp of God, however, is never the end-product of scientific reasoning and demonstration. Whatever arguments we employ either show only that faith is at least not impossible or absurd, or else they are arguments which are themselves drawn from sources (especially Sacred Scripture) whose divine authority is, in turn, accepted on faith.

Thus, even though Aquinas emphasized the intellectual dimension of faith, he never lost sight of faith's close relationship with hope and charity, and therefore with the will as well as the intellect. Faith is directed to the good as well as to the true: "Faith is the substance of things to be hoped for" (Hebrews 11:1). Without hope, faith has no direction or goal. Without charity, faith is simply dead (II-II, q. 4).

For Aquinas, faith is essentially and absolutely supernatural. Its source is God; its motive is God; its goal is God. If there are certain external signs of the truth of faith (e.g., miracles and prophecies), they are without force in the absence of the internal cause of belief, which is the Holy Spirit (II-II, q. 6). Unless the grace of the Spirit is present, elevating the intellect above its own limited natural capacities, we cannot truly believe in God.

Council of Trent (1545-1563)

Just as Augustine influenced the decrees of the Second Council of Orange, so did Aquinas influence those of Trent, a major ecumenical council held in northern Italy in the immediate aftermath of the Protestant Reformation and for the purpose of confronting, however belatedly, the crisis created by the Reformation.

The Council of Trent's decrees on faith were formulated against the Protestant, and especially Lutheran, notion of trusting faith (*fides fiducialis*). Recently, Catholic theologians such as Karl Rahner and Hans Küng have argued that the differences between Trent and the Reformers on this question were more verbal than substantive, but they were not perceived that way at the time, nor for centuries thereafter.

The council's teachings on faith are to be found in the *Decree on Justification* which was formulated during one of the most important sessions of the council, the sixth, which lasted from June 21, 1546, until January 13, 1547. It described justification as "a passing from the state in which man is born a son of the first Adam, to the state of grace and adoption as sons of God through the second Adam, Jesus Christ our Savior." The process of justification begins with God's grace through Jesus Christ. This call to justification is completely unmerited. We remain free to reject it, but apart from divine grace we could not take one step toward justification and salvation (a clear echo of the teaching of the Second Council of Orange).

Trent also insisted on the objective content of faith. Faith is not exclusively fiducial, as Luther implied, but includes also some assent to revealed truths. Furthermore, in the spirit of the Epistle of James, faith without works is dead. Faith is not a saving faith apart from hope and charity.

Finally, Trent clarified the meaning of the statement: The sinner is gratuitously justified by faith. "We may be said to be justified freely, in the sense that nothing that precedes justification, neither faith nor works, merits the grace of justification; . . . otherwise . . . grace is no longer grace."

In summary: Without furnishing a formal definition of faith, the Council of Trent taught that faith is *strictly supernatural* and at the same time a *free* act; taught that faith is *necessary for justification and salvation*, and not simply a matter of intellectual acceptance of truths; and taught that faith *can coexist with sin*, contrary to the position of some sixteenth-century Protestants.

First Vatican Council (1869-1870)

Whereas Protestantism had posed the primary challenge at Trent, it was *Rationalism* (the belief that nothing can be accepted as true unless reason can perceive it to be true) and, to a lesser extent, *Fideism* (the belief that reason is of no value at all in the understanding of Christian truth), and *Traditionalism* (the belief that one must rely upon faith alone as communicated in the traditions of the Church) which provided the stimulus for Vatican I's additional official teachings on this question.

On April 24, 1870, Vatican I promulgated its doctrine on faith in the Dogmatic Constitution *Dei Filius* (the first two Latin words of the document, which mean literally "the Son of God"). *Against Rationalism*, the council taught that our belief in revealed truth is "not because its intrinsic truth is seen with the light of reason, but because of the authority of God who reveals them," and that saving faith is impossible without "the enlightenment and inspiration of the Holy Spirit. . . ." *Against Fideism and*

Traditionalism, the council taught that the "submission of faith" must be "consonant with reason" and that that is why God provided various signs, especially miracles and prophecies, whereby the revelation itself might be recognized as being of divine origin. The assent of faith, therefore, is "by no means a blind impulse."

Beyond that, the council also widened the Scholastic notion of faith, which focused so much on its intellectual aspect. Vatican I spoke of the act of faith as one by which we offer ourselves to God in "free obedience." The council also repeated the teaching of Trent on the essential link between faith and justification and on the priority of faith in the supernatural order.

The force of the council's arguments, therefore, was more strongly placed against Rationalism than against Fideism—so much so, in fact, that one bishop suggested that the council add a note to canon 6 to the effect that the council did not intend to deter the faithful from at least examining the motives of credibility. It is perhaps all the more surprising that Catholic apologetics after Vatican I continued on a somewhat rationalistic course, leaving Catholics with the impression that good arguments make conversion to the Church inevitable, except for those persons too indifferent to consider them or too perverse to accept their moral consequences. Nothing could be farther from the teaching of Vatican I, or indeed of the entire Catholic tradition.

Second Vatican Council (1962-1965)

Despite what is occasionally said uncritically and without historical perspective, the Second Vatican Council did not revolutionize or set aside the Catholic tradition as we knew it before 1962. Vatican II's teaching on faith, for example, is entirely consistent with the record we have been tracing and examining thus far. Faith is essentially supernatural: ". . . the grace of God and the interior help of the Holy Spirit must precede and assist . . ." (*Dogmatic Constitution on Divine Revelation*, n. 5). It requires assent to revealed truth but also a giving of oneself to God as well in an "obedience of faith." Its supernatural character notwithstanding, there are signs and wonders which can lead us to faith under the impulse always of divine grace.

Nevertheless, there are at least two new emphases in Vatican II's teaching on faith. Both were prompted by the modern discovery of, and appreciation for, pluralism. *First*, there is a recognition that the freedom of the act of faith means just that. Faith is a free gift of God, and ours is a free response to that gift. Neither God's hand nor ours can be forced. In a world of increasingly diverse religious and non-religious convictions, we must learn to respect the consciences and the motives of those who do not, or cannot, accept Christian faith (*Declaration on Religious Freedom*, n. 2). *No one is to be penalized, socially or politically, for his or her convictions about religious matters.*

The *second* new emphasis is similar to the first. Just as the Church has grown to respect diversity in the human community at large, so has it grown to respect diversity within the Body of Christ itself. The *Dogmatic Constitution on the Church* (n. 15) and the *Decree on Ecumenism* (n. 3) both acknowledge that *Christian faith exists outside the Catholic Church*, that it is a justifying faith, and that it relates one not only to Christ but to the Church as well.

Faith: A Synthesis

Earlier in the chapter we were satisfied, "for the moment," to define faith as personal knowledge of God, and Christian faith as personal knowledge of God in Christ. In the light of the preceding historical and theological discussion, it is clear that faith is indeed personal knowledge of God, but there is much more to it than that.

1.   Although faith is personal knowledge of God, that knowledge is always achieved and activated within a given community of faith, whether the Church as we know it or some other religious body, and beyond that within the whole human family.

2.   This knowledge of God is not merely knowledge in the cognitive or intellectual sense, although it *is* that, too. It is a knowledge which implies trust and a total commitment of the self to God, a commitment of heart as well as of mind.

3.   Faith is not just the knowledge of God in general, but the knowledge of God which comes through the reception and acceptance of God's word. In the Christian sense, faith is the acceptance

of God's Word-made-flesh in Jesus Christ, and then of the preaching of that Word by the Apostles and the Church.

4. The acceptance of God's word in Christ and in the Church demands not only intellectual assent but also obedience—obedience to the Commandments and to the New Law of the Gospel, which calls us to work for social and political liberation as well as personal transformation of the individual.

5. If there is to be genuine obedience, there must be some acknowledgement of past failures, a conversion (*metanoia*, or change of mind), and repentance.

6. Faith always remains free. The "evidence" for faith is never overwhelming. There are signs and witnesses. But these are always external and never finally persuasive in themselves. The only motive of faith that ultimately counts is internal: the presence of the Holy Spirit.

7. On the other hand, faith and reason are not absolutely separate. Even if one does not "reason to" faith, faith must always be "consonant with reason." Thus, St. Paul urges us to worship God "in a way that is worthy of thinking beings" (Romans 12:1). A fuller statement of this relationship will be developed in chapter 5, where the problem of nature and grace is taken up.

8. Faith is a matter of the highest human importance, because without it we cannot be justified or saved. But since God wishes the salvation of all persons, faith must be available in principle even to those outside the Church.

THEOLOGY
Theology and Faith

There can be no theology without faith. By definition, theology is "faith seeking understanding" (Anselm). It is, as we defined it earlier in this chapter, "the interpretation of one's faith." Theology is not the interpretation of someone else's faith, but of one's own, or of one's own community of faith. It is possible, in other words, to subject the Bible to very careful literary scrutiny and to come to the highest appreciation of its style, content, and message, without at the same time accepting it as the very Word of God. So, too, it is possible to write and speak of Jesus of Nazareth in the most admiring terms without at the same time accepting him as Lord and Savior, the very Son of God in our midst. None of this is theology.

Theology is not simply talk *about* God, or *about* Christ, or *about* the Bible, or even *about* faith. Theology happens only when someone is trying, in a more or less systematic and critical manner, to come to a better, clearer, more refined understanding of his or her own faith *in* God and *in* Christ, as it has become available to us *in* the Bible, *in* the Church, or wherever else.

When "theology" is done without faith, it is really a *philosophy of religion*. The theologian reflects on his or her own faith-commitment; the philosopher of religion reflects on the faith-commitment of others. The injunction of Augustine, *"Crede ut intelligas"* ("Believe that you might understand") makes no sense to the non-believer. We do not go to theology for our faith. Theology is there to give us a greater understanding of what we already believe.

Theology and Belief

On the other hand, theology has an important critical function to perform. It does not simply take what is believed and try to put the best face possible on it. Theology has the responsibility of measuring what is believed against established *criteria*.

1. Is the belief rooted in, or at least consistent with, the Bible?

2. Has the belief been expressed and defended, at least in substance, by the Fathers and doctors of the Church?

3. Has the Church officially proposed this belief in council or through some other magisterial forum?

4. Conversely, has the official Church ever rejected this belief in whole or in part, indirectly or by implication?

5. Is the belief consistent with the official teachings of the Church on other related matters of faith?

6. Is the belief consistent with the present consensus of theologians on this or related matters of faith?

7. Is the belief consistent with scientific knowledge?

8. Is the belief consistent with our corporate experience of faith?

What happens, however, when those beliefs become official? Theology retains its critical function even in the face of official beliefs, such as doctrines and dogmas, not to mention disciplinary decrees of Vatican congregations. Theology still must ask if the official belief is consistent with the Bible, the teaching of the Fathers and doctors of the Church, previous official pronounce-ments, other recent or contemporary official pronouncements, the present consensus of theologians, the findings of other sciences, and finally the experience of Christians themselves.

This critical process occurs not only after a belief has been made official, but also and always before. *The very formulation of a doctrine is a work of theology.* Before a belief is officially adopted and proposed for wider acceptance in the Church, a decision has to be made about its truth and the appropriateness of commending it to the larger community at this time and in this manner. The decision about its truth cannot be made apart from the theological criteria outlined above. Insofar as a particular belief is elevated to the level of a doctrine, it is regarded as consistent with the biblical message, the writings of the Fathers and doctors of the Church, and other ecclesiastical pronouncements of past and present, and it presumably represents the best fruits of contemporary theology and related sciences. Finally, it is not only consistent with the present experiences of Christians, but its promulgation will in fact enhance and enrich that experience.

Accordingly, the question is not *whether* theology will exer-cise a critical function in the formulation and subsequent reflec-tion upon doctrine, but rather *which* theology will. Sometimes it is not clear for decades, even centuries, if the Church has employed the best theology in its doctrinal pronouncements.

Origin and Development of Theology

Self-Conscious Faith in God

Theology is as old as self-conscious faith in God. As soon as human beings began thinking about the ultimate meaning of life, about their relationship to the whole cosmos, about the direction of history (although the notion of "history" as such is a relatively modern development), about the experience of the holy and the sacred, they were beginning to do theology. Theology precedes not only Christianity but even Judaism as well.

The Apostles

Christian theology begins with the Apostles. It developed for two reasons: (1) because the Apostles had to reconcile for themselves the message of Jesus Christ with their own religious experience as Jews; and (2) because the Apostles had to preach the "Good News" that Jesus had bequeathed to them, and this meant interpreting and translating the Gospel for diverse communities and cultures.

Why are there, for example, *four* Gospels in the New Testament? If the Gospels are nothing more than objective accounts of what Jesus said and did, why the need for four? Why not only one? The answer is that the Gospels are more than historical narratives or biographies. They are, first and foremost, *testimonies of faith*: the faith of the evangelist himself and the faith of the community to which he belonged. Each Gospel is an interpretation of the significance of Jesus Christ, directed to different audiences (e.g., Luke's is Gentile, Matthew's is Jewish). As such, each is a work of *theology*. Indeed, the whole of the New Testament is theological to one degree or another.

But *New Testament theology* is more *catechetical* than speculative (with the obvious exceptions of the Fourth Gospel and some of the Pauline letters). Theology became more deliberately *systematic* as the first serious intellectual challenges were raised against Christian faith. There developed in the second and third centuries an *apologetical* theology. The Apologists (e.g., Justin, Clement of Alexandria, Origen, Irenaeus) tried to speak to the cultured in their own language. Technical theological terms were created. Specific theological problems were defined. In the struggle against Gnosticism, for example, the continuity between Old Testament and New Testament had to be established and clarified. In the controversy over the necessity of rebaptizing those who had left the Church and later returned, a theology of the Church (ecclesiology) began to take shape. The need to distinguish inspired from noninspired literature forced the question of the canon of Sacred Scripture ("canon" = the list of books accepted by the Church as inspired and, therefore, as part of the Bible).

Neo-Platonism; Roman Juridical Thought

With the Edict of Constantine in 313 the Church acquired legal status, and its theology began to show the marks of the Church's new situation: It was strongly influenced by neo-Platonism, the last of the great Graeco-Roman philosophies, and by Roman juridical thought. Given this combination, reality was increasingly perceived in hierarchical terms, with God as the remote, other-worldly, "supreme Being." It was within this intellectual framework that some of the great theological issues of the times were faced: the inner life of the Trinity, the divine-human status of Christ, and the necessity and effects of grace. Terms and concepts taken over from contemporary Greek culture were employed against *Arianism* in the formulation of the doctrine that in Christ there is one divine person (*hypostasis*), with two natures (*physis*), the one human and the other divine. Those natures are united, without confusion or division, in the one divine person, i.e., hypostatically. (Arianism had taught that Christ was more than a man but less than God.) Similar concepts were applied to the Trinity: circumincession, procession, generation, spiration. And these, in turn, were incorporated into official teachings and creeds of the Church of the fifth century: the *Council of Chalcedon* (451) and the *Athanasian Creed*.

Monasteries

As circumstances changed, so, too, did the character of Catholic theology. With the dissolution of the Roman Empire in 476 and the breakdown of traditional social and political institutions, intellectual and cultural leadership within the Church passed from the great bishop-theologians (Augustine, Athanasius, Basil, Gregory of Nyssa, d. 394, Gregory Nazianzen, d. 390) to the monasteries and to such monastic theologians as Anselm of Canterbury, who began as an abbot and later became an archbishop,

Bernard of Clairvaux (d. 1153), Hugh of St. Victor (d. 1141), Bonaventure (d. 1274), and others. Theology assumed a *devotional* character consistent with its new monastic environment.

Universities

Indeed, those who had been formed in the spiritual theology of the monasteries found it most difficult to accept, much less adapt to, the new theology coming out of the universities, as represented by Albert the Great, Thomas Aquinas, and their intellectual disciples who were known as the Schoolmen, or Scholastics (thus, the term *Scholasticism*). It was Anselm who provided the bridge between the two approaches: the one emphasizing the sufficiency of faith as expressed in Sacred Scripture, and the other insisting on the need for critical reflection on that faith, using not only Sacred Scripture, but the writings of the Fathers, theologians, and philosophers, even non-Christian philosophers such as Aristotle. Theology, Anselm argued, is "faith seeking understanding."

Although there were clear differences among the Schoolmen, one could also distinguish a certain common mentality in their approach to theology. All agreed on the power of reason to come to some basic, albeit imperfect, understanding of the mysteries of faith and to construct some overarching synthesis of the whole Christian doctrinal system (thus, Thomas' own *Summa Theologica*). The pessimism of Augustinianism, with its emphasis on the depravity of the human condition and the corresponding weakness of human powers, such as reason, gave way to a new intellectual optimism. Things were seen to have natures of their own which do not consist simply of their reference to God. We come to a knowledge of God and of our faith, therefore, not only through direct spiritual illumination but more usually through our sense experience of the visible and the concrete. To this end we are aided by the use of *analogy*, a way of explaining the meaning of one reality by showing its similarity to another (e.g., God is not a "father" in the strict sense of the word, but God's relationship to us is *like* that of a father to his children). But the Schoolmen also agreed on the authority of the Bible as a kind of textbook from which proofs could legitimately and necessarily be drawn. Reason, in other words, was not without guides and limits.

The Scholastic position was embraced neither immediately nor universally. Resistance continued from those still suspicious of the powers of reason (Bonaventure, in particular). Parallel approaches were also developed, e.g., by John Duns Scotus (d. 1308). And inevitably others took the new emphasis on reason to apparent extremes, as may have been the case with Nominalism, which tended to reduce theology to a kind of word-game. The theologian is a manipulator of terms and concepts, none of which can lead us to, much less put us in touch with, the reality of God. The movement, identified in large part with William of Ockham (d. 1347), is regarded as the forerunner of such modern philosophical schools as Logical Positivism, which also denies the possibility of getting beyond words to the reality of things in themselves.

Scholastic theology had certain inherent *weaknesses* as well as strengths. *First*, it relied too heavily on reason and logic. The Bible and the writings of the Fathers very often took second place to Aristotle and Scholastic colleagues. *Secondly*, theological questions were regularly studied apart from their historical context. The Bible was read not, as we insist today, according to its original setting and literary meaning, but rather as if it were primarily a collection of independent sayings or principles which could be used independently of one another to support particular theological and even philosophical arguments. *Thirdly*, Scholastic theology tended to invent distinctions and sub-distinctions unnecessarily ("How many angels can dance on the head of a pin?" is a caricature, of course, but it suggests the kind of useless subtlety that occasionally emerged at the time). *Finally*, Scholastic theology too quickly constructed systems of thought and then elevated these systems to the status of self-contained authorities. Theology became for many a matter of competition between or among systems.

Seminaries; Religious Orders

As controversy followed controversy and subtlety piled upon subtlety, the role of the universities as centers of theological thought declined, and they were replaced by the seminaries and the schools of religious orders. Manuals of theology bore the words "dogmatic-scholastic" in their title, thus expressing the intention to wed the positive, historical element with the speculative, rational element. The format and structure of these new seminary textbooks was the same as of those used by future priests in Catholic seminaries up to, and in some cases beyond, the Second Vatican Council. First, the thesis was given (e.g., "The Church is the Body of Christ"). This was followed by the *status quaestionis* ("state of the question"), in which various current opinions on the thesis were presented. Next came the proofs: from the Bible, the Fathers and doctors of the Church, and the teachings of the Church. There were additional arguments of much less weight, drawn from theological reason and from "convenience" (e.g., "It is *fitting* that God should have done such-and-such; but God is all powerful and *could have done* such-and-such; therefore, God *did* such-and-such.") The defense of the thesis concluded with various corollaries, or *scholia*, which applied the thesis to some related minor questions.

Episcopal theology of the earliest Christian centuries had been concerned with a defense of the faith against non-believers and heretics; *monastic* theology, with its spiritual and devotional implications; and *university* theology, with giving the whole body of Christian faith some coherent, logical unity and structure. *Seminary* theology, on the other hand, was concerned primarily with preparing future priests for the service of the Church as preachers, teachers, and confessors. From the end of the seventeenth century until the first half of the twentieth century, Catholic theology focused its attention on questions that would likely confront the priest in the course of his ministry. And because the priest is an official of the Church, it was important that he should have access to, and communicate, the official teaching of the Church rather than his own private opinions. Accordingly, the emphasis was always on the authoritative sources by which a given thesis was shown to be true. Reverence for the Bible notwithstanding, the primary authority was always the teaching of the official Church, i.e., papal statements, conciliar declarations, and Vatican decrees.

Möhler, Newman, Scheeben

The seeds of yet another major theological transformation (indeed, the one in which we now find ourselves) were already being sown in the late eighteenth and nineteenth centuries. The outstanding theologian of this period was Johann Adam Möhler (d. 1838), who recovered a sense of theological development, a sense of history, and a sense of viewing the Christian message as an organic whole rather than as a collection of theses. He rejected the rationalistic spirit of much contemporary Catholic thought and reunited dogmatic and moral theology. In 1879 Pope Leo XIII's encyclical *Aeterni Patris* sounded the call to reconnect Catholic theology with its own best tradition: Thomas Aquinas in particular, but also Augustine, Bonaventure, and others. Unfortunately, much of the restoration assumed a diffident, defensive, and frequently hostile attitude to the new intellectual trends of its own time. But the idea of genuine historical development continued to gain strength. Cardinal John Henry Newman (d. 1890) constructed his own celebrated theory of doctrinal development, linking it with the faith of the community itself down through the centuries. Another major contributor to the new historical and wholistic approach to Catholic faith was Matthias Scheeben (d. 1888).

Modernist Crisis

The Modernist Crisis of the late nineteenth and early twentieth centuries, however, interrupted the course of this new historical and integrated approach to Catholic theology. From today's perspective the interruption was only temporary, but "temporary" meant that it spanned the entire theological careers of many twentieth-century scholars and the entire intellectual formation period of the overwhelming majority of priests ordained in this century. Like most movements and systems in the history of the Church, Modernism is more nuanced and more complex than first appears, either to its devoted defenders or to its tenacious critics. One might suggest, at the risk of oversimplification, that the Modernists (Alfred Loisy, d. 1940, and others) took the new nineteenth-century emphasis on history and opposition to abstractionism too far to the left. Like the Nominalism of the post-Scholastic era, Modernism held that there can be no real continuity between dogmas and the reality they presume to describe. Dogmas have a negative function at best. They warn against false notions. They are above all practical. A dogma is a rule of conduct more than a rule of truth. Thus, to say that "Jesus is risen" means that we must regard him as we would have done before his death, or as we would a contemporary.

It is fair to say that the Modernists, in their commendable effort to bring some historical realism to the interpretation of Christian faith, adopted too uncritically certain common notions of history abroad during the nineteenth century, along with that century's "dogmatic" and ideological rejection of values (including the supernatural) that cannot readily be observed and tested apart from a study of concrete persons and events. Modernism, therefore, began, as all heresies do, with a partial truth and inflated it into a comprehensive, and therefore radically flawed, system of thought which denied the capacity of the human mind to grasp and express the supernatural in ways that are open to objective examination, in accord with objective criteria of truth and appropriateness.

Because it was so vehemently condemned by Pope Pius X (d. 1914) in his encyclical *Pascendi* (1907) and then made the subject of a negative oath that every future priest, bishop, and professor of religious sciences had to take from 1910 until 1967, Modernism stalled the progress which Catholic theology had been making under the impact of such scholars as Möhler, Scheeben, and Newman. It would not be until the Second Vatican Council (1962-1965) that Catholic theologians would feel free once again to depart from the traditional textbook approach and study theological questions in their wider historical and even ecumenical contexts. In the meantime, there were several fits and starts.

Twentieth-Century Renewal

Even as the atmosphere in all Catholic seminaries and religious houses remained tense and their intellectual spirit exceedingly cautious, there were all the while signs of extraordinary renewal:

the biblical work of Marie-Joseph LaGrange (d. 1938), later endorsed, for all practical purposes, by Pope Pius XII's encyclical on biblical studies, *Divino Afflante Spiritu* (1943); the ecumenical and ecclesiological work of Yves Congar, later confirmed by Vatican II's *Dogmatic Constitution on the Church* and its *Decree on Ecumenism*; and the philosophical and systematic work of Karl Rahner, recognized generally today as this century's leading Catholic theologian.

Each of these scholars and many others had been condemned, or at least severely restricted, at some point in their careers by Vatican authorities who appealed to guidelines laid down in Pope Pius XII's encyclical *Humani Generis* (1950). This document rejected what it called "the new theology" as it had been developing on the Continent just after the Second World War. This "new theology" was linked with Modernism because of its presumed downplaying of the supernatural order and of the teaching authority of the official Church. But a few of the practitioners of the "new theology," unlike their putative predecessors in the Modernist movement, have come to enjoy the approval even of the official Church itself. They served as experts (*periti*) at the Second Vatican Council, or as members of the new Theological Commission established by Pope Paul VI (d. 1978), and some continue to fill important and influential positions in seminaries and universities, on editorial boards of theological journals, and as consultants to diocesan, regional, national, and even international bodies.

Divisions of Theology

Faith-Community

There are different kinds of theology. The interpretation of faith differs on the basis of the faith-community in which, and for which, that interpretation occurs. Thus, there is Christian theology, and within that, Catholic theology, Protestant theology, Anglican theology, Orthodox theology, and so forth. Then, of course, there are Jewish theology, Moslem theology, and as many other kinds of theology as there are religions. Every self-conscious attempt to come to a better understanding of what one believes about God, about the ultimate meaning of life, about our hopes for the future, and so forth, is a work of theology at one level or another.

Content

There are differences even *within* Christian and Catholic theology. Theology differs according to content. There is *dogmatic theology*, which interprets faith as it has been expressed in official teachings of the Church (since not every official teaching is a dogma, this theology should more accurately be called *doctrinal* rather than dogmatic). There is *moral theology*, which interprets the impact of faith on our attitudes, motives, values, and behavior. The division between doctrinal and moral theology is not a happy one. The latter was separated from the former in the sixteenth century for the convenience of priest-confessors, as we shall see in chapter 25.

There is also *spiritual* or *ascetical theology*, which focuses on the inner transformation effected by the presence of faith and grace in the human mind and heart. There is *pastoral theology*, which seeks to understand the implications of faith for the actual situation of the Church, specifically for preaching, ministry of various kinds, counseling, and the like. There is *liturgical theology*, which interprets the meaning of faith as expressed in the rituals and devotions of the Church. And some have spoken recently of a *structural theology*, which seeks to understand the faith in its various institutional expressions within the Church, thus combining the insights of the Church's canon law with its theological self-understanding, or ecclesiology.

Methods

Catholic theology also differs according to its various methods. There is *positive* or *historical theology*, which seeks to understand and interpret the faith as that faith has been articulated already in some principal historical source, such as the Bible, the writings of the Fathers and doctors of the Church, the ecumenical councils, or the great theological controversies of past centuries. *Biblical theology*, therefore, is a subdivision of historical theology. It attempts to come to an understanding of the faith as expressed and communicated in the pages of Sacred Scripture. Until the twelfth century Catholic theology was, for the most part, biblical theology. *Patristic theology*, too, is a kind of historical theology. It attempts the same task as biblical theology, but in reference to the writings of the Fathers of the Church rather than the Bible. *Doctrinal theology* can also be viewed as a subdivision of historical theology insofar as the quest for understanding is limited to an examination of official teachings of the Church.

On the other hand, theology may be *speculative* rather than historical; such theology seeks an understanding of the faith in light of the best of contemporary knowledge and experience and without limiting the historical inquiry to any given source, such as the Bible or doctrines.

Finally, there is *systematic theology*, which embraces every kind of theology mentioned thus far. It is comprehensive in its method. It seeks to understand and articulate the Christian whole by examining each of its parts in relation to one another and to the whole. Anglican theologian John Macquarrie has called it a work of "architectonic reason." Some schools of theology refer to it as *constructive theology*. This book, in fact, is an attempt at a systematic theology.

Catholics have often confused *doctrinal* or *dogmatic theology* with the whole of Christian theology, as if theology were always and only our critical (and sometimes not so critical) reflection on, explanation, and defense of the official teachings of the Church. Protestants, on the other hand, have sometimes confused *biblical theology* with the whole of Christian theology, as if theology were always and only our critical (and sometimes not so critical) reflection on the biblical message.

But if all theology were biblical theology, then there could not have been any theology at all before the Bible was written. But if there were no theology before the Bible, how did the Bible get written? The very process by which the Bible came into being is itself a theological process. For the same reason, if all theology were doctrinal or dogmatic, so that there can be no real theology without doctrines to understand, explain, and defend, how could there have been any theology at all before the first doctrinal pronouncement was issued? And if there was no theology before doctrine, how did doctrine even begin to exist? For doctrines are beliefs that have received official approval. And beliefs, in turn, are expressions of faith. But expressions of faith emerge from a process known as theology, which is the interpretation of faith.

Perspective

One final division: Theology may also be distinguished according to its perspective. These various perspectives, however, are not scientific divisions, as are those based on content or method. But it may be helpful to the reader to be advised of the differences among theologies as they are likely to be reported in the press and other popular media. *Liberal theology* (with the capital *L*) is not the same as *liberal theology* (with the lower-case *l*). The former refers to a specific movement in Protestant theology, beginning in the nineteenth century and continuing, with considerably diminished force, to the present. Like Catholic Modernism, Protestant Liberal theology "reduces" the supernatural content of faith to its least common denominator and, for all practical purposes, eliminates that supernatural content entirely from consideration. Lower-case liberal theology refers to a progressive *style* of theology. The adjective *liberal* is entirely relative in its meaning. Thus, it may be regarded as "liberal" to favor the ordination of women. Others may consider support for the ordination of *anyone* as "reactionary."

There is also *orthodox theology* and *conservative theology*. Orthodox theology is the interpretation of faith which confines the process of interpretation to sources generated by the Church itself: the Bible, or the Fathers and doctors of the Church, or doctrinal pronouncements and creeds. Orthodox theology may also be known as *confessional theology* (more of a Protestant term, since it refers to the confessions of faith adopted by the Church not only outside but also inside the Protestant Reformation). Conservative theology, on the other hand, refers to a *style* of doing theology, a style that is cautious in the face of proposed change. Again, it is a highly relative term. There are also variations on the orthodox theme. Within Protestantism there is *neo-orthodoxy*, associated with the names of Karl Barth (d. 1968) and Reinhold Niebuhr (d. 1971), which challenged Liberalism to reconnect itself with the long-standing themes of Reformation thought on the sinfulness of humankind and the need for the redemptive grace of God.

Other approaches to theology include *radical theology*, which usually refers to the "death-of-God" movement of the mid-1960s; *secular theology*, another mid-1960s movement, which emphasized the this-worldly character of Christian existence and the Church's abiding responsibility to transform the world; *liberation theology* (whether Latin American, black, or feminist), which stresses the motif of liberation from economic, racial, and cultural oppression and reinterprets the sources of Christianity in accordance with that motif; *political theology*, which insists on the connection between theory and practice and, therefore, suggests that every statement about God and salvation must be translatable into a statement about the human condition in its total social and political situation; *existential theology*, at the other side of the spectrum from political theology, which emphasizes the individual believer as the *locus* for God's saving activity so that all theological reflection is reflection about one's own personhood and the meaning of one's own human existence; and *process theology*, developed against the presumably static traditional theology of the mainstream churches, which understands God and all reality as in a constant "process" of change and movement forward—nothing is fixed or immutable; and hence, process thought bears some family resemblance to Liberalism and Modernism.

Theology: A Synthesis

We defined theology earlier in the chapter as the interpretation of one's faith or, with Anselm, as faith seeking understanding. In the light of the preceding historical and systematic discussion, it is clear that theology is indeed the interpretation of faith, but that it is also much more complex than that.

1. *Not all interpretations of faith are theological.* Theology happens when there is *an interpretation of one's own faith.* Apart

from that faith, the exploration of faith is a philosophy of religion rather than a theology.

2.   On the other hand, theology has an important *critical function* to perform. It must ask if the various expressions of faith (beliefs) are *true*, or at least *appropriate*, to the Christian tradition. Do they conform with Sacred Scripture, the writings of the Fathers and doctors of the Church, the Church's official creeds and teachings, the consensus of the faithful, and scientific knowledge?

3.   *Theology is as old as self-conscious faith in God.* Christian theology began with the awareness that God was present in Christ, reconciling the world to himself (2 Corinthians 5:19). The *Apostles* and *Evangelists* were the first Christian theologians. The *Apologists* were the first to systematize theology.

4.   Almost from the beginning Christian theology has drawn from *contemporary thought-forms and culture* to express, explain, and even to defend the faith: from contemporary Greek philosophy during the controversies of the fourth and fifth centuries, from Aristotelianism during the Middle Ages, and from modern philosophy in the present age.

5.   Theology also changed its character as it has moved from one *pastoral need* to another and from one *environment* to another: The theology done by the great bishops of the fourth and fifth centuries was different from the theology of the monasteries around the end of the first Christian millennium, and that theology differed, in turn, from the medieval theology of the universities, and that from the seminary theology of the seventeenth and eighteenth centuries, and that from the historical and ecumenical theology of today, done again in universities, but more distinctively in the public forum, i.e., through books, articles, and lectures.

6.   *There are as many kinds of theology as there are religious faiths.* Theology also differs according to *content* (doctrinal, liturgical, etc.), *method* (historical, speculative, etc.), and *perspective* (Liberal, liberational, etc.).

7.   In the end, *Christian theology is a more or less systematic effort to come to terms with, and to express, our experience (knowledge) of God in Christ.*

BELIEF
Dimensions of the Question

When there has been a movement from faith to understanding, and from understanding to expression, we are in the realm of belief. It may be the belief of a single person or of many persons. It may be a belief that is manifestly in error or at least not yet accepted by the community at large, or it may be a belief that the Church proposes to the whole community for acceptance, even under pain of excommunication from the group. We shall be speaking in this last section of the chapter about official belief, i.e., about expressions of faith which have been accepted by the community at large as having authoritative, even normative and binding, force for every member of the Church. At one level of belief, we have the Bible. At another level, we have doctrines and dogmas. At a third, we have liturgies. At a fourth, we have catechisms and other instruments of Christian education.

The Bible

Canonicity

The word *bible* is derived from Latin and Greek words (*biblia*) which mean "books." The Bible is a *collection of books* rather than a single literary composition. The books of the Bible are called "sacred" because they are regarded as inspired by God and are not simply the product of ordinary human creativity and effort, although they are that as well. They are considered "canonical" because they are on the list, or *canon*, of books which the Church officially regards as inspired. The canon was definitively and solemnly determined by the Council of Trent in 1546.

Old Testament, New Testament

The Bible is also divided into Old Testament and New Testament. The former is centered on the old covenant of Sinai; the latter is centered on the new covenant of Jesus Christ. One of the earliest heresies, *Marcionism*, denied the revelatory character of the Old Testament. In its rejection of Marcionism, the Church has insisted from the earliest days on the essential continuity between the two testaments. There is no basis at all, in other words, for the once-common belief that the Old Testament is the law of fear and the New Testament, the law of love. The call to mercy and love (*ḥesed*) is at the core of Jewish faith as it is of Christian faith. The two testaments have a common theological focus: the *Kingdom of God*, i.e., the reign or rule of God that is already present in the world and is destined to be realized in all of its perfection at the end of human history when God will be "all in all" (1 Corinthians 15:28).

Inspiration

Because the Bible is believed to be inspired by God, it has an authority equaled by no other written source. It is, in the theological sense, the *norma normans non normata* ("the norm which is the standard for all other norms but is not itself subject to a higher norm"). The understanding of the Bible's authority is rooted, as we have said, in its inspired character.

Inspiration signifies in general the divine origin of the Bible. Already in the Old Testament there was the conviction that certain books are sacred because they are inspired by God. This belief was carried over into the New Testament, where the Old Testament is cited some 350 times in such a way as to show that Jesus and the New Testament writers shared the conviction that the Old Testament was indeed inspired by God. "All Scripture is inspired by God and is useful for teaching..." (2 Timothy 3:16). The New Testament itself does not claim inspiration, but the Fathers of the Church from the very beginning included the New Testament with the Old Testament in the inspired corpus of books.

The question of inspiration did not become a theological issue until the nineteenth century, after the First Vatican Council's formal definition. Subsequently, a vigorous debate developed, not over the *fact* of inspiration but over its *manner*. In 1893 Pope Leo XIII issued an encyclical, *Providentissimus Deus*, in which he declared that "God so moved the inspired writers by His supernatural operation that he incited them to write, and assisted them in their writing so that they correctly conceived, accurately wrote down and truthfully expressed all that He intended and only what He intended; and only thus can God be the author of the Bible." The teaching of Vatican I and Leo XIII is reaffirmed at Vatican II in its *Dogmatic Constitution on Divine Revelation:* "...Sacred Scripture is the word of God inasmuch as it is consigned to writing under the inspiration of the divine Spirit" (n. 9).

Inerrancy

Closely linked with the belief about inspiration is the belief about inerrancy. If the Bible is of God, it cannot be in error since God is the author of truth, not lies. A consensus of biblical and theological scholars favors the following principles: (1) The words of the Bible are true only in the sense in which the human authors conveyed them. Therefore, we must determine how they thought, what influenced them, and so forth. (2) The human author himself was not necessarily without error. Many of his personal opinions and even convictions may have been wrong. But inerrancy means that these opinions and convictions did not affect the message itself. (3) Inerrancy does not rule out the use of common literary devices, such as poetry, figures of speech, paradox, approximation, compressed narratives, inexact quotations, folklore, legend, song. (4) The human authors were Oriental, not Western. They did not think metaphysically or according to the rules of Scholastic logic. (5) Insofar as the principle of inerrancy applies, it applies to those essential religious affirmations which are made for the sake of salvation. "The Books of Scripture must be acknowledged as teaching firmly, faithfully, and without error that truth which God wanted put into the Sacred Writings for the sake of our salvation" (Vatican II, *Dogmatic Constitution on Divine Revelation*, n. 11).

Tradition as Criterion

But how do we know that the Bible is inspired and immune from error in those matters which pertain to our salvation? This is not an easy question to answer. As we mentioned earlier, the New Testament makes no claim about itself. The Catholic Church has always maintained that *there is no other criterion except its own traditions*, and that these, in turn, are vehicles of divine revelation. The inspiration of the Bible has been believed from the beginning and, beyond that, has been the subject of an official definition by the Church. Even as we try to understand its meaning in the light of modern notions of authorship, of history, and of psychology and sociology of knowledge, we recognize that the fact of inspiration is a given. One cannot be true to the Catholic and Christian faith without affirming at the same time the inspired, and therefore finally normative and authoritative, character of the Bible.

But what about the authority of *tradition*? Does not the Catholic Church teach that there are two separate *sources of divine revelation*, Sacred Scripture and Tradition, and that the latter is more authoritative than the former? The simplest answer is "No." It is true, on the other hand, that the Council of Trent did speak of two sources of revelation, the one written and the other unwritten. And it is also true that many Catholic theologians interpreted the Council of Trent to mean that Scripture and Tradition are two separate streams of revelation and that the one (Tradition) is the final measure of the other (Scripture). It seemed for a time that this position was about to be endorsed at the Second Vatican Council, but Pope John XXIII (d. 1963) in November 1962 sent the draft of the *Dogmatic Constitution on Divine Revelation* back to the Theological Committee of the council. When the document returned, it spoke not of two separate and independent sources of divine revelation but of a single divine revelation expressed and available in different forms: "It is clear that sacred tradition, sacred Scripture, and the teaching authority of the Church, in accord with God's most wise design, are so linked and joined together that one cannot stand without the others, and that all together and each in its own way under the action of the one Holy Spirit contribute effectively to the salvation of souls" (n. 10).

A more accurate formulation of the Scripture/Tradition relationship than the usual explanation offered before Vatican II would underscore the principle that *Scripture is itself a product of Tradition*. It is not as if you first have Scripture and then you have Tradition which is, among other things, the Church's reflection on Scripture. Tradition comes before and during, and not just after, the writing of Sacred Scripture. In fact, careful study of the various books of the Bible, including the Gospels themselves, discloses several layers of tradition from which the individual books have emerged and taken final form. Those traditions may be oral (preaching), liturgical (prayer formulae), narrative (recollection of important events, especially Jesus' passion), and so forth.

In the *wider meaning* of the word, tradition refers to *the whole process by which the Church "hands on"* (the literal meaning of the word *tradition) its faith to each new generation.* This handing on occurs through preaching, catechesis, teaching, devotions, gestures (e.g., the sign of the cross), doctrines, and indeed the Bible itself. In the *narrow meaning* of the term, tradition refers to *the content of the Church's post-apostolic teaching.* The Second Vatican Council opts for the *wider meaning* of the term: "The Church, in her teaching, life and worship, perpetuates and hands on to all generations all that she herself is, all that she believes" (*Dogmatic Constitution on Divine Revelation,* n. 8). The Church's tradition is its lived and living faith.

One final distinction: There is Tradition (upper case) and tradition(s) (lower case). Tradition (capitalized) is the living and lived faith of the Church; traditions are customary ways of doing or expressing matters related to faith. If a tradition cannot be rejected or lost without essential distortion of the Gospel, it is part of Tradition itself. If a tradition is not essential (i.e., if it does not appear, for example, in the New Testament, or if it is not clearly taught as essential to Christian faith), then it is subject to change or even to elimination. It is not part of the Tradition of the Church. It is a perennial temptation for Catholics to confuse traditions (e.g., obligatory priestly celibacy) with Tradition: on the one side of the spectrum, to make a non-essential tradition a matter of orthodoxy; or, on the other side, to treat a matter essential to faith (e.g., the Real Presence of Christ in the Eucharist) as if it were non-essential and therefore dispensable. The process of sorting out Tradition and traditions is ongoing, and involves the teaching authority of the official Church, the scholarly authority of theologians, and the lived experience of the Christian community itself.

Doctrine/Dogma

Meaning of Terms; Promulgation

A belief that receives the official approval of the Church, whether through a pronouncement of an *ecumenical* council (literally, a council drawn from "the whole wide world"), a pope, or a body of bishops in union with the pope (as at an international *synod* or at a *general* council, i.e., representative of segments of the Church universal), is called a *doctrine*. A doctrine that is taught with the fullest solemnity, i.e., so that its rejection is heresy, is called a *dogma* (literally, "what seems right"). The promulgation of doctrines and dogmas is the prerogative and responsibility of the pope alone, acting as head of the Church; the pope and bishops acting together in ecumenical council or international synod; or a body of bishops, subject to the (at least implicit) ratification of the pope—e.g., as in the case of the publication of a national catechism.

New Testament

One finds official beliefs already in the New Testament. Paul, for example, uses the word *tradition* in 1 Corinthians 11:23 (the words of Eucharistic institution) and 1 Corinthians 15:3-5: "I handed on to you first of all what I myself received, that Christ died for our sins in accordance with the Scriptures; that he was buried and, in accordance with the Scriptures, rose on the third day; that he was seen by Cephas, then by the Twelve. . . ." The clear suggestion is that Paul is using fixed formulae for these recitals, i.e., expressions of belief which had received the official approval of the Church and were widely accepted as normative statements of Christian faith.

Present Meaning

It was not until the eighteenth century, however, that the term *dogma* acquired its present meaning, namely, a teaching (doctrine) which the Church explicitly propounds as revealed by God. The notion was formally adopted by the First Vatican Council and in the Church's *Code of Canon Law* (see canons 1323, #2; 1325, #2; and 2314, #1). According to Vatican I, *a dogma must meet the following conditions*: (1) It must be contained in Sacred Scripture or in the post-biblical Tradition of the Church, and as such considered part of God's revelation. (2) It must be explicitly proposed by the Church as a divinely revealed object of belief. (3) This must be done either in a solemn decree or in the Church's ordinary, universal teaching. Such teachings are "irreformable," i.e., they are not subject to review by a higher authority in the Church.

Magisterium

A *solemn decree* could have only one of two sources: an ecumenical council whose head is always the pope, or the pope speaking as head of the universal Church but apart from a council. *Ordinary, universal teaching* may be communicated in a papal encyclical, a synodal declaration, a decree of a Vatican congregation with the approval of the pope, or an ecumenical council. In the *widest sense* of the term, *teaching authority belongs to the whole Church*. The Second Vatican Council taught that the whole People of God participates through Baptism in the threefold mission of Christ as Prophet, Priest, and King (*Dogmatic Constitution on the Church*, n. 30). In the *more restricted sense, magisterium* applies to *particular groups of teachers whose authority is grounded in their office* (as in the case of the pope and the bishops) *or in their scholarly competence* (as in the case of the theologians). The charism of teaching, after all, is not linked exclusively with the office of bishop or superior in the New Testament (see Romans 12:6-8 and 1 Corinthians 12:28-31). In the Middle Ages Thomas Aquinas distinguished between the magisterium of the cathedral chair, i.e., the teaching authority of the bishop, and the magisterium of the professorial chair, i.e., the teaching authority of the theologian. In the *strictest sense* of all, however, the term *magisterium* has been *applied exclusively to the teaching authority of the pope and the bishops.*

Historical Summary

Without a *historical perspective*, Catholics will continue to understand the concept of *magisterium* according to its early twentieth-
century meaning. In apostolic times there were many different
charisms and ministries involved in the teaching process: Those of
apostles, prophets, evangelists, teachers (*didaskaloi* = theologians), and administrators. Already in the days of the Fathers of
the Church there were tensions among prophets, teachers, and
pastors. From early in the third century the prophets receded as a
recognized group within the Church, and teachers were increasingly subordinated to the bishops. Irenaeus, in his fight against
Gnosticism, insisted on the primacy of the bishops' teaching as a
sure guide to Christian truth, while Clement of Alexandria and
Origen argued that the teachers are, in a way, part of the apostolic
succession and that the Church need not look only to the hierarchical magisterium for pure apostolic doctrine. Tertullian (d. 225),
in fact, tended to reduce the role of bishops to a purely disciplinary
function. But in the third and fourth centuries the onslaught of
new heresies solidified the magisterial standing of the bishops.
Indeed, most of the principal theologians were themselves bishops.
Juridical authority and intellectual competence resided in the
same person.

The bishops lost ground in the Middle Ages when laymen,
especially political rulers, came to the fore. From the tenth to the
thirteenth centuries, the papacy in combination with religious
orders assumed magisterial leadership. In the later Middle Ages,
ecumenical councils such as Constance (1414-1418) and general
councils such as Basle (1431-1439) included theologians in their
ranks, but with the Protestant Reformation the juridical and clerical character of councils and of the *magisterium* generally was
underscored. Teaching became less a matter of insight and
enlightenment and more a matter of the imposition of approved
formulae. The Church divided according to those who taught
(and presumably no longer had to learn) and those who learned
(and presumably had nothing to do with teaching). That hard and
fast distinction between the teaching Church (*ecclesia docens*) and
the learning Church (*ecclesia discens*) has only recently begun to
disappear.

Recent Practice

The change in thinking is reflected in the *different style of teaching* recently adopted by the hierarchy. It tends to be less authoritarian, less absolutist, and less closed to other points of view. The change in thinking is also reflected in the more sophisticated process by which such teaching is formulated. Collegiality has introduced a spirit of collaboration or cooperation which is the antithesis of unilateral decision-making.

There is also a greater respect for the *historical context* of doctrinal or dogmatic pronouncements. Fundamentalism in the interpretation of dogma is no less objectionable than fundamentalism in the interpretation of Sacred Scripture. *Mysterium Ecclesiae*, a 1973 declaration of the Congregation for the Doctrine of the Faith (formerly the Holy Office, and, before that, the Inquisition), acknowledged in principle the historical conditioning of dogma. Not only do the mysteries of faith transcend the powers of the human intellect, it said, but the very expressions of revelation are historically conditioned and therefore their meaning is not always self-evident to those in some other historical setting. The meaning of dogmatic language may change from one historical period to another. The truth itself may be expressed incompletely (even if not falsely). The original dogmatic teaching may have been directed at specific questions or certain errors, and these may not be the same questions or errors at issue in some later period of the Church's history. And the dogmatic formulae themselves inevitably bear the marks of the philosophical and theological universe in which they were first constructed. The formulae may not always be the most suitable for every time and place. Indeed, they must sometimes give way to new expressions which present the same meaning more clearly and more completely. At the same time, of course, *Mysterium Ecclesiae* rejects the Modernist notion that a dogma can never express Christian truth in a determinate way (see the Appendix of this book for excerpts from this document).

Dogma and Its Development

Two major questions remain: (1) How do we know the difference between a dogma and a doctrine? and (2) What is the relationship between the Church's official teaching and the contributions of theologians?

The determination of what constitutes a dogma is always a theological problem. Surprising though it may seem to many, *there is no list of dogmas to which all Catholic theologians or even pastoral leaders would agree.* Some criteria for determining what constitutes a dogma are: (1) The teaching is explicitly identified with the essence of Christian faith. (2) It is the clear intent of the teaching Church to bind the whole Church on the matter. (3) The teaching is contained in Sacred Scripture and/or is unmistakably present in the various doctrinal pronouncements of the Church through the centuries.

Beyond that, the actual formulation must be scrutinized to see to what degree the dogma *as expressed* is authoritative. The following criteria may be helpful: (1) The argument supporting the teaching must be internally coherent and persuasive to those competent to judge. (2) There must be evidence that various legitimate schools of thought on the matter were taken into account in the drafting of the dogmatic statement and that their arguments, even if rejected, were evidently understood. (3) The dogmatic teaching must be received by the Church at large and accepted as an accurate, appropriate, and unerring expression of its faith. (This last criterion, "reception," has only recently been recovered as part of authentic Catholic tradition.)

Dissent is never possible against a dogma, assuming that the preceding criteria have been taken into account—in other words, if there is no question that it is a dogma, and if its meaning is clear to all. *To reject such a dogma*, however sincere or well-intentioned the act, *places one outside the Catholic Church and technically makes one a heretic.* On the other hand, the Church itself acknowledges that a development of dogma is possible, sometimes even necessary. Not every dogma was originally expressed in the best form. A dogma can reflect "the changeable conceptions of a given epoch" (*Mysterium Ecclesiae;* see Appendix). Although always subordinated to the living magisterium of the Church, theologians have an important contribution to make to the clarification and even improvement of such dogmatic formulations. Without the possibility of raising questions about the meaning and the suitability of certain dogmatic expressions, however, theologians could never make their full contribution to the faith of the whole Church.

The impression is sometimes left that theologians are presenting themselves as a co-equal teaching body with the hierarchy (the so-called "double magisterium" theory). This is not being proposed here. The teaching Church (which is also part of the learning Church) has the responsibility and, therefore, the authority to articulate the faith for the whole Church, whereas the learning Church (among whom all teachers, official and unofficial alike, are numbered) is bound to articulate its faith in light of, and in fidelity to, the official teaching.

But if theologians are to serve the Church not only by explaining and defending its official teachings but also by recommending better ways of expressing and of understanding some of those teachings, then it is entirely possible that theologians will, on occasion, find themselves at odds with other theologians, ecclesiastical leaders, and laity who just as sincerely believe that the official teachings are perfectly acceptable as formulated and as traditionally interpreted. If the theologian's view happens to conflict with that of a pope or the bishops, the theologian's view may take on the character of dissent. Such dissent is almost inevitable over the long run of the Church's history and particularly in periods of great change, such as our own (see the *Pastoral Constitution on the Church in the Modern World*, nn. 4-10).

To be sure, some of the Church's major theologians in the past found themselves in disagreement with official positions at one time or another—e.g., Thomas Aquinas, some of whose theological opinions were formally condemned by the bishop of Paris in 1277 and later by two successive archbishops of Canterbury, one a fellow Dominican and the other a Franciscan. Biblical scholars such as Marie-Joseph LaGrange, O.P., drew scholarly conclusions contrary to the directives of the Pontifical Biblical Commission, but at least some of those views came to be adopted by Pope Pius XII in *Divino Afflante Spiritu* (1943). Henri de

Lubac, S.J., was undoubtedly one of the "new theologians" criticized in the same pope's *Humani Generis* (1950), and yet de Lubac was singled out for special praise by Pope John Paul II during the pope's visit to France in 1980.

Two of the twentieth century's leading Catholic theologians, Karl Rahner, S.J., and Yves Congar, O.P., were for a while forbidden to publish their research because of suspicions in Rome that they were insufficiently orthodox. And the case of John Courtney Murray, S.J. (d. 1967), is particularly well known to Catholics in the United States. Forbidden by the Holy Office to publish articles on the subject of Church and State because his interpretations of papal teachings differed from those of more traditional theologians and canonists and especially of Cardinal Alfredo Ottaviani (d. 1980), prefect of the Holy Office, and excluded from the first session of the Second Vatican Council, Murray became one of the council's leading consultants (*periti*) and the architect of its *Declaration on Religious Freedom*.

This is not to suggest, of course, that most theological criticisms of an official teaching of the Church are correct or that the critics are usually destined for the kind of rehabilitation and recognition these aforementioned theologians were to enjoy. The point is that development of dogma (and of doctrine as well) goes hand in hand with the possibility of some measure of dissent. Although the Catholic's first and proper instinct is to be guided by the official teachings as presently understood and interpreted, one must nonetheless take into serious account the theological work that continues to be produced alongside, and sometimes even over against, these conventional interpretations.

To reproduce only the official teachings in a work such as this without also presenting the theological discussion of those teachings is to leave intelligent readers unprepared for any development which might conceivably—and legitimately—occur in the future. It would also leave them without the necessary resources and guidance to make sense of those controversies which eventually reach them through the press and the electronic media. The challenge for the theological critic is always to formulate and express any disagreements according to objective and recognizable criteria and in a pastorally sensitive way—i.e., without polemics and in a non-adversarial manner. Furthermore, the discussion should be engaged, in the first instance, with the theologian's own peers and then, as circumstances warrant, in dialogue with the wider Church, especially with those who have particular competence in the areas under examination.

Liturgy and Christian Education

Basically the same principles apply here as were applicable above. Creeds, prayers, and other formulae of worship are expressions of belief that are officially approved and proposed for general acceptance and use. They, too, are always subject to theological scrutiny according to the criteria already enumerated. The same is true of catechisms and other instruments of Christian education. Insofar as they reproduce dogmatic formulae, they assume the authority of the formulae. Insofar as they express doctrine, the doctrine is no more and no less authoritative in the catechism than it is in its original setting. Insofar as the catechism or educational instrument expresses theological opinions, those opinions are as strong or as weak as the arguments which support them. And that applies, of course, to this book as well.

It is precisely through our eucharistic and sacramental celebrations, on the one hand, and through the religious instruction process, on the other, that the vast majority of Catholics come into contact with the beliefs of the Church.

Belief: A Synthesis

1. A *belief* is any *expression of faith* and, more immediately, of theology. The belief, however, may be accurate or inaccurate, appropriate or inappropriate, in accordance with the authoritative sources of Christian Tradition (Bible, ecumenical councils, writings of the Fathers and doctors of the Church, papal encyclicals, general councils, synods of bishops) or with the actual experience of the community of faith.

2. The *Bible* (as well as the other "authoritative sources" mentioned above) is itself an expression of belief. It has an eminence among all other sources because it alone is inspired by God.

As such, it is protected from fundamental error in matters pertaining to salvation.

3. The process of formulating authoritative beliefs continued after the biblical period, and in a much more systematic fashion in order to meet the challenges of non-believers and believers alike. The assorted post-biblical expressions of belief have been called *Tradition*.

4. It is inexact to speak of *Tradition* as if it were simply opposed to Sacred Scripture as a separate and independent source of divine revelation. *The Bible is itself the product of Tradition— of many traditions, in fact.*

5. In the *wider meaning* of the term, Tradition refers to *the whole process of "handing on" the faith* from Christian generation to Christian generation, through preaching, catechesis, teaching, devotions, gestures, doctrines, and the Bible itself.

6. In the *strict sense* of the term, Tradition refers to *the content of the Church's post-apostolic teaching*, written and unwritten alike.

7. There is also a distinction to be made between Tradition and tradition(s). Tradition (with a capital T) is the living and lived faith of the Church; traditions are customary ways of acting or expressing matters related to faith which may or may not be essential to that faith. (Benediction of the Blessed Sacrament is a non-essential tradition; the celebration of the Eucharist is an essential tradition.)

8. *A doctrine* is *a belief that is officially taught by the Church*; a *dogma* is *a doctrine taught with the highest solemnity and is immune from fundamental error.* One might reject a doctrine, but not a dogma, and remain within the communion of Catholic faith.

9. The distinction between a dogma and a non-dogmatic doctrine, however, is not completely helpful because *there is no list of dogmas to which all Catholic theologians or even pastoral leaders would agree.*

10. Insofar as *dogmas* are human expressions of belief, they are *subject to the same limitations of language, style, structure, and even appropriateness as any human expression.* To say, therefore, that dogmas are *irreformable* (as the First Vatican Council taught)

is to say that they are *not subject to review by some higher authority in the Church.*

11.   The *official beliefs* of the Church are communicated by an authoritative teaching body known as the *magisterium.* The term *magisterium* also applies to the teaching authority residing in that body of teachers.

12.   In the *widest sense* of the term, *magisterium* may also apply to *the whole People of God,* whose authority is rooted in Baptism; in the *narrower sense,* to *the hierarchy and the theologians,* whose authority is rooted in office and competence respectively; and in the *narrowest sense,* to *the hierarchy alone.*

13.   *In principle, dissent against a dogma is impossible for a Catholic.* It is an act of heresy, and as such separates one from communion with the Church. *In practice, it is often difficult to decide when, in fact, a doctrine has acquired dogmatic status.*

14.   Although the official teachings of the Church remain normative for faith, theologians have a special responsibility to help the Church come to a better understanding and even clarification of those teachings. This may, on occasion, place the theologian at odds with certain traditional interpretations of those teachings.

15.   *Liturgy* and *Christian education* embody and communicate beliefs. Indeed, *it is through these two channels that most Catholics come into immediate contact with the beliefs of their faith-tradition.*

SUMMARY

1.   If Catholicism is in *crisis* today, it can be explained in part by the persistent failure of many Catholics to understand the differences among faith, theology, and belief: *Faith is not theology; theology is not belief; faith is not belief.*

2.   *Faith* is personal knowledge of God gained through the experience of God (revelation), mediated by a community of faith. *Theology* is the interpretation of one's own faith, from within a community of faith. *Belief* is an expression of faith and, as such, is a work of theology.

3.   Beliefs take many different *forms*: the Bible, doctrines and dogmas, writings of the Fathers and doctors of the Church, decrees of

ecumenical councils, general councils, synods of bishops, papal encyclicals, creeds, liturgies, catechisms, and other instruments of Christian education.

Thus:

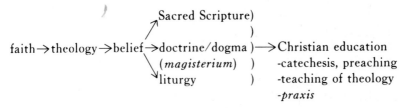

4.   *Faith* is at the same time individual and communal, of the mind and of the heart, free and certain, reasonable and supernatural.

5.   *Theology* is the interpretation of one's own faith in God; *Christian* theology is the interpretation of one's own Christian faith—that is, of one's own perception of God in Jesus Christ.

6.   *Belief* is an expression of faith and a work of theology. The most authoritative expression of faith (because it is inspired by God) is the *Bible.* After that, there is *dogma* (a teaching proposed by the official Church with the highest degree of solemnity). After that, there is *doctrine* (or any official teaching of the Church proposed by the pope alone, an ecumenical council, a general council, or a synod of bishops). After that, there are the *writings of the Fathers and doctors of the Church.* Each of these expressions of belief is a work of *magisterium,* i.e., of teaching authority (whether of office or of competence or of both).

7.   Other forms of belief are contained in creeds, the liturgy, catechisms, and other instruments of Christian education. Each is as authoritative as the source or sources from which it is drawn or which now sanction and commend it to the Church at large.

8.   The whole process of handing on the faith (as outlined in the schema above) is called Tradition. Theology begins at the point where a person begins to reflect on his or her faith. Tradition begins at the point where such reflections are communicated to others.

9.   Fidelity to Tradition (capitalized to exclude all non-essential and non-binding customs and opinions) is not inconsistent with dissent, so long as that dissent is formulated and expressed in a responsible manner, i.e., derived from one's area of competence.

SUGGESTED READINGS

Congar, Yves. *A History of Theology.* New York: Doubleday, 1968.

Dulles, Avery. *Apologetics and the Biblical Christ.* Westminster, Md.: Newman Press, 1963.

_____. *The Survival of Dogma.* New York: Doubleday, 1971.

Moran, Gabriel. *Scripture and Tradition: A Survey of the Controversy.* New York: Herder & Herder, 1963.

Moroux, Jean. *I Believe: The Personal Structure of Faith.* New York: Sheed & Ward, 1959.

Rahner, Karl. "The Development of Dogma." *Theological Investigations.* Baltimore: Helicon, 1961, vol. 1, pp. 40-77; "Considerations of the Development of Dogma." 1966, vol. 3, pp. 3-35.

Schillebeeckx, Edward. *The Understanding of Faith: Interpretation and Criticism.* New York: Seabury Press, 1974.

PART ONE

HUMAN EXISTENCE

HUMAN EXISTENCE

INTRODUCTION

The first theological question we ask ourselves is "Who am I?" or "Who are we?" It is precisely in our attempt to come to terms with the meaning of our own lives that we raise the question of God, of Christ, of Church, and of Christian moral behavior.

We raise the question of *God* because we seek the deepest and surest foundation of meaning that we can find.

We raise the question of *Christ* because we seek some concrete, personal, historical expression of that foundation of meaning. Christ is our way of getting in touch with God.

We raise the question of the *Church* because we seek some institutional and communitarian expression of Christ as the personification of ultimate meaning. The Church is our way of getting in touch with Christ.

And we raise the question of *Christian existence* because we seek some experiential verification of the meaning we embrace. Christian living is the way we express our relationship with the Church, with Christ, and ultimately with God.

But we start with the question of ourselves, with the question of *human existence*. It is, after all, *we* who have come to a belief in God, in Christ as the Word of God, and in the Church as the Body of Christ. It is *we* who seek to find meaning and order in our lives and in our world. Since all theological questions *begin* with us, as the ones who raise them in the first place, theology cannot afford to take for granted the *questioner* if it really hopes to understand both the questions we ask and the answers we have been fashioning in response.

Accordingly, chapter 3 offers a *description* of the human situation today, a situation which poses particular kinds of questions and demands particular kinds of answers. We live in a so-called *modern world*. In what does *modernity* consist, and how does it affect our self-understanding?

Chapter 4 explores the range of answers which have emerged in the modern world. Under the umbrella term of *anthropology*, the chapter considers in sequence the understandings of human existence which have been developed in the natural and social sciences, in modern literature, in philosophy, in theology, and in the official teachings of the Catholic Church.

Chapter 5 actually attempts a coherent *theology of human existence* (or theological anthropology) by examining the biblical, doctrinal, and theological meaning of the human person, and specifically an understanding of *nature, grace,* and *Original Sin.*

A theological anthropology sums up the whole of theology, for in our understanding of human existence we progressively articulate our understanding of God, of Christ, of redemption, of Church, of the moral life. No aspect of theology is untouched by our anthropology. Therefore, no theology can begin without immediate attention to the question of human existence.

·III·

THE HUMAN CONDITION
TODAY

"THE SIGNS OF THE TIMES"

Like most ecclesiastical declarations emanating from the Vatican (the tiny political entity which houses the Catholic Church's central administrative offices), the documents of the Second Vatican Council are known by the first two words in the original Latin text. Thus, the *Dogmatic Constitution on the Church* is called *Lumen gentium* ("Light of Nations") and the *Dogmatic Constitution on Divine Revelation* is called *Dei verbum* ("The Word of God"). But the conciliar documents are also identified by their general titles (the other designation given in the preceding examples).

The general title for the council's only "pastoral" constitution is of particular significance. Known on the one hand as *Gaudium et spes* ("Joy and Hope"), it is also commonly cited as the *Pastoral Constitution on the Church in the Modern World.* The preposition *in* is exceedingly important. The constitution is not about the Church *and* the modern world, but about the Church *in* the modern world. The former construction would have emphasized the over-againstness of the Church in relation to the world, as if the Church were somehow different from, and even at odds with, the human community at large. The latter construction emphasizes the integration of Church and world. The Church is not the non-world. The Church is not something completely apart from the world. Rather, the Church is in the world and the world is in the Church.

Even here, in so seemingly a trivial matter, one can perhaps appreciate a basic difference in the traditional theological approaches of Catholicism and Protestantism. Protestantism emphasizes the *dialectical*. Affirmation is set against negation, "Yes" against "No"; e.g., in society individuals are set against the larger community. Catholicism, on the other hand, emphasizes the *analogical*. Realities are more similar than different; e.g., society is like a human body; the parts are not at odds with the whole nor the whole with the parts.

The *Pastoral Constitution* itself emerged from the deliberate collaboration of two of the most important Catholic leaders in the twentieth century, Pope John XXIII and Cardinal Leo–Jozef Suenens, Archbishop of Malines-Brussels in Belgium. On Christmas day, 1961, Pope John formally convoked the council in a constitution entitled *Humanae Salutis* ("Of Human Salvation"). The document used the phrase "signs of the times" (previously limited, by reason of its biblical origins, to the frightening events that are to precede the end of the world) in an entirely optimistic sense. Pope John would employ the term in the same positive manner more than a year later in his encyclical letter *Pacem in Terris* ("Peace on Earth"). Developments are occurring in human history, it said, which the Christian ought not necessarily shrink from, fear, or resist. They are perhaps instruments of divine revelation. God may be summoning us to recognize new challenges and to devise new ways of meeting these challenges. God may be calling us to conversion in its deepest meaning, a "change of mind" (Mark 1:15).

"Indeed," the pope wrote, "we make ours the recommendation of Jesus that one should know how to distinguish the 'signs of the times' (Matthew 16:4), and we seem to see now, in the midst of so much darkness, a few indications which augur well for the fate of the Church and of humanity."

Soon after the pope's official convocation of Vatican II, Cardinal Suenens issued a pastoral letter for the Catholics of his archdiocese on the state of the Church and the opportunities open to it. Pope John saw the letter and advised Suenens that it represented his own views exactly. The influence of the Suenens letter on the pope's opening speech to the council on October 11, 1962, was pronounced. Pope John dismissed the worries of those "prophets of gloom, who are always forecasting disaster, as if the end of the world were at hand." Divine Providence, he declared, is "leading us to a new order of human relations" in accordance with "God's superior and inscrutable designs." This new order is one founded on unity: the unity of the entire Church and of all humankind. The council, therefore, must be attentive to both kinds of unity. Its focus cannot be exclusively on the Church.

Less than two months later, on December 4, Cardinal Suenens addressed the council as its first (of four) sessions moved toward adjournment. We need to do more, he urged, than examine the mystery of the Church as it is in itself (*ad intra*). We must also reflect on its relationship with the world at large (*ad extra*). Commentators have interpreted this speech by Cardinal Suenens to have been a crucial moment in the history of the council, and certainly for the genesis of the *Pastoral Constitution on the Church in the Modern World*. They also suggest that the cardinal made his speech with the knowledge and approval of the pope.

And so a unique kind of ecclesiastical document was produced, a "pastoral constitution," in which the Church is said to have the "duty of scrutinizing the signs of the times and of interpreting them in the light of the Gospel . . . . We must therefore recognize and understand the world in which we live, its expectations, its longings, and its often dramatic characteristics"(n. 4).

What is that world like? What is the state of the human community today? What is the present human condition, of which the Church is an integral part and for which it has an abiding missionary responsibility?

THE MODERN WORLD
A World of Change

It has been observed that if the last fifty thousand years of human existence were divided into lifetimes of approximately sixty-two years each, there have been about eight hundred lifetimes. Of these eight hundred, six hundred and fifty were spent in caves. Only during the last seventy lifetimes has it been possible to communicate through the written word, and only during the last six lifetimes has the human community had access to the printed word. Only during the last four lifetimes have we been able to measure time precisely, and only in the last two have we had the use of an electric motor. And within the same lifetime, our own, we have seen part of the world pass successively from agriculture as the primary form of human labor, to the manual labor of factories, and then to the so-called white-collar labor of salespersons, administrators, educators, communicators, and so forth.

In the meantime the world's population has experienced explosive, almost incomprehensible, growth in this century. More than one hundred years ago only four cities had a population of a million or more. By 1900 there were nineteen; by 1960, one hundred and forty-one. Just over ten years later the urban population had doubled again.

The same kind of accelerated change has occurred in the area of transportation. In the year 6000 B.C. the camel caravan provided the fastest transportation over long distances: about eight miles per hour (what a moderately quick jogger covers in about the same time). It was not until about 1600 B.C. that, with the invention of the chariot, the speed of travel increased from eight to twenty miles per hour. This "record" was to stand for several thousand years. The first steam locomotive, introduced in 1825, reached a speed of only thirteen miles per hour, and the great sailing ships of the same period were half again as slow. Not until the nineteenth century, with improvements in the steam engine, did we attain speeds of one hundred miles per hour. And it had taken the human race thousands upon thousands, even millions, of years to do it. What is perhaps more remarkable is that it then took only fifty-eight years to quadruple that limit, so that by 1938 planes were breaking the four-hundred-miles-per-hour figure. In another twenty-five years even that seemed modest, as the new jets doubled the mark. And then by the 1960s rockets approached speeds of four thousand miles per hour, and astronauts in space capsules were circling the earth at eighteen thousand miles per hour. The next frontier was the moon, and who knows where after that?

The whole dizzying process has generated what social commentator Alvin Toffler calls "future shock...the shattering stress and disorientation that we induce in individuals by subjecting them to too much change in too short a time"(*Future Shock*, p. 4). Sociologists differ among themselves on the interpretation of this phenomenon. Many agree that such rapid changes as these have led inevitably and inexorably to a breakdown of traditional values and traditional human relationships. Others have argued, with just as much conviction, that the human effects have been much less radical than is supposed.

The Elements of Change

That the world has undergone major change is a fact beyond reasonable debate. And the process of change continues. That, too, is clear. The causes and elements of change are less obvious, if only because many people, even those with some special responsibility for the quality of human life on our planet, have not attended to them in any coherent, systematic way. What follows represents just such an attempt. Its limited and schematic character should be readily apparent. The outline may serve, nonetheless, as a useful framework for our subsequent studies on what it means to be human, how we experience God in the midst of life, the role of Jesus Christ in making sense of existence, and the place and function of the Church in and for the world.

Science and Technology—Mobility and Communications

It is generally agreed that the so-called *modern period* of world history begins around 1500. Not coincidentally, it is just about the time of the *disintegration of Christian unity* in the West and of the rise of *critical reasoning* and *skepticism.* For whatever social, economic, political, cultural, or philosophical and religious reasons, our world has been decisively shaped by the development of science and technology. *Science* understands the way things work; *technology* applies science to practical problems. Both together have generated the kinds of extraordinary (and extraordinarily rapid) changes to which we referred earlier in this chapter. The two most significant developments have been in the areas of *transportation* and *communication.*

The automobile and the jet airplane have given the average person in economically advanced countries a *mobility* of the most unprecedented kind. The world of direct human experience is no longer geographically confined. We can meet people, talk with them, hear their points of view, argue with them, learn from them, teach them, influence them, be influenced by them on a scale unthinkable for those whose means of transportion were limited to the horse, the sailing ship, or one's own two legs.

But neither are our human contacts limited any longer to the direct and the immediately tactile. Because of the correlative revolution in *communications* we have access to one another through television, radio, telephone, films, newspapers, magazines, paperback books, and tapes. Ideas and opinions have countless outlets, and they circulate more freely than ever before in human history. The modern person is a person in constant *dialogue* with others. And through that dialogue he or she is conscious more than ever before of human *interdependence* and of the importance, even the urgency, of human *unity*.

Material and Educational Growth

If increased mobility and communications are the most significant effects of the scientific and technological revolutions, those effects have become, in turn, instruments of the same scientific and technological revolutions which produced them. They are two of the principal factors in *material and educational growth*.

Unlike those who lived before us—fifty years ago or fifty *thousand* years ago—most people in the economically advanced and politically liberal countries of the world can take for granted those *material goods* that were once the constant preoccupation and anxious concern of every man, woman, and child: adequate food, comfortable housing, sufficient clothing, necessary medicines, productive work, and opportunities for leisure. We have created what some philosophers have called a "meta-cosmos"—something over and above the natural order of things given ultimately by God. We have taken the raw material of the world (*cosmos*) and given it an order and a shape beyond (*meta*) what was there.

To summarize: *Communications* make it possible for us to know where and how our material needs can be met, and *mobility* makes it possible either to gain access to material goods or to have others deliver them to us.

Educational progress is another major by-product of the scientific and technological revolutions. We are no longer limited in our choice of beliefs, because we are exposed to a whole range of them. We are no longer limited in our choice of life-styles and values, because we are brought in touch with a whole spectrum of expressions and convictions. We are no longer limited to our own commonsense wisdom or that of our relatively small circle of family, relatives, and friends to make sense of the meaning of human existence, because we are linked with the greatest minds and greatest discoveries of present and past alike.

Education is indeed liberating in that it frees us from illusions, from decision-making based on insufficient or erroneous information, from boredom, from dependence on the sensate and the tangible, from limited choice of occupation and recreation, and especially from the dark suspicion that things cannot be other than they are.

To summarize again: *Communications* make it possible to expand our narrow individual universe of human experience by putting us in touch with persons, institutions, and scientific findings that widen our range of choice and our opportunities for growth; *mobility* makes it possible for us to reach people and institutions, and to be reached by them in turn, for our mutual enrichment.

Ambivalence of Progress

But material and educational progress is not without ambiguity, even ambivalence. As a minority of the world's population is lifted to the heights of material satisfaction, the view from the top can be sobering. The gap between rich and poor is sharpened. (That is not to say, however, that material progress in itself creates the gap, as if the poor did not exist before the scientific and technological revolutions of the last century.) We see, too, how many problems are not only left unattended by this rapid progress, but also how many problems are themselves the product of that material growth: the nuclear arms race and the stockpiling of nuclear weapons, international conflicts, civil wars, economic crises, inflation, pollution, traffic congestion, health hazards in our food, water, air, and manufactured products, crime of all varieties, and the rejection of spiritual values.

Educational growth discloses the same kind of gaps and contradictions. On the one hand, education helps the individual to understand his or her dignity as a person, his or her uniqueness, and the meaning and opportunities of freedom and personal responsibility. Moreover, education not only broadens but sharpens one's *vision of reality*. Even as it expands the range of possibilities open to personal choice, it also exposes the countlessly subtle and sometimes blatant assaults upon that freedom through the manipulation by certain kinds of advertising, through outright deception by those in government, business, or even religion, and through psychic and social conditioning. The recent popularity of books which summon the individual to greater assertiveness (looking out for Number One, playing a power game, monitoring your erroneous zones, pulling your own strings, being your own best friend) is itself an indication that many people feel themselves to be less and less in control of their own lives.

Education also expands our *social horizons*, disclosing that economic, cultural, and societal structures and patterns need not be as they are or have been. The whole affirmative action movement for women and minorities is a direct outgrowth of this discovery.

But there have been *counter-trends* as well. Even as we perceive anew the reality of our interdependence, we find ourselves living in an age of increasingly bitter racial and international conflicts, of the proliferation of the most heinous sorts of crimes, especially against the elderly, and of increasing pressures against the integrity and cohesiveness of families and of neighborhood communities.

Education, finally, expands our *political vision*, yielding for many a much greater measure of sophistication in the use (and abuse) of power: whether on the left (in various liberation movements, some of which are dedicated to violence as a normal means

of effecting change), on the right (in various resistance movements, expressed either in civil repression by totalitarian governments or bloodlessly in the Proposition 13-type tax revolts of the
late 1970s), or in the center (where many adopt a so-called "moderate" position, not out of philosophical conviction but simply to
gain time and see which way the wind is blowing).

Religion and Change

We live in a time of accelerated change. The moving forces behind
that change have been science and technology; their primary products have been material and educational growth. And mobility
and communications have made those products widely available.

Religion has not escaped the effects of such change, both good
and bad. The Second Vatican Council's *Pastoral Constitution on
the Church in the Modern World* acknowledged this. There has
been an extraordinarily significant change in attitudes and in
human structures in our time and, as frequently happens, many
accepted values have been called into question. This is especially
true of the young, who often feel less responsible to the past
because they have had little, if anything, to do with its shaping and
direction. Consequently, they grow impatient with, even rebel-
lious toward, traditional norms and customs. They want a more
direct and effective hand in the development of policies for the
present and for the future, and particularly of those decisions
which have an immediate impact on their own lives.

These new conditions in the world today have had an effect,
therefore, on religion as well, and on a scale not limited to the
experience of the young: "On the one hand a more critical ability
to distinguish religion from a magical view of the world and from
the superstitions which still circulate purifies religion and exacts
day by day a more personal and explicit adherence to faith. As a
result many persons are achieving a more vivid sense of God.

"On the other hand, growing numbers of people are abandoning religion in practice. Unlike former days, the denial of God
or of religion, or the abandonment of them, are no longer unusual
and individual occurrences" (*Pastoral Constitution*, n. 11).

At first, therefore, the scientific and technological revolutions of this century and the major changes they produced seemed to move religion, including Christianity, off its accustomed foundations. Belief in a supernatural order of reality was shaken. Many Christians in the mid-1960s shifted from a sacred to a secular perspective in the hope of saving the credibility of the Gospel. Some were influenced in this new course by the prison writing of a young German theologian.

The world has "come of age," Dietrich Bonhoeffer (executed by the Nazis in 1945) asserted in his now-celebrated *Letters and Papers from Prison*. The world no longer takes the religious premise for granted, he said. It no longer assumes that God is "up there," ready at every moment to intervene in our human affairs, to rescue or to punish. We must learn today that only a "suffering God" can help us, one who allows us to share the pain and agony and risk of creation and to be, like the Son of God, a "man for others."

The challenge for the Church, Bonhoeffer argued, is to find a way to preach the Lordship of Jesus Christ to a world without religion, to present a kind of "religionless Christianity" that not only makes sense but may even be persuasive. By "religionless Christianity" he did not mean a religion without prayer, without worship, without doctrine, without formal institutional structures. He meant rather a Christianity that does not *confuse* the faith itself with these institutions and structures. They are embodiments, expressions, and even carriers of faith, but they are not themselves identical with faith. To be Christian, in other words, is not to perform certain devotional or ascetical practices, but to live in a fully human way, in the service of others, as Jesus lived and served.

The second challenge for the Church, Bonhoeffer maintained, is to find a way to be a servant community in the spirit of Jesus, the Suffering Servant of God (a discussion of this and other Christological titles will be taken up in chapter 12). What is to be the place of the Church (literally, "those who are called forth") in a world without religion? Can the Church continue to appeal to humankind as if the world were in some perpetual foxhole, the bullets and mortar shells whizzing overhead? Science and technology have changed the human situation. We no longer ascribe every bolt of lightning and every burst of thunder to the anger of God. As we continue to gain a certain amount of mastery over the material world, we are less and less inclined to accept a supernatural explanation of events when a purely scientific explanation will do.

But that traditional apologetic, Bonhoeffer insisted, was ignoble in any case. The Church cannot rest its preaching of the Gospel and its invitation to Christian faith on the premise that humankind is incapable of governing its daily affairs without constant attention to, and direct assistance from, the God of the heavens above. God, on the contrary, is to be found not on the borders of our life where human powers give out, but at its center. God is indeed the "the beyond in the midst of life." That is the Church's peculiar task and challenge in this age: to model itself on the servant presence of God in the midst of life, to use whatever resources it has in the service of those most in need.

Bonhoeffer's fundamentally straightforward insights were taken up by Anglican bishop-theologian John A. T. Robinson, Baptist theologian Harvey Cox, and various Protestants who became known as "death-of-God" theologians. In each instance (although with substantially different conclusions) these younger theologians accepted Bonhoeffer's remarkable starting-point —that the world has changed dramatically, that it no longer takes the reality of God and the supernatural order for granted (if it ever fully did anyway), and that it sees no necessary connection in any case between religious faith and formal affiliation with a religious community. Bishop Robinson's analysis appeared in a best-selling book, *Honest to God*, published in 1963; Harvey Cox's in a similarly successful work, *The Secular City*, published in 1965; and the "death-of-God" theologians in various articles and books, the most important of which was Thomas Altizer's *The Gospel of Christian Atheism* in 1966.

All these writers agreed that theology now had to be done according to a secular motif. (The word *secular* is from the Latin *saeculum*, meaning "world.") The Church is in and for the *world*, not above or apart from it. And Christ is a "man for others," not simply God in human form, remote from us and our human concerns. For Robinson and Cox this did not mean the denial of God or of spiritual realities (although the latter were not very strongly underscored in Cox until some of his later writings). It meant rather a new way of thinking and speaking about God, a new way of understanding the mission of the Church, and a new style of Christian existence. For the "death-of-God" group, however, it *did* mean the denial of God, the rejection of the Church, and the development of humanism without belief in the Lordship of Christ.

The Robinson-Cox approach prevailed over the "death-of-God" approach. The theology of Christ, of the Church, and of Christian morality was recast by many writers in the light of the changed human condition. The "human face" of Jesus, the servanthood of the Church, and the freedom and social responsibility of Christian existence were all emphasized, but without denying the abiding importance and religious value of each in itself.

But the Robinson-Cox approach did not prevail over *all* other approaches. With the social and political dislocations of the latter part of the decade, typified by the anti-Vietnam war protests and the dissolution of President Lyndon Johnson's "Great Society" program for domestic economic reform, Christian activism yielded in some quarters to a new Christian asceticism. There was a withdrawal from social and political involvement into new forms of spirituality represented in the Catholic Charismatic renewal, a movement begun in the aftermath of Vatican II as a way of better expressing and experiencing the Church as a community of prayer, rooted in the Bible and motivated by the power of the Holy Spirit.

By the mid-1970s the pendulum swung again, this time closer to the center. The response to the apparent eclipse of God and the supernatural, so abruptly perceived after the Second World War, was increasingly formulated on a "both/and" rather than an "either/or" basis. Jesus Christ is indeed fully human and totally sensitive to, and involved in, our personal concerns, but his sensitivity and involvement are of significance to us only because he is in the first instance the Son of God and the Lord of history. The Church is indeed called to be a servant community, but its service is of significance because it is in the first instance the Body of

Christ. And Christian existence is indeed a life of freedom and social responsibility, but it is a freedom given by the Holy Spirit and a responsibility for the Kingdom of God, or the realization of unity through the transforming presence of God's love and justice.

Chapter 6 will be devoted entirely to the problem of belief and unbelief. The preceding exposition and analysis, therefore, has been deliberately brief.

THE CHURCH IN THE MODERN WORLD

Sociologists describe the modernization process in different ways. Many insist that it has happened in spite of, or even over against, the Church; others, far fewer in number, insist just as strongly that Christian faith has made the scientific and technological revolutions possible in the first place. The former interpretation is offered by Talcott Parsons and his school of disciples; the latter view, by Andrew Greeley and, to some extent, Harvey Cox.

Parsons notes the growth of competing institutions alongside the Church and the family (governmental bureaucracies, business organizations, universities). Productive and economic functions shifted away from the family unit to the new corporations, while the Church yielded many of its legal, economic, and welfare roles to the new state bureaucracies. Greeley has argued, over against this view, that certain uniquely Christian notions led to the conclusion that science is not merely for knowledge but also for action: History is a process rather than a cycle; the universe is purposeful and therefore understandable; the world is a sacrament of God's presence, and we are called by God to collaborate with the divine plan by vigorous action in and for the world.

Harvey Cox had made a similar point in *The Secular City*. Secularization (i.e., the process of moving away from a religious answer to *every* human problem and toward the acceptance of substantial responsibility for the quality of human life) is not the enemy of the Gospel. On the contrary, the Bible's own sense of history requires it, starting with the Lord's command to Adam and Eve to name the animals in the Garden of Eden (Genesis 2:19-20). Unfortunately, humankind has frequently shrunk from the responsibility, starting with the moment in the same Garden of Eden when Adam and Eve allowed a serpent to dictate their action (Genesis 3:1-7).

Whatever the sociological explanation of the modernization process, it is clear that the world has changed markedly over the past few centuries, and has changed even more rapidly over the past several decades. We have already reviewed those changes. It is evident that science and technology have contributed mightily, not to say decisively, to them. Whether science and technology have developed in reaction to the Church and its faith, or whether science and technology have developed because of, and under the inspiration of, the Church and the Church's faith is a matter of sociological debate. From a purely theological point of view, however, the Greeley/Cox position is readily sustained, as we shall argue in the next two chapters.

The principal products of the scientific and technological revolutions, as we have seen, have been material and educational progress. These, in turn, have been supported by advances in transportation and communications. And these, in turn, have accentuated an essential aspect of human existence which was perhaps not sufficiently understood before the so-called modern period—namely, that men and women are persons in *dialogue*, that we grow by dialogue, that through dialogue we become increasingly aware of our interdependence, and that through our new awareness of interdependence we become increasingly sensitive to our responsibility for *the unity of the human race*.

The Church, therefore, need not be threatened by modernization. On the contrary, the modernization process only confirms what Christ and the Church have consistently taught: We are brothers and sisters, children of one Father in heaven, and we are to love one another as the Father has first loved us (John 15:9-17; 1 John 4:7-21). Modernization has disclosed that we cannot live isolated lives, that we can be fully human only insofar as we are open to the other in dialogue and in mutual support. Unfortunately, the principle is too often honored in the breach.

The Second Vatican Council, in the same *Pastoral Constitution*, correctly saw the crisis of modernization as a special opportunity for the Church. In the face of such developments, it said, more and more people are raising the most basic questions about the meaning of life or raising those questions with a new sharpness: "What is man? What is this sense of sorrow, of evil, of death, which continues to exist despite so much progress? What is the purpose of these victories, purchased at so high a cost? What can man offer to society, what can he expect from it? What follows this earthly life?" (n. 10).

These are the kinds of questions which are addressed in the next chapter.

SUMMARY

1.   The Catholic Church's first official *positive* acknowledgement of modernization (as opposed to the vehemently negative assessments of Pope Pius IX in his *Syllabus of Errors,* for example) came in the Second Vatican Council's *Pastoral Constitution on the Church in the Modern World*, known also by its Latin title, *Gaudium et spes* ("Joy and Hope"), drawn from the first words of the Latin text.

2.   The document is significant for its title: the Church *"in"* rather than *"and"* the modern world. The Church is not over against the world or apart from it. *The Church is in the world, and the world is in the Church.*

3.   The document is also significant for its positive emphasis on the "signs of the times," i.e., *those events of history through which God continues to speak to us and summon us to respond for the sake of the Kingdom*, which is the reign of God's love and justice throughout the whole of creation.

4.   The world in which the Church lives and for which the Church exists is *a world of change* at once profound and rapid. The change is evident in the growth of the world's population and in the improvement in the means of transportation and communication.

5.   Improvements in *transportation and communication* have been made possible by *science* (understanding how things work) and *technology* (applying science to practical problems). Their principal products have been *material growth* and *educational progress*. And these, in turn, have been enhanced by the aforementioned improvements in transportation and communication.

6.   But material and educational progess have *not* been *unmixed blessings.* The former has also produced a nuclear arms race, wars, pollution, health hazards in food, crime of all kinds. The latter has made more people aware of, and therefore troubled by, the gaps between

appearance and reality on a whole range of important human issues: personal freedom, sexual and racial identity, the use of power.

7. *Modernization* has also had a strong impact on religion in general and on Christianity in particular. *Positively*, religion has been increasingly purified of magical and superstitious overtones; *negatively*, many have abandoned the practice of religion as they have embraced rational and scientific explanations for problems once resolved by formally religious principles.

8. Christian theology responded to the "world come of age" (Bonhoeffer) in the mid-1960s by stressing the *secular or worldly aspects of Christian faith*: Jesus is a "man for others," the Church is a servant community, and Christian existence is one of freedom and social responsibility.

9. A *swing away from Christian activism* developed in the late 1960s and early 1970s. This new mood (represented, for example, in the Catholic Charismatic movement) emphasized spontaneity of prayer rooted in the Bible and in an unshakable confidence in the Holy Spirit.

10. The pendulum, however, swung again back toward the *center* by the mid-1970s. Christian activists increasingly recognized the need for prayer and other traditional spiritual values and practices, while charismatics and others acknowledged the abiding importance of social justice in the life and mission of the Church.

11. Whether the modernization process happened in spite of, or over against, the Church and its faith (Parsons and others), or whether it happened because of the Church and its faith (Greeley and others) is primarily a matter of *sociological debate*. On the basis of theological principles alone, however, the argument seems weighted in favor of the latter position.

12. In any case, modernization has italicized the necessity of dialogue for human growth and the fact of interdependence within the entire human community. The Church, therefore, need not be threatened by modernization. *It is a process which confirms, rather than undermines, the Church's historic message: that we are all brothers and sisters under God in Christ and that we must love one another and work unceasingly for the unity of the world.*

SUGGESTED READINGS

Berger, Peter. *The Heretical Imperative: Contemporary Possibilities of Religious Affirmation*. New York: Doubleday, Anchor, 1979.
Cox, Harvey. *The Secular City*. New York: Macmillan, 1965.

Geertz, Clifford. *The Interpretation of Cultures*. New York: Basic Books, 1973.

Greeley, Andrew. "Modernization." *No Bigger Than Necessary*. New York: New American Library, Meridian, 1977, pp. 29-43.

Robinson, John A. T. *Honest to God*. Philadelphia: Westminster Press, 1963.

Toffler, Alvin. *Future Shock*. New York: Random House, 1970.

Vatican Council II. "The Church in the Modern World" (*Gaudium et spes*). *The Documents of Vatican II*. Ed. Walter M. Abbott. New York: America Press, 1966, pp. 199-308.

·IV·

UNDERSTANDINGS OF HUMAN EXISTENCE

THE QUESTION: WHO ARE WE?

There can be no reasonable doubt that we live in an age of rapid and substantial change. However, some will argue that the changes have been, for the most part, beneficial to the human community. Others will insist that they have been harmful, even destructive. Each side takes its stand on the basis of some (often unstated) understanding of what it means to be human. One cannot, after all, have an opinion about what contributes to human progress unless one first has an opinion about what human beings need and identifies such needs in the light of one's perception of the fundamental structure and purpose of the human person and of the larger human community in which the person lives. Similarly, one cannot have an opinion about what impedes human progress unless one also has some antecedent opinion about what makes us "human" in the first place, and about what might threaten the "human" in all of us.

Anthropology is the umbrella term we use to embrace all of the scientific and disciplinary ways in which we raise and try to answer the question, "Who are we?" *Anthropology is our explanation of ourselves.* It means etymologically "the study of humankind" (*logos* and *anthropos*). What makes the anthropological question unique is that we are at once the questioner and the questioned. Consequently, our answers are always inadequate. They can only lead to further questions and further attempts at answers.

Indeed, if we could really get to the bottom of the matter and answer the question of ourselves without remainder, we would at that moment cease to be human. But even to draw that conclusion one has to have some prior understanding of human existence. Implied in that judgment (i.e., that we would cease to be human if we were to answer the question of ourselves finally and forever) is the conviction that freedom and openness to the future are intrinsic to the human condition. If we knew exactly what makes us what we are, what makes us act the way we act and think the way we think, every human thought and action would be programmable to achieve the precisely desired and/or intended effect.

We would marry only those whom our calculations revealed to be completely compatible with us. We would choose as friends only those with similar computerized clearance. We would associate ourselves professionally or occupationally only with those who could work with us most efficiently and effectively and who could best enhance the development of our careers. There would be no more risks, no more taking of chances. Everything and everyone would be plotted on a grid.

Life would no longer be a mystery to be faced and experienced with love, trust, hope, wonder, and not a little anxiety and fear. Decisions would no longer be provoked by crises of any kind. We would not have to choose between compelling alternatives. Motives would be unmistakably clear. Projections would be mathematically established.

Our freedom would be the freedom to bow to the evidence, or the freedom to be irrational and deny the undeniable (but even that display of irrationality would have been calculated and anticipated). As for the future, it would no longer be open. We would know it as we know the present and the past. Only physical and natural disorders (disease, famine, earthquakes, hurricanes, and the like) could disrupt our calculations, and even those would come increasingly under human control to the extent that human weakness, error, or lack of foresight was responsible for them in the first instance.

Even humor would disappear, for it essentially rests on our capacity to see discrepancies (things are not what they seem). The pompous general, in full uniform, slips on a banana peel in the midst of a military parade. The neighborhood bully is discovered to be terrified of spiders. An overbearing tightwad loses a ten-dollar bet after boasting loudly that he would be a sure winner. Indeed, there could be no real discrepancies at all. Things would always be as they seemed, for the motives and inner psychic forces governing the action of others would be apparent to all. Nothing would, or could, catch us off guard or by surprise. Laughter, which according to some philosophers is our way of defying the darkness of doubt and ignorance about the future, would be reduced to the sardonic chuckle of one "in the know."

Some, at first glance, might find the prospect of a totally calculable society positively exciting. Most others, it can fairly be assumed, would be frightened and appalled by the thought. In any case, the point remains moot for the time being. The emergence of test-tube babies, computer dating services, and various forms of behavior modification notwithstanding, we are still a long way from that kind of world. In the meantime, all of us continue to "make do" with what we have, to make decisions laden with risks, and to place our trust in people we are never fully and finally sure of.

We are, as the German philosopher Friedrich Nietzsche (d. 1900) put it, an "as yet undetermined animal." We can look back in history at the way we have used our freedom and then draw inferences about who we really are, about our motives and our actions. And since that history is *not yet finished*, our understanding of ourselves is always tentative, subject to revision. Since that history is also *multi-faceted*, our understanding of ourselves is possible only if we use a variety of approaches: biology, ethology, sociology, economics, politics, psychology, literature, philosophy, and theology.

The rest of this chapter will be taken up with the views on human existence of such disciplines as these. Given the nature of this book, major emphasis will be placed on philosophical and theological positions.

A SPECTRUM OF ANSWERS
The Natural Sciences:
Biology, Ethology, and Anthropology

For centuries our self-understanding as human beings had been expressed in terms of the *Ptolemaic world view:* The earth is the center of the whole universe, and we are the center of the earth by the design and will of God. With the *Copernican revolution* the sun displaced the earth as the center, and so we, too, were pushed closer to the margin of the cosmic order. But there endured a tenacious confidence in the powers of reason and in the intellectual faculty as the great line of demarcation between human beings and the rest of life. This conviction, too, would be put to the test in the middle of the nineteenth century.

Darwin

Charles Darwin (d. 1882) was a *biologist* who, in his early years, was at the same time a believing Christian. He accepted the fixity of species and their special creation as depicted in the book of Genesis. But doubts began to emerge in 1835 when he visited the Galápagos Archipelago, where he noticed that very small differences were present in the so-called species inhabiting separate islands. His original doubts were only reinforced by additional observations of flora, fauna, and geological formations at widely separated points of the globe. All living things, he tentatively concluded, have developed from a few extremely simple forms, through a gradual process of descent with modification. He developed a theory of natural selection to account for the process, and especially for the adaptations of living things to their often hostile environments. His findings were published in *The Origin of the Species* (1859).

At first there was strong opposition to his views from biologists themselves. They insisted that directly observed phenomena must somehow be brought under general laws. But before long all scientific opposition collapsed under the weight of arguments of the kind and force marshaled in a later work, *The Descent of Man,* published in 1871. The field of battle was left entirely to his newly aroused enemies in the ranks of Christianity. Darwin himself was a modest man, not given to polemics. His public image as an enemy of the Bible and the Church was as much caused by the activities of T. H. Huxley ("Darwin's bulldog"), who delighted in crossing swords with theologians, as by his own scientific hypotheses. But Darwin himself eventually grew away from his traditional faith. He concluded that "the whole subject is beyond the scope of man's intellect ....The mystery of the beginning of all things is insoluble for us; and I for one must be content to remain an Agnostic."

We cannot easily overestimate the importance of Darwin's work. No longer can any serious person reflect on the meaning of human existence as if each one of us lived in an environmental or cosmic vacuum. We are not disembodied spirits. We are bodily creatures, materially linked with the rest of creation, and especially with other living beings. Reason may indeed set us on a qualitatively different level of reality, but so, too, do our will, our emotions, our sexuality, our esthetic sense, and our total bodiliness.

Other natural scientists carried Darwin's insights forward. Harvard University *sociobiologist* Edward O. Wilson suggests that "the genes hold culture on a leash. The leash is very long, but inevitably values will be constrained in accordance with their effects on the human gene pool." Nature's first commandment, Wilson argues, is to do what is genetically advantageous. In two of his principal works, *Sociobiology: The New Synthesis* (1975) and *On Human Nature* (1978), he advances the thesis that aggression, sexual differences, religious impulses, and even altruism are biologically based products of natural selection. But unlike other sociobiologists he does not go so far as to justify either war or male dominance as the inevitable outcome of our biological destiny. On the contrary, we have seen only a small portion of the human behavior that is possible. The cultures which enhance or impede this genetic potential represent only a fraction of what is possible.

Lorenz

Konrad Lorenz, an Austrian *ethologist* (ethology is that branch of biology which focuses primarily on behavior), also pursued a path similar to Darwin's. From early childhood he recorded his observations of waterfowl and noted the impact of environment on their behavior. The essence of his thought is contained in his book *The Evolution and Modification of Behavior* (1953), but he is perhaps best known for his later work, *On Aggression*, published in 1966. Although he concedes that some behavior is environmentally conditioned (the extreme form of this view is proposed by the psychologist B. F. Skinner), he holds that other behavior is genetically programmed or "imprinted." Environmental factors, of course, develop what is innately present. But it is never sufficient to change the environment if one is to change behavior. In this he strongly opposes those who seem to argue that society, not the criminal, is responsible for crime.

Every person has what Lorenz calls a *nonrational sense of values*. This alone, he says, can prevent a retrograde evolution of civilized society because we have managed to eliminate in the meantime all other selective factors in human evolution. Included among these nonrational senses of values is *human love*. Lorenz argues that the abuse of sex through gross commercialization may be at least as harmful as excessive violence in the media. The destruction of the higher emotions, the disappearance of love (falling in love, being in love), may present more of a danger to the survival of culture than violence as such. Accordingly, Lorenz has relatively little enthusiasm for the popularization efforts of such writers as Robert Ardrey (d. 1980), *The Territorial Imperative* (1966), and even less for Desmond Morris, *The Naked Ape* (1967). The latter, he insists, treats culture as if it were biologically irrelevant. If one is to call human beings apes, then let them at least be culture-apes or the "ideal conception of all apes." That human beings are naked is irrelevant. We might just as well be furry.

Eiseley

Still other natural scientists interpret human existence in grim and pessimistic terms. *Anthropologist* Loren Eiseley's *The Firmament of Time* (1962) speaks of the evolution of the human being as if it were some kind of natural disaster drowning out the ancient sounds of nature "in the cacophony of something which is no longer nature, something instead which is loose and knocking at the world's heart, something demonic and no longer planned —escaped, it may be—spewed out of nature, contending in a final giant's game against its master."

The Social Sciences: Psychology, Sociology, Economics, Politics

Freud, Jung, Fromm

Whereas natural scientists have been interested in the interaction of human behavior and the world outside the person, *psychologists* have been concerned with the interaction of human behavior and the world *inside* the person. But even this statement has to be qualified. It may apply in large measure to the founder of modern psychology, Sigmund Freud (d. 1939), but to a much less extent to those who have followed in his path and/or developed courses of their own, such as Carl Jung (d. 1961) and Erich Fromm (d. 1980).

Freud, like Darwin, made his discoveries about human existence through direct observation. Darwin examined non-human life; Freud examined the human. He concluded that human behavior is shaped by unconscious drives and motivations and that these, in turn, have some sexual correlation. Our psychic lives consist in the inner struggle of conflicting drives for power and sexual gratification, on the one hand, and the psychic and social inhibitions against the fulfillment of those drives, on the other. One of his earliest works is also perhaps his most original, *The Interpretation of Dreams* (1900). Therein, he proposed the principle of wish fulfillment, the Oedipal complex, and the influence of infantile life in conditioning the human adult.

Strongly influenced by the *mechanical materialism* of his day, Freud's basic theories were highly quantitative. Even culture he regarded as a quantitative activity in which civilization is more or less determined by the degree or intensity of the *repression of instincts*. But Freud was no biological determinist. He saw that in history the only alternative to having no culture at all and no neuroses is having civilization with the repression and neuroses it necessarily entails. He looked upon the whole process of repression as a result of the social development of humankind. Unfortunately, he was innocent of the major sociological writings of the late nineteenth and early twentieth centuries: those of Marx, Durkheim, and Weber. He remained primarily interested in the psychological and physiological, even though he was considerably shaken by the events of the First World War and became noticeably less optimistic and rationalistic about human nature.

Nor was Freud a psychological determinist. On the contrary, he was trying to liberate us from those hidden psychic forces which direct our actions. If he had been a determinist, he would not have vested any hope in *therapy* as a means of changing motivation and behavior by making the person aware of the unconscious forces at work in his or her psychic life.

Freud, of course, will always have a cloud over his head in religious circles. Religion, for him, is the product of *wish-fulfillment*. God in heaven replaces the fallible and weak human father. By becoming and remaining religious, a person can prolong the status of a child into adult life. Religion, therefore, perpetuates infantile behavior patterns, especially those having to do with guilt and forgiveness. For that reason, religion is a particularly damaging species of illusion because it militates against our necessary efforts to distinguish always between what is and what we want reality to be.

One of Freud's colleagues, Carl Jung, tempered this harsh attitude toward religion. It was Jung who introduced the distinction between the individual and the *collective unconscious*. The latter originates in those patterns of behavior (archetypes) which are determined by the human race itself and which show themselves in dreams, visions, and fantasies, and are expressed in myths, religious stories, fairy tales, and works of art. Consequently, the many images which abound in human history are more than primitive expressions. They are a necessary and profound expression of a communal experience. And this is especially true of Christianity and its rich symbol system.

Erich Fromm, a German psychoanalyst, is in the tradition of Freud (in fact is often referred to as a "neo-Freudian") but, by his own account, wishes to liberate Freud's most important discoveries from his somewhat narrow libido theory. Unlike Freud, Erich

Fromm insists that much human behavior is *culturally* rather than biologically conditioned. Culture structures persons to conform to the social mold. We are what we have to be, in accordance with the requirements of the society in which we find ourselves. Depending upon our response to these social exigencies, we can be either productive persons or automatons.

Productive persons, Fromm says, are individuals who are relatively independent of others in producing what they need for themselves as they function in society, not just economically but emotionally and intellectually as well. A productive person has a sense of his or her own authority, and the courage of his or her convictions. This is what authenticity means. Automaton conformists, on the other hand, yield to the dictates of others, faithfully obeying every signal designed to control human behavior.

Clearly, Fromm holds, the second kind of individual is the one closer to the norm of humanity. We are indeed freaks of nature in that we represent "the only case of a living organism having awareness of itself." We are beings, therefore, who seek an answer to the question of why we were born and why we are living. But we can progress or regress. We progress by increasing our powers of reason, love, and relatedness to others. We regress by seeking only security. In Fromm's judgment, we seem to be losing the battle, although compelling human figures like Pope John XXIII are encouraging reminders of the deep reservoir of strength still present within the human community.

Marx

Karl Marx (d. 1883) is, of course, *sociologist, economist,* and *political theorist* wrapped up in one. Best known for his *Communist Manifesto* (1847) and *Capital* (1867), Marx, like Darwin, argued that human beings are definable only in relation to other realities. For Darwin, human beings are part of the larger natural order. For Marx, they are part of the larger *social* order. "The essence of man is no abstraction inherent in each separate individual," he wrote. "In its reality it is the ensemble of social relations." And Marx, like Freud, insisted that human problems are traceable to conflicts produced by *alienation.* For Freud, the alienation is from one's true self; for Marx, the alienation is from the fruits of one's labors and thus from the industrialized world and from other people. We are distinguished from the rest of the animal kingdom by the way we express our lives: by our work, by our various activities, by our changing of the environment, and especially by our producing our own means of subsistence.

But no individual human being, Marx holds, can sufficiently express himself or herself without benefit of society. Only in society, by joint effort, can we express ourselves in the complex way we do. Human beings, therefore, do not really appear on the historical scene until there is society, for *it is only in and through society, the collective, that we are who and what we are.* It is already there when we are born, and it conditions the kind and quality of lives we lead. The individual is derived from society and, therefore, is secondary and subordinate to it.

However, Marx maintains, if each person is essentially social, then each person should enjoy and share in all of the fruits of social collaboration. But because of the structure of capitalist societies, we are divided into the haves and the have-nots, masters and slaves, capitalists and proletarians. The great mass of humankind is alienated or separated from the products of its labors. Instead of expressing themselves through their labor (as in a work of art), most human beings are forced to sell their products to some entrepreneur in order to survive. Moreover, instead of expressing themselves fully through a variety of activities, they are forced to perform only one monotonous task all day long while someone else performs another (a process Marx called the "division of labor").

The solution to this unhappy state of affairs lies in changing the economic base on which society is built, Marx argues. It is not enough, in other words, to *interpret* the world (as Marx accused Feuerbach (d. 1872) of doing), but we must also struggle to *change* it. The way to free human beings from alienation is to destroy its causes: private property and the division of labor. We shall once again enjoy the fruits of our own labors and the labors of our fellow human beings in a society he called "communist." In such a society, *each contributes according to ability and receives according to need.* When we have all we need, there will be no envy, theft, or other crimes against our fellow human beings. The world, one might suggest, awaits the evidence.

Important elements of Marxist theory have, of course, been adopted generally, even in the West. There is a greater recognition of the need to change social and economic structures to achieve justice. We have become more fully aware of the impact of economic factors in the history of ideas and on our accumulation of knowledge. And *laissez-faire* liberalism, of the sort Marx himself faced, has been rejected as an unacceptable and ultimately unjust expression of economic values. On the other hand, there is an unmistakable conflict between Marxist theory and human freedom: freedom of expression, freedom of worship, freedom of movement, freedom of communication, freedom of thought. The crude and cruel suppression of the uprisings in Hungary (1956) and Czechoslovakia (1968), the harassment of Alexander Solzhenitsyn and other Soviet dissidents, and the human slaughter that followed the Communist "liberation" of Cambodia in 1975 are only a few cases in point.

There have been recent efforts to extricate Marxism from its almost obsessive preoccupation with economics and use it instead as an all-embracing critical social theory, with some emphasis on cultural criticism and even psychoanalysis. A noteworthy example is the so-called Frankfurt School of social criticism, composed of such figures as Herbert Marcuse (d. 1979), Jürgen Habermas, and others. They have tended to explain very well what has to be changed in human society to maximize freedom but less well what has to be preserved. The objectives of the change also remain vague. From its very beginning, in fact, this group of theorists has resisted the temptation to develop a coherent philosophical system. It has always functioned instead as a kind of gadfly of other existing systems and points of view.

The Humanities: Literature

The implications of the Marxist image of human beings were explored by Arthur Koestler in *Darkness at Noon* (1961). The novel's subject is the great Soviet purges of the 1930s and the imprisoning, interrogation, and trial of Rubashov, one of the old guard of the Russian revolution. Rubashov now feels a sense of guilt for some of his actions on behalf of the Party, including even the sacrifice of his own secretary. He had done it unquestioningly. The Party was clearly supreme over every individual need or want. But looking back over his behavior, Rubashov now sees how inhuman it was. In his fidelity to an abstract idea, he had effectively denied the reality of human beings.

John Steinbeck's *Grapes of Wrath* (1939) offers a different approach. Tom Joad, whose family has been uprooted from Oklahoma to work in the fields of California, devotes himself to the fight for social justice through the organization of the workers and the strikes. His response to alienation is not filtered through an abstract philosophical system but through personal dedication to real people caught in inhuman conditions. Yet even Tom Joad is not free of further torment. He kills the man who has killed his friend, Jim Casy, and has to leave his family.

Both novels show how socialized we are. The sources of alienation are in society itself, and our common challenge is their removal.

T. S. Eliot (d. 1965) begins with life as it is experienced today: empty and inauthentic. In the *Love Song of J. Alfred Prufrock* (1917) we find social consciousness almost completely inverted. Prufrock thinks only of what others think of him (Fromm's "automaton conformity"). For Prufrock as for Sartre, hell is other people. It is the world of the *Waste Land* (1922), dry and lifeless, a kind of death in life. In the latter part of *Waste Land* the thunder brings rain, but it signifies the rebirth of an individual, not the salvation of humankind. The landscape remains desolate. In his later writings, however, Eliot draws from Christian mysticism, which requires prayer, silence, and ritual. But that mysticism is also for a community, not just for an individual. The community he describes is hierarchically structured, and so Eliot's image of the human race is of one that is divided into classes. Meaningfulness is derived from one's sense of place within the hierarchy. There is a kind of "high Church" elitism here that is barely concealed.

Georges Bernanos' (d. 1948) *Diary of a Country Priest* (1936) poses a contrast with Eliot's Becket in *Murder in the Cathedral*

(1935). The country priest is young, inexperienced, and pastorally awkward. Beset by a lack of self-confidence and illness, the priest nonetheless assumes the burdens of his people, identifying readily with their suffering and pain. His clumsiness and ineptitude remain with him to the end. But unlike too many of our contemporaries torn by inner conflicts, self-hate, and insecurity, the country priest deals with life in a manner that is at once honest, humble, and self-accepting. And so he dies at peace.

We have, to be sure, only lightly touched the surface in this brief exploration of the meaning of human existence in literature. A more thorough investigation would take us through Shakespeare, Milton, Dostoevsky, Tolstoy, and countless other recent and modern works.

Philosophy

The distinction between philosophy and theology is not easily discerned. The old explanation will simply not do, namely, that philosophy proceeds from reason, while theology proceeds from revelation and faith. On the other hand, it is almost impossible to define philosophy. Any attempted definition proves to be itself one of the many philosophies which now exist. The question of the distinction between philosophy and theology is further complicated by the fact that theology and at least some philosophies claim to be concerned with the whole of reality and, therefore, universal in scope. The solution offered by the First Vatican Council—that truth comes from the same God and cannot be contradictory—is not sufficient. It is not clear, for example, whether one can be both a philosopher and a theologian at the same time, or whether such a choice has to be made at all.

Why, then, will the traditional explanation not do, namely, that philosophy proceeds from reason, and theology from revelation and faith? Because reason itself enters into the process of understanding faith and of identifying criteria and signs of revelation. On the other hand, revelation and grace are universally available, even to the philosopher. No matter how hard he or she might try, the philosopher is inevitably influenced by the faith (Christian or not) which he or she brings to the investigation of a

problem. Indeed, the problems themselves are often as much theological as they are philosophical: What does it mean to be human?
How are we free? What does happiness consist in? What is justice?
What is the measure of truth? How and why are we propelled in
the pursuit of truth? Philosophy clearly points itself and its practitioners in the direction of God, and so onto the course marked out
by theology itself.

But there is no single philosophy nor only one point of view
on the ultimate meaning of life. "Philosophical" understandings of
human existence cover a wide range on the spectrum: existentialist, phenomenological, processive, positivist, and pragmatic.

Existentialism

The Danish Lutheran Sören Kierkegaard (d. 1855) is perhaps the
founder of modern *existentialist* thought. He was the first to
emphasize the *subject* as a responsible person who must always be
ready to stand alone before God without benefit of some social,
even ecclesiastical, shield. By thus stressing individuality and
authenticity, Kierkegaard challenged the Hegelian emphasis on
the abstract and the universal. Our individuality, Kierkegaard
argued, is bound up with the awareness of our limitations and
especially our awareness of impending death. Therefore, it is our
relationship with the Absolute that finally counts, not our relationships with one another. "Sickness unto death" and "dread" are
characteristic of "existential man." But Kierkegaard does not
interpret them as Freud had. In his *Fear and Trembling* (1843)
Kierkegaard contrasts the "ethical man" with the "religious
man." The former is one who subordinates himself to universal
moral imperatives (as Kant would have it); the latter obeys divine
commands made directly to him as a person, as Abraham did when
he was commanded to slay his son Isaac. For Kierkegaard, Abraham is a model of the responsible individual, who obeys the call of
faith without seeking to be justified before anything less than the
presence of God. His responsible bond with God is maintained,
not by means of the categorical imperative, but by reason of his
personal, inward dedication of self to God.

Friedrich Nietzsche, in the same spirit but with far different results, also wanted to do away with externally imposed values. We can recover our lost freedom only through internally created values, he held. Like Kierkegaard, Nietzsche rejected Hegel's system of universals and abstractions. In *Thus Spake Zarathustra* (1883) the transcendent no longer has any effective power and is submerged in the evils of the times. Under the circumstances man has to deify himself (Nietzsche's superman), but is aware of his own impotence in the face of a hostile world. Meaning is not out there, waiting to be perceived and appropriated. It is something we have to create by ourselves. And since this process is carried on by many men and women, the real image of the human person will emerge only through the struggle of various groups in value-creating acts. But, of course, Nietzsche had to assume some of the values that he insisted had to be created.

Unlike Jean Paul Sartre (d. 1980), for whom human existence is hell, Albert Camus (d. 1960) eventually finds meaning in life, especially in such later works as *The Rebel* (1952). Although we must rebel against the absurd, against tyranny, and even against God, our rebellion must be controlled or it can lead to disaster. We can never justify the harming of other human beings. There must, in fact, be *dialogue* among us. It is only through dialogue that we discover values together. Such values come not from abstract principles but from reflection on concrete life-situations. Modern persons must struggle against those forces in the world which war against dialogue: oppression, injustice, fear, and the like.

Martin Buber (d. 1965), the Jewish theologian and philosopher, took dialogue a step beyond Camus. He wrote of the paradox inherent in every dialogue, where each party remains himself or herself even as he or she draws very close to the other. The principal expression of his view is contained in his *I and Thou* (1958). Our relationships are of two kinds: I-thou and I-it. There is nothing wrong with the latter unless they dominate and eventually suppress the former. The opposite of I-thou dialogue is monologue, which implies selfishness and manipulation. Buber is clearly more positive than Kierkegaard about the value of interpersonal relations with other human beings. We accept God precisely insofar as we accept God's creation.

The existentialist philosopher who has exercised the greatest influence on modern theology is Martin Heidegger (d. 1976). His *Being and Time* (1927) may be the most significant philosophical book published in this century. He provides, in fact, a bridge between existentialist thought and *phenomenology*. If we are to come to an understanding of what it means to be human, Heidegger argues, then we must reflect on what it is that we are and do. This requires some preliminary descriptive steps.

We must first of all look to see what shows itself (*phenomenon*) or lets itself be seen in human existence. The test of such description is to compare it with what we ourselves actually know of existence through our own firsthand participation in it. But it is not a simple matter. Existence is not an object we can set before us and describe from the outside. We ourselves are the existents that are to be described, and self-knowledge is exceedingly difficult. Indeed we all have a tendency to conceal the truth not only from others but even from ourselves. We have to strip away the cover. When we do, we find that selfhood is not ready-made but rather is always on the way and always incomplete at any given moment. We can either attain to authentic selfhood by realizing the possibilities open to us, or we can fall below the standard of authentic existence.

An analysis of human existence discloses certain tensions or polarities. First, there is the polarity between *existence and facticity,* that is, between freedom and finitude. We exist in a world. Our possibilities, therefore, are not unrestricted. They are limited by the concrete situation in which we find ourselves, including all the "givens" of human existence such as intelligence, race, temperament, environment, heredity.

A second polarity exists between *rationality and irrationality.* Our minds move toward truth, and at the same time toward untruth, error, and deception. Freud, as we have already noted, helped us see the frightening extent to which our lives are governed by dark and irrational forces.

A third polarity exists between *responsibility and impotence.* We recognize what we "ought" to be doing and yet cannot bring ourselves to do what is demanded. In the words of the Epistle to the Romans: "What happens is that I do, not the good that I will to do, but the evil I do not intend. This means that even though I want to do what is right, a law that leads to wrongdoing is always ready at hand. My inner self agrees with the law of God, but I see in my body's members another law at war with the law of my mind; this makes me the prisoner of the law of sin in my members" (7:19–23).

A fourth polarity exists between *anxiety and hope.* In a sense, this polarity sums up all the rest. A life lived in the midst of tensions generated by such polarities as these can never be free from anxiety, i.e., from a sense of the threat of absurdity and negativity. On the other hand, such a life can be lived only on the basis of the hope that life is somehow worthwhile. Anxiety springs from the sense of the radical difference that separates us from the totality of reality, while hope springs from the sense of belonging to that totality and having some affinity with it.

A fifth polarity exists between the *individual and society.* Human beings realize themselves and their varied possibilities only in and through interaction with other human beings. *Sexuality* and *language* make this unmistakably clear. Every human being is incomplete insofar as the reproductive function is concerned, and the existence of language shows that we are essentially beings in need of communication with one another.

But it is *death* that sets the framework of human existence. When one becomes aware of the boundary or limit of human existence, then one also has recognized that this is one's *own* existence. If there is no thought of death and if the future is regarded as stretching out indefinitely, then there is no great sense of urgency or responsibility. In the inauthentic mode of existence, death is covered up. We employ euphemisms and treat the whole matter impersonally. We acknowledge that everyone must die, but we somehow manage to put our own death off into the indefinite future.

Authentic existence, however, requires that we come to terms with our own death and recognize it for what it is: the boundary and limit of our own personal existence. We are thus compelled to think of all the possibilities that are open to us this side of death and to try and bring these possibilities into some kind of overarching unity. (Recent discussions of the stages of human development—mid-life crisis, etc.—are consistent with Heidegger's perspective.) Death, therefore, is not simply the end of life, but the force that introduces a wholeness and unity into life.

Phenomenology

If existentialism is primarily concerned with the human person as a source of freedom and spontaneous activity, *phenomenology is concerned chiefly with the person as knower.* The connection, however, between knowing and deciding is very close, and so, too, is the connection between these two philosophical movements.

Edmund Husserl (d. 1938) is the founder of modern phenomenology, and the publication of his *Logical Investigations* in 1900 and 1901 marks the beginning of this movement. This work attacked what Husserl called "psychologism," which in its extreme forms is found in behaviorism. Consciousness, Husserl argued, is not materially explainable. It has a structure and rules proper to itself. Consciousness is never closed in upon itself, however. It has an intentionality; i.e., it is always conscious of something, of *phenomena.*

Phenomenology studies such phenomena, not as things in themselves (as other sciences do) but as objects of intentionality. But it does not revert to psychologism because phenomenology maintains that there is a fundamental and irreducible duality between consciousness and the world. The two are correlated as the eye is correlated with the field of vision. There can be no field of vision without the eye, and yet the two remain distinct. For the same reason there can be no reality without consciousness. The task of phenomenology is to describe the various regions of reality in the way they appear to consciousness, and to show what activity consciousness must carry out in order to allow such regions of reality to appear.

For Husserl, as for Heidegger, we are beings in time. Our past experiences enter into our present consciousness and personality. A material thing like a stone can pass through innumerable events and not be changed at all by them. A human person, on the other hand, is changed by what happens. The past is borne within the person because present consciousness retains what is past. And yet we are never imprisoned by the past. We never entirely lose the possibility of changing or redeeming the past, because the present is also open upon the future.

And what applies to the person as individual applies to the human community as a whole. Human temporality, therefore, is not a passive reality. We are not simply caught up in the flow of time. Through our consciousness we look forward to the future and retain the past. We are thereby empowered to engage in a process of inquiry into who and what we really are.

Maurice Merleau-Ponty (d. 1961) is in the same philosophical tradition as Husserl. He differs from him, however, by reducing consciousness to the lived corporeal experience. We are *embodied* spirits.

Process Thought

Alfred North Whitehead (d. 1947) began as a mathematician but turned to philosophy. His mathematical penchant for order, generalization, and systematization, however, never left him. He insisted on the interrelatedness of all reality and on human knowledge's exclusive concern with relatedness. The perceiver is a natural organism reacting to the world around him. But our experience of that world is of durations (events), not of point-instants. Change is otherwise unintelligible. In change the past flows into the present, as durations can but instants cannot. The past remains fixed and determined, however, while the future is open and indeterminate. Because of freedom we can "clutch at novelty" and alter the course of events. Religion, in the meantime, helps us maintain some sense of the importance of our individual experience within the social relationships and flowing experience of life.

One commentator has suggested that no one will ever succeed in writing a short account of Whitehead's work. That is undoubtedly true. It is a very complicated system of thought. On the other hand, the recent, almost inordinate, popularity of "process thought" in Catholic educational circles suggests that complexity is no obstacle. If the truth be told, it is only the *general notion* of process rather than the actual body of process philosophy which has been appropriated and applied.

Positivism

The starting-point of positivism is that *the only possible source of knowledge is our sense experience.* If we have no tangible data, we can make no judgments and reach no conclusions. We can deal only with what is there. The sociological counterpart of philosophical positivism is August Comte (d. 1857), who argued that science can be concerned only with facts, not values. Ludwig Wittgenstein (d. 1951) is the principal exponent of philosophical positivism. The task of philosophy, for him, is not the investigation of facts (which is the task of the exact sciences) but the logical analysis of language-units (words, propositions, speech as a whole) by which we speak of the world. There are only two kinds of meaningful propositions: those about factual relationships stemming from experience and verifiable by experience, and those about purely logical relationships which provide no factual knowledge and hence are valid independently of experience.

Positivism provides little in the way of a philosophy of human existence. Positively, it underlines our responsibility to reality as it is, not as we would like it to be. Negatively, it lacks openness to experience in all its dimensions including the religious and metaphysical, which means that positivism, in spite of its humane intentions, is silent in the face of the great human problems. "And so it is impossible," Wittgenstein writes in his *Tractatus Logico-Philosophicus* (1921) "for there to be propositions of ethics."

Pragmatism

John Dewey (d. 1952) is in the tradition of Darwin and process philosophy. The leading characteristic of his thought is its evolutionary emphasis. Many of Dewey's criticisms, in fact, are directed against the older traditional metaphysics which stressed the unchanging essence of humankind and of the universe. Human thought, therefore, is not for constructing great cosmic systems of reality but for solving problems in an intelligent and reflective way. Experience is something to be reconstituted. There is nothing beyond experience. We have to take reality as we find it and reconstruct our goals in keeping with our situation and our environment.

There is, of course, a strong similarity not only between Dewey and Darwin but also between Dewey and Marx. All three hold that it is not enough to theorize about reality; we are called upon to change it. A concept without practical consequences has no real meaning. Thus, the term *pragmatism* describes this school of thought. Dewey also used the term *instrumentalism*. Ideas, hypotheses, and theories are only so many tools for attaining concrete goals in life. But if there are no metaphysical principles independent of practical content, there can be no absolute moral norms by which one can determine the good. An ethical relativism follows.

Philosophies of Human Existence: A Synthesis

Modern philosophy is essentially a reaction against classical philosophy (Aristotle, Plato, Aquinas) on the one hand, and Idealism (Hegel) on the other. In modern philosophy there is an emphasis on the *subject*, on the *changeable*, on the *particular*, and on the *practical*, as opposed to the objective, the unchanging, the universal, and the theoretical. Thus, *Existentialism* stresses the individual's obligation to take responsibility for his or her life, and, along with *Phenomenology, Positivism, Process thought*, and *Pragmatism*, it stresses the individual's obligation to attend to reality and to history as they are, not as we would wish them to be or as we would abstractly conceive them to be. Neither reality nor the history within which human reality is framed is static and unchanging; they are in process, from a past that is fixed because complete to a future that is as yet open, undetermined. We are called upon to shape that future by reconstructing our experience and reforming our environment to the extent that consciousness and practicality allow. Human existence, therefore, is not a given to be examined, but a potential in process of realization.

Theology

Existentialism

The major existentialist theologian of this century is Rudolf Bultmann (d. 1976), a German Lutheran. It was he who applied the philosophy of Heidegger to the interpretation of the New Testament. And it was he who initiated on the Continent and in the United States a whole school of theological reflection characterized by an emphasis on the faith and consciousness of the individual believer. Nowhere is his approach expressed more simply or more succinctly than in his *Jesus Christ and Mythology* (1958).

"The question of God and the question of myself," he wrote, "are identical." Accordingly, when the Bible tells me about God, he says, it really is addressing me about myself, about the meaning of human existence. For Bultmann, existentialist philosophy offers the most adequate perspective and conceptions for understanding human existence. It does not say to me "In such and such a way you must exist." It says only "You must exist" or at least says what it means to exist.

Every person has his or her own history, Bultmann goes on. Always the present comes out of the past and leads to the future. We realize our existence if we are aware that each "now" is the moment of free decision: What is the element in the past to be retained? What is our responsibility toward the future? No one can take another's place, since every one of us must die his or her own death. In our loneliness we realize our existence.

Christian existence (or "eschatological existence") is not a worldly phenomenon but is realized in our new *self-understanding*. I encounter God not in the other nor even in myself but in the divine Word. So focused, in fact, is Bultmann's thought on the individual believer that some critics (e.g., Johannes Metz) have described his theology as "privatized." The socio-political dimension is all but lost.

Paul Tillich (d. 1965), another German Lutheran existentialist theologian who spent many years lecturing in the United States, stressed the anxiety *(Angst)* of moderns, not as something neurotic or pathological, but as something intrinsic to the human condition. Such anxiety has several sources. First, every person must have *meaning* in life, or the power of self-affirmation and integration is lost. Secondly, each has to struggle constantly with the burden of *guilt*, whether from specific actions or as a vague, general backdrop. Without some means to deal with guilt, we are led into moral confusion and aimlessness. Finally, there is the underlying *fear of death*, which poses the greatest threat of all to the self. Only by coming to terms with the world can we deal with this anxiety about death.

It is by our participation in God, who is the infinite power to resist the threat of nonbeing, that we acquire the "courage to be" fully, even in the face of these three forms of anxiety. Similarly, when we become deeply aware of historical existence as full of ambiguities, we become filled with perplexities and despair. The Christian answer is the notion of the *Kingdom of God*, which is the meaning, fulfillment, and unity of history.

Reinhold Niebuhr (d. 1971), an American Protestant theologian, also centered his attention upon the category of *anxiety*. Anxiety arises from our recognition of the limitations and contingencies of our existence and from our imagining a life infinitely better than this one. Such anxiety generates sin because we seek to bring anxiety under control by pretending to have power or knowledge or virtues or special favors from God, and this pretense leads, in turn, to pride, cruelty, and injustice. Or else we seek to escape our anxieties by turning inward and pursuing a life of sensuality.

Though not inevitable, sin is universal and existed even before we became sinners. The condition of sin and anxiety, however, leaves us in a state of despair. We sense ourselves as being at once bound and free. We are bound insofar as we are involved in the flux of time; we are free insofar as we stand outside of time. We are aware of this capacity to stand apart because we know ourselves as object, we can judge ourselves as sinners, and we can survey the past and the future. We also know that nothing actually operating in history can ever sufficiently deliver us from despair, despite our optimistic illusions to the contrary. Only a divine, forgiving, timeless love beyond history, such as has been revealed in Jesus Christ, gives meaning to human life.

Phenomenology

A Dutch Catholic theologian, Edward Schillebeeckx, adopts a phenomenological approach to the meaning of existence, consistent with the basic approach he followed earlier in his treatment of the sacraments, in *Christ the Sacrament of Encounter with God* (1960). Rejecting both positivism on the one hand and the classical definition of human nature on the other, Schillebeeckx proposes a theology of human existence based on what he calls "anthropological constants" (see his "Questions on Christian Salvation of and for Man," in *Toward Vatican III: The Work That Needs to Be Done*, David Tracy, ed. New York: Seabury Press, 1978, pp. 27-44). These constants point in a general way toward lasting human impulses, orientations, and values. Among these constants are the following: (1) the relation of the human person to his or her own bodiliness (a human being *is* and *has* a body); (2) our coexistence with other persons (the human face is an image of oneself *for others*); (3) our relation to social and institutional structures (they are not something added but are intrinsic to our existence); (4) our relation to space and time; (5) our capacity, even our drive, to imagine an ideal state (*Utopia*) which becomes the impulse of hope for the future.

Since the human condition is inevitably characterized by suffering, all action which seeks to conquer suffering presupposes at least an implicit and vague anticipation of a possible, future universal meaning (Kingdom of God). We refuse, therefore, to submit to the absolute reign of technocracy (which is itself one of the causes of suffering). Schillebeeckx's phenomenological approach is akin to, and certainly highly sympathetic with, the liberation approach summarized below in the subsection on theological pragmatism.

Process Thought

The most celebrated theological exponent of process thought is Teilhard de Chardin (d. 1955). His influence on recent and contemporary Catholic thinking is difficult to calculate but impossible to deny. Some have suggested, in fact, that his spirit hovers over the Second Vatican Council's *Pastoral Constitution on the*

Church in the Modern World, particularly its assertion that "the human race has passed from a rather static concept of reality to a more dynamic, evolutionary one" (n. 5).

Teilhard's basic premise is that all of reality, the whole of the cosmic order, is moving toward a goal (the *Omega Point*), gradually progressing from one state of development to another, each one more unified than the preceding. The highest stage of material development is life. The highest stage in the development of life is human life. With human life, consciousness achieves a level of self-reflection. We not only *know*; we *know that we know.* Human existence, therefore, represents a new and unique order of being.

Although it may appear that the "cosmic involution" (the movement toward unity) has been halted, this is not true. *Hominization,* or the progressive development of human life to higher and higher levels, continues with even greater vigor than before. We can observe this in the increasingly powerful thrust toward *socialization.* As a result of socialization, humankind is continuing to advance towards the supreme degree of consciousness. The conclusions of physics, biology, and psychology confirm this judgment, Teilhard insists. As a result of humankind's standing on its own feet, life is here and now entering a new era of autonomous control and self-orientation. We are beginning to take over the biological forces which heretofore have determined our growth. The whole evolutionary process is moving constantly toward unification and spiritualization, with the whole cosmic system rising unmistakably toward a critical point of final convergence. We shall have reached such a level of self-consciousness that no further growth will be possible. This he calls the Omega Point.

As a Christian, Teilhard equates the Omega Point with Christ. *History, therefore, is in movement toward Christ.* But Christ is already present in the world. There is even now a Christic dimension to the cosmic order. The Church, in this schema, is the "reflexively Christified portion of the world," the focal point at which human socialization based on charity occurs. Indeed, this is the whole impulse of creation. "To create is to unite," Teilhard declares. The whole of history is the story of the progressive unification of reality and of the human community in particular.

But an inevitable consequence of creation is *sin* (here, of course, Teilhard's thought runs counter to traditional Catholic doctrine on Original Sin, to which we shall return in the next chapter). Because created reality is multiple, it is essentially subject in its arrangements to the operation of chance, and therefore is "absolutely barred from progressing towards unity without sporadically engendering evil, and that as a matter of statistical necessity."

Just as sin is inevitable, so, too, is *incarnation*. There can be no creation without union of Creator with the created. For in order to create, God must be immersed in the multiple, and is even forced into war with the evil element in the multiple. The coming of Christ—another inevitable requirement and effect of the evolutionary process—maintains the evolutionary effort toward hominization by providing a focus of biological involution (involution meaning here again the movement toward unification). In Christ-Omega the universal comes into exact focus and assumes a personal form.

For the person who sees what is happening, who perceives the whole evolutionary process in the light of Christ, everything becomes animate and a fit object for love and worship. *Christian charity*, far from being simply a soothing lotion poured over the world's suffering, *is the most complete and the most active agent of hominization.*

Theological Positivism

For anyone who has been following the argument very closely thus far, this may seem a curious, if not a dubious, category. How can there be a *positivism* that is at the same time *theological?* Is not positivism a denial of what is not directly observable? And does that not include God above all else? The answer is, "Yes, of course. But ...." We are referring here not to positivism in its technical philosophical sense (such as we described in the brief section on Wittgenstein) but to positivism as a general method or approach.

Positivism limits the study of a reality to that reality's appearance in a given source or sources. A *theological* positivist is one who equates theology with the study of a given source or sources. Thus, theology is not (as we defined it in the second chapter) the process of giving expression to our experience of God, but rather the study of *documents* in which the experience of God has been recorded and interpreted (especially the Bible or the official teachings of the Church). The theological positivist understands theology as the study of the Bible (which is really equating all of theology with biblical theology) or with the study of doctrines and dogmas (which is to equate all of theology with dogmatic theology). Theology is either "the testing of Church doctrine and proclamation . . . by the standard of the Holy Scriptures" (Karl Barth, d. 1968) or is the transmission of the teaching of the Church (the methodological assumption of many Catholic theology textbooks in use prior to Vatican II).

The similarity between Wittgenstein and Barth, for example, is at least superficially apparent in the latter's definition of theology with which he begins his massive, multi-volume *Church Dogmatics*: Theology is "the scientific test to which the Christian Church puts herself regarding the language about God which is peculiar to her." For Wittgenstein, the task of philosophy is the logical analysis of language-units (words, propositions, etc.) by which we speak of the world. It does not get beyond the language to deal with the reality so described or talked about.

In theological terms, the Word of God in Sacred Scripture is taken as a given. It is simply there. One does not question it or challenge it. One comes to terms with it. For some Catholics, the same attitude prevails regarding the pronouncements of the official magisterium. Our understanding of human existence, therefore, is to be derived totally from the Bible or from the official teachings of the Church. Philosophy, or anthropology in the widest sense, is of no significant account in the inquiry.

Pragmatism: Liberation Theology

The parallel between philosophical and theological pragmatism is the same as the parallel between philosophical and theological positivism. In the strict sense of the terms, there is no theological pragmatism, just as there is no theological positivism. But there are similarities in method and approach. It is those similarities which engage our attention here.

The closest approximation of philosophical pragmatism in contemporary Christian theology is in the *Latin American liberation school*. We have already referred briefly to liberation theology in the second chapter. Its principal exponents are, on the Catholic side, Gustavo Gutierrez of Peru and Juan Luis Segundo of Uruguay, and, on the Protestant side, Hugo Assmann of Brazil. They reject both the traditional Catholic and traditional Protestant approaches to theology, the one emphasizing doctrine and intellectual assent, and the other emphasizing the Bible and trusting faith. Theology is faith seeking understanding, the liberation theologians admit, but faith is "the historical *praxis* of liberation."

The Word of God is mediated, they insist, through the cries of the poor and the oppressed. Theology, therefore, can only be a form of *praxis*; i.e., it must always be directed toward the changing of the existing social order. It cannot simply interpret it without reference to the practical consequences of the theory of interpretation. Only by participating in the struggles of the poor and the oppressed, Gutierrez argues, can we understand the implications of the Gospel message and make it have an impact on history. This, in turn, imposes a specific method on theology, which Juan Luis Segundo calls a "hermeneutic circle." This requires that our interpretation of the Bible change continually with the continual changes in our present-day reality, both individual and social.

The similarity not only to pragmatism but to positivism as well should be apparent. For the liberation school, theology's reflection on *praxis* is grounded in the Bible. Theology is essentially the study of the Bible insofar as it can be interpreted according to a liberation motif. That motif is, in turn, communicated through actual participation in the struggle for liberation. The affinity, finally, with the Marxist view of human existence is too obvious to draw out here.

Transcendental Thomism

For Karl Rahner the problem of human existence is not simply one theological question among many others. The "question of man," he insists, "must be looked upon, rather, as the whole of dogmatic theology." He argues that such a view is entirely consistent with Thomas Aquinas' teaching that God is the formal object of theology. As soon as it is understood that the human person stands alone in the whole of creation as the one being who is absolutely oriented toward God and whose very essence is determined by this orientation, then it becomes clear that a thorough study of the human person necessarily involves the study of God, and vice versa. Whatever we might say about the ultimate meaning of human existence is something said at the same time about God, who is the author, support, and destiny of human existence. And whatever we might say about God, therefore, is something said also about human existence.

Such an anthropology, Rahner suggests, must be a *transcendental* anthropology. The word *transcendental* is not easily defined. It means literally that which is capable of going beyond or above or over something else. The "transcendent," therefore, is that which is actually above, beyond, and over the tangible, the visible, the immediately available. God is *the* Transcendent, in that God is above, beyond, and over everything else. God is the one to whom all reality is oriented. Anthropology is transcendental, therefore, when the human person is seen, not simply as a collection of biological and behavioral responses, but as a being whose meaning is to be found beyond the purely corporeal and beyond the satisfaction of physical, social, psychological, political, economic, and cultural needs. The person is transcendental insofar as the person is oriented beyond himself or herself toward God as the source, sustainer, and final perfection of the person's existence.

If you wish to understand human existence, you must seek to discover the conditions in the human person which make it possible for the person to arrive at knowledge of God, to whom the person is oriented. For Rahner the *a priori* condition (i.e., the condition that must be present before any other if there is to be any knowledge of God at all) is *grace*, which is the presence of God in the knowing subject. In other words, *the human person is capable of transcending himself or herself in the knowledge of God, to whom his or her whole life is oriented because God is already present in the person as the transcendent force or condition which makes such knowledge possible.*

This *transcendental method* has been at work in theology, Rahner notes, at least since Thomas Aquinas, but it has been given a new and stronger impulse by modern philosophy, i.e., the philosophy which has developed *after* Descartes (d. 1650), Kant (d. 1804), and the existentialist movement. Much of this philosophy is deeply un-Christian, insofar as it begins *and ends* with the autonomous personal subject which has closed itself to the experience of God. But this philosophy is also most deeply Christian (more, in fact, than its traditional critics in the Catholic Scholastic philosophy of recent decades have understood) because in the Christian understanding of human existence the human person is not one element in a cosmos of things, subordinated to some abstract, impersonal system of reality based on *things*. On the contrary, the human being is the personal subject upon whose freedom as a subject the fate of the entire cosmos depends.

And indeed this has been the direction modern philosophy has been taking us in recent years. The human person is seen not simply as part of a larger cosmic mosaic, but as the most active agent, under God, in the forward movement of history itself. That is why the principal themes of today's philosophy (and correspondingly of much of today's theology) include hope, society, the critique of ideology, freedom, and planning for the future.

And that is why there is also so much emphasis today, in theology as well as in philosophy, on the anthropological dimension of all statements about the ultimate meaning and direction of life and of history. We cannot accept teachings as "truths revealed by God" if they have no apparent connection with our own understanding of ourselves, an understanding derived from our experience as human beings. A proper understanding of the relation between nature and grace would make this clear (a point to which we shall be returning in the next chapter).

To put the matter more simply (assuming at the same time the obvious risk of *over*simplifying): God is not "a" Being separate from the human person. God is Being itself, permeating the person but transcending the person as well. Because God permeates as well as transcends us, there is no standpoint from which we can "look at" God objectively, in a detached manner, as it were. God is always present within us, even before we begin the process, however tentatively and hesitatingly, of trying to come to terms with God's reality and our knowledge of God.

Accordingly, everything we say about God can be translated into a declaration about our own existence. God is a constitutive dimension of our existence. To talk about God is to talk about ourselves as well. The Word of God is not some message given from some heavenly perch, but rather it *is* God. And this is the distinctiveness of Jesus' preaching, namely, that God is present to us, not as some abstract power, but as the very core of our being (what the Scholastics called "uncreated grace"). God, therefore, enters into the very definition of human existence.

We are alive by a principle that transcends us, over which we have no power, and which summons us to surpass ourselves and frees us to be creative in the shaping and redirection of history. History is not determined by inanimate forces or by causes which already exist. Tomorrow can be different from today because God is present to history through the free human persons who are at history's center. Nowhere is this principle more sharply focused or more effectively realized than in Jesus Christ, who is the Word of God-made-flesh, the point at which the human community becomes fully conscious of itself as human and assumes full responsibility for the shaping of its future under God.

Another way of expressing this in a manner consistent with the basic lines of Transcendental Thomism has been proposed by Bernard Lonergan, author of the widely influential *Insight* (1957) and *Method in Theology* (1972). Lonergan, too, breaks away from the classical philosophical doctrine that the human person is static, unchanging, unaffected by the movement of history and variations in the environment. The human person is, on the contrary, "constituted by meaning."

Take the example of a family. On the one hand, we are convinced that families exist. We talk about them. We think we see them. We feel ourselves part of one or more. And yet no one can really touch a family or even see a family, for that matter. A family is a reality "constituted by meaning." We *interpret* a particular collectivity of human beings (a man, a woman, children) to be something *more than* what appears on the purely physical level.

We are living at a time, furthermore, when the family is under severe stress. Scientists and other social commentators distinguish among the so-called traditional family, the nuclear family, the single-parent family, the extended family, the communal family, and so forth. The reality itself changes as the meaning changes. And because meanings change, so, too, can the reality of human existence change.

We human beings, insofar as we are constituted by meaning, are, like the family, not directly available to scientific investigation or to "seeing" and "touching" in the usual sense of those words. We see and touch ourselves and other bodies that have specific characteristics and modes of behavior. But our judgment that we and they are "human" is exactly that, a *judgment*. It is a judgment that follows *understanding*, and that understanding, in turn, follows *insight*.

Such an understanding of the human person as "constituted by meaning" stands in striking contrast to the traditional classical and Scholastic definitions of the human as "rational animal." The "constituted-by-meaning" view is a *dynamic* understanding of the human, seeing the human as open to development and change, whereas the classical definition assumes a *static*, once-and-for-all given nature. Furthermore, the "constituted-by-meaning" view takes the concrete and the historical seriously, whereas the classical view is abstract. Indeed, according to Lonergan, it is precisely our new *historical-mindedness* (the distinctive feature of the modern, as opposed to the classical, mentality) which has allowed us to move beyond the earlier formulation of human existence without rejecting its own measure of truth.

But the newer view also provides a firmer philosophical, and also theological, basis for the notion of *responsible* human existence. The human person as "subject" is one who is conscious, oriented toward interrelationship with others, and capable of becoming something other than he or she presently happens to be (i.e., is capable of becoming "self-constituting"). Through increasing degrees of consciousness—from unconscious sleep to dreaming

consciousness to experiential consciousness to intelligent consciousness to rational consciousness and finally to rational self-
consciousness—the human person as "subject" arrives at the level
of deliberating, evaluating, choosing, and finally acting. The subject is a *doer*, not just a thinker. As a doer, the subject has the
potential for self-formation, for effecting changes in others or in
the environment.

All the while, the subject is conditioned by the fact that one *is*
a human subject: in particular places and times, in particular
circumstances shaped by tradition and culture, under the impact
of specific historical events, and shaped by one's own free decisions
and the free decisions of others. One develops a biography which
discloses the self. It is as a "subject," therefore, with all of these
historical contingencies, that one *becomes* what one is.

Theologies of Human Existence: A Synthesis

The emphasis on the subject, the changeable, the particular, and
the practical that we see in modern philosophy is carried over into
theology. The theological *existentialism* of Bultmann, Tillich,
and Reinhold Niebuhr focuses on the anxiety which characterizes
human existence: anxiety in the face of meaninglessness, sin, and
death. God alone allows us to overcome the contingency of human
existence.

The theological *phenomenology* of Schillebeeckx explores the
dimensions of that contingency and suggests that we experience
transcendence in the struggle to conquer the suffering which characterizes the human condition. In this regard, Schillebeeckx's position is akin to that of the *liberation theologians* (whom I have
placed in parallel with the philosophical pragmatists), in that
human existence is marked by economic conflict, disparity, and
oppression—and the suffering this generates. Theology, therefore,
is not reflection on God or human existence as such; it is a form of
praxis, i.e., it is a form of participation in the struggle on behalf of
the poor and the oppressed. It is reflection on the human condition
as an oppressor-oppressed condition of human relationships and is
a formulation of ways in which that condition can be transformed
by justice. There is a sense, therefore, in which existentialism and

liberation theology are at cross purposes, although there are also important points of convergence: particularly their common rejection of the principle that things are necessarily the way they are and we must accept them and deal with them as they are.

Process theology is not necessarily inconsistent with either of these two approaches. It stresses the dynamic movement of history and the changeability of all reality, including God. Conservative process thinkers might stress the inevitability of the process, whereas left-of-center process thinkers would stress the responsibility of human agents in the direction and construction of history. The latter are, of course, in tune with the concerns of the liberation school.

Transcendental Thomism would seem, at first glance, to be closer to existentialism than to the more politically conscious liberation approach. But Rahner's insistence on the intimate connection between nature and grace, and between theology and anthropology, provides a foundation for an essential link between the two approaches: the emphasis on the subject (as in Bultmann) and the emphasis on the socio-political order (as in liberation theology). Indeed, even within existentialism itself (especially with Reinhold Niebuhr) we have a politically refined sense of social justice. History, for the Transcendental Thomist, is not something to be taken for granted, something inevitable, but something to be shaped and directed by free human persons in whom God, the author of creation, is present as the One who makes the new ever possible, and whose Word, in fact, provides the critique by which the old can be corrected and changed. It is in the context of history, in fact, that we *become* who we are.

Insofar as Transcendental Thomism comprehends and preserves the best that is present in the aforementioned philosophical and theological approaches, it will serve as the integrating principle of our own theology of human existence, developed in the next chapter.

Official Teachings of the Church

Official pronouncements (i.e. by popes, ecumenical councils, and general councils) have advanced the following points on the meaning and context of human existence:

1.   God is the Creator of the whole world, material as well as spiritual, and remains present to it through Providence.

2.   All created things, therefore, are good because they come from the creative hand of God. But human persons are the crown of divine creation.

3.   The dignity of the human person resides in the person's intimate relationship with God. The human person has a soul. (This is the transcendental dimension of human existence.)

4.   We are, at the same time, essentially oriented to other people. Human existence is social existence.

5.   The human condition is also characterized by a split. We are plagued by weakness and sin. We experience ourselves as limited creatures, and this generates a sense of anxiety.

6.   Nonetheless, we are called by God to master ourselves and our environment, and we are empowered to do so by grace and especially by the grace of Jesus Christ.

7.   Death is not the end of human existence. Life is changed, not taken away (to use a line from the Preface of the Mass for the Deceased). We are destined for glory.

These teachings are synthesized from the following sources:

1.   The provincial Council of Constantinople (543), which condemned certain positions associated with followers of Origen, namely, that the human body is a degrading place of exile to which preexisting souls have been consigned.

2.   The provincial Council of Braga, in Portugal (561), which also rejected the anti-matter, anti-body teaching borrowed the Origenists.

3.   Pope Innocent III's "Profession of Faith" (1208), prescribed for all those returning to the Church from the heresy of *Albigensianism*, a French offshoot of the ancient heresy of *Manichaeism*, which taught that matter is evil, and from *Waldensianism*, another French-based movement which assumed the same

dualistic notion of spirit and matter but which had as well an anti-clerical dimension directed against the display of worldliness and power in the Church.

4.   The Fourth Lateran General Council (1215), which spoke the final word against the Albigensian and Waldensian errors. Its teaching was later adopted by the First Vatican Council (1869-1870).

5.   Similar condemnations can be found in the Council of Vienna (1311-1312), the Council of Florence (1442) in its *Decree for the Jacobites*, the Fifth Lateran Council (1513), the *Syllabus of Errors* promulgated by Pope Pius IX (1864), the First Vatican Council, as mentioned above, and Pope Pius XII's encyclical letter, *Humani Generis* (1950).

6.   Nowhere is the official teaching more succinctly expressed—and without the intrusion of polemical intent—than in the *Pastoral Constitution on the Church in the Modern World* of Vatican II (1965). The principal elements of that teaching follow:

> a.   We are created in the image of God, capable of knowing and loving God and appointed by God to master all of the earth for the sake of God's glory (n. 12; see also Genesis 1:26; Wisdom 2:23; Sirach 17:3-10; Psalm 8:5-6).
>
> b.   But God did not create us as solitary creatures. We are created male and female, and, therefore, as essentially social beings (n. 12).
>
> c.   "The call to grandeur and the depths of misery are both a part of human experience" (n. 13).
>
> d.   We cannot, however, despise our bodies nor the created world in which we find ourselves, even though both may be the source of pain and anxiety. For by our interior qualities we outstrip the rest of creation. God is present to our hearts, awaiting our discovery (n. 14).
>
> e.   "In fidelity to conscience, Christians are joined with the rest of men in the search for truth, and for the genuine solution to the numerous problems which arise in the life of individuals and from social relationships" (n. 16).
>
> f.   Only in freedom—not from blind internal impulse nor from mere external pressure—can we direct ourselves toward goodness. But since our freedom has been damaged

by sin, only with the help of God's grace can we bring our relationship with God and thereby with the whole of creation to full flower (n. 17).

g.   In the face of death the riddle of human existence becomes most acute. Technology cannot calm our anxiety about death, for the prolongation of biological life cannot satisfy that desire for a higher life which is inescapably lodged in the human heart (n. 18).

h.   "Although the mystery of death utterly beggars the imagination, the Church has been taught by divine revelation, and herself firmly teaches, that man has been created by God for a blissful purpose beyond the reach of earthly misery" (n. 18).

7.   A similarly positive statement on human dignity and freedom in light of the redemption is set forth in Pope John Paul II's first encyclical, *Redemptor Hominis* (1979).

SUMMARY

1.   In a time of rapid and substantial change, the meaning of human existence assumes new and urgent force. Various attempts have been made to answer the question "Who are we?" These efforts can be subsumed under the generic term *anthropology.*

2.   Answers have been proposed by the *natural sciences* and by *Charles Darwin*, in particular. We are creatures linked biologically with the rest of creation. Human existence is not simply given. It is something to be worked out through the process of evolution and adaptation to the environment.

3.   If the natural scientists have been concerned with the interaction of human behavior and the world outside the person, one of the *social sciences, psychology*, has been concerned as well with the interaction of human behavior and the world *inside* the person. This is the special contribution of *Freud.* Human existence is not simply a matter of knowing what to do (intellect) and then deciding to do it (will). There are unconscious drives, forces, and motives that influence, probably even determine, our choices and our behavior.

4.   Other social sciences, i.e., *sociology* and *economics*, focus on the social, economic, and political context in which human persons find themselves. *Karl Marx*, like Freud, insisted that human problems are

traceable to conflicts produced by alienation. For Freud, the alienation is from one's true self; for Marx, the alienation is from the fruits of one's labors and thus from the industrialized world and from other people. It is only in and through society that persons can live as human beings. The collective defines who and what we are.

5. The *humanities*, too, and especially *literature*, disclose an understanding of human existence, but one that is inevitably broad and diverse. Persons are seen as people at odds with themselves and with others, struggling to work out their identity in the resolution of conflicts.

6. *Philosophical* understandings of human existence similarly cover a wide range of approaches: the *existentialist*, the *phenomenological*, the *processive*, the *positivistic*, and the *pragmatic*. There is a *common emphasis* on the *subjective*, the *changeable*, the *particular*, and the *practical*, over against the objective, the unchanging, the universal, and the abstract. Human existence is not a given to be examined, but a potential in process of realization.

7. There are similar emphases in contemporary *theology*, although one can detect two apparently opposed orientations: the one (*existentialist*) which focuses on the subject and the importance of achieving sufficient self-understanding, and the other (*liberationist*) which focuses on the subject's responsibility to criticize and to change an unjust social order. *Transcendental Thomism*, at first glance closer to existentialism than to the liberation approach, may provide a bridge between the two.

8. For the *Transcendental Thomist* history is not something to be taken for granted, something inevitable, but something to be shaped and directed by free human persons in whom God is present as the One who makes the new ever possible, and whose Word provides the critique by which the old can be corrected and changed.

9. The *Church* over the centuries has *officially taught* that God is the Creator of the whole world, material as well as spiritual, and that all reality, including the bodily, is good. Our dignity resides in our intimate relationship with God, in spite of which we experience anxiety about the meaning of life, sin, and death. We are called, nonetheless, to master ourselves and our environment and are empowered to do so by grace. Death is not the end of life but the beginning of a new phase of life. We are destined for glory.

SUGGESTED READINGS

Baum, Gregory. *Man Becoming.* New York: Herder & Herder, 1970.

Ferkiss, Victor. *Technological Man: The Myth and the Reality.* New York: New American Library, 1969.

Moltmann, Jürgen. *Man.* Philadelphia: Fortress Press, 1974.

O'Grady, John F. *Christian Anthropology.* New York: Paulist Press, 1975.

Pannenberg, Wolfhart. *What is Man?* Philadelphia: Fortress Press, 1970.

Rahner, Karl. "Theology and Anthropology." In *The Word in History.* Ed. T.P. Burke. New York: Sheed & Ward, 1966, pp. 1-23.

Rousseau, Richard W. "Secular and Christian Images of Man," *Thought* 47 (Summer 1972), 165-200.

·V·

TOWARD A THEOLOGY OF HUMAN EXISTENCE

THE QUESTION

The preceding chapter surveyed a relatively wide range of scientific and disciplinary areas—e.g., biology, psychology, sociology, philosophy. This chapter is explicitly theological. It offers an actual position on the question of human existence, one that strives to be consistent with the Catholic tradition which provides the focus for this entire book.

This question, it must be reasserted here, is as fundamental for Christian theology and for Christian faith as is the question of God. Indeed, the question of human existence and the question of God, as we pointed out in the preceding chapter, are two sides of the same coin. Our statements about God and Jesus Christ, about creation and salvation history, about life and death, about sin and judgment, about the Church and Christian morality, are always in some important measure a reflection of our understanding of human existence and of the human condition.

For example, if I think of myself as utterly without worth, I am saying something about the divine estimation of God's own handiwork, about the effectiveness of Jesus Christ's redemptive work on my behalf, about the power and impact of Original Sin, about the value of being a member of the Church and of having access to its sacraments, about the meaningfulness of my life as a Christian, and about the basis of our common hope in the coming of God's Kingdom.

Correspondingly, if I think of myself and others as nothing more than a collection of neurological responses to be conditioned and programmed at will, then that, too, says something about my understanding of a whole schema of theological questions, not least of which are the questions of sin and redemption.

THE HUMAN PERSON
Biblical Views

Old Testament

In the Old Testament the human person is, before all else, a *creature* of God, formed out of the clay of the ground (Genesis 2:7). The word which designates "man/woman" in the concrete sense is *adam*. The word for "clay" is *adamah*. This etymological connection is crucial. We are not composite beings, made of body and soul as two separate parts (as the medieval Scholastic philosophers had it). Soul and flesh are not contrasted in the Old Testament. Unlike the Greeks, who look upon a human being as an incarnated spirit, the Hebrews regarded the human person as an animated body. We do not *have* a soul and a body; we *are* soul and body.

The hope of salvation, therefore, is expressed in terms of the *resurrection of the body* ("But your dead shall live, their corpses shall rise . . . "—Isaiah 26:19; see also Daniel 12:2-3, and 2 Maccabees 7:14), and this is taken up and developed in the New Testament (" . . . if the dead are not raised, then Christ was not raised; and if Christ was not raised, your faith is worthless" — 1 Corinthians 15:16-17; see the entire fifteenth chapter as well as Mark 12:18-25; John 6:39-40; and Acts 24:15). The idea of the *immortality of the soul*, on the other hand, is *not* developed in the writings of the later Old Testament period nor in the New Testament. The notion of immortality reflects a world view fundamentally different from the Bible's anthropology. Indeed, it is more akin to Greek philosophy (i.e., the human person as incarnated spirit) than to the Hebrew mentality (i.e., the human person as animated body).

Bodiliness is also the basis of our relationship with one another. Human existence, in the Old Testament, is *coexistence with other persons*. That coexistence is, in turn, founded on our primary relationship with God. Each of us is equally powerless in the face of God's transcendence, and at the same time of equal value before God. We are commanded by God to love our neighbor (yes, even in the *Old* Testament!): "You shall love your neighbor as yourself" (Leviticus 19:18; see also 19:9-18,34; and 25:35-38). Our responsibility for one another is underlined by the prophets as well: "But if you would offer me holocausts, then let justice surge like water, and goodness like an unfailing stream" (Amos 5:23-24; see also 8:4-6, and Isaiah 3:13-15).

Coexistence with, and even interdependence upon, one another is highlighted in a special way in the *sexual relationship*. Created male and female, human persons are most deeply themselves in a relationship of intimate mutual love (Genesis 1:27). "The Lord God said: 'It is not good for the man to be alone' . . . . That is why a man leaves his father and mother and clings to his wife, and the two of them become one body" (Genesis 2:18,24).

Human existence—at once dependent upon God and interdependent in relationship with others—is, therefore, *responsible existence*. The Lord gave Adam an order, not to eat from the tree of knowledge (Genesis 2:16). Human existence is a life of responsibility to the will of God. Fulfilling that responsibility need not be a matter of fear and drudgery; it can be one of merriment and joy (1 Kings 4:20; Psalm 43:4). Unfortunately, we are not always faithful to God's will.

The Old Testament also sees human existence as *sinful existence*. Although there is no fully developed notion of Original Sin, we are presented as sinners whose hearts are filled with pride and are thereby closed to the call of God and the cry of our neighbor (e.g., Genesis 8:21; Psalm 143, Psalm 2). Sin is portrayed as something breaking out in the world and harming not only the individual but history itself (Genesis 3-11). And that consciousness of sin deepens as the history of salvation unfolds. "Can the Ethiopian change his skin? The leopard his spots? As easily would you be able to do good, accustomed to evil as you are" (Jeremiah 13:23). But the same prophet assures us of the Lord's forgiving spirit: "The days are coming, says the Lord, when I will make a new covenant with the house of Israel and the house of Judah . . . . I will be their

God, and they shall be my people ... for I will forgive their evildoing and remember their sin no more" (Jeremiah 31:31-34).

Human existence, therefore, is or can be *hope-filled existence*: hopes for a savior and a time of salvation, for resurrection of the body and new life, for the fulfillment of the promises of the new covenant.

New Testament

The New Testament's understanding of human existence is consistent with, and develops from, the Old Testament's. Thus, we find no abstract or speculative "philosophy" of human existence, with elaborate divisions of soul and body, or of intellect and will. As in the Old Testament, human existence is *historical existence*, life emerging from, and shaped by, the concrete experiences of everyday happenings.

Accordingly, *Jesus* does not formulate some universal doctrine of fraternal charity, replete with criteria and conditions. Instead he tells the story of the Good Samaritan and asks, "Which ... was neighbor to the man who fell in with the robbers?" (Luke 10:25-37). All of us, he insists, are sinners, in need of *conversion* or of a fundamental change of mind and of heart: "This is the time of fulfillment. The reign of God is at hand! Reform your lives and believe in the gospel!" (Mark 1:15). The reform must be, in fact, so radical that we are required even to love our enemies: "My command to you is: love your enemies, pray for your persecutors ... If you love those who love you, what merit is there in that? ... In a word, you must be made perfect as your heavenly Father is perfect" (Matthew 5:43-48).

In the end, we shall be judged by the quality of our response to those in need, friend and enemy alike: " ... as often as you did it for one of my least brothers, you did it for me ... as often as you neglected to do it to one of these least ones, you neglected to do it to me" (Matthew 25:31-46). Just as Jesus' own existence is an existence in the service of others (Mark 10:45), so must every person's be *a coexistence of service*.

Paul's understanding of human existence is developed in the light of the death and resurrection of Christ. As such, it draws out some of the anthropological implications of Jesus' own preaching. Paul, like Jesus and the Old Testament before him, refuses to speculate about the philosophical nature and properties of the human person. He, too, rejects the body-soul dualism of contemporary Greek thought. For him the resurrection in which we all hope will be a *resurrection of the body* (1 Corinthians 15), because the body *(soma)* is intrinsic to the being of the human person (1 Corinthians 15:15-19). "Body" is not just that through which the spirit acts; it is the whole person. This notion of the body does not eliminate the traditional idea of the soul. Rather it emphasizes the unity of the human person.

But we find ourselves *sinners* in the world, in the hands of alien forces, i.e., the domain of the "flesh" *(sarx)* which is in rebellion against God (Romans 8:6-8, 10:3; 2 Corinthians 10:5). When Paul considers the human person as alienated from himself and from God, he speaks of the person as flesh, as sinner. Flesh must be "put off" at Baptism (Romans 8:9-13), while body, i.e., the person as a whole, is to be transformed at the resurrection (1 Corinthians 15:44; Philippians 3:21). The "old man" is to yield to the "new man" in Christ (Ephesians 2:5; 2 Corinthians 4:16; Galatians 1:11-12; 1 Corinthians 3:3).

But even the "new man" in Christ lives in a state of tension, between the "already" of Christ's saving work on our behalf and the "not yet" of its final perfection in the Kingdom of God. By *faith*, and through a life based on faith, we work out our salvation in the midst of this tension: "But now that faith is here, we are no longer in the monitor's charge [i.e., the law's]" (Galatians 3:25; see also Romans 3:14; Colossians 2:12,20). In this faith there is no longer any fear of death ("O death, where is your victory? O death, where is your sting?"—1 Corinthians 15:55), but rather *hope* for the appearance of Christ when we "shall appear with him in glory" (Colossians 3:4). But over all these virtues, including even faith and hope, we put on *love*, "which binds the rest together and makes them perfect" (Colossians 3:14).

For *John*, as well as for Paul, the "world" is prone to evil, not because God created it evil, but because it is populated by men and women who are sinners. Indeed, the world would be lost if it were not for Jesus Christ; by sending the Son, God brings the world to a crisis or turning point, but out of a motive of love (John 3:16-17).

God sends the Son not to judge the world but to save it (1 John 4:9,14). Without an act of liberation from on high (John 3), we are imprisoned within a domain of evil. By having faith in Jesus Christ, we receive a fresh possibility of life from a new source. This *new life* is an eschatological existence, i.e., an existence between our situation as it is—imperfect, limited, prone to sin—and the Kingdom of God as it has been promised to us. In the meantime, we find a new home in the community of the faithful and in the *love of the brethren* by which we prove our sinlessness (1 John 3:14-18; 4:19-21).

It is not for us to decide whether or not we shall be "born again." On the contrary, no one comes to the Father unless the Father draw that person (John 6:44). But as a believer, the person must abide in Jesus' word and act according to his command (1 John 1:6-7; 2:3-6). The hope that is in all of us for a life completely fulfilled is, for John, to be directed to the *present* rather than to the future. We find the "new life" here and now by faith (1 John 1:2-3; John 17:3). To be human is, in the deepest sense, to live by grace, i.e., by the presence of God in our hearts and in our midst.

Patristic Views

There are no real breakthroughs in the writings of the Fathers of the Church beyond the anthropological perspective of the Bible. What the patristic period contributes is an element of systematization (Tertullian's *De Anima* is the beginning) around certain fundamental principles—e.g., the human person as the *image of God*, and the history of the universe as *the history of divinization and salvation*. These themes are expressed nowhere more clearly or more forcefully than in Irenaeus's *Adversus Haereses* (literally, "Against the Heresies" of Gnosticism and other related errors).

At the heart of Irenaeus' theology is his theory of *recapitulation*, borrowed from Paul but expanded considerably. Recapitulation, for Irenaeus, is taking up in Christ of all that is or has been from the beginning. God gathers up everything which had been sidetracked by the fall of Adam and renews, restores, and reorganizes it in Jesus Christ, who becomes the Second Adam. Since the whole human race was lost through the sin of the First Adam, the Son of God had to become a human being in order to bring about the re-creation of humankind. "When he became incarnate and was made man," Irenaeus wrote, "he recapitulated in himself the long history of man, summing up and giving us salvation in order that we might receive again in Christ Jesus what we had lost in Adam, that is, the image and likeness of God" (III,18,1).

But the tendency to dichotomize remained. In the writings of the Eastern, Greek Fathers (e.g., Gregory of Nyssa) the tension between matter and spirit endured. Human fulfillment is possible because on one side of human nature, the spiritual, the human person stands already on God's side. Our goal is the vision of God after death. This vision comes only after purification and restoration to our original purity. For Western, Latin theology (e.g., Augustine) the tension is between the person as sinner and the merciful God. "Every man is Adam, every man is Christ" (cited by Henri Rondet, *The Grace of Christ*, p. 136). The history of the world, therefore, is seen essentially as the history of reuniting what was divided rather than "the free history of God himself in the world" (Rahner).

The Medieval Period

That there is still no decisive breakthrough even after the passage of many centuries should not be too surprising. As we pointed out in the preceding chapter, the most significant scientific, philosophical, and eventually theological advances in our understanding of human existence did not occur until the eighteenth and especially the nineteenth centuries, with the discoveries of Darwin and Freud, the new social analysis of Marx, and the new focus on the human person as subject in the philosophy of Kant, in existentialism, and in Transcendental Thomism.

There is no independent theological anthropology in any of the medieval treatises in theology. "Man" is simply listed among the various creatures: lower than the angels but higher than the animal kingdom. (Darwin, of course, would later undermine the assumption that some inviolable gap exists between human beings and the animal world.) This "objective" view of human existence could not, and did not, do justice to the special character of the person. Little or no attention at all was given to the history of salvation. Human beings do not grow and develop; they simply are, with an unchanging essence.

The medieval distinction between mortal and venial sin, for example, did not even set contemporary theologians to wondering about the basis for such a distinction in human action itself. There was still no real theological analysis of such fundamental human experiences as anguish, joy, and death. The world and its history were merely the ready-made scene for the unfolding of each individual human drama. Would the person finally save his or her soul, or not? There was nothing new to be added to the world and its history. If the world and history were not in process, neither were human beings.

And yet there were also some counter-indications in medieval theology—evidence of some initial movement toward a genuine anthropology. If reflections on salvation had a non-historical cast to them, their strongly individual focus also prepared the way, however unwittingly, for the modern period's subsequent emphasis on the person as subject. Medieval theology stressed the importance of the *Beatific Vision,* i.e., the direct, unobstructed experience of God after death by the saved individual. It provided also for non-sacramental possibilities of salvation, i.e., the so-called *votum sacramenti* (desire for the sacrament). If an individual's basic good will could, under some circumstances, replace the need for Baptism, then there must be something of fundamental and enduring importance about the activities and processes of the human mind, will, and subjective consciousness. This assumption was also reflected in medieval theology's remarkably provident teaching on the inviolability of conscience, even when it is in opposition to ecclesiastical law.

Scholastic philosophy, and the theology which flowed from it, provided what proved to be a true basis for the later recognition of genuine subjectivity, in that it noted, as Rahner says, that "anything is or has being in proportion to the degree in which it is subjectivity in possession of itself." Or, in the spirit of Teilhard de Chardin, life moves to higher and higher levels of self-reflection. The highest forms of life not only "know"; we "know that we know." The more conscious we are of ourselves, of our knowing powers, of our powers of decision, of the implications of our thoughts, our judgments, and our actions, the more we are in possession of ourselves. And the more we are in possession of ourselves, the greater is the level of "genuine subjectivity." The point, therefore, is that although medieval theology was not particularly attentive to the subjective side of human existence (on the contrary), there were elements and orientations in medieval thought which already anticipated the modern movement in the direction of subjectivity.

The Modern Period

Because of the scientific, philosophical, and theological developments outlined in the preceding chapter, the time for an anthropological recasting of all the traditional doctrines is at hand. But the task is as yet uncompleted. Early indications of a trend, however, are evident in the emergence of historical theology, in the recognition of religious pluralism and of the universality of God's saving grace, in the new regard for the world as something to be transformed by the Church, and in the recent renewal of interest in spirituality for the individual in his or her personal relationship with God.

The Second Vatican Council, to which reference was made also in the preceding chapter, also fails to construct a theological anthropology, but there are elements present therein which are consistent with the trends just noted: (1) the insistence on conscience as the guide to truth and to genuine solutions to current problems; (2) the declaration that "only in freedom ... can we direct ourselves toward goodness"; and (3) the reference to our desire for a higher life, a desire which is "inescapably lodged in the human heart" and which makes it possible for us to transcend our anxiety about death (*Pastoral Constitution on the Church in the Modern World*, nn. 16-18).

Theology of the Human Person:
A Synthesis

The *Bible* views the human person as a creature of God, as animated body. Our *bodiliness* is the basis of our relationship with one another. *Human existence is coexistence.* But such existence is also fraught with as many risks as opportunities. Human existence is at once responsible, sinful, and hope-filled. The focus of its hope is the resurrection of the body, and the ground of that hope is the preaching, ministry, and saving death and resurrection of Jesus Christ, whom we accept in faith and to whom we manifest our fidelity in love. To live according to this dynamic of faith, hope, and love is to enter a new life, to become *a new creature in Christ.* This new life and new creaturehood is, as always, shared with others, in accordance with our social nature and the coexistent character of human existence. The immediate context of the sharing is the community of the faithful, which is the Church.

Until modern times, there was little or no significant development of a theology of human existence beyond that already expressed in the Bible. The *Fathers of the Church*, especially Irenaeus, spoke of the human person as the image of God, and of human history as the history of salvation—a process in which all things are being recapitulated in Christ. The *medieval period*, consistently with the prevailing philosophy of the times, viewed human existence "objectively," i.e., as an unchanging form of created life essentially unaffected by the process and vicissitudes of history. There were, however, some elements in medieval theology which anticipated, to some extent, the modern turn toward the "subjective." Medieval theology's emphasis on the inviolability of conscience is one example to which we earlier referred.

Under the impact of scientific and philosophical developments, *modern theology* focuses its attention on the consciousness of the human person, on the person's freedom and responsibility, not only to co-create himself or herself but to co-create the world and its history under God. The *Second Vatican Council's* insistence on the importance of conscience, freedom, and the innate desire for a higher life reflects this modern shift to the subject.

NATURE AND GRACE
Nature

Until this century, the formal concept of "nature" served only as a basis of contrast with "grace" in Catholic theology. "Nature" is a concept, however, which is still almost totally absent from the Eastern Orthodox theology of grace and has generally been resisted by Protestant theology.

The Catholic tradition has always been insistent that *the grace of God is given to us, not to make up for something lacking to us as human persons, but as a free gift that elevates us to a new and unmerited level of existence.* Hypothetically, we could have a *natural end.* This would be something akin to *limbo,* a state of "natural happiness" reserved for those who die in infancy without the grace of Baptism and without, of course, the possibility of having ever expressed even an implicit desire for Baptism (*votum sacramenti,* again) through free choices which happen to be consistent with the will of God. The real, historical order, however, is already permeated with grace, so that a state of "pure nature" does not exist. In other words, if grace supposes nature, nature in its own way supposes grace, insofar as the grace of Christ sustains us in our actual existence and orients us toward a supernatural end, the Kingdom of God. This emphasis on the importance of the natural and of the natural order is historically and theologically characteristic of Catholicism.

Eastern Orthodoxy, on the other hand, stresses the spiritual side of human existence to such an extent that the natural foundation is sometimes all but lost. *Much of Protestantism,* meantime, has so emphasized the depravity of the natural human condition apart from the grace of God that the natural order can only be viewed in thoroughly negative terms.

"Nature," to be sure, is not directly a biblical concept but arises from subsequent theological reflection on the New Testament's (especially John's and Paul's) proclamation of "the grace of God through Christ." *We infer who we are as creatures of God by reflecting on who we have become through Christ.* By the grace of Christ we enter into a new relationship of communion with God, and we are transformed interiorly by the Spirit of Christ. As we have already suggested, the Fathers of the Church, from Irenaeus on, understood this participation in the life of God through Christ as a true *divinization*. The Latin Fathers, especially Augustine and Pope Leo the Great (d. 461), adopted this concept and made it the foundation of the whole theology of grace in the medieval period, as is particularly evident in Thomas Aquinas.

But the emphasis is not upon divinization alone, but upon its *gratuitous* character as well. We neither deserved nor needed grace. We would not have been less than human without it. Although, in fact, God created us and the world in and through Christ, God could have created us without including the communication of grace (or better: God's *self*-communication.)

Hence, the theological concept of "nature" means that we are bodily creatures who are intelligible (i.e., whose existence makes sense) and who would have been open to full human growth apart from the grace of divinization. The creation of humankind and of the world is theoretically possible without the incarnation of the Son of God in Jesus Christ. The whole self-communication of God—in creation and in the incarnation—is free. Human existence non-divinized by grace is a possible hypothesis.

"Nature," therefore, is neither a purely positive nor a purely negative concept. It is *not purely positive* because it is a concept one *derives* from reflecting on something higher, namely, grace. It is *not a purely negative* concept because it implies the rationality of the human person and the person's fundamental relationship to God, to other persons, to the world, and to its history apart from grace.

The theological concept of nature is, of course, very different from the philosophical or the naturally and socially scientific (as we have already seen in the preceding chapter), because theology views the human person as having *a radical capacity (potentia obedientialis) for the divinizing grace of Christ.* This fundamental aspect of the theological concept of nature is not derived from Darwinian or Freudian experimentation, nor from Marxist analysis, nor even from philosophical reflection, but from inferences drawn from the revelation that we are, in fact, called to a participation in the very life of God through Jesus Christ. (The notion of "revelation," which is so obviously crucial in the preceding sentence, will be explained in chapter 7.)

It is important to add here, by way of conclusion, that the traditional Catholic emphasis on "nature" is not without its dangers—dangers of which Protestants and Orthodox have been mindful. One might easily be led to the exaggerated view that the purely natural person does, in fact, exist and that grace is something merely "added" to, or superimposed upon, nature. It cannot be denied that the introduction of the concept of nature in the explanation of grace can lead, and has led, to a dualistic vision of human existence in relation to God. God is, on the one hand, our creator, and, on the other hand, our Savior through Christ—with a different relationship to the human person in each case. Hence the importance of the problem of "nature and grace" to which we are now attending in this section of the present chapter.

Grace

Old Testament

In the Old Testament the Hebrew noun *ḥēn* designates a quality which arouses *favor*. The word appears most frequently in the phrase "to find favor in the eyes of" God or other persons. One who seeks favors throws himself or herself completely on the good will of the one from whom the favor is sought. The verb *ḥānan*, "to show favor," designates an attitude which is proper toward the needy, the poor, the widow, the orphan, and so forth. One shows favor by gifts, by assistance, and by refraining from punishment. Yahweh shows favor by giving prosperity (Genesis 33:11), by giving children (Genesis 33:5), by accepting sacrifice (Malachi 1:9). Most frequently Yahweh shows favor by delivering from distress (e.g., Psalms 4:2; 6:3; 9:14; 25:16; 26:11; 27:7). Yahweh delivers Israel from its enemies (2 Kings 13:23; Isaiah 30:18-19; 33:2), even when Israel deserves punishment for its sins. Such favor is also forgiveness (Psalms 41:5,11; 51:3; Isaiah 27:11; Amos 5:15). Yahweh's favor is shown *freely*. It can be given or withheld (Exodus 33:19).

New Testament

In the New Testament the corresponding noun for *grace* is the Greek *charis*. It becomes a key word in the Christian message. The word occurs frequently in the introductory and final greetings of the various epistles, usually accompanied by the word *peace*. Thus: "To all in Rome, beloved of God and called to holiness, grace and peace from God our Father and the Lord Jesus Christ" (Romans 1:7). The word designates the *good will of God*, sometimes in a general sense (e.g., Acts of the Apostles 14:26; 15:40) and most frequently in reference to the saving will of God executed in Jesus Christ and communicated to humankind through Christ. Such grace makes us *righteous* (Romans 3:24; Titus 3:7). By grace Paul (and others) are called (Galatians 1:15). Grace appears in Christ for our salvation (Titus 2:11). By it Jesus suffered death for all (Hebrews 2:9). Faith and love are fruits of grace (1 Timothy 1:14).

Elsewhere in the New Testament the emphasis is less on the saving will of God and more on *that which is given* (James 4:6; 1 Peter 5:5). The Word is full of grace (John 1:14,16). It is a store to which we have full access through Christ (Romans 5:2). It abounds more than sin (Romans 5:15,20; 6:1). It is given us in Christ (1 Corinthians 1:4). It is within the Christian (2 Corinthians 9:14), and extends to more and more people (2 Corinthians 4:15). The prophets foretold it (1 Peter 1:10). Christians are its heirs (1 Peter 3:7), called to grow in the grace and knowledge of Jesus Christ (2 Peter 3:18).

Grace stands in opposition to *works*, which lack the power to save (Romans 11:5-6; Ephesians 2:5,8-9; 2 Timothy 1:9). Grace stands also in opposition to the *law* (Acts of the Apostles 15:11; Galatians 2:21; 5:4). The Christian is not under the law but under grace (Romans 6:14-18). Grace is a gift, not something owed (Romans 4:4).

The *Gospel* itself can be called grace, in which the Christian should stand and remain steadfast (1 Peter 5:12; Acts of the Apostles 13:43). It is indeed the Gospel of the grace of God (Acts of the Apostles 20:24), or the word of God's grace (Acts of the Apostles 14:3; 20:32).

Grace is also *the principle of Christian life, action, and mission.* The first martyr, St. Stephen, was full of grace and power (Acts of the Apostles 6:8). Paul's apostolate was an apostleship of grace (Romans 1:5, and other passages). His hearers partake of it (Philippians 1:7). It is the *power* by which the apostle performs his apostolic functions (Romans 12:3; 1 Corinthians 3:10, 15:10; Ephesians 3:7-11). It produces good works (2 Corinthians 8:1). The grace of God, not earthly wisdom, guides our conduct (2 Corinthians 1:12).

Its only appearance in the Synoptic Gospels is in Luke. It refers to the heavenly reward, hence to a *salvation that is to come* (6:32-34). In 1:30 and 1:52 the Old Testament use of the word survives. But when Luke employs the term to express his own theological insights, he identifies it with the salvation wrought by God in Christ and since Christ, particularly through the words of the Gospel and the preaching thereof (4:22). On the whole, the terminology which Luke uses is not derived from Paul but reflects a wider tradition which may be pre-Pauline.

One final note regarding the meaning of the word *grace* in the New Testament: The Greek noun *charis* is to be distinguished from the noun *charisma* (a term popular today in the so-called charismatic renewal as well as in popular political terminology, as in "charismatic candidate"). The *charismata* (plural of *charisma*) are a particular type of spiritual gift which enable the recipient to perform some office or function in the Church. Such offices or functions are enumerated in Romans 12, 1 Corinthians 12, and Ephesians 4.

Apostolic Fathers

The Apostolic Fathers (Irenaeus and others) and the theologians of the *first two centuries* repeat the doctrine of Sacred Scripture, initially stressing its moral demands and then focusing more sharply on the effect of divinization, as we saw earlier in the chapter. The first theological reflections are made on the possibility of losing and then recovering the grace of Baptism (*The Shepherd of Hermas* and Tertullian). *The first major controversy* erupted in the second and third centuries under the impact of

Gnosticism, a heresy which made salvation both non-universal and non-historical. Salvation was given instead to a select few, and it consisted of a special knowledge (thus, the term *gnosis*). Its principal opponents were Irenaeus, Tertullian, and Hippolytus (d. 235).

"We need not mention how necessary it is to do again the work that Saint Augustine and Saint Thomas once did," Henri Rondet has written. "It is most probable that the genius who could attempt such an enterprise has not yet been born" (*The Grace of Christ*, p. 384).

Greek Fathers; Western Fathers

The Greek Fathers (from Origen on) developed a doctrine of grace in keeping with the Trinitarian questions of the period. Because the Spirit is truly God, we are truly *divinized* by the presence of the Spirit; and because we are truly divinized, the Spirit must be divine. It is through the incarnation of the divine *Logos* (word) that the Spirit enters the world. Therefore, the Greek doctrine of grace is optimistic about salvation.

The Western Fathers (Augustine, and others) were less interested in the intellectual and cosmic aspects of divinization and more *moralistic* in tendency. They also oriented their theology of grace toward the history of salvation and of the individual because of their struggle against *Pelagianism* (the fifth-century heresy which held that human beings can, without the grace of God, achieve supernatural salvation). Grace is a free gift of God and, because of sin, is necessary for salvation. But there is some trace, even in Augustine, of a denial of the universal salvific will of God. Some are *predestined* to salvation, others to damnation.

Later Patristic Period; Early Middle Ages

The later Patristic period and the early Middle Ages overcame the tendency toward predestinationism. The great age of Scholasticism gave precise formulation by means of Aristotelian categories and terminology (*habitus*, "disposition," "accidents") to the nature and effects of grace. The concept of the strictly supernatural character of salvific grace was slowly elaborated. It was a free, unmerited gift of God, for saint and sinner alike.

Reformation

With the Reformation in the sixteenth century and the emergence of new heresies within the Catholic Church (e.g., Jansenism), it was necessary for theologians—and eventually the Council of Trent—to defend the freedom of the human person under grace, the truly inward new creation of the human person by habitual grace, the strictly supernatural character of grace, and the universality of God's saving will. The controversy over precisely *how* we can reconcile human freedom with divine power (the debates between the Molinists and the Banezians, for example) was left undecided in 1607 and remains so even today.

Official Church Teachings

The major formulations of official Church teachings were drafted in response to the two principal distortions of the nature and effects of grace: *Pelagianism* on the left (because it was too optimistic about human freedom) and *Protestantism* on the right (because it was too pessimistic about human freedom). Against the first tendency toward complete self-reliance, the Church officially affirmed at the Second Council of Orange (529) the necessity of grace in every person's life, from beginning to end. Against Protestantism, the Council of Trent (1547) asserted that we are interiorly transformed by the grace of Christ.

During the post-Tridentine period, attention was centered on the relationship between human freedom and divine help (*actual* grace), but, as we have just noted, the issue was never resolved. In the meantime, the biblical and patristic perspective tended to be pushed to the background. Catholic theology (and Catholic spirituality, too) was so much influenced and shaped by existing controversies, on the one hand, and by the response of the official teaching authority, on the other, that we had, in effect, begun to lose sight of the inner renewal all of us experience through the indwelling of the Holy Spirit and through our concomitant personal union with Christ. The return to biblical and patristic emphases began under Pope Leo XIII and reached new levels of emphasis in the Second Vatican Council.

Principal examples of this official teaching follow.

1. Second Council of Orange (529): "If anyone asserts that by his natural strength he is able to think as is required or choose anything good pertaining to his eternal salvation, or to assent to the saving message of the Gospel without the illumination and inspiration of the Holy Spirit . . . , he is deceived by the heretical spirit . . . " (canon 7; see also canons 3-6,8).

2. Council of Trent (1547): "Thus, not only are we considered just, but we are truly called just and we are just, each one receiving within himself his own justice, according to the measure which 'the Holy Spirit apportions to each one individually as He wills' (1 Corinthians 12:11), and according to each one's personal disposition and cooperation" (chapter VII; see the entire "Decree on Justification").

3. Pope Leo XIII, encyclical letter *Divinum Illud* (1897): ". . . by grace God abides in the just soul as in a temple, in a most intimate and singular manner . . . . Now this wonderful union, which is properly called indwelling . . . is most certainly produced by the divine presence of the whole Trinity: 'We will come to him and make our home with him' (John 14:23); nevertheless it is attributed in a particular manner to the Holy Spirit."

4. Second Vatican Council, *Dogmatic Constitution on the Church* (1964): "The Spirit dwells in the Church and in the hearts of the faithful as in a temple . . . " (n. 4).

The Problem of Nature and Grace

"Grace" is essentially God's *self-communication to us men and women, and, secondarily, the effect(s) of that self-communication.* "Nature" refers to *human existence apart from God's self-communication and the divinizing effect of that self-communication.* Theology, however, carries the concept of "nature" one step beyond philosophy or anthropology, namely, to mean human existence without grace but at the same time as radically open to, and capable of receiving, grace (*potentia obedientialis*).

What is the *relationship* between the two realities of nature and grace? *The problem of the relationship between nature and grace is as fundamental a problem as one will ever come upon in all of Christian theology.* The nature-grace issue underlies the following relationships: creation and incarnation, reason and faith, law and Gospel, human freedom and divine sovereignty, the history of the world and the history of salvation, human progress and the Kingdom of God, natural law and the law of Christ, humanity and the Church, and so forth.

The problem of nature and grace is focused in the questions: *Does grace really change human nature, and if so, how is human freedom preserved? How is the human person able to accept freely the self-communication of God in grace?*

The Catholic theological tradition works its way through two extreme positions, to which reference has just been made: the extreme left of *Pelagianism*, which emphasizes so much the superiority of nature over grace that it effectively submerges the transcendental, supernatural dimension of salvation; and the extreme right of *Protestantism* (at least Protestantism as perceived and condemned by Trent), which emphasizes so much the superiority of grace over nature that it effectively submerges the dimension of human freedom and cooperation in salvation. The parenthetical qualification is necessary because subsequent historical studies have shown that the positions of Luther, Calvin, and Melanchthon were more nuanced than first appeared.

The Catholic theological tradition is grounded, first of all, in the New Testament's perspective of a Christocentric universe (1 Corinthians 8:6; 15:24-28,44-49; Romans 8:19-23,29,30; Ephesians 1:9-10,19-23; 3:11; Colossians 1:15-20; 3:4; Philippians 3:21; Hebrews 1:2-3; John 1:3; 12:32). All *creation* is oriented toward the *Covenant* between God and the People of God, and the Covenant, in turn, toward the *New Covenant* grounded in the incarnation of the Son of God in Jesus Christ. The human community and the entire world in which the human community exists is oriented toward Christ and is sustained by him. Although hypothetically it could have been otherwise, it in fact has not been otherwise. There is no creation except in view of Christ. There is no Covenant except in view of Christ. There is no human existence, therefore, except in view of Christ and of our New Covenant in Christ.

This intrinsic orientation of the human person and of the entire human community in Christ radically excludes any dualism, or sharp separation, between nature and grace. Although *in principle* we could know God apart from revelation and apart specifically from the revelation of God in Christ, *in fact* we cannot and do not know God apart from this revelation (Romans 1:18-28; Acts of the Apostles 17:24-27).

Sin is an exercise of human freedom *against* the relationship. Grace, however, is not destroyed by sin. The sinner remains radically open to the possibility of conversion and of forgiveness. If grace were not still available to the sinner, conversion and forgiveness would be impossible. The call of God to conversion and repentance (1 Corinthians 1:9; Galatians 2:20; Romans 8:28-30) would be meaningless unless there were some basis in the human person for responding to the call. Grace supposes even in the sinner the capacity to receive it. This capacity is what Karl Rahner and other Transcendental Thomists call our "limitless openness to being and ultimately to the Absolute," which openness constitutes the human person as "spirit in the world" (the title of one of Rahner's earliest works).

Grace supposes the nature of the human person. Theologically, nature includes the radical capacity for grace. That radical capacity is called, more technically, a *"supernatural existential."* This "supernatural existential" is *a permanent modification of the human spirit which transforms it from within and orients it toward the God of grace and glory.* This "supernatural existential" is not grace itself but only *God's offer of grace* which, by so modifying the human spirit, enables it freely to accept or to reject grace. *Every human person has this radical capacity* and many, perhaps most, have actualized it by receiving grace. That does not mean that they are conscious of grace as grace. On the contrary, Rahner argues," . . . the possibility of experiencing grace and the possibility of experiencing grace *as* grace are not the same thing" (*A Rahner Reader*, p. 185).

If grace supposes nature, so, too, does *nature suppose grace*, to the extent that the grace of Christ orients and sustains us in our very human existence. Catholic theology, from Augustine through Aquinas to the Transcendental Thomists of the present century, has argued, in fact, for a "natural desire" for direct union with God. It is only in the vision of God that the human mind can satisfy fully and definitively its desire to know. No finite reality can satisfy that desire. It is only in the encounter with God, the Absolute, that its deepest spiritual aspirations are fulfilled.

By ourselves, however, we could never go beyond the knowledge of the limited and the created. Such knowledge, on the other hand, is consonant with human existence. We would not thereby be less than human because we could know only the limited and the created. In fact, however, God gives us the radical capacity to transcend the limited and the created. There is now a radical capacity in nature itself, and not merely superadded to nature, by which we are ordained to the knowledge of God. Thus, all dualism between nature and grace is eliminated. There are not in the human person two separate finalities, the one oriented toward the vision of God, and the other oriented toward human fulfillment apart from the vision of God. *Human existence is already graced existence.* There is no merely natural end of human existence. *Human existence in its actual condition is radically oriented toward God.*

This means, too, that the whole universe is oriented to the glory of God (Romans 8:19-23). *The history of the world is, at the same time, the history of salvation.* It means also that authentic human progress in the struggle for justice, peace, freedom, human rights, and so forth, is part of the movement of, and toward, the Kingdom of God (Vatican II, *Pastoral Constitution on the Church in the Modern World*, n. 39). It means as well that human freedom is never to be conceived totally apart from grace, because it is always modified and qualified by grace; so, too, the grace of God is operative only insofar as it interacts with, and radically transforms, the natural order of the human person. The movement and dynamism of human freedom, on the one hand, and divine sovereignty, on the other, will converge perfectly at the end, in the vision of God and the final realization of the Kingdom. Each person and all of history will then achieve their definitive meaning.

ORIGINAL SIN
The Problem

There are three common misunderstandings of Original Sin. The *first* assumes that the doctrine denies human freedom and therefore exempts us from responsibility for the condition of the world and of human relationships. This first school of thought rejects such a doctrine and insists instead that with the right technology, politics, and education, we can and must strive to overcome social and individual evils.

The *second* identifies Original Sin with the absurdity of human existence. We can do nothing about our situation. We are radically and thoroughly flawed. This is the view of pessimistic existentialism, e.g., Sartre.

The *third* misunderstanding equates Original Sin with personal sin—a personal sin which somehow is imposed on our otherwise innocent shoulders. Such a view of Original Sin forces us to accept it, or write it off, simply as a "mystery" or to reject the doctrine as an intrinsic contradiction. How can one be really guilty of something that someone else committed?

Accordingly, the doctrine of Original Sin does not play a very large part in contemporary Catholic theology and even less in liberal Protestant theology. It no longer enters into our theology of human existence. We assume, for example, that Baptism annuls it in any case, so that it remains a vital problem only for unbaptized babies.

Biblical Notion

Old Testament

Contrary to a popular belief within the Church, the Old Testament has no formal concept of Original Sin. Clearly it is aware of sin and especially of its corrupting effects (Genesis 6:12). But Genesis 2:8-3:24 (the account of the first sin of Adam and Eve) should not be read apart from chapters 4-11. Genesis 3 is only an introduction to what amounts to a series of anecdotes intended to show how sin, once admitted into the world, spreads everywhere, bringing death and destruction in its wake.

New Testament

In the New Testament, and especially in *Paul*, we find the substance of a doctrine of Original Sin (1 Corinthians 15:21-23, and Romans 5:12-21). In the latter passage Paul speaks of Original Sin by first drawing a parallel (verse 18) between Adam and Christ. Because of Adam we are sinners without the Spirit (verse 19), but because of Christ we are sought by God's saving will and are, therefore, in a state of objective redemption. And both these effects—the one from Adam's sin and the other from Christ's saving work—are antecedent to human freedom and personal decision. What *we* do is to ratify the deed of Adam by personal sin (verse 12) or the deed of Christ by faith.

Paul, of course, does not, nor can he, explain *how* this is so, how it is that we are affected by the sin of Adam without any personal decision. He insists only *that* it is so, and he argues from the universality of *death*. Because we all die, we are all implicated in sin, since death is the effect of sin. This sense of our corporate involvement in sin cannot be separated from the biblical belief in the solidarity of the human community and in its notion of corporate personality, sometimes linked with the Suffering Servant of God in Isaiah 40-55.

But since death is the effect of sin, death (the death of Christ) can also be the instrument of its destruction. It is by dying to sin with Christ that we are liberated from it (Romans 6:1-23). Through Christ's death comes new life. In dying with Christ we rise also with him (1 Corinthians 15:3,17; Galatians 1:4). Our dying and rising with Christ does not eliminate the enduring conflict between the spirit and the flesh, but we can achieve the final victory through Christ and the Spirit (Romans 8:1-17).

Post-biblical Theological Developments

Augustine

The biblical teaching on Original Sin, which as we have noted is exceedingly brief, was not developed until Augustine. The Greek Fathers (Irenaeus, Basil, Gregory of Nyssa, *et al.*) were too much involved against the heresies of Gnosticism and Manichaeism (both of which insisted that all matter is evil) to lay stress on such a doctrine. They were trying to show, on the contrary, how the incarnation elevated and transformed the whole created order. But the situation was just the opposite for Augustine. He faced not those who rejected the goodness of nature but those who glorified nature to excess, i.e., the Pelagians. Unfortunately, Augustine portrayed Original Sin as a situation in which every human being finds himself or herself, but from which only some are rescued. Although God desired the salvation of all in Christ, only those who are justified by faith and Baptism are actually saved.

Furthermore, Augustine linked Original Sin with *concupiscence* (i.e., the human person's *spontaneous desire* for material or sensual satisfaction). It is an effect of Original Sin and is transmitted by the libido in the parents' love by which a person first comes into existence. To the extent that concupiscence infects every human act, all of our deeds are in some sense sinful. Augustine did not suggest that every such deed is a *new* sin, but he never worked out the intrinsic difference between Original and personal sin because, for him, the consequences of both kinds of sin are the same in the next world.

Middle Ages; Trent; Post-Trent

In the Middle Ages, from Anselm of Canterbury onward, the essence of Original Sin was increasingly equated with the *lack of sanctifying grace* (medieval theology's new term for the divine indwelling) brought about by Adam's actual sin. Concupiscence now appeared simply as a consequence of Original Sin (Aquinas). Thus, it became possible to explain how Baptism blotted out Original Sin without at the same time canceling all of its effects, including concupiscence.

The Council of Trent (to which greater attention will be devoted below) agreed with the Protestant Reformers that Original Sin, caused by Adam's sin, affects all (except Mary) and that it is really overcome by justification. But *against* the Reformers, Trent insisted that Original Sin does not consist in concupiscence itself, since this remains even in the justified. Rather, Original Sin is the lack of original righteousness (justice) and holiness. Post-

Tridentine theology tried to answer the obvious difficulties associated with the traditional doctrine of Original Sin—e.g., How is it possible to translate blame from Adam to ourselves?

Contemporary Theologians

Contemporary theologians (especially Rahner) reject the notion that Original Sin is simply the sinful act of the first man or is a matter of collective guilt, since both of these views lead to contradictions and are not required by the dogma of Original Sin in any case. It is a mystery because grace itself is a mystery. The self-communication of God is antecedent to our free decision or proof of our worthiness (*ante praevisa merita*). Just as there is a state of holiness which is antecedent to our personal decision and which nonetheless qualifies and conditions our moral lives, so there is a lack of holiness which ought not to be, and that lack posits a state of unholiness which is also antecedent to our personal decision and which qualifies and conditions our moral lives. The fact that the mystery of Original Sin is subordinate to the mystery of grace explains why the actual doctrine of Original Sin appears in the Bible only when our divinization by the Spirit is explicitly grasped (as in Paul).

Contemporary theologians also reject the notion (suggested by Augustine and others) that Original Sin is more pervasive and more universal than is redemption, since everyone is affected by Original Sin but some are not effectively touched by the cross and resurrection of Christ. On the contrary, Original Sin and being redeemed are two constitutive components of the human situation in regard to salvation, which at all times determine human existence. "It may be assumed that sin was only permitted by God within the domain of his unconditional and stronger salvific will, which from the beginning was directed towards God's self-communication in Christ" (K. Rahner,"Original Sin," *The Concise Sacramentum Mundi*, p. 1151).

A *positive* statement of contemporary theology (especially Rahner) comprises the following principles:

1. All human beings are offered grace and, therefore, redemption *through Christ*, and not simply insofar as they are

human beings or members of the human community. This grace is given us as the *forgiveness of sins*. Indeed, Jesus himself thought of his own death on the cross as an expiatory death "for all." (More on this, of course, in Part III on Christ, especially chapter 12.)

2. The human person lacks God's grace precisely because he or she *is* a person and a member of the human community. At the same time God wills that we should have grace. Thus, if it is not present, this must be because of some guilt freely incurred (otherwise it contradicts God's will). Yet the absence of grace (a condition incurred freely by sin) is also against God's will, even when the individual is not at all responsible for its absence. This lack of grace, which ought not to be, has in an *analogous* sense the character of sin: It is very much *like* sin, in that it is contrary to the will of God, but it is at the same time *unlike* sin, in that it does not involve a free decision against God's will. But God remains attached to us in spite of the sin of Adam. God bestows grace freely now, not in view of Adam, but in view of Christ. As children of Adam, we do not have grace. As sons and daughters of God in Christ, we do.

3. The lack of grace is an inner condition of each one of us in that we are all human, but it is also *situational*. We are born into a "situation" in which, because of Adam's sin, grace is not at our disposal in the manner and measure which God intended. Accordingly, we now have to make our decision about salvation under the impact of both *concupiscence* and *death*, each of which is an effect of Original Sin. For that reason, and in spite of the work of Christ on our behalf, all of us are still directly concerned with Original Sin in our daily lives. We are, to that extent, "wounded" or weakened in our natural powers.

4. On the other hand, this does *not* mean that death and concupiscence are totally unnatural, that we would not have experienced them were it not for Adam's sin. It means, rather, that both are in contradiction to what we are in the concrete. They are indications of the as-yet-incomplete victory of grace. The process of history begins at the point where neither death nor concupiscence has been eliminated.

5. Our human situation in the face of a free moral decision is always *dialectically* determined: We are in Original Sin through

Adam and at the same time are oriented toward Christ and the God of glory. Either we freely ratify our state of Original Sin by personal sin, or we freely ratify our redeemed condition by faith, hope, and love. Our situation is one in which our decision to ratify is always qualified by concupiscence and death, on the one hand, and by the fact of our having been redeemed, on the other. Our moral standing before God, however, is always and finally determined by our free choice, weakened though it be.

6. The doctrine of Original Sin remains always pertinent to our lives as Christians and to Christian theology. It indicates (a) that grace is given historically, and not as a necessity of human existence; (b) that it comes from Christ, not from Adam at the beginning of history; (c) that the goal of history is greater than it was at the beginning of history; (d) that our situation of death, concupiscence, and other experiences of human limitation cannot simply be abolished in history, because they were there from the beginning; and (e) that our efforts, therefore, to overcome the effects of Original Sin (injustice, war, etc.) constitute a duty that cannot be completed in this world and, therefore, a duty that is never done.

Official Teachings of the Church

Sixteenth Council of Carthage

The Sixteenth Council of Carthage (418), a gathering of two hundred bishops, condemned the errors of the British monk *Pelagius*, who reduced Adam's sin to one of bad example and insisted that grace is not absolutely necessary for salvation. The canons (or principal doctrinal formulations) of the council were later approved by Pope Zosimus (d. 418).

Indiculus

The *Indiculus* (between 435 and 442), a summary of the doctrine of grace, was composed probably by Prosper of Aquitaine (d. 460), a disciple of Augustine and the strongest opponent of *semi-Pelagianism*, which held that none of us requires grace at the beginning but that God grants it as needed later. This document subsequently received papal approval and was used as the standard exposition on grace by the end of the fifth century.

Second Council of Orange

The Second Council of Orange (529) finally settled the matter against the *semi-Pelagians.* This local council accepted the teachings of Caesarius of Arles (d. 542), another of Augustine's disciples, plus material from Prosper of Aquitaine. Pope Boniface II (d. 532) approved Orange's action.

Council of Trent

The Council of Trent (sixth session, 1547), "Decree on Justification," said: We have lost innocence through the sin of Adam, and have inherited not only death but also sin. Nevertheless, we are redeemed by Christ interiorly and not just by a divine decree which leaves us unchanged within. Although we still suffer from the effects of Original Sin, God's justice inheres in us (see especially chapter 16 of the decree).

Humani Generis

Pope Pius XII's encyclical letter *Humani Generis* (1950) insisted on the truly gratuitous character of the supernatural order (i.e., God was not *required* to create us for glory) and on the importance of our common descent from one pair of parents.

SYNTHESIS: TOWARD A THEOLOGY OF
HUMAN EXISTENCE

It is obvious by now that theology does not follow the same clear lines of direction that one might find in such disciplines as accounting, law, chemistry, or the statistical sides of political science and economics. Like all of the humanities, theology is concerned with the question of human existence. But human existence can only be studied by human beings. We ourselves raise the question *about* ourselves. We have already noted in the preceding chapter that there is no standpoint from which we can "look at" God objectively, in a detached manner, as it were. This is so because God permeates as well as transcends us. For the same reason, there is no standpoint from which we can "look at" ourselves objectively, in a detached manner. We are at once the subject and the object of the inquiry. Consequently, our answers are always inadequate. They lead to further questions and to further attempts at newer answers.

The Christian "standpoint" is inevitably qualified by the conviction that God is real, that the real God is available to us, and that the real, available God is a principle of consciousness, knowledge, and moral action within each one of us, even within those who do not explicitly advert to God's presence as well as within those who explicitly reject the possibility of a divine principle of human existence.

We are persons who are self-aware (i.e., we not only *know*; we *know that we know*, and we know ourselves *as knowers*). *We are beings in possession of ourselves as subjects.* And this is the case even before we have had an opportunity to reflect on our existence from various disciplinary points of view (all of which we have placed under the umbrella of *anthropology*).

The knowledge that we have of ourselves before any of us has had an opportunity for systematic investigation and reflection is called *a priori* knowledge (as opposed to *a posteriori* knowledge, i.e., the knowledge of objects which is disclosed to us through study and examination). For the Christian, and indeed for every religious person, our *a priori* knowledge of ourselves as persons includes the light of faith as a "supernatural existential." In other words, *God is present in us from the beginning as the principle and the power of self-knowledge.* We are, "from the very circumstance of (our) origin, . . . already invited to converse with God" (*Pastoral Constitution on the Church in the Modern World*, n. 19). We do not come to the knowledge of God by a step-by-step investigation of data, arguments, and evidence. Rather, *our knowledge of God begins at the very moment when we become really conscious of ourselves as personal subjects*, as human beings, with all that this implies.

The Christian knows himself or herself as a creature, and a limited, flawed creature at that. But *the Christian also knows himself or herself as a person addressed by God in history, as a person touched by God's presence (grace).* What the Christian hears about himself or herself from the corpus of religious doctrines, especially in Sacred Scripture, the Christian recognizes as something of what he or she already knows about himself or herself in faith. *In the presence of some authentic statement about the meaning of human existence, the human person recognizes its truth almost spontaneously.* Aquinas called this "knowledge by connaturality." It "rings true," as it were. What is proposed is seen as consonant with what is immediately experienced in the act of self-consciousness.

Grace makes possible human nature's capacity for the connatural reception of God's self-communication in the Word (biblical, preached, theological, personal, and especially incarnate). *Hypothetically*, human nature could exist without the capacity for God. *Historically*, human nature has the capacity and cannot be without it. However, because of what is hypothetically true about human nature, one can explicitly reject God's presence without, at the same time, denying or destroying oneself *as human.*

Human nature is open to, but cannot absolutely demand, God's self-communication in grace. Grace remains always *grace* ("gift"). We have no title to it, and yet, given the present historical order and the intention of God, we are not fully human without it. But within that set of principles governing human existence there is an extraordinarily wide range of possibilities for the realization of our humanity. *Our historicity* (or situation in the world and within the process of human events) *means that we are significantly affected, and changed, by our environment, our bodiliness, our race, our sexuality, our social institutions, our interpersonal relationships, and so forth.* We discussed these and other factors in the preceding chapter.

But even though theological anthropology includes in principle all of the rest of theology, each of the other major doctrinal elements of Christian theology, and especially the question of

God, requires separate (though not unconnected) treatment. We are not retreating from our previous assertion that reflection on human existence is inevitably reflection on God, and vice versa. But because we are beings who by our very nature have the center of our existence outside ourselves, in God, our statements *about* God are more properly made outside of theological anthropology as such.

For the same reason we must keep theological anthropology and Christology apart, not absolutely, but for purposes of study and reflection. This does not mean that our theological statements about human existence can prescind from what we have come to know about Jesus Christ. On the contrary, a number of such statements (e.g., about the resurrection of the body) are possible only because of Christology. In that sense, Christ does not fit himself into some preexisting notion of human existence, but human existence itself is qualified and illuminated by God's grasp of it in Christ. *Christology is the recapitulation of theological anthropology.*

On the other hand, we do already know something about ourselves before Christ and apart from Christ, so that when we encounter Christ in history, we recognize him as human. Theological anthropology, therefore, cannot be pursued solely from within Christology, but must always be pursued in relation to it.

SUMMARY

1.   The *Old Testament* understands the *human person* primarily as a *creature* who *is* a *body* (and does not simply *have* a body) and whose hope of salvation is expressed in terms of the *resurrection of the body*. Bodiliness implies *coexistence* with other "bodies," especially in *sexual* relationships. That coexistence must be *responsible*, but because human freedom can be abused, human existence is also *sinful*. In spite of the spread of sin, human existence is *hope*-filled.

2.   The *New Testament* also understands human existence as *historical*. It is limited existence, qualified by sin. *Jesus* calls us all to *conversion* and *repentance*, to a working out of our salvation through a change in our relationships with others. *Paul*, too, speaks of the *bodily* condition of human existence and of our common hope in the resurrection of the body, a hope based on the saving work of Christ and the power

of the Holy Spirit. For *John*, to be human is to live by *grace*, i.e., by the presence of God in our hearts and in our midst. Our sinful selves and our sinful world would be lost if it were not for Christ and the *new life* that he brought us and that we enjoy even now.

3. The *Fathers of the Church* made no real breakthroughs in our understanding of human existence. There was some strong emphasis on the human person as the *image of God* and on human history as the *history of divinization and salvation* (Irenaeus, and others). It is Christ who *recapitulates* within himself all that is human in the individual and in history. But a tendency to *dichotomize* between matter and spirit perdures.

4. The *medieval period* focused principally on the person as *object*, a creature among creatures: lower than the angels, higher than the animal kingdom. "Man" was an unchanging essence, unchanged by environment and by history. But at least the beginnings of a turn to the *subject* can be found here, e.g., in medieval theology's concession that one could receive the grace of Baptism by *desire*, a subjective rather than objective principle.

5. Under the impact of scientific, philosophical, and theological developments outlined in the preceding chapter, a fundamental shift in our understanding of human existence has occurred in the so-called *modern period*. Emphasis is placed on our self-awareness as persons, and on our freedom and responsibility. This new direction in thought is reflected to some discernible extent in the *Second Vatican Council's Pastoral Constitution on the Church in the Modern World*.

6. "*Nature*" refers to the human condition apart from grace, but with the radical capacity to receive grace. "*Pure nature*" is a *hypothetical* concept. It refers not only to human existence apart from grace, but to human existence without the radical capacity to receive grace as well (known as the *potentia obedientialis* in medieval Scholastic theology, and as the "supernatural existential" in modern Transcendental Thomist theology).

7. Until this century, "nature" served only as a point of contrast with "*grace*", i.e., God's self-communication. *Grace supposes nature*, but *nature* in its own way *also supposes grace*, insofar as the grace of Christ sustains us in our actual, historical existence and orients us toward our one supernatural end, the Kingdom of God.

8. Nature is not directly a biblical concept. It is one that is inferred from subsequent reflection on the New Testament's proclamation of the new order of grace in Christ. We infer who we are as *creatures* of God by reflecting on who we have become through the grace of Christ.

9.   The concept of "nature" also underlines the essentially *gratuitous* character of God's self-communication. We are bodily creatures who are fully intelligible and fully open to human growth apart from grace. *In historical fact*, however, we have been given the radical capacity for grace, and therefore *the fullness of our growth is linked inextricably with our growth in the grace of Christ as well.*

10.   The concept of "nature" is not without dangers. Its use easily leads one to a *dualistic* understanding of human existence, as if grace were something merely *added* to, or superimposed upon, nature.

11.   The reality of *grace*, on the other hand, is fully and deliberately expressed in the Bible. In the *Old Testament* it means literally a "favor." It has to do with our attitude toward the needy, with the experience of liberation from distress and from sin. As a "favor," it is always given, or withheld, *freely.*

12.   In the *New Testament* the word for grace, *charis*, becomes a key word in the Christian message, designating the *good will of God*, expressed in Christ and producing such *effects* as righteousness, faith, love, and new life. Grace stands in opposition to *works* and *law*; not that works and law are of no account, but only that they do not of themselves save us. *Salvation* is from *grace*. It is a free gift, something not owed us because of our performance of works or our observance of laws.

13.   The *doctrine of* grace developed systematically under the impact of certain major heresies: *Gnosticism*, which challenged the *universality* of grace and of salvation; *Pelagianism*, which challenged the *necessity* of grace for salvation; and historic *Protestantism*, which challenged the *effectiveness* of grace in transforming us interiorly. Major opposition to each of these views was mounted by *Irenaeus, Augustine*, and the *Council of Trent*.

14.   The *relationship between nature and grace* is a fundamental issue for theology because it underlies so many other important relationships: creation and incarnation, reason and faith, law and Gospel, human freedom and divine sovereignty, the human community and the Church, and so forth. How does grace change nature without destroying human freedom and responsibility? How is the person able to accept freely the self-communication of God in grace?

15.   The *Catholic theological tradition* avoids two extreme positions: the one which emphasizes nature so strongly that it effectively diminishes the significance of grace, and the other which emphasizes grace so much that it effectively suppresses nature. Thus, on the question of the Kingdom of God, the extreme left would make of it the work of human effort alone, with subsequent divine approval, and the extreme

right would make of it the work of divine power alone, accepted in trusting faith by God's people.

16. The Catholic theological tradition is rooted in a *Christological* and, therefore, *incarnational* and *sacramental* perspective. There is no creation except in view of Christ. And whatever there is in the visible, created order is itself, at least in principle, the expression of the invisible presence and power of God. Although, *hypothetically*, we could know God apart from the "supernatural existential" (i.e., the radical capacity which God gives us from the beginning), *in fact* we do not know God apart from that *a priori* condition.

17. This *"supernatural existential"* is not grace itself, but only God's offer of grace. It is an offer given to every person. *Grace, therefore, supposes nature, i.e., the radical capacity to receive grace. But nature also supposes grace. There is a kind of "natural desire" for direct union with God.* It is only in that union that we can finally and fully satisfy our desire to know and to become what we sense we are called to become.

18. The *whole universe, too, is oriented by grace to the Kingdom of God. The history of the world is, at the same time, the history of salvation.* Therefore, the struggle for justice, for example, is part of the movement of, and toward, the Kingdom (*Pastoral Constitution on the Church in the Modern World*, n. 39). *Grace transforms not only persons but the whole created order* (Romans 8:19-23).

19. Our understanding of the relationship between nature and grace, however, must also contend with the reality of *sin*, both *personal* and *Original*. Sin does not destroy the relationship of communion with God once and for all, but it modifies it once and for all.

20. The *Old Testament* has no formal concept of Original Sin. It is aware of sin and of its widespread corrupting effects.

21. The *New Testament*, and especially *Paul*, develops the notion of "original" sin by drawing a parallel between the sin of Adam and the saving work of Christ (Romans 5:12-21). *We either ratify the sin of Adam and make it our own by personal sin, or we ratify the work of Christ and make it our own by faith.* Just exactly *how* we are affected by the sin of Adam, Paul cannot say. *That* we are affected by the sin of Adam is clear from the fact that we all *die*, and death, he perceives, is a consequence of sin. Only by dying with Christ can we overcome the destructive effects of sin.

22. This biblical teaching remained undeveloped until *Augustine*. Faced with those who exaggerated the goodness of nature (Pelagianism),

he stressed the sinful and wounded condition of every person. Unfortunately, he also insisted that while everyone is affected by sin, not everyone is rescued from it in fact. A certain theological disposition toward *predestinationism* followed from such an emphasis. Furthermore, Augustine linked Original Sin with *concupiscence* so strongly that he suggested that the sin (and one of its principal effects, concupiscence) was transmitted in the sexual union of our parents.

23.   By the *Middle Ages*, and especially with *Aquinas*, concupiscence was viewed simply as a consequence of Original Sin, and the sin itself as simply *the lack of sanctifying grace*. Thus, by Baptism the sin is completely blotted out (sanctifying grace is bestowed), although the effects of sin remain.

24.   *Contemporary theologians*, especially *Rahner*, reject the notion that Original Sin is simply the sin of the first human being or is a matter of collective guilt. These views, they hold, cannot be sustained biblically nor theologically. They also reject the Augustinian notion that Original Sin is more pervasive and universal than is redemption.

25.   Positively, contemporary theologians argue that (1) every human person is *offered* grace; (2) the *absence* of grace follows from some *guilt* freely incurred by the *person*; (3) the absence of grace also follows from the human *situation* itself; i.e., because of Adam's sin we are born into a situation in which grace is not at our disposal in the manner and measure that God first intended; it is a situation, too, in which the *effects* of that sin weaken our capacity to decide in favor of salvation; (4) death and concupiscence, however, are not totally unnatural, since history begins at the point where neither is absent; (5) our human situation, therefore, is *dialectically* determined; i.e., we are, at the same time, wounded by the effects of sin and oriented toward Christ and the God of glory; and (6) all of our efforts to overcome the effects of Original Sin (injustice, war, etc.) constitute a duty that cannot be completed in this world, and, therefore, a duty that is never done.

26.   The *official teachings of the Church* insist on the reality of Original Sin, on the absolute necessity of grace for salvation, and on the interior effects of such grace: the Sixteenth Council of Carthage (418), the *Indiculus* (435-442), the Second Council of Orange (529), the Council of Trent (1547), and Pope Pius XII's encyclical *Humani Generis* (1950).

27.   The difficulty in constructing a theological anthropology is rooted in the inescapable fact that we are at once the investigators and the ones investigated. *We cannot achieve a standpoint from which a pure, unobstructed, completely objective understanding of human existence is possible.*

28. *Neither can we Christians reach a standpoint from which we can prescind from the effects of God's grace on our consciousness and on the very process of inquiry and self-reflection.* God is available from the beginning. There is in every one of us a radical capacity to know ourselves as persons in the light of the reality of God, and to know God as the ultimate object of our every striving toward human growth and fulfillment. *Hypothetically,* human nature could exist without grace; *in fact,* however, we do not exist without it.

29. *Our theological statements about human existence cannot prescind from Christology, since much of what we know about ourselves we know because of what we know about Christ. On the other hand, we already know something about ourselves before Christ and apart from Christ,* in that our existence is *historical* existence and the reality of God is disclosed therein.

30. When we encounter Christ in history, we recognize him as human because we already have some understanding of what it means to be human. This is not to say, on the other hand, that the humanity we encounter in Christ does not far surpass our previous expectations and assumptions.

SUGGESTED READINGS

Barth, Karl. *Church Dogmatics.* III/2. New York: Scribner, 1960.

Baum, Gregory. *Man Becoming: God in Secular Experience.* New York: Herder & Herder, 1970.

Fichtner, Joseph. *Man the Image of God: A Christian Anthropology.* New York: Alba House, 1978.

Haight, Robert. *The Experience and Language of Grace.* New York: Paulist Press, 1979.

Macquarrie, John. *Principles of Christian Theology.* 2d rev. ed. New York: Scribner, 1977, chapter 3.

Rahner, Karl. *Foundations of Christian Faith.* New York: Seabury Press, 1978, chapters 1-5.

_____. *Hominisation: The Evolutionary Origin of Man as a Theological Problem.* New York: Herder & Herder, 1965.

_____. *A Rahner Reader.* Ed. Gerald A. McCool. New York: Seabury Press, 1975, chapters 1-4,9.

Rondet, Henri. *Original Sin: The Patristic and Theological Background.* New York: Alba House, 1972.

——————. *The Grace of Christ: A Brief History of the Theology of Grace.* Westminster, Md.: Newman Press, 1967.

Tavard, George. *Woman in Christian Tradition.* Notre Dame, Ind.: University of Notre Dame Press, 1973.

PART TWO

GOD

GOD

INTRODUCTION

We move now from the question of human existence to the question of God because the reality of God enters into the very definition of what it means to be human.

But if God is so fundamental and so central to human existence, why is it that many of us reject or practically ignore the reality of God? Why is it so difficult to *believe* in God? Why do any of us, Christian or non-Christian, believe in God at all (chapter 6)?

Belief in God must arise from some experience of God, clear or obscure. How, when, where, and under what circumstances is the reality of God made available to us? Are there recognizable signs of God's self-communication, or *revelation*? What is it that is communicated in the first place (chapter 7)?

To whom is God revealed? What are the effects of revelation on the individual, on society, and on institutions (the question of *religion*)? How do the religions of the world differ, one from another? To what extent are they similar? To what extent are non-Christian religions signs and instruments of God's saving love toward the whole human family? Does Christianity have a special place in salvation history nonetheless (chapter 8)?

Our understanding of God enters into our understanding of ourselves. We believe that God has somehow been made available to us in Jesus Christ. As a particular people with a particular history, we have developed a highly structured response to the revelation of God in Jesus Christ. At the core of the Christian religion, as of any other religion, is our doctrine of God. Who is *the Christian God*, and how is that God related to us and to human history at large (chapter 9)?

How has the Christian doctrine of the *triune* God developed, from its biblical origins to the present day? What are the principal elements of the Christian doctrine of the Trinity? What place and importance does it hold in the total exposition and practice of the Christian faith, and in the comprehensive statement of Christian theology (chapter 10)?

In addressing the question of God, Part II comes to the heart of the matter, both of this book and of theology itself. All else converges here. Our understanding of God is the foundation and context for our understanding of creation, redemption, incarnation, grace, the Church, moral responsibility, eternal life, and each of the other great mysteries and doctrines of Christian faith.

Every theological question is a variation on the *one* theological question: the God-question. But the invisible reality of God is mediated through the visible created order. The gracious and merciful God is at work in Jesus Christ. The Church is, as the late Pope Paul VI expressed it, "a reality imbued with the hidden presence of God." In the end God will be "all in all" (1 Corinthians 15:28).

This notion of God-in-all is closely linked with the distinctively Catholic emphasis on *sacramentality* (a notion that will be developed more fully in Part IV and recapitulated in chapter 30). The Catholic tradition has always insisted on the principle of mediation: The invisible depths of reality are manifested in visible ways. God, the foundation of all that is, is disclosed through signs: the cosmos, history, persons, mystical experience. Jesus Christ is the great sign or sacrament of God's presence and saving activity among us. The Church is, in turn, the sign or sacrament of Christ's and the Holy Spirit's healing and reconciling presence in the world.

But from beginning to end, it is God who is mediated through each and all of these signs: not the God of philosophy, not an abstract God, but the triune God.

The mystery and doctrine of the Trinity means that the God who created us, who sustains us, who will judge us, and who will give us eternal life is not a God infinitely removed from us. Our God is a God of absolute closeness, a God who is communicated truly in the flesh, in history, within our human family, and a God who is present in the spiritual depths of our being and in the core of our unfolding human history as the source of enlightenment and of community.

The doctrine of the triune God is what Christian faith is all about.

·VI·

BELIEF AND UNBELIEF
TODAY

THE PROBLEM

The reality of God enters into the very definition of what is means
to be human. Human existence is qualified from the beginning by
the God-given radical capacity ("supernatural existential," *potentia obedientialis*) to get beyond ourselves and to reach out toward
that which transcends us, the Absolute, and toward that which
raises us to a new level of existence, a sharing in the life of the
Absolute (grace). The question of God, in other words, is implied
in the question of human existence. And the opposite holds true as
well. As soon as we address the problem of God, we are confronted
with the problem of human existence.

But if the divine is so central to the existence of human
persons, why do so many of us reject or ignore the reality of God?
How is it that our radical capacity for grace is not universally
actualized? In short, why are there unbelievers as well as
believers?

The problem of unbelief is complicated by the fact that *unbelief is always relative.* Unbelief is a negative concept. It presupposes something positive which it negates. From the point of view
of religious faith (whether Christian, Jewish, or Moslem, for example), unbelief is a denial of or at least an avoidance of God. But
from another point of view, these religious traditions themselves
may be forms of unbelief. To the ideological Marxist, religious
faith may be a refusal to believe in the dialectical historical process or the classless society. To the positivist, religious faith may

represent a stubborn refusal to believe in the conclusions of scientific experimentation.

The term unbelief is being used in this chapter to mean *the denial or at least disregard of the reality of God* (whether God is named "ultimate concern," the Transcendent, the Absolute, the "beyond in our midst," the ultimate dimension of secular experience, the other dimension, Being, or whatever else). There are, of course, different *kinds* and different *degrees* of unbelief. There are also different *sources*. (We treated the question of belief more technically, of course, in chapter 2.)

According to the Second Vatican Council, *atheism* (which we are equating here with unbelief) has many forms. The *Pastoral Constitution on the Church in the Modern World* summarizes these: *classical atheism*, or the outright denial of God; *agnosticism*, or the refusal to decide whether to believe in God or not (a decision wherein one effectively decides *not* to believe in God); *positivism* (which rejects all reality which cannot be verified by scientific testing); an excessive *humanism* (which exaggerates the human capacity to control the universe through technology and which emphasizes freedom to the detriment of order); the rejection of *false notions* of God which the atheist assumes to be official doctrine; the transfer of ultimate concern from God (the Transcendent) to material things (the totally immanent); and the transfer of blame for social evil from individual, institutional, environmental forces to God as the One who thwarts the struggle for *liberation* by shifting our attention from this world to the next.

"Undeniably," the *Pastoral Constitution* declares, "those who willfully shut out God from their hearts and try to dodge religious questions are not following the dictates of their consciences. Hence they are not free of blame." But then the council proceeds to an extraordinary admission: "Yet believers themselves frequently bear some responsibility for this situation . . . .To the extent that they neglect their own training in the faith, or teach erroneous doctrine, or are deficient in their religious, moral, or social life, they must be said to conceal rather than reveal the authentic face of God and religion"(n. 19).

Some major *sociologists of religion* would agree with the main lines of the council's explanation, but their analyses are more broadly based. Thus, at a 1969 symposium in Rome, cosponsored by the Vatican's Secretariat for Non-Believers, University of California sociologist Robert Bellah noted that the phenomenon of unbelief was limited to relatively small groups of intellectuals and cultural elites until the eighteenth century. With the expansion of these classes (especially through education and the concomitant rise in literacy) in the nineteenth century, a new spirit spread to a larger public: a fuller appreciation for the dignity of the individual and the importance of free inquiry, on the one hand, and a reaction against authority (or at least authoritarianism), on the other. This was accompanied, as we already saw in the two previous chapters, by a shift in *philosophical* emphasis from the objective to the *subjective* orders. Belief became less an imposed system than a matter of personal decision.

So widespread was this change that many nineteenth-century rationalists and positivists predicted the demise of religion. But that never happened. Why not? Because the anti-religious forces made the same mistake that many religious people have committed: they confused religious belief with *cognitive* belief. Thus, with the collapse of cognitive belief, religious belief as such was sure to follow.

But this assumption about the collapse of religious belief was never verified by the facts. The large portion of religious people had never regarded cognitive, intellectualized belief as essential to their religious lives. What they embraced instead was an *embodied* truth, transmitted not through definitions and logical demonstrations, but through narratives, images, and rituals. This insight is fully consistent with the *Pastoral Constitution's* insistence that "the witness of a living and mature faith ... penetrating the believer's entire life ... activating him toward justice and love ... " is even more important in overcoming unbelief than is "a proper presentation of the Church's teaching" (n. 21).

Faith, according to Bellah and other sociologists, is deeply embedded in our existential situation and is part of the very structure of human experience—an insight which Bellah correctly attributes to Pascal (d. 1662) and Kierkegaard (d. 1855), and which we might also link with Rahner and Lonergan as well. Religion, therefore, is not "a matter of objective-cognitive assertion which might conflict with science, but a symbolic form within which one comes to terms with one's fate" (see *The Culture of Unbelief*, p. 46). Faith, consequently, is an *inner* reality, and the belief which follows from faith is inner-directed. But that does not mean that faith and belief are purely private. Such faith and such belief relate us to others, to the total human community, and indeed to the whole universe—bringing us even to the point of sacrificing our lives for others.

How widespread is the opposite, unbelief? Again, it depends on how you define it. In one sense at least, everyone is a believer; everyone believes in something important. And insofar as people express their belief, they are "religious." In the context of the United States, for example, such beliefs may issue forth in what Bellah has called "civil religion." It is the linking of one's search for personal authenticity with a sense of national identity and national purpose. The Peace Corps would be one major instance of it. It had something of the character of a secular monastic order, complete with a vow of poverty and a heroic devotion to the service of others.

But if you take belief to mean some *explicit* affirmation of the reality of God, then unbelief is considerably more prevalent, and certainly more in evidence than in previous centuries—again, because of advances in education generally, in literacy particularly, and because of the modern philosophical shift to the "subject."

And that is why the obverse side of the problem of God is the problem of the unbelieving person. Indeed, the problem of God—of belief and unbelief—becomes a problem only when it is concretely stated in such terms. According to the Bible and to the kind of philosophical theology represented by Transcendental Thomism, the presence of God is integral to the very structure of our historical existence. Therefore, the person who does not "fear God" (in the biblical sense of responding obediently to the presence and call of God) somehow does not exist, and that person's nature is somehow less than, or other than, human. On the other hand, the unbeliever *does* exist. He or she is there. And that is the problem.

We shall not, in this chapter or anywhere else in this relatively ambitious book, solve that problem. There are some things that we can do no more than accept as part of our historical situation (a "given" of reality) and deal with as intelligently and as constructively as possible.

The problem of belief and unbelief, therefore, is not primarily the problem of communicating the correct information about God so that everyone will be able to know it, and in knowing it perceive at once its truth. Nor is it simply a problem of laziness or bad will on the part of those to whom the information is directed. Rather, *the problem of belief and unbelief is*, once again, *the problem of human existence.* Is human existence finally and ultimately worthwhile? Is it meaningful? Is it purposeful? Is it intelligible? Is it directed to some end beyond itself? Or is it simply "full of sound and fury, signifying nothing"? And the problem of human existence is but the other side of the *problem of God.* For the question of the intelligibility, purposefulness, and worthwhileness of human existence is always answered, positively or negatively, in terms of God or some verbal surrogate for God.

SOME CONTEMPORARY VIEWS OF THE PROBLEM

Hans Küng

Swiss theologian Hans Küng, professor at the University of Tübingen in West Germany and author of many influential and controversial books on the Church, has perhaps made his deepest impression thus far with his massive volume *On Being a Christian.* He discusses the problem of belief and unbelief early on in the book, in the section on God.

His approach is consistent with the one adopted in this book. "In order to answer the question of God," he insists, "it must be assumed that man accepts in principle his own existence and reality as a whole ... " (p. 70). Our attitude to reality, if we are ever to reach God, has to be one of fundamental trust and confidence. Not that such trust automatically eliminates uncertainty of every kind. Reality is there as a fact, and yet it remains always enigmatic, without any clearly visible support or purpose. The challenge is to find some kind of satisfactory answer, and in this quest the believer is in competition with the unbeliever. Which one can more convincingly interpret the basic human experiences?

Even someone who does not think that God exists could at least agree with the hypothesis that *if* God existed, a fundamental solution to the problem of human existence would be provided. God would be seen as the ultimate reason for all that is, as reality's ultimate support, ultimate goal, and ultimate core. Threats of death, meaninglessness, rejection, and nothingness would be overcome. But we cannot proceed from the *hypothesis* of God to the *reality* of God.

Besides, it is also possible to formulate the *opposite* hypothesis: If God does *not* exist. One must concede that it is indeed possible to deny the reality of God. Atheism (or unbelief in its most explicit form) cannot be refuted on the face of it. There is more than enough *uncertainty* about reality to justify, or at least explain, why someone might decide to deny the reality of God. On the other hand, atheism is also incapable of positively excluding the alternative. If it is possible to deny God, it is also possible to affirm God. Just as atheism rests on a *decision* about the ultimate meaning (or meaninglessness) of reality, so, too, does belief. Just as there is enough *uncertainty* about reality to explain, and perhaps even justify, unbelief, so, too, there is enough *clarity* in reality to explain, and perhaps even justify, belief.

And so the terms of the problems become clear. *If* God is, God is the answer to our most fundamental questions about reality and about human existence. *That* God is cannot be proved or demonstrated or otherwise established beyond all reasonable doubt. It can ultimately be accepted only in a confidence founded on reality itself. Since the "evidence" is so uncertain, it cannot be imposed upon us conclusively. There remains room for human freedom. We are free to decide: to affirm the fundamental worthwhileness of reality and of human existence, or to deny it. Each path is fraught with risks. The decision not to decide (agnosticism) is itself a decision against the intelligibility and purposefulness of reality. It is a vote of no confidence, and *confidence* is what belief and unbelief are really all about.

Michael Novak

The American philosopher Michael Novak, a disciple of Bernard Lonergan, has written several popular books on an extraordinarily diverse range of subjects (fiction, sports, Vatican II, politics, as well as philosophy and theology). None is more pertinent to our discussion here than his *Belief and Unbelief: A Philosophy of Self-Knowledge.*

Although Novak would not disagree with Küng's analysis of the problem, Novak proceeds from a more explicitly philosophical starting point than Küng does. That starting point is Lonergan's approach to human understanding and the structures of consciousness. Religion is based on the drive to understand. Even when all the goods of health, education, security, and wealth are in our possession, we still hunger to know who we are. And we infer from this hunger to know that there is some intelligent source of this hunger. "Belief in God based on fidelity to understanding is based upon fidelity to oneself. In discovering one's own identity, one discovers God" (p. 182).

How, then, does belief differ from unbelief? The believer is attentive to the data of his or her own consciousness, and the unbeliever is not, or at least interprets the data differently. Since no one has ever seen God (John 1:18), one stands always before a silent and invisible God. One "sees," and another does not "see." Being irreligious is like being tone-deaf or color-blind. At least that is how the believer looks at it. But perhaps the believer perceives what is not there. The believer, therefore, can never be certain that his or her belief is accurate and true. "He is held in darkness by a hidden God" (p. 23).

On the other hand, it is in believing that reality assumes intelligibility. If one believes in God, one understands why one is inclined to pay respect to other persons and why one is inclined to be faithful to understanding, to friendship, and to creativity. In the end, however, "The serious nonbeliever and the serious believer . . . share a hidden unity of spirit. When both do all they can to be faithful to their understanding and to love, and to the immediate task of diminishing the amount of suffering in the world, the intention of their lives is similar, even though their conceptions of what they are doing are different" (p. 191).

Gregory Baum

Following not Lonergan but the French philosopher and theologian Maurice Blondel (d. 1949), Gregory Baum pursues a similar line of analysis. Belief is not a matter of accepting as true certain elements of some unlikely story about God, but a matter of interpreting human experience in a particular way. Blondel named his approach "the method of immanence." The Christian message reveals the hidden (supernatural) dynamism present in human life everywhere. The message is not foreign to life; it explains what has been going on in life and where it is leading us.

In his book *Faith and Doctrine*, Baum carries Blondel's apologetical approach one step further. He identifies the elements of ordinary human experience which contribute to a believing as opposed to an unbelieving response. He calls them "depth experiences," i.e., ordinary human experiences that are memorable, that are the source of many decisions, and that tend to unify human life. Those depth experiences may be specifically religious, or they may be secular. In the final accounting, however, they are all religious in that they ultimately put us in touch with God.

The specifically *religious* experiences are the experience of the holy and the experience of contingency. The so-called *secular* depth experiences are the experience of friendship, encounter, conscience, truth, human solidarity, and compassionate protest.

The religious literature of the world abounds in testimonies to the experience of the *holy*. It is what William James (d. 1910) described in his *The Varieties of Religious Experience* (1902) as a "sense of reality, a feeling of objective presence, a perception of what we may call 'something there,' more deep and more general than any of the special and particular 'senses' by which the current psychology supposes existent realities to be originally revealed."

Rudolf Otto (d. 1937), another major analyst of religious experience, insisted in fact that the sense of the sacred or of the transcendent is a purely *a priori* category. It is not something derived from sense experience, he argued in his classic work, *The Idea of the Holy* (1917). The experience of the sacred is rooted instead in "an original and underivable capacity of the mind implanted in the 'pure reason' independently of all perception." (The similarity to Rahner's notion of the "supernatural existential" is difficult to miss.)

The experience of *contingency* is our feeling of radical dependency, our sense of limitation, even of insignificance, and our concomitant sense of insecurity. At the same time we are profoundly aware that we belong to another who is vast, strong, caring, eternally reliable, that we are part of a larger unity which has meaning and in the context of which we find the strength to face life. It is an experience alluded to many times by Jesus himself (the parables of the lilies of the field and the birds of the air, for example) and systematically developed in the works of the great nineteenth-century Protestant theologian Friedrich Schleiermacher (d. 1834).

The experience of *friendship* gives us a new kind of self-possession. We become reconciled with ourselves as we are accepted by another. And since we become more ourselves, we have more energy available for the mission of life. Closely related to the experience of friendship is the experience of *encounter* (as in a teacher–student relationship) that profoundly changes and shapes our lives. The Jewish philosopher and theologian Martin Buber (d. 1965) is one of the principal systematizers of encounter experiences.

Conscience, too, is a depth experience. It is the experience of moral responsibility. We realize the call to transcend ourselves and our own self-interest and to act on behalf of others. In so doing we sense that we are acting in accordance with what is deepest in us and thus opening ourselves to reality and to life as it is and as it is meant to be. A thinker who has assigned to conscience a central place in Christian theology is Cardinal John Henry Newman (d. 1890).

Truth is another depth experience. At certain moments in our lives, whether in conversation, research, or reading, our resistance to truth is overcome and we experience a conversion of the mind to a higher level of consciousness. We suddenly see the picture. And because we see, we are able to plan and redirect our lives differently, make decisions in a new way, and enter more deeply into personal unity. St. Augustine stands out among those who have understood life as a series of conversions to truth. Bernard Lonergan's notion of conversion is also pertinent here, as we shall see in chapter 26.

The experience of *human solidarity* makes us aware of the unity of the human family and its common destination to growth and reconciliation. The experience transcends our ideologies and even shatters them. We realize our interdependence. We share in the joys and sufferings of people everywhere. We recognize the deathly, inhuman character of prejudice, hatred, and discrimination. Baum names Pope John XXIII as one in whom this experience bore astounding fruits. One could add the work of Methodist theologian James Fowler, who, building on the psychological theories of Harvard professor Lawrence Kohlberg, speaks of the sixth stage of faith-development as "universalizing faith."

Connected with the sense of human solidarity is yet another depth experience, that of *compassionate protest*. It is the experience of those who become deeply disturbed by the misery in life, who are burdened by the presence of injustice, exploitation, and war. They identify with those who have no hope in this world. Such persons speak out as prophets, as accusers, as critics, even at the risk of their reputations, their physical safety, and their lives. Martin Luther King, Jr. (d. 1968), personifies this experience. And so, too, perhaps do some of the *theologians of liberation* in Latin America.

Depth experiences such as these bring us in touch with reality at its deepest level, and in so doing they bring us in touch with ourselves. Or to put the matter differently, as we reflect on the content and meaning of our human experiences, we begin to see that there is more to life than meets the eye, that there is an intelligibility (to use the Lonerganian term) which grounds, explains, and directs all that is. *To believe means to affirm the intelligibility of reality.* Or, in Baum's terms, *to believe means to recognize the significance of our depth experiences.* They put us in touch with the God who is immanent to human life. They explain our lives and give them direction.

Peter Berger

A sociologist of religion in the Lutheran tradition, Peter Berger has developed an apologetic similar to Baum's. He, too, argues for an anthropological starting point in his *A Rumor of Angels.* What is there, if anything, in ordinary human experience which gives rise to belief in transcendental reality? What Baum called "depth experiences" Berger calls "signals of transcendence." He defines them as "phenomena that are to be found within the domain of our 'natural' reality but that appear to point beyond that reality" (pp. 65-66). As such, they express essential aspects of our being. They are not the same as Jung's archetypes, because they are not unconscious and do not have to be excavated from the depths of the mind. They belong to ordinary, everyday experience.

Berger identifies five: our propensity for order, our engagement in play, our unquenchable spirit of hope, our sense of outrage at what is thoroughly evil, and our sense of humor.

Our propensity for *order*, Berger argues on the side of philosopher of history Eric Voegelin, is grounded in a faith or trust that ultimately all reality is "in order." This transcendent order is of such a character that we can trust ourselves and our destiny to it. Human love—parent for child, man for woman—defies death. Death cannot annihilate the reality and fruits of love. There is an order which banishes chaos and which will bring everything to a unity at the end. And belief in God vindicates that order.

Play also mediates transcendence. When one is playing, one is on a different time, no longer measured by the standard units of the larger society but by the peculiar ones of the game itself. In the "serious" world it may be Tuesday, 11:00 A.M., March 5, 1981. But in the universe of play it may be the second inning, the fourth round, the fifth match, or two minutes before the half. The time structure of the playful universe takes on its own specific quality, a kind of eternity. Religion—belief in God—is the final vindication of childhood and of joy, and of all the playful gestures that replicate these.

Even the Marxist philosopher Ernst Bloch (d. 1978) has argued that our being cannot be understood adequately except in connection with our unquenchable propensity to *hope* for the future. We realize ourselves in projects, as we seek to overcome the difficulties and the limitations of the here and now. The artist, in failing health, strives to finish her creative work. A man risks his life to save another. Herein, we have a kind of depreciation or even denial of the reality of death. And it is precisely in the face of the death of others, and especially of those we love, that our rejection of death asserts itself most loudly. It is here, above all, that everything we are calls out for a hope that will refute the empirical fact. So deeply rooted is this attitude that one might conclude it is part of the very essence of human existence. Belief in God vindicates the gestures in which hope and courage are embodied.

The argument from *damnation* or *outrage* is the other side of the argument from hope. Some evils (e.g., the Nazi war crimes) are so obscene that we are convinced they cry to heaven for vengeance. And we are equally convinced they *will* be condemned and punished. Belief in God validates our deeply rooted conviction in a retribution that is more than human.

Finally, there is the argument from *humor*. By laughing, we transcend the present, the given, what is. We see discrepancies. The neighborhood bully is in deathly fear of spiders. A fastidious writer makes an egregious mistake in grammar. So we see that our imprisonment in the conditions of the present is not final. Things are not always what they seem. They can be other. Belief in God vindicates our laughter.

OFFICIAL TEACHINGS OF THE CHURCH

The preceding apologetical approaches do not seem to be inconsistent with the official teachings of the First Vatican Council and are certainly not inconsistent with those of the Second Vatican Council. The former council declared that "God, the beginning and end of all things, can be known with certainty from the things that were created through the natural light of human reason, for 'ever since the creation of the world His invisible nature has been clearly perceived in the things that have been made' (Romans 1:20) . . . " (*Dogmatic Constitution on the Catholic Faith*, chapter 2).

Nor is the First Vatican Council's teaching a denial of the necessity of grace. The same council insists on the necessity of faith for salvation, and faith is always the work of grace (chapter 3 of the *Constitution*). Furthermore, we have already argued, with Rahner and others, that human reason does not exist in an historical vacuum. Our history is the history of salvation. Our reason, indeed our whole consciousness, has been radically modified by God's offer of grace. There is no such order of reality as a purely natural order. Likewise there is no such reason as a purely natural reason. Hypothetically, that could have been the case. But in fact it is not. Thus, when Vatican I argues that we can know God through the power of human reason alone, that teaching is not necessarily inconsistent with the view that all of our knowledge of God is, in the first instance, made possible by God, by the offer of grace, by the "supernatural existential."

The Second Vatican Council, we pointed out earlier in this chapter, acknowledges that there are many reasons for unbelief, at least one of which is the failure of the Church to live up to its own teaching. If we are to persuade the world of the reality of God, it will not be done simply through a more effective communication of doctrine. It will happen chiefly through our putting the Gospel into practice (*Pastoral Constitution on the Church in the Modern World*, n. 21).

The council also seems to be pursuing the same theological course outlined above. The Church knows "that her message is in harmony with the most secret desires of the human heart . . . .Far from diminishing man, her message brings to his development light, life, and freedom . . . .'Thou has made us for Thyself, O Lord, and our hearts are restless till they rest in Thee' (*Confessions of St. Augustine*)" (n. 21). For that reason we must be prepared always to enter into dialogue with one another, believers and unbelievers alike, in order to learn from one another's human experiences and to assist one another in the interpretation of those experiences (nn. 21 and 23).

What is to be said, finally, of the abiding presence of *unbelief* in the world? According to Vatican II (the *Pastoral Constitution*, nn. 19-22; the *Dogmatic Constitution on the Church*, n. 16; and the *Decree on the Church's Missionary Activity*, n. 7), not every instance of positive atheism, i.e., explicit rejection of God, is to be regarded as the result and the expression of personal sin. Even the atheist can be justified and receive salvation if he or she acts in accordance with his or her conscience. Over against the earlier teaching of the textbooks, the council assumes that it is possible for a normal adult to hold an explicit atheism for a long period of time, even to life's end, without this implying moral blame on the part of the unbeliever.

The council also seems to rule out the notion that those who die without explicit faith in God but who live good lives are destined for some form of natural happiness alone. The council, in the *Decree on the Church's Missionary Activity*, implicitly affirms our thesis that the natural order is already graced and that there can be no purely and distinctly natural end of human existence. Even the so-called nonbelievers can reach a saving faith without having accepted the explicit preaching of the Gospel.

CONCLUSION

Belief and unbelief are two sides of the same human coin. They represent different interpretations of the mystery of human existence. *The believer interprets reality and human existence as finally worthwhile, intelligible, and purposeful.* The unbeliever interprets reality and human existence as finally without intelligibility or purpose and, therefore, without ultimate worth. *Neither belief nor unbelief can be established or disproved by arguments alone.* The believer sees what the unbeliever does not see. Still, the believer's perception is not arbitrary. There are dimensions of human experience which cannot be explained fully apart from the God-hypothesis—call them "depth experiences," "signals of transcendence," or whatever else. This does not mean that the case for belief is clearly the stronger of the two, but only that *the case for belief is not without warrants.*

Michael Novak expresses the problem movingly in his *Belief and Unbelief* (p. 24):

> The believer need not forgive God for the suffering of this world; like Job, he may accuse God to his face. But he does not cease to remain faithful to the conscience which cautions him not, finally, to be dismayed. Belief in God, he knows, could be an empty illusion, even a crime against his own humanity. He knows the stakes. If he is faithful to his conscience and thinks clearly concerning what he is about, he has no place in his heart for complacency or that sweet pseudoreligious 'peace' that sickens honest men. His belief is not unsteady—quite the contrary—though he knows that the thread supporting it, however firmly, is so slender that in the night it cannot by any means be seen. This commitment to conscience keeps him faithful, and his daily experience may make his commitment as plausible as Sartre's experience made his, but there is no final way short of death of proving who is right. Each man has but a single life, during which his choice may go either way. That choice affects many things in his life, but one thing it does not affect: his reliance on his own conscience (formed, no doubt, in friendship with other men) as his sole concern and comfort.

No one has seen God.

SUMMARY

1. The *"problem"* of belief and unbelief is focused in these questions: If God is so central to human existence, why do so many apparently reject or ignore God? How is it that their radical capacity for grace is not actualized? Moreover, "unbelief" is a relative concept. "Unbelief" in relation to whom or what? In this chapter the term refers to the denial or at least the disregard of the reality of God.

2. There are different *sources* or reasons for unbelief: a refusal to decide (*agnosticism*), a rejection of all scientifically unverifiable reality (*positivism*), an exaggeration of the human capacity to control the universe (excessive *humanism*), *false notions* of God, substitution of material goods for God (*materialism*), transfer of blame for social evil from human and institutional failure to the stunting effects of religious faith.

3. The *Second Vatican Council* acknowledged that the failure of believers to live up to their beliefs is one of the chief causes of unbelief.

4. *Sociologists of religion* attribute the growth of unbelief to the expansion of the naturally critical intellectual classes through *education*, the rise in *literacy*, and a *philosophical shift* to the *subject*. Belief becomes more a matter of personal decision and less a matter of socially imposed doctrine.

5. The collapse of belief in the nineteenth century, however, did not bring with it the collapse of religion because the sort of belief that collapsed was *cognitive* belief, not religious belief (in God). That noncognitive belief is deeply embedded in our existential situation and is part of the very structure of human experience.

6. For that reason, some would argue that pure unbelief does not exist. Everyone believes in something important insofar as everyone is in quest of personal authenticity. If, on the other hand, belief is understood to mean explicit acknowledgment of the reality of God, then there is as much unbelief around as there are people and institutions which say, or imply, that they prescind completely from the reality of God.

7. In the end, the problem of belief and unbelief is at once the problem of God and the problem of human existence, for reasons which we have already spelled out in Part I. Belief in God is belief in the worthwhileness, the intelligibility, and the purposefulness of human existence.

8. This approach which unifies belief in God and the affirmation of human existence is adopted widely in contemporary Christian theology. *Hans Küng* admits that neither belief nor unbelief can be finally proved, but the hypothesis of God answers more questions about the meaning and purpose of reality and of human existence than does unbelief. To believe is to approach reality with *confidence. Michael Novak*, following Bernard Lonergan, argues that belief follows from reflection on the structures of our own consciousness and the process of human understanding. Our unrestricted desire to know implies some intelligent source of this hunger for understanding. *Gregory Baum*, following Maurice Blondel, adopts a method of immanence. Belief in God explains and gives direction to our deepest human experiences: of the holy, of our

contingency, of friendship, of conscience, of human solidarity, and so forth. We begin to see that there is more to life than meets the eye, that God is present to life as the source of life's meaning and as the principle of life's movement. *Peter Berger* has a similar approach. He calls the "depth experiences" of Baum "signals of transcendence" —namely, our propensity for order, our engagement in play, our unquenchable spirit of hope, our sense of outrage at what is thoroughly evil, and our sense of humor. Belief in God vindicates each of these universal human experiences.

9. The *First Vatican Council* taught that we can come to the knowledge of God through natural reason alone. This teaching is not inconsistent with our present understanding of the relationship of nature and grace (see the previous chapter). Since this is already a graced order of existence, reason does not operate in a historical vacuum. God is already present to it, elevating it to a higher order of existence. It is *graced reason* which, according to Vatican I, can know God as the beginning and end of all things.

10. The *Second Vatican Council* insists, furthermore, that the Church's message is in harmony with the most secret desires of the human heart. There is a correlation, in other words, between belief in God and self-knowledge, which is exactly the point contemporary theologians are making. It is erroneous, therefore, to assume, as our earlier textbooks did, that all those who explicitly reject or ignore God are culpable and subject to damnation. Even the unbeliever can attain a saving faith implied in his or her commitment in conscience to those values and activities which are reflections of divine reality.

SUGGESTED READINGS

Baum, Gregory. "A Modern Apologetics." *Faith and Doctrine: A Contemporary View.* New York: Newman Press, 1969, pp. 51-90.

Berger, Peter. "Theological Possibilities: Starting with Man." *A Rumor of Angels: Modern Society and the Rediscovery of the Supernatural.* New York: Doubleday, 1969, pp. 61-94.

Caporale, Rocco, and Grumelli, Antonio, eds. *The Culture of Unbelief.* Berkeley: University of California Press, 1971.

Küng, Hans. *Does God Exist? An Answer for Today.* New York: Doubleday, 1980.

_____. "The Other Dimension." *On Being a Christian.* New York: Doubleday, 1976, pp. 57-88.

Marty, Martin. *Varieties of Unbelief.* New York: Doubleday, Anchor Books, 1966.

Novak, Michael. *Belief and Unbelief: A Philosophy of Self-Knowledge.* New York: Macmillan, 1965.

Shea, John. *Stories of God: An Unauthorized Biography.* Chicago: Thomas More, 1978.

Whelan, Joseph, ed. *The God Experience: Essays in Hope.* New York: Newman Press, 1971.

·VII·

REVELATION

THE PROBLEM

The Bible itself admits that "no one has ever seen God" (John 1:18). And yet we talk *about* God and *in the name* of God all the time. Where do we derive our "information" about God? How does God communicate with us? Under what conditions and circumstances does such communication occur? How can we be sure that we have, in fact, been "in touch with" God rather than with our own wish-projections and imaginings? Does God communicate with others besides ourselves? Or is God hidden, almost as a matter of principle, from great segments of the human family? Is the *form* of communication verbal, pictorial, dramatic, mystical, historical, social, political, natural, or what? *What* is communicated or disclosed? Is it facts about God and the "other world"? Is it God's own self-communication? Would we have "known" that which is revealed even if it were not revealed? If God does indeed reveal, why is it that so many creatures of God seem either indifferent to, or ignorant of, God's revelation? Or is it perhaps very difficult to pick up God's signals?

The "problem" of revelation, therefore, is the same as the "problem" of belief and unbelief. In this chapter we are addressing ourselves to the question once again, but this time from a more deliberately biblical, historical, doctrinal, and theological point of view.

BIBLICAL NOTIONS OF REVELATION
Old Testament

At the heart of the faith of Israel is the conviction and affirmation that God has intervened in history, modifying the course of Israel's historical experience and the lives of individuals within Israel. Although the Old Testament does not use the technical term *revelation* to describe this process, the expression "word of Yahweh" seems to come closest in meaning. Even in the case of the *theophanies* (e.g., Yahweh's appearance in human form to Abraham to announce the birth of Isaac and the destruction of Sodom, Genesis 18:1-33), it is not the fact of seeing God that is primary in importance but rather the fact of hearing God's word. This is particularly evident in the call of Abraham (Genesis 12:1-3) and in God's dealings with Moses (Exodus 33:11,21-23).

Theophanies and Oracles

The earliest stage of revelation in the Old Testament is characterized by the predominance of theophanies and oracles. Yahweh appears in order to conclude an alliance and changes the name of Abram to Abraham (Genesis 17:1-22; for other appearances to Isaac and Jacob see Genesis 26:2, 32:25-31; 35:9). It is impossible, however, to determine precisely the nature of such manifestations. At times they are presented as if they were external visions, and at other times as internal ones. In general, the Old Testament reflected its own Oriental milieu. The Bible, therefore, employs techniques that were characteristic of its cultural environment: e.g., divination, dreams, omens. They were, of course, purified of their polytheistic or magical connotations. Before a war or the conclusion of a treaty, Israel would "consult" God through its seers and especially its priests (1 Samuel 14:36; 22:15). Israel acknowledged that God could be revealed in dreams (Genesis 20:3; 28:12-15; 37:5-10; 1 Samuel 28:6; 1 Kings 3:5-14). Joseph excelled in the interpretation of dreams (Genesis 40-41). Gradually Israel began to distinguish between dreams by which God truly communicated with the prophets (Numbers 12:6; Deuteronomy 13:2) and those of the professional seers (Jeremiah 23:25-32; Isaiah 28:7-13).

Sinai Covenant

The Sinai Covenant is a decisive movement in the history of revelation, but it can be appreciated only in the light of the entire history of salvation. Through the Covenant, Yahweh became head of the nation and delivered Israel from Egypt. In return, Yahweh exacted a pledge of fidelity to the Law (Exodus 20:1-17) or to the "ten commandments" (Exodus 34:28). The Law discloses the divine will. Obedience brings blessings; transgression brings malediction. The whole destiny and subsequent history of Israel was now tied inextricably to the will of God as manifested in the event by which Israel was liberated from the bondage of Egypt. The prophets never ceased to apply to the events of their own day the implications of the Sinai Covenant. Whatever legislation followed was considered a prolongation of the Decalogue, or Ten Commandments.

Prophecy

The phenomenon of prophecy also enters into the Old Testament's basic notion of revelation. Moses is the prototype of the prophets (Deuteronomy 34:10-12; 18:15,18), but it is only with Samuel that prophecy becomes a frequent occurrence in the history of Israel (1 Samuel 3:1-21). Amos, Hosea, Micah, Isaiah, the prophets who preceded the Exile (which lasts from the destruction of Jerusalem by the Babylonians in 587 B.C. to the Edict of Cyrus in 538 B.C.), conceived themselves as guardians and defenders of the moral order prescribed by the Covenant. Their preaching is always a call to justice, to fidelity, to the service of the all-powerful God. But because of Israel's frequent infidelity to the Covenant, the divine word uttered by the prophets more often than not brought condemnations and warnings of punishment (Amos 4:1; 5:1; 7:10-11; Hosea 8:7,14; 13:15; Micah 6-7; Isaiah 1:10-20; 16:13-14; 28:13; 30:12-13; 37:22; 39:5,7).

Jeremiah occupies a particularly important place here because he attempted, as the others did not, to determine the criteria by which the authentic word of God could be recognized: (1) the fulfillment of the word of the prophet, i.e., what the prophet says will happen, happens (Jeremiah 28:9; 32:6-8; Deuteronomy 18:21-22); (2) the prophecy's fidelity to Yahweh and to the traditional religion (Jeremiah 23:13-32); and (3) the often heroic witness of the prophet himself (Jeremiah 1:4-6; 26:12-15). For Jeremiah the word of Yahweh is always superior to himself and to everything else. Yahweh places the word in his mouth as if it were a material object (Jeremiah 1:9). At times it provides delicious nourishment (15:16); at other times, it is a source of torment (20:9,14). Through the word, Israel is summoned to fidelity to the Law and the Covenant. It is a word of independent and irresistible dynamism and force: "Is not my word like fire, says the Lord, like a hammer shattering rocks?" (23:29).

Deuteronomy

With the book of Deuteronomy the two currents, legal and prophetic, converge. The connection between *Law and Covenant* is emphasized more than ever. The history of Israel is the history of its fidelities and infidelities to both. If Israel wishes to live, it must put into practice every word of the Law (Deuteronomy 29:28), for this Law from God is the source of all life (32:47). Deuteronomy also enlarged upon the meaning of the "word of Yahweh" already given in Exodus. It no longer applies only to the Ten Commandments but to every clause of the Covenant (28:69), i.e., to the whole corpus of moral, civil, religious, and criminal laws. It placed everything under the heading of the Mosaic Law (28:69; 30:14; 32:47). The word of the Law is something to be interiorized: "No, it is something very near to you, already in your mouths and in your hearts; you have only to carry it out" (30:14). The Law consists precisely in this: " . . . you shall seek the Lord, your God; and you shall indeed find him when you search after him with your whole heart and your whole soul" (4:29).

Historical Literature

Parallel to the prophetic and deuteronomic currents is the historical literature (Joshua, Judges, Samuel, Kings), which places the word of God in an even more thoroughly historical context. Hereafter, Israel would never think of its religion apart from the category of history. It is the word of God which makes history and renders it intelligible. Throughout the long history of the kings, the words of Yahweh penetrate the course of events and express their religious significance (e.g., 1 Kings 2:41; 3:11-14; 6:11-13; 2 Kings 9:7-10; 21:10-15). A particularly significant text is the prophecy of Nathan (2 Samuel 7) which provides the foundation for royal messianism. By reason of this prophecy the dynasty of David became directly and forever allied to Yahweh (2 Samuel 7:16; 23:5). This prophecy, furthermore, is the point of departure for a theology, elaborated by the prophets, which is eminently one of promise, turned always toward the future, in contrast to the theology built on the Sinai Covenant, whose demands are meant to apply to the present moment.

Exile

At the time of the *Exile*, the prophetic word, without ceasing to be a living word, became increasingly a *written* word. The word confided to Ezekiel is inscribed on a scroll which the prophet had to assimilate before he could preach its contents (Ezekiel 3:1-3). It remains always a word of *judgment*. Ezekiel repeats the refrain that Yahweh does acts of judgment in order that Israel might know that he is Yahweh, that it is Yahweh who acts, and that Yahweh is holy (6:14; 7:9,27; 11:12; 12:20; 13:23). Ezekiel meantime attempts to form a new Israel during its period of Exile. His word is also a word of comfort and hope (33:1-9). But it is never enough simply to hear the word; one must live it (33:32). In Deutero-Isaiah (Isaiah 40-55) the word is boldly personified as a dynamic reality which creates history itself. It dominates history (45:19; 48:16). "So shall my word be that goes forth from my mouth; It shall not return to me void, but shall do my will, achieving the end for which I sent it" (55:11).

Wise Conduct of Israelites; Creation

Yahweh is revealed, finally, in the wise conduct of the faithful of Israel. The wise person is the one who fulfills the Law of God (Sirach 15:1; 19:20; 24:23; Ecclesiastes 12:13), for all *wisdom* comes from God (Proverbs 2:6). The wisdom of God is manifested in the works of God and is communicated to those who love God (Sirach 1:8-10; Wisdom 9:2; Job 28:12-27). Wisdom comes forth from the mouth of God from the very beginning of the world (Sirach 24:3-31). Thus, wisdom is itself identified with the word of God. It is at once creative and revealing (Wisdom 7-9).

Indeed, *creation* itself discloses the reality of God. The whole created order gives echo to the word of the One who named its creatures, and these created beings manifest the divine presence, majesty, and wisdom (Psalm 19:2-5; Job 26:7-13; Proverbs 8:23-31; Sirach 42:15-25,43; Wisdom 13:1-9).

New Testament

The major themes of the Old Testament—creation, history, prophecy, law, wisdom—are recapitulated in the New Testament in the person of Jesus Christ: "In times past, God spoke in fragmentary and varied ways to our fathers through the prophets; in this, the final age, he has spoken to us through his Son, whom he has made heir of all things and through whom he first created the universe. This Son is the reflection of the Father's glory, the exact representation of the Father's being, and he sustains all things by his powerful word" (Hebrews 1:1-3). *Christ is the summit and fullness of revelation.*

Synoptics

In the Synoptic tradition (Matthew, Mark, and Luke) Christ is the one who reveals insofar as he proclaims the Good News of the Kingdom of God and teaches the word of God with authority (Mark 1:14-15; Matthew 23:10, 5:21—7:29; 24:35). *His authority* to reveal is based on his sonship. As Son, he knows the secrets of his Father: "No one knows the Son but the Father, and no one knows the Father but the Son—and anyone to whom the Son wishes to reveal him" (Matthew 11:27; see also Luke 10:22). The Apostles, in turn, have been commissioned by Christ to pass on what they have heard from him and what they have seen in him (Mark 3:14). They are to preach the Gospel and invite men and women to accept it in faith (Mark 16:15-16). The essential *content* of the revelation is the salvation that is being offered to humankind under the form of the Kingdom of God, which is announced and definitively realized by Christ (Mark 1:15). The time is fulfilled. The reconciling power of God (which is what the symbol "Kingdom of God" means) is in our midst. Be open to it. Let it transform your consciousness and your behavior. Christ reveals the Kingdom, therefore, in his word, in his works, and in his presence.

Acts of the Apostles

The Acts of the Apostles describe the apostolic activity as in continuity with the action of Christ. The Apostles have heard Christ speak, preach, and teach, and they have received a commission to give witness to his resurrection and his work (1:1,22; 10:39), to preach and to teach what he prescribed and taught (2:42). Their function, therefore, is that of *witnesses* and *heralds*. They preach and teach what they have seen and received (e.g., 8:5; 9:20), namely, the word of God (15:35; 18:11), the word of Christ (18:25), and the word about Christ (28:31). More specifically, they proclaim the Good News of salvation through Christ (10:36; 13:26; 20:21), that Jesus is risen (2:32), and that he is the Messiah, the Lord, and the Savior.

Paul

For Paul revelation is the *free and gracious action of God by which he offers us salvation in and through Christ* (Romans 16:25-27; Colossians 1:26). The mystery that revelation communicates is God's plan of recapitulating all things in Christ (Ephesians 1:8-10). Because it *is* a mystery (i.e., because the invisible is manifested through the visible but remains all the while invisible), what is disclosed or unveiled (the root meaning of the word *revelation*) remains all the while hidden (1 Corinthians 2:7). Nonetheless, certain witnesses have "seen" it—namely, the Apostles and the prophets (Ephesians 3:5), and it is concretely realized in the Church (Ephesians 3:8-11).

But nowhere is revelation more fully personified or embodied than in Jesus Christ (Romans 8:3; Galatians 4:4; Philippians 2:7). The Epistles look forward as well to an *eschatological revelation,* i.e., the final and complete outpouring of God. When Jesus comes again, God will be revealed more clearly than in the incarnation itself (1 Corinthians 1:7; 2 Thessalonians 1:7; 1 Peter 1:7,13). So, too, will the glory of the Christian be revealed (Romans 8:18-21; 1 Peter 1:5; 4:13; 5:1).

Paul also seems to speak of what theologians once called "natural revelation" (although, in light of our earlier reflections on nature and grace and on the historical impossibility of a state of pure nature, "natural revelation" must be a hypothetical concept, if not entirely meaningless). In the Old Testament, Yahweh is manifested through *nature* (Wisdom 13:1-9, e.g.); so also for Paul: "Since the creation of the world, invisible realities, God's eternal power and divinity, have become visible, recognized through the things he has made" (Romans 1:20).

And he speaks, finally, of "private" revelations to himself (2 Corinthians 12:1-7; Galatians 2:2) and expects that other Christians will experience revelations which will give them a deeper understanding of the Gospel (Ephesians 1:17; Philippians 3:15). These personal revelations are *mystical insights* which are given to the individual alone.

John

John conceives revelation as the *Word of God-made-flesh* (John 1:1-18). This Word is manifested in creation itself (1:3), through the Law and the prophets (1:11), and finally through the incarnation. The whole life of Christ gives testimony to the Father, and this testimony is perfect in its content and in its expression (17:4,6,26). He is the Word of God (1:1-2) and the Son of the Father (1:18). What he has seen and heard of the Father he communicates to us (8:38; 8:26,40). The Word is acceptable to us because the Father gives testimony regarding the Son: in the works of Christ by which he is acknowledged as the Son, sent by the Father (5:36; 10:25) and through the interior action of the Father by which he draws us to Christ (6:44-46). In the Johannine theology of revelation, *Christ is both God revealing* (1:18; 4:23) *and God revealed* (1:1; 14:5-6). For John, the Word of God appears in the flesh (3:6; 1 John 1:1-2). It is both light and life (John 9:5; 8:12; 12:46; 17:3). Whoever sees Jesus Christ, therefore, sees the Father (14:10-11).

The Holy Spirit will complete the revelation of Jesus and insure the accuracy of the apostolic teaching (14:26; 16:13)—an emphasis no doubt prompted by the rise of pseudo-revelation and pseudo-prophecy in the primitive Church.

Theological Note

We cannot forget here what we acknowledged in the preceding chapter. Belief cannot be demonstrated beyond all reasonable doubt, nor can unbelief be positively disproved. And the same limitations hold true for unbelief. What, then, are we to say about the biblical views of revelation just summarized? *First,* the Bible does not prove the *fact* of revelation. The Bible only testifies to its own belief that God is a living God and that the living God has been disclosed to us in various ways at various times and nowhere more fully than in Jesus Christ. *Secondly,* the Bible presents an *interpretation* of history. It *infers* from the experience of Israel and the early Church that God was active in our corporate and individual lives through the Law, the prophets, the wisdom of Israel, and supremely through Christ. But such a view is always an inference. The presence and saving action of God in Christ, or anywhere else, was not self-evident. It was possible for someone to "look" and yet not "see." What we have in the Bible, therefore, is an understanding of revelation which follows from certain presumed experiences of God but is not necessarily revelation itself. The Bible reports various revelatory experiences along with its interpretation of those experiences. To return to the schema in chapter 2: (1) our experience of God, at once individual and communal, is recognized as an experience of the divine reality (*faith*); (2) from within a community of faith, we reflect on the nature and meaning of that experience (*theology*); (3) we articulate what we have reflected (*belief*), and are drawn more deeply into that experience of God through the community's teachings; and (4) we reflect further on the ways in which that original experience of God occurred in our lives (*theology of revelation*). What we have been doing thus far in this chapter is working at that fourth level, namely, trying to identify and synthesize the Bible's understanding not of revelation as such but of the meaning of the very *notion* of revelation.

What we have to remember at the same time is that revelation does not emerge as a major theological question until after the Enlightenment. What follows immediately in this chapter, therefore, is very schematically presented because there is relatively little historical data with which to work.

PATRISTIC NOTIONS OF REVELATION
Apostolic Fathers

For the Apostolic Fathers (Clement of Rome, d. ca. 96; Polycarp, d. ca. 155; Ignatius of Antioch, d. ca. 107), revelation is the "Good News" of salvation. Christ is its supreme herald and embodiment. The Apostles are its messengers, just as were the prophets before them, and the Church receives and transmits their teaching. Ignatius of Antioch, following John and Paul, insisted that the Word of God was manifested first of all in creation (*Epistle to the Ephesians* 15:1) and then in the Old Testament through the prophets (*Epistle to the Magnesians* 9:1-2; *Epistle to the Philadelphians* 5:2). All of these earlier manifestations of the Word pointed to, and culminated in, the supreme manifestation of the Word in Christ. Jesus Christ is the one and only Master, and he alone can provide the knowledge of the Father (*Epistle to the Ephesians* 15:1; 17:2; *Epistle to the Magnesians* 9:1). Ignatius' writings frequently lashed out against heretics and false doctrines (Judaism, Gnosticism, Marcionism). The triple criteria of true doctrine for him were Christ, the Apostles, and the Church as represented in the bishop and his presbyterate (or group of priests). Fidelity to the Church in the person of the bishop insures fidelity to Christ (*Epistle to the Smyrneans* 8:1).

Apologists

The Apologists (Justin, and others) shared the same understanding of revelation, but they were inclined to focus more sharply on its philosophical aspects. Because they wrote for, and in dialogue with, the contemporary intellectual community, they wanted to show that the *Logos* (truth) which all philosophers lovingly pursued was embodied in the *Logos*-made-flesh, Jesus Christ. Christians are his pupils and disciples, members of his school. Irenaeus' view is especially significant. Irenaeus stressed the dynamic and historical character of revelation, underlining its movement, its progress, and its profound unity. He saw the Word of God in creation, in the theophanies of the patriarchal period, in the Law, the prophets, Christ, the Apostles, and the Church. Revelation is a movement from God to God: from Trinity to the Beatific Vision (our unobstructed experience of God in heaven). Christ is at the center of the movement. *Revelation is the epiphany or manifestation of God in Christ.* And, over against Marcionism, Irenaeus argued that it is in Christ that the two Testaments are joined: The Old Testament proclaims Christ-announced; the New Testament proclaims Christ-in-fact. Revelation is the teaching of the Son of God, the Gospel message, the apostolic tradition, the faith of the Church, the Christian mystery, the truth, the rule of salvation, the norm of life, Christ himself. Revelation, therefore, is not a human doctrine but a gift of love, which invites the response of faith and leads to eternal life.

Greek Fathers

Among the Greek Fathers there were two major schools: the *Alexandrians* and the *Cappadocians*. The *Alexandrians* (Clement, Origen, Athanasius, Cyril) developed an understanding of revelation very similar to the Apologists'. For Clement, Christ is the answer to our quest for truth. But true knowledge can be obtained only through charity, the life to which the *Logos*-made-flesh calls us. Christ reveals the Father and the mysteries of eternal life. The Apostles share in his teaching authority and are commissioned to preach the Gospel to the whole world. They have transmitted to the Church the deposit of faith which they have received and preserved intact.

The *Cappadocians* (Basil, Gregory of Nyssa, Gregory Nazianzen) were engaged primarily in repelling the Trinitarian and Christological heresies (especially *Arianism*), but in the process they also indirectly developed a theology of revelation. We have two means of access to the Father: visible creation and the teaching of faith. Understanding of the divine mysteries comes only through Christ, under the illuminating force of the Holy Spirit. Christ is the Word-in-person who witnesses to, and instructs us in, the divine mysteries. The Apostles have the mission to proclaim the mystery as the Good News.

Latin Fathers

The Latin Fathers (Tertullian, Cyprian, Augustine) were on the whole less speculative than the Greek Fathers in their treatment of revelation. Augustine's theology of revelation, developed in his commentary on the Fourth Gospel and in his *De Gratia Christi* (*On the Grace of Christ*), is closely linked with his doctrine of *illumination*, which centers on God as the light of truth. Revelation is understood, therefore, more as *an inner light by which we are able to believe than as that which is proposed for belief.* The one Word of God is at once invisible (the illumination and inspiration of the Spirit) and visible (Christ). In Christ we have God revealing and God revealed. The prophets and the Apostles participate in the light of Christ and give witness to what they have seen and heard. That apostolic witness and word are contained in Sacred Scripture and in the proclamation of the Church. Here below we walk in faith, but our faith aspires to the vision of God.

Augustine's teaching dominated the remainder of the Patristic period in the West. Revelation continues to be understood as any kind of divine illumination. Only in the high Scholasticism of the thirteenth century does the term *revelation* become restricted to "supernatural knowledge" and eventually to the content of Church doctrine.

MEDIEVAL NOTIONS OF REVELATION

The Augustinian tradition is especially strong in the theology of Bonaventure, who also identified revelation with the illuminative action of God or with the subjective illumination which results from God's action. Bonaventure did not clearly distinguish between the notion of revelation and that of inspiration, often confusing the two. On the other hand, Bonaventure did understand the mystery of revelation in its larger historical and processive context: relating it first to the Trinity, to the history of salvation, to the disclosure of God in the natural order, to contemplation, and finally to the Beatific Vision.

The cognitive emphasis emerges particularly in Thomas Aquinas. *Revelation is that saving act by which God furnishes us with the truths which are necessary for our salvation.* Revelation occurs in history, moving us toward a greater and greater understanding of the revealed truths. The sacred deposit of these truths is built up gradually from the time of the patriarchs and prophets in the Old Testament to the time of the Apostles. The incarnation marks the fullness and consummation of revelation. Although Aquinas acknowledged that revelation had no other purpose than to proclaim the Good News of salvation, he was interested primarily in the process by which the recipient and bearer of revelation (especially the prophet) assimilated the revelation and handed it on. He portrayed such a process as essentially *cognitive.* Thanks to a special illumination from God, the prophet judges with certitude and without error the various objects presented and seizes the truth which God intends to communicate. The majority of humankind does not have such direct access to revelation. It is always mediated through preaching, and this preaching, in turn, has been authenticated by the miracles and other signs which God provides (*Summa Contra Gentiles,* book 3, ch. 154). Revelation, however, does not achieve its perfection until the Beatific Vision (*Summa Contra Gentiles,* book 4, ch. 1).

The opening of Part II-II of his *Summa Theologica* is where Aquinas provides his fullest discussion of the *content* of revelation. What is it that we discover in and through revelation? It is "the First Truth insofar as it is manifested in Sacred Scripture and in the doctrine of the Church" (q. 5, a. 3). How is the *First Truth* made known? Through statements or propositions which are presented to the human mind for acceptance or rejection (q. 1, a. 2). The principal expressions of revelation are contained in the articles of the Church's creeds (q. 1, aa. 6-9).

Aquinas follows Augustine to the extent that, like Augustine, he insists on the absolute necessity of an interior illumination from

God which elevates the mind to perceive and accept what God reveals. But unlike Augustine, he does not identify this interior divine illumination with revelation itself. For Aquinas and his school, revelation assumes a more *objective* character.

It is always important, of course, to view Aquinas' theology of revelation in the context of his whole system of philosophical and theological thought. For Aquinas, all knowledge is achieved only in the act of *judgment*. Revelation, which is *the highest type of knowledge*, implies the reception of some data and a light by which to pronounce judgment on the data's truth or falsity. This is the case with "natural knowledge"; so, too, is it the case with "supernatural knowledge." Truths are proposed to the mind, and we *assent* to those truths. In revelation, divine truths are proposed through preaching and are authenticated by miracles. We give supernatural assent to those truths under the light of faith (q. 173, a. 2).

And, thus, for Aquinas reason is an ascending movement of the mind from creatures to God, while revelation is a descending action by which the divine truth enters the human mind by a free communication. Revelation, in turn, has two stages: In this life we accept the divine truth on God's word in faith; in the next life we see God face to face, without the need for faith.

For many centuries this was to be the standard Catholic view on the relation between faith and reason.

THE COUNCIL OF TRENT

The Council of Trent has no explicit teaching on revelation as such. It develops its position indirectly, by what it says about the *sources* of revelation and by what it says about *faith*. The Gospel, which is "the source of all saving truth and rule of conduct," is contained "in the written and unwritten traditions which have come down to us, having been received by the Apostles from the mouth of Christ himself, or from the Apostles by the dictation of the Holy Spirit, and have been transmitted as it were from hand to hand ... and preserved in continuous succession in the Catholic Church" (*Decree on Sacred Books and on Traditions to Be Received*, Session IV, 1546).

This teaching was set against the newly emerging *Protestant* view that the Word of God is available in Sacred Scripture alone, and that the Bible is self-authenticating and self-interpreting by the power of the Holy Spirit.

We saw already in the chapter on faith (chapter 2) that this council opposed also the Protestant, and especially Lutheran, emphasis on *trusting* (fiducial) faith. "Adults are awakened for that justice," the council declares in its *Decree on Justification* (Session VI, 1547), "when, awakened and assisted by divine grace, they conceive faith from hearing (cf. Romans 10:17) and are freely led to God, *believing to be true what has been divinely revealed and promised* ... " (my italics).

FROM TRENT TO VATICAN I

Influenced by the new rationalistic climate of the day, both Catholic and Protestant theologians moved in the sixteenth and seventeenth centuries in the direction of a new and more rigid Scholasticism. The post-Tridentine Scholastics (Suarez, d. 1617, and de Lugo, d. 1660) stressed the objective character of revelation. God reveals through legates or intermediaries. Revelation is some static reality which one receives from others. And with increasing attacks on the whole concept of revelation, the defenders of traditional Christian faith became more, not less, inflexible on the issue.

The names of the opposition include some of the most important figures in the history of philosophy: Benedict Spinoza (d. 1677), who argued that revelation can add nothing to our knowledge that has not already been attained by reason; John Locke (d. 1704), for whom revelation makes available truths which are knowable to reason alone but which the great bulk of humankind is nonetheless ignorant about; Immanuel Kant (d. 1804), for whom the knowledge of God is impossible for speculative or theoretical reason but is accessible to practical reason alone, i.e., the voice of conscience; Georg Hegel (d. 1831), for whom revelation is the necessary self-generation of Absolute Spirit through the dialectic of historical process rather than the free intervention of a personal and gracious God in history; and Ludwig Feuerbach (d. 1872), for whom the idea of God is nothing more than a human projection.

Under the impact of both Rationalism (Spinoza, Locke, *et al.*) and Idealism (Kant, Hegel, *et al.*), Catholic theology began to grapple anew with the problem of revelation. Some of the early efforts failed because they imbibed too much of the errors they hoped to correct.

Thus, we had Catholic *semi-Rationalists* (Georg Hermes, d. 1831; Anton Günther, d. 1863; and Jacob Frohschammer, d. 1893), who accepted revelation as valid but who maintained, at the same time that reason could also independently establish all the truths of revelation. At the other extreme, we had Catholic *Fideism* (Louis Bautain, d. 1867), which underrated the powers of reason, and Catholic *Traditionalism* (Louis de Bonald, d. 1840; Félicité de Lammenais, d. 1854; and Augustin Bonnetty, d. 1879), a particular form of Fideism which held that God made a general revelation at the beginning of time and that the human race has been "living off" this general revelation ever since.

Mainstream Catholic attempts at coming to terms with the new spirit of Rationalism and Idealism, but without falling into semi-Rationalism on the left or Fideism and Traditionalism on the right, were fashioned by certain Jesuit theologians at the Roman College (now the Pontifical Gregorian University), Giovanni Perrone (d. 1876) and Johannes Franzelin (d. 1886), the Tübingen theologian Johannes Adam Möhler (d. 1838), England's John Henry Newman (d. 1890), and the German scholar Matthias Scheeben (d. 1888).

Scheeben, with commendable theological balance, emphasized both the external (historical) and internal (supernatural) dimensions of revelation, which culminates in Christ as the fullness of all revelation. Christ is at once the sign and reality of God's revealing presence. Scheeben also distinguished among three different levels or forms of revelation: revelation of *nature* (*revelatio naturae*): God is manifested through the works of creation; revelation of *grace* (*revelatio gratiae*): God is manifested through the divine word expressed by the prophets, Christ, the Apostles, and the Church; and revelation of *glory* (*revelatio gloriae*): God is fully manifested in direct vision at the end. Revelation in all three senses is destined for the totality of humankind.

THE FIRST VATICAN COUNCIL

The teaching of Vatican I had both a negative and a positive side. *Negatively*, the council's teaching was formulated against *Rationalism* (which proclaimed the complete autonomy of human reason), *Materialism* (which denied immaterial and spiritual reality), *Pantheism* (which spoke of everything as being not only a manifestation of God but identical with God), *semi-Rationalism* (which accepted the fact of revelation but affirmed the power of reason to apprehend the truths of revelation without divine assistance), *Fideism* (which accorded no significant role at all to reason), and *Traditionalism* (a form of Fideism).

Positively, the council taught that revelation can include truths of the *natural order* and that there are *mysteries* (truths of faith which are entirely beyond the natural powers of reason to apprehend) which can and have been revealed. Revelation comes implicity through the natural order of created things, and explicitly through the teachings of Christ, the prophets, the Apostles, and the Church. What is revealed is God and the eternal decrees of the divine will. The content is accepted on the authority of God, with the help of divine grace, not on the basis of rational argument. The whole human race is the recipient of revelation. There are some truths we could have grasped apart from revelation, but only with the greatest difficulty. There are others which we could never have grasped apart from revelation. Accordingly, revelation is *morally necessary* for the majority of humankind to come to a knowledge of religious truths of the natural order (e.g., the immortality of the soul); and it is *absolutely necessary* for all with regard to truths of the supernatural order (e.g., the Trinity). The Church's task is faithfully to guard and officially—and sometimes infallibly—interpret the revelation entrusted to it by Christ and the Apostles. On the other hand, the assent of faith is not blind or arbitrary. It must be "consonant with reason."

The doctrine of Vatican I must be understood, of course, against the background of the period. The *Dogmatic Constitution on the Catholic Faith* was intended not as a full statement on the meaning of revelation but as an answer to the various philosophical and theological systems which were threatening the integrity of the faith. Vatican I's teaching on revelation is less concrete and less historical than was Trent's, and certainly more abstract. What it lacks in biblical and personalist tones (something to be contributed by Vatican II) it compensates for in its remarkable conceptual clarity.

MODERNISM AND EARLY TWENTIETH-CENTURY CATHOLIC THOUGHT

But the Vatican Council's clarity did not hold for a group of theologians within the Catholic Church who were still trying to meet the Liberal enemy halfway. The movement was called *Modernism* because its adherents sought to adapt Catholicism to what was valid in modern thought, even at the risk of introducing some discontinuity between new forms of belief and the Church's past teachings. The principal Modernists were Alfred Loisy (d. 1940), George Tyrrell (d. 1909), and Edouard Le Roy (d. 1954). Drawing from the Liberal Protestant writings of the late nineteenth century, they identified revelation with a universal human experience—an ever-evolving personal knowledge of God attained in the ordinary course of life. Accordingly, they downplayed both the dogmatic content of revelation and its supernatural origin and process of communication.

Modernism was condemned in three separate ecclesiastical documents: the decree *Lamentabili* of the Holy Office (1907), the encyclical letter *Pascendi* of Pope Pius X (1907), and the *Oath Against Modernism* (1910). Over against Modernism, these documents declared that (1) revelation has a transcendental as well as immanent character; (2) it proceeds from a special intervention on the part of God; (3) it has a doctrinal aspect; and (4) it is a free gift of God, and not something demanded by, or already present in, the human person.

By present standards, these anti-Modernist documents seem excessively narrow in their own theological perspective. They tended to settle the issues on a purely disciplinary basis (removing Modernists from teaching positions, censoring writings, etc.) instead of trying to provide some good, solid answers to the various difficulties with which the Modernists were struggling. It is clear today that the Church could concede many points to the Modernists without at the same time undermining the traditional notion of revelation or indeed of the whole supernatural order.

The most constructive Catholic response to Modernism was formulated by Maurice Blondel (d. 1949), who, as we have already seen, anticipated the work of such theologians as Karl Rahner and Gregory Baum. He rejected both the excessive immanentism of Modernism (which excluded any transcendental dimension) and the excessive extrinsicism of the anti-Modernist documents (which tended to portray revelation as something coming totally from outside). Blondel called his mediating position the "method of immanence." An analysis of human action, he suggested, shows a dynamism which moves us toward a goal lying beyond our power to achieve it, but which, if it were offered as a supernatural gift, would be a genuine fulfillment of the human. The Transcendental Thomist movement of the early twentieth century was itself directly indebted to Blondel: Joseph Marechal (d. 1944), Henri Bouillard, and others.

THE SECOND VATICAN COUNCIL

The Second Vatican Council, in its *Dogmatic Constitution on Divine Revelation* (1965), reaffirms the various elements of the doctrine of revelation as proposed by earlier councils and in earlier official papal documents. It is Vatican II's *perspective* which differs from that of these other teachings. (1) It places the problem and mystery of revelation in the context of the history of salvation. (2) It views revelation not simply as divine speech, or as the communication of specific truths, but as something comprising both word and deed: "This plan of revelation is realized by deeds and words having an inner unity: the deeds wrought by God in the history of salvation manifest and confirm the teaching and realities signified by the words, while the words proclaim the deeds and clarify the mystery contained in them" (n. 2). (3) The "word" (*dabar*, the Hebrew root) is dynamic, and not merely conceptual: "God ... through the word creates all things and keeps them in existence" (n. 3). (4) Revelation is both cosmic and historical; i.e., it is communicated through the works of creation and in the course of the history of Israel, of Christ, and of the early Church. (5) Christ reveals, not only through his words and teachings, but also through his redemptive work itself and especially through his passion, death, resurrection, and glorification. (6) The deposit of faith is not simply a static entity. There is true growth of understanding on the part of the Church: "For, as the centuries succeed one another, the Church constantly moves forward toward the fullness of divine truth until the words of God reach their complete fulfillment in her" (n. 8). (7) Although the Church authentically interprets the word of God, the teaching office is "not above the word of God, but serves it, teaching only what has been handed on, listening to it devoutly, guarding it scrupulously and explaining it faithfully in accord with a divine commission and with the help of the Holy Spirit ... " (n. 10). (8) Finally, there is a much stronger and more general emphasis on the place of Sacred Scripture in the Church (" ... all the preaching of the Church must be nourished and ruled by (it)" (n. 21).

While Vatican II subtracts nothing from the earlier official teachings, it does add a new and fuller theological dimension more in keeping with advances in biblical studies and in Catholic theology accomplished in this century alone. We turn now to an outline of that contemporary Catholic theological terrain.

CONTEMPORARY THEOLOGICAL VIEWS OF REVELATION

Contemporary theological positions fall into three general categories: (1) those which continue to emphasize the *objective* and/or *cognitive* aspect of revelation; (2) those which work primarily out of *subjective* and/or *personalist* categories; and (3) those which *combine* elements of both.

Revelation As Objective and/or Cognitive

Although the purely *cognitive* understanding of revelation was the common notion of revelation in textbooks of Catholic theology throughout most of this century, it is no longer seriously proposed. Even relatively conservative approaches such as John Hardon's *The Catholic Catechism* (1975) and the joint effort known as *The Teaching of Christ* (1976), edited by Ronald Lawler, Donald Wuerl, and Thomas Lawler, reflect the broader biblical, historical, and personalist perspective of the Second Vatican Council, even as they continue to underline the objective character of revelation and the assent aspect of faith.

The so-called objective emphasis continues today in more surprising places: in Wolfhart Pannenberg, a German Lutheran theologian, in particular. God is made known indirectly, through those mighty acts by which divine sovereignty over history is exhibited and exercised. Indeed, one of Pannenberg's principal works is entitled simply *Revelation as History* (1968). Pannenberg contends that revelation in history can be recognized by anyone, even without faith. In effect, he falls back into Rationalism or at least semi-Rationalism.

A modification of the revelation-as-history approach is offered by Catholic theologian Edward Schillebeeckx in his *Revelation and Theology*, vol. 1 (1967). God is revealed in history, but the word of God in both Old and New Testaments is necessary to illuminate and clarify the revelatory character of those historical events. This is a compromise position which bears striking resemblance to Vatican II's *Dogmatic Constitution on Divine Revelation*, summarized above.

Another variation is advanced by those in the so-called *liberation theology* school. God is disclosed in the historical *praxis* of liberation. It is the situation, and our passionate and reflective involvement in it, which mediates the Word of God. Today that Word is mediated through the cries of the poor and the oppressed. According to Gustavo Gutierrez, the liberation school's principal exponent, "History is the scene of the revelation God makes of the mystery of his person. His word reaches us in the measure of our involvement in the evolution of history" ("Faith As Freedom,"

Horizons 2/1, Spring 1975, p. 32). The Word of God is distorted and alienating unless one is committed to change for the sake of the Kingdom. Such a commitment to liberation gives rise to a new way of being human and of believing, of living and thinking the faith, of being called together as Church. Revelation, therefore, happens when we recognize and accept God's summons to us to participate in the historical struggle for liberation.

Revelation As Subjective and/or Personal

If the preceding theories of revelation define revelation almost entirely from the viewpoint of God, others focus on the believing subject—in keeping with the fundamental orientation of modern philosophy. It is an approach strongly proposed on the Protestant side by Rudolf Bultmann. Revelation happens when our eyes are opened to the possibilities of authentic human existence and when we begin to respond to the transforming power of the Word of God. Preaching summons us to decision. *In the dynamic of the preaching and of the decision which the preaching evokes we have the event of revelation.*

A similarly subjective emphasis is given on the Catholic side by Karl Rahner, following in the philosophical tradition of Transcendental Thomism and, at least partially, in that of Heideggerian existentialism. The call of grace (the "supernatural existential" to which we referred in chapters 4 and 5) renders us restless for God. God is present to everyone of us and is offered in grace to whoever is freely open to the divine presence. For Rahner, revelation is either transcendental or predicamental.

Transcendental revelation is the change of horizon or world view which the presence of God effects in the person. *Predicamental* revelation is what is given in historical events and formal teachings (Bible, doctrines, etc.). But predicamental revelation is always secondary to transcendental revelation. Once grace has been given and accepted into the inner life of the person (transcendental revelation), it inevitably tends toward expression in the believer's ideas, beliefs, and moral action (predicamental revelation). Christ is the high point of both kinds of revelation. He is one in whom God is fully present, and he is at the same time the fullest expression of that presence in history. In Rahner's words, Christ is *"at once God himself as communicated, the human acceptance of this communication and the final historical manifestation of this offer and acceptance"* ("Revelation," *The Concise Sacramentum Mundi*, p. 1462; italics are Rahner's).

Variations on the subjective/personalist approach to revelation from within the Catholic tradition are provided by Gregory Baum in *Man Becoming* (1970) and Gabriel Moran in *The Present Revelation* (1972).

"Mediating" Views of Revelation

Without denying that theologians like Rahner embrace both sides of the objective/subjective dialectic, one might also note other efforts in contemporary theology to achieve a self-described mediating position between the two poles. It is a position characteristically adopted by Catholic theologian Avery Dulles. Revelation and faith dialogically interact so that the believer responds creatively to the self-manifestation of God, not simply in the depths of his or her own subjectivity, but in the cosmos and in history. Revelation, therefore, is neither an external datum that imposes itself on any alert and open-minded observer (Pannenberg) nor a free expression of one's own subjectivity (Bultmann), but a disciplined response that unfolds under the aegis of faith within a community and a tradition.

Dulles and others who seem to follow this "mediating" position are themselves in the tradition of Rahner, but they assert that they place greater emphasis on Rahner's concept of predicamental revelation (revelation as externally expressed) than Rahner himself does. Transcendental revelation, Dulles insists, never exists except in dialectical combination with its predicamental counterpart. There is no such thing as revelation in general, just as there is no faith in general, nor religion in general. Revelation occurs, and is expressed, within a given historical situation, community, and tradition. In that sense, there is a Christian revelation, a Moslem revelation, an Islamic revelation, a Hindu revelation.

TOWARD A THEOLOGY OF REVELATION
Some Theological Elements:
Creation, History, Prophecy, Mystery

Like every major part of the Christian theological network of doctrines, revelation can only be comprehended in terms of its relationship with other doctrines and symbols of Christian faith. Thus, our notion of revelation is impacted by our understanding of God, of human existence, of Christ, of Church, of grace, of nature, of history. Indeed, one can point to any major component of the Christian doctrinal system and legitimately suggest that all of theology is embodied and/or implied therein, whether it be the theology of human existence, of history, of Jesus Christ, or indeed of revelation itself.

A complete synthesis of the theology of revelation, therefore, would demand some substantive reference to each and all of the other major doctrines. This is impractical, and unnecessary in any case, since this whole book is itself an attempt at a comprehensive and systematic statement of the whole Catholic tradition. What is included in the synthesis which follows, therefore, is only those important doctrinal elements which are not formally treated elsewhere in this book. *Human existence* has already been examined in Part I. We are at this point about the task of developing a theology of *God*. Our attention will soon turn to the questions of *Jesus Christ* and the *Church*. Accordingly, we shall limit ourselves here to a consideration of the relationship between revelation and *creation, history, prophecy,* and *mystery*.

Creation

It must be said, first of all, that creation has to do with more than the beginning of all reality. Even if we were to assume that the world has always existed co-eternally with God, the question of creation would still present itself. Creation, in other words, has to do also with the *lasting relationship between God and reality*, and between God and us in particular. (There will, of course, be a further discussion of this relationship in chapter 9 in connection with the question of *Providence*.)

The doctrine of God, and the doctrine of revelation as well, presupposes a doctrine of creation. How would we know that there *is* a God unless God were somehow available to us? And how can God be available to us except through the created order? And how can we even begin to express our understanding of God except in terms of our perceived relationship with God? That relationship is a creaturely relationship. God is the source and sustainer of our very being.

The doctrine of creation is also intimately allied with the question of *nature*, to which we have already addressed ourselves in chapter 5. "Nature" is that which is. The nature of a being is what it is, as distinguished from other beings. In terms of human existence, "pure nature" is what we are apart from our call to divinization, apart even from our radical capacity to hear and to respond to that call (the "supernatural existential" or *potentia obedientialis*, again). But pure human nature does not exist. We are, from the beginning, open to divine grace.

In terms of the whole created order, "nature" means "being" (our word *nature* is derived from the Greek *physis*, which means not only "being" but also "becoming"). Thus, in the Heideggerian sense, nature is "the process of arising, of emerging from the hidden" (*An Introduction to Metaphysics*, pp. 13-15,17). Every created being stands between nothing and being and is at various degrees of proximity to the one or to the other. There is, in other words, a hierarchy of beings. Those are higher which display a wider range of being and a greater unity: increasing complexity without fragmentation.

We humans are at the highest level of created material/spiritual being. We are both distinct from nature (we alone know that we know) and at one with nature in that we, too, are part of the whole created order. Matter is not evil, as some of the earliest heresies (Gnosticism, Manichaeism) insisted. It comes from the creative hand of God, in one and the same creative act by which God brought forth spiritual realities: "God looked at everything he had made, and he found it very good" (Genesis 1:31).

Among those spiritual realities are *angels*. The word itself is derived from the Greek *angelos*, which, in turn, is the translation of the Hebrew *mal'ak*, which means "messenger." The existence of angels is of theological relevance here for two reasons: (1) angels remind us that there is more to the created order than what we actually see, feel, hear, and taste; and (2) all such spiritual forces other than God are less than God; i.e., they, like us, are part of the *created* order and are not themselves rivals of God in the production of good or the insertion of evil into the world. (The official teaching *that* angels exist as *creatures* of God is given by the Fourth Lateran Council in 1215 and by the First Vatican Council in 1869-1870.) In the Bible, angels function as their name suggests—as messengers of God (2 Samuel 14:17; 2 Kings 19:35; Exodus 14:19; and in the Book of Revelation generally).

Since they are intelligent creatures with freedom, angels have the capacity to reject God, as we do. Those angels which have rejected God are portrayed as demons in league with Satan (1 Corinthians 15:24; Ephesians 2:2). In other words, not every "signal" from the world of the numinous necessarily bears a "message" *from God*. The world of the numinous is as ambiguous and as fraught with sin as is the world of the tangible. Occasional bizarre happenings and behavior associated with various religious cults only reinforce that principle (e.g., the murder of a United States Congressman, other members of his investigative party, and nearly a thousand members of the People's Temple religious group in Guyana, South America, in 1978 is only one of many such cases).

Creation, we must repeat, is already an *act of grace*. It is *an act of divine self-giving*. The being of God is poured out so that there might be beings who can share in the being of God. The supreme act of self-giving occurs in the incarnation when God is so identified with a created reality (the humanity of Christ) that God and the created reality are uniquely one. (We shall return to the theology of the incarnation in Part III.) Indeed, the whole of the creative process is directed toward, and therefore culminates in, the union of the divine and the human in Jesus Christ.

If there were no creation, we could not know God, because there would be no one there to know God. If there were no creation, there would be no *nature*, for nature is the product of creation. Nature arises from the creative act which itself moves from nothing to being. *Creation also makes history possible*, not just in the sense that there must be reality before there can be history, but in the deeper sense that reality must be in movement before there can be history. And creation is a continuous process of movement toward higher and higher levels of being. It is within that progressive movement of history that God "speaks" to us.

Creation, in fact, is considered to be the first chapter in the history of salvation. Creation as ongoing reality underlies the whole of the saving process. God is disclosed not only by the emerging of reality from nothing, but by its continuation and dynamic movement "before our eyes," as it were. We take a look at reality as it is and see how marvelously structured and ordered it is (natural scientists should appreciate this even more than theologians and philosophers do). That does not in itself "prove" the existence of God, but it certainly makes it easier to attribute purposeful intelligence to reality than to ascribe its structure and order to chance. "For from the greatness and the beauty of created things their original author, by analogy, is seen" (Wisdom 13:5).

It is the *Church's official teaching* that God created the whole world, spiritual as well as material realities (against all forms of dualism, Gnosticism and Manichaeism especially); that the world is distinct from God (against Pantheism); that God created the world in freedom, to manifest divine goodness and glory. All created things, therefore, are good. Indeed, they have their own rightful autonomy and are not simply means to some spiritual end.

This teaching is contained in the documents of the Fourth Lateran Council (1215), the Council of Florence's *Decree for the Jacobites* (1442), the First Vatican Council's *Dogmatic Constitution on the Catholic Faith* (1870), the encyclical letter of Pope Pius XII, *Humani Generis* (1950), and the Second Vatican Council's *Pastoral Constitution on the Church in the Modern World* (1965). The latter document is especially important because it underscores the autonomy of the created order and draws out the principal practical implication of such autonomy, namely, ". . .if methodical research in any branch of learning is carried out in a truly scientific manner. . ., it will never really conflict with the faith, because both secular things and the realities of faith derive from the same God. . ." (n. 36).

For the same reason, we might add here, if we discover God through the created order, we need not underestimate the revelatory character of that discovery by referring to it as "natural" revelation (and, therefore, not truly revelation in the strict theological or doctrinal sense). On the contrary, there is only one Creator, who is available to us in a variety of ways and under a variety of forms. Just as there is no such reality as "pure nature," neither is there any such reality as "natural revelation." All revelation, whether through created things or through the prophets, Christ, the Apostles, and the Church, is derived from the same God.

History

For the Christian, history is not simply the place or context wherein God communicates eternal truths to humankind. History is itself the creative act of God through which God is manifested and continues to be manifested to us. The climactic moment of history is always the event of Jesus Christ.

Because God is disclosed in and through creative acts, and because these creative acts (to which we respond and with which we cooperate) constitute history, *we come to a knowledge of God as we reflect on the principal events of our history*. Israel did this before us, fixing its attention constantly on the Exodus in particular (Deuteronomy 6:20-25; Judges 6:8,13; Isaiah 10:26; Jeremiah 2:6; Ezekiel 20:5-6; Psalms 78:12-16; 105:23-38 and other passages too numerous to list). We do so as Christians by reflecting not only on the mighty acts of God in the Old Testament period, but also by reflecting on the supreme creative act of God in Christ, and other "signs of the times" which continue to characterize the world of human experience and history. Nowhere is this perspective more fully developed in the Bible than in the Gospel of Luke and the Acts of the Apostles.

The question whether there are two histories or one, i.e., whether there is a history of salvation alongside of, or even emerging from within, the history of humankind, has been debated since the seeds of a separate theology of *salvation history* were planted in the work of Irenaeus. Irenaeus' basic understanding reappeared in

Augustine's *City of God*. Other formulations were constructed by Joachim of Flora (d. 1202), who spoke of the three ages of history corresponding to the work of each of the Persons of the Blessed Trinity. But not until the seventeenth century did these notions receive explicit development, in the work of Johannes Cocceius (d. 1669), a Calvinist who contrasted the covenant of grace with the covenant of works. The covenant of grace is recounted in Sacred Scripture, with all historical events therein leading up to, and proceeding from, Jesus Christ. Cocceius was the forerunner of the theological movement of the nineteenth century, in which a formal school of salvation history thought (*Heilsgeschichte*) emerged in the writings of a group of scholars at Erlangen University in Germany: Johann Hofmann (d. 1877) and Martin Kahler (d. 1912), in particular. The Erlangen school, in turn, provided a basis for twentieth-century developments in the work of Old Testament scholar Gerhard von Rad (d. 1971) and Lutheran theologian Oscar Cullmann, who is responsible, more than anyone else, for the full-scale construction of a salvation-history perspective, especially in his *Christ and Time* (1946; revised edition, 1964).

The salvation-history perspective is clearly assumed by the Second Vatican Council in its *Dogmatic Constitution on the Church* (nn. 2-4,9) and also in its *Dogmatic Constitution on Divine Revelation* (nn. 2-4).

When it is set over against the dogmatically existentialist views of Rudolf Bultmann, against whom Cullmann waged so many theological battles over this issue, the salvation-history approach is strongly persuasive. Whereas Bultmann and others tend toward the ancient heresy of Marcionism, which denied the revelatory character of the Old Testament (it was completely replaced by the New, they argued), Cullmann, von Rad, and others insisted on the essential connection between the two Testaments and on their coequal status as revelatory documents, linked together by Jesus Christ, toward whom the one leads and from whom the other proceeds.

But to the extent that the salvation-history approach tends to introduce a dualism of nature and grace, of the profane and the sacred, to that same extent is it less acceptable as a theological tool.

History—whatever the adjective placed before the noun—is from the creative hand of God. Insofar as God is knowable through creation and through the creative events which constitute history, God is knowable through history—the whole history of the world, the whole history of humankind, and not simply the history of Israel, of Jesus Christ, and of the Church. For the history of which the Bible speaks will be radically transformed (1 Corinthians 15:35-58) and God will be "all in all" (15:28). Only death remains in history as its "last enemy" (15:26), but history itself is bound for glory, not death. This has been revealed definitively in the incarnation and especially in the resurrection of Jesus Christ (1 Peter 1:3-4; 2 Corinthians 4:14; Philippians 3:10; 2 Timothy 2:11; John 11:25; 6:39-44,54; 1 Corinthians 15).

Prophecy

The prophet is one who, literally, is called to *speak on behalf of another*, in this case on *behalf of God* (Hebrew, *nābi'*). The prophet, as opposed to the institutional figure, stands over against his or her own society, as critic and judge. The prophet proclaims a message which makes demands. Insofar as the prophet claims to speak on behalf of God, the prophet is the bearer of revelation as well as its interpreter. What he or she speaks is the word of God. The word of God comes to the prophet, not for the prophet's own good, but for the community's.

Accordingly, prophecy is not primarily a matter of predicting the future (that is the function of an oracle or clairvoyant). But insofar as the prophet offers an interpretation of events and discusses the consequences of one form of action or another, or of a failure to act, the prophet is indeed concerned with the future.

There are many prophetic voices in the Old Testament: Samuel, Gad, Nathan, Elijah, Elisha, Abraham, Aaron, Miriam, Isaiah, Ezekiel, Jeremiah, Amos, Hosea, Micah, *et al.* None, of course, is greater than Moses. There are also "false prophets" (Isaiah 3:1-3; Jeremiah 5:31; Ezekiel 13:1-23, e.g.). The true prophet is one who speaks on behalf of God in spite of the great difficulty and severe personal risk (Jeremiah 1:7; 6:11; 20:9; Amos 3:8). The New Testament is insistent that God spoke through the prophets (Matthew 1:20; 2:15; Luke 1:70; Acts of the Apostles 3:18,21; Romans 1:2). John the Baptist was accepted as a prophet, but there is some question whether or not Jesus understood himself as a prophet. In one sense, of course, Jesus had to be the supreme prophet, for who could speak on behalf of God more clearly or with more authority? And yet Jesus speaks, unlike the prophets, on *his own* authority. That there were prophets in the early Church is attested to by a number of passages (Acts of the Apostles 11:27; 21:10-11; 13:1-3; 1 Corinthians 13:2; 14:3-5, 24-25; Ephesians 3:5, e.g.). Prophets are listed among the officers of the Church (Romans 12:6; 1 Corinthians 12:10, 28-29; Ephesians 2:20; 3:5; 4:11).

Since revelation is given for all and not for the few, prophecy can be found outside of Israel and the Church. And since revelation is not limited to a particular time in history but occurs within the total historical process itself, prophecy cannot be regarded as if it were completed. God continues to be disclosed through events (the "signs of the times") and through persons who embody the divine presence and who speak boldly on behalf of the God who is present to them.

The signs of true prophecy are never so clear that all persons of good will must agree on who is or is not a prophet. What are some criteria by which to judge one who claims to be, or is regarded as, a prophet? (1) The prophet will claim to speak on behalf of God, particularly on behalf of the Kingdom of God, and will show himself or herself transformed by the word that is communicated to others. (2) The prophetic word will ultimately work for the unity of the Church and for the human family. A prophetic word that destroys unity is automatically suspect. (3) A prophetic word uttered by someone who does not live by that word is almost totally without force. (4) A prophetic word that is so unusual that it bears no visible connection with ordinary life is similarly situated on the borders of credibility. Prophecy is never for display. (5) Prophecy is never so garbled that it cannot be communicated to more than a few. It is always public and community-oriented. Otherwise, we have lapsed into Gnosticism once again.

Formal teachings of the Church on prophecy are exceedingly sparse. The most explicit is given by the First Vatican Council's *Dogmatic Constitution on the Catholic Faith*, in which prophecies

are linked with miracles as "exterior proofs of (God's) revelation
. . . joined to the interior helps of the Holy Spirit." If, for example,
we could accept the late Pope John XXIII as a prophet in the true
sense of the word, then his word, his ministry, and the example of
his whole life would make it easier for us—and indeed for many
outside the Church—to believe that God is real and that the real
God was disclosed to us in this kind, jovial, and pastorally courageous priest.

Mystery

At the opening of the second session of the Second Vatican Council
in 1963, Pope Paul VI spoke of the Church as a mystery, that is, "a
reality imbued with the hidden presence of God." No definition of
the word *mystery* can easily improve upon this one. Because God is
totally other than we are, because God is totally of the spiritual
order, because God, therefore, is not visible to our bodily senses,
our experience of God is always *mediated*. We experience the
reality of God through our experience of created things, or particular persons, or particular events, or through a psychic sense of
divine presence (mysticism). Consequently, every contact with
God is mysterious, or sacramental. The *hidden* God imbues a
visible reality. In grasping that visible reality we grasp the hidden
God.

All revelation, therefore, is mysterious, or *sacramental*, in
character. (*Sacramental* is understood here in its Augustinian
sense, as a "visible sign of an invisible reality.") God is disclosed
mediately, not immediately. We may indeed come to a true knowledge of God, but that knowledge is always mediated. To use
Bernard Lonergan's expression, we know the world as "mediated
by meaning." Thus, Jesus did not primarily bring new truths to us,
new "information" about the other world. He illuminated reality
in new ways, disclosing new meanings.

But God always remains ineffable and beyond comprehension. The Lord dwells "in unapproachable light, whom no human
being has ever seen or can see" (1 Timothy 6:16). Many of the
Fathers of the Church referred to the darkness on the mountain
into which Moses entered when he went to speak with God. And

Thomas Aquinas had to write that "man's utmost knowledge of God is to know that we do not know him" (*De Potentia*, 7,5, *ad* 14). The Protestant Reformers' theology of the cross (*theologia crucis*) included a protest against our tendency to domesticate God by making God a topic among topics in our theological and philosophical systems.

In the nineteenth century, as we have already seen, the Catholic Church confronted two essentially opposed positions: the one which denied the possibility of any knowledge of God apart from revelation in the narrow sense of the word (some form of direct communication from God), and the other which insisted that everything we know about God we know through reason alone. The First Vatican Council rejected both Fideism on the right and Rationalism on the left. In modern theological terms, Vatican I insisted that God is knowable through the created order (history, events, persons, prophecies) and yet always remains hidden and incomprehensible. Our knowledge of God, therefore, is always sacramental, at the level of mystery.

Since we are persons whose openness to God is without limit because God is without limit, our progress in knowledge and freedom can keep advancing to higher and higher levels, closer and closer to the reality that is God. But it is only because God is already somehow available in the tangible, the visible, the finite, the worldly, the personal, the historical, that we can continue to press for the fullest grasp of God. Indeed, our radical capacity for God (which God has implanted in us as part of our historical nature) makes possible our knowledge and our freedom.

Christ is a mystery insofar as he is the great sacrament of God's presence to us and of our response to that presence (Ephesians 1:9-10). The Church, too, is a mystery, and for similar reasons (Ephesians 5:32). The sacraments and the truths of faith are mysteries of which the Apostles are stewards (1 Corinthians 4:1). The Christian message, therefore, has an all-embracing, comprehensive unity. It is not simply a collection of truths placed side by side, to be believed as they are proposed. The Christian message is about one mystery, the mystery of God, who is revealed sacramentally: in the order of nature, through historical events, through charismatic figures (prophets), through Jesus Christ, who is the great mystery, through the Apostles, through the early Church, and indeed through all those events, objects, and persons which constitute and profoundly shape human experience and human history.

We are never certain, of course, *that* God is present to us in a special way in this or that person or event. We can never be certain either of *what* God calls us to do through particular persons or events. God remains at the same time veiled and unveiled. We cannot escape the realm of ambiguity. The challenge of belief and unbelief confronts us relentlessly. Some "see" and others do not. As we suggested in the preceding chapter, there are no absolute proofs for or against belief, for or against unbelief. On the other hand, belief is not without reason. And therein lies the question of mystery. And therein, too, lies one of the distinguishing characteristics of Catholic theology and of the Catholic tradition: its commitment to the principle of *sacramentality*.

Synthesis: Toward a Theology of Revelation

Revelation is the self-communication of God. It is a process which God initiates and which we recognize and accept because of our radical capacity to be open to the presence and action of God in our history and in our personal lives. *God is disclosed always sacramentally*, mysteriously. Revelation, or the unveiling of God, occurs in nature itself, in historical events, through the words and activities of special individuals (prophets, Apostles, *et al.*), of special communities (the Church in particular), and supremely in and through Jesus Christ, who is at once God-revealing and God-revealed. All of history, and therefore all of revelation, is oriented toward the Christ-event as history's center and core.

But how do we avoid the two extremes of Modernism on the left and a decadent Scholasticism on the right, i.e., the (Modernist) view that God is so thoroughly immanent to the world that revelation constitutes nothing more than ordinary human experience and ordinary human knowledge, and the (Scholastic) view that makes of revelation the transmission of certain truths from one party to another (prophet to Israel, Christ to Apostles, Apostles to Church, Church to members and to the world at large)? To answer this question we must draw again upon our understanding of human existence and of nature-and-grace in particular.

Revelation is God's self-communication, and as self-communication it has a history. The communication is supernatural (i.e., not due to human nature or to human history in its hypothetically "pure" state) and available in principle to every person. Revelation is transcendent (i.e., beyond the material, created order), but it is always and only operative in history. If it were not operative in history, we could not know it, because we are historical beings and the historical is the only context we have for the quest for knowledge and the exercise of freedom. *Revelation, therefore, is always mediated, and always mediated historically.* In other words, we never experience God directly. We only experience God in and through something or someone other than God and other than ourselves.

Revelation has *two aspects. First,* it is the *process* by which God is communicated to us. *Secondly,* it is the *product(s)* of this communication, since God's self-communication is always mediated. That product might be a person (thus, Christ is revelation), or it might be a conceptual formulation (the Bible, a dogma of the Church). The mediating product of God's self-communication is revelatory in that it brings about and witnesses to the individual's or community's experience of God. *Christ always remains the supreme moment of revelation, both as process and as product, because in Christ alone God's self-communication totally transforms the mediator, so that the mediator and the mediated are one and the same.* Christ is not only our "go-between" with God. He is also "very God of very God," to cite one of the ancient creeds. Christ is at once the one who mediates for us and the divine reality which is mediated to us.

There is no sharp separation, therefore, between the history of the world and the history of revelation, just as there is no sharp separation between the history of the world and the history of salvation. In other words saving revelation is available within the ordinary fabric of human existence. "Nor does divine Providence deny the help necessary for salvation to those who, without blame on their part, have not yet arrived at an explicit knowledge of God, but who strive to live a good life, thanks to His grace"

(Vatican II, *Dogmatic Constitution on the Church*, n. 16). But salvation is impossible without faith (Hebrews 11:6; Council of Trent; First Vatican Council), and faith is impossible without revelation, since faith is personal knowledge of God, and we can know God only to the extent that God is disclosed to us.

The Church's official teachings and the New Testament's own conviction about the universality of salvation (1 Timothy 2:4; 4:10) assume, but do not formally articulate, a theological position, namely, that every human being is elevated by grace in the very depths of consciousness. Even when grace is not adverted to, it is present and operative as a fundamental orientation to God. *Thus, every human person is already the recipient of divine revelation in the very core of his or her being in that God is present to every person in grace.*

But more than that is given in revelation. The "more than" is what we profess in the articles of the Creed: the saving activities of God in Israel, in Christ, and in the Church. The "more than" is also given in the various persons and events of history as well as in the natural created order itself. Revelation over and above that which is given to every person in the core of the person's consciousness, and apart from Christ himself and the infallible teaching of the Church, is inevitably mixed with error, distortion, misinterpretation, exaggeration, abuse, and the like.

Indeed, those who try to work out a theology of revelation on an extrinsicist basis alone (i.e., revelation is the communication of certain truths from on high) must eventually come to terms with the interior, transcendental side of revelation. Like the proverbial tree falling with no one within earshot, there is no revelation unless there is someone to receive it as such in faith. A person, an event, a natural phenomenon is perceived as mysterious or sacramental, i.e., as bearing and mediating the presence of God, only insofar as it actualizes our innate capacity for God. It is known by what Aquinas called "knowledge by connaturality."

The Modernist, therefore, was wrong to ignore or reject the inevitable historical expressions of God's inner presence to every human being. And the extrinsicist was wrong to limit revelation to what occurs outside the person and outside human consciousness.

It is not enough, however, to say that revelation is always mediated. There are at least *two levels of mediation: the person or the event which mediates, and the interpretation of what is mediated*. Only in Christ do we have what is mediated and an interpretation of what is mediated in one and the same person. The Exodus event, for example, mediates the presence of God. The prophets mediate what has been mediated: They interpret what has happened, and they call it an act of saving revelation. So, too, the dogmas of the Church do not themselves mediate the presence of God. They interpret what has been mediated. In some cases, they interpret the interpretations of what has been mediated. And in still other cases, they may interpret the interpretations of interpretations of what has been mediated (e.g., Vatican II may definitively interpret Trent, which was definitively interpreting Paul, who was trying to interpret Jesus Christ). *Christ remains always the one mediator who definitively interprets all other mediators and mediating events*. The Church, as the continuation of Christ in history, participates in Christ's work of mediation. *The Church is the definitive interpreter of Christ, the Mediator*.

SPECIAL QUESTIONS: PRIVATE REVELATION AND THE CLOSING OF REVELATION

Private revelation is, by exclusion, whatever is not available to the general community, be it the Church or any other segment of the human family. Private revelation is, in principle, possible at all times. Indeed, even public revelation is given to specific individuals such as prophets or Apostles. To speak, therefore, of *"the closing of revelation"* with the death of the last Apostle means only that the Christ-event, which is the definitive and normative self-communication of God by which all other communications are to be measured and tested, has happened in all of its essential parts.

An analogy might be helpful. Christ is like a *master key*. *In principle*, our knowledge of God in Christ is totally adequate: There is nothing to be discovered about God (about God's mercy, love, fidelity, justice, etc.) which we do not already know through Christ. *In fact*, however, many (indeed most) who know God in

Christ do not know God as fully as they might. Other persons who do not know God in Christ might know God more fully nonetheless. They may not have access to Christ, the master key, but they have keys of their own, some of which open many doors and some of which open a few or only a single door. But these persons do have some measure of access. *In principle*, it is better to have the master key than a key that opens only some doors. *In fact*, however, the revelation of God in Christ does not insure a fuller measure of knowledge of, or love for, God on the part of those who receive it. Others who have access to God's self-communication apart from explicit faith in Christ may exceed their Christian brothers and sisters in both knowledge and love. (The obvious question "Why, then, be a Christian?" will be addressed more directly in chapter 20.)

God continues to be disclosed not only to individuals but also to communities and to the world at large in the same way as before: through natural phenomena, through historical events, through prophetic figures, through the lives of truly holy people. On the other hand, the more private those disclosures, the less subject they are to critical scrutiny and testing and the more prone they are to distortion, illusion, projection, and misinterpretation. Some private revelations have, of course, attracted public interest and some measure of public acceptance: e.g., those to Joan of Arc, Margaret Mary Alacoque (the nine first Fridays), the appearances of the Blessed Virgin Mary at Lourdes and Fatima. Others are clearly bizarre and are quickly condemned even by ordinarily cautious ecclesiastical officials, although such "revelations" often continue to attract a following.

In any case, private revelations have to be tested if they are to influence the Church. What criteria can the Church, at the universal and local levels, apply to the claim that one has received a revelation from God? (1) Is the revelation consistent with the public revelation of Sacred Scripture and of the official interpretations of that revelation by the Church, officially and through the Fathers and theologians? (2) Does the private revelation work toward building up the Body of Christ and the human family, or is it finally divisive? (3) Does the private revelation contribute to our knowledge of God and of our human responsibilities, or is it merely concerned with the unusual and the bizarre ("The Blessed Mother has ordered all nuns to wear their religious habits once again and all lay women to wear blue berets")? (4) Are the bearers of the private revelation themselves good examples and witnesses of integral Christian and human existence, or are they finally odd, eccentric, difficult to communicate with, and in direct opposition to the Church's social doctrine in their public and political views? (5) Is the devotional practice approved by the local bishop, who has responsibility for the faith and good order of the diocese?

SUMMARY

1.   The "problem" of revelation is the same as the "problem" of belief and unbelief. How do we come to "know" God? With whom does God communicate? How does such communication occur? What is communicated? Why do so many apparently miss God's signals?

2.   Central to Israel's faith is the conviction that *God has intervened in history*, taking a personal interest in the fortunes of Israel and ultimately of the whole of humankind. God's communications take many forms: created things, theophanies, oracles, dreams, prophecies, laws, wise sayings, historical events, and particularly the Covenant with Moses and the Exodus from Egyptian bondage. The *Covenant/Exodus theme* runs throughout the *Old Testament* and shapes Israel's fundamental understanding of God and of the "word" of God.

3.   All of the Old Testament themes are recapitulated in the *New Testament* but are now focused in *Jesus Christ*, through whom God has spoken the final word (Hebrews 1:1-3). Jesus reveals the Kingdom of God and is himself the "Word made flesh" (John 1:1-18). The Apostles and the early Church are witnesses and heralds of Christ, and look forward to the day when the "unveiling" of God (the literal meaning of the word *revelation*) will be completed with the Second Coming of the Lord.

4.   The Bible—the Old Testament and New Testament taken together—does not *prove* the *fact* of revelation; it only *testifies* to its belief that God is a living God and that the living God has been disclosed to us in various ways at various times and nowhere more fully than in Jesus Christ. Secondly, the Bible offers an *interpretation* of history: its own history and the history of humankind at large. The Bible *infers* from the history of Israel, of Christ, and of the early Church that God is active in our lives, summoning us to lives of fidelity to the divine word of love

and mercy: ". . .only to do the right and to love goodness, and to walk humbly with your God" (Micah 6:8).

5. For the earliest *Fathers of the Church* revelation is simply the Good News of salvation. Christ is its supreme herald and embodiment, and the prophets, Apostles, and Church are its messengers. Some, such as *Irenaeus*, stressed the historical and developmental character of revelation, culminating always in Christ. Others, such as *Clement of Alexandria*, emphasized the overlapping of the Christian idea of revelation (Christ is the *Logos*) and the notion of truth (*Logos*) in contemporary Greek philosophy. The Latin Fathers, such as *Augustine*, were inclined to be less speculative than their Greek counterparts. Their theology of revelation was closely linked with Augustine's doctrine of *divine illumination; i.e., revelation is something that happens inside rather than outside the person.*

6. The Augustinian tradition dominates Catholic theology until the thirteenth century, when there is a turn, in the writings of *Thomas Aquinas*, toward the *cognitive* or *intellectual* side of revelation. *Revelation is the truth that God communicates through the prophets, Christ, the Apostles, and the Church.* Revelation, therefore, is the highest form of *knowledge.* Thanks to a special illumination from God, we are capable of *judging* this knowledge to be true.

7. The *Council of Trent's* teaching on revelation is indirectly formulated; i.e., it has to be inferred from the council's explicit teaching on *faith.* Over against the Protestant notion of trusting faith, the council insisted on the *objective* character of what has been revealed and to what we must assent in faith.

8. After Trent, i.e., in the *sixteenth and seventeenth centuries*, Catholic theology and contemporary secular thought move in diametrically opposed directions: The former becomes rigidly Scholastic and the latter, rationalistic.

9. In the *nineteenth century*, Catholic theology finally attempts to come to terms with the Enlightenment. Some were judged to go too far in their efforts to accommodate Catholic theology to modern secular thought. These were the *semi-Rationalists* (Hermes, Günther, Frohschammer). Others resisted modern secular thought to the end. These were the *Fideists* (Bautain and others). Both positions were rejected by *Vatican I.* Middle positions were developed, in the meantime, by Möhler, Scheeben, and Cardinal Newman.

10. The teaching of *Vatican I* is formulated against various forms of Rationalism on the left and various forms of Fideism on the right. Revelation, the council said, comes through the natural order of created

things (and to that extent is within the range of our rational powers) and also through the mediation of the prophets, Christ, the Apostles, and the Church (and to that extent is beyond the range of unaided reason alone). Revelation is morally necessary for the majority of humankind to know revelation of the first type, and absolutely necessary for all to know revelation of the second type. (*Morally* here has nothing to do with ethics or correct behavior: It is a technical word in theology meaning a little less than absolute, as in "moral certitude.")

11.   The Rationalist spirit reemerges in *Modernism* (Loisy, Tyrrell, LeRoy), which tries to adapt Catholic thought once again to contemporary philosophy. Its emphasis was on the natural rather than the supernatural, and on the subjective rather than the objective. Although Modernism was condemned by *Pope Pius X,* its legitimate concerns and questions were carried forward in a more balanced manner by *Maurice Blondel,* who himself anticipated the development of Transcendental Thomism and the work of such present-day theologians as *Karl Rahner* and *Gregory Baum.*

12.   *The Second Vatican Council* returns to a more biblical, more personalist, more historical understanding of revelation as opposed to the highly conceptual approach of Vatican I. Revelation comprises both word and deed, is not static but dynamic, and communicates not conceptual truths but God and the will of God.

13.   In *contemporary theology* three basic approaches are identifiable: those which continue to emphasize the objective and cognitive aspect of revelation, those which stress the subjective and personalist aspect, and those which try to mediate between the two.

14.   But any *complete theology of revelation* can only be constructed in terms of the whole network of Christian doctrines, so central is revelation to theology. Since this is impossible in a single chapter (and is being attempted, in any case, in the book as a whole), we restricted ourselves to additional discussion of four important theological elements: creation, history, prophecy, and mystery.

15.   Revelation would be impossible without *creation.* The creative act is already revelation, the self-communication of God. *"Nature"* is what arises from the creative act. It is through nature that God continues to be disclosed in a progressive movement through the Christ of history to the Second Coming of Christ. Through an examination of the created order, we infer that all reality emerges from some purposeful intelligence rather than by chance. Accordingly, the discovery of God through creation is not something less than revelation but is a form of revelation itself. All revelation, whether from creation or from the

prophets, Christ, the Apostles, and the Church, is derived from the same Creator-God.

16. Because God is disclosed in and through creative acts, and because these creative acts constitute *history*, we come to a knowledge of God as we reflect on the principal events of our history, as Israel did before us. There are not two histories, the one sacred and the other profane. All history, like all creation, is from the hand of the one God. It is through history—all of history—that God is communicated.

17. *Prophecy* is the act of speaking on behalf of God. Prophecy is related to history as interpretation is related to event. The prophet is less the instrument of revelation than the interpreter of revelation. Insofar as Christ can be considered a prophet, he alone is both revelation and the interpreter of revelation.

18. It is apparent, given the nature of our human condition, that our experience of God is always *mediated*. This means that all revelation, i.e., every form and manner of God's self-communication, is *mysterious* or *sacramental* in character. God, the invisible One, is known always and only through what is visible: e.g., created things, historical events, persons. Insofar as any visible reality contains and communicates the presence of God, it can be called a *mystery*. Christ, therefore, is the great mystery. The Church, too, is a mystery. God remains at the same time hidden and disclosed. The presence of God is never so clear that belief is inevitable, nor ever so obscure that belief is impossible.

19. This commitment to the *principle of sacramentality* is one of the distinguishing characteristics of Catholic theology and of the Catholic tradition generally. Historically, the "Protestant principle" (Paul Tillich) has been wary of identifying God with some finite reality lest such an identification give rise to idolatry. The ecumenical movement of recent decades, however, has seen the Catholic and the Protestant positions come closer together.

20. Revelation is the self-communication of God. It is both the *process* by which God is disclosed and is one or another of the *products* of that process (the Bible, a dogma of the Church, e.g.). In Christ alone do we have the convergence of process and product. He is at once the reality communicated and the sign of the reality.

21. A *balanced theology* of revelation has to avoid the extremes of Modernism on the left and extrinsicism on the right. *Revelation has its origin and foundation outside the human subject, but if it happens at all, it happens within the consciousness of the human subject.*

22. *Revelation,* understood as God's self-communication, is *available in principle to everyone.* All are called to salvation, but salvation is

impossible without faith, and faith, in turn, is impossible without revelation of some kind.

23.   Revelation is *closed* only in the sense that Christ, who is the fullness of revelation, *has already been present to us in history.* Revelation *continues,* on the other hand, in that *God is a living God and remains available to us. But God will not fundamentally alter, and certainly not revoke, the self-communication that has already occurred in Christ.*

SUGGESTED READINGS

Dulles, Avery. *Revelation Theology.* New York: Herder & Herder, 1969.

Jastrow, Robert. *God and the Astronomers.* New York: W. W. Norton, 1978.

Latourelle, René. *Theology of Revelation.* New York: Alba House, 1966.

Moran, Gabriel. *The Present Revelation: In Quest of Religious Foundations.* New York: Herder & Herder, 1972.

Niebuhr, H. Richard. *The Meaning of Revelation.* New York: Macmillan, 1962.

Rahner, Karl. "The History of Salvation and Revelation." *Foundations of Christian Faith.* New York: Seabury Press, 1978, pp. 138-175.

Schlette, Heinz. *Towards a Theology of Religions.* New York: Herder & Herder, 1966.

Schnackenburg, Rudolf. "Biblical Views of Revelation." *Theology Digest* 13 (1965), 129-134.

Vatican Council II. *Dogmatic Constitution on Divine Revelation (Dei verbum),* 1965.

·VIII·

RELIGION AND ITS VARIETIES

THE PROBLEM

There is always a debate about the meaning of the word *religion*. With the growth of many small sects, cults, and movements in the United States, even governmental agencies like the Internal Revenue Service are hard pressed to decide which group can legally be classified as a religion for tax-exemption purposes, and which cannot. Etymology helps us only a little bit.

Religion is derived from the Latin noun *religio*, but it is not clear which of three verbs the noun is most closely allied with: *relegere* ("to turn to constantly" or "to observe conscientiously"); *religari* ("to bind oneself (back)"); and *reeligere* ("to choose again"). Each verb, to be sure, points to three possible religious attitudes, but in the final accounting a purely etymological probe does not resolve the ambiguity.

Let us assume for the moment, however, that religion has something to do with our perception of, and response to, God. Why is it, then, that we have not one religion but many? And of the many, why is it that sociologically marginal, even bizarre, types abound?

And what of the mainstream religions, the so-called major world religions? Does their very existence, not to mention their numerical strength, undermine Christianity's traditional claim to uniqueness and supremacy? If we are to regard them as more or less legitimate signs and instruments of God's saving grace (as does the Second Vatican Council's *Declaration on the Relationship of the Church to non-Christian Religions*), does not that imply they have received divine revelation of some kind and have interpreted it with some measure of clarity? Under what circumstances and through what forms of mediation do the non-Christian religions encounter God in revelation? According to what criteria do they interpret their revelation-experience(s) accurately and adhere to them faithfully?

And what of Judaism? Undoubtedly, the Church's relationship with Judaism is different from its relationship with all other non-Christian religions. Christianity emerges from Judaism. Jesus was himself a Jew. The Church accepts the Old Testament, or Hebrew Scriptures, as just as much the Word of God as the New Testament. Indeed, the Church condemned the heresy of Marcionism early in its history, and has never retreated from that doctrinal insistence on the fundamental unity of the two Testaments. Has Judaism now been superseded completely? Are Jews no longer the People of God? Does Christianity have anything still to learn from Judaism?

And what of the general relationship between religion—*any* religion—and the society in which it finds itself? Is religion, of its very nature, inimical to human interests? Is religion the enemy of freedom, of rationality, of political responsibility? Why have so many regarded religion in this light? Are recent trends in the direction of greater religious involvement in the social and political processes of history consistent with, or opposed to, religion's essential purposes and functions?

And what, finally, of the general relationship between religion and institutionalism? Is religion, of its very nature, so private and so spiritual that it can and must avoid structural expression? Can one be "religious," in other words, without belonging to, and actively participating in, a specific religious group? Can there be such a thing as a "religionless Christianity" (Dietrich Bonhoeffer)?

The subject of religion and its varieties is treated at this point in Part II and in the book as a whole because (1) religion is an immediate product of revelation; and (2) religions embody singly and collectively human understandings of God which are rooted in God's own offer of grace to every person. We cannot fully appreciate the Christian answer to the question of God apart from the spectrum of answers previously or concomitantly provided by others. The same, of course, held true for our exploration of the Christian, and specifically the Catholic, understanding of human existence. That is why the method and content of this chapter bear some modest resemblance to that of chapter 4.

THE NOTION OF RELIGION
Defining Religion

Over the centuries the notion of religion has been defined philosophically, anthropologically, psychologically, sociologically, phenomenologically, culturally, and theologically. It would seem that the best definition would incorporate elements from all rather than from only one or two of these disciplines. But that has not been the case, for the most part.

Some have restricted themselves to an *abstractly philosophical* approach. They have prescinded from all the particularities of the various religions and have tried instead to identify the pure essence of religion as such.

Others have taken a *purely phenomenological* approach, searching for certain visible characteristics common to each of the world's religions.

Others have adopted a *narrowly theological* approach, insisting that there is, and can be, only one true religion, Christianity.

Others have isolated the *psychological* dimension of religious experience (the feeling of absolute dependence; the experience of the holy) and limited the nature and scope of religion accordingly. Some indeed make of religion a mere projection of human wishes, a phenomenon that emerges at the point where human beings can no longer bear their sense of dependence, their anxieties, or even their poverty.

Still others have defined religion *functionally*, locating it at the intersection of *sociology and culture*. Religion is a "given" of the human situation, something to be observed and studied in its total structural composition and defined in terms of its role in meeting social needs and shaping culture.

It is the conviction of this chapter that no definition of religion can ignore any of these methods. Thus, religion requires a *philosophical* analysis if we are to attain any kind of definition at all. Philosophy is concerned with the nature of things, with principles, with theories and laws that transcend the particular and the specific but, at the same time, help to illumine and explain them.

But that philosophical analysis must also be *phenomenologically* developed. Not even in the most narrow medieval philosophies were essences plucked from thin air. All inquiry after truth begins with sense experience. One must first take a look at what is out there before coming to a conclusion about what it is at its core. So, too, with religion. If we hope to define religion as it is and not simply as it might be in one or another philosopher's mind, then we have to take account of religion in all of its varieties.

That very phenomenological exploration will disclose the obviously social and cultural dimensions of religion, its impact on interpersonal relationships, social, political, and economic institutions, art, music, architecture, and the like. No attempt at a definition of religion that is at once philosophical and phenomenological will lack an explicitly *sociological* dimension.

But a closer look at the social aspects of religion will reveal that its varied social expressions are only a reflection of the conversion of mind and heart—for good or for ill—that has occurred in a religion's individual adherents. Religion clearly meets a deeply rooted human need to find meaning in life, as well as the corresponding social need to find a community which shares and sustains that meaning. And so the *psychological* dimension is indispensable to any useful and comprehensive definition of religion.

In the end, however, a definition of religion must be *theological* unless we are to sever all connection between religion and revelation, or between religion and God. Most people, in fact, who would describe themselves as religious or who would be identified as religious according to standard philosophical, sociological, and psychological categories, attest to their own firm conviction that God is on the "other side" of their religious relationship and that somehow God has managed to reach across the "infinitely qualitative distance" (Kierkegaard) between the divine and the human to communicate with them in revelation.

Even if these religious persons' perception of God were in error, and beyond that, even if God did not exist, the psychologist and the sociologist would still have to take the "experience of God" into account, trying to determine its origins, its modes of actuation, and its psychic and social implications.

But for the theologian God *is* real, and so, too, is the corporate experience of God in the world's great religions, however imperfect or even distorted those experiences might be. How, then, is religion to be defined?

As we have noted before, the earliest Fathers of the Church (e.g., Justin, Tertullian, Irenaeus, Clement of Alexandria, Origen) emphasized the link between the *Logos* (truth) of contemporary Greek philosophy and the *Logos*-made-flesh of Christian faith. Whenever human thoughts and actions are determined by, and directed toward, the *Logos*, we are at least at the threshold of religion. But for these Fathers, as for *Augustine* later, there were not many religions, but only one, just as there are not many *Logoi*, but only one *Logos*. And since the Son of God is coeternal with the Father, the *Logos* whom the philosophers and others sought even before the coming of Christ was the same *Logos* who became flesh *in* Christ. The one, true, religion, therefore, "has been expressed outwardly and carried on under one set of names and signs in times past and [under] another set now; it was more secret then and more open now; . . . yet it is one and the same true religion . . . . The saving grace of this religion, the only true one, through which alone true salvation is truly promised, has never been refused to anyone who was worthy of it . . . " (*Letter #102*).

Thomas Aquinas adopted this same positive estimation of the religious orientation of non-Christians. The knowledge of God, through the recognition of the effects of God's action in the world, is possible for every person. Such knowledge is one of the "preambles of faith" (i.e., those truths which can be known apart from the explicit teaching of Christ and the Church and which are a necessary foundation for Christian faith itself).

For Aquinas, religion is one of the "potential parts" of the virtue of *justice*, in that religion bears many of the characteristics of justice but at the same time falls short of the full meaning of the virtue of justice. The essence of justice consists in rendering to another his due. When one has been rendered what is due, equality has been established or restored. But there can be no equality between God and ourselves. Therefore, religion will always be something like the virtue of justice but is not exactly the same.

Thomas agrees that a purely etymological exploration will not finally disclose the meaning of religion. It is simply not clear from which verb the noun is derived. But no matter, because each of the possible sources is consistent with the view that religion "denotes properly a relation to God" (*Summa Theologica*, II-II, q. 81, a. 1).

Is religion for God's benefit or our own? "We pay God honor and reverence, not for His sake (because He is himself full of glory . . .), but for our own sake, because by the very fact that we revere and honor God, our mind is subjected to Him; wherein its perfection consists, since a thing is perfected by being subjected to its superior . . . " (a. 7).

The Thomistic and earlier patristic perspectives were themselves linked together by the *Transcendental Thomists* in this century. Because we are alive by a principle which transcends us, we are not merely *capable* of reaching beyond ourselves to God, which is what an act of religion is all about. We are actually *summoned* to do so. And this is also the position adopted by the *Second Vatican Council*, namely, that we are "at once impelled by nature and also bound by a moral obligation to seek the truth, especially religious truth" (*Declaration on Religious Freedom*, n. 2).

Religion, therefore, has to do with the whole of human existence, and not merely with some special sector of it. God's presence touches the whole person in the totality of the person's relationships not only with God but with all other persons, and with the whole cosmic order as well. *Religion is the whole complexus of attitudes, convictions, emotions, gestures, rituals, beliefs, and institutions by which we come to terms with, and express, our most fundamental relationship with Reality (God and the created order, perceived as coming forth from God's creative hand).* That relationship is disclosed by a process we have called *revelation*. Religion, therefore, is our (more or less) structured response to revelation.

The word *Reality* has been capitalized to insure that religion will not be confused with any "philosophy of life." In the act of religion we deliberately reach out toward God. We perceive God in the persons, events, and things we see, that is to say, sacramentally. Religion presupposes and flows from *faith*. One is not religious who does not think there is more to reality than meets the eye. The religious person believes himself or herself to be in touch with another dimension, with "the beyond in the midst of life" (Bonhoeffer).

This does not mean, however, that every person of faith is also religious. It is possible to have only *implicit* faith in God. Even a person who thinks of himself or herself as an atheist might be a person of faith. Such persons might be rejecting false notions of God, as the Second Vatican Council admitted. In any case, they may be oriented to God through their firm commitment to love, justice, and the like. It is not *explicit* faith in God which saves, but only that faith, explicit *or* implicit, that issues forth in obedience to God's will (Matthew 7:21; see also the Parable of the Sheep and the Goats in Matthew 25:31–46). On the other hand, the actions of a person with *implicit* faith only cannot be called religious except in the widest sense of the word. Religion is an individual, social, and institutional manifestation of some *explicit* faith in God.

Characteristics of Religion

1.   The most basic characteristic of religion is its sense of the *holy* or the *sacred*. For the sociologist Emile Durkheim (d. 1917) the sacred, unlike the secular or the profane, has *no utilitarian purpose* at all. It is something revered for its own sake. It elicits from us what the phenomenologist of religion G. van der Leeuw (d. 1950) has called *awe*. Religious rites are not performed to achieve something so much as to express an attitude. Awe, in other words, develops into *observance*.

Other characteristics of the sacred, for Durkheim, are its being perceived as a *power* or *force*, its *ambiguity*, its *invisible* or *spiritual* quality, its *non-cognitive* dimension, its *supportive* or *strength-giving* nature, and the *demands* it makes upon believers and worshipers. (See *The Elementary Forms of the Religious Life*, 1954.)

Rudolf Otto (d. 1937) has also analyzed what he calls *The Idea of the Holy* (1917), referring to it as the "numinous," i.e., as something beyond rational and ethical conceptions. It embodies a mystery that is above all creatures, something hidden and esoteric, which we can experience in feelings. The holy is the *mysterium tremendum et fascinosum* (a mystery which at the same time overwhelms and fascinates us). It is "wholly other" (which is how the Protestant theologian Karl Barth also referred to God), quite beyond the sphere of the usual, the intelligible, and the familiar. The experience of the holy, according to Otto, arouses a feeling of unworthiness in the believer.

Durkheim and Otto agree, therefore, on the extraordinary character of the phenomenon (the experience of the sacred), its implication of power, its ambiguity in relation to us, its awesome character, and the feeling of dependence it evokes.

2. Religion not only has to do with the impact of the holy upon us but with our *response to the holy* as well. Religion necessarily includes *faith*. The content of that faith may differ from religion to religion, and there will even be sharp differences of interpretation within the same religion, but there can be no religion to begin with unless there is some self-consciousness and reflective awareness of the holy, the sacred, the ultimate, of God. And that is faith, which we defined in chapter 2 as a way of knowing God.

3. Religion inevitably gives rise to *beliefs* of various kinds: some popular, some official (doctrines, creeds). And the more sophisticated the religion, the more likely the emergence of a *theological* tradition, even of *systematic* theology. (We have already outlined, again in chapter 2, the connections among faith, theology, and belief.)

4. Religion is also expressed in various *actions*: *moral behavior* consistent with the beliefs, and *liturgy*, or the ritualization of beliefs.

5. Religion, finally, generates a *community* of shared perceptions, meanings, and values. Each such community has at least some rudimentary *structure*.

It is important to note the connection between the original religious inspiration and the community it eventually generates.

The foundational religious experience is *charismatic* in nature. Max Weber (d. 1920) defines *charisma* as " . . . a certain quality of an individual personality by virtue of which he is set apart from ordinary men and treated as endowed with supernatural, superhuman, or at least specifically exceptional powers or qualities. These are such as are not accessible to the ordinary person, but are regarded as of divine origin or as exemplary, and on the basis of them the individual concerned is treated as a leader" (*The Theory of Social and Economic Organization*, 1947, pp. 358–359). The three chief characteristics of a charisma are that it is unusual, spontaneous, and creative.

A second stage is reached when the charisma is "routinized." Pure charisma can only exist in the act of originating. When the leader dies, his or her disciples face a crisis. Are they to disband, or continue? If they decide to continue, then the charismatic element will somehow have to share the stage with the institutional and the structural. Otherwise, there can be no permanence to the charisma. There has to be stability of thought, of practice, and of organization.

Every religious group that hopes to endure, even those groups which describe themselves today as "charismatic," assumes abiding organizational forms. No group is completely charismatic if it agrees to meet at a certain time, in a certain place, to engage in certain activities, however spontaneous those activities turn out to be. The holding of national meetings, of conventions, the publication of magazines, the circulation of newsletters—all of these represent a routinization of the original charismatic impulse.

The routinization process becomes a serious problem only when the organizational interests overtake the charismatic or even replace them. A religious community must constantly reflect on its original purposes, the values of its founder, the convictions about God and human life which originally set the community apart. It must take care that each of its institutional forms and patterns of behavior facilitates rather than impedes those basic purposes. The challenge to a religious community that would remain faithful to its original charisma is not to find ways to *de*institutionalize itself but to *re*institutionalize itself according to its abiding faith. A religious community without any institutional forms at all, on the other hand, is a religious community which no longer exists, or is on the verge of extinction. By their very nature, charisms die out unless they are somehow routinized, i.e., unless they find adequate institutional expression.

Criticisms of Religion

The very notion of religion can be, and has been, criticized from within as well as from without. *From within*, religion has been characterized as the product of human effort to assert itself over against God. But in revelation it is God who approaches us. We do not approach God. We are simply overtaken by the revelation and accept it as God's word. Anything beyond this, any attempt to "deal with" God from our side, places religion above revelation. This is the view of Karl Barth and, to some similar extent, of Emil Brunner (d. 1966), both of whom insisted on the exclusivity of Christian revelation and, therefore, the intrinsic error of every other kind of "religion."

Religion has also been criticized from within, but with much less negative force, by Paul Tillich ("The divine No to religion is only perceptible where religion exists") and by Dietrich Bonhoeffer, who rejected the Christian tendency to make religion a separate compartment of life. Earlier, of course, we have internal criticisms of *religion-in-practice* by the *prophets* of Israel. Indeed, most of the other major religions (e.g., Islam, Hinduism, and Buddhism) have had reform movements designed to purify the structured manner in which their brothers and sisters in faith had responded to the presence and call of God. The history of the Church is also replete with examples of reformist movements: e.g., the reform of spirituality, of monasteries, of clerical life-styles, of ecclesiastical authority, of canon law, of the liturgy, of seminaries. Significantly, Christianity itself suffered its most severe division in an event known as the Reformation.

Religion is also criticized *from without*. It is perceived as a projection of the human spirit. For Ludwig Feuerbach God is the highest projection of our selves in the objective order. A similar position is taken by John Dewey. For Freud religion is an illusion, a regression to the helplessness and insecurity of childhood, the product of wish-fulfillment. For Marx it is the opiate of the people, numbing their capacity for outrage at the gross inequities of the economic order. Others, like Albert Camus, insist that religion is not the *only* response to a limit-situation, one in which all of our most basic values are put to the test. In his novel *The Stranger* Camus writes of a man condemned to die the next day, achieving a sense of serenity in the face of an impersonal and indifferent cosmos. He displays at the limit-situation the same incapacity for relationships that he had in his daily experiences.

In our earlier chapters on belief and unbelief and on revelation we have already addressed ourselves to such challenges as these from without. The criticisms are not without force. It is not impossible that they are correct. But neither is it obvious that they are correct. On the contrary, there are good and solid reasons for affirming the truth of religion (seen as our structured response to God's revelation), even when in practice religion merits the severest of internal, as well as external, criticisms.

There is, finally, a criticism of religion which defies easy categorization. It is not the criticism of a non-believer, but neither is it the criticism of an internal reformer. It is rather the anti-religious critique of those who insist that they believe in God, perhaps also in Jesus Christ and the Holy Spirit, but who reject the necessity of any ordered, structured, and institutionalized expression of their faith and belief.

One might suggest that there is a subtle pride in this point of view. It assumes a kind of angelic self-understanding. We are not angels but "bodies" in the biblical sense (see chapter 5). We cannot shrug off the facticity of human existence. We are in history. We are constituted by relationships, not only with other persons but with institutions, the natural order, and the whole cosmos. Just as revelation must be embodied somehow if it is to be known, just as God must be sacramentalized if God is to be experienced, so our response to God must find some concrete expression consistent with our nature and our human situation. That expression is religion. It is impossible to respond to God in any way whatsoever without that response being religious. It may be a very primitive, superficial, or simple expression, but if it is expressed at all, it is religious.

This does not deny in the least that religion is abidingly open to distortion, that it can obscure rather than illuminate revelation, that it can crush rather than generate the life of faith in God. Religion is subject to such distortions because it is a response to the invisible God. Since no one has ever seen God, and since no one can ever be absolutely certain (in an empirical or scientific sense) that one has truly experienced God in revelation, we can never be sure that our structured response to the God who reveals accurately reflects, or does justice to, the Object of that experience. But the abuse of religion does not destroy its very use.

Types of Religion

Although the question is not directly addressed until the last section of this chapter, it should be clear by now that a *plurality* of religions is being assumed here. Revelation, saving grace, and the capacity to respond to both are not limited to Israel of old or to Christians from New Testament days to our own. There are as many religions as there are theologically and institutionally distinctive and self-contained responses to the presence of God. On the other hand, because there is but one God, each particular religion participates to one degree or another in the single, universal notion of religion as such. "Religion as such," it must be added, does not exist. There are *religions.* For that reason, the adjective *religious* is helpful in expressing a fundamental attitude or characteristic, but it is insufficiently precise to qualify such nouns as *community, education,* and the like.

Taking as our starting-point the principle that God is at once transcendent and immanent, "the beyond in our midst," religions can be differentiated from one another on the basis of the relative stress they place on the transcendent or the immanent nature of God. The division, of course, is based on our Christian perspective. It is in the central Christian doctrine of the incarnation that God is revealed as *both* transcendent and immanent, the Word made flesh.

We can discern, therefore, two basic types of religions: those which stress the transcendence of God, and those which stress immanence. Within each type there are degrees of emphasis.

Thus, a religion in the transcendence series may stress the otherness of God so much that God's relationship with the world of beings is all but lost, as in *Deism*. A religion in the immanence series, on the other hand, may stress the worldliness of God so much that God's relationship with the world of beings becomes one of complete identity, as in *Pantheism*.

Religions in the *transcendence series* are interested in history and eschatology, their worship tends to be objective and highly verbal, they have a sense of ethical demands following from their faith in God, and they have some measure of rational reflection on that faith (theology). Religions in the *immanence series*, on the other hand, tend toward a timeless, ahistorical understanding, their worship is more elaborately ritualistic, their personal goals are not so much obedience to God's will as absorption into God, and they favor mystical experience over rational reflection.

Among religions in the transcendence series are Judaism, Islam, and Confucianism. Among religions in the immanence series are Buddhism and Hinduism. When pushed to their ultimate extremes, religions in the transcendence series lapse into atheism; religions in the immanence series lapse into fetishism, of which "black magic" is a form. In the first extreme God is pushed so far beyond the reality of this world that the divine disappears altogether. In the second extreme God is so identified with the reality of this world that this world's goods take on the character of the divine itself.

THE NON-CHRISTIAN RELIGIONS
Religions of the Past

Egypt, Canaan

Taking as our starting-point that religion has something to do with our experience of, and response to, God (even if and when our perception of God is faulty and thoroughly distorted), we find that religion has always been part of the human landscape. In ancient Egypt (c. 2778–2263 B.C.) the king was worshiped. Later, when divinity was transferred from the royal throne to the Sun (*Re*), the king was regarded as the son of the Sun-God. Later still, during the period of the Middle Kingdom (2052–1786), monotheism came more fully to the front. *Amon* was the supreme God, not only during the Middle Kingdom but during the New Kingdom as well (1580–1085). Perhaps the most distinctive feature of ancient Egyptian religion was its preoccupation with the afterlife, a belief most visibly manifested in the construction of the pyramids and the laying in of ample provisions for the entombed king to use in the next life.

Another important religion of the ancient East (important because it was part of the religious scene at the time when Israel took possession of the land) was that of the Canaanites. Myth and ritual in Ugarit (present-day northern Syria) centered on the effort to secure the *fertility* of nature. The supreme God, *El*, was nonetheless surpassed in power by *Baal*, who displayed his might in the thunderstorm and the bestowal of fertility.

Ancient Greece

Ancient Greece was another major home of religions. For the Greeks there were many gods (polytheism), "higher powers" possessing all of the Greek ideals of beauty, wisdom, and power. The gods alone are immortal. *Zeus* is the father of the gods and, as such, is supreme. He reigns with the other gods on Mount Olympus, from which point he takes in all reality, including the future. Hence he is a great source of oracles. One of Zeus' two brothers is *Hades*, lord of the underworld; the other is *Poseidon*, whose palace is in the depths of the sea (the "inspiration" also of the American film *The Poseidon Adventure*). *Apollo* is the son of Zeus; he always appears in the prime of youth. He has the power of healing and forgiveness. Among his many functions, he is the source of justice, law, and order in the State, and is as well the god of wisdom. *Dionysius*, on the other hand, inspires wild enthusiasm and frenzy in his followers, and he himself celebrates his feasts among satyrs and beasts. Some Christian theologians in the theology of festivity and fantasy school of recent years have used these two gods as a way of contrasting elements even within the Christian religion. Their argument has been that Christians have been too Apol-

Ionian (too orderly, sedate, rational) and insufficiently Dionysian in their religious mentality and practice.

Greek sacrificial rites, centered on the sacrificial meal, had one primary purpose, fellowship. The central place of worship was the temple, where the images of the gods were kept, and the temple was served, in turn, by a priesthood.

Ancient Rome

Ancient Rome was similarly religious. Triads of gods headed the Roman pantheon: first *Jupiter, Mars,* and *Quirinus*, and then Jupiter, *Juno,* and *Minerva*. Jupiter dwelt on mountaintops, was the source of storms, and gave warriors strength in battle. He prized loyalty and justice. Mars was the god of war, and Quirinus was very much like him. Juno, Jupiter's wife, was the guardian of marriage, as Zeus' sister *Hera* had been in Greece, and other parallels with the ancient Greek gods were obvious (Minerva = Athena, Neptune = Poseidon, Venus = Aphrodite, Mercury = Hermes, e.g.). Just as in Greece, the most important religious act was the sacrifice. The gifts were animals or corn, and there were set prayers and rituals. The high priest of the Roman State was called the *Pontifex Maximus*, a title assumed eventually by the pope and only recently disavowed by Popes John Paul I (d. 1978) and John Paul II. The Vestal Virgins were women priests. Piety (reverent devotion) was the key to a correct relationship with the gods, and on the human level it required the honoring of obligations between persons and especially the obligation of love for one's parents. Worship of the emperor was a later development.

Mayans, Aztecs, Incas

Other ancient and now-defunct religions were to be found in the Orient and in certain parts of Europe. In what is present-day Latin America there were the Mayans (focused, it seems, on the rain-god *Chac*), the Aztecs (with their human sacrifices), and the Incas (with their sun and moon gods, *Inti* and *Mama Quilla*). As usual, the temple was the place of worship and contained a golden disc representing the sun; it also contained the mummies of dead kings. There was a well-organized priesthood and, as with the other religions of Central and South America, there was a belief in survival after death.

Religions of the Present

Zoroastrianism

Zoroastrianism, the ancient religion of Iran (Persia), has been preserved to the present in the form of the preaching and teaching of its prophet *Zarathustra* (Hellenized as *Zoroaster*), who lived sometime between 1000 and 600 B.C. It is a religion marked by dualism (the struggle between good and evil) and eschatology (the individual is rewarded or punished after death, depending on his or her behavior in this life). Both principles are said to have influenced Judaism, Islam, and Christianity.

Hinduism

Hinduism, one of India's ancient religions, is obscure in its origins—an obscurity linked undoubtedly with a certain sense of timelessness in Indian history itself. What we do know of its earliest period comes from the sacred book of the *Veda* (meaning *"knowledge"*), which tells of magical cults and priestly powers. The priests (Brahmans) gradually became supreme, and their wisdom is reflected in the *Upanishads* (*Upa* = *near*; *ni-shad* = *sitting down*). The title of these texts indicates the position of the pupil in receiving the sacred knowledge imparted by the teacher. Unlike the Veda, the Upanishads are pessimistic in outlook. The sadness of life is reflected in the belief in a cycle of rebirths which is the necessary consequence of each person's *karma* or "work" of good or evil deeds in life. Salvation is possible only through mystical absorption in the knowledge of the one true reality, the Absolute, *Brahma*. Although Hinduism has no doctrine of God, it is an intensely ascetical and meditative religion, as in the practice of *Yoga*. As Hinduism developed, other figures joined Brahma, now perceived as the creator: *Vishnu*, the preserver, and *Shiva*, the destroyer. Of the various forms in which Vishnu appears on earth (*avatāra* = "descent"), that of *Krishna* has great importance. It is as Krishna that Vishnu appears in the *Bhagavad-Gita* (*The Song of the Majestic*). Here he proclaims religious and moral truths. Along with the Sermon on the Mount, the *Bhagavad-Gita* was *Gandhi's* (d. 1948) favorite reading. The persistent influence of Krishna in the United States and other Western countries is evident in the *Hare Krishna* movement, which has proved attractive to many college-age men and women.

Buddhism

Buddhism, also Indian in origin, is derived from the title *Buddha*, which means "enlightened one." *Siddharta Gautama* (d. 480 B.C.) was the first Buddha. He was a member of a princely line who encountered human misery during his frequent trips from his father's palace. He eventually chose to live like a beggar-monk, a homeless ascetic. He is said to have received the *bodhi* ("enlightenment") one night while sitting under a fig tree. He proclaimed the revelation in a sermon. The content is called *dharma*, the doctrine of Buddhism. It teaches that we can break out of the grim cycle of rebirths and attain *Nirvana* ("dissolution") by following the "middle way," avoiding both total, hedonistic absorption in the world and excessive self-torment. *Nirvana* implies the overcoming of all desires and gives salvation according to one's deeds. At first the movement was limited to male monks; then nuns were allowed in, and finally lay persons. There were inevitably strict and less strict observances. *Hinayana* Buddhism allowed entry into *Nirvana* through monasticism alone. *Mahayana* Buddhism, in which lay persons were prominent, holds that salvation is open to all who faithfully revere the many earlier Buddhas and the Buddhas yet to come. It is this latter form of Buddhism which is to be found in *Tibet*, where the *lamas*, and especially the *Dalai Lama* and the *Panchen Lama*, are regarded as reincarnations of a Buddha.

Taoism

Taoism, an ancient Chinese religion, is derived from the term tao, which means "the way." The *tao* comprises a male, active principle (*yang*) and a female, passive principle (*yin*), representing heaven and earth. We must all live in harmony with the order of the universe as determined by the *tao*. Wisdom consists in knowing the will of heaven. One of the principal exponents of *Taoism* was Cung-fu-tse (d. 479 B.C.), whose name was Latinized by the Jesuit missionaries of the seventeenth century as *Confucius*. Confucius collected the ancient writings and added his own interpretations, which had an ethical bent to them. His naturalistic ethics centered on *jen* ("humaneness," "benevolence"). The right order of the *tao* is maintained by the rites (*li*) performed by the emperor, who is the Son of Heaven. Rome strictly forbade the Jesuit missionaries, however, from equating "heaven" or the "supreme ruler" with God.

Shintoism

Shintoism, an ancient Japanese religion, also focuses on the way (*to*) of numinous beings (*shin*). It is essentially a polytheistic religion with a simple worship of nature. Eventually it was amalgamated with Buddhism, which was introduced into Japan in the sixth century A.D. Entrance into paradise is insured for those who trust in the grace of Buddha. Buddhist doctrine is assimilated through meditation on the *Lotus of the Good Religion* (*Hokkekyo*). The practice of meditation, of course, remains central in the many schools of *Zen Buddhism* which reached Japan from China.

Islam

Islam, an ancient Arabic religion, means literally "total surrender to the will of Allah." Its origins lie with its Prophet *Mohammed* (d. 632), who experienced a call from Allah to proclaim monotheism. He began to preach in Mecca, laying emphasis on judgment, the resurrection on the last day, and faith in Allah as the one God. Encountering hostility from the Meccan aristocracy, Mohammed moved to Yathrib. The flight was known as his *hegira* ("abandonment of kindred"), and with it the Moslem era begins. Yathrib's name was changed to Medina, and it was here that Mohammed broke with Judaism, orienting his prayers now to Mecca rather than Jerusalem. He saw his task as reviving the monotheism of Abraham. His early disciples recorded or memorized his teachings, and after his death they were collected into the *Koran*, composed of 114 chapters (*sura*) divided into verses (*ayat*). There is no logical or chronological order to them. There *is* a division between the Meccan and the Medinese *suras*: The Meccan convey the traditional emphases on Allah as creator and judge, on the resurrection, and on hell, while the Medinese contain authoritative directives. Successors of Mohammed are known as *caliphs*, who are responsible for the temporal interests of the community.

In Islam Allah is eternal, simple, omnipotent, supreme over all. There is no distinction between the spiritual and the temporal. Whatever Allah does is completely just. Whatever happens, Allah causes. We freely choose between good and evil, and Allah creates the human act which corresponds with the choice. Allah has sent prophets to speak in his name (Abraham, Moses, Jesus, and lastly Mohammed). He is the creator of angels, devils, and even the *jinn* (genies). There is a future life (paradise and hell). Allah will forgive all sins except apostasy. The faithful are urged to care for the needy, orphans, pilgrims, prisoners, and the like. They are to pray, be loyal to contractual obligations, and be resigned to misfortunes. The "pillars of Islam" are prayer (recited five times each day), profession of faith, alms, fasting, and pilgrimage to Mecca at least once in one's lifetime. *Sari*, the religious law of Islam, is derived from the Koran, the *sunna* (Mohammed's own example), analogy (*qiyas*) and prudent judgments (*ra'y*), and the common opinion of the learned or the customary practice of the people (Islam's principle of flexibility).

In the eighth century Islam suffered a division between the *Sufi* and the more orthodox *Sunnites*. The word *sūf* means "wool" and refers to the coarse wool garments which the ascetics wore in imitation of the Christian monks. For the Sunnites, to love God is simply to worship and obey him according to established rules. For the Sufi, *union* with Allah is possible—a teaching that was detestable to the Sunnites, who insisted there can be no equality and therefore no reciprocity between Allah and ourselves. By the ninth century Sufism was flourishing, and it remains at the base of Moslem ethics today.

Christians at first regarded Islam as a heretical movement within Judaism (the view of St. John Damascene, for example). Later, after the Moslem penetration of the West and the West's penetration of the East in the Crusades, extensive dialogue followed contact. Evidence of the dialogue can be found in various writings, especially Thomas Aquinas' *Summa Contra Gentiles*. The dialogue, however, was to cease (and not to reopen until the post-Vatican II period) with the wars against the Turks and the downfall of the Ottoman Empire.

Judaism

Judaism has its origins in the formation of the Twelve Tribes of Israel, which some (especially Martin Noth) identify with the covenant of Shechem described in Joshua 24. Other Old Testament scholars insist that the Israel which worshiped Yahweh existed before Shechem, and that the Shechem covenant enlarged but did not create Israel. More immediately, Judaism emerges from the period when the exiles returned from Babylon in the sixth century B.C. Most of these exiles were recruited from the tribe of Judah (see Ezra 1-2). They saw themselves as the purified "remnant of Israel," i.e., as that portion of the Twelve Tribes which had survived the catastrophe of captivity and submitted to it as the judgment of God upon their guilt (see especially Ezra 6:13–18).

Among the *principal characteristics* of Judaism are its sense of the Covenant, the land, the past, and the Kingdom of God.

The most fundamental conviction of the Jewish people has always been that they are a people of the *Covenant*: Yahweh is the God of Israel, and Israel the people of Yahweh (Exodus 19:4–6; Joshua 24). God is present among the people of Israel as a powerful God (Isaiah 45:14). The promises of descendants to the patriarchs are to be understood in the light of this Covenant (Genesis 13:16; 15:5; 26:4,24; 28:14; 32:13, e.g.). The God of the Covenant, however, is not the object of systematic theological reflection, as in Christianity. The God of Israel is a holy God who calls the people of Israel to be a holy people, faithful to the divine commands linked with the Covenant: the observance of the Sabbath and feast days, the recital of prayers, the keeping of purity laws, circumcision, the maintenance of ancient Jewish tradition, the hope of salvation. The holy God of Israel is ever a God of mercy and justice, concerned with the people, giving them instruction and reproof, inspiring them to right conduct, and inhibiting their impulses to infidelity. As in Islam, even the most ordinary and profane activities of everyday life are to be penetrated by the kingship of God, who is always present and whose presence becomes increasingly effective in its power.

A second major characteristic of Judaism is its *respect and reverence for the past.* Judaism finds courage to live through the hardships of the present by recalling and reflecting upon the glories of the past and God's promises to the patriarchs (Genesis 24:7; 50:24; Exodus 13:5,11; Numbers 14:16; Deuteronomy 4:31; 6:23, e.g.).

There is also Judaism's close relationship to *the land* of Israel as promised by the God of the Covenant. The claim to the promised land has never been abandoned by Israel even to the present day: "Keep all the commandments, then, which I enjoin on you today, that you may be strong enough to enter in and take possession of the land into which you are crossing, and that you may have long life on the land which the Lord swore to your fathers he would give to them and their descendants, a land flowing with milk and honey" (Deuteronomy 11:8–9).

Finally, there is the conviction of faith which sums up and incorporates all of the others, namely, belief in the coming of the *Kingdom of God.* Sometimes, the notion of God's kingship is exceedingly nationalistic, as in the time of the Maccabees (170 B.C.-70 A.D.) or in the rebellion of Bar Kochba (132-135 A.D.). At other times, the hope of a Messiah to deliver them from captivity into salvation is more universal in outlook. The Book of Ruth, for example, was written to praise a foreign Moabite woman as the ancestress of King David. The Book of Jonah was similarly inspired by universalistic motives. And the Old Testament generally makes clear that Israel was not chosen by God because of its holiness but in spite of its obstinacy and rebelliousness (Deuteronomy 7:6-9; 9:4-9). One should not confuse Judaism's hope in salvation, however, with the traditional Christian hope in eternal life for each person. Judaism's generally optimistic sense of what we can accomplish in this life with God's help (Psalm 8; Zechariah 1:3; Malachi 3:7) has no corresponding sense of any individual call to happiness in some life beyond. It is the people of Israel that will survive and prosper, and not any particular person within it.

The *sources* of Judaism are the *Torah* (literally, divine oracle revealed "by the lot"), which is the most general word for law in Judaism. The Torah has both a written and an oral form. The written Torah is the *Tanak* (Old Testament), consisting of twenty-four books. The oral Torah is to be found above all in rabbinical literature, especially the *Mishnah* (literally, "tradition," "repetition"), which is the official commentary on the Old Testament law and the traditions. The Mishnah is the core of a larger collection of rabbinical opinions known as the *Talmud* ("teaching"). Talmudic interpretation may be literal or practical. The practical interpretations are known as *Midrash* ("searching"), and this, in turn, can be ethical (*halakhah*) or narrative and homiletical (*haggadah*). The former is more important in the religious life of Jews than the latter, which is mostly legend.

Judaism, like all of the great religions of the world, has endured change throughout history. The Old Testament provides a full and rich account of Israel's and of Judaism's historical experiences before the coming of Christ. After the destruction of the Temple at Jerusalem in 70 A.D. Judaism entered a new period of religious life. The *synod of Jamnia* (c. 90) provided a new basis for a religion which now sought to maintain itself without a temple, without political independence, and in a newly pluralistic situation, surrounded by other peoples and other religions, especially Christianity and Gnosticism. It was in the exchange between Judaism and Greek philosophy that the first stirrings of Jewish "systematic theology" occurred, and in the medieval period Jewish thought assumed an Islamic cast, when Jewish Neo-platonism and Aristotelianism appeared on the scene. Among the great philosopher-theologians of the period are Jehudah Halevi (d. 1140), who insisted on the superiority of revelation over reason, and Moses Maimonides (d. 1204), who insisted on the essential conformity between revelation and reason (philosophy) and on the necessity of the latter to apprehend the former. Just as there had been a strong Catholic reaction against Thomas Aquinas for his vigorous use of reason in the understanding of faith, so was there a vehement protest against Maimonides from within contemporary Judaism. It was the Halevian attitude of reserve toward the pretensions of reason that was to dominate until the middle of the eighteenth century, when a sharply rationalistic orientation reasserted itself in the writings of Moses Mendelssohn (d. 1786). Judaism was not to recover its intellectual bearings until the latter part of the nineteenth and the early twentieth centuries with the work of Franz Rosenzweig (d. 1929) and Martin Buber (d. 1965).

CHRISTIANITY AND THE OTHER RELIGIONS

For reasons already summarized in chapter 3 (mobility, communications, e.g.), the modern world is marked in an unprecedented way by the experience of *pluralism*. We are more aware than ever before of the diversity which characterizes the human community. Just as Copernicus helped us see that our earth is not at the center of the universe, and Darwin helped us see that our species did not spring up independently of other life-forms, so our belated recognition of pluralism is helping us see that the world is filled with "heresies", i.e., selective perceptions of reality and selective apprehensions of truth. In such a world, even the Christian faith appears "heretical."

Why, then, are there many religions rather than one? Just as God is in principle available to every person (Rahner's "supernatural existential") and to every people (since we are essentially social), so also religion, as the structured response to the experience of God, is available in principle to every person and people. But since "no one has ever seen God" (John 1:18), we can never be absolutely certain that we have had an actual experience of God or that we have correctly perceived, interpreted, and expressed that experience. Furthermore, God can become available to us only on terms consistent with our bodily existence, i.e., sacramentally. Every experience of God or, from the other side, every self-disclosure of God, is inevitably conditioned by the situation of the person or community to which God has become available in a special way. Those communities are differentiated by time, place, culture, language, temperament, social and economic conditions, etc. Revelation, therefore, is always received according to the mode of the receiver, to cite a central Thomistic principle (*"Quod enim recipitur in aliquo recipitur in eo secundum modum recipientis," Summa Theologica,* I, q. 79, a. 6). Since religion is our structured response to the reception of God in revelation, our response will be shaped by that mode of reception. Indeed, the Son of God became incarnate in a particular time and place, in a particular cultural and religious situation, in a particular man of a particular family, nation, and race.

When one scans the spectrum of religions, past and present, as we have done in outline-form earlier in this chapter, one begins to appreciate the striking similarities between Christianity and the other great religions of the world: their common sense of the supreme majesty of God, their ethical codes, their rites of worship, their priesthoods, their call to judgment, conversion, and reform. Suddenly for many Christians the old skepticism toward the non-Christian religions ("How can anyone seriously believe in them?") is redirected toward Christianity itself ("Why should we think that we're any better than any other religion?"). On the opposite side, some Christians assume a militant posture. They call for renewed efforts at "evangelization" understood not in the broad and comprehensive manner of Pope Paul VI's 1975 Apostolic Exhortation *Evangelii Nuntiandi* ("On the Evangelization of the Modern World")—the proclamation of the word, the celebration of the sacraments, the offering of corporate witness to Christ, and participation in the struggle for justice and peace—but in the narrow sense of "making converts" or of bringing "fallen-away" Catholics back to church.

The first group is victimized by a loss of nerve and/or a lapse of theological balance. It feels that Christianity has lost its intrinsic power to persuade and to convince the non-believer, and so it is better to lift the oars out of the water and let the currents take us where they will. Or this group forgets that the questions of exclusiveness and uniqueness are separate questions. The Christian faith can still be a compellingly *unique* expression of divine revelation in Jesus Christ without at the same time being the *exclusive* sign and instrument of revelation.

The second group seems to be afflicted with historical and sociological naivete. The present state of Christian missions can not be changed simply through the application of more aggressive techniques or through the commissioning of more dedicated Christian preachers. Decisions were rendered by the Catholic Church some centuries ago which have had the effect of closing off whole countries, indeed whole continents, to the effective presence of Christianity. (For example, the initially successful sixteenth-century mission to China under the leadership of Jesuit Father Matteo Ricci (d. 1610) was aborted when Rome rejected the development of native rites and opposed other cultural adaptations.)

Beyond that, the other great world religions are too intricately enmeshed in the social, political, ethnic, and cultural elements of their geographical settings: Islam with the Arab world, Judaism with a specific people, Hinduism and Buddhism with Asian culture, Taoism and Shintoism with the Oriental experience. There is a relative permanency to the present condition of religious pluralism, it would seem. Less than one percent of the people of China and Japan are Christian, and only two percent of the people of India. We are, in the words of Catholic theologian Yves Congar, "a small church in a large world." This is a fact that we can either wring our hands over or respond to thoughtfully and constructively.

The Second Vatican Council's approach has been strikingly positive: "The Catholic Church rejects nothing which is true and holy in these religions. She looks with sincere respect upon those ways of conduct and of life, those rules and teachings which, though differing in many particulars from what she holds and sets forth, nevertheless often reflect a ray of that Truth which enlightens all people. Indeed, she proclaims and must ever proclaim Christ, 'the way, the truth, and the life' (John 14:6), in whom everyone finds the fullness of religious life, and in whom God has reconciled all things to Himself (cf. 2 Corinthians 5:18-19)" (*Declaration on the Relationship of the Church to Non-Christian Religions,* n. 2).

Theologians have tried to come to terms with the challenge of religious pluralism in a similarly constructive fashion. There are various approaches, three of which are given here. *First,* there is the view that there is still but one true religion and that insofar as other "religions" embody authentic values and even saving grace, they do so as "anonymously Christian" communities. All grace is grace in Christ, who is the one Mediator (1 Timothy 2:5). Therefore, all recipients of grace are at least in principle new creatures in Christ, people whose lives are governed implicitly by the new life in Christ that is at work within them. This is a position which has been identified with Karl Rahner and others.

A *second* position acknowledges the salvific value in each of the non-Christian religions and underscores, as the preceding view does, the universality of revelation and of grace. It does not speak of the other religions as "anonymously Christian," but instead accepts them for what they are: lesser, relative, and extraordinary means of salvation. This is the teaching, for the most part, of the Second Vatican Council and perhaps of the majority of Catholic theologians today.

Without prejudice to the uniqueness and truth of Christian faith, a *third* view affirms the intrinsic religious value of the other great religions of the world and insists, beyond the preceding position, on the necessity and worthwhileness of dialogue with them. These other religions are not only to be tolerated or even respected; they are to be perceived as having something to teach us, not only about themselves but about God, about life, even about Christ. They are not simply deficient expressions of Christianity. This is the approach of Hans Küng, Heinz Robert Schlette, and others.

It should be evident that these three positions are not mutually exclusive, although the second and the third are closer together than either is to the first. Each respects the uniqueness of Christianity and the salvific value of the other religions. However, each assesses the uniqueness of Christianity and the salvific value of the other religions differently. But the differences are matters more of degree than of kind.

Insistence on the uniqueness of Christianity is not an unimportant matter. There are, after all, significant differences between Christianity and the other religions. Islam is clearly a book religion. Christians, for example, do not have to wash their hands before reading the Bible as Moslems do before reading the Koran. Love of neighbor does not mean the same thing in the teaching of Confucius as it does in the teaching of Jesus. Christianity, far from validating holy wars against its enemies, preaches love of one's enemies. Christianity does not worship sacred cows nor countenance a caste system.

To say, therefore, that other religions are also instruments of salvation is not to say that they are all equally good. On the contrary, there are serious deficiencies in some of them. No religion has as fully developed a theology as Christianity, and some have practically no theology at all. Dialogue, therefore, is exceedingly difficult, if not impossible, in some cases. Because of their lack of any critical component, the other religions are often impotent in the face of modernity. They have no rational weapons against the enemies of the human spirit in our time, and their own world view is frequently naive and unhistorical.

Islam, for example, believes the Koran to have been dictated word for word to Mohammed by an angel. It allows no room at all for an historical understanding of its evolution and composition. Hinduism and Buddhism share a generally cyclical view of reality. Everything is predetermined. Passivity is the favored posture. In Hinduism, a rigid caste system is assumed to be part of the necessary order of things. Confucianism and Taoism are steeped in traditionalism, with ancestor worship and an exceedingly patriarchal notion of society and of the family. Such basic liabilities hamper these religions in their effort to bring meaning into the lives of people and to change the world in accordance with the will of God.

Judaism, of course, poses a special challenge to Christianity. Jesus was himself a Jew, of a Jewish family. His preaching was directed first of all to the Jewish people. The Old Testament was the Bible of the early Christian community. The Gospel presupposed the Law and the prophets: There were common values and common structures in the two religions. And yet from the beginning they were at odds with each other. The anti-Jewish polemic in John's Gospel has been noted by New Testament scholars, and the second-century rabbinical prayer (*Shemoneh 'Esreh*), recited daily, including a curse against "heretics and Nazarenes."

The post-biblical history of Christian-Jewish relations has been, until very recently indeed, a record of hostility, alienation, and atrocities. Jews were slaughtered during the Crusades and exiled from their homes in England, France, Spain, and Portugal in the fourteenth and fifteenth centuries. But, of course, no episode affecting the Jews has had a more profound effect on the Christian conscience than the Nazi extermination of six million Jews at the time of the Second World War. "After Auschwitz there can be no more excuses," Hans Küng has written. "Christendom cannot avoid a clear admission of its guilt" (*On Being A Christian*, p. 169).

Because the persecution of Jews has too often been explained, even defended, on the basis of Jewish involvement in the crucifixion of Jesus, the Second Vatican Council clearly and unequivocally condemned such thinking: " . . . what happened in His passion cannot be blamed upon all the Jews then living, without distinction, nor upon the Jews of today. Although the Church is the new people of God, the Jews should not be presented as repudiated or cursed by God, as if such views followed from the holy Scriptures. . . . Moreover, mindful of her common patrimony with the Jews, and motivated by the gospel's spiritual love and by no political considerations, (the Church) deplores the hatred, persecutions, and displays of anti-Semitism directed against the Jews at any time and from any source" (*Declaration on the Relationship of the Church to Non-Christian Religions*, n. 4).

Is there any sense, furthermore, in which the Jews can still be regarded, from the Christian perspective, as part of the People of God? Yes, insofar as they are "the people to whom the covenants and the promises were given and from whom Christ was born according to the flesh (cf. Romans 9:4-5). On account of their fathers, this people remains most dear to God, for God does not repent of the gifts He makes nor of the calls He issues (cf. Romans 11:28-29)" (*Dogmatic Constitution on the Church*, n. 16). And at the end of history the Jewish people will join with us and all others to address the Lord "in a single voice and 'serve him with one accord' (Zephaniah 3:9; cf. Isaiah 66:23; Psalm 65:3; Romans 11:11-32)" (*Declaration on the Relationship of the Church to Non-Christian Religions,* n. 4).

We are left, then, with an agenda for dialogue: to encourage other religions, including Judaism, to bring out what is best and deepest in their own traditions and to encourage them in self-criticism and purification. And since dialogue is by definition a two-way process, it means also that the Church is to be stimulated into appreciating anew its own traditions and into seeing them in a fresher, more critical light. We can learn from the strict simplicity of Islam, the breadth of understanding of the Asian religions, the this-worldliness of Confucianism, the mysticism and commitment to peace of the Oriental religions. We can attempt a Christian theology of Judaism and learn from a Jewish theology of Christianity. Christianity in dialogue will not shrink from emphasizing its own uniqueness, but dialogue will make it increasingly open to the religious richness and salvific value of the other great traditions.

OFFICIAL CATHOLIC TEACHING ON
RELIGIOUS PLURALISM

Since the fact of pluralism has struck the consciousness of the Church only recently, especially since the Second World War, the official teachings of the Catholic Church before Vatican II are of a considerably different orientation from those of the council itself and thereafter. There are four historical stages in the development of this teaching. In the first stage the Church's attitude toward other religions was primarily negative. It was taken for granted that they cannot lead to salvation. Positively, the Church was teaching that Jesus Christ is the only Mediator between God and humankind, in keeping with 1 Timothy 2:5: "And the truth is this: God is one. One also is the mediator between God and men, the man Christ Jesus, who gave himself as a ransom for all."

The second stage occurred in the medieval period when the Church felt threatened by the continued presence of distinct Jewish communities in the West and by Moslem military aggressiveness. For the first time, the official Church issued pronouncements on the subject, and these were generally negative.

A third stage developed in the nineteenth century when the enemy was no religion in particular but Liberalism and its egalitarian philosophy that one religion is as good (or as bad) as another. Indifferentism is condemned.

A fourth stage has only recently emerged under the impact of the recognition of pluralism. The centerpiece of this stage is the Second Vatican Council's 1965 *Declaration on the Relationship of the Church to Non-Christian Religions (Nostra Aetate)*.

The official doctrine of the Church may be summarized as follows: All religions are related somehow to the Christian economy of salvation; apart from this relationship they have no salvific power; yet their adherents can find salvation, even though their religions are not on an equal footing with Christianity. These other religions contain many authentic values, although they also are mixed with error, and hence need to be purified. But they do contain elements of the supreme truth and seeds of God's word, and divine grace works in them. They deal, therefore, with the one God and with ultimate questions about human existence. Accordingly, we must support true religious freedom, tolerance, and respect. Our relations with other religious bodies should be characterized by acceptance, collaboration, and dialogue. Christians can learn from the values of other religious traditions. And there should be charity in any case.

Examples of these teachings follow:

The Second General Council of Nicea (787) insists that only those Jews who sincerely wish to convert to Christianity should be received into the Church. Otherwise, they should be allowed to "be Hebrews openly, according to their own religion" (canon 8).

Pope Gregory VII's letter to Anzir, Moslem King of Mauritania (1076), acknowledges that Christians and Moslems worship the same God: " . . . for we believe and confess one God, although in different ways, and praise and worship Him daily as the creator of all ages and the ruler of this world."

The General Council of Florence, *Decree for the Jacobites* (1442), refers for the first time in an official document to non-Christians as "pagans." Earlier that designation had been reserved to schismatics and heretics. On the other hand, the document does not deny the presence of grace beyond the borders of the Church. It also affirms that Christian freedom makes all human customs lawful if the faith is intact and edification attended to. The key negative teaching, however, is contained in this declaration:

"(The Holy Roman Church) ... firmly believes, professes and preaches that 'no one remaining outside the Catholic Church, not only pagans', but Jews, heretics or schismatics, can become partakers of eternal life; but they will go to the 'eternal fire prepared for the devil and his angels' (Matthew 25:41), unless before the end of their life they are received into it."

Religious indifferentism was explicitly condemned in the following: Leo XII's encyclical letter *Ubi Primum* (1824), Gregory XVI's encyclical letter *Mirari Vos Arbitramur* (1832), Pius IX's encyclical letter *Qui Pluribus* (1846), his allocution *Singulari Quadam* (1854), his encyclical letter *Quanto Conficiamur Moerore* (1863), and his *Syllabus of Errors* (1864). On the other hand, *Singulari Quadam* acknowledges that individuals outside the Church may simply be in ignorance of the truth through no fault of their own and so "are not subject to any guilt in this matter before the eyes of the Lord." Furthermore, his *Quanto Conficiamur* reminds us that we should bear no enmity against those outside the Church. "On the contrary, if they are poor or sick or afflicted by any other evils, let the children of the Church endeavor to succour and help them with all the services of Christian love."

Pope Leo XIII marks another shift in the Church's official teaching, a shift which anticipates the later doctrine of Vatican II on religious freedom. In his encyclical letter *Immortale Dei* (1885) he recognizes that a government may, for the sake of a greater good or of avoiding some evil, "tolerate in practice and by custom" various other forms of worship. Furthermore, ". . . nobody (is to) be forced to join the Catholic faith against his will. . . ."

In the First Plenary Council of India (1950), held in Bangalore, convoked by a papal legate, Cardinal Gilroy, and approved by Pope Pius XII in 1951, indifferentism is once again rejected, but for the first time in an official document of the Catholic Church a clearly positive statement is made regarding the spiritual values of the world religions. "We acknowledge indeed that there is truth and goodness outside the Christian religion, for God has not left the nations without a witness to Himself, and the human soul is naturally drawn toward the one true God. . . . But the inadequacy of all non-Christian religions is principally derived from this, that, Christ being constituted the one Mediator between God and men, there is no salvation by any other name."

The teaching of the Second Vatican Council on the subject is contained in the *Dogmatic Constitution on the Church* (1964), the *Declaration on the Relationship of the Church to Non-Christian Religions* (1965), the *Decree on the Church's Missionary Activity* (1965), and the *Pastoral Constitution on the Church in the Modern World* (1965). The council's teaching can be summarized as follows: The council stresses what unites us with other people rather than what divides us (*Declaration*, n. 1). It mentions other religions with respect: Hinduism, Buddhism, Islam, Judaism, and the primitive religions (*Decree*, n. 10; *Declaration*, nn. 2-4; *Dogmatic Constitution*, n. 16). They provide not only human answers to life's problems but also precious religious values (*Pastoral Constitution*, n. 12). They represent goodness intrinsic to the human heart which finds expression in rites and symbols, and are a true preparation for the Gospel (*Dogmatic Constitution*, n. 16; *Decree*, n. 9). They also contain treasures of ascetical and contemplative life (*Decree*, nn. 15,18). Thus, their faith is a response to the voice and self-communication of God (*Pastoral Constitution*, nn. 36, 22).

Indeed, the Holy Spirit was at work in the world even before Christ (*Decree*, n. 4). Religious traditions outside the Church have their place in God's saving design (*Decree*, n. 3), with values that are intimately related to the divine mystery (*Dogmatic Constitution,* n. 16; *Declaration,* n. 2). The Church, therefore, must adopt a wholly new attitude toward non-Christian religions (*Declaration*, nn. 1-5). We are to reject nothing of the truth and holiness we find in them (*Declaration*, n. 2) and should respect even those doctrinal elements which differ from our own because they may also contain a ray of truth (*Declaration*, n. 2; *Pastoral Constitution*, n. 57). We must learn to appreciate the riches of the gifts of God to all the peoples of the world (*Decree*, nn. 11,18).

While the right to freedom from coercion in civil society is inviolable, our moral duty toward the one Church of Christ remains untouched (*Declaration on Religious Freedom,* nn. 1-4). We must oppose every form of discrimination based on creed as well as on sex and race (*Declaration on the Relationship of the Church to Non-Christian Religions*, n. 5, hereafter again referred to simply as *Declaration*). We must be open to all forms of dialogue, imbued with the spirit of justice and love, and must engage in a common search for moral and spiritual enrichment (*Pastoral Constitution*, n. 92; *Decree*, nn. 11, 12,16,18,34; *Declaration*, nn. 2,3,5). This will require discernment, but it is part of the Church's task and can be done without compromise of its faith in Christ (*Dogmatic Constitution*, nn. 16,17; *Decree*, n. 9; *Declaration*, nn. 2,5; *Pastoral Constitution*, n. 28).

Pope Paul VI's encyclical letter *Ecclesiam Suam* (1964) insists, on the one hand, that "there is one true religion, the Christian religion, and that we hope that all who seek God and adore Him, will come to acknowledge this. . . . Yet we do, nevertheless, acknowledge with respect the spiritual and moral values of various non-Christian religions, for we desire to join with them in promoting and defending common ideals in the spheres of religious liberty, human brotherhood, teaching and education, social welfare and civil order. On these great ideals that we share with them, we can have dialogue, and we shall not fail to offer opportunities for it whenever, in genuine mutual respect, our offer would be received with good will." The same spirit permeates Pope Paul's letter *Africarum Terrarum* (1967) to the hierarchy and the peoples of Africa.

SUMMARY

1.   *Religion* is not easy to define. In fact, there is no single definition agreed upon by all, even within the religious sciences themselves. It is not even clear from which word or words the term *religion* is derived.

2.   We have *defined religion* here as the whole complexus of attitudes, convictions, emotions, gestures, rituals, beliefs, and institutions by which we come to terms with, and express, our most fundamental relationship with Reality (God and the created order, perceived as coming forth from God's creative hand).

3.   That relationship is disclosed by a process we have called *revelation*. Religion, therefore, is our (more or less) structured response to revelation.

4. Other definitions will differ from ours to the extent that they focus more sharply on one or another aspect of religion: the philosophical, the phenomenological, the psychological, the sociological, the anthropological, or finally its peculiarly Christian form.

5. Although the early Christian writers stressed the truth of the Christian religion, they also acknowledged that the saving grace of the Christian faith has never been refused to anyone who was worthy of it (Augustine). It is possible for every person to know God by seeing evidences of God in the created world (Aquinas). Insofar as religion is our response to God's presence, religion is in principle available to every person. And insofar as God *is* present to every person, we are not only capable of reaching beyond ourselves to God; we are actually summoned to do so (Transcendental Thomism, Rahner, Vatican II).

6. But not every person of faith is religious. There is such a thing as *implicit faith*. Implicit faith is sufficient for salvation but insufficient for religion. Religion is an individual, social, and institutional manifestation of some *explicit* faith in God.

7. Every authentic religion has, to some degree, the following *characteristics*: (1) a sense of the *holy* or the sacred (a totally other power or force which at once overwhelms and fascinates us); (2) some self-conscious response to the experience of the holy, i.e., *faith*; (3) the articulation of that response in the form of *beliefs*; (4) *moral behavior* and *ritual* consistent with the perception of the holy; and (5) the emergence of a *community* of shared perceptions, meanings, and values, with at least some rudimentary *structure*.

8. In every religion there is an intrinsic tension between *charism* and *institution*. Charisms are unusual, spontaneous, and creative. But unless they are "routinized," they will have no effect beyond the life and/or presence of the charismatic leader or founder. Routinization is institutionalization. Institutions, however, must also serve the original purposes of the community and reflect the original spirit of the founder's charism.

9. Religion's *critics* are both inside and outside organized religion. *From within*, religion is perceived as the enemy of faith (Barth) or as its false substitute (Bonhoeffer). Religion is also criticized from within by its prophets and reformers who challenge not the very concept of religion but its performance record. *From without,* religion is perceived as a projection of the human spirit, an expression of wish-fulfillment, an illusion, an opiate numbing our capacity for outrage against social injustice (Freud, Marx, and others). Still others criticize religion not because

they reject faith but because they reject institutionalization of any kind ("I don't have to go to church; I have a personal relationship with God").

10.   The prophetic and reformist criticism is alone acceptable to our understanding of religion. The Barthian critique assumes that Christianity is the exclusive recipient of revelation. The humanistic critique assesses the signals of transcendence differently from people of faith, or ignores those signals entirely. The anti-institutionalists are sociologically naive.

11.   For Christianity God is at once transcendent (beyond the world of created reality) and immanent (within the world). Other religions seem to differ from Christianity to the extent that they stress transcendence more than immanence, or vice versa. Religions in the *transcendence series* (emphasizing history, eschatology, objective, verbal worship, ethics, and some measure of rational reflection) include Judaism, Islam, and Confucianism. Religions in the *immanence series* (emphasizing the timeless, the ritualistic, the mystical) include Buddhism and Hinduism. Pushed beyond its outer limits, transcendentalism issues forth in atheism, and immanentism in fetishism.

12.   Among the non-Christian religions, there are religions which no longer exist (in ancient Egypt, the ancient East, ancient Greece, ancient Rome, e.g.) and religions which continue to exist. The *ancient religions* have run the gamut from polytheism to monotheism. All have some sense of divinity, some practice of worship, some form of priesthood, and some sense of moral obligation flowing from their relationship to the divinity or divinities. Several believed in life after death.

13.   *Religions of the present* include: (1) *Zoroastrianism*, with its emphasis on the struggle between good and evil (dualism); (2) *Hinduism*, which teaches that salvation is possible only through absorption in the knowledge of the one true reality, the Absolute, *Brahma*; (3) *Buddhism*, which teaches that we can break out of the grim cycle of rebirths and attain *Nirvana* (dissolution) by overcoming all desires; (4) *Taoism*, which calls us to live in harmony with the universe as determined by *tao* (the way); (5) *Shintoism*, which is essentially a polytheistic religion with a simple worship of nature; (6) *Islam*, which emphasizes the oneness of God (Allah) and his supremacy over every detail of human existence, and also emphasizes judgment, resurrection, prayer, fasting, and almsgiving; and (7) *Judaism*, which stresses the Covenant, the land, the past, and the coming Kingdom of God.

14.   There has always been a plurality of religions in the world, but the recognition of *pluralism* is a peculiar phenomenon of modern times. Why are there many religions rather than one alone? Because God is

available to all peoples, widely *differentiated* as they are by time, by geography, by culture, by language, by temperament, by social and economic conditions, etc. Revelation is received according to the mode of the receiver, and the response to revelation (religion) is necessarily shaped by that mode of reception.

15.   The *similarities* of religions among themselves pose an opposite question: If religions all have the same source, why are they not all equally valid? Because perceptions of revelation are subject to distortion, and so, too, are the modes of response. Common sense, though not a highly refined philosophy of human values, would tell us that a religion which worships through a communal meal is superior to one which practices human sacrifice.

16.   What is to be said, finally, of the *"validity"* of the non-Christian religions? (1) They are "valid" religions insofar as they implicitly share and practice the values inherent in the one true religion of Christianity (the theory of "anonymous Christianity"); (2) they are "valid" religions but are also lesser, relative, and extraordinary means of salvation; (3) they are "valid" in varying degrees, to be sure, but Christianity has much to learn from them and they from Christianity. Dialogue, therefore, must characterize our relationships with each other. The call to dialogue, however, does not require us to withhold criticism of other religions. The question of truth is always pertinent.

17.   *Judaism* always has a special relationship with Christianity for obvious historical and theological reasons. The Jews can still be regarded as part of the People of God insofar as the Covenant and the promises were given them, Christ was born of them, God has not withdrawn his gifts from them, and they, like all of us, are called to the final Kingdom.

18.   The *official teaching* of the Catholic Church on the question of non-Christian religions has passed through various stages. In the beginning the attitude was basically negative, since Christ was perceived as the one Mediator between God and us; in the medieval period negative teachings were formulated under the impact of the threat of continued Jewish presence in the West and of Moslem military aggressiveness; in the nineteenth century the enemy was religious indifferentism, and so emphasis had to be placed on the uniqueness and even superiority of Christianity; but with the recognition of pluralism and the changing consciousness of the Church represented by Pope John XXIII and Vatican II, the official teachings moved in a more positive direction.

19.   Present official teaching acknowledges the salvific value of non-Christian religions (without prejudice to the unique and central

place of Christianity in the economy of salvation) and calls for religious liberty for all and dialogue among all.

SUGGESTED READINGS

James, William. *The Varieties of Religious Experience.* New York: New American Library, Mentor, 1958.

Macquarrie, John. "Religion and Religions." *Principles of Christian Theology.* 2d ed. New York: Scribner, 1977, pp. 149-173.

O'Dea, Thomas F. *The Sociology of Religion.* Englewood Cliffs, N.J.: Prentice-Hall, 1966.

Otto, Rudolf. *The Idea of the Holy.* Baltimore: Penguin Books, 1959.

Rahner, Karl. "History of the World and Salvation-History" and "Christianity and the Non-Christian Religions." *Theological Investigations.* Baltimore: Helicon, 1966, vol. 5, pp. 97-134.

Robertson, Roland, ed. *Sociology of Religion: Selected Readings.* Baltimore: Penguin Books, 1969.

Schlette, Heinz. *Towards a Theology of Religions.* New York: Herder & Herder, 1966.

Smith, Huston. *The Religions of Man.* New York: Harper & Row, 1965.

Smith, William C. *The Meaning and End of Religion.* New York: Harper & Row, 1978.

·IX·

THE CHRISTIAN UNDERSTANDING OF GOD

THE PROBLEM

Nothing in this chapter retracts what has already been noted, namely, that the reality of God can neither be proved nor disproved by rational arguments. The judgment that God has been revealed in a particular person, event, or mystical experience is always precisely that, a judgment, however reasonable and informed it might be. Indeed, as we suggested in the previous chapter, there are many religions rather than one because, among other things, "no human being has ever seen or can see" God (1 Timothy 6:16). We can never be absolutely certain that we have had an experience of God or whether we have correctly perceived, interpreted, and expressed that experience. Since God can become available to us only in some bodily or sacramental way, the self-communication of God will always be conditioned by the historical situation of the person or community to which God is disclosed. Revelation is received, in other words, according to the mode of the receiver. And that is why we must also carry forward here what has already been proposed in the section on human existence, for the God-question is to a very great extent the reverse side of the question of human existence.

What follows in this chapter is a statement and description of the uniquely Christian experience of God. Because Christians are no less human, no less historically situated than others, the Christian perception, interpretation, and expression of God is also, in principle, subject to ambiguity, error, and distortion. On the other hand, it is the *distinctively Christian conviction* that God has been disclosed so clearly and so definitively in Jesus of Nazareth that there is no possibility of *fundamental* error in the perception, interpretation, or formal doctrinal expression of the reality of God. Fundamental distortion is possible only in *secondary* matters of belief. *Ambiguity*, however, is always possible because of the ineffable character of God and the inherent limitations of language.

But this distinctively Christian conviction raises a major problem for theology: If God is one, how is it that Sacred Scripture and the Church's creeds affirm a pluralism within God, that in God there is Father, Son, and Holy Spirit? *The Christian confession of the Lordship of Jesus is inextricably linked with the Christian belief in the Trinity,* for Jesus' place in saving history makes sense only insofar as he has been sent by the Father and, together with the Father, sends the Holy Spirit to heal, to renew, and to reconcile all that has been wounded by sin. The Christian understanding of God, in other words, cannot be expressed fully, let alone explained, apart from the doctrine of the Trinity and the person and work of Jesus Christ.

We shall focus even more sharply on the doctrine of the Trinity in the next chapter (although it is fully integrated into the discussion of God in this chapter), and Part III of the book will be devoted exclusively to Christology.

THE GOD OF THE BIBLE
Old Testament

Given the undeniably intimate relationship between Judaism and Christianity, represented by the unity of the two biblical Testaments, an historical unfolding of the Christian understanding of God must begin with the Old Testament.

It is by now almost an axiom of theology that the People of God in the Old Testament were not interested in philosophical speculation. Their view and grasp of reality tended to be earthy and concrete. This principle applies to their understanding of God. The medieval distinction between essence and existence, for example, was totally foreign to the Hebrew mind. Their God was

a living God, known to them through the name *Yahweh* given to
Moses and his descendants (Exodus 3:13-15). For the Israelites
Yahweh is present and active wherever the name of Yahweh is
known, recognized, and invoked. To call upon Yahweh is to summon Yahweh. Yahweh's name is glorious (Psalm 72:19), great
(1 Kings 8:42), awful (Deuteronomy 28:58), exalted (Psalm
148:13). The name is also the source of deliverance (Psalm 54:3)
and exaltation (Psalms 33:21; 89:25). Yahweh's name is at once
supportive (Psalm 124:8) and trustworthy (Psalm 33:21; Isaiah
50:10). To know Yahweh's name is to know Yahweh (Isaiah 52:6;
64:1). And so it was crucial to the success of Moses' mission that he
should discover the name of God:

> "But," said Moses to God, "when I go to the Israelites
> and say to them, 'The God of your fathers has sent me to
> you,' if they ask me, 'What is his name?' what am I to tell
> them?" God replied, "I am who am." Then he added,
> "This is what you shall tell the Israelites: I AM sent me
> to you."

> God spoke further to Moses, "Thus shall you say to the
> Israelites: The Lord, the God of your fathers, the God of
> Abraham, the God of Isaac, the God of Jacob, has sent
> me to you.

> "This is my name forever; this is my title for all genera-
> tions." (Exodus 3:13-15)

What the name *Yahweh* actually means is difficult to
determine. There is no unanimity among scholars regarding its
derivation. There seems to be general agreement, however, that
the name has some etymological connection with the archaic form
of the verb *to be* (*hawāh*). The distinguished biblical archaeologist
W. F. Albright (d. 1971) links the name with the causative form
and suggests that it is only the first word of the entire name,
yahweh-'aser-yihweh, "He who brings into being whatever comes
into being." The name would, therefore, signify the creative
power of God. Still others have suggested that the name means "I
am who I will be," thereby revealing a God in process, one who
summons us to collaborate in the building of the future.

Whatever the precise linguistic source, the name *Yahweh* clearly distinguished the God of Israel from every other claimant to the divine title (the other gods, or *Elohim*). Yahweh alone is the creator. Yahweh alone is the revealer. Yahweh alone governs history and humankind. Yahweh alone judges and saves. Yahweh alone possesses the kingdom which is as wide as creation itself. Yahweh alone is a living God (Joshua 3:10; 1 Samuel 17:26,36; 2 Kings 19:4,16; Psalms 42:3; 84:3; Isaiah 37:4,17; Jeremiah 10:10; Hosea 2:1). Yahweh alone gives life (Job 12:10; Deuteronomy 32:39; 1 Samuel 2:6; Psalm 133:3). Indeed, life is given to those who keep the divine commandments (Deuteronomy 30:15-20). One lives by heeding the word of Yahweh (Isaiah 55:3; Ezekiel 20:11,13,21).

New Testament

As we have already seen in the chapter on the religions of the world, monotheism is not peculiar to Judaism alone, nor finally to Christianity. What is *original* about the Christian understanding of God, however, is its *identification of God with Jesus of Nazareth*. The revelation of God in Jesus Christ does not occur merely in the prophetic word he uttered as was the case with the Old Testament prophets. Rather, God is communicated in the very person of Christ. There is an identity between God and Jesus Christ. The Prologue of John's Gospel makes this as clear as does any passage in the New Testament:

> There was a man named John sent by God, who came as a witness to testify to the light, so that through him all men might believe, but only to testify to the light, for he himself was not the light. The real light which gives light to every man was coming into the world.
>
> He was in the world, and through him the world was made, yet the world did not know who he was. To his own he came, yet his own did not accept him. Any who did accept him he empowered to become children of God....

The Word became flesh and made his dwelling among us, and we have seen his glory: the glory of an only Son coming from the Father, filled with enduring love. (John 1:6-12,14)

There is a kind of parallel "prologue" in the Epistle to the Hebrews:

In times past, God spoke in fragmentary and varied ways to our fathers through the prophets; in this, the final age, he has spoken to us through his Son, whom he has made heir of all things and through whom he first created the universe. This Son is the reflection of the Father's glory, the exact representation of the Father's being, and he sustains all things by his powerful word. (1:1-3)

In Jesus, therefore, the reality of God is manifested in visible, personal form. And yet the New Testament generally reserves the Greek title *ho theos* ("God") to the Father of Jesus Christ. Jesus is the *Son* of God. We said "generally," because the title "God" *is* bestowed on Jesus here and there, e.g., in the opening verse of John's Gospel ("and the Word was God") and in the Apostle Thomas' confession of faith upon seeing the risen Lord ("My Lord and my God"—John 20:28). Furthermore, the "glory of the great God and of our Savior" which is to appear can be the glory of no other than Jesus (Titus 2:13), and Jesus identifies himself with the Father (John 10:30).

In Jesus Christ not only is the Word made flesh, but all of the saving attributes of Yahweh in the Old Testament are actualized. God pardons through Christ (Ephesians 4:32) and reconciles the world through him (2 Corinthians 5:19). God gives the Spirit through the Son (John 15:26; 16:7). The Christian belongs to Christ, and Christ belongs to God (1 Corinthians 3:23).

The God who acts in and through Jesus Christ and the Holy Spirit is a forgiving God (Matthew 6:14; Mark 11:25; Luke 15:1-32), a merciful God (Luke 1:72,78; 6:36; 2 Corinthians 1:3; Ephesians 2:4; 1 Timothy 1:2; Titus 3:5; 1 Peter 1:3), a kind God (Matthew 19:17; Luke 11:13; 18:19; James 1-5), a loving God

(John 3:16; 16:27; Romans 5:5; 8:37,39; Ephesians 2:4; 2 Thessalonians 2:16; Titus 3:4), a faithful God (1 Corinthians 1:9; 2 Thessalonians 3:3), a patient God (Romans 15:5), the God of all grace (Acts of the Apostles 20:24; Romans 5:15; 1 Corinthians 1:4; 3:10; 15:10; 2 Corinthians 1:12; Ephesians 3:2,7), the God of hope (Romans 15:13), the God of peace (Romans 15:33; 16:20; 1 Corinthians 1:3; 2 Corinthians 1:2; Galatians 1:3; Ephesians 1:2; Philippians 4:9), the God of comfort (Romans 15:5; 2 Corinthians 1:3-4; 2 Thessalonians 2:16), the God of salvation (Luke 1:47; 1 Timothy 1:1; 2:3; 4:10; Titus 2:11; 2 Peter 3:9), a compassionate God who desires the salvation of all (Matthew 18:14; 1 Timothy 2:3,4; 4:10; Titus 2:11; 2 Peter 3:9).

THE GOD OF THE EARLY CHURCH FATHERS
The Apostolic Fathers

The doctrine of *the one God*, the Father and Creator of all things, was a fundamental premise of the Church's faith from the very beginning. Inherited from Judaism, monotheism provided Christianity's first line of defense against pagan polytheism, Marcionite dualism (reality comes from the hands of two opposite but equal forces, the one good, the other evil), and various other contemporary heresies. And yet Christian theology was still in an exceedingly undeveloped state in this earliest of its historical periods. What is to be gleaned from the Fathers of the first century of Christian existence is relatively meagre indeed. The fourth bishop of Rome, Clement of Rome (d. 100), in urging the Christians of Corinth to end their quarrels, divisions, schisms, and other internal hostilities, declared: "Do we not have one God and one Christ and one Spirit of grace, a Spirit that was poured out upon us?" (*Letter to the Corinthians*, 42). The identity of Father, Son, and Spirit with God and their distinctiveness, one from the other, are also suggested by Ignatius of Antioch in his *Letter to the Ephesians*: "You consider yourselves stones of the Father's temple, prepared for the edifice of God the Father, to be taken aloft by the hoisting engine of Jesus Christ, that is, the Cross, while the Holy Spirit serves you as a rope; your faith is your spiritual windlass and your love the road which leads up to God" (par. 9).

The Apologists

Although his writings are not without some ambiguity because of his Platonist philosophical background, Justin insists that "we worship and adore" the Father, the Son, and the prophetic Spirit, and that our faith is fixed on Jesus Christ as "the only proper Son who has been begotten by God, being His Word and first-begotten..." (*First Apology*, chapters 6 and 23). The generation of the Son is conditioned by, and is a product of, the Father's will. But this does not suggest any separation between the Father and the Son. On the contrary, Justin, like the other Apologists, never tired of trying to safeguard the *oneness* of God.

No theologian, however, summed up so authoritatively the thought of the second century as Irenaeus. He approached the mystery of God from two directions: as God exists internally, or immanently, and as God is manifested in the economy of salvation. What is disclosed in history (namely, the trinitarian pluralism of the Godhead) was actually there from all eternity. And over against Marcionite dualism and Gnosticism, Irenaeus declared that "there is only one God, the Creator—He who is above every Principality, and Power, and Dominion, and Virtue; He is Father, He is God, He the Founder, He the Maker, He the Creator.... He is the Father of our Lord Jesus Christ: through His Word, who is His Son, through Him He is revealed and manifested to all to whom He is revealed; for those (only) know Him to whom the Son has revealed Him" (*Against Heresies*, II,30). And not only is God the Creator of all things; God is their provident sustainer as well, ruling with goodness, mercy, patience, wisdom, and justice (III,25).

Third-Century Fathers: Tertullian, Origen, Dionysius of Rome

The doctrinal preoccupation of the Church's earliest theologians had been, until now, the oneness and unity of God. As challenges to the oneness of God subsided, the Fathers turned their attention to the plural manifestation of God in creation, in redemption, and in reconciliation (known as "economic Trinitarianism"— *economic* because it refers to the measurable "household" activities of God in the world of our experience, i.e., in our "household," as opposed to the unobservable, and therefore unmeasurable, activities within the inner or *immanent* life of God). But this deliberately Trinitarian shift in the understanding of God generated its own set of problems and questions: principally, How is the ancient doctrine of God as *Pantokrator* ("the Almighty") to be maintained if we are to confess that Jesus Christ is equal to the Father as *Pantokrator?*

Tertullian tried to resolve the problem through the use of analogies, the one biological, the other anthropological. First, the Father and the Son are parts of the same organism, but the organism itself is undivided and its power is one. Secondly, the Father and the Son, although distinct from each other, are in complete harmony of mind and will. Neither analogy solved the problem. Both are at the level of imagination, while the problem is at the level of thought. (See his *Apology* and his *Against Praxeus.*)

Origen (d. 254), the greatest of the third-century theologians and certainly one of the most gifted theologians of all time, approached the problem at a higher level. Borrowing from contemporary Platonist philosophy, Origen insisted that there is only one God, but that there is also the Logos which emanates from the One and participates in the One as the image of the divine Goodness. The Father is *the* God (only of the Father does Origen use the definite article). The Logos is not *the* God; he is simply God, and he is God by emanation and participation in a Platonist sense. He is a God "of the second order." As such, he is a diminished deity, since in the Platonist scheme emanation involves some measure of degradation of being. (See his *Principles, Against Celsus,* and *Commentary on John.*) Unfortunately, Origen's solution did not do justice to the actual faith of the Church, namely, that the Logos is God in an undiminished divine sense. The best philosophical instrument at his disposal, Platonism, simply could not supply an answer. Origen's attempt, however, paved the way for the forthright, although finally heretical, solution of Arius (d. 336), a priest of Alexandria, who argued that the Logos is a creature of

God, even though a perfect creature. He came to be out of nothing. "There was when he was not."

Dionysius of Rome (d. 268), twenty-sixth bishop of Rome, provides yet another indication of the mind of leading contemporary theologians on the developing Trinitarian problem. By the time of his pontificate, there were already three clearly distinguishable heresies on the scene: *Sabellianism* (also known as *Modalism*), which taught that God is one person who appears in three different roles according to three different functions: Creator, Redeemer, and Sanctifier; *Subordinationism*, which recognized the trinity of Persons, but made the Son less than the Father and the Spirit less than the Son; and *Tritheism*, which so emphasized the distinction of Persons that there were now three gods instead of one. Dionysius called a synod in Rome and in a letter to the Bishop of Alexandria, also named Dionysius, about whom there had been some rumors of unorthodox teaching, he insisted that all three points of view mentioned above were wrong. Positively, we must hold: (1) there is one *Pantokrator*; (2) Jesus Christ is the Lord; i.e., he is the *Pantokrator;* and (3) Christ, the *Pantokrator*, is the Son, and as such is distinct from the Father who is *the* God, the *Pantokrator*. The bishop of Rome, of course, did not solve the problem, but like most authoritative interventions his at least clarified the limits of the discussion and underlined the principles of orthodoxy which are to be maintained, whatever the proposed explanation or solution.

ARIANISM, THE COUNCIL OF NICEA, AND THE COUNCIL'S AFTERMATH

In every period of the Church's history, theologians have confronted mysteries of faith in one of three ways: first, they in effect eliminate the mystery and reduce everything to what reason can grasp (the Liberal or Rationalist approach); secondly, they throw up their hands and insist that the mystery is so impenetrable that we should ask no further questions of it (the Fideist or anti-intellectual approach); or thirdly, they acknowledge that the mystery never can be resolved, but they press ahead nonetheless, hoping at least to clarify the problem and reach some greater measure of understanding (the mainstream, orthodox approach). Arius pursued the first course. How can we preserve the oneness of God without denying the preeminence of the Son over the entire created universe? Simple enough. The Son, despite his exalted status in the economy of salvation, is a creature like us. He is no more a mystery than you or I.

That is not to say, however, that Arius' attempt at a solution to the mystery of God was simply frivolous in its origins and arbitrary or irresponsible in its conclusions. Given the nature of human intelligence, it was inevitable that someone would eventually ask the questions of how and why. We move always from *description* (the way things look to us) to *definition* (the way things are in themselves). The Bible describes the creative, redemptive, and sanctifying activities of God: Father, Son and Holy Spirit. How are these Persons really related to one another, and in particular the Son to the Father? Can we really safeguard the oneness of God if we insist at the same time on the complete equality of the Son with the Father?

On the other hand, the Arian controversy was more than an intellectual debate. At stake was the very practical matter of our salvation in Christ, to which the same Sacred Scriptures clearly attest. If the Son is not God, fully the *Pantokrator*, wholly situated within the Godhead on an equal footing with the Father, then he is not our Savior and we are not saved. For if the Son is a creature like us, he has no special standing before the Creator against whom we creatures have sinned. His act of reparation on our behalf has no ultimate effect.

It was the Council of Nicea, summoned in 325 by the Emperor Constantine in the hope of restoring unity to the Church, that gave a definitive answer to the Arian question. "We believe in one God the Father, the *Pantokrator* ('the Almighty'), Maker of all things visible and invisible; and in one Lord Jesus Christ, the Son of God, begotten out of the Father, the Only-begotten." Thus far, the affirmation of faith is entirely traditional, fully consistent with earlier creeds and with the biblical formulae as well. But then the council comes to the heart of the Arian controversy: ". . . the only-begotten generated from the Father, that is, from the being of the Father, God from God, Light from Light, true

God from true God. . . ." Thus, the Son does not emanate from the Father's *will*, as a creature, but out of the Father's *substance*, by a unique mode of origination radically different from the creative act. The Son, therefore, is "begotten, not made." He is not the perfect creature outside the divine order. He is begotten within the divine order and he remains within it. His being is untouched by createdness. Finally, he is "one in being (*homoousios*) with the Father."

The Council of Nicea, therefore, did not simply describe the reality of God; it defined it. It defined what the Son is, in himself and in his relation to the one God the Father. The Son is from the Father in a singular, unshared way, begotten as Son, not made as a creature. The Son is all that the Father is, except for the Name of Father. This is what "one in being," or "consubstantial" (*homoousios*), means. That is what the Son is. "A passage has been made," John Courtney Murray, S. J. (d. 1967), wrote, "from a conception of what the Son is-to-us to a conception of what the Son, Christ, is-in-himself. The transition is from a mode of understanding that is descriptive, relational, interpersonal, historical-existential, to a mode of understanding that is definite, explanatory, absolute, ontological. The alteration in the mode of understanding does not change the sense of the affirmation, but it does make the Nicene affirmation new in its form" (*The Problem of God*, p. 46).

Opposition to the Nicene creed came from both extremes: not only from the Arians on the left but also from the conservative party on the right, those who gathered around Eusebius of Caesarea (d. ca. 340), who is also generally regarded as the first serious Church historian. This party wanted to say no more than Sacred Scripture seemed to be saying, namely, that the Son is "like" (*homoios*) in all things to the Father. The same position appears in the formula of the Synod of Constantinople in 361. *Homoousios*, they insisted, is not a biblical word; therefore, the Nicene formula cannot be a formula of faith. The deeper issue, of course, was the *development of doctrine*. The Eusebians, like many traditionalists down through the centuries, refused to acknowledge the possibility, not to say the appropriateness, of progress in doctrinal understanding. They were at heart fundamentalists, biblical positivists.

The Eusebians' affection for their particular reconstruction of the past (*archaism*) would give rise to the opposite tendency, i.e., the notion that no affirmation of faith can ever be final (*modernism*).

The Nicene formula avoids both extremes. It rejects archaism by transposing the biblical affirmations concerning the Son into a new mode of understanding, but always consistent with the biblical. And it also rejects modernism because the notion "consubstantial" (*homoousios*) sets a final limit in the understanding of faith. There can, and must, be further growth in our understanding of this mystery, but the direction and dimensions of that growth are forever conditioned by the finality of the Nicene formula. And the Nicene formula, in turn, provides a charter and a precedent for the later councils of Ephesus and Chalcedon, which also had to transcend the biblical formulae and attempt an expression of the internal makeup of Christ in the philosophical categories of nature and person. (We shall be returning to the Christological debates and doctrines in greater detail in Part III.)

Through the efforts of Athanasius and Hilary of Poitiers (d. 367), the Eusebians (the so-called *homoiousion* party) were eventually reconciled with the orthodox *homoousions*. Hilary contended in his *On the Councils* that both sides were right and had an obligation to recognize the essentially orthodox concerns of the other side. Since the Nicenes acknowledged the distinction of persons in the Godhead, they could not really deny the *homoiousion* principle. The *homoiousions*, for their part, had to allow unity of substance (*homoousios*) if they believed seriously in the perfect likeness of substance. At the Council of Alexandria in 362 the reconciliation was sealed. With Athanasius in the conciliar chair, the assembly legitimated the "three *hypostases* (persons)" formula of the Eusebian party, provided it merely expresses the separate subsistence of the three Persons in the Trinity. From this emerged a new orthodox formula: "one *ousia* (being, substance), three *hypostases* (persons)."

FOURTH-CENTURY CAPPADOCIAN FATHERS: BASIL, GREGORY OF NYSSA, AND GREGORY OF NAZIANZUS

There remained only the problem of the relationship between the Holy Spirit and the Godhead in general, and between the Holy Spirit and the Son in particular. Since Origen's day theological reflection had not kept pace with the considerable devotional practice centered on the Holy Spirit. Under the impact of denials of the divinity of the Spirit (a group of Egyptian Christians, for example, argued that the Spirit was a creature brought into existence out of nothing), the specifically theological task of articulating the divine equality of the Spirit with the Father and the Son was begun by Athanasius and taken up even more systematically by three major Fathers of the Church, known together as the Cappadocians: Basil (d. 379), his brother Gregory of Nyssa (d. 394), and his friend Gregory of Nazianzus (d. 390). It was Basil who urged that the Spirit must be accorded the same glory, honor, and worship as the Father and the Son; Gregory of Nyssa who emphasized the oneness of nature shared by the three Persons of the Trinity; and Gregory of Nazianzus who insisted that the Spirit, like the Son, is consubstantial, or one in being (*homoousios*), with the Father. (This point would be developed even more fully by Cyril of Alexandria, d. 444, in his *Thesaurus on the Holy and Consubstantial Trinity*.) For Basil the Spirit issues from God not by way of generation (as in the case of the Son) but "as from the breath of his mouth"; for Gregory of Nazianzus the Spirit simply "proceeds" from the Father, as John's Gospel has it; but for Gregory of Nyssa the Spirit is "out of God" and is "of Christ." The Father is uncaused, and the Son and the Spirit are caused. The Son is directly produced by the Father, while the Spirit proceeds from the Father through the Son, but without any trace of subordinationism (i.e., the heresy that the three Persons of the Trinity are somehow unequal).

The essence of the Cappadocian doctrine of God (as expressed in Basil's *On the Holy Spirit*, Gregory of Nyssa's *Letter #38, On the Holy Spirit: Against the Followers of Macedonius*, and *On "Not Three Gods,"* and Gregory of Nazianzus' *The Fifth*

Theological Oration) is that the one God exists simultaneously in three ways of being or *hypostases*. Each of the divine *hypostases*, or Persons, is the *ousia* or essence of the Godhead; these Persons are distinguished from one another only by their relationships to one another, and those relationships are determined, in turn, by their origins. Thus, the Father is different from the Son in that the Father is unbegotten, while the Son is begotten by a process of generation; the Son is different from the Spirit in that the Son is generated while the Spirit is spirated by, or proceeds from, the Father and the Son.

Gregory of Nazianzus' expression of the mystery is fully representative of the Cappadocian position:

> But the difference of manifestation,...or rather of their mutual relations to one another, has caused the difference of their Names. For indeed it is not some deficiency in the Son which prevents His being Father (for Sonship is not a deficiency), and yet He is not Father. According to this line of argument there must be some deficiency in the Father, in respect of His not being Son. For the Father is not Son, and yet this is not due to either deficiency or subjection of Essence; but the very fact of being Unbegotten or Begotten or Proceeding has given the name of Father to the First, of the Son to the Second, and of the Third, Him of whom we are speaking, of the Holy Ghost, that the distinction of the Three Persons may be preserved in the one nature and dignity of the Godhead. For neither is the Son Father, for the Father is One, but He is what the Father is; nor is the Spirit Son because He is of God, for the Only-begotten is One, but He is what the Son is. The Three are One in Godhead, and the One Three in properties.... (*The Fifth Theological Oration*)

The whole Greek theological approach to the mystery of the triune God would later be summed up by John of Damascus (d. ca. 749) in his *The Source of Knowledge*, part III, "On the Orthodox Faith."

THE COUNCILS OF
CONSTANTINOPLE (381) AND OF ROME (382)

This post-Nicean theology received official endorsement at two councils, the one ecumenical and the other provincial. The First Council of Constantinople (May-July, 381) was called by the Emperors Theodosius (d. 395) and Gratian (d. 383), the one ruling the East, the other the West. The one hundred and fifty bishops attending the council reaffirmed the faith of Nicea. Against the *Macedonians*, who denied the divinity of the Holy Spirit, they held the consubstantiality (oneness-in-being) and the coeternity of the Spirit with the Father and the Son. From this council there emerged the *Nicaeo-Constantinopolitan Creed*, recited in every Sunday Mass throughout the Catholic world (see the Appendix for the full text). The bishops of Constantinople had not themselves composed the creed. They accepted one that was already available and which they deemed entirely consistent with the doctrinal formulations of Nicea.

Pope Damasus (d. 384) did not participate in the Council of Constantinople, and there is no historical evidence that he officially accepted its decisions. The following year, however, he summoned a provincial council in Rome, which issued a set of anathemas or condemnations against those who held false teachings about the Father, Son, and Holy Spirit. The collection of condemnations was subsequently known as the *Tome of Pope Damasus I*. Positively, the council of Rome taught that there is one God of three divine, coequal, coeternal Persons, each distinct from the other, but not so distinct that we have three separate gods.

AUGUSTINE

There was no comparably sophisticated theology in the West (i.e., the Christian world of Latin rather than of Greek) until Augustine, although important contributions had already been made by Irenaeus, Tertullian, Hilary, and others. Influenced by the writings of the neo-Platonist convert to the Church, Victorinus (d. ca. 380), Augustine accepted without question the doctrine that there is one God in whom Father, Son, and Holy Spirit are at once distinct and consubstantial (or "co-essential," as he preferred). Significantly, nowhere does Augustine try to prove this doctrine. He accepts it as a datum of revelation which, in his view, Scripture proclaims almost on every page. His concern is not with proof but with understanding, which is consistent with his fundamental notion of theology as belief seeking understanding. (I believe in order that I might understand.)

Unlike the Greek Fathers, Augustine does not begin with the three Persons as they function in history for our salvation and then work backwards, so to speak, to the unity of the Godhead. He begins rather with the one divine nature itself and tries to understand how the three Persons share in that nature without dividing it. Subordinationism of every kind is rejected. Whatever is affirmed of God is affirmed equally of each of the Persons (*On the Trinity*, Book 5, chapter 9). "Not only is the Father not greater than the Son in respect of divinity, but Father and Son together are not greater than the Holy Spirit, and no single person of the Three is less than the Trinity itself" (8,1). Thus, we are not speaking here of three separate individuals as we would of three separate human beings. There are not three wills, but one. There are not three sources of divine action, but one. Against the obvious objection that Augustine is destroying the several roles of the three Persons (and, therefore, is lapsing into Modalism), he argued that, even though it was the Son and not the Father who was born, suffered, and died, the Father cooperated fully with the Son in bringing about the incarnation, the passion, and the resurrection. It is fitting, however, for the Son to have been manifested and made visible in those events, since each of the divine Persons possesses the divine nature in a particular manner and since, in the external operation of the Godhead, roles which are *appropriate* to a particular Person in view of that Person's origin within the Godhead are fittingly attributed to that Person. And yet all three Persons are always fully involved as one in every external action.

One of Augustine's original contributions to the Christian doctrine of God (and his most effective rebuttal of the charge of Modalism) was his notion of real or *subsistent relations*. Anticipating the teaching of Anselm and then of the Council of Florence that in the Trinity all things are one except what is differentiated by reason of an opposition of relations (e.g., the Father, who is *unbegotten*, is not the Son, who is *begotten*), Augustine opposed the Arian notion that distinctions within the Godhead are either substantial (in which case there are three separate gods) or accidental (in which case God is not purely simple). Whatever the Father, the Son, or the Holy Spirit is, he is in relation to one or both of the others (see *On the Trinity*, Books 5-7). Threeness in God, therefore, is not rooted in threeness of substance or threeness of accidents but in threeness of relations: of begetting, of being begotten, and of proceeding.

What is perhaps Augustine's most original contribution to Trinitarian theology, however, is his use of analogies drawn from human consciousness to explain the inner life of God. (This is not to say that his argument is easy to follow, or in fact can be deemed entirely helpful today.) In every process of perception there are three distinct elements: the external object, the mind's sensible representation of the object, and the act of focusing the mind. When the external object is removed, we rise to an even higher trinitarian level, superior to the first because the process occurs entirely now within the mind and is therefore "of one and the same substance," namely, the memory impression, the internal memory image, and the focusing of the will. In his *On the Trinity* Augustine elaborates the analogy at length in three successive stages, with the following resulting trinities: (1) the mind, its knowledge of itself, and its love of itself, (9, 2-8); (2) memory, or the mind's latent knowledge of itself, understanding, and love of itself (10, 17-19); and (3) the mind as remembering, knowing, and loving God (14, 11-end). Augustine regarded the last of the three analogies as the most satisfactory. It is only when the mind has focused itself on its Creator with all its powers of remembering, understanding, and loving that the image it bears of God can be fully restored. "Since these three, the memory, the understanding, and the will, are, therefore, not three lives but one life, not three minds but one mind, it follows that they are certainly not three substances, but one substance" (10, 11).

Augustine himself was realistic about the limitations of this analogical approach. Analogies, as the saying goes, always limp.

They tell us how things are *like* other things, but they warn us at the same time that the things being compared are also *unlike* one another. Thus, the operations of human consciousness are by no means identical with the inner operations of the Trinity. Remembering, understanding, and loving are three separate faculties of the human mind. In the Godhead there are no distinct faculties. God is absolutely one. Furthermore, in the human mind these three faculties operate independently. In God every act and operation is indivisible (15, 43). Furthermore, why are there only two processions and only three Persons?

We are left, in the end, with the mystery: Scripture and Christian doctrine portray God as acting in three Persons, but Scripture and Christian doctrine also insist firmly and unequivocally on the oneness of God.

Augustine's influence on subsequent Christian belief and theology is, to be sure, enormous. Apart from Boethius (d. ca. 525), who bequeathed the definition of *person* as "an individual substance of a rational nature," no one competes with him for theological impact on later centuries. But the more immediate effect of his approach was also considerable. The so-called *Athanasian Creed (Quicumque)* of the late fifth century clearly bore the stamp of Augustinian thought. Falsely attributed to St. Athanasius, the creedal formula has stood ever since as the Western Church's classical statement of Trinitarian faith. Augustine's influence was also operative in the deliberations of the Eleventh Council of Toledo (675), which drew upon the *Quicumque* creed as well as Augustine's writings for the construction of its own profession of faith, in which it declares that God is both One and Three.

ANSELM OF CANTERBURY

Although no complete history of the Christian understanding of God can ignore the watershed figure of John Scotus Erigena (d. 877), the most famous scholar and teacher of his day and one of the last who tried to reconcile ancient Greek philosophy with the faith (see his *On the Division of Nature*, in which he seems to propose a pantheistic notion of God), our attention turns here to

Anselm, the single most important theologian between Augustine and Aquinas.

Anselm's contribution to the Christian understanding of God is at least threefold: the so-called ontological argument for God's existence; the debt-satisfaction theory of atonement; and the principle that in God everything is one except for the opposition of relationships among the three Persons. Only the last seems to have survived subsequent critical analysis. On the first point, Anselm insisted that God is "a being than which nothing greater can be conceived." But, he said, if such a being exists only in the mind or in the realm of understanding, "the very being, than which nothing greater can be conceived, is one, than which a greater can be conceived. Hence, there is no doubt that there exists a being, than which nothing greater can be conceived, and it exists both in the understanding and in reality" (*Proslogium*, chapter 2). The argument was later rejected by Aquinas and Kant alike. What may be true in the order of the mind is not necessarily real in the order of objective reality. On the second point, Anselm argued that the sin of Adam could be forgiven only if sufficient satisfaction for the sin were offered to the Father. But only a divine person could adequately resolve the debt incurred by human sin. Therefore, God had to become human if we were to be restored to God's friendship. (We shall return to this theory of atonement in Part III on Christology.) On the third point, Anselm argued, following in the tradition of Augustine, that God is absolutely one except for the pluralism of persons created by the opposition of relationships among them. The Father, Son, and Holy Spirit are one God, except insofar as the Father is unbegotten and the Son is begotten, and insofar as the Spirit proceeds whereas the Father and the Son spirate (see his *On the Procession of the Holy Spirit*, chapter 1). This principle is the theological basis for the doctrine of the *mutual indwelling of the three divine Persons*: The Father is always in the Son and the Holy Spirit; the Son is always in the Father and the Spirit; the Spirit is always in the Father and the Son. The mutual indwelling is also known as *circumincession*. The Council of Florence (1442) adopted the principle in its "Decree for the Jacobites": "The Father alone begot the Son out of His substance; the Son alone was begotten from the Father alone; the Holy Spirit alone proceeds from both Father and Son. These three persons are one God and not three gods, for the three are one substance, one essence, one nature, one Godhead, one infinity, one eternity, and everything (in them) is one where there is no opposition of relationship."

In the final accounting, Anselm believed that the mystery of the triune God is "so sublime" that it "transcends all the vision of the human intellect. And for that reason I think it best to refrain from the attempt to explain how this thing is." It is enough for Anselm to be secure in the knowledge *that* God is, and that what we *do* know of God is "without contradiction of any other reason" (*Monologium*, chapter 64). For theology itself is "faith seeking understanding."

THE FOURTH LATERAN
GENERAL COUNCIL (1215)

When a new pope is elected to the office of "supreme pastoral ministry" in the Church, one of his first official acts is to take possession of the Lateran Basilica, the cathedral church of the diocese of Rome. It is as bishop of Rome, of course, that the pope serves as head of the Church Universal. The Lateran has also been the scene of five general or ecumenical councils. It was the fourth such council of the Lateran, during the pontificate of Innocent III (d. 1216), which produced a profession of Trinitarian faith as well as a formal doctrinal statement on the reality of the triune God. The council confessed that "there is only one true God...Father, Son and Holy Spirit: three persons indeed but one essence, substance or wholly simple nature:...the Father generating, the Son being born, the Holy Spirit proceeding; consubstantial, co-equal, co-omnipotent and co-eternal; one origin of all things: the Creator of all things visible and invisible, spiritual and corporal." This creedal affirmation was directed explicitly against *Albigensianism*, one of the most serious heresies in the history of the Church.

Indeed, the late Monsignor Philip Hughes (d. 1967), one of the best known English-speaking Church historians of this century, regarded the seventeen years (1181–1198) that separated Pope Innocent III from Pope Alexander III as "the most critical period of the Middle Ages. . . . Of all the dangers that threatened, the greatest of all was the revival of Manicheeism which, beginning a hundred years before this, had by now made its own all the south of France (Provence) and much of northern Italy" (*A Popular History of the Catholic Church*, New York: Doubleday Image, 1949, p. 115). The sect was called Albigenses after the city of Albi, Provence. Its theological position was that matter is evil, that it comes from some source other than the true God. Because matter is evil, we must abstain from food, from marriage, and especially from conception. The sect was well-organized and was extraordinarily successful in gathering adherents from the cultured nobility and from the wealthy merchant class. At first the pope tried to combat the heresy with persuasion and preaching, but when those failed, he adopted more aggressive measures: One was the calling of the Fourth Lateran Council, and another was the establishment of the Inquisition to root out this heresy and others. (For an excellent case-study of how the Church went about this task, see Emmanuel LeRoy Ladurie's *Montaillou: The Promised Land of Error*, New York: Braziller, 1978.)

The council taught, therefore, that God is the author of both matter and spirit and that Christ is fully God, with a human as well as a divine nature.

In its second document, the council addressed itself to a bitter dispute between Joachim of Flora (d. 1202) and Peter the Lombard (d. 1160). The dispute was a kind of microcosm of the historic difference between the Eastern and Western approaches to the mystery of the Trinity. The Eastern approach, as noted earlier, was centered on the saving activity of the three Persons in history. The Western approach, with its roots principally in Augustine, was centered on the one divine nature which subsists as Father, Son, and Holy Spirit. Peter the Lombard had systematized this latter approach in his *Sentences*, making the divine essence the center of his speculation. Joachim attacked Peter, accusing him of producing a fourth Person, the "divine essence." The council defended Peter against the accusation that he had produced a quaternity, and sanctioned the doctrine which became the basis of the Trinitarian theology of most Scholastics thereafter: ". . . in God there is only Trinity, not a quaternity, because each of the

Persons is that reality, viz., that divine substance, essence or
nature which alone is the beginning of all things, apart from
which nothing else can be found. This reality is neither generating
nor generated, nor proceeding, but it is the Father who generates,
the Son who is generated and the Holy Spirit who proceeds, so that
there be distinctions between the persons but unity in nature.
Hence, though 'the Father is one person (*alius*), the Son another
person, and the Holy Spirit another person, yet there is not another
reality (*aliud*),' but what the Father is, this very same reality is
also the Son, this the Holy Spirit, so that in orthodox Catholic faith
we believe them to be of one substance."

THOMAS AQUINAS

Aquinas' understanding of God is too precise and detailed to
summarize in so brief a subsection as this. Its major components,
however, are twofold: (1) the identification of essence and existence in God; i.e., God's essence is "to be"; and (2) the participation of the created order in the Being of God, who is the First
Cause of all that is.

For the first, he rests his case on the Exodus text (3:14)
wherein Yahweh "responds" to Moses' question: "I am He Who
Is." For Aquinas, "He Who Is" is the most suitable name for God
(*Summa Theologica*, I, q. 13, a. 11). "Every thing," he writes,
"exists because it has being. A thing whose essence is not its being,
consequently, is not through its essence but by participation in
something, namely, being itself. But that which is through participation in something cannot be the first being, because prior to it is
the being in which it participates in order to be. But God is the
first being, with nothing prior to Him. His essence is, therefore,
His being" (*Summa Contra Gentiles*, I, 22).

From this follows the principle that every created reality
participates in the Being of God. God is perpetually and immediately present to the world of beings, for God is Being itself, the
condition for the existence of any beings at all (*Summa Theologica,* I, q. 8; q. 104). Unlike the God of *Deism*, who creates the world
in the beginning and then allows it to work on its own thereafter
(much like the clockmaker's relation to the clock), the God of

Aquinas is at once transcendent and immanent to the world (*Summa Contra Gentiles*, II, 21; III, 67–68). But God's intimate involvement in the created universe does not thereby destroy the integrity of free agents. "God works in things in such a manner that things have their proper operation." Otherwise, "the operative powers which are seen to exist in things would be bestowed on things to no purpose, if things produced nothing through them. Indeed, all created things would seem, in a way, to be purposeless, if they lacked an operation proper to them, since the purpose of everything is its operation" (*Summa Theologica*, I, q. 105, a. 5).

Aquinas' understanding of the Being and action of God is consistent with his famous "five ways" to prove the existence of God: the argument from *motion* (there must be a prime mover), the argument from *causality* (every effect must have a cause), the argument from *necessity* (all beings are possible, but one must be necessary if there are to be any beings at all), the argument from gradation or *exemplarity* (our ideas of more or less, of better or worse, presuppose some standard of perfection), and the argument from *design* (the consistent and coherent operation of the whole universe demands some intelligent and purposeful designer). (See *Summa Theologica*, I, q. 3, a. 3). These arguments were not original with Aquinas. He was largely indebted to Plato, Aristotle, Avicenna, Augustine, and especially the Jewish philosopher Moses Maimonides. All of the arguments are reducible to one: the argument from causality. No one argument "proves" the existence of God. They are simply ways in which the believer can begin to "make sense" of his or her belief in God after the fact. (We touched already upon this problem in chapters 5 and 6, with regard to the relationship of nature and grace and the teaching of the First Vatican Council on our knowledge of God.)

Insofar as God ordains all things to their goal, God is *provident*; i.e., God "foresees" and insures what is necessary for the fulfillment of the end of the world and all that is in it (*Summa Theologica*, I, q. 22, a. 1). The human being, as the creature endowed with reason, "is under God's providence in the special sense of sharing in providence inasmuch as he is provident with regard to himself and other things" (I-II, q. 91, a. 2). This sharing of the rational creature in the reason of God (I-II, q. 19, a. 4) is called the "natural law" (q. 91, a. 2). Alongside the natural law is the new law of the Gospel and of the Holy Spirit which is imparted to those who believe in Christ (q. 106, a. 1). There can be only one goal, God, of both the created and the recreated universe, i.e., of the order of nature and the order of grace (I, q. 103, a. 2).

Finally, with regard to the doctrine of the Trinity, Aquinas completed the psychological explanation of the relations of Persons which Augustine initiated and Anselm developed. He was the first to argue that there are two distinct processions (generation and spiration) because a spiritual being has two operations: intellection and volition. These processions produce, in turn, four real relations: paternity, filiation, spiration, and procession, but only three of them are really distinct from one another by reason of their mutual opposition: paternity, filiation, and (passive) spiration (I, q. 28, aa. 1–4). And so there are three Persons, and only three, in God (I, qq. 27–43). Other important medieval theologians, like Duns Scotus (d. 1308), agreed with the conclusion but not with the argument. Anticipating the Greek Orthodox position, Scotus argued that not only opposite relations but also disparate relations (e.g., passive generation and active spiration) distinguished divine persons. Therefore, it was not necessary that the Spirit proceed also from the Son (see *Commentary on the Sentences*, I, d. 11, q. 2).

SECOND COUNCIL OF LYONS (1274); COUNCIL OF FLORENCE (1438–1440)

What these two ecumenical councils had in common was their concern for the split between the Eastern and Western Churches, by now already two centuries old. Both tried to effect some kind of reconciliation, but neither succeeded for very long. Insofar as the schism involved divergent understandings of God, and of the Trinity in particular, the conciliar texts are of interest to us here.

Lyons II adopted as its own a so-called "Profession of Faith of Michael Palaeologus." It was taken from a letter written by the Byzantine Emperor Michael VIII Palaeologus (d. ca. 1282), in which the emperor merely reproduced, without modification, the text of a profession of faith proposed to him by Pope Clement IV (d. 1268) as early as 1267. Clement believed this to be required of the Greeks if reunion was to occur. Insofar as Michael desired reunion, he himself subscribed to it. Not surprisingly, the text reflects the Latin approach to the doctrine of the Trinity: It begins with the oneness of the divine nature and then proceeds to the trinity of Persons, with the Holy Spirit proceeding from the Father *and* the Son (not *through* the Son, as the Greeks would have it). In another document, the *Constitution on the Holy Trinity and the Catholic Faith*, the council explains the Latin doctrine on the origin of the Holy Spirit, insisting, against its Eastern detractors, that the origin of the Holy Spirit from the Father *and* the Son does not imply a double principle in God.

The Council of Florence's teaching on God is contained in two documents: the *Decree for the Greeks* (1439) and the *Decree for the Jacobites* (1442). In the former, the council explains the procession of the Holy Spirit from Father *and* Son, but allows also for the formula cherished by the East, namely, procession from the Father *through* the Son, with the understanding, however, that the Son, just as fully as the Father, is the "cause" or "principle" of the subsistence of the Holy Spirit. The *Decree of Union* was signed by both groups, but when the Greeks returned to Constantinople, public opinion forced them to repudiate it. The Churches remain separated to this day.

Representatives of the Syrian Jacobite Church came to Rome afterwards and engaged in similar negotiations leading to a consensus statement, in this case the *Decree for the Jacobites*, important for its emphasis on the concept of *circumincession* or *perichoresis*, namely, that each Person is always present to the other two Persons: ". . . the Father is wholly in the Son and wholly in the Holy Spirit; the Son is wholly in the Father and wholly in the Holy Spirit; the Holy Spirit is wholly in the Father and wholly in the Son." The Decree is also significant for its articulation of the principle, to which we have already referred in this chapter, that in the Trinity all things are one except what is opposed by the opposition of relations.

PROTESTANTISM AND THE COUNCIL OF TRENT
(1545–1563)

The Council of Trent's doctrinal formulations on God (to which we have already referred in Part I on human existence) cannot be understood apart from the theology of the Reformers. For Martin Luther (d. 1546) the difficulty is not with the immanent Trinity (i.e., the Trinity from the viewpoint of life within the Godhead) but with the economic Trinity (i.e., the Trinity from the viewpoint of the action of God in the world, and specifically in the lives of human beings). Luther believes in, and confesses, the mystery of the Blessed Trinity. But he cannot accept the Catholic principle that God desires the salvation of all, that God is essentially a gracious God, and that God wills us to cooperate freely with divine grace in the working out of our salvation. For Luther, on the contrary, we can do nothing on our own. God has mercy on whomever he wills (Romans 9:18). "He wills that his power should be magnified in man's perdition" (*Lectures on Romans*, chapter 8). But Luther also insisted that the true God says " . . . I take no pleasure in the death of the wicked man, but rather in the wicked man's conversion, that he may live" (see Ezekiel 33:11). "God is the same sort of God to all men that He was to David, namely, one who forgives sins and has mercy upon all who ask for mercy and acknowledge their sins" (*Lectures on Psalms, On Psalm 51:1*). In *Bondage of the Will*, however, Luther stressed God's foreknowledge and omnipotence so much that practically no room is left for our free response. In Christ, of course, we have access to the Father's will and heart. If God be for us in Christ, who or what can be against us (Romans 8:31)? (See his commentary on the First Commandment in *The Large Catechism*.)

John Calvin (d. 1564), the other great Reformer, carries the doctrine of predestination even further. Taking Romans 9:13 very literally, he concludes that God loves some and hates others: "It is just as Scripture says, 'I have loved Jacob and hated Esau'." On the other hand, Calvin acknowledges in his *Institutes of the Christian Religion* that "God has destined all things for our good and salvation . . . nothing that is needful for our welfare will ever be lacking to us" (chapter 14). And yet "By God's bidding . . . salvation is freely offered to some while others are barred from access to it. . .he does not indiscriminately adopt all into the hope of salvation but gives to some what he denies to others" (Book III, chapter 21). Salvation is owed to no one; therefore, God does no one an injustice by denying it to anyone. Furthermore, if God cannot punish, how is his mercy to be made manifest (chapter 23)?

The Reformers' attitude toward God's salvific intentions underscores again one of the principal historic differences between Protestant and Catholic theology and spirituality. The former tradition, as we suggested in the earlier discussion of the problem of nature and grace in chapters 4 and 5, has tended to emphasize the radical unworthiness of the person, even after God's redemptive activity on our behalf. The Catholic tradition, on the other hand, insists that God not only makes a declaration of our worthiness for salvation, but actually transforms us and makes us new creatures in Christ and the Holy Spirit. God offers this inner transformation to every person, without exception. No one is excluded beforehand. Only a free act of the will, rejecting the divine offer of grace, can impede God's saving designs. The alternate view—predestination to hell as well as to heaven—has been described by the Anglican theologian John Macquarrie as a "fantastic exaggeration of the divine initiative into a fatalism [which] is repugnant not merely because it dehumanizes man but also because it presents us with a God who is not worthy to be worshipped" (*Principles of Christian Theology*, p. 341).

The Council of Trent's *Decree on Justification* teaches that "all men" have been called to the status of adopted sons of God in Christ (chapter 2), but that they can freely reject the grace of adoption (chapter 5). Insofar as we do open ourselves to the divine presence, it is because our hearts have been touched through the illumination of the Holy Spirit (*ibid.*). The process of passing from the condition of sin as a child of the first Adam to a condition of adopted sonship in Christ is called justification (chapter 4). Justification "is not only a remission of sins but also the sanctification and renewal of the inward man through the voluntary reception of the grace and the gifts whereby an unjust man becomes just" (chapter 7). God wills the salvation of all, and God will achieve that purpose "unless men themselves fail in his grace" (chapter

13). Indeed, the council's sixth canon explicitly anathematizes, or condemns, those who say "that it is not in man's power to make his ways evil, but that God produces the evil works just as he produces the good ones, not only by allowing them but properly and directly, so that Judas' betrayal is no less God's work than Paul's vocation."

BLAISE PASCAL (d. 1662)

Pascal, mathematician, scientist, and spiritual writer, is perhaps best known for his unique apologetical argument on behalf of belief in God, namely, the famous wager. First, he says, there is no clear evidence for the existence of God. "What meets our eye denotes neither total absence nor manifest presence of the divine, but the presence of a hidden God" (*Pensées*, #12). God is or is not. Which is it? A game is on. If one gambles that God is not, that person has nothing to gain and everything to lose should God exist. If, on the other hand, one wagers that God is, that person has everything to gain and nothing to lose. For if God exists, faith in God will have its infinite reward. If God does not exist, the person has lost nothing, since there would be no infinite reward in any case. So to "bet on" God is to enter a game weighted in the gambler's favor, for the gambler wagers finite stakes with the possibility of infinite returns.

More significant for our purposes here is Pascal's relatively balanced understanding of the God of faith. Christianity, he declares, teaches us twin truths about this God: "that there is a God whom men can reach, and that there is a corruption in their nature which renders them unworthy of Him." It is crucial that we keep both truths before us. "Knowledge of one alone causes either the pride of philosophers who have known God but not their misery, or the despair of atheists who know their misery but not their Redeemer." It is only in our knowledge of Jesus Christ that we grasp both truths at once, namely, that we have access to God and that we are creatures in need of forgiveness and reconciliation. The Christians' God, therefore, is like the God of Abraham, of Isaac, and of Jacob, "a God of love and consolation, a God who fills the soul and heart of those whom He hath purchased, a

God who makes them deeply conscious of their misery and of His infinite mercy; who makes His home in their heart, filling it with humility, joy, confidence and love; who renders them incapable of any other object than Himself" (*ibid.*). This God is always a "hidden God," but there is an escape from our blindness through Jesus Christ, "apart from Whom all communication with God has been cut off. . ." (#246).

A fuller statement of Pascal's importance in the history of the Church and of Christian theology generally would require a more complete description of the cultural and ecclesiastical situation in seventeenth-century France, of the development of *Gallicanism* (a movement of French nationalism which, among other things, insisted on the autonomy of the local Church over against Rome and the papacy), of *Jansenism* (with which Pascal was once associated at Port-Royale), and of various other contemporary spiritual movements associated with the names of Fénelon (d. 1715), Bossuet (d. 1704), and others.

FIRST VATICAN COUNCIL (1869–1870) AND ITS ANTECEDENTS
Kant

Immanuel Kant (d. 1804) in his *Critique of Pure Reason* rejected the traditional arguments on behalf of the existence of God, having been awakened from his own "dogmatic slumber" by David Hume's (d. 1776) analysis of causality. Since God is by definition in a totally different order, God's "objective reality cannot indeed be proved, but also cannot be disproved, by merely speculative reasoning" (section 7). Since God operates in the moral order, it is there that God is to be apprehended, if at all. Insofar as we all seek the highest good, we must be able to presuppose that the quest is possible in the first place. "Granted that the pure moral law inexorably binds every man as a command (not as a rule of prudence), the righteous man may say: I will that there be a God, that my existence in this world be also an existence in a pure world of the understanding outside the system of natural connection, and finally that my duration be endless" (*Critique of Practical Reason*, section 8). Since our idea of the highest good in the world leads to the postulation of a higher, moral, most holy, and omnipotent Being which alone can unite our quest for happiness with our obedience to duty, morality thus leads ineluctably to religion. God becomes the powerful moral Lawgiver whose will is the final end of creation and of all human activity (*Religion Within the Limits of Reason Alone*, Preface to the first edition). We feel ourselves at once impelled to seek the highest good, even duty-bound to seek it, but powerless on our own to reach it. We discover ourselves to be living in an ethical commonwealth under the governance of a moral Ruler who is creator, guardian, and administrator. The Lawgiver's beneficence, however, is limited by human cooperation with the holy law. To say that "God is love" means that God approves us insofar as we obey the law. To speak of a *triune* God, however, is to exceed the limits of reason alone, for we cannot grasp God in himself but can only grasp God insofar as he is for us as moral beings (Book III).

Hegel

Georg W. F. Hegel (d. 1831), on the other hand, did posit the reality of the Trinity, but he grounded the reality of the Trinity on a purely philosophical basis. Central to his whole system (expressed most fully in his *Phenomenology of Spirit*) is the insight that all reality develops *dialectically*, moving through contradictions to a resolution thereof; *thesis* (initial knowledge), *antithesis* (contradiction), and *synthesis* (unification). The reality of God proceeds in the same way. The Absolute Spirit, which is God, posits its own opposite other, Matter, and resolves the difference in an eternal return to itself. The Father is Being-in-and-for-itself; the Son is the Other, the finite particularization of the universal; the Spirit is the singleness, the unity of the universal and the particular. The Trinity provides the paradigm for what occurs in all of reality, which moves inexorably through dialectical processes of universality and particularity, and of identity and distinction. Everything is moving finally to the Kingdom of the Spirit, where alone God becomes personal. (See *The Philosophy of Religion, Part III*.)

Once again, only a fuller historical, philosophical, and theological discussion can begin to do justice to the extraordinary impact which both Kant and Hegel have made upon, and continue to make upon, Christian thought, not to say secular thought—e.g., Marxism: Kant in the realms of ethics and fundamental theology, and Hegel in the realm of systematic theology. Indeed, the influence of Hegel upon much of present-day German theology, of both Catholic and Protestant varieties, cannot easily be overestimated. It is particularly strong in Rahner, Metz, Pannenberg, and Moltmann. The impact of Kant on the revision of our traditional notions of our knowledge of God in revelation and faith and of our apprehension of truth generally is also broadly ecumenical. There is no serious theologian working in the area of fundamental theology who has not been affected by the Kantian revolution. On the other hand, Kant's influence in moral theology or Christian ethics has tended to be restricted to Protestantism.

Schleiermacher

Friedrich Schleiermacher (d. 1834) carried forward the now traditional Protestant insistence on the inability of the human mind to grasp the reality of God—a position consistent, of course, with classical Protestantism's understanding of the relationship between nature and grace. Schleiermacher taught that faith is essentially our feeling of absolute dependence. If we find God at all, we find God in our consciousness. Since the Trinity does not emerge from an analysis of human consciousness, it cannot be regarded as a primary datum of Christian faith. (See his *The Christian Faith*, where the Trinity is relegated to an appendix.) It is perhaps fair to say that Schleiermacher is the principal forerunner of Liberal Protestantism of the nineteenth and early twentieth centuries. Together with Adolf von Harnack (d. 1930), who rejected the doctrine of the Trinity as an unacceptable Hellenization of the essential Christian message, he is one of the principal targets of the neo-orthodox revival initiated by Karl Barth around the time of the First World War. For Barth, the Trinity is utterly fundamental and central to God's revelation in Jesus Christ (see the "Prolegomena" of the *Church Dogmatics*).

Kierkegaard

Sören Kierkegaard (d. 1855) constructed a position at odds with both Hegel and Schleiermacher. Against Hegel, Kiekegaard argued that "an infinitely qualitative difference" separates us from God, that we are not in fact absorbed into the universal Spirit but retain our individual selfhood before God. Indeed, so strongly did Kierkegaard insist upon the importance of the individual's responsibility before God that he is generally regarded as the father of modern existentialism. For Kierkegaard God is utterly transcendent, without any need at all for us. On the contrary, it is we who need God if we are to become authentic persons. We are called to an interior conversion of the heart so that we become fixed entirely on the will of God. Against the liberalism represented by Schleiermacher, Kierkegaard argues that "the fundamental error of modern times. . . lies in the fact that the yawning abyss of quality between God and man has been removed. . . before God man is nothing (*Journals*, #712). Furthermore, Kierkegaard retains the doctrine of the Trinity as central to Christian faith. Kierkegaard's impact upon Karl Barth, especially in the latter's development of the notion of God as "wholly Other," is exceedingly profound. Through Barth, Kierkegaard would have a part in shaping the direction of neo-orthodox, neo-Reformation Protestant thought in the early and mid-twentieth century, with its emphasis on the transcendence of God and our personal relationship with God, and its corresponding caution regarding the sociopolitical dimensions of the Christian faith.

Feuerbach

Ludwig Feuerbach (d. 1872) regarded God as simply our projection of our own nature into the ethereal world beyond this one. God possesses all of the ideal attributes of humankind (see *The Essence of Christianity*, chapter 2). Feuerbach urged his readers to recognize what we had done and to reclaim our responsibility for the course of the world. Accordingly, he prepared the way not only for Karl Marx but, within the Christian community, for an excessively anthropological method of doing theology in which the study of God is really our own self-study. Within contemporary Catholic theology, Gregory Baum comes as close to that model as any other, without, however, lapsing straightaway into atheism or the complete denial of transcendence. In recent Protestant theology, the so-called "death-of-God" movement associated with Thomas J. J. Altizer and others even more clearly adopted Feuerbach's approach, with a good measure of Hegel and Nietzsche thrown in.

Nietzsche

Friedrich Nietzsche (d. 1900) attributed the development of the idea of God to primitive ancestor worship. As certain ancient tribes prevailed over others, their members credited their ancestors with their victories. While religious beliefs and practices have changed considerably since then, the feeling of owing something to God has continued among human beings. Behind this view, Nietzsche contended, is a will for self-torture. We attribute to God the opposite of the qualities which arouse guilt in ourselves. The presence of a holy God makes us feel sinful, and this tortures us. God also represents the best qualities of a nation. The God of dominant nations is powerful and pitiless. The Christian God, therefore, is despicable because to Christians goodness and mercy are the dominant divine attributes. Indeed, "The Christian concept of God . . . is one of the most corrupt concepts of God that has ever been attained on earth. . . . In God, nonentity is deified, and the will to nonentity is declared holy!" (*The Antichrist*, #18). Nietzsche, with his emphasis on the notion of the "superman," influenced not only the development of "death-of-God" theology in the 1960s but, more menancingly, the emergence of Nazism in the Germany of the 1930s and 1940s.

Vatican I

The First Vatican Council confronted these and other approaches to the question of God: materialism, rationalism, pantheism, and the like. In its *Dogmatic Constitution On the Catholic Faith*, the council taught that "there is one God, true and living, Creator and Lord of heaven and earth, mighty, eternal, immense, incomprehensible, infinite in His intellect and will and in all perfection. As He is one unique and spiritual substance, entirely simple and unchangeable, we must proclaim Him distinct from the world in existence and essence...ineffably exalted above all things that exist or can be conceived besides Him." All contrary positions are explicitly anathematized.

SECOND VATICAN COUNCIL (1962–1965) AND ITS ANTECEDENTS
Twentieth-Century Understandings of God

A complete survey of pre-Vatican II understandings of God within the Christian community would require a comprehensive outline of twentieth-century theology. John Macquarrie has attempted something like this in his *Twentieth-Century Religious Thought* (New York: Harper & Row, 1963), and John Cobb has produced a similar work, although more limited in scope, in *Living Options in Protestant Theology* (Philadelphia: Westminster Press, 1962). The reader already has the barest framework for such an outline in chapters 2 and 4 of this book: In the former chapter there is a descriptive listing of various kinds of contemporary theology, and in the latter chapter there are sketches of various contemporary understandings of human existence. What follows here is a brief survey of the various theological approaches insofar as they embody a particular understanding of God.

First, there are *liberal* and *neo-liberal* theology which tend to reduce the supernatural content of faith to its lowest common denominator. The emphasis in the divine/human relationship is always on the human, particularly in its social and political dimensions. A formal doctrine of the Trinity is marginal to the liberal schema. In this regard, liberal theology draws upon Schleiermacher (from within the Church) and upon Feuerbach and Nietzsche (from outside the Church). Liberalism in theology is primarily, although no longer exclusively, a Protestant phenomenon.

Secondly, there are *orthodox* and *neo-orthodox* theology. Both are also known as *confessional* theology. On the Catholic side, this theology stresses the otherness, the unchangeability, and the providential power of God manifested in and through Jesus Christ and the Holy Spirit. On the Protestant side, this theology stresses divine judgment and the wholly otherness of God. But given the historic emphases on justification-as-transformation in Catholicism and on justification-as-declaration in Protestantism, the otherness of God tends to be more strongly stressed in Protestantism than in Catholicism, while the sacramental availability of God in our ordinary everyday lives tends to be more strongly stressed in Catholicism than in Protestantism.

Thirdly, there is *radical* or *"death-of-God"* theology which, in the spirit of Feuerbach, Hegel, and Nietzsche, insisted that the transcendent God is dead, that transcendence itself has collapsed into total immanence, that what we call divine or supernatural is just another way of describing the human and the natural. This was a mid-1960s exaggeration of the liberal and neo-liberal reductionist understandings of God which have persisted throughout the twentieth century.

Fourthly, there is *secular* theology, another 1960s development, which, like liberal and neo-liberal theology, emphasized the this-worldly character of God and of Christian faith, but without setting aside the content of the Christian tradition. On the contrary, a strong insistence on the social and political dimensions of Christianity is portrayed as consistent with, even demanded by, the principles of the Old and New Testaments and of post-biblical Christian doctrine: God calls us to a life of responsibility in and for the world through the servant Christ ("man for others") and the reconciling Holy Spirit. Indeed, it is in experiencing the "gracious neighbor" that we experience the "gracious God" (John A.T. Robinson).

Fifthly, there is *liberation* theology which also bears a general resemblance to liberal and neo-liberal theology insofar as it stresses the social and political dimensions of the faith, but also resembles orthodox and neo-orthodox theology insofar as it stresses the biblical notion of God as judge and liberator from sin. The God of liberation theology (whether of the Latin American, black, or feminist kind) is a God whose primary, if not sole, passion is the freeing of the oppressed from the bondage of economic, racial, or sexist exploitation. Although rooted in pre-Vatican II insights, liberation theology is in large measure a post-conciliar phenomenon.

Sixthly, there is *political* theology, a more comprehensive category than liberation theology, in which God, and more specifically the Kingdom of God, is seen as the critical principle by which all human, social, and political realities are judged. God is the limit against which all of our notions of justice, humaneness, peace, love, and so forth are finally measured.

Seventhly, there is *existential* theology, which emphasizes the individual believer as the place where God's saving activity occurs in its most concentrated and even in its normative form. Consistent with the position outlined by Kierkegaard in the nineteenth century and subsequently developed by Tillich, Bultmann, and others in the twentieth century, existentialist theology understands God as the source of authentic human personhood. To be exposed to the Word of God is to be open to the principle of conversion and growth. God is not "a" being, but Being itself. God is, more precisely, "holy Being," i.e., Being which *lets be* (Macquarrie). Except for Macquarrie, a formal doctrinal understanding of the Trinity tends to be either obscured or less than central to contemporary existentialist theology.

Eighthly, there is *process* theology, which clearly owes much of its inspiration to the Hegelian understanding of reality but, more immediately, to such twentieth-century theologians and philosophers as Whitehead and Teilhard. God is always in a state of flux, moving forward, co-creating history with us. God is neither static nor fixed. God is a dipolar God, in process of becoming other than what God is now, a process which involves a dialectical relationship between all that is meant by "God" and all that is meant by "world." God is at once absolute (as the one whose *existence* depends on no other being) and relative (as the one whose *actuality* is relative to all other beings). Indeed, God alone is relative to all other beings. God alone affects and is affected by all others (Charles Hartshorne). History is moving inexorably toward the Omega Point, when the Kingdom of God will have been brought to perfection.

Ninthly, there is *Transcendental Thomism,* most notably represented by Karl Rahner, which understands God as *the* Transcendent, above, beyond, and over everything else. God is the one to whom all reality is oriented, by a principle which is itself interior to all of reality. That principle is God. God is the "supernatural existential" which makes possible the knowledge of, and the movement toward, the Absolute. In the completion of that movement, both individually and corporately, we find our human perfection. God, therefore, is not "a" Being separate from the human person, but is Being itself, at once permeating and transcending the person. Because God permeates as well as transcends us, there is no standpoint from which we can get a "look at" God objectively. God is so fully constitutive of our human existence that almost everything we say about God can be translated into a declaration about our own existence as well. This is not to reduce all God-talk to philosophy, but simply to highlight the intimate connection between theology and anthropology in Transcendental Thomism. God is present to history in Jesus Christ and in a special way in the Church, where the human community has become explicitly conscious of itself in its ultimate relationship with God. The similarities with the Hegelian scheme are apparent, but so, too, are the differences.

Tenthly, there are various combinations of the above, some of which possess a measure of internal consistency and coherence while others are arbitrarily or uncritically eclectic.

The Second Vatican Council

The council, it must be noted, did not set out to produce a full-scale theology of God. On the contrary, insofar as it developed a more or less systematic theology of anything, that reality was the Church, as we shall see in Part IV. The council's understanding of God has to be inferred from what it says about other questions: the salvific value of non-Christian religions, the nature of the Church and its mission in the world.

The council's overriding concern was for unity, not only the unity of the Church but of the whole human race. "For all people comprise a single community, and have a single origin, since God made the whole race of men dwell over the entire face of the earth (cf. Acts 17:26). One also is their final goal: God. His providence, His manifestations of goodness, and His saving designs extend to all men (cf. Wis. 8:1; Acts 14:17; Rom. 2:6-7; 1 Tim. 2:4) against the day when the elect will be united in that Holy City ablaze with the splendor of God, where the nations will walk in His light (cf. Apoc. 21:23 f.)" (*Declaration on the Relationship of the Church to Non-Christian Religions,* n. 1).

"The Church knows that only God...meets the deepest longings of the human heart, which is never fully satisfied by what this world has to offer," the *Pastoral Constitution on the Church in the Modern World* declares. Thus, "only God, who created man to His own image and ransomed him from sin, provides a fully adequate answer" to the various questions about human existence. "This He does through what He has revealed in Christ His Son, who became man. Whoever follows after Christ, the perfect man, becomes himself more of a man" (n. 41). The theology of God and the theology of human existence converge at the point of the theology of Christ.

What does most to reveal God's presence in the world is "the brotherly charity of the faithful who are united in spirit as they work together for the faith of the gospel and who prove themselves a sign of unity" (n. 21). This community of faith, the Church, is itself the product of trinitarian action. The Church is called forth by the Father to carry forward the work of the Son with the sanctifying power of the Holy Spirit *(Dogmatic Constitution of the Church,* nn. 2–4). "Thus, the Church shines forth as 'a people made one with the unity of the Father, the Son, and the Holy Spirit'" (n. 4). (The quotation is derived from Saints Cyprian, Augustine, and John of Damascus.)

The call to unity is theologically grounded on the mystery of the Trinity itself. There is "a certain likeness between the union of the divine Persons, and in the union of God's sons in truth and charity" (*Pastoral Constitution on the Church in the Modern World,* n. 24).

GOD AND HISTORY:
SYSTEMATIC REFLECTIONS
Providence

The question of Providence is exceedingly difficult because it is at once comprehensive and complicated. It is comprehensive because it sums up God's relationship to the world and to all of history. It is complicated because it raises the problem of the interaction between divine sovereignty and human freedom. The former can never satisfactorily be described, and the latter can never satisfactorily be explained. With the question of Providence, therefore, we come as close to the heart of the problem of God as we possibly can. And the closer we come, the more deafening the silence.

Providence, first of all, refers to God's "foresight." It has to do with the way God shapes and directs history. Providence is not an exclusively Christian concept, nor even an exclusively religious concept. There are many *secular notions* of "Providence." We find the term first used in the fifth century B.C. and especially in Stoic philosophy. There is a cosmic harmony in the universe insured by some non-personal divinity or divinized rationality. Leibniz invoked a similar notion of a preestablished rational harmony. The Enlightenment's concept of inevitable progress in history is a secular variant of the Christian understanding of Providence, and so, too, are the Hegelian notion of world-reason and the Marxist interpretation of the dialectical movement of history.

The term appears only in the later part of the *Old Testament*, and then under Hellenistic influences (Job 10:12; Wisdom 6:7; 14:3; 17:2). But more important than the term itself is the concept it represents. The Old Testament clearly portrays Yahweh as a powerful, wise, merciful, and caring God. Creation, the election of Israel, the Exodus—all of these and more are manifestations of God's abiding concern for the world and especially for the Chosen People. History is itself the arena of God's saving action (Psalms 9:2; 26:7; 40:6; 71:17; 72:18; Isaiah 9:5; 28:29; 29:14).

The *New Testament* also attests to a basic faith in God's loving regard for the world, but now it is linked explicitly with faith in Christ as the great sign of God's love and concern. Jesus admonishes his listeners for their inordinate anxiety about material needs. "Look at the birds in the sky....Learn a lesson from the way the wild flowers grow....Your heavenly Father knows all that you need" (Matthew 6:26-34; see also 10:29-31). A notion of Providence is also embodied in the New Testament's understanding of *salvation history*. God has a "set purpose and plan," and it has been manifested in the death and resurrection of Christ (Acts of the Apostles 2:22-24). Indeed, even the villains of the piece are seen as instruments of the divine intervention: "They have brought about the very things which in your powerful providence you planned long ago" (Acts of the Apostles 4:28). The salvation-history perspective is more fully developed in Ephesians 1:3-14, where Christ is identified as the center-piece of the divine plan to "bring all things in the heavens and on earth into one under Christ's headship." We were chosen in him by God "who administers everything according to his will and counsel." And all of this has been "sealed with the Holy Spirit" who is "the pledge of our inheritance, the first payment against the full redemption of a people God has made his own, to praise his glory."

The conviction of faith in a provident God has been held consistently within the Church from the beginning. It is central, of course, to Irenaeus' theology of history (e.g., *Against Heresies*, chapter 25), to Augustine's polemic against the Pelagians, who insisted too strongly on the power of unaided human freedom, and to Thomas Aquinas' "sacred doctrine" about God (*Summa Theologica*, I, q. 22). It is as well the straightforward teaching of the First Vatican Council's *Dogmatic Constitution on the Catholic Faith* (chapter 1): "God protects and governs by his Providence all things which he has made...." Finally, the Second Vatican Council urges us to discern in the "signs of the times" evidence of "God's presence and purpose" (*Pastoral Constitution on the Church in the Modern World*, n. 11).

Christian *belief* in the reality of Providence is not in doubt. Christian *understanding* of Providence is another matter entirely. Once again, we are confronted with the relationship of nature and grace (to which we referred in some detail in the preceding Part of the book). Some Catholic solutions have tended to overemphasize divine power at the apparent expense of human responsibility and freedom. We become mere actors in a play written wholly by God, with an ending already precisely determined regardless of our flubbing our lines and missing our cues. We need not trouble ourselves, therefore, about this world's injustices. God will take care of everything in the end. At the other extreme, some solutions have tried so hard to uphold the enduring value of human effort that God becomes little more than a play's producer, backing it with his money and influence but depending utterly upon the ability of the actors for its eventual success. Thus, if we do not overcome injustice by our political efforts, it will simply swallow us up in the end. And still others have attempted a compromise position, assigning divine and human activity on a fifty-fifty basis (we are completely free in our actions, but God must simultaneously *concur* with our free decisions and invest them with efficacy).

The later medieval, post-Tridentine theological debates *de auxiliis* (concerning helps) were not so much about the broad issue of Providence as about the narrower, although related, question of *actual grace*. They were essentially fruitless controversies. The Church never took an official stand on behalf of either party, the Banezians or the Molinists, because both took for granted that every act of free consent was itself from God's grace (anything less than that would have been Pelagian, and thus unorthodox).

Karl Rahner's view is representative of the Catholic theological and doctrinal tradition as it is understood today: We begin from where we are. We profess a faith and practice a religion which comprises prayer for God's intervention, miracles, an understanding of history as saving history, persons invested with authority from on high, an inspired book which comes from God, ritual acts which mediate the presence of God, and so forth. On the other hand, our theological starting point seems to say that "God is everywhere insofar as he grounds everything, and he is nowhere insofar as everything that is grounded is created, and everything which appears in this way within the world of our experience is different from God, separated by an absolute chasm between God and what is not God" (*Foundations of Christian Faith*, p. 82).

Rahner follows the Thomistic principle that God works through secondary causes; i.e., God is the ultimate cause, but not just one cause among many. God-as-cause is in the world as a totality, but not in any particular things within the world. That is, God does not "intervene" in the world in the sense that God acts now here and now there; now in this event, now in that; now in this person, now in that. God "intervenes" in the sense that *God is always there.* The world is fundamentally and radically open to God. "Consequently, every real intervention of God in his world, although it is free and cannot be deduced, is always only the becoming historical and becoming concrete of that 'intervention' in which God as the transcendental ground of the world has from the outset embedded himself in this world as its self-communicating ground" (p. 87).

And so we come back to the fundamental problem for the Christian understanding of God: How can God be God, i.e., totally other, and at the same time in the world, e.g., in Christ, in the Church, in the sacraments? We can exaggerate the first at the expense of the second, and vice versa. With the hope of avoiding both extremes, Rahner offers an example. We get a "good idea." It seems to come "out of the blue." We can interpret it in a purely physiological and psychological way and conclude that it is not in any sense an intervention of God. Or we can experience ourselves as a subject radically open to God (i.e., as a "transcendental subject"). At the moment we accept that experience, the "good idea" becomes a part of that total network of historical and worldly relationships whose meaning and unity are given by God. In that sense, the "good idea" is an "inspiration" from God.

Rahner writes: "Of course it could be objected against this that in this way everything can be regarded as a special providence, as an intervention of God, presupposing only that I accept the concrete constellation of my life and of the world in such a way that it becomes a positive, salvific concretization of my transcendental relationship to God in freedom. But against this objection we can simply ask the counter-question: Why, then, may this not be the case?" (p. 89). He continues: "Because the subject's response in freedom is itself really and truly for the subject himself something given to him, without it losing thereby the character of the subject's own responsible and accountable action, a good decision along with everything which it presupposes as its mediation correctly has the character of an intervention of God, even though this takes place in and through human freedom, and hence can be explained functionally to the degree that the history of freedom can be explained, namely, insofar as it is based on elements objectified in time and space" (*ibid.*).

There is never, therefore, a salvific act of God on our behalf which is not also and always a salvific act of our own. Our actions are truly free, and they are at the same time grounded in the grace or presence of God. We can never even begin to have anything to do with God or to approach God without already being moved by God's grace. On the other hand, this movement toward salvation never takes place without our involvement and our freedom.

To be sure, we have not solved the problem of nature and grace, of divine sovereignty and human freedom, or of Providence as such. But we have at least identified the problem as it is, and taken note of the limits within which all attempted solutions must be developed. No explanation of Providence satisfies the biblical, theological, and doctrinal traditions of the Church if it takes history out of God's hands (Pelagianism, Deism, e.g.). And no explanation suffices which takes history out of human hands (extreme Augustinianism and Calvinism). God is present to every person and to history itself as an inner principle which makes forward movement possible without sacrifice of freedom. Precisely *how* that is done, we do not know. We can, like Rahner and others, propose answers based on specific philosophical premises. But these are always explanations "after the fact," so to speak. And that, after all, is what theology is: faith seeking understanding. Theology does not produce the given, but reflects upon it. Theology does not make "possible" the given, but reflects on the terms of its "possibility." Theology, in the end, is not faith.

Miracles

Few theological questions are treated so unsatisfactorily as the question of miracles. Discussion moves from one extreme to the other: from the extreme right, where miracles are simply accepted in a fundamentalistic sense (they happened in exactly the way they are described in the Bible or by the people in post-biblical times—e.g., the appearances of the Blessed Virgin Mary at Lourdes, France), to the extreme left, where miracles are rejected in principle because they are presumed to be disruptions of the inflexible laws of nature and of physics. In between there are also other sorts of inadequate explanations. We are assured that the *fact* of miracles is not important, only their significance. Or we are reminded, following the Rahnerian approach outlined above, that God is already everywhere as the principle of free action and that, therefore, whatever happens, happens through the grace of God; in that sense everything is a miracle.

All of these explanations fail because they cannot be reconciled with certain clear principles which emerge from the New Testament:

Miracles were as important to the ministry of Jesus as his preaching. They express the saving *power* of God shown in Jesus' healing, feeding the hungry, curing the sick, even raising the dead. Indeed, when the disciples of John the Baptist came out to the desert to ask Jesus if he was the One who was promised, Jesus told them to go back and tell John what they had seen and heard: "The blind recover their sight, cripples walk, lepers are cured, the deaf hear, dead men are raised to life, and the poor have the good news preached to them" (Luke 7:22).

Miracles are linked with faith. "If I do not perform my Father's works," Jesus said, "put no faith in me" (John 10:37; see also 15:24). On the other hand, it is possible to be present at the performance of a miracle and not see it as a miracle at all (notice, e.g., the inability or refusal of many to believe in Jesus even after the multiplication of the loaves and fishes—John 6:26). Indeed, it happened that Jesus could not work miracles in his home country "so much did their lack of faith distress him" (Mark 6:5). Instead he devoted himself to teaching.

The miracle stories are meant to evoke faith, but not all of the stories are on the same plane. The fundamentalist forgets that the biblical accounts are not eyewitness reports, nor scientifically tested documentation, nor historical, medical, or psychological records. They are rather unsophisticated popular narratives, entirely at the service of the proclamation of the Lordship of Jesus. Recent biblical scholarship discloses that there are many different levels at work in the various accounts: Some are patterned after Old Testament models; others follow the narrative styles common to Jewish and Hellenistic stories; others are simply collected accounts (redactional summaries) of the evangelists which give the impression of a continuous and widespread miracle-working activity on the part of Jesus.

But certain events apparently did take place, and they were taken, by friend and foe alike, as marvelous in their own right. The sick were cured, for example. Jesus' enemies did not challenge the fact of the cure but the propriety of curing on the Sabbath.

In the accounts of several of the miracles, too many details are given which have too little interest to have been invented and yet which are so human and true to life that they suggest the presence of an eyewitness. The cure of the possessed boy is a case in point (Mark 9:14-29).

We are left, in the end, with more questions than answers. Did Jesus really walk on water to calm the waves during a sudden storm, or was the story constructed after the fact as a sign that God hears our prayers for help in times of distress? Were those "possessed by the devil" simply suffering from temporary mental illness, or did the impact of Jesus' kindly personality perhaps effect a momentary remission of a more serious emotional problem? Did the story of the coin in the fish's mouth simply answer Jesus' request to catch a fish in order to pay the temple tax? Did other stories, such as the raising of Jairus' daughter from the dead, simply anticipate the resurrection of Christ in order to present Jesus as the Lord of life and death (keeping in mind, all the while, that when the Gospels were written, they were removed from the historical Jesus by a few decades)?

At the very least, something significant and impressive occurred in the life and ministry of Jesus, over and above his preaching and teaching. He had an impact upon people—the sick, the troubled, the bereaved—in a way that clearly set him apart from his contemporaries. Indeed, he himself pointed to his good works as moments in which the power of God operated in him and through him.

That Jesus performed miracles as signs of revelation is certainly the belief of the New Testament Church and of the official

Church of the post-biblical period. The First Vatican Council teaches this in its *Dogmatic Constitution on the Catholic Faith* (chapter 3), and the Second Vatican Council acknowledges their existence at least in passing in its *Dogmatic Constitution on the Church*: "The miracles of Jesus also confirm that the kingdom has already arrived on earth..." (n. 5).

Just *what* those miracles were, from a scientific, empirically verifiable, objective point of view (i.e., apart from faith), is difficult to say. We can at least exclude the too-simple solutions of the extreme left and the extreme right, and reject the practical avoidance of the problem in some of modern theology.

Miracles are manifestations of the power of God and as such are consistent with divine Providence. They were central to Jesus' ministry. They enter into the formation of our own faith. Beyond that, many questions remain open.

Evil

We move from a very difficult problem to a nearly impossible one: *the mystery of evil*. Again, simple answers abound. At the extreme left, God is portrayed as not involved at all in evil because God is not much involved in good either. At the extreme right, God is directly and immediately implicated in evil. God deliberately, almost callously, inflicts suffering and pain upon us in order to teach us a lesson or gain some unknown greater good. And in the middle, we have the usual traditional explanations that God does not cause evil; God only permits it. Or that evil is nothing in itself; it is simply the absence of good. For many, of course, the very existence of evil (natural disasters, the terminal illness of a young child, the sudden death of a father or a mother, a brutal murder, an act of terrorism, Auschwitz) is the single most persuasive argument *against* the existence of God, or at least against the existence of the God of Christianity. They cannot readily explain, on the other hand, how there can also be so much goodness and heroic charity in a world *without God*.

In the preceding discussion, we noted that it is easier to accept the meaning of miracles than it is to accept the fact of their existence. In the case of evil, just the reverse is true: It is easier to accept the fact of evil than it is to understand its meaning.

Evil, like a miracle, is *power*. But unlike a miracle, it is a power against life, not for it. So intense and so focused may this power be that it can be personified as *Satan* (from the Hebrew word *sātān*, which means "adversary"). The New Testament carried over the general Jewish teaching about evil spirits and the devil. He is the evil one (Matthew 13:19), the enemy (Luke 10:19), the father of lies (John 8:44), etc. He is especially opposed to Jesus Christ, and their enmity reaches a fever pitch in the passion (Luke 22:3,31; John 13:27; 1 Corinthians 2:8), but therein the devil is also finally defeated (1 Corinthians 2:8; John 12:31; Revelation 12:7-12). This opposition continues, however, in the history of the Church until it is overcome once and for all at the end (Revelation 20:8,10).

Again, *that* there is evil in the world is obvious. That such evil is often collective and at the same time very personalized is also evident. *What* this evil is in its core is not so clear. To the extent that the Church has addressed itself officially to the question, the official magisterium has affirmed the existence of the devil and of evil spirits, has acknowledged their negative effect on the course of history, and has insisted that they, like all of creation (material and spiritual), come under the sovereignty of God. Contrary to the impression one might gain from some recent novels and films, evil spirits do not control us to the point of suppressing human freedom and responsibility (see, for example, the Council of Trent's *Decree on Original Sin*).

If it is clear *that* evil exists, it is also clear that God wars against it and that we are called to participate with God in the struggle against evil in every form: social injustice, oppression, infidelity, dishonesty, e.g. "Caught in this conflict, man is obliged to wrestle constantly if he is to cling to what is good" (Second Vatican Council, *Pastoral Constitution on the Church in the Modern World*, n. 37). Indeed, God sent his Son to save us from "the power of darkness and of Satan" (*Decree on the Church's Missionary Activity*, n. 3).

The fact of evil is undeniable, but why is there evil at all? If it is any comfort, the reader should be assured that he or she has not missed the definitive explanation somewhere along the line. None of the greatest minds of human history, whether Christian or not, has devised a compelling answer. Nor are we about to do so here, succeeding where all others have failed. We can only identify some of the principal options we have in response to evil, and especially to innocent suffering, and then try to decide which is the most intelligent and which conforms best to Christian faith.

First, we can rebel and revolt, shaking an angry fist if not at the real God then at some conventional idea of God. This is the way of Ivan Karamazov in Dostoevsky's *The Brothers Karamazov* and of Albert Camus in his *Rebel*. Secondly, we can try to bear up stoically, tight-lipped, avoiding the question "Why?" We simply accept what we can neither understand nor change. Or, thirdly, we can stand with *Job*, placing our complete trust in God even in the face of the incomprehensible, and with *Jesus*, from whom we have received the "good news" that God wishes to deliver us from all evil, and indeed that suffering itself can be as redemptive for us individually as it was for all humankind in the passion and death of Christ.

But even Jesus did not *explain* suffering. He endured it, an innocent Lamb in the sight of God (1 Peter 1:19). But in the resurrection his suffering and death acquired meaning beyond themselves. Such meaning is not always, nor even often, apparent. Christ teaches us that suffering *can* have a meaning, or can *acquire* a meaning. We can learn from it. We can be ennobled by it. We can grow through it. For the God who encounters us in suffering is a God who knows suffering from the inside, as it were, in Jesus Christ. God is literally a *sympathetic* ("suffering with") God. The reality of evil and suffering notwithstanding, God is a God of mercy, of forgiveness, of compassion for all. Furthermore, God has promised the Kingdom to those of us who remain steadfast and faithful even in the midst of evil and suffering, a Kingdom where "he shall wipe away every tear from [our] eyes, and there shall be no more death or mourning, crying out or pain, for the former world has passed away" (Revelation 21:4).

In the end, the problem of evil and of innocent suffering reveals as well as conceals the God of love. For if it were not for our faith in God as a God of justice and mercy, of love and peace, of truth and loyalty, we would not recognize the reality of evil in all its depths; nor, what is more important, would we be impelled to do something about it, risking even our lives for the good of others. (Indeed, many who deny God do evil and call it good.) Corruption in government, for example, would not bother us very much, and certainly we would do very little about it, if we did not have at the same time a highly refined sense of moral and political idealism. For some, corruption mocks and negates the ideals (the reaction of the cynic). For others, corruption makes the ideals even more urgently attractive and worthwhile.

But the fact of evil and of innocent suffering remains. We can do nothing about evil in general (i.e., we cannot completely elimi-nate it from the world) and relatively little about it in the concrete (as our everyday experience attests). But what *is* under our control is the manner in which we respond to what is so frequently inevi-table. We are *free*, and our freedom is, in turn, a condition which makes some forms of evil possible. Will our free response be one of rebellion and passivity, or will it be a response of trust and renewed growth? Apart from faith in God, the problem of evil (which presumably *destroys* faith in God!) is unresolvable. And apart from faith in Christ and in the redemptive value of his passion and death, evil and innocent suffering can have no positive meaning at all.

The Church insists on the meaning of miracles, and some-times stammers a bit regarding their factuality. In the case of evil, however, the Church joins the rest of humankind in acknowledg-ing evil's wretched factuality, but it shares with others the agony of interpretation. Nevertheless, it does not stammer here. The Church's faith and trust are as forthright as Job's, built as they are upon the rock of Christ, and strengthened as they are by the power of the Holy Spirit.

Prayer

Can we change the course of events through prayer? Can we alter God's will and so receive some blessing that otherwise might pass us by? Can we fend off some evil occurrence by specifically implor-ing God to save us from it?

The problem of prayer is difficult because it is a component of the difficult problems of Providence and of evil. Prayer has to do with the interaction between divine sovereignty and human freedom. Just as we can distort the meaning of Providence by exaggerating the one over the other, so we can distort the meaning of prayer by seeing it, on the one hand, as a method of manipulating the mind and heart of God, or, on the other hand, as a completely useless activity no more sublime or mysterious than autosuggestion or the power of positive thinking.

In accord with the theological position we have already taken, prayer is a conscious, deliberate coming to terms with our actual situation before God. When we explicitly advert to that relationship, we are praying. Every action we perform as a way of expressing our sense of that relationship with God is a prayer. Every act whereby we sacrifice our own personal interests for a higher purpose because of our explicit faith in God is a prayer. Prayer is a *response* to, not an initiation of dialogue with, God. It is an act by which we accept ourselves as subjects radically open to the Transcendent, Who is God. Prayer is, therefore, always an act of faith and of hope, which is fulfilled in our surrender to the love of God.

In prayers of *praise* and *thanksgiving*, we give more explicit and deliberate form to our sense of the majesty and sovereignty of God and of our own place within the total scheme of reality. In prayers of *contrition*, we acknowledge our failure to respect this fundamental relationship with God and deliberately open ourselves anew to God's abiding presence within us, a presence which makes it possible for us to become someone other than we are, someone better than we are. In prayers of *petition*, we explicitly come to terms with our needs and those of other people. We make ourselves ever more sensitive to our obligations to do whatever is possible to fulfill those needs, whether for ourselves or for others. And insofar as those prayers of petition are public (as in the Eucharist), we put other members of the community on notice and draw them into the process of identifying and meeting needs, and they, in turn, enlarge our own horizons and make us more fully aware of the plight of others besides ourselves and our loved ones.

Prayer, in other words, does not effect a change in God but in ourselves. To that extent, prayer affects the course of history indirectly rather than directly.

SPECIAL QUESTIONS: PERSONHOOD AND FATHERHOOD OF GOD
God As Person

Is God "a person"? We are not asking here the question of the Trinity, whether there are three Persons in the one Godhead. We raise instead the question whether God is a separate Being among beings. Putting the question that way, the answer is "Of course not. God is not *a* person because God is not any one thing or being." But if the noun *person* is taken analogically, the answer has to be different. Does the reality we name "God" have qualities which we also attribute to persons? Yes, insofar as we understand persons as centers of intelligence, love, compassion, graciousness, fidelity, and the like. What we mean by the noun *God* certainly must comprehend such qualities as these. In other words, it is better to attribute "personality" to God than to deny it entirely and to look upon God as some impersonal, unconscious cosmic law. And yet the attribution is always analogical; i.e., God is *like* a person, but God is also very much *unlike* a person. In the end, the revelation of God in the person of Jesus Christ must tip the balance in favor of attributing personality to God than of denying it.

God As Father

If Jesus were still with us in his fleshly, historical existence today, would he be speaking of his relationship to God as one of Son and Father and of our relationship to God as one of children and Father? Or would the raising of our consciousness about sexuality and the oppressive character of sexist language have also affected Jesus' preaching and teaching? This is an entirely speculative question, of course, but it would seem reasonable to suppose that Jesus would have modified substantially his references to God. During his own life-time, Jesus mingled freely with women and emphasized their fundamental human equality before God.

Indeed, even the most vigorous exponents of a feminist point of view exempt Jesus himself from their standard criticisms of institutional religion and of Christianity in particular.

But the facts are that Jesus did live at a certain time, in a certain place, among certain people, within a certain social, cultural, economic, and political context. He was at once a product of, and a prophet to, his own age. But having granted the principle that Jesus' references to the Fatherhood of God are historically conditioned, we must nonetheless come to terms with the transhistorical meaning of those references. Even if Jesus had spoken of God as our Mother, he would still have had the same essential message to communicate about God. What is that message implied in the Fatherhood of God?

God is a loving and caring God (Matthew 6:5-8, 26-34; 7:11; 10:29-31; 18:14; Luke 11:13). God's love must inspire us to love even our enemies (Matthew 5:48). God is likewise a forgiving God, even a model of forgiveness (Matthew 6:14-15; 18:35; Mark 11:25). Nowhere is this more movingly expressed than in the parable of the prodigal son, also known as the parable of the forgiving father (Luke 15:11-32).

Furthermore, Jesus' references to his own relationship with his Father in heaven simply underscore the intimacy of Jesus with God (whether God is spoken of as Father or as Mother, as Husband or Wife, as Son or as Daughter). Jesus' will and God's are one (Matthew 26:39-43; Mark 14:35-39; Luke 22:41-42; 23:34,46). God is the source of Jesus' power and authority (John 1:14,18; 16:15). To know Jesus is to know God (John 14:7-9) because Jesus and God are one (John 10:30). Jesus is in God, and God is in Jesus (John 10:38; 14:10). Whatever Jesus teaches, he has learned from God (John 8:28-38). Whatever Jesus does, he does as the work of God (John 10:32; 14:10). No one comes to God except through Jesus (John 14:6), but God is greater than the historical Jesus (John 14:28). Jesus sends his disciples forth with the same fullness of power with which he was sent (John 20:21).

In each of the preceding texts it is *the Father* and not the more generic noun *God* that is used. But the fact that we can so easily substitute *God* for *Father* suggests that it is not the Fatherhood of God that is important to Jesus but the Godhood of the Father.

SUMMARY

1.   The problem of God is, as we have pointed out before, the other side of the problem of human existence. This chapter, therefore, must be correlated with chapter 5, which outlines a Christian understanding of human existence consistent with Catholicism's perception of the fundamental relationship of nature and grace.

2.   Although Christians are no less conditioned in their understanding of God by history and by factors of various sorts (economic, political, cultural, social, e.g.), it is clear nonetheless that there is a *distinctively Christian conviction about God*, namely, that God has become incarnate in Jesus of Nazareth, and that God is triune. God is Father, Son, and Holy Spirit; i.e., God is creator of all that is, is intimately identified with all that is, and is the principle of life and unity of all that is.

3.   But this distinctively Christian understanding of God raises a major problem: If God is one, how is it that Jesus is also invested with divinity, and how is it, further, that God is also portrayed as triune? These are the questions which largely shaped the history of Christian theology in the first four or five centuries.

4.   Because of the undeniably intimate religious link between Judaism and Christianity, the Christian understanding of God has its roots in the *Old Testament*, where God (Yahweh) is a living God, i.e., is present and active in the history of Israel, is the Lord of all humankind, the giver of all life. One lives by heeding Yahweh's word.

5.   The *New Testament* identifies Jesus with God (especially the Prologue of John's Gospel). All of the saving attributes of the God of the Old Testament are actualized anew in Christ. God pardons and reconciles through Christ. God continues to bestow life through Christ. And God bestows the Spirit through Christ.

6.   Over against pagan polytheism, the earliest *Apostolic Fathers and apologists* stressed the doctrine of the one God, creator and sustainer of all things.

7.   In the *third century*, emphasis shifted from the oneness of God to the triune pluralism of God, when the Church could no longer avoid the difficult questions posed by the apparent discrepancy between its uncompromising monotheism, on the one hand, and the clear testimony of Sacred Scripture and of its liturgical and prayer life that God is Father, Son, and Holy Spirit.

8.   This fundamental confession of faith in the Trinity did not first emerge from philosophical speculation about the inner life of God (the

so-called "immanent Trinity") but from a response to the activity of God in the world (the so-called "economic Trinity").

9. One of the earliest attempts at a solution to the problem of the-one-and-the-three proved unorthodox, namely, the *Arian* solution, which made Christ something more than a man but less than God the Almighty (*Pantokrator*). The implications were serious: If Christ is a creature like us, he has no special standing before God, and we are still in our sins.

10. The *Council of Nicea* (325) gave the definitive answer to Arius. The Son does not "emanate" from the Father's will, as a creature. The Son is "begotten, not made." He is "of the same substance" (*homoousios*) as the Father. For the first time, the Church moved officially from biblical to speculative categories to define its faith.

11. This transition did not occur without opposition. The Eusebians (followers of Eusebius of Caesarea) preferred to say no more than what Scripture seemed to be saying, namely, that the Son is "like" (*homoiousios*) the Father. Through the efforts of Athanasius and Hilary of Poitiers, the *homoousion* and *homoiousion* parties were reconciled. The agreement was sealed at the *Council of Alexandria* (362), from which emerged a new orthodox formula: "one substance, three Persons."

12. Attention shifted in the *fourth century* to the question of the Holy Spirit's relation to the Father and the Son. It was the so-called *Cappadocian* theologians (Basil, Gregory of Nyssa, and Gregory of Nazianzus) who established the coequal divinity of the Spirit with the Father and the Son, without prejudice to the oneness of substance in the Godhead.

13. By the end of the fourth century the Church was in a position to synthesize and officially express its newly systematized trinitarian faith in creedal form. The *First Council of Constantinople* (381) endorsed the so-called *Nicaeo-Constantinopolitan Creed*, which is recited each week in the Catholic Eucharist.

14. *Augustine* approached the mystery of the Trinity from a different starting point. Instead of beginning with the saving activity of the three Persons in salvation history (as the Greek Fathers did) and working back to the unity of the Godhead, Augustine began with the one divine nature and tried to understand how the three Persons share in that nature without dividing it. Threeness in God is not rooted in threeness of substance (essence, being) but in threeness of *relations*: of begetting, of being begotten, and of proceeding. Augustine employed analogies drawn from human consciousness to explain this inner life of the Trinity (remembering, understanding, loving), and this is perhaps his most original contribution to trinitarian theology. He also anticipated the teaching

of the Council of Florence in the Middle Ages that everything in God is one except what is differentiated by the opposition of relations; i.e., the Father and the Son are one God, except insofar as the Father begets and the Son is begotten, and so on.

15. *Anselm*, most famous for his ontological argument for the existence of God (God is an idea than which nothing greater can be thought), carried forward the Augustinian principle that God is absolutely one except for the opposition of relations between and among the three Persons. This, in turn, provided the theological basis for the principle of the mutual indwelling of the three divine Persons: The Father is always in the Son and the Holy Spirit; the Son is always in the Father and the Spirit; and the Spirit is always in the Father and the Son.

16. The *Fourth Lateran Council* (1215) repudiated *Albigensianism*, one of the most dangerous errors ever to attack the Church because of its rejection of the intrinsic goodness of created matter. The council taught that God is the author of both matter and spirit, and that Christ is fully God, with a human as well as a divine nature. The council also produced a doctrinal formulation on the Trinity which became the basis of most of Scholastic theology.

17. *Thomas Aquinas* insisted on the identity of essence and existence in God (God's essence is "to be") and on the participation of the created order in the Being of God, Who is the First Cause of all that is. Insofar as God ordains all things toward their goal, God is a provident God. And insofar as there is only one goal for all reality—created and recreated alike—the order of nature and the order of grace are radically one. Aquinas, too, carried forward the Augustinian approach to the mystery of the Trinity, employing similar psychological explanations of the relations between and among the three Persons.

18. The *Second Council of Lyons* (1274) and the *Council of Florence* (1438–1440) both were concerned with the schism between East and West, and insofar as the split was traceable to the divergent ways in which East and West interpreted the procession of the Holy Spirit in the Trinity, both councils helped clarify the Church's trinitarian faith. *Lyons* reflected the Latin approach in stressing the procession of the Spirit from the Father *and* the Son (*Filioque*). *Florence* reaffirmed the Latin approach, but allowed also for the Greek approach, namely, that the Holy Spirit proceeds from the Father *through* the Son (*per Filium*). For the Greeks the *Filioque* implied a double principle in God; for the Latins the *per Filium* implied a subordination of Son to Father. Neither side intended what the other side thought was implied, and much of the controversy was, in fact, unnecessary.

19.   The *Council of Florence* also enshrined the principle, to which reference has already been made, that *in God all things are one except what is differentiated by the opposition of relations between and among the Persons.*

20.   Insofar as the *Council of Trent* (1545–1563) addressed itself directly to the problem of God, it did so in reaction against the insistence of the major Reformers (*Luther* and *Calvin* in particular) that God deliberately and explicitly excludes some people from salvation (predestination to reprobation, to use the technical term). The Catholic tradition, articulated at Trent, argues that God not only makes a *declaration* of our worthiness for salvation but actually *transforms* us from within by the indwelling of the Holy Spirit and offers this transformation to every person, without exception. Only a free act of the will on our part can negate God's universal salvific will.

21.   The Christian understanding of God tended to zig-zag in the post-Reformation period between Trent and Vatican I (1869–1870). *Blaise Pascal* gave a strongly spiritual or ascetical cast to the theology of God in the seventeenth century, but by the next century serious challenges against traditional theology were mounted by such Protestant philosophers as *Kant, Hegel, Feuerbach*, and *Nietzsche*. The first two proposed new ways of understanding the reality of God (the former, as Supreme Lawgiver; the latter, as historical Process); the other two in effect denied the reality of God altogether. The influence of all four, but especially of Kant and Hegel, on subsequent Christian theology is undeniably strong. Meanwhile, Protestant theologians were also introducing new modes of understanding God. *Schleiermacher*, the forerunner of Liberal Protestantism of the late nineteenth and early twentieth centuries, devalued the doctrine of the Trinity and focused instead on our feeling of absolute dependence on the God of our consciousness. *Kierkegaard*, who anticipated the Barthian neo-orthodox, neo-Reformation reaction of the First World War period, insisted on the "infinitely qualitative difference" between God and ourselves and underlined the individual character of our relationship with God.

22.   The *First Vatican Council* (1869–1870) rejected some of these positions (rationalism, pantheism, and the like), insisting on the uniqueness and the difference of God over against the world.

23.   The *Second Vatican Council* (1962–1965) taught that God is the origin of all that is; therefore, the human race is called to unity. God also meets our deepest human longings, if only we open ourselves to the divine presence, especially in Christ. The most effective sign of God's presence among us is our fellowship with one another. The Church is

called to be a sacrament of God in the world, a sign of the same unity which is to be found in the Trinity.

24.   *Contemporary Christian understandings of God* are many and varied. Some emphasize the divine side of the God/human relationship; others emphasize the human side. The latter propose more transcendental understandings of God (God as "wholly other"); the former propose more immanentist understandings of God (God is to be met in the needs of the world).

25.   *Transcendental Thomism*, which comes closest to the perspective of this book, understands God as *the* Transcendent—above, beyond, and over everything else—who is at the same time within everything as the principle of life and movement (God as the "supernatural existential"). God is present to history in a particular way in Jesus Christ and in the Church. In the Church the human community has become explicitly conscious of itself in its ultimate relationship with God through Christ and the Holy Spirit.

26.   *Providence* is, literally, God's "foresight" in relation to the created order and to history. Both Old and New Testaments present God as a provident, caring, concerned, powerful God. History is God's history as well as ours. It is salvation history. God's plan and design is centered on Christ, and the sending of the Holy Spirit is the "first payment" against the full redemption offered in Christ.

27.   *Belief* in Providence has been consistent throughout the entire post-biblical history of the Church, but there have been different *understandings* of that belief, some stressing the divine power at the apparent expense of human freedom, and vice versa.

28.   Transcendental Thomism, represented by Karl Rahner, notes with Thomas Aquinas that God works through *secondary causes*. God does not "intervene" in the world in the sense that God interrupts and interferes with the normal course of human events. God "intervenes" in the sense that God is there from the beginning and that the world is radically open to the presence of God from its beginning. Our actions remain completely free, but they are at the same time grounded in the grace or presence of God. Precisely how this is the case we do not know, but we can exclude clearly unsatisfactory solutions which diminish the sovereignty of God or human freedom. We are left, then, with attempted explanations based on specific philosophical premises, such as those identified with Transcendental Thomism.

29.   *Miracles* pose yet another difficult problem, a variation really on the question of Providence. We can come to some understanding of what miracles might mean and what they might signify, but we find it far

more difficult to know what, if anything, actually happened. What is clear, however, is that: (1) miracles were important to the ministry of Jesus; (2) they were challenges to faith; (3) they vary considerably in the way they are "reported" in the New Testament; (4) the factuality of some of them was not challenged, even by the enemies of Jesus; and (5) some "reports" of miracles are too detailed and too true to life simply to be dismissed.

30.   *That* Jesus performed miracles is certainly the belief of the New Testament and of the post-biblical Church. Just *what* those miracles were from an objective point of view is difficult to say. We exclude at once, however, two extreme explanations: the one which rejects miracles of any kind as a matter of principle, and the other which accepts the reality of miracles in an uncritical, fundamentalistic way. Miracles, in the end, are manifestations of the presence and power of God and are consistent with the doctrine of Providence. Beyond that, many questions remain open.

31.   *Evil*, like a miracle, is power. But unlike a miracle, evil is a power against life, not for it. Sometimes evil is so intense that it can be personalized. The word *Satan* is derived from the Hebrew word which means "adversary." There is a special enmity between Satan and Christ, but Satan is definitively vanquished in the passion and death of Jesus; the triumph of Christ over evil will be made manifest finally and perfectly when the Kingdom of God appears in all its fulness.

32.   The problem of evil is the reverse of the problem of miracles. We have a problem with the factuality of miracles, but not at all with the factuality of evil. We find it relatively easy to offer explanations of the meaning of miracles, but we find it very difficult indeed to find meaning in evil.

33.   Human response to evil may take three forms: (1) rebellion, (2) resignation, or (3) trust and hope. The third course is that of *Job* in the Old Testament and, of course, of *Jesus Christ* in the New Testament. For the Christian, suffering can have meaning, or at least can acquire meaning. Because of Christ, suffering can be redemptive, even enriching. Furthermore, in Christ God knows what it is to suffer. God is literally a sympathetic ("suffering with") God. God wars against evil and seeks our collaboration in the struggle against the powers of darkness.

34.   Indeed, if it were not for our faith in a loving God, the existence of evil would not be so much of a problem. We might not even acknowledge evil as evil (and, in fact, many who do not believe in God do evil and call it good).

35.   *Prayer* is a conscious, deliberate acknowledgment of, and coming to terms with, our actual situation before God. Through prayer we accept our relationship with God and become more fully aware of the implications of that relationship. Our understanding of prayer, however, cannot be prejudicial to the sovereignty of God or to human freedom and responsibility.

36.   Is God "a *person*"? No and yes. No, because God is not *an* anything. God is not even *a* Being. Yes, in an analogical sense. God is *like* a person in that God is loving, caring, compassionate, faithful, forgiving. It is better to attribute personality to God than to deny it to God.

37.   God is also Father, but not in the sexist sense. God has no sex. Our God is not a male. On the other hand, the Fatherhood of God embodies truths about God which transcend sexual identity. God is loving, caring, forgiving, etc. And Jesus' relationship with God is as intimate as the relationship of child with parent, and more! Jesus is the way to God. All his power and authority are derived from God. God is in him, and he in God. It is the Godhood of the Father that counts, not the Fatherhood of God.

SUGGESTED READINGS

Baum, Gregory. *Man Becoming*. New York: Herder & Herder, 1970.

Dupré, Louis. *The Other Dimension*. New York: Doubleday, 1972.

Fortman, Edward J., ed. *The Theology of God: Commentary* . Milwaukee: Bruce, 1968.

——————, ed. *The Triune God: A Historical Study of the Doctrine of the Trinity*. Philadelphia: Westminster Press, 1972.

Gilkey, Langdon. *Naming the Whirlwind: The Renewal of God–Language*. Indianapolis: Bobbs-Merrill, 1969.

——————. *Reaping the Whirlwind: A Christian Interpretation of History*. New York: Seabury Press, 1976.

Kehoe, Kimball, ed. *Theology of God: Sources*. Milwaukee: Bruce, 1971.

Küng, Hans. *On Being a Christian*. New York: Doubleday, 1976. pp. 57–88; 214–65; 295–318.

Lewis, C.S. *The Problem of Pain*. New York: Macmillan, 1945.

Monden, Louis. *Signs and Wonders: A Study of the Miraculous Element in Religion*. New York: Desclee, 1966.

Murray, John Courtney. *The Problem of God: Yesterday and Today*. New Haven: Yale University Press, 1964.

Rahner, Karl. *Foundations of Christian Faith*. New York: Seabury Press, 1978, pp. 44–89.

——————. *A Rahner Reader*. Ed. Gerald A. McCool. New York: Seabury Press, 1975, pp. 23–45; 132–136.

· X ·

THE TRINITY

THE PLACE AND IMPORTANCE
OF THE DOCTRINE

The whole of Christian theology is trinitarian in origin and in content. In terms of *origin*, Christian theology is made possible by the self-communication of God the Father in the Word-made-flesh, and our apprehension of God-in-Christ occurs only because we have been drawn by the Holy Spirit who dwells within our hearts and elevates our whole consciousness. In terms of *content*, Christian theology is concerned with creation, sin, grace, redemption, reconciliation, salvation, and the re-creation of the whole cosmic order in the Kingdom of God. All of these, and more, are component parts of the doctrine of the Trinity. "It is impossible to believe explicitly in the mystery of Christ," Thomas Aquinas wrote, "without faith in the Trinity, for the mystery of Christ includes that the Son of God took flesh, that He renewed the world through the grace of the Holy Spirit, and, again, that He was conceived by the Holy Spirit" (*Summa Theologica*, II-II, q. 2, a. 8).

Because the mystery of the Trinity is at once fundamental and central to Christian theology, the doctrine can be placed either at the beginning or at the end of a comprehensive statement of Christian faith. At the *beginning*, it anticipates the exploration of the whole theological terrain and provides the inquirer with a view of what is to come. At the *end*, it summarizes and synthesizes what has preceded it and provides the inquirer with a substantial review.

A third possibility occurs, however, and it is the one pursued in this book. The doctrine of the Trinity is placed somewhere nearer to the middle, consistent with the process of human discovery operative in the individual consciousness and in history itself. The doctrine of the Trinity presupposes some awareness of God and of God's active and gracious presence in Jesus Christ. That awareness, in turn, presupposes some experience of the Transcendent Other as the generator of this awareness. But the judgment that we have indeed had an experience of God also presupposes some understanding of what it means to be human and of the limits of ordinary human experience (for the experience of God is, by definition, that which carries us to, and beyond, the limits of ordinary, everyday, "objective," empirically verifiable experience).

Accordingly, the doctrine of the Trinity appears in this book as a focal or integrating principle. This doctrine is the way we Christians systematically account for the deepest meaning of human existence and systematically express our experience of the ultimate source of that meaning, which is the triune God, disclosed through Jesus Christ and abidingly active as the instrument of reconciliation and unification in the Holy Spirit.

If the doctrine of the Trinity *presupposes* a theology of human existence and of revelation, and even a Christology, it also *implies* a theology of Christ, as it does a theology of the Church and of Christian existence. Thus, our discussion of the Trinity both sums up what we have been doing from the beginning and sets the agenda for the more explicitly Christological as well as ecclesiological and moral discussions that follow.

Because of the peculiar doctrinal relationship between the mystery of the Trinity and the mystery of Christ, one might persuasively argue that the Trinity ought to be treated systematically *after*, rather than before, Christology. But in a sense, we are doing that. The preceding chapter has, in fact, provided a synthesis of the whole Christian doctrine of God. We have already noted there that the formal doctrine of the Trinity developed under the pressure of confronting the apparent contradiction between the Church's consistent affirmation of monotheism and its simultaneous confession of faith in the Lordship of Jesus. In that sense,

Christology generates the doctrine of the Trinity and must be presupposed by it.

On the other hand, Christianity has not been immune from a certain *Christomonism,* a kind of "unitarianism" of the Second Person, in which God as Creator and Judge and God as Reconciler and Sanctifier are effectively replaced by the God who is at our side in the service of the neighbor as the "man for others." Christomonism has also diminished our understanding of the Church and of Christian life. How else explain the recent extraordinary rediscovery of the presence and power of the Holy Spirit by the West, if not as an acute reaction to the practical exclusion of the Spirit from Latin Christian consciousness, devotion, and even theology?

There *is* a sense in which our discussion follows rather than precedes Christology, since the basic elements of a Christology have already been presented in the previous chapter. But there is another sense in which a Christology cannot fully be developed except within the larger context of trinitarian doctrine if we are not to lapse into Christomonism. Indeed, the uniqueness of Christ is rooted in his consubstantial union with God the Father. An understanding of that uniqueness must, in turn, presuppose an understanding of God, the one *triune* God.

Furthermore, we have deliberately and intentionally rejected the traditional textbook division between the one God (*De Deo Uno*) and the triune God (*De Deo Trino*), rooted in the medieval syntheses and favored in Catholic theology ever since. *It is theologically impossible to reflect on the mystery of God from the perspective of Christian faith without reflecting at the same time on the mystery of the Trinity.* There is only one God, and that one God is triune. There is no "one God" who is not always and at the same time triune. The only circumstance under which Christians reflect deliberately on the "one God" who is not perceived as triune is in the comparative study of various non-Christian religions, such as we provided in chapter 8, or in a systematic meditation on the God of Abraham, of Isaac, and of Jacob as manifested in the pre-Christian history of Israel. But even in these cases, the trinitarian perspective inevitably shapes the theological process, dictating not only the answers we propose but, what is more important, the questions we raise.

HISTORY OF THE DOCTRINE
Biblical Foundations

Old Testament

The Old Testament is pre-Christian and as such does not provide any trinitarian understanding of God. This is not to say that the Old Testament's understanding of God (summarized briefly in the preceding chapter) is utterly *inconsistent* with the subsequent trinitarian development of the Christian era. The God of the Old Testament is a living God, intimately involved in the history of the people of Israel, sending forth a word through the prophets and the "signs of the times" — a word so identified with its source that it is called the very word of Yahweh. While it would be theologically unjustifiable to suggest some "foreshadowing" of the Trinity in the Old Testament, the personification of certain divine forces (the "word," the "wisdom," and the "spirit" of God) which are distinct from God and yet not simply intermediate powers between God and the world provides a certain prelude to the Christian understanding of God as triune.

New Testament

Even if it is evident that the doctrine of the Trinity is *not* in the Old Testament, it does not follow, by some process of elimination, that the doctrine of the Trinity *is* clearly and unequivocally in the New Testament. As we noted in the preceding chapter, the New Testament speaks simply of "God," the same God who was at work in the Old Testament: the God of Abraham, of Isaac, and of Jacob. The New Testament writers do not even ordinarily speak of Jesus as "God" (except in the rarest of cases, e.g., the Prologue of John's Gospel), since this would be for them an identification of Jesus with the Father. On the other hand, the New Testament recognizes the divinity of the Son. Where the Son appears as pre-existent, he is in the realm of the divine (John 1:1; Philippians 2:6-11). He is the presence of the Kingdom (Matthew 12:28; Luke

11:20), has lordship over the Sabbath (Mark 2:23-28; 3:1-6), and possesses the fullness of the Spirit (Luke 4:18).

But the New Testament does not specify the terms of the relationship between Father and Son, nor among Father and Son and Holy Spirit. It assumes only that there *is* some relationship (Matthew 11:27; John 1:1; 8:38; 10:38; 1 Corinthians 2:10). The Father "sends" the Son and the Spirit (John 14:16,26; 17:3; Galatians 4:6) and gives the Spirit through the Son (John 15:26; 16:7). Many other texts focus more explicitly on the Father-Son relationship (e.g., Mark 12:1-12; John 1:1,14; 2 Corinthians 4:4; Hebrews 1:3). But none of these texts individually, nor all of them together, express a theology of the Trinity as such. They refer to the impact of God upon the primitive Church. They have to do with the actions of God in the world outside of the inner life of God, i.e., with the "economic Trinity" of salvation history as opposed to the "immanent Trinity." It took three or four hundred years before the Church began to make the proper distinctions, to go beyond the formulations of the Bible and the creeds alone, and to see how the "economic Trinity" and the "immanent Trinity" are one and the same.

The God whom we *experience* as triune is, *in fact*, triune. But we cannot read back into the New Testament, much less into the Old Testament, the more sophisticated trinitarian theology and doctrine which slowly and often unevenly developed over the course of some fifteen centuries.

Post-biblical Theological Reflections

The reader is referred again to the historical material outlined in some detail in the preceding chapter. What follows here is a recapitulation and a reshaping of that material.

Patristic Age

The main question facing the Church in the immediately post-biblical period concerned the relationship of the Son to God the Almighty (*Pantokrator*). Statements about the Spirit tended to appear as a consequence of Christological statements. The Spirit was regarded as a synonym for God. But that could be not true of the Son, since the Son had specific roles and was perceived to have a distinctive identity apart from the Almighty. Is the Son subordinate to the Father and, therefore, not "true God of true God" (Nicea), or is he "consubstantial" (*homoousios*) with the Father, "true God of true God" indeed?

Consequently, the trinitarian theology of the Fathers had its starting point in their reflection on the history of salvation, i.e., on soteriology, or the theology of redemption. The coequal divinity of Christ was of the highest urgency, not because doctrinal purity had to be preserved but rather because our salvation was at stake. If Christ is not truly divine, then he is a creature like us and has no special standing before God. We are still in our sins.

The basic unity of the patristic approach notwithstanding, there is also a discernible difference between the theology of the Greek Fathers and the theology of the Latin Fathers. The Greeks were oriented toward the "economic Trinity" (Father, Son, and Holy Spirit as they are experienced in the history of salvation); the Latins, toward the "immanent Trinity" (Father, Son and Holy Spirit as they exist and interrelate within the inner recesses of the Godhead).

Greeks

The Greeks distinguished *hypostasis* (a term close to, but definitely not identical with, the term *person*) from *ousia*, or being. The distinction underscored for them the truth that God (*theos*, the Father, the Almighty) has come to us through the Son and the Spirit. God is revealed through the Son, and through the Son God reaches us in the Holy Spirit. Therefore, our "contact" with God, or more properly God's "contact" with us, is *historically definite* (through the Son) and *immediate* (in the Spirit), contrary to the various heresies of the day—e.g., Modalism, Sabellianism, Arianism.

The Greek Fathers were content, however, to define the relation between the one divine being, or nature, and the three *hypostases* (not quite "persons" in the modern sense of the word) in terms of traditional philosophical categories. The concrete character of these *hypostases* was then deduced from their function in the history of salvation.

Augustine

Augustine fully exemplified the Latin approach, which was to try to explain the nature of the triune God without deriving or inferring the "content" of the Godhead from the way in which the three Persons function for us in the history of salvation. He began not with the three Persons but with the one nature, or substance. Employing a psychological analogy, Augustine argued that the inner life of God is, in effect, necessarily trinitarian. *Ad extra*, i.e., outside of the inner life of God, however, divine activity is common to all three Persons since it proceeds from the one divine nature. Thus, for example, the Father could have become a human being if the Father so willed. (Some Catholic theologians today, such as Karl Rahner, would strongly resist this hypothesis, however, because the significance of the economy of salvation is proportionately diminished.) The importance and usefulness of the Augustinian approach notwithstanding, it obscured the connection between the "immanent Trinity" and the "economic Trinity" and made of the doctrine, at least in much of the Western Church, a matter of abstract speculation alone, of no real pastoral importance, having no place in the pulpit, for example, except perhaps once a year on Trinity Sunday.

Medieval Scholasticism

Augustine's impact on medieval Scholasticism was enormous, and it was only reinforced, not essentially modified, by Thomas Aquinas. Another type of trinitarian theology, more in keeping with the Greek approach and stressing the psychology of love rather than of understanding, was promoted by Richard of St. Victor (d. ca. 1173), Alexander of Hales (d. 1245), and Bonaventure (d. 1274). In his *On the Trinity*, Richard, unlike Augustine, begins with person rather than nature, looking to the unselfish love of human friendship as the reflection of the unselfish love of divine friendship (since we are, after all, made in the image of God). In God there is one infinite love and three infinite lovers: lover produces beloved, and lover and beloved are the productive principle of an equal co-beloved. Alexander of Hales explains the divine processions through the principle that "goodness diffuses itself." The inner life of the Trinity is characterized by perfect charity. In Bonaventure we find this same emphasis on "pure goodness" and "mutual love" as principles underlying the dynamism and plurality of the God-head (see his *Commentaries on the Four Books of Sentences*). Perhaps because they were less precise than the Augustinian and Thomistic expositions, the so-called Franciscan contributions to trinitarian theology did not succeed in establishing themselves. Attempts at some constructive synthesis of these two approaches are only recently being made, so long has the theology of the Trinity been under the influence of Scholasticism.

Official Teachings on the Trinity

In the preceding chapter we have already presented the principal doctrinal contributions of the official Church to the developing theology of the triune God. Each of the major formulations was placed in its proper historical context. Here we review and summarize those doctrinal pronouncements in a more deliberately *systematic* way. The reader is cautioned, however, not to forget the original historical situation in which the official teaching authority exercised its magisterial duties. Apart from that context, the doctrinal statements become so many "proof texts" of relatively equal importance and authority, their terminology carrying the very same meaning they bear today (e.g., the notion of "person"). Dogmatic and/or doctrinal fundamentalism, we noted in chapter 2, is as much a temptation and a danger for the Church as is biblical fundamentalism.

On the other hand, if we are to have confidence in our theology of the triune God as one that is consistent with, and faithful to, the authentic teachings of the Church, we must take serious account of the doctrinal clarifications and limitations which have accumulated over the centuries.

The Trinity as Absolute Mystery

The Trinity is an *absolute mystery* in the sense that we do not understand it even after it has been revealed. It is a *mystery* in that it is "hidden in God (and) cannot be known unless revealed by God." It is an *absolute* mystery in that it remains forever such. This is the teaching of the First Vatican Council's *Dogmatic Constitution on the Catholic Faith* (1870). The concept of "mystery," however, is left undetermined by the council. A mystery is at least something which clearly transcends the capacity of our ordinary rational and conceptual powers and exceeds, beyond all human imagination, the range and resources of our everyday knowledge. (For a fuller discussion of the notion of "mystery," see again chapter 7.)

God as Triune

That (as opposed to *how*) God is triune is the clear and consistent teaching of the official magisterium of the Church. The Council of Nicea (325) testifies to the Church's official faith in "one God, the Father almighty...and in one Lord Jesus Christ, the Son of God...and in the Holy Spirit." The Council of Constantinople (381) confirmed the faith of Nicea and gave us the so-called Nicaeo-Constantinopolitan Creed which Catholics recite each week at the Eucharist. The teaching of Constantinople was verified the following year at a provincial council in Rome from which appeared *The Tome of Pope Damasus* (d. 384), which declared that there is one God of three, coequal, coeternal Persons, each distinct from the other, but not to the point where we have three separate gods. Against the heretical assault of Albigensianism, which regarded all matter as evil and therefore was led logically to the denial of the incarnation, the Fourth Lateran Council (1215) confessed that "there is only one true God...Father, Son and Holy Spirit: three persons indeed but one essence, substance, or wholly simple nature...." And against certain charges made against Peter the Lombard, the council also taught that "...in God there is only Trinity, not a quaternity...." In response to the great schism of East and West the Second Council of Lyons (1274) and the Council of Florence (1438–1440) both reaffirmed the doctrine of the Trinity, by now almost taking it for granted, and concentrated instead on the ecumenically sensitive matter of the procession of the Holy Spirit from the Father (*and? through?*) the Son. Thereafter the doctrine, indeed the *dogma*, of the Trinity is assumed by official Church sources rather than intrinsically developed and formally restated. A minor exception would be Pope Paul VI's profession of faith, "Credo of the People of God" (1968) which begins with the words "We believe in one God, Father, Son and Holy Spirit...."

God as Father

These same confessions of faith in the Trinity are at once confessions of faith in the divinity of each of the three Persons of the Trinity and, at the same time, in the oneness of the Godhead. From Nicea (325) to Pope Paul VI (1968) professions of faith regularly begin with the words, "We believe in one God...." God the Father is the Lord of salvation history and Creator of all that is. The Father is "unbegotten" but acts, and can only act, in the unity of the Son and the Holy Spirit. The Father generates the Son, and with the Son sends forth the Holy Spirit.

Although not an ecumenical council, the Eleventh Council of Toledo (675) in Spain, attended by only seventeen bishops, gave the Church a profession of trinitarian faith that was cherished and revered for many centuries thereafter. Its profession of faith in God the Father is as succinct and doctrinally precise a formulation as one might discover anywhere in the entire history of the Church:

> And we profess that the Father is not begotten, not created, but unbegotten. For He Himself, from whom the Son has received His birth and the Holy Spirit His procession, has His origin from no one. He is therefore the source and origin of the whole Godhead. He Himself is the Father of His own essence, who in an ineffable way has begotten the Son from His ineffable substance. Yet He did not beget something different from what He Himself is: God has begotten God, light has begotten

light. From Him, therefore, is "all fatherhood in heaven and on earth"(cf. Ephesians 3:15).

God the Son

The Son is begotten by the Father and not made out of nothing, like a creature (as the Arian heresy asserted). The Son is of the same substance with the Father. Thus, the Son is coequal in divinity and coeternal with the Father. It is through the Son as the Word, or *Logos*, of the Father that the Father is expressed in salvation history and within the inner life of the Trinity as well. Because the Son is consubstantial (*homoousios*) with the Father, his Sonship is not simply like that of any other son or daughter of God in the conventional sense of the expression "We're all God's children." Within the human family, of Jesus Christ alone can it be said that he is of the same substance with the Father. In the words of Nicea:

> We believe... in one Lord Jesus Christ, the Son of God, the only-begotten generated from the Father, that is, from the being (*ousia*) of the Father, God from God, Light from Light, true God from true God, begotten, not made, one in being (*homoousios*) with the Father, through whom all things were made, those in heaven and those on earth. For us men and for our salvation He came down, and became flesh, was made man, suffered, and rose again on the third day. He ascended to the heavens and shall come again to judge the living and the dead.

God the Holy Spirit

The Holy Spirit is the Father's gift through the Son. It is through the Spirit that the Father is communicated to us with immediacy, and it is through the Spirit that we are able to accept the self-communication of the Father. As the self-communication of God, the Holy Spirit is God given in love and with the reconciling and renewing power of that love. The Spirit has the same essence as the Father, and yet is distinct from the Father and the Son. The

Spirit proceeds from the Father through the Son (despite the bitter
East-West dispute on this point, the Council of Florence *did* allow
for the preposition *through* as a legitimate alternative to the preferred conjunction *and*). The procession is not a begetting, since
this would lead to the supposition that there are two Sons, nor is
the Spirit merely a mode in which the Son communicates himself
to us. The Spirit originates from the Father and the Son and has a
distinct relationship to the Father and the Son which accounts for
the Spirit's distinct hypostatic existence within the Godhead and
the Spirit's distinct salvific mission in history (without prejudice to
the principle of the mutual indwelling of the three Persons, each
one in the others). From the First Council of Constantinople:

> We believe...in the Holy Spirit, the Lord and
> Giver of life, who proceeds from the Father (and the
> Son), who together with the Father and the Son is wor-
> shipped and glorified, who has spoken through the
> prophets. (And) in one Holy Catholic and apostolic
> Church. We acknowledge one baptism for the forgive-
> ness of sins. We expect the resurrection of the dead and
> the life of the world to come.

Two observations: first, the words *and the Son* (*filioque*) were
added later in Spain in the sixth century, and from there the usage
spread to Gaul and Germany. It was eventually introduced into
the Roman liturgy by Pope Benedict VIII (d. 1024). The Greeks
ignored the *filioque* and denied the Church's right to make any
addition to the ancient creed of Constantinople, as we have
already noted. Secondly, the realities of the Church, the forgiveness of sins, the resurrection of the dead, and the life of the world
to come are a constitutive part of our affirmation of the Holy Spirit
because these are directly attributed to the Spirit's role in salvation history, again without prejudice to the principle of the mutual
indwelling of the three Persons (circumincession).

Processions, Relations, Persons, and Nature

From the point of view of our "discovery" of the triune character
of God, we first experience the divine *processions*, or missions (we

experience the Spirit who has been *sent* by the Father and/through the Son, and we experience the Son as the one *sent* by the Father). The processions, in turn, suggest *relations* between and among *persons* (or distinct *hypostases*) which nonetheless participate coequally, coeternally, and consubstantially in the *nature* of the Godhead, namely, the *divinity*. The official Church provides no final definitions of any of these key doctrinal terms. The magisterium does, however, provide certain fundamental dogmatic principles regarding them:

1. There are two *processions* and only two processions in God: generation and spiration.

2. There are four *relations*, (paternity, filiation, active spiration, passive spiration), but only three *subsistent relations*, i.e., three relations which are mutually opposed and, therefore, distinct from one another (without, however, being distinct from the very Being of God): paternity, filiation, and passive spiration. Active spiration (which involves Father and Son) is not opposed to either paternity or filiation, and, thus, does not constitute a fourth subsistent relation.

3. In God all things are one except what is opposed by the opposition of relations. Those relations which are opposed and, therefore, distinct one from the other are called, as noted above, subsistent relations, or *hypostases*. They give rise, in turn, to the trinity of *Persons* within the Godhead: Father, Son, and Holy Spirit.

4. Because of the unity of the divine essence, of the processions and of the relative oppositions, which constitute the Persons, there is a *mutual indwelling* (circumincession) of the Persons, one in the other two, the other two in the one, so that the Son is for all eternity in the Father, and the Father from all eternity in the Son, and so on.

These teachings are set forth explicitly, but not exclusively, in the Council of Florence's *Decree for the Greeks* (1439) and *Decree for the Jacobites* (1442).

We must take care, however, not to confuse the terminology of the Fathers and of the ecumenical councils of the past with the meanings presently associated with those same words today. This is especially true of the term *person*. It is a notion which for us today is inextricably linked with *consciousness*. A person is an individual center and subject of consciousness. But there exists in God only one power, one will, one self-presence, one activity, one beatitude, and so forth. Insofar as the individual Persons can even be described as "self-conscious" (which at best is an analogical attribution), it is a self-consciousness which derives from the one divine essence and is common to the divine Persons. Our modern psychological and philosophical notions of subjectivity, therefore, must be kept strictly away from the concept of person as applied to the Trinity. The activity of the three Persons is one and the same and can be ascribed to any one of the Persons only by *appropriation*. This axiom, however, deals only with the efficient causality of God. It does not affect the truth that the *Logos* or Son alone became human, or the theory of uncreated grace in which each of the three divine Persons has a special relation to us. To say otherwise would reduce the doctrine of the Trinity to mere words and the Christian understanding of God to an unqualified monotheism.

THEOLOGICAL SYNTHESIS

For too many Christians, the doctrine of the Trinity is only a matter of intellectual curiosity, on the one hand, or a somewhat arbitrary test of faith, on the other. It is as if Jesus at some point in his teaching ministry called the disciples aside and said, "By the way, there *is* just one more thing you should know. In God there are three divine Persons: Father, Son, and Holy Spirit. And yet there is still only one God. It's quite important that you believe what I'm telling you. Your readiness and willingness to believe will be a sign of your faith in me and in my word." Accordingly, the mystery and doctrine of the Trinity is often relegated to an entirely marginal place in the total Christian schema. Even theologians as sober as Karl Rahner have suggested that, as far as many Church members are concerned, the doctrine could be erased completely from the Christian treasury of faith and that many spiritual writings, sermons, pious exercises, and even theological treatises could remain in place with little more than minor verbal adjustments.

A proper theological and pastoral understanding of the Trinity depends upon our perception of *the identity between the so-called "economic Trinity" and the so-called "immanent Trinity."* The two have, in effect, been separated, and the former has been practically forgotten. The doctrine of the Trinity is received as if it were merely an arcane description of the inner life of God—a life that we cannot observe at first hand, in any case. In that view, it has to do with a network of divine relationships which concerns only God and not ourselves, except insofar as Christ asks us to believe his "revelation" about the mystery as a sign of our faith in him and in his total message.

But that, in fact, is not the way the mystery of the Trinity was revealed to us. Nowhere do we find the Lord calling his disciples aside, and "revealing" the Trinity as if it were this week's catechetical lesson. On the contrary, the Church gradually and painstakingly came to certain conclusions about the inner reality of God on the basis of its experience of God within its own human experience. In other words, the Church began to wonder theologically and doctrinally whether there is more to God than traditional monotheism suggests, or whether, at the other extreme, there might be three gods, or two, or perhaps a small community of unequal gods. The Church came to the knowledge of God as triune as it progressively reflected on its experience of the triuneness of God's dealings with us in history. And then the Church concluded that the God whom we experience as triune in history (the "economic Trinity") must also be triune in essence, i.e., within the inner life of the Godhead (the "immanent Trinity").

In traditional categories, the revelation of the economic Trinity *is* the revelation of the immanent Trinity. We did not first "hear about" the immanent Trinity and then search for signs of its activity in our lives. In that case the revelation of the immanent Trinity would have been a merely verbal, highly abstract communication. Rather, our "understanding" of the immanent Trinity came about precisely as a result of our reflection on the very practical, saving activities of the triune God in our lives. Therefore, the doctrine of the Trinity is not a speculative doctrine alone. *It is the way we express our most fundamental relationships with the God of our salvation as well as God's relationships with us.*

We must keep in mind, all the while, that we would not even know about the economic Trinity if its activities on our behalf were not "called to our attention" (the process of *revelation*, already discussed in chapter 2). For those of us living after the biblical, foundational period of the Church, the Bible itself and subsequent creedal statements of the Church serve to "call our attention" to the trinitarian character of God's dealings with us. Those of us reflecting on the mystery of the Trinity today do so because the doctrine is already there, as a given of our Christian experience, consciousness, and faith. In the primitive Christian community—the disciples, the Apostles, the evangelists, the first faithful members of the Church—the seeds of the doctrine were also "given." But not by the Bible, since it did not yet exist. And not by creedal statements, although some of these were already circulating and some few found their way into the New Testament. The earliest Christians were "alerted" to the trinitarian dimension of divine salvation by Christ, first of all, and then by the preaching of the Apostles, and then by attentiveness to their own unusual experience of the triune God (e.g., at Pentecost) in this most unusual period in the history of the Church. But having conceded all of that, the mystery of the Trinity remains precisely that: a mystery, and absolute mystery at that.

If the communication of God in Jesus Christ, the Son, and in the Holy Spirit is really the communication *of God*, then these communications must be attributed to God as God is, immanently, within the Godhead. The divine self-communication, therefore, has two basic modes: of truth (the *Logos*, or Word) and of love (the Spirit). As *truth*, the self-communication takes place in history, through a particular person. As *love*, it brings about the openness of human beings to the presence of God in Christ and makes possible our acceptance of that divine presence. Without being simply identical, these two forms of divine self-communication constitute together the one divine self-communication which manifests itself in truth and love. And yet there is a real distinction between the two forms of self-communication (or processions, or missions): In the one, the Father is expressed as truth; in the other, the Father is received and accepted in love.

One of the most obvious *difficulties* with the doctrine of the Trinity arises from the Church's *use of the word person* to identify the various terms of the divine relationships. We take it to be a theologically non-negotiable matter as well. There is simply no other way of talking about the triune God except in terms of the "one God and the three divine Persons." And yet the New Testament does not use the term *person*. Indeed, it was introduced only very gradually into ecclesiastical language. And even when the Church passed beyond the biblical formulations, its theologians and official magisterium did not immediately fasten upon the term *person* (*prosopon*). The initial preference was for *hypostasis*. *Hypostasis* can be predicated of any being, not merely of rational beings. It applies to whatever exists in itself. *Persona* always means the *intellectual* subsistent. Moreover, our modern notion of "person" further complicates the problem, since the modern notion is so much tied in with the idea of a separate and independent subject or center of consciousness. Applying the modern concept of "person" without any modification to the doctrine of Trinity would leave us with three consciousnesses, three free wills, eventually three gods. The word *person*, therefore, is almost inevitably misunderstood today.

Where does that leave us? Can we simply reject the traditional formula first proposed by the Council of Alexandria (362), "one substance, three persons"? We cannot erase history, nor are we really in a position today to produce a better formula which could be universally intelligible, acceptable, and binding on the whole Church.

At least we can, with renewed determination, follow the pattern given from the beginning by the New Testament itself. We can speak of the Trinity always in the context of salvation history, using the names of Father, Son, and Holy Spirit, without forgetting that one God is spoken of throughout. We can also speak of *three distinct ways of God's being present in the history of salvation and three different ways of God's subsisting within the Godhead itself.*

The word *ways* has its strengths and weaknesses, to be sure. One of its strengths is that it can help us to see that the Persons are there as in relation to one another and that where the relationships are different, one from the other, we have put our finger, so to speak, on what constitutes difference in God. Father, Son, and Holy Spirit are one and the same God, but subsisting in different ways. It is only with respect to the ways of subsistence that the number three can be applied to God. A way of subsisting is *distinct* from another way of subsisting by its relation of opposition, and is *real* by virtue of its identity with the divine being. "He Who" subsists in such a way is truly God.

But there is an obvious risk in the use of the word *ways*. It is a short step indeed from that term to Modalism, which effectively denies the reality of the Trinity, economic or immanent. We have to be particularly attentive to the reminder of Bernard J. F. Lonergan that a subsistent is *that which is*, whereas a mode of being is *a way in which it is*. Thus, in God paternity is not a mode of being; it is God the Father. There are three in God to whom we can say "You" (*Divinarum Personarum Conceptionem Analogicam*, Rome: Gregorian University, 1957, pp. 172-175).

Finally, what of the so-called *psychological explanation* of the doctrine of the Trinity, the one proposed by Augustine and further developed by Thomas Aquinas? It uses the pattern of the human mind and an analysis of human consciousness in attempting to illustrate the two immanent processions of generation and spiration within the Godhead. Although it is not the official teaching of the Church, at least not directly, the approach can still be helpful. "It appears all the more legitimate in the light of a metaphysical anthropology which demonstrates that there are only two fundamental acts of spiritual existence, knowledge and love. The obvious thing is to regard these basic acts as paralleled in the two divine processions" (Karl Rahner, "Trinity," *The Concise Sacramentum Mundi*, p. 1764).

On the other hand, the psychological approach is not without its own difficulties. There is some measure of circular reasoning involved. The approach "postulates *from* the doctrine of the Trinity a model of human knowledge and love, which either remains questionable, or about which it is not clear that it can be more than a *model* of human knowledge precisely as *finite*. And this model it applies again to God. In other words, we are not told why in God knowledge and love demand a *processio ad modum operati* (as Word or as 'the beloved in the lover')" (Rahner, *The Trinity*, pp. 117–118). And without such a procession there is no real trinity of ways of subsistence.

What the mystery and doctrine of the Trinity mean, when all is said and done, is that the God who created us, who sustains us, who will judge us, and who will give us eternal life is not a God infinitely removed from us. On the contrary, our God is a God of absolute proximity, a God who is communicated truly in the flesh, in history, within our human family, and a God who is present in the spiritual depths of our existence as well as in the core of our unfolding human history, as the source of enlightenment and community.

That mystery and doctrine is, in its turn, the beginning, the end, *and* the center of all Christian theology.

SUMMARY

1. The whole of *Christian theology* is trinitarian in origin and content. In *origin*, because theology itself is made possible by the self-communication of God the Father in the Word-made-flesh, and because our apprehension of God-in-Christ occurs only after we have been drawn by the Holy Spirit who dwells within our hearts and elevates our whole consciousness. In *content*, because every major Christian doctrine is an expression of the mystery and doctrine of the Trinity.

2. Consideration of the Trinity might conceivably occur at the beginning of theology, as a preview, or at the end of theology, as a review and synthesis. Our *method* places the doctrine nearer to the center of the systematic presentation, since an understanding of the Trinity presupposes some understanding of human existence (theological anthropology), some notion of transcendence and of the process and signs by which the Transcendent is disclosed and/or discovered (revelation), and even some grasp of God's active and gracious presence in Jesus Christ (Christology and grace). On the other hand, certain mysteries and doctrines seem to presuppose so much the mystery and doctrine of the Trinity that they cannot easily be considered *before* the Trinity, namely, the mystery

of the Church, the sacraments, Christian existence, and, to a very large extent, Christology itself.

3.　In any event, there can be *no separation* between theological reflection on the one God and theological reflection on the triune God. The God of Christian theology is always and only the triune God.

4.　The mystery and doctrine of the Trinity is not foreshadowed in the *Old Testament*, but the elements for such a doctrine (e.g., the closeness and active presence of Yahweh among the people of Israel) are there as a kind of prelude to the Christian understanding of God as triune. At the very least, there is no inconsistency or contradiction between the two Testaments.

5.　But neither is the doctrine of the Trinity clearly in the *New Testament*. Again, certain elements are present: the special status and role of Jesus Christ, the Son of God, in particular. The New Testament does not specify the nature or the terms of the relationship between and among the Persons of the Trinity; indeed, it does not even use the word *person* in reference to the Father, Son, or Holy Spirit.

6.　The first questions posed *after the foundational period* of the New Testament were "How can there be one God, the Almighty, when Jesus Christ is also invested with divinity?" or, conversely, "How can Jesus be true God of true God if there is only one God?" Only later did the question of the divinity of the Holy Spirit arise.

7.　The *Greek Fathers* started with our experience of the triune God in salvation history (the economic Trinity), whereas the Latin Fathers, and especially Augustine, began with a more speculative analysis of the inner life of the Godhead, moving from nature or essence to Persons (the immanent Trinity).

8.　It was mainly through the achievement of the Greek Fathers that the principal conciliar formulations of trinitarian faith were constructed: Nicea, Constantinople, etc. *The councils* insisted that the Son is of the same substance (*homoousios*) with the Father, and is, therefore, an effective instrument of our redemption. The Holy Spirit, too, is divine, a separate *hypostasis* alongside the Father and the Son, without prejudice to the oneness of divinity itself.

9.　*Medieval Scholasticism*, especially as exemplified in Thomas Aquinas, adhered to the Augustinian approach, although there were certain "minority reports" being written, namely, by the Franciscan school represented by Richard of St. Victor, Alexander of Hales, and Bonaventure, who were closer to the approach of the Greek Fathers. Their contributions to trinitarian theology, however, did not attract a very wide constituency until recently.

10. *Official teachings of the Church* on the Trinity have advanced the following principles: (1) The Trinity is an *absolute mystery*; i.e., it transcends our ordinary human capacity for understanding even after we know it as revealed; (2) God is triune: Father, Son, and Holy Spirit, coequal and coeternal, and yet each distinct one from the other, but not to the point where we have three gods; (3) the Father alone is unbegotten, begets or generates the Son, and sends forth or spirates the Holy Spirit (with or through the Son); (4) the Son is begotten by the Father, but not as a creature (Arianism); he is of the same substance as the Father, "true God of true God" (Nicea); (5) the Holy Spirit proceeds from the Father (and or through) the Son and has a distinct salvific mission in history: creating the community of faith (Church), forgiving sins, giving new life, etc.

11. There are two *processions*, or missions, in God: generation and spiration; i.e., both the Son and the Holy Spirit are "sent."

12. The processions, in turn, are the basis of the *relations* between and among the Persons or *hypostases* (which do not mean exactly the same, since *persons* are *rational hypostases*). There are four relations: paternity, filiation, active spiration, and passive spiration. But there are only three *subsistent relations*: paternity, filiation, and passive spiration. Active spiration is not really distinct from paternity or from filiation, since there is no opposition of relations between them.

13. These subsistent relations are relatively opposed one to another, and thus are *hypostases* or Persons (again, the two terms are not exactly identical). The *hypostases* or Persons have names: Father, Son, and Holy Spirit.

14. Although there are three Persons, there is only one divine nature or essence. Because of the unity of essence, there is a *mutual indwelling* of the Persons, i.e., of one in the other. This is also called *circumincession*.

15. Such teachings as these are to be found throughout the history of the Church, particularly in the first fifteen centuries, but they are comprehensively proclaimed by the *Council of Florence* (1438–42).

16. Despite this abundant corpus of official teachings on the mystery of the Trinity, many *fundamental difficulties* remain, especially the ambiguity that continues to revolve around the notion of "person," a term the New Testament does not use. The modern understanding of a person as an independent center or subject of consciousness does not apply to the Trinity. And yet we do not have a better term to replace it, and we cannot erase centuries of slow and painstaking debate and doctrinal formulations.

17. A proper theological, not to say pastoral, understanding of the Trinity requires that we perceive the identity between the *economic Trinity* and the *immanent Trinity*. The God who is active on our behalf in salvation history is the triune God of the Godhead. It is not the immanent Trinity which is first revealed, but the economic Trinity. The constitution of the immanent Trinity is inferred from our experience of, and reflection upon, the functions of the economic Trinity.

18. Since the notion of *"person"* continues to create ambiguity, confusion, even heresy at the rank-and-file level (*tritheism*, belief in three gods), and since we cannot simply abandon it, we should follow the pattern set by the New Testament and speak of the Trinity always in the context of salvation history. God deals with us in three distinct *ways* of being present to our history: As Father, as Son, and as Holy Spirit. There is a danger, of course, that an explanation of this sort might lapse into Modalism.

19. The so-called *psychological analogy* first employed by Augustine also has its advantages and disadvantages, but, like the notion of "person," it cannot simply be set aside. It helps us see the basic parallel between the life of the Trinity, which is governed by the twin processes of truth and love, and our own lives, or at least the ideal expression of our own lives.

20. *In the end*, the mystery and doctrine of the Trinity means that the God who created us, who sustains us, who will judge us, and who will give us eternal life is not infinitely removed from us, but is absolutely close to us, communicated in the flesh and present in our hearts, our consciousness, and our history as the source of enlightenment and community.

SUGGESTED READINGS

Bracken, Joseph. *What Are They Saying About the Trinity?* New York: Paulist Press, 1979.

Fortman, Edward J., ed. *The Triune God: A Historical Study of the Doctrine of the Trinity*. Philadelphia: Westminster Press, 1972.

Kelly, J. N. D. *Early Christian Creeds*. London: Longmans, Green, 1950.
_____. *Early Christian Doctrines*. New York: Harper & Row, 1965.

Lonergan, Bernard J. F. *The Way to Nicea: The Dialectical Development of Trinitarian Theology*. Philadelphia: Westminster Press, 1976.

Panikkar, Raimundo. *The Trinity and the Religious Experience of Man*. New York: Orbis Books, 1973.

Rahner, Karl. *A Rahner Reader.* Ed. Gerald A. McCool. New York: Seabury Press, 1975, pp. 132-144.

_____. *The Trinity.* New York: Herder & Herder, 1970.

Sloyan, Gerard. *The Three Persons in One God.* Englewood Cliffs, N.J.: Prentice-Hall, 1964.

PART THREE

JESUS CHRIST

JESUS CHRIST

INTRODUCTION

What is distinctively Christian about the Church's faith is its understanding of God as triune. But it is only because we first knew God in Jesus Christ that we came to know God as triune. Thus, it is equally true that the distinctively Christian element in Christian faith is the confession of the Lordship of Jesus. Christianity alone identifies Jesus of Nazareth with God. Jesus Christ is "true God of true God." He is of one substance with the Father.

A separate section on the mystery of Jesus Christ, therefore, requires little justification. Christian theology, not to say Catholic theology, focuses on him. Our understanding of, and response to, God is a function of our understanding of, and response to, Jesus Christ.

Why, then, is there not also a separate section on the Holy Spirit, if the Christian God is a triune God? First, there is no such separate "section," as it were, even in the New Testament, nor in the earliest tradition of the Church. The preoccupation of the New Testament is with God, the Almighty, and with Jesus Christ, who comes among us to manifest and to do the Father's will: to proclaim and practice and hasten the coming of the Kingdom of God. The Holy Spirit is never an object of that proclamation, whether of Jesus or of the Church. Rather, the Holy Spirit is the power through which that proclamation is uttered and fulfilled.

We do not have in this book a separate treatment of the Holy Spirit because the Holy Spirit is at issue in every major theological discussion: the divinization of humankind by grace, the renewing and reconciling presence of God in history, the mystery of the

Church, the celebration of the sacraments, the exercise of Christian witness. "The Holy Spirit cannot become a formula, a dogma apart," the Orthodox theologian Nikos Nissiotis writes. "Pneumatology is the heart of Christian theology, it touches all aspects of faith in Christ. It is a commentary on the acts of the revealed triune God, the life of the Church, and of the man who prays and is regenerated . . . orthodox pneumatology does not allow the doctrine of the Holy Spirit to become a separate chapter of dogmatic theology" (cited by Patrick Corcoran, *Irish Theological Quarterly,* vol. 39/3, July 1972, p. 277).

In this Part on Jesus Christ we examine first how he is understood, interpreted, and accepted today—whether as teacher, holy man, liberator, brother, etc.—and how he variously relates with contemporary culture (chapter 11).

The heart of the matter, of course, is the New Testament. We would know practically nothing about Jesus Christ (apart from the barest of biographical details) if it were not for the testimony of the Church preserved in the pages of the New Testament. And here we are confronted with the central problem of connecting the Jesus of history and the Christ of faith. Does the Church's testimony about Jesus conform with what Jesus thought, said, and did? What was the significance of his life and death? Did he rise from the dead (chapter 12)?

But the New Testament record was open to various interpretations, and the missionary needs of the early Church required it to communicate the Gospel across cultural lines. The supposedly straightforward, uncomplicated message of the Bible had to be reinterpreted, recast, reformulated. And it was: by the Fathers of the Church, by the early ecumenical councils, and by the theologians of the Middle Ages. The story of that process is not easily reviewed, but the Church's present and future understanding of the meaning and purpose of Jesus Christ is forever shaped by that story and by its dogmatic residue (chapter 13).

The discussion about the mystery of Jesus Christ has been, in a sense, reopened in the twentieth century, first because of the renewal of biblical studies and, secondly, because of a development in our understanding of the meaning of human existence and of human history. Both of these factors have generated a fresh outpouring of Christological writings, the first such outpouring since the medieval period. Who are the principal contributors? How do their contributions compare, one with another? How consistent are those contributions with the biblical and dogmatic traditions (chapter 14)?

Christology can be abstract unless it is always related to soteriology. In other words, we are ever concerned about the nature and person of Jesus Christ because we are ever concerned about his effectiveness in bringing about our salvation. If he is not truly God, then he could not *save* us. If he is not truly a human being, then he could not save *us*. If divinity and humanity are not united in a single person, then *he* could not save us. Certain practical questions help focus the central dogmatic issues: The questions of the virginal conception of Jesus and his sinlessness help focus the truth of his divinity, and the questions of his knowledge and sexuality help focus the truth of his humanity (chapter 15).

In the final accounting, how can we even begin to differentiate between Christologies which are consistent with the broad Catholic tradition and those which are not? The same fifteenth chapter proposes five theological criteria.

Chapter 16 elaborates upon one of those five criteria, namely, the principle that our Christological belief must correspond always with our worship. The "Christ of the Liturgy" is as much a norm of Christological orthodoxy as is the Christ of the New Testament, of the Fathers, of the councils, of medieval theology. The liturgy is Christology-as-worship-and-prayer.

Although the mystery of Jesus Christ is not the most fundamental doctrine of Christian faith (it is rooted, after all, in the mystery of the triune God), it is unquestionably at the heart of Christian faith. And so, too, is Part III in relation to the rest of the book.

·XI·

CHRIST AND
CONTEMPORARY CULTURE

THE PROBLEM

We have said that what is distinctively Christian about the Church's faith is *the understanding of God as triune.* The God who created us and who sustains us, the God who will judge us and give us eternal life, is a God who has entered our history in the flesh and who continues to enter and dwell in our hearts and our minds as the principle of understanding and of love.

On the other hand, it is because we first knew God in the *Logos*, the Word that is Jesus Christ, that we eventually came also to know God as triune. So it is equally true that the distinctively Christian element in Christian faith is *the confession of the Lordship of Jesus.* Christianity alone identifies Jesus of Nazareth with God. Jesus Christ is "true God of true God." He is of the same substance as the Father.

But who is this Jesus whom we proclaim as Lord? How do we know him? How can we be sure that our picture of him is true to the facts? On what basis do we connect the Jesus of our prayers and devotions with the Jesus who lived in Palestine some two thousand years ago? Who is to say that we are really teaching and preaching as Jesus did? Does our present understanding of Christian faith accurately reflect the intentions and consciousness of the Lord himself? Is the Church truly faithful to the mission God has given it in Christ and in the Holy Spirit? Is Christianity as Christ meant it to be?

Such questions as these arise because of the gap between the so-called "Jesus of history" and the "Christ of faith." The distinction between the names "Jesus" and "Christ" is important. "Christ," after all, is not Jesus's last name. "Jesus" (literally, "Yahweh is salvation") is the name given him at birth.

Insofar as he lived at a certain time, in a certain place, with certain parents, was engaged in certain occupations, associated with certain persons, established a certain reputation among his contemporaries, and died a certain death, in a certain place, at a certain time, under certain circumstances, he, this "Jesus," is an *historical fact*.

But insofar as some of his contemporaries reacted to him in a particular way and estimated his significance in a particular fashion, and insofar as subsequent generations have readily affirmed with Paul that "God. . .reconciled us to himself through Christ" (2 Corinthians 5:18), this man "born of a woman" (Galatians 4:4), this "carpenter's son" (Matthew 13:55) bears *a meaning which transcends the historical fact* of his existence, although never disconnected from it. This "Jesus of Nazareth" is the "Christ" (literally, the "anointed one") who has been promised and whom we now accept in "faith."

Jesus, therefore, is a matter of historical record; *Christ* is a matter of meaning or of interpretation, an interpretation that we call "faith." To affirm the historicity of Jesus without affirming his Christhood is to take Jesus as a human being and no more, the greatness of his humanity notwithstanding. To affirm the Christhood, on the other hand, without identifying the historical Jesus with the Christ is to make of "Christ" a cosmic idea, an abstraction, a universal principle of growth and progress, a kind of theological yeast with no identity of its own.

Neither affirmation is true to the Christian faith. For Christians confess, as we shall see in some detail, the identity of Jesus with the Christ. Jesus *is* the Christ. He is indeed *Jesus Christ*, and he is "the same yesterday, today, and forever" (Hebrews 13:8).

But the Jesus Christ of the New Testament, of the creeds, of the dogmatic formulae, of the liturgy, and of the living faith of the whole Church is not always recognizable in the world about us, and sometimes not even in portions of the Church itself.

Too often the Christ of our personal faith bears little resemblance to the Jesus of history or to the Christ of the Church's faith. We make of Jesus Christ what *we* would like him to be for us. Consequently, he no longer challenges us from the outside to conform to him, but rather we project on him all that we are or would like to be. The affirmation of the Lordship of Jesus becomes, then, a form of *self*-affirmation.

JESUS CHRIST TODAY

There has been an extraordinary resurgence of interest in, even enthusiasm for, Jesus in recent years. He made the cover of *Time* magazine twice in one year (June 21 and October 25, 1971), at the high point of the so-called "Jesus movement." We had the "Jesus People," even "Jews for Jesus." He was celebrated on Broadway and in film: *Jesus Christ Superstar* and *Godspell*. Bumper stickers advertised his name: "Honk if you love Jesus," "Jesus is the answer," and "Jesus is Lord." The revival of Evangelical Christianity and the charismatic incursion into Roman Catholicism ran almost a parallel course to Jesus' sudden popularity in the "outside world."

But *which* Jesus was it who won the hearts of a new generation of young people and inspired the spiritual rebirth of young and middle-aged alike, including even a man destined to become president of the United States? And which Jesus was it who continued to be taught, and honored, and appealed to in the official churches? Which Jesus was preached from the pulpits? Which Jesus was the centerpiece of the catechisms and college textbooks? Which Jesus was the norm of conscience? Which Jesus set the example for a truly human, and therefore truly Christian, life?

One can detect at least five such Jesuses:

Jesus, Teacher: Gnosticism, insofar as it was a heretical exaggeration of the importance of knowledge (*gnosis*) for salvation, is not dead. There are still many in the Church who sincerely believe that orthodoxy is all that really counts in the end, and that, therefore, no greater threat to Christ exists in the world today than the internal "subversion" of the Church by dissident theologians. The primary duty of pastors (pope and bishops in particular) is to safeguard the faith and protect it from the impurities of so-called progressive thought. (We have already alluded to the confusion of "faith" with "theology" in chapter 2.)

Such views have several roots, of course. They reflect a particular ecclesiology, a particular understanding of God and of human existence, a particular notion of the redemption, and so forth. But they reflect as well a particular Christology, and that is what interests us here. Jesus Christ is perceived primarily as a *teacher*, as one who came among us, sent by the Father, in order to communicate certain truths about God and about ourselves that we must know if we are to achieve the ends for which we were created. We noted in the previous chapter how this mentality helped to marginalize the doctrine of the Trinity, as if it were some abstract concept which makes little or no real difference in our lives but which is set before us nonetheless as a test of our readiness and willingness to believe the word of God in Christ, "who can neither deceive nor be deceived" (from the "Act of Faith").

But the preceding attitude is an extreme one. It must not be allowed to obscure the fact that Jesus was indeed a *teacher*. This was a title, in fact, given him more frequently than any other. He was regarded as a teacher (Matthew 10:24; Luke 20:21; John 3:2). He gathered a group of disciples and acted as their rabbi, or teacher (Matthew 8:18-22; 21:1-11; 26:17-19; Mark 4:35-41; 11:1-11, e.g.). He is asked the type of questions a teacher would be asked (Matthew 22:36; Luke 10:25). His place for teaching was often the synagogue (Matthew 4:23; 9:35; 13:54; Mark 6:2; Luke 4:15,31; 6:6). He taught "with power" and as one having authority (Matthew 7:29; Mark 1:22; 11:18). His teaching is that of the one who sent him (John 7:16), and Jesus teaches whatever he himself was taught by the Father (John 8:28).

Not surprisingly, the early Church continued the ministry of teaching in fidelity to its charge from the Lord. Teachers appeared among the lists of officers in the Church (1 Corinthians 12:28; Ephesians 4:11), and teaching is regarded as part of the office of Apostles (1 Timothy 2:7; 2 Timothy 3:10) and of the bishop (2 Timothy 4:2). With the death of the last of the Apostles, the Church was particularly concerned that the apostolic traditions be preserved and that whatever was taught should be "sound doctrine" (1 Timothy 1:10; 2 Timothy 4:3; Titus 1:9, 2:1). Ultimately, the object of the Church's teaching, then as now, was the same as it was in Jesus' own teaching: the Kingdom of God (Mark 1:15). But after the resurrection of Christ, the Church increasingly saw Christ as the personification of the Kingdom, and so the Church's teaching centered more and more on Christ himself (Ephesians 4:21).

Jesus, Ruler, Judge, and King: Others have distorted the reality of Jesus by exaggerating his function as *ruler*, or shepherd, and as *judge*. How else explain why so many apparently sincere Christian leaders have adopted the life-styles of princes or of millionaires, have governed their communities in severe, authoritarian ways, and have gloried in the pomp and circumstance of ecclesiastical titles and ceremonies and public events? How else explain such institutionalized cruelties as the *Inquisition*, the imprisonment of *Galileo* (d. 1642), the suppression of the free access to the great works of literature and philosophy, the banishment of persons from their professional careers without due process, the harshness and rigidity of life in religious communities, the intricate ecclesiastical legal system of crimes and penalties? How else explain the bitterness of official denunciations of Protestants and others, and the literal insistence that no one can be saved outside the Catholic Church?

And yet Jesus was indeed a *ruler,* or shepherd, and a *judge*. But he is the shepherd who leaves the ninety-nine to search out for the one stray, and whose rejoicing over its recovery is beyond measure (Matthew 18:12-14; Luke 15:3-7). He is, in fact, the good shepherd (John 10:1-6,10-16) and the door of the sheepfold (10:7-9). He is concerned with the unity of the flock (an echo of Ezekiel 34:11-22).

The title of *shepherd* was applied to ministers of the Church as well. Pastors (etymologically "shepherds") are included on the lists of officers (Ephesians 4:11). The elders are addressed as shepherds of the flock (Acts of the Apostles 20:28; 1 Peter 5:2-4). Peter is given the distinctive ministry of shepherd (John 21:15-17).

Jesus is also accorded the title *king* in Matthew 2:2, where his royal character is the key to understanding the entire narrative, whose purpose is to present the true kingship of Jesus as free of external pomp. Jesus simply accepts the designation in his conversation with Pilate (Matthew 27:11; Mark 15:2; Luke 23:3). The longer version of the dialogue (John 18:33-39) makes even clearer the unworldly character of the kingship of Jesus. Indeed, the kingship of Jesus is mentioned only once in the post-resurrection period (1 Corinthians 15:24-26) and the reference there is eschatological. Jesus will be king only after the conquest of all his enemies.

The title of *judge* is also sparingly applied to Jesus. On the "day of wrath" Jesus will come to judge the living and the dead (2 Timothy 4:1). But Jesus' role as judge is at best paradoxical in John's Gospel. On the one hand, we are assured that God did not send his Son to judge the world but to save it (John 3:17), and Jesus himself says the same thing (John 12:47). Yet he also says that he has come into the world for judgment (John 9:39). Some biblical scholars explain the apparent discrepancy by noting that the *believer* is not judged, whereas the *unbeliever* is already judged by his or her very unbelief (3:18; 5:24). Jesus is the judge in the sense that he presents himself as the object of decision. He becomes the standard by which the world will, in a sense, judge itself.

Meanwhile, the disciples are warned that they themselves should not judge others (Matthew 7:1; Luke 6:37). Those who are merciless will be judged mercilessly (James 2:13).

Jesus, Holy Man of God: The Jesus of icons and holy cards, of songs and prayers and devotional literature, is often a Jesus almost totally removed from the ordinary currents of human life on this planet. This "holy man of God" is unmarried, because there is something inherently inferior about the married state (a "lawful remedy for concupiscence," the older moral theology textbooks conceded). Marriage is a less exalted state because there is something inherently evil about the flesh and in particular about genital expressions of love and affection. Pleasure, therefore, is to be kept in its place (how many "portraits" of Jesus have him smiling, not to say laughing?). To be virtuous is to act *against* one's natural inclinations and desires. "If it's not difficult, it's probably not virtuous," many assumed in the past. This attitude, of course, admits of degrees. For some Christians, the anti-pleasure, anti-flesh principle leads to prohibitions against alcohol, even against card-playing, for example.

Meanwhile, the more dignified, highly artistic representations of the Lord, as in the icons of Eastern Orthodox Christianity, tell also of an other-worldly Jesus, his expressionless facial features distorted to emphasize that his true home and his true interests are somewhere else. The gaze, untouched by even a hint of compassion, suggests a Being supremely uninterested in involving himself in this world, much less in changing its structures.

This is the Jesus, too, of the charismatic (the word in lower case to indicate a generic reference only, with no necessary application to adherents of the Catholic Charismatic Movement). He is totally consumed with the praise of God in word and song. He came among us for no other reason than to alert us to the presence and power of the Holy Spirit and to open our minds and our hearts totally to the God who heals and forgives, who affirms and confirms us in our individual existence.

Jesus is, to be sure, a *holy man of God*. But holiness is not the same as an other-worldliness which calls us to deny the radical goodness of the created order (see again chapters 5 and 7). Holiness is *wholeness*, according to the title of one of Josef Goldbrunner's works (*Holiness Is Wholeness*, Notre Dame: University of Notre Dame Press, 1964). The holy person is the one who is fully what God created that person to be, and who has indeed been re-created in the Holy Spirit. To be fully what God intends us to be is to live by the principle of the divine indwelling, to be open truly to the Transcendent, and to know and love by the light and power of that principle (see again chapter 5). Holiness, in its deepest biblical meaning, is simply the life of God. God alone is holy: "There is no Holy One like the Lord; there is no Rock like our God" (1 Samuel 2:2). God's name (which is equivalent to God's "person") is holy (Leviticus 20:3; 22:2; Ezekiel 20:39; 36:20). Persons, places, even seasons become holy by being touched with the divine presence (see, e.g., Deuteronomy 26:15; Exodus 3:5; 28:41; Psalm 46:5; Leviticus 25:12; Isaiah 65:5; Haggai 2:12).

Where the holiness of God is mentioned in the New Testament, the Old Testament roots are clear, as in the Lord's Prayer ("hallowed be your name"—Matthew 6:9; Luke 11:2) and in

1 John 2:20, for example. Jesus, too, is called the holy one of God (Mark 1:24; Luke 1:35; 4:34; John 6:69; Acts of the Apostles 3:14; Revelation 3:7) and the holy servant of God (Acts of the Apostles 4:27,30).

It is to the Church and its members that the term is more frequently applied. The Church is a temple holy to the Lord (Ephesians 2:21), made so by the indwelling of the Spirit (1 Corinthians 3:17). The principal effect and sign of Christian holiness, however, is a life lived according to Christian moral standards (2 Peter 3:11). Just as the holiness of Jesus was the principle of his life of servanthood (Mark 10:45), so the holiness of the Church and of the Christian is for the sake of Christian witness and service.

Jesus, Liberator: If the first three Christological types suggest a right-of-center or conservative understanding of Christian faith and mission, these last two reflect a left-of-center or liberal emphasis.

Given our new sensitivity to previously hidden or ignored pockets of injustice and oppression (see again chapter 3), the image of Jesus as instrument of liberation has become increasingly attractive. He is the one "who came into the world to preach the Gospel to the poor and liberate the oppressed" (Gustavo Gutierrez, Foreword to Hugo Assmann's *Practical Theology of Liberation*, London: Search Press, 1975, p. 11). He is indeed "the Liberator of the poor and the wretched of the land," and in that sense he may even be described as "black" (James Cone, *God of the Oppressed*, New York: Seabury Press, 1975, pp. 2, 133-137). For similar reasons and according to a similar theological method, Jesus is perceived as "red," "gay," or "feminist." Today, as in his own lifetime, Jesus is to be found in "bad company" (see Adolf Holl, *Jesus in Bad Company*, New York: Holt, Rinehart and Winston, 1973). But this is not to say that Jesus' whole life and work were that of a political revolutionary. His message of the Kingdom of God was directed not only against the existing order but against the Zealots as well, the political revolutionaries of his own day. "My kingdom does not belong to this world" (John 18:36).

That Jesus identified with the poor and the oppressed of his own day is without question, however. He himself belonged to the lower class and made it clear that wealth is an obstacle to entrance into the Kingdom of God (Matthew 19:16-30; Mark 10:17-31; Luke 18:18-30). He employs Isaiah 61:1 in responding to the Pharisees regarding his mission, a mission which includes preaching the good news to the poor (Matthew 11:5, Luke 4:18). He praises Zacchaeus for his generosity to the poor (Luke 19:1-10). Later Paul would propose that the wealthy should give away their superfluous goods so that some measure of equality might be established between themselves and the poor (2 Corinthians 8:14). And even if we cannot be absolutely certain that Jesus ascribed to himself the title "Suffering Servant of God" (with its roots in the Servant Songs of Deutero-Isaiah, chapters 40-55), it is clear that the early Church so interpreted his mission (Acts of the Apostles 3:13,26; 4:27,30). The words of the baptism of Jesus (Matthew 3:17; Mark 1:11; Luke 3:22) are almost an exact quotation from Isaiah 42:1. The various descriptions of the passion are probably a development of the idea of the Servant as well (Matthew 26:28; Mark 14:24; Luke 22:20). Jesus took the form of a slave on our behalf (Philippians 2:5-11). He touches lepers (Mark 1:40-41), feeds the hungry (Mark 6:34-44), converses frequently with women (Mark 7:24-30; John 4:4-30), has women in his company (Luke 8:1-3), cures on the Sabbath (Luke 13:10-17), defends an adulteress (John 8:1-11), condemns the hypocrisy of religious officials (Matthew 23:1-36), blesses those who are poor, hungry, mournful, persecuted, who seek peace (Matthew 5:1-12), places love of neighbor on par with the love of God (Mark 12:28-31), and insists that our attitude toward our neighbor in need will be the principal measure of judgment on the last day (Matthew 25:31-46).

Jesus, Our Brother: Others who are reluctant to acknowledge the Lordship of Jesus are satisfied to describe him as a kind of exemplary human being, one who inspires us to treat our fellow human beings as brothers and sisters. The great message of Christianity is summed up by Adolf Harnack as consisting of the fatherhood of God and the brotherhood of man. Jesus shows us what brotherhood is all about. This is the romanticized Jesus of *Jesus Christ Superstar* and *Godspell*. He is the symbol of joy and true life, a victimized figure who is nonetheless universally admired.

"He's a man—he's just a man. He's not a king—he's just the same as anyone I know" (*Jesus Christ Superstar*).

Brotherhood is important to the New Testament conception of the Christian life. That is undeniable. Christians are called brothers about one hundred and sixty times, and Jesus himself said that one who does the will of the Father is his (Jesus') own brother—and sister and mother (Matthew 12:50; Mark 3:35; Luke 8:31). But a Christology which goes no farther than that cannot be reconciled with the dogmatic development already outlined in the two preceding chapters. Such purely humanistic interpretations of Jesus recall a question the late Anglican Archbishop William Temple put to their adherents: "Why any man should have troubled to crucify the Christ of Liberal Protestantism has always been a mystery" (*Readings in St. John's Gospel*, New York: Macmillan, 1942, p. xxix).

CHRIST AND CULTURE

Each of these "Jesuses," when taken alone, represents a selective reading of the historical record. The principle of selection is an expression, in turn, of some cultural perspective. A given *culture* is the interlocking network of products which arises from the human activities of particular societies and communities: language, customs, ideas, beliefs, social organization, art, technology, values, and the like.

But Jesus, or at least our idea of Jesus, is not only a *reflection* of our cultural perspective. Jesus is also seen as having a *relationship* to culture, whether positive, negative, or some combination thereof. Protestant theologian H. Richard Niebuhr (d. 1962) identified five such relationships: Christ *against* culture; Christ *of* culture; Christ *above* culture; Christ and culture *in paradox*; and Christ as *transformer* of culture. The first two represent extreme views; the third, fourth, and fifth are variations on the mainstream, centrist position of the Church at large.

Christ Against Culture

Although it cannot simply be conceded that this was the original attitude of the Christian community toward the world, it surely was an answer which appeared very early in the history of the Church. The First Letter of John counsels the faithful against loving the world, for the world is under the power of evil, full of lies, hatred, murder, and lust. It is a dying world, destined to pass away (1:6, 2:8-9,11,15,17; 3:8,11-15; 5:4-5,19). The same negative orientation is to be found in the writings of Tertullian (*Apology* and *On Idolatry*), and later was significantly present in the monastic movement of the Catholic Church and in the sectarian movement within Protestantism (the Mennonites and the Quakers, for example).

The witness of radical Christianity is a perennial gift to the whole Church. Jesus alone is Lord. We cannot compromise our faith with the kingdoms of this world. On the other hand, the Christ-against-culture position denies in action what it affirms in word. The radical Christian uses the very language, thought-patterns, scientific understandings, sociological analyses, and so forth which are themselves expressions of culture. Even the writer of 1 John used the terms of the Gnostic philosophy to which he objected. Tertullian was a Roman to the core. And monasticism actually *contributed* to the advancement of culture. At the edges of the radical position, furthermore, is at least a touch of the Manichean heresy, which rejects the goodness of matter. But nature has been elevated by grace. God is present to the creation. Indeed, God took on human flesh.

The Christ of Culture

The opposite extreme is entirely comfortable with culture. There is no tension at all between Christ and the world. For those holding this view, Jesus may be a great educator, or philosopher, or reformer, or humanist. He comes not to challenge the world or to pronounce a judgment upon it but to bless and embrace it. In the earliest period this seemed to have been the position adopted by the *Judaizers*, i.e., those who sought to maintain loyalty to Christ without abandoning any important element of their Jewish traditions, and by the *Gnostics*. In more recent times, the Christ-of-culture approach is identified most closely with what Niebuhr called "culture-Protestantism" of the nineteenth and early twentieth centuries, of Friedrich Schleiermacher, Albrecht Ritschl (d. 1889), Harnack, and Walter Rauschenbusch (d. 1918), father of the Social Gospel movement in American Protestantism. The Kingdom of God for them was, for the most part, the realization of human brotherhood in this world. We are all God's children. The Lord calls us to accept and love one another.

There is much to be said about the Christ-of-culture view, just as there is much to admire in the Christ-against-culture stance. Earlier generations of non-Christians were not only impressed with the constancy and uncompromising behavior of the young Church; they were also attracted by the harmony of the Christian message with the moral and religious philosophy of their best teachers and by the agreement of Christian conduct with that of their exemplary heroes. Furthermore, the word of God *is* expressed in culturally diverse ways. The coherence of Christ with culture is rooted in the incarnational principle itself. Jesus is relevant to every time and place and people.

But the Christ-of-culture perspective is also too selective in its reading of the New Testament. Jesus does in fact stand over against the world, as the Christ-against-culture position convincingly argues. Sin is in the world—everywhere. Education alone will not produce justice or goodness or peace. The oppressed, once liberated from their oppression, too often become, in turn, the oppressors. Jesus' kingdom is not of this world (John 18:36).

Christ Above Culture

This approach and the next two share the conviction that nature, on which all culture is founded, is good and rightly ordered by the Creator—indeed, that it has been re-created by Christ and the Holy Spirit. These three positions also recognize the universality and radical character of sin. Culture is possible because of grace, i.e., God's presence; and grace has to be expressed sacramentally, in cultural forms. Nonetheless, there are three variations within this centrist point of view. We have *synthesists*, *dualists*, and *conversionists*.

The *synthesist* ("Christ above culture") confesses a Lord who is both of this world and of the other. Jesus is both God and a human being, one person with two natures, divine and human. As a human being, Jesus is very much *of* culture. As God, he is very much *above* culture. As a human being *and* God, he is at once *of* culture and *above* it.

This motif runs through the New Testament. Indeed, New Testament faith is a radically incarnational one. Christ insists, for example, that he has not come to abolish the Law and the Prophets, but to fulfill them (Matthew 5:17-19), that we should render to Caesar the things that are Caesar's and to God the things that are God's (Matthew 22:21). Justin Martyr and Clement of Alexandria were among the principal patristic synthesizers, but Thomas Aquinas and the Catholic theological tradition generally have been particularly strong representatives of this approach.

The position is attractive because it is consistent with our abiding human quest for achieving balance and for unity, a unity grounded in the unity of the Godhead itself. We shy away from single-minded, extreme positions. But some have worried that the synthesist view leads to a cultural conservatism. God is perceived by the synthesists to have been embodied very well in a particular culture; therefore, that culture (identified with "Christian civilization") should be preserved at all costs. But no culture is perfect. Does a synthesist approach take sufficient account of the radical evil which is everywhere present, or of the multiplicity of cultural ways in which the Lord can be expressed?

Christ and Culture in Paradox

The *dualist* view is identified especially with Paul and Luther. We dwell now in an "earthly tent," Paul reminds us. But when it is destroyed, as inevitably it will be, we shall have "a dwelling provided for us by God, a dwelling in the heavens, not made by hands but to last forever. We groan while we are here, even as we yearn to have our heavenly habitation envelop us" (2 Corinthians 5:1-2). For Luther there are two kingdoms, the one of God and the other of the world. God's kingdom is a kingdom of grace and mercy, but the kingdom of the world is a kingdom of wrath and severity. We cannot confuse the two, thereby putting wrath into God's kingdom or mercy into the world's, as the fanatics do. And yet the two kingdoms are closely related, and the Christian must affirm both in a single act of obedience to the one God of mercy and wrath, not as a divided soul with a double allegiance and duty. Living between time and eternity, between wrath and mercy, we find life at once tragic and joyful. There is no solution to this until the Kingdom of God comes in all its perfection at the end (see his *Treatise on Good Works*, for example). A twentieth-century variation on the Lutheran position has been expressed by Reinhold Niebuhr, especially in his *Moral Man and Immoral Society* (New York: Scribners, 1932).

The strengths of the dualist position are reasonably clear. Sin exists not only in the individual but in communities, in institutions, in laws. On the other hand, such dualism has also led Christians to a certain disdain for law and even toward the same kind of cultural conservatism we detected in the preceding view. The dualists seem to rest content with the quality of political and economic life. For the dualist, laws, institutions, the state are only restraining forces, without positive purpose and impact. All of our work in the temporal order, therefore, is transitory. However important cultural duties might be for us, the Christian's heart is simply not in them.

Christ the Transformer of Culture

This position emphasizes the participation of the Word in creation itself and of the Creator in the incarnation of the Son and in the redemption wrought through the Son's work. God brings order out of chaos in the act of creation, and Christ brings new order out of the chaos of sin in the act of redemption. History, therefore, is the dramatic interaction between God and humankind. It is the story of God's mighty deeds and of our response to them. We live "between the times." The future is already being realized in the present. The Kingdom of God is even now.

This *conversionist* motif is most clearly indicated in the Fourth Gospel, especially in its Prologue (1:1-18). "Yes, God so loved the world that he gave his only Son, that whoever believes in him may not die but may have eternal life. God did not send the Son into the world to condemn the world, but that the world might be saved through him" (3:16-17). John's sacramental vision, particularly his emphasis on the Eucharist and Baptism, stresses the conversion of ordinary elements and symbols into signs and instruments of God's redeeming and sanctifying presence. Christ is the one who transforms human actions. Indeed, when Christ is lifted up, he will draw all to himself (1:29; 3:14-17; 12:32,47).

The same conversionist motif can be found in Augustine's classic work, *The City of God*, and in his *Confessions*. Christ transforms culture in that he redirects, reinvigorates, and regenerates human life as expressed in human works which are at once perverted and corrupted by sin although of a radically good and holy nature. Whatever is is good. Jesus Christ has come to heal and to renew what sin has tarnished.

Calvin, unlike Luther and more like Augustine, also saw a positive role for social and political institutions. God's sovereignty must be made manifest in the whole network of human relationships, even in the public domain.

In the end, of course, there is no fundamental opposition between Christ and culture. The work of culture is the work of grace, and the power of grace is expressed in culture (as the *synthesists* hold). And yet we live as if in two worlds simultaneously: in *this* world, but not completely *of* it (as the *dualists* remind us). But if the world we live in is destined for the Kingdom of God, we are called to collaborate with God in its ongoing re-creation and renewal (as the *conversionist* position states). Meanwhile, the witness of the radicals helps to sharpen our sense that the Kingdom is not *of* this world, and the witness of the harmonizers or cultural Christians encourages us to commend the eternal message of Christ to those who might otherwise ignore it.

Who is the Christ of contemporary culture, then? He is all of these Christs, yet no one of them alone. But if he is to be the Christ of *history* and of Christian *faith* as well as the *contemporary* Christ, each of our modern versions of Jesus must be measured against the

standards of the biblical texts and the Church's subsequent interpretations of those texts.

"One of the strange features of Christianity," George
MacRae, Stillman Professor of Roman Catholic Studies at
Harvard Divinity School, has observed, "is that its adherents are
so often dissatisfied with the Jesus whom tradition has bequeathed
to them. New theories about Jesus, new discoveries that present
him in a different light, whatever their historical plausibility,
never lack an eager reception among the curious. And it was
always so—that is what we sometimes fail to recognize" (*Commonweal*, vol. 99, January 25, 1974, p. 417).

MacRae notes that Paul himself was frequently preoccupied
with rejecting divergent images of Jesus and cites, by way of
example, a passage in Second Corinthians:

> My fear is that, just as the serpent seduced Eve by his
> cunning, your thoughts may be corrupted and you may
> fall away from your sincere and complete devotion to
> Christ. I say this because, when someone comes preach-
> ing another Jesus than the one we preached, or when you
> receive a different spirit than the one you have received,
> or a gospel other than the gospel you accepted, you seem
> to endure it quite well. (11:3–4)

We move in the next chapter to a fuller discussion of those
New Testament texts and of the Church's faith which they
express.

SUMMARY

1. Christianity alone proclaims that Jesus of Nazareth is Lord,
that he is "true God of true God." But even within the Christian
community there are apparently widely divergent notions of Christ. Is
the Christ of *faith* the same as the Jesus of *history*? Is the Christ of *our*
faith the Christ of the Church's faith as well?

2. Popular views of Jesus Christ, both within and without the
Church, range from one end of the theological spectrum to the other.
Some see Jesus principally as a *teacher*, which he is, but as one principally
concerned with the communication of doctrine and with its purity of
expression. Others perceive Jesus as *ruler*, *judge*, and *king*, which he is,

but as one who lays down the law and who reigns over us enveloped in pomp and circumstance. Others know Jesus as the *holy man of God*, which he is, but it is a holiness that separates Christ from the world, that places him high on some pedestal removed from the everyday world of ordinary people. Still others understand Jesus as a *liberator* or revolutionary, which he is, but as one who is concerned primarily with overcoming economic and political exploitation and with renovating *this* world alone. Finally, there are those who can accept Jesus as no more, or no less, than their *brother*, a human being like us in all things. Jesus is our brother, to be sure, but he is also the Son of God, the Lord of history, the only one about whom it can be said that he is of the same substance as the Father, the Almighty.

3.   Whatever our concept of Jesus Christ, that Christ has some relationship, whether positive, negative, or some combination thereof, with the world around him. This is the problem of Christ and culture. Culture here is understood as the interlocking network of products which arises from the *human activities* of particular societies and communities: language, customs, beliefs, art, technology, social organizations, etc.

4.   Christ has been portrayed as standing entirely *against* culture. The world is evil, and we must keep our distance from it (monasticism, sectarianism, pacifism, e.g.). Although there is much that is true in this position, it tends to deny the goodness of creation as well as the inevitability of employing some cultural forms in the expression of the Word and the Kingdom of God.

5.   The Christ *of* culture is always at home wherever he finds himself. He is the fulfillment of our heart's desires and aspirations. He calls us to acknowledge God as our Father and all human beings as our brothers and sisters under God. Although this view does show the harmony that exists between the Gospel and human life, it neglects the prophetic and judgmental aspects of Christ's mission and pays too little heed to the universal presence of sin.

6.   Three other positions are generally part of the mainstream of the Church's attitude toward Christ and culture. The *synthesists* ("Christ above culture") stress the incarnational principle, namely, that Jesus is both God and a human being. As such, he is at once *above* culture and *of* it. The *dualists* ("Christ and culture in paradox") stress the fact that we live in two cities simultaneously and that complete synthesis can come only after death and the fullness of the Kingdom. The *conversionists* ("Christ the transformer of culture") emphasize the doctrines of creation and redemption. God did not send the Son to condemn the

world, which came forth from the divine hand in the first place, but to save it. When Christ is lifted up, he will draw all things to himself.

7.   The work of culture is the work of grace, and the power of grace is expressed in culture (as the *synthesists* hold). And yet we live in this world of culture while not being completely of it (as the *dualists* declare). But this world is itself destined for the Kingdom of God, and we are called to facilitate its movement toward the Kingdom (as the *conversionists* insist). All the while, the radicals ("Christ against culture") remind us that the Kingdom ultimately is not of this world, and the harmonizers or cultural Christians ("Christ of culture") encourage us to commend the eternal message of Christ to those who might otherwise ignore it.

8.   The Christ of contemporary culture is all of these Christs, yet no one of them alone.

SUGGESTED READINGS

Boff, Leonardo.   *Jesus Christ Liberator: A Critical Christology for Our Time.* New York: Orbis Books, 1978.

Cullmann, Oscar.   *Jesus and the Revolutionaries.* New York: Harper & Row, 1970.

Frei, Hans.   *The Identity of Jesus Christ: The Hermeneutical Basis of Dogmatic Theology.* Philadelphia: Fortress Press, 1975.

McFadden, Thomas R., ed.   *Does Jesus Make a Difference?* New York: Seabury Press, 1974.

Niebuhr, H. Richard.   *Christ and Culture.* New York: Harper & Row, 1951.

O'Grady, John J.   *Jesus, Lord and Christ.* New York: Paulist Press, 1972.

·XII·

THE CHRIST OF THE NEW TESTAMENT

THE PROBLEM

Jesus of Nazareth really lived. No one questions that fact today. He was born at a certain time, in a certain place, of a certain family. He passed through various stages of human development just like anyone else: infancy, childhood, adolescence, young adulthood, adulthood. He had certain convictions, and he expressed them in a certain way, to certain audiences, at certain places. He engaged in certain activities, in certain ways, in certain company, in certain places. His words and deeds had a certain impact, on certain people, under certain circumstances. And he died at a certain time, in a certain manner, at a certain place, in the presence of certain people.

But if that were all there were to the matter, Jesus Christ would not be a problem, or indeed a matter of very great concern to us today. Indeed, he is called Jesus *Christ* and not simply Jesus *of Nazareth* because a certain meaning or interpretation was given the otherwise bare historical facts of his existence some two thousand years ago. It is clear, in fact, that a special value was placed on the life and death of Jesus of Nazareth even during the first century of Christianity, immediately after his death by crucifixion at the hands of the local Roman government and at the instigation of the local religious establishment.

To be specific: It was very early asserted that this Jesus of Nazareth, who "was crucified under Pontius Pilate, suffered and was buried," did not remain in the state of death but rose from the dead "on the third day." Furthermore, that he is now "seated at the right hand of the Father," and that "he shall come again in glory to judge the living and the dead" and that his Kingdom shall have "no end." This is so because Jesus is Lord; he is "true God from true God,...one in being with the Father."

The question arises: Was the Christ whom the Church confessed in faith, both within the New Testament and beyond it, the same Jesus of Nazareth whose sheer historical factity no one seriously challenges? In other words, *Did the primitive and post-biblical Church create a Christ who is divine from a Jesus who was purely human?* And what of Jesus himself? How did he estimate his own significance? Were the words and claims which the New Testament places on the lips of the carpenter's son really the words and claims of Jesus, or were they the words and claims of the Church read back into the life and ministry of Jesus? In other words, *What connection, if any, can we establish between the Church's evaluation of Jesus and Jesus' own evaluation of himself?*

It is, once again, *the problem of the Jesus of history and the Christ of faith.*

THE SOURCES AND THEIR INTERPRETATION
Non-Christian Sources

The few non-Christian sources for the life of Jesus provide us with very little information. They do confirm the argument, however, that from the earliest days it never occurred even to the bitterest enemies of Christianity that the historical existence of Jesus should be challenged. Tacitus (d. ca. 116) reported that Jesus was condemned to death by Pontius Pilate under Tiberius (*Annals* 15,4). Suetonius (d. ca. 120) wrote of a certain "Chrestus" who caused disturbances in Rome (*Claudius* 25,4). Pliny the Younger (d. ca. 110) acknowledged in a letter to Trajan that Christ was revered as a God (*Epistola* 10,96). Josephus the historian (d. ca. 93) referred to James as the brother of Jesus who is called the Christ (*Antiquities*, 20,200). The Talmud references and the apocryphal gospels (e.g., the Gospel of Thomas) likewise add nothing to our knowledge of Jesus. Again, at best this non-Christian material provides independent evidence for the actual existence of Jesus.

Christian Sources

New Testament

The most important source for the life of Jesus, therefore, remains the New Testament itself, and the four Gospels in particular. But when one dips into the Gospels, one finds that they do not present history as we generally understand that word today. In other words, they would not stand up alongside a lengthy obituary essay in the *New York Times* as a work of objective reporting and interpretation. They provide us instead with a testimony of faith. *Their purpose is not to reconstruct the life of Jesus in every chronologically accurate detail, but to illustrate the eternal significance of Jesus through selected examples of his preaching, his activities, and the impact of both upon his contemporaries.*

The Gospels were written by men of faith for men and women of faith. They are the product of subsequent reflection on the life of Jesus—a process that required anywhere from thirty-five to sixty years. They are complex documents because of their peculiar purpose, because of the diversity of their origin and the audiences to which they were initially addressed, and because of the various stages of development they passed through before reaching the form in which we have them.

There are at least *three stages of development* culminating in the actual writing of the Gospels: (1) the original words and deeds of Jesus; (2) the oral proclamation of the Apostles and disciples (catechesis, narratives, testimonies, hymns, doxologies, and prayers); and (3) the writings themselves. These are specified as such by the Instruction of the Pontifical Biblical Commission, *The Historical Truth of the Gospels*, 1964. (An excerpt is given in the Appendix. The full text and a commentary by Joseph Fitzmyer appear in *Theological Studies*, vol. 25, 1964, pp. 386-408.)

Depending upon one's point of view, one might expand the number of stages to five; for example: (1) the period of direct contact and communication between Jesus and the disciples and others; (2) the emergence of an oral tradition following the resurrection, a period in which there were no significant writings because the expectation of the Second Coming or return of Christ was intense and vivid; (3) the hardening of the oral tradition into the shape of accepted doctrine communicated through letters (Epistles), which were written for specific occasions and audiences and not for posterity; (4) the writing of the Gospels as soon as it became clear that the Lord was not about to return very soon, a period in which the first generation of Christians was dying out and a new generation, with no direct contact with, or memories of, Jesus was coming on the scene (much like the situation today when many young people have no personal recollection of a 1960s figure such as John F. Kennedy); (5) the completion of the New Testament canon (official collection of books accepted by the Church as inspired) with the composition of the pastoral Epistles (Timothy and Titus) and 2 Peter, a period in which the Church is newly conscious of itself as a society, still threatened from without and from within.

Development

How many stages of development there were is a matter of choice, but *the fact of development is beyond question today*. Indeed, we cannot easily overestimate the significance of the Pontifical Biblical Commission's Instruction of 1964 on the historicity of the Gospels. The Commission calmly and openly admits that we do not have in the written Gospels the words and deeds of Jesus as exactly and as completely as they were first uttered or performed, nor do we even have the full and exact record of what was communicated orally between the death and resurrection, on the one hand, and the actual composition of the Gospels, on the other. What we have, rather, is *the finally edited version* given by the evangelists. This imposes upon us all the responsibility of trying to get behind and beyond the written Gospels, and to identify and sort out the various *levels of tradition* through which the evangelical process moved.

The *first layer* of tradition is made accessible through *historical criticism*. Historical criticism is a relatively late development in the history of Christian theology and of biblical interpretation. Until the Enlightenment of the eighteenth century it was generally assumed that the Gospels gave a clear and reliable account of the life of Jesus, that there was no discrepancy at all between the faith of the primitive Church and the facts upon which that faith was built. Herman Reimarus (d. 1768), a German professor of oriental languages, was the first to challenge this assumption with the rallying cry "Back from the Christ of dogma to the real Jesus." The immediate reaction to Reimarus' thesis was strongly negative. Many different versions of the "life of Jesus" appeared, as if in rebuttal of Reimarus. But the differences among the several "lives" of Jesus were glaringly obvious. As we pointed out in the preceding chapter, many authors portrayed Jesus as they would like him to have been rather than Jesus as the early Church knew him to be. The biographical confusion generated an attitude of fundamental skepticism about the whole project. Albert Schweitzer (d. 1965) slammed the door once and for all on Liberal efforts at reconstructing the life of Jesus with his own *The Quest of the Historical Jesus*, published right at the turn of the century. The historical Jesus, it now seemed, could not be recovered scientifically from the New Testament documents. But this, too, proved to be an over-reaction, and since Schweitzer's time there has, in fact, been a steady return of confidence in the scholar's and the Church's capacity to get behind the testimonies of faith and identify at least the basic historical foundation of Jesus' life and ministry.

The *second layer* of tradition is discovered through a method known as *form criticism*. This method was developed in Germany between the two world wars and was concerned primarily with the formation of the Gospel tradition which occurred through catechesis and liturgical expressions, roughly between 35 and 60 A.D. It is essentially a means of analyzing typical features of biblical texts (hymns, acclamations, confessions, sermons, instructional material, editorial remarks, descriptive narratives, sayings of Jesus, dialogues, Old Testament allusions and quotations, etc.) in order to relate them to their original "situation-in-life." It was the development of form criticism which brought out the fact that a long period of *oral* tradition preceded any writing of the New Testament.

The *third layer* of tradition is examined through the method of *redaction criticism*, whose origin is the most recent of all, i.e., the mid 1950s. Redaction criticism tries to discover the dominant ideas which governed the final editing of the Gospels as we have them today (e.g., What was the "peculiar purpose" of each evangelist mentioned by the Biblical Commission's 1964 Instruction?). Just as form criticism discloses the existence of an *oral* tradition prior to the formulation of the New Testament, so redaction criticism stresses the antecedent existence of *both* oral *and written* traditions from which the New Testament authors worked and which they creatively transformed to suit their particular theological and catechetical intentions.

Different Cultures

Furthermore, there are different cultures at work in the production of the New Testament, and these, in turn, generate distinctive theological viewpoints regarding the meaning of Jesus. These are the cultures of the Palestinian communities of Aramaic/Hebrew-speaking Jewish Christians, of the Syrian communities of Greek-speaking Jewish Christians, of the communities of Asia Minor and Greece with their Greek-speaking Gentile Christians, and finally of the particular communities influenced by major individual Christians like Paul and John. One might also classify these cultures more broadly as Palestinian, Jewish-Hellenistic, and Hellenistic-Gentile.

Only in the past century has biblical scholarship acquired the linguistic and historical data necessary for even recognizing such theological and cultural diversity within New Testament Christianity. Previous scholarship, for example, had known Aramaic, the language which Jesus apparently spoke. But the only forms of Aramaic which it had at its disposal came from several centuries before Jesus (Imperial Aramaic) or from several centuries after Jesus (Syriac and Talmudic Aramaic). "To reconstruct the language of Jesus from such evidence," Catholic biblical scholar Raymond Brown writes, "was not unlike trying to reconstruct Shakespearian English from Chaucer and the *New York Times*" (*Horizons*, vol. 1, 1974, p. 43). The situation improved over the past one hundred years through such relatively recent discoveries as the Dead Sea Scrolls in 1947. (For a good summary of their contents and significance, see John L. McKenzie, "Qumran Scrolls," *Dictionary of the Bible*, pp. 710-716.)

Sayings of Jesus

In spite of the plurality of stages, layers, forms, and so forth, biblical scholars have reached a consensus regarding criteria for establishing authentic sayings of the historical Jesus: (1) Sayings which contain Aramaicisms characteristic of the Palestine of Jesus' day are more likely to have their origin in Jesus. (2) The shorter or shortest of two or three different accounts of the same incident is probably the one closer or closest to the source, since authors tend to expand and explain. (3) Sayings or principles attributed to Jesus which are contrary to the developing traditions of the early Church are usually more authentic than those which clearly give support to current attitudes. (4) The same is true of elements in the message of Jesus which make a break with the accepted traditions and customs of Judaism. (5) Words and deeds which are attested to by many different sources probably have a strong historical basis. (6) Negatively, sayings which reflect the faith, practices, and situation of the post-resurrection Church cannot be taken always at face value.

Interpretations of the Sources

Until the eighteenth century, as we noted above, there was no New Testament problem. All Christians—Catholic, Anglican, Orthodox, and Protestant alike—assumed that the Christ of the New Testament and the Jesus of history were exactly one and the same. But once the assumption was challenged, Christians began dividing over the question of the relationship between the Christ of faith and the Jesus of history, i.e., between the Church's interpretation of Jesus and Jesus' own self-understanding.

Those positions move all the way from the conservative right, which posits a real relationship between Jesus' self-evaluation and the New Testament Church's Christology, to the liberal left, which denies any real relationship or continuity between the two. Those positions are also distinguished by their scholarly or non-scholarly bases of support. *Scholarly* conservatism and *scholarly* liberalism are expressed by reputable scholars who have produced a body of articles that meet the publishing standards of the professional biblical journals or whose books have been reviewed favorably in such journals. It is not enough, therefore, that a point of view be expressed and defended by someone holding a biblical degree or a teaching position in biblical studies. *Non-scholarly* conservatism and *non-scholarly* liberalism are the product of those who either hold no biblical degrees and/or no teaching position in biblical studies or who have not published a body of articles in serious professional journals or books which have been reviewed favorably in such journals. The distinction is important for making sense of such comments as "Scripture scholars are divided over this question," or "Not all Scripture scholars agree with this position," or "Scripture scholars tell us that...," or "Scripture scholars can't make up their minds about...."

What follows is a summary, with some modifications, of Catholic biblical scholar Raymond Brown's schematization of twentieth-century views on the Christology of the New Testament:

Non-scholarly Conservatism

This view *identifies* the Christology of the New Testament with Jesus' own self-evaluation. Even though the Gospels were written some thirty to sixty years after the ministry of Jesus, this conservative position maintains that there had been *no significant Christological development* in that time. Thus, when Jesus accepted Peter's confession that Jesus was indeed the Messiah, the Son of the living God (Matthew 16:13-20), that acceptance reflects the self-understanding of Jesus—despite the fact that Peter's confession and Jesus' reaction are very different in the *earlier* Gospel of Mark (8:27-30). And if in the Gospel of John, Jesus speaks as a pre-existent divine figure (8:58; 17:5), he must have actually spoken that way during his lifetime—despite the fact that there is no indication of this in the three synoptic Gospels.

This view was first held defensively (i.e., over against the views of the scholars of the major Protestant denominations) by Protestant fundamentalists and other less-than-fundamentalist

Christians, particularly in various main-line Reformation churches of the American South. Catholics generally also held this position, but not defensively. After the condemnations of Modernism there was strict supervision over Catholic biblical studies from 1910 until Pope Pius XII's encyclical *Divino Afflante Spiritu* in 1943. Before 1943, the non-scholarly conservative position was the only view taught, accepted, and preached in the Catholic Church; it was simply taken for granted. Once the principles of modern biblical criticism were approved by Rome and assimilated by Catholic scholars, however, some Catholics did become exceedingly defensive about the traditional approach.

In light of the fact that the Gospels do not provide a literal account of what Jesus said and did, and in light of the evidence for development in the production of the New Testament, the non-scholarly conservatives should have asked, "How much development?" Instead they asked, "How do we know that any of it is true?" And rather than risk the loss of faith itself, they simply rejected the whole network of scholarly premises, even those formally and explicitly endorsed by the pope in the encyclical of 1943 and by the Pontifical Biblical Commission's Instruction of 1964.

Non-scholarly Liberalism

As on a political spectrum (Stalin at the extreme left, Hitler at the extreme right), the extremes touch. If the non-scholarly conservative asked the wrong question ("How do I know any of it is true?"), so, too, did the non-scholarly liberal. The only difference is in the answers given. The conservative rejects the scholarship in order to "save" the Christ of faith. The non-scholarly liberal rejects the Christ of faith in order to "save" his or her favorite notion of the Jesus of history.

The non-scholarly liberal concludes that there is no continuity at all between the Christology of the New Testament and Jesus' self-evaluation. He was nothing more than an ordinary man, except that he was more brilliant, more charismatic, more of a revolutionary, or take your pick. It is not finally important that Jesus was or was not the Son of God. It is what he taught us about life that counts, and what he taught us is that we have to love one another.

Although non-scholarly liberalism began as a Protestant phenomenon, enjoying wide popularity during the early decades of this century before it was effectively challenged by scholars and by declining membership rolls, it has made a belated entrance into Catholicism as a reaction to the exaggerated dogmatism of the pre-Vatican II period.

Scholarly Liberalism

Scholarly liberalism, unlike its non-scholarly counterpart, does not dismiss the Christology of the New Testament as unimportant, nor does it deny that the New Testament writers claimed far more than that Christianity was a "way of life." On the other hand, scholarly liberalism shares with its non-scholarly cousin the conviction that the Christology of the New Testament is a mistaken evaluation of Jesus which does not stand in real continuity with the self-evaluation of Jesus. For the liberals, New Testament Christology is a *creation* of the early Church.

Unquestionably, modern biblical studies owe a great debt of gratitude to the previous work of the liberal scholars. They were the ones, after all, who first challenged the non-scholarly conservatism which dominated all Christian churches until the eighteenth century. It was the liberals who discerned developmental patterns in the New Testament and who laid the groundwork for many of our present principles of biblical interpretation. Perhaps the best example of this scholarly liberalism in terms of both method and content was Wilhelm Bousset (d. 1920), whose book *Kyrios Christos* was first published in German in 1913 and in English translation in 1970 (Nashville: Abingdon).

For the scholarly liberals the historical Jesus was a preacher of stark ethical demand who challenged the religious institutions and who cut through the false ideas of his time. If the early Church had not turned him into the heavenly Son of Man, the Lord and Judge of the world, or indeed the Son of God, his ideals and insights might otherwise have been lost. But now that the crutch of New Testament Christology is no longer necessary (Christ's place in history and in our collective memories is secure), it can be discarded.

Bultmannian Existentialism

World War I undercut the optimism of liberal theology, and of liberal biblical scholarship as well. The war created a need for a God who saves us in Jesus, rather than for a Jesus who taught us how to live and, in effect, to save ourselves. In theology the anti-liberal movement was headed by Karl Barth. In the area of biblical studies it was led by Rudolf Bultmann.

Some mistakenly place Bultmann in the liberal camp because so many of his views were regarded as radical when he first proposed them. Yet his New Testament theology is a rejection of pre-World War I liberalism. Without discarding the legitimate methodological achievements of liberalism, Bultmann nevertheless denied the liberal thesis that New Testament Christology was a creation of the early Church. That is not to say that Bultmann's own view is clear and unequivocal. Brown regards it "difficult to characterize exactly" and suggests that "in some of his writing at least he is agnostic about the self-evaluation of Jesus" (*Horizons* article, p. 45). But Bultmann definitely did not think that the Christology of the New Testament distorted the import of Jesus, as the liberals maintained. Rather, there is a *functional equivalence* between the Church's Christological proclamation and Jesus' own proclamation of the Kingdom.

It is in this functional equivalence that Bultmann's existentialist philosophy can be found at work (see chapter 4, where Bultmann's existentialist philosophy is mentioned in the context of various theologies of human existence). If we are to escape from the vicious circle of futile existence, it will only be through the saving action of God in Jesus. We are called upon to accept this action of God. Where Jesus preached the Kingdom, the Church preached Jesus. Functionally, this preaching was equivalent. Dispensing, therefore, with the Church's proclamation would be to dispense with the challenge that is at the core of Christianity, a challenge that is primarily based on what God has done for us, rather than what we can do for ourselves.

Moderate Conservatism

Just as Bultmann's position was somewhat to the right of the scholarly liberals, so most contemporary biblical scholarship is somewhat to the right of Bultmann. This does not ignore the fact that Catholic scholarship has moved decidedly *to the left* since the 1940s, but it has moved "to the left" in relation to the non-scholarly conservatism which controlled Catholic theology and biblical studies beforehand.

This moderate conservatism posits a *discernible continuity* between the self-evaluation of Jesus and the Christology of the early Church. Nonetheless, there is some difference of opinion within the moderate conservative group. On one side, there are those for whom the Church's Christology is *explicit* in Jesus' self-evaluation, and, on the other, those for whom the Church's Christology is only *implicit* in Jesus' self-understanding. Neither side, however, holds that Jesus applied to himself or accepted the so-called "higher" titles of later New Testament Christology, e.g., "Lord," "Son of God," or "God." Both sides regard the application of these titles to have been the result of later Christian reflection on the mystery of Christ. Where the two sides differ, therefore, is on the matter of the so-called "lower" titles that were known to the Jews from the Old Testament or inter-testamental writings—e.g., "Messiah," "Prophet," "Servant of God," or "Son of Man."

The *explicit* school was popular in the 1950s and early 1960s and is still respectable today. Among its adherents are such Protestant scholars as Oscar Cullmann, C. H. Dodd (d. 1973), Joachim Jeremias, and Vincent Taylor (d. 1968). Most Roman Catholic scholars writing on the subject in the 1960s were in the same camp.

In the 1970s, however, in Protestant and Catholic writing alike, the *implicit* school gained acceptance. According to this approach, Jesus did not express his self-understanding in terms of titles or accept titles attributed to him by others. Rather he conveyed what he was by speaking with unique authority and by acting with unique power. This view of Jesus' attitude does not necessarily detract from his greatness. If Jesus did not find the title "Messiah" acceptable, for example, it may mean only that the title simply did not match his uniqueness. The Church was able to call him "Messiah" successfully only after it reinterpreted the title to match Jesus' greatness. Thus, the ultimate tribute to Jesus may have been that every term or title in the theological vocabulary of Israel had to be reshaped by his followers to do justice to him, including even the title "God" itself. Even the Second Vatican Council, as early as 1965, anticipated this shift: "...Jesus perfected revelation by fulfilling it through His whole work of making Himself present and manifesting Himself: though His words and deeds, His signs and wonders, but especially through His death and glorious resurrection from the dead and final sending of the Spirit of truth" (*Dogmatic Constitution on Divine Revelation*, n. 4). Among the scholars holding to the *implicit* opinion are, on the Reformation side of the line, F. Hahn, Reginald Fuller, Norman Perrin (d. 1977), some of the post-Bultmannians in Germany, and Roman Catholic authors of the 1970s such as Bruce Vawter and Raymond Brown (it would seem).

Brown and others expect that for the rest of this century biblical scholarship will move back and forth between these two moderate conservative positions. But regardless of whether one detects explicit or implicit Christology in the self-evaluation of Jesus, the line of *continuity* between his self-understanding and the early Church's subsequent proclamation is more firmly secure than was ever thought possible earlier in the century.

(For a summary, see the chart on page 437.)

WHERE FROM HERE?
THE QUESTION OF METHOD

From this point we can proceed in one of two directions. We can adopt the more traditional approach and take up the life and teachings of Jesus, beginning with the Gospel accounts. Thereafter, we would present the early Church's estimation of Jesus. But there are problems with this alternative. The fact is that the New Testament contains no biography of Jesus written during his lifetime nor even shortly after his death. What we have, as noted earlier, are testimonies of faith, constituted from fragments of the oral and written traditions which developed after Jesus' death and resurrection. It is Jesus *as he was remembered* by the earliest Christians and *as he was experienced* in their communities of faith whom we meet in the Gospels.

A second course is open to us, one that *begins* with the faith of the Church as expressed in the New Testament and moves from there to the message, mission, and person of Jesus as the source of that faith. The faith of the Church is centered on the *resurrection* of Jesus from the dead. The *kerygma*, or proclamation, is by definition a testimony to the resurrection, the earliest witness to which is given in Paul's First Letter to the Corinthians (15:3-8), written sometime in the year 56 or 57. Paul is obviously incorporating a creedal formula that he had previously been taught:

> I handed on to you as of the greatest importance
>   what I myself received:
> that Christ died for our sins
>   in accordance with the Scriptures,
> and that he was buried,
> and that he was raised on the third day
>   in accordance with the Scriptures,
> and that he was seen by Cephas,
>   then by the Twelve.
> After that he was seen by five hundred brothers at
>   once, most of whom are still alive, although some
>   have fallen asleep.
> After that he was seen by James,
>   then by all the apostles.
> Last of all he was seen by me. . . .

Paul explicitly states that he is drawing on tradition, and certain internal evidence suggests this—e.g., the stylized structure of the passage and the use of such terms as "the Twelve," which is not an expression he uses otherwise. Clearly, he had some ready-made text at hand. And this would have been an entirely normal practice in the composition of the various books of the New Testament. Authors like Paul would draw upon existing liturgical formulations, as Paul had done earlier in the same letter when he quoted from a traditional eucharistic prayer (1 Corinthians 11:23-26).

We begin, therefore, where the New Testament begins, not with the nativity scene in Bethlehem but with the Church's proclamation of the risen Christ.

THE RESURRECTION
Its Meaning and Importance

The resurrection has been understood poorly. We refer here not only to the question of its facticity (whether it was a bodily, historical happening) but to the question of its place and significance in the whole Christ-event. For Roman Catholic theology the resurrection has long been viewed as simply the strongest possible corroboration of Jesus' messianic claims. It had no importance in itself in the work of redemption. We were redeemed by the cross, and by the cross alone. This relatively narrow perception of the resurrection was not a peculiarly Catholic failing. Even so great a biblical scholar as C. H. Dodd lends unwitting support to such an approach in his book *The Founder of Christianity*, where the resurrection comes at the end, as "the sequel" to the whole story about Jesus. "Liberation Christology" has the same tendency, for reasons already suggested (e.g., Jon Sobrino, *Christology at the Crossroads: A Latin American Approach*, Maryknoll, N.Y.: Orbis Books, 1978).

Christian theology today, in keeping with the results of modern New Testament studies, more commonly understands the resurrection as central to, not simply confirmatory of, Christian faith, and as the beginning, not the end, of the story.

Three men died on crosses in occupied Palestine sometime during the fourth decade of the Christian era. The executions were relatively routine. And so, too, was the mode of execution. Without question the Roman authorities regarded all three as trouble-makers, disturbers of the Roman peace. Over the head of one of them, however, the Romans affixed a sign "The King of the Jews," obviously in a spirit of derision and contempt. If we could return to Calvary on that Good Friday, that is all we would have seen: three men being put to death by crucifixion. And yet one of the three, the one they called "King of the Jews," would not be swallowed up forever by his death. At some point soon after his death, his closest followers would become convinced that he had, in fact, risen from the dead and that he lived again in their midst in a new and more powerful way than before. On the basis of their experience of the resurrection, these disciples would see the life and death of Jesus in a whole new light. They would reinterpret everything that he had said and done, recalling and reconstructing it all to the best of their ability. The message of the New Testament was always the message of the resurrection:

> Men of Israel, listen to me [it is Peter who speaks]! Jesus the Nazorean was a man whom God sent to you with miracles, wonders, and signs as his credentials. These God worked through him in your midst, as you well know. He was delivered up by the set purpose and plan of God; you even made use of pagans to crucify and kill him. God freed him from death's bitter pangs, however, and raised him up again, for it was impossible that death should keep its hold on him. . . .
>
> This is the Jesus God raised up, and we are his witnesses. . . .
>
> Therefore let the whole house of Israel know beyond any doubt that God has made both Lord and Messiah this Jesus whom you crucified. (Acts of the Apostles 2:22-24,32,36)

Paul was even more explicit about the centrality and utterly crucial importance of the resurrection for Christian faith: "And if Christ has not been raised, our preaching is void of content and your faith is empty too" (1 Corinthians 15:14).

The ambiguity that surrounded the life and death of Jesus now disappears. Under the impact of the resurrection everything falls into place. For the first time the Apostles look upon the figure of Jesus with confidence and self-assurance. His relationship with the Father, the Almighty, is now clearer than ever before. Jesus is without doubt the Christ, the Anointed One, of God. He is the Son of Man, the Suffering Servant, the Son of God, the Lord, the Son of David, the Word. At first such titles as these were *functional*; i.e., they described what Jesus had done. Then they became *confessional*; i.e., they were used in prayer and worship. They specified what it meant to be a Christian, i.e., one who confesses that Jesus is Lord. And eventually the titles were to assume a *metaphysical* and *theological* character; i.e., they would become intellectual tools to probe the inner reality of Jesus Christ: his person, his natures, and their relationships.

It was because of the early Church's faith in the resurrection that it came to acknowledge the *divinity* of Jesus. And once the Church acknowledged the divinity of Jesus, it began laying the foundations for the doctrine of the *incarnation*, which sees Jesus as the Word made flesh (John 1:14). From the doctrine of the incarnation the Church was led ineluctably to the *preexistence* of Jesus (John 1:1; Philippians 2:5-9) and to the question of his relationship to the whole of *creation* and to the *history of salvation* (Colossians 1:15-20; Romans 8:19-22; Ephesians 1:9-10,22,23). He is indeed the "first fruits" (1 Corinthians 15:20) of the "new creation" (2 Corinthians 5:17), which is the *Kingdom of God*.

Varieties of Interpretation Within the New Testament

As noted earlier in this chapter, there are different cultures at work in the production of the New Testament, and these, in turn, generate distinctive theological viewpoints regarding the meaning of Jesus. In each case, however, it is the Easter experience which provides the foundation for Christology.

Palestinian Community

In the Palestinian community, the closest to the events of the life, death, and resurrection of Jesus, there is a keen sense of the *imminence* of the Second Coming of Jesus. Jesus is identified as the *Son of Man* (Acts of the Apostles 7:55-56), who will return in power and glory—an identification which has apparent roots in Jesus' own sayings about the Son of Man (Mark 8:38; Luke 12:8-10). The return of Jesus as the Son of Man is the final act of vindication for all that Jesus said and did during his lifetime. Indeed, this hope shaped the liturgy of the Palestinian Church. At the center of its eucharistic worship is the *Maranatha* prayer, "O Lord, come!" (1 Corinthians 16:22), "Come, Lord Jesus!" (Revelation 22:20).

More important and certainly more central to the Palestinian Christology was its confession of Jesus as *the Christ* (Acts 3:20), or the *Messiah* (literally, "the anointed"). And because Jesus is the Messiah, he is also seen as the *Son of David* (Revelation 3:7; 5:5) and the *Son of God* (Luke 1:32), who will appear at the Second Coming, or *Parousia*. This explains, too, why such stress is placed in Matthew and Luke on the genealogies (Matthew 1:1-17; Luke 3:23-38). It was necessary that Jesus be able to trace his ancestry all the way back to David, for it had to be a descendant of the house of David who would inaugurate the messianic era (Mark 11:10). The Son of God title, on the other hand, expressed the closeness between Jesus and God, but not necessarily his divinity, as many might think. In the Old Testament, for example, various individuals and groups are called sons of God (e.g., Exodus 4:22-23; Hosea 11:1; Isaiah 1:2; Jeremiah 3:19). Subsequently, the title came to have messianic significance, but it was not until the much later Hellenistic stage that the title signified divinity.

Among other titles applied to Jesus by the Palestinian community were *Prophet* (Acts of the Apostles 3:22-24) and *Servant* (3:26), fused as the Mosaic prophet-servant of Yahweh. But the *Christ* title remained the focal point for all the rest.

Jewish-Hellenistic Community

The Jewish-Hellenistic community, composed of Greek-speaking Jewish converts to Christianity, had to translate such Palestinian categories into intelligible Hellenistic ones. The delay of the *Parousia* seemed to require a major theological shift away from emphasis on the Second Coming of Jesus in the future to the *present exalted state* of Jesus. Thus, Jesus is the one who is *already* Lord (*Kyrios*) and Christ (Acts of the Apostles 2:36), for he is even now "exalted at God's right hand" (2:33). Indeed, that becomes the central confession of faith: "Jesus is Lord" (Acts of the Apostles 11:20; 16:31; Philippians 2:11). It is in the name of the "Lord Jesus" that Christians are baptized (Acts of the Apostles 8:16; 19:5). In using the title *Lord*, the Greek-speaking Jews were attributing divine status to Jesus, for it was a title employed in the Greek Old Testament (the *Septuagint*) to translate the Hebrew equivalent for Yahweh. And so the various Palestinian titles are recast in the light of this new and distinctive emphasis on the exaltation of Jesus: Christ, Son of Man, Son of David, Son of God (Acts of the Apostles 2:36; 11:17; Romans 1:3-4). At an even later stage, the Jewish-Hellenistic Church projects these titles back into the earthly life of Jesus as well.

Hellenistic-Gentile Community

The final stage of Christological development occurs within the Hellenistic-Gentile community, under the impact of the missionary activity of the Pauline and Johannine schools of theology. The Church now fully accommodates itself to the conceptual categories of the Greek world. The classic expression of this Christology is contained in the great hymn of Philippians 2:5-11, complete with the three-deckered Hellenistic cosmology: heaven, earth, and the underworld (v. 10). Correspondingly, there is a threefold division of Jesus' existence: his pre-existence (v. 6), his becoming flesh in the incarnation (vv. 7-8), and his exaltation following his death and resurrection (vv. 9-11). Variations on this threefold pattern can be found in Colossians 1:15-20 and the Prologue of John's Gospel (1:1-14).

Furthermore, what was only hinted at in the early stages of Jewish-Hellenistic Christology is fully developed in Hellenistic-Gentile Christology: The earthly life of Jesus is itself already an exalted form of existence, although veiled. In the synoptic Gospels we have evidence of this in the infancy narratives, the accounts of Jesus' baptism by John, and the Transfiguration (e.g., Luke 1:5—2:52; 3:21-22; 9:28-36). In John's Gospel, of course, this so-called "high Christology" is full-blown.

And there is a correlative reinterpretation of the titles as employed by the earlier Christologies. The *Son of Man* is portrayed as "the One who came down" from heaven (John 3:13), and when he ascends, it will be "to where he was before" (6:62). The title *Christ* becomes, for all practical purposes, a proper name for Jesus. *Son of God* takes on a higher meaning than it once enjoyed in the Old Testament, and *Lord* becomes entirely central. Thus, for the Hellenistic-Gentile Church God is even now present exercising lordship over the universe in and through Jesus Christ, who is the risen and exalted Lord.

Its Redemptive Effects

The resurrection is a saving event because it is not until Jesus has received the fullness of life which is properly his as Son of God and Son of Man that his redemptive work is complete. He is the firstborn of those who rise (Colossians 1:18). Jesus "was handed over to death for our sins and raised up for our justification" (Romans 4:25). Those of us who die and are buried with him will also rise with him to new life (6:3-11). He was in fact raised from the dead "so that we might bear fruit for God" (7:4). To be "in Christ" who is risen is to be "a new creation" (2 Corinthians 5:17). We have been born anew "unto hope...from the resurrection of Jesus Christ from the dead" (1 Peter 1:3). Indeed, the Spirit cannot be given until Jesus has been raised and glorified (John 7:39; 16:7), and the first thing the risen Lord does when he appears to the disciples behind locked doors is to breathe the Holy Spirit upon them (20:19-23). Our very bodies are given life through the Spirit which now possesses us (Romans 8:11).

The resurrection, therefore, is the principle of our own new being. The Father who raised Jesus will also raise us (2 Corinthians 4:14). Those who die with Christ will live with him (2 Timothy 2:11). Jesus is the resurrection and the life. Those who believe in him will be raised on the last day (John 11:25-26; 6:39-44,54). Nowhere is this theme more fully elaborated than in 1 Corinthians 15: "...if Christ was not raised, your faith is worthless. You are still in your sins, and those who have fallen asleep in Christ are the deadest of the dead" (vv. 17-18). But Christ was raised. And just as "death came through a man," so "the resurrection of the dead comes through a man also. Just as in Adam all die, so in Christ all will come to life again" (vv. 21-22).

Its Historicity

Did It Happen?

Something happened after the death of Jesus. The tomb was found empty on Easter morning, many claimed to have seen the risen Jesus, and many more were marvelously transformed by the event and its aftermath. Certainly from the very earliest days of Christianity, Jesus' followers were convinced that he had indeed been raised from the dead. The Pauline confession to which we referred earlier (1 Corinthians 15:3-8) has its origins at least as early as 35 A.D., the year of Paul's own conversion to Christ. The construction of these verses reflects an Aramaic or Hebrew background, which tends to confirm the hypothesis that it comes from a very primitive tradition indeed.

What Happened?

But the problem, of course, is that no one actually saw the resurrection. We have no eyewitnesses. To the extent that we know anything at all about it, we know it through its effects. Is it an historical event, therefore? The answer has to be "No" if by "historical" one means an event that could have been photographed as it was occurring or that a disinterested person could have observed happening. There is no indication in the New Testament record that the early Church believed the resurrection to have been in the very same category of history as the crucifixion, for example. Even the enemies of Jesus could see what was taking place on Calvary. On the contrary, Jesus is said to have entered an entirely new mode of life, a Spirit-filled existence in which he becomes the source of life for all humankind (2 Corinthians 3:17; 1 Corinthians 15:43). If Jesus had simply resumed the kind of bodily existence he had before his death, then he would not have been the risen Lord. On the contrary, for him there could be no return to the realm of ordinary space and time. His history was over. He had moved into the final and definitive state of existence and would never die again (unlike, for example, Lazarus whom Jesus had raised from the dead). And yet to concede that the resurrection was not an historical event in our ordinary sense of historical event (something open to scientific investigation and verifiable by neutral witnesses) does not mean that the resurrection was not a *real* event for Jesus with *historical implications* for others.

Behind the apostolic confession of faith in the risen Lord lies the experience of having witnessed him at some time and in some way. The disciples were convinced that they had indeed seen him, so that *for them* the appearances *are* historical. And it would have been very difficult from a purely psychological point of view to synchronize such a wide range of individual experiences of the risen Lord unless there was some basis in reality for them. Furthermore, the appearances are not to people in general, but to particular individuals, in particular places, at particular times.

Nonetheless, it would seem better to speak of the resurrection as *trans-historical* rather than *unhistorical*. The average person will translate *unhistorical* simply to mean that it never happened at all. It is trans-historical in the sense that it refers to an event that took place on the other side of death and, therefore, which lies beyond the confines of space and time. Similarly, the reality of the risen Lord is also a reality which transcends history as we know it. By the resurrection Jesus enters a completely new universe of being, the end-time of history, beyond the control of history and beyond the reach of historians.

To Whom Did It Happen?

Was the resurrection truly something that happened *to Jesus*? Some have argued that it did not happen to Jesus but to his disciples. In other words, the mystery of the resurrection means that the early Church and in particular the Apostles and disciples were suddenly enlightened regarding the meaning of Jesus' life and death. The resurrection was an evolution of their consciousness as they gradually began to understand what Jesus was all about, much as some Americans might have been inspired to work diligently in the cause of civil rights following the assassination of Martin Luther King, Jr. (d. 1968).

The question of the *bodiliness* of the resurrection, therefore, is a very important one. If it *was* a bodily occurrence, then it was something that *did* happen to Jesus, and not just to his disciples. It was a sovereign act of God the Father glorifying Jesus of Nazareth and making him the source of new life for all of us.

The bodily element is clear in the description of some of the post-resurrection appearances of Jesus to his disciples. The evangelists speak of touching (John 20:27), eating (Luke 24:41-43), and conversing (John 21:15-22). This drives home the underlying unity between the Jesus of history and the risen Lord. It also counteracts the Greek tendency to spiritualize everything, to make of the resurrection, therefore, an abstract, non-corporeal event. The physical emphasis also challenges certain Gnostic interpretations of Jesus that were already beginning to appear in the second half of the first century.

On the other hand, there had to be something radically different about Jesus' "bodiliness" following the resurrection. The resurrection, after all, was not the resuscitation of a corpse. The disciples, for example, sometimes did not recognize him as he stood before them (Luke 24:16; John 20:14; 21:4), and some even doubted that it was he (Matthew 28:17; Luke 24:41). The risen Jesus is portrayed as coming and going in a manner unlike that of any mortal body (Luke 24:31; John 20:19,26). Mark says explicitly that he appeared "in another form" (Mark 16:12). This contrary emphasis on the difference between Jesus' historical existence and his risen existence safeguards against a too-physical understanding of the resurrection, and stresses the Pauline teaching that Jesus underwent a marvelous *transformation* (1 Corinthians 15:42-44).

Therefore, in trying to determine what really happened and to whom, we have to avoid two extreme answers: one which denies all bodily reality to the resurrection and makes of it something that happened to the disciples alone; and the other which exaggerates the bodily character of the resurrection and makes of it an event that was equally available to the disinterested observer and to the person of faith. The first extreme can be called *subjectivist*; the second, *objectivist*.

The *subjectivist* has to ignore the accounts of the appearances and the empty tomb. He or she has to explain away the extraordinary change and conversion in the lives of a small group of ordinary men whose faith had just been shattered by the crucifixion, who had abandoned Jesus on Calvary, and who had apparently begun returning to their everyday lives. Suddenly, they begin to believe in the resurrection, go out and preach it, develop a whole new way of understanding human existence on the basis of it; then even lay down their lives for it. And what is the subjectivist to make, finally, of the whole network of doctrines developed by the Church in direct response to its faith in the resurrection: the doctrine of the Holy Spirit, the Church, the sacraments, eternal life? If the resurrection is not something that really happened to Jesus, then what foundation do the principal doctrines of Christianity have?

The *objectivist*, or fundamentalist, on the other hand, oversimplifies the New Testament and simply ignores the manner in which it was put together. He or she ignores the metaphorical character of New Testament language about the resurrection and the symbolic imagery used by Paul, who describes the risen Jesus in terms of "a spiritual body" (1 Corinthians 15:20,23). He or she also cannot make sense of the fact that even Jesus' closest disciples did not at first recognize the risen Lord when he appeared to them. Why not, if the resurrection was essentially the resuscitation of the corpse of Jesus?

Who Saw It Happen?

No one actually saw the resurrection happen, as we have already noted. But many claimed to have seen the risen Lord. The Gospels do not agree, however, regarding the places where Jesus *appeared after the resurrection*, nor regarding the persons to whom he appeared. (Compare Mark 16:1-8; Matthew 28; Luke 24; Mark 16:9-20; John 20; and John 21.)

It is better not to attempt an artificial harmonization of the accounts, but to accept the discrepancies as inevitable in view of the lateness of the reports, the nature of the events in question, and variations in authorship, audience, and theological purpose. In spite of these differences there is something *common* to all accounts of the appearances. *First*, those to whom he appears are in a state of depression or at least keen disappointment (Luke 24:21). *Secondly*, it is always Jesus who initiates the appearances

(John 20:19; Luke 24:15; Matthew 28:9,18). *Thirdly*, Jesus gives some form of greeting—e.g., "Peace be with you" (John 20:19; Matthew 28:9). *Fourthly*, a moment of recognition follows (John 21:7; 20:20; Matthew 28:9,17). And, *finally*, Jesus gives a word of command to go forth and make disciples (Matthew 28:19; John 20:21; 21:15-17; Luke 24:46-49).

Regarding the last item: Did Jesus actually speak during these appearances? Some Christians have thought, for example, that Jesus spent forty days after the resurrection instructing the Apostles in theology, ethics, and canon law. There is a self-contradictory character, for example, to the Lucan account of Paul's conversion experience on the road to Damascus (Acts 9:7 and 22:9). In one text the companions of Paul are reported to have heard the voice from heaven, but in the other they did not. Did the risen Lord communicate with the Apostles verbally, or did he communicate intuitively? It is a question that one cannot really answer with certitude. An increasing number of scholars, however, do doubt that the risen Jesus used words.

But some form of communication is said to have taken place. What was it? Raymond Brown's hypothesis, which is gaining favor among his colleagues, is as follows: After the crucifixion, the Twelve fled Jerusalem and made their way back to Galilee, thoroughly discouraged by recent events. If, in fact, they had heard of the empty tomb before leaving Jerusalem, their puzzlement and fright must have been only heightened all the more. As Peter returned to his fishing, Jesus appeared to him on the shores of the Sea of Tiberias (John 21:1-14), and faith in the resurrection was born. Subsequently, Jesus appeared to the rest of the Twelve, confirming perhaps the inchoate faith stirred by Peter's report. It was on the occasion of his appearance to the Apostles that he breathed the Holy Spirit upon them and commissioned them to proclaim that the Kingdom of God had come among them in a new and definitive way through what God had accomplished in Jesus.

The Apostles would gradually discover on their own that the proclamation of the Kingdom of God would involve bearing witness to the Lord in word and in deed, baptizing people and forgiving their sins, and forming a new community, a new Israel, the Church. By the time the Gospel narratives themselves were written, all this was already happening. Accordingly, certain words of

Jesus were incorporated into the actual commission, as if Jesus himself on that occasion had instructed them in detail.

One final point about the appearances: In the various accounts, the post-resurrectional confession is not "We have seen Jesus" but "We have seen the Lord" (John 20:18,25; 21:7; Luke 24:34). Since *Lord* is a "high" Christological evaluation of Jesus, the evangelists are telling us that the witnesses enjoyed not only the *sight* of Jesus but also and even primarily *insight*. They saw that Jesus had been transformed, that he was now in the realm of God (Acts of the Apostles 2:32,36). Thus, the appearances involve a sight that is revelatory, i.e., an experience of God within ordinary human experience.

Where Did It Happen?

Jesus was buried in a tomb owned by Joseph of Arimathea, "a distinguished member of the Sanhedrin" (Mark 15:43). Two days later the tomb was discovered to be empty. Those are the barest details.

Like reports of the appearances, the *empty tomb* accounts are full of inconsistencies and embellishments. (Compare Mark 16:1-8; Matthew 28; Luke 24; and John 20.) It is very curious indeed that in Mark's account the women flee the empty tomb out of fear and astonishment and "said nothing to anyone" about it (Mark 16:8). In Luke's account, when the women inform the Apostles, ". . . the story seemed like nonsense and they refused to believe them" (Luke 24:11), although Peter did get up and run out to the tomb to see for himself. But these indicate that *the fact of the empty tomb* proves nothing in itself. It simply raises questions like "What happened to Jesus' body? Did someone steal it? Did Jesus in fact rise from the dead?"

And yet an empty-tomb tradition did develop, and the nature of the evidence lends a high degree of probability to it. No author, for example, would have used female witnesses in a fabricated story, since women were simply not accepted at the time as witnesses. Furthermore, the early Jewish controversies about the resurrection all supposed that the tomb was empty. The arguments were over the question of how. Some charged that the disciples had stolen the body (Matthew 28:11-15; 27:64). Others said the gardener had taken it away (John 20:13-15). Indeed, if the tomb were still intact, it would have been impossible to propose the story in the first place.

What of the significance of the empty-tomb tradition? At best it is a secondary piece of evidence, second certainly to the appearances. *We do not make an act of faith in the empty tomb but in the resurrection.* There are plenty of empty tombs in the world. The publicity surrounding the King Tut exhibitions conducted throughout the United States in 1978–9 only dramatized that fact. He was one of the very few ancient figures whose tombs were discovered with the body and other artifacts still there. Does that mean all of the other Pharaohs rose from the dead?

The empty tomb was more important for the first Christians than it is for us today. For them it was yet another safeguard against the Gnostic denial of the bodiliness of Jesus and of his resurrection. In the actual genesis of faith in the resurrection, it was the appearances of the risen Lord that first brought the disciples to believe; this belief, in turn, made sense of the empty tomb. Having seen him, the Apostles now understood the reason why the tomb had been empty. He was raised and then appeared to them (1 Corinthians 15:4-5; Luke 24:34). The first Christians, therefore, proclaimed a bodily resurrection in the sense that they did not think that Jesus' body had corrupted in the tomb. On the other hand, that risen body was now a spiritual body and not simply a resuscitated corpse, as we noted earlier (1 Corinthians 15:42-44).

THE PASSION AND DEATH

Although the doctrine of the cross was not the earliest Christology to emerge from faith in the resurrection but was something developed only by degrees, it is inextricably linked with resurrection faith and is at the same time entirely central to the New Testament's evaluation of the life, message, and mission of Jesus. Already in the primitive creedal formula in 1 Corinthians 15:3-8, there is the confession of faith "that Christ died for our sins."

On the other hand, the connection between the crucifixion and the resurrection had not always been so explicitly drawn. The great Christological hymn of Philippians 2:6-11 is one of the earliest attempts to make sense of the death of Jesus, not as Paul would usually have it, i.e., "for our sins," but as the culmination of a life of obedient humiliation within the human condition:

> Though he was in the form of God,
>> he did not deem equality with God
>> something to be grasped at.
>
> Rather, he emptied himself
>> and took the form of a slave,
>> being born in the likeness of men.
>
> He was known to be of human estate,
>> and it was thus that he humbled himself,
>> obediently accepting even death,
>> death on a cross!
>
> Because of this,
>> God highly exalted him
>> and bestowed on him the name
>> above every other name,
>
> So that at Jesus' name
>> every knee must bend
>> in the heavens, on the earth,
>> and under the earth,
>> and every tongue proclaim
>> to the glory of God the Father:
>> Jesus Christ is Lord!

However we finally interpret this text (regarding, for example, its origin, its proper punctuation, its structure, the Christological model upon which it is based), there is no question that it is a very early Christology indeed (pre-56 or 57 A.D., when Paul wrote to the Philippians), one that was inspired by the resurrection and pieced together from various available images of Jesus. Yet it did not attempt an interpretation of the death of Jesus, nor did it concern itself with his historical existence. The words "death on a cross" in verse 8c are not part of the original hymn but were added by Paul or by a Pauline editor. The addition was consistent with a growing trend within the early Church to work back from the resurrection experience to the death and life of the one who had been raised.

Indeed, his death makes sense only if the Gospel portrait of the historical Jesus is accepted as basically reliable. To suggest that he was executed because of his political attitudes and behavior toward the Roman government, whether as a Zealot or as a Zealot sympathizer, does not correspond with his preaching against violence and his almost-studied indifference to specifically political questions, and his central teaching about love for one's enemies. His problem was with the Jews, not with the Romans. That is how the Gospels present it, and that is how early Jewish antagonists of Christianity recalled it as well.

He was periodically locked in controversy with the Jewish men of power: the chief priests, the Pharisees, and their Scribes. Unfortunately, the portrayal of Jewish hostility to Jesus and of direct Jewish involvement in his condemnation and death has allowed many Christians down through the centuries to justify a virulent anti-Semitism ("Christ-killers" and all that). But the counter-reaction has also been unfortunate. In playing down Jewish complicity in the death of Jesus, even transferring it entirely to Roman shoulders, we remove the very basis for the Gospel traditions. In effect, the credibility of the event we seek to explain is undermined, perhaps destroyed completely. If Jesus has been remembered as he was, then his confrontation with the religious establishment was practically inevitable. But if that confrontation did not exist to the extent it is reported in the New Testament and with the effect it is also reported to have had, then the portrait of Jesus itself is open to question and to challenge.

Jesus functioned as a prophet greater than Moses. He claimed to forgive sin. He initiated a new form of table fellowship between God and humankind. He promised salvation. And he, of course, sharply criticized the religious situation as he found it in contemporary Israel. "The reason why the Jews were even more determined to kill him was that he not only was breaking the sabbath but, worse still, was speaking of God as his own Father, thereby making himself God's equal" (John 5:18). "He commits blasphemy!" they charged. "Who can forgive sins except God alone?" (Mark 2:7). When Jesus was asked by the high priest of the Sanhedrin whether or not he considered himself the Messiah, the Son of the Blessed One, Jesus answered, "I am; and you will see the Son of Man seated at the right hand of the Power and coming with clouds of heaven." With that the high priest tore his robes and said, "You have heard the blasphemy" (Mark 14:61-63).

But Jesus had been on a collision course from the beginning of his preaching ministry. He preached the Kingdom of God in a wholly new way, as a reality now "at hand" and demanding repentance and faith (Mark 1:15). "Do you think I have come to establish peace on the earth? I assure you, the contrary is true; I have come for division . . . . father will be split against son and son against father, mother against daughter and daughter against mother . . ." (Luke 12:51-53; see also Matthew 10:34-36). He had to know, as many prophets before him knew, that his life was at stake because of his preaching.

But did he explicitly connect his death with our redemption? If he did, why did the earliest New Testament Christology not make the same connection? Presumably it would have done so if it had some basis for it in the sayings of Jesus. And yet eventually, within the New Testament, Jesus' death *is* interpreted in redemptive categories, as a work of atonement for our sins. Such a conviction evidently had to develop, not at once but over a period of time, as the life and death of Jesus continued to be contemplated in the light of the resurrection. But as we noted earlier, resurrection faith first inspired the Church to look forward to the Second Coming, not backward. Only later did it reverse direction and display greater interest in the actual historical existence of Jesus, an interest which produced the Gospels. But where the older Christologies of the Epistles worked out of contemporary thought patterns, the Gospels remained more or less faithful to Old Testament thinking. It was this kind of thinking which accommodated itself most readily to the notion of redemptive sacrifice.

The idea of *vicarious atonement,* i.e., the sufferings of an innocent person having redeeming value for the sins of others, was already well accepted in the Judaism of Jesus' day. The best-known expression of this concept occurs in the Servant songs of Deutero, or Second, Isaiah (42:1-4; 49:1-6; 50:4-9; 52:13—53:12), where the Servant, probably Israel itself, becomes an instrument of divine salvation through his/its passion and death. Jesus himself is identified with the *Servant of the Lord* in the early Christian proclamation (Acts of the Apostles 3:13,26; 4:27,30) and is taken into the Gospel accounts themselves (Matthew 8:17; 12:18-21; Luke 22:37). The Second Isaian imagery is clearly woven through the passage of 1 Peter 2:22-25:

> He did no wrong; no deceit was found in
>   his mouth.
>
> When he was insulted, he returned no
>   insult.
> When he was made to suffer, he did not
>   counter with threats.
> Instead, he delivered himself up to the One
>   who judges justly.
>
> In his own body he brought your sins to the
>   cross,
> so that all of us, dead to sin, could live in
>   accord with God's will.
> By his wounds you were healed.
>
> At one time you were straying like sheep,
> but now you have returned to the Shepherd,
>   the Guardian of your souls.

But the Servant role, at first eagerly attributed to Jesus, was later abandoned as being too Jewish and, therefore, not readily understandable within the Gentile world. Other, more flexible Old Testament figures came to the surface, particularly the notion of *ransom* and the associated idea of *redemption*. A Marcan saying (10:45) is taken up by the Gospels (Matthew 20:28), with parallels elsewhere (1 Timothy 2:6) to show that Jesus understood his own mission as giving his life as a ransom for many.

In the New Testament world of commerce, a ransom was the price that had to be paid to buy back a pawned object or to liberate a slave. Thus, Christ is seen as the ransom given to liberate us all from the slavery of sin. But it has been an extraordinary misunderstanding to view this act of ransoming in more than *metaphorical* terms, as if it were some necessary payment demanded by God. On the contrary, "the redemption wrought by Christ" is itself "the gift of God" (Romans 3:24). We have no reason for supposing that the New Testament intended to press the metaphor any farther than did the Old Testament.

We do not pay a ransom to God (Psalm 49:8); it is God who is our redeemer (Psalm 78:35; see also Psalm 19:14; Isaiah 63:5). The metaphor means that forgiveness of sin is not some casual or arbitrary act of God. Sin is truly a bondage leading to death. It "costs" God much to forgive and to deliver us from that bondage. In speaking of the blood of Christ as the "price" he had to pay, the New Testament is trying to emphasize that the risen Lord's life and death somehow served God's salvific purposes in history. *There is no exact "commercial" description of what actually occurred in Jesus' passion and death.*

What does it mean, therefore, to speak of Jesus as having become a "curse" for us, and as having shed his blood in *expiation* of our sins?

First, what does it *not* mean? It does *not* mean that Jesus was accursed of God like the *scapegoat* of the Old Testament (Leviticus 16:20-28), which was burdened with the sins of all the people and then driven away to die in the desert, the abode of the demons. Christ is never likened in New Testament Christology to the scapegoat of the Old Testament. It does *not* mean, therefore, that Jesus was marked out for death by the Father in expiation for offenses against the divine majesty, for neither is there any Old Testament model for such a notion.

What we have is an exercise in Pauline paradox (Galatians 3:13, with a quotation from Deuteronomy 21:22-23). Christ has brought us back from the "curse" of the Law by himself becoming a "curse" for us. As in the case of the word *ransom*, the usage here is *metaphorical*. He mixes proper and improper senses of the same word in order to make a point. The cross, which is "folly" to us, is the "wisdom" of God, who "saves those who believe through the absurdity of the preaching of the gospel" (1 Corinthians 1:20-21).

What of the blood sacrifices? When they were employed as a means of atonement, the death of the animal was entirely incidental. Blood in itself was regarded as a purifying and sacred element (Deuteronomy 12:23). Insofar as the shedding of Christ's blood is clearly associated with the establishment of a new covenant (Hebrews 9:12-14; Mark 14:24; Matthew 26:28; Luke 22:20), the allusion is always to the enactment of the Old Covenant on Sinai (Exodus 24); namely, the blood of a *peace offering*, not a sacrifice of expiation. It is not that God was so enraged by the world's sin that a price was to be exacted (the prevalent idea of God among the pagans), but that God "so loved the world that he gave his only Son . . ." (John 3:16).

In summary, the Church's faith in the saving power of Christ's death emerged from its initial faith in his resurrection, and not from any general sense of need for deliverance from sin or from some wide-ranging exploration of Old Testament texts. *Jesus' death assumes meaning within the context of his resurrection:* "Unless the grain of wheat falls to the earth and dies, it remains just a grain of wheat. But if it dies, it produces much fruit. The man who loves his life loses it, while the man who hates his life in this world preserves it to life eternal" (John 12:24-25).

THE LIFE AND MESSAGE OF JESUS
The Historical Situation

Basic introductions to the New Testament abound. The more one knows about and understands the social, economic, political, and religious situation at the time of Jesus, the more intelligently one will be able to interpret the New Testament's faith in him as well as the import and impact of Jesus' words and deeds upon his contemporaries. We can do no more here than outline that situation in the broadest of strokes. And that may not be particularly unfortunate. On the contrary, the late Protestant New Testament scholar Norman Perrin acknowledged that in his own experience as a teacher, students tend either to skip the introductory material on the Hellenistic, Roman, and Jewish "background" of the New Testament or to forget its content by the time they actually begin dealing with the texts themselves, just when the material is most necessary. So in his own book, *The New Testament: An Introduction*, to which I am greatly indebted for this last section of the chapter, Perrin places all this material at the end, in two appendices, and discusses the background materials when and where they are relevant to understanding the texts themselves.

Since 63 B.C. the Jews had been politically subject to Roman power. Although by present standards that power was exercised with some measure of tolerance for national and religious diversity, there was in Jesus' time a widespread expectation of a political messiah. The Jewish party known as the *Zealots* wanted to throw off the yoke of Roman domination, and by violent revolutionary means. Although some latter-day political leftists have tried to portray Jesus as a member of the Zealot party, there is no real evidence that he even took a stand on the political issues of his time. Indeed, the New Testament seldom mentions a political group hostile to him, with the exception of the discussion about taxation (e.g., Matthew 22:15-22). On the other hand, much attention is given his religious controversies with the Pharisees.

How closely Jesus is to be identified with the *Essenes* is a matter of dispute, although recent scholarship seems to suggest that the points of contact were substantially fewer than was thought soon after the Dead Sea Scrolls were discovered. The Essenes, or Qumran community, were a sect within Judaism which separated itself from regular commerce with the world and established hierarchically structured communities of salvation wherein members could follow the Law of God perfectly until the end of history. Jesus, on the other hand, addressed himself explicitly to the whole nation of Israel and not simply to this "remnant" within the nation.

The Jews of his day were exceedingly jealous of their religious and national traditions, and so, unlike their brothers and sisters living outside of Palestine, they tended, as least in Palestine, to resist the pervasive influence of Greek culture. Jesus, therefore, shows no sign of Hellenistic influence. He probably speaks in Aramaic. His parables are drawn from ordinary Jewish life; his theological arguments, from the Old Testament.

If it were not for the near universality of Hellenistic culture in this ancient world, Christianity might not have spread so rapidly and so widely. In most cities public instruction in the Greek language was available to anyone interested in acquiring it. And, of course, there was a real incentive to do so because people were needed to fill various positions in business and government. For a movement, therefore, that was composed primarily of "the world's lowborn and despised" (1 Corinthians 1:26-31), it was crucial to communicate its message in spoken and written form far beyond its own particular circle.

Life

We know relatively little about the actual life of Jesus. He was baptized by John the Baptist, and the beginning of his ministry in Galilee was in some way linked with that of the Baptist. His ministry centered on the proclamation of the Kingdom of God, with a sharp edge of challenge to it. His preaching was reinforced by an apparently deserved reputation as an exorcist (Mark 1:27; Luke 4:36). In a world that readily believed in the powers of good and evil, in demons and evil spirits, Jesus was able to help many who thought themselves to be possessed by such forces.

One of his fundamental concerns was to bring together a group of respondents to his proclamation of the Kingdom of God, regardless of their sex, status, or background. Central to the life of this group was sharing a common meal that celebrated their unity in their new relationship with God. Jesus, therefore, set himself and his group against the Jewish tendency to permit the fragmentation of the religious community and to engage rather freely in "excommunications" of certain undesirables. He spoke as one having great authority (Mark 1:22; John 7:46; Matthew 5:21-22). He forgave sins (Mark 2:10; Matthew 9:6; Luke 5:24). And he addressed God as Abba, or Father (Mark 10:36). These activities provoked severe opposition—an opposition which reached a climax during a Passover celebration in Jerusalem when he was arrested, tried by Jewish authorities on a charge of blasphemy, and by the Romans on a charge of sedition, and then crucified. Indeed, his decision to go up to Jerusalem and to end his Galilean ministry proved to be the major turning point. He definitively rejected a political mission, even though the hopes of some of his followers were still oriented in this direction to the very end (Luke 19:11; 24:21).

During his lifetime he had chosen from among his followers a small group of disciples who thereafter exhibited in their own activities something of his power and authority.

Message

Proclamation of the Kingdom of God

There is general agreement among New Testament scholars that four sayings concerning the Kingdom of God have very strong claims to authenticity: "This is the time of fulfillment. The reign of God is at hand!" (Mark 1:15); "But if it is by the finger of God that I cast out devils, then the reign of God is upon you" (Luke 11:20); "You cannot tell by careful watching when the reign of God will come. Neither is it a matter of reporting it is 'here' or 'there.' The reign of God is already in your midst" (Luke 17:20-21); and "From John the Baptizer's time until now the kingdom of God has suffered violence, and the violent take it by force" (Matthew 11:12). Nor is there any doubt at all that the proclamation of the Kingdom of God is at the very center of the message of Jesus.

To speak of the Kingdom of God is to speak of the exercise of divine power on our behalf. The Kingdom is an apocalyptic symbol referring to God's final act of redemption at the end of the world, and so it is a symbol filled with hope. God, acting as King, visits and redeems his people. This is the central theme of Jesus' preaching.

In the light of the four sayings listed above, there is obviously some tension between present and future in Jesus' understanding of the Kingdom. It is at once "in the midst of you" and "at hand"; i.e., it is imminent but still in the future. To the extent that the Kingdom is present, it comes about in the healings and exorcisms (Luke 11:20) and in the endurance of suffering (Matthew 11:12). On the other hand, Luke denies the possibility that the Kingdom comes about through any one experience (17:20-21), such as the prophet Daniel describes, for example (Daniel 11:3-35).

What, then, does Jesus mean when he says that the Kingdom is "in the midst of you"? If he is not speaking of the history of kings, wars, and persecutions, as Daniel was, then he is speaking of the history of the individual and of the individual's experience of reality. But, of course, individual reality is never divorced from its larger social and political context (which is the interpretation Bultmann's thoroughgoing existentialism gives), and so the power of God also realizes itself in our relationships with one another and in the many institutional expressions of those relationships.

The Parables

The following points seem to be agreed upon by modern New Testament scholars:

1.   Jesus taught in parables, but the early Church translated them into *allegories*. In parables, the whole story counts as a totality; in allegories, each detail is important and has to be interpreted to detect its special meaning. Once the allegory has been deciphered, it can be set aside, for it has achieved its purpose. Not so with a parable, which keeps yielding new meanings. An example of allegory in the New Testament is the interpretation of the parable of the Sower in Mark 4:13-20.

2.   Both the allegorizing of the parables and their placement and application within the Gospels are the work of the Church and the evangelists. To interpret a parable of Jesus, therefore, one must first reconstruct it in its original nonallegorical form and then interpret it as a parable in the context of the message of Jesus without reference to its place or function in the Gospels.

3.   The fundamental element in a parable is the element of *metaphor*. The Kingdom of God, which is the unknown, is compared to something that is known. Thus, "The Kingdom of God is like..." (see, for example, Matthew 13:44-46).

4.   There is in every parable, therefore, a *literal* point (what it means in itself) and a metaphorical point (what it refers to).

5.   The purpose of a parable is normally *pedagogical*. But Jesus used parables not only for instruction but also for *proclamation*. An example is provided by the parable of the Good Samaritan (Luke 10:30-36). If the parable were merely exemplary, illustrating by way of example the principle of neighborliness, then it would have been more effective to have the hated Samaritan the injured man and the Israelite the one who gives aid. But the way Jesus tells it, the story in itself focuses attention not on the needs of the injured man but on the deed of the Samaritan, from whom no Jew would expect hospitality (see Luke 9:52-56). Thus, the para-

ble asks the listener to conceive the inconceivable: that the Samaritan is "good." The listener is thereby challenged to reexamine his or her most basic attitudes and values. The parable has become not instruction but *proclamation*.

The parable of the Unjust Steward (Luke 16:1-9) may be even more challenging, for Jesus commends a man who compounds his dishonesty (having cheated his master) by committing additional acts of dishonesty (cutting the debts owed his master so he will have friends after he loses his job). The point of the parable is to admit the presence of an order of reality that challenges all accepted norms of behavior and rules of human relationships. And that is how other parables function as well—i.e., by turning our worlds upside down and challenging us to reconsider our whole perspective on life (e.g., the Rich Man and Lazarus in Luke 16:19-31; the Pharisee and the Publican in Luke 18:10-14; and the Wedding Guest in Luke 14:7-11). That experience of sudden reversal is one experience of the inbreaking Kingdom of God.

But Jesus also used the parables for *instruction*. Examples are the Hidden Treasure and the Pearl (Matthew 13:44-46), the Tower Builder and the King Going to War (Luke 14:28-32), the Friend at Midnight (Luke 11:5-8), and the Unjust Judge (Luke 18:1-8).

The Proverbial Sayings

A proverb is a saying that gives insight into ordinary human situations—e.g., "No prophet is without honor except in his native place, among his own kindred, and in his own house" (Mark 6:4). Sometimes proverbs have an imperative ring to them—e.g., "Do not give what is holy to dogs or toss your pearls before swine. They will trample them under foot, at best, and perhaps even tear you to shreds" (Matthew 7:6). Some proverbs are formulated as questions—e.g., "Which of you by worrying can add a moment to his life-span?" (Matthew 6:27). In general, proverbs are affirmations of faith in God's rule over the world—i.e., faith in the Kingdom of God.

The most radical proverbial sayings of Jesus are the injunction to let the dead bury their own dead (Luke 9:60) and the

command to turn the other cheek, to give away one's cloak (the
only garment hiding sheer nakedness), and to walk the extra mile
(Matthew 5:29-41). Again, they challenge the hearer not to radical
obedience but to radical questioning. They jolt the hearer out of
his or her routine existence and force him or her to see human
existence in a new light. As such, proverbial sayings are a form of
proclamation of the Kingdom of God.

Other proverbial sayings carry forward this technique. Jesus
tells his listeners that the first will be last and the last first (Mark
10:31), that whoever would save his life must lose it (Mark 8:35),
that it is easier for a camel to get through the eye of a needle than
for a rich man to enter the Kingdom (Mark 10:23-25), and that the
one who exalts himself will be humbled, and vice versa (Luke
14:11). Still other sayings highlight the element of *conflict*: A
kingdom divided against itself cannot stand (Mark 3:24-26), and
no one can plunder the house of a strong man without first binding
him (Mark 3:27).

Finally, there are the *instructional* sayings: No one who puts
his hand to the plough and looks back is fit for the Kingdom (Luke
9:62); entrance into the Kingdom is by a narrow gate (Matthew
7:13-14); nothing outside of a person is defiling; only what is inside
defiles (Mark 7:15); one must receive the Kingdom like a child
(Mark 10:15); and we must love our enemies if we are to be perfect
(Matthew 5:44-48).

Always it is the Kingdom of God which is being proclaimed.

The Lord's Prayer

The Lucan version (11:2-4) is generally recognized as being close
to the prayer which Jesus actually taught his disciples:

> Father,
> hallowed be your name,
> your kingdom come.
>
> Give us each day our daily bread.
>
> Forgive us our sins
> for we too forgive all who do us wrong;
> and subject us not to the trial.

The simplicity and brevity of this prayer suggest a very special, intimate relationship between the petitioner and God. For the person who can pray the Lord's prayer, the Kingdom has already come. On the other hand, this prayer also asks that the Kingdom might yet come. It looks to the future as well as to the present, just as some of the parables challenge Jesus' hearers to look to the future (the Sower in Mark 4:3-9; the Mustard Seed in Mark 4:30-32; the Leaven in Matthew 13:33; and the Seed Growing of Itself in Mark 4:26-29).

It does not follow, however, that Jesus' conception of the future is the same as ours, namely, temporal and historical. On the contrary, Jesus rejected tendencies in first-century Judaism to exaggerate the importance of signs and wonders. Perhaps the future that Jesus spoke of is the future that emerges as the consummation of the present, the fulfillment of what is already available to those who respond to the challenge of his proclamation of the Kingdom of God.

FROM JESUS TO CHRIST

The one who proclaimed the Kingdom of God in his own lifetime became, after his death, the one *proclaimed*. The historical details of this transition are probably lost to us forever. What we have is what we began with in this chapter, namely, the early Church's testimony of faith in the risen Lord. All else in the New Testament flows from that—forward and backward alike.

SUMMARY

1. No one questions that Jesus of Nazareth really lived. There is ample historical evidence of this. What is at issue is whether this same Jesus of history is also the Christ of faith proclaimed by the New Testament.

2. The Gospels, however, do not provide us with the kind of biographical information which we are accustomed to receive from such "papers of record" as, for example, the *New York Times*.

3. What we have in the Gospels, according not only to New Testament scholars but also according to the Pontifical Biblical Commis-

sion, is the finally edited version of the oral and written proclamation of the early Church regarding Jesus Christ. In order to reconstruct the process of development and come to a greater understanding of what the New Testament proclaims, we must employ *historical criticism* (What is the nature of documents we have in hand?), *form criticism* (What are the various units out of which the Gospels were put together?), and *redaction criticism* (What was the peculiar purpose of each evangelist?).

4.   Furthermore, the Gospels are products of different Christian communities with distinctive theological perspectives: *Palestinian, Jewish-Hellenistic,* and *Hellenistic-Gentile.* The first emphasized the imminence of the Second Coming of Jesus and his fulfillment of the role of the Christ, or the Messiah; the second shifted emphasis away from the future to the present exalted state of Jesus, who is now proclaimed as Lord; the third combines present and future with past, dividing Jesus' existence into pre-existence, the incarnation, and the exaltation.

5.   Until the eighteenth century there was no "New Testament problem." All Christians accepted the New Testament as an accurate and literal account of the life, teachings, ministry, death, and resurrection of Jesus. Ever since the assumption was challenged on the Protestant side by Reimarus and others, Christians have been divided across a broad spectrum of views, some scholarly and some non-scholarly.

6.   In *non-scholarly conservatism* the Christology of the New Testament is *identified* with Jesus' self-evaluation. Jesus knew and expressed from the beginning what the Church affirmed of him after the resurrection. It is a view held by Protestant fundamentalists and others, and was the common view of Roman Catholics before Pope Pius XII's encyclical on biblical studies, *Divino Afflante Spiritu* (1943).

7.   *Non-scholarly liberalism* concludes that there is *no continuity* at all between the Christ of faith and the Jesus of history. Once the fashion in Protestantism, it now enjoys some favor with Catholicism as well. Jesus is confessed as everything except what the New Testament confessed him to be.

8.   *Scholarly liberalism* insists that New Testament Christology is a *creation* of the early Church. The creative act was necessary at the time; otherwise, Jesus might have faded from memory. But since that is no longer possible, we can dispense with the theological overlay.

9.   *Bultmannian Existentialism* acknowledges a *functional equivalence* between the early Church's Christology and Jesus' own proclamation of the Kingdom. What the Church was proclaiming about Jesus is functionally the same as what Jesus was proclaiming about the Kingdom. The two proclamations made the same practical demands upon the hearers.

10.   *Moderate Conservatism* posits a *discernible continuity* between the Christ of faith and Jesus' self-evaluation. One branch suggests that the Church's Christology was *explicit* in Jesus' self-understanding with regard to the so-called "lower" titles (e.g., Messiah, Prophet, Servant, Son of Man), while another indicates that such titles are at most *implicit* in Jesus' self-evaluation. That is, he conveyed what he was saying by speaking with unique authority and by acting with unique power. The explicit school was more popular in the 1950s and 1960s, although it is still respectable today, while the implicit school has tended to gain acceptance among Catholics and Protestants alike more recently.

11.   One can proceed with a presentation of the Jesus of the New Testament in one of two ways: by the *traditional approach*, which views the resurrection as a kind of capstone of his whole ministry and mission; and by the *New Testament's own approach*, which is to begin with the resurrection and work forward and backward, viewing all that Jesus did and said in the light of the early Church's fundamental conviction of faith that he is indeed risen. This chapter follows the second approach.

12.   The *resurrection* of Jesus from the dead is both the *starting-point* and the *center* of the early Church's faith in him as the Christ and Lord of history. This is evident in such primitive sources as the creedal formula in 1 Corinthians 15 and in the apostolic proclamation of Peter in the Acts of the Apostles 2.

13.   In the light of the resurrection everything else falls into place and begins to make sense: Jesus' special relationship with the Father, Jesus' fulfillment of the hopes of Israel, the preaching of the Kingdom, the crucifixion, the empty tomb.

14.   The interpretations and connections, however, differed from Christian community to Christian community. (See #4 above.)

15.   The resurrection is perceived as a saving event in that it is the necessary step by which Jesus receives the *fullness of life* that he is destined to share with us. He is the *first-born of those who rise* (Colossians 1:18). To be "in Christ" is to be a "new creation" (2 Corinthians 5:17). Indeed, the Holy Spirit cannot be given until Jesus has been raised and glorified (John 7:39; 16:7). Jesus breathes the Spirit upon his disciples as soon as he first appears to them (20:19-23).

16.   *Did it happen? Something* happened, we can be sure of that much. The tomb was found empty, many claimed to have seen the risen Jesus, and his followers were marvelously transformed. But there are *no eyewitnesses* to the actual event of the resurrection itself.

17.   *What happened*, therefore? By modern scientific standards, the resurrection is not *historical*. It was not available to the disinterested

observer and the person of faith alike. But even by New Testament standards, neither is it an historical event in the sense that it involved simply the resuscitation of Jesus' corpse. That would not have been a saving event in that case. Jesus entered into an entirely *new mode of existence.* The fact that the disciples did not easily recognize him is significant. The resurrection was something *real, although trans-historical, for Jesus*; but it was something *real and historical* from the side of *the disciples*, so profoundly were they affected by it and by the appearances.

18.   *To whom did it happen?* Did it happen to Jesus, or did it happen to the disciples? The extreme liberal or *subjectivist* answer is that the resurrection, understood as a breach of the most fundamental laws of life and nature, could not have literally happened to Jesus. Therefore, it was something that happened to the disciples alone; i.e., it is the "miracle" of the sudden and wondrous transformation of the disciples as they reflected on the meaning of the life and death of Jesus. The extreme conservative or *objectivist* solution is that the resurrection was so literally real that a photographer could have captured the event on film had he or she been present. The *subjectivist* ignores the accounts of the appearances and the empty tomb, and has to explain away the whole network of doctrines which directly express the early Church's faith in the resurrection *of Jesus.* The *objectivist* has to treat the New Testament in fundamentalist categories, denying all that we know about it from historical, form, and redaction criticism, and ignoring Paul's teaching that Jesus rose with a "spiritual body," one not readily recognized even by some of his closest friends.

19.   *Who saw it happen?* No one. And yet many claimed to have seen Jesus *after* it happened. Those to whom he appeared were always in a state of depression or at least keen disappointment. Jesus always initiates the appearances. He gives some form of greeting—e.g., "Peace be with you." A moment of recognition follows. Then Jesus communicates some missionary command. The last, however, is not to be confused with formal, lengthy theological and canonical instruction, such as some of our earlier textbooks imagined. An increasing number of scholars, in fact, deny that Jesus actually spoke. Rather, they say, he communicated without the mediation of language—i.e., through direct mystical experience.

20.   *Where did it happen?* We know only that Jesus was buried in a tomb owned by Joseph of Arimathea and that two days later it was discovered to be empty. Like the accounts of the appearances, the accounts of the *empty tomb* are filled with inconsistencies. Nonetheless, all—even the earliest Jewish polemicists against Christianity—agree that the tomb was found empty. If it had not been empty, how could the

story of its empty status have been proposed in the first place without rebuttal? At best, however, the empty-tomb tradition is a *secondary piece of evidence*, secondary certainly to Jesus' appearances. We do not make an act of faith in the empty tomb. It is the early Church's faith in the resurrection, a faith generated by the appearances, which compelled it to take another look at the empty tomb and judge its significance. Although Jesus now enjoyed a spiritual body, his resurrection was indeed a *bodily* resurrection of some kind. The tomb *was* empty, after all.

21.   Again, contrary to the impression given by some of our traditional textbooks and catechisms, the early Church did not at first focus on the redemptive significance of the *crucifixion* and then see the resurrection as simply Jesus' reward for suffering death or as the Father's way of proving Jesus' claims about himself. It was the other way around.

22.   Did Jesus die "for our sins," or did he die because of his political views and activities? If one chooses the second possibility, the New Testament portrait of Jesus—and of the Jews of his time—no longer hangs together. He claimed to forgive sin. He initiated a new form of table fellowship. He promised salvation. And he sharply criticized the religious establishment of his day. In the end, the Jews rejected him and brought about his death because he *blasphemed* (Mark 14:61-63).

23.   Did Jesus explicitly connect his death with our redemption? If so, why is that connection not made explicit in the New Testament? Eventually, however, the connection *is* made by the early Church as it contemplated the meaning and implications of the resurrection.

24.   When the New Testament did develop a theology of the redemptive value of the cross, where did it derive its notion of *vicarious atonement*? The initial source is the Servant songs in Deutero-Isaiah, but that was later abandoned as being too Jewish. The notion of *ransom* came to the fore. But this, too, has been misunderstood, as if it were a commercial term alone. It is used *metaphorically* in the New Testament. Thus, it is not something we give to the Father or to anyone else in payment for our sins, nor even something Jesus is compelled to give to the Father or to anyone else on our behalf. Rather, it is something the *Father gives to us* (Romans 3:24).

25.   Did Jesus die in *expiation* for our sins in any sense at all? Not in the sense of his becoming a scapegoat. The New Testament never likens him to that. The shedding of Christ's *blood* is not a sacrifice of expiation but, in the biblical sense, a *peace offering*. It was never necessary that the animal offered should die, but only that blood be shed as a sign of purification. So, too, with Christ. To say, on the other hand, that the Father somehow demanded the death of his Son in expiation for our sins

is to deny such fundamental principles as God's love for the world (John 3:16). Again, the redemptive value of the cross assumes meaning always in the light of the resurrection: "...unless the grain of wheat falls to the earth and dies..." (John 12:24-25).

26.   The more one understands the social, economic, political, and religious *situation* at the time of Jesus, the more intelligently one will interpret the New Testament's faith in him as well as the import and impact of his words and deeds upon his contemporary world. Jesus was a Jew, but neither a Zealot nor an Essene. His parables are drawn from ordinary Jewish life, his theological arguments are rooted in the Old Testament, and his political interests are minimal.

27.   We know very little about his actual *life*: He was baptized by John the Baptist, began his ministry in Galilee, and focused all his preaching and teaching on the Kingdom of God. He had a well-deserved reputation as an exorcist and healer, and attracted much attention because of it. He gathered a group of disciples around him, without regard for sex, status, or background, and celebrated their unity through the sharing of meals. He, therefore, set himself and his followers at odds with the more sectarian, excommunicating mentality and practice of contemporary Judaism. Opposition to him reached a climax during a Passover celebration in Jerusalem, when he was arrested, tried, and crucified.

28.   His *message* centered on the *Kingdom of God*. He announced it as something "at hand" (Mark 1:15). The final redemptive power of God is already at work, realizing itself in the individual's experience of reality, in his or her relationships with other persons, and with social and political institutions, broadly understood.

29.   Jesus' message was communicated principally through *parables, proverbial sayings*, and the *Lord's Prayer*. Always it is the Kingdom which is proclaimed and/or explained.

30.   The one who proclaimed the Kingdom in his lifetime is himself proclaimed after his resurrection. God's final redemptive act has been exercised in and through the risen Lord. And so we end where we began: with the early Church's faith in the resurrection. All else in the New Testament flows forward from the resurrection to the exaltation of Christ and backward from the resurrection to the crucifixion, passion, ministry, early life, birth, and even pre-existence of Jesus. Faith in the resurrection is always at the center of the New Testament's witness to Jesus Christ.

SUGGESTED READINGS

Bornkamm, Gunther. *Jesus of Nazareth.* New York: Harper & Row, 1960.

Brown, Raymond. *The Virginal Conception and Bodily Resurrection of Jesus.* New York: Paulist Press, 1973.

——————. "'Who Do Men Say That I Am?'—Modern Scholarship on Gospel Christology." *Horizons. Vol. 1 (1974), pp. 35-50.*

Bultmann, Rudolf. *Jesus Christ and Mythology.* New York: Scribner, 1958.

Crossan, John D. *In Parables: The Challenge of the Historical Jesus.* New York: Harper & Row, 1973.

Dodd, Charles H. *The Founder of Christianity.* New York: Macmillan, 1970.

Fuller, Reginald. *The Foundations of New Testament Christology.* New York: Scribner, 1965.

Hengel, Martin. *Son of God.* Philadelphia: Fortress Press, 1976.

Lane, Dermot A. *The Reality of Jesus: An Essay in Christology.* New York: Paulist Press, 1975.

Neill, Stephen. *The Interpretation of the New Testament, 1861-1961.* London: Oxford University Press, 1964.

O'Collins, Gerald. *The Resurrection of Jesus.* Valley Forge: Judson Press, 1973.

Perrin, Norman. *The New Testament: An Introduction.* New York: Harcourt Brace Jovanovich, 1974.

Price, James. *Interpreting the New Testament.* 2d ed. New York: Holt, Rinehart & Winston, 1971.

Senior, Donald. *Jesus: A Gospel Portrait.* Dayton: Pflaum-Standard, 1975.

Sloyan, Gerard. *Jesus on Trial.* Philadelphia: Fortress Press, 1973.

Vawter, Bruce. *This Man Jesus: An Essay Toward a New Testament Christology.* New York: Doubleday, 1973.

TWENTIETH-CENTURY VIEWS ON THE CHRISTOLOGY OF THE NEW TESTAMENT

(A survey of opinions of the relationship between the evaluation of Jesus during his ministry and the christological evaluation of him in the NT writings composed some twenty to one hundred years later—from *Horizons*, vol. 1, 1974, p. 38.)

Non-Scholarly Liberalism	Views Within The Domain Of Scholarship			Non-Scholarly Conservatism
	Scholarly Liberalism	Bultamannian Existentialism	Scholarly Conservatism	
This view regards the christological question as unimportant, for Christianity is primarily concerned with how man should live. Jesus came to teach man a way of life centered on love. It was his followers who first gave any importance to evaluating him. Liberalism was popular in the Protestantism of the late 1800's and early 1900's. It has revived today in Catholicism as a reaction to the dogmatic strictness of the past.	(Early 1900's) Liberal scholars developed a scientific methodology for detecting precise states of growth in NT christology. They judged this growth to be a creation, distorting the historical Jesus. Christology was once necessary in order to preserve the memory of Jesus, but now modern scholarship can give us the historical Jesus without christology, which should be dispensed with. Exemplified in W. Bousset's *Kyrios Christos* (1913).	(1920's through the 1950's) A reaction to liberalism. He further refined the scientific methodology, but rejected the liberal judgment on the invalidity of christology. Bultmann is indefinite and even agnostic on how Jesus evaluated himself. But the NT christology is functionally equivalent to Jesus' message about the kingdom, since both are a demand to accept what God has done through Jesus. Christology cannot be dispensed with.	(1960's and 1970's) Most scholars today are less agnostic than Bultmann about the historical Jesus and admit a continuity between the evaluation of Jesus during the ministry and the evaluation of him in the NT. Yet they continue to use with refinement the methodology for detecting growth in NT christology. The dominating motif is development in continuity. A division exists as to whether to posit an explicit christology in the ministry of Jesus (he used or accepted some titles: Son of Man, Suffering Servant, Messiah) or an implicit christology (Jesus did not use or accept christological titles). Implicit Christology Scholars such as Hahn, Fuller, Perrin; some post-Bultmannians; many Catholics of the 1970's. Explicit Christology Scholars such as Cullmann, Jeremias, Dodd, Taylor; most Catholics of the 1960's.	A failure to allow any development from the ministry to the NT. This theory posits that Jesus was christologically evaluated during his ministry exactly as he is portrayed in the Gospels (which are literal accounts of the ministry). A view held defensively by fundamentalist Protestants. Also held by Catholics until Church changes in the approach to the Bible began to affect Gospel study in the 1960's.

·XIII·

THE CHRIST OF THE FATHERS, THE COUNCILS, AND MEDIEVAL THEOLOGY

THE PROBLEM

Jesus is at the center of Christian faith. But not just the carpenter's son, Jesus of Nazareth; Christians confess that Jesus is the Christ, the Promised One of God, the risen Lord. An understanding of Jesus Christ, therefore, implies and/or presupposes some understanding of a dynamic God who is involved in our history, indeed of a God who became one of us in order that the whole world, first created through the Word, might be restored fully through the same Word-made-flesh. That is why the chapters on God and on the Trinity (9 and 10) preceded this one.

An understanding of Jesus Christ also implies and/or presupposes some understanding of what it means to be human, for we are a new creation in Christ. That is why the chapters on human existence (4 and 5) also preceded this one.

Christians confess that the one God—the God who created us, sustains us, and providentially guides us toward our eternal destiny in the Kingdom—identifies with us, accepts us, and redeems us in Jesus Christ. Jesus has this unique role in our salvation because he is at the same time divine and human. If he were not divine, by what power and authority does he redeem us from our sins? If he were not human, what does his redemptive work have to do with us or for us?

Soteriology ("the study of salvation") and Christology ("the study of Christ") are intimately connected, therefore. We inquire into the nature(s) and person of Jesus Christ because who he is *in himself* is the foundation of what he is *for us*. If he is not at once human and divine, how does he redeem us? But if he *is* at once human and divine, how is that union to be understood?

AN HISTORICAL AND THEOLOGICAL OVERVIEW

Development in the Church's understanding of faith occurred for various reasons: (1) the naturally inquisitive and probing impulse of the human mind; (2) the challenge of dissident opinions; and (3) the need to communicate the Christian message across cultural lines. Each of these factors was already at work even in the New Testament period. Christological development occurred as the early Church made contact with the wider Hellenistic world around it, and as the heresy of Gnosticism tested the limits of Christian orthodoxy. There was an acceleration of Christological development after the New Testament period as the Church extended its missionary outreach, and as the need increased to translate, clarify, and refine the inherited Jewish categories found in Sacred Scripture.

From the earliest stage of this theological development, the concept of Word, *Logos*, was at the center. For the *Jews*, the Word had been present and operative at creation (Genesis 1), in the utterances of the prophets, and in the Wisdom literature. For the *Greeks*, the Word was identified with reason and with the Truth of the philosophers. If for the Jews the Word was a form of God's presence in *history*, for the Greeks it was an all-pervasive principle of rationality within the *universe*. Christianity united and transformed these two understandings of the Word, as is evident in the Prologue of John's Gospel (1:1-18). By the second century the *Apologists* made the connection even more explicit. Jesus is the key to both history and the universe. The Christ-event is one of unlimited significance because through it the Word itself became flesh.

But exaggerations of the divinity or of the humanity of Jesus soon appeared within the Church itself. For the *Docetists* (from the Green verb, *dokein* = "to seem, to appear"), the body of Jesus only appeared to be real, and for the *Gnostics* it was at best incidental to our salvation. Over against these views, Ignatius of Antioch insisted that if Jesus was not fully human like us, then he could not have saved us. At the other extreme there were approaches which undermined the divinity in favor of the humanity of Jesus—e.g., the *Adoptionism* of the *Ebionites*, a Jewish-Christian sect. Such Fathers of the Church as Irenaeus argued that if Jesus is not "of God," then he could not have saved us. Note, again, that it is concern for our *salvation* which inspires these earliest rebuttals of Christological deviation.

Others attempted mediating positions—Tertullian, Origen, Paul of Samasota, Arius—but these proved unsatisfactory because they tended, in divergent ways to be sure, to make of Jesus something more than human but less than God. The Word is of one substance with the Father, but not of the same nature. Or the Word is within the Godhead, but lower in rank than the Father. Or the Word is a semi-divine creature. Such views fall under, or at least come close to, the general category of *Subordinationism*. It was at the Council of Nicea in 325 that Subordinationism of every kind was rejected. Jesus Christ is "true God of true God ... begotten, not made."

In the aftermath of Nicea two major theological schools emerged: one in Alexandria, Egypt, and the other in Antioch, Syria. The *Alexandrian school* was interested principally in preserving the *divinity* of Jesus and focused on the *unity* of the humanity with the Word, while the *Antiochene school* was concerned principally with his *humanity* and so adopted a looser approach to the unity of the human and the divine. Thus, standard histories of Christology refer to the Alexandrian approach as *Logos-sarx* (literally, "Word-flesh"), and the Antiochene as *Logos-anthropos* (literally, "Word-human being"). The former stresses that *the Word* took on flesh; the latter, that the Word became *a human being*. As this theological and doctrinal history was to unfold, each school of thought would generate extremes. From the Alexandrian school there would be those like Apollinaris (d. 390) who would insist so strongly on the divinity of Jesus, i.e., on the unity of the humanity with the Word, that they would deny him a human soul. And from the Antiochene school there would be those like Nestorius (d. ca. 451) who would insist so strongly on the humanity of Jesus, regarding it as a separate and distinct personal entity, that they would deny that Mary was truly the Mother of God.

If one is to make any sense of the otherwise complicated and often confusing history of the controversies and the councils, one has to keep the tensions between these two schools always in mind. The mystery of Jesus Christ has to do with the way in which divinity and humanity come together in one and the same person. Stress the divinity too much, and you run the risk of supplanting his humanity. Stress the humanity too much, and you run the risk of denying his divinity. In either case, not only is orthodoxy lost, but our salvation in Christ as well.

That orthodoxy was first articulated and defended, not without ambiguity, by the Council of Nicea (325). As we noted above and in the earlier chapters on God and the Trinity, Nicea rejected every solution which made Jesus Christ anything less than divine. Next came the First Council of Constantinople (381), which condemned Apollinaris and, therefore, struck a doctrinal blow for Jesus' humanity. After that, the Council of Ephesus (431), which condemned Nestorius and reinforced the Church's conviction that the one person, Jesus, is "true God of true God" and that Mary, his mother, is not only the mother of Christ but the Mother of God as well (*Theotokos*). There followed the Council of Chalcedon (451), which balanced Nicea's "of one substance with the Father" with its own formula, "of one substance (being) with us as to the humanity, like unto us in all things but sin," thereby achieving some measure of synthesis between the Alexandrian and Antiochene schools. Still another doctrinal statement was provided by the Second Council of Constantinople (553), which to a great extent repeated the definition of Chalcedon, reiterating its condemnation of Nestorianism. Finally, there was the Third Council of Constantinople (680-681), which in fidelity to Chalcedon condemned *Monothelitism* (the view that in Jesus there is only *one will*, the *divine* will).

Since Constantinople III there has been no significant *doctrinal* development to this very day. What we have had are some refinements of concepts and terminology in the Scholastic period, but without the same concern for the soteriology as the New Testament and the Fathers and councils of the Church had. At the risk of oversimplifying, one might suggest that the medieval theologians were more interested in Jesus Christ as he is *in himself* (e.g., his consciousness, his knowledge, his freedom, his sinlessness, the mode of the divine-human union) than as he is *for us*, as our Savior. This same heavily speculative, not to say abstract, approach to Christology has governed the production of seminary textbooks and catechisms, and accounts in part for Christology's general lack of pastoral usefulness for preaching, religious education, social ministry, and spirituality.

For all practical purposes, it was not until the occasion of the fifteen hundredth anniversary of the Council of Chalcedon that Catholic theologians, in any concerted way, took a fresh look at their own doctrinal tradition. Not surprisingly, it was Karl Rahner who led the way with a highly influential article, "Chalcedon—End or Beginning?" (which appears in a still-untranslated work *Das Konzil von Chalkedon*, A. Grillmeier and H. Bacht, eds. Würzburg, 1954, 3 volumes). Rahner argued that every conciliar definition is *both* an end and a beginning: an *end* of one phase of a discussion and the settling of certain points of controversy, but the *beginning* of a whole new phase of questioning, leading to deeper insights. Doctrinal formulations must constantly be rethought, not because they are false or radically imperfect, but precisely because they are true and, as such, can yield further truth and shed new light on other, related matters. Indeed, doctrinal pronouncements remain alive only insofar as they are continually elucidated. Consistent with his own theological starting point (i.e., the human person as radically open to God), Rahner developed an understanding of the incarnation as the unique and supreme instance of the essential completion of human reality. Anthropology is fulfilled in Christology. (We shall return to his position, and several others', in the next chapter.)

THE THEOLOGICAL AND DOCTRINAL
DEVELOPMENT: PATRISTIC ERA
Before Nicea

The *earliest Christological heresies* came from opposite extremes: *Docetism* and *Gnosticism* on the right (denying the humanity of Jesus for the sake of the divinity) and *Adoptionism* on the left (denying the divinity of Jesus for the sake of his humanity). Neither extreme, perhaps because they were so obviously extreme, required any kind of official condemnation such as a general council of the Church might render. Certain of the early theologians and Fathers were quick to identify the fundamental errors in these positions, and especially their implications for our salvation.

"There is only one physician," Ignatius of Antioch wrote in his *Letter to the Ephesians*, "both carnal and spiritual, born and unborn. God became man, true life in death; sprung both from Mary and from God, first subject to suffering and then incapable of it—Jesus Christ our Lord" (n. 7). Ignatius hereby testifies to both the divinity and the humanity of Jesus united in a single person. Against the Docetists and Gnostics, he insists that Jesus is the son of Mary and is subject to suffering.

Later in the same epistle (nn. 18-19) Ignatius speaks of Jesus as the epiphany or manifestation of God. Jesus' purpose is "to mold 'the newness' (Romans 6:4) of eternal life." He is the Word who breaks God's silence in order to destroy death and bring new life. To accomplish this he was "really born and ate and drank, really persecuted by Pontius Pilate, really crucified and died ... really rose from the dead" (*Letter to the Trallians*, nn. 9-11). If, however, all of this was "make-believe," then his saving work on our behalf is all for naught, and the Eucharist that we celebrate together is of no account (*Letter to the Smyrnaeans*, n. 7).

The Word, or *Logos*, concept is also central for *Justin* as he tries to show the connection between the Greek philosophers' pursuit of Truth and our common human quest for the fullness of life and for salvation. "The Christ who has appeared for us represents the *Logos* principle in its totality, that is both body and *Logos* and soul" (*Second Apology*, nn. 10,13). Only in him is the Word fully present. And yet that particular expression or embodiment of the Word is available in principle to all and for all, just as the Word already contains whatever truth is to be found apart from the particularity of the Christ-event and of Christian faith: "The truths which people in all lands have rightly spoken belong to us Christians. . . . Indeed, all writers, by means of the engrafted seed of the Word which was implanted in them, had a glimpse of the truth." The same approach is developed several decades later by Clement of Alexandria.

An early indication of what Scholastic theology calls the *communicatio idiomatum* is provided by Bishop Melito of Sardis (d. ca. 190), who testifies not only to the divinity and humanity of Jesus but also to their *mutuality*: ". . .he who suspended the earth is suspended; he who fixes the heavens in place is himself fixed in place; he who fastened all things is fastened to the wood; . . .God is murdered. . ." (*Homily on the Pasch*).

Since the "communication of the idioms" (the mutual predication of properties) is a matter of some importance in interpreting the later history of Christology, it might be appropriate to explain it now, where it first appears. Because there is only one person, Jesus Christ, who acts through two natures, one divine and one human, we may legitimately predicate, or affirm, of this one person attributes which are both human (e.g., the ability to suffer) and divine (e.g., unlimited knowledge). But even beyond that, one can also predicate of his humanity what is his by virtue of the divinity, and vice versa. Thus by the "communication of idioms," one can say that "Mary's son is all-knowing" or that "God was born of Mary." Rejection of the personal unity of Jesus led Nestorius, for example, to reject the "communication of idioms" with reference to Jesus' birth and the motherhood of Mary. The Council of Ephesus would insist that Mary is the Mother of God, and precisely on the theological principle that she gave birth not to a nature alone but to a person, a *divine* person. As a consequence of the union by which divinity and humanity are united in one person, we can predicate of the one person what is rooted in either nature.

The great third-century theologian Irenaeus carried forward the defense of Christological faith against the extremists. The balanced quality of his position is striking. Jesus was human and truly suffered, but he was also "our only true master. . .the Word of God." More to the point: "Had he not as a human being overcome our adversary, the enemy would not have been justly overcome. Again, had it not been God who bestowed salvation, we should not have it as a secure possession. And if we had not been united to God, we could not have become partakers of immortality. For the mediator between God and humankind had to bring both parties into friendship and concord through his kinship with both; both to present humankind to God, and make God known to humankind" (*Against Heresies* 3.18.6,7). Jesus Christ, therefore, *recapitulates* everything in himself, restoring all reality to fellowship and communion with God.

Irenaeus is well in advance of the formulation of a classic Christological principle, one to be fashioned and refined by Athanasius and Gregory of Nazianzus—namely, "What is not taken up (by the Word) is not healed; but what is united with God is also saved."

Subsequent efforts at preserving orthodoxy while opening new lines of communication with contemporary non-Christian philosophy led inevitably to some Christological ambiguity. If Jesus Christ was to be believable as the fullness of truth, then his identification with the world of ordinary intellectual experience had to be secure. Accordingly, such theologians as Origen, Tertullian, and Paul of Samasota struggled to find new formulations of the relationship between Jesus and God the Father, concerned as they were both about the intellectual skepticism of their colleagues outside the Church and about the Gnostic and Docetic tendencies of many of their brothers and sisters within the Church. And they were concerned as well with reconciling their faith in one God with their confession of Jesus as Lord. Accordingly, their language at times suggested a *Subordinationist* orientation, i.e., one that made the Son of God less than or "subordinate to" the Father.

Thus, Origen's *First Principles* speaks of the necessity for some "intermediate instrument" between God and flesh to make their union possible. And there is at least a hint of Nestorianism (the positing of two separate persons in Christ) in his *Commentary on John*, where he distinguishes perhaps too sharply between Christ as the Word and Christ as human, a distinction that is not overcome, according to Origen, until after the exaltation. So "spiritual" is Origen's approach that much of his Christology is open to misinterpretation. This will explain why the official Church reached back beyond Origen to Irenaeus to find theological grounding for its teachings on the unity of God and man in Jesus Christ.

Tertullian, on the other hand, anticipated by more than two centuries the Christological formulation of the Council of Chalcedon. In his *Against Praxeas* (n. 27) he insists that Jesus, who is truly God and truly human, is at the same time a single subject: "Jesus is one person, God and man." Such union does violence to neither the divinity nor to the humanity: "Flesh does not become spirit nor spirit flesh. . . ." Unfortunately, Tertullian's understanding of the redemptive significance of the incarnation is not so penetrating or balanced. True to his Roman legalistic spirit, he focused entirely on the cross as the price of our salvation. Jesus came into this world, taking on our humanity, for one purpose only: to suffer the death of the cross. There is no corresponding emphasis on the rest of Jesus' human life, nor on the significance of the Word's taking on our flesh. Jesus stands as our representative, therefore, in a juridical sense alone. It was this legalistic approach that would influence much of Western theology for centuries thereafter.

Paul of Samasota, perhaps in reaction to Origen's tendency to shake Jesus loose from his human roots, seems to have professed some kind of adoptionist Christology. The Father dwells in the human being Jesus, thereby making of him his son. Paul of Samasota's view was condemned by the Synod of Antioch, which declared in 268 that "the divine Word is in (Jesus) what the interior man is in us." But did the synod also mean that Jesus did not have a *human* soul? Precisely that implication would be drawn within the century, and it would create a storm of theological controversy and political conflict.

The Council of Nicea (325)

It was Arius (of whom we wrote in chapter 9) who carried these *Subordinationist* tendencies to their extreme. The Son is a creature, created in time by the Father and then used by the Father in the creation of the world. Thus, Christ was neither God nor a human being. Rather, he was less than God but more than a human being. He was a kind of composite intermediary being, but not the mediator spoken of by Irenaeus and others.

Against the Arian view, the Council of Nicea solemnly proclaimed the oneness in being ("consubstantiality") of the Son with the Father. He is "God from God, Light from Light, true God from true God, begotten, not made, one in being (*homoousios*) with the Father. . . . For us men and for our salvation He came down and became flesh, was made man, suffered, and rose again on the third day."

The First Council of Constantinople (381)

Its ambiguities still unresolved, the controversy generated by Paul of Samasota and by the Synod of Antioch's response to him surfaced again around 360, almost a century later. Apollinaris of Laodicea, a faithful supporter of Athanasius and a strong defender of the Council of Nicea, made the *denial of the human soul* in Jesus the very heart of his Christology. For Apollinaris the Word is the unique principle of the flesh of Jesus. If Christ also had a human soul, or mind, then the Word would have been *in* a man, as Paul of Samasota seemed to be saying, but the Word itself would not have been made flesh. "How can God become a human being without ceasing to be God except by taking the place of the mind in a human being?" Apollinaris asked.

As a reaction against perduring adoptionist tendencies in the Church, the position of Apollinaris was understandable. But it failed to safeguard the transcendence of the Word and the integrity of Jesus' human nature. And in failing to safeguard the latter in particular, it undermined the effect of Christ's saving activity on our behalf. Accordingly, the position had to be condemned, as it was, by the First Council of Constantinople in 381 and again the next year at a Council of Rome convened by Pope Damasus I (d. 384). The "heresy" of the "Apollinarists" was censured by name in Canon I of the former council's declarations, and in Canon VII of the latter's, the text of which follows: "We condemn those who say that the Word of God dwelling in human flesh took the place of the rational and spiritual soul, since the Son and the Word of God did not replace the rational and spiritual soul in His body but rather assumed our soul (i.e., a rational and spiritual one) without sin and saved it."

The Council of Ephesus (431)

The controversy which had broken out in Antioch around the year 360 saw the emergence of two distinct and opposed parties. The debate between them was of major moment because it would set the stage for, and shape the terms of, the landmark Christological definitions of both Ephesus and Chalcedon.

On the one side, there were those who regarded the unity of the Word and the human in Christ rather loosely and who were intent upon defending his full humanity. This was the Antiochene school, and Nestorianism was its extreme expression. On the other side, there were those who tended to exaggerate the unity of Christ to the point where, as in Apollinaris, the human soul was entirely supplanted. They were intent upon defending Christ's divinity. This was the Alexandrian school, and Monophysitism was its extreme expression.

Two of Apollinaris' opponents, Diodore of Tarsus (d. ca. 394) and Theodore of Mopsuestia (d. 428), launched their own counter-protest and proclaimed the complete fullness of the humanity of Jesus. But the aggressiveness of their disciple Nestorius (d. 451) provoked resistance from Cyril of Alexandria (d. 444), who, in turn, allowed himself to use Apollinarian expressions. The Council of Ephesus condemned Nestorius.

More specifically: Diodore of Tarsus, like almost every exponent of a heterodox or even heretical point of view, was not intent upon *denying* some aspect of Christological truth. He was concerned rather with *preserving* something which he feared to be in danger of denial from the other side, namely, the transcendence of the Word. Diodore, therefore, did not deliberately set out to divide the human Jesus from the divine Word, but that was the effect of his position that the human being Jesus was son of Mary in the flesh and of God *by grace*, whereas the Word is the Son of God (not of Mary) *by nature*: "The man born of Mary is son by grace; God the Word is Son by nature" (Syriac Fragments 31-32; cited in Carmody and Clarke, *Word and Redeemer*, p. 83).

Theodore, bishop of Mopsuestia, joined forces against the *Logos-sarx*, or Word-flesh, approach of the Alexandrians, namely, the view which emphasizes *the drawing of all that is of the flesh into the Word* (as against the Antiochene *Logos-anthropos*, or Word-human being, approach which emphasizes *the Word's becoming human*). It was important for Theodore, and for others of the *Logos-anthropos* school, that Jesus be an agent and model of our liberation from sin and death, and he could be such only to the extent that he was truly one of us and with us. "Therefore it was necessary," Theodore wrote in his *Catechetical Homilies*, "that he should assume not only the body but also the immortal and rational soul; and not only the death of the body . . . but also that of the soul, which is sin" (n. 5). And so the human being Jesus, body and soul, ascended into heaven beyond Satan's reach. We, too, ascend beyond Satan's power insofar as we participate in the death and resurrection of Jesus. Mary, therefore, *is* the Mother of God, but Theodore seemed to understand the title in a weakened sense, as Diodore had before him. The human being born of Mary is not identically God, but only has God (the Word) dwelling in him.

Nestorius, patriarch of Constantinople (until deposed by the Council of Ephesus in 431), carried these views to their extreme. He fully represented the Antiochene insistence on the *Logos-anthropos*, or Word-human being, approach. The Word really and truly *became human*. Accordingly, such expressions as "God has suffered" or "God was nursed at his mother's breast" were offensive to him. (See "communication of idioms," referred to earlier in this chapter.) They smacked of Arianism and of Apollinarianism, both of which in their own way rejected the full incarnation, or becoming flesh, of the Word.

For Nestorius there are two natures in Christ, one divine and the other human, and each has its own *personal* manifestation.

These, in turn, form a third "person of union." The Nestorian position demands, of course, a special understanding of the motherhood of Mary: "If anyone wishes to use this word *theotokos* (literally, "mother of God") with reference to the humanity which was born, joined to God the Word, and not with reference to the parent, we say that this word is not appropriate for her who gave birth, since a true mother should be of the same essence as what is born of her . . . none gives birth to one older than herself" (*Letter to Pope Celestine*, n. 2).

Cyril, bishop of Alexandria, brought the *Logos-sarx*, or Word-flesh, Christology to its peak in this controversy, as Nestorius had brought the opposite *Logos-anthropos*, or Word-human being, Christology to its own logical heights. As a bishop (and most of the participants were men in pastoral office, not academicians), Cyril was principally concerned with the effects of the debate on our understanding of salvation and, more immediately, of the Eucharist. If the divine and the human are not really and fully united in Jesus Christ but are, as Nestorius would have it, separate and divided, then the flesh of the Word could not be the life-giving instrument of our own divinization—neither in salvation history nor in Holy Communion. In an almost classic expression of the Alexandrian *Logos-sarx* approach, Cyril writes that "the flesh does not bring the Word down to its own level; for divinity can in no wise be diminished. Of itself the flesh is incapable of imparting life . . ." (*Commentary on John*, n. 4).

Cyril was to address three letters to Nestorius, the *second* of which (written in 430) the Council of Ephesus formally accepted as a statement of orthodox faith. Therein, Cyril explicitly disavowed any Apollinarian interpretation of his position. The Word truly became flesh through a real hypostatic union. The Word *is* truly human, and not merely *in* a human being. Therefore, Mary can be called the Mother of God, and not the Mother of Christ, because "It was not an ordinary man who was first born of the holy virgin, and upon whom afterwards the Word descended, but he himself, united to humanity from the womb, who is said to have undergone fleshly birth, as making his own the birth of his own flesh." Thus, we worship "one Christ and Lord," and not a "human being along with the Word." What was born of Mary was "his rationally animated body to which the Word was hypostatically united."

The Council of Ephesus, convened by the emperor Theodosius II (d. 450), was formally opened by Cyril on June 22, 431, before the arrival of the delegates from Rome, representing Pope Celestine (d. 432). Cyril's second letter to Nestorius was approved by the council Fathers. Nestorius' views were condemned, and Nestorius was deposed as patriarch of Constantinople. When the Roman delegation finally arrived, they ratified in the name of the pope what had already been decided and done.

Neither the council nor the pope's representatives, however, officially accepted the so-called twelve anathematizations, or condemnations, contained in Cyril's *third* letter to Nestorius. Nonetheless, the document was read to the council, and it created a great measure of dissatisfaction among the Eastern bishops, i.e., those close to the Antiochene school of thought. Some of Cyril's language, as we noted earlier, was at least suggestive of an Apollinarian approach, particularly his characterization of the union of the divine and the union in Christ as a "physical" one (third anathema). The council ended with the mutual excommunication of the two great patriarchs of the East, John of Antioch and Cyril of Alexandria.

At the invitation of the emperor Theodosius II, John of Antioch (d. 441) provided a profession of faith to which Cyril was able to subscribe in 433. It expressed better than Cyril had the reality of Christ's distinct human nature, and the distinction between the two natures united in one person. Pope Sixtus III (d. 440) congratulated both parties and by implication accepted the so-called *"Formula of Union"* (also known as the "Symbol of Union" and the "Edict of Union") between Cyril and the bishops of Antioch. It was chiefly through this formula that the Antiochene school made its contribution to the subsequent development of the Christological dogma at Chalcedon.

Because this formula is so important a bridge between Ephesus and Chalcedon, a relatively generous excerpt is reproduced here.

> We confess therefore our Lord Jesus Christ, the only-begotten Son of God, perfect God and perfect human

being composed of rational soul and body, begotten before all ages from the Father as to his divinity, and the same in the last days born of the Virgin Mary as to his humanity for us and for our salvation, consubstantial with the Father in divinity and consubstantial with us in humanity. For a union of two natures has taken place; hence we confess one Christ, one Son, one Lord. In accordance with this union without confusion, we profess the holy Virgin to be Mother of God (*theotokos*), for God the Word became flesh and was made human and from the moment of conception united to himself the temple he had taken from her.

As for the words of the gospels and of the apostles concerning the Lord, we know that theologians have considered some as common because they are said of the one person (*prosopon*), while they have distinguished others as applying to the two natures (*physeis*), reserving those which befit God to Christ in his divinity while assigning those which are lowly to Christ in his humanity.

The Council Of Chalcedon (451)

The *Formula of Union*, however well-intentioned and well-conceived, did not hold the parties permanently together. Cyril's successor as bishop of Alexandria, Dioscorus (d. 454), would interpret some of Cyril's ambiguous formulations too literally. In the heat of struggle against Nestorianism, he tended to understand the hypostatic union as something achieved at the level of nature (*physis*) rather than of person. Thus, the divine and the human come together in Christ in *one divine nature (Monophysitism)*. Eutyches (d. ca. 454), the aged head of a monastery in Constantinople, carried the position to an even greater extreme. Better known for his sanctity than for his theological scholarship, Eutyches denied that Christ was consubstantial with us. Christ's human nature was completely absorbed by the divine nature.

Eutyches was brought to trial and condemned at a synod in Constantinople in 448. Although temporarily rehabilitated by

Dioscorus, Eutyches was also subsequently condemned by Pope Leo the Great (d. 461), to whom he had appealed. In a letter (the *"Tome of Leo"*) addressed in June 449 to Flavian (d. 449), patriarch of Constantinople, the pope gave the clearest expression to date of the doctrine of the incarnation. In Christ there are two distinct natures united in one person: "For he who is truly God is the same who is also truly human and there is no deception in this unity in which the lowliness of a human being and the divine majesty coincide. . . . For each of the two natures performs the functions proper to it in communion with the other: the Word does what pertains to the Word and the flesh what pertains to the flesh."

With his Augustinian stress on Christ as Mediator and on the saving power of the miracles and mysteries of the life of Christ, the pope clearly linked Christology with soteriology. Because of the union of the divine and human natures in the one divine person, all of the activities of the human Jesus are rooted in, and spring from, the one divine person and are, therefore, of infinitely salvific value. And yet they also remain fully human actions and fully representative of the whole human community, for the Lord was "born with the complete and perfect nature of a true human being; he is complete in his nature and complete in ours."

But Pope Leo's letter did not settle the matter once and for all, at least not so far as Dioscorus and Eutyches were concerned. They exercised their considerable local influence and succeeded in having a synod convened at Ephesus in August of 449 at which, under very strong political pressure, the bishops approved Eutyches' doctrine and deposed two of his episcopal opponents. Pope Leo labeled the synod a "robbery" (*latrocinium*), and it is still known today as the "robber synod" of Ephesus. Its proceedings were condemned by a Roman synod which met the very next month. It also asked that the emperor, Theodosius II, convoke a general council in Italy. He refused. It was left to his successor, Marcion (d. 457), to summon the Council of Chalcedon in October, 451. With nearly six hundred bishops, including three papal legates and two representatives of Latin Africa, this was by far the largest and most important council of the early Church.

At the first sessions the legality of the "robber synod" of Ephesus was examined and found wanting. Eutyches' doctrine was once again rejected, and Dioscorus was condemned for his part in the synod and for his complicity in bringing such unwarranted pressure to bear on the bishops. But the Fathers of Chalcedon were not initially interested in drafting yet another confession of faith. They were satisfied with the formulations of Nicea (325), Constantinople (381), and the "Tome of Leo" (449). The emperor's representatives, however, insisted on something more. They prevailed. A commission of bishops drafted a schema, but it was so ambiguous about the union of natures in Christ that the papal legates rejected it and threatened to move the council back to Italy. The emperor's delegates sided with the pope's and ordered the bishops to face up to the issue. They would have to choose between Dioscorus and Pope Leo.

A new commission, whose members now also included the Roman delegates and the emperor's, composed a profession of faith which the council accepted. Borrowing freely from Cyril of Alexandria's second letter to Nestorius, the "Formula of Union," and the "Tome of Leo" (the reading of which had elicited cries of "Peter has spoken through the mouth of Leo"), the Chalcedonian symbol of faith repudiated *both* Nestorianism and Monophysitism.

The *Alexandrian* school had clearly triumphed in the central formula, "one and the same Lord Jesus Christ." It is the "one and the same Lord Jesus Christ" who appears and lives in the man Jesus of Nazareth. The *Arians* were once again repudiated for having seen in the incarnation the "proof" that the Son is not truly God; and so, too, were the *Nestorians*, who sacrificed the unity of Jesus Christ in order to "save" the complete humanity.

The *Antiochene* school also triumphed in the formula "the same truly God and truly man composed of rational soul and body...like unto us in all things but sin...." The Antiochenes had fought for these principles against the old *Docetism* and also against certain tendencies in the disciples of *Origen*. Jesus of Nazareth was truly one of us and of our human family, but through the hypostatic union he is, at the same time, the source of our redemption and sanctification.

The older Christologies of Irenaeus and Tertullian were also represented in the Chalcedonian definitions. It was Irenaeus who provided the formula "one and the same" and who insisted that "had it not been God who bestowed salvation, we should not have it as a secure possession. And if we had not been united to God, we could not have become partakers of immortality." And it was Tertullian's formula, one person in two natures, which the council took over and made its own, although without any detailed elaboration. The "person" is the "who" of the union, namely, the eternal Son of God. The "natures" are the "what" of the union. Accordingly, Jesus Christ is consubstantial with the Father and also substantially one with us.

The definition follows:

> Following therefore the holy Fathers, we unanimously teach and confess one and the same Son, our Lord Jesus Christ, the same perfect in divinity and perfect in humanity, the same truly God and truly man composed of rational soul and body, the same one in being (*homoousios*) with the Father as to divinity and one in being with us as to humanity, like unto us in all things but sin (cf. Hebrews 4:15). The same was begotten from the Father before the ages as to the divinity and in the latter days for us and for our salvation was born as to his humanity from Mary the Virgin Mother of God.

> We confess that one and the same Lord Jesus Christ, the only-begotten Son, must be acknowledged in two natures, without confusion or change, without division or separation. The distinction between the natures was never abolished by their union but rather the character proper to each of the two natures was preserved as they came together in one person (*prosopon*) and one hypostasis. He is not split or divided into two persons but he is one and the same only-begotten, God the Word, the Lord Jesus Christ, as formerly the prophets and later Jesus Christ himself have taught us about him and as has been handed down to us by the Symbol of the Fathers.

The Second Council of Constantinople (553)

The solemnity of the conciliar definition notwithstanding, some bishops in Syria and Egypt who were inclined to Monophysitism expressed concern that Chalcedon had contradicted Ephesus (the council that had condemned the opposite heresy of Nestorianism). In 519 some Monophysite monks sought from Pope Hormisdas (d. 523) approval of their own formula, "one of the three (Persons in the Trinity) has suffered in the flesh." They were not satisfied with the pope's response. Several years later the emperor Justinian (d. 565), himself sympathetic to the Monophysite cause, for political rather than theological reasons, asked Pope John II (d. 535) for papal approval of the formula. He gave it, more or less, in a letter to the Senate of Constantinople in 534, but he also reaffirmed the Church's rejection of *both* Nestorianism and Monophysitism.

The controversy continued. A so-called "neo-Chalcedonian" current developed, giving many the hope that somehow the Chalcedonian formula might be reconciled with Monophysitism. The current's supporters urged the condemnation of the first opponents of Monophysitism: Theodoret of Cyr (d. 466), Ibas of Edessa (d. 457), and Theodore of Mopsuestia (d. 428), Nestorius' teacher. All were accused of Nestorian tendencies, and their works were lumped together under the heading of *"Three Chapters."* Again, the emperor Justinian, concerned about the politically divisive effects of these disputes, asked a pope, this time Pope Vigilius (d. 555), to take a public stand against these three opponents of Monophysitism. At first the pope refused, insisting that the three were orthodox by Chalcedonian standards. Only after he had been taken by force to Constantinople in 548 did he issue the condemnation. The reaction in the West was severe. Relations between the emperor and the pope were broken off, and Vigilius published a strong anti-Monophysite profession of faith (552).

At Justinian's call the Second Council of Constantinople opened in May of 553, condemned the "Three Chapters," adopted vehemently anti-Nestorian positions, and embraced the newly popular Monophysite formula, "One of the three has suffered in the flesh." The Council never won acceptance in the West, nor did it achieve the union Justinian hoped for in the East. The pope did eventually approve it, but the doctrinal scope of that approval is not entirely clear. It seems to have been restricted to the three canons which were directly concerned with the "Three Chapters" of Theodoret, Ibas, and Theodore. To the extent that the council has any longer-term doctrinal significance for Catholic faith, its importance may consist simply in its reaffirmation of the earlier condemnations of Nestorianism. Otherwise, it is not an exceptionally bright moment in the conciliar history of the Church.

The Third Council of Constantinople (681)

By now Islam, a new and powerful threat to the unity of Christendom, had made its entrance upon the world scene. These internal theological divisions within the Church were a luxury it could now afford even less than before. A new emperor, Heraclius (d. 641), offered his support to Sergius (d. 638), patriarch of Constantinople, in the latter's attempts at some theological reconciliation. Unfortunately, Sergius only succeeded in producing yet another Christological deviation, this one called *Monothelitism* (one will), or *Monenergism* (one action). In one of those interesting cases of history where a pope seems to have come down on the side of a heretical position, Pope Honorius (d. 638) agreed with Sergius that the expression "one will" could be used, but then Sergius carried it one step further: If one will, then one nature. And so he was back to Monophysitism. It was inevitable that Monothelitism and its companion, Monenergism, would be condemned. The first conciliar blow against Monothelitism was delivered at a non-ecumenical Council of the Lateran (649), convoked by Pope Martin I (d. 655) and attended by one hundred and five bishops from Italy and Africa. The definitive thrust, however, came from the Third Council of Constantinople, convoked by the emperor Constantine IV (d. 685) with the consent of Pope Agatho (d. 681). The council accepted the doctrinal formulation which the pope had previously expressed in a letter to the emperor (March, 680), and it condemned Monothelitism and all of its supporters, even chastizing the late Pope Honorius for his unwitting approval of the heresy. One year later Pope Leo II (d. 683),

Pope Agatho's successor, formally approved the council's proceedings.

The definition follows:

> . . . believing that one of the holy Trinity, who after the incarnation is our Lord Jesus Christ, is our true God, we say that his two natures shine forth in his one hypostasis. In it, throughout his entire human existence in the flesh, he made manifest his miracles and his sufferings, not in mere appearance but in reality. The difference of natures in that same and unique hypostasis is recognized by the fact that each of the two natures wills and performs what is proper to it in communion with the other. Thus, we confess two natural wills and actions concurring together for the salvation of the human race.

Subsequent Councils

Doctrinal development stopped at this point. To the extent that Christological dogma was touched upon by subsequent councils of the Church, it was always simply a matter of reiterating the teachings of one of these earlier councils—Nicea, Ephesus, and Chalcedon in particular. This is the case with the Fourth Lateran Council (1215) in its profession of faith; in the profession of faith given at the Second Council of Lyons (1274); in the *Decree for the Jacobites* at the Council of Florence (1442); in the *Decree on Justification* at the Council of Trent (1547); and in various papal encyclicals and decrees of Roman congregations in more recent years. As we shall see in Part IV, the Second Vatican Council focused its attention principally on the mystery of the Church, not on Christology. Vatican II's Christology, therefore, is to be inferred from its ecclesiology. All is fixed on the goal of unity. The Church is called to be a sign and instrument of unity: of the unity of humankind with God and of humankind within itself. This call to unity is grounded in the mystery of Christ and of the Kingdom of God. Just as Christ came to proclaim the Kingdom, to personify it, and to bring it about, so, too, the Church is summoned to carry forward Christ's mission for the sake of the Kingdom (see the

Dogmatic Constitution on the Church, n. 5, and the *Pastoral Constitution on the Church in the Modern World*, n. 45).

Synthesis

Against assorted Christological errors—especially Arianism, Nestorianism, and Monophysitism—the official teachings of the Church preserved an essential balance in its understanding of the mystery of Christ, at once God and a human being. The Word of God, who became human, suffered, died, and rose for our salvation, is truly God, of the same substance as the Father (*Nicea*). But he is also fully human, of one nature with us (*Constantinople I* and *Chalcedon*). In spite of the irreducible difference between his divine and his human natures, he is one and the same, the eternal Son of God, who as a human being is born of the Virgin Mary, the Mother of God (*Ephesus, Chalcedon*, and *Constantinople II*). Because he is a human being, he leads a truly human life in all things but sin: a life of truly human actions, of truly human freedom, of truly human consciousness (*Constantinople III*).

MEDIEVAL CHRISTOLOGY
Some Antecedents

Augustine

Augustine died in 430 and therefore had no direct role in any of the major Christological councils. And yet he remains, alongside Thomas Aquinas, as one of the most influential of all Christian theologians. For Augustine, Christ is the *Mediator* between God and humankind. He is the Word incarnate, a teacher of infinite knowledge and wisdom, who leads us to eternity through temporal realities. By identifying completely with our human condition, Jesus Christ shows us how to live and gives all of us hope for life without end. On the other hand, " . . . we would not be redeemed by the one mediator of God and man, the man Jesus Christ (1 Timothy 2:5), if he were not also God" (*Enchiridion*, n. 137). Christ, therefore, is the new head of the human race. We are predestined to glory through him, and we are joined to him even now as members of his Church.

Boethius

Boethius (d. 525) is the one generally credited with refining the meaning of the terms *person* and *nature* as they function in Christological discussion. It was his definition of *person* which carried over into medieval thought and which provided some verbal leverage for clarifying the preceding conciliar doctrines: "an individual substance of a rational nature." The definition was slightly modified by Thomas Aquinas (who spoke of an "incommunicable" substance as well) and especially by Richard of St. Victor (d. 1173), for whom person is "an incommunicable existence of an intellectual nature." Person, therefore, is the reality of a being which belongs to itself and is its own end. But personhood is never grasped as it is, directly. We are persons who act as persons and who come to the knowledge of our personhood only by reflecting on the meaning of what we do. But this is getting us into modern conceptions of "person," well beyond Boethius' pioneering efforts.

Anselm

Anselm of Canterbury's place in the history of Christology is insured by his distinctive *theory of satisfaction*. It is an understanding of redemption, however, which seems to distort rather than illuminate the meaning of Christ's mission, so far does it appear to be from the New Testament's theology of the cross and resurrection (see chapter 12).

   According to Anselm's argument, as expressed in Book I of *Cur Deus Homo*? (*Why Did God Become Man*?), sin disturbed the order of the universe. Some compensation had to be offered to restore what had been disrupted. But we were simply not up to the task. The offense was against an infinite God, and we are finite. Only infinite satisfaction would do, and only God could provide it (chapter V). But not just God. It had to be one who is at once God and a human being, a God-man. This answered the question: Why did God become a human being? But it did not answer the question: Why did Jesus have to die?

Anselm proposed that satisfaction required more than the incarnation. Jesus had to do something which he as a human being was not otherwise bound to do. Because he was sinless, he was not bound to die. But he endured death nonetheless as a voluntary payment of the debt incurred by our sins, and so he satisfies for those sins (Chapters IX-XII).

Anselm's theory is to be understood against the background of the Germanic and early medieval feudal system. There is a bond of honor between feudal lord and vassal. Infringement of the lord's honor is tantamount to an assault upon the whole feudal system. A demand for satisfaction, therefore, is not for the sake of appeasing the lord's personal sense of honor but for the sake of restoring order to the "universe" (feudal system) in which, and therefore against which, the "sin" was committed. The feudal lord cannot simply overlook the offense, because the order of his whole economic and social world is at stake. So, too, with God (Chapters XIII-XV).

Aquinas would later modify Anselm's theory, arguing that it was *fitting* for God to act in that way, but it was not *necessary*, as Anselm had insisted (*Summa Theologica*, III, q. 1, a. 2). Thus altered, Anselm's theory entered the wider stream of medieval and then post-medieval theology. It was never made an official teaching of the Church, however. Over the years, many Catholics have incorrectly assumed it to be a matter of doctrine, if not even of dogma. Through Calvin and Luther, Protestants, too, ingested the theory in its more severe form (Christ died as our *substitute*, in punishment for sin).

Thomas Aquinas

Aquinas followed in the tradition of Augustine in formulating his own answer to the question at hand, "Why did God become a human being?" The incarnation occurred because ". . . it belongs to the essence of goodness to communicate itself to others. . . (and) to the essence of the highest goodness to communicate itself in the highest manner to the creature" (III, q. 1, a. 1). Thus, the incarnation deepens our faith in goodness, strengthens our hope, enkindles charity, sets us an example, divinizes us, turns us from evil, heightens our sense of human dignity, destroys our presumption about grace and salvation, removes our pride, and frees us from sin (q. 1, a. 2). Given the last effect, it was "fitting" that Jesus Christ serve as our Mediator between God and us since in him alone are God and humankind united.

Thomas turned his attention quickly, however, to the *mode of union*, and it is here, in question 2, that he defines and distinguishes the meanings of *nature* and *person*. *Nature* signifies *what* a thing is, as distinct from some other species of reality. *Person* signifies *who* it is, i.e., an individual substance of a rational nature (Boethius again). "If the human nature is not united to God the Word in person, it is not united to him at all; and thus belief in the incarnation is altogether done away with, and Christian faith wholly overturned" (q. 2, a. 2). He also insists, with Chalcedon, that the union is truly *hypostatic*, against those who would continue to argue that there are two hypostases in the incarnation, the one of God, the other of a human being, while there is but one person, Christ. "Person," Thomas notes, "only adds to hypostasis a determinate nature, i.e., rational" (q. 2, a. 3). To say otherwise is to lapse once more into Nestorianism, thereby destroying the unity of the God-human being and undermining his salvific work on our behalf.

The medieval discussion about the meaning of *person* would demand more effort and space than the purpose of this book requires or allows. It is sufficient simply to note that three discernible schools of opinion developed: The *Thomist* school, represented especially by the Dominican Banez (d. 1604); the *Scotist* school, represented by Duns Scotus himself (d. 1308); and a mediating *Jesuit* school, represented by Francis Suarez (d. 1617). The first insisted that Christ's human nature participates in the same act of existence by which the Word itself exists. The "act of human existence" is subtracted from it, without loss of human dignity. On the contrary, Christ's human nature receives an even higher dignity in being alive by the same principle of existence by which the

Word is alive. The second (Scotist) view preferred to define personality in a negative way, as an incapacity for dependence (conversely, a capacity for independence). In the hypostatic union the power of God brings to fulfillment this capacity for independence by fully orienting the human nature of Christ to God. Finally, the Suarezian position says, against the Thomists, that nothing is "subtracted" from the human nature of Christ. The two natures are joined by what Suarez called a created mode of union. Against the Scotists, Suarez argued that personality is a positive, not a negative, reality. It is an essentially necessary form in which a nature is manifested.

Three observations should be made about this discussion. (1) It showed how far medieval theology had veered from the historical, soteriological, and pastoral interest of New Testament and patristic thought in favor of an exceedingly speculative analysis of "how" the divine and the human are united in Jesus Christ. (2) The debate itself defies easy summarization, as the preceding paragraph shows. (3) Since the Church has never officially and finally defined its understanding of the mode of union, the matter is still open to debate. There is no one orthodox explanation, although there have been some unorthodox ones.

Much of the remainder of Thomas' Christology dwells on questions which have to do with the *inner makeup* of Christ: his intellect, his soul, the presence of grace, the virtues, his knowledge, his grasp of the Beatific Vision, his powers, his bodily integrity, his capacity for suffering, the unity of wills, his ability to merit, his subjection to the Father, and so forth. Principal exceptions, beyond the opening statement on the fittingness of the incarnation, are provided by the discussion of Christ's headship over the Church (q. 8), his role as Mediator (q. 26), and then the sequential treatment of the various mysteries of Christ's life, death, resurrection and exaltation (qq. 35-59). But these "exceptions" did not govern the Christologies of subsequent centuries. They remained focused on the so-called "constitutive" questions, i.e., Christ as he is *in himself* rather than *for us*. Christology and soteriology drew farther and farther apart.

Post-medieval Scholasticism

Catholic Christology from the medieval period to the middle of the twentieth century (specifically, the fifteen hundredth anniversary of the Chalcedonian definition) is really a history of commentaries on Thomas Aquinas' *Summa Theologica*, retaining all the while the *Summa's* basic structure. One can take up practically any Latin textbook from this vast period and find this verified. Thus, Charles Boyer, for many years professor at the Pontifical Gregorian University in Rome, the academic training ground of many Catholic bishops and theologians, patterned his own work almost exactly on the *Summa*. His *De Verbo Incarnato* discusses in sequence the fittingness of the incarnation, the mode of union, the two wills, and the redemptive work. Several other subsidiary questions appear almost exactly where Thomas himself treated them—e.g., the priesthood of Christ, the adorability of the humanity of Christ, the headship of Christ. On the other hand, Boyer, like many other post-medieval theologians, failed to carry forward some of Thomism's stronger biblical and patristic insights, especially the discussion of the mysteries of Christ's life and the more comprehensive understanding of the redemption. On the latter point, for example, Thomas does not completely limit Christ's saving work to the cross; Boyer and most others do. In this they reflect a Latin tradition which goes back even before the Middle Ages, to the time of Tertullian (d. 220). For them, the resurrection and exaltation are a *reward* for Christ's obedient death and a *proof* in support of his claims to divinity. As we saw in the last chapter, such a view brings us a considerable distance indeed from the theological perspective of the New Testament.

SUMMARY

1. Development in the Church's understanding of Jesus Christ occurred for three reasons: (1) the naturally inquisitive and probing impulse of the human mind; (2) the challenge of dissident opinions; and (3) the need to communicate the Christian message across cultural lines.

2. Distortions of the Church's Christological faith appeared at opposite ends of the theological spectrum. At the *extreme left* there were denials of the divinity in favor of the humanity (*Adoptionism*), and at the

extreme right there were denials of the humanity in favor of the divinity (*Gnosticism, Docetism*). These were opposed by such early Church Fathers as *Ignatius of Antioch, Justin, Melito of Sardis*, and *Irenaeus*. The connection between Christology (Christ in himself) and soteriology (Christ for us) is always firmly maintained by these Fathers. For Irenaeus, what is not taken up by the Word is not healed, and what is united to God is saved.

3. Subsequent theological formulations, however, began to skirt the edges of orthodoxy. In their efforts to commend Christian faith to their philosophical contemporaries and, at the same time, to deal effectively with the Gnostic and Docetic threats from within the Church, some of the early Church theologians (*Origen*, in particular) came close to *Subordinationism*, making the Son of God less than, or subordinate to, the Father.

4. It was *Arius*, however, who carried these tendencies to their logical conclusion. The Son is a *creature*, neither God nor a human being, but a composite intermediary being. Against the Arian view the *Council of Nicea* (325) defined the "consubstantiality" of the Son with the Father, insisting that the Son was "begotten, not made."

5. Some pressed the Nicean definition too far in the other direction. *Apollinaris of Laodicea*, a member of the *Alexandrian school*, emphasized so much that the Word is the unique principle of the flesh of Jesus that Jesus was left with *no human soul* at all. Apollinarianism was condemned by the *First Council of Constantinople* (381). If the Word did not assume a human soul as well as a human body, then he did not save us in soul as well as in body.

6. In the meantime, a theological approach opposite from Apollinaris' developed within the *Antiochene school*. Apollinaris had been concerned primarily with the *unity* of Christ's humanity with the Word. For *Diodore of Tarsus* and *Theodore of Mopsuestia*, however, Apollinaris' insistence on the unity of the Word with the humanity in effect suppressed the humanity altogether. The Antiochenes, therefore, preferred to regard the unity of Christ more loosely in order to protect the integrity of his humanity. Their position was carried forward, to an extreme, by *Nestorius*. There are two separate persons in Christ. Mary, therefore, is not the Mother of God (*theotokos*) but only the Mother of Christ, the human being. Nestorius was opposed by *Cyril of Alexandria* and then condemned by the *Council of Ephesus* (431).

7. A *"Formula of Union"* was worked out after the Council of Ephesus between Cyril and some of the bishops of Antioch, who still were not satisfied with the results of the council nor with some of Cyril's

preconciliar expressions. But the "Formula" did not hold the parties together permanently. Indeed, Cyril's views were carried to their own extreme by *Eutyches*, a monk in Constantinople, who argued that Christ's human nature was completely absorbed by the divine nature so that we have not only one divine person but also one divine nature (*physis*). Thus, *Monophysitism*. The *Council of Chalcedon* (451) condemned Monophysitism and reaffirmed the condemnation of Nestorianism. The *Alexandrians* were satisfied with the council's formula, "one and the same Lord Jesus Christ," and the *Antiochenes* with the formula, "the same truly God and truly man composed of rational soul and body...like us in all things but sin...."

8.   Monophysitism continued, however, in Syria and Egypt, and charges and counter-charges were exchanged. Given the political as well as theological dimensions of the controversies, the situation was complicated by the intervention of the emperor, on the one side, and then by the pope, on the other. The *Second Council of Constantinople* (553) was convened by the emperor (and subsequently approved by the pope) to see if a pro-Monophysite "tilt" might contribute to political unity. It did not, and the council is of theological significance for us today only insofar as it repeated the earlier condemnations of Nestorianism.

9.   Monophysitism reappeared in the next century in slightly altered form. *Sergius*, patriarch of Constantinople, argued that there is only one divine will in Christ (*Monothelitism*). At first even the pope (*Honorius*) saw no problem with this, but then Sergius carried his position to *its* logical extreme: If only one will, then only one nature. Monothelitism was condemned at the *Third Council of Constantinople* (681).

10.   There has been no *doctrinal* development since Constantinople III. Subsequent councils have merely repeated the earlier conciliar definitions whenever they turned their attention to Christological issues: *Lateran IV* (1215), *Lyons II* (1274), *Florence* (1442), *Trent* (1547), and *Vatican II* (1962-1965).

11.   Subsequent *theological* development culminated in the medieval synthesis of *Thomas Aquinas*, which held sway in Catholic education until the middle of the twentieth century. That synthesis was rooted in the Patristic era generally, and in *Augustine* particularly. For Augustine, Christ is primarily our *Mediator* with God.

12.   Anselm of Canterbury is best known for his theory of satisfaction. Sin disrupted the balance of the universe, and at the same time imposed a debt upon the human race. Only a God-man could restore that balance and make adequate payment of that debt. Often misunderstood,

Anselm's theory entered the mainstream of medieval and post-medieval thought only after it was modified by Aquinas, who insisted that it was fitting but not necessary that God should have acted in that particular way.

13. *Aquinas'* own Christology reflected the concerns and preoccupations of medieval theology. Although he does speak of Christ's headship, his role as Mediator, the fittingness of the incarnation as a manifestation of divine goodness, and of the mysteries of Christ's life, the principal emphasis of Thomas' Christology is on the *inner makeup* of Jesus Christ: the union of natures with the one divine person, the knowledge of Christ, the operation of his wills, his powers, his consciousness, etc. The focus is on Christ as he is *in himself* rather than on Christ as he is *for us.*

14. Post-medieval Scholastic Christology follows that same pattern, but often without carrying forward some of Thomas' peculiar strengths, namely, his more comprehensive understanding of the redemption (to include the resurrection and exaltation) and his attention to the mysteries of Christ's life. By 1951, the fifteen hundredth anniversary of the Council of Chalcedon, the distance between the New Testament's Christological perspective and that of the Church's theologians was very considerable indeed.

SUGGESTED READINGS

Carmody, James, and Clarke, Thomas. *Word and Redeemer: Christology in the Fathers.* Glen Rock, N.J.: Paulist Press, 1966.

Hardy, E., and Richardson, C., eds. *Christology of the Later Fathers.* Library of Christian Classics, vol. 3. Philadelphia: Westminster Press, 1954.

Grillmeier, Aloys. *Christ in Christian Tradition: From the Apostolic Age to Chalcedon (451).* New York: Sheed & Ward, 1965.

Kelly, J. N. D. *Early Christian Doctrines.* New York: Harper & Row, 1960.

Neuner, J., and Dupuis, J., eds. "Jesus Christ the Savior." *The Christian Faith in the Doctrinal Documents of the Catholic Church.* Westminster, Md.: Christian Classics, 1975, pp. 135-190.

Smulders, Piet. *The Fathers in Christology: The Development of Christological Dogma from the Bible to the Great Councils.* De Pere, Wis.: St. Norbert Abbey Press, 1968.

· XIV ·

THE CHRIST OF
TWENTIETH-CENTURY
THEOLOGY

CATHOLIC CHRISTOLOGY BEFORE 1950

Catholic Christology from the time of Aquinas to the middle of the
twentieth century remained essentially the same in structure and
in content. The approach taken by the "Spanish Summa" (*Sacrae
Theologiae Summa*, Madrid: Library of Christian Authors, 1953,
vol. III) was typical of the textbooks in general use in Catholic
seminaries and colleges throughout this period. The material was
divided into two main parts: the mystery of the incarnation (Christ
as he is in himself), and the redemptive work of Christ (Christ as
he is for us). The two "Christs" are brought together by the sin of
Adam. If Adam had not sinned, the Word would not have become
flesh.

But the discussion immediately turned from the "fittingness"
of the incarnation to a metaphysical analysis of the way in which
the union of Word and flesh occurred and the conditions under
which it was sustained. Herein, the treatment followed the conciliar teaching outlined in the previous chapter: The union occurs at
the level of person, or hypostasis, not at the level of nature, and so
forth. The residual medieval influence was particularly evident in
the raising of various subsidiary questions—e.g., whether Christ
could have been called a human being or the Christ while he lay in

the tomb between Good Friday and Easter Sunday; the reconciliation of the "sadness" of Christ with his sinlessness; the legitimacy of devotion to the Sacred Heart.

The limitations of early twentieth-century Catholic Christology, however, were even more apparent in its treatment of the redemption. The exposition was shaped by the medieval focus upon *merit*, i.e., something which is or ought to be accepted by another, for which the one accepting ought to give something in return. By his passion Christ merited all the gifts of grace and of glory for humankind. He rendered more-than-adequate reparation for sin and, therefore, satisfied the "vindictive justice" of God. The resurrection and exaltation of Christ were mentioned in these Christologies, but their redemptive significance remained unclear. Indeed, what Christ accomplished through his passion was taken as fully sufficient for our salvation. A marked change in this approach was signaled by the publication of Catholic scholar Francis X. Durwell's *The Resurrection* (New York: Sheed & Ward, 1960). This book argued that the resurrection was the center, not an adjunct, of Christ's redemptive work.

WHY THE CHANGE?

There is a pronounced difference between medieval Christology and the Christology of the twentieth-century manuals, on the one hand, and the Christologies of contemporary Catholicism (Rahner, Küng, Schillebeeckx, Kasper, *et al.*), on the other. How account for this? There are two principal reasons: (1) *the shift from an uncritical to a critical reading of the New Testament;* and (2) *the shift from a static to an evolutionary understanding of human existence.* Both of these changes were, for the most part, products of the major transformation of human consciousness connected more or less with the *Enlightenment* of the eighteenth century. These developments, in turn, lay underneath the theological reexamination of the Council of Chalcedon, on the occasion of its fifteen hundredth anniversary, to which reference was made in the previous chapter.

There is no need here to retrace our steps. The significance of the shift in the way we read the New Testament was explained in the previous chapters. The shift in our understanding of human existence was described in Part I, chapters 3–5. Thus, the Jesus of the New Testament is neither the Jesus of traditional piety, based on a fundamentalist interpretation of the Bible, nor the Jesus of liberal revisionism, based on an anti-dogmatic, anti-supernatural, anti-transcendental interpretation of the biblical message and testimony. Since almost all Catholic Christologies before 1950 fell into the first category, these Christologies had to be reconstructed in the light of the biblical renewal.

And with few exceptions, before mid-century the Catholic theology of human existence was similarly untouched by the Enlightenment and its several products: the emergence of historical and political consciousness, and the corresponding development of processive and liberational modes of thinking. Thus, the Jesus of historically-minded Christian faith is neither the omniscient, omnipotent God-in-human-form of traditional piety, based on a static, classical concept of human existence, nor the flat, one-dimensional human being-with-the-aura-of-God of liberal piety. Catholic Christology assumed a new shape, therefore, as it assimilated the findings of twentieth-century New Testament scholarship, on the one hand, and of recent theological anthropology, on the other.

CURRENT AND RECENT CATHOLIC CHRISTOLOGY

Pre-note: The distinction between Christology "from above" and Christology "from below" must be clear at the outset because it recurs throughout this chapter.

Christology "from above" begins with the pre-existent Word of God in heaven, who "comes down" to earth to take on human flesh and to redeem us by dying on the cross, rising from the dead, and returning to enjoy an exalted state as Lord in heaven. This was the emphasis, as the reader may recall, of the Alexandrian School in the age of the great Christological controversies, as it was of the Fourth Gospel and of Paul.

Christology "from below" begins with the Jesus of history, a human being like us in all things except sin, who stands out from the rest of the human race by his proclamation of, and commitment to, the Kingdom of God. His life of dedicated service of others led him to the cross, from which point God raised him up and exalted him. This was the emphasis of the Antiochene School in the age of the Christological debates, as it was of the Synoptic Gospels.

Carried too far, a Christology "from above" becomes Monophysitism or Docetism: Jesus is not really human, but only appears to have taken on our human condition. Carried too far, a Christology "from below" becomes Nestorianism or Adoptionism: Jesus is not really divine, but fulfills a unique role in the history of the human race, calling attention to the demands of God's Kingdom among us.

Karl Rahner

Because he is the most important and most influential Catholic theologian of this century, Karl Rahner's Christology has to be taken with the greatest measure of seriousness. Although expressed in assorted articles in the various volumes of his *Theological Investigations*, the most comprehensive and systematic statement of Rahner's Christology is available in his *Foundations of Christian Faith* (New York: Seabury Press, 1978). The reader must be forewarned: The material is not easy to grasp. But its complexity does not diminish its importance.

Jesus Christ is what is specifically Christian about Christianity, Rahner insists at the outset. This is said without prejudice to the principle that someone who has no concrete, historical contact with the explicit preaching of the Church can nevertheless be justified and saved in virtue of the grace of Christ. The transcendental self-communication of God is available in principle to every person, as we noted in chapter 5. But for the Christian the process of divine self-communication reaches its goal and its climax in Jesus Christ. He or she alone is Christian who explicitly professes in faith and in Baptism that Jesus is the Christ, that he is the decisive and climactic moment in God's transcendental self-communication to humankind.

Contrary to the complaints of some of his critics, Rahner does not propose an ahistorical Christology. The basic and decisive point of departure for Christology, he argues, lies in an encounter with the historical Jesus of Nazareth, and hence in an "ascending Christology." On the other hand, he warns against placing too much emphasis on this approach. The idea of God coming into our history "from above" also has its power and significance. Both an ascending and a descending Christology have to be taken into account even if, in the light of modern evolutionary consciousness, our *starting point* is "from below" rather than "from above."

Rahner's notion of *evolution* is heavily influenced by Hegel. Matter and spirit, Rahner suggests, are intrinsically related to each other. They spring from the same creative act of God, and they have a single goal in the fullness of God's Kingdom. The world and its history are moving, i.e., are in evolution, toward a unity of matter and spirit, which Rahner (like Hegel) conceives as a *becoming* higher. The capacity for becoming something higher is called the capacity for "self-transcendence."

Since the free gift of God's grace, i.e., God's self-communication, was incorporated into the world from the beginning, the history of the world is really also the history of salvation. At the point (or points) where we realize that the direction of history is toward the Kingdom of God, we can speak of the experience of *revelation*. But whether we realize it or not, i.e., whether we are formally and explicitly religious, even Christian, or not, does not change what is in fact going on. God is always present to the world and to persons within the world as the principle of self-transcendence. We have the capacity to move beyond ourselves, to become something higher and better than we are, because "the Absolute Beyond" is already in our midst, summoning us forward toward the plenitude of the Kingdom.

There are, of course, other, relative causes at work in the world and in our individual histories. These, too, have to be taken into account when we strive to understand the course and direction of history. We have the human capacity to better ourselves by means of human resources already available to us. But even those mundane resources, or causes, are made possible in the first instance by God.

For Rahner, "The permanent beginning and the absolute guarantee that this ultimate self-transcendence, which is fundamentally unsurpassable, will succeed and has already begun is what we call the 'hypostatic union'" (p. 181). In other words, the unity of matter and spirit, which is what the movement of history achieves, reaches its climax in the union of Word and flesh in Jesus Christ. With the incarnation, history has entered its "final phase." The divinization of the world is underway but not yet complete. The further course of this phase and its final result remain "shrouded in mystery."

In light of the mystery of Jesus Christ, therefore, it is clear that the human person is neither purely matter (as the behaviorists believe) nor purely spirit (as the Platonists contend) but a single reality which comprehends both matter and spirit. Indeed, it is only in the human person that both of these elements can be experienced in their real essence and in their unity. The person is *spirit* insofar as he or she is conscious of himself or herself as one who lives in the presence of God and whose whole being is oriented toward God. The person is *matter* insofar as he or she is an individual whose concreteness as an individual is experienced as something inescapably given. Apart from matter the human person cannot experience the world, other persons, or even himself or herself. Indeed, apart from matter the human person cannot even experience the *spiritual* reality that is present in ourselves and in others. Thus, there is a fundamental *reciprocity* between matter and spirit. Together they constitute the world and human persons within the world.

On the other hand, there is an essential difference between matter and spirit. Influenced also by Teilhard de Chardin, Rahner argues that the whole historical process involves a movement from lower to higher, from the simple to the complex, from unconsciousness to consciousness, and from consciousness to self-consciousness. Everything is in a state of *becoming*, and becoming is a process of *self-transcendence*, and self-transcendence is possible because God is present to life as the principle of growth and development.

Human persons, therefore, are the self-transcendence of living matter. Apart from human persons, matter would never have achieved consciousness, much less self-consciousness. The history of the material world is thus intertwined with, even dependent upon, the history of humankind. Through humankind the material world reaches its goal by reaching beyond itself. Because we are not only observers of nature but a part of nature as well, our history is also a history of the active transformation of the material world itself. It is through such free action, arising from the spiritual dimension of the human person, that both we and nature reach our single and common goal.

However, since we act in freedom, both the history of the material world and human history are in a state of guilt and trial. We can reject God's self-communication and refuse to enter this historical movement toward God. But our freedom always remains grounded in the reality of God. The religious person, and the Christian in particular, knows that the history of the world will find its fulfillment in spite of, as well as in and through, human freedom.

The human person, consequently, is not an accident of evolution but a necessary part of it. The world in fact becomes conscious of itself, of its essential unity, and of its purpose and goal by means of humankind. But this coming to consciousness is possible only because God is immediately present to reality in grace. In that sense, the end, or goal, of history is also its beginning. The history of the cosmos from the beginning is always and basically a history of the human spirit, a desire to become conscious of itself and of its ground, who is God.

It is from this *evolutionary perspective*, Rahner argues, that we must understand the place of Jesus Christ. The process of divine self-communication to the world and the process of our free acceptance of that self-communication of God reach a point in history which makes these acts, from God's side and ours, both irrevocable and irreversible. Since the goal of the whole historical movement is present to history from the beginning (as its *final cause*, the Scholastics would say), that event by which movement toward the goal of history becomes irrevocable and irreversible must also be part of that historical process from the beginning. Thus, all of history has a unity, and that unity is focused in the event of Jesus Christ.

Consequently, the doctrine of the hypostatic union is not a speculative doctrine alone. Jesus is truly a human being; i.e., he is truly part of the earth, truly a moment in this world's biological process of becoming, a human being in human history, for he was "born of a woman" (Galatians 4:4). He, too, has received God's self-communication, and he, too, accepts it and lives out that acceptance. That principle cannot be stressed too much. The Word *became flesh*. The Word did not simply draw near to flesh, and, therefore, affect the world indirectly, through affecting the spirit of the world, as the Gnostics contended. The Word takes hold of flesh and is expressed in its materiality. It is through the flesh that the Word is present to the world. Spirit and flesh are one in the Word-made-flesh.

Such an understanding of the incarnation, Rahner insists, in no way denies that God could also have created a world without an incarnation. In other words, God could have denied to the self-transcendence of matter that ultimate culmination which takes place in grace and incarnation. For every movement from a lower to a higher stage is always unexpected and unnecessary. Self-transcendence occurs as a kind of leap from one level to the next because it is only the presence of God to life which makes such leaps possible.

And that brings us to the other side of the doctrine of the incarnation. It is *God* who takes on flesh. But not in the sense that God simply enters our history from the outside, moves us a step further along the road to fulfillment, and then leaves us behind. Rather the incarnation is an intrinsic moment in the whole historical process by which grace is communicated to all persons. And because that divine self-communication occurs at a particular time and in a particular person, the self-communication becomes unconditional and irrevocable from God's side, and irrevocable and irreversible from our side, insofar as that divine self-communication is definitively accepted by a human being, Jesus Christ.

In Christ, the communication of grace is not only established *by* God; it *is* God. That which is offered is inseparable from the offerer. Here we have a human reality, Jesus of Nazareth, who belongs absolutely to God. And this is what the *hypostatic union* means: *God once-and-for-all, in a specific human individual, is communicated to us, and that communication is absolutely, unequivocally accepted.*

Because of the incarnation, God is in humankind and remains so for all eternity, and humankind is for all eternity the expression of the mystery of God because the *whole* human race has been assumed in the individual human reality of Jesus. For this reason Christology is the beginning and the end of anthropology. The finite is no longer in opposition to the infinite. Christ is a human being in the most radical way, and his humanity is the most autonomous and the most free not in spite of its being assumed, but because it has been assumed, because it has been created as God's self-expression. The humanity of Christ is not simply the "form" of God's appearance on earth. *God* ex-ists (literally, "stands out from") in Christ. The Church has consistently condemned every heretical attempt to say otherwise: whether Gnosticism, Docetism, Apollinarianism, Monophysitism, or Monothelitism.

Christian faith, therefore, is the acceptance of Jesus Christ as the *ultimate* word of God to humankind. But there are many who in effect have accepted Jesus Christ but do not *explicitly* acknowledge him as God's ultimate word. What of them? Anyone who fully accepts his or her own humanity and the humanity of others has at least *implicitly* accepted Christ because Christ is in all of us and God is in Christ. On the one hand, God accepts us and loves us in the neighbor. And, on the other hand, we accept and love God in the neighbor, as the parable of the Sheep and the Goats (Matthew 25) shows. Just as our love for our neighbor must always take some concrete form in the love of a specific individual, so must our love for God. "One who has no love for the brother he has seen cannot love the God he has not seen" (1 John 4:20).

For the same reason, a transcendental Christology (summarized above) requires that the self-communication of God occur in a particular, concrete individual, Jesus Christ. That is why Christology today begins "from below." It does not start by saying "God became a human being" but by saying that in Jesus God's merciful and absolute self-communication to the world is finally accomplished and made present to us. The incarnation must be historical because it must touch historical beings and the total actual history of the world. We can realize our humanity nowhere else except in history.

Jesus of Nazareth understood himself, however incompletely and gradually, to be this savior, and his resurrection established and manifested that he is such. He did not regard himself simply as another prophet, but he made our reaction to him decisive for our entrance into the Kingdom of God. Indeed, Jesus is himself the Kingdom.

Hans Küng

If Karl Rahner is the most important and most influential theologian in the Catholic Church today, Hans Küng is the best known and most controversial. His major Christological work, *On Being a Christian* (New York: Doubleday, 1976), was preceded by books on Church reform, papal infallibility, priesthood, and other practical topics. In *On Being a Christian* Küng shifts his attention from questions about the movement Jesus initiated to questions about Jesus himself.

The book is less philosophical and less speculative than Rahner's. Although Küng and Rahner share the same "from below" starting-point for their Christologies, Küng never ascends so far as Rahner, who establishes an eventual connection between the newer "from below" Christology and the traditional "from above" Christologies of the great councils of the Church and of the medieval theologians. Küng is also much less inclined to see the significance of Jesus in Rahner's larger historical and cosmic terms. Küng's Jesus is a man born to ordinary parents, with brothers and sisters, who grew up to become a wandering, uneducated Jewish layman, supremely indifferent to sacred traditions and institutions. Our knowledge of him comes from the earlier New Testament writings, Mark and the authentic letters of Paul, as interpreted by modern German scholarship.

Jesus addresses God as *Abba* (Father), organizes feasts in anticipation of the Kingdom of God, and makes the human person the center of biblical religion. He is condemned for blasphemy and put to death. His followers experience his "new life" as God's *representative* among us and as our representative before God. For

Küng, the various New Testament titles given to Jesus are only honorific. There is no pre-existence, no incarnation, and no redemption in any traditional sense of the words. Those doctrinal assertions which claim otherwise are the product of Greek speculation.

The main lines of the book's arguments are summarized in the form of twenty theses in a later work, *Signposts for the Future* (New York: Doubleday, 1978, pp. 2–40; see also *The Christian Challenge*, New York: Doubleday, 1979). The Christ of Christian faith, Küng argues, is no other than the historical Jesus of Nazareth (thesis #4). He was not interested in proclaiming himself. He was totally subordinated to God's cause, the Kingdom of God, the direct, unrestricted rule of God over the world. Jesus, therefore, preached the will of God as the one supreme norm of human action. And God's will is none other than humankind's total well-being (thesis #5). It was for the sake of our well-being that Jesus challenged and thereby relativized sacred institutions, law, and cult. In their place he preached love, even of one's enemies. He identified himself with the poor and the wretched of the earth, proclaiming all the while the forgiveness of God (thesis #6).

Because of his words and deeds, Jesus proved a divisive figure. Some hated and feared him; others showed him spontaneous trust and love. Jesus demanded of all a final decision: to direct one's life for God's cause or for our own. In claiming to be above Moses and the prophets and in forgiving sin, Jesus exposed himself to the charge of blasphemy (thesis #7). Indeed, Jesus so identified himself with God's cause that he even addressed God as Father (*Abba*), *his* Father. It became impossible to speak of Jesus without speaking of this God and Father, and it was difficult thereafter to speak of this God and Father without speaking of Jesus. "When it was a question of the *one true God*, the decision of faith was centered not on particular names and titles but on this *Jesus*" (p. 19). The way in which one came to terms with Jesus decided how one stood with God. Jesus acted and spoke in God's name, and for the sake of God he allowed himself to be slain (thesis #8).

Jesus did not simply accept his death. He actively provoked it. He appeared as the personification of sin and as the representative of all sinners. And the God with whom Jesus had identified himself throughout his public life did not identify with Jesus at the end. Jesus was "forsaken." Everything seemed to have been in vain (thesis #9). But Jesus' death was not the end. After his death his followers experienced him as alive. The death of Jesus, like the death of any one of us, is transition to God, retreat into God's hiddenness, into that domain which surpasses all imagination. It is significant, of course, that Küng describes the resurrection as primarily something that happened to the disciples: "...there remains the *unanimous testimony of the first believers,* who regarded their faith as based on something that really happened to them..." (p. 21; thesis #10).

Therefore, the cause of Jesus continued. His followers were convinced that he was still alive. He became the content of the Church's own proclamation (thesis #11). But, for Küng, it is not the resurrection which is at the heart of the Christian proclamation, but the crucifixion. It is the great distinctive reality which distinguishes this faith and its Lord from other religious and irreligious faiths and ideologies: the cross in the light of the resurrection, and the resurrection in the shadow of the cross (thesis #12). The crucifixion is "the permanent signature of the living Christ" (*On Being a Christian,* p. 400).

Walter Kasper

Walter Kasper has produced yet another Christology "from below" in his *Jesus the Christ* (New York: Paulist Press, 1976). According to his own introductory account, the book is indebted to the Catholic Tübingen School, and in particular to the Christological approaches of Karl Adam (d. 1966) and Joseph Geiselmann. Their theology focused on a study of the origins of Christianity in Jesus Christ which they knew were accessible only through biblical and ecclesiastical tradition. So, too, does Kasper begin there, with the New Testament, and with the historical Jesus who is proclaimed as the risen Christ.

Kasper develops what he calls an historically determined, universally responsible, and soteriologically determined Christology. It is *historically determined* in that it begins with, and is oriented to, the specific history and unique life and destiny of Jesus

Christ. It narrates the story of Jesus of Nazareth and asks: Who is he? What did he want? What was his message and mission? This means that Christology today must deal with problems of modern historical research: the quest for the historical Jesus, the quest for the origins of Easter faith, and the quest for the earliest Christological formulation of belief. These historical questions have to be answered if faith in Christ is to be taken seriously.

Christology must also be *universally responsible*, i.e., philosophically sophisticated. Christology inquires not just into this or that existent, but into existence in general. Christian faith claims that "the ultimate and most profound means of reality as a whole has been revealed only in Jesus Christ, in a unique and at the same time finally valid way" (p. 21). But such an understanding of Christ implies a specific understanding of reality. Thus, there can be no question of playing off an ontological or philosophical Christology (such as the Fathers and councils of the Church left us) against a non-ontological or functional Christology. We have to do both: to take seriously both the history and the deeper philosophical questions which the history provokes.

Finally, Christology must be *soteriologically determined*. Christology and soteriology form a whole. There are soteriological motives behind all the Christological pronouncements of the early Church. Both the defense of the true divinity and the defense of the true humanity were intended to protect the reality of the redemption. Kasper, therefore, rejects two extremes: the one which subordinates soteriology to Christology (as the medieval theologians did), and the other which reduces Christology entirely to soteriology, as the Reformers did and as Friedrich Schleiermacher did, arguing from the present experience of redemption back to the Redeemer, and making all Christological propositions an expression of Christian self-consciousness. Schleiermacher's influence, Kasper notes, can be seen in Tillich, Bultmann, and the Bultmannian school of thought. For Kasper, therefore, being and meaning are indissolubly joined. "What is believed can be known only in the exercise of belief. The exercise of belief, however, is meaningless if it is not directed to a something which is to be believed" (pp. 23-24).

The Jesus whom Kasper finally presents is the historical Jesus as mediated to us by conservative New Testament scholarship, in contrast, for example, to the more liberal exegesis upon which Küng relies. Jesus preached the Kingdom of God as "the coming to power in and through human beings of the self-communicating love of God" (p. 86). The Kingdom must be seen, therefore, "in the context of mankind's search for peace, freedom, justice and life" (p. 73). Through his miracles Jesus showed that in him "God was carrying out his plan, and that God acted in him for the salvation of mankind and the world" (p. 98). That preaching and activity include an "implicit Christology." Jesus went beyond the Law in his teaching. He made no distinction between his word and God's. And he summoned people to make a decision for or against him as the touchstone for their decision for or against the Kingdom of God. His summons to decision and his gathering of disciples underlined his authority and his (and his disciples') break with their past. Jesus, therefore, was reluctant to accept certain titles, not because they exceeded his own claims, but because he was more than those titles could express (p. 103). Jesus understood himself and functioned as our *representative*. He foresaw and accepted his death in that light, even though his disciples did not see the significance of his death until the resurrection.

Unlike Rahner, Kasper does not perceive the incarnation as an integral part of historical evolution. Whether the incarnation happened because of sin, or whether sin happened in order to make the incarnation possible, Kasper says is unanswerable. Whatever the case, the cross and resurrection of Jesus Christ are the climax of God's self-revelation for the salvation of the world. They are that "than which nothing greater can come to be" (p. 192). Insofar as he attempts an answer of his own, Kasper comes close to Anselm's. "The order of the universe (peace and reconciliation among men) is possible only if God himself becomes man, the man for others, and so establishes the beginning of a new human solidarity" (p. 225).

Kasper understands the hypostatic union, in the end, pneumatologically. The Father communicates himself in love to the Son. It is in the Spirit that this love can be communicated outside the Trinity. The Spirit is also involved in the reverse movement.

"The creature filled with God's Spirit becomes in freedom an historical figure through which the Son gives himself to the Father. In this all-consuming dedication to the point of death, the Spirit as it were becomes free; he is released from his particular historical figure, and consequently Jesus' death and resurrection mediate the coming of the Spirit (cf. John 16:7; 20:22). And thus Jesus Christ, who in the Spirit is in person the mediator between God and man, becomes in the Spirit the universal mediator of salvation" (p. 252).

Edward Schillebeeckx

Edward Schillebeeckx subtitles his 767-page book on *Jesus* "An Experiment in Christology" (New York: Seabury Press, 1979). And it is only the first, and shorter, of two volumes. The sequel treats of the Christ of Pauline and Johannine faith, whereas this one presents the historical figure we know as Jesus of Nazareth. So Schillebeeckx, too, constructs a Christology "from below." He is interested in discovering what is "peculiar, unique, about this person Jesus," for it was this Jesus who succeeded in touching off a religious movement that has become a world religion asserting that he, Jesus, is the revelation, in personal form, of God.

"Thus the question of his ultimate identity governs the whole of this enquiry," Schillebeeckx writes. "My purpose is to look for possible evidences in the picture of Jesus reconstructed by historical criticism . . ." (p. 34). The volume confines itself, however, to the period of primitive Christianity, "a period that brings us closest to Jesus and is still very reticent over the matter of identifying Jesus of Nazareth, in whom followers of Jesus, after his death, found final and definitive salvation" (p. 35). The subtitle, therefore, is deliberate. The book is a prolegomenon. It clears the ground for the fuller argument.

The presentation is heavily exegetical. The aim is to discover the historical Jesus, and the historical Jesus is available to us only in the pages of the New Testament. Part I addresses the problem of how we get in touch with the historical Jesus. Schillebeeckx's alternative to other quests for the historical Jesus is to examine the actual movements (Christian communities) which Jesus set in motion, and especially their confessions of faith in him, all of which were based on some historical facet of Jesus' life and work.

Part II synthesizes what can be reconstructed: Jesus' message, the rejection, his death, and the response of his disciples after his death. The Easter experience is portrayed as one of receiving forgiveness and grace from a Jesus known to have died, and this experience of forgiveness, in turn, provided the basis for the disciples' coming back together again.

Part III describes and analyzes the growth of the early creeds, each of which was founded on some remembered experience of the historical Jesus. The various Christological titles were expanded and transformed by these historical memories. So we have here again a Christology "from below." It begins with "the encounter with and recollection of Jesus of Nazareth, the prophet of the near approach of God's rule and the praxis of the kingdom of God, who turns our human way of living upside down and thus is able to touch off some explosive situations..." (p. 570). But from the Council of Nicea onwards, Schillebeeckx contends, one particular Christological model ("from above"), the Johannine, developed as the norm of all reflection on Christ. Thus, the history of the Church has never done justice to the possibilities inherent in the Synoptic model, which he presents here.

Part IV of his book is an attempt at a beginning of such a Christology, developed out of a mixture of Thomism, existentialism, and some elements from linguistic philosophy. Here he underlines the universality of Jesus as the definitive salvation from God. Jesus is the parable of God and the paradigm of humanity, the one who realizes that human concerns and God's coincide and that we must realize that we are "of God" even when death seems to contradict this. "Through his historical self-giving, accepted by the Father, Jesus has shown us who God is: a *Deus humanissimus*" (p. 669). But precisely *how* the man Jesus can be for us at the same time the form and aspect of a divine Person, the Son, is in Schillebeeckx's view "a mystery theoretically unfathomable beyond this point."

What we affirm, however, is that what Jesus preached, what he lived and died for, the Kingdom of God, was in the end the person of Jesus Christ himself, the eschatological man, Jesus of

Nazareth, who is exalted to the presence of God and who of his plenitude sends us the Spirit of God, to open up "communication" among human beings. "Jesus' being as man is 'God translated' for us. His pro-existence as man is the sacrament among us of the pro-existence or self-giving of God's own being. . . . The unique universality lies, therefore, in Jesus' eschatological humanity, sacrament of God's universal love for human beings. . . . Jesus is the firstborn of the kingdom of God. The cause of God as the cause of man is personified in the very person of Jesus Christ" (p. 670). And this is the sole heart and center of Christianity. Jesus brought no new system or set of doctrines. Rather he came to put the Kingdom of God into practice. He had the wonderful freedom "to do a good deed" (Mark 3:4). In his dealings with people he liberated them and made them glad. He was a warm companion at table. His eating and drinking with his own and with outcasts brought freedom and salvation. He showed, in other words, that it *is* possible to put the Kingdom into practice in this world, in our history.

Jesus' unique universal significance is, in turn, historically mediated through the Church's own practice of the Kingdom: a work of service, carried out in faith, as we are led by the Spirit of Christ. "Thus it is in the power of Jesus' Spirit that the Church mediates the manner in which God is concerned with all human beings" (p. 672). And, thus, we are invited today to combine the theoretical theology with *orthopraxis* (literally, "right practice") i.e., "the practice of the kingdom of God, without which every theory and every story loses its credibility—certainly in a world calling in its impotence for justice and liberation" (p. 673).

James Mackey

Professor of Divinity at New College, Edinburgh, James Mackey sets out on a new quest of the historical Jesus, but without the presuppositions of those who engaged in earlier quests (*Jesus the Man and the Myth: A Contemporary Christology*, New York: Paulist Press, 1979). For Mackey, faith and history must be kept together, but the history we are concerned with is present-day history, not something recovered from the past. Indeed, we must be able to move from past history about Jesus to the present influence of Jesus in our historical experience. This he does by focusing on the experience of the spirit and power of Jesus which enables us, through its contagiousness, to continue in the faith of Jesus (pp. 188, 196, 259). It is Jesus' own faith in human existence as sheer gift from God, as belonging to God, and as binding us to God. In Jesus and in his faith we meet the one true God.

In search of the historical Jesus, Mackey begins with the most certain piece of evidence we have about him, namely, his death. But the fact of Jesus' death is overladen with theological interpretation, or myth. What do we know about his death apart from theology? That Jesus was put to death because he challenged the practices and institutions of Judaism and had tried to reform it. The myth grew up that Jesus not only died because of his political and religious confrontation but also because of our sins. This particular myth emerged from the conviction that Jesus was not finally contained by death, but that his power and his spirit lived on, enabling his disciples to overcome evil, to live in faith and love, and to defy death in a spirit of hope (p. 99). This experience of Jesus was at once "deep and infectious." That the experience was rooted in any particular, "objective" appearances of the risen Christ Mackey will not concede.

From the resurrection Mackey moves to the life and preaching of Jesus, both centered on the Kingdom of God, as the rediscovery of life as precious gift and absolute grace. The Kingdom of God is our experience of the contingency of life, of its giftedness, of the reality of God as Father. Jesus expressed this myth about God in his prayer, in his fellowship meals, and through his good works.

With Paul we see the movement of Jesus' own myth about the Kingdom of God to the Church's myth about Jesus. The fullgrown myth about Jesus is given in the Nicene definition which states that Jesus is "one in being" with the Father. Such a doctrine is grounded, Mackey argues, in Jesus' own faith, namely, that God is immediately present as Father in everything around us, in the "very contingency of our existence" (p. 231). But the Nicene achievement became over-simplified with time, and people began speaking of the divinity of Jesus as if he were some kind of divine person or thing. The Council of Chalcedon, therefore, had to insist upon his humanity as well.

What is distinctive about Mackey's Christology is his choice of Jesus' own faith as its starting point. According to Mackey, Jesus was, before all else, a man of faith in God and in the giftedness of human existence. Christian faith is a sharing in the faith of Jesus. The symbol linking Jesus' faith with our own is the Kingdom of God.

The Kingdom, however, is very much a present-oriented reality for Mackey. The symbol refers to the reality of life-as-grace (gift), but without any real socio-political dimension. Nor is there any reversal of values in Jesus' preaching of the Kingdom. There is no apparent need for repentance and conversion in response to Jesus' proclamation (see our earlier discussion of these issues in chapter 12). There is no yet-to-be-realized future transformation of the cosmos and of the individual human being (topics to be discussed in chapter 29). Indeed Mackey professes impatience even with the word *eschatological*, calling it "the most abused word in contemporary theology, a kind of pseudo-verbal escape mechanism from all kinds of conceptual difficulty[;]. . .[it is] not easy to say what it means" (p. 287, n. 8). It is this uncertainty about eschatology that theological critics are most likely to fix upon.

Process Theologians

Teilhard de Chardin

Unlike the five major Catholic theologians just presented, Teilhard de Chardin (d. 1955) never produced a systematic Christology. Indeed, he was not primarily a theologian at all but a paleontologist and archaeologist. But because he was a convinced Christian and a priest, he felt a special need to reconcile somehow his work as a natural scientist with his faith and his vocation. He did this, as noted earlier in chapter 4, by placing Christ within an evolutionary framework.

Christ is both the bearer and the goal of the upward movement of the universe toward the divine. Christ is the Omega Point, the focus of union needed by the "noosphere" in order that the noosphere might achieve a creative breakthrough into a new and final state of complexity and convergence. All of history, therefore, is a movement toward Christ, and yet Christ is at the same time already present in the world. His presence gives all of reality a Christic dimension. The Church is that place where that Christification is explicitly understood and acknowledged. Insofar as the Church practices Christian charity, the Church injects the most active agent of hominization into the world. The world thereby becomes a commonwealth of persons united in selfless love.

This intimate link between Christ and the perfection of the universe Teilhard believed to be justifiable on New Testament grounds, specifically on the basis of the Fourth Gospel and the Epistles to the Colossians and the Ephesians. (For a fuller statement of Teilhard's Christology, see Christopher Mooney, *Teilhard de Chardin and the Mystery of Christ*, New York: Harper & Row, 1965.)

Teilhard's principal contribution to Christology is his insistence on an historically evolutionary framework for understanding the mystery of Christ. That Christology, however, is very much a Christology "from above," an approach more typical of the time in which he wrote. His influence on Karl Rahner has already been noted. He had an even more direct influence on Ansfried Hulsbosch, a Dutch Augustinian theologian.

Ansfried Hulsbosch

Hulsbosch's basic evolutionary position is expressed in his *God in Creation and Evolution* (New York: Sheed & Ward, 1965). A more formal expression of his Christology appeared the next year in a Dutch theological journal, *Tijdschrift voor Theologie* ("Jezus Christus, gekend als men, beleden as Zoon Gods"—"Jesus Christ, Known as Man, Confessed as the Son of God"—vol. 6, 1966, pp. 250-273; the article is summarized by Robert North in "Soul-Body Unity and Man-God Unity," *Theological Studies*, vol. 30, 1969, pp. 27-60).

Hulsbosch was principally concerned with accounting for the real unity of Christ. The traditional teaching, he argued, tends to leave us with the image of Christ divided into "two layers." A better way is offered by Teilhard's evolutionary perspective. The unity of Christ is an expression of the unity of the spiritual and the material in the human person. We are not composed of body and soul as if they were separate components of the human condition. We are absolutely indivisible subjects. So, too, Jesus is not man-plus-God but a divinized human being. Jesus is *known* as a human being and is *confessed* as the Son of God. This means that Jesus is God by being human in a special way; i.e., "... the divine nature of Jesus is relevant to the saving mystery only insofar as it alters and elevates the human nature. And whatever that is, it must be called a new mode of being man." To attribute divinity to a divine nature distinct from his human nature is just as alien to his truly unified being, therefore, as a separate spiritual soul would be alien to the human person's unity. Something would be brought in from the outside, making the person of Jesus "a juxtaposition of two realities."

Does this make Jesus a mere human being? Hulsbosch wants to avoid this conclusion. He insists that Jesus is a human being in a new and higher way. Through Jesus, humanity itself has been brought to a new threshold, and Jesus himself has crossed that threshold. He is "the image of God" (Colossians 1:15) in a unique and supreme way. He is in a very real sense the presence of God to human beings and to the entire cosmos, and hence divine. But his divinity is not in virtue of anything distinct from his humanity. It is there precisely in virtue of his humanity itself. What we have in Jesus is the "unfolding of the capabilities which lay latent within matter." He is not God who became a human being, but *a human being who became God*.

This is a Christology "from below" of a most radical kind, and yet very different from Küng's or Schillebeeckx's, for example. The latter two begin with, and focus fully upon, the historical Jesus as disclosed to us in the Gospels and the authentic Pauline letters. Hulsbosch, like Teilhard, focuses not upon the historical Jesus of Nazareth, the preacher and agent of the Kingdom of God, but upon the historical Christ, the yeast which makes history's evolution toward the Kingdom possible. The process Christologists are, in a sense, less historical than the others even though their stated intention is to propose a fully historical understanding of Christ and of salvation.

Piet Schoonenberg

Dutch Jesuit theologian Piet Schoonenberg follows a similar Christological course in his own contribution to the same special issue of the *Tijdschrift voor Theologie* and in his full-length *The Christ: A Study of the God-Man Relationship in the Whole of Creation and in Jesus Christ* (New York: Herder & Herder, 1971). We cannot point to anything divine in Jesus that is not realized in and from what is human. More deliberately than Hulsbosch, Schoonenberg confronts the question of the *pre-existence* of Christ. He argues that the Second Person of the Trinity is none other than the human person of Jesus, who came to exist at a specific moment in time. God is initially a single Person, therefore, but as history unfolds God becomes two Persons, and then three. Christ is God's ultimate revelation, however, and not simply a fortuitous climax to history. In him the fullness of what it is to be human is realized, just because the fullness of the Godhead dwells in him.

But as Schillebeeckx has pointed out, the idea of human transcendence is not so straightforward as might appear. It assumes that we know precisely what "humanness" is, so that starting from there we can come to realize what transcendental humanness is. According to Schillebeeckx, it is clearly true that God is revealed in humanity and that if we are to know Christ as God, we know this only out of his mode of being man. But it is also true, following Thomas Aquinas (III, q. 16, a. 11), that we encourage confusion when we say that "the man Jesus is God." Christ, insofar as he is human, has the grace of union, but one cannot say that Christ, *insofar as he is human*, is God. A more proper formula would be: Jesus Christ is the Son of God in humanity.

The most extreme statement of a process view of Christ thus far has come from outside the Roman Catholic tradition. Norman Pittenger, an Anglican theologian, concludes that Jesus is different from the rest of us in degree, not in kind. Jesus realized to an unsurpassed degree the possibilities open to us as human beings. Christ is divine only in the sense that the Love which is God is at work in and through him. If human beings have the capacity to live in love, it is Jesus Christ who fully actualizes that capacity. And so Christ and God are one with the other in Love. (See *Christology Reconsidered*, London: SCM Press, 1970.)

Liberation Theologians

Leonardo Boff

Another set of Christologies "from below" has emerged from the Latin American liberation school of theology. The most systematic effort thus far is offered by Leonardo Boff, a Brazilian Franciscan, in *Jesus Christ Liberator: A Critical Christology for Our Time* (Maryknoll, N.Y.: Orbis Books, 1978). Liberation Christology, he writes, stresses the historical Jesus over the Christ of faith. The historical Jesus, not the Christ of faith, speaks to our situation today. He did not present himself as the explanation of reality but as an urgent demand for the transformation of that reality (p. 279).

Accordingly, Jesus preached not himself but the Kingdom of God, which is "the realization of a utopia involving complete liberation, a liberation that is also structural and eschatological" (p. 280). The Kingdom is a reality that is at once present and still to be completed in the future. It is to the poor, the suffering, the hungry, and the persecuted that Jesus preaches, because it is they who must directly challenge the justice of the messianic king. Through Jesus, God has sided with them.

Everything about Jesus' words and deeds must be interpreted in this light. He was not merely a reformer but a liberator: "You have heard...but I tell you." He preaches a God to whom we have access not primarily through prayer and religious observance but through service to the poor, in whom God lies hidden and anonymous. Jesus establishes fellowship with society's outcasts (Matthew 11:19). He rejects wealth (Luke 19:9) and dominative power (Luke 22:25-28). Jesus' own praxis, in other words, establishes a new way of looking at God and at reality, i.e., through the prism of the struggle for liberation.

The conversion demanded by Jesus is not simply a change of convictions but a change of practice. And it is concerned not just with individuals but with social and political structures as well. "In the conditions of history, then, the kingdom of God does not come unless human beings accept it and enter into the whole process of conversion and liberation" (p. 287).

But Jesus chose to die rather than impose the Kingdom by violence. Indeed, he provoked his death by his call for conversion, his proclamation of a new image of God, his freedom from sacred traditions, his prophetic criticism of those in power. "His preaching and his outlook brought him close to the liberation project of the Zealots" (p. 289). On the other hand, he renounced the political messianism of the Zealots and their confidence in the use of force.

Through the resurrection the life that was hidden in Jesus was unveiled. The resurrection shows that it is not meaningless to die for another, that the murderer will not triumph over his victim. "Thanks to his resurrection, Jesus continues to exist among human beings, giving impetus to their struggle for liberation" (p. 291). Thereafter, to follow Jesus is to "follow through with his work and attain his fulfillment" (p. 292).

In effect, what we think of Christ, how we understand the meaning of the hypostatic union, the resurrection, and so forth is not primary. "Life is more important than reflection" (p. 157). Liberation Christology, therefore, is not so much a contribution to our understanding of the nature and mission of Jesus Christ as it is a way of understanding the meaning and demands of liberation. Liberation Christology has a prophetic, even messianic task, i.e., to move Christians outside Latin America to hear the painful cry of their oppressed brothers and sisters and to bring justice to those who fight to regain their freedom (p. 295).

Jon Sobrino

A Jesuit theologian from El Salvador, Jon Sobrino has produced a similarly comprehensive Christological statement in his *Christology at the Crossroads* (Maryknoll, N.Y.: Orbis Books, 1978). It is written from the same liberational framework and with the same "from below" starting-point: "If the *end* of Christology is to pro-fess that Jesus is the Christ, its *starting point* is the affirmation that this Christ is the Jesus of history" (p. xxi). And this means also giving priority to the praxis of Jesus over his own teaching and over the teaching of the New Testament theologians regarding Jesus' praxis. "Thus the New Testament will be viewed primarily as *history* and only secondarily as *doctrine* concerning the real nature of that history" (p. xxii).

Furthermore, Jesus' past can be recovered in the present only to the extent that it pushes us toward the future. The convergence of these three tenses occurs in the symbol of the Kingdom of God, and that is understood, in turn, in a trinitarian sense. It is the Father who is "the ultimate horizon of human existence and history" (p. xxiv), the Son who practices the Kingdom, and the Holy Spirit who makes possible life in accordance with the exam-ple of the Son. "Liberation theology is concentrated in Christology insofar as it reflects on Jesus himself as the way to liberation" (p. 37).

The emphasis remains functional; i.e., what is finally impor-tant is what Christ is for us, not what he is in himself. This functional emphasis runs the risk, to be sure, of collapsing com-pletely into functionalsim. Sobrino suggests, for example, that if at any point Christ ceased to be of interest to people or to serve as the path to salvation, he "would cease to be the revelation of what human beings are, and hence the revelation of who God is" (p. 388).

CURRENT AND RECENT PROTESTANT CHRISTOLOGY

Since the central interest of this book is in the Roman Catholic tradition, the description of current and recent Protestant (and Orthodox) Christologies will be abbreviated. Some general intro-ductory remarks, however, are in order: (1) The "from below" approach began at an earlier historical point for Protestants than for Catholics because Protestants were first to feel the impact of biblical criticism. Indeed, until the liberating encyclical of Pope

Pius XII, *Divino Afflante Spiritu* (1943), the field of biblical criticism was left almost entirely to Protestants. (2) Protestantism, in its very origins, has been a liberal rather than a conservative modification of historic Catholicism. The "Protestant principle" to which Paul Tillich referred in his book *The Protestant Era* (Chicago: University of Chicago Press, 1948) has rejected attempts to identify the divine with the finite, whether in sacraments, sacramentals, dogmas, or ministries. He called this attempted identification the temptation to idolatry. Some Protestants, not surprisingly, carried this principle to its logical extreme in Christology. For them, Jesus was a human being like us in all things, including sin, except that he was better than the rest of us. (3) Protestant Christology, however, is not unremittingly liberal. On the contrary, much of Protestant Christology in this century has been developed in reaction against the previous liberal, even reductionist, spirit of the nineteenth and early twentieth-century theology, just as much, indeed most, of present-day Catholic Christology has been developed in reaction against the ahistorical, metaphysical Christology "from above" which prevailed in the Catholic Church until the middle of this century.

Rudolf Bultmann (d. 1976)

The first sustained challenge to this thoroughly humanistic approach came in our century from Rudolf Bultmann, a German Lutheran. For Bultmann," . . . we can know almost nothing concerning the life and personality of Jesus" (*Jesus and the Word*, New York: Scribners, 1958, p. 8). What we do know is what the early Church believed him to be, and, secondarily, that he actually existed and was crucified. At the center of Jesus' proclamation is the Kingdom of God, but not as a power outside of ourselves but as a power given to us to be authentically human in our existence. Jesus summons us to a decision to think deeply about our lives, to attend to the limit set to our lives by death, and to assume responsibility for our lives in view of our impending deaths.

Bultmann's *existentialist interpretation* does not commend itself to the more activist interpreters of Jesus Christ—the Latin American liberation school in particular—because it denies our capacity to get back to, much less reconstruct, the Jesus of history. But neither is Bultmann attractive to more conservative interpreters. For Bultmann, "...*faith in the resurrection is really the same thing as faith in the saving efficacy of the cross*" ("New Testament and Theology," in *Kerygma and Myth*, Hans Bartsch, ed., New York: Harper & Row, 1961, p. 41; author's italics). It is not something that happened to Jesus. It is something that happened to the disciples. It is also incorrect, according to Bultmann, to speak of Christ as divine. In Christ God speaks to the depths of the human person. The early councils of the Church, therefore, illegitimately Hellenized the primitive faith of the New Testament and turned from an existentialist to a metaphysical interpretation of the Christ-event.

Oscar Cullmann

At odds with Bultmann's approach is that of Oscar Cullmann, another German Lutheran. Where Bultmann placed little confidence in history, Cullmann placed almost total confidence there. What the New Testament presents is not primarily an existentialist interpretation of the Christ-event but a *salvation-history interpretation*. Unlike the Jewish and Greek conceptions of history, Christian historical understanding views history in linear rather than circular terms. History begins with creation and ends with the Second Coming (*parousia*). At the mid-point stands Jesus Christ. Over against the abiding temptation to Docetism, Cullmann insists that redemption occurs in time. It is not an abstraction. The redemptive events which culminate in Jesus Christ are historical events, and not just a mythological process of salvation, as Bultmann proposed. Jesus is the definitive revelation of God's redemptive love for humankind.

But if Cullmann's approach is different from, even opposed to, Bultmann's, so is it different from the more traditional ontological, metaphysical, "from above" approaches which have been common to Catholic theology since the medieval period. Cullmann offers a functional Christology in the sense that we discover who Jesus is by discovering what he has actually done for us in history. This was the approach of the New Testament, he argues. All of the titles of Christ, for example, are in virtue of what Christ does for us, rather than in virtue of what Christ is in himself. Each title signifies a specific function of Christ in salvation history. (See *Christ and Time*, Philadelphia: Westminster Press, 1964, rev. ed., and *The Christology of the New Testament*, Philadelphia: Westminster Press, 1963, rev. ed.)

Karl Barth (d. 1969)

The most direct rebuttal of Liberal Protestantism came from the Swiss Calvinist theologian Karl Barth. Over against both Liberalism and one of Liberalism's notable opponents, Rudolf Bultmann, Barth argued that our knowledge of God does not arise from our knowledge of the human condition but from revelation, i.e., from the Word of God given to us without predisposition, preunderstanding, or pre-anything else. There is only one God, the God of the Gospel, and that God can be known in only one way, through the Word which is Jesus Christ.

Theology, for Barth, is Christology. Christ tells us at once who God is and who we are. Christology frames our theology and our anthropology as well. Furthermore, the Jesus of history and the Christ of faith are one and the same. And the Christ as he is in himself is the same as the Christ as he is for us. He is the reconciling Christ. He is God for us. On the other hand, Jesus is "man totally and unreservedly as we are," uniting to himself and in himself all that is human. Although Barth's Christology tries to work both "from below" and "from above," the emphasis is clearly on the latter. (See *Church Dogmatics*, Edinburgh: T. & T. Clark, 1956, vol. IV/1; for a briefer summation of Barth's basic theological approach, see *Evangelical Theology: An Introduction*, New York: Doubleday, 1963.)

Paul Tillich (d. 1965)

A German Lutheran and an existentialist like Bultmann, Paul Tillich begins his Christology "from below" through an analysis of the human condition. We are beings marked by anxiety, faced as we are by the abiding threat of non-being. We are conscious of ourselves as alienated beings, as beings now separated from the ground of all being. It is a separation which implies an original union, a ruptured union which demands to be healed. This awareness leads us to seek "New Being," the Being who gives us "the courage to be." Christianity affirms that Jesus of Nazareth, who has been called the Christ, is the one who brings the new state of things, the New Being (see *Systematic Theology*, Chicago: University of Chicago Press, 1957, vol. 2, p. 97). What is significant about Jesus is "not that essential humanity includes the union of God and man (but) that in one personal life essential manhood has appeared under the conditions of existence without being conquered by them" (p. 94).

Tillich says that it makes no sense at all to speak of Jesus as divine. He argues that "the only thing God cannot do is to cease to be God. But that is just what the assertion that 'God has become man' means" (p. 94). The traditional teaching is to be discarded and replaced with "the assertion that in Jesus as the Christ the eternal unity of God and man has become historical reality" (p. 148). Indeed, there are Adoptionist overtones in Tillich's statement that essential God-manhood means that "there is one man in whom God *found* his image undistorted, and who stands for all mankind—the one, who for this reason, is called the Son or the Christ" (*The Eternal Now,* New York: Scribners, 1963, p. 76; my italics). For Tillich, Christ brings to all of us the hope that the existential anxiety and estrangement which characterizes and mars our situation can be healed and that unity with the ground of our being can be restored.

Dietrich Bonhoeffer (d. 1945)

Another German Lutheran theologian, influenced by Harnack on the left and Barth on the right in his years of academic formation, Dietrich Bonhoeffer marked out a course somewhere between their two approaches. He moved progressively through three phases of theological development: a liberal phase rudely shattered by the First World War, a confessional (Barthian) phase similarly undermined by the rise of Nazism in Germany, and an ecumenical phase prompted by the devastating experience of the Second World

War. Bonhoeffer never produced a formal, systematic Christology, but what we have of his Christology comes from class notes taken by his students in the second, confessional phase (see *Christ the Center*, New York: Harper & Row, 1966). Thus, Jesus is God for us (p. 107). God chose to come among us and to address us in weakness. He reconciled us with God through the crucifixion and rose for our justification. Christ is known to us today in the community of saints. He is present there *"pro me"* (for me). Christology and ecclesiology are, therefore, inseparable. Christ is really present only in the Church (*Communio Sanctorum*, New York: Harper & Row, 1964, p. 100). He is disclosed to us there as the new human being, or as new humanity itself (*Act and Being*, New York: Harper & Row, 1963, p. 121).

Jesus, and the God whom he reveals, is not at the borders of life where our human powers give out, but at its very center. And he is there only for others, as "the man for others." In fact, "His 'being there for others' is the experience of transcendence," i.e., the experience of God's transforming presence (*Letters and Papers from Prison*, New York: Macmillan, 1962, pp. 209-210).

With Bonhoeffer the emphasis within Protestant theology shifts once again to "the below" of human experience. But it is not simply a reproduction of the Liberal Protestant approach. He insists in *Christ the Center*, for example, that Jesus is important in what he does *for us* because of who he is *in himself*. Nor is it simply a slightly altered version of the "from below" existentialist analysis of Bultmann and Tillich. Bonhoeffer, on the contrary, laid the foundation for the development of the secular and radical theology of the 1960s. If Jesus is "the man for others," Christian existence must be existence for others, the Church must be a servant Church, and so forth. We meet this Jesus in one another. To use a Catholic phrase, Jesus is sacramentalized in the neighbor.

It is a theme that would be taken up by Bishop John Robinson, on the more conservative wing of secular theology (see *The New Reformation?*, Philadelphia: Westminster Press, 1965, and *The Human Face of God*, Philadelphia: Westminster Press, 1973), and by the so-called "death-of-God" theologians, on the more radical wing of the movement. Robinson would remain closer to the traditional Christology, although with a humanistic and then

Teilhardian leaning, while the "death-of-God" theologians, like Thomas Altizer and Paul Van Buren, would press the humanistic tilt all the way to the ground (see Altizer's *The Gospel of Christian Atheism*, Philadelphia: Westminster Press, 1966, and Van Buren's *The Secular Meaning of the Gospel*, New York: Macmillan, 1963). To believe in Christ is to stand at his side in the service of the neighbor.

Wolfhart Pannenberg

Still another German Lutheran, Wolfhart Pannenberg, provided one of the first modern systematic Christologies in his *Jesus: God and Man* (Philadelphia: Westminster Press, 1968). For several years, in fact, it was the only textbook available on the subject, even for Roman Catholic use. Following in the theological tradition of both Barth and Bonhoeffer, Pannenberg insisted that we can know God "only as he has been revealed in and through Jesus" (p. 19). We do not first know God and then come to a knowledge of Jesus as one with the God of Israel.

The God of Jesus Christ is a God who is revealed in and through *history*. But such revelation takes place not at the beginning of history but at its end. Jesus Christ is the end of history, and therefore it is only in the light of the revelation in Jesus Christ that everything that preceded him in the history of Israel assumes the character of revelation as well, "in the totality of events" (p. 388). Indeed, the end that stands before all of us has actually occurred already in Jesus Christ, in his death and resurrection. The latter is "the actual event of revelation" which establishes the divinity of Jesus and confirms God's self-revelation in him (p. 129).

The resurrection is, for Pannenberg, an utterly historical event. It is not something accessible only through the eyes of faith (p. 99). All of the biblical data regarding the resurrection (the empty tomb, the appearances, etc.) converge so that the assertion that Jesus really rose from the dead is to be presupposed until contrary evidence appears (p. 105). Significantly, Pannenberg pays almost no attention to the cross.

Using Hegelian categories (a practice, as we have seen, not at all uncommon among German theologians, Catholic and Protestant alike), Pannenberg locates the identity of Jesus with the Father in Jesus' *dedication* to the Father. And the Father is, in turn, dedicated to the Son (p. 332). Jesus' unity with the Father is not fully given at the incarnation, however. Rather, it is through the process of his life of dedication to the Father that Jesus' existence is integrated with the divine and his identity as Son of God becomes established (pp. 337, 344).

Pannenberg's Christology does not readily fit under either of our two working categories: "from above" or "from below." It may be more accurate to characterize his as a Christology "from ahead." It is an approach peculiar to Pannenberg, and no theologian of substance has taken it up sinᵣ he first proposed it.

Jürgen Moltmann

A German Reformed theologian, Jürgen Moltmann is, among Protestant Christologists, closest to the perspective and interests of the Latin American liberation school. His position is expressed in his influential *Theology of Hope* (New York: Harper & Row, 1967) and, later, in *The Crucified God* (New York: Harper & Row, 1974). In the first book Moltmann's focus was, like Pannenberg's, on the resurrection. Influenced by the Marxist philospher Ernst Bloch, Moltmann concentrated on the themes of the future and of hope. Even though he left room for a prophetic role for Christian faith and for the Church (see his last chapter on "The Exodus Church"), Moltmann concluded that his approach was still abstract, bearing too little relationship to praxis. The Frankfurt School of social critical theory replaced Bloch as his philosophical inspiration. His thinking came to center on the cross of Jesus, shifting from hope in Christ's future to the following of the historical Jesus.

Christian existence is itself praxis. The following of the crucified God transforms us and our situation. If Christology is to be truly responsible, it must consider the psychic and political implications of its words, images, and symbols. It must be a political theology of the cross. The history of human suffering, focused on

Calvary, has to do in the end with justice. Human sympathy is insured only when the murderer does not finally triumph over the victim.

A central question posed by *The Crucified God* is "How can God himself be in one who has been forsaken by God?" (p. 190). His answer: "In the passion of the Son the Father himself suffers the pains of abandonment" (p. 192). The Good News of human hope and liberation is all contained in that proclamation. God is now inseparable from the Godforsaken of the earth. The Church, therefore, is called to identify in the same way with society's outcasts, the oppressed, the poor. "The glory of God," Moltmann insists, "does not shine on the crowns of the mighty, but on the face of the crucified Christ" (p. 327).

John B. Cobb

Methodist theologian and Whiteheadian, John B. Cobb, Jr., of the Southern California School of Theology at Claremont, California, acknowledges that his earlier Christological efforts were really exercises in Jesusology (*Christ in a Pluralistic Age*, Philadelphia: Westminster Press, 1975). Under the influence not only of process thought but of the writings of Pannenberg and Thomas Altizer, Cobb insists that "Christ" is not just Jesus but any incarnation of the Word of God. Christians, therefore, must be open to the possibility of "radical creative transformation" in light of the insights of other religious traditions. The Christian view must lose itself in other traditions in order to find itself.

The vision remains Whiteheadian from beginning to end. Christ is not so much a person as a process, although Christians name Christ only in "responsible relation" to Jesus. But "Christ" cannot name the process if the process leads to nothing. If there is no hope, then all that is said becomes pointless. The content of that hope is that we shall all transcend our separate individuality to enter "a fuller community with other people and with all things. In this community the tensions between self and Christ decline, and in a final consummation they would disappear. This is the movement of incarnation. Christ is the name of our hope" (p. 258).

A CONTEMPORARY ORTHODOX CHRISTOLOGY

Russian Orthodox theologian John Meyendorff provides a useful statement of Orthodox Christology in his *Christ in Eastern Christian Thought* (Washington: Corpus Books, 1969). It is his firm conviction that Byzantine Christological thought—far from being, as is sometime supposed, a crypto-Monophysitic, Hellenized form of Christianity—is in fact consistent with some of the most fundamental concerns in contemporary theology, the approach of Karl Rahner in particular. What has always been central to the whole Eastern patristic understanding of salvation is the principle that "Man is truly man when he participates in God's life. This participation. . . is not a supernatural gift, but the very core of man's nature" (p. viii). We must realize in ourselves the image and likeness of God, and this participation diminishes in no way our authentically human existence, energy, and will. And so it was with Jesus Christ.

By assuming humanity hypostatically, the *Logos* "becomes" what he was not before, and even "suffers in the flesh." This openness of God to the creature actually "modifies" God's personal existence. Such an understanding of the incarnation, according to Meyendorff, excludes all Docetism or Monophysitism, and it affirms that the salvation of humankind was a matter serious enough to bring the Son of God to the cross (p. 164). This, of course, represents a Christology "from above."

Meyendorff insists, however, that one can begin as well "from below." The notion of *participation* implies not only openness in the divine being but also a dynamic, open, teleological concept of the human. Since Gregory of Nyssa, the destiny of humankind is viewed, in Greek patristic thought, as an ascent in our knowledge of God through greater participation in the divine life itself. It is precisely at this point that post-Chalcedonian Byzantine Christology meets the modern Christological concerns. By basing Christological thinking on anthropology, as Rahner does, one is necessarily led to the other major conclusions of Greek patristics: The human being does not disappear in contact with God but, on the contrary, becomes more truly and more freely human, not only in the human being's similarity to God, but also

in what makes the human being radically different from the Creator. "And this is the very meaning of the hypostatic union of
divinity and humanity in Christ" (p. 165).

Nestorianism had argued the opposite, insisting on the idea of
competition between, and mutual exclusion of, divinity and
humanity. A proper understanding of Christ, Meyendorff continues, requires that we consider the *Logos* as the hypostasis, the
"uniting unity" and the source of Christ's human existence. And
this, in turn, challenges the traditional Scholastic notion of God's
absolute immutability. God *became* human. A sound Christology,
Meyendorff argues in concert with Rahner, implies "the return to
the pre-Augustinian concept of God, where the three hypostases
were seen first of all in their personal, irreducible functions, as
Father-God, Son-Logos, and the Spirit of God, and not only as
expressions of the unique immutable essence" (p. 166). The *being*
of God, therefore, cannot simply be identified with the *essence* of
God, as has been done in the West ever since Augustine.

Meyendorff is encouraged by the present movement in Western theology, represented in Rahner's work, because it implies not
only a return to pre-Augustinian thought but also a return to the
basic presuppositions of the Christological thought analyzed
throughout Meyendorff's own book. This coincidence shows "the
astonishing relevance, for our own time, of the patristic view of
the Christian message. . . . The ecumenical significance of this
discovery is incalculable" (p. 166).

SYNTHESIS

So broad and diverse a sampling of recent and current Christologies is not easily synthesized. They range all the way from the
Christomonism (Christ *alone* manifests the presence and word of
God) of Karl Barth to the bland universalism of Norman Pittenger, for whom Jesus Christ differs from the rest of humankind
in degree only. On what basis, for example, does one categorize
the various positions: (1) their understanding of the resurrection as
an objective, or subjective, event? (2) their understanding of the
divinity of Jesus? (3) their "from below," or "from above," or
"from ahead" starting points? (4) their emphasis on the political

implications of Jesus' preaching and practice? (5) their use of conservative, or liberal–to–radical, New Testament scholarship? (See Summary, n. 33.)

Taking all of these together and no one of them alone, certain relationships do begin to emerge. At the *far left* one might place the *process theologians* (Hulsbosch, Schoonenberg, and Pittenger—Teilhard himself is too complex for categorization, and so, too, perhaps is Cobb), Küng, Bultmann, Tillich, Altizer, and Van Buren. To their right, but still clearly *left-of-center* on the total spectrum, are Schillebeeckx, Mackey, the *liberation theologians* (Boff and Sobrino), Bonhoeffer, Robinson, and Moltmann. At the *center* is Rahner. Slightly to his right, Kasper, Cullmann, and Meyendorff. Further to the right, Pannenberg. Fully to the right, Barth.

Thus, none on the *far left* understands the resurrection in clearly objective as well as subjective terms. None unequivocally affirms the divinity of Jesus in the sense defined by the great Christological councils. All begin their Christologies "from below." The uniformity breaks down with items (4) and (5). Bultmann and Tillich do not emphasize the political dimensions of Jesus' preaching. On the contrary, Bultmann in particular resists a political interpretation of Jesus' preaching. Nor are political accents clearly discernible among the process Christologists. And some (e.g., the process theologians and the "death-of-God" theologians) do not employ any recent or current New Testament scholarship at all.

On the other hand, Barth and (to a lesser extent) Pannenberg offer a reasonably clear example of the *right-of-center* emphasis: The objectivity of the resurrection is affirmed; Jesus' divinity is accepted (although somewhat idiosyncratically in Pannenberg); the starting point is not "from below"; and conservative rather than radical New Testament scholarship is employed. One major divergence between Barth and Pannenberg, however, is on the matter of political implications. Pannenberg allows greater room for them in his understanding of the Kingdom of God than does Barth.

Rahner stands somewhere near the *center* in that he understands the resurrection in both objective and subjective categories, understands the divinity of Jesus in a way consistent with the councils but revised according to our modern evolutionary consciousness, reconciles his "from below" starting point with the abiding doctrinal concerns and principles of the "from above" Christologies, underlines the political implications of the Kingdom without exaggerating them or setting them off against other, non-political implications, and makes use of both conservative and liberal–to–radical New Testament scholarship, although here Rahner is more right-of-center than centrist.

But how does one even begin to evaluate such a wide array of theological positions? Legitimate diversities notwithstanding, some Christological views must be more (or less) consistent with the broad Catholic tradition than others. What should one look for in these various expressions of the mystery of Jesus Christ? The following principles should facilitate that critical process. A Christology which incorporates these principles is more consistent with the Catholic Christological tradition than is a Christology which overlooks or rejects one or several of them:

1. Jesus Christ is what is specifically Christian about Christianity.

2. As both truly human and truly divine, Jesus Christ is the decisive and climactic moment in God's transcendent self-communication to humankind and of humankind's acceptance of God's self-communication. This "moment" is focused in the events of his crucifixion and his bodily resurrection from the dead.

3. The center of Jesus' preaching and the goal of all history is the Kingdom of God. The Kingdom is at once present and future.

4. Our reaction to Jesus (conversion) and to his proclamation and practice of the Kingdom of God is decisive for our entrance into the Kingdom, for Jesus is the sacrament of God's universal love for human beings; and human beings (neighbors) are, in turn, the sacrament of Jesus' presence among us. Thus, love of God and love of neighbor are intimately linked.

5. The Kingdom of God, therefore, has to do with the fulfillment of our humanity. *In that sense*, salvation is humanization, and humanization occurs through authentic liberation.

6. Christology and soteriology are inextricably connected. Jesus Christ as he is in himself is the same as Jesus Christ as he is for us. On the other hand, his *being-for-us* is rooted in his *being* (i.e., as Word of God made flesh).

SUMMARY

1. *Catholic Christology* from the time of Aquinas to the middle of the twentieth century remained essentially the same. It focused principally on the so-called ontological questions (i.e., Who is Christ *in himself*?) and only secondarily on the soteriological questions (i.e., Who is Christ *for us*?). But even in its treatment of the redemption, the discussion was limited to the crucifixion as the act by which our indebtedness to God for sin was fully satisfied. The resurrection and exaltation were seen as appendices rather than as constitutive elements of the redemption.

2. The *change* from the medieval approach to the so-called modern approach occurred for *two principal reasons:* (1) the shift from an uncritical to a critical reading of the New Testament; and (2) the shift from a static to an evolutionary understanding of human existence. Both of these changes were among the products of the eighteenth-century Enlightenment, which introduced an historically critical element in human reasoning and understanding. The spark which ignited the change for Catholic Christology was the occasion of the fifteen hundredth anniversary of the Council of Chalcedon.

3. *The principal Catholic Christologies today* are those produced by *Karl Rahner, Hans Küng, Walter Kasper,* and *Edward Schillebeeckx.* All four are generally consistent with the new approach of developing a Christology "from below," i.e., by starting with the Jesus of history rather than with the Word who became flesh ("from above"). Rahner and Kasper are generally more conservative in their Christologies than Küng and Schillebeeckx. Küng is the most liberal of the four. He stresses the humanity of Jesus more than the others do, and is least concerned with preserving the divinity.

4. *Karl Rahner,* the most influential of the four, calls his approach an *ascending* Christology. His point of departure is our encounter with the historical Jesus. On the other hand, he holds, there is also a *descending* course in Christology. The idea of God coming into our history "from above" also has power and significance. But in the light of modern evolutionary consciousness, the *starting point* is "from below."

5. Rahner's Christology is, of course, a function of his basic theological *method of transcendence.* The whole world is moving in evolution toward becoming something higher than it now is. It is called to self-

transcendence. Since the capacity for self-transcendence is rooted in the presence of God (grace, the self-communication of God), and since this presence has been there from the beginning, the history of the world is also the history of salvation.

6.   For Rahner the permanent beginning and absolute guarantee of this self-transcendence is the *hypostatic union*, where matter and spirit are climactically united in the union of Word and flesh in Jesus Christ. Ever since that union, *history is in its final phase*.

7.   But Christ does not exclude the possibility of *sin* or of short-term failure. *Human freedom* allows us to participate in the progressive transformation of the world, but it also allows us to reject God's self-communication and to refuse to enter the movement toward God.

8.   The world becomes conscious of itself through humankind, which alone unites matter and spirit in itself. The world moves forward toward its goal, *the Kingdom of God*, insofar as we actualize our capacity for self-transcendence. Thereby we become more than we are, and more than we could ever be if we were matter alone.

9.   From the beginning, *the whole evolutionary process is centered in Jesus Christ* as its final cause. The process towards the Kingdom becomes *irrevocable* and *irreversible* in him. The Word became flesh. The Word takes hold of the world by taking hold of flesh and materiality. Christ, because he is the Word-made-flesh, not only offers grace; he *is* grace. This is why the hypostatic union is not a purely speculative doctrine. *Jesus is the Kingdom which he proclaims*.

10.   *Hans Küng's* Jesus is not the cosmic figure of Rahner's Christology. He is an entirely ordinary historical figure who happened to say and do some extraordinary things and who made an extraordinary impact not only upon his contemporaries but upon much of the human race ever since.

11.   Küng's Jesus proclaims *the Kingdom*, but is not himself the Kingdom. Everything (laws, traditions, cult, etc.) is to be subordinated to the Kingdom, i.e., to human well-being. *Salvation is humanization*. Through his death, Jesus appeared as the personification of sin and as the *representative* of all sinners. After his death, his followers experienced him as alive (the resurrection). They felt a change in themselves.

12.   According to Küng, the cause of Jesus continued in the Church, which now proclaimed him, the crucified one, as the heart of the message about the Kingdom.

13.   *Walter Kasper's* Christology begins with the specific history of Jesus of Nazareth, but moves beyond that to philosophical reflection which history itself provokes. Finally, his Christology is *soteriologically determined*. The redemptive implications of what we believe about Jesus Christ are always uppermost in the minds of the New Testament writers,

the Fathers of the Church, and the ecumenical councils. On the other hand, soteriology is not the whole of Christology.

14.   Kasper *differs from Küng*, for example, in that Kasper follows a more conservative school of biblical interpretation and posits an implicit Christology in the thinking of Jesus. Jesus was reluctant to accept titles because he was greater than what those titles could express. Kasper, however, agrees with Küng in seeing Jesus as our *representative* before God.

15.   Kasper *disagrees with Rahner*, who perceives the incarnation as an integral part of historical evolution. Kasper adopts a position closer to *Anselm's*. Thus, God became man to restore order and balance to the universe.

16.   If there is anything distinctive about Kasper's Christology it is perhaps his *pneumatological* interpretation of the hypostatic union. It is the Holy Spirit who makes possible the movement of the Son outside the Trinity, and it is the Holy Spirit, released from the historical figure of Jesus after his death and resurrection, who makes possible the coming together of all humankind in saving unity.

17.   *Edward Schillebeeckx* argues that there are two ways of doing Christology: "from above" according to the Johannine model, or "from below" according to the Synoptic model. It is the latter which he presents in his book on *Jesus*. The historical Jesus is the parable of God and the paradigm of humanity. "His pro-existence as man is the sacrament among us of the pro-existence or self-giving of God's own being." He is "the sacrament of God's universal love for human beings. . . ."

18.   Jesus brought no new doctrine or religious system, according to Schillebeeckx. Rather he proclaimed and *practiced the Kingdom of God*. He showed that it is possible to put the Kingdom into practice. It is the Church which is called to mediate Christ's praxis of the Kingdom. The Church is led by the Spirit of Christ in doing this.

19.   *James Mackey* begins with Jesus' own faith in the Fatherhood of God and the giftedness of all human existence. The central symbol in Jesus' preaching (i.e., the Kingdom of God) means that life is graced. Christian faith is a sharing in Jesus' faith. To share Jesus' faith is to encounter the one true God who is immediately present to Jesus as to us.

20.   *Teilhard de Chardin, Ansfried Hulsbosch*, and *Piet Schoonenberg* share an evolutionary perspective. For *Teilhard*, all history is a movement toward Christ, the *Omega Point*, and yet Christ is also already present in and to the world, giving it a Christic (love-oriented) dimension. For *Hulsbosch*, Jesus is God by being human in a special way. He is *known* as a human being and *confessed* as God. He is not God who became a human being but a human being who became God. What we have in Jesus is the "unfolding of the capabilities which lay latent within

matter." *Schoonenberg*, finally, follows essentially the same approach but lays more emphasis on the question of Christ's pre-existence, which he rejects. The Second Person of the Trinity is none other than the human person of Jesus, who came into existence at a particular moment in time.

21. The Christology of the *Latin American liberation school* is represented in the work of *Leonardo Boff* and *Jon Sobrino*. Both stress the historical Jesus over the Christ of faith. Jesus preached not himself but the *Kingdom of God*, which is the realization of *complete liberation*. It is to the poor, the suffering, and the oppressed that he preaches, for these are the people who challenge the justice of God. Through Jesus, God has sided with them. The *conversion* he seeks is not only of convictions but of practice, and it is concerned not just with individuals but with social and political structures as well.

22. *Protestant Christology* has generally been more sympathetic to the "from below" approach and for a longer time because (1) biblical criticism developed first within Protestantism; and (2) Protestantism has characteristically been skeptical of identifying any human reality within the divine. On the other hand, much of twentieth-century Protestant Christology has been developed in reaction against extremely liberal or reductionist tendencies within Protestantism. On a relative scale, therefore, Protestant Christologies have been moving to the right, and Catholic Christologies to the left.

23. Thus, *Rudolf Bultmann* challenged Liberalism's assumption that we can know the historical Jesus with confidence. What the New Testament offers us is a philosophy of human existence. Bultmann's existentialist interpretation, focusing as it does on the private sphere of the individual person, puts him at odds also with the liberationist and political Christologies. Bultmann is also suspect on the right because of his refusal to accept the divinized Jesus of traditional theology.

24. *Oscar Cullmann*, to the right of Bultmann, makes salvation history the context for understanding Jesus Christ. He is the center of linear time and the definitive revelation of God. Cullmann prefers, however, a functional Christology (what Christ did for us) over an ontological Christology (what Christ was in himself). All of the New Testament titles applied to Jesus in a functional, not an ontological, way.

25. *Karl Barth* mounted the strongest and most direct assault upon Liberalism, opposing Bultmann at the same time. Jesus is the Word of God. All theology is Christology. There is no other point of access from and to God except through Jesus Christ.

26. *Paul Tillich* was for systematic Christology what Bultmann was for biblical Christology. Both offered an existentialist interpretation of the message and mission of Jesus. For Tillich, Christ is the "New

Being" who allows us to overcome the anxiety and estrangement which characterize human existence because he conquered both in his own life.

27. *Dietrich Bonhoeffer* marked a course somewhere between Liberalism and Barth. Jesus is the "man for others." He is Christ "for me." He exists for us today in and through the community of saints.

28. Bonhoeffer's "man for others" Christology laid the foundation for a more thoroughly secular interpretation of Jesus in the so-called secular theology of the 1960s: *Bishop John Robinson*, insisting that Jesus is to be discovered in the neighbor and that he shows us the "human face" of God; *Thomas Altizer* and *Paul Van Buren*, making Jesus the model and inspiration of our service of others.

29. *Wolfhart Pannenberg*, like Cullmann, emphasizes history as the vehicle of divine revelation. Revelation, however, takes place at the *end* of history, in Jesus Christ. It is only in the light of Christ that antecedent events become revelatory. Jesus' divinity is rooted in his complete dedication to the Father, and it is fully and finally established in the resurrection, which is a literally historical event. Pannenberg's Christology might appropriately be characterized as neither "from above" nor "from below" but rather "from ahead."

30. *Jürgen Moltmann* is, of all the modern Protestant Christologists, closest to the Latin American liberationist point of view. For him the cross is central and is a political event. Through the passion and death of Jesus, God actually suffers with us and identifies with the oppressed of the human race. It is only in the practice of the Kingdom of God that we truly follow the way of Christ, a practice which involves the same identification with the outcasts, the poor, and the persecuted of society.

31. *John Cobb* is difficult to categorize because he is influenced not only by the process thought of Whitehead but by Pannenberg and Altizer as well. The Christ is in Jesus, and yet not exclusively so. It is only in losing itself in other traditions that Christian faith can find itself. What Jesus represented and proclaimed is the common hope of all: full community with other people and with all things.

32. *John Meyendorff* is representative of Eastern Christian thought, with its historical emphasis on our participation in the divine life accomplished through the passion and death of Christ. Meyendorff insists that Karl Rahner's Christology, based as it is on an understanding of human existence as open to the transforming presence of God, is closest to the Orthodox way of understanding the mystery of Christ. Meyendorff and Rahner, in turn, reflect the pre-Augustinian thought of the Greek Fathers.

33. *Differences* among and between the preceding theologians can be determined on the basis of the following criteria: (1) What is their

understanding of the *resurrection*? Is the resurrection purely objective, purely subjective, or both? (2) How do they understand the *divinity* of Jesus? Is their understanding a literal appropriation of the councils, a rejection of the councils, or a critical reappropriation of the conciliar teaching? (3) What is their *starting point*? "From above"? "From below"? "From ahead"? (4) How do they understand the *political* implications of the Kingdom of God which Jesus preached? Is it totally political? Completely apolitical? Political within a larger context? (5) What kind of New Testament scholarship do they rely upon in constructing their understanding of Jesus Christ? Conservative? Liberal-to-radical? A broad cross-section?

34.   Contemporary Christologies which are consistent with the broad Catholic Christological tradition incorporate the following principles: (1) As both truly human and truly divine, Jesus Christ is the specifically Christian element in Christianity; (2) through the events of his crucifixion and bodily resurrection from the dead, he is the decisive moment in God's self-communication and of our definitive acceptance of God; (3) the Kingdom of God, at once present and future, is at the center of Jesus' preaching; (4) we make a decision for the Kingdom when we make our decision for Jesus Christ, the sacrament of God; and our decision for Jesus is linked, in turn, with our decision for the neighbor; (5) the Kingdom, therefore, has to do with humanization, and humanization, with liberation; and (6) Christology and soteriology are intimately connected: Jesus Christ-in-himself is Jesus Christ-for-us, and vice versa.

SUGGESTED READINGS

In addition to the titles already cited in this chapter:

Dulles, Avery. "Jesus as the Christ: Some Recent Protestant Positions." *Thought* 39 (1964), 359–379.

_____. "Contemporary Approaches to Christology: Analysis and Reflections." *Living Light* 13 (Spring 1976), 119-144.

Lane, Dermot A. *The Reality of Jesus: An Essay in Christology.* New York: Paulist Press, 1975.

May, William E. *Christ in Contemporary Thought.* Dayton: Pflaum, 1970.

O'Collins, Gerald. *What Are They Saying About Jesus?* New York: Paulist Press, 1977.

Schillebeeckx, Edward. *Christ: The Experience of Jesus As Lord.* New York: Seabury Press, 1980.

Schillebeeckx, Edward, and Van Iersel, Bas, eds. *Jesus Christ and Human Freedom*. New York: Herder & Herder, 1974.

Van Beeck, Frans Josef. *Christ Proclaimed: Christology As Rhetoric*. New York: Paulist Press, 1979.

· XV ·

SPECIAL QUESTIONS IN CHRISTOLOGY

This chapter addresses four specific questions in Christology: the *virginal conception* of Jesus, his *sinlessness*, his *knowledge*, and his *sexuality*. The first two underscore the *divinity* of Jesus Christ; the third and fourth, his *humanity*.

The chapter concludes with a list of criteria by which one might differentiate between Christologies which are consistent with the broad Catholic tradition and those which are not.

Section One: Special Questions

THE VIRGINAL CONCEPTION OF JESUS

It is the official teaching and the universal belief of the Church that Jesus was "born of the Virgin Mary," as the Nicene Creed proclaims. The truth and validity of that teaching and belief are not in question here, but biblical scholars and theologians have been asking what that belief might mean and how it might be understood today, in light of developments in New Testament exegesis and our understanding of human existence. It must also be clear at the outset that what is at issue here is the belief that *Jesus was conceived in the womb of a virgin, Mary, without the intervention of a human father (virginitas ante partum)*. The issue is *not* the related belief that Mary remained a virgin during the childbirth (*in partu*) and for the rest of her life (*post partum*). We shall be treating the question of Mary's *in partu* and *post partum* virginity in chapter 24. Our concern in the present chapter is Christological rather than Mariological.

There are five sub-questions to be considered: (1) Is the belief in the virginal conception of Jesus truly a belief of the New Testament Church? (2) Is that belief rooted in historical fact? I.e., was Jesus actually conceived without a human father? (3) Does the Church officially impose belief in the historicity of the virginal conception of Jesus? (4) Can New Testament scholarship and the official teaching of the Church be reconciled? (5) What does the belief finally mean in relation to Jesus Christ?

Is It a Belief of the New Testament Church?

Belief in the virginal conception of Jesus *is* to be found in the New Testament, and, given the nature of the New Testament, that belief was held by at least some Christian communities of the first century. The references are twofold: Matthew 1:18-25 and Luke 1:26-38, the so-called Infancy Narratives.

Matthew reports that Mary conceived before she and Joseph lived together, that "he had no relations with her at any time before she bore a son, whom he named Jesus" (v. 25). The child was conceived "through the power of the Holy Spirit" (v. 18). "All this happened," Matthew writes, "to fulfill what the Lord has said through the prophet: 'The virgin shall be with child and give birth to a son, and they shall call him Emmanuel' " (vv. 22-23).

No one questions the authenticity of the narrative. There is a difference of opinion on whether it is Matthew's own conviction that Jesus was virginally conceived, or whether Matthew was drawing upon a tradition which preceded him. The current weight of scholarship seems to be on the latter side. One major reason for saying so is that the other infancy account, Luke 1:26-38, also speaks of a virginal conception by the power of the Holy Spirit (v. 35). Since this is one of the few points on which they agree, scholars conclude that this tradition antedated both accounts. In fact, this tradition must have been old enough to have developed into narratives of very diverse character and to have circulated in different Christian communities.

The rest of the New Testament is silent about the virginal conception. Biblical exegetes, Catholic and Protestant alike, generally reject the hypothesis that implicit references to the virginal conception are given in Mark 6:3, John 1:13, 6:42, 7:42, and 8:41

(see Raymond E. Brown, *et al.*, eds., *Mary in the New Testament: A Collaborative Assessment by Protestant and Roman Catholic Scholars*, p. 289).

Is the Virginal Conception Historical?

This question cannot be answered with a clear "Yes" or a clear "No," at least not on the basis of scientifically controllable evidence from the New Testament.

The arguments *in favor* of historicity are twofold: (1) One searches in vain for exact parallels in non-Jewish religions, societies, and mythologies which might explain how early Christians happened upon the idea of a virginal conception without even a male deity or element to impregnate Mary, because apparent parallels (e.g., the births of Buddha, Krishna, the Pharaohs, *et al.*) all involved a divine male in some form or other. (2) There were rumors abroad that Jesus was conceived illegitimately. Matthew's account acknowledges this gossip, and it is implied also in Mark 6:3, where Jesus is referred to as the "son of Mary" —an unusual designation unless paternity is uncertain or unknown—and in John 8:41, where the Jews sneer, "*We* were not born illegitimate." In early Jewish polemics against the new Christian faith the charge persisted that Jesus was born of an adulterous union since he was obviously not the son of Joseph.

But the arguments *against* historicity are also strong. (1) If Joseph and Mary knew that their son had no human father but was conceived in truth by the Holy Spirit alone, why would they have kept this secret from Jesus? And if they had not kept the secret, why could he not have known and affirmed from the very beginning that he was the Messiah and the unique Son of God? Our consideration of the Christological development of the New Testament (chapter 12), however, disclosed a movement from a lower to a higher Christology within the New Testament period itself. Jesus may have had only an implicit Christology of his own. (2) The Infancy Narratives themselves, in both structure and content, suggest a non-historical rather than historical accounting of the conception of Jesus. The two basic stories are virtually irreconcilable; e.g., compare Matthew 2:14 with Luke 2:39. There is an artificiality in format—e.g., Matthew's genealogy with its three groupings of fourteen generations. There is folklore—e.g., the appearance of angels in dreams, guiding stars, treasures from the East. (3) The rest of the New Testament is completely silent about the virginal conception. (4) How could one have verified the historicity of the virginal conception in the first place? It would have been known to Mary and Joseph alone, and those to whom they told it.

The scales seem to tip in favor of the theory that the belief in the virginal conception of Jesus is the result of what is technically called a *theologoumenon*. A theologoumenon stands between a theological interpretation that is normative for faith (a doctrine or a dogma) and an historically verifiable affirmation. In other words, a theologoumenon is a non-normative, non-doctrinal theological interpretation that cannot be verified on the basis of historical evidence. In the case of the virginal conception of Jesus, the word *theologoumenon* means that the early Church, in the writings of Matthew and Luke, read back into the earthly origins of Jesus an historically unverifiable element that was designed to say something about the significance of Jesus for our salvation: Jesus did not *become* one with God as time went on; *Jesus was one with God from the moment of his conception.*

Does the Church Officially Teach the Historicity of the Virginal Conception?

Creedal and doctrinal references to the virginal conception ("born of the Virgin Mary") can be found in: (1) the Apostles' Creed (date uncertain); (2) the Nicene Creed (325); (3) the Nicene-Constantinopolitan Creed of the First Council of Constantinople (381); (4) the Athanasian Creed (end of fifth century); (5) the Fourth Lateran Council (1215); (6) the Second Council of Lyons (1274); and other less authoritative sources (for those references, see *The Christian Faith in the Doctrinal Documents of the Catholic Church*, J. Neuner and J. Dupuis, eds., Westminster, Md.: Christian Classics, 1975, p. 137).

Given the original setting and purpose of those creedal and doctrinal formulations, their primary concern would seem to have been with preserving the unity of the divine and the human in

Jesus Christ, rather than with affirming the historicity of his virginal conception. The Church was teaching, against the Gnostics, Docetists, Monophysites, and others, that Jesus was truly human, that he was truly born of a woman. And it was teaching, against the Adoptionists, the Nestorians, and others, that he was truly divine.

Nowhere, however, did the Church define the "how" of Jesus' conception. Clearly, his origin is in God, and the Holy Spirit is directly operative in his conception. But whether the Holy Spirit's involvement positively excluded the cooperation of Joseph is not *explicitly* defined.

One can assume, on the other hand, that the Fathers of the Church themselves believed the virginal conception to be historical. They simply presupposed it. And until the beginning of the nineteenth century the virginal conception of Jesus, even in this biological sense, was universally believed by Christians.

What happened to change that virtual unanimity of belief? The same factors which generated a change in our understanding of Jesus Christ and of Christian faith itself, namely, a newly critical way of reading the New Testament, and a newly evolutionary way of perceiving human existence and human history. Both of these developments are linked with that philosophical watershed known as the Enlightenment.

Can New Testament Scholarship and Official Church Teaching Be Reconciled?

There is no contradiction between the two. Even if it were clear that the official Church had explicitly defined the historicity of the virginal conception of Jesus, it would not follow that such a teaching is contradicted by biblical criticism. New Testament scholarship does not claim that the historicity of the virginal conception can be *disproved* exegetically.

Admittedly, there *is* some measure of discrepancy between the traditional teaching and belief, on the one hand, and the general drift of some contemporary New Testament scholarship, on the other. If all Catholic theologians were somehow to reach agreement on the normative character and binding force of the constant and ordinary magisterium on this important matter,

Catholic biblical scholars assure us that they could "live with it" (Joseph Fitzmyer, "The Virginal Conception of Jesus in the New Testament," *Theological Studies*, vol. 34, December 1973, p. 574). But such scholars also insist on taking the critical position toward the New Testament text itself which their discipline demands. The Matthaean annunciation scene and possibly the Lucan account assert the virginal conception of Jesus, "but the question as to whether they make of that assertion an affirmation of faith or a theologoumenon is still a vital question," according to Fitzmyer.

It must be stressed, however, that Catholic exegetes and theologians who have been involved in this discussion have not denied the virginal conception of Jesus. They have raised questions about it, as is their responsibility as scholars, and they have been trying to draw the line between "what is of the essence of Catholic faith and what has been uncritically associated with it in pious and unquestioning assumptions." They cannot ascribe to the biblical sources, therefore, what the texts themselves will not allow, nor would the official Church want to base its arguments for the doctrine on an uncritical reading of those texts.

What Is the Meaning of the Belief?

The virginal conception has been understood from the very beginning as a statement about Jesus first, and about Mary only secondarily. Through this belief, the Church clearly taught that Jesus is from God, that he is unique, that in Christ the human race truly has a new beginning, that the salvation he brings transcends this world, and that God works through human instruments, often weak and humble instruments at that, to advance the course of saving history.

If in denying the historicity of the virginal conception, one is also denying such principles as these, then one has indeed moved outside the boundaries of the Christian, and certainly the Catholic, tradition. However, a more traditional understanding of the doctrine remains an integral part of belief and devotion for a great many Catholics.

THE SINLESSNESS OF JESUS

Belief in the sinlessness of Jesus Christ is a direct implication of belief in the hypostatic union, i.e., the belief that the human nature of Jesus Christ is perfectly united with the Second Person of the Trinity. The dogma of the hypostatic union, in turn, is a product of the Church's reflection on the intimacy and communion between Jesus and the Father, to the extent that Jesus spoke of God as his "Daddy" (*Abba*). Belief in the virginal conception of Jesus establishes the basis of this intimacy in Jesus' origin. He is from God, having been conceived by the power of the Holy Spirit. It is in this context that the question of Jesus' sinlessness must be answered.

There are five sub-questions to be considered here also: (1) Is the belief in the sinlessness of Jesus Christ truly a belief of the New Testament Church? (2) Is that belief rooted in historical fact? I.e., was Jesus actually without sin throughout his entire lifetime? (3) Does the Church officially teach not only the sinlessness of Christ but his impeccability as well? (4) Can our understanding of the New Testament be reconciled with the official teaching of the Church? (5) What does the belief in the sinlessness of Jesus Christ mean?

Is It a Belief of the New Testament Church?

Belief in the sinlessness of Christ *is* rooted in the New Testament—more widely, in fact, than belief in the virginal conception. The pertinent texts are John 8:46, 14:30; 2 Corinthians 5:21; 1 Peter 2:22; and Hebrews 4:15. Jesus declared that Satan had no hold on him (John 14:30) and challenged his opponents to convict him of sin if they could (John 8:46). Paul, in very early testimony, proclaims that Jesus "did not know sin...that in him we might become the very holiness of God" (2 Corinthians 5:21). "He did no wrong," the author of 1 Peter writes (2:22). Finally, the Epistle to the Hebrews commends Jesus Christ to us as our great high priest "who was tempted in every way that we are, yet never sinned" (4:15).

Significantly, nowhere is it asserted that Jesus could not have sinned, that he was absolutely incapable of sin (*impeccabilitas*).

The New Testament declares that, in fact, Jesus did not sin (*impeccantia*). Indeed, he was genuinely *tempted* to sin (Mark 1:12-13; Luke 4:2-13; Matthew 4:1-11). It was Scholastic Christology, on the contrary, which concluded to the impeccability of Jesus. And since Scholastic Christology has prevailed in Catholic teaching until the middle of the twentieth century, as we noted in the previous two chapters, the understanding of the sinlessness of Christ as impeccability has simply been taken for granted for the past five or six centuries.

Is That Belief Rooted in Historical Fact?

Did Jesus, in fact, never sin? It is a claim which is even more difficult to verify historically than the claim for the virginal conception. It is, for all practical purposes, impossible to verify. No one could have read into the mind and heart of Jesus to detect any sinful attitudes and wishes, even if he had them. And no one could have been with Jesus every moment of the day or night to notice his doing something sinful, even if he had committed a sinful act.

But neither do we have any evidence that Jesus *did* sin. Not even his gravest enemies could make the accusation, and even less make it stick. This is one of the most remarkable aspects of the belief in, and the claim of, the sinlessness of Christ. If the moral gap between Jesus' words and deeds had been apparent to anyone at all, it would have been brought to public attention, so threatening and so revolutionary was his message. Indeed, it would not have taken much to twist the Zacchaeus episode (Luke 19:1-10) into one of consorting with the oppressing class. Nor, as John A.T. Robinson has observed, "would most ministers today be able to survive three circumstantial (and, I believe, independent) reports that he had his feet (or head) kissed, scented and wiped with the hair of a woman, whether or not of doubtful repute" (*The Human Face of God*, p. 98; the references are to Mark 14:3-9; Luke 7:36-50; and John 12:1-8).

Does the Church Officially Teach
the Impeccability of Jesus?

The official Church certainly teaches as much as the New Testament does, namely, that Jesus Christ was without sin. In fact, where the Church formulates its belief, it simply repeats biblical expressions, especially the Hebrews text. This is true in the following instances: (1) the Council of Chalcedon (451), which defines that Jesus Christ is "one in being with us as to the humanity, like unto us in all things but sin;" (2) the Lateran Council (649), "sin only being excepted;" and (3) the Eleventh Council of Toledo (675), "without sin."

The work of interpretation becomes difficult when moving to the Third Council of Constantinople (681), which condemned *Monothelitism* (in Christ there is only *one will*, and that divine). The council taught that there are two wills, the one human and the other divine, just as there are two natures. The human will, however, is "compliant, it does not resist or oppose but rather submits to the divine and almighty will." On the other hand, the same doctrinal formulation declares that the human will "has not been destroyed by being divinized. It has rather been preserved...."

Although one could reasonably infer from the teaching of Constantinople III that Jesus Christ was incapable of sin, that precise point is not explicitly made. Indeed, one could also reasonably argue that if Jesus were utterly incapable of sinning, his human will was not after all preserved. Rather, it would have become so "compliant" to the divine will as to be indistinguishable from it. But that is precisely the heresy of Monothelitism which the council condemned.

It seems better to conclude that *it is the clear and constant belief and teaching of the Church that Jesus Christ was perfect in his humanity, that he was so completely in union with the Father that he was in fact absolutely without sin.* It is not that Jesus Christ was absolutely *incapable* of sin, but rather that he was *able not to sin* and, in fact, *did not sin.* However, both views—the one favoring impeccability and the one that does not—are within the range of Catholic orthodoxy.

Can the New Testament Witness Be Reconciled with the Official Church's Teaching?

This question, in the light of the preceding, answers itself. The New Testament does not enter the realm of theological speculation. There is no analysis of the operation of Jesus' human will, nor is there any philosophical reflection on the dynamics of human consciousness or of human freedom. But neither is there very much of this in the Church's doctrines, not to say dogmas. On the contrary, where the official Church formulates its teaching, it simply builds on the biblical testimony, relying in particular on the expression from the Epistle to the Hebrews, namely, that Jesus is completely like us in everything except sin. The text does not say—nor does the Church—that Jesus is different because sin is metaphysically impossible for him, but that he is different because, in fact, he was *without sin.*

What Does the Sinlessness of Jesus Christ Mean?

The fact that Jesus Christ is without sin makes him the supreme expression of communion between God and humankind. It is because he is utterly, completely, and perfectly holy in his very humanity that he is able to disclose the divine to us through that same humanity. Jesus Christ, the sinless one, shows us not only the human but the divine. He is "the reflection of the Father's glory, the exact representation of the Father's being" (Hebrews 1:3).

THE KNOWLEDGE OF JESUS

The question of the knowledge of Jesus is important for two reasons: (1) Many problems of New Testament interpretation cannot be solved if there is no possibility of development, even error, in the knowledge of Jesus (see again the discussion in chapter 12); and (2) Hebrews 4:15 and the Council of Chalcedon assert that Jesus is like us in all things "yet never sinned." How much like us is Jesus if he knew exactly what the future held for him, down to the finest detail? We face the future with wonder and hope, and sometimes with fear and dread. Jesus would have experienced none of these human emotions if he knew, with factual certitude, precisely what the Father had in store for him, and especially that the Father would raise him from the dead "on the third day."

At issue in the first two special questions were the origin of Jesus in God (the virginal conception) and the intimate communion of Jesus with God (the sinlessness of Jesus). Both italicize the *divinity* of Jesus Christ. At issue here, and in the next question, is the *humanity* of Jesus Christ. Is he really one with us—in all things except sin?

There are three sub-questions to be considered: (1) Does the New Testament attribute ignorance and even error to Jesus? (2) Does the official Church admit of ignorance and error in the mind of Jesus? (3) Can the New Testament record be reconciled with the official teaching of the Church?

Does the New Testament Attribute Ignorance and Even Error to Jesus?

Although there are indications in the New Testament that the early Church thought Jesus to be in possession of unlimited and infallible knowledge, the weight of the evidence seems to be on the other side.

Indications in Favor of Unlimited Knowledge

Given the development from a low (Jesus-as-human) to a high (Jesus-as-divine) Christology within the New Testament and within the Gospels themselves (e.g., from Mark to John), it is not surprising that the later New Testament material should have suppressed any suggestion of Jesus' ignorance. For example, Matthew 9:22 reports the same incident found in Mark 5:30-33, where a woman "afflicted with a hemorrhage for a dozen years" touched Jesus' garment and "healing power had gone out from him." In the earlier Marcan account, however, Jesus does not know who touched him. In Matthew's account, Jesus turns and immediately identifies the woman.

In John's report of the miracle of the loaves, Jesus asks Philip where they could find enough bread to feed such a "vast crowd" (John 6:5). But John quickly adds that Jesus already "knew well what he intended to do but he asked this to test Philip's response" (verse 6). Later in John 6:64 we are assured by the author of the

Fourth Gospel that Jesus knew that some of his disciples would be unfaithful, and Judas in particular (6:71; 13:11).

All of the Gospels attribute to Jesus the ability to know what others are thinking (Mark 2:6-8; Mark 9:33-34; Luke 9:46-47; John 2:24-25; 16:19,30). But it is not always clear whether this reflects Jesus' own keen perception of human nature or whether it is really a form of superhuman knowledge.

Finally, there are several examples where Jesus is portrayed as having knowledge of events taking place somewhere else. In John 1:48-49 he knew that Nathanael had been under the fig tree. In Mark 11:2 he knew that there would be a colt at the entrance of a nearby village. In Mark 14:13-14 and Luke 22:10 Jesus sends two of his disciples to the city with the instruction that they would come upon a man carrying a water jar and that he would provide a room for them in which to celebrate the Passover feast. But the Old Testament prophets also were believed to have had this kind of knowledge. Thus, Ezekiel had visions of events in Jerusalem although he was still in Babylon (Ezekiel 8; see also 1 Samuel 10:1-8).

Indications Against Unlimited Knowledge

In Mark 5:30-33 (= Luke 8:45-47), to which we referred above, Jesus does not know who in the crowd touched his garment. In Luke 2:46 he asks questions of the teachers of the Law in the Temple. In Luke 2:52 he is described as having "progressed steadily in wisdom." Both these texts are significant because they are part of the Lucan Infancy Narrative, where Jesus is presented unequivocally as God's Son from the moment of his conception.

Even in the specifically religious realm Jesus is shown to have been ignorant about certain matters. He reflects the inadequate and sometimes erroneous biblical views of his contemporaries. He cites an Old Testament text which apparently does not exist (John 7:38). He is wrong about the identity of the high priest at the time David entered the house of God and ate the holy bread which only the priests were permitted to eat (Mark 2:26); it was Ahimelech (1 Samuel 21:1-6) and not Abiathar, as Jesus thought. He was in error, too, about the fact that Zechariah, son of Jehoiada, was killed in the Temple (2 Chronicles 24:20-22); it was not Zechariah son of Barachiah, as Jesus said (Matthew 23:35). And Jesus mistakenly attributed Psalm 110 to David, making it a messianic psalm besides (Mark 12:36), even though there was no expectation of a Messiah at the time it was composed.

Jesus also shared the primitive ideas of his contemporaries about demons, confusing demon possession with epilepsy and insanity (Mark 5:4, 9:17-18; Matthew 12:43-45; Luke 11:24-26). He drew upon the same limited religious concepts of his day to describe the afterlife and the end of the world (Mark 9:43-49; 13). There is nothing new, superhuman, or unique about such declarations. Jesus simply employed ideas and imagery that were already current.

We cannot even take at face value his foreknowledge and predictions of his passion, death, and resurrection (Mark 8:31; 9:31; 10:33-34; and parallels). Among other exegetical problems, one has to account for the exceedingly curious attitude of the disciples who, if they had really heard Jesus make such predictions, should not have been taken by such complete surprise by the crucifixion even when it was imminent; nor, of course, should they have been so totally unprepared for the resurrection (Luke 24:19-26).

Much the same can be said of Jesus' predictions of the destruction of the Temple at Jerusalem (Mark 13:2). He insisted, for example, that "not one stone will be left upon another." And yet they are still there, even today!

The biblical and theological discussions about Jesus' knowledge of the date of the Second Coming (*parousia*) cannot usefully be summarized here. But all those who favor a so-called maximalist position (namely, that Jesus knew everything, and everything about everything) have to contend with the stark assertion: "As to the exact day or hour, no one knows it, neither the angels in heaven nor even the Son, but only the Father" (Mark 13:32).

Did Jesus, finally, know himself to be the unique Son of God? It is true that Jesus spoke of God as his Father in such a way as to suggest a special, intimate relationship. But there is no incontrovertible proof that he claimed a unique sonship not open to other persons. "Why do you call me good?" he asks a man who kneels before him to inquire about everlasting life. "No one is good but

God alone" (Mark 10:18). And when he teaches his disciples to pray, he instructs them, and all of us, to address God just as he addresses God, as "Our Father" (Luke 11:2). The Fourth Gospel, of course, clearly shows Jesus claiming to be the Son of God, but that book was written precisely to prove that point (20:31). It is difficult, to say the least, to find the historical basis for Jesus' explicit claim to unique Sonship.

The Firm Convictions of Jesus About the Kingdom

To suggest that Jesus did not have unlimited knowledge, that he was ignorant of many things and in error about others, is not to suggest at the same time that Jesus was a man without extraordinary intellectual strength and vision. On the contrary, Jesus displayed an exceedingly novel and courageous degree of *conviction* on the most central matter of all, the Kingdom of God. He was obviously convinced that the reign of God was active even now in his preaching, in his actions, and in his very person. He interpreted it with complete authority. Six times in the fifth chapter of Matthew he says to his disciples, "You have heard...," and follows each with the assertion, "What I say to you is...." He puts demands upon others. He forgives sins. He changes the Law of Moses. He violates the Sabbath ordinances. He offends against proprieties—e.g., by eating with sinners. He forbids divorce. He urges us to turn the other cheek, and so forth. All of this implies a unique conviction and, therefore, a unique human consciousness about himself and his relationship to God, a relationship without parallel in the lives of any of the Old Testament prophets. Moreover, there is no indication anywhere in the New Testament that Jesus only gradually developed this particular conviction. On the contrary, as he begins his public ministry, that conviction is at the heart of his proclamation (Mark 1:15).

Does the Official Church Admit of Ignorance and Error in Jesus?

The gap between the New Testament and the official teaching of the Church is greater here than on the first two special questions, the virginal conception and the sinlessness of Jesus. On the other hand, the magisterial sources are less authoritative (nothing

approaching an ecumenical council, for example), and their dependence upon the medieval synthesis is even more pronounced.

Medieval Christology had argued, on the basis of the hypostatic union, that no perfection is to be denied Jesus if it was at all
possible for him to have had it. Therefore, he not only knew
everything, but he knew everything about everything. He had
beatific knowledge, i.e., God's knowledge of all things; *infused*
knowledge, i.e., angelic knowledge requiring no learning effort;
and *experimental* knowledge, i.e., what he inescapably encountered within the particularities of his earthly life. An extreme form
of the medieval position was expressed by certain seventeenth-
century commentators on Thomas Aquinas, known as the
Salmanticenses (theologians associated with the University of Salamanca, in Spain). In their view, Jesus' knowledge was so unlimited that he could accurately be described as the greatest
mathematician, the greatest doctor, the greatest painter, the
greatest farmer, the greatest sailor, the greatest philosopher, and
so forth.

Not all medieval theology was so narrowly focused. Thomas
himself acknowledged that "if there had not been in the soul of
Christ some other knowledge besides his divine knowledge, he
would not have known anything. Divine knowledge cannot be an
act of the human soul of Christ; it belongs to another nature"
(*Summa Theologica* III, q. 9, a. 1). The official declarations of the
post-medieval Church, however, have tended to carry forward the
spirit, if not the letter, of the Salmanticenses rather than the
frequently more-nuanced approach of Thomas.

In 1907 the Holy Office, under the direction of Pope Pius X,
issued its anti-Modernist decree *Lamentabili*, in which it rejected
certain contemporary assumptions about the knowledge and consciousness of Jesus, namely, that he was in error about "the proximity of the Messianic advent" and that his human knowledge was
limited.

In 1918 the same Holy Office, this time under the direction of
Pope Benedict XV, categorized certain propositions as being
"unsafe" for teaching in Catholic seminaries and universities,
namely, the opinion that Christ may not have had the beatific
vision during his lifetime, that he would not have known "from

the beginning...everything, past, present and future, that is to say everything which God knows with the 'knowledge of vision.'"

Finally, in 1943 Pope Pius XII declared in an encyclical letter on the Church as the Mystical Body of Christ (*Mystici Corporis*) that Jesus enjoyed the beatific vision "from the time He was received into the womb of the Mother of God." Consequently, "...the loving knowledge with which the divine Redeemer has pursued us from the first moment of His incarnation is such as completely to surpass all the searchings of the human mind."

There are also two pre-medieval pronouncements. The first comes from the *Constitutum* of Pope Vigilius (553), in which certain Nestorian propositions are condemned: "If anyone says that the one Jesus Christ who is both true Son of God and true Son of man did not know the future or the day of the Last Judgment and that He could know only as much as the divinity dwelling in Him as in another revealed to Him, *anathema sit*."

The second comes from a letter of Pope Gregory the Great to Eulogius (d. 607), Patriarch of Alexandria, in which the pope commends the patriarch for his treatise against the *Agnoetes*, a sect which inverted the Monophysitism of the day by teaching that the divine nature was absorbed into the human. Resting their case on the passage in Mark's Gospel to which we referred above (13:32), the Agnoetes argued that Jesus was ignorant about the Day of Judgment. Gregory affirmed Eulogius' argument that the passage in question applied not to Christ as Head but to Christ as Body, i.e., Christ as Church. What Jesus knew *in* his human nature he did not know *from* his human nature. Because he is one in being with the Father, he has a knowledge which surpasses all others', including even that of the angels. Therefore, no ignorance was present in him, much less error.

Can We Reconcile the New Testament Record and the Teachings of the Church?

No; at least not *these* teachings. But then, what precisely are these teachings excluding, and what authority do they have?

The difficulty with answering the first of these two questions is compounded by the variety of theological universes which are operative in the New Testament, the medieval period, and in contemporary thought. On closer examination, the three universes are not mutually opposed. The medieval position is the "odd man out." The New Testament and modern theology are in closer harmony, one with another.

The teachings in question reflect certain assumptions about the meaning of knowledge which may be open to challenge today. The teachings assume, first, that God is not involved in human consciousness or in the growth of human knowledge except as a divine supplement. Thus, ordinary human beings (i.e., everyone except Jesus Christ) begin with absolutely nothing (*tabula rasa*) and proceed to accumulate knowledge experimentally, i.e., through human experience. Insofar as ordinary human beings know anything beyond what they can gather through experience, they receive it from God, as a revelation. Revelation, in this conception, is knowledge which is given over and above human knowledge. But we have already addressed in chapters 4 and 5 the problem of nature and grace, and in chapter 7 the question of revelation as such. The medieval approach to the problem of Jesus' knowledge is merely consistent with the medieval understanding of the relationship between nature and grace and of the meaning of revelation. Those same medieval conceptions of nature-and-grace and of revelation were immediately operative in the anti-Modernist documents and in *Mystici Corporis*.

The medieval understanding of Jesus' knowledge also reflects a pre-Enlightenment concept of history as something essentially static, as if history were simply the record of human actions in the world (e.g., comparable to a jet stream or the wake of a ship) rather than the evolutionary context in which human actions assume their meaning, significance, and direction (e.g., comparable to water as the element in which sea creatures live and develop). In the modern, as opposed to classical, understanding of history, an exact foreknowledge of all events (such as Christ is supposed to have had) would make truly free human action impossible. Human freedom is not simply the negative absence of contraints but the positive capacity to venture one's own future for something greater. It involves risk-taking, trust, hope, mystery.

Accordingly, to identify the human consciousness of Jesus with the divine consciousness, or to make Jesus' human consciousness something completely directed by the divine consciousness, is to relapse into Monophysitism. This sets clearly one limit to our understanding of Jesus' human consciousness and knowledge. However, we must continually remind ourselves that we are dealing ultimately with a mystery, which does not readily yield to theological analysis. It may be helpful to distinguish, as some contemporary theologians do, between the *unreflexive consciousness* in the depths of Jesus' being and the *objectifying and verbalizing consciousness* which had a history and which fully shared in the human situation (concepts, ideas, etc.) of Jesus' time, encompassing processes of learning, surprising experiences, crises of self-identity, etc.

In his *unreflexive conciousness* Jesus was aware of himself as a subject in whom God was fully present and as one who was fully present in God. The *immediacy* of this contact with God was unique, based as it is on the hypostatic union, and it explains the extraordinary *conviction* with which Jesus proclaimed and practiced the Kingdom of God. Similarly, his sense that his own relationship with God is something *exemplary* for all other human beings generated the *conviction* that he was himself the personification of the Kingdom which he proclaimed and practiced.

In his *objectifying and verbalizing consciousness* Jesus understood and expressed *less* than the "content" of his unreflexive consciousness. In other words, Jesus, like the rest of us, knew more than he was capable of saying. Through dialogue with others he, like the rest of us, came to a fuller understanding of who he was and what or who he was for. He went to his death knowing at least that it was the fate of a prophet, and he accepted his death in the light of his conviction that God would vindicate what he had said, done, and been. Such a theological explanation does not at all deny that Jesus Christ was, in his very being and from the beginning, the Word made flesh, nor does it deny that through his death and resurrection he fully realized and achieved for us all that God intended to realize and achieve through him.

It is readily admitted that this theological explanation is not the one operative in the magisterial documents under consideration. But is this explanation positively excluded by those documents? And if so, what authority do these documents have?

The *Constitutum* of Pope Vigilius was directed specifically against Nestorian errors. Even if one were to grant *dogmatic* status to the *Constitutum*—and no one can—it does not explicitly exclude the position outlined above (proposed by Rahner, Schoonenberg, and others). The two Holy Office decrees of 1907 and 1918 also have to be interpreted carefully: The first rejected certain Modernist theses but contained no distinct censure of the view outlined above; the second simply called views like it "unsafe." *Mystici Corporis* raises the question of Jesus' knowledge almost in passing. The encyclical is not directed at contemporary Christological aberrations. Insofar as the passage is doctrinally pertinent, it applies more properly to the glorified Savior who now acts as the risen Head of the Body, which is the Church.

Even if one were to grant, however, that these documents do condemn the position advanced here, and by Rahner and other Catholic theologians elsewhere, one would still have to raise the question of the authoritative status of such condemnations. The reader is referred again to chapter 2, and is alerted as well to the ecclesiological discussion in Part IV of this book. It is sufficient here to note that, on a scale of authoritative value, decrees of Vatican congregations and even papal encyclicals fall well below infallible pronouncements of ecumenical councils. And one might, finally, make a reasonable case that they fall below the doctrinal pronouncements of an international synod of bishops or of a general council of the Church, i.e., one involving several national churches but not "the whole wide [Christian] world," which is the literal meaning of the word "ecumenical."

Moreover, the teaching authority of the Church—at whatever level of exercise—is "not above the word of God, but serves it..." (Vatican II, *Dogmatic Constitution on Divine Revelation*, n. 10). The word of God, as proclaimed in the New Testament and as interpreted in the light of present theological principles, calls into question the apparent intent of the magisterial pronouncements on this question of the knowledge of Jesus. Finally, this newer approach is not without precedent even in the patristic period. It was Cyril of Alexandria (d. 444), whose anti-Nestorian writings were officially adopted by the Council of Ephesus (431), who wrote of Jesus Christ: "We have admired his goodness in that for love of us he has not refused to descend to such a low position as to bear all that belongs to our nature, included in which is ignorance" (*Thesaurus on the Holy and Consubstantial Trinity*, thesis 22).

THE SEXUALITY OF JESUS

Here again the issue is the *humanity* of Jesus, but it is posed even more sharply than in the preceding question. Is he really like us in all things except sin, or is he so much an exception to the rule of human existence, indeed of *sexually* human existence, that he can scarcely be *one of us*, let alone the representative of *all of us*?

Our discussion will make its way through four sub-questions: (1) How does the New Testament portray the sexuality of Jesus? (2) How has the sexuality of Jesus been understood in the tradition and official teachings of the Church? (3) Can the New Testament record be reconciled with that tradition and those teachings? (4) Can our own contemporary understanding of sexuality be reconciled with either or both: the New Testament and the tradition, on the one hand, and teachings of the Church, on the other?

How Does the New Testament Portray the Sexuality of Jesus?

One is struck at once by the almost total silence of the New Testament about the sexuality of Jesus. The New Testament reports that he knew hunger and thirst. He even knew anger, as on the occasion of his driving the money-changers from the Temple (Mark 11:15-17). He was tempted to pride, idolatry, and the desire for power (Matthew 4:1-11). And he endured rejection, betrayal, physical abuse, and finally death itself. But nowhere is he sexually tempted, much less engaged in sexual activity. Was he, in fact, sexless? And if sexless, how was he fully human?

There are a few references to sexual morality which do convey something of Jesus' attitude toward sexuality: "You have heard the commandment, 'You shall not commit adultery.' What I say to you is: anyone who looks lustfully at a woman has already commited adultery with her in his thoughts" (Matthew 5:27-28).

He accentuates his point: "If your right eye is your trouble, gouge it out and throw it away. . . . if your right hand is your trouble, cut it off and throw it away. Better to lose part of your body than to have it all cast into Gehenna" (verses 29-30).

Jesus moves immediately from adultery to divorce: "What I say to you is: everyone who divorces his wife. . .forces her to commit adultery. The man who marries a divorced woman likewise commits adultery" (verses 31-32). He also tells his audience that "when people rise from the dead, they neither marry nor are given in marriage but live like angels in heaven" (Matthew 22:30). (The meaning, force, and applicability of Jesus' ethical teaching will be examined more fully in Part V of the book, Christian Existence.)

On the other hand, the Gospels also present Jesus as a man known for his conviviality, his readiness to bless matrimonial unions, as one who even refers to the wedding feast as a symbol of the Kingdom of God (Matthew 22:1-14).

But how account for the obvious paucity of material on his sexuality? One plausible explanation is that Jesus deliberately wished to disassociate his proclamation of the Kingdom of God from the standard attitude toward human existence one finds in the other contemporary religions, where sex consistently played a large, if not even central, part. Some idealized sex as a sign of power that had to be replenished from on high; others condemned sex as a pollution to be purged from our lives. Jesus simply refused to sanction the religious status of sex. He is neither Dionysian nor anti-Dionysian.

Interpretations, beyond this one, vary widely. Hugh Montefiore, now an Anglican bishop, once suggested that Jesus may have had homosexual tendencies ("Jesus the Revelation of God," in *Christ for Us Today*, Norman Pittenger, ed., London: SCM Press, 1968, pp. 108-110). William Phipps, a Protestant theologian at Davis and Elkins College in West Virginia, has advanced the thesis that Jesus was married and that the post-resurrection encounter with Mary Magdalene can best be understood in light of his marital relationship with her (*Was Jesus Married?*, New York: Harper & Row, 1970). John 20:17 had been rendered by the Latin Vulgate as *"Noli me tangere"* ("Do not touch me"). The Greek,

"*Me mou haptou,*" is much stronger: "Do not cling to me." The physical relations she had previously had with Jesus and which she desired to continue were no longer appropriate or possible in his risen life.

There are, however, at least three arguments against the suggestion that Jesus was married: (1) The Gospels say nothing at all about a marriage; (2) the anti-erotic bias of the New Testament churches came very early into Christianity, and it can be supposed that if Jesus had been married, that tendency would have been checked; and, most decisively, (3) when Paul invoked his right to marry a believing woman "like the rest of the apostles and the brothers of the Lord and Cephas" (1 Corinthians 9:5), why did he not appeal to Jesus' own marriage to support his argument?

How Has the Sexuality of Jesus Been Understood in the Tradition and Teachings of the Church?

In a word, poorly. The influence of idealistic Greek philosophy, and the thought of Plato in particular, has been profound. Plato's true philosopher does not concern himself with sexual pleasure (*Phaedo*, 64, 82). Sexual desire is referred to as a diseased aspect of the personality (*Republic*, 402-405). The well-balanced person is the one who sublimates his sexual energies in intellectual pursuits (*Republic*, 485). Aristotle is at least as negative. A woman, he noted, is "a mutilated male" (*On the Generation of Animals*, 737a). The male is by nature superior. He commands; the female obeys (*Politics* 1254b, 1260a).

This same spirit was carried forward into the patristic and medieval periods by such men as Gregory of Nyssa and Augustine, for whom the sexual impulse is a sin and a shame (*City of God*, 14:17-18). Indeed, the genital organs are indecent and dishonorable (*partes inhonestae*, Scholastic theology would call them). They are the bodily instruments for the transmission of Original Sin (*On Marriage and Concupiscence*, 1:13). The ideal society for Augustine was a society without passion, where male and female would join for reproduction not through the "eager desire of lust, but the normal exercise of the will" (*City of God*, 14:26). The highest ideal, therefore, is consecrated virginity.

Thomas Aquinas was more moderate, but his views were also influenced by Greek philosophy and Augustinianism. The celibate life is to be preferred, he argued, because it is "unseared by the heat of sexual desire" (*Summa Theologica* II-II, q. 152, a. 1). He quoted with approval Augustine's injunction that sexual contact proper to the married state pulls down the mind from its heights (q. 151, a. 3). Following Augustine's theory on Original Sin, Thomas also argued that Jesus had to be conceived virginally because sin is transmitted by the male seed (III, q. 31, a. 3). Aquinas' attitude toward women was similarly appalling by present standards: The woman is an entirely passive agent in the act of love, and is less than a man on nature's scale (I, q. 99, a. 2; II-II q. 26, a. 10; III, q. 32, a. 4). Comparably negative attitudes toward sexuality can be found in the major Protestant Reformers: Luther, Zwingli, and Calvin (see W. Phipps, *The Sexuality of Jesus*, New York: Harper & Row, 1973, pp. 95-104).

Not surprisingly, this same attitude found expression in religious art and a counter-reaction in secular *literature*. Mass-produced paintings, statues, and holy cards depicting Jesus in one form or another (the Infant of Prague, the Sacred Heart, e.g.) are unrelievedly sexless. It is an art style called *Kitsch*, something one instantly recognizes but cannot define. "*Kitsch* is weak, save in two respects," Bruno Brinkman, S.J., writes. "It encourages submission and obedience, and it is strong in repressing or infantilizing sex, which is different from sublimating it. It has been unmistakably powerful and popular. We must not forget that in religious houses such statues were for decades the object of regular private, if not community, *cultus* [worship]" ("The Humanity of Christ: Christ and Sexuality," *The Way*, vol. 15, 1975, p. 210). *Kitsch* expresses fear of the human body and of sexuality. It is patently Docetic in tendency. It preaches and teaches a Jesus who is not recognizably human.

This vehemently anti-sexual bias has brought forth a variety of reactions. The most celebrated is D. H. Lawrence's (d. 1930) short story "The Man Who Died" (reprinted in *Christian Faith and the Contemporary Arts*, Finley Eversole, ed., New York: Vintage Books, 1959). Lawrence makes Jesus' resurrection his awakening to sensual love. On the other side is Nikos Kazantzakis'

(d. 1957) *The Last Temptation* (New York: Simon and Schuster, 1960), in which Jesus' spiritual struggle, his final battle with Satan, is defined by his carnal desire for Mary Magdalene, even as he hangs on the cross. But Jesus is shaken out of his dream and overcomes the Devil's power: "The moment he cried ELI ELI and fainted, Temptation had captured him for a split second and led him astray. The joys, marriages and children were lies . . . illustrations sent by the Devil" (p. 496).

Just as Lawrence had read into Jesus' life his own exceedingly permissive approach to sexuality, so Kazantzakis had projected upon *his* Jesus a mixture of late Western asceticism and Buddhism.

And what of the *official teachings* of the Church? The Church is nearly as silent as the New Testament. The only direct reference is to be found in the documents of the Second Council of Constantinople (553), not one of the more authoritative of the Church's ecumenical councils, as we pointed out in chapter 13. A condemnation of Theodore of Mopsuestia is issued and is subsequently approved by Pope Vigilius. Among Theodore's allegedly *Nestorian* views is one which holds that "God the Word is one while Christ is another who, disturbed by the passions of the soul and the desires of the flesh, freed himself gradually from inferior inclinations. . . ." The issue at hand was not Jesus' sexuality, but the unity of the two natures in the one divine Word. In any case, it is not a *dogmatic* definition nor, as given there, is it even clearly a *doctrine* of the Church.

Can the New Testament and the Tradition and Teachings of the Church Be Reconciled?

On this precise point, i.e., whether or not Jesus had an active sexual life or was sexually tempted, there is no possibility of contradiction, since the New Testament says nothing about either. The larger question, i.e., whether the patristic and medieval traditions are fundamentally consistent with the whole of the New Testament message and of Christian faith, will be addressed by implication, at least, in the next section.

What Does Our Contemporary Christian Consciousness Disclose About Sexuality in General, and About Jesus' Sexuality in Particular?

It seems entirely consistent with Christian faith in the *humanity* of Jesus Christ that Jesus should have known sexual temptation. Temptation itself is no sin; therefore, it would not violate the previous principle that Jesus was indeed sinless. Moreover, the New Testament does explicitly acknowledge that Jesus was tempted by Satan in the areas of power and wordly acclaim. To accept a Jesus who is at once fully human and yet immune from sexual desires is to stretch not only one's imagination but also one's theological convictions about the incarnation and the fundamental goodness of creation, the human body, and human sexuality.

It would not necessarily follow, however, that Jesus, as a necessary expression of his humanity, actually did engage in sexual activities. Neither would it follow that sexual activity within marriage would have been inconsistent with Jesus' *divinity*. Although it is true of a small minority of the world's population, it is true nonetheless that there are well-integrated, courageous, forceful, responsible, and thoroughly dedicated human beings who do not marry. One has only to point to a random sample of such persons within the past few decades alone: Pope John XXIII, Dag Hammarskjold (d. 1961), Mother Teresa of Calcutta, Theodore Hesburgh, and many others.

But to think and speak of Jesus as if he—and they—were asexual, if not anti-sexual, not only does an injustice to God's creation of sexuality but may finally undermine the humanity of Jesus as well, and would thereby remove an indispensable basis for our redemption and salvation.

Sexuality is not to be understood in a biological sense alone. Even celibates are sexual beings. The sexual difference between a man and a woman is constitutive of human nature itself, and that constitutive dimension finds expression in the psychological as well as the physiological levels of human existence. Sexuality, therefore, is not something added on to a neutral human nature. It determines a person as man or as woman. The "human person" is neither man alone or woman alone. Man and woman together constitute what we mean by the human. The need for communication and complementarity is self-evident. In sexuality a man and a woman experience their individual insufficiency and their dependence upon each other. And each one depends not just on the other but on the other as his or her sexual complement.

Sexuality, even when fulfilled in marriage, still points beyond itself to its perfect fulfillment in God. In the "already" and the "not yet" experience of fulfillment in sexual union, we come to a certain understanding of the transcendental relationship we have with God. Jesus was fully a human being, with sexual desires and with an understanding of sexual struggle. But he subordinated (not "suppressed") the *genital* expression of that sexuality in order to leave himself completely free for the proclamation of the Kingdom of God. Freud called this "sublimation." It is not something negative, like "repression." On the contrary, it represents a change in the goal as well as the object of the powerful sexual drive, putting its enormous energies at the service of some other value. This happens when there has been a free choice by which this drive is accepted and redirected. In the absence of a consciously free decision, however, repression occurs and personal maturity is blocked. This leads, in turn, to false attitudes, compensations, and/or an exaggerated quest for power for its own sake. None of these effects of repression was ever attributed to Jesus. Jesus, the perfect human being, was a sexually integrated human being.

Section Two: Christological Criteria

What follows here is not offered as an easy way of indentifying unorthodox or even heretical understandings of Jesus Christ. Very few deficient Christologies are expressed so unequivocally as, e.g., "I begin with the premise that it makes no sense at all to speak of Jesus of Nazareth as divine." At the serious academic and scholarly levels, even views which may be *reductively* unorthodox are first proposed as bona fide efforts to explain real difficulties in the mystery of Christ. That could undoubtedly have been said of each of the theologians of the first seven centuries who, in the end, found their explanations condemned by one or more of the great Christological councils.

On the other hand, there *is* an objective and objectifiable Christian and Catholic tradition. It is carried forward in the New Testament, in the dogmatic formulations of the ecumenical councils, the theological writings of the Fathers and doctors of the Church, the doctrinal assertions of other, non-ecumenical councils and of popes, and in the Church's liturgy. In listing criteria by which to differentiate between Christologies which are consistent with this broad tradition from those which are not, I do not suggest that the content of that tradition is always readily identified and understood. But the opposite impression also has to be checked, namely, that, when it comes to expressing our faith in Jesus Christ, one Christian's ideas are as good as another's, that we somehow begin afresh in each generation, taking or leaving what history bequeaths to us or what the Church universal proclaims, celebrates, and teaches today.

1.   The Catholic Christological tradition, *synthesized at the Council of Chalcedon (451)*, has *three principal dogmatic components:* (1) *Jesus is divine;* (2) *Jesus is human;* and (3) *the divine and the human are united in one person, Jesus Christ.*

a.   These principles are *not* purely metaphysical. They are primarily *soteriological.* If Jesus is not *at once* divine *and* human, then he did not save us. Both the divinity and the humanity are fully operative and effective in the redemption because they are indeed *united* in one person.

Christological explanations which explicitly or implicitly deny any of these three principles are inconsistent with the Catholic tradition. *Examples:* (1) "Jesus was not an ordinary human being, to be sure. He was the greatest of human beings. He achieved the highest *degree* of humanity." (2) "Jesus could not have been tainted in the least by ignorance, error, or, dare we say it, sexual appetites. That would be demeaning to the Son of God present in the human body of Jesus." (3) "Jesus is the Christ, to be sure. But there are other expressions of 'the Christ' as well.

Indeed, 'the Christ' is a cosmic process carrying the world toward its final perfection, and Jesus is one of his/its principal carriers and instruments."

b. The need for constant reinterpretation notwithstanding, no Christological interpretation can prescind from the objective data of this tradition in its biblical, dogmatic, doctrinal, theological, and liturgical expressions.

On the other hand, any such reinterpretation must be initiated and sustained by the most serious biblical, theological, and historical scholarship. Idiosyncratic interpretations, without any recognizable connection with, or even awareness of, the scholarly discussions are to be rejected.

2. *The object of Christian faith is not Christology, i.e., the dogmatic or even the biblical formulae, but Jesus himself. There is no radical separation, therefore, between the Jesus of history and the Christ of faith.*

This criterion is an elaboration of the third dogmatic component listed above, namely, that the divine and the human are united in one person, Jesus Christ. No processive or evolutionary Christology is consistent with the Catholic tradition which breaks the unique and definitive connection between Jesus of Nazareth and the Christ of the cosmos. This principle does not, on the other hand, exclude evolutionary or processive Christologies. Karl Rahner's Christology is one which reflects an evolutionary perspective, yet, by the standards proposed here, his is eminently consistent with the Catholic tradition.

3. *Jesus' life, death, and resurrection are redemptive. However they are finally explained, no explanation is consistent with the Catholic tradition if the explanation makes them merely exemplary or inspiring, or if it so divorces them from the human situation that they are simply divine disruptions of physical and natural laws.*

This criterion is an elaboration of the first two dogmatic components given in criterion #1 above, namely, that Jesus is divine *and* human. A merely exemplary or motivational explanation effectively denies the first dogmatic principle; a purely interventionist explanation effectively denies the second. No explanation, from whatever side of the theological spectrum, is consistent with the Catholic tradition if the *redemptive* significance of the life, death, and resurrection of Jesus is simply ignored. Thus, the resurrection is not simply a proof of Jesus' divinity or a reward from the Father.

4. *Christological explanations which contradict the central affirmations of the Church's liturgy are in violation of the long-standing theological norm: "The rule of prayer is the rule of belief" ("Lex orandi, lex credendi").*

The applicability of this criterion to Christology will be explored in the next chapter. For the moment it is sufficient to note its probable origin in the *Indiculus,* composed sometime between 435 and 442 by Prosper of Aquitaine (d. 460), a disciple of Augustine. The axiom is cited throughout the history of the Church, and in such recent documents as Pope Pius XII's encyclical on the Sacred Litury, *Mediator Dei* (1947). Pope Pius XI attributes the formula to Pope Celestine I (d. 432). In any case, it goes back at least to the early fifth century.

5. *Christological explanations which deny or are completely silent about the social implications of Jesus Christ's saving work misunderstand or supplant what was central to Jesus' proclamation and practice, namely, the Kingdom of God.*

Although this principle was not central to the conciliar debates of the first seven centuries, it is a clear implication of Jesus' preaching and activity on behalf of the reign of God. It also follows from the second major criterion above.

We addressed ourselves already to this issue in chapter 12, and will return to it again and again throughout the rest of the book: in the discussion of the Church's mission, of Christian existence, and, in chapter 29, of the Kingdom of God as such.

SUMMARY

1. The chapter addresses four specific questions as a way of elaborating upon the Christological discussion contained in chapters 12-14; it also offers a list of theological criteria by which Christologies which are consistent with the broad Catholic tradition can be differentiated from those which are not.

2. The *virginal conception of Jesus* refers to the belief that *Jesus was conceived in the womb of a virgin, Mary, without the intervention of a human father (virginitas ante partum)*. It does *not* refer to the virginity of Mary during or after the birth of Jesus (*in partu* or *post partum*).

3. Belief in the virginal conception of Jesus *is* to be found in the *New Testament*, specifically in the Infancy Narratives of Matthew and Luke. The rest of the New Testament is silent about it.

4. It cannot be determined, on the basis of the New Testament evidence, whether the virginal conception of Jesus was an *historical fact*. There are exegetical arguments for and against its historicity. Belief in the virginal conception, therefore, may have been a *theologoumenon*, i.e., a theological belief that is read back into the historical life of Jesus in order to make a point of faith: *Jesus was one with God from the moment of his conception.*

5. The *official Church* presupposes the virginity of Mary ("born of the Virgin Mary"). Given the original setting and purpose of the creedal and doctrinal affirmations, however, their primary concern would seem to have been with preserving the unity of the divine and the human in Jesus Christ, rather than with affirming the historicity of his virginal conception. Belief in the historicity of the virginal conception, however, remained universal within the Church at least until the Enlightenment, and is still held by a great many in the Church today.

6. Rejection of the historicity of the virginal conception does not necessarily imply rejection of the *divinity* of Jesus Christ. *The Word could also have become flesh with the human cooperation of Joseph.*

7. Belief in the virginal conception, apart now from the question of historicity, means that Jesus is from God, that Jesus is unique, that in him the human race has had a new beginning, that the salvation he brings transcends this world, and that God works through the weakness and even powerlessness of human instruments to advance the course of salvation history. If in denying the historicity of the virginal conception one also denies one or more of these principles, then one has effectively moved outside the Christian, and certainly the Catholic, tradition.

8. Because Jesus Christ is believed to be "from God," he is also believed to be *without sin*.

9. Belief in the *sinlessness* of Jesus is rooted in the *New Testament*, and especially in Hebrews 4:15. The New Testament affirms only that Jesus was without sin (*impeccantia*), not that he was absolutely incapable of sin (*impeccabilitas*).

10. The sinlessness of Christ cannot be *historically verified* because no one could have read the thoughts and heart of Jesus nor observed him in his every waking moment. But neither do we have any historical evidence or even accusations that Jesus *did* sin, and this is remarkable in view of Jesus' extremely controversial and threatening public image.

11. The *official Church* teaches at least as much as the New Testament; namely, that Jesus was de facto without sin. It would appear that *Constantinople III* (681) also taught that Jesus was incapable of sin, but that point is not explicitly formulated. In any case, such teaching would rest on the assumption that Jesus' human will was effectively absorbed or absolutely directed by the divine will. But this was precisely what the council was trying to combat (*Monothelitism*). The official teaching of the Church, taken comprehensively, is that Jesus Christ was perfect in his humanity and so completely in union with the Father that he was absolutely without sin. He may also have been incapable of sin, but he was at least able not to sin and, in fact, did not sin.

12. The belief in the sinlessness of Jesus underscores the more fundamental belief that he is the *supreme expression of communion between God and humankind*, that he is "the reflection of the Father's glory, the exact representation of the Father's being" (Hebrews 1:3).

13. The question of Jesus' *knowledge* is important because, unless we can admit to ignorance and perhaps even error in Jesus, certain problems of New Testament interpretation cannot be solved. Secondly, a Jesus who knows all things, and everything about all things, is not apparently the same human Jesus who the Council of Chalcedon confessed is like us in all things except sin.

14. On the basis of the *New Testament* evidence alone, one finds arguments on both sides of the question. Some texts, reflecting a later, higher Christology, attribute unlimited knowledge to Jesus, while many other texts, reflecting an earlier, lower Christology, reveal both ignorance and error in Jesus.

15. In any case, Jesus displayed a novel and courageous degree of *conviction* about the Kingdom of God, seeing his preaching, his actions, and his very person as signs and instruments of its inbreaking. He spoke with unprecedented *authority*. He put *demands* on others. He *forgave sins*. He *changed the Law of Moses*, and so forth. Indeed, he *began* his public ministry with this conviction already in place, so to speak (Mark 1:15).

16.   The *medieval tradition* and the *twentieth-century decrees of the Holy Office* clearly favor the "unlimited knowledge" side of the argument, but this tradition and these teachings reflect a particular understanding of knowledge, of revelation, of history, and of the relationship between nature and grace. In the light of our *modern understanding* of these philosophical and theological issues, Jesus would not have been a free human being, and therefore would not have really been one like us in all things except sin, if he knew exactly what lay ahead for him.

17.   Theologians distinguish between (a) Jesus' *unreflexive consciousness* which was the source of his unshakable conviction about his role in the coming of the reign of God—in other words, his unarticulated, not-yet-objectified sense of himself as a distinct subject with a uniquely intimate relationship with God—and (b) his *objectifying and verbalizing consciousness* which gradually reached the level of clear and precise self-understanding and expression, especially through dialogue with other people.

18.   The few *doctrinal pronouncements* which have addressed the issue of Jesus' knowledge, of course, support the view that Jesus did have unlimited knowledge. But the preceding explanation was not current at the time of these magisterial formulations, nor is it exactly clear which Modernist understandings were condemned, and to what extent they were condemned. In any case, none of these ecclesiastical documents has *dogmatic* status, which is not to say they have no authority at all for Catholics.

19.   The issue of Jesus' humanity is posed even more sharply by the question of his *sexuality*. If Jesus was sexless, how was he human?

20.   The *New Testament* is silent about the matter. It reports other basic human emotions (anger, hunger, temptations to power, etc.) but affords no indications of sexual desires or sexual activities. Is it perhaps because Jesus did not want his proclamation of the Kingdom of God confused with other contemporary religious attitudes? Other religions accorded religious status to sexuality, either exaggerating its importance or fundamentally rejecting its goodness.

21.   The *tradition* of the Church on this question has been influenced, in a decidedly negative way, by Greek and especially *Platonic* philosophy, as mediated by *Augustine* and other Fathers. Sexuality is evil. Indeed, it is the means through which Original Sin is transmitted. This same negative attitude toward sexuality in general, and toward women in particular, was carried forward in popular art and spirituality and, in

turn, evoked strong counter-reactions among secular artists such as D. H. Lawrence.

22.   The *official Church* is nearly as silent as the New Testament on Jesus' sexuality. *Constantinople II* (553) alone refers to the matter, but it is in the context of its anti-Nestorian thrust. The issue was not directly the sexuality of Jesus but the unity of the two natures in the one divine Word. In any case, the formulation is not a *dogmatic* definition, nor is it even clearly a *doctrinal* pronouncement.

23.   In conclusion, it would seem entirely consistent with Christian faith in the *humanity* of Jesus to believe that he knew *sexual desires and sexual temptations*. The contrary view seems to undermine his full humanity in all things except sin. Temptation and desires are not in themselves sinful.

24.   One need not, on the other hand, attribute *overt genital sexual activity* to Jesus on the grounds that his humanity could not have been fulfilled without it. Sexuality has to do with more than the biological. It has to do with the way we are, with the way we understand ourselves as male or female, and with the way we relate to the other, male or female, to complement our humanity. Even Freud acknowledged the importance of *sublimation*, as distinguished from *repression*. Sublimation involves a free acceptance of our sexual drives and a free redirection of those drives for other values. Repression, on the other hand, leads to false attitudes, compensatory behavior, and inordinate quests for power over others. Jesus was never accused of any of these traits. He was a sexually integrated man.

25.   The following *criteria* may be helpful in differentiating between Christologies which are consistent with the broad Catholic tradition and those which are not.

(1)   The Catholic Christological tradition, synthesized at the Council of Chalcedon (451), has three principal dogmatic components: (1) *Jesus is divine*; (2) *Jesus is human*; and (3) *the divine and the human are united in one person, Jesus Christ.*

(1-a)   These principles are primarily *soteriological*; i.e., unless the one Jesus is at once human and divine, we are not saved.

(1-b)   The need for *constant reinterpretation* notwithstanding, no Christological interpretation can ignore the *objective data* of this tradition, as appropriated and understood by modern scholarship.

(2)   *The object of Christian faith* is not Christology, i.e., the dogmatic or even the biblical formulae, but *Jesus himself.* There is *no radical separation*, therefore, *between the Jesus of history and the Christ of faith.*

(3) *Jesus' life, death, and resurrection are redemptive.* However they are finally explained, no explanation is consistent with the Catholic tradition if it makes them merely exemplary or inspiring, or if it so divorces them from the human situation that they are simply divine disruptions of physical and natural laws.

(4) Christological explanations which contradict the central affirmations of the Church's *liturgy* are in violation of the longstanding theological norm: *"The rule of prayer is the rule of belief" (Lex orandi, lex credendi).*

(5) Christological explanations which deny or are completely silent about the *social implications* of Jesus Christ's saving work misunderstand or supplant what was central to Jesus' proclamation and practice, namely, the *Kingdom of God.*

SUGGESTED READINGS

Brinkman, Bruno. "The Humanity of Christ: Christ and Sexuality." *The Way* 15 (1975), 209–224.

Brown, Raymond E. "How Much Did Jesus Know?" *Jesus, God and Man: Modern Biblical Reflections.* Milwaukee: Bruce, 1967, pp. 39–105.

————. et al., eds. *Mary in the New Testament: A Collaborative Assessment by Protestant and Roman Catholic Scholars.* New York: Paulist Press, 1978.

————. *The Virginal Conception and Bodily Resurrection of Jesus.* New York: Paulist Press, 1973, pp. 21–68.

Driver, Thomas F. "Sexuality and Jesus." *New Theology No. 3.* Eds. Martin Marty and Dean Peerman. New York: Macmillan, 1966, pp. 118–132.

Malatesta, Edward, ed. *Jesus in Christian Devotion and Contemplation.* St. Meinrad, Ind.: Abbey Press, 1974.

Phipps, William E. *The Sexuality of Jesus: Theological and Literary Perspectives.* New York: Harper & Row, 1973.

Rahner, Karl. "Dogmatic Reflections on the Knowledge and Self-Consciousness of Christ." *Theological Investigations.* Baltimore: Helicon, 1966, vol. 5, pp. 193–215.

Robinson, John A. T. *The Human Face of God.* Philadelphia: Westminster Press, 1973, pp. 1–98.

Schoonenberg, Piet. *The Christ: A Study of the God-Man Relationship in the Whole of Creation and in Jesus Christ.* New York: Herder & Herder, 1971, pp. 104–152.

· XVI ·

THE CHRIST OF THE LITURGY

This chapter is by way of an appendix to the preceding Christological reflections (chapters 11-15). More specifically, it provides a fuller exposition of the fourth criterion given at the end of the previous chapter, namely, that Christological explanations which contradict the central affirmations of the Church's liturgy are in violation of the longstanding theological axiom: "The rule of prayer is the rule of belief" (*Lex orandi, lex credendi*).

The *thesis* of this chapter is that *the eucharistic and other sacramental rites* of the Catholic Church, especially as they have been revised by decree of the Second Vatican Council and Pope Paul VI, *at once express and confirm the major Christological principles* which have been set forth thus far, namely, the centrality of the *resurrection* of Jesus to redemption; the centrality of the *Kingdom of God* within the message and mission of Jesus; the centrality of the same Kingdom of God for the *Church's* message, mission, and hope within the *history of salvation*; and the empowerment of the Church by the *Holy Spirit* to carry forward that mission in history *until the Lord returns*.

This chapter has a limited purpose and scope. It does not attempt to do in advance the work of chapters 21 and 22, on the sacraments. It proposes only to show that the Christology of the Church's liturgy is consistent with the main Christological principles of contemporary Catholic theology, and to suggest that contemporary Christology, in turn, has shaped and guided the revision process mandated by Vatican II.

Accordingly, the chapter examines the prayers used in the seven sacraments of the Church, beginning with the new Rite of Christian Initiation (Baptism, Confirmation, and Eucharist). Because the Eucharist is the supreme Christian sacrament, special attention is given to it: the introductory rite, the service of the word, the canons, or Eucharistic Prayers, and the Communion rite. The chapter then moves to the sacraments of Penance, Marriage, Holy Order (the latter consisting of diaconate, priesthood, and episcopate), and the Anointing of the Sick. The focus of interest in each instance is the specifically Christological content of the various prayers and sacramental formulae.

The liturgy, after all, is Christology as worship and prayer; Christology, in turn, is worship and prayer as theological and doctrinal formulation. Indeed the very word *orthodoxy* means, in the Greek, "right praise," and the Church's historic Christological creeds are, for the most part, liturgical formulae or are derived therefrom.

THE SACRAMENTS OF CHRISTIAN INITIATION
Baptism

First Stage: Rite of Becoming Catechumens

Although "God enlightens every person who comes into the world," the celebrant reminds the candidate for Baptism, "you are called to walk by the light of Christ and to trust in his wisdom. He asks you to submit yourself to him more and more and to believe in him with all your heart. This is the way of faith on which Christ will lovingly guide you to eternal life. Are you ready to enter on this path today under the leadership of Christ?" The candidate responds, "I am."

The celebrant then turns to the candidate's sponsors and to the entire assembly and asks if they are "ready to help (him/her) come to know and follow Christ." Faith in him, in other words, is never a purely individual matter. The Church mediates Christian faith.

There follows a brief rite of *exorcism* in which the celebrant lightly breathes toward the face of the candidate and says:

"Breathe your Spirit, Lord, and drive out the spirits of evil: command them to depart, for your kingdom is drawing near." From the very beginning, the candidate's attention is focused on what was in fact central to Jesus' own preaching and mission: the coming Kingdom of God. (See chapter 12.)

The primitive biblical and patristic *distinction* between God, the Almighty (*Pantokrator*), and Jesus, the Christ ("anointed") of God, is preserved in an optional rite in which the candidate renounces non-Christian worship and spirits or magical arts: "With the help of God and in response to his call, you have indicated your intention to worship and serve God alone and his Christ." And immediately thereafter: "Do you reject every power which sets itself up in opposition to God and his Christ?" (See chapter 13.)

Then the sponsors are asked to assure the celebrant that the candidate has indeed "chosen Christ as Lord and wishes to serve him alone." The candidate and sponsors come forward, and the celebrant makes the sign of the cross on the candidate's forehead: "Receive the cross on your forehead: by this sign of love (or: of his triumph) Christ will be your strength. Learn now to know and follow him."

There follows the signing of the various senses and parts of the body: ears, eyes, lips, breast, shoulders, each accompanied by an appropriate formula: "May you hear the voice of the Lord"; "May you see with the light of God"; "May you respond to the word of God"; "May Christ dwell in your heart by faith"; and "May you accept the sweet yoke of Christ." And then the general blessing: "I sign you in the name of the Father, and of the Son, and of the Holy Spirit: may you live for ever and ever."

Then the celebrant prays that the candidate may be kept safe by the "power" of the cross of Christ. An optional form of the prayer is even more soteriologically comprehensive: "Almighty God, you have given life to your people by the death *and resurrection* of your Son. . ." (italics mine).

A service of the Word follows: readings, homily, and presentation of the Gospels. Then the sponsors and the whole assembly pray that "God the Father reveal his Christ to (him/her) more and more with every passing day," and that, with the support of the community, the candidate may be "found ready, in due time, to receive the new birth of baptism and life from the Holy Spirit." The ceremony concludes with the prayer that those "who have listened to the word in this community be renewed by its power and come to reflect the image of Christ who lives and reigns for ever and ever. Amen."

During the course of the catechumenate minor *exorcisms* are celebrated to show the candidate the true nature of the spiritual life as a battle between flesh and spirit, and to underline both the importance of self-denial in order to gain the blessings of the Kingdom of God and the continuing need of God's help. "Even when (we) sinned against you, you did not abandon (us), but in love and wisdom you chose to save (us) by the coming of your Son as man." And again: "Lord Jesus Christ, when ascending and preaching from the hillside you led your followers from the path of sin and made known to them the way of happiness of the Kingdom. . . . May they work for peace among men and joyfully endure persecution. May they come to share in your Kingdom and in the forgiveness you promised them."

Second Stage: Rite of Election or Enrollment of Names

The celebrant extends his hands over the candidate(s) and prays: "God our Father, you created the human race that you might also be the One who makes it ever new. Count these adopted children as sons and daughters reborn to your new covenant. Make them children of the promise. Although they cannot reach eternal life by their own nature, they may come to share it by the power of your love. We ask this through Christ our Lord. Amen." The close connection between Christology and Christian anthropology is evident. Our humanity is good because it comes from the creative act of God. We are all alive by a principle which transcends us. The presence of God in us enters into the very definition of what it means to be human (see chapter 5). Through the redemptive work of Jesus Christ the goodness of our humanity is reconfirmed. We are renewed. Evident, too, is the priority of God's work over our own in the coming of the Kingdom: "Keep them faithful to their calling, help them *to be built into* the Kingdom of your Son..."(italics mine)

In a later rite of exorcism, the *uniqueness* of Jesus is attested to in the words: "Lord Jesus, you are the fountain we thirst for, you are the teacher we seek; you alone are the Holy One." And again: "Lord Jesus, you are the true light that enlightens all men." And again: "Father of eternal life, you are a God, not of the dead, but of the living: you sent your Son to proclaim the good news of life, to rescue men from the kingdom of death and to lead them to resurrection. Free these chosen people from the power of the evil spirit who brings death. May they receive new life from Christ and bear witness to his resurrection."

The *miracles* of Jesus are portrayed for what they are: not interruptions of the laws of nature in order to overwhelm, but signs given in order to teach. "Lord Jesus, you raised Lazarus from death as a sign that you had come to give men life in fullest measure." (See chapters 9 and 12.)

A profession of faith follows in which the candidate confesses faith in "Jesus Christ, his only Son, our Lord. He was conceived by the power of the Holy Spirit and born of the Virgin Mary. He suffered under Pontius Pilate, was crucified, died, and was buried. He descended to the dead. On the third day he rose again. He ascended into heaven, and is seated at the right hand of the Father. He will come again to judge the living and the dead."

Third Stage: Celebration of the Sacrament

The celebrant blesses the baptismal water with these words: "We ask you, Father, with your Son to send the Holy Spirit upon the water of this font. May all who are buried with Christ in the death of baptism rise also with him to newness of life." There follow a renunciation of Satan, an anointing, a profession of faith, and then the actual rite of Bapitsm "in the name of the Father, and of the Son, and of the Holy Spirit." A post-baptismal anointing is accompanied by the prayer: "As Christ was anointed Priest, Prophet, and King, so may you live always as a member of his body, sharing everlasting life." Then the new Christian is clothed in a white garment to symbolize his or her having become "a new creation," clothed in Christ.

Confirmation

Baptism is completed through the rite of Confirmation, in which the Church prays in a special way that the Spirit might be poured forth upon the new Christians "to strengthen them with his abundant gifts and anoint them to be more like Christ his Son." The candidates are called "to witness to his grace by [their] manner of life."

Eucharist

Christology-as-worship is most fully expressed, of course, in the Eucharist. Here more than anywhere else in the Church's liturgical and devotional life, the Church's perception of Jesus Christ is expressed in a manner at once comprehensive and precise.

Introductory Rites

The third penitential rite is filled with explicit Christological references: "You were sent to heal the contrite"; "You came to call sinners"; "You plead for us at the right hand of the Father"; "You came to reconcile us to one another and to the Father"; "You heal the wounds of sin and division"; "You raise the dead to life in the Spirit"; "You bring pardon and peace to the sinner"; "You bring light to those in darkness"; "You raise us to new life"; "You forgive us our sins"; "You feed us with your body and blood"; "You healed the sick." Jesus is a healer of spiritual *and* bodily sickness. He brings truth that enlightens the mind. He gives us himself in the Eucharist. And through all of these activities, he reconciles us with God the Father (see chapter 12).

In the "Glory to God" (*Gloria*) the Church prays: "Lord Jesus Christ, only Son of the Father, Lord God, Lamb of God, you take away the sin of the world: have mercy on us; you are seated at the right hand of the Father: receive our prayer. For you alone are the Holy One, you alone are the Lord, you alone are the Most High,

Jesus Christ, with the Holy Spirit, in the glory of God the Father. Amen." The reconciling work of Christ, therefore, continues. Even now he pleads for us "at the right hand of the Father." The Jesus of history, the Nazarene who died on the cross, is our living Lord.

Liturgy of the Word

Herein there are readings from both Testaments. The selections from the New Testament, of course, are regularly focused on Jesus Christ, but since they are not the same from Eucharist to Eucharist, they cannot be cited here. What is constant on Sundays and major feasts is the "Profession of Faith," or Nicaeo-Constantinopolitan Creed, to which reference has been made several times already: "We believe in one Lord, Jesus Christ, the only Son of God, eternally begotten of the Father, God from God, Light from Light, true God from true God, begotten, not made, one in Being with the Father. Through him all things were made. For us men and for our salvation he came down from heaven: by the power of the Holy Spirit he was born of the Virgin Mary, and became man. For our sake he was crucified under Pontius Pilate; he suffered, died, and was buried. On the third day he rose again in fulfillment of the Scriptures; he ascended into heaven and is seated at the right hand of the Father. He will come again in glory to judge the living and the dead, and his kingdom will have no end." We have here, of course, a summary of the Church's historic faith in Jesus Christ. This summary is the fruit of centuries of controversy and doctrinal clarification (see chapter 13).

Liturgy of the Eucharist

As the celebrant pours wine and a little water into the chalice, he prays: "By the mystery of this water and wine may we come to share in the divinity of Christ, who humbled himself to share in our humanity." The Christological perspective here is "from above," but it is also decidedly incarnational. Jesus is truly one with us.

The *prefaces* of the Eucharistic Prayer, or canon, also vary from season to season. The regular weekday preface, however, expresses its Christology with commendable leanness: "With love we celebrate his death. With living faith we proclaim his resurrection. With unwavering hope we await his return in glory." Jesus Christ is situated at the center of salvation history. He alters its course by his death; he renews it by his resurrection; and he will bring it to perfection at the Second Coming.

Eucharistic Prayer I sounds the purpose of the Mass from the very beginning. It is an act of "praise and thanksgiving (of the Father) through Jesus Christ (his) Son." The consecratory prayer cites the words of Jesus in which he speaks of "the blood of the new and everlasting covenant" which is shed for all for the forgiveness of sins. The memorial acclamations which immediately follow the consecration declare that "Christ has died, Christ is risen, Christ will come again"; "Dying you destroyed our death, rising you restored our life. Lord Jesus, come in glory"; "Lord, by your cross and resurrection you have set us free. You are the Savior of the world." And all four Eucharistic Prayers conclude with the words: "Through him, with him, in him, in the unity of the Holy Spirit, all glory and honor is yours, almighty Father, for ever and ever. Amen." The trinitarian dimension remains central always (see chapters 9 and 10). The reconciling work for which the Son is sent is completed by the Holy Spirit.

Eucharistic Prayer II has its own *preface* which speaks of Jesus Christ as "the Word through whom you [the Father] made the universe, the Savior you sent to redeem us. By the power of the Holy Spirit he took flesh and was born of the Virgin Mary. For our sake he opened his arms on the cross; he put an end to death and revealed the resurrection. In this he fulfilled your will and won for you a holy people." The consecratory prayer is introduced with the words "Before he was given up to death, a death he freely accepted. . . ."

Eucharistic Prayer III begins with the words "All life, all holiness comes from you [the Father] through your Son, Jesus Christ our Lord, by the working of the Holy Spirit." After the consecration, the Church calls "to mind the death your Son endured for our salvation, his glorious resurrection and ascension into heaven," and expresses its readiness "to greet him when he comes again." We pray that the Father will look with favor on the

Church's offering "and see the Victim whose death has reconciled us to yourself." Finally, we express the "hope to enjoy for ever the vision of your glory, through Christ our Lord, from whom all good things come."

Eucharistic Prayer IV acknowledges the goodness and mercy of the Father in not abandoning us to the power of death. "Father, you so loved the world that in the fullness of time you sent your only Son to be our Savior. He was conceived through the power of the Holy Spirit, and born of the Virgin Mary, a man like us in all things but sin. To the poor he proclaimed the good news of salvation, to prisoners, freedom, and to those in sorrow, joy. In fulfillment of your will he gave himself up to death; but by rising from the dead, he destroyed death and restored life. And that we might live no longer for ourselves but for him, he sent the Holy Spirit from you, Father, as his first gift to those who believe, to complete his work on earth and bring us the fullness of grace." And, as in all the Eucharistic Prayers, there is a recalling (*anamnesis*) of the redemptive work of Christ on our behalf, through his death, resurrection, exaltation, and coming again in glory. But this Eucharistic Prayer, more than the other three, underlines the redemptive significance of Jesus' earthly ministry *before* the crucifixion: his proclamation of the good news to the poor and the oppressed (see chapters 11 and 12).

Communion Rite

The Communion rite begins with the Lord's Prayer, and that, in turn, is introduced with such formulae as "Jesus taught us to call God our Father, and so we have the courage to say..." or "Let us pray for the coming of the kingdom as Jesus taught us...." Afterwards, we pray to the Father to "Keep us free from sin and protect us from all anxiety as we wait in joyful hope for the coming of our Savior, Jesus Christ." We pray also *directly to Christ*, asking him to "look not on our sins, but on the faith of your Church, and grant us the peace and unity of your kingdom, where you live for ever and ever. Amen." Jesus Christ is not only our brother but our Lord as well. We pray not only with him but *to* him.

The eucharistic bread is broken, and the community prays: "Lamb of God, you take away the sins of the world, have mercy on us." Then the celebrant prays privately before Communion: "Lord Jesus Christ, Son of the living God, by the will of the Father and the work of the Holy Spirit your death brought life to the world." As the celebrant raises the host before the general distribution of Communion, he proclaims: "This is the Lamb of God who takes away the sins of the world." Again, Jesus' life and ministry, indeed his place in history, make no sense apart from the forgiveness of sins and the reconciliation of God and humankind.

THE OTHER SACRAMENTS
Penance

After the penitent's confession of sins, he or she makes an act of contrition which concludes with "Our Savior Jesus Christ suffered and died for us. In his name, my God, have mercy." Then the priest extends his hands over the penitent's head and pronounces the absolution: "God, the Father of mercies, through the death and resurrection of his Son has reconciled the world to himself and sent the Holy Spirit among us for the forgiveness of sins; through the ministry of the Church may God give you pardon and peace, and I absolve you from your sins in the name of the Father, and of the Son, and of the Holy Spirit."

One of the suggested prayers to be recited by a deacon or other minister within a public rite of reconciliation (to be followed by individual confession and absolution) focuses on the earthly life of Jesus, in keeping with the more recent "from below" Christologies (see chapter 15): "You were sent with good news for the poor and healing for the contrite"; "You came to call sinners, not the just"; "You forgave the many sins of the woman who showed you great love"; "You did not shun the company of outcasts and sinners"; "You carried back to the fold the sheep that had strayed"; "You did not condemn the woman taken in adultery, but sent her away in peace"; "You called Zacchaeus to repentance and a new life"; "You promised Paradise to the repentant thief." Each prayer is followed by the response "Lord, be merciful to me, a sinner" or simply "Lord, have mercy."

The entire public rite is concluded with a common prayer: "You sent your Son into the world to destroy sin and death by his passion, and to restore life and joy by his resurrection....You have shown us your mercy and made us a new creation in the likeness of your Son."

Marriage

The Nuptial Blessing, recited after the Lord's Prayer of the Mass, refers to the newly wedded man and woman as "married in Christ." The marriage "symbolizes the marriage of Christ and his Church." Otherwise the distinctively Christological content of this sacrament is meagre.

Holy Order

Ordination of Deacons

In the instruction at the beginning of the rite, the bishop reminds the candidates that they are to be "ministers of Jesus Christ who was recognized among his disciples as the one who served." In the course of the examination of the candidate, the bishop asks if the new deacon will shape his way of life "according to the example of Christ." In the prayer of consecration itself, through which (in connection with the imposition of hands) the diaconate is conferred, the bishop speaks of Jesus Christ as the Father's Word, power, and wisdom. The deacons are to be "steadfast in Christ. Just as your own Son came not to be served but to give himself in service to others, may these deacons imitate him on earth and reign with him in heaven." Jesus Christ is at once Lord and *servant*.

Ordination of Priests

In the opening instruction by the bishop, he refers to Jesus Christ as "our high priest...sent by the Father," who, in turn, "sent the Apostles into the world so that through them and their successors, the bishops, he might continue forever his work as Teacher, Priest and Pastor." It is Christ's ministry "to make his own body, the

Church, grow into the people of God, a holy temple." Although priests are called to a ministry of instruction, it is always "in the name of Christ who is the chief Teacher." (See chapter 11.) The mystery of the death and resurrection of Jesus Christ is to provide the pattern for the priest's own ministry. All that the priest does as a priest, he does in the name of Christ and to carry on the work of Christ, who is "Head of the Church and its Pastor." The priest is to lead the faithful together like a unified family "through Christ and in the Holy Spirit to God the Father." Finally, the priest is always to "remember the example of the good shepherd who came to serve rather than to be served, to seek out and save what had gone astray."

In the course of the Examination, the bishop asks if the candidate is "resolved to unite [himself] more closely every day to Christ the first priest who offered himself for us to the Father as a perfect sacrifice." The consecratory prayer itself is only tangentially Christological. The bishop prays that "the gospel may reach the farthest parts of the earth, and [that] all nations, gathered together in Christ, may become one holy people of God."

As the newly ordained priest's hands are anointed, the bishop refers to Christ's own anointing by the Father through the power of the Holy Spirit. While the new priest is being invested in stole and chasuble, Psalm 100 may be sung, with the antiphon "Christ the Lord, a priest for ever according to the order of Melchisedech, offered bread and wine." Christ's redemptive and reconciling work on our behalf is a *priestly* work.

Ordination of a Bishop

The principal consecrator addresses the clergy, people, and bishop-elect on the duties of a bishop, and uses words to this effect: "Our Lord Jesus Christ, who was sent by the Father to redeem the human race, sent in turn twelve apostles into the world." The Apostles selected helpers for themselves and "passed on to them the gift of the Holy Spirit they had received from Christ." The Lord Jesus Christ is called "high priest for ever," one "present among you." This same Christ continues to proclaim the word of God and to unfold the mysteries of faith through the ministry of the bishop, and he adds to his Body and incorporates new members into it in the paternal functions of the bishop. Finally, through the bishop's wisdom and prudence Christ guides the Church in its earthly pilgrimage toward eternal happiness. (For a more detailed statement on the relationship between Christ and the Church, see chapters 17 and 20.)

The principal consecrator recalls the example of Christ himself. A bishop, like Christ, must serve rather than rule. "Such is the counsel of the Master that the most important should behave as if he were the least, and the leader as if he were the one who serves." (For a contrast, see chapter 11 on the image of Jesus as ruler, judge, and king.) The grace that the priest draws upon for the people has its source in the "the overflowing holiness of Christ." Christ is the good Shepherd "who knows his sheep and is always known by them and who did not hesitate to lay down his life for his sheep." The instruction refers, finally, to Christ's triple office of Teacher, Priest, and Pastor.

In the Examination the bishop-elect is also asked if he is resolved "to show kindness and compassion in the name of the Lord to the poor and to strangers and to all who are in need" and to be a good shepherd and "seek out the sheep who stray and to gather them into the fold of the Lord."

In the consecratory prayer all the bishops present, their hands joined, pray that "the perfect Spirit" who was given to Jesus Christ should flow out upon the bishop-elect.

Anointing of the Sick

As the priest enters the sickroom, he addresses those present in these or similar words: "We have come together in the name of our Lord Jesus Christ, who restored the sick to health, and who himself suffered much for our sake." He says a prayer of thanksgiving over the holy oil: "Praise to you, almighty God and Father. You sent your son to live among us and bring us salvation. Praise to you, Lord Jesus Christ, the Father's only Son. You humbled yourself to share in our humanity, and you desired to cure all illnesses." And then, as the priest anoints the sick person, he says, "May the Lord who frees you from sin save you and raise you up." An alternate prayer after the anointing reads: "Lord Jesus Christ, you shared in our human nature to heal the sick and save all mankind."

After the giving of Communion, the rite concludes with this prayer: "Father, your son, Jesus Christ, is our way, our truth and our life. Our brother (sister) entrusts himself (herself) to you with full confidence in all your promises. Refresh him (her) with the body and blood of your Son and lead him (her) to your kingdom in peace. We ask this through Christ our Lord. Amen." Finally, the priest imparts a blessing in the name of "the Father, and the Son, and the Holy Spirit."

SUMMARY

1. The eucharistic and other sacramental rites of the Catholic Church at once express and confirm the major Christological principles: the redemptive significance of the death and resurrection, the centrality of the Kingdom of God in Jesus' preaching and in our own mission and hope, the centrality of Jesus Christ to all of salvation history.

2. Christian initiation occurs over the course of three sacraments: Baptism, Confirmation, and the Eucharist. In *Baptism*—and in the catechumate rites leading up to it—Christ is "the light" for our way to eternal life: He is our leader and example for Christian existence; by the power of the Holy Spirit, he drives out the spirits of evil and makes the Kingdom draw nearer; he is the Christ of God, the Almighty; his death and resurrection are the source of our life from God; he does not abandon us even when we sin, but offers us the peace and forgiveness of the Kingdom.

3. Christ is our teacher (prophet), priest, and king; he alone is the Holy One, the true light that enlightens all; he proclaims the good news of life to rescue us from the kingdom of death and lead us to the resurrection; his miracles, especially the raising of Lazarus, are signs that he had come to give us life in the fullest measure.

4. *Confirmation* completes the baptismal rite. The Church prays that, through the working of the Holy Spirit, the new Christian might be strengthened to be more like Christ, the Son of God, through the witness of his or her life.

5. Christology-as-worship is most fully expresed in the *Eucharist.*

6. The *third penitential rite* speaks of Christ healing the contrite, calling sinners, pleading for us at the right hand of God, reconciling us to

the Father, healing the wounds of sin and division, raising the dead to life in the Holy Spirit, bringing pardon and peace, forgiving sins, healing the sick. The *Gloria* continues these themes and addresses Christ as "alone...the Holy One,...the Lord,...the Most High."

7. *The Nicaeo-Constantinopolitan Creed* encapsulates the whole conciliar tradition, which culminates eventually in the dogmatic decrees of the Council of Chalcedon. Jesus Christ is the eternal Son of God, begotten, not made, who became a human being for our salvation and who accomplished that salvation through his passion, death, and resurrection. He will come again in glory, and his kingdom will have no end.

8. *Eucharistic Prayer I* emphasizes that the Mass is an act of praise and thanksgiving to the Father *through* Jesus Christ, that we have a new and everlasting covenant in his blood, which was shed for the forgiveness of sins.

9. *Eucharistic Prayer II* has its own *preface* which speaks of Christ as the Word through whom the Father made the universe and the Savior he sent to redeem us. He put an end to death and revealed the resurrection, and so won for the Father a holy people. Indeed, he freely accepted the death by which he conquered sin and death.

10. *Eucharistic Prayer III* begins with "All life, all holiness comes from [the Father] through [the] Son, Jesus Christ our Lord, by the working of the Holy Spirit." It asks, after the consecration, that the Father will look upon the Church's offering and "see the Victim whose death has reconciled us" to the Father. Finally, it expresses hope that we shall enjoy the vision of his glory, through Christ.

11. *Eucharistic Prayer IV* explicitly employs the text from Hebrews 4:15 and the Council of Chalcedon which says that Jesus was like us in all things except sin. It puts Christ's saving work in an historical context and refers more directly than the other Eucharistic Prayers to Jesus' earthly ministry of proclaiming the good news to the poor, freedom to prisoners, joy to those in sorrow. By rising from the dead, he destroyed death and restored life, and then sent us the Holy Spirit to complete his work on earth and to bring us the fullness of grace.

12. In all of the Eucharistic Prayers there are the *memorial acclamations* following the consecration which declare that Christ died, rose, and will return; that he destroyed death through *his* death and restored life through his resurrection; that he set us free by both; and that he is the Savior of the world.

13. In each of the Eucharistic Prayers there is also the *anamnesis*, or recalling, of what Christ did to accomplish our redemption: He died, rose, was exalted, and will come again.

14. Finally, all of the Eucharistic Prayers end with the words "Through him, with him, in him, in the unity of the Holy Spirit, all glory and honor is yours, almighty Father, for ever and ever. Amen."

15. The *Communion Rite* begins with the Lord's Prayer, and that, in turn, is introduced by formulae which recall that Jesus taught us to address God as Father, to pray for the coming of the Kingdom, to forgive sins against us. Christ keeps us free from sin and anxiety now, and he will come again in a final act of salvation. His death brought life to the world, we are reminded as Communion is about to be distributed.

16. The same themes are sounded in the sacrament of *Penance*: Christ suffered, died, and rose for our salvation, and sends the Holy Spirit for the forgiveness of sins. One of the suggested prayers for a public celebration of Penance underlines the earthly ministry of Jesus: his concern for the poor, the outcasts, sinners.

17. *Marriage* establishes a union "in Christ" akin to the union of Christ and the Church.

18. *Holy Order* is conferred at three ministerial levels: the diaconate, the priesthood (or presbyterate), and the episcopacy. In all, the example of Christ who came to serve, and not to be served, is held up as a model.

19. In the ordination to the *priesthood*, the priesthood of Christ himself is emphasized. He is teacher, priest, and pastor. He is also head of the Church. He seeks to unify the whole human family in the Holy Spirit. The same themes are reiterated in the ordination of a *bishop*.

20. The sacrament of the *Anointing of the Sick* highlights Jesus' concern for healing of body as well as of soul, and recalls that he suffered much for our sake. Indeed, he shared our human nature in order to heal the sick and save all humankind, that all might be led to the Kingdom.

SUGGESTED READINGS

The Rites of the Catholic Church as Revised by Decree of the Second Vatican Ecumenical Council and Published by Authority of Pope Paul VI. New York: Pueblo Publishing Co., 1976.

The Roman Missal: Revised by Decree of the Second Vatican Council and Published by Authority of Pope Paul VI. Washington: National Conference of Catholic Bishops, 1970.

The Roman Pontifical: Revised by Decree of the Second Vatican Council and Published by Authority of Pope Paul VI. Washington: National Conference of Catholic Bishops, 1973.

PART FOUR

THE CHURCH

THE CHURCH

INTRODUCTION

We come now to the heart of the distinctively Catholic understanding of Christian faith. Catholics have always more strongly emphasized the place of the Church in mediating salvation than have other Christian traditions. And within the mystery of the Church, Catholics have always stressed the mediating function of certain ministries, structures, and institutional forms. Thus, Catholics have insisted on the importance of the ordained ministries of the bishop, priest, and deacon, and the special role of the bishop of Rome, the pope. Catholics have underlined, too, the essentially sacramental character of Christian existence and have taken care to define precisely the nature, meaning, and number of the sacraments, as well as the conditions under which they are celebrated. Catholics have also accorded a prominent position to Mary, the mother of Jesus Christ, a theological and devotional emphasis that is in keeping with three characteristically Catholic principles: the principle of *mediation*, the principle of *sacramentality*, and the principle of *communion* (see chapter 24).

Consistently with the historical method of this entire book, Part IV begins with an examination of the nature, structure, and mission of the Church and the churches in the New Testament (chapter 17) and traces their development and growth through subsequent centuries (chapter 18). Special emphasis is given the event which, more than any other, has shaped, and continues to shape, contemporary Catholic thought and practice, the Second Vatican Council (chapter 19).

In light of this history, from the New Testament to the present, there is offered a systematic definition of the Church and a description of its mission (chapter 20). An ecumenical spectrum of contemporary ecclesiological views is also outlined. Given the sacraments' significance in expressing the nature of the Church and in fulfilling its mission, the sacraments are accorded separate and relatively extensive treatment: first, the sacraments of initiation, i.e., Baptism, Confirmation, and Eucharist (chapter 21); and then the sacraments of healing, i.e., Penance and the Anointing of the Sick, and the sacraments of vocation and commitment, i.e., Matrimony and Holy Order (chapter 22). Special ecclesiological questions are identified and examined: authority, papacy, ministry, ordination of women, and intercommunion (chapter 23). The chapter on Mary (chapter 24), which illustrates three characteristically Catholic principles—mediation, sacramentality and communion—brings Part IV to a conclusion.

In this book generous attention is given the mystery of the Church, but not because it is the most fundamental of the mysteries of Christian faith. It is not. Nor is our extensive treatment of the Church prompted simply by the view that the mystery of the Church is itself a synthesis of all of the other mysteries of faith. It is that, of course. What is more important, however, is that with the mystery of the Church we come at last to the point at which the distinctively *Catholic* understanding and practice of Christian faith most clearly emerges. So if this book is to be successful in its purpose of identifying, examining, and explaining the reality of Catholicism, sustained study of the mystery of the Church is both imperative and inevitable.

·XVII·

THE CHURCH OF THE NEW TESTAMENT

FROM CHRISTOLOGY TO ECCLESIOLOGY

The interlocking character of Christian doctrine is by now unmistakably clear. Our understanding of Jesus Christ is a function of our understanding of God, and our understanding of God is, in turn, a function of our understanding of human existence. Jesus, after all, has meaning and value for us because he is no ordinary person; he is hypostatically one with the Word of God. And God has meaning and value for us because God is the source, the core, the sustenance, and the destiny of our being as individual human persons and as members of the total human community. God enters into the very definition of our humanity. We are alive by a principle which transcends us.

There is also a connection, therefore, between our understanding of human existence, of God, and of Jesus Christ, on the one hand, and our understanding of the Church, on the other. Or more immediately, our understanding of the nature and mission of the Church depends upon our understanding of the meaning and value of Jesus Christ, who reveals to us at one and the same time who God is and who we are.

This presupposes, of course, that there is some vital link between Jesus Christ and the Church, that the Church somehow issues forth from Christ and is identified with his person and work. It is precisely for the sake of examining and establishing that connection that we turn first to the question of the Church in the New Testament. In keeping with the historical method employed throughout this book, we begin at the beginning and then follow the course of the Church's development down to the present time.

THE PROBLEM

The Church exists. No one questions that fact, even though many would differ when it comes to defining what we mean by *Church*. The initial problem is not with the *existence* of the Church but with its *origins*: (1) *When* did the Church *begin* to exist? (2) Did *Jesus intend* that the Church should exist? (3) Did the Church remain *faithful* to Jesus' intentions even during the so-called foundational period encompassed by the New Testament writings?

These three questions are reducible to one: *What connection, if any, can we establish between the Church's evaluation of itself and Jesus' evaluation of the Church?* This is only a variation of the question which framed the parallel chapter (The Christ of the New Testament) in Part III, namely, the question of the Christ of faith and the Jesus of history.

It requires just as much care and delicacy to answer the question in its ecclesiological form as it did to answer it in its Christological form. The New Testament is the same primary source for both. That source can only be interpreted *developmentally*. The New Testament itself emerged through a three-stage process: (1) the original words and deeds of Jesus; (2) the oral proclamation of the Apostles and disciples (catechesis, narratives, testimonies, hymns, doxologies, and prayers); and (3) the writings themselves. Insofar as the New Testament reports sayings of Jesus on the Church (e.g., Matthew 16:18; 18:17), we have to ask: (1) What did those sayings mean when, and if, spoken by Jesus himself? (2) What did they mean in the earliest stage of the apostolic preaching? (3) What did they mean to the communities which preserved them and to the New Testament author(s) who recorded them?

The writings, in turn, reflect a progressive theological movement as the Gospel is proclaimed and accepted in one setting and then in another: (1) in the *Jewish-Christian* community of Palestine, which was closest to the events of the life, death, and resurrection of Jesus and which was most concerned with establishing the connection between Jesus and the house of David; (2) in the *Jewish-Hellenistic* community, which, in the light of the obvious delay of the Second Coming (*parousia*), stressed the present exalted state of Christ ("Jesus *is* Lord!"); and (3) in the *Hellenistic-Gentile* community, which, under the impact of the missionary activity of the Pauline and Johannine schools of theology, declared that God is even now exercising lordship over the universe in and through Jesus Christ, who is the risen and exalted Lord.

Recognizing such developments in both composition and theological content is one thing; interpreting the finally developed material is another. We should not be surprised, therefore, to discover a diversity of ecclesiological approaches not only *within* the New Testament but also within the present-day body of biblical exegetes and theologians. And since the conclusions of scholars are part of the public domain, a diversity of non-scholarly opinion about the Church is also to be expected.

JESUS AND THE CHURCH: A SPECTRUM OF INTERPRETATIONS
Non-scholarly Conservatism

This view *identifies* the whole of New Testament ecclesiology with Jesus' own evaluation of the Church. Even though the New Testament books were composed over a period of some fifty to eighty years and were addressed to diverse audiences of diverse circumstances, this non-scholarly conservative position maintains that there had been *no significant ecclesiological development* in all of that time. Thus, when Jesus accepted Peter's confession that Jesus was indeed the Messiah and made Peter the rock upon which he would build his Church (Matthew 16:13-20), that acceptance and that designation reflected the self-understanding of Jesus—despite the fact that Peter's confession and Jesus' reaction are very different in the earlier Gospel of Mark (8:27-30). Indeed, the next scene in Mark's Gospel has Jesus reprimanding Peter, "Get out of my sight, you satan!" (8:33).

According to the non-scholarly conservative view, Jesus left the Twelve Apostles a detailed blueprint for a Church: seven sacraments with precise matter and form, the papacy vested with supreme and universal jurisdiction, the monarchical episcopate, doctrines, liturgies, and laws. Indeed, the whole purpose of his "coming down from heaven" was to pay humanity's "debt" to the Father by his death on the cross and then to leave a Church behind in order to communicate the benefits of that saving act to as many people as possible. The view was commonly held by Catholics until the Second Vatican Council and the application of biblical scholarship to ecclesiology in the 1960s. Traces of it continue to be found in the Catholic Church today, sometimes even among its pastoral leaders.

Non-scholarly conservatism cannot withstand biblical criticism. There is no evidence in the New Testament that Jesus indicated in detail the where, the how, or the when of ecclesial development. Not even the Acts of the Apostles presents this type of continuity. On the contrary, the great advances in ecclesiastical life and organization which are reported there are responses to new and unprecedented challenges. One of the first great crises to confront the Church centered on the question of whether Gentiles might also be admitted to membership in the Christian community (Acts of the Apostles 10:1—11:18). When Peter was compelled to justify his eating with, and then baptizing, uncircumcised persons (namely, the Roman centurion Cornelius, his relatives, and close friends), he appealed not to some specific doctrinal or legal directive of Jesus but to the prompting and instruction of the Holy Spirit (11:12). Thus, if we are to speak of *continuity* in New Testament ecclesiology, it must be in terms of the Spirit of Christ who dwells within the Church, in every circumstance, time, and place. There was no institutional master plan.

But continuity does not mean *uniformity*, as if there were some unbroken line of development within the New Testament period. There are strong differences in outlook found among the various New Testament writers. For example, Matthew's attitude toward the Law (5:18; 23:2-3) is clearly not the same as Paul's in Galatians (3) and Romans (2-4; 7; 13). And Luke in the Acts of the Apostles makes no attempt to hide the fact that the Hellenistic Christians vehemently objected to the type of ecclesiastical organization which had begun to prevail among the Jewish Christians (15:1-29).

Non-scholarly Liberalism

The non-scholarly liberal concludes that there is *no continuity* at all between the Church's self-understanding and Jesus' evaluation of the Church. Jesus came to teach us a way of life centered on love and based on freedom from institutional oppression of every kind. He proclaimed the Kingdom of God, but his followers gave us the Church instead.

Although non-scholarly liberalism began as a Protestant movement, it has made a delayed entrance into Catholicism as a reaction against the ecclesiastical authoritarianism and the dogmatic and ethical fundamentalism of the pre-Vatican II period.

Scholarly Liberalism

Scholarly liberalism, unlike its non-scholarly counterpart, does not dismiss the ecclesiology of the New Testament as non-existent or unimportant. On the other hand, scholarly liberalism shares with non-scholarly liberalism the conviction that the ecclesiology of the New Testament is a mistaken evaluation of what Jesus intended. For the liberals, New Testament ecclesiology is entirely a creation of the early church.

The liberals hold that Jesus himself did not intend a Church because he expected the Kingdom of God as imminent: at first within his own lifetime, and then as something that would come about immediately after his death. The disciples, therefore, expected the Second Coming in the very near future. They perceived themselves as the ultimate Messianic Community of the Saints, the elect of the final generation who would soon enter a new form of being in the new aeon. With the further delay of the *parousia*, the post-apostolic Church abandoned this Pauline view and assumed organizational form of a type that suggested some historical permanence.

This view is expressed in Martin Werner's *The Formation of Christian Dogma* (Boston: Beacon Press, 1957) but goes back to earlier figures like Johannes Weiss, Albert Schweitzer, and Adolf Harnack.

Bultmannian Existentialism

Over against the Weiss-Schweitzer-Werner point of view, Rudolf Bultmann argued that Jesus did link entrance into the Kingdom with affiliation with a community, the Jewish people. "Do not live in fear, little flock. It has pleased your Father to give you the kingdom" (Luke 12:32). For Bultmann, the individual will find deliverance "only because he belongs to the eschatological community, not because of his personality" (*Jesus and the Word*, London: Collins, 1958, p. 41). Furthermore, he rejected the scholarly liberal's assertion that Jesus' expectation of the Kingdom of God led to his enunciating only an interim ethic. Jesus was unconcerned with the human future; he was concerned only with God's. Every person *now* stands under the judgment of God's word and will. This is the hour of decision; this is the *final* hour (p. 96).

On the other hand, Bultmann rejects the sacramentalism of the Fourth Gospel and of Hellenistic Christianity in general. For Jesus, it is not sacramental washings or meals that make a person pure, but only a pure heart, i.e., a good will (Mark 7:15). "The teaching of Jesus and that of the oldest group of his followers contained no trace of any such sacramental conception" (p. 111).

Scholarly Conservatism

Most scholars today admit *continuity within development*. They reject the fundamentalistic assumptions of their non-scholarly cousins who deny development and inflate continuity into identity. They also reject the Liberal's stress on discontinuity to the point where there is no discernible connection at all between what Jesus said and did and what eventually emerged as Church.

This so-called scholarly conservative position has its *Protestant* and *Catholic* wings, but their differences have perhaps had less to do with exegesis than with theological and doctrinal commitments. Catholics are more likely than Protestants to underline the Church's role in mediating salvation. Thus, Catholic biblical scholars such as Rudolf Schnackenburg, Anton Vögtle, and Raymond Brown affirm a stronger sacramental and ministerial character to the New Testament Church than Protestant biblical scholars such as Ernst Käsemann, Eduard Schweizer, or Hans Conzelmann. For the Catholics, this structure is constitutive or essential to the Church. For the Protestants, it is at best functional and, therefore, not absolutely necessary to the Church's integrity.

Catholic scholars have tended to emphasize *continuity*; Protestant scholars have tended to emphasize *development*. In recent years, however, the Catholic and Protestant wings of the scholarly conservative school have moved closer to each other. Catholics continue to underline continuity, but without prejudice to development. And Protestants continue to underline development, but without prejudice to continuity. An example of this remarkable ecumenical convergence is provided by the joint exegetical and theological study, *Peter in the New Testament* (New York: Paulist Press, 1973), sponsored by the United States Lutheran-Roman Catholic Dialogue.

(The chart on page 603 summarizes the various approaches to the question of Jesus' relationship with, and attitude toward, the Church.)

DID JESUS INTEND TO FOUND A CHURCH?

The answer is "No" if by "found" we mean some direct, explicit, deliberate act by which Jesus established a new religious organization. The answer is "Yes" if by "found" we mean "lay the foundations for" the Church in various indirect ways. In this second case, it is preferable to speak of the Church as having its *origin* in Jesus rather than as having been founded by Jesus.

Jesus Did Not "Found" the Church

In his preaching Jesus never addressed himself merely to a *select group* of people, even though such groups existed in his day—e.g., the Qumran community which understood itself as God's holy remnant, the chosen of the new Covenant. The Kingdom of God, he insisted, is open in principle to everyone: "Mark what I say! Many will come from the east and the west and will find a place at the banquet in the kingdom of God with Abraham, Isaac, and Jacob, while the natural heirs of the kingdom will be driven out into the dark" (Matthew 8:11-12; see also Luke 13:28-29). He is aware that his mission is not to gather together all of the just and the righteous but to "go instead after the lost sheep of the house of Israel" (Matthew 10:6). It is the whole of Israel, and no group or sect within it, which is called to be God's people in the last days. To the very end, despite the experience of failure, Jesus addressed himself to the whole of the people.

Even the call of *the Twelve* has to be seen in this light. The Twelve were to represent Jesus' call to all of the twelve tribes of Israel, and they were to serve as rulers and judges "when the Son of Man takes his seat upon a throne befitting his glory" (Matthew 19:28; Luke 22:30). So, too, the wider circle of disciples were entrusted with the mission to Israel as a whole (Luke 10:1-20).

Although the missionary mandate makes particular demands upon the disciples, Jesus imposes no specific rule of life, nor is membership in the company of his disciples a condition of salvation. On the contrary, "None of those who cry out, 'Lord, Lord,' will enter the kingdom of God but only the one who does the will of my Father in heaven" (Matthew 7:21). And the will of the Father is often done without explicit awareness: "Lord, when did we see you hungry and feed you...?...I assure you, as often as you did it for one of my least brothers, you did it for me" (Matthew 25:31-46). Neither the disciples nor those Israelites who were disposed to hear his message and repent were ever organized formally into a religious group.

One should not be surprised, therefore, to find no evidence of a specific act of founding a Church or of gathering together a community of the elect. Had Jesus done this, his gesture would have been interpreted as the founding of a separate synagogue and would have minimized and even destroyed the uniqueness of his proclamation. Indeed, the only time in all of the Gospels where Jesus is reported to have made explicit reference to the founding of the Church is given in Matthew 16:18. Apart from the problem of its clashing with Mark 8:27-30, to which we referred above, Jesus speaks here not of the present but of the future. Indeed, not until Jesus is risen from the dead do the first Christians even speak of a "Church."

Jesus Laid the Foundations for the Church

First, Jesus did gather disciples around him. They participated in his healing power, which was a sign for Jesus that the Kingdom of God was breaking through: "He sent them forth to proclaim the reign of God and heal the afflicted" (Luke 9:2). On the other hand, the message of the Kingdom which he preached and which he commissioned them to preach was a divisive one. They would be like "sheep among wolves" (Matthew 10:16). "Brother will hand over brother to death, and the father his child; children will turn against parents and have them put to death. You will be hated by all on account of me" (10:21-22). Consequently, those Israelites who would accept his proclamation of the Kingdom would inevitably be distinguished from those who rejected it.

Secondly, he anticipated an interim period between his death and the *parousia*, even though, as we saw in our discussion of Jesus' knowledge in chapter 15, it is difficult to determine just what his understanding of this time-period was. He foresaw that Jerusalem would reject the call to salvation and that instead the pagans would be invited to the heavenly banquet as a new People of God, without regard for ethnic origins (Matthew 8:11-12).

Thirdly, the community of disciples did in fact stay together after the rejection of Jesus by the majority of the Jewish people. It is from this perspective that one must understand the Last Supper, with the Lord's injunction: "Do this in remembrance of me" (1 Corinthians 11:24). Likewise the word to Simon Peter suggests that the disciples understood Jesus as having intended them to stay together (Luke 22:31-34). In fact, there never was a churchless period in the New Testament following the resurrection.

DID THE EARLY CHRISTIAN COMMUNITY UNDERSTAND ITSELF AS CHURCH?
The Word Church

The Greek word *ekklēsia* originally signified a legislative assembly of citizens. Only those citizens who enjoyed full rights could belong to this assembly, and so the word implies both the dignity of the members and the legality of the assembly. The word, however, had no religious usage. It was adopted by the Septuagint (the Greek version of the Old Testament) to render the Hebrew word *kāhāl*, which, with the Hebrew word *'ēdāh*, signifies the religious assembly of the Israelites. The word appears about one hundred times in the Septuagint, often qualified by the phrase "of the Lord" (*kāhāl yahweh*). Because in its earliest phase the young Christian community did not view itself as distinct from Judaism, the Christians simply took over the term to apply to their own gatherings of prayer. *Not until the admission of Gentiles to the community did the distinction between the Church and Judaism become acute.* Thereafter, the work *ekklēsia* applied to the Christian community alone.

The word appears only twice in the *Synoptic Gospels* (Matthew 16:18; 18:17). Of the first, we have already spoken. The second reference (18:17) may have been to the Jewish synagogue, since the distinction between Jesus' disciples and Judaism had not yet become clear.

The word occurs twenty-three times in the *Acts of the Apostles*. In no passage does it certainly refer to anything except the local church, and usually the Church of Jerusalem, the parent and prototype of the other churches (5:11; 8:1,3). These churches outside of Jerusalem are organized with their own bishops, presbyters, and deacons, and they are founded by the Apostles (e.g., 20:28). Entrance is not by Jewish birth but by rite of Baptism. And it is God who gathers the people together (20:28 again).

The word *ekklēsia* occurs sixty-five times in the *Pauline material*—more frequently, therefore, than anywhere else in the New Testament. In most instances the word signifies a local church. Paul is also the first to use the *plural* form of the word (1 Corinthians 11:16; 14:33; 2 Corinthians 8:18; 12:13; Galatians 1:2,22; Romans 16:4,16; and so forth). In *Ephesians* and *Colossians* the word applies to the whole worldwide assembly of Christians. Christ is the head, and the Church is the fullness of his body (Ephesians 1:22-23; Colossians 1:18-20). It is through the Church that the mystery of salvation is revealed (Ephesians 3:10). The relationship between Christ, who is the great sacrament of salvation, and the Church, which is his body, is a great mystery (Ephesians 5:22-32). The figure of the Church as the body of Christ is the basis of Paul's appeal for Christian unity and fellowship (1 Corinthians 12:12-26; Romans 12:4-5). This unity is symbolized by the one bread of the Eucharist (1 Corinthians 10:17).

On the other hand, sometimes the *ekklēsia* is just a small house community (Romans 16:5; Philemon 2), listed alongside larger communities (1 Corinthians 16:19). It often has a specifically liturgical meaning (1 Corinthians 11:18; 14:23,24), and refers also to particular congregations (1 Corinthians 11:18,20,33-34; 14:23). The churches of the New Testament, whether local or universal, are congregations gathered in the name of Jesus Christ. Indeed, they are churches of Jesus Christ (Romans 16:16; 1 Thessalonians 2:14; Galatians 1:22). The Church is the true Israel and the legitimate heir of the Covenant promises (Romans 9-11).

The word *ekklēsia* appears in the *Johannine writings* in 3 John 6, 9, and 10, and twenty times in Revelation, always referring to particular churches. In the Fourth Gospel the Christian community is described as a flock gathered into a sheepfold (10:1-5), and Jesus, as the Good Shepherd. He is also the true vine; his followers, the branches united to him (15:1-8). He commits the flock to Peter (21:15-17) and prays that all of his followers may be one, as he and the Father are one (17:20-21).

In the *other New Testament writings* the word occurs once in James 5:14, where it probably signifies a particular church. There also appears a clearly defined body of followers of Jesus which is called a synagogue (James 2:2).

The Church of the New Testament is no uniform or monolithic reality. It is at once local and universal, but not in the sense that the local church is simply a subdivision of the Church universal, nor that the Church universal is simply the sum total of local churches. Although the precise relationship between the Church universal and the local church(es) is not made clear in the New Testament, it *is* clear that what is excluded in the preceding sentence is excluded also by the New Testament. There is not a Corinthian division of the Church, for example, but "the church of God which is in Corinth" (1 Corinthians 1:2; see also 2 Corinthians 1:1). On the other hand, the Church universal is a living, integrated organism: "the fullness of him who fills the universe in all its parts" (Ephesians 1:23).

The early Christian community did, in fact, appropriate to itself the title "Church" in both senses. It knew itself to be the community of Jesus the Messiah, whom God raised to his right hand (Acts 2:32-36; 3:13-15,20-26; 5:30-31; 7:55-56; 9:4-5; 10:37-43; 13:27-31). That the original Jerusalem Church traced itself back to Jesus is evident in its maintenance of the circle of the Twelve, listed once again by name (less Judas) in Acts 1:13, and completed at the election of Judas' replacement (1:25-26). The celebration of the Eucharist, in fidelity to the Lord's own command, is yet another crucial link with the company of Jesus' disciples (1 Corinthians 11:23-25).

Thus, a purely individualistic Christianity is unthinkable for the earliest Christians. Belief in Christ and life in Christ are to be found only within the community of believers joined to the Lord. All of the New Testament writers write as members of the one Church of Jesus Christ. There is no fragmentation. All of the particular churches are built on the foundation of the Apostles and prophets, and Christ is always the cornerstone (Ephesians 2:20).

The Coming of the Holy Spirit

The descent of the Holy Spirit upon the Church at *Pentecost* did not inaugurate the Church. It already existed (Acts of the Apostles 1:15). But Pentecost was the moment when the Church was specifically endowed with power from on high (Luke 24:49; Acts of the Apostles 1:18). For the early Church the outpouring of the Spirit upon the Church was an established fact, and the manifestations of the Spirit's gifts were not in doubt (1 Corinthians 12-14). Even in Thessalonica those gifts were perceptible (1 Thessalonians 5:19), and so, too, in the Galatian churches (Galatians 3:2-5) and in Rome (Romans 12:6-8). The Spirit is the gift of God to all who believe and are baptized (Acts of the Apostles 2:38; Galatians 4;6; Romans 5:5). The Spirit is the firstfruits of the final Kingdom (1 Thessalonians 4:8; 1 Peter 1:2; Hebrews 6:4; Jude 19-20; 1 John 3:24; 4:13).

The coming of the Holy Spirit makes Christ's community the temple of God (1 Corinthians 3:16; 2 Corinthians 6:16; Ephesians 2:22), a spiritual building where true spiritual sacrifices are offered (1 Peter 2:5) and where true worship in spirit and in truth occurs (John 4:23-24). Through the Spirit all members of the Church have access to the Father and become fellow citizens of heaven with the saints (Ephesians 2:18-19). It is the Spirit who guides the Church in mission (Acts of the Apostles 5:3,9; 8:29,39; 9:31; 10:19; 13:2; 15:28; 16:6-7; 20:23; 21:11) and who speaks to the churches (Revelation 2:7,11,17,19; 3:6,13,22).

The early Church, therefore, did not understand itself simply as another sect within Judaism or even as another religious organization. The Church of the New Testament proclaimed the Gospel "in the Holy Spirit" (1 Thessalonians 1:5). Its message and preaching were given through "the convincing power of the Spirit" (1 Corinthians 2:4). It was a community transformed by the presence of the Spirit, the firstfruits of redemption (Romans 8:23; 2 Corinthians 1:22), and sealed with the Spirit (Ephesians 1:13). The Church is a community saved "through the baptism of new birth and renewal by the Holy Spirit . . . that we might be justified by his grace and become heirs, in hope, of eternal life" (Titus 3:5,7).

HOW DID THE EARLY CHRISTIAN COMMUNITIES EXPRESS THEMSELVES AS CHURCH?
The Original Jerusalem Community

The religious life of the original Jerusalem Church is summarized in the Acts of the Apostles 2:43-47; 4:32-35; and 5:12-16. We find apostolic activity, supported by healing and miracles, which, in turn, increased the membership of the community; the sharing of goods among the members; and a rich liturgical and prayer life both in a special meeting place in the Temple and in the houses of members themselves. They gathered for the breaking of the bread (2:46; 20:7,11), clearly the eucharistic meal of 1 Corinthians 11:20 which was the central and common worship of all the Christian churches.

This original Jerusalem community maintained its close links with Judaism: the strong attachment to the Temple (a point clearly opposed by the Hellenists, see Acts of the Apostles 6:13-14; 7), the continuation of Jewish practices, and the voluntary community of goods. The Jerusalem Church was not without inner conflict and tension, however. The dispute between the Jewish and Greek members over the care of widows (6:1-6) and, of course, the great debate over the need for circumcision and the observance of Jewish dietary laws (15:1-31) were major cases in point.

The Church at Antioch in Syria

Antioch was at this time the third-largest city in the Roman Empire. The Christian community here was a mixed group: former Jews and former pagans ("Greeks") alike. The Antiochene Church was a model of harmony between Jews and Gentiles, a fact indirectly confirmed by Paul in Galatians 2:1-14. Here, for the first time, the followers of Jesus Christ were called "Christians." They had regular meetings at which the large congregation was "instructed" (Acts of the Apostles 11:26). Prophets and teachers were active here (13:1-3), and the gifts of the Spirit were evident (11:27; 15:32).

It was from this community that Paul and Barnabas were sent to carry the case against the Judaizers at the Council of Jerusalem (15:1-29). Both attested to the marvelous work of God among the Gentiles (15:12). The Council of Jerusalem resolved the crisis with a principle that has remained normative for the Church ever since (if sometimes more in the breach than in the observance): no burden is to be imposed "beyond that which is strictly necessary"(15:28).

The Church of Corinth

This was a church of predominantly pagan origin whose life is disclosed through the two letters of Paul. What is striking about the church in this busy port city is its charismatic character (1 Corinthians 1:5-7; 12:8-11) and its human weaknesses. The charismatics often created confusion (1 Corinthians 14). Serious disorders arose at the celebration of the Eucharist because of the behavior of the rich (1 Corinthians 11:20-34). Partisan groups attached to particular missionaries emerged (1 Corinthians 1:11;

see also 3:4-5, 22). Many sided with opponents of Paul, as his second letter suggests. Pagan vices, especially of a sexual kind, still prevailed (1 Corinthians 5; 6:12-20).

On the other hand, there was also a flourishing church life at Corinth. The apostolic preaching and instruction were sounded in the assemblies (2 Corinthians 3:4—4:6). Worship occupied a central place (1 Corinthians 11:17-34). Baptism and Eucharist were sources of deep religious experience (1 Corinthians 1:13-16; 6:11; 10:1-11,16-22). They understood themselves as the Church of God (1 Corinthians 1:2; 10:32; 11:22; 2 Corinthians 1:1) which honors the Lord (1 Corinthians 1:2,9; 8:6; 10:21; 12:3; 2 Corinthians 3:17-18; 4:5). It was a church in fellowship with the Church of Jerusalem (for which the great collection was taken up) and with the other churches (1 Corinthians 1:2; 7:17; 11:16; 16:1,19; 2 Corinthians 1:1; 8:24; 12:13; 13:12).

Unity in Diversity

Despite all local differences among the Jewish-Christian, Jewish-Hellenistic, and Hellenistic-Gentile communities, *common elements* stood out clearly: faith in Jesus as Messiah and Lord; the practice of Baptism and the celebration of the Eucharist; the apostolic preaching and instruction; the high regard for communal love; and the expectation of the coming Kingdom of God. Great freedom was allowed in all other matters—a freedom which, when exercised, manifested the limitations as well as the spiritual grandeur of God's Church.

HOW DID THE EARLY CHURCH UNDERSTAND ITS MISSION?
Church and Kingdom of God

Just as Jesus' message and mission are centered on, and framed by, the coming Kingdom of God, so, too, are the Church's. It is indeed what Jesus instructed his disciples to pray for: "your kingdom come" (Luke 11:2; Matthew 6:9). It is the reality signified in the many parables attributed to Jesus. But the Church lives "between the times," i.e., between the decisive inbreaking of the Kingdom of

God in Jesus Christ and the final outpouring of the Holy Spirit at the end. As such, the Church is both a Church of glory and a Church of the cross.

It is a *Church of glory* insofar as it has been sanctified from within: "He gave himself up for her to make her holy, purifying her in the bath of water by the power of the word, to present to himself a glorious church, holy and immaculate, without stain or wrinkle or anything of that sort" (Ephesians 5:25-27). "It was in one Spirit," Paul writes elsewhere, "that all of us, whether Jew or Greek, slave or free, were baptized into one body. All of us have been given to drink of the one Spirit" (1 Corinthians 12:13). Indeed, "There is but one body and one Spirit, just as there is but one hope given all of you by your call" (Ephesians 4:4).

But the Church is also a *Church of the cross*. Although it is to the risen body of Christ that Christians are joined (Romans 7:4), within this age that body continues also to be a *suffering* body. "Continually we carry about in our bodies the dying of Jesus, so that in our bodies the life of Jesus may also be revealed" (2 Corinthians 4:10; see also Galatians 6:17; 1 Corinthians 15:31; Romans 8:36). Being joined to the risen Christ means being baptized "into his death...If we have been united with him through likeness to his death, so shall we be through a like resurrection" (Romans 6:3-5). We share "in the blood of Christ" (1 Corinthians 10:16), and by our own suffering, joined to his, we "fill up what is lacking in the sufferings of Christ, for the sake of his body, the church" (Colossians 1:24).

The glory that, in one sense, is *already* in the Church, is *not yet* revealed. We are "heirs of God, heirs with Christ, if only we suffer with him so as to be glorified with him" (Romans 8:17). The tension between glory and suffering is clearly stated in Philippians: "I wish to know Christ and the power flowing from his resurrection; likewise to know how to share in his sufferings by being formed into the pattern of his death. Thus do I hope that I may arrive at resurrection from the dead" (3:10-11). The process is ongoing: "We do not lose heart, because our inner body is renewed each day even though our body is being destroyed at the same time. The present burden of our trial is light enough, and earns for us an eternal weight of glory beyond all comparison" (2 Corinthians

4:16-17). "This means," Paul continues, "that if anyone is in Christ, he is a new creation. The old order has passed away; now all is new!" (5:17).

As a Church both of glory and of the cross, *the Church is both a sign and an instrument of the Kingdom of God*. Peter receives the keys of the Kingdom (Matthew 16:19). He and the other Apostles are given the power of binding and loosing, of forgiving and of withholding forgiveness (Matthew 18:18), of sharing in Jesus' own power (Mark 2:10; John 20:23), even over the demons (Mark 3:15; 6:7). This is indeed the deepest meaning of Jesus' authority: to break the rule of Satan (Luke 11:20; Matthew 12:28; Mark 11:28, 33) and thereby to establish the Kingdom of God. The Church understands itself as having been sent by Christ to make disciples of all nations and to baptize them in the name of the Father, the Son, and the Holy Spirit (Matthew 28:19). This is the grandeur and the burden of the Church. Not all who are called prove worthy of the call (Matthew 22:11-14). Nonetheless Jesus promises to be with the Church for all ages (Matthew 28:20). In the meantime, healings and other signs of renewal will show that the powers of the future age are already present in the Church (Luke 10:17,19; Mark 16:17).

Nowhere is the orientation of the Church toward the Kingdom more explicitly revealed than in the Eucharist, which anticipates the eating and drinking at the Lord's table in the Kingdom (Luke 22:30). "I solemnly assure you, I will never again drink of the fruit of the vine until the day when I drink it new in the reign of God" (Mark 14:25; see also Matthew 26:29).

Proclamation of the Word

That the Church understood itself as having been commissioned to proclaim the Word of God is beyond any reasonable doubt. To *evangelize*, or to announce the good news of salvation, is a favorite word in Luke, occurring ten times in his Gospel and twenty-five times in the Acts of the Apostles. So, too, does it occur frequently (twenty-one times) in the Pauline material, where he speaks also (sixty times) of "the gospel." The evangelist delivers not his own word but the word of God (1 Thessalonians 2:13). It is a Gospel to be proclaimed throughout the world (Mark 13:10). After Easter it becomes the message of salvation about Jesus crucified and risen (Acts 8:5; 9:20; 1 Corinthians 1:23; 15:12). The preaching itself shows forth "the glory of Christ, the image of God" (2 Corinthians 4:4). It has been announced "to every creature under heaven" (Colossians 1:23). It is "a message about God's reign" (Matthew 13:19).

The proclamation also takes the form of *teaching* (Acts of the Apostles 4:2,18; 5:21, 25, 28, 42; 11:26; 15:35; 18:11; 20:20; 28:31). It takes place publicly in the Temple and in houses (5:42; 20:20). The proclamation applies Sacred Scripture to the daily life of the community as a word of instruction, of encouragement, and of consolation (14:22; 15:30–32; 1 Thessalonians 2:2; 1 Corinthians 14:3,31). It is sometimes *prophetic* (1 Corinthians 14). The prophets are listed even before the teachers (1 Corinthians 12:28; Ephesians 4:11), and the faithful are said to be built on the foundation of the Apostles and the prophets (Ephesians 2:20; 3:5). On the other hand, there were false prophets or pseudo-prophets against whom the Church had to act (1 Thessalonians 5:21; 1 Corinthians 12:3; 1 John 4:1-3).

Worship and Sacraments

Baptism

Even Rudolf Bultmann acknowledged that there never was a time in the life of the Church when there was no Baptism. The testimony of Paul is particularly important. In the spring of 56 or 55 or perhaps even 54, he wrote from Ephesus to the Church of Corinth that "it was in one Spirit that all of us, Jew or Greek, slave or free, were baptized into one body" (1 Corinthians 12:13). This testimony takes us back biographically to about the year 33, just after Jesus' death. Baptism has its roots, therefore, not in the later Hellenistic churches but in the Jewish-Christian Church, and the Gospels themselves point to the prototype, *the baptism of John.*

John's baptism is characterized by eschatological expectation; it involves a call to repentance; it is administered only once; and it does not introduce one into a sect but is demanded for the whole people. Jesus himself was baptized by John (Mark 1:9-11), and because of that the community was convinced that he approved "a baptism of repentance which led to the forgiveness of sins" (Mark 1:4). The Church baptized not only in memory of John's baptism but also in memory of Jesus.

Easter gave Baptism a completely new meaning. Jesus is now perceived as the risen Lord (Acts of the Apostles 2:36). Salvation is through his death and resurrection. Even though Baptism is still a baptism of repentance for the forgiveness of sins, repentance is seen as a turning to Christ, and the forgiveness of sins occurs on the authority of Christ and by his power. Baptism is administered "in the name of Jesus" (Acts of the Apostles 2:38; 8:16; 10:48; 1 Corinthians 1:13-15; Galatians 3:27; Romans 6:3). By being baptized in the "name" of Jesus, a person becomes subject to him and is committed to his rule and care. The word "name" is a legal concept, signifying authority and competence.

That Baptism is closely linked with the proclamation of the Word is evident in the meeting between the deacon Philip and the Ethiopian court official (Acts of the Apostles 8:26-40), where Baptism follows an instruction on the Scriptures. The content of that Word is the death and resurrection of Christ. Baptism is a Baptism into his death and resurrection (Colossians 2:11-13; 3:1-4; Ephesians 2:5). And just as the Holy Spirit is released through the resurrection, so, too, is the Spirit given in a special way at Baptism (Acts of the Apostles 19:2-6; Titus 3:6). But the effect is not automatic. Baptism without faith is empty, and without openness to the Spirit there is no holiness (1 Corinthians 10:1-13; Hebrews 6:4-8; and all of 1 Peter).

Eucharist

Like Baptism, the Eucharist, or Lord's Supper (the term used in the oldest account in 1 Corinthians 11:20), is rooted in the very beginning of the Church. The Last Supper tradition is ancient and is given in four variant versions: 1 Corinthians 11:23-25; Mark 14:22-25; Matthew 26:26-29; and Luke 22:15-20. The Pauline account dates from the years 54-56 and refers to the fact that Paul handed on this tradition to the Corinthians at the beginning of his missionary activity in Corinth (about 49). But Paul also states that this tradition comes directly from the Lord. Peter was still alive and could have repudiated Paul's account if it were inaccurate. Paul himself lived for many years with members of the Jerusalem Church (Barnabas, Mark, Silas) and took part in the Lord's Supper in various communities. His account must have agreed with those of eyewitnesses.

The more strongly Semitic flavor to Mark's account has led some exegetes to conclude that his is even older than Paul's. The differences between the two accounts are too great, in any event, to assume a common Greek source. On the other hand, the agreement between them in content is so great that we must assume a common Aramaic or Hebrew source.

The meal that Jesus shared with his Apostles was the last of a long series of daily meals he had with his disciples. For Orientals, shared meals have always signified peace, trust, and community. But Jesus also shared meals with sinners, outcasts, and tax collectors, as a sign that the reign of God had begun and was open to all and demanded love of all. The Last Supper, however, was a special meal. It was either a Passover meal or perhaps a farewell meal on the night before the Passover feast. Whichever it was, it was celebrated with a view to the coming Kingdom of God. Indeed, the Kingdom was the focus of everything Jesus did and said, not only at this meal but in his whole life and ministry.

The structure was obviously taken over from the Jewish ritual meal: the words over the bread, followed by its breaking and sharing, and the blessing over the wine. But now Jesus identifies himself with the bread and wine. It is his body which is broken and his blood which is poured out in atonement for sin and for the establishment of a new Covenant. All four texts agree on this. The Jews regarded every death, but particularly the death of an innocent one, as having the character of atonement. And so Jesus could have easily seen his own innocent suffering in this way, without necessarily tying it to the more fully developed theology of the post-resurrection Church.

By distributing the bread and wine as his flesh and blood, Jesus gave his disciples a share in the power of his death to make atonement and to establish a new Covenant. This, too, is a familiar Oriental idea: Eating and drinking communicated divine gifts.

After the resurrection the disciples gathered again and again for these shared meals, but now with the conviction that the risen Christ was in their midst as they gathered in his name (Matthew 18:20). There was joy in their new fellowship: joy over the presence of Christ and joy over the approach of the Kingdom of God (Acts of the Apostles 2:46). It is important to note that the celebration of the Lord's Supper after the death and resurrection of Christ was not an arbitrary act on the part of the Church. The Church was convinced it was following the Lord's own injunction, and indeed it referred to the actions of Jesus at the Last Supper as the pattern and authority for what it did.

The Eucharist, therefore, is a meal of remembrance and thanksgiving, of fellowship, and of anticipation. It looks at once to the past, the present, and the future. "Every time, then, you eat this bread and drink this cup, you proclaim the death of the Lord until he comes!" (1 Corinthians 11:26).

Through the Eucharist, therefore, the Church proclaims its faith in the Lordship of Jesus and in the coming of the Kingdom. Through the Eucharist the Church manifests and more fully recognizes and deepens its unity in Christ (1 Corinthians 10:16-17). Through the Eucharist the Church sets a pattern for its own ministry to those in need (1 Corinthians 11:17-34) and exposes itself thereby to judgment (11:34).

(We shall, of course, be returning to the sacraments of the Church in chapters 21 and 22.)

Mission to All and for All

The Church always understood itself as a missionary community. It reached out, first, to the whole people of Israel (Acts of the Apostles 3:11; 4:1; 5:25, 40, 42), even beyond Jerusalem (9:32-43; Galatians 2:8; 1 Corinthians 9:5), and then to the Gentiles (Matthew 8:11 = Luke 13:28). The transition, however, from the mission to the Jews to the mission to the Gentiles as well did not occur without difficulty, as we have already noted. There was hesitation, to say the least, on the part of the Jewish Christians of

Jerusalem, including the Apostles. Luke, on the other hand, gives a theological foundation for broadening the mission (Acts of the Apostles 28:25-28) and points to an intervention from God and the authority of Peter as factors in changing the situation (10:1—11:8). The differences, however, were not irreconcilable. The Jerusalem Church still had very close ties with the Jews and Jewish ways of thought and customs (1:6; 10:14), and yet James, the leader of the Jerusalem community, declared himself in agreement with the Pauline approach, which dispensed with the absolute need of circumcision and with Paul's mission to the Gentiles (Acts of the Apostles 15; Galations 6:10). Previously, Barnabas, the representative of the Jerusalem Church, had approved the conversion of Greeks in Antioch and indeed had accompanied Paul on his first missionary journey (Acts of the Apostles 13-14).

On the other hand, Jerusalem's privileged position is upheld. The mission to "the ends of the earth" begins from Jerusalem (Acts of the Apostles 1:8; Luke 24:47; Romans 9-11). Israel was to be given its last opportunity for repentance through the apostolic preaching (Acts of the Apostles 2:38; 3:19; 5:31; Mark 7:27; Romans 1:16; 2:9). Historically, the Hellenistic Christians, who had a freer and more open attitude toward paganism, were probably the first to proclaim the Gospel to the Gentiles.

Paul sees the conversion of the Gentiles as a mystery of the history of redemption, after which all of Israel will be saved (Romans 11:25). That the Gentiles are co-heirs of Christ and sharers in the promise Paul sees as a matter of recent revelation in the Spirit (Ephesians 3:5-6). Through their incorporation into the Church, "God's manifold wisdom is made known" (3:10).

HOW DID THE EARLY CHURCH ORGANIZE ITSELF FOR MISSION?

First, there is *no uniform order or structure* to the Church of the New Testament. This varied from place to place. It is not clear, for example, how the Twelve function even in the Jerusalem Church, and why they seem to recede into the background after Acts of the Apostles 6:2, or why the elders are mentioned with them at the Council of Jerusalem, or what rank and position "the

Seven" held (6:6). There is no doubt about Peter's special position, but what of the importance of James, the "brother of the Lord," who assumes a position of pastoral leadership in Jerusalem alongside Peter (12:17; 15:13-21; Galatians 1:19; 2:9) and after Peter leaves (Galatians 2:12; Acts of the Apostles 21:18)?

Secondly, however, there is *some* order and structure which shapes the life and mission of the Church. The Church is never without it, nor can it be without it. In this sense, that order is said to be *constitutive* rather than merely functional. This is not to say that all authority and missionary responsibility were given to the hierarchical few to be exercised in the name of, or for the sake of, the many. On the contrary, the whole congregation was involved in important decisions in this earliest of periods (Acts of the Apostles 15; 1 Corinthians 5). But there were also members who served in some leadership capacity. Local churches were guided by presbyters, and others were appointed as overseers (the original meaning of the word for *bishop, episcopos*; see Acts of the Apostles 20:28). And that is not only Lucan theology. A hierarchically structured community is also at the basis of Paul's listing of the various ministers and ministries in 1 Corinthians 12:28, and he derives these various offices from the Lord himself (Ephesians 4:11). Mention of the Apostles first, and then prophets and teachers, cannot be by chance. There is a sacred order of ministers and pastors who are responsible to their heavenly chief shepherd (1 Peter 5:2-4).

Thirdly, there is *no radical opposition between the charismatic and administrative ministries,* as some Protestant scholars had argued in the past. All of the gifts and charisms have the same source, the Holy Spirit (1 Corinthians 12:11). Some of these gifts are clearly "charismatic"—e.g., the gift of tongues. Others are clearly "administrative" or "institutional"—e.g., teaching and presiding (Romans 12:7-8; Ephesians 4:11-12).

Fourthly, *neither is there any radical opposition between the order of the Jerusalem Church and the order of the Pauline communities.* Despite his absence from Corinth, Paul decides the cases of the incestuous man (1 Corinthians 5:3-5), gives directives for the divine service (11: 17, 33), admonishes and gives concrete prescriptions (7:17; 16:1; Titus 1:5), and gives definite moral guidance

(1 Thessalonians 4:11; 2 Thessalonians 3:4,6,10,12). The Church of Corinth must have recognized his apostolic authority. Why else would they have submitted certain questions to him for decision (1 Corinthians 7:1, and following chapters)? Nor is the picture presented by the Pastoral Epistles (1 and 2 Timothy, and Titus) improbable for the period of consolidation of the Pauline communities.

Fifthly, whatever the office or ministry, it is also for the sake of *service*, never for domination. The model is Jesus, who lays down his life for others (Mark 10:45). The one who humbles himself will be exalted, and vice versa (Luke 14:11; Matthew 23:12). Paul consistently refers to his own office as that of a servant (1 Corinthians 4:1, 9-13; 2 Corinthians 4:5,12,15; 6:4-10; Philippians 2:17).

Sixthly, the chief ministry in the Church is the *Petrine ministry*, i.e., a ministry for the universal Church. Indeed, even if one were to conclude that Jesus did not say "You are Peter and upon this rock I will build my church..." in July of the year 29 at Caesarea Philippi, we still have to contend with the clear fact that this tradition, embedded in Matthew 16:18, was maintained somewhere in the first-century Church and represents a Christian evaluation of Peter's position with which every serious Christian must cope.

Peter was one of the first called, and remained prominent thereafter among Jesus' disciples. He is the most frequently mentioned disciple in all four Gospels. Even the distant Gentile converts of Paul in Galatia know of Peter. He functioned as the spokesman of the Apostles and is always placed first on lists of Apostles (Matthew 10:2). Indeed, he was probably the first to whom the Lord appeared after the resurrection (1 Corinthians 15:5; Luke 24:34; Mark 16:7). This fact alone may explain the prominence of Peter in the early Church, not all of which is explicable in the light of his role during the life of Jesus. That Peter served as the spokesman of the Apostles after the resurrection is clear in the Acts of the Apostles, but it was never a unilateral or unaccountable sort of role. He is also portrayed as consulting with the other Apostles and even being sent by them (8:14). He and John act almost as a team (3:1-11; 4:1-23; 8:14). It was Peter who took the decisive step in ordering the Baptism of the Gentile Cornelius (Acts of the Apostles 10). And although Paul spoke of Peter's ministry as being directed to the circumcised (Galatians 2:7), Peter's influence in Gentile areas is obvious (1 Corinthians 1:12; 1 Peter 1:1).

Whatever the minimal facts of Peter's life and ministry, it is also clear that he became a symbol for Christian thought. He is portrayed as having played many different roles in the life of the Church. Modern New Testament scholars speak of a *trajectory* of biblical images of Peter. It begins with Peter as the great Christian *fisherman* (Luke 5; John 21), then as the *shepherd*, or pastor, of the flock (John 21), then as the Christian *martyr* (John 13:36; 1 Peter 5:1), then as the *receiver of special revelation* (Mark 9:2-8, and parallels; 2 Peter 1:16-18; Acts of the Apostles 5:1-11; 10:9-16; 12:7-9), then as the *confessor of the true faith* (Matthew 16:16-17) and as its *guardian* against false teaching (2 Peter 1:20-21; 3:15-16). He is portrayed also as a weak and sinful man, but a *repentant sinner*. He is reproached by Paul (Galatians 2:11-14), misunderstands Jesus (Mark 9:5-6; John 13:6-11; 18:10-11), is rebuked by Jesus (Mark 8:33; Matthew 16:23) and denies Christ (Mark 14:66-72). But he is rehabilitated. The risen Lord appears to him (John 21:15-17), and he becomes again a source of strength to the Church (Luke 22:32).

Other Apostles were also subjects of similar trajectories, but no trajectory outdistanced Peter's, not even the Twelve's or Paul's. This is even implied already in 2 Peter, where the image of Peter is evoked to correct those who are appealing to Paul.

WHAT IS THE CHURCH OF THE NEW TESTAMENT?
People of God

According to Hebrew ways of thinking, the people forms a whole, a *corporate personality*. The individual takes on meaning, importance, and even destiny insofar as the individual is involved with the people. Israel understood itself as the people of God, by God's own call (Exodus 19:5; 23:22; Deuteronomy 7:6; 14:2; 26:18). "I will take you as my own people, and you shall have me as your

God" (Exodus 6:7). The call to peoplehood is linked with the *Covenant:* "I will look with favor upon you...as I carry out my covenant with you...I will set my Dwelling among you, and will not disdain you. Ever present in your midst, I will be your God, and you will be my people..." (Leviticus 26:9-12). The same connection is to be found in the major prophets (e.g., Jeremiah 32:38-41).

The early Church appropriated this image to itself: "You, however, are 'a chosen race, a royal priesthood, a holy nation, a people he claims for his own to proclaim the glorious works' of the One who called you from darkness into his marvelous light. Once you were no people, but now you are God's people..." (1 Peter 2:9-10). The allusions to the Old Testament are evident: in particular Isaiah 43:20-21, and Exodus 19:6. Undoubtedly, the passage intends to show that the Church is the new People of God purchased by the redemptive work of Christ.

That fundamental text from the Old Testament, "I will take you as my own people, and you shall have me as your God," is cited several times throughout the New Testament and applied to the Church itself, as the new eschatological community. Paul quotes it in 2 Corinthians 6:16 from Ezekiel 37:27 in order to distinguish the Church from the unbelievers. In Hebrews 8:10 it occurs in the lengthy quotation from Jeremiah 31:31-34 to show that this great prophecy has been fulfilled in the new Covenant. And the formula appears finally in Revelation 21:3 in the vision of the future Jerusalem. Indeed, the notion of the Church as the new eschatological People of God is the guiding theme of the Epistle to the Hebrews.

This new People of God, formed out of the remnant of Israel and from many Gentiles, arises out of the love and grace of God: "Once you were no people, but now you are God's people; once there was no mercy for you, but now you have found mercy" (1 Peter 2:10). But, again, it is a "purchased" people, "acquired at the price of his own blood" (Acts of the Apostles 20:28). God makes a new beginning for the human community in grace. The Church is itself the new People of God (Titus 2:14, where the reference again is to Ezekiel 37:23).

Nowhere is the Church spoken of explicitly as the "new" People of God, but there *is* explicit mention of the *new* Covenant

(Luke 22:20; 1 Corinthians 11:25; 2 Corinthians 3:6; Hebrews 8:13; 9:15; 12:24), and that Covenant is connected, at least implicitly, to a new community (Hebrews 8:8-12 cites Jeremiah 31:31-34, where such a link is made). But it is no longer a covenant signed by circumcision, but by faith in Jesus Christ and the "circumcision of Christ" (Colossians 2:11), i.e., Baptism.

A tension between the old and new People of God remains, however, and it is most strongly portrayed in Paul, especially in Romans 9-11. Unbelieving Israel is "Israel according to the flesh" (1 Corinthians 10:18), but believing Israel is "the Israel of God" (Galatians 6:16). God calls us, Jew and Gentile alike. "There does not exist among you Jew or Greek, slave or freeman, male or female. All are one in Christ Jesus. Futhermore, if you belong to Christ you are the descendants of Abraham, which means you inherit all that was promised" (Galatians 3:28-29).

But even in the New Testament the new People of God are not identical with the community of the elect. In other words, membership in the Church is no guarantee of participation in the Kingdom of God. There are false prophets in the Church who will be repudiated by the Lord at the end (Matthew 7:22-23). All evildoers will be cast out (13:41-43). On the other side, many who did not belong to the Church will be acknowledged by the Son of Man as his brothers and sisters (25:31-46). "He will dispatch his angels and assemble his chosen from the four winds, from the farthest bounds of earth and sky" (Mark 13:27). The final test will be a just life. No one will enter the marriage feast without a wedding garment (Matthew 22:11-13).

Body of Christ

If the People-of-God image underlines the Church's intimate connection with Israel and with God's call to a covenant relationship, the Body-of-Christ image underlines the Church's intimate connection with Jesus Christ and with God's call to a communal relationship, one with another in Christ.

The image is, of course, distinctively Pauline, although it bears some affinity with the Johannine allegory of the vine and the branches (John 15:1-8). The Church in the New Testament is the

People of God, but a people newly constituted in Christ and in relation to Christ. The two images, therefore, are not mutually opposed. The Church is the People of God insofar as it is the Body of Christ, and it is the Body of Christ insofar as it is the People of God. In principle, both images are rooted in the Old Testament idea of *corporate personality*.

The conception of the Church as Body of Christ is grounded in the union that exists between the Christian and the *risen* body of Christ. Just as the resurrection is central to New Testament Christology, so is it central to New Testament, and especially Pauline, ecclesiology. When the Christian shares in the bread of the Eucharist, he or she becomes one body with Christ (1 Corinthians 10:16-17). Thus, the one who eats or drinks unworthily profanes the body of the Lord (11:27) and eats and drinks unto his or her own condemnation (11:29). It is in one body that Christ has reconciled us to the Father by his death (Ephesians 2:16-17; Colossians 1:22). The Church has become one body, his own, in which the Holy Spirit dwells (Ephesians 4:4). Christians are called one body (Colossians 3:15).

The physical realism of the union between Christ and the Church lies behind the development from the notion of one body "in" Christ (Romans and 1 Corinthians) to one Body "of" Christ (Ephesians and Colossians). But it *is* a development. In Romans 12:4-21 and in 1 Corinthians 12:4-27, for example, the application of the image refers more to the union of Christians with each other than with Christ. It speaks of a diversity of charisms and offices which, despite their multiplicity, do not compromise the fundamental unity of the Church. The members are one because they are baptized by one spirit into one body (1 Corinthians 12:13). They are called not one body "in" Christ but one body "of" Christ (12:27). The same identity is presupposed in 1 Corinthians 6:15: "Do you not see that your bodies are members of Christ?" Indeed, it is because the Christian is really a member of the body of Christ that he or she can also be called metaphorically a temple of the Holy Spirit (6:19).

The ideas of these earlier letters are presupposed as the Body of Christ image is introduced, with seeming abruptness, in Ephesians 1:23 and Colossians 1:24. Christ is now called the head of his

Body the Church (Ephesians 5:23; Colossians 1:18; 2:19). As head of the Church, Christ is the principle of union and growth (Ephesians 4:16; Colossians 2:19). The Body of Christ is something that is to be built up (Ephesians 4:12,16).

With some measure of urgency, the Pauline author of Ephesians pleads with the community to "live a life worthy of the calling...(to) make every effort to preserve the unity which has the Spirit as its origin and peace as its binding force. There is but one body and one Spirit" (4:1-4; see also Colossians 3:12-15).

Temple of the Holy Spirit

Because the Church is the Body of Christ it can also be called the Temple of the Holy Spirit. Here again the *resurrection* is central. The Spirit proceeds from the "Lord of the Spirit," who through his resurrection has become "a life-giving spirit" (1 Corinthians 15:45). There is, of course, a special outpouring of the Spirit at Pentecost, as the fruit of Christ's saving action (Acts of the Apostles 1:8; 2:3-4,38; 4:8,31; 6:8; 9:17; 11:24; 13:52; 19:2). This thought is particularly clear in John where it is asserted that the Spirit could not be given until the Lord had been glorified (7:39; 6:63). The risen and exalted Lord releases the Spirit and with the Spirit builds his Church. The Body of Christ "takes shape as a holy temple in the Lord...to become a dwelling place for God in the Spirit (Ephesians 2:21-22). Jew and Gentile alike have "access in one Spirit to the Father" (2:18).

Just as Jesus identified himself with the Temple, so the Body of Christ is itself the new Temple (1 Corinthians 3:9, 16-17; 2 Corinthians 6:16; Ephesians 2:19-22). The Church is now the place of God's dwelling. It is, in the theological sense of the word, a *mystery*, i.e., "a reality imbued with the hidden presence of God" (Pope Paul VI, at the opening of the second session of Vatican II, September 1963).

The Spirit is manifested in various ways, witnessing to the presence and activity of God in the Church (Acts of the Apostles 2:3-13; 10:47; 11:17; 15:8). The Spirit teaches the disciples what to say (Luke 12:12), reveals the mysteries of God (Luke 1:41,67; Acts of the Apostles 11:28; 13:9), inspires prophecy (2:18), is the source of wisdom (6:3), faith (6:5; 2 Corinthians 4:13), encouragement (Acts of the Apostles 9:31), joy (13:52), hope (Romans 15:13; 1 Corinthians 14:14-16; 2:4-5; Galatians 3:5), and love (Romans 5:5; Colossians 1:18; Galatians 5:13-36).

The Spirit directs the officers of the Church in important decisions (Acts of the Apostles 13:2; 15:28; 20:28). The Spirit is conferred upon all of the members at Baptism (19:2,6; 2:38-39; 15:8-9; 8:16-18; 9:17; 10:44; 11:16-17) and at the imposition of hands (8:14-17; 19:6). The gifts of the Spirit are for the building up of the Church (1 Corinthians 14:12,26). By his or her union with the Spirit of the risen Christ, the Christian rises in a spiritual body (1 Corinthians 15:35-50). The Christian's and the Church's present possession of the Spirit is a foretaste (Romans 8:23) and a pledge (2 Corinthians 1:22; 5:5) of the salvation, i.e., of the Kingdom of God, that is to come.

SUMMARY

1.   The mystery of the Church flows directly from the mystery of Christ. The Church is the Body of Christ and carries forward his mission.

2.   Did Jesus found the Church? Was his evaluation of the Church identical with the Church's evaluation of itself? There is a spectrum of answers to these questions: *non-scholarly conservatism*, which insists on continuity (between Jesus' intentions and the Church's self-understanding) without development within the New Testament itself; *non-scholarly liberalism*, which denies all continuity and ignores even the ecclesiology of the New Testament; *scholarly liberalism*, which does not ignore the ecclesiology of the New Testament but denies its origin in Jesus because he expected the Kingdom of God as imminent; *Bultmannian existentialism*, which acknowledges some continuity between Jesus' proclamation of the Kingdom and membership in the community of faith here and now, but rejects the development toward sacramentalism in the Fourth Gospel and in Hellenistic Christianity; and *scholarly conservatism*, which admits continuity within development, but which divides Catholic from Protestant on the degree of sacramental and ministerial structure that is necessary or "constitutive" for the life and mission of the Church.

3.   Jesus did *not* intend to found a Church if by *found* we mean some direct, explicit, deliberate act by which he established a new religious organization. He never addresses a select group of people; he

imposes no specific rule of life; he makes no connection between membership in his circle with salvation.

4. Jesus *did* found a Church, at least indirectly; i.e., he laid the foundations for it. First, he gathered disciples around him for the proclamation of the Kingdom of God. Secondly, he anticipated an interim period between his death and the final coming of the Kingdom. Thirdly, at the Last Supper and in the injunction to Peter, he looked toward the disciples' staying together even after his death.

5. The word *church* is from the Greek *"ekklēsia,"* which refers in its original political meaning to an assembly of citizens who enjoy full civil rights. It was taken over by the Greek-speaking Jews to translate the Hebrew word *kāhāl*. Not until the admission of Gentiles to the community did the word *ekklēsia* apply to the Church alone, over against Judaism.

6. Did the early Christian community understand itself as Church? Yes, in both local and universal senses. *Church* as *local* church is mentioned twenty-three times in the Acts of the Apostles and in most of the sixty-five references to Church in the Pauline literature. In Ephesians and Colossians, however, *Church* is used in its *universal* sense, as the fullness of Christ. At other times, *Church* refers to a small *house* community (as in Romans 16:5 and Philemon 2) or to *particular congregations* (1 Corinthians 11:18,20,33-34; 14:23). All references in the Johannine literature (at least twenty-three) are to particular churches.

7. The local Church is not simply a subdivision of the Church universal, nor is the Church universal simply the sum total or composite of local churches. There is not a Corinthian division of the Church, for example, but "the church of God which is in Corinth" (1 Corinthians 1:2).

8. *There is no individualistic Christianity in the New Testament.* Belief in Christ and life in Christ are to be found only within the community of believers joined to the Lord. All of the New Testament writers write as members of the one Church of Jesus Christ.

9. The Church did not begin at *Pentecost*. It already existed by that time. But Pentecost was the moment when the Church was endowed in a special way with power from on high, i.e., the power of the Holy Spirit, as the firstfruits of the Kingdom of God.

10. The early Church did not understand itself as just another Jewish sect or a new religious organization. It was a community transformed by the presence of the *Holy Spirit*.

11. The Jewish-Christian Church of *Jerusalem* maintained many links with Judaism: strong attachment to the Temple, continuation of certain Jewish practices, and a sharing of goods. It was eventually marked by conflict over the need for circumcision and the observance of

the dietary laws. As in all of the churches, the Eucharist was its central act of worship.

12.   The Jewish-Hellenistic Church of *Antioch* was a model of harmony between Jews and Gentiles. Here the followers of Christ were called "Christians" for the first time. Prophets and teachers were active here, and the gifts of the Spirit were evident.

13.   The Hellenistic-Gentile Church of *Corinth* was also marked by the gifts of the Spirit, but they were often sources of division rather than unity. On the other hand, the apostolic preaching and instruction were carried on, as was the worship of God in the Eucharist.

14.   Despite the differences among these three different types of churches, certain *common elements* remain: faith in Jesus as Messiah and Lord, the practice of Baptism and the celebration of the Eucharist, the apostolic preaching and instruction, regard for communal love, and the expectation of the Kingdom of God. Freedom was allowed in most other matters.

15.   The *mission* of the Church, like the mission of Jesus, centered on the *Kingdom of God*. The Church lives between-the-times, between the Kingdom as promised and the Kingdom as realized fully. As such the Church is at once a *Church of glory* (the firstfruits of the Kingdom, i.e., the Holy Spirit, are already present in the Church), and a *Church of the cross* (it continues to be joined to the sufferings and death of Christ).

16.   The Church, therefore, is both *sign* and *instrument* of the Kingdom. It is sent by Christ to proclaim the Kingdom of God, to make disciples of all nations, to baptize them in the name of the Father, the Son, and the Holy Spirit, to forgive sins, and thereby to break the power of Satan. The orientation of the Church to the Kingdom is explicit in the Eucharist.

17.   The mission of the Church, more specifically, includes the *proclamation* of the Word (evangelization): a message about the crucifed and risen Jesus, about the reign of God. It may also take the form of teaching and prophecy.

18.   The mission also includes *worship and sacraments* , especially Baptism and the Eucharist. *Baptism* is always into the death and resurrection of Jesus. As such, it is an act of repentance and forgiveness of sins. The *Eucharist*, or Lord's Supper, whose structure is taken over from the Jewish ritual meal, is an act of remembrance and thanksgiving, of fellowship, and of anticipation of the Kingdom.

19.   The mission is *to all* and *for all*. This did not happen without some reluctance, even sharp conflict. But eventually the Church understood itself as having a mandate to reach out to the Gentiles, who are co-heirs of Christ and sharers in the promise given to Israel in the past.

20.   There is *no uniform order or structure* in the New Testament Church. It varied from place to place. On the other hand, all churches had *some* order and structure. Some members served in leadership roles as presbyters, bishops, elders, etc. All ministers were responsible to the chief shepherd in heaven.

21.   There is no radical opposition between the charismatic and administrative ministries. All have the same source: the Holy Spirit.

22.   Neither is there any radical opposition between the Jerusalem Church and the Pauline churches. Paul's apostolic authority was recognized and exercised even in the freer communities of the Hellenistic world.

23.   All offices and ministries are for the sake of *service*, never for domination. Jesus is always the model.

24.   The chief ministry in the Church is the *Petrine* , a ministry to and for the universal Church. Even if Jesus did not say, "You are Peter...," it is clear that the early Church believed in the primacy of Peter. Among other things, he was probably the first to whom the risen Lord appeared. There is a trajectory of images about Peter (fisherman, shepherd, guardian of the faith, etc.) which tend to support the special status he came to enjoy in the eyes of the New Testament and post-biblical Church.

25.   The Church of the New Testament is also portrayed according to various *images*, the most important of which are three: People of God, Body of Christ, and Temple of the Holy Spirit.

26.   The Church is *People of God*. The image is linked with the Old Testament notions of *corporate personality* and *covenant*. The former reminds us that the destiny of the individual is wrapped up with the fortunes of the whole people, and the latter reminds us that the people are constituted as a people by reason of God's covenant with them: "I will be your God, and you will be my people" (Leviticus 26:12). The Church is founded on a *new Covenant* in Christ. Entrance into the new People of God is not by circumcision but by faith and Baptism. The new People of God are not entirely separate from the old Israel. Many in Israel have come to believe; the rest will enter in God's own good time. All are called as one in Christ.

27.   The Church is the *Body of Christ*. Here, too, the notion of *corporate personality* is significant. Christians are united to the *risen* Christ and therefore to one another "in Christ." We are baptized into his body, and become one with the body by partaking of the body and blood in the Eucharist. Christ is *head* of the body, as principle of unity and growth. All must live according to the calling, to manifest the unity that is the Church.

28.   The Church is the *Temple of the Holy Spirit*. It is "a dwelling place for God in the Spirit" (Ephesians 2:21–22). The risen and exalted Lord releases the Spirit and with the Spirit builds the Church, as a temple. The Spirit is manifested in various ways and is the source of wisdom and strength. The gifts of the Spirit are for the building up of the Church. And the Spirit is itself a foretaste and a pledge of the Kingdom that is to come.

SUGGESTED READINGS

Brown, Raymond E., et al. *Peter in the New Testament: A Collaborative Assessment by Protestant and Roman Catholic Scholars*. New York: Paulist Press, 1973.

Minear, Paul. *Images of the Church in the New Testament.* Philadelphia: Westminster Press, 1960.

Robinson, John A. T. *The Body: A Study in Pauline Theology* . London: S. C. M. Press, 1952.

Schnackenburg, Rudolf. *The Church in the New Testament* . New York: Herder & Herder, 1965.

Schweizer, Eduard. *Church Order in the New Testament*. London: S. C. M. Press, 1961.

Zehnle, Richard. *The Making of the Christian Church*. Notre Dame, Ind.: Fides Press, 1969.

TWENTIETH-CENTURY VIEWS OF THE ECCLESIOLOGY OF THE NEW TESTAMENT

Non-Scholarly Liberalism	Scholarly Liberalism	Bultmannian Existentialism	Scholarly Conservatism	Non-Scholarly Conservatism
There is no continuity at all between the Church's evaluation of itself and Jesus' evaluation of the Church. Jesus came to teach us a way of life centered on love and based on freedom from institutional oppression. Jesus did not intend to found a Church in any sense. He came only to preach the Kingdom of God. Liberalism has emerged within Catholicism in recent years as a reaction against ecclesiastical authoritarianism and doctrinal and moral fundamentalism.	Because of Jesus's own expectation of the Kingdom as imminent, bringing an end to this world order, he did not intend to found a Church. With the delay of the *parousia* until after the death and resurrection of Jesus, the Church perceived itself as the ultimate Messianic Community of the Saints, the elect of the final generation, Jews and Gentiles alike, who would soon enter a new form of being in the new aeon. With the delay of the *parousia* well beyond the death and resurrection, the post-apostolic Church abandoned this Pauline view and assumed some organizational form suggesting some historical permanence. Expressed by Johannes Weiss (1892) and especially in Martin Werner's *The Formation of Christian Dogma* (1941).	In reaction to Liberalism, Bultmann insisted that Jesus linked entrance into the Kingdom of God with affiliation with the Jewish people, as the eschatological community. He rejects the Liberal view that Jesus' expectation of the Kingdom as imminent led him to expound only an interim ethic. On the other hand, Jesus never thought of a mission to the Gentiles, nor would he have countenanced the sacramentalism of the Fourth Gospel and of Hellenistic Christianity.	Most scholars today admit a stronger and broader continuity between the Church's self-evaluation and Jesus' evaluation of the Church. Yet they recognize growth and development in New Testament ecclesiology. But there is continuity in development. Differences between Catholic and Protestant scholars are more a reflection of theological and doctrinal commitments than of exegetical differences. Catholics emphasize the Church's role in mediating salvation more than Protestants do, and this accounts for some differences in approach toward questions of sacramental and ministerial order. Recent ecumenical dialogues, however, suggest a growing convergence of views.	Jesus left the Twelve Apostles a detailed blueprint for a Church: seven sacraments with precise matter and form, the papacy as vested with supreme and universal jurisdiction, the monarchical episcopate, doctrines, liturgies, and laws. The Church's evaluation of itself (as given in Counter-Reformation and pre-Vatican II theology) and Jesus' evaluation of the Church are identical. A view held by Catholics until the Second Vatican Council and the application of biblical studies to ecclesiology in the 1960s.

·XVIII·

THE CHURCH IN HISTORY

THE PROBLEM

This chapter is deliberately entitled "The Church in History" rather than "The History of the Church." Even from a practical point of view, the second project would have been impossible, given the limitations of both purpose and space. But the second project would also have been less appropriate on ecclesiological grounds as well. We are not so much interested here in the accumulated past of the Church as in the impact history itself has had upon the Church, and the Church upon history. *The relationship between the Church and history is a theological one.* It has to do with the presence of grace in the world, with the direction and destiny of the world toward the Kingdom of God, and with the role of the Church in proclaiming, celebrating, exemplifying, and serving that reality of grace, as personified in Jesus Christ, by which the world is alive and in movement toward perfection. (The reader is referred again to the discussion of revelation and history in chapter 7.)

But whether one is discussing the history *of* the Church or the Church *in* history, some logical order must be imposed upon the massive amount of data one confronts. To talk at all about the Church from an historical point of view is to talk about *something* historical. What should that be, and in what context(s)? What should be passed over, and why? On what basis can the selected material be systematized (for if not systematized, it is unusable)? Which divisions are to be employed, and why? Who, after all, "consecrated" the usual tripartite structure: ancient, medieval, and modern? What is the "early Church"? If the Church (and the world) is still in existence in the year 20,000, will not the late twentieth century look very much like the "early Church" to our brothers and sisters of that future period? And from the vantage point of the year 20,000, what possible meaning can the term Middle Ages have?

The earliest Christian historians divided history in various ways. Some used the *six world-ages,* analogous to the six days of creation, each world-day the equivalent of one thousand years. "In the Lord's eyes, one day is as a thousand years and a thousand years are as a day" (2 Peter 3:8). The seventh day, the universal Sabbath, would bring the *millennium,* when all those who had died "for their witness to Jesus and the word of God" would come "to life again and (reign) with Christ for a thousand years" (Revelation 20:4-5). *Millenarianism* has always had a sympathetic hearing in the Church, albeit at the fringes rather than at the center of the Christian community: Anabaptists, Adventists, Mormons, Jehovah's Witnesses, and others.

Other historians used the *four world-empires*—Assyrian-Babylonian, Persian, Macedonian, and Roman—by way of interpreting Daniel 2:36-45 and 7:2-27. The fourth of these empires, the Roman, is now Christianized and will last until the end of the world. This explains why so many Christians clung to the Roman "way" well into the Middle Ages.

Still other historians have employed the threefold *Augustinian schema*: before the law (*ante legem*), under the law (*sub lege*), and after the law (*post legem*). There were variations. Some substituted *grace* for *law,* and Joachim of Flora (d. 1202) imposed a trinitarian perspective: the Old Testament as the age of the Father, the New Testament as the age of the Son, and the post-New Testament period as the age of the Holy Spirit. Joachim prophesied that in the year 1260 the Petrine hierarchical Church would be replaced by the new Johannnine Church of the Spirit.

Theologically, the Church has had two major historical moments and is now moving into a third. The *first* was its *Jewish* moment. The Christ-event was proclaimed in the beginning within and to Israel. This is the period of Jewish Christianity, centered in Jerusalem. The *second* is, or was, its *culturally-determined* moment, when the Church became the Church of

Hellenism, of Europe, of North America, and so forth. The *transition* or, perhaps more accurately, the *break* between the first and second moments was signaled by the decision (or series of decisions) to carry the Gospel to the Gentiles without imposing circumcision or other Jewish laws and customs on the new Christians.

As we noted in the previous chapter, Jesus did not explicitly anticipate this widening of the mission. When Peter had to justify his baptizing of Cornelius, the Roman centurion, he appealed not to some specific directive of Jesus but to the prompting and instruction of the Holy Spirit (Acts of the Apostles 11:12). Paul made exactly the same appeal (Acts of the Apostles 16:9; 18:9; 20:22; 22:21; *et passim*; see also Ephesians 3:5-6). But if something as "essential" as circumcision could be set aside, what can and must be retained from the Old Testament? Moreover, the Church would also change the Sabbath, move the center from Jerusalem to Rome, and modify various ethical and disciplinary principles. We simply do not have, at this point, a clear theology of explanation for this substantial, perhaps even radical, break between Jewish Christianity and Gentile Christianity.

The *third* moment, whose inauguration was heralded by the Second Vatican Council, is the movement from a Church of cultural confinement (especially of European and North American confinement) to a genuine *world Church*. There is as much misunderstanding of, and resistance to, this transition to a world Church as there was to the transition to a Church of the Gentiles in the first century. Today's resistance has ample precedent: in the rites controversy of the seventeenth century (to which brief reference will be made later in this chapter), in the insistence on the Latin language in liturgy and in all official communications, in the imposition of canon (Roman) law on the whole Church, in the enforcement of certain culturally conditioned styles of Christian life (e.g., clerical celibacy), and in the rejection of the religious experiences of non-European cultures.

Given this theological schema, which Karl Rahner in particular has proposed, the material in this chapter is not so much an outline of the Church's course throughout all of its history thus far as it is an outline of the Church's course in the *second moment* of its still-very-young history. Even within that second moment, i.e., the period of the Church's cultural confinement especially within European culture, there are transitions and breaks to which attention is given here.

We shall be relying, with some modifications, on the divisions proposed by H. Jedin and August Franzen: (1) the Church within Graeco-Roman civilization (first through the seventh centuries); (2) the Church as the dominant presence in the West (about 700-1300); (3) the disintegration of Christian unity and the transition to a wider mission (1300-1750); and (4) the Church in the period of industrialization and technology (nineteenth and twentieth centuries). The transition from one period to the next has always involved a crisis or series of crises, which we spoke of in chapter 1. Choices had to be made about abandoning older approaches and structures and selecting new ones. We are obviously in another period of crisis today, but one far more profound than any of those which marked the life of the Church within its *second moment* alone.

THE CHURCH AND HISTORY

But the question "*How* shall we organize the data?" is less important than the question "*What* is it that we are organizing?" What do we mean by *Church* and *history?*

If the *Church* is principally a hierarchical society, with the pope at the top of the pyramid and the bishops just below him, then the history of the "Church" is the history of the popes, of ecumenical councils, of heresies and schisms, of contests with the secular government, and the like. And that is precisely what many (indeed, too many) histories of the Church appear to be.

If, on the other hand, the Church is primarily the People of God—laity, religious, and clergy alike—then its history includes more than papal initiatives, conciliar definitions, and struggles for power, whether from the outside or from within. History has to take into account the lives and achievements of the vast majority of the Church's membership: its laity, its religious, and its so-called lower clergy.

If, furthermore, the Church is the Body of Christ, it must be incarnate in history and affected by history, as Jesus was (see especially chapter 15). It is not like some gust of wind that blows through a house, scattering loose items but without any effect upon itself.

And if the Church is, finally, the Temple of the Holy Spirit, it must be infinitely adaptable to the changing circumstances of history, without compromise of its fundamental identity or without loss of the radical unity given by the Spirit.

Here, of course, we raise again the issue of classicism versus historical consciousness. The *classicist* perceives the Church as a static, essentially unchanging reality, by divine decree and guidance immune to process. The Church moves through history, but is affected by it only at the most external levels. Change is always cosmetic, or, as some are fond of saying, "semantic." The *historically conscious* approach understands history as a human as well as a divine phenomenon. What occurs is also the result of human passions, human decisions, and human actions. And just as each person is different from the other, so is each event and each culture. But not only are the "events" of history contingent. So, too, are the *interpretations* of those "events." The historian himself or herself is a particular person, of a particular family and nation, of a particular economic and social status, with particular intellectual strengths and limitations, with particular theological and philosophical commitments, with particular associations and experiences.

We cannot define *history*, therefore, as simply the residue or sum total of "what happened." *Data* have to be translated into *facts,* and facts have to be *interpreted* by reason of their *interrelationship* with other facts. But who, apart from God, has access to all the data? And who, apart from God, knows all the facts? And who, apart from God, sees all the facts in their exact interrelationship with one another?

Consequently, history is always written by those with limited data, fewer facts, and faulty perspective. That is why histories of the same reality can differ so markedly, not only in terms of how facts are interpreted, but even in terms of *which facts* are considered. Thus, we have had histories of the Church which pay no attention at all to the development of spirituality or to the social, political, economic, and cultural impact of Christian faith on the emergence and maintenance of such units as neighborhoods.

The history of the Church is reflection on the *mystery* of the Church, i.e., on the active, continuous, and purposive presence of God in the world through the Christian community. God calls and moves the world to the Kingdom of God. The Church is the sign and instrument of that call and movement. The Church itself is called and is in movement toward the Kingdom. The whole process by which the world, and the Church within the world, is moving toward the Kingdom is what we know as *history*.

Since the call requires a *free response* (see again chapter 5 on the fundamental relationship between nature and grace), history is not only the history of God's interventions in human affairs, as the classicist believes. Furthermore, since both the call and the movement toward the Kingdom are given in *grace*, history is not only the history of contingent human events, as the historicists have contended. (We distinguish here between *historicism* and historical consciousness. Historicism is a form of historical consciousness, but it is not the only form.)

THE CHURCH IN THE GRAECO-ROMAN PERIOD
(FIRST THROUGH SEVENTH CENTURIES)
The New Testament Period

This comprises at least the first two generations of Christians, and probably carries forward into the middle of the second century. It is the period already considered in the previous chapter. It is marked, first, by the preaching and ministry of Jesus and his impact on his disciples and those beyond the circle of his followers; secondly, by the preaching and teaching of the disciples and by the prayers and practices of the earliest converts; and, thirdly, by the formation of stable communities, or churches, from which the various New Testament writings emerged.

The principal crisis of this earliest period was the decision to extend the mission to the Gentiles without, at the same time, imposing Jewish law and practice upon them (as the *Judaizers* insisted). This first great controversy was adjudicated at the

Council of Jerusalem (ca. 50), thanks to the "decision of the Holy Spirit" (Acts of the Apostles 15:28), and the leadership of Peter and James (15:1-29).

Second and Third Centuries

As the young Church progressively detached itself from Judaism and entered the mainstream of Graeco-Roman civilization, it confronted the challenge of communicating the message of Jesus across diverse social, intellectual, and cultural lines. This task fell in the beginning upon the *Apostolic Fathers* (so called because they were themselves pupils of the Apostles) and the *Apologists,* or defenders of the faith. By the end of the century a major theological center was established in *Alexandria*, Egypt. Less than a hundred years later, another such center would be founded in *Antioch,* Syria. The two schools, as we pointed out in chapter 13, would become principal competing forces in the great Christological debates of the fourth and fifth centuries.

A correct understanding of the Gospel was a problem not only for those still outside the Church, but for some inside as well. Already the community, summoned to unity by its Lord (John 17:20-23), was wracked by heresy: principally *Gnosticism* (salvation is through "knowledge" available only to an elite few), *Adoptionism* (Jesus was not truly divine), and *Docetism* (Jesus only "seemed" to be human). It was because of the challenge of Gnosticism, with its appeal to private sources of revelation, that the Church was compelled to establish the *canon,* or list, of Sacred Scripture as the sole norm of faith and to underscore the role of the bishops, standing in *apostolic succession* to the Apostles, as official interpreters or guarantors of the apostolic tradition.

From the latter half of the second century, the bishops began meeting in *synods* to present a common defense against these heresies, now including the *purist* (holier than the Church) extremes: *Manichaeism* (material realities, including marriage, are to be renounced), *Montanism* (no sins committed after Baptism can be forgiven) and *Donatism* (a sacrament is not valid if the minister of the sacrament is in the state of mortal sin). The more widespread the heresy, the more broadly based were the synods.

Local synods were replaced by provincial synods. It would not be until the beginning of the fourth century that the Church would hold its first *ecumenical* council (literally, a council representing the "whole wide world") at Nicea.

Once Christianity began making an impact upon society, it came to the notice of those completely uninterested in such internal theological disputes. As one Catholic historian has written, "The established state cult of the emperor could hardly be expected to favor a religion founded by an executed criminal" (John P. Dolan, *Catholicism*, p. 11). But more offensive even than the character of its "founder" was Christianity's absolute claims. It was not proposed as just one new religion among many, but as the *true* religion. "In a culture and civilization toward which they had contributed nothing, the Christians, by rejecting the religious pluralism of the Roman state, made themselves public enemies" (Dolan, p. 11).

Until the middle of the second century, however, the *persecution* of Christians was of a local nature with a relatively small number of victims. It is important to remember that all accounts of the persecutions were written by Christians, whose characterizations of the emperors were not entirely disinterested. On the other hand, there would be many instances of severe repression and cruelty in later years, especially in the reigns of Decius (d. 251) and Diocletian (d. 305), with a forty-year period of peace and missionary success in between, under the emperor Gallienus (d. 268).

Fourth Century

The conversion of Constantine (d. 337) in the year 312 marked another great turning point in the historical progress of the Church. As noted in chapter 1, the new emperor pursued a vigorous campaign against pagan practices and lavished money and monuments upon the Church. Roman law was modified to accommodate Christian values, and the clergy were accorded privileged status. Opinions differ about the long-term effects of this display of imperial favor. For some historians it signaled the beginning of a sort of *Caesaro-papism* (Caesar is pope), with the Church utterly dependent upon the state and forced eventually to subordinate its spiritual interests to political considerations. For others, the conversion of Constantine provided the Church with extraordinary opportunities for proclaiming the Gospel to all nations and for bringing necessary order into its doctrinal and liturgical life. It also allowed the Church to be less defensive about pagan culture, to learn from it and be enriched by it. On the other hand, the end of the age of persecutions and "least favored status" also meant the end of a certain quality of Christian commitment, a development not without parallel today.

The protest against this development gave rise to the *monastic movement*. Although the roots of monasticism reach back into the pre-Constantinian period, the great monastic exodus from society coincided with the era of Constantine. When the multitudes entered the Church, the monks went into the desert, not as an escape but as an encounter with the demons who inhabited those waterless places. Anthony of Egypt (d. 356), generally regarded as the founder of monasticism, had withdrawn into the desert in 285 and remained there for twenty years living a hermit's existence. Only under Anthony's contemporary Pachomius (d. 346) did the movement to the desert (the root meaning of the word *hermit*) become communal, according to organized patterns of life.

Monasticism had an almost-immediate impact on the Church. Bishops began to be recruited from among those with some monastic training. Athanasius, for example, was a disciple of Anthony. According to August Franzen, "The strong missionary impetus, the remarkable development of pastoral care, the effort to Christianize the Roman State, and above all the theological work of the great councils of the 4th to the 7th century are inconceivable without monasticism" ("Church History," *The Concise Sacramentum Mundi*, p. 264). On the other hand, when monks were transferred to episcopal sees, they also tended to bring with them some of their monastic mores, particularly celibacy and a certain disdain for ordinary human experiences. The separation between leaders and the general membership of the Church, therefore, was not only on the basis of office and power but also on the basis of spirituality.

The Doctrinal Controversies
of the Fourth and Fifth Centuries

We have already reviewed in chapters 9, 10, and 13 the history of the doctrinal controversies regarding the Trinity and the mystery of Jesus Christ. All of these occurred in the Greek-speaking East.

Over against pagan polytheism, the Apostolic Fathers and the Apologists had consistently stressed the doctrine of the one God, the Father, the Almighty. In the third century the emphasis shifted to the triune pluralism of God when the Church could no longer avoid the difficult questions posed by the apparent discrepancy between its uncompromising monotheism and the clear testimony of Sacred Scripture and of the Church's liturgical life that Jesus Christ is also Lord, and that upon rising from the dead he gave the Church his Spirit.

One of the earliest attempts at a solution to the problem of the one-and-the-three proved unorthodox, namely, the *Arian* solution, which made Christ something more than man but less than God, the Almighty. The implications were serious: If Christ is a creature like us, he has no special standing before God as savior, and we are still in our sins.

The first general, or ecumenical, council in the history of the Church was called by the emperor Constantine in 325. Over two hundred and fifty bishops assembled at *Nicea,* the imperial summer residence. Representation from the West was negligible: five priests. The pope was not present, nor did he send any special legates. Nonetheless, the council gave what the Church has subsequently accepted as the definitive answer to Arius. The Son does not "emanate" from the Father's will, as a creature. The Son is "begotten, not made." He is "of the same substance" (*homoousios*) as the Father. For the first time, the Church moved officially from biblical to speculative categories to define the faith.

This transition did not occur without opposition. Followers of Eusebius of Caesarea preferred to say no more than what Scripture seemed to be saying, namely, that the Son is "like" (*homoiousios*) the Father. Through the efforts of Athanasius and Hilary of

Poitiers, the two sides were reconciled at the Council of Alexandria in 362, from which emerged a new orthodox formula, "one substance, three persons."

Meanwhile, others pressed the Nicean definition too far in the opposite direction. Apollinaris of Laodicea, a member of the Alexandrian School, placed so much emphasis on the Word as the unique principle of life in Jesus Christ that Jesus was left with no human soul at all. *Apollinarianism* was condemned at the First Council of Constantinople in 381. This was also the council that approved the so-called *Nicaeo-Constantinopolitan Creed*, expressing faith in the fullness of the Blessed Trinity: Father, Son, *and* Holy Spirit. It was the so-called *Cappadocian Fathers* (Basil, Gregory of Nyssa, and Gregory of Nazianzus) who established the co-equal divinity of the Spirit with the Father and the Son.

Still another theological approach developed at Antioch. Concerned with the emphasis of the Alexandrians on the divinity of Christ and intent upon preserving the humanity of Jesus, the Antiochenes preferred to regard the relationship between Jesus and the Word more loosely, to the point where Jesus seemed to be divided in two. Thus, Mary was said to be the Mother of Jesus the man but not the Mother of God. This was the position of Nestorius, and of *Nestorianism*. Nestorius was opposed by Cyril of Alexandria and then condemned by the Council of Ephesus in 431.

But Cyril's views were themselves carried to an extreme by Eutyches, a monk in Constantinople, who argued that Christ's human nature was completely absorbed by the divine nature so that we have not only one divine person but also one divine nature (*physis*). Thus, the heresy was known as *Monophysitism*. The Council of Chalcedon in 451 condemned Monophysitism and reaffirmed the earlier condemnation of Nestorianism. The Alexandrians were satisfied with the council's formula, "one and the same Lord Jesus Christ," and the Antiochenes were pleased with the formula, "the same truly God and truly man composed of rational soul and body...like us in all things but sin...."

During this same period theological activity in the Latin West was significantly less pronounced. *Augustine,* of course, was the principal figure and *Pelagianism* the principal heresy. Here the concern was with the doctrines of justification and grace. It was Augustine who led the fight against those who assumed that salvation is the result of human effort alone.

The "Barbarian Invasions"

By the beginning of the fifth century, the West was also caught up in the great Germanic migrations: The Visigoths in southern France (Gaul) and Spain, the Vandals in North Africa, and the Ostrogoths and Lombards in Italy. Augustine died in 430, while the Vandals were besieging Hippo, his episcopal city. Those migrations were to last for six hundred years and were to come in three waves: the continental Germans in the fifth and sixth centuries, the Saracens in the seventh and eighth centuries, and the Scandinavians and Vikings in the ninth and tenth centuries. Although their disruptive effect on the social, political, and religious scenes was serious enough, it has often been exaggerated.

Most of those who turned to Christianity after entering the Roman Empire turned to Arianism. Many of the conversions were tribal rather than individual and deeply personal. Such was the case of the Frankish tribes under Clovis (d. 511). In many cases, therefore, there was only a superficial appreciation of the doctrinal and moral content of the new religion. Hence, superstitious practices and vestiges of pagan worship remained for many centuries.

The position of women among these tribes was extremely low, much lower, in fact, than in Roman society. Divorce was only gradually abolished. Legal matters were settled by ordeal, either by fire or water or combat rather than by the Roman system of proof substantiated by witnesses. Compensation, a practice whereby money was given to make satisfaction for crimes, was encouraged by the Church since at least it avoided bloodshed. It also proved to be the forerunner of the medieval system of indulgences.

The strongly militaristic and feudal elements in Germanic culture influenced Germanic Christian devotion and spirituality: Christ was the *Heiland*, the most powerful of kings; the place of worship was the *Burg-Gottes*, God's fortress; monks were the warriors of Christ; the profession of faith was regarded as an oath of fidelity to a feudal lord.

Since the conversion of the northern lands was largely the work of laymen (Olaf, Erich, Canute), ecclesiastical authority was usually reserved to the warrior chief. The anointing of kings was regarded as a sacramental act. Unlike the ancient Christian-Roman law which had guarded the independence of the Church, German law held to a more political idea of church office and, therefore, was less concerned with the moral qualifications of the officer, whether a bishop or an abbot of a monastery. By the eighth century, politically controlled churches of this kind far outnumbered those under the authority of the local bishops. With the development of feudalism, the system was solidified, preparing the way for the great investiture struggle in the eleventh century between the popes (especially Gregory VII, d. 1085) and the rulers of state, i.e., the struggle about whether ecclesiastical leaders would be appointed by the Church or by the state.

On the other hand, credibly strong ecclesiastical leadership *was* exercised at this time by Pope Gregory the Great (d. 604), who inaugurated the mission to the Anglo-Saxons in the British Isles. He also displayed imaginative and resourceful administrative skills in his distribution of church funds: to ransom captives from the Lombards, to charter vessels to bring grain to Rome from the islands, to ship lumber to churches in Egypt or blankets to the monks at Mount Sinai. The emperor at Constantinople did not like this papal usurpation of imperial power, but the pope was, after all, paying the bills. The rise of the temporal power of the papacy (in response to a vacuum of civil leadership, following the collapse of the Western Empire) is commonly assigned to the middle of the eighth century, but it had its origins here, during the pontificate of Gregory the Great (590-604).

THE CHURCH AS THE DOMINANT FORCE IN THE WEST (700-1300)
The Germanization of Christianity

When, in the middle of the eighth century, the exarchate of Ravenna fell to the Lombards and the Eastern emperor proved unable to assist the papacy, Pope Stephen II (d. 752) turned to the Franks. In 754 Pepin (d. 768) was consecrated king and given the title of patriarch of the Romans. The process was completed on Christmas day, 800, with the crowning of Charlemagne (d. 814) by Pope Leo III (d. 816) as emperor of the Romans and protector and defender of the papacy. He was to see to it that Roman liturgy and Roman disciplinary practices were introduced and observed throughout his new empire. He appointed all bishops and abbots and presided over all synods. The role of pope receded far into the background. The line between Church and state dissolved.

With the collapse of the Carolingian empire, however, the papacy was plunged into even worse straits. The attacks of the Normans and the Saracens and the absence of any strong personalities among the successors of Leo reduced the papacy to a plaything of the Roman nobility. Throughout the tenth and much of the eleventh centuries the office languished in what historians have called the *saeculum obscurum* (dark age).

Western Monasticism

Eastern monasticism was transferred to the West by St. Martin of Tours (d. 397), who established a monastery near Poitiers in 362. Distinctive shape was given Western monasticism by St. Benedict (d. ca. 550) in the middle of the sixth century. After a period as a hermit, he established a community at Monte Cassino, imposing a sensible rule with vows of poverty, chastity, obedience, and stability. The purpose of the monastery was to honor God by worship and to benefit the community by prayer. Since the monastery was to be self-sustaining, the monks were required also to work in the fields. Thus, the essence of the Rule of St. Benedict: *Ora et labora* (pray and work).

The role of the monastery as a center of scholarship developed only gradually. Benedict thought it desirable that his monks be literate enough to read the Bible and the Fathers of the Church. Later, with the Carolingian renaissance, many of the monks were relieved of manual labor and were able to devote themselves to scholarly pursuits. One of the most practical was the copying of the texts of the classics of Western civilization.

Western monasticism, thus transformed, was to play a crucial part in the Gregorian Reform of the late eleventh century. By the ninth century most monks were drawn almost exclusively from the nobility, and the monasteries had become one of the most important social institutions. Monastic schools were the only effective replacements for the municipal schools of the late Roman Empire. In spite of their personal poverty, the monks had vast landholdings and agricultural enterprises that played an important role in the economy and government. After the eighth century the monks became part of the feudal system. Abbots were made vassals of the king.

The Gregorian Reform

By the middle of the eleventh century, however, sufficient social, economic, and political stability had returned to Europe. There appeared an elite who studied philosophy, theology, and law outside of monasteries. Monks had less and less to do with temporal matters, and the impulse to return to the realm of the spiritual became increasingly strong. Men like Peter Damian (d. 1072) and Cardinal Humbert (d. 1061) were among the leading reformers, carrying their cause even as high as the papal office itself. Not content with purifying the monasteries, they devised a program for the entire Christian world.

Avoiding some extreme proposals, Pope Gregory VII (d. 1085) focused his attack upon three evils: simony (the buying and selling of ecclesiastical offices and/or spiritual goods), the alienation of property (the passing of church property into the private hands of a bishop's or a priest's offspring), and lay investiture. Each reform was designed to free the Church from political control and to restore the authority of the pope over the whole Church. Gregory proclaimed in 1075 that the pope held supreme power over all Christian souls. He was the supreme judge, under God alone. All prelates (bishops and abbots) were subject to him, and his powers of absolution and excommunication were absolute.

This *Dictatus Papae*, alongside the systematic establishment of the Roman Curia as the central organ of Church government, gave one of Gregory's successors, Innocent III (d. 1216), a unique position of authority and leadership among all the Western nations. This was to find expression in the new Western general, or ecumenical, councils (Lateran I-IV; Lyons I-II) and was supported by the Church's canonists, or lawyers. (For an English text of the *Dictatus*, see Dolan, *Catholicism*, pp. 72-73.)

Indeed, this was the beginning of the dominance of canon law in the medieval Church. Because of the systematizing efforts of the monk Gratian (d. ca. 1159), a concordance of ecclesiastical laws appeared about the year 1150, entitled *The Concord of Discordant Canons*. Like the *Sentences* of Peter Lombard (d. 1160) which systematized theology as it existed up to that time, this work was to become the basic text of a new branch of theological studies, canon law. Legal decrees rather than the Gospel became the basis for moral judgments. Even the sacraments assumed a legal cast, and a whole sacramental jurisprudence developed. (Who can administer a sacrament? Who is eligible to receive a sacrament? When? Under what circumstances?) Baptism was portrayed less as a moment of rebirth in Christ than as a juridical act by which a person becomes a member of the Church, with full rights, privileges, and obligations. Matrimony was considered a legal contract whose validity depended upon the absence of any one of a whole list of impediments drawn up by Rome. A knowledge of canon law became the requisite for ecclesiastical advancement, and it remained so until the post-Vatican II period.

By 1234 all former collections of papal decisions were combined and codified by Pope Gregory IX (d. 1241) into *The Five Books of Decretals*. The classical juridical doctrine of the Church was now clearly established. The Church is a visible, hierarchically structured organization with supreme power vested in the pope. The place of the laity and all religious and lower clergy is to obey the directives of the Church's lawfully constituted authority. Indeed, many rights formerly exercised by bishops and synods were now reserved to the pope. Even the election of a new pope was reserved to cardinals who were themselves appointed by the pope. Bishops meanwhile were obliged to take an oath of obedience to the pope that resembled the feudal oaths binding a vassal to his lord.

The pope was no longer only consecrated. He was crowned with a tiara, a helmet-shaped head covering used originally by the deified rulers of Persia. The coronation rite, so redolent of imperial prerogatives, was used in the conferral of the papacy from that time until 1978, when Pope John Paul I (d. 1978) chose simply to be "installed" into his new "supreme pastoral ministry." Pope John Paul II, who succeeded to the papacy the following month, also refused the crown.

The Monastic Renewal

The Gregorian Reform (also known as the *Hildebrandine* Reform, since Gregory VII had been Cardinal Hildebrand before election to the papacy) was not an unqualified success. Emperor Henry IV (d. 1106) sacked the city of Rome, Gregory died a prisoner in Salerno, and the investiture struggle continued for many centuries. On the other hand, simony was effectively prohibited, and celibacy was imposed upon the Latin-rite clergy as a way of dealing with the alienation of property. Concurrently, the same ascetic impulse that worked so powerfully to produce a reform of the central administration of the Church also found a natural outlet in the renewal of monasticism. New orders appeared: Camaldolese (founded by Romuald, d. 1027), Carthusians (Bruno, d. 1101), Cistercians (Robert of Molesme, d. 1111, and Bernard of Clairvaux, d. 1153), and the religious Orders of Chivalry (Knights of Malta, 1099, Templars, 1118, and Teutonic Knights, 1189). The ongoing reform of the clergy was carried forward by the Canons Regular movement: Augustinians, Premonstratensians or Norbertines, the latter founded by Norbert of Xanten (d. 1134). The laity formed Bible groups, and many dedicated themselves to lives of evangelical poverty. The Crusades, for all the negative results they generated (especially the fourth crusade), also released extraordinary religious energy, solidifying the sense of community and widening the horizons of Western Christians through contact with the great Byzantine and Islamic cultures. The development of Western philosophy and theology in the medieval period could not have occurred as it did without this encounter with the East.

Outstanding in all of this movement was St. Bernard of Clairvaux, described as an "admonisher of popes and preacher of Crusades." "If you are to do the work of a prophet," he told the pope, "you will need a hoe rather than a sceptre." Although he believed in the theory of the two swords (namely, that the pope had power not only in the spiritual realm but also in the temporal), he insisted that the temporal power was always to be used for spiritual purposes alone. The pope was a minister, not a lord.

From this point of view, Bernard was a reformer, a progressive by modern standards. But there was another side to him. His approach to spirituality might be summed up in the Latin phrase, *credo ut experiar* (I believe that I might experience), in contrast to Augustine's *credo ut intelligam* (I believe that I might understand) or Anselm's *fides quaerens intellectum* (faith seeking understanding). Bernard, therefore, heralded a turn toward subjective, even individualistic, piety that began to surface throughout Europe. His mysticism was founded on the union of Christ and the soul, and his devotional life was focused on the Blessed Virgin, to whom all Cistercian churches were dedicated. The once-popular Catholic formula, *Ad Jesum per Mariam* (To Jesus through Mary), is ascribed to Bernard. And his opposition to the use of dialectics in the study of revelation is also well known.

Theological Renewal

Bernard's attitude notwithstanding, there was indeed a significant turn in the theological posture of the Church at the outset of the second Christian millennium. The early medieval theology of the monastic schools, so closely wedded to the biblical texts, no longer satisfied the increasingly critical minds of the mid-eleventh century. Independent schools appeared which sought new ways of doing theology. Anselm of Canterbury was himself part of this movement. At the beginning of the thirteenth century several such schools in Paris united to form the first *university*. Other universities followed in Bologna, Padua, Naples, Montpellier, Oxford, Cambridge, Salamanca, and Valencia. Not until a century later did a similar development occur in Germany.

There were also new assaults upon orthodoxy, e.g., the Albigensians, or Cathari, and the Waldensians, to which reference has already been made. The Inquisition was founded at this time, and in 1252 Pope Innocent IV (d. 1254) authorized the use of torture to secure proof of heresy. By all reasonable standards, the Inquisition was one of the shabbiest chapters in the entire history of the Church.

Others found alternate ways of combatting heresy. St. Francis of Assisi (d. 1226) and St. Dominic (d. 1221) founded the Franciscans and Dominicans respectively to express, by way of their example of voluntary poverty and their straightforward preaching of the Gospel, what the true faith required. These new religious movements, in turn, inspired a resurgence of theological scholarship. On the Dominican side: Albert the Great (d. 1280), Thomas Aquinas (d. 1274), and Master Eckhart (d. 1328). On the Franciscan side: Alexander of Hales (d. 1245), Bonaventure (d. 1274), and Duns Scotus (d. 1308). Perhaps equally important, if not more important, was the *pastoral* orientation of these new mendicant (begging) orders. In the older forms of monasticism, people entered religious life for their own spiritual welfare: the glory of God through personal sanctification. But the Franciscans and Dominicans centered their activities in the preaching of the Gospel and the care of souls, i.e., ministry "out in the world."

The East-West Schism

From the time of the Council of Chalcedon (451), when Rome rejected the proposal (canon 28) to grant major jurisdictional powers to Constantinople, relations between the two sees were marked by sporadic tension and conflict. The subsequent controversy over Monothelitism (one divine will in Christ) saw the Roman view triumph over the Constantinopolitan at the Third Council of Constantinople in 680, but even a deceased pope, Honorius, came in for censure (see again chapter 13). The Eastern emperors' attempt to enforce a policy of *iconoclasm* (the abolition of all religious images) in the eighth century widened the gap. The West, which by now no longer understood the Greek language, could not distinguish between *veneration* and *adoration*. Where the Easterners recommended the former, the Westerners thought they meant the latter. And the refusal of the East to send military assistance to the pope in 753 prompted Rome's turning to the Franks, as we have already noted.

The next breach occurred in 858 when the patriarch of Constantinople was deposed by the emperor and replaced by Photius (d. 895), against the wishes of Pope Nicholas I (d. 867). Nicholas sent delegates to Constantinople, who decided in favor of Photius. But then Photius insisted that he did not accept the pope's supremacy, so the pope withdrew his support. After much negotiation, a reconciliation between the patriarchate and the papacy was achieved at a council held in Constantinople in 879. Peace was maintained throughout the tenth century, but it came apart in the middle of the eleventh century and has not been healed even to this day.

Michael Cerularius (d. 1058), patriarch of Constantinople, assumed office in 1043. He brought with him an exceedingly low opinion of the papacy and some measure of ignorance about recent Roman reforms. Because the pope had been insisting that Easterners conform to Latin usage in the West, Michael, in turn, ordered the Latin churches in Constantinople to adopt Greek usages. When they refused, he closed them down and ordered the head of the Bulgarian Church to write to the bishop of Tani in southern Italy, where the Eastern Christians were living, and denounce such Latin customs as the use of unleavened bread in the Eucharist. The letter was to be forwarded thereafter to the pope. It arrived at an inopportune moment. Pope Leo IX (d. 1054) had just been defeated by the Normans and was being held in captivity. His cardinal-secretary, Humbert of Moyenmoutier, also known as Humbert of Silva Candida (d. 1061), with little knowledge of Greek, probably mistranslated some of the letter, thereby exaggerating its offensive tone. Legates were dispatched to Constantinople, Humbert among them.

To compress the story: The legates botched their diplomatic mission, dealing heavy-handedly with the patriarch. On July 16, 1054, they marched into the Church of Santa Sophia just before the afternoon liturgy and laid on the altar a bull excommunicating Michael Cerularius, the emperor, and all their followers, and then departed, ceremoniously shaking the dust from their feet. The general populace, already annoyed at the emperor's concessions to the Latins in their midst, rioted and could be calmed only after a public burning of the bull. A synod condemned the legates, but significantly not the pope. The door was left ajar for still another reconciliation. In the meantime, Pope Leo died, leaving his successor with the option and the opportunity for making peace. Unfortunately, Leo's successors and others in Rome believed Humbert's account of the sorry events, and no peace initiatives were taken.

With the election of Urban II (d. 1099) in 1088, hopes rose. The new pope was a man of good will and calmness. He reopened negotiations with the Byzantine court and lifted an earlier excommunication of the emperor. When the Pope called for a crusade at Clermont in 1095, one of his motives was to bring help to Eastern Christians. But the crusade had the opposite effect. Quarrels between the emperor and the crusaders developed over the status of the reconquered city of Antioch. The conduct of the Western knights disgusted the people, and the situation became inflamed when the crusade leader drove the Greek patriarch out of the city and replaced him with a Latin patriarch. Though no one can give an exact date for the beginning of the East-West Schism, it was this Fourth Crusade (1202-1204) which probably drove the last wedge in. In 1203 the crusaders sacked the city of Constantinople, not even sparing the churches. Two later attempts at bringing the two sides back together—at the Council of Lyons in 1276 and at the Council of Florence in 1439—did not have lasting results. The climate has only just recently begun to change, under the impact of Pope John XXIII and the Second Vatican Council.

THE DISINTEGRATION OF WESTERN CHRISTIAN UNITY AND THE TRANSITION TO A WIDER MISSION (1300-1750)

The unity of the Christian West rested on two universally recognized forces: the papacy and the empire. When the papacy fell from its position of temporal power and the empire was overwhelmed by the growth of national states, the twin supports of "Christendom" buckled and collapsed. The process began in the fourteenth century, continued in the fifteenth, and reached its climax in the Protestant Reformation in the sixteenth century. Not until the middle of the eighteenth century was it arrested.

Church and State in Conflict

With the defeat of the Hohenstaufen emperors after the middle of the thirteenth century, the papacy found itself in mortal conflict with the new dominant powers in France. Philip the Fair (d. 1314) claimed a royal power to tax the Church. Pope Boniface VIII (d. 1303) retaliated with a papal bull, or manifesto, entitled *Clericis Laicos*, threatening excommunication upon anyone interfering with the collection of papal revenues. The situation worsened when Philip demanded the degradation of the bishop of Parmiers, a demand that was calculated as an open affront to ecclesiastical authority. Boniface issued another bull, *Unam Sanctam* (1302), asserting papal authority over the French national state. It has been described as the most absolute theocratic doctrine ever formulated:

> "We are taught by the evangelical works," the document declares, "that there are two swords, the spiritual and the temporal, in the control of the Church. . . . Certainly he who denies that the temporal sword was under the control of Peter, misunderstands the word of the Lord when he said: 'Put your sword into the sheath.' Therefore, both the spiritual and material sword are under the control of the Church, but the latter is used for the Church and the former by the Church. One is used by the hand of the priest, the other by the hand of the kings and knights at the command and with the permission of the priest. . . . We therefore declare, say, affirm, and announce that for every human creature to be submissive to the Roman pontiff is absolutely necessary for salvation."

Boniface was arrested by Philip at Anagni in September, 1303, and died soon thereafter. The action sent shock waves throughout Catholic Europe. Boniface's successors Benedict XI

(d. 1304) and Clement V (d. 1314) came increasingly under French influence until the latter moved the papacy in 1309 to Avignon, where it remained until 1378. The period was known variously as the Avignon Exile and as the Babylonian Captivity of the Church. It was not a time of unrelieved disaster for the Church, however. On the contrary, there was much evidence of renewed interest in missionary activity. But this was also a period of intensified financial abuses, and perhaps more than anything else these prepared the way for the eventual breakup of the Church at the Reformation. Those appointed to ecclesiastical office were expected to pay a benefice tax. There seems to have been a price tag on everything. In 1328, for example, Pope John XXII (d. 1334) announced in a public audience that he had excommunicated, suspended, or interdicted one patriarch, five archbishops, thirty bishops, and forty-six abbots for failure to make their appropriate payments. As the financial burden rested more and more heavily on the so-called upper clergy, they, in turn, were forced to seek ways of supplementing their own income to pay these enormous taxes. The money came somehow from the laity. Both groups, the upper clergy and the laity, developed a contempt for the system of taxation. The laity became increasingly anti-clerical, and the clergy increasingly nationalistic.

Conflicts Within the Church

Trouble began brewing as well on the theological front. Two major challenges were pressed against the prevailing ecclesiological and canonical notions of ecclesiastical, and especially papal, authority: one by William of Ockham (d. 1347), an English Franciscan, and the other by Marsilius of Padua (d. 1343), former chancellor of the University of Paris.

Ockham accepted the pope's supreme authority over the Church, but only if exercised in a ministerial, not dominational, way, and for the good of the whole Church, not for the temporal power of the papacy or the ecclesiastical bureaucracy. Placing the pope above all law and placing everyone else under his absolute authority is a direct violation of the principle of Christian liberty. Although the pope was now elected by the College of Cardinals, that system could readily be changed since the responsibility rests on the entire body of the faithful.

Marsilius of Padua was even more radical in his opposition. In his *Defensor Pacis* (1324), which some have characterized as the dividing line between medieval and modern notions of political and religious theory, he argued that the Church is a spiritual and sacramental community, united by a common faith and a common celebration of the sacraments. Relying on Aristotle, Marsilius argued that the clergy-laity distinction had been overdrawn. Each cleric and each lay person is a citizen with inherent rights to participate in the affairs of state. Ordination has nothing at all to do with it. The Church should be governed by those closest to the scene: local bishops and priests, rather than the pope. And sanctions such as excommunication should be ignored since coercive power is foreign to the Gospel. The pope is no more than the executor of the wishes of the whole Christian community. Supreme authority rests with a representative council of all Christians. However, despite his apparently democratic leanings, Marsilius seemed to hold that actual power in the governance of the Church should be exercised by the civil ruler.

The Great Western Schism (1378-1417)

The papacy returned to Rome in 1378. In April of that year the College of Cardinals, long since predominantly French in composition, elected the archbishop of Bari, Bartolomeo Prignano, who took the name Urban VI (d. 1389). Within a few months the same electoral body declared their previous decision null and void and proclaimed a new pope, Clement VII (d. 1394). Now the Church had two claimants to the papacy, and schism resulted. To resolve the terrible ambiguity, key churchmen turned to *conciliarism*, a theory originally developed by canonists in the twelfth century and carried forward by Marsilius of Padua in the fourteenth. According to this theory, the Church is a vast corporation, with some members exercising leadership roles. All power resides ultimately in the whole body of the faithful, but that power is transferred to certain representatives, as in the case of the College of Cardinals in the election of the pope. There are in effect two churches: the Universal Church (the Body of Christ, in the New Testament sense) and the Apostolic Church, the administrative arm of the Universal Church. The latter, however, is always subordinate to the former. The theory was later refined by such theologians as Jean Gerson (d. 1429), who insisted that the pope is subject to the judgment and legislation of a general council, which is the only true representative of the Universal Church.

By 1409 the situation worsened. At a council held in Pisa a third pope was elected, Alexander V (d. 1410). Meanwhile, Benedict XIII (d. 1428) had succeeded Clement VII, and Gregory XII (d. 1415) was in office in the Roman line. By the end of his reign, however, Benedict had no support outside a small Spanish town where he lived, and Gregory had the allegiance only of certain Italian princes. The one who, according to some, had the least claim on the papacy, Alexander V, actually had the widest measure of support. Upon the death of Alexander, the Pisan party elected Baldassare Cossa, who took the name John XXIII. He proved such a poor choice that he alienated most of his original backers. The emperor Sigismund (d. 1437) forced John XXIII to call a new council, which met at Constance in November, 1414. More than one hundred thousand people descended upon the city: one hundred eighty-five bishops, three hundred theologians and canon lawyers, and vast numbers of priests, monks, lay persons, and politicians. Not only the bishops but also the doctors of theology and law were voting members of the assembly. The dominant figure, however, was the emperor.

Realizing that he was about to be condemned and deposed, John XXIII fled Constance but was arrested and placed under guard while the council continued. On May 29, 1415, John XXIII was formally deposed after a trial, and six days later he accepted his sentence. Meanwhile, the Roman Pope, Gregory XII, now eighty-nine years of age, was still holding out at Rimini, where he refused the emperor's invitation to the council. He decided to abdicate, but first sent his representatives to Constance formally convoking the council and then formally announcing his resignation. The third claimant, Benedict XIII, was also condemned, but he refused to accept the judgment and died, as one put it, "excommunicated and excommunicating." On St. Martin's day, November 11, 1417, the conclave, consisting of twenty-three cardinals and five prelates from each of the five nations represented at the council (Italy, France, England, Germany, and Spain), elected a new pope, Martin V (d. 1431). The schism was over.

Conciliarism

Two important pieces of legislation were produced by the Council of Constance, and they have been the subject of much discussion and debate ever since. The one, *Haec Sancta* (1415), espoused the supremacy of a general council and the collegiality of the bishops; the other, *Frequens*, decreed a kind of parliamentary government for the Church, requiring the calling of general councils at specified intervals. Although the new pope generally approved the decrees insofar as they were truly conciliar and did call a council at Pavia five years later, it was obvious that he and his immediate successors were determined to resist the onslaught of conciliarism in the Church. In fact, Eugene IV (d. 1447) suspended the next general council at Basle and transferred it to Florence in 1431. It was at Basle that conciliarism reached its highest development, inspired undoubtedly by the work of a German priest, Nicholas of Cusa (d. 1464). In a work published during the council entitled *De Concordantia Catholica* (On Catholic Concord), Cusa argued for the supremacy of a general council over the pope. The council, in turn, governs the Church only through the consent of the faithful.

In 1460 Pope Pius II (d. 1464) issued a decree condemning the "deadly poison" of conciliarism and forbidding under pain of excommunication any appeal beyond the pope to a general council. The prohibition was repeated by Popes Sixtus IV (d. 1484) and Julius II (d. 1513). Among the strongest opponents of the pope's negative stance toward general councils were members of the reformed monastic groups, especially the Carthusians. The pope's resistance to the conciliar principle, they argued, was rooted in the Roman Curia's fear of being held to account for centuries of evil practices. That was not the first attack upon the Curia, nor would it be the last, as the history of the Second Vatican Council shows.

The Reformation

"The Reformation" is the all-embracing term which describes the disintegration of Western Christianity in the sixteenth century. Like all other major developments in the history of the Church, including even the decision to carry the Gospel to the Gentiles, this one did not occur in a single event and through the efforts of a single person, such as Martin Luther (d. 1546). It was instead an extremely complex process in which religious, intellectual, political, and social forces converged.

Insofar as one can identify specific *causes* of the Reformation, they are as follows: (1) the corruption of the Renaissance papacy; (2) the divorce of piety from theology, and of theology from biblical and patristic tradition; (3) the aftereffects of the Western Schism; (4) the rise of the national state; (5) the close connection between Western Christianity and Western civilization; and (6) the vision, experiences, and personalities of Luther, Ulrich Zwingli (d. 1531), and John Calvin (d. 1564).

1.   The *Renaissance* (literally, "rebirth") of the fifteenth century tried to recapture the literary and artistic achievements of Latin and Greek antiquity. The focus was not upon ideas but upon the aesthetic and the emotional. The movement was, by many accounts, excessive in its celebration of the human. Not only were the works of art of the ancient civilizations brought forward, but so, too, were the mores and morals of those civilizations. Although there were instances of real, substantial advancements in this period (e.g., the establishment of the Vatican Library by Pope Nicholas V, d. 1455), it was also a period marked by nepotism, simony, military expeditions, financial manipulation, political intrigue, and even murder. The year America was "discovered" by Columbus (1492), the notorious Alexander VI (d. 1503) ascended to the papal throne.

2.   At the same time Catholic *piety* grew increasingly away from sound theology, and theology, in turn, from its own best tradition. Religious art and spirituality appealed directly, almost blatantly, to the emotions. Emphasis on the sufferings and wounds of Christ in excruciatingly physical detail became commonplace. Statues of Christ with blood dripping down from his crown of

thorns appeared everywhere. Attention was riveted on the Last Judgment, not as the day of redemption but as the day of reckoning and of terror.

Catholic *theology* also drifted along an anti-intellectual course. In reaction against the excessive abstractions of Scholasticism, a new style of theology known as *nominalism* rejected all forms of mediation between God and humankind: sacraments, Church authority, meritorious deeds, and so forth. Nothing can bridge the gap between God and us except the mercy of God manifested in Christ. Since we are utterly corrupt, justification is exclusively God's work. The rapidity with which this new theological approach spread through Europe—influencing Luther, Calvin, Zwingli, and others—indicates the intensity of dissatisfaction with the status quo of late medieval Catholicism. There was an "alluring simplicity" to the Protestant message, and it caught on almost immediately. And it had its Catholic counterparts—e.g., in the *Imitation of Christ* of Thomas à Kempis (d. 1471), who insisted, among other things, that "it is better to feel compunction than to be able to define it."

3.   The debilitating effects of the *Great Western Schism* are obvious enough. The pope's ability to function as a symbol and instrument of unity was seriously undermined even within the Church of the West. The *East-West Schism* had weakened the office's credibility and effectiveness one to two centuries earlier.

4.   The rise of the *national states* made independence from the influence of the papacy increasingly possible, likely, and then certain. The new slogan was *Rex imperator in regno suo* (The king is emperor in his own kingdom). That political perspective gradually widened to embrace even authority over the Church.

5.   The insistence of the Western Church on tying its identity too intimately to *Western civilization* denied the Church a necessary measure of flexibility and adaptability. The papacy, and ecclesiastical authority in general, had taken on an imperial cast. The Church was less the People of God than a hierarchical, indeed an absolutely monarchical, society. Its rulers tried to impose as a matter of faith what we have since come to recognize all too clearly to be only a matter of culturally-conditioned political theory and churchcraft. (Compare, for example, Boniface

VIII's *Unam Sanctam* with the Second Vatican Council's *Dogmatic Constitution on the Church*.)

6. In the final accounting, no one can ever ignore the direct *impact of personalities* themselves on the course of events, no matter how much we talk of larger social, political, and economic forces. The Reformation took hold in Europe and in the forms it assumed because of the peculiar strengths and weaknesses of specific men: Luther, Calvin, and Zwingli in particular.

Luther was a monk who, like most medieval Christians, took the "last things" very seriously: death, judgment, heaven, and hell. He was tormented by the thought of God's judgment as he reflected on his creatureliness and unworthiness. Traditional modes of mortification and penance did not work for him. He was still without peace. He concluded that he had to relinquish all forms of self-reliance. God alone would save him if only he would trust in God's power and readiness to save him. All other devices of mediation, including *indulgences* (the remission of a temporal punishment in purgatory still due to sins which have already been forgiven), are contrary to the simple, unadorned message of the Gospel. The charging of fees for indulgences brought the matter to a head, and on October 31, 1517, Luther posted his now famous Ninety-five Theses on the door of the castle church at Wittenberg. The rest is history.

Zwingli was a Swiss humanist who became vicar of the cathedral at Zurich in 1519, whereupon he announced that he would preach the entire Gospel of Matthew and not only the excerpts available in the liturgy. He would thereby carry the Church back to its simpler, primitive, non-Roman origins. He abolished fast days, removed images, and banned all church music. Zwingli's system of church polity, not surprisingly, was well suited to the city of Zurich, which had a representative government. His ecclesiology was also considerably more democratic, anti-clerical, and anti-institutional than Luther's, who was satisfied to introduce the vernacular into the liturgy and eliminate religious vows and celibacy.

Calvin, a French theologian who left the Catholic Church in 1533, provided Protestantism with its first integrated doctrinal system: *The Institutes of the Christian Religion* (1536). Calvin was especially noted for his theory of *predestination*. We can do nothing at all about our salvation. God has already determined our destiny. Since the fall of Adam, all of us deserve to be damned. And God indeed allows many to be damned to manifest divine justice. But some are saved to manifest divine grace. There are signs in a person's life by which one can tell if he or she is destined for salvation or reprobation: profession of the true faith, an upright life, and attendance upon the sacrament of the Lord's Supper. The Church, therefore, is the company of the elect.

Calvin's ecclesiology was somewhere between the still essentially "Catholic" Luther on the right and the strongly "Protestant" Zwingli on the left. Where Luther still employed the crucifix (with the figure of Christ upon the cross), and where Zwingli abandoned it altogether, Calvin allowed the cross but without the corpus. Calvinism was to become the most international form of Protestantism.

Other Reformation movements included the *Anabaptists* on the far left (to the left even of Zwingli) and the *Anglicans* on the right (to the right even of Luther). The *Anabaptist* movement is often referred to as the "radical Reformation." They were called *ana*baptists (literally, "baptized again") because they held as invalid the Baptism of infants ("dipping in the Romish bath"). For them the Church is a completely voluntary society of convinced believers. Only those who are truly converted and repentant can be baptized.

Anglicanism, on the other hand, is the result of a fusion of nationalism and religious upheaval. The quarrel with Rome was not over doctrine nor even over morality and finances, but over a royal wedding. Pope Clement VII (d. 1534) refused to allow King Henry VIII (d. 1547) to divorce his first wife and take a second. What followed was a moral course of action in search of theological justification. The writings of Marsilius of Padua and others proved useful to this purpose. The state "acquired" the Church, and Henry became in effect his own pope. Even today, the reigning monarch of Great Britain is at the same time the head of the Church of England.

The Counter-Reformation

By the 1530s all of Scandinavia, the British Isles, and much of Germany, Austria, and France had severed the bonds of communion with Rome. In spite of the fact that Luther himself had called for a general council to examine his doctrine, nothing of the sort was done until 1545. The reasons for the delay were for the most part political. The pope as a temporal ruler was caught between the territorial designs of the Hapsburgs, on the one hand, and the king of France, on the other. The threat of conciliarism still hung over Europe. There was a general fear in Rome that should a general council be called, the very office of the papacy might be abolished. Another reason for the delay was the simple failure of the Church's leadership to recognize the seriousness of the Protestant movement, and especially how much opposed it really was to traditional Catholic doctrine. Luther was looked upon at first as a sincere reformer who was merely expressing dissatisfaction with the abuses in contemporary Catholicism.

Not until the election of Paul III (d. 1549) in 1534 did the situation begin to change. Surrounding himself with bona fide reformers, he mandated steps to eliminate the abuses. A call was issued for the reform of the Roman Curia, particularly its financial dealings. When a council finally convened in 1545 in the northern Italian town of Trent, its attendance was skimpy: less than forty bishops, mostly Italian. There was a long debate about the representative character of the assembly, and then about the relative importance of dogmatic over against disciplinary issues. In early 1546 the opposed forces within the council reached a compromise, deciding to deal simultaneously with both matters.

Although its composition was slight in comparison with Chalcedon (about 630 delegates) and Vatican I (about 700), not to mention Vatican II (over 2000), and although its proceedings were twice suspended (from 1548 to 1551, and again from 1552 to 1561), the Council of Trent (1545-1563) is perhaps second only to the Second Vatican Council (1962-1965) in terms of disciplinary decrees and the clarification of Catholic doctrine. Until Vatican II, twentieth-century Catholicism was shaped more by the Council of Trent than by any other historically tangible event or force.

The council definitively articulated Catholic doctrine on the matter of faith and grace against Luther, Zwingli, Calvin, and their followers. Following a middle course between Pelagianism (everything depends on human effort) and Protestantism (everything depends on God), the council insisted that salvation comes from God as a pure gift, but that it requires some measure of human cooperation (see again chapter 5). It has been asserted that "had Trent's decree on justification been decreed at the Lateran Council at the beginning of the sixteenth century, the Reformation would not have occurred and the religious unity of the Middle Ages would have endured" (John P. Dolan, *Catholicism,* p. 149).

The council also clearly and decisively defined the meaning and number of the sacraments, especially the Eucharist, thereby confirming a tradition which first emerged about 1150 and achieved conciliar formulation at Florence in 1439. Its decree on marriage, *Tametsi,* required that a wedding be celebrated before a priest and two witnesses, and held as invalid marriages between Catholics and Protestants. The council also created the Index of Forbidden Books (not abolished until the pontificate of Paul VI, d. 1978) and established seminaries for the training of future priests. Both of these actions, conceived as temporary measures, proved to have lasting effects on the life of the Church: The first kept both the laity and the clergy separated from the major intellectual works of modern times, and the second tended to sharpen the distinction between clergy and laity by encouraging an academic and spiritual formation for priests in isolation from the ordinary workday world of the rest of the People of God. Again, those effects have only recently begun to change under the impact of Vatican II.

At the heart of the Catholic Counter-Reformation was the newly established Society of Jesus, founded by St. Ignatius of Loyola (d. 1556), a former soldier, and approved by Pope Paul III in 1540. Although it was only one of several new communities in the Church, the Jesuits stand out because of their dedication to various forms of the apostolate, especially the education of the young and of future priests, their sense of solidarity as a community and with the pope, their scholarship and learning, and their rapid expansion, growing as they did to more than 13,000 within fifty years of Ignatius' death. To the extent that the Counter-Reformation succeeded, it did so primarily through the worldwide efforts and missionary imagination of the Society of Jesus.

There was a concurrent resurgence of art, piety, and theology in the so-called *Baroque age* (1550-1750). Baroque scholasticism replaced the more obscure pre-Reformation, nominalistic theology. Spanish and Italian theologians like Bellarmine, Soto, Suarez, Cano, and others, distinguished themselves. Suarez (d. 1617) made a particularly strong impact, influencing every branch of theology and philosophy. Theology became exceedingly systematized. The authority of each theological position was precisely identified. Suarezianism had its spiritual effects as well: especially on the Spanish mystics (St. Teresa of Avila, d. 1582, and St. John of the Cross, d. 1591), who, in turn, influenced French spirituality.

But by and large the post-Tridentine Church continued to emphasize those practices which came under particular attack by the Protestants: veneration of the saints, Marian devotions, and eucharistic adoration. The first and second tended, unwittingly or not, to diminish the role of Christ, and the third, the role of the laity in the Church and at the Eucharist. The liturgy was still the affair of the clergy. In 1661 Pope Alexander VII (d. 1667) forbade any translation of the missal into the vernacular under pain of excommunication. The anti-vernacularists wanted instead to preserve the aura of "mystery." Recitation of the rosary at Mass became common, and preaching, when it occurred at all at the Eucharist, was divorced from the biblical readings. The reception of Communion took place after the Mass. The sacrament was primarily to be worshiped rather than taken as spiritual nourishment. Thus, this period saw the spread of eucharistic processions, forty hours devotions, and benediction of the Blessed Sacrament. The baroque character of the age was also manifest in architecture and in sacred music (the works of Mozart, Haydn, and Beethoven, and the growth of polyphonic song). The liturgy became as much a grand spectacle as an act of community worship.

At the same time the seventeenth and eighteenth centuries were marked by religious fervor and holiness. The seventeenth century has been called the century of saints: St. Vincent de Paul (d. 1660), St. Jean Eudes (d. 1680), Jean Jacques Olier (d. 1657),

Jacques Bossuet (d. 1704), and others. Of particular importance was St. Francis de Sales (d. 1622), bishop of Geneva, who was considerably ahead of his time as an ecumenist, a pastoral leader, an encourager of the lay apostolate and of lay spirituality. He gave particular expression to the latter in his *Introduction to the Devout Life* (1590). The section on marriage is the very antithesis of the monastic prejudice which characterized so many earlier treatments of the married state.

Jansenism

By the beginning of the seventeenth century, the papacy was as strong as it had been since the thirteenth. But doctrinal controversy continued to hamper the Church's quest for a unified missionary effort. Michael de Bay of Louvain (d. 1589), also known as Michael Baius, considered grace, immortality, and freedom from concupiscence as due to us and given in creation; they were not gifts freely bestowed by God. Thus, by Original Sin we lost not only goods that were "extra" to begin with, but goods that are constitutive of our human condition. Therefore, the wound of Original Sin is radical.

Baianism was less important in itself than in a movement it influenced, namely, *Jansenism,* generated by one of Michael's pupils at Louvain, Cornelius Jansen (d. 1638). Jansen wrote a defense of Baius entitled *Augustinus,* in which he attacked Thomism and the theology of the Jesuits and argued that Augustine, not Thomas, is the true representative of Christianity. The book appeared two years after Jansen's death and evoked a strong reaction. Protestants were pleased. Jansen had laid bare the Pelagianism of Rome. But Pope Urban VIII (d. 1644) placed the book on the Index. Jansenism spread nonetheless, especially through France, where it influenced the training of large numbers of priests. It promoted the theory of predestination and a morally rigorous style of Christian life.

Since Original Sin has so radically corrupted human nature, everything purely natural is evil. Grace is given only to the few. Reception of Communion, therefore, is to be experienced only rarely, as an occasional reward for virtue. (Since Jansenism was from the outset an anti-Jesuit movement, its stand on reception of Communion was not surprising in view of the Jesuits' promotion of frequent reception.) Much of pre-Vatican II American Catholicism's obsession with sexual morality and its relatively narrow eucharistic piety (e.g., infrequent reception of Communion and then only after "going to Confession") is directly traceable to this Jansenist influence.

Gallicanism

The condemnation of Jansenism by Rome fueled the fires of independence in France. In 1682 the French clergy declared that the pope had only spiritual authority, that he is subject to the decrees of the Council of Constance, and that henceforth all of his pronouncements would have to be approved by the consent of the entire Church. This latter point is especially important because it would be a matter of specific condemnation at the First Vatican Council (1869-1870) when, on the matter of papal infallibility, the Church would officially declare that a pope's authoritative teachings are *not* subject to the consent of the entire Church. Some Catholics in the twentieth century interpreted that to mean that the pope has absolute teaching authority, that can in no way require the consent of the Church. But as we shall see when returning to the question of papal infallibility in chapter 24, Vatican I meant here to rule out the juridical necessity of some subsequent formal vote taken by a general council or other representative agency in the Church. Infallible teachings, on the other hand, do require the consent of the Church in the sense that what the pope teaches must really be consistent with the actual faith of the whole Church.

Gallicanism (so-called because of its French, or Gallic, origins) persisted in France even beyond the Revolution at the end of the eighteenth century. As transplanted to Germany it was called *Febronianism* or *Josephism* (after the emperor Joseph II, d. 1790).

The Enlightenment

Conditions grew substantially worse as the intellectual atmosphere also changed. It was at this time that the West was to undergo the most revolutionary of all movements in Western history. The *Enlightenment* began in the Netherlands and in England in the mid-seventeenth century and reached its highwater mark in French rationalism (Voltaire, d. 1778, *et al.*). Its fullest philosophical expression occurred in Germany (Leibniz, d. 1716, Lessing, d. 1781, and Kant, d. 1804). It had relatively little effect in southern and eastern Europe.

The Enlightenment was characterized by its confidence in reason, its optimistic view of the world and of human nature, and its celebration of freedom of inquiry. It had a decidedly hostile attitude toward the supernatural, the notion of revelation, and extrinsic authority of every kind. It was chiefly in the Protestant countries that a distinctively Enlightenment Christianity took hold in the form of dogmatic reductionism and an anti-sacramentalism. The reconciliation of science and culture, on the one hand, and Christianity, on the other, was facilely achieved.

But there was also a Catholic Enlightenment which brought about a renewal of Church life as early as the eighteenth century, particularly in the Catholic states of Germany. It took the form of advances in historical and exegetical methods, improvements in the education of the clergy, the struggle against superstition, reform of the liturgy and catechesis, and the promotion of popular education. In many ways, its reforms paved the road for the renewal of the nineteenth century.

In the final accounting, the Enlightenment marks the division between an often pre-critical, authority-oriented theology and a critical, historically sophisticated, and philosophically mature theology. The fact that much Catholic theology was written *after* the Enlightenment does not mean that all of it was truly a post-Enlightenment theology. On the contrary, much Catholic theology before Vatican II was still largely unaffected by the Enlightenment.

The Missions

The transition from a culturally confined Church to a genuine world Church might have begun also at this time, but it did not. With the discovery of new territories by the Spanish and Portuguese in the early fifteenth century and with the continuing geographical expansions of the sixteenth and seventeenth centuries, the Church had an opportunity to be enriched not only quantitatively but qualitatively as well. But *colonialism* compromised the missionary efforts on the political side, and *controversies over methods* compromised those efforts on the ecclesiastical side. The debate over the Chinese and Malabar rites (1645-1692, 1704) brought the promising Jesuit missions in China and India to an end. Rome insisted on the Latin way. The movement to a world Church would have to wait.

THE CHURCH IN THE INDUSTRIAL AND TECHNOLOGICAL AGE (NINETEENTH AND TWENTIETH CENTURIES)

The French Revolution (1789)

The crisis that precipitated yet another qualitative leap in the Church's historical course was the *French Revolution,* the Enlightenment's political carrier. It brought about the end of the feudal, hierarchical society that had been so much a part of medieval Catholicism. But it tried to do more than that. It tried to destroy Catholicism itself, and not just its organizational structure. The French Revolution's extremism generated a counter-reaction among some European intellectuals, who once again turned to the basic principles of Catholicism. The Revolution also destroyed Gallicanism by uprooting the clerical system upon which it had been based. The clergy were forced to look to Rome and the papacy for direction. In a few words, the French Revolution gave the Catholic Church the "grace of destitution." It no longer had much to lose. It was free once again to pursue the mission for which it had existed from the beginning.

Nineteenth-Century Renewal

In France and Germany *Romanticism* extolled Catholicism as the mother of art and the guardian of patriotism. Catholic revival groups as well as new theological schools came into existence. Georg Hermes (d. 1831) in Bonn tried to overcome the new rationalism by using the very concepts of Kant and of Fichte, but he was condemned in 1835 as a semi-rationalist. Similar efforts were made by A. Günther (d. 1863) and J. Frohschammer (d. 1893), with similar results. More successful theological ventures were undertaken by the Tübingen school (J. Möhler, d. 1838, *et al.*). The French priest Félicité Lamennais (d. 1854) and the French Dominican preacher Jean Lacordaire (d. 1861) also attempted a reconciliation between Catholic faith and modern freedoms. Thousands who had been alienated from the Church returned to Catholicism. In Italy, Antonio Rosmini's (d. 1855) *The Five Wounds of the Church* called attention to the need for internal ecclesiastical reform and renewal. And in England John Henry Newman (d. 1890) centered his interests on the problems of faith in the modern world, e.g., in his *Grammar of Assent*, and thereby anticipated by many decades the modern theological and philosophical return to the subject, as in the work of Rahner, Lonergan, and Transcendental Thomism. But Newman was not typical of nineteenth-century theology which, for the most part, was *neo-Scholastic*, an essentially *restorative* theology.

Nineteenth-Century Reaction

For every authentic attempt to deal constructively with the new intellectual currents there seemed to be as many, if not more, forces moving in the opposite direction. A rigid traditionalism developed in France (going by the names of *Integralism* and *Fideism*), distrustful of all rational reflection in theology and excessively dependent upon papal direction (*Ultramontanism*, literally those who look *beyond the mountains*, the Alps, to Rome). The papacy, under Gregory XVI (d. 1846) and Pius IX (d. 1878), set its face against the winds of Liberalism, and nowhere more defiantly than in the latter's *Syllabus of Errors* (1864), where he proclaimed that the pope "cannot and should not be reconciled and come to terms with progress, liberalism, and modern civilization."

At the First Vatican Council Pope Pius IX also secured the dogmatic definition of papal primacy and papal infallibility, but at the same time lost the Papal States (September 1870) and with them his remaining political power. Indeed, the pope became "the prisoner of the Vatican." It was not until the Lateran Treaty of 1929 that the pope's temporal rights to the Vatican territory were acknowledged, and then it was not until 1958 that a pope, John XXIII, made pastoral visitations outside that tiny principality. Paul VI was the first pope in modern times to leave Italy while serving as pope. He did so on several occasions: to visit the Holy Land, India, Latin America, the United States, Australia, and the Philippines. Pope John Paul II has continued that practice, traveling to such countries as Mexico, Poland, Ireland, and the United States.

The Social Question

The *second phase of the Enlightenment* occurred at the economic level. Just as the first phase had disclosed how conditioned our thinking is by extrinsic "authorities" (revealed or otherwise), the second phase disclosed how conditioned our very lives are by extrinsic economic and social forces. With the rapid development of industrialism in the nineteenth century, the condition of the workers worsened. Marxism stepped into the gap. The workers were now alienated not only from the fruits of their labor but from their historic faith as well. Religion, Marx had warned them, was but an opiate, designed to make them forget their oppressive situation. By the time the Church responded at the official level in 1891, especially in Pope Leo XIII's (d. 1903) encyclical *Rerum Novarum (On the Condition of the Workingman)*, it was for many already too late.

With the accelerated growth in the population, the move to the industrial cities, the increase of literacy, the dissemination of news, and dramatic improvements in health care, especially in the decline of infant mortality, the Church found itself unable to meet the pastoral needs of its people and to reiterate, without provoking dissent, its traditional moral teaching on birth control and divorce. This new human situation was only the forerunner of what has been described more fully in chapter 3.

Modernism

If Protestantism's initial impulse is to embrace modernity, Catholicism's has always been to repudiate it. Eventually, however, the Catholic Church comes to terms with modernity, sometimes making a few of the same mistakes Protestantism has already made many years before. Accordingly, the Church's first reaction to the continued industrial, social, and intellectual upheavals of the late nineteenth century was to pronounce a condemnation upon them. That was done, for the most part, by Pope Pius X (d. 1914). The enemy this time was not Liberalism but *Modernism*.

Modernism was not a single movement but a complex of movements. It assumed many very different forms: some clearly unorthodox, others clearly orthodox by today's standards. Unfortunately, the distinction was not often recognized or made. The term *Modernism* was applied to all who refused to adopt a strictly conservative standpoint on debatable matters. Indeed, many of the positions eventually taken by the Second Vatican Council would have been characterized as Modernism had they been expressed by individual theologians or church persons in the early twentieth century, and, in fact, that was precisely what sometimes happened.

In its *unorthodox* form, Modernism was so subjectivist and existentialist as to be anti-intellectual. There could be no fixed doctrinal positions. Everything was always in a state of flux. The new methods of interpreting the Bible accentuated this trend. The French biblical exegete Alfred Loisy (d. 1940) insisted that one must study the Bible as any other historical document, without doctrinal or dogmatic presuppositions. The movement found expression in England in the work of the ex-Jesuit George Tyrrell (d. 1909), who insisted that Christ did not present himself as a teacher of orthodoxy and that dogma is just a human effort to put into intellectual terms the divine force working in all of us. Some of his disciples carried the point a step further, coming close to pantheism. In Italy the movement took social and political form, favoring the establishment of society in complete freedom from hierarchical control.

As noted in chapter 7, Modernism was condemned in various documents issued by the authority of Pope Pius X: the Holy Office decree *Lamentabili* (1907), the encyclical *Pascendi* (1907), and the Oath Against Modernism (*Sacrorum Antistitum, 1909*). Although all the clergy were required to take this oath, its imposition produced such a strongly negative reaction in Germany that the German bishops secured an exemption for Catholic university professors.

Much of twentieth-century Catholic theology in the years before Vatican II was written while authors were looking back over their shoulders at the Modernist crisis. Church officials sustained this atmosphere by continuing to equate most deviations from Scholastic or neo-Scholastic theology with Modernist unorthodoxies. But Modernism in its more sophisticated theological forms was *right* about several important matters: (1) The inner religious experience *is* an essential element of the life of the spirit and, in large measure, generates and supports the act of faith; (2) dogmatic formulae are always inadequate to their object, which is God; (3) revelation is first and foremost for the sake of salvation and the quality of human life rather than for the satisfaction of intellectual curiosity; (4) revelation was only gradually unfolded in the life of the Church, and with many fits and starts; and (5) the Bible, and indeed all the sources of Christian tradition, must be studied according to the most scientifically critical methods at hand.

On the other hand, (1) inner religious experience is not the only way to come to a knowledge of God; (2) dogmatic formulae are not completely devoid of objective content; (3) the development of dogma and of our understanding of revelation is not a completely natural process which can just as easily distort the meaning of the Gospel as illuminate it; and (4) the Bible and other authoritative sources are not just historical documents, but are expressions and products of the Church's collective faith and must also be read and interpreted as such.

The Church's official magisterium may have oversimplified the Modernist position and prematurely condemned it, without really understanding its inner substance and its fundamental truth. But the Modernists themselves often exaggerated their partial grasp of that truth, uncritically adopted late nineteenth-century positivist views of history, and individualized theology by tearing it from its broader ecclesial context.

Between the Two World Wars (1918-1939)

Although Catholic theology and its official interpretation remained conservative in the aftermath of the Modernist crisis, the period between the two World Wars was one of unusual progress on several major fronts, each of which would reach a fuller flowering at the Second Vatican Council in the 1960s:

1. The *liturgical movement* worked to bridge the gap between altar and people by emphasizing the liturgy as an act of communal worship in and through Christ, the head of the Church, and by recovering the Thomistic principle, taught at the Council of Trent, that the sacraments are both signs and causes of grace. As *signs* of grace, they must be intelligible.

2. The *biblical movement* prudently carried forward the work of critical interpretation without provoking additional papal or curial condemnations. Père Marie-Joseph Lagrange (d. 1938) continued his scriptural studies in Jerusalem and trained a corps of scholars who were available for service to the Church when, in 1943, Pope Pius XII issued the so-called Magna Carta of Catholic biblical scholarship, *Divino Afflante Spiritu*.

3. The *social action* movement continued to apply the social teachings of the Church, including Pope Pius XI's major encyclical *Quadragesimo Anno (Forty Years After [Rerum Novarum])* in 1931. In the United States, for example, this movement was centered in the drive for the recognition of labor unionism in American industry.

4. The *lay apostolate* under Pius XI and especially Pius XII sought to involve larger and larger numbers of the laity in the work of the Church ("Catholic Action").

5. The *ecumenical movement*, in spite of the negative tone of Pius XI's encyclical *Mortalium Animos*, on the occasion of the

Faith and Order Conference of 1927 at Lausanne, began attracting the scholarly attention of such major Catholic theologians as Yves Congar in his pioneering work, *Divided Christendom* (1939).

6.   The *missionary movement* was now increasingly carried out with a minimum of colonial and European influence. The first native bishops in the new mission territories were consecrated in 1926, and Pius XII furnished the mission countries with their own hierarchies.

7.   A *theological renewal* was signaled by the emergence of a theology inspired by the Catholic Church's renewed respect for Thomas Aquinas but not uncritically wedded to his system. Because of the preceding six items, the new theological approach was more biblically, historically, pastorally, socially, and ecumenically oriented. Prominent among the varieties of developing Catholic theologies was Transcendental Thomism, whose principal and most celebrated exponent has been the Austrian Jesuit Karl Rahner. The new understanding of the mystery of Church as People of God with a mission to the whole world was anticipated in the writings of the century's most important ecclesiologist, the French Dominican Yves Congar.

The Second World War and Its Aftermath (1940-1962)

The change in official Catholicism is evident in the encyclicals that were produced during this period. The *liturgical movement* was given a major push in Pius XII's *Mystici Corporis* (1943) and *Mediator Dei* (1947), and in the restoration of the Easter Vigil (1951) and the rites of Holy Week (1955). The *biblical movement*, as we just noted, received remarkable endorsement in Pius XII's *Divino Afflante Spiritu* (1943)—remarkable certainly in the light of the exceedingly restrictive directives of the Pontifical Biblical Commission at the turn of the century. The *social action movement* and the *lay apostolate* in general were warmly endorsed in John XXIII's *Mater et Magistra* (1961) and *Pacem in Terris* (1963) and in Paul VI's *Populorum Progressio* (1967). The *ecumenical movement* had to await the pontificate of John XXIII before it could surface with official blessing. John XXIII established in 1960 the Secretariat for the Promotion of Christian Unity and invited non-Catholic Christians as official observers at Vatican II. The *missionary movement,* and particularly the need for adaptation and enculturation, was strongly approved in Pius XII's encyclicals *Summi Pontificatus* (1939), *Evangelii Praecones* (1951), and *Fidei Donum* (1957). Finally, the *theological renewal,* after a glaring setback in Pius XII's *Humani Generis* (1950), found itself at the center, not the margin, of the deliberations of the Second Vatican Council.

The next chapter is devoted entirely to that extraordinary event, a moment comparable in historical significance to the early Church's abandonment of circumcision as a condition for membership.

SUMMARY

1.   The relationship between the Church and history is a theological one. It has to do with the movement of the world, and the Church within the world, toward its destiny in the Kingdom of God, and with the presence of God to the world here and now through the Church.

2.   Dividing the history in which the Church has been present and active, however, always reflects certain theological presuppositions. We use here *three major divisions:* the Church of *Jewish Christianity* (a very brief period); the Church of *cultural confinement* (Hellenistic Christianity, European Christianity, etc.); and the Church of the world, or the period of the *world Church.*

3.   The transition, or break, between the first and second periods occurred at the point (or points) at which the Church carried the Gospel to the Gentiles and decided at the same time not to impose circumcision as a condition for membership. The transition, or break, between the second and third periods has only just begun to occur with the Second Vatican Council.

4.   This chapter, therefore, is concerned with the *second period* of the Church's historical pilgrimage, namely, its movement through, and consecutive identification with, various cultures, especially the European.

5.   The historical material of this second period is further divided as follows: (1) the Church within Graeco-Roman civilization (first to seventh centuries); (2) the Church as the dominant presence in the West

(about 700-1300); (3) the disintegration of Christian unity and the transition to a wider mission (1300-1750); and (4) the Church in the period of industrialization and technology (nineteenth and twentieth centuries).

6.   By the word *Church* we mean here not just the pope and the bishops, but the whole People of God. By *history* we mean the whole process by which the world, and the Church within the world, is moving toward the Kingdom of God. History is also the *interpretation* of that process. God alone can "interpret" history without error: comprehending all the data, knowing all the facts, and perceiving all the facts in their proper relationships one with another to constitute the whole.

7.   *Classicism*, in effect, denies the reality of history as a process as well as the element of human cooperation with the grace of God. *Historicism*, in effect, denies the reality of history as the work of God and as the sign of God's presence in grace. *Historical consciousness* understands history as a process that is grounded in, and sustained and guided by, the grace of God, but which also emerges through human decisions and events according to an often-unpredictable pattern.

8.   The Church of the *Graeco-Roman civilization* (first through seventh centuries) began with the transition from Jewish Christianity to Christianity of and for Gentiles, and that, of course, was an occurrence within the New Testament period itself. Overlapping with the latter part of this period was the age of the *Apostolic Fathers* (pupils of the Apostles) and the *Apologists* (defenders of the faith). Early challenges to the faith in this period included *Gnosticism, Adoptionism,* and *Docetism*, and these, in turn, moved the Church to determine its *canon* (list) of Sacred Scripture as the norm of faith and to articulate an understanding of *apostolic succession*, by which the witness of the Apostles as authoritatively interpreted by the bishops is an additional norm and guarantee of faith.

9.   By the *latter half of the second century* organizational complexification occurred: local synods, regional synods, and then, in 325, an ecumenical council (Nicea). This development was in response to continuing challenges to the purity of faith from *Montanism* (no sins committed after Baptism can be forgiven) and *Donatism* (a sacrament is invalid if administered by one in mortal sin).

10.   *Persecutions* began also at this time as Christianity increasingly set itself at odds with the religious pluralism of contemporary society. Major persecutions occurred under the emperors *Decius* and *Diocletian*.

11. A major event at the beginning of the *fourth century* was the conversion of the emperor *Constantine* and his edict of 313 granting legal status to Christianity.

12. The *monastic movement* began at this time at least partially in protest against the lessening of Christian fervor in this new atmosphere of legal status. It originated as a retreat of individuals (hermits) into the desert but soon became a communal movement. Bishops and leading theologians of the period were trained in the monastic way. It shaped their scholarship (and hence influenced the great ecumenical councils of the fourth and fifth centuries) and their spirituality as well.

13. The *fourth and fifth centuries* were also preoccupied with dogmatic controversies in the East about the relationship between the one God and Jesus Christ, and then about the Holy Spirit in relationship to both. *Arianism* (Christ is a creature, greater than we but less than God) was opposed by the *Council of Nicea* in 325; *Apollinarianism* (Christ had no human soul) was condemned by the *First Council of Constantinople* in 381; *Nestorianism* (the man Jesus is separate from the Word; the two are not united in one person) was condemned by the *Council of Ephesus* in 431; and *Monophysitism* (Christ's human nature was completely absorbed by the one divine person) was rejected by the *Council of Chalcedon* in 451.

14. In the West, meanwhile, the theological challenge came from *Pelagianism* on the issue of nature and grace (salvation is through human effort alone), and its chief opponent was *Augustine*.

15. By the beginning of the fifth century also, German tribes began migrating through Europe without discernible control. This movement has been called the *Barbarian Invasions*. These invasions were to last some six hundred years and were to change the character of Christianity from a largely Graeco-Roman religion to a broader European religion. Except for the Franks, most of the tribes converted to Arianism, carrying with them many of their former pagan and superstitious practices. The strongly militaristic and feudal character of Germanic culture was to influence Christian devotion, spirituality, and organizational structure.

16. The tradition of the warrior chief in these tribes led eventually to the great *investiture struggle* between the rulers of state and the popes, especially *Gregory VII* (d. 1085): Shall ecclesiastical leaders be appointed by the Church, or by the state?

17. Meanwhile, a mission to the Anglo-Saxons in the British Isles was inaugurated by *Pope Gregory the Great* (d. 604), who also imagina-

tively employed undeniably strong financial resources to draw temporal power to the papacy.

18.   The Church entered another major historical period at the beginning of the *eighth century*. Because the Eastern emperor proved incapable of coming to the aid of the papacy when it was under attack from the Lombards in northern Italy, the pope turned to the Franks for help. This was the start of ther Holy Roman Empire, which reached its climactic moment in the year 800 with the crowning of *Charlemagne*. The line between Church and state disappeared, for all practical purposes.

19.   When the Carolingian empire collapsed, however, the papacy was left at the mercy of an essentially corrupt Roman nobility. Throughout the *tenth and eleventh centuries* the papacy languished in its "dark age."

20.   Meanwhile, *monasticism* was imported into the West from the East, reaching its high point in the middle of the sixth century with the founding of Monte Cassino by *St. Benedict*. In spite of its simple purposes of work and prayer, Western monasticism became the principal carrier of Western civilization during the early Middle Ages. No other institution had comparable social or intellectual influence.

21.   Some measure of stability returned to Europe by the *middle of the eleventh century*. Monks, no longer required to bear so many temporal burdens, returned to their monasteries. A spirit of renewal and reform prevailed. *Pope Gregory VII* attacked three evils: simony, the alienation of property, and lay investiture. Each reform was designed to liberate the Church from lay control. The powers of the papacy were enormously strengthened, especially in the pontificate of *Innocent III* (1198-1216).

22.   *Canon law* was codified to support the new network of papal authority. Legalism replaced theology in the self-understanding of the Church and in its sacramental life, especially concerning marriage. The classical, juridical, papal-hierarchical concept of the Church was firmly established by the *middle of the thirteenth century*. By now the pope was crowned like an emperor, a practice observed until 1978, when newly elected Pope John Paul I abandoned the coronation rite.

23.   Although the Gregorian Reform was not a complete success (the investiture struggle continued, and Gregory himself died a prisoner), there was a renewal of religious life, of the life of the clergy, and even of the Church's central administration. *Bernard of Clairvaux* (d. 1153) was

one of the principal instruments of the renewal, although he also introduced a highly personal, subjectivist, almost anti-intellectual approach to spirituality and theology.

24. With the consolidation of independent schools at the beginning of the thirteenth century, theology moved from the monasteries to the emerging *universities* and assumed the speculative character of university disciplines.

25. New assaults upon orthodoxy came from purist groups: The *Albigensians*, or *Cathari*, and the *Waldensians*. The *Inquisition* was founded at this time to deal with these movements. Its excesses are well known. Others combatted the new heresies through preaching, example, and pastoral care: *Francis of Assisi* and *Dominic* in particular, and the mendicant orders they founded. A renewed theological scholarship also grew out of these communities: *Aquinas, Bonaventure, Duns Scotus, et al.*

26. Concurrently, through a series of unfortunate and complicated political and diplomatic maneuvers, the historic bond of union between the Church of Rome and the Church of Constantinople came apart. In 1054 the patriarch of Constantinople, *Michael Cerularius*, was heavy-handedly excommunicated by papal legates, but the death blow to East-West unity was dealt by the *Fourth Crusade* (1202-1204) and the sack of Constantinople by Western knights. Thus began the *East-West Schism.*

27. The Church moved into another major period of its history at the beginning of the *fourteenth century*, a period of *disintegration* which reached its climax in the *Protestant Reformation* of the *sixteenth century.*

28. Events which prepared the way for the Reformation included: the confrontation between *Pope Boniface VIII* and *Philip the Fair*, leading to the Pope's imprisonment and death; the proliferation of serious financial abuses during the papacy's Babylonian Captivity at Avignon, in France (1309-1378); the rise of nationalism and anti-clericalism in resentment against papal taxes; the new theological challenges to the canonical justifications of papal power, especially in *Marsilius of Padua's* advocacy of a conciliar rather than a monarchical concept of the Church (1324); the *Great Western Schism* (1378-1417) with, at one point, three different claimants to the papacy; and the turn to the principle of *conciliarism* to resolve the problem at the *Council of Constance*, which decreed the supremacy of a general council and the collegiality of the bishops.

29. Among the *causes of the Reformation* are: (1) the corruption of the Renaissance papacy of the fifteenth century; (2) the divorce of piety from theology, and of theology from biblical and patristic tradition; (3) the debilitating effects of the Great Western Schism; (4) the rise of the

national state; (5) the too-close connection between Western Christianity and Western civilization; and (6) the vision, experiences, and personalities of *Luther, Zwingli,* and *Calvin.*

30.   The *Reformation* itself took *different forms:* On the *right,* it retained essential Catholic doctrine but changed certain canonical and/or ecclesiological forms (Lutheranism and Anglicanism); on the *left,* it repudiated much Catholic doctrine as well as much of Catholicism's sacramental life (*Zwinglianism* and the *Anabaptist* movement); nearer to the *center,* it modified both doctrine and practice but retained much of the old (*Calvinism*).

31.   The Catholic response was belated. When it came, it was vigorous. Known as the *Counter-Reformation,* it began at the *Council of Trent* (1545-1563) and especially under the leadership of *Pope Paul III* (1534-1549). The council, which perhaps did more than any other event or historical factor to shape Catholicism from that time until the Second Vatican Council in the mid-1960s, articulated Catholic doctrine on faith and grace, following a middle course between Pelagianism (it all depends on us) and Protestantism (it all depends on God). The Council also defined the sacraments, created the Index of Forbidden Books, and established seminaries. There were good and bad effects of the council's work.

32.   At the heart of the Catholic Counter-Reformation was the *Society of Jesus* (Jesuits), the strongest single force in helping the Church regain the initiative on several fronts: missionary, educational, and pastoral. Spiritual renewal in the form of Spanish mysticism also occurred at this time in the work of *Teresa of Avila* and *John of the Cross.*

33.   But by and large the post-Tridentine Church continued to emphasize those practices so vehemently attacked by the Protestants: veneration of the saints, Marian devotions, and eucharistic adoration. The centrality of Christ, the communal character of the Eucharist, the responsibility of the laity in the Church—all of these were muted. Exceptions, of course, existed, as in the work and writings of *Francis de Sales* (d. 1622).

34.   Although by the *beginning of the seventeenth century* the papacy was as strong as it had been since the thirteenth, the Church was wracked again by doctrinal and moral controversy, this time provoked by *Jansenism.* The movement drew its inspiration from Augustine, who had always emphasized the priority of grace over nature. Jansenism took Augustine's emphasis many steps further, portraying nature as totally corrupt and promoting a theory of predestination. From these principles there emerged a life-style that was exceedingly rigorous and puritanical.

35. *Gallicanism* developed as a result of Rome's efforts to combat and suppress Jansenism, which was largely a French movement. Gallicanism affirmed that the pope lacks supreme authority in the Church. That belongs only to a general council. Therefore, all papal decrees are subject to the consent of the entire Church, as represented in such a council.

36. These internal problems were complicated by the most fundamental external challenge to traditional Christianity, the *Enlightenment*. It displayed enormous (indeed exaggerated) confidence in reason; it had an optimistic view of human nature and the world (inevitable progress); and it celebrated freedom of inquiry. It made inroads particularly in Protestant countries.

37. A counterpart to the Englightenment occurred within the Catholic Church of the eighteenth century, with advances in scholarship, education of the clergy, reform of the liturgy and catechesis, and so forth.

38. Missionary expansion at this time, especially by the Spanish and Portuguese, was marred by colonialism and Romanism; i.e., the Gospel was tied too closely to certain political, cultural, and legal forms. Flexibility and adaptation were not in order. This was the period of the great controversy over the Chinese rites.

39. The Church was catapulted into the final period of its second great historical moment (i.e., its moment of cultural confinement) by the *French Revolution* (1789), which ended medieval Catholicism once and for all.

40. Catholic reactions to the excesses of the French Revolution included a *romanticist* movement (an attempt at recovering the glories of the Church's past) and a *theological* movement designed to come to terms constructively with the Enlightenment. But the *nineteenth century* does not present a uniform picture. Although *Cardinal Newman*'s interest in the problem of faith anticipated the major theological developments of the twentieth century, the Church also witnessed the spread of *Integralism*, *Fideism*, and *Ultramontanism*, all of which found support in the pontificates of *Gregory XVI* and *Pius IX*. The spirit of the leadership's attitude to this period of pronounced change is captured in the latter Pope's *Syllabus of Errors* (1864), which condemned "progress, liberalism, and modern civilization."

41. The official Church's response to the *social question* was more positive, though belated. *Pope Leo XIII* initiated a series of teachings on behalf of social justice that have remained largely pertinent even to the present day.

42.   The Enlightenment continued to pound at the Church's door, but now in the form of *Modernism* at the turn of the twentieth century. Not a single school of thought so much as a cluster of movements, Modernism emphasized the inner religious experience in the genesis of faith, and correspondingly downplayed the role of revelation, of dogma, and of ecclesiastical authority. The reaction of the Pope, *Pius X*, was unmistakably negative. It was at this time that the *Oath Against Modernism* was imposed upon all priests (1909).

43.   Between the two World Wars, Catholicism lived at once under the impact of the Modernist crisis and under the power of new movements within the Church: liturgical, biblical, social action, lay, ecumenical, missionary, and theological.

44.   These movements were to surface, now with official approval, in the years during or just following the Second World War. They were forerunners of the renewal and reforms of the Second Vatican Council.

SUGGESTED READINGS

Bainton, Roland. *Christendom: A Short History of Christianity and Its Impact on Western Civilization*. 2 vols. New York: Harper & Row, 1966.

Barry, Colman. *Readings in Church History*. 3 vols. Westminster, Md.: Newman Press, 1960-1965.

Bausch, William J. *Pilgrim Church: A Popular History of Catholic Christianity*. Notre Dame, Ind.: Fides Press, 1973.

Bettenson, Henry, ed. *Documents of the Christian Church*. New York: Oxford University Press, 1967.

Dillenberger, John, and Welch, Claude. *Protestant Christianity: Interpreted Through Its Development*. New York: Scribner, 1954.

Dolan, John P. *Catholicism: An Historical Survey*. Woodbury, N.Y.: Barron's Educational Series, 1968.

Franzen, August. *A Concise History of the Church*. New York: Herder & Herder, 1969.

Ruether, Rosemary, and McLaughlin, Eleanor, eds. *Women of Spirit: Female Leadership in the Jewish and Christian Traditions*. New York: Simon & Shuster, 1979.

· XIX ·

THE CHURCH OF THE
SECOND VATICAN COUNCIL

THE SIGNIFICANCE OF VATICAN II

The Second Vatican Council was only the twenty-first general or *ecumenical* (literally, "the whole wide world") council of the Church. To a great extent it was convened, organized, and governed by the same laws and processes which shaped its predecessor, Vatican I (1869-1870), and, to a slightly lesser extent, the Council of Trent (1545-1563). This is not to say, however, that all of the councils have followed the same pattern as Trent, Vatican I, and Vatican II. The eight ancient ecumenical councils of the Byzantine East, for example, were convened not by the bishop of Rome but by the emperor. In an official statement released on the eve of Vatican II's opening (September 1962), Pope John XXIII expressed the judgment that "by virtue of the number and variety of those who will participate in its meetings [Vatican II] will be the greatest of the councils held by the Church so far." Why should this have been so?

First, the total number of delegates to this council greatly exceeded the number attending any of the preceding twenty. The largest previous ecumenical council had been Vatican I, with 737 in attendance. Vatican II had more than 2600 bishops from all over the world (2908 would have been eligible to attend the first session). Counting theologians and other experts on hand, the number of participants approached 3000.

Secondly, and more significantly, this council was not only the largest in number but also the most representative in terms of nations and cultures. Even Vatican I, with its 737 delegates, was dominated by Europeans, including European bishops of missionary lands. But between Vatican I and Vatican II a major change occurred in the composition of the hierarchies of mission countries. In his encyclical letter *Maximum Illud* (1919), Pope Benedict XV insisted on the primary importance of establishing a native clergy and a native hierarchy in mission lands, of the disinterestedness required from foreign missionaries, and of their full adaptation to their adopted country. The same stress on developing a native clergy and native bishops was carried forward in subsequent encyclicals by Popes Pius XI and Pius XII. Consequently, most of the bishops from mission countries in attendance at Vatican II were themselves natives of those lands and products of those cultures. Among eligible bishops, 1089 were from Europe, 489 from South America, 404 from North America, 374 from Asia, 296 from Africa, 84 from Central America, and 75 from Oceania.

Thirdly, the council was also more representative than earlier councils in terms of non-Catholic and lay observers. With the arrival of three representatives of the Russian Orthodox Church, sixty-three non-Catholic observers were in attendance by the beginning of the second session (1963), an increase of eighteen over the first session. Almost every major Christian church was represented. In addition, eleven laymen were invited to attend the second session. This number was to increase to fifty-two lay auditors by the beginning of the fourth session (1965), twenty-nine of whom were men and twenty-three women, including ten nuns.

Fourthly, this was the first ecumenical council to have available to it electric lights, telephones, typewriters, and other modern means of communication and transportation. It was also the first to be covered by newspapers and magazines from all over the world, as well as by radio and television.

Finally, the council was also unique in its intended purpose. Unlike so many councils before it, it was not called to confront a serious attack upon the doctrinal or organizational integrity of the Church. It was not called simply to repeat ancient formulas or to condemn dissidents and heretics. On the contrary, Pope John XXIII, in his opening address of October 11, 1962, said that the council's goal was to eradicate the seeds of discord and promote peace and the unity of all humankind. Insofar as it would attend to doctrine, the council was to keep in mind the basic distinction between the substance of doctrine and the way in which it is presented. The Church must employ, to this end, the best methods of research and the literary forms of modern thought. The council would thereby prepare "the path toward that unity of mankind which is required . . . in order that the earthly city may be brought to the resemblance of that heavenly city. . . ."

In a word, Vatican II was a council unique in the history of the Church because it was the first really *ecumenical* council. As such, it signaled the Catholic Church's movement from a Church of cultural confinement, particularly of the European variety, to a genuine world Church.

TWENTIETH-CENTURY CATHOLIC THEOLOGY BEFORE VATICAN II

One must be careful about a purely pejorative understanding of the expression "pre-Vatican II theology." There is no uniform preconciliar theology. In the early and mid-twentieth century we find not only the theology of the textbooks, or manuals, but also the theology of individual theologians whose work was not yet accepted at official levels but who were, in fact, laying the foundation for the documents of Vatican II. Included among these theologians were Karl Rahner, Yves Congar, Henri de Lubac, Edward Schillebeeckx, Hans Küng, and the American Jesuit John Courtney Murray.

Textbook Theology

Nowhere is the traditional pre-Vatican ecclesiology more faithfully or more responsibly set forth than in Joachim Salaverri's *"De Ecclesia Christi"* ("On the Church of Christ") in the first volume of the so-called *Spanish Summa (Sacrae Theologiae Summa,* Madrid: Library of Christian Authors, 1962, 5th ed.). The basic approach is clear in the organization of the material. Salaverri divides his ecclesiology into three main parts, or books. The first is on the "social constitution" of the Church. Here he explains, in chapter 1, Christ's "institution of a hierarchical Church." He suggests that the Church is the visible, earthly, external form of the Kingdom of God and that it is governed by the college of the Apostles, by mandate of the Lord himself. The Apostles were granted the power of teaching, ruling, and sanctifying, with the understanding or proviso that every person would submit himself or herself to this power.

Salaverri argues in his second chapter that the Church is not only a *hierarchical* Church; it is also a *monarchical* Church. This is rooted in Christ's conferral of the primacy on Peter, which the author proves on the basis of the New Testament (employing a form of exegesis not consistent with that accepted and practiced by Catholic scholars today, as already suggested in chapter 17 of this book). According to Salaverri, after the resurrection Christ gave Peter "direct and immediate" authority over the universal Church. Peter is, therefore, the Vicar of Christ and the "superior" of the Apostles. The permanence of this monarchical-hierarchical Church is insured through the act of succession: apostolic in the case of the bishops, Petrine in the case of the pope. The papal primacy, Salaverri argues in his tenth thesis, is "universal, ordinary, immediate, truly episcopal, supreme and full, and is subject to no higher judgment on earth." There is, of course, much here that is reminiscent of the papal claims in the Middle Ages, especially as represented in the *Dictatus Papae* of Gregory VII (1075) and the bull *Unam Sanctam* (1302) of Boniface VIII. Salaverri concludes Book I with the assertion that "the Roman Catholic Church alone is the true Church of Christ" and he "demonstrates" this on the basis of the necessity of a permanent hierarchy and primacy to insure the permanence of the Church as Christ instituted it.

In Book II, Salaverri moves to a thorough discussion of the teaching authority (*magisterium*) of the Church and the sources of that authority. He argues that Christ established in the Apostles a teaching authority that is authentic (i.e., attached to an ecclesiastical office) perpetual, and infallible (immune from error). The pope is infallible when he speaks *ex cathedra* ("from the chair") on matters of faith and morals with the intention of binding the whole Church. The bishops share in this infallibility when they define a dogma of faith in union with the pope either at an ecumenical council or through some other vehicle of common teaching. Doctrinal decrees of the various Vatican administrative offices (the Curia) express the intention of the pope and therefore are to be received with "internal and religious assent of the mind." The source for the Church's official teaching authority is the divine apostolic tradition, including Sacred Scripture, the Fathers of the Church, and theological consensus (especially the opinion of Thomas Aquinas).

In Book III, Salaverri turns finally to the "supernaturality" and "properties" of the Church. But here, too, the discussion is largely in terms of the hierarchical, the organizational, and the juridical. Thus, thesis 23 asserts: "The Church is a perfect and absolutely independent society with full legislative, judicial, and coercive power." When he speaks of the Church as Mystical Body of Christ, the focus is upon conditions for membership. One gains entrance through valid Baptism, and one may be subsequently excluded by heresy, apostasy, schism, or excommunication. The Church, in any case, is necessary for salvation even by "necessity of means." (A distinction was drawn in the older theology between "necessity of means" and "necessity of precept." "Necessity of precept" refers to a condition that "ought" to be fullfilled because the Lord asked us to do so, but it is possible nonetheless to reach a particular end without fulfilling the condition. "Necessity of means" refers to a condition that "ought" to and "must" be fulfilled if the end is to be reached.)

Regarding the properties of the Church, Salaverri proposes that the Roman Catholic Church alone possesses the "notes" of unity, holiness, catholicity, and apostolicity. All other churches, insofar as they lack one or more of these notes, are "false churches." The whole treatise on the Church concludes with the thesis that Christ gave the Apostles and their successors the threefold power of teaching, ruling, and sanctifying, and that this is the primary law for the whole Church.

"Progressive" Theology

Yves Congar

The most important ecclesiologist of this century, Yves Congar perhaps did more than any other single theologian to prepare the way for the Second Vatican Council. The council's major themes are already anticipated in Congar's books. He wrote of the Church as the People of God in his *Mystery of the Temple* (1958). Within the People of God the laity are called to full participation in the mission of the Church (*Lay People in the Church*, 1953). The Church is more than the Roman Catholic Church alone (*Divided Christendom*, 1937). The mission of the Church is not to grow and multiply but to be a minority in the service of the majority. Like the French Underground during the Second World War, the Church is a small community which prepares the way for the salvation of all in the coming of the Kingdom. The Church exists in itself but not for itself (*The Wide World, My Parish*, 1961). This Church, ecumenically conceived, is always in need of reform, even institutional and structural reform, in head as well as in members (*Vraie et fausse reforme dans l'Eglise*, 1950). This book, whose title means *True and False Reform in the Church,* was never translated into English, and in fact was withdrawn from circulation because of its controversial content.

Karl Rahner

Although Rahner's principal theological contributions have not been in the area of ecclesiology as such, he, too, prepared the way for Vatican II with his fundamental notion of the universality of grace (already discussed at length in our earlier chapters on human existence, 4 and 5) and the correlative notion of the *diaspora* Church. In an essay published in 1961 but written earlier than that, "A Theological Interpretation of the Position of Christians in the Modern World" (*Mission and Grace*, London: Sheed & Ward, 1963, pp. 3-55), Rahner notes that some events in the history of salvation "ought not" to be, but are and "must" be so (e.g., the crucifixion, the existence of poverty, etc.) The minority, scattered (*diaspora*) condition of the Church is one of those "musts" of salvation history. This diaspora situation, he argues, is not only permitted by God but positively willed by God. And we must draw our conclusions from this.

It means that the Church is no longer "in possession" and cannot act as if it were. The age of "Christendom" is over. The Church must attract people on the basis of choice, not on the basis of social convention or political pressure. Those who belong to the Church will belong to it as a matter of conviction, not of habit. "Just where is it written that *we* must have the whole 100 per cent? God must have all. . . . Why should we not alter to our use, quite humbly and dispassionately, a saying of St. Augustine's: Many whom God has, the Church does not have; and many whom the Church has, God does not have?" (p. 51).

Edward Schillebeeckx

Another major theological influence before the council was Edward Schillebeeckx's *Christ the Sacrament of Encounter with God*, first published in Dutch in 1960, and translated into English in 1963 (New York: Sheed & Ward). Schillebeeckx's argument is easily summarized: Apart from the sacramental principle, there is no basis for contact (encounter) between God and the human community. God is totally spiritual, and we are bodily creatures. Thus, it is only insofar as God adapts to our material condition that God can reach us and we can reach God. The embodiment of the spiritual in the material and the communication of the spiritual through the material is the sacramental principle. Christ is the great sacrament of God, because God addresses us through the flesh of Christ and we respond through that same fleshly Christ. The Church, in turn, is the sacrament of Christ, who otherwise would be removed from our range of daily, bodily existence. The seven sacraments are, finally, the principal ways by which the Church communicates the reality of Christ and of God, and by which we respond to Christ and to God in worship.

The essence of the Church, therefore, "consists in this, that the final goal of grace achieved by Christ becomes visibly present in the *whole* Church as a visible society" (p. 56). The Church is not only a means of salvation; it is the principal sign, or sacrament, of salvation. It is not only an institution but a community. Indeed, it is an institutionalized community. The important missionary implication is not whether the whole world enters the Church but whether the Church itself gives credible witness to the presence of Christ and of God within the community.

Henri de Lubac

A similarly sacramental perspective was advanced by the French Jesuit Henri de Lubac in his influential work *Catholicism* (New York: Sheed & Ward, 1950). "Humanity is one, organically one by its divine structure; it is the Church's mission to reveal to men that pristine unity that they have lost, to restore and complete it" (p. 19). The Church, de Lubac insisted, is "not merely that strongly hierarchical and disciplined society whose divine origin has to be maintained. . . . If Christ is the sacrament of God, the Church is for us the sacrament of Christ. . ." (p. 29). Indeed, "it is through his union with the community that the Christian is united to Christ" (p. 35).

John Courtney Murray

John Courtney Murray was not formally an ecclesiologist, although his best-known writings touched upon the relationship between Church and state and on the correlative question of religious freedom. Not invited to the first session of the council because of his views on these issues, Murray proved to be the major influence in the composition of the council's *Declaration on Religious Freedom*. His pre-Vatican II contributions were done through scholarly articles in *Theological Studies* in which he subjected certain traditional teachings, especially of Pope Leo XIII, to historical and theological reinterpretation. He argued not that the Leonine doctrine was false but that it was archaic. It was based on a paternalistic rather than a constitutional concept of political authority. Leo's position was also formulated in the context of the Continental laicist state, and Leo confused society with the state just as they were confused in the philosophies of pagan antiquity. But given developments in Catholic social philosophy and in the political character of much of the world, the Leonine teaching can no longer obtain.

Over against this teaching, Murray argued for the four truths which came to be accepted in essence by the council: the dignity of the human person (a principle which pervaded the doctrinal work of Pope Pius XII), our endowment with natural rights and duties (also in Pius XII, but developed by John XXIII in *Pacem in Terris*), the juridical nature of the state, i.e., its primary commitment to the protection of human rights and the facilitation of duties (Pius XII again), and the limitation of the powers of government by a higher order of human and civil rights (Pius XII, as elaborated upon by John XXIII). A brief summary of Murray's position, in light of Vatican II's statement on religious liberty, is available in *Council Daybook, Vatican II, Session 4,* pp. 14-17.

Hans Küng

Hans Küng was only 33 when he published his *The Council and Reunion* (London: Sheed & Ward, 1961). It was undoubtedly the single most influential book in the council's preparatory phase because it alerted so many people in the Catholic world to the possibilities for renewal and reform through the medium of Vatican II. For Küng, reunion of the churches depends upon their prior reform, including the reform of the Roman Catholic Church. This is always necessary because the Church consists not only of human beings but of sinful human beings. Although his book is remarkably comprehensive, its basic ecclesiological point is that "the chief difficulty in the way of reunion lies in the two different concepts of the Church, and especially of the concrete organizational structure of the Church" (p. 188). The difference is most sharply focused in the question of ecclesiastical office: its origin, powers, scope of authority, and forms. And the heart of the matter is the Petrine office: "Do we need a pope?" Pope John XXIII, Küng noted, was giving the papacy a whole new style and perhaps in the process eliminating or diminishing many of the historic objections to the office from the Protestant side.

Almost all of the reforms Küng argued for were eventually adopted—e.g., the establishment of episcopal conferences, the abolition of the Index of Forbidden Books, simplification of the liturgy.

POPE JOHN XXIII

It is difficult to exaggerate the role played by Pope John XXIII in the total event known as the Second Vatican Council, even though he was to die between the first and second sessions (1963). When elected in 1958 Pope John insisted that his was a "very humble office of shepherd" and that he intended to pattern his ministry after that of Joseph in the Old Testament story, who greeted the brothers who had once sold him into slavery with the compassionate and forgiving words, "I am Joseph, your brother" (Genesis 45:4). When the new pope took possession of the Lateran Basilica in Rome, he reminded the congregation that he was not a prince surrounded by the signs of outward power but "a priest, a father, a shepherd." From the beginning he broke the precedent of centuries and visited the sick in the Roman hospitals, the elderly in old-age homes, the convicts at Regina Coeli prison. Every day he celebrated what was then known as the dialogue Mass (i.e., with responses from the people). On Holy Thursday he washed the feet of selected members of the congregation, and on Good Friday he walked in the procession of the cross.

This new-style pope first announced the council on January 25, 1959, and officially convoked it on December 25, 1961, with the hope that it would be a demonstration of the vitality of the Church, a means of rebuilding Christian unity, and a catalyst for world peace. In his address at the council's solemn opening on October 11, 1962, the pope revealed again his fundamental spirit of hope and even optimism about the future. He complained openly about some of his advisers who "though burning with zeal, are not endowed with much sense of discretion or measure. In these modern times they can see nothing but prevarication and ruin." He called them "prophets of gloom, who are always forecasting disaster, as though the end of the world were at hand." On the contrary, "Divine Providence is leading us to a new order of human relations. . . ."

To carry out its purposes, the council would have to remain faithful to the "sacred patrimony of truth received from the Fathers. But at the same time she must ever look to the present, to the new conditions and new forms of life introduced into the modern world which have opened new avenues to the Catholic apostolate." But a council was unnecessary at this time, the pope insisted, if the preservation of doctrine were to be its principal aim. "The substance of the ancient doctrine. . . is one thing, and the way in which it is presented is another." This is not the time for negativism. The Church counteracts errors by "demonstrating the validity of her teaching rather than by condemnations." The council and the Church in council are like Peter who said to the beggar, "Silver and gold I have none; but what I have, that I give you. In the name of Jesus Christ of Nazareth, arise and walk" (Acts of the Apostles 3:6).

Thus, the Church of Vatican II will spread everywhere the fullness of Christian charity, "than which nothing is more effective in eradicating the seeds of discord, nothing more efficacious in promoting concord, just peace and the brotherly unity of all." This means that the council must work for the unity of the whole Christian family and for the unity of the whole human family. "The council now beginning rises in the Church like daybreak, a forerunner of most splendid light. It is now only dawn."

THE COUNCIL DOCUMENTS IN GENERAL

There are sixteen council documents in all. Two were produced in the second session (1963): *The Constitution on the Sacred Liturgy* and the *Decree on the Instruments of Social Communication.* Three were produced in the third session (1964): the *Dogmatic Constitution on the Church (Lumen gentium),* the *Decree on Ecumenism,* and the *Decree on Eastern Catholic Churches.* Eleven were produced in the fourth and final session (1965): the *Decree on the Bishops' Pastoral Office in the Church,* the *Decree on Priestly Formation,* the *Decree on the Appropriate Renewal of the Religious Life,* the *Declaration on the Relationship of the Church to Non-*

Christian Religions, the *Declaration on Christian Education,* the *Dogmatic Constitution on Divine Revelation,* the *Decree on the Apostolate of the Laity,* the *Pastoral Constitution on the Church in the Modern World (Gaudium et spes),* the *Decree on the Ministry and Life of Priests,* the *Decree on the Church's Missionary Activity,* and the *Declaration on Religious Freedom.*

Their Authority

These documents are unequal in juridical standing, in content, and in effect. They vary in *juridical standing* in that the dogmatic constitutions are more "authoritative" than decrees and declarations. *Constitutions* touch substantively upon doctrinal matters which pertain to the very essence, or "constitution," of the Church. *Decrees* and *declarations* are directed at practical questions or specific pastoral concerns. As such, they presuppose the doctrine and the theology of the constitutions. Two of the four constitutions (on the Church and on revelation) are called "dogmatic" in that they do indeed touch upon matters which are themselves part of the dogmatic content of Christian faith. One of the constitutions is called "pastoral"—a designation unprecedented in the history of the Church—in that it touches upon the fundamental, "constitutive" relationship of the Church to the world at large. And a fourth constitution, on the sacred liturgy, has no special designation at all. Liturgy is part of the Church's constitutive nature, but it is not part of the dogmatic content of its faith. Rather it is dogma in practice (*Lex orandi, lex credendi* again).

These documents vary also in *content.* Some are substantive—e.g., the *Dogmatic Constitution on the Church,* and others are remarkably thin—e.g., the *Declaration on Christian Education.* Some reflect the progressive theological currents of the preconciliar period—e.g., the *Decree on Ecumenism,* and others reflect the more traditional currents—e.g., the *Decree on the Instruments of Social Communication.*

These documents vary, finally, in their *effect* upon the Church. How a teaching is "received" by the Church is one of the important criteria by which we judge the teaching's authority. It is not enough, in other words, that a document should have issued forth from an ecumenical council. Just as there is a hierarchy of sacraments (Eucharist being the most important, according to the Council of Trent) and a hierarchy even of biblical books (the Epistle to the Romans, for example, is certainly more important than the Epistle to Philemon), so there is a hierarchy of official pronouncements.

Theologians judge the *degree* of any official pronouncement's authority, therefore, by a variety of standards: (1) *What is the nature of the document?* Is it an encyclical? An address to a group of pilgrims to Rome? A disciplinary decree from a Vatican congregation? A declaration of an ecumenical council? A dogmatic constitution of an ecumenical council? (2) *What is the source of the pronouncement?* A pope? An ecumenical council? A synod of bishops? (3) *How representative was the process by which the document was written?* Were all those with competence and a legitimate interest in the question under discussion actually consulted, and did they effectively participate in the formulation of the pronouncement? (4) *Do the concepts and language of the final formulation reflect the current state of the discussion on the topic?* Are the terms of the current debate and the rejected positions clearly understood? (5) *How is the pronouncement received by those with competence on the topic,* either by reason of their academic and scientific qualifications or by reason of their experiential knowledge of the subject? Does the pronouncement, in other words, have any significant impact on the life of the Church?

It is this fifth criterion that is most pertinent to our evaluation here. According to this norm of *reception,* the following seven documents of Vatican II have emerged in this post-conciliar period as the most important: the *Dogmatic Constitution on the Church (Lumen gentium),* the *Pastoral Constitution on the Church in the Modern World (Gaudium et spes),* the *Decree on Ecumenism,* the *Constitution on the Sacred Liturgy,* the *Dogmatic Constitution on Divine Revelation,* the *Declaration on Religious Freedom,* and the *Declaration on the Relationship of the Church to Non-Christian Religions.* In other words, most of the significant changes in thought and practice since Vatican II are traceable to the teachings and orientations of these seven documents rather than to the other nine.

Their Relationship to the Church

All of the documents are concerned, in one way or another, with the mystery of the Church:

The Church in General: Nature and Place in History
  Dogmatic Constitution on the Church

The Inner Life of the Church
  Proclamation and Teaching
    Dogmatic Constitution on Divine Revelation
    Declaration on Christian Education
  Worship
    Constitution on the Sacred Liturgy
  Ministries and Forms of Christian Existence
    Decree on the Ministry and Life of Priests
    Decree on Priestly Formation
    Decree on the Bishops' Pastoral Office
    Decree on the Appropriate Renewal of Religious Life
    Decree on the Apostolate of the Laity
  Interrelationships among Churches
    Decree on Ecumenism
    Decree on Eastern Catholic Churches

The Church and the World Beyond the Church
  Other Religions
    Declaration on Non-Christian Religions
  The World at Large
    Pastoral Constitution on the Church in the Modern World
    Decree on the Church's Missionary Activity
    Declaration on Religious Freedom
    Decree on the Instruments of Social Communication

THE COUNCIL DOCUMENTS IN PARTICULAR
The Major Documents

Dogmatic Constitution on the Church

The first draft of this document, prepared by the council's Theological Commission in 1962, resembled the standard textbook treatments of the mystery of the Church which were in general use in seminaries, colleges, and universities throughout most of the twentieth century. The successive drafts (there were four in all) disclose the extraordinary development which occurred in the council's self-understanding. Whereas at the beginning the emphasis was on the institutional, hierarchical, and juridical aspects of the Church, with special importance assigned to the papal office, the finally approved and promulgated constitution speaks of the Church as the People of God and of its authority as collegial in nature and exercise.

According to *Lumen gentium*, the Church is a *mystery* before all else, i.e., "a reality imbued with the hidden presence of God" (Pope Paul VI). It is, to use an almost identical theological term, a *sacrament*, "a visible sign of an invisible grace" (Augustine). "By its relationship with Christ, the Church is a kind of sacrament of intimate union with God, and of the unity of all humankind, that is, it is a sign and an instrument of such union and unity" (n. 1). The Church is the visible embodiment of the triune God. It is called by the Father (n. 2) to union with and in Christ (n. 3) through the power of the Holy Spirit (n. 4). It is inaugurated by Jesus' preaching of the Kingdom of God, which he also personified and brought into being by his good works. The Church, too, is called to proclaim, embody, and serve the coming Kingdom of God (n. 5). As such, the Church is the pilgrim People of God in movement through history, sharing in Christ's threefold mission as Prophet, Priest, and King (chapter II).

Not until the council had described the Church as People of God did it direct its attention to the Church's hierarchical structure. An earlier draft of the constitution had the chapter on the hierarchy before the chapter on the People of God. In one of the most crucial arguments waged during the entire council, the point was urged upon the Fathers that the chapters should be reversed.

To speak of the Church's hierarchy before speaking of the Church as People of God would simply carry forward the textbook tradition that the Church is, first and foremost, a hierarchical institution to which people belong for the sake of certain spiritual benefits. The argument prevailed, and the chapters were reversed. The Church is presented in *Lumen gentium* as the whole People of God (chapter II), which happens to have a certain hierarchical structure to help the People of God fulfill its mission in history (chapter III).

The third chapter on the hierarchical structure of the Church, however, is important not only for the position it finally occupies in the dogmatic constitution but also for its content. The governance of the Church is no longer portrayed in purely monarchical terms, as it was in the theology textbooks and in the first draft of *Lumen gentium* itself. Authority is given not just to Peter and his successors but to the whole college of the Apostles and to those who succeed to the apostolic commission: "Together with its head, the Roman Pontiff, and never without its head, the episcopal order is the subject of supreme and full power over the universal Church" (n. 22). This collegial union is especially apparent in an ecumenical council, but it is also manifested "in the mutual relations of the individual bishops with particular churches and with the universal Church....In and from such individual churches there comes into being the one and only Catholic Church. For this reason each individual bishop represents his own church, but all of them together in union with the Pope represent the entire Church joined in the bond of peace, love, and unity" (n. 23). The Church, therefore, exists in each legitimate local congregation, as was the case in the New Testament, and also in the communion of all these local congregations (n. 26). The Church is at once local and universal.

The Church is also at once lay, religious, and clerical. The Church is the whole People of God, not just the hierarchy. "Everything which has been said so far concerning the People of God applies equally to the laity, religious, and clergy" (n. 30). Pastors were not intended by Christ to shoulder the whole mission themselves. On the contrary, their task is one of coordination of the gifts, charisms, and ministries which in fact exist within a given local church, to see to it that "all according to their proper roles may cooperate in this common undertaking with one heart" (n. 30). The laity, therefore, do not simply participate in the mission or the ministry of the hierarchy: "The lay apostolate, however, is a participation in the saving mission of the Church itself. Through their baptism and confirmation, all are commissioned to that apostolate by the Lord himself" (n. 33). And because the laity are as much a part of the Church as religious and clergy, and because the Church is called to holiness in order to be a credible sign of Christ to the world, everyone in the Church—laity, religious, and clergy alike—is called to holiness (chapter V). But this is always an imperfect realization. The Church is still on pilgrimage. "She herself dwells among creatures who groan and travail in pain until now and await the revelation of the sons of God" (n. 48). In the meantime, Mary serves as "a model of the Church in the matter of faith, charity, and perfect union with Christ" (n. 63). She is "a sign of sure hope and solace for the pilgrim People of God" (n. 68).

Pastoral Constitution on the Church in the Modern World

As we pointed out in chapter 3 of this book, the impetus for this unprecedented "pastoral" constitution came from Pope John XXIII and Cardinal Leo-Jozef Suenens of Belgium. With the prior knowledge and approval of the pope, Cardinal Suenens rose at the end of the first session (December 4, 1962) and urged the council to do more than examine the mystery of the Church in itself (*ad intra*). The council must also attend to the Church's relationship with the world at large (*ad extra*). The document (*Gaudium et spes (Joy and Hope)* is the principal result of that important intervention. (It was Pope John Paul II, then a bishop delegate at the council, who suggested the adjective "pastoral" for this unusual constitution.)

The pastoral constitution recapitulates the Church's social teachings as they had developed from Pope Leo XIII's encyclical *Rerum Novarum* (1891), through Pope Pius XI's *Quadragesimo Anno* (1931), and Pope John XXIII's *Mater et Magistra* (1961) and *Pacem in Terris* (1963). But it correlates this teaching with intellectual and scientific developments outside the Church as well: "...the Church has always had the duty of scrutinizing the signs of the times and of interpreting them in the light of the gospel" (n. 4). The ecclesiological theme is sounded at the outset: The Church exists not alongside the world but within the world, and not in domination over the world but as its servant. "Inspired by no earthly ambition, the Church seeks but a solitary goal: to carry forward the work of Christ himself under the lead of the befriending Spirit. And Christ entered this world to give witness to the truth, to rescue and not to sit in judgment, to serve and not to be served" (n. 3). (The reader is referred again to chapters 3 and 6 of this book, where some attention was already devoted to this conciliar document.)

Even though the Church will not fully attain its saving and eschatological purpose except in the age to come, the Church is called even now "to form the family of God's children during the present history of the human race..." (n. 40). The Church is "at once a visible assembly and a spiritual community (and) goes forward together with humanity and experiences the same earthly lot which the world does" (n. 40). In trying to imbue the world and its history with deeper meaning and importance, "...the Church believes it can contribute greatly toward making the family of humankind and its history more human" (n. 40). On the other hand, the Church is not a political party. It has "no proper mission in the political, economic, or social order" (n. 42). Nor is the Church bound to any "particular form of human culture, nor to any political, economic, or social system" (n. 42).

The pastoral constitution nevertheless recognizes and underlines the connection between religious faith and temporal activities. It characterizes the split between the two realms as "among the more serious errors of our age.... Therefore, let there be no false opposition between professional and social activities on the one part, and religious life on the other. The Christian who neglects his temporal duties neglects his duties toward his neighbor and even God, and jeopardizes his eternal salvation" (n. 43). The document acknowledges that this dichotomy between faith and action can occur within the Church as well as outside it, and the council calls upon Christians to close the gap between message and performance wherever it exists. In all, "...the Church has a single intention: that God's kingdom may come, and that the salvation of the whole human race may come to pass" (n. 45). The Church is in fact the universal sacrament of salvation. It is the sign of that fellowship "which allows honest dialogue and invigorates it" (n. 92). This means that life inside the Church must be governed always by the principle "Let there be unity in what is necessary, freedom in what is unsettled, and charity in any case" (n. 92). Insofar as the Church offers a credible witness to the truth, it will arouse the world to a "lively hope" in the coming of the Kingdom of God (n. 93).

Decree on Ecumenism

The quest for Christian unity is a missionary responsibility, for the Church is called to be a sacrament of Christ and of the unity of the triune God who is present within the Church (n. 2). The decree is remarkable for a variety of reasons: It describes the ecumenical movement as one of seeking the *restoration* of Christian unity rather than as a *return* of non-Catholics to the already-existing unity of the Catholic Church; it acknowledges the ecclesial reality of other Christian communities, which share the same Sacred Scriptures, the same life of grace, the same faith, hope, and charity, the same gifts of the Holy Spirit, the same Baptism, and many other common elements which constitute the Church; and it admits, finally, that both sides were to blame for the divisions that ruptured the Church at the time of the Reformation (nn. 3,20-23).

The immediate path to unity is through reform and renewal (n. 6). "There can be no ecumenism worthy of the name without a change of heart" (n. 7). This change of heart (which the council calls "spiritual ecumenism") may express itself at times even in joint celebration of the Eucharist. Although it is not simply a means of unity to be employed indiscriminately, eucharistic sharing may at times be necessary for the gaining of the grace of unity (n. 8). In the meantime, ecumenism also requires theological collaboration, dialogue, and joint study, as well as cooperation in social action (nn. 9-12).

Constitution on the Sacred Liturgy

This document is based on the ecclesiological assumption that the liturgy is "the outstanding means by which the faithful can express in their lives, and manifest to others, the mystery of Christ and the real nature of the true Church" (n. 2). It underscores the Church's mission to be a sign, or sacrament, of Christ and of God's presence in and for the world. The Church is called to proclaim the Gospel not only in word but also in ritual: in the sacraments and in the Eucharist particularly (n. 6). Through the liturgy the Church continues Christ's worship of the Father, which Christ achieved principally by the paschal mystery of his passion, resurrection, and exaltation to the right hand of God (n. 5). Through our participation in that same worship, we have a foretaste of the heavenly liturgy that is to come (n. 8). Although the liturgy does not exhaust the entire activity of the Church (n. 9), it can be described as "the summit toward which the activity of the Church is directed; at the same time it is the source from which all her power flows" (n. 10).

Because the Church is the whole People of God, everyone must be encouraged to participate actively in the celebration of the Eucharist and the other sacraments (nn. 26, 28, 29, 31, 47-55). But this is impossible if the liturgy, which is a world of signs and symbols, is not intelligible to those who participate in it (n. 21). And so this principle must govern the reform and renewal of the Church's liturgical life: If the sign is to cause the grace it signifies (as the Council of Trent declared), then the sign must be understandable. Otherwise it is not a sign at all, and, if not a sign, it cannot cause the grace for which it exists. That is why the language of the Eucharist and the other sacraments is once again the language of the people, and that is why the rites or ceremonies have been restructured and simplified since Vatican II. The latter process has been guided by the principles that there should be "legitimate variations and adaptations to different groups" and that there be no "rigid uniformity in matters which do not involve the faith or the good of the whole community" (nn. 37-38).

Dogmatic Constitution on Divine Revelation

The Church is commissioned to preach the Gospel to the whole of creation. What the Church is called upon to proclaim today it draws from Sacred Scripture and from the tradition "which comes from the apostles...with the help of the Holy Spirit. For there is a growth in the understanding of the realities and the words which have been handed down....the Church constantly moves forward toward the fullness of divine truth until the words of God reach their complete fulfillment..." (n. 8). The teaching office of the Church interprets the word of God as it is communicated in Scripture and in the successive interpretations of the Scriptures (tradition). "This teaching office is not above the word of God, but serves it....It is clear, therefore, that sacred tradition, sacred Scripture, and the teaching authority of the Church...are so linked and joined together that one cannot stand without the others, and that all together and each in its own way under the action of the one Holy Spirit contribute effectively to the salvation of souls" (n. 10).

Declaration on Religious Freedom

This document was at first to be a chapter of the *Decree on Ecumenism*, and later an Appendix of that same decree. Finally, it was given independent status as a declaration of the council. Although it is hardly a milestone in the history of the world (the principle of religious liberty had long since been recognized and defended by others inside and outside the Church), the declaration was a major event in the history of the Catholic Church and of the Second Vatican Council. It was by far the most controversial document produced by the council, because it raised in a special way the underlying question of *doctrinal development*. In light of so many seemingly unequivocal condemnations of the principle of religious freedom in earlier papal documents, how could the Church now turn around and endorse the principle? The distance between Pope Pius IX's *Syllabus of Errors* (1864) and Vatican II's *Declaration on Religious Freedom* (1965) is more than chronological. They inhabit two different theological universes.

This declaration ends the so-called double standard by which the Church demands freedom for itself when in a minority position but refuses to grant freedom to other religions when they are in the minority. The council declares as a matter of principle that the dignity of the human person and the freedom of the act of faith demand that everyone should be immune from coercion of every kind, private or public, in matters pertaining to the profession of a particular religious faith (n. 2). No one can be compelled to accept the Christian faith, nor can anyone be penalized in any way for not being a Christian (n. 9). The supreme model is Jesus himself and, after him, the example of the early Church (n. 11).

Declaration on the Relationship of the Church to Non-Christian Religions

This document, too, was originally planned as a chapter in the *Decree on Ecumenism*. It was also to be concerned principally with the Jews. Its vision, however, is considerably broader than that. It acknowledges, first of all, that the whole human community comes from the creative hand of the one God, and that variations in religious faith and expression are a reflection of the diversity that characterizes humankind itself. "The Catholic Church rejects nothing which is true and holy in these religions. . . . [They] often reflect a ray of that Truth which enlightens all persons" (n. 2). And so the Church encourages dialogue and collaboration with the followers of other religions in order to promote common spiritual and moral values.

The declaration recounts the many basic elements the Church has in common with the Jews. Since there is such a close union between Christians and Jews, we must pursue the way of mutual understanding and respect. Specifically, we must eschew the notion that Jews can be blamed as a race for the death of Jesus. Furthermore, the Jews are not repudiated or accursed by God (n. 4). Every form of persecution is to be condemned, and so, too, every kind of discrimination based on race, color, condition of life, or religion (n. 5).

The Minor Documents

Decree on the Church's Missionary Activity

This document presupposes the dogmatic constitution *Lumen gentium* and the pastoral constitution *Gaudium et spes*. It differs from both of them in that they speak of the "mission" of the Church in its total sense of preaching the Gospel in word, sacrament, witness, and service to the whole human community, Christians and non-Christians alike, whereas the *Decree on the Church's Missionary Activity* is concerned with one important aspect of that total mission, namely, "evangelization and the planting of the Church among those peoples and groups where it has not yet taken root" (n. 6). The distinction is between the "mission of the Church" and "the missions."

The decree does not restrict its vision to the de-Christianized West. The Gospel is to penetrate Asia, Africa, and Oceania as well. But wherever missionaries go, they are not to impose an alien cultural reality from outside. They are to recognize and preserve "whatever truth and grace are to be found among the nations, as a sort of secret presence of God. . . .And so, whatever good is found to be sown in the hearts and minds of men and women, or in the rites and cultures peculiar to various peoples, is not lost" (n. 9). This pastoral principle is rooted in the theological principle of the incarnation (n. 10). Finally, "the whole Church is missionary, and the work of evangelization is a basic duty of the People of God. . ." (n. 35).

Decree on the Apostolate of the Laity

This document also presupposes what is contained in *Lumen gentium* and *Gaudium et spes*. Moreover, its subject matter is treated in various other pronouncements of the council—e.g., the aforementioned *Decree on the Church's Missionary Activity*. This decree makes clear, as the *Dogmatic Constitution on the Church (Lumen gentium)* also made clear, that the laity are full members of the People of God and, as such, share directly in the mission of the Church, not simply by leave of the hierarchy but "from their union with Christ their Head. Incorporated into Christ's Mystical

Body through baptism and strengthened by the power of the Holy Spirit through confirmation, they are assigned to the apostolate by the Lord himself" (n. 3). This apostolate is located principally, but not exclusively, in the temporal order: the world of family, culture, economic affairs, the arts and professions, political institutions, and so forth (n. 6).

Decree on Eastern Catholic Churches

This decree is really a complement to the *Decree on Ecumenism.* It relates to the six main Eastern Catholic rites (i.e., to those Eastern churches in union with Rome as distinguished from those Eastern Orthodox churches which are still separate from Rome ever since the East-West Schism at the turn of the thirteenth century): Chaldean, Syrian, Maronite, Coptic, Armenian, and Byzantine. They are also known as "Uniate" churches. They have been sources of much friction between Rome and the Orthodox world because the "Uniate" churches were originally conceived as "substitutes" for, rather than as "bridges" to, the Orthodox East, and as such have always been resented by the latter.

Although the decree proclaims the equality of the Eastern and Western traditions of Christianity (n. 3) as well as the importance of preserving the spiritual heritage of the Eastern churches (n. 5), the decree itself is still very much a Latin text about the Eastern tradition (nn. 7-23). It clearly manifests, however, an ardent desire for reconciliation with the separated churches of the East and opens the door from Rome's side to common eucharistic sharing (nn. 24-29).

Decree on the Bishops' Pastoral Office in the Church

In its earlier stages this document reflected the pre-conciliar ecclesiology which tended to make bishops entirely subordinate to the pope and the Curia and to make the office of bishop more a jurisdictional than a sacramental reality. The finally approved decree, however, reflects the teaching of *Lumen gentium* on collegiality. Thus, bishops exercise their episcopal office "received through episcopal consecration" (n. 3). They exercise that office at three levels: over their own diocese, or "particular church," in collaboration with other bishops on a regional or national level (episcopal conferences), and as a worldwide body in union with the pope (college of bishops). Bishops, therefore, are not simply delegates or vicars of the pope in a diocese, as an exceedingly hierarchical model of the Church once proposed. They are "the proper, ordinary, and immediate pastors" of their own dioceses (n. 11). That pastoral office, which includes preaching the Gospel, presiding at worship, and ministering to those in need, must always be exercised in the mode of a servant (n. 16). The bishop must carry out his episcopal, or supervisory, duties in a manner that encourages communication and integration among the various apostolates (n. 17). Indeed, the decree contains a kind of job description and list of qualifications for the office of bishop (nn. 11-21).

Decree on the Ministry and Life of Priests

This decree emerged as a separate document because many bishops at the council thought there was too little said about priests in the *Dogmatic Constitution on the Church*. The essence of the decree's teaching follows: "Established in the priestly order by ordination, all priests are united among themselves in an intimate sacramental brotherhood. In a special way they form one presbytery in a diocese to whose service they are committed under their own bishop." Whether they are in parish work, teaching, or some other special activity, priests are "united in the single goal of building up Christ's Body" (n. 8). This work includes the proclamation of the Gospel, the celebration of the Eucharist and other sacraments, governance of a community, and ministering to those in need (nn. 4-6).

Decree on Priestly Formation

For four centuries the training of Catholic priests had been shaped by the directives of the Council of Trent, which was itself originally a reform council. Prior to Trent, priests were ordained with little or no theological or spiritual formation. But eventually the reforms of Trent developed into rigid rules, and seminaries tended to become increasingly isolated from the world around them. The essence of the present-day reform, encouraged in such large measure by Vatican II, is the impulse to combine the theological and the spiritual with the pastoral, and thereby to allow seminary training to be adapted to the particular social and cultural circumstances in which priestly service will be rendered. Such a reform required some measure of decentralization of authority, so that national churches could also have a direct hand in determining what is required for effective priestly service. Therefore, the decree proposes the principle of adaptation (n. 1) and insists on a close connection of seminary formation with pastoral realities (n. 4). Meanwhile, theological studies should be biblical, ecumenical, historical, and personally formative (nn. 16-17). Special attention must be given to the relationship between theory and practice (n. 21). Continuing education programs for the clergy are also of great importance (n. 22).

Decree on the Appropriate Renewal of the Religious Life

"Religious life" refers to a corporate form of Christian existence in which members of the Church gather together in common pursuit of the evangelical counsels: poverty, chastity, and obedience (see Matthew 19:10-12, 21). We have already referred to the origins and growth of religious life in the preceding chapter. Renewal of such a life depends on two principles: "(1) a continuous return to the sources of all Christian life and to the original inspiration behind a given community and (2) an adjustment of the community to the changed conditions of the times" (n. 2). Such communities must always see themselves as part of the Church and as participants in its mission, whatever their composition, structure, and apostolate. The generally traditional tone and spirit of the decree have been recognized and embraced by an American-based organization of religious men and women devoted to the preservation of traditional forms of religious life, e.g., traditional religious clothing (habits), traditional places of residence (convents and other religious houses), and traditional modes of exercising authority (more directive than collegial or participative). That organization, *Consortium Perfectae Caritatis*, took for its name the Latin title of this decree.

Declaration on Christian Education

This declaration is different from most of the other council documents in that it deals only with a few fundamental principles and leaves further development to the postconciliar process, particularly in the various conferences of bishops. The focus is on the education of the young as it occurs in the home, the school, and the church. Emphasis is placed most strongly on schooling. Insofar as the declaration does reflect something of the spirit of the council itself, it insists that education must be broadly humane, in keeping with advances in all of the sciences, and with a concern for nurturing personal maturity and social responsibility (nn. 1-2).

Decree on the Instruments of Social Communication

This decree was one of the first two documents approved by Vatican II, on December 4, 1963, at the end of the first session. That may explain why it is so clearly out of touch with the theological and pastoral character of the council as a whole. It is indeed, alongside the aforementioned *Declaration on Christian Education*, one of the two weakest documents produced by Vatican II. The language employed in the opening paragraphs is typical of the spirit which informs the decree: "As a Mother, the Church welcomes and watches such inventions with special concern.... Such would be the press, the cinema, radio, television, and similar media, which can be properly classified as instruments of social communication" (n. 1). "Mother Church...is also aware that men can employ these gifts against the mind of the divine Benefactor, and abuse them to their own undoing. In fact the Church grieves with a motherly sorrow at the damage far too often inflicted on society by the perverse use of these media" (n. 2).

THE ECCLESIOLOGY OF VATICAN II

The council's distinctive understanding of the nature and mission of the Church is a reflection and embodiment of the following theological and pastoral principles:

1.   *The Church is, first and foremost, a mystery or sacrament*, i.e., "a reality imbued with the hidden presence of God" (Pope Paul VI). This principle, articulated in the first chapter of *Lumen gentium*, supplants the pre-Vatican II emphasis on the Church as *means* of salvation.

2   *The Church is the whole People of God.* This principle, expressed in the second chapter of *Lumen gentium*, replaced the pre-Vatican II emphasis on the Church as hierarchical institution, which tended to make the study of the Church more akin to "hierarchology" than to "ecclesiology."

3.   *The whole People of God—laity, religious, and clergy alike—is called to participate in the mission of Christ as Prophet, Priest, and King.* This principle, presented in the fourth chapter of *Lumen gentium* (especially nn. 30,33) and reaffirmed in the *Decree on the Apostolate of the Laity*, replaces the pre-Vatican II notion of "Catholic Action," wherein the laity participates only in the mission of the hierarchy.

4.   *The mission of the People of God includes service (diakonia) to human needs in the social, political, and economic orders as well as the preaching of the Word and the celebration of the sacraments.* This principle is especially set forth in *Gaudium et spes* and is reiterated in more abbreviated form in such documents as the *Decree on the Apostolate of the Laity,* the *Decree on Ecumenism*, the *Decree on Bishops' Pastoral Office in the Church*, the *Decree on the Ministry and Life of Priests*, and the *Decree on the Church's Missionary Activity*. The principle supplants the pre-Vatican II notion of "pre-evangelization," wherein such service is, or may be, a necessary preparation for the preaching of the Gospel (evangelization) but is not itself essential to the Church's mission in the same way as the preaching or the celebration of the sacraments.

5.   *This Church*, so composed and with such a mission, *is realized and expressed at the local as well as the universal level. The Church is indeed a communion of churches (=* collegiality). This principle is articulated especially in *Lumen gentium* (n. 26), and is also expressed in the *Decree on the Bishops' Pastoral Office in the Church*, the *Decree on the Church's Missionary Activity*, the

Decree on Eastern Catholic Churches, and the *Decree on the Ministry and Life of Priests*. The principle supplants the common pre-Vatican II notion that the Church is, for all practical purposes, always understood as the Church universal, centralized in the Vatican under the supreme authority of the pope, with each diocese considered only as an administrative division of the Church universal, and each parish, in turn, an administrative subdivision of the diocese.

6. *This Church*, at once local and universal, *embraces more than the Catholic Church. It is the whole Body of Christ: Catholics, Orthodox, Anglicans, and Protestants alike.* This principle is to be found in the *Decree of Ecumenism* and in the *Dogmatic Constitution on the Church (Lumen gentium)*. It sets aside the pre-Vatican II concept that the Roman Catholic Church alone is the one, true Church, and that the other Christian communities (never called "churches" before Vatican II) are somehow "related" to the Church but are not real members of it. This is not to say, however, that all churches are equal.

7. *The mission of the whole Church is* (a) *one of proclamation of the Gospel that is always subordinate to the Word of God*; (b) *one of celebration of the sacraments in a way that always fully engages the intelligent participation of the worshiping community or individuals*; (c) *one of witnessing to the Gospel through a life-style that is marked by humility, compassion, respect for human rights, etc; and* (d) *one of service to those in need, both inside and outside the Church.* This multiple principle is grounded (a) in the *Dogmatic Constitution on Divine Revelation*; (b) in the *Constitution on the Sacred Liturgy*; (c) in the *Pastoral Constitution on the Church in the Modern World*, the fifth chapter of the *Dogmatic Constitution on the Church* ("The Call of the Whole Church to Holiness"), the *Decree on the Bishops' Pastoral Office in the Church*, the *Decree on the Ministry and Life of Priests*, the *Decree on the Church's Missionary Activity*, and the *Decree on the Appropriate Renewal of the Religious Life*; and (d) for the service aspect of mission, in the same documents. This multiple principle expands upon a narrower view of mission in pre-Vatican II ecclesiology, namely, one that tended to restrict the mission to the preaching of the Word and the celebration of the sacraments, and one which perhaps paid too

little attention to the missionary responsibility of corporate witnessing to the Gospel. In other words, it is an essential part of the Church's mission to practice what it preaches.

8. *All authority in the Church is to be exercised as a service and in a collegial mode.* The principle is particularly proposed in *Lumen gentium* (chapter III) and is reaffirmed in such other documents as the decrees on bishops, priests, and religious life. The principle is intended to transform the exercise of authority from one of domination and unilateral decision-making, as prevailed in the pre-Vatican II period.

9. *Religious truth is to be found outside the Body of Christ and should be respected wherever it is discovered. In no instance is anyone to be coerced to embrace either the Christian or the Catholic faith.* This dual principle is set forth in the *Declaration on the Relationship of the Church to Non-Christian Religions* and in the *Declaration on Religious Freedom.* It replaces a too-exclusive understanding of revelation as "Christian revelation," as well as the formula "Error has no rights."

10. *The nature and mission of the Church are always to be understood in relationship and in subordination to the Kingdom of God.* This principle is expressed in article 5 of *Lumen gentium* and again in article 45 of *Gaudium et spes.* It replaces what was perhaps the most serious pre-Vatican II ecclesiological misunderstanding, namely, that the Church is identical with the Kingdom of God. If it is, then it is beyond all need for institutional reform, and its mission is to bring everyone inside lest salvation elude them.

SUMMARY

1. The Second Vatican Council was the largest and most representative council in the Church's history. It was perhaps the Church's first really *ecumenical* council in that its bishops were drawn from every major continent and culture. With this council, the Church began its movement from a Church of cultural confinement to a geniune world Church.

2. Twentieth-century *ecclesiology before Vatican II* was of two kinds: *textbook* ecclesiology, which stressed the institutional, juridical,

and hierarchical aspects of the Church (Salaverri), and *progressive* eccle-siology, which understood the Church as the whole People of God, including laity and other Christians (Congar). Since this Church is not yet the Kingdom of God, it is always in need of renewal and reform (Congar, Küng). It does not exist primarily to grow and multiply but to be a credible and effective sign or sacrament of Christ's and God's presence in the world (Rahner, Schillebeeckx, de Lubac). The state owes the Church no special privileges, nor can the Church use the state to compel Catholic faith (Murray).

3. The single most influential personality associated with the event of Vatican II was *Pope John XXIII.* He called and opened the council and set its tone by the style he himself adopted as pope, namely, that of a servant-shepherd. The council, he insisted, was not for condem-nations but for moving the Church into the future for the sake of its own vitality, Christian unity, and world peace.

4. There were *sixteen council documents* of varying authority, content, and effects. The most authoritative in the *juridical sense* were the four *constitutions*: on the Church, on the Church in the modern world, on revelation, and on the sacred liturgy. The most authoritative in terms of their *reception* in and by the Church have been the four constitutions, plus the *Decree on Ecumenism*, the *Declaration on Religious Freedom*, and the *Declaration on the Relationship of the Church to Non-Christian Religions.*

5. The major documents in summary form are:

> a. *Dogmatic Constitution on the Church:* The Church is a mys-tery, or sacrament, the whole People of God, in whose service the hierarchy is placed. The authority of pope and bishops is to be exercised as a service and in a collegial mode. Bishops are not simply the vicars of the pope, and the laity participate fully and directly in the Church's mission.
>
> b. *Pastoral Constitution on the Church in the Modern World:* The Church must read the signs of the times and interpret them in the light of the Gospel. The Church does not exist alongside or apart from the world; the Church is part of the world, and its mission is to serve the whole human family in order to make the human race's history more human.
>
> c. *Decree on Ecumenism:* Christian unity is a matter of restora-tion, not of a return to Rome; other Christian communities are churches within the Body of Christ; and both sides were to blame for the divisions of the Church.

d. *Constitution on the Sacred Liturgy*: The Church proclaims the Gospel not only in word but also in sacrament, or by sacred signs. Since the whole People of God is involved in this worship, the signs must be intelligible.

e. *Dogmatic Constitution on Divine Revelation*: The Word of God is communicated through Sacred Scripture, sacred tradition, and the teaching authority of the Church, all linked together and directed by the Holy Spirit. The sacred realities are always open in principle to a growth in understanding.

f. *Declaration on Religious Freedom*: No one is to be forced in any way to embrace the Christian or the Catholic faith. This principle is rooted in human dignity and the freedom of the act of faith.

g. *Declaration on the Relationship of the Church to Non-Christian Religions*: God speaks also through other religions, so we should engage in dialogue and other collaborative efforts with them. The Jews have a special relationship to the Church. They cannot be blamed as a people for the death of Jesus.

6.   The minor documents in summary form are:

a. *Decree on the Church's Missionary Activity*: The Gospel is to be preached also and always to non-Christians, but not as a culturally alien reality. Evangelization is an obligation for every member of the Church.

b. *Decree on the Apostolate of the Laity*: The laity participates in the mission of the Church, but especially in the temporal order.

c. *Decree on Eastern Catholic Churches*: The Eastern Catholic, or "Uniate," churches can be a bridge to the Orthodox East. The integrity of Eastern traditions of liturgy, spirituality, and discipline is to be restored.

d. *Decree on the Bishops' Pastoral Office in the Church*: Bishops are the pastors of their own local churches, and beyond that collaborate with other bishops through episcopal conferences and with the pope and all other bishops through the episcopal college. Authority is always for service.

e. *Decree on the Ministry and Life of Priests*: Priests are members of a presbytery in union with a bishop, and with him serve the building up of Christ's body.

f. *Decree on Priestly Formation*: There must be a closer connection between seminary training and the pastoral situation.

g.   *Decree on the Appropriate Renewal of the Religious Life*: The renewal of religious life (a life lived according to the evangelical counsels of poverty, chastity, and obedience) must be based on the Gospel, the original purposes of the community, and the changed conditions of the times.

h.   *Declaration on Christian Education*: Education must be broadly humane and up-to-date, with a concern for personal maturity and social responsibility.

i.   *Decree on the Instruments of Social Communication*: The Church must be vigilant toward the media because of the ever-present danger of their abuse, but must also use the media where opportune.

7.   The *distinctive ecclesiology* of Vatican II is based on the following principles:

a.   The Church is a mystery, or sacrament, and not primarily a means of salvation.

b.   The Church is the whole People of God, not just the hierarchy.

c.   The whole People of God participates in the mission of Christ, and not just in the mission of the hierarchy.

d.   The mission of the Church includes service to those in need, and not just the preaching of the Gospel or the celebration of the sacraments.

e.   The Church is truly present at the local level as well as at the universal level. A diocese or parish is not just an administrative division of the Church universal.

f.   The Church includes Orthodox, Anglicans, and Protestants, as well as Catholics.

g.   The mission of the Church includes proclamation of the Word, celebration of the sacraments, witnessing to the Gospel individually and institutionally, and providing service to those in need.

h.   All authority is for service, not domination.

i.   Religious truth is to be found outside the Church as well. No one is to be coerced to embrace the Christian or the Catholic faith.

j.   The Church is always for the sake of the Kingdom of God and is not itself the Kingdom.

SUGGESTED READINGS

Abbott, Walter, and Gallagher, Joseph, eds. *The Documents of Vatican II*. New York: America Press, 1966.

Anderson, Floyd, ed. *Council Daybook: Sessions 1 and 2*. Washington, D. C.: National Catholic Welfare Conference, 1965; *Session 3* (1965); and *Session 4* (1966).

Kloppenburg, Bonaventure. *The Ecclesiology of Vatican II*. Chicago: Franciscan Herald Press, 1974.

Lindbeck, George. *The Future of Roman Catholic Theology: Vatican II—Catalyst for Change*. Philadelphia: Fortress Press, 1970.

Miller, John H., ed. *Vatican II: An Interfaith Appraisal*. Notre Dame, Ind.: University of Notre Dame Press, 1966.

Outler, Albert. *Methodist Observer at Vatican II*. Westminster, Md.: Newman Press, 1967.

Pawley, Bernard C., ed. *The Second Vatican Council: Studies by Eight Anglican Observers*. New York: Oxford University Press, 1967.

Rynne, Xavier. *Vatican Council II*. New York: Farrar, Straus & Giroux, 1968.

Vorgrimler, Herbert, ed. *Commentary on the Documents of Vatican II*. 5 vols. New York: Herder & Herder, 1967-1969.

THE CHURCH TODAY:
ITS NATURE AND MISSION

As noted in the preceding chapter, many of the progressive features of the Second Vatican Council were anticipated in the work
of theologians writing *before* Vatican II. Some of these theologians
continued to exercise leadership in the postconciliar period as
well. The spirit of the council has also been reflected in official
ecclesiastical statements, in pastoral developments of various
kinds, in ecumenical dialogues, and in the work of individual
Protestant theologians where a new sense of the sacramentality of
the Church has begun to emerge alongside a deepened emphasis on
its servanthood toward the world. We have perhaps reached a
point in the evolution of twentieth-century ecclesiology where
consensus has nearly been achieved, both inside and outside the
Catholic Church, on the question of the nature and mission of the
Church.

ECCLESIOLOGY SINCE VATICAN II
Catholic Ecclesiology

Karl Rahner

Rahner's understanding of the Church is consistent with his fundamental approach to the theology of *grace*. The Church is the
sacrament of God's universal saving activity on our behalf. It is
"the historically real and actual presence of the eschatologically
victorious mercy of God," or "the sign of the grace of God definitively triumphant in the world in Christ" (*The Church and the*

Sacraments, London: Nelson, 1963, pp. 14,18). The Church is not itself the Kingdom of God. "It is the sacrament of the kingdom of God in the eschatological phase of sacred history which began with Christ, the phase which brings about the kingdom of God" ("Church and World," *The Concise Sacramentum Mundi*, p. 239).

The relationship of Church and world is a function of the relationship of Church and Kingdom. The Kingdom, which is the redemptive presence of God, is not purely otherworldly, spiritual, meta-historical. It is also this-worldly, concrete, and historical. Accordingly, the Church must understand its mission in a way that falls between two extremes: *integrism*, which regards everything in the world as evil or worthless unless and until it is somehow "integrated" with Christianity, and *esotericism*, which regards everything in the world, apart from Christianity, as unrelated to salvation, and therefore to be shunned. Provided that the spirit of detachment from the world, of penance, contemplation, and renunciation remains alive in the Church, there need be no mistrust of the Church's present and recent course in announcing the unity of the love of God and love of neighbor (i.e., we manifest our love of God precisely in and through our love for others), in taking up the cause of the poor and the oppressed, in speaking and acting on behalf of human rights and freedom, and in opening dialogue with the rest of humankind.

Rahner insists that we can never forget that we are sinners, not only we ourselves as individuals but also as a society which creates or tolerates inhuman social conditions and institutions. "The danger of debasing Christianity by confining the struggle with sin to the wholly private sphere is imminent and menacing," because so much sin has been institutionalized and has become part of our taken-for-granted world (*The Shape of the Church to Come*, New York: Seabury Press, 1974, p. 124). If the Church avoids the task of challenging institutionalized sin, it will be regarded as a "merely conservative power, devoted to the defence of things as they are" (p. 125). On the other hand, if the Church is to be outwardly credible, it must allow its commitment to justice and freedom to become more effective in its internal life as well. The Church of the future will be an open Church, ecumenical from its very roots, democratized, and especially declericalized.

Edward Schillebeeckx

Sacramentality is also the key to Edward Schillebeeckx's understanding of the nature and mission of the Church. The key idea which inspired the fundamental change of emphasis at Vatican II, he argues, is that of the Church as the *sacramentum mundi* ("sacrament of the world"). In this context "world" means fellowship, community, or other-oriented existence. It is a way of being human in the world, i.e., of being in dialogue with one's fellow human beings (*God the Future of Man*, New York: 1968, p. 123). The Church is committed to the coming Kingdom of God, but it is not yet in possession of the Kingdom. The Church is still on the way, in history, searching tentatively for solutions to the problems of human existence. Its message is not "This is precisely how the world can be fully humanized" but "Humanity is possible." The task of humanization, in other words, "is not a labor of Sisyphus" (p. 156). The hope of the final Kingdom, where all things will be brought to perfection, stimulates the Church never to rest satisfied with what has already been achieved in this world. The promised future has not yet been given. Therefore, nothing that now exists is beyond prophetic criticism. On the other hand, "The Church's critical function is not that of an outsider, pursuing a parallel path, but rather that of one who is critically involved in the building of the world and the progress of the nations" (p. 161).

Schillebeeckx's post-Vatican II turn in the direction of a more socially and politically critical function for the Church is consistent with his discovery and/or renewed appreciation of socio-critical theory (see his *The Understanding of Faith*, New York: Sheed & Ward, 1974) and with his more recent work in Christology, referred to in chapter 14.

Hans Küng

Hans Küng's major post-conciliar work on the Church is entitled simply *The Church* (New York: Sheed & Ward, 1968). It is a significant book in that it is the first major volume in ecclesiology which attends at some length to the subordinate relationship of Church to the Kingdom of God. Standard Catholic textbooks, as we noted in the previous chapter, usually identified the two. The

Church, for Küng, is first and foremost an historical reality. It is the pilgrim People of God. As such, its essential reality is embodied in changeable forms. Adaptation occurred even within the New Testament period itself. The Church emerged not from the direct mandate of Jesus but as a product of his preaching of the Kingdom of God. The Church's own mission is similarly oriented toward the coming Kingdom.

It is here perhaps that Küng's close contacts with the churches of the Reformation, especially Lutheranism, shape his theology in a manner that is not unequivocally Catholic. Specifically, Küng insists very strongly on the discontinuity between Church and Kingdom. The Church does not bring about the Kingdom but is "its voice, its announcer, its *herald*. God alone can bring his reign; the Church is devoted entirely to its service" (p.96). The emphasis is at least reminiscent of Martin Luther's *Alleinswirksamkeit Gottes* ("God's working-aloneness").

On the other hand, Küng does not want to dissociate completely the Church from the Kingdom. It is the anticipatory sign of the Kingdom. The Church is also the Body of Christ and the Creation of the Holy Spirit, as well as the pilgrim People of God. It is a community constituted by Baptism and the Lord's Supper, and it exists at both local and universal levels. A local church is not merely a section of the universal Church, nor is the universal Church merely an accumulation of local churches. Each local church is a manifestation of the Body of Christ in that place, and the Church universal is a dynamic communion of local churches, something more than the sum total of those churches.

A persistent emphasis in Küng's post-Vatican II books and essays on the Church is the need for ongoing institutional reform. The Church is a credible proclaimer and witness of the Kingdom only if it also follows the way of Jesus as a provisional, serving, guilty, and determined Church. It must be a community marked not only by faith, hope, and charity, but also by truthfulness and freedom (*On Being a Christian*, New York: Doubleday, 1976, pp. 481-484). All authority in the Church must always be ultimately in the service of the Kingdom and immediately in the service of the Church itself. We should speak, as the New Testament did, of service (ministries) rather than of offices. The Petrine ministry (papacy), as important as it is, cannot be the sole criterion of orthodoxy or for identifying what and where the Church is (pp. 829-842). The dividing line between Catholic and Protestant is less sharp than we have traditionally thought. For Küng, the names represent basic attitudes. *Catholic* expresses a preference for the whole, for continuity, and for universality; *Protestant* embraces a concern for the Gospel (Sacred Scripture) and for constant reform. These two attitudes are not necessarily mutually exclusive at all.

Avery Dulles

Avery Dulles, one of the leading Catholic theologians in the United States, has made his principal contributions to post-Vatican II ecclesiology in his *The Dimensions of the Church* (Westminster: Newman Press, 1967) and *Models of the Church* (New York: Doubleday, 1974). The former book, subtitled *A Postconciliar Reflection*, notes that the council moved beyond Robert Bellarmine's (d. 1621) highly institutional notion of church as "a group of men bound together by the profession of the same Christian faith and by the communion of the same sacraments, under the rule of the legitimate pastors, and especially of the one vicar of Christ on earth, the Roman pontiff" (cited, p. 4). Indeed, the great weakness of Bellarmine's view is that it omits "precisely what makes the Church the Church, namely, the communion of minds and hearts through sharing in the same divine life" (p. 5). The council's understanding of the Church as People of God and as sacrament carried our ecclesiology forward, Dulles suggests, and its refusal to identify the Church of Christ exclusively with the Roman Catholic Church broadened that ecclesiology's base (p. 10).

A more mature expression of Dulles' theology of the Church is presented in his widely read and influential *Models of the Church*. Here he insists that the mystery of the Church is too rich and diverse to be confined to any single theological category. It is not just an institution, or a mystical communion, or a sacrament, or a herald, or a servant. It is all these. The *institutional model* makes it clear that the Church must be a structured community, including pastoral officers bearing authority to direct and guide it, to preside over worship, to determine the limits of dissent, and to represent the community in an official way. The *community model* makes it evident that the Church must be united to God by grace, and that its members must be united to one another in Christ. The *sacramental model* reminds us, especially in the community's prayer and worship, that the Church must be a sign of the continuing vitality of Christ's grace and of our hope for the redemption he promises. The *kerygmatic model* underlines the Church's abiding call to herald the Gospel and to summon people to faith in Jesus as Lord and Savior. The *servant model* stresses the importance of the Church's contribution to transforming the world and impregnating human society with the values of the Kingdom of God.

Taken in isolation, however, each model can distort the reality of the Church, Dulles warns. Thus, the institutional model can exaggerate the importance of structures, of official authority, of obedience to rules. The community model can generate an unhealthy spirit of enthusiasm, leading to false expectations and impossible demands. The sacramental model can lead to a sterile aestheticism and to an almost narcissistic self-contemplation. The kerygmatic model can exaggerate the importance of merely verbal faith at the expense of social action. And the servant model can lead to an uncritical acceptance of secular values and a completely this-worldly view of salvation.

Dulles expresses a clear preference for the sacramental model, because it preserves and integrates the values and strengths of the other four models. (1) Official structures give a certain vivid character to the *community*. (2) The Church is an authentic *sacrament* of Christ when it is also a community of *love*. (3) The Church bears witness to Christ through the *preaching of the Word*. (4) And its devotion to worldly *service* testifies to the presence and concern of the servant Christ (pp. 182-188). Although Dulles is least disposed to the institutional model (p. 187), some subsequent writings would suggest that his spirit of caution is more directly focused on the servant model than on the institutional. This is clear in his *The Resilient Church* (New York: Doubleday, 1977, pp. 9-27). Therein, he also reaffirms his preference for the sacramental model, "the universal sacrament of salvation" (*Lumen gentium*, n. 48). He concludes, "After some years of work in ecclesiology, I am inclined to think that there is no better definition" (p. 26). A sacrament is a sign, but not an empty sign. It must always be, or strive to be, what it signifies. Thus, the Church is always summoned to greater perfection and to greater fidelity to its mission, to "bear witness to the wonderful deeds of God and attract others to share in the peace and freedom that Christ alone can give" (p. 27).

Johannes Metz

Metz is best known for introducing the concept of "political theology," i.e., a theology which relates theory and practice. Liberation theology, as already noted in chapter 2, is a form of political theology. Political theology measures all reality in the light of the promised Kingdom of God. And because the Kingdom has not yet come in all its perfection, there is nothing, including the Church, which escapes the critical gaze of political theology (see *Theology of the World*, New York: Herder & Herder, 1969, pp. 107-140).

The Church itself is not exempt from criticism, because the Church is also part of the world. "For it is *that world* which attempts to live from the promised future of God, and to call *that world* in question which understands itself only in terms of itself and its possibilities. . . . The Church is the eschatological community and the exodus community. . . . The Church is not the goal of her own strivings; this goal is the Kingdom of God" (p. 94). The Church has a hope and witnesses to a hope, but its hope is not in itself. The hope is in the Kingdom as the world's future. The Church is the universal sacrament of hope for the salvation of the whole world. It is precisely because of this that the Church must be "the liberating and critical force of this one society" (p. 96). Hope is living for the other.

Gregory Baum

Canadian theologian Gregory Baum recapitulates the central themes already contained in these other theologies, especially Rahner's. The distinctive mission of the Church today is one of dialogue. Proclamation includes listening and learning. It is a way of becoming more aware of the ambiguity of the Church's own situation in the world and of entering more deeply into what is God's will for us. Indeed, it was dialogue with the secular world that taught the Church to cherish religious liberty, pluralism, critical interpretation of texts, etc., as religious values (*Faith and Doctrine*, New York: Newman Press, 1969).

But dialogue is not simply a missionary tactic imposed by circumstances. Dialogue is imperative because God's saving presence is everywhere. Ecclesiology studies the manner in which salvation comes to everyone, and hence it has to do with human life in community. In that sense, ecclesiology may be regarded as "the theological study of human society" (*Man Becoming*, New York: Herder & Herder, 1970, p. 69). The Church is people insofar as they are touched by grace. That grace offers and creates community. Such community is the Church, which comes into being "whenever and wherever people become friends through God's presence to them" (*The Credibility of the Church Today*, New York: Herder & Herder, 1968, p. 47).

This is not to say, however, that the Church has no specific character of its own. "The universality of grace does not obliterate the distinction between Church and humanity. The Christian Church is the community in which Jesus Christ, in whom God reveals himself unconditionally and definitively, is proclaimed and celebrated" (p. 48). The mission of such a Church is a movement of humanization. It serves humankind "to help the redemptive presence of God...triumph in terms of unity, reconciliation, social justice, and peace" (p. 198).

Gustavo Gutierrez

The principal theologian of the Latin American liberation school, Gustavo Gutierrez, of Peru, also embraces the Second Vatican Council's sacramental perspective. The Church's existence is not for itself but for others. On the one hand, the Church rescues the world from anonymity and enables it to know the ultimate meaning of its historical future. On the other hand, the Church must listen to the world and be evangelized by it. As the universal sacrament of salvation, the Church must signify in its own structures the salvation it announces. "As a sign of the liberation of man and history, the Church itself in its concrete existence ought to be a place of liberation.... The break with an unjust social order and the search for new ecclesial structures...have their basis in this ecclesiological perspective" (*A Theology of Liberation*, Maryknoll, N.Y.: Orbis Books, 1972, p. 261).

Although the "primary task of the Church ... is to celebrate with joy the salvific action of the Lord in history" (p. 265), the Church must reflect on and live the Gospel in light of the situation in which it finds itself. Thus, in Latin America the Church must take a clear stand against social injustice and in favor of the revolutionary process which seeks to abolish that injustice and build a more human order. The first step is to recognize how much the Church itself is tied to that unjust system. The Church must truly announce the good news of the Kingdom which "reveals, without any evasions, what is at the root of social injustice: the rupture of the brotherhood which is based on our sonship before the Father..." (p. 269). And the Church must also make its own members aware of their oppressed condition, to affirm their humanity, and to motivate them to take responsibility for the quality of their lives ("The oppressed themselves should be the agents of their own pastoral activity"). "Universal love is that which in solidarity with the oppressed seeks also to liberate the oppressors from their own power, from their ambition, and from their selfishness" (p. 275). In the meantime, the unity of the Church cannot be achieved apart from the unity of the world. "In a radically divided world, the function of the ecclesial community is to struggle against the profound causes of the division among men. It is only this commitment that can make of it an authentic sign of unity" (p. 278).

Protestant Ecclesiology

Jürgen Moltmann

For Moltmann, a Reformed (or Calvinist) Protestant, the Church is "the community of those who on the ground of the resurrection of Christ wait for the kingdom of God and whose life is determined by this expectation" (*Theology of Hope*, New York: Harper

& Row, 1967, p. 326). The Church is the body of the crucified and risen Lord "only where in specific acts of service it is obedient to its mission to the world. . . . it is nothing in itself, but all that it is, it is in existing for others. It is the Church of God where it is a Church for the world" (p. 327). The Church's service of the world and of humanity is not such that it strives to keep everything as it is; its service is rather for the sake of helping the world and humankind transform themselves and become what they are promised to be. "For this reason 'Church for the world' can mean nothing else but 'Church for the kingdom of God' and the renewing of the world" (p. 328). The Church's mission is reconciliation with God, forgiveness of sins, peace. The salvation it proclaims is not merely salvation of the soul but also "the realization of the eschatological *hope of justice*, the *humanizing* of man, the *socializing* of humanity, *peace* for all creation" (p. 329).

Following an approach very close to Metz's, and having also in mind the classic Marxist critique of the Church, Moltmann insists that "mission means not merely propagation of faith and hope, but also historic transformation of life" (p. 330). Christian hope calls everything in question by measuring everything against the future Kingdom. The hope of resurrection, therefore, brings about a new understanding of the world as not yet finished. Our world is a world of unfinished possibilities. "To disclose to it the horizon of the future of the crucified Christ is the task of the Christian Church" (p. 338).

The same themes are carried forward, but with more deliberate attention to the place and role of the Holy Spirit, in Moltmann's more recent *The Church in the Power of the Spirit* (New York: Harper & Row, 1977). The Church is, before all else, the Church of Jesus Christ. "Every statement about the church will be a statement about Christ. Every statement about Christ also implies a statement about the church; yet the statement about Christ is not exhausted by the statement about the church because it also goes further, being directed towards the messianic kingdom which the church serves" (p. 6). The Church's mission "embraces all activities that serve to liberate man from his slavery in the presence of the coming God, slavery which extends from economic necessity to Godforsakenness" (p. 10). It is an ecumenical Church;

the whole Church is present in each church. Therefore, the concerns of one are the concerns of all others, and vice versa. So, too, the Church is a political Church, committed to and ever engaged in the struggle for liberation, in liberation's most comprehensive sense.

Wolfhart Pannenberg

Pannenberg, a German Lutheran, also places the Church in the context of the coming Kingdom of God. It is an eschatological community, "a community of high expectation and hope" (*Theology and the Kingdom of God*, Philadelphia: Westminster Press, 1969, p. 74). It is true to its vocation "only as it anticipates and represents the destiny of all mankind, the goal of history." Protestantism, Pannenberg suggests, has focused too much on the piety and salvation of Church members themselves ("the congregation of saints wherein the gospel is rightly preached and the sacraments rightly celebrated"). The doctrine of the Church begins not with the Church but with the Kingdom of God, "the utterly concrete reality of justice and love" (p. 79).

The mission of the Church is to proclaim the universal significance of Jesus, to be a community through which contemporary men and women can participate in the hope for the ultimate fulfillment of humanity, to witness to the limitations of any given society, to stir the imagination for social action and to inspire the visions of social change (pp. 83-85). But in the end it is the Kingdom of *God*. The Church's function is always and only "preliminary." "Any effort to make man appear to be more than he can be in his historically preliminary moment inevitably makes man less" (p. 82).

Carl Braaten

An American Lutheran, Carl Braaten acknowledges his own indebtedness to Pannenberg's vision of the Church. He defines the Church as "the prolepsis of a new world that is coming into being through the power of God's creative future in Christ" (*The Future of God*, New York: Harper & Row, 1969, p. 109). The Church is not itself the Kingdom of God, but only the "sacramental sign of

the new world that is emerging in, with, and under the manifestations of the present, visible world" (p. 111). He, too, criticizes the
traditional Protestant notion of the Church as the "congregation
of saints." The definition leaves out the Kingdom of God and the
Church's missionary function in world history. That missionary
imperative arises itself from the universal vision of the Church's
eschatological faith (p. 133).

George Lindbeck

Another American Lutheran, George Lindbeck similarly stresses
the sacramental character of the Church. Indeed, the Church's
"essence" is "to be a sacramental sign or witness to God's saving
work in all that it is and does. It exercises this witnessing or
missionary function in its *diakonia* or secular service of the
world. . ., its *leitourgia* or worship of God. . ., and its *koinonia* or
communal unity expressed both interpersonally and in institutional structures. . . and in common faith and dogma" (*The Future
of Roman Catholic Theology*, Philadelphia: Fortress Press, 1970,
p. 5). Apart from this mission to be a sacramental sign and anticipation of the Kingdom of God, there is nothing which differentiates the Church from the rest of humankind (p. 27).

Ecumenical Ecclesiology

In addition to the theological work done by individual theologians, the post-Vatican II period has also witnessed the production
of a new form of theological communication: consensus statements
of bilateral, trilateral, or multilateral groups composed of theologians from various Christian traditions. Reference has already
been made to the work of those groups, and even more detailed
references will be made again, later in this chapter and in the next
three chapters.

In the United States alone remarkable progress has been
recorded since the council on such specific questions as the Eucharist, ministry, even the papacy. A measure of consensus on the
general topic of the Church and its mission has also been achieved

by such bilateral consultations as the Presbyterian-Reformed/Roman Catholic, the Orthodox/Roman Catholic, the United Methodist/Roman Catholic, the Lutheran/Roman Catholic and the Anglican/Roman Catholic. The last may usefully represent the others as an example of the nature and degree of ecclesiological consensus.

It its "Agreed Statement on the Purpose of the Church" (*Documents on Anglican-Roman Catholic Relations III*, Washington, D.C.: United States Catholic Conference, 1976, pp. 1-11), the Anglican/Roman Catholic Consultation in the U.S.A. defines the Church as "that community of persons called by the Holy Spirit to continue Christ's saving work of reconciliation. As Christ proclaimed the Kingdom, so the Church serves the Kingdom..." (p. 2). This mission is carried out in various ways: by the proclamation of the Good News, in the context of the fellowship of believers, in the witness of individual members and in its own structures and agencies, and in its service to those in need. The mission, therefore, is threefold: proclamation, worship, and service.

The proclamation must also be a word of challenge, at times even of confrontation. "The imperative of evangelism...has many dimensions" (p. 6). The Eucharist is the summit and source of the Church's mission, for it "testifies to the dependence of all people upon God and it affirms God's action for humanity in the death and resurrection of Jesus Christ, in the promise of the gift of the Spirit, and in our ultimate destiny of union with the Father" (p. 6). But the witness of worship is "only fully complete when it results in a commitment to service" (p. 7). The contemporary reexamination of mission has emphasized the call of the Church to be an agent and forerunner of God's Kingdom of justice and peace. "Human liberation, we agree, is that aspect of the Church's mission of service which is most challenging for our time" (p. 8).

The statement concludes: "We, as Roman Catholics and Episcopalians charged by our churches to explore the possibility that there is a fundamental unity between us, find that we are in substantial agreement about the purpose or mission of the Church as we have set it forth above. We have uncovered no essential points on which we differ" (p. 9).

The Ecclesiology of Official Church Documents

The Third International Synod of Bishops (Rome, 1971)

An international synod of bishops is second only to an ecumenical council in collegial authority. It is an entirely modern phenomenon, a direct outgrowth of the Second Vatican Council, designed to give structure to the council's desire to draw the bishops of the world into the ongoing governance and direction of the Church. The 1971 synod issued two statements, one on "The Ministerial Priesthood" and the other on "Justice in the World" (Washington, D.C.: United States Catholic Conference, 1972, pp. 33-52).

It is this latter document which contains, in its introduction, the assertion which has been so frequently cited ever since: "Action on behalf of justice and participation in the transformation of the world fully appear to us as a constitutive dimension of the preaching of the Gospel, or, in other words, of the Church's mission for the redemption of the human race and its liberation from every oppressive situation" (p. 34). This document dwells, too, upon the changed circumstances in the world wherein human life is marked by interdependence: "Never before have the forces working for bringing about a unified world society appeared so powerful and dynamic; they are rooted in the awareness of the full basic equality as well as of the human dignity of all" (p. 35). On the other hand, there are now technological forces at work (arms race, nuclear power, e.g.) which also threaten the very survival of the human community. The division between rich and poor only exacerbates that danger. Dialogue among peoples is a matter of urgency today, and not simply a desirable goal. The Church has a special role and obligation.

Its mission is to preach the Gospel, a message of universal brotherhood and sisterhood and a consequent demand for justice in the world. The Church is not alone responsible for justice, but nonetheless "has proper and specific responsibility which is identified with her mission of giving witness before the world of the need for love and justice contained in the Gospel message, a witness to be carried out in the Church institutions themselves and in the lives of Christians" (p. 42). The latter point is highlighted in the document's third chapter: "While the Church is bound to give witness to justice, she recognizes that anyone who ventures to speak to people about justice must first be just in their eyes. Hence we must undertake an examination of the modes of acting and of the possessions and life style found within the Church herself" (p. 44). Everything has to be touched by this overriding concern for justice: the exercise of ministry, education, liturgy, etc. And everything is, in turn, placed in the context of the coming Kingdom of God, a kingdom of justice and love, a kingdom rooted in "the radical transformation of the world in the Paschal Mystery of the Lord . . ." (p. 52).

Papal Statements

Ecclesiam Suam (*His Church*, 1964):   Pope Paul VI's inaugural encyclical stressed the fundamental need for *dialogue*. Although the encyclical is not precisely post-conciliar, the council had already established clear ecclesiological lines, and the encyclical itself reflects them. The Church is called to dialogue with humankind at various levels. The pope sketches four concentric circles: The first and widest comprises all men and women, with whom dialogue must be initiated and sustained on each of the great problems of the world; the second circle embraces all religious people; the third, all Christians; and the fourth, all Catholics.

Populorum Progressio (*On the Development of Peoples*, 1967):   This encyclical, so strong in its insistence on the social and political character of the Church's mission, is generally credited with inspiring the growth of Latin American liberation theology and of shaping the remarkable documents of the Second Latin American Bishops' Conference, which met in Medellin, Colombia, in 1968. The pope points immediately to the teachings of the Second Vatican Council on the Church's responsibility to the world at large and especially to those in need, and ultimately to the example of Jesus himself, who preached the Gospel to the poor as a sign of his mission (n. 12). "Sharing the noblest aspirations of men, and suffering when she sees them not satisfied, she wishes to help them attain their full flowering, and that is why she offers men what she possesses as her characteristic attribute: a global vision of man and of the human race" (n. 13).

Octagesima Adveniens (A Call to Action, 1971*):* This "Apostolic Letter" to Cardinal Maurice Roy, President of the Council of the Laity and of the Pontifical Commission, Justice and Peace, recapitulates the social doctrine of the Catholic Church from *Rerum Novarum* (1891), whose eightieth (*octagesima*) anniversary provided the occasion for the document. What is distinctive about *A Call to Action* is its shift of focus from economics to politics (n. 46). Politics is more comprehensive than economics, the pope declares. It has to do with the common good. Such power, however, is to be exercised in a way that maximizes shared responsibility (n. 47).

And what of the place of the Church in this wider political context? The Church is called "to enlighten minds in order to assist them to discover the truth and to find the right path to follow amid the different teachings that call for their attention; and secondly to take part in action and to spread, with a real care for service and effectiveness, the energies of the Gospel" (n. 48).

Evangelii Nuntiandi (On Evangelization in the Modern World, 1975*):* This is technically an "Apostolic Exhortation" on the occasion of the Fourth International Synod of Bishops in Rome (1974). The document links the mission of the Church with Jesus' proclamation of the Kingdom of God, as "liberation from everything that oppresses man, but which is above all liberation from sin and the Evil One..." (n. 9). Just as Jesus accomplished this proclamation in works as well as in word, so is the Church called to be a servant as well as a herald of the Gospel. "Evangelization would not be complete if it did not take account of the unceasing interplay of the Gospel and of man's concrete life, both personal and social" (n. 29). Thus, "... the Church strives always to insert the Christian struggle for liberation into the universal plan of salvation which she herself proclaims" (n. 38).

Redemptor Hominis (Redeemer of Humankind, 1979*):* This inaugural encyclical of Pope John Paul II focuses more on Christology, anthropology, and the ethical implications of both than it does on the mystery of the Church. The document is primarily concerned with human dignity, rooted in the saving work of Christ. The Church must be a constant champion of human dignity, consistent with the teachings of the Second Vatican Council and especially of its *Declaration on Religious Freedom.* The person with whom the Church is concerned is "man in the full truth of his community and social being" (n. 14). The Church's commitment to humankind is shaped by its participation in the threefold mission of Christ as Prophet, Priest, and King. Every member of the Church, not just the hierarchy, shares in this mission: teaching, worshiping, and serving. "The Church's fundamental function in every age and particularly in ours is to direct humankind's gaze . . . toward the mystery of God, to help every person to be familiar with the profundity of the redemption taking place in Christ Jesus . . ." (n. 10). What is finally "amazing" is the "good news" that we are indeed worth something. "This amazement determines the Church's mission in the world. . . ."

Bishops' Statements

The Church in the Present-Day Transformation of Latin America in the Light of the Council (Second General Conference of Latin American Bishops, Medellin, Colombia, 1968):   Inspired by the Second Vatican Council and by *Populorum Progressio*, the so-called Medellin documents describe the Church as an instrument of liberation, an agent of social justice, a defender of the poor and the oppressed. This understanding of the Church's mission must penetrate every major area of Church life: education, youth ministry, the family, catechesis, and so forth. "No earthly ambition impels the Church, only her wish to be the humble servant of all men" (XIV,18).

Message to the People of God (Third General Conference of Latin American Bishops, Puebla, Mexico, 1979):   The same sense of integration characterizes the work and final message to the people of Latin America in this Third General Conference as in the preceding one: Christ assumed humanity and its real conditions, except for sin. Therefore, the Church must be concerned with the whole person, with the matter of human rights, economic justice, the use of power and force, and so forth. "What interests us as pastors is the integral proclamation of the truth about Christ."

Political Responsibility (Administrative Board, United States Catholic Conference, 1976):   "Christians believe," the statement declares, "that Jesus' commandment to love one's neighbor should extend beyond individual relationships to infuse and transform all human relations from the family to the entire human community." The bishops cite a classic text, Luke 4:18: "He has sent me to bring glad tidings to the poor, to proclaim liberty to captives, recovery of sight to the blind and release to prisoners." The call to feed the hungry, clothe the naked, care for the sick and the afflicted, comfort the victims of injustice (Matthew 25) requires more than individual acts of charity. We must understand and act upon "the broader dimensions of poverty, hunger and injustice which necessarily involve the institutions and structures of economy, society and politics."

Sharing the Light of Faith: National Catechetical Directory for Catholics of the United States (Washington, D.C.: United States Catholic Conference, 1979):   The ecclesiology of this document is essentially that of the Second Vatican Council. The Church is described first as a mystery, and then as People of God, servant, sign of the Kingdom, pilgrim, and hierarchical society. The explanation of each descriptive term is consistent with the council's. Thus, the Kingdom is understood also as a Kingdom of justice, love, and peace, as well as of holiness and grace, and authority is to be exercised collegially and in the spirit of service. Christians are called to be a community of shared beliefs, experiences, ideals, and values. The Church is to be missionary. Every member is called to proclaim the Gospel "to the whole of creation" (Matthew 16:15). The marks of the Church—one holy, catholic, and apostolic—are gifts which the Church must "strive to realize ever more fully in its life" (p. 39). The interpretation of each mark differs in some discernible measure from the pre-Vatican II textbooks. Catholicity, for example, means that "the gospel message is capable of being integrated with all cultures. It corresponds to all that is authentically human" (p. 40). Apostolicity is not portrayed in a purely *chronological* sense—i.e., that the Catholic Church's bishops can trace their episcopal orders all the way back, in an unbroken chain, to the Apostles, but in a *dynamic* sense as well—i.e., as "the continuing fidelity to Christ's loving and saving work and message, to ministry and service inspired by the evangelical vision and teaching of the original apostles" (p. 41).

The Church is also a communion of local churches, of East and West alike. "The Church's unity is not based on a particular language, rite, spiritual tradition, or theological school, but upon the one cornerstone, Jesus Christ" (p. 41). It must always be a Church in dialogue and collaboration with others. First, there must be dialogue and collaboration within the Body of Christ between and among separated Christians. Then there must be dialogue and collaboration with Jews, Moslems, and representatives of other religions. Finally, there must be dialogue and collaboration with those who profess no religion because "the Church is confident that its message is in harmony with the most authentic and profound desires of the human heart" (p. 44).

The Impact of Post-Vatican II Ecclesiology on Pastoral Developments

As a result of the ecclesiological self-understanding of Vatican II and the development of that understanding in post-conciliar theology, the following changes in the life, mission, and structure of the Catholic Church have occurred and continue to occur:

Because the Church is perceived more clearly as the whole People of God, and not just the hierarchy, and because all participate directly in the mission of Christ by Baptism and not simply in the mission of the pope and the bishops ("Catholic Action"), the Catholic Church functions now in a more deliberately *conciliar* mode, emphasizing shared responsibility—e.g., parish councils, diocesan pastoral councils, national advisory boards, priests' senates, leadership conferences of religious.

Because the Church is perceived more clearly as a communion of local churches and not just as a single Church subdivided for organizational purposes, the responsibility of bishops and of the body of bishops, representing as they do the local churches in communion with one another, has increased—e.g., national episcopal conferences, international synods of bishops, the expansion of bishops' authority of dispensation without recourse to Rome.

Because the Church's mission includes as an essential component the call to service (*diakonia*), even in the political realm, the

Church is increasingly attentive to the needs of the wider community in its allocation of resources (e.g., the Campaign for Human Development in the United States) and in its formulation of ecclesiastical priorities (e.g., the "Call to Action" Conference in Detroit, Michigan, October, 1976).

Because the Church's mission also includes as an essential component the call of the whole Church to holiness, the Church is marked today by an extraordinary renewal of interest in Christian *spirituality* (e.g., the Catholic Charismatic movement, directed retreats, Marriage Encounter, cursillos).

Because the Church is perceived to include Orthodox, Anglicans, and Protestants, as well as Catholics, the post-Vatican II period has been one of expanding and deepening ecumenical contacts and cooperation—e.g., theological dialogue at the international and national levels, seminary and divinity school consortia, common prayer.

(For a fuller statement of the relationship between ecclesiology and ecclesiastical structures, see my *The Remaking of the Church: An Agenda for Reform*, New York: Harper & Row, 1973).

THE NATURE OF THE CHURCH: TOWARD A DEFINITION

Models of the Church

The word *model* has, first, an *evaluative* meaning—e.g., "She is a model educator" or "He is a model student," in which the term conveys some notion of excellence. A model is an exemplar of some value. The word may also be used in a more *neutral* sense—e.g., "model home" or a "fashion model." Here it means "This is about how you or your own home might look." A model can also be a *philosophical* category, describing a fundamental perspective or way of understanding some complex reality. It may in that instance be either evaluative or neutral. The word *model* is employed here in the philosophical, or perspectival sense, and in its neutral, rather than evaluative, sense.

There are at least three dominant models of, or ways of perceiving, the Church, and they are presented below not in order of importance but in the chronological sequence in which they have entered the recent history of the Catholic Church.

Institution

This model perceives the Church *primarily* (which is not to say exclusively or exhaustively) as a hierarchically structured, visible society which mediates salvation to its individual members through the preaching and teaching of the Word and the administration of the sacraments. This was, of course, the dominant model in Roman Catholicism before Vatican II, and it inspired the first draft of the council's *Dogmatic Constitution of the Church.* Perhaps the most sophisticated expression of this model is contained in Joachim Salaverri's tract *De Ecclesia Christi* in the so-called *Spanish Summa* (summarized in the preceding chapter).

Strengths: This model was and remains attractive because it affords a strong sense of ecclesiastical *identity* (the Church is a specific, visible, clearly defined reality, rooted in the will of God, the mandate of Jesus Christ, and the power of the Holy Spirit); it gives the members a sense of their *place* and *role* within the Church, even if it be a subordinate one (some have clearly defined authority, others do not); and it is attentive to historical *continuity* (the Church has definite origins and has passed through specific points of development in which its identity was further clarified and determined, and both of these—origins and points of passage—connect the Church of the present with the Church of the past).

Weaknesses: On the other hand, the institutional model tended to exaggerate the hierarchical or societal aspect of the Church at the expense of the communitarian. That indeed was the point of the debate at Vatican II over the placement of chapters two and three in *Lumen gentium.* Is the Church first the People of God with a particular structure, or is is a hierarchical reality which happens to provide spiritual benefits to a particular people? *Secondly,* the institutional model may have also exaggerated the role and importance of the ordained, and especially of bishops, at the expense of the missionary responsibility of the entire community of the baptized. Thus, the mode of decision-making was monarchical and/or oligarchical rather than collegial or democratic. *Thirdly*, the institutional model tended to limit the scope of the Church to the Roman Catholic Church, at the expense of the Christian and ecclesial reality of the other churches (Orthodox, Anglican, and Protestant). *Fourthly*, this model tended to limit the scope of the Church's mission to the preaching of the Word and the celebration of the sacraments, at the expense of the Church's broader social and political responsibilities. *Finally*, this model tended to identify the Church with the Kingdom of God on earth, at the expense of the abiding need for renewal and reform not just of its individual members but of the whole Church, structures and persons, head and members.

Community

This model perceives the Church primarily as a community, or a people, whose principal task is the promotion and sustaining of personal growth through interpersonal relationships. This model was at least partially embraced by Vatican II in its central teaching on the Church as the People of God. It is an understanding of the Church proposed at the beginning of the 1960s by Edward Schillebeeckx in his *Christ the Sacrament of Encounter with God* and at more popular levels by Catholic lecturers with a psychological orientation—e.g., Eugene Kennedy and Henri Nouwen. It is a model that was warmly endorsed by those favoring a theology of festivity and fantasy in the late 1960s and early 1970s—e.g., Harvey Cox in *The Feast of Fools* (New York: Macmillan, 1969). This was also the dominant model in the early years of the Catholic Charismatic movement, and it is consistent with the recent emphasis in contemporary American culture on personal growth and development (the so-called Human Potential movement).

Strengths: The community model emphasizes the reality of the Church as a people and the responsibility of the Church to provide a context for human growth in Christ. Specifically, this model avoids some of the problems associated with the institutional model and conforms better than the institutional model to the bibilical, patristic, and Vatican II stress on the Church as the

People of God. Secondly, this model stresses the responsibility of the Church not only to make certain spiritual benefits available to its members, as in the sacraments, but to contribute positively to the human growth of its members. Thirdly, this model underlines the Church's abiding missionary responsibility to be a sign of Christ's presence by the mutual love shown within the community of his disciples.

Weaknesses: On the other hand, the community model is not always clear in identifying those elements which make such a community distinctive. Is "community" the private preserve of Christianity? Is the Church the only real "community"? If not, what makes the Christian community different from other communities? Secondly, this model tends to concentrate on the value of the individual's growth at the expense of the social and political responsibilities of the whole community and at the expense of the community's abiding commitment to the renewal and institutional reform of the Church itself.

Servant

This model perceives the Church primarily as an agent of social change whose task is the wise and courageous allocation of its own moral and material resources for the sake of the coming of the Kingdom of God among humankind—a Kingdom of justice and peace as well as of holiness and grace. It is a model supported by Vatican II's *Pastoral Constitution on the Church in the Modern World*, the Third International Synod of Bishops' *Justice in the World*, and similar official documents of the Catholic Church. It is also articulated in recent theological writings on the Church—e.g., those of Metz, Moltmann, Schillebeeckx, and Gutierrez.

Strengths: The servant model properly emphasizes the social and political responsibilities of the Church, insisting that the Kingdom of God is indeed a Kingdom of justice, peace, and freedom. Furthermore, this model underscores the principle that *diakonia*, which includes service in the socio-political order, is as essential, or constitutive, to the mission of the Church as are proclamation and sacramental celebration.

Weaknesses: But this model, too, is not always clear in identifying those elements which make such an agent of social change distinctive. Why belong to the Church if one can work more effectively for justice and peace outside of it? *Secondly*, some of those who have emphasized the servant model have also tended to identify the Church with the Kingdom of God, as the institutional model's proponents have sometimes done. Thus, wherever God, or the Spirit of God, is redemptively present as the source of justice and reconciliation, there is the Church. But since, as we shall indicate again below, the redemptive presence of God is the Kingdom of God, such an assertion effectively identifies the Kingdom with the Church.

A balanced theology of the Church would have to incorporate the distinctive strengths of all three models without, however, carrying over their individual weaknesses and especially their common liability, namely, their tendency to absolutize themselves, i.e., to equate the whole mystery of the Church with their own particular perspective. Thus, the Church is an institutionalized servant-community.

Definition of Church

The Church is the whole body, or congregation, of persons who are called by God the Father to acknowledge the Lordship of Jesus, the Son, in word, in sacrament, in witness, and in service, and, through the power of the Holy Spirit, to collaborate with Jesus' historic mission for the sake of the Kingdom of God.

The definition embraces all Christians: Catholics, Orthodox, Anglicans, and Protestants. Thus, although the noun *Church* is singular, it is always to be understood at the same time as having a pluralistic character. There is "the Church" and there are "the churches." Again, this is not to say that all churches fully satisfy the criteria implied in the definition.

But the distinction between the Church and the churches is not only ecumenical. There is also the distinction between the Church as "Church universal" and the church as "local church."

Church refers at once to the whole Body of Christ and the whole People of God, as well as to the congregation of Christians in a particular place (a parish, a diocese, e.g.). Indeed, the Church universal is itself a *communion of local churches*, as noted earlier.

When does a group of persons at a local level become a church? When the following theological and pastoral conditions are verified: (1) a corporate confession of the Lordship of Jesus; (2) ratification of that confession of faith in Baptism, the Eucharist, and other sacraments; (3) regular nourishment on the biblical word of God as a force that summons the community of faith; (4) a sense of fellowship (*koinonia*) within the group—i.e., a common awareness of the call to become a community; (5) an acceptance of the Gospel of Jesus Christ as the conscious motivation for one's values and ethical commitment; and (6) the existence and exercise of certain formal ministries designed to assist the community in remaining faithful to its mission and providing order, coherence, and stability to its internal life so that it really can be a sacrament of Christ and of the Kingdom. For the Catholic Church this last item also implies union with the pope and the college of bishops, who are themselves related by succession to Peter and the other Apostles.

Each of these ecclesial elements is a matter of degree. On the other hand, the noun *church* is not applicable to a particular group except where all of these elements are present, to one degree or another. Thus, we always have to distinguish between movements and associations within the Church (even *within* a local church), and "the Church" itself (whether universal or local).

The definition and brief explanation presuppose, of course, all that has gone before, in this chapter and in chapters 17-19.

THE MISSION OF THE CHURCH

The mission of the Church is focused, as is Jesus' mission, on the *Kingdom of God*. By *Kingdom of God* is meant *the redemptive presence of God actualized through the power of God's reconciling Spirit*. Literally, the Kingdom of God is the reign, or rule, of God. The Kingdom happens whenever and wherever the will of God is fulfilled, for God rules where God's will is at work. And since God's will is applicable to the cosmos, to nature, to objects, to history, to institutions, to groups as well as to individuals, the Kingdom of God is as broad and as overarching as the claims and scope of the divine will itself.

More precisely, one might argue that the Kingdom of God is indistinguishable from God as such. The Kingdom is not something other than God. The Kingdom *of* God *is* God insofar as God is redemptively present and active in our midst through the power of the Holy Spirit. The Kingdom is the divine redemptive presence, reconciling, renewing, healing, and liberating. (A fuller discussion of the Kingdom of God will be provided in chapter 29.)

The mission of the Church is unintelligible apart from the Kingdom of God. The Church is called, first, to proclaim in word and in sacrament the definitive arrival of the Kingdom in Jesus of Nazareth; secondly, to offer itself as a test-case or sign of its own proclamation—i.e., to be a people transformed by the Spirit into a community of faith, hope, love, freedom, and truthfulness; and thirdly, to enable and facilitate the coming of the reign of God through service within the community of faith and in the world at large.

Each of these three missionary responsibilities generates, or is the foundation of, one of the three models of Church given above. The call of the Church to proclaim the Gospel in word and in sacrament in an organized and authorized manner is consistent with the concerns of the institutional model. The call of the Church to proclaim the Gospel by the quality of its own life is consistent with the concerns of the community model. And the call of the Church to proclaim and apply the Gospel through the struggle for social justice, peace, and human rights is consistent with the concerns of the servant model. Just as no one aspect of the Church's mission is the whole of its mission, so no one model of the Church captures the whole of the mystery of the Church.

Missionary Responsibility	Corresponding Model
Proclamation of the Gospel in *word* and in *sacrament*, in an *organized* and *authorized* manner.	Institution
Proclamation of the Gospel by the *quality* of the *Church's own life.*	Community
Proclamation of the Gospel by *application* of the Gospel to the struggle for *social justice*, *peace*, and *human rights.*	Servant

Proclamation in Word and Sacrament (Kerygma and Leitourgia)

The Church is that segment of humankind which hopes in the future of the world because of its fundamental faith in the unique significance of the life, death, and resurrection of Jesus of Nazareth, and in the abiding power of the Holy Spirit. Its first task is to keep alive the memory of Jesus Christ in word and in sacrament, to call attention to his and the Spirit's continued presence in history, and to profess its hope in his and the Spirit's totally new, creative manifestation in the future Kingdom.

Whatever changes in form and structure this Church assumes in the years ahead, it will always be that community which explicitly and publicly identifies Jesus Christ as the focal point of the whole historical process. The Church will not only announce this in word (preaching, catechesis, teaching), but it will celebrate that faith in sacrament. Through the *Eucharist* in particular the Church gives thanksgiving to God for the confirmation and validation of God's promises of reconciliation and peace in Jesus Christ (2 Corinthians 1:20). Through the Eucharist the Church keeps alive Christ's memory in order to make clear that he is indeed the hinge of history, that he is the final measure of all that is good and human. And finally, through the Eucharist the Church fixes the eyes of the world on the future, where the world's final meaning and destiny reside.

The Church, therefore, is a community of *faith* in the significance of what has already happened in and through Jesus Christ; it is a community of *love* as an expression of the effects of that Christ-event; and it is a community of *hope* in the power of the God of Jesus Christ to re-create all things anew in Christ and the Holy Spirit. The celebration of the Eucharist is the "summit and source" of the Church's mission, to use the terms of Vatican II.

But the Church is not commissioned to proclaim the Kingdom of God in an uncritical or naive manner. The Church can never equate any earthly reality, including itself, with the Kingdom of God. The Pauline appeal to flee the world and not be conformed to it (Romans 12:2) means that we should never forget the relative character of everything this side of the Kingdom. The Church, therefore, proclaims the Gospel with a consciousness of sin in the world and in its own household as well. Its proclamation is always prophetic.

Prophecy means, literally, *speaking on behalf of God.* A prophetic Church is a Church that speaks always on behalf of God, measuring everything against the coming Kingdom of God. The Church's preaching, however, is effective and credible to the extent that the Church itself has been converted by it. And this leads to the second missionary task.

Signification (Koinonia, or Fellowship, and Marturia, or Witness)

The Church must also be a sign of what God *is* actually doing in history and of what the human community *should* be doing in response to God's saving action. Men and women should be able to look upon this Christian community and thereby take courage with regard to the future course of history. They should be filled with confidence in the core of reality—affirming its intelligibility and its worthwhileness—because the ordinary men and women who belong to this community and maintain close affiliation with that core of reality are constantly being transformed by the Spirit of love, justice, intelligence, compassion, fortitude, and so forth. The Church has the responsibility, therefore, to be so open itself to Jesus, the reconciling Word of God, and to the reconciling power of the Spirit that the Church becomes the unmistakably clear sign of Jesus' and the Spirit's presence in the world. The Church must be a community marked by faith, hope, love, freedom, and truthfulness, not only in its official proclamations but in its life-style as well.

But the Church cannot be a sacrament of God's Kingdom unless the Kingdom exists somehow within the community. A sacrament is both sign and reality. The two are distinct but inseparable. Thus, *the Church is not itself the Kingdom of God*, yet *the Church must be inseparable from the Kingdom.* If indeed the Church were in no way imbued with the hidden presence of God, its preaching would have no force and its service no lasting effect. The Church would not be a mystery, or sacrament, at all.

But insofar as the Kingdom *is* present within the Church, that fact imposes upon the Church the missionary obligation to make the Kingdom's presence visible and instrumental for others. It means that the Church must *be* what it is; it must practice what it preaches. It means, too, that the Church must continually reform itself in fidelity to the Gospel. Accordingly, the question of institutional or structural reform is always an important one. The issues that have been on the Church's agenda in recent years— e.g., the ordination of women, the election of bishops, coresponsibility through diocesan and parish councils, papal and episcopal authority—may not be the issues on tomorrow's agenda. But the underlying problem will always be there: How can the Church best express in form and structure the inner reality which it embodies? The question is a missionary question, because the Church is called to be a sign as well as an instrument of the Gospel and of the Kingdom of God.

It would be illogical, therefore, to argue that the Church should be a vigorous agent of liberation and yet to be indifferent to the processes by which the Church selects its leadership or reaches important decisions regarding the allocation of its limited material and human resources. If the Church is called to be a sacrament of Christ, then how it organizes itself for mission and how it practices the virtue of justice within as well as without the community of faith become matters of some practical consequence.

Service (Diakonia)

Because the Kingdom of God is also a Kingdom of justice, peace, and freedom, and because the Church exists for the sake of the Kingdom, the Church's mission must also include responsibility for humanization in its fullest sense. The Church's activities on behalf of social justice or human rights are not merely preparatory to the real mission of the Church, as the notion of "pre-evangelization" had it before Vatican II. Apart from the official church documents already cited (*Gaudium et spes*, the synodal document *Justice in the World*, and various papal statements), the Church's involvement in the social and political orders is justified on the basis of the social and institutional character of sin itself. Since the Church is called to combat sin of every kind, the Church has responsibility in all areas where sin appears. More positively, the Church is called to uphold and practice virtue. Justice is one of the cardinal, or "hinge," virtues (along with prudence, fortitude, and temperance), and social justice is one of the principal kinds of justice (alongside commutative, distributive, and legal justice). Therefore, the Church's commitment to, and involvement in, the struggle for social justice, peace, and human rights is an essential, or "constitutive," part of its mission.

On the other hand, that intervention in the social and political orders must always be responsible, never arbitrary, particularly in the light of the Church's limited resources. Accordingly, such intervention must be governed by the following criteria: (1) The issue must be clearly *justice-related*. (2) The ecclesiastical agency or cluster of churches should have the *competence* to deal with the issue. (3) There should be *sufficient resources* within the particular church(es) to deal with the problem effectively. (4) The issue should have a *prior claim* over other justice-related problems which compete for the Church's attention. (5) the *form* of ecclesiastical action should not unnecessarily or unduly polarize the Church itself, since the Church is always called to be a sign of the Gospel and of the Kingdom of God. A diversity of viewpoints is to be expected and tolerated, so that agreement with the specific form of social or political action selected by the church(es) should not become itself a test of authentic Christian faith and commitment. This is not to say, on the other hand, that the mere risk of *conflict* within the Church should discourage such intervention. Conflict is essential to growth. But *excessive* conflict can be corrosive and finally destructive of the unity of the Church itself.

THE NECESSITY OF THE CHURCH

Do we need the Church? We have already indicated what we mean by *Church*. The question here is, What do we mean by *need?* The need may be *psychological* (the need for meaning), *sociological* (the need for a community of shared meaning), or *theological* (the need for direction in life, and ultimately the need for salvation). The question of the necessity of the Church takes in all three levels of meaning.

Who has the need? *First*, every human being, insofar as he or she needs to find some meaning for life and some sense of community of shared meaning, has at least a fundamental openness to religion of some kind (see chapter 8). *Secondly*, the world at large needs religious communities which testify to values which otherwise might be forgotten and lost, to the detriment of the human community itself. *Thirdly*, insofar as Jesus Christ is the Lord of history and the Savior of all humankind, the world at large also needs a particular religious community which testifies to the significance of Jesus Christ and which somehow carries forward his saving work on behalf of all, members and non-members alike. *Finally*, individuals who are convinced in faith of the Lordship of Jesus need a community where this fundamental conviction can be shared in word, in ritual, and in communal living, and through which it can be applied to the world at large for the sake of the world's salvation.

Accordingly, (1) the Church is necessary *for the world* as a sacrament, an efficacious sign and instrument of God's redemptive activity in Jesus Christ, leading toward the final Kingdom of God. The necessity of the Church *for the world* is an *historically contingent* necessity; i.e., *hypothetically* the Kingdom of God could come about without the Church or even without Jesus, but *in fact* it does not and will not. (2) The Church is necessary *for those individuals* who are in fact called by God to acknowledge the Lordship of Jesus and to collaborate with him in the coming of the

Kingdom of God. The necessity of the Church *for the individual* is similarly *contingent*, but contingent this time on the call of God to belong to *this* community rather than to another. Personal salvation, in other words, is not inextricably linked with one's membership or non-membership in the Church. It is existence within the Kingdom of God, not within the Church, that finally determines our relationship with God and our reception of salvation. It is not the one who says, "Lord, Lord!" who will enter the Kingdom, but "only the one who does the will of [the] Father in heaven" (Matthew 7:21). Where is it said, Rahner asked, that we must have the whole one hundred percent?

THE ROMAN CATHOLIC CHURCH

What is different about the Roman Catholic Church? If the Church is necessary to the world and to individuals within the world, is the Roman Catholic Church also necessary to the Body of Christ as a whole and to individuals inside and outside the Body of Christ?

One must distinguish between what is *characteristic* of Roman Catholicism and what is *distinctive* about it. What is characteristic may also be found in different shape or form in other churches, but what is distinctive will be found in Roman Catholicism alone.

What is *characteristically* Catholic? Its conviction that *grace* is finally triumphant over sin, not only as the declaration of God that we are just but through a real interior transformation by the power of the Holy Spirit. *Secondly,* its sense of *tradition*, of *doctrine*, and of the importance of maintaining *continuity* not only with the Church's origins but with its principal points of passage from its beginnings to the present. *Thirdly*, its sense of *peoplehood*, of *community*, and of *church*. *Fourthly*, and most significantly, its sense of *sacramentality* and its correlative sense of the importance of *mediation*. God is present to us through signs and symbols, and the presence of God is effective for us through these same visible signs and instruments.

What is *distinctively* Catholic? Here the answer given earlier by Hans Küng in his *Council and Reunion* still applies: The ecumenical question is the question of ecclesiastical office, and of the Petrine ministry in particular. It is true that Catholic ecclesiology posits a collegial understanding of the Church—i.e., that it is a communion of churches. But, so, too, does the Orthodox tradition. But Roman Catholicism alone insists on the role of the Petrine minister, the pope, as the "perpetual and visible source and foundation of the unity of the bishops and of the multitude of the faithful" (*Dogmatic Constitution of the Church*, n. 23).

One may become, be, and/or remain a Catholic for any number of reasons which have something to do with what is characteristic about Roman Catholicism but nothing to do with what is distinctive about it. But that fact does not negate Catholicism's distinctive *ecclesiological* feature, namely, the importance it assigns to the place and function of the Petrine ministry exercised by the bishop of Rome.

This is not to say, however, that belief in the Petrine ministry is the *only* distinctive feature of Catholicism. Although the Catholic Church is not alone among Christian churches in affirming the triumph of grace over sin, is not alone in its sense of tradition and doctrine, in its commitment to the principles of sacramentality and mediation, or in its emphasis on the peoplehood of the Church, one can argue that there is within Catholicism a particular configuration of such values as these—a configuration which one does not discover elsewhere in the Body of Christ. (A fuller statement on this central question of Catholic identity is provided in chapter 30.)

It is with this distinction in mind between what is characteristic and what is distinctive about Roman Catholicism that we must confront the question, "Do we need the Roman Catholic Church?"

For one thing, the Catholic Church is a part, and a very large and significant part indeed, of the whole Body of Christ. Therefore, the Roman Catholic Church is necessary *for the world* for the same reason that the Church as a whole is necessary for the world, namely, as a sacrament of Jesus Christ and of the Kingdom of God.

Secondly, The Roman Catholic Church is necessary *for the whole Body of Christ* because the Roman Catholic Church alone has all the institutional elements which are necessary for the integrity of the Body of Christ (e.g., the Petrine ministry, the seven sacraments) as well as the many characteristic values which serve to enrich the rest of the churches (e.g., its regard for community, its confidence in God's grace as transformative, its sacramental perspective, its spiritualities, its systematic approach to the Christian theological and doctrinal tradition).

Finally, the Roman Catholic Church is necessary *for the individual* who is called to the Church as such and who is, beyond that call to confess the Lordship of Jesus, persuaded that the fullness of ecclesial union with Christ requires participation in that church within the Body of Christ, whose unity is expressed not only through faith and its sacraments, but also through the ministry of the Petrine minister, the pope, who stands in the midst of the Church as the "source and foundation" of the unity of the communion of churches.

In light of the teaching of the Second Vatican Council, especially the *Decree on Ecumenism* and the *Declaration on the Relationship of the Church to Non-Christian Religions*, a common pre-Vatican II answer to the question of the Roman Catholic Church's necessity—namely, that the Roman Catholic Church alone is the one, true Church of Christ, outside of which authentic religious truth does not exist and salvation can be attained only with the greatest difficulty—is subject to some modification. This position is challenged by the following theological principles: God is present in grace to every human being; revelation is available apart from the Church; and within the Church itself there are many churches which, to one degree or another, "are brought into a certain, though imperfect, communion with the Catholic Church...are incorporated into Christ...have a right to be honored by the title of Christian, and are properly regarded as brothers in the Lord by the sons of the Catholic Church" (*Decree on Ecumenism*, n. 3). The *Decree on Ecumenism* complements the teaching of the *Dogmatic Constitution on the Church* that the Church of Christ "subsists in" the Roman Catholic Church, which gives it a certain normative status in relation to the other churches.

SUMMARY

1. *Catholic ecclesiology* since Vatican II has carried forward the basic theological insights of the council itself. The greatest emphasis is on the *sacramentality* of the Church ("the universal sacrament of salvation"). This emphasis is seen especially in *Rahner, Schillebeeckx, Dulles,* and *Gutierrez*. Secondly, there is a stress on the subordination of the Church to the *Kingdom of God* and a wider understanding of the Kingdom to include the coming of peace, justice, and freedom *(Rahner, Schillebeeckx, Küng, Dulles, Metz, Baum,* and *Gutierrez)*. Thirdly, there is renewed attention to the need for ongoing institutional reform as a way of fulfilling the Church's sacramental mission *(Rahner, Küng,* and *Gutierrez)*. Finally, because of the universality of grace, all the foregoing theologians stress the abiding need for dialogue with others and for collaboration in the task of humanizing the world.

2. A sampling of *Protestant ecclesiology* since Vatican II suggests a new emphasis also on the *sacramentality* of the Church *(Braaten, Lindbeck)* and a movement away from the traditional Protestant notion of the Church as the "congregation of saints wherein the gospel is rightly preached and the sacraments rightly celebrated" *(Pannenberg, Braaten)*. There is an insistence, too, on the subordination of the Church to the *Kingdom of God* and on the Church's correlative responsibility to participate in the struggle for *liberation, social justice,* and *humanization (Moltmann, Pannenberg, Braaten, Lindbeck)*.

3. Similar convergences have been noted in recent *ecumenical dialogues*—e.g., in the *Agreed Statement on the Purpose of the Church* by the Anglican/Roman Catholic Consultation in the U.S.A.

4. *Official documents* of the Catholic Church have also reaffirmed the principal teachings of the Second Vatican Council; those documents focus particularly on the Church's responsibility for social justice and liberation, e.g., *Justice in the World* (Third International Synod of Bishops, 1971), *Populorum Progressio* (Pope Paul VI, 1967), *Octagesima Adveniens* (Paul VI, 1971), *Evangelii Nuntiandi* (Paul VI, 1975), *Redemptor Hominis* (John Paul II, 1979), the Medellin and Puebla statements of the Latin American Bishops Conference, and recent statements from the United States Catholic Conference, including the *National Catechetical Directory*.

5. This post-Vatican II ecclesiology has had a *practical impact* on the life of the Catholic Church: on parish and diocesan councils (reflecting the principle that the Church is the whole People of God), national episcopal conferences and international synods of bishops (the Church is

a communion of churches), the development of various social action and social ministry projects (the mission of the Church includes the struggle for justice, peace, and human rights), the emergence of new movements and forms of spirituality (all are called to holiness since the whole Church is to be a sign of the Gospel), and ecumenical dialogues and common prayer (the Church is the whole Body of Christ).

6.   There are at least three basic perspectives (models of the Church) in ecclesiology today: Church as *institution,* as *community,* and as *servant.* The first was the dominant perspective in the pre-Vatican II period (Church as a hierarchically structured, visible society, means of salvation, through word and sacrament); the second was encouraged by the council itself (Church as people, fellowship, community); and the third was impelled by the activist concerns of the 1960s and a renewed appreciation of the Church's social doctrine (Church as agent of social change, instrument of liberation, etc.).

7.   *Institutional model:*

strengths: clear sense of Christian identity, of each member's place and role within the Church, and of the continuity of the Church's present faith with the past.

weaknesses: too hierarchical, too clerical, too Roman, too much focused on word and sacrament, and too disposed to identifying Church and Kingdom.

8.   *Community model:*

strengths: consistently with Bible, Fathers of Church, and Vatican II, stresses responsibility of Church for human growth of members, and underlines call to be a sign to others through mutual love and concern.

weaknesses: not always clear on distinctiveness of Christian community, and may exaggerate growth of the individual at the expense of social and political mission.

9.   *Servant model:*

strengths: recognizes wider meaning of Kingdom of God as a Kingdom of justice and peace, and incorporates *diakonia* into the essence of mission.

weaknesses: not clear on distinctiveness of Church, and can lead to identification of Church and Kingdom also.

10.   A balanced theology of the Church must incorporate all three models.

11.   *Definition:* The Church is the whole body, or congregation, of persons who are called by God the Father to acknowledge the Lordship of Jesus, the Son, in word, in sacrament, in witness, and in service, and,

through the power of the Holy Spirit, to collaborate with Jesus' historic mission for the sake of the Kingdom of God.

12.   The definition embraces Catholics, Orthodox, Anglicans, and Protestants alike, and applies at once to the Church universal and to the local church. The Church is, in fact, a communion of churches. This is not to say that all churches fully satisfy the criteria implied in the definition.

13.   Church comes into being where there is (1) a confession of Jesus as Lord, (2) sacramental ratification of that faith, (3) reverence for the Bible, (4) a sense of fellowship, (5) a readiness to apply the Gospel to life, and (6) some ministerial structure to insure stability and direction to the community.

14.   The *mission* of the Church is directed to the *Kingdom of God,* which is the redemptive presence of God actualized through the power of God's reconciling Spirit. The mission is threefold: *proclamation* in word and sacrament *(kerygma* and *leitourgia),* signification *(koinonia* and *marturia),* and service *(diakonia).*

15.   *Proclamation* focuses on the significance of Jesus Christ and is principally expressed in the *Eucharist,* which looks to the past (when God acted in Christ), the present (where God continues to act in Christ and the Spirit), and the future (when God will bring all things to perfection in Christ, by the power of the Spirit). That proclamation, whether in word or sacrament, is always *prophetic* (prophecy means speaking on behalf of God). Everything is measured against the standard of the coming Kingdom of God.

16.   *Signification* emphasizes the sacramentality of the Church. The Church is called to be a sign of what it proclaims and of what it embodies (mystery). Accordingly, the Church must be holy and must engage in continuing institutional reform.

17.   *Service* even in the socio-political order is required by the social and institutional character of sin, and by the Church's obligation to practice and uphold virtue, including social justice.

18.   *Intervention* in the political arena must meet the following criteria: (1) justice-related issue, (2) competence of the Church to deal with it at all, (3) sufficient resources within the Church to deal with it effectively, (4) priority of this issue over other issues, and (5) form of action that is not unnecessarily or unduly polarizing.

19.   The Church is *necessary* insofar as it helps answer the quest for meaning (the psychological need), for a community of shared meaning (the sociological need), and for guidance and example in the pursuit of

salvation (the theological need). This need is incumbent on every human being in principle and on the world at large, but specifically upon those individuals in the world who are persuaded by the proclamation of the Lordship of Jesus.

20. The Church is a *sacrament for the world,* to disclose what God is doing for all. Its necessity for the world is *historically contingent;* i.e., the Kingdom hypothetically could come about without the Church or even without Jesus, but *in fact* it will not come about without them.

21. The Church is necessary for those *individuals* who are called by God to confess Jesus as Lord, but that necessity is also *contingent* on the call of God to this community (the Church) rather than to some other community.

22. Roman Catholicism *characteristically* emphasizes the triumph of grace over sin as a transforming presence; tradition, doctrine, and continuity; peoplehood, community, and church; and especially the principles of sacramentality and mediation. Roman Catholicism is *distinctive* in its conviction regarding the fundamental importance of the Petrine ministry to the life and mission of the Church and in its comprehensive (catholic) grasp of the preceding characteristics.

23. Roman Catholicism is as *necessary* for the *world* as the whole Church is necessary, namely, as a sign and instrument *(sacrament)* of the world's salvation. It is necessary for the whole *Body of Christ* because Roman Catholicism alone has all the institutional elements necessary for the integrity of the Body of Christ as well as the many characteristically Catholic values which enrich and enhance the life and mission of the whole People of God. Finally, Roman Catholicism is necessary for the *individual* who is called not only to confess the Lordship of Jesus but also to enter into explicit union with that communion of churches whose visible center of unity is the Petrine minister within the college of bishops.

24. This understanding of the necessity of Roman Catholicism differs from the common pre-Vatican II understanding of the Roman Catholic Church as the "one, true Church of Christ." The deeper theological reasons for the shift in understanding are the renewed appreciation of the universality of grace and revelation, and the recognition that the Church (i.e., the whole Body of Christ) is composed of many churches, some of which are not in communion with the bishop of Rome. The Roman Catholic Church, however, retains a certain normative status in relation to the other churches.

SUGGESTED READINGS

Dulles, Avery. *Models of the Church*. New York: Doubleday, 1974.

Gilkey, Langdon. *Catholicism Confronts Modernity: A Protestant View*. New York: Seabury Press, 1975.

Gutierrez, Gustavo. *A Theology of Liberation*. Maryknoll, New York: Orbis Books, 1972.

Küng, Hans. *On Being a Christian*. New York: Doubleday, 1976.

McBrien, Richard P. *Church: The Continuing Quest*. New York: Newman Press, 1970.

_____. *Do We Need the Church?* New York: Harper & Row, 1969.

_____. *The Remaking of the Church: An Agenda for Reform*. New York: Harper & Row, 1973.

_____. *Who Is a Catholic?* Denville, N.J.: Dimension Books, 1971.

_____. "On Being a Catholic." *Why Catholic?* Ed. John Delaney. New York: Doubleday, 1979, pp. 115-136.

Pannenberg, Wolfhart. *Theology and the Kingdom of God*. Philadelphia: Westminster Press, 1969.

Schineller, Peter, et al. *Why the Church?* New York: Paulist Press, 1977.

·XXI·

THE SACRAMENTS OF INITIATION: BAPTISM, CONFIRMATION, AND EUCHARIST

THE PLACE OF SACRAMENTAL THEOLOGY

As has been noted several times throughout this book, a major theological, pastoral, and even aesthetical characteristic of Catholicism is its commitment to the *sacramental principle*. Catholicism has never hesitated to affirm the "mysterious" dimension of all reality: the cosmos, nature, history, events, persons, objects, rituals, words. Everything is, in principle, capable of embodying and communicating the divine. God is at once everywhere and all-powerful. There is no finite instrument that God cannot put to use. On the other hand, we humans have nothing else apart from finite instruments to express our own response to God's self-communication. Just as the divine reaches us through the finite, so we reach the divine through the finite. The point at which this "divine commerce" occurs is the point of *sacramental encounter*. For Christians, *the* point of a sacramental encounter with God is Jesus Christ.

Catholicism has also historically emphasized the notion of peoplehood and of church as a *mediating* principle. God's relationship to us and our relationship to God is not exclusively, nor even primarily, individual and personal. It is corporate and communal. "In Adam's fall, we sinned all." If indeed our relationship with God were not primarily corporate and communal, rather than individual and personal, the doctrines of Original Sin and of redemption would make no sense. But the principle of human solidarity is not only a theological principle. It is also firmly grounded in modern social science (e.g., Max Scheler, Alfred Schutz, Emile Durkheim, George Herbert Mead, Georges Gurvitch) and, beyond that, in the contemporary human experience of *interdependence* (see chapter 3).

Those points of encounter between God and humankind, therefore, are never simply "transactions" between the divine and *this* person, although they are also clearly that as well. God touches all of humankind, and the human community as a whole responds to its experience of the divine through a sacramental mode. The word *sacramental* is being used here in its *widest sense*, of course. It applies to *any finite reality through which the divine is perceived to be disclosed and communicated, and through which our human response to the divine assumes some measure of shape, form, and structure.* (We cannot go into any detail regarding this wider understanding and manifestation of sacramentality. The interested reader should consult the work of Mircea Eliade—e.g., *Patterns in Comparative Religion*, New York: Sheed & Ward, 1958, and *Myths, Rites, Symbols: A Mircea Eliade Reader*, W. C. Beane and W. G. Doty, eds., New York: Harper & Row, 1976.)

Taken in the more *specific* sense as *those finite realities through which God is communicated to the Church and through which the Church responds to God's self-communication,* sacraments are directly ecclesiological in character. This is not to say that sacraments are not also linked closely with theological anthropology, with Christology, with eschatology, or with Christian moral life. But their immediate context is the Church. The redeemed human person (theological anthropology) is made visible in the Church. Christ is mediated through the Church. The Church is the sign and instrument of the Kingdom of God (eschatology). Christian moral life is Christian existence, i.e., our way of being Church.

The Church is the *fundamental sacrament* of God's promise and deliverance of the Kingdom of God in Jesus Christ. It is the "sacrament of universal salvation" (*Lumen gentium*, n. 48). The sacraments, i.e., those seven specific actions which the Church has defined to be sacraments (Eucharist, Baptism, Confirmation, Penance, Anointing of the Sick, Marriage, and Holy Order), are acts of God, to be sure. They are acts of Christ, to be sure. But they are immediately *acts of the Church*. They are expressions of the nature and mission of the Church. The sacraments are not simply actions which the Church performs, or means by which the Church makes grace available. They are moments when the Church becomes Church, manifesting itself as Church to itself and to others.

Correspondingly, those who receive the sacraments are not only related anew to God or to Christ. The sacraments immediately relate the recipient to the Church. The *lasting effect* of the sacrament (the *res et sacramentum*, to be explained in due course) is one of *relationship with the Church*. Thus, the sacrament of Penance has as its immediate purpose and effect not the restoration of friendship with God but reconciliation with the Church. Why else, for example, is a penitent who has committed a serious sin but who has made an act of perfect contrition (which restores union with God) still required to seek forgiveness in the sacrament? The reason is that serious sin compromises the mission of the Church to be a holy people, a credible and effective sacrament of Christ and of the Kingdom of God. It is not just God who is "offended" by the sin. The Church, too, has been violated. Its sacramentality has been tarnished. The sinner also has to "make up" with the Church.

This is not to say that sacramental theology is not at the same time closely connected with Christology, with which it has usually been placed in the past. It is Christ who is encountered in the sacraments. It is Christ who acts in the sacraments. It is Christ's worship of the Father that is carried forward in the sacraments. On the other hand, a too-close connection between sacramental theology and Christology tends to lead to an exaggeration of such questions as the "institution" of the sacraments by Christ and the power of the sacraments to "infuse" the grace of Christ, earned on Calvary, to the individual recipient, even when that individual is a seven-day-old infant. Doing sacramental theology as part of Christology rather than ecclesiology also tends to ignore the sacramental principle itself. We do not encounter Christ directly, but in the Church, which is his Body. Although it is Christ who is present and active in every sacramental celebration, it is the Church which makes that celebration available and which mediates the presence and action of Christ.

SACRAMENTS IN GENERAL
Signs of Faith

It is not an exaggeration to suggest that Catholic sacramental theology and practice, from the time of the Reformation until the full flowering of the liturgical renewal at the Second Vatican Council, concentrated too much on the *causality* of the sacraments and too little on their role as *signs*. Accordingly, it seemed to make little difference if the congregation failed to grasp the meaning of the words and rituals of the Eucharist and the other sacraments, so long as the sacraments were validly administered by an authorized minister using the prescribed matter and form, to a properly disposed recipient (i.e., someone not placing an obstacle in the way, such as lack of faith or serious sin). But it was the clear teaching of the Council of Trent (*Decree on the Sacraments,* Session VII, 1547), and before that of Thomas Aquinas (*Summa Theologica* III, qq. 60-65), that *sacraments cause grace insofar as they signify it*. Indeed, the twentieth-century renewal of sacramental theology is essentially a rediscovery of that Thomistic perspective.

Before the time of Aquinas, moreover, the emphasis had been on the sign. It was Augustine who gave the first technical definition of a sacrament as a sign of grace ("a visible sign of invisible grace"). The priority of sign over cause continued until the scholastic revival of the twelfth century. Its thinking was climaxed and balanced by Thomas, who added the notion of *efficacious* sign of grace; i.e., the sacraments *cause* what they signify. Thomas' own great contribution lay in his exposition of *how* the sacraments cause grace. Although Thomas himself was exceedingly well balanced in his understanding of the relationship between sign and cause, post-medieval theology was not. The sign aspect of sacraments receded from the center of ecclesial consciousness. The sacraments were perceived as instruments of grace, producing their spiritual effects by the very performance of the ritual according to the prescribed manner (*ex opere operato*, "from the work worked").

Thomas devoted his entire first question in sacramental theology (III, q. 60) to the sign, and it is a motif that runs through his whole treatment of the sacraments. The purpose of a sign, he insisted, is to instruct, to call to mind the reality that it signifies. In using the sign, we, from our side, express our *faith* in the unseen reality hidden underneath the sign. Sacraments, then, are signs which proclaim faith.

Secondly, sacraments are signs which express *worship*. Through the sacraments we participate ritually, i.e., through signs, in Christ's own worship of the Father. The Lord's Supper, or Eucharist, is linked from the beginning with the Passover meal, at which Israel gratefully (eucharistically) relived its deliverance from the bondage of Egypt and prayed for the coming of the Messiah. The early Church spoke of Christ as its Passover who had been sacrificed (1 Corinthians 5:7) and related its own fellowship meals to Christ's sacrificial action (1 Corinthians 10:16-17).

Thirdly, sacraments are signs of the *unity of the Church*. The faith that is expressed in each sacrament is the faith *of* the Church and the faith mediated to the individual *by* the Church. Insofar as the celebrants (recipients, ministers, congregation) of a sacrament have a common faith in what they do and in whom they encounter through what they do, the sacrament is also a sign of the Church's faith and of its unity.

Fourthly, sacraments are signs of *Christ's presence*, and ultimately of God the Father's. Since Christ is neither God alone nor a human being alone, but the God-man, the human actions of Christ which are memorialized and represented in the sacraments, especially in the Eucharist, are not confined to the actual time in which they were first expressed (e.g., at the Last Supper, on a particular occasion, in a particular room, during a particular moment in human history). Because Christ himself is also a sacrament, indeed the *primordial* sacrament (or sacrament of the "first order"), God is present in and through him. And since God transcends time as well as space, the saving presence and action of God in Christ is mediated every time the sacrament is celebrated. The risen Lord lives now, at this moment. His presence is signified in every sacrament.

Causes of Grace

The traditional (i.e., post-Trent, pre-Vatican II) explanation of sacramental causality stressed the teaching of Trent's canon 6: "If anyone says that the sacraments of the New Law do not contain the grace which they signify, or that they do not confer that grace on those who place no obstacles in the way...let him be anathema." Neither the merit (holiness) of the minister nor that of the recipient is causally involved, except in a negative way (i.e., the recipient must not put an obstacle in the way). What the Council of Trent was trying to safeguard was the basic truth that the grace of the sacraments is caused not by human forces but by God acting in and through Christ and the Church. We do not merit saving grace; it is a pure gift of God. The phrase *"non ponentibus obicem"* ("for those not placing an obstacle") was taken from Augustine, who had used it to support the argument that infants receive the grace of Baptism because they are clearly not capable of placing any moral obstacle to it. Trent applied the principle across the sacramental board: *It is not the personal merit of the recipient that causes the grace received.* On the other hand, God does not force the human will.

Its balance and good intentions notwithstanding, the teaching of the council was more often misunderstood than understood. Many Catholics came to believe that the graces of the sacraments were theirs if only they placed no obstacle, i.e., were not in mortal sin. The measure of preparation, the intensity of faith, the awareness of the sign's meaning—none of these counted in the end. So long as there is no moral obstacle, the sacrament "works."

Thomas Aquinas, on the other hand, never used the phrase "not placing an obstacle." He refers always to the sign of the sacrament as serving to dispose one more perfectly for receiving sacramental graces (*ex opere operantis,* "from the work of the worker"). He calls for an interior conversion to God, for a personal encounter between the Christian and Christ. Rarely does he speak of "valid reception" of the sacrament. He emphasizes instead the "right disposition" which is worthy of a Christian: faith and devotion.

In fact, this Thomistic stress on the right disposition is so much a part of authentic Catholic tradition that a present-day theologian, Karl Rahner, argues that there is always an element of uncertainty about the effect of the sacrament. "With the sacrament a person knows just as little as he does with his merely 'subjective' actions performed in faith, whether it has really given him God's grace. Just as little and just as much" (*The Church and the Sacraments*, p. 25). The popular notion has been just the opposite, of course. The belief has prevailed among Catholics that they are always more certain that their sins have been forgiven in the sacrament of Penance than are Protestants and others who have to rely solely on the precarious path of personal contrition. "Falsely, therefore, do some accuse Catholic writers as if they maintained that the sacrament of penance confers grace without any good disposition on the part of those receiving it; this is something which the Church of God never taught or accepted" (Trent, *Doctrine on the Sacrament of Penance*, chapter IV, Session XIV, 1551).

But this is looking at the matter from the point of view of the individual who is free and, therefore, has no certain knowledge that his or her own life will end victoriously in the Kingdom of God. On the other hand, it is the faith and hope of the Church as a whole that the world has been redeemed and that history itself will reach final salvation because of what God has already revealed and achieved in Christ. At least to this extent, the individual is assured that the grace of salvation is present and available in and through this sign (*ex opere operato*). We also know that each one of us remains free to give a "Yes" or a "No" (and this is the *opus operantis*).

The sacraments do not cause grace magically. They are free acts of God, and they are free acts of ours. They "work" only to the extent that we bring faith and devotion to them. "Sacraments are nothing but God's efficacious word to man, the word in which God offers himself to man and thereby liberates man's freedom to accept God's self-communication by his own act" (Karl Rahner, *Foundations of Christian Faith*, p. 415).

Effects of Sacraments

The sacraments do not cause grace in the sense that the redemptive grace of God in Jesus Christ is otherwise unavailable. Grace is already present to the individual, to the Church, and to the human community at large in God's original self-communication, as we noted in chapter 5. The sacraments shape and "channel" that original communication of grace so that the divine presence may be effective for this individual or for this group insofar as they are members of the Church and responsible for its mission.

Thus, everybody does not strictly "need" Baptism to become a child of God and an heir of heaven. Every human person, by reason of birth and of God's universal offer of grace, is already called to be a child of God and an heir of heaven. Unbaptized infants do not go to limbo, a state of "natural happiness" without the vision and company of God. We do not "need" the sacrament of Holy Order to minister to others. Every person, by reason of his or her graced humanity, is called and empowered to minister to others. We do not "need" the sacrament of Matrimony to commit ourselves to another for life. And so on. *The sacraments signify, celebrate, and effect what God is, in a sense, doing everywhere and for all.* But the sacraments also mandate and equip specific members of the human community, i.e., disciples of Jesus Christ, to be the corporate sign and instrument of God's presence and saving activity in Christ. Once again, sacraments establish a relationship ultimately with God and with Christ but immediately with the Church.

Thus, in every sacrament there is, in addition to the sign or ritual (*sacramentum tantum*, "the sign alone") and the grace, or immediate effect (*res tantum,* "the reality alone"), the lasting effect (*res et sacramentum*). It is that which is signified by the *sacramentum tantum* (the rite) and, in turn, disposes the recipient to grace (the *res tantum*). Why did this distinction arise in sacramental theology? As a way of dealing with one of the major medieval challenges to the Real Presence of Christ in the Eucharist.

According to Augustine, "A good man receives the sacrament and reality of the sacrament, but a bad man receives only the sacrament and not the reality" (*Commentary on John*, 26,11). What Augustine had in mind by "reality" was the grace of the sacrament. Berengar of Tours (d. 1088) accepted the reality of the sacrament, i.e., the grace of union with Christ, but he denied that Christ's true body was present in the Eucharist. For him there were only two elements in the sacrament: the external sign, or symbol, and the ultimate effect, the grace. Theologians did not agree upon a third eucharistic element for almost a century. Not until Hugh of St. Victor (d. 1142) and Peter Lombard (d. 1160) did the concept of the *res et sacramentum* finally emerge. The bread and wine (*sacramentum tantum*) signify the body and blood of Christ (*res et sacramentum*); the body and blood of Christ, in turn, are the basis for union with Christ (*res tantum*) insofar as the body and blood are received worthily. But whether they are received worthily or not, the body and blood of Christ are really present because they have been signified and made present by the *sacramentum tantum* (the rite of the Eucharist).

Only gradually was the triple distinction applied to all of the sacraments, and only more recently, in the closing decades of the nineteenth century, was the *res et sacramentum* understood in a consistently ecclesiological sense, namely, in Matthias Scheeben's (d. 1888) *The Mysteries of Christianity*. For Scheeben, the *res et sacramentum* of the Eucharist is not just the risen body of the Lord, but the whole Christ, the Church.

By tradition the Church does not repeat three sacraments: Baptism, Confirmation, and Order. They are received only once. The *res et sacramentum* for those three sacraments is also called the "*character*." The term was taken over from pagan antiquity, where it referred to the seal by which a soldier or a slave might be identified as belonging to the service of the emperor or an owner. When used by Christians like Tertullian and Augustine, the term was intended to apply to the sacramental rite alone. It was the rite of sealing by which a person became a Christian for life, even if he or she were to lapse into heresy or schism. Only later, in the medieval period, did the word "character" become identified with the *res et sacramentum*, i.e., the lasting effect which is distinguishable from the rite itself as well as from the grace produced by the sacrament. The term *character* does not refer to an indelible mark on the soul, as some catechisms had it. It is simply the word used to describe the permanent effect of three sacraments: Baptism, Confirmation, and Holy Order. These sacraments are not, in fact, administered more than once to the same person during the course of his lifetime. Therefore, they must produce some effect that is permanent (= "the character").

The *res et sacramentum* of *Baptism* and *Confirmation* is membership in the Church and responsibility for its mission. For *Holy Order* it is the abiding responsibility for pastoral service to the Church. For the non-character sacraments, explanations vary: *Matrimony* (the bond of union between man and woman, symbolizing the union of Christ and the Church), *Penance* (reconciliation with the Church), *Anointing of the Sick* (a healing of the separation between the individual and the Church created not by sin but by sickness), and the *Eucharist* (the real presence of Christ). In each instance, the *res et sacramentum* is signified by the rite itself (*sacramentum tantum*) and disposes the recipient(s) for the grace that is appropriate to the special relationship with the Church which is called for in this particular sacrament.

Intention of Minister and Recipient

The Minister

The sacraments do not achieve their intended effect if certain conditions are not fulfilled on the part of the minister of the sacrament and on the part of the recipient. The sacraments are acts of the Church. *The minister represents the Church and acts in its name.* Since everything the Church does, it does as the Body of Christ, the minister of a sacrament also acts in the name of Christ. On the other hand, the sacramental act is not automatic in its effect. The minister must voluntarily carry out the intention of the Church. He or she must intend what the Church intends. This does not mean, however, that the minister must also be a person of profound faith or even of moral probity, although both of these are eminently desirable. But if those qualities were demanded of each minister in every instance, the Church would never know when and to what extent its sacraments were properly celebrated and administered.

It is precisely because the sacraments are acts of the Church, and not simply acts of personal devotion, that the role of the minister is so important. There has been much controversy in the history of Catholic theology over this question of the minister's intention. Is it possible, for example, for a Jewish nurse to baptize validly a dying person who wishes to be baptized? The standard answer has been "Yes, so long as he or she intends to do what the Church intends." The theological problem with this approach is that it tends to conceive of the sacraments as indispensable means of achieving some spiritual effect. But they are not any more "indispensable" than the Church itself. People can be saved without Baptism (unless they know themselves to be called to the Church and deliberately reject the call), and in extraordinary cases people can even enter the Church without Baptism (as in the case of the dying person who wishes to be associated with the Body of Christ in some explicit way but is physically incapable of passing through the normal rite of initiation). Indeed, a catechumen is already in some real sense a part of the Church even before receiving Baptism itself.

It is the official teaching of the Catholic Church that the minister must have at least "the intention of doing what the Church does" (Council of Florence, *Decree for the Armenians*, 1439; and also Council of Trent, *Decree on the Sacraments*, canon 11). The validity of the sacrament is independent of the worthiness of the minister (condemnation of Wyclif by the Council of Constance, 1415; Council of Trent, *op. cit.*, canon 12). But not every member of the Church is qualified to administer every sacrament (Council of Trent, canon 10: "If anyone says that all Christians have the power (to preach) the word and to administer all the sacraments, *anathema sit*").

The Recipient

The *fruitful reception* of the sacraments (in contradistinction to their valid celebration) depends, as noted earlier, on the *disposition* of the recipient. Again, the sacraments are not magic. Sacraments are acts of the Church. The reception of sacraments draws one more fully into the life and mission of the Church. A sacrament can have no ecclesiological impact if the intended recipient has no faith in it or in the reality it symbolizes, or if he or she is morally unprepared for it.

What of a person who receives Baptism, Confirmation, or Holy Order in a state of mortal sin? The traditional answer would have it that the sacrament is validly received but that the grace is not communicated unless and until perfect contrition occurs. The answer is still correct in principle, but the case presupposes that "mortal sin" is relatively common even among active members of the Church who frequent the sacraments and who would be deemed fit candidates for one of the character sacraments. On the contrary, mortal sin involves a fundamental rejection of God and the reorientation of one's whole life away from all that is good and just. It is not something that one "commits" frequently. Certainly it will be rare, even non-existent, in the life of a sincere and active member of the Church (see also chapter 26). Furthermore, this assumption that mortal sin may often obstruct the grace of a character sacrament also seems to forget the principle reaffirmed by the Second Vatican Council's *Dogmatic Constitution on the Sacred Liturgy*: "(The sacraments) do indeed impart grace, but, in addition, the very act of celebrating them most effectively disposes the faithful to receive this grace in a fruitful manner, to worship God duly, and to practice charity" (n. 59). This does not make conversion inevitable, however.

This raises, finally, the question of the *Baptism of infants*, since we have here the case of persons who are manifestly incapable of being "disposed" for a fruitful reception of a sacrament. Two extremes are to be avoided: one which assumes that the primary purpose of Baptism is the "washing away of Original Sin" so that the Baptism of infants is a matter of highest priority no matter what the circumstances; the other which assumes that sacraments are only for adults and that life in the Church is within reach only of adults or of mature young people. Just as one enters a family by birth and is really a part of that family even though for a long period of time there is no real capacity for giving human love but only for receiving it, so one may be brought into the family of the Church before he or she is capable of understanding its significance or of expressing the love that marks this community out as the Body of Christ and the Temple of the Holy Spirit. In the case of infants, the intention is expressed not by the child but by those who bring the child for Baptism—e.g., parents, sponsors, relatives, and friends (*Summa Theologica*, III, q. 68, art. 9). There is a coresponsibility here that is also not foreign to sacraments even for adults. One thinks, e.g., of the role of sponsors and of one's family and friends at Confirmation, of the witnesses and one's family and friends at Marriage, of one's loved ones and others at the Anointing of the Sick.

Institution of the Sacraments

Were the sacraments "instituted" by Christ? Here again, the question is to be answered in its larger ecclesiological context. Just as the Church was not "founded" by Christ in the sense that he immediately and directly established a new religion, with specific organizational structure, doctrines, moral codes, and so forth (see chapter 17), neither do the sacraments issue from some precise mandate of the Lord. On the other hand, the Church does have its origin in Jesus Christ, especially in his proclamation of the Kingdom of God and the call to discipleship; and the sacraments, in turn, have their origin in the Church.

The question is also to be answered in terms of Christology. If one adopts exclusively a Christology "from above" (as in the Johannine writings), then, of course, every possibility is open. The omniscient *Logos* came down from heaven with his program and mission already marked out. He intended the Church as we know it, with the full sacramental life as exists in it. But if one starts instead with the historical Jesus (Christology "from below"), it becomes historically improbable that Jesus would have explicitly determined more than the Synoptic Gospels indicate. *Jesus willed the sacraments to the same degree and extent as he willed the Church.*

The rapidity with which Catholic theology, under the impact of recent developments in ecclesiology, in Christology, and in biblical studies, is moving away from the standard textbook treatments of the institution and the number of sacraments is very remarkable. In 1960 the Dutch theologian Edward Schillebeeckx argued in his important and influential work, *Christ the Sacrament of Encounter with God*, that "Christ...must himself have established the sevenfold direction of grace..." (p. 116).

Just three years later Karl Rahner was beginning to move beyond that cautious view, arguing that "the institution of a sacrament can...follow simply from the fact that Christ founded the Church with its sacramental nature" (*The Church and the Sacraments*, p. 41). And then in a later book (published originally in German in 1976), Rahner questioned even the possibility of tracing Baptism back to the words of Jesus, leaving the Lord's Supper as the only sacrament directly instituted by Christ ("Do this in remembrance of me," Luke 22:19; 1 Corinthians 11:24). He continues to link the "institution" of the sacraments with the "founding" of the Church, in an analogous way. The Church is in its essence sacramental, i.e., "the irreversible presence of God's salvific offer in Christ. This sacramentality is interpreted by the church in the seven sacraments, just as the church developed its own essence in its constitution. From this perspective, an individual Christian can accept without hesitation and live out this seven-fold sacramental order as it in fact exists" (*Foundations of Christian Faith*, p. 413).

The Number of Sacraments

What is essential is not the number seven, but the affirmation that there are certain ritual actions through which the saving presence and activity of God, on the one hand, and the sacramental nature of the Church, on the other, are visibly and effectively engaged. Even according to the most stringent interpretation of the teaching of the Council of Trent that there are seven sacraments, one could say that there are nine, taking diaconate and the episcopate as separate sacramental stages of the sacrament of Holy Order. Or one could say there are only six, considering Baptism and Confirmation as one sacrament. Or one could say that there are eight, combining Baptism and Confirmation but expanding Holy Order from one sacramental order to three.

It was and always is up to the Church to determine whether certain acts flowing from its nature as a sacrament of universal salvation are fundamentally and unconditionally a realization and expression of that nature. Before the number seven was finally settled upon during the medieval period (at Lyons II in 1274, at Florence in 1439, and at Trent in 1547), the Church lived through its entire first millennium and then some without ever having settled upon even a final definition of *sacrament*, let alone their precise number. On the contrary, there were literally hundreds of sacred rites (what we call today "sacramentals") which were simply referred to as "sacraments." These included Sacred Scripture, the mysteries of faith, cultic rites, and even allegory and typology.

Today *sacramentals* are understood as sacred signs which bear a resemblance to the sacraments. Insofar as the sacramentals cause grace, they do so not *ex opere operato*, primarily through the power of the rite itself, but *ex opere operantis*, primarily through the faith and devotion of those who are using, receiving, or celebrating the sacramental. Examples of sacramentals are baptismal water, holy oils, blessed ashes, candles, palms, crucifixes, statues, and medals.

THE RITE OF INITIATION

Most Christians are baptized shortly after birth, but Confirmation and Eucharist are postponed for several years. What is the usual practice is far from the ideal, however. The norm, as set down in the new *Rite of Christian Initiation*, is that a person should receive all three sacraments during the annual celebration of the Easter Vigil, following a suitable period of formation known as the *catechumenate*. But even when the norm cannot be observed, i.e., when Baptism is not followed immediately by Confirmation, or when the sequence of Confirmation and Eucharist is reversed, the ritual still calls for some post-baptismal anointing to replace Confirmation, and at Confirmation itself, the Baptism is renewed and reaffirmed and the Confirmation rite leads to eucharistic Communion.

The doctrine of Christian initiation is summed up in the "General Introduction" to the rite in the revised Roman Ritual:

1.   Through the sacraments of Christian initiation men and women are freed from the power of darkness. With Christ they die, are buried and rise again. They receive the Spirit of adoption which makes them God's sons and daughters and, with the entire people of God, they celebrate the memorial of the Lord's death and resurrection.

2.   Through baptism men and women are incorporated into Christ. They are formed into God's people, and they obtain forgiveness of all their sins. They are raised from their natural human condition to the dignity of adopted children. They become a new creation through water and the Holy Spirit. Hence they are called, and are indeed, the children of God.

Signed with the gift of the Spirit in confirmation, Christians more perfectly become the image of their Lord and are filled with the Holy Spirit. They bear witness to him before all the world and eagerly work for the building up of the body of Christ.

Finally they come to the table of the eucharist, to eat the flesh and drink the blood of the Son of Man so that they may have eternal life and show forth the unity of God's people. By offering themselves with Christ, they share in his universal sacrifice: the entire community of the redeemed is offered to God by their high priest. They pray for a greater outpouring of the Holy Spirit so that the whole human race may be brought into the unity of God's family.

Thus the three sacraments of Christian initiation closely combine to bring the faithful to the full stature of Christ and to enable them to carry out the mission of the entire people of God in the Church and in the world.

(*The Rites of the Catholic Church*, New York: Pueblo Publishing Co., 1976, pp. 3-4)

It is clear from this "General Introduction" and from the introductions to the other separate rites, including the Baptism of children and Confirmation by bishops, that *the premier rite is that of full initiation of adults.* All the other initiatory rites are to be understood in the context of this *Rite of Christian Initiation of Adults*, and their various details often refer back to the full rite of adult initiation as the governing norm of them all.

This represents a major shift in theological and pastoral understanding from the sacramental theology and liturgical practice of the pre-Vatican II Church and those of the post-Vatican II Church. In the pre-Vatican II period, many theological explanations of the sacraments began with the Baptism of infants, as if to underline the principle that the sacraments really do confer grace *ex opere operato*, by the power of Christ alone and not by the faith of the recipient (as some Protestants had insisted). Adult Baptisms were essentially modifications of the rite of infant Baptism (in much the same way as adult religious education was regarded as the exception, and the religious education of youth the norm).

A second major change suggested by the new rites, especially of adult initiation, is the explicit recognition that *the sacraments are closely related one to another.* Baptism is not simply the "ticket" which gives one entrance into the Church's sacred grounds, nor is Confirmation the first moment when the Holy Spirit is conferred (see *The Rites*, n. 34, p. 30). Baptism, Confirmation, and the Eucharist are all of a piece. One is not simply handed a membership card. One is fully introduced into the Spirit-filled life of the community which is God's people and Christ's body.

Thirdly, the sacraments are seen less as means of personal sanctification and more as *empowerments "to carry out the mission of the entire people of God in the Church and in the world."* The broader ecclesial vision is sharpened by the directive that the rite of Christian initiation should normally occur during the Easter Vigil which "speaks" about initiation in terms of the evangelization of the cosmos: fire, wind, wax, bees, light and darkness, water, oil, nakedness, bread, wine, aromas, words, and gestures. The full paschal sweep of God's intentions and accomplishments in Jesus

Christ is sketched out. All of the other sacraments and sacramentals find their meaning and purpose only within this salvation-history context (the work of the "economic Trinity" to which we referred in chapters 9 and 10).

Finally, therefore, with the restoration of the catechumenate (the process of pastoral formation of candidates for entrance into the Church), the point is reinforced that membership in the Church is *not simply for individual salvation but for participation in the saving work of God, in Christ, through the Church.* One does not assume this missionary responsibility lightly. The Church, both universal and local, has to take care that those who present themselves for membership understand that missionary responsibility and are properly equipped to fulfill it. All must share in the candidate's growth in faith: the community at large, relatives, friends, the sponsors, catechists, the bishop or his delegate, priests, and deacons.

It is important to note, however, that the catechumenate does *not* apply to those who are seeking entrance into the Catholic Church from some other Christian community. Eastern Orthodox Christians need only make a simple profession of faith, but only after recourse to Rome may they enter the Latin rite. In other cases the admission to the Catholic Church consists of the profession of faith, ordinarily with the Catholic community as a part of the eucharistic celebration, followed by Confirmation (if the person has not already been confirmed in his or her own church), and climaxed by eucharistic Communion for the first time within the Catholic community. No abjuration of heresy is required, as in the past, nor is the candidate to be absolved from any penalty of excommunication. Conditional Baptism ("If you are not already baptized, I baptize you...") is not permitted "unless there is reasonable doubt about the fact or validity of the baptism already received. If after serious investigation it seems necessary—because of such reasonable doubt—to confer baptism conditionally, the minister should carefully explain beforehand the reasons..., and he should administer it in the private form" (*Directory on Ecumenism*, 1967).

BAPTISM
New Testament Origins

Pre-Christian Ablutions and Baptisms

There were already many different kinds of ritual acts in Judaism, including those practiced by the Qumran sect, or Essenes. There were purification rites associated with food preparation and diet, and there were initiatory rites associated with water. This practice of *proselyte baptism* (by which Gentiles became Jews) seems to have developed with the expansion of Judaism outside Palestine. It had three phases: instruction concerning Judaism's persecuted condition and the commandments of the Law, circumcision for males, and a water bath for all. The central element of this ritual process was circumcision, by which solidarity was established with the holy nation of kings and priests (Exodus 19:6). Gradually, the water bath began to absorb the initiatory aspects of circumcision, and finally displaced it altogether. By the Christian era, therefore, proselyte baptism had assumed an increasingly initiatory rather than purificatory character.

This is not to suggest that Christian Baptism was derived from proselyte baptism. What evidence there is leads us to conclude, on the contrary, that Christian Baptism was patterned after the baptism of Jesus by John the Baptist in the Jordan river. There is no hint of a death-resurrection theme, no initiatory motif, no notion of admission to a new community. The emphasis is instead upon repentance as a preparation for messianic work. John's baptism was also a baptism in water. It would give way to another baptism in water and the Holy Spirit (Matthew 3:11; Luke 3:16). John himself regarded his baptism as a temporary rite. In submitting to it, Jesus established his solidarity with those who were the objects of John's preaching, the faithful remnant of Israel.

Baptism in Transition: From Judaism to Christianity

The Fourth Gospel says at one point that Jesus himself baptized, and at another that he did not but authorized his disciples to do so (John 3:22-23; 4:1-4). In any case, baptism continued to be practiced outside Jesus' circle, and it eventually widened the rift between his disciples and the followers of John. These pre-paschal baptisms were no longer Jewish, but neither were they as yet fully Christian. Not until the gathering at Pentecost is the outpouring of the Holy Spirit associated with baptism (Acts of the Apostles 2:1–39). There can be little doubt that the Pentecost occurrence influenced the ways in which the evangelists later interpreted the baptism of Jesus by John and the subsequent initiatory practice of the Church. Both water baptism and the outpouring of the Spirit are necessary as a follow-up to the proclamation of Jesus' resurrection and exaltation. Thus, the normal sequence: proclamation of the Gospel, conversion in faith, water bath, and post-baptismal teaching, fellowship in the Spirit, breaking of the bread, and prayers (Acts of the Apostles 2:42).

Baptism in the New Testament Churches

The relatively sparse data from the Synoptics, the Acts of the Apostles, and the Fourth Gospel is summarized in the preceding paragraph. More detail is provided by non-canonical writings (i.e., writings which were written at the same time as the New Testament but which were not subsequently included on the list, or canon, of inspired books): in the *Didache* (literally, *The Teaching*, composed about the year 100), in the *Apology* of Justin, and later in Tertullian and the *Apostolic Tradition* (ca. 200) of Hippolytus (d. ca. 236). The *theology* of Baptism is worked out later, in the Pauline corpus, in 1 John, and in 1 Peter.

Baptism incorporates us into the death, burial, and resurrection of Jesus, into "life with him" (Colossians 2:12; Ephesians 2:1, 4–6; Philippians 3:10–11). It is a Baptism of repentance (Acts of the Apostles 2:38) and an expression of belief in the Good News (8:37). Baptism purifies (Ephesians 5:26), cleansing our hearts from an evil conscience (Hebrews 10:22). We become "dead to sin but alive for God in Christ Jesus" (Romans 6:11). And what does it require of us? We must lead a wholly different kind of life, no longer "under the law but under grace" (6:12–23). (See also the discussion of Baptism in the New Testament in chapter 17.)

Baptism in Controversy

Donatism

Named after Donatus (d. 347), a false claimant to the episcopal chair at Carthage, this movement was an early rigoristic movement (much like Jansenism in the post-medieval period) which maintained that church membership was restricted to those who are free from sin. Sacraments administered by priests in sin were regarded as invalid. Those who left the Church and then reentered must be rebaptized. Rome's answer was that Baptism should not be readministered; a solemn laying on of hands would suffice. This difference in practice led to an open conflict between Cyprian (d. 258), bishop of Carthage, and Pope Stephen I (d. 257). The two agreed that Baptism could not be repeated. The question was whether or not heretics could validly baptize to begin with. Eventually Roman law prevailed, and the principle (to which we referred earlier in this chapter) was established that the personal holiness of the minister is not required for the efficacy of the sacrament.

Pelagianism

Since Pelagianism (see chapter 5) affirmed that we can attain salvation by our own efforts because we are naturally good, and since, in effect, Pelagianism denied the reality of Original Sin, it denied at the same time the necessity and even the propriety of infant Baptism. Augustine mounted the principal counter-attack, arguing in his treatise *On Baptism* (I,24,34) that we must be in sacramental communion with Christ's redemptive act if we are to reach the Kingdom of God and salvation. On the other hand, Augustine also inveighed against a purely mechanical concept of the sacrament. Without faith there is no sacrament. Thus, against the Donatists he argued that Christ, and not the sinful priest, is the true minister of Baptism; against the Pelagians, that Baptism is necessary for salvation; he also insisted that the fruitfulness of the sacrament depends on the dispositions of the recipient, i.e., the recipient's faith and love.

Thus, by the late fourth and early fifth centuries the theology of Baptism reached a certain level of maturity, weaving together various strands of New Testament and classic patristic theologies. What once happened to Christ now happens to us in Baptism. We are reborn to a new life, and we are given the Holy Spirit as an empowerment to live in Christ and in his body, the Church. (For a fuller treatment of the history of the rite of initiation, see J. D. C. Fisher, *Christian Initiation: Baptism in the Medieval West*, London: S.P.C.K., 1965, and Leonel Mitchell, *Baptismal Anointing*, London: S.P.C.K., 1966. Some of this material is summarized in *Made, Not Born*, pp. 50-98, cited in the Suggested Readings at the end of this chapter.)

The Doctrine of Baptism

The theological development is summed up in the Council of Trent's canons on the sacrament of Baptism (Session VII, 1547): that Baptism is valid even if administered by heretics, that it is necessary for salvation, that it imposes obligations to live a holy life, that its grace can be lost through serious sin, that it can never be repeated, that it can be administered to infants and children, etc. The Second Vatican Council's *Dogmatic Constitution on the Church* notes that Baptism incorporates us into the Church, orients us to the worship of God, and gives us a rebirth as sons and daughters of God (n. 11).

"Baptism of Desire"

The Church has always taught that Baptism is necessary for salvation. On the other hand, we have seen in the chapters 19 and 20 (and also in chapter 8 on the question of religious pluralism) that grace and revelation are universally available. Accordingly, the doctrine that Baptism is necessary for salvation can mean that for those called explicitly to the Church, Baptism is necessary for their salvation. In other words, if we are convinced in conscience that Jesus is Lord and Savior, we are obliged to seek admission to his Church, for there is no other place that we can go where the Lordship of Jesus is proclaimed and celebrated, and where we can collaborate in his historic mission for the sake of the Kingdom of God.

This understanding of the necessity of Baptism for salvation has also been known as "Baptism of desire." A widely held position, taught by Thomas Aquinas, was that prior to Christ it was sufficient to believe in God and in providence. This was tantamount to implicit faith in Christ. After the coming of Christ, however, explicit faith was necessary. It was generally assumed in the Middle Ages, we must never forget, that the world as a whole had already been evangelized. This is long before the geographical discoveries and before the development of modern means of transportation and communication described in chapter 3. After the discoveries of America and the Far East, the question of human salvation was posed with much greater urgency. Some theologians taught that people across the sea who had not yet been evangelized were like those who were alive before the coming of Christ. They, too, could be saved by implicit faith. These theologians were convinced of two principles: Christ is the one mediator of salvation, and every person is touched somehow by the grace of Christ.

This general understanding of a "Baptism of desire" received its most formal expression in the so-called Boston Letter sent by the Holy Office (now called the Congregation for the Doctrine of Faith) to Cardinal Richard Cushing (d. 1970) in 1949. A controversy had developed in the Archdiocese of Boston, Massachusetts, because of the literal interpretation given the principle "Outside the (Catholic) Church, no salvation" by Father Leonard Feeney, S.J. (d. 1978). According to the letter, it is Catholic doctrine that "it is not always required that a person be incorporated in reality (*reapse*) as a member of the Church, but it is required that he belong to it at least in desire and longing (*voto et desiderio*). It is not always necessary that this desire be explicit.... God also accepts an implicit desire, so called because it is contained in the good disposition of soul by which a man wants his will to be conformed to God's will." This teaching is reaffirmed by Vatican II's *Dogmatic Constitution on the Church*, n. 16 (see also n. 9). (See my *Do We Need the Church?*, New York: Harper & Row, 1969, and Gregory Baum, "Baptism of Desire," *The Concise Sacramentum Mundi*, pp. 75-78.)

The Church and Baptism

The sacraments not only signify and communicate grace for the recipient. They also disclose something fundamental about the Church which celebrates them. Thus, Baptism incorporates one into the Church, associates one with the death and resurrection of Christ unto new life, effects a forgiveness of sins, and orients one to the worship of God and the wider mission of the Church. In baptizing, the Church reveals itself to itself and to the rest of the world primarily as a *community*, the Body of Christ, and only secondarily as an institution; the Church identifies itself with the sufferings and death of Christ and so points the way to a share in his resurrection and glorification; it shows itself a forgiving community and, at the same time, a community in need of forgiveness; and its whole life is directed to the glory of God which is achieved in and through the humanization of the world. The Church which baptizes and is baptized has been given "a new birth by water and the Holy Spirit" and as such is a "holy people . . . (anointed) with the chrism of salvation" just as "Christ was anointed Priest, Prophet, and King" unto "everlasting life" (*Rite of Baptism*).

CONFIRMATION
Historical Considerations

In light of what has been noted already regarding the rite of initiation in general and Baptism in particular, the following historical points are pertinent to an understanding of Confirmation and to its relationship with Baptism:

1. There is no separate rite of Confirmation in the New Testament. Where the Spirit is given, the Spirit is given in connection with Baptism.

2. The East has never separated Baptism and Confirmation (chrismation). Theologically, the East has viewed them as essentially a single sacrament and, juridically, the East has always

regarded the presbyter as the legitimate minister of Baptism and the post-baptismal rites (including anointing).

3.   In the West, however, the post-baptismal rites (including the anointing) were reserved to the bishop. Two developments eventually led to the separation of Baptism and Confirmation: (a) the sense of urgency about the now-universal practice of infant Baptism (a development linked with Augustine's elaboration of the doctrine of Original Sin against the Pelagians), and (b) the unavailability of bishops to attend immediately to the post-baptismal rites. The bishop now came to those who had already been baptized sometime earlier. Here, too, we have the starting point for the later episcopal visitations, mainly for Confirmation. The prerogative of the bishops as ministers of the post-baptismal rites in the West did not presuppose, but in fact created, two independent sacraments.

4.   At first, the separation of the two rites was regarded as abnormal and less than ideal. Consequently, efforts were made to administer the post-baptismal rites as soon as possible after Baptism, including the Baptism of infants, as was the practice in the East. It was not until the thirteenth century that opposition to the separation of rites began to relax and official allowance was made for the concrete pastoral situation. A provincial council at Cologne in 1280, for example, postponed Confirmation until at least the age of seven. A minimum instead of a maximum age was now imposed. Adults continued to follow the older tradition and received the post-baptismal rites immediately after Baptism. Originally, these rites were relatively simple, as in the baptismal anointing today. From the ninth century on, however, a second anointing which had been known only in Rome was expanded to a self-contained "rite of confirmation."

5.   It was only in the high Middle Ages that a specific theology of Confirmation was developed in order to justify, *after the fact*, the now-autonomous rite carried out only by the bishop. The notion emerged that Confirmation provides a *gratia ad robur* ("grace for strength"), the armor of the soldier of Christ. The False Decretals of Gratian, which formed the basis of all medieval

law, treated Confirmation as a greater sacrament even than Baptism. Peter Lombard, whose *Sentences* influenced much of medieval theology, including Aquinas, followed the same line and described Confirmation as the gift of the Spirit "for strengthening" (*ad robur*) in contrast with baptismal grace, which is "for forgiveness" (*ad remissionem*). Even though this distinction had no basis in Sacred Scripture, the liturgy, or the Fathers of the Church, it was retained in the theology textbooks until the present time (see, for example, *Sharing the Light of Faith, National Catechetical Directory for Catholics of the United States*, p. 68). The distinction was definitively established by the Council of Florence in its *Decree for the Armenians* in 1439, and was confirmed without further reflection by the Council of Trent against Luther. Always the difference between the two ordinary ministers of the sacrament is emphasized: the presbyter for Baptism, the bishop for Confirmation.

6.   Today, of course, the rite of Confirmation is often administered, even in the West, by priests rather than bishops. This is to insure that, in the case of a newly baptized adult or a young person capable of being catechized, the full rite of initiation can be given all at once.

Theological Implications

1.   *Baptism and Confirmation are*, in essence and in light of their origins and history, *one sacrament*.

2.   Confirmation, which comprises the post-baptismal rites of anointing, the laying on of hands, and the words "Be sealed with the gift of the Holy Spirit," is a *ratification* of Baptism. For those who were baptized as infants, Confirmation provides an opportunity to ratify freely and deliberately what was done for them at Baptism. It helps to focus their minds and the minds of the whole community on the essentially *missionary* dimensions of the baptismal commitment.

The Church and Confirmation

As a continuation and/or ratification of the Christian's baptismal commitment, Confirmation expresses the essentially missionary character of the Church and its nature as the Temple of the Holy Spirit. It is a community called to manifest "the spirit of wisdom and understanding, the spirit of right judgment and courage, the spirit of knowledge and reverence . . . the spirit of wonder and awe in (God's) presence" (*Rite of Confirmation*). It is not only a sacred, grace-bearing sign for the good of the recipient, therefore, but it is also a principal moment when the Church reveals itself to itself and to the rest of the world as a particular kind of community, filled with the Holy Spirit and committed to the Spirit's release for the transformation of the whole of creation.

EUCHARIST
General Introduction

Our reflections on the Eucharist are framed by two basic doctrinal principles: the one enunciated by the Council of Trent and the other by the Second Vatican Council. Trent taught that the Eucharist is not simply one of the sacraments but is pre-eminent among them because Christ is present in the Eucharist even before the sacrament is used (*Decree on the Most Holy Eucharist*, chapter III, Session XIII, 1551); Vatican II declared that "the Liturgy . . . , most of all in the divine sacrifice of the Eucharist, is the outstanding means whereby the faithful can express in their lives, and manifest to others, the mystery of Christ and the real nature of the true Church" (*Constitution on the Sacred Liturgy*, n. 2). The Eucharist is indeed the "the source and summit of the entire Christian life" (n. 11).

Biblical Origins

The term *eucharist* is derived from the Greek word which means "thanksgiving." Jesus himself "gave thanks" at the Last Supper (Luke 22:19; 1 Corinthians 11:24; Mark 14:23; Matthew 26:27). The more strongly Semitic flavor of Mark's account has led some

biblical interpreters to conclude that its wording is even closer to
the original than Paul's. The differences between the Marcan and
Pauline accounts are too great for us to assume a common Greek
source. On the other hand, there is sufficient measure of agreement between them to assume a common Aramaic or Hebrew
source. The essential kernel of the various reports, however, is
clearly part of a unanimous tradition in the New Testament
churches.

The *meal* which is the object of these reports was only the
last in a long series of daily meals which Jesus shared with his
disciples. In the Oriental world of his day, a shared meal was
always a sign of peace, trust, and communality. Jesus, of course,
proclaimed the Kingdom by sharing meals with outcasts, tax-
collectors, and the like. But this last meal was special. According
to the Synoptics it was a ritual Passover meal, a festive farewell
meal. Whether it was a Passover meal or not (John says otherwise),
it had the same basic structure: the words over the bread, its
breaking and sharing; the words over the wine, and its sharing.
But Jesus identified the bread and wine with his own body and
blood. And sensing his own impending death, he speaks of himself
as a sacrifice. Just as the unleavened bread is broken, so will his
body be broken. And just as the wine is poured out, so will his
blood. All four texts agree that Jesus' death is an atonement and
establishes a new Covenant. The Jews, in fact, regarded every
death of an innocent person as an atoning death, and Jesus saw his
own death in this light.

There are connections here also with the Old Testament:
first, with the idea of the sacrifice of the old Covenant in Exodus
24:8,11 and of the new Covenant in Jeremiah 31:31-34; and, secondly, with the idea of the atoning sufferings of the servant of God
in Isaiah 53:12. Thus, the New Testament interprets the death of
Jesus as an atoning death which establishes a new Covenant in his
blood and brings redemption to all. By distributing the bread and
wine, his body and blood, Jesus was indicating that his disciples
were to share in his sacrifice and in the power of his atoning death.
This, too, is a familiar idea in Oriental thinking: that eating and
drinking communicate divine gifts.

With the resurrection the disciples now see the Last Supper and their own subsequent meals together in a new light. They eat and drink with the assurance that Christ will make good his promise to be present among those who are gathered in his name (Matthew 18:20). The new fellowship is now characterized by eschatological joy, a fundamental confidence in the coming of the Kingdom (Acts of the Apostles 2:46).

There are, of course, arguments among New Testament scholars and theologians of various Christian churches regarding the precise meaning and implications of Jesus' words at the Last Supper. We are not going into detail here. It is sufficient for our purpose to note that there is an undeniable continuity between what happened at the Last Supper and what the disciples did together at meals after the resurrection. There is no other explanation for the fact that the disciples repeated this meal and that later communities always referred to the actions of Jesus at the Last Supper to explain and justify what they did at the eucharistic table. The post-Easter Church was convinced that it was doing what Jesus intended it to do when he said: "Do this in remembrance of me" (1 Corinthians 11:24-25).

As an act of remembrance (*anamnesis*) the Eucharist not only recalls to mind what Jesus did but also effectively makes it present again. Thus, Paul affirms the bodily presence of Jesus: "Is not the cup of blessing we bless a sharing in the blood of Christ? And is not the bread we break a sharing in the body of Christ?" (1 Corinthians 10:16). Indeed, to eat and drink unworthily is to sin "against the body and blood of the Lord" (11:27). Because we partake of the same bread, "we, many though we are, are one body" (10:17).

The Lord's Supper establishes and celebrates the communion that exists not only between the Church and Christ but also within the Church—i.e., not only "with Christ" but also "in Christ." And it is a communion that looks always not only to the past—i.e., to the Last Supper and to the redemptive events that followed it—but also to the future, "until he comes" (11:26). Jesus himself had said that he would not drink again of the fruit of the vine until that day when he would drink it new in the Kingdom of God (Mark 14:25; Matthew 26:29; Luke 22:18). Christ's presence in the Eucharist, therefore, is the presence not only of the crucified and risen one, but also the presence of one who is yet to come.

On the other hand, that presence comes about not through some magical formula, but through the proclamatory words of faith. John places a clear warning at the end of Jesus' words about the bread of life: "It is the spirit that gives life; the flesh is useless. The words I spoke to you are spirit and life" (John 6:63). The word is ultimately effective, however, only if it is creative of a sense of community. Where there is no fellowship, where there are divisions, where there is insensitivity to those in need, there is no real community and the Lord's Supper brings judgment, not grace (1 Corinthians 11:17-34). What is proclaimed must be lived (11:26). (See also the discussion of the Eucharist in the New Testament in chapter 17.)

History of the Eucharist

General Structure

As we have just seen, the Eucharist, or Lord's Supper, was celebrated in the beginning as a *meal*. (The term *Mass* is derived from the Latin word *missa*, which meant "dismissal," the closing blessing at any ecclesiastical celebration. The term was eventually applied only to the Eucharist.) During the second and third centuries the meal disappeared. The prayer of thanksgiving (formerly known as the "canon" and now once again called the "Eucharistic Prayer") became the central feature of the rite. It was during this prayer that the bread and wine were consecrated, after which the people responded "Amen" to ratify what had been said and done. Communion followed. The same introductory prayers that are recited today ("The Lord be with you." "And also with you." "Lift up your hearts." "We lift them up to the Lord." "Let us give thanks to the Lord our God." "It is right to give him thanks and praise.") are to be found in the account of Justin about the year 150 and in a text put forward as a model by Hippolytus about 215. Though the details of the service were left to the discretion of the celebrant, especially the phrasing of the prayers (another practice recently restored), the whole Christian world must have celebrated the Eucharist in much this form until well into the fourth century.

In the earliest centuries, too, the Eucharist was celebrated every Sunday, but on few other occasions. Daily Mass was not the rule. The Eucharist was attended by the whole Christian community of the neighborhood, early in the morning (now that it was separated from the supper meal at the end of the day) and before work (since Sunday was still an ordinary workday). Part of the traditional synagogue service survived and was incorporated into these liturgies. The memoirs of the Apostles or the writings of the prophets were read, and these were followed by a sermon from the president of the assembly and a prayer for the general needs of the community. There are also various indications of an Offertory procession (also since restored) as early as the third century. This ceremony in which bread and wine and other gifts were brought forward to the altar may have been a conscious reaction against Gnosticism, which denied the goodness of matter.

As the Church was liberated from persecution and spread more easily through the empire, cultural diversification set into the liturgy. The entrance rite was expanded to include prayers at the foot of the altar (since eliminated and now incorporated into the introductory greetings and penitential rite). Readings from Scripture, however, formed the core of the early part of the Mass in every celebration, and hence this part of the liturgy was simply called, as it is today, the liturgy of the word. Responses were developed for each reading—songs which survive today in the form of psalm verses and the alleluia. Much solemnity attended the reading of the Gospel: e.g., candles and incense. There followed the recitation of the creed, except in non-Roman rites, where the creed occurred just before the Eucharistic Prayer itself. After the creed came the intercessory prayers (as we have them again today), then the preparation of the gifts (the prayers which are still recited silently over the gifts were not introduced until the ninth century). Finally, the Eucharist itself.

Eucharistic Prayer

For many centuries the canon, or Eucharistic Prayer, was recited in the West in an undertone not audible to the congregation. Today it is once again proclaimed aloud. In the East it was always proclaimed in that manner. The admonition "Do this in remembrance of me" was followed, in all liturgies, by the *anamnesis*: "We remember, we do this to commemorate you." The prayer ends, as it did from Hippolytus' day, with the solemn doxology: "Through him, with him, in him, in the unity of the Holy Spirit, all glory and honor is yours, almighty Father, forever and ever." After Communion there was the blessing (*missa*), and the sacred vessels were cleansed after the liturgy itself.

This basic, straightforward structure was progressively interrupted by the insertion of a variety of petitions for the living and dead, and then by the *epiclesis*, or solemn invocation of the Holy Spirit. Even the breaking of bread came to be embroidered with prayers. The canon was rendered inaudible by the Carolingian liturgists, who wished to make it a sort of sanctuary which the priest alone could enter. To compensate for this, the elevation of the host and chalice after the consecration was introduced in the thirteenth century so that the whole congregation could look upon and adore the sacrament. It was only at the close of the canon that the priest resumed contact with the people. (In the pre-Vatican II Latin Mass, the *per omnia saecula saeculorum* just before the *Pater Noster*, or Our Father, was the first generally audible sound made by the celebrant since the recitation of the preface.)

Congregational Participation

By the seventeenth century frequent Communion had fallen into disrepute, partly through the influence of Jansenism. Not until the early years of the twentieth century was frequent Communion encouraged again, by Pope Pius X. As recently as 1960 most people were still not making responses at Mass. What responses there were the "altar boy," or server, made in their name. The "dialogue Mass" was introduced in the late 1950s just before the Second Vatican Council, but the Latin language was still used. During the Romanticist eighteenth century, choirs had begun to

supplant the congregation, singing elaborate polyphonic rendi-
tions of the various parts of the Mass: *Kyrie* ("Lord have mercy"),
Gloria, Credo, Sanctus ("Holy, Holy"), and *Agnus Dei* ("Lamb of
God"). As a concession, the congregation was encouraged to sing
vernacular hymns not taken from the Eucharist itself, but this was
stopped in the nineteenth century.

Private Masses

The practice of private Masses, i.e., Masses celebrated by a priest
without a congregation, appeared about the sixth century, chiefly
in the form of votive Masses, or Masses for the necessities of the
faithful. The Mass was perceived increasingly as an act of petition, something to be performed to receive some particular benefit
from God, or it was often regarded as a rite, however complicated,
to produce hosts for the tabernacle. And since private Masses
became so frequent, they were also regarded eventually as the
norm rather than the exception. The Second Vatican Council,
however, declared the communal celebration preferable to individual and quasi-private celebrations *(Constitution on the Sacred
Liturgy,* n. 27).

Eucharistic Doctrines

Catholic eucharistic doctrine has been focused on two issues: the
sacrificial nature of the Mass and the real presence of Christ in the
consecrated elements of bread and wine.

It is official Catholic teaching (Council of Trent) that the
Mass is a true *sacrifice,* not only of praise and thanksgiving and of
commemoration but also of expiation for the living and the dead,
without diminishing the value of the sacrifice of Calvary. Christ is
the same victim and priest in the Eucharist as he was on the cross,
although the mode of offering is different at Mass. The sacrifice of
the cross was a bloody sacrifice; the sacrifice of the Mass is
unbloody. Nonetheless, the fruits of the latter sacrifice are the
same as those of the former. The sacrifice of the Mass, Trent
declared, is "properly offered not only for the sins, penalties, satis-
factions, and other needs of the faithful who are living but also for
the departed in Christ who are not yet fully cleansed" *(Decree on
the Mass,* chapter II).

It is also official Catholic teaching that Christ is *really present* in the consecrated elements of bread and wine. By the Middle Ages the real presence of Christ was being reduced by many (especially Berengar of Tours, d. 1088) to a merely spiritual presence, in reaction to a crudely physical notion (represented, for example, in the belief that if one were to scratch the consecrated host, it would bleed). For the first time in the history of Catholic doctrine, the Fourth Lateran Council (1215) spoke of *transubstantiation*, i.e., the belief that the substance of bread and wine is changed into the body and blood of Christ. This teaching was reaffirmed and made more precise by the Council of Constance (1415) and the Council of Trent (1551). Zwingli and Calvin, however, denied transubstantiation completely, while Luther held to *consubstantiation*, i.e., the belief that the bread and wine become the body and blood of Christ but that they remain also bread and wine.

The traditional medieval teaching on the real presence was repeated in Pope Paul VI's *Mysterium Fidei* (1965), an encyclical written against the views of certain Dutch Catholic theologians who were attempting to explain the real presence without employing the Scholastic concept of transubstantiation. A mere "transignification or transfinalization," he insisted, is not sufficient to explain the real presence. Rather, the consecrated elements bear not only a new meaning (transignification) and a new purpose (transfinalization) but a new substantial, or ontic, reality as well (transubstantiation). The pope also reaffirmed the teaching that the real presence continues after Mass, and he defended eucharistic adoration and private Masses.

The scope of Christ's presence has been subject to controversy as well. According the the same medieval doctrine of transubstantiation, the whole Christ is present under each form, the consecrated bread and the consecrated wine. For that reason, Trent insisted, it is unnecessary to receive the Eucharist under both species as John Hus (d. 1415) and his disciples in Bohemia had argued. (The practice of Communion under both kinds has recently been reintroduced into the Catholic Church of the Latin rite.) But if Christ is present under each form, that is not to say that he is present *only* there. The Second Vatican Council has taught that the presence of Christ in the Eucharist is not confined to the consecrated elements of bread and wine. Christ is present, first, in the community which has assembled for worship. Secondly, he is present in the person of the minister who presides in his name. Thirdly, he is present in the biblical word which is proclaimed. Finally, he is present in the sacred species themselves (*Constitution on the Sacred Liturgy*, n. 7).

The real presence of Christ in the sacred species comes about through the ordained priest, who "confects" the Eucharist (Lateran Council IV). The power of the priest to consecrate the bread and wine is not dependent upon his personal holiness (Council of Constance). Under the impact of the twentieth-century renewal, this traditional Catholic emphasis on the role of the ordained priest was broadened to include the participation of all the faithful who are present at the celebration of the Eucharist. Both Pope Pius XII's *Mediator Dei* (1947) and the Vatican II's *Constitution on the Sacred Liturgy* insisted that the faithful participate not merely through the priest but along with him (*Constitution*, n. 48). This is not to say, however, that their function is the same as the priest's.

Ecumenical Consensus Today

Eucharist as Sacrifice

It was once assumed that Catholics alone (with the usual exception of the Orthodox) believed in the sacrificial nature of the Eucharist. The ecumenical dialogues and consultations at both international and national levels since 1965 have almost completely undermined that common assumption. The sacrificial nature of the Eucharist is affirmed in varying degrees by the Anglican-Roman Catholic Consultation, Orthodox-Catholic, Lutheran-Catholic, Presbyterian-Reformed-Catholic, and in a 1970 consensus statement of a study commission of the National Council of Churches in the United States. The Lutheran-Catholic dialogue provides the fullest treatment of the subject in its "The Eucharist: Joint Statement" (*Lutherans and Catholics in Dialogue*, vol. 4, Washington D.C.: United States Catholic Conference,

1970, pp. 7–33). The Lutherans join with the Catholics in acknowledging that the Eucharist is also the sacrifice of the Church to the Father through the power of the Holy Spirit. The Eucharist is also a propitiatory sacrifice, "efficacious for the forgiveness of sins and the life of the world." A more recent statement from the International Roman Catholic-Lutheran Commission (*Origins* 8/30, January 11, 1979, pp. 465,467-478) also notes "growing convergence" on this matter.

Real Presence

Here the consensus is even wider and stronger. Every consultation in which Roman Catholics have been involved affirms some measure of basic agreement on the real presence of Christ in the Eucharist. In addition to those mentioned in the paragraph above, there is the Disciples of Christ-Catholic consultation. The Lutheran-Catholic consultation again is emphatic: "We affirm that in the sacrament of the Lord's supper, Jesus Christ, true God and true man, is present wholly and entirely, in his body and blood, under the signs of bread and wine." As to the time or duration of the real presence, the statement declares: "The true body and blood of Christ are present not only at the moment of reception but throughout the eucharistic action" (p. 193). The Lutherans do not reject everything implied in the medieval term *transubstantiation*, but they shy away from it because it is "misleading" (pp. 195-196).

From the other side of the Reformation, i.e., the Presbyterian and Reformed, the same affirmation is made: "The real presence of Christ in the Eucharist...does not depend upon the belief of each individual, but on the power of Christ's Word...and upon his promise to bind himself to the sacramental event as the sign of his person given to us" (*The Unity We Seek*, New York: Paulist Press, 1977, p. 39). This is not to say that there is also fundamental agreement on the "how" of the real presence. But there is agreement on the "that" of it (p. 40). Needless to say, agreement between Catholics and Anglicans and Catholics and Orthodox on this point is clear and unequivocal.

Reflection

What emerges from these consensus statements is the principle
that the doctrine and celebration of the Eucharist can make sense
only when understood in the context of the doctrine and life of the
whole Church as People of God, Body of Christ, and Temple of
the Holy Spirit. What also emerges is a general readiness (except
among the Orthodox) to call for some eucharistic sharing, or
intercommunion, on the basis of these remarkable convergences
on eucharistic doctrine. On the other hand, the more sophisticated
consultations (especially the Anglican-Roman Catholic and the
Lutheran-Roman Catholic) admit that they have not yet solved
the fundamental ecclesiological question, "What is minimally
required before there can be full ecclesiastical communion and
sacramental sharing?" The question of intercommunion will be
taken up again in chapter 23.

(For a reliable synthesis and interpretation of the various
ecumenical statements on the Eucharist, see John F. Hotchkin,
"Christian Dialogue and the Eucharist," *Catholic Mind* 75,
March 1977, pp. 11-32.)

The Eucharist and the Church

The first effect of the Eucharist is a more profound incorporation
into the unity of the Church. St. Thomas himself regarded the
Eucharist as the sacrament of the Church's unity (III, q. 82, a. 2).
According the Karl Rahner, the Church is "most manifest and in
the most intensive form, she attains the highest actuality of her
own nature, when she celebrates the eucharist" (*The Church and
the Sacraments*, p. 84). The Church at the Eucharist is a structured community, a community listening to the word of God, a
community in continuity with the preaching, ministry, death, and
resurrection of its Lord, a community looking forward to the
coming of the Kingdom, a community conscious of its sinfulness
and repentant of its sins, a community convinced of the power of
God's grace, a community ready to serve others, i.e., to carry out
"the breaking of the bread" beyond the Church, and a community
here and now open to the presence of the Lord and his Spirit.

"Only a person who is prepared in principle to entrust himself to the whole activity of the Church that takes place in the eucharist . . . will share even in the blessings and graces of this sacrament for the individual," Rahner suggests. "For ultimately these are nothing but that deeper and deeper union with the Church, her action and her lot" (p. 87).

SUMMARY

1. A major theological, pastoral, and even aesthetical characteristic of Catholicism is its commitment to the *sacramental principle*, namely, the conviction that everything is capable of embodying and communicating the divine, that all reality has a "mysterious" dimension insofar as it is imbued with the hidden presence of God.

2. Just as God reaches us through the finite and the visible, so we reach God through the finite and the visible. The point at which this occurs is the point of *sacramental encounter*. For Christians, *the* point of sacramental encounter with God is *Jesus Christ*.

3. For Catholics especially, the *Church* also plays an important sacramental, or *mediating*, role in salvation history. Just as Christ is the sacrament of encounter with God, so the Church is the sacrament of encounter with Christ, and, ultimately, with God.

4. In its *widest sense*, the word *sacrament* applies to any finite reality through which the divine is perceived to be disclosed and communicated, and through which our human response to the divine assumes some measure of shape, form, and structure.

5. In a *more specific sense*, sacraments are those finite realities through which God is communicated to the Church and through which the Church responds to God's self-communication. As such, sacraments are directly *ecclesial* in character. Although they are certainly the acts of God and of Christ, sacraments are immediately *acts of the Church*, expressions of the nature and mission of the Church.

6. Since the medieval period, the sacraments have been understood primarily as *causes of grace*. Their function as *signs of faith* was subordinated to concerns about causality. A recovery of the sacramental perspective of *St. Thomas Aquinas* in recent decades has restored balance to Catholic sacramental theology. Sacraments cause grace insofar as they signify it. If they are not intelligible and effective *signs*, then they are not effective *causes*.

7. Sacraments, therefore, are signs of faith, acts of worship, signs of the unity of the Church, and signs of Christ's presence. They are *signs*

of faith insofar as they express and proclaim belief in the unseen reality of God. They are *acts of worship* insofar as they draw us ritually into Christ's paschal worship of the Father. They signify the *unity of the Church* insofar as all who participate in them share a common faith and enjoy a common fellowship. And they signify *Christ's presence* insofar as the incarnate Word is not confined by time and space but is made available here and now, as he is, the risen Lord.

8.   The *Council of Trent* taught, on the other hand, that the sacraments also *cause* grace for those who place no obstacle to it. The point of the council's teaching was that it is not the personal merit of the recipient that causes the grace received. Nevertheless, God does not force the human will.

9.   Trent's teaching, however, was frequently misunderstood. "Not placing an obstacle" was interpreted to mean that the absence of mortal sin was enough to have the sacrament "work." St. Thomas, on the other hand, insisted on the "right disposition" of the recipient—i.e., interior conversion, faith, devotion. The "fruitfulness" (as opposed to the mere "validity") of the sacrament depends on this.

10.   Sacraments do not cause grace in the sense that grace is otherwise unavailable. Grace is already present to the world in God's original self-communication. Sacramental grace shapes and "channels" that original communication of grace for the sake of the Church's mission. The sacraments signify, celebrate, and effect what God is, in a sense, doing everywhere and for all.

11.   In every sacrament there is the sign or ritual (*sacramentum tantum*—e.g., the pouring of the water and the recitation of the formula "I baptize you . . ."), the fruit, or immediate effect (*res tantum*—i.e., the grace of the sacrament), and the lasting effect (*res et sacramentum*—e.g., the permanent membership bond with the Church in Baptism).

12.   The distinction arose as a way of dealing with the challenge posed by *Berengar of Tours*, who acknowledged that the Eucharist is a sign of and causes the grace of union with Christ (*res tantum*) but who denied the real presence of Christ in the sacrament. Theologians insisted that there is a third element that comes into being whether the sacrament is worthily received or not: It is still the body and blood of Christ, even if it does not cause grace in this particular recipient.

13.   Those sacraments which, by tradition, the Church does not repeat are known as "character" sacraments. The term *character* conveys the notion of a "sealing" of the Christian, either as a member of the Church (*Baptism-Confirmation*) or in its service (*Holy Order*).

14. The lasting effects of the non-character sacraments are the bond of union between a man and a woman (*Matrimony*), a healing of the separation between an individual and the Church caused by sin (*Penance*), a healing of the separation of an individual and the Church caused by sickness (*Anointing of the Sick*), and the real presence of Christ (*Eucharist*).

15. The *minister* of the sacrament acts in the name of the Church and therefore must intend to do what the Church wishes to be done (Councils of Florence and Trent). But the validity of the sacrament does not depend on the holiness of the minister (Councils of Constance and Trent). Not every member of the Church is qualified to administer every sacrament (Council of Trent).

16. The *recipient* must be disposed properly (faith, conversion, devotion). If he or she is not, "the very act of celebrating" the sacrament may produce the proper disposition (Vatican II).

17. *Infant Baptism* is the exception rather than the rule of sacramental reception. Two extremes are to be avoided in explaining it: the one which assumes that Original Sin cannot be "removed" without Baptism, and the other which assumes that sacraments are only for adults or for mature young people. The community's "intention" supplies for the infant's, and it is the community which nurtures the baptized member's faith.

18. The sacraments were "*instituted*" by Christ in the same way that the Church was "instituted" by Christ. They have their origin in Jesus' proclamation of the Kingdom of God and in his call to discipleship. Jesus willed the sacraments to the same degree and extent as he willed the Church.

19. There are many sacramental actions celebrated and/or used by the Church to mediate the presence of God. Some few of these so fully engage the nature and mission of the Church that they are placed in a special category. By definition of the Councils of Lyons II, Florence, and Trent, the Catholic Church recognizes *seven* such signs as sacraments in the fullest sense: Baptism, Confirmation, Eucharist, Penance, Anointing of the Sick, Matrimony, and Holy Order. The number seven, however, is not absolute. Thus, one might consider Baptism and Confirmation as one sacrament, or the sacrament of Holy Order as three (diaconate, priesthood, episcopate).

20. The *rite of Christian initiation* includes three sacraments: Baptism, Confirmation, and Eucharist. It follows a suitable period of formation known as the *catechumenate*. The initiation of *adults* is the pastoral norm, not the exception. All other baptismal rites are referred to

this one. The new rite also underscores the *unity among the sacraments*, their close relationship with the *mission of the Church*, and the *responsibility of the local church* to share in the candidate's growth in faith.

21.   Those entering the Catholic Church from some other Christian church do not become catechumens, nor are they rebaptized, nor do they abjure "heresy." They are already members of the Body of Chirst.

22.   The sacrament of *Baptism* is not without pre-Christian origins—i.e., the purification and initiation rites of Judaism, and the baptism of John the Baptist. Baptism was practiced outside of Jesus' circle during his lifetime, but it was not until Pentecost that the outpouring of the Holy Spirit was associated with it, along with conversion, repentance, the forgiveness of sins, and the call to mission.

23.   The New Testament data on the *practice of Baptism* even in the post-resurrection period is sparse. More detail is provided in the noncanonical writings (*Didache*, Justin's *Apology*, and the *Apostolic Tradition* of Hippolytus). The *theology of Baptism*, however, is worked out in Paul, 1 John, and 1 Peter. Baptism incorporates us into the death, burial, and resurrection of Jesus, into "life with him" (Colossians 2:12, e.g.).

24.   The *post-biblical theology of Baptism* developed under the pressure of the *Donatist* and *Pelagian* controversies: The former insisted on the holiness of the minister for validity, and the latter rejected the necessity of the sacraments for salvation. In each case, the key theological figure was *Augustine*, who insisted, on the one hand, that the sacraments do require faith, but that, on the other hand, Baptism is necessary for salvation. Thus, infants are fit subjects of Baptism, and furthermore they place no obstacle to its effectiveness.

25.   These principles were gathered up and definitively taught by the *Council of Trent*. A wider ecclesiological vision, however, was provided by *Vatican II*, which emphasized our incorporation into the Church and our call to worship.

26.   Many are never baptized during their lifetime, and yet God intends the salvation of all in Christ. With the geographical discoveries of the Middle Ages, theologians were compelled to confront this apparent dilemma. Their solution was the concept of *"Baptism of desire,"* which was tantamount to *implicit faith* in Christ. This approach was adopted by the Holy Office in 1949 in its response to the so-called Feeney case in Boston, Massachusetts, where the principle "Outside the (Catholic) Church, no salvation" had been pushed to extremes.

27.   *Confirmation* is also a sacrament, but it may be regarded as part of the sacrament of Baptism. There is no separate rite of Confirmation in the New Testament. The separation of the rites of Baptism and

Confirmation in the West occurred because the post-baptismal rites (= Confirmation) were reserved to bishops, and bishops were often unavailable when Baptism was administered. An elaboration of this separate rite of Confirmation began in the ninth century, and it was only in the high Middle Ages that a specific theology of Confirmation developed. The distinction was ratified by the Councils of Florence and Trent.

28.   Recent reforms of the rite of initiation restore the unity of Baptism and Confirmation, especially by authorizing priests to be the ministers of Confirmation.

29.   The separate rite of Confirmation allows one who was baptized as an infant to ratify that Baptism and to embrace freely and deliberately his or her missionary responsibilities within the Church.

30.   The *Eucharist* is the preeminent sacrament because Christ is present in it even before it is used. It is also the "source and summit" of the entire Christian life.

31.   The term *eucharist* means "thanksgiving." It has its origins in the meal which Jesus celebrated with his disciples, known as the *Last Supper*, at which he directed them to "do this in remembrance" of him. It was one of a long series of meals which Jesus shared with his friends as a sign of fellowship, peace, and trust.

32.   At this meal, however, Jesus identified himself with the bread and wine ("This is my body . . ."). He also ate and drank with his disciples with the knowledge that his own death was imminent. Consistently with Jewish consciousness, he perceived innocent death as *atoning* death.

33.   The disciples and the early Church came to interpret this meal as establishing a new Covenent in the blood of Christ for the redemption of all. They continued the practice of shared meals after the death and resurrection in this light and with fundamental confidence in his promises and with hope in the coming Kingdom of God.

34.   The Eucharist, or Lord's Supper, became an act of remembrance (*anamnesis*) of what Christ had done, an act of fellowship and communion not only "with Christ" but also "in Christ," and an act of eschatological anticipation.

35.   By the second and third centuries the meal aspect of the Eucharist had disappeared. The prayer of thanksgiving (canon, Eucharistic Prayer), introduced by readings and followed by Holy Communion, became central. At first the Eucharist was celebrated only on Sundays.

36.   As the persecutions lifted and the Church moved more freely throughout the empire, the Eucharist assumed many different cultural

forms. The rite became more elaborate. In some cases, there were distortions of its original purpose. E.g., the congregation no longer participated actively, the canon was recited quietly by the celebrant, frequent Communion declined, private Masses for special intentions multiplied. The liturgical reforms mandated by Vatican II restored the Eucharist to its original purpose and structure.

37.   The *real presence* of Christ became a doctrinal preoccupation of the medieval Church because it had been challenged, in particular by Berengar of Tours. Lateran IV, Constance, and Trent all definitively affirmed the doctrine, especially against the Reformers. And Trent also affirmed the doctrine of the *sacrificial* nature of the Eucharist and its *expiatory* value. These traditional themes were sounded again in 1965 by Pope Paul VI's *Mysterium Fidei*. Pope Pius XII's *Mediator Dei* (1947) and Vatican II's *Constitution on the Sacred Liturgy*, however, insisted on the active participation of all the faithful not merely through the priest but along with him. Vatican II also noted that Christ is present at the Eucharist not only in the consecrated elements of bread and wine, but also in the community, the word, and the minister.

38.   There is a remarkable *ecumenical convergence* today on such previously controverted questions as the sacrificial nature of the Eucharist and the real presence of Christ in the Eucharist. The various Christian traditions have come increasingly to perceive the Eucharist in the context of the mystery and mission of the Church.

39.   The first *effect* of the Eucharist is *a more profound incorporation into the Church*. The Church is most manifest and most fully itself in the Eucharist, where the Church is visible as a structured community, listening to the word of God, breaking bread and sharing the cup "until he comes."

SUGGESTED READINGS

Bausch, William J. *A New Look at the Sacraments*. Notre Dame, Ind.: Fides/Claretian, 1977.

Cooke, Bernard. *Christian Sacraments and Christian Personality*. New York: Doubleday, Image Books, 1968.

Davis, Charles. *Sacraments of Initiation: Baptism and Confirmation*. New York: Sheed & Ward, 1964.

Hellwig, Monika K. "New Understanding of the Sacraments." *Commonweal* 105 (16 June 1978), 375-380.

Jungmann, Josef. *The Mass: An Historical, Theological, and Pastoral Survey*. Collegeville, Minn.: Liturgical Press, 1976.

Kavanagh, Aidan. *The Shape of Baptism: The Rite of Christian Initiation.* New York: Pueblo Publishing, 1978.

Murphy Center for Liturgical Research, The. *Made, Not Born: New Perspectives on Christian Initiation and the Catechumenate.* Notre Dame, Ind.: University of Notre Dame Press, 1976.

Rahner, Karl. *The Church and the Sacraments.* New York: Herder & Herder, 1963.

Schanz, John P. *The Sacraments of Life and Worship.* Milwaukee: Bruce, 1966.

Schillebeeckx, Edward. *Christ the Sacrament of Encounter with God.* New York: Sheed & Ward, 1963.

Sullivan, C. Stephen, ed. *Readings in Sacramental Theology.* Englewood Cliffs, N.J.: Prentice-Hall, 1964.

·XXII·

THE SACRAMENTS OF HEALING, VOCATION, AND COMMITMENT

We are initiated into the Christian community by Baptism-Confirmation and the Eucharist, but initiation is only the beginning of a *process*. We are not already fully mature in Christ by the mere fact of having been baptized, anointed, and invited to share the Lord's Supper. We are human. Hence we are prone to sin and vulnerable to illness, physical incapacity, and finally death. And yet the call to Christian existence is a call to perfection: "In a word, you must be perfect as your heavenly Father is perfect" (Matthew 5:48). It is God's will that we be sanctified (1 Thessalonians 4:3; Ephesians 1:4), that we become as saints (Ephesians 5:3). We are to love God with all our mind and all our strength, and our neighbor as ourselves (Mark 12:30). Jesus' proclamation of the Kingdom of God, which shaped his own ministry as well as the mission of the Church, is a call to conversion: "This is the time of fulfillment. The reign of God is at hand! Reform your lives and believe in the gospel" (Mark 1:15).

Two sacraments are celebrated by the Church as a sign and instrument of God's and of Christ's abiding *healing* power. The sacrament of *Penance*, or of *Reconciliation*, is for those whose bond with the Church, and ultimately with God and Christ, has been weakened or even severed by sin. The sacrament of the *Anointing of the Sick* (formerly called *Extreme Unction*) is for those whose bond with the Church has been weakened by illness or physical incapacity. In either case, the purpose of the sacrament is to heal and to restore the morally and/or physically sick member to full communion with the Church so that once again he or she can participate in its life and mission.

Beyond that, the Church itself is disclosed in these sacraments as an essentially healing and forgiving community, as the sacrament of the healing and forgiving Lord. The Church is also the penitent Church, ever bathing the feet of Christ with its tears and hearing his words, "Nor do I condemn you" (John 8:11). And because of its unshakable confidence in the triumph of God's mercy and grace in Christ, when night falls the Church holds high the lamp of hope and reveals itself as the sacrament of *universal* salvation, the community which gives up on no one and no situation, no matter how seemingly hope-less.

All Christians are initiated into the Church through the same essential process, but not all Christians are called to live as Christians in the same mode of existence. Most are called to live in intimate union with another in marriage. Some few others may (also) be called to a life of service of the Christian community itself, specifically through a ministry which attends directly to the order and mission of the Church. So fundamental are both the call to human life itself and the call to the life of the Church that each of these calls and its corresponding commitment is celebrated as a sacrament: the one, the sacrament of *Matrimony*; the other, the sacrament of *Holy Order*.

Like all the sacraments, both these sacraments are directed to the nature and mission of the Church. In Matrimony the Christian community is itself built up and manifested at its most natural and local level. The union of Christ and his Church is symbolized (Ephesians 5:22-32). In Holy Order the Christian community is provided structure and direction for the exercise of its mission. These are the sacraments of *vocation* and of *commitment*. The Church is revealed in them as a community called forth (the root meaning of the word *church — ekklesia*) and committed to a life of love and service.

Section One: Sacraments of Healing

PENANCE
History

New Testament Period

The text to which Catholic doctrine has appealed in asserting the sacramentality and divine origin of Penance is John 20:22-23, which records one of Jesus' post-resurrection appearances: "Receive the Holy Spirit. If you forgive men's sins, they are forgiven them; if you hold them bound, they are held bound" (see also Matthew 16:19, 18:18). By itself, the text does not "prove" that Jesus instituted the sacrament of Penance as we know it today or that he conferred the power to forgive sins only on the Apostles, their successors, and their chosen delegates. We have no basis even for concluding that these are the "very words" of Jesus, given the different approach to history in the Fourth Gospel, over against the Synoptics.

On the other hand, the text *is* entirely consistent with Jesus' abiding concern about sin and his readiness to forgive and to heal (Matthew 9:2-8; Mark 2:5-12; Luke 5:20-26). In all three reports of Jesus' cure of the paralytic at Capernaum there is mention of the forgiveness of sins. The forgiveness of sins is also prominent in the preaching of the Apostles (Acts of the Apostles 2:38; 5:31; 10:43; 13:38; 26:18). Accordingly, even though John does not tell us how or by whom this power was exercised in the community for whom he wrote, the very fact that he mentions it shows that it was exercised.

Second and Third Centuries

The material for this period is scant. What evidence there is suggests that Penance was available for the baptized. *The Shepherd of Hermas* (ca. 150), an important para-scriptural document, takes for granted the practice of post-baptismal forgiveness, although it balks at the possibility of a third opportunity for forgiveness. The first to deny the Church's and the bishop's right to forgive those guilty of serious sins were the *Montanists* and the *Novatians*, both arguing that certain sins (e.g., apostasy, murder, adultery) were outside the Church's powers.

Fourth, Fifth, and Sixth Centuries

The purists were condemned by the *Council of Nicea* (325). It explictly directs that the dying are to be reconciled and given *Viaticum* (literally, "on the way with you"; it is the term used for Holy Communion for those at the point of death—i.e., "on the way" to heaven).

During this period Penance was public in character and came to be known as "Canonical Penance" because local councils devoted a number of canons, or juridical decisions, to regulating its practice. Canonical Penance was administered only once in a lifetime, since Baptism was normally received late in life and was seen as calling for a deep conversion, neither easily nor frequently set aside. The Church demanded proof of reconversion before restoring the grace of Baptism through Penance.

Canonical Penance was always reserved for serious sins, e.g., apostasy, murder, heresy, adultery. These were matters of common, public knowledge. The offender would receive a form of liturgical excommunication and was forced to leave the celebration of the Eucharist at the Offertory, along with the catechumens. For less serious offenses there were other forms of penance: almsgiving, fasts, charity to the poor and the sick, and prayers.

Public penance required the sinner's demonstrating a change of heart, presenting himself or herself before the bishop and the local community, and joining the local group of penitents. Then, after a suitable period of probation, he or she would be readmitted to the Christian community by a rite known as the "reconciliation of the penitent." As the needs of the people and the circumstances of the Church changed, private penance became more the rule and so, too, the actual "confession" of sins. By the end of the sixth century Canonical Penance came to be known simply as *Confession*.

Seventh to Eleventh Centuries

This period is marked by a pronounced Celtic influence as the missionary efforts of the Church reached into the British Isles, far removed from the influence of Rome and from all of Europe. (The Irish monks themselves were to bring this Celtic influence to bear upon the Continent in the seventh century.) Since the liturgical life of the Celtic church was monastically oriented, private penance became normative for priests and religious, and under their direction it spread among the laity as well. It was imposed even for trivial offenses and became increasingly divorced from the larger community of faith. In fact, a person could be restored to the Eucharist even before completing the penance. If the penance were deemed too onerous, the penitent could ask for a *commutation* to a lighter penalty. It was also possible to substitute the payment of a sum of money instead of performing the actual penance. This practice was known as *redemption*. Furthermore, Penance was administered by priests as well as the bishop. In order to help the priests in the selection of appropriate penances, a codification of penitential practices was developed, the so-called penitential books (*libri poenitentiales*). These were lists of every kind of sin, with the exact type of penance attached. The minister of the sacrament was no longer the healer and the reconciler. He was now the *judge*. A formula of absolution was also developed at this time.

Eleventh to Fourteenth Centuries

Four principal changes occur in this period. Penance becomes satisfaction, confession, contrition, and absolution. In the ancient Church the emphasis was on the *reconciliation* of the sinner with the Church and ultimately with God. Now the emphasis shifts to the doing of a penance, or the making of *satisfaction*, for sin. When this became too strenuous, the practices of commutation and redemption were introduced. Secondly, *confession* of sins originally served the purpose of insuring that adequate satisfaction was being imposed, but gradually confession came to be considered as having its own efficacy, its own power to reconcile the sinner. Thus, we find at this time the development of arguments urging the necessity of confessing to a priest. Thirdly, in the writings of Abelard (d. 1142) and Peter Lombard there was a shift to *contrition*, i.e., the conversion of heart. The sinner, if truly contrite, was already forgiven even before confession. So pronounced was this new stress on contrition that the purist Albigensians and Waldensians denied any efficacy whatsoever to confession to a priest, a view condemned by the Fourth Lateran Council in 1215. All orthodox theologians and canonists came to the defense of the role of the priest, and this led to a fourth shift: to *absolution* by a priest. Since absolution was *not* part of the practice and teaching of Penance in the early Church, there was some dispute among the medieval authors about its place in the sacrament. By the time of Thomas Aquinas, however, absolution came to be regarded as essential, along with confession and contrition.

From the Middle Ages to Vatican II

Thomas' theology was endorsed in the Council of Florence's *Decree for the Armenians* (1439): (1) Penance is a sacrament; (2) it consists of contrition of the heart (including the resolution not to sin in the future), oral confession to the priest, satisfaction (e.g., prayer, fasting, almsgiving), and absolution by the priest; (3) the effect of the sacrament is the forgiveness of sins.

The Reformers, and Luther in particular, rejected this teaching. Although Luther accepted the sacramentality of Penance, he believed there was an abiding danger of regarding the works of the penitent as more important than faith in God's mercy. He also rejected the reservation of the power of forgiveness to priests. The first official reaction to Luther's views came in a bull of Pope Leo X (d. 1521), *Exsurge Domine* (1520). Calvin also accepted private confession and absolution as a means of arousing faith and confidence in God's mercy, but he denied its sacramentality.

The definitive response to the Reformers came from the Council of Trent (*Doctrine on the Sacrament of Penance*, Session XIV, 1551). It taught that Penance is a sacrament instituted by Christ; that it is distinct from Baptism; that the three acts of the penitent are contrition, confession of all serious sins in number and kind, and satisfaction; that absolution is reserved to priests alone; and that the priest must have jurisdiction, since absolution is a juridical act.

The Tridentine doctrine remained normative in Catholic theology and practice down to the Second Vatican Council. What is to be said of that teaching in light of our present understanding of the historically conditioned character of all doctrinal pronouncements (as acknowledged, for example, by the 1973 declaration *Mysterium Ecclesiae*, from the Sacred Congregation for the Doctrine of the Faith)?

1. The council taught that the *confession of grave, or serious, sins* is necessary by divine law (*iure divino*). In no way, however, does divine law canonize any concrete form which this confession may have taken in history—e.g., the private confession of sins to a priest. None of those varieties of forms which have been employed in the history of the Church can be said to contradict the intention of Christ. Hence, there are always, in principle, liturgical alternatives to private confession as we have known it from the Middle Ages to the present.

2. The *detailed* confession of all serious sins was also affirmed by Trent as being *iure divino*. However, this is not to be understood in the strict sense. It was the council's purpose only to defend against the Reformers' teaching that integral confession was manifestly contrary to the venerable tradition of the Church. The council did not intend to make the integral confession of sins the only way in which the sacrament may be received. It is the *normal* form. Other forms are possible according to needs and circumstances.

3. The council also affirmed that the confessor is a judge and that the sacrament is a tribunal. But this, too, must be seen in light of the council's concerns about the Reformers' new teaching, namely, their utter rejection of the power of the keys and their insistence that the proclamation of the word alone is efficacious in the remission of sins. The council also wished to maintain that absolution is to be given not in an arbitrary fashion but as a result of a working knowledge of the case.

4. The council's model of judge and tribunal must be understood, finally, in light of the figure employed by the council, namely, that the sacrament resembles more the judgment made by

a physician on a sick person who comes to him for help than by a civil judge who denounces and punishes a guilty person. So somebody whose sorrow is in its initial stages, or is imperfect, can be reconciled through the healing grace of the sacrament.

Vatican II

The Second Vatican Council called for a revision of the rite and formulae for the sacrament of Penance "so that they more clearly express both the nature and effect of the sacrament" (*Constitution on the Sacred Liturgy,* n. 72). The sacrament's purpose, the council's *Dogmatic Constitution on the Church* declares, is to "obtain pardon from the mercy of God" and to be "reconciled with the Church whom (sinners) have wounded by their sin, and who, by her charity, her example and her prayer, collaborates in their conversion" (n. 11).

The New Rite of Reconciliation

Although not on a par with the new *Rite of Christian Initiation of Adults* (to which we referred in the previous chapter), the new *Rite of Penance* does bring out the ecclesial dimension of the sacrament more fully than does the traditional (i.e., post-Tridentine) practice of private confession. In the new rite, the effect of the sacrament is identified as reconciliation with God and with the Church. The minister functions more as a healer than as a judge. Emphasis is placed on conversion inspired by the Church's proclamation of God's word. And communal celebration of the sacrament is provided for and encouraged.

"The celebration of this sacrament is thus always an act in which the Church proclaims its faith, gives thanks to God for the freedom with which Christ has made us free, and offers its life as a spiritual sacrifice in praise of God's glory, as it hastens to meet the Lord Jesus" (Introduction to the new *Rite,* n. 7).

The Church and Penance

In its celebration of the sacrament of Penance, the Church reveals itself as the sacrament of God's mercy in the world, but also as a sinful community, still "on the way" to the perfection of the

Kingdom. Those who sin and who must avail themselves of the sacrament are just as much "the Church" as are those who, in the name of the Church, act to reconcile the sinner with God and the Church. The Church knows what it is both to forgive and to be forgiven, mindful always of the Lord's own prayer, "Forgive us our sins for we too forgive all who do us wrong" (Luke 11:4).

A Church which cannot admit its sin is not the Church of Christ. A Church which cannot forgive the sins of others against itself is not the Church of Christ. *How* the liturgical process of conversion, repentance, and forgiveness is to be structured is always of less importance than *the fact that* it goes on continually within the Church.

ANOINTING OF THE SICK
History

New Testament

Apart from James 5:14 there is no mention of *Anointing* as a sacred rite in the New Testament. The pertinent text is as follows: "Is there anyone sick among you? He should ask for the presbyters of the church. They in turn are to pray over him, anointing him with oil in the Name [of the Lord]." It continues: "This prayer uttered in faith will reclaim the one who is ill, and the Lord will restore him to health. If he has committed any sins, forgiveness will be his. Hence, declare your sins to one another, and pray for one another, that you may find healing" (5:15-16).

The "elders" or "presbyters" are those appointed and ordained by Apostles or disciples of Apostles (Acts of the Apostles 14:23; Titus 1:5). The presbyters are described by James as having extraordinary spiritual gifts which enable them to heal the sick. Sickness, it must be noted, was attributed to sin, as in the Old Testament and contemporary Judaism, and so it posed a problem for the early Church. At the sickbed it is the task of the presbyter to pray for the sick person and to anoint him or her with oil in the name of the Lord. The oil is regarded as a vital substance, a restorative. There is nothing magical implied, however. It is not the oil but the prayers to the Lord which provide the hope of recovery and the forgiveness of sins. (The recommendation that

Christians declare their sins "to one another" is not without relevance to our previous discussion of the sacrament of Penance.)

Although this text by itself does not "prove" the sacramentality of the Anointing of the Sick, it does indicate that there was such a practice in the early Church, that it required the presence of some leader of the community, that it involved prayers, anointing, and the forgiveness of sins, and that its purpose was the restoration of the sick member not only to physical health but also to spiritual health within the community of faith.

Second Century to the Middle Ages

There is, for all practical purposes, no evidence in the early centuries for the actual rite of Anointing. Since it was not a public liturgical act like the rite of initiation, it was passed over in the liturgical books. The first documentary item is provided by a letter of *Pope Innocent I* (d. 417) to Decentius, bishop of Gubbio, in which certain practical points are clarified regarding the administration of the rite of Anointing. It links the Anointing with the text of James and notes that the oil is blessed by the bishop and applied to the sick person by the bishop or a priest. This letter became a basic source for the late Roman and early medieval period inasmuch as it was incorporated into the most important canonical collections and thus became the starting point for theological discussion of the sacrament.

In the first part of the eighth century Bede the Venerable (d. 735), author of the earliest extant commentary on the Epistle of James, states that it has been the custom of the Church from apostolic times for presbyters to anoint the sick with consecrated oil and to pray for their healing. Nowhere in the early tradition does one find mention of the Anointing as a sacrament of *preparation for death*. Where mention *is* made of a "sacrament of the dying," the reference is always to the Eucharist, administered as Viaticum.

The Early Medieval Period

With the Carolingian Reform at the beginning of the ninth century—i.e., the effort guided by the emperor Charlemagne to

impose Roman liturgy and Roman disciplinary practices throughout his new Holy Roman Empire—Anointing becomes established
among the "last rites." By the middle of the twelfth century the
association between Anointing and dying was so taken for granted
that it came to be called *sacramentum exeuntium* ("the sacrament
of the departing") or in the words of Peter Lombard, *extrema
unctio* ("last anointing"). By the close of the twelfth century
Extreme Unction was in fact appropriating to itself the function
and effects previously associated with Viaticum. Thus, Anointing
became more and more a sacrament of the dying, although its
original purpose was to be a remedy against sickness, with the real
hope of recovery. Even in the early medieval period the Church
did not require that a sickness be terminal before the sacrament
could be administered.

Thirteenth and Fourteenth Centuries

In this period the doctrine of the seven sacraments came to its full
development, and Anointing of the Sick was counted among them.
It was understood as the sacrament of spiritual help for the time of
grave illness unto death. Restoration to bodily health was
regarded as a subordinate and conditional effect only. Theologians began to exaggerate the sacrament's spiritual powers: The
Franciscan school argued that all venial (i.e., non-serious) sins
were forgiven as well as serious sins, and the Dominican school
argued that the sacrament removed even the consequences of sin
and anything which lessened a soul's capacity for the life of glory
in heaven. To die immediately after Extreme Unction, in other
words, guaranteed an unimpeded journey to God.

Fifteenth and Sixteenth Centuries

This theological understanding of the sacrament as a sacrament
for the dying was endorsed by the Council of Florence's *Decree for
the Armenians* (1439), which declared that the sacrament could
"not be given except to a sick person whose life is feared for." The
Council of Trent's *Doctrine on the Sacrament of Extreme Unction*
(1551) was formulated as a complement to the council's teaching
on the sacrament of Penance. It defined the Anointing of the Sick

as a true sacrament. The first draft of its doctrinal formulation, however, had directed that the sacrament be given "only to those who are in their final struggle and who have come to grips with death and who are about to go forth to the Lord." The final draft introduced important modifications, declaring that "this anointing is to be used for the sick, particularly for those who are so dangerously ill as to seem at the point of departing this life." It speaks of the sacrament's effects as purification from sin as well as from the effects of sin, comfort and strength of soul, the arousal of confidence in God's mercy, readiness to bear the difficulties and trials of illness, and even health of body, where expedient for the welfare of the soul. Trent's teaching is remarkable not only for what it contains about the spiritual, psychological, and bodily effects of the sacrament but also for what it omits about the sacrament as a last rite. The council thereby struck at the root of a growing abuse which delayed the sacrament until the very last moment of life.

Twentieth Century

The Tridentine doctrine shaped the theological, canonical, and pastoral understanding and practice of this sacrament for centuries thereafter. In the twentieth century some tentative advances were suggested. Theologians and liturgists alike suggested that insofar as this is a sacrament of the dying it is essentially an "anointing for glory." Others, however, pointed out that the prayers of the ritual made no mention of death, and that the sacrament was really a sacrament of the sick. The "last sacrament" is not the Anointing, but Viaticum. Indeed, it was only in the middle of the twelfth century, these theologians argued, that the stress on preparation for death had emerged.

Vatican II

The Second Vatican Council endorsed this second line of thought, recommending that the sacrament be called the Anointing of the Sick rather than Extreme Unction and noting explicitly that it "is not a sacrament reserved for those who are at the point of death"

(*Constitution on the Sacred Liturgy*, n. 73). Indeed, the *last* sacrament to be administered to the dying is Viaticum (n. 68). The *Dogmatic Constitution on the Church* places the sacrament in its larger ecclesial context: "In the holy anointing of the sick with the prayer of the priest, the whole Church recommends the sick to the Lord, who suffered and has been glorified, asking him to give them relief and salvation. She goes further and calls upon them to associate themselves freely with the passion and death of Christ, and in this way to make their contribution to the good of God's people" (n. 11).

The New Rite of Anointing and Pastoral Care of the Sick

The new rite acknowledges that sickness prevents us from fulfilling our role in human society and in the Church. On the other hand, the sick person participates in the redemptive sufferings of Christ and provides the Church with a reminder of higher things and of the limitations of human life. The Church's concern for the sick is in fidelity to Christ's command to visit the sick and is consistent with a wholistic understanding of salvation as reaching the total person (see chapter 5 of this book).

This sacrament is a sacrament of faith: the faith of the Church which looks back to the death and resurrection of Christ and looks ahead to the future kingdom which is pledged in the sacraments. The sacrament provides the grace of the Holy Spirit, heightens trust in God, strengthens us against temptation and anxiety, and may even restore physical health. The sacrament may also provide forgiveness of sins, as a complement to the sacrament of Penance. Anointing is not just for the dying but for anyone who is seriously ill. That judgment is always a prudential one, of course. The last sacrament is Viaticum, received during Mass where possible.

The Church and the Anointing of the Sick

The Church discloses itself in this sacrament as the community of those who are on pilgrimage to the Kingdom of God, with eschatological faith and hope. The Church is a sacrament of Christ the healer, the one who saves us in our human wholeness, body as well as soul. It is at the same time a community always in need of healing, a community subject to physical as well as spiritual reverses.

A Church which is not interested in healing and in the total health of the whole human person and of the human community at large is not the Church of Christ. A Church which abandons those who, by certain of the world's standards, are no longer of practical use is not the Church of Christ. The Church which anoints the sick is the Church of the "Lord Jesus Christ, (who) shared in our human nature to heal the sick and save all mankind" (Prayer After Anointing).

Section Two: Sacraments of Vocation and Commitment

MATRIMONY
History

Old Testament

The Church's understanding of the sacredness of marriage is rooted in the *creation* narrative in Genesis. "The Lord God said: 'It is not good for the man to be alone'.... That is why a man leaves his father and mother and clings to his wife, and the two of them become one body" (2:18,24). The Lord blesses their union and orders them to "be fruitful and multiply" (1:28). Marriage functions primarily in the Old Testament, however, as an institution for the preservation of the husband's clan. That is why children, especially sons, are regarded as a blessing and a gift from God (Genesis 24:60; Psalm 127:3) and why childlessness is a disgrace and a chastisement (Genesis 30:1-6; 1 Samuel 1:6-11). The highest honor paid to marriage in the Old Testament is the application to it of the symbol of the *Covenant* between Yahweh and Israel (Hosea 2; Isaiah 54:4-5; Jeremiah 2:2; 3:20).

New Testament

Jesus deepens the Hebrew concept of marriage, insisting on the oneness that exists between the man and the woman. The woman is not to be cast aside at will. He speaks, therefore, against divorce, so strongly in fact that the one who marries a divorced woman commits adultery (Matthew 5:31-32; 19:3-12). But the early Church adds an "exceptive clause" as a softening of Jesus' demands: " . . . lewd conduct is a separate case" (5:32). On the other hand, Jesus also consistently regards marriage as a state in life proper to this age; in heaven there will be no marrying (Mark 12:25). All of the concerns of marriage must yield to the claims of the Second Coming (Luke 14:20; see also Matthew 24:38-39; Luke 17:27). As always with Jesus, everything is to be seen in light of the Kingdom of God.

This ambivalent view of marriage comes through even more forcefully in the Pauline writings. On the one hand, marriage is a symbol of Christ's union with his Church (Ephesians 5:21-33). The union of man and woman in marriage is not only compared with the union of Christ with the Church; it is actually based on the union of Christ with the Church. When husbands love their wives as their own flesh, they are only doing what Christ does with the Church. On the other hand, Paul in 1 Corinthians wishes that the faithful would renounce marriage in favor of virginity *because he thinks the Lord will soon return* and because he worries about the risk of distraction in the meantime (7:32-35). Paul reduces marriage to something of secondary importance *in view of the Second Coming*. Whereas the creation narrative cautions that it is not good for man to be alone, Paul insists that "a man is better off having no relations with a woman" (7:1). But he does not go so far as to condemn marriage. There are several passages in fact in the New Testament where the messianic period is described as a wedding feast (Matthew 9:15; 25:1-13; Mark 2:19; John 3:29).

Second Century to the Middle Ages

This ambivalence toward marriage continues beyond the apostolic age. Marriage is viewed more and more as the justification of the use of sex which has been infected by sin (a "lawful remedy for concupiscence," the Scholastic textbooks would call it). This trend reached its fullest development in Augustine, who influenced the Church on this subject more profoundly than any other single individual did. Augustine (as we noted in chapter 15 in connection with our discussion of the sexuality of Jesus) linked sexuality with animality. The purpose of marriage is none other than the begetting of children. Indeed, our sexual desires are nothing more than the unfortunate effects of Original Sin. Every child is literally born of his or her parents' "sin" because procreation is possible only with the seductive aid of physical lust. But it is a tolerable "sin" because God wills that we should be fruitful and multiply, and it provides a legitimate way of keeping "perverse desire within its proper bounds."

Why this altered view of marriage developed is not completely clear. It may be because of the influence of Greek philosophy, especially the Stoic insistence on keeping oneself fully under control, and the Gnostic-Manichaean rejection of the goodness of matter. But the Fathers of the Church never went so far as to deny the basic value and sanctity of marriage as upheld, for example, in 1 Timothy 4:1-5 ("Everything God created is good; nothing is to be rejected...").

The Middle Ages to Vatican II

Discussion of marriage continued along a similarly ambivalent course into the medieval period. Abelard acknowledged its sacramentality but insisted that it did not "avail unto salvation .... For to bring home a wife is not meritorious for salvation, but it is allowed for salvation's sake because of incontinence." The goodness of marriage meanwhile was affirmed against the Waldensians and Albigensians, the medieval counterparts of Manichaeism, in the Profession of Faith prescribed by Pope Innocent III in 1208, and marriage itself was accounted a true sacrament in the Council of Florence's *Decree for the Armenians* (1439) and then, most definitely, at the Council of Trent *(Doctrine on the Sacrament of Matrimony,* Session XXIV, 1563).

The Protestant Reformers upheld the sacredness of marriage in the order of creation, but they denied that marriage belonged to the order of grace as a sacrament. They also rejected the Church's authority over marriage, and approved the practice of divorce as a lesser of two evils. Trent affirmed the opposite position in each instance. Among the council's more "historically conditioned" canons is the tenth: "If anyone says that the married state surpasses that of virginity or celibacy, and that it is not better and happier to remain in virginity or celibacy than to be united in matrimony, *anathema sit.*"

The Tridentine perspective remained normative for Catholic theology, canon law, and pastoral practice until the Second Vatican Council. Meanwhile, Trent's teaching was vigorously reaffirmed by Pope Pius XI's *Casti Connubii* in 1930, which set forth as marriage's primary purpose the propagation of life, calling the "mutual faithfulness of husband and wife" the "second blessing" of marriage.

Vatican II

As happened with so many other theological and pastoral questions, the Catholic Church's perspective on marriage was significantly modified by the Second Vatican Council. In contrast with previous official pronouncements and conventional theological and canonical insights, the council adopts a remarkably personalistic standpoint. It no longer uses the traditional term *contract* to describe the marriage bond. Instead, the council speaks of the "marriage covenant" which is sealed by an "irrevocable personal consent" (*Pastoral Constitution on the Church in the Modern World,* n. 48).

Secondly, neither does the council continue to employ the old distinction between primary and secondary ends in which the begetting of children is always more important than the mutual love of husband and wife. "Hence, *while not making the other ends of marriage of less account,* the true practice of conjugal love, and the whole tenor of family life resulting from it, tend to dispose the spouses to cooperate generously with the love of the Creator and Savior who through them day by day expands and enriches His family" (n. 50, italics mine).

Thirdly, the sacrament of marriage is not something added to the marriage union established through mutual human love. "Authentic married love is taken up into divine love and is ruled and enriched by the redemptive power of Christ and the salvific action of the Church ... " (n. 48). This new emphasis in the theology of marriage is consistent with the claims of contemporary sociology that this is the first age in which people marry and remain in marriage because they love each other. And so there is this stress on the mutual exchange of love as constituting the sacrament of marriage, on married love as the source of the institution of marriage, on the need for growth in this love in order to bring the sacrament to its full realization, and on the need for the Church constantly to bring forth the witness value of this sacrament to the whole community of faith. As husband and wife are called to be faithful, generous, and gracious to each other in fulfillment of their marriage covenant, so is the whole Church called to be faithful to its covenant with God in Christ. "When Christian marriage flounders," Father John T. Finnegan, former President of the Canon Law Society of America has written, "the witness of fidelity in all Christian vocations flounders" ("Marriage/Pastoral Care," *Origins* 5/10, August 28, 1975, p. 152).

Fourthly, the council emphasizes the necessity of a faith commitment for the sacrament of marriage (see *Constitution on the Sacred Liturgy,* n. 59). It is no longer sufficient that the two parties be baptized. Marriage is not just a ceremony by which two people are legally bound together. As a sacrament, it is an act of worship, an expression of faith, a sign of the Church's unity, a mode of Christ's presence (as we noted in the previous chapter). Vatican II moves beyond the Code of Canon Law (canon 1012, par. 2, in the present Code; canon 242, par. 2, in the newly proposed revision), which says that there is no valid marriage between the baptized which is not by that very fact a sacrament. The council uses the term *christifideles.* Marriage is not just a union between *baptized* Christians; it is a union between *faithful* Christians.

Fifthly, the full consummation of marriage is more than a biological act. The old theology and the old canon law asserted that a marriage between two baptized Christians, once performed according to the rite of the Church *(ratum)* and once consummated by a single act of physical union *(consummatum)*, can never be dissolved, not even by the pope.

But according to the council, the expression of the mutual love which is at the heart of the sacrament consists of more than biological union. "It involves the good of the whole person. Therefore it can enrich the expressions of body and mind with a unique dignity, ennobling these expressions as special ingredients and signs of friendship distinctive of marriage . . . . Such love pervades the whole of [the spouses'] lives" (n. 49; see also Pope Paul VI's *Humanae Vitae,* 1968, nn. 8-9). Consummation without love is without meaning. It would be difficult to see, in light of the council's teaching, how such purely biological consummation could have a sacramental character. Rather, the council speaks of the "intimate partnership of married life" *(consortium vitae conjugalis,* n. 48).

Finally, the broader ecclesial dimension of the sacrament is maintained. "Christian spouses, in virtue of the sacrament of matrimony, signify and share in the mystery of that union and fruitful love which exists between Christ and the Church (see Ephesians 5:32)" *(Dogmatic Constitution on the Church,* n. 11).

The New Rite of Marriage

The council's theology of matrimony is carried over into the new *Rite of Marriage.* The "Introduction" to the rite speaks of the union of Christ and the Church (n. 1), of the covenantal nature of the marriage bond (n. 2), of the essential element of mutual affection in body and mind (n. 3), of the importance of the procreation and education of children without prejudice to the other purposes of marriage (n. 4), of the virtue of faith required ("for the sacrament of matrimony presupposes and demands faith," n. 7), and of the significance of the eucharistic setting for marriage (n. 6).

Some Canonical Considerations

Indissolubility

The Catholic Church teaches (canon 1013) that marriage is *monogamous* (one husband, one wife at a time) and *indissoluble* (permanent). On the other hand, the Church's own pastoral practice over the years has tolerated certain limited measures of ecclesiastical reconciliation where the rigorous imposition of the full demands of Christian law would require moral heroism. Origen (d. 254) had proposed a formula that was widely quoted throughout the first thousand years of the Church's history: "The matter of divorce and remarriage was contrary to what has been handed down, but not entirely without reason." It was a kind of "lesser-of-two-evils" principle. The Eastern Orthodox churches developed and continue to maintain the principle of *economy* (similar to the Catholic notion of *dispensation),* by which the unintended harshness of a given law is removed. Thus, the Orthodox churches have permitted remarriage after divorce. "Because the risen Christ has entrusted to the church a stewardship of prudence and freedom to listen to the promptings of the Holy Spirit about today's problems of church unity, a proper understanding of economy involves the exercise of spiritual discernment" (Orthodox-Roman Catholic Consultation, "Unity and Divine Economy," *Origins* 6/9, August 12, 1976, p. 144). The teaching of the Council of Trent (Session XXIV, canon 7, 1563) on indissolubility was formulated against the Reformers, not against the Orthodox. While the official position of the Catholic Church is clear—i.e., that marriage is permanent—it does not absolutely exclude the kind of pastoral flexibility embodied in the principle of economy.

Canonical Form

The Catholic Church requires that all Catholics marry before a priest or deacon, and two witnesses. This is known as the requirement of "canonical form." Before 1966 there were serious penalties incurred by Catholics who married "outside the Church" and before a Protestant minister. Between 1966 and 1970 Pope Paul VI retroactively lifted and abolished all such penalties. Catholics are now permitted to marry in a Protestant church before a Protestant minister with permission from the local bishop. Protestants and Orthodox may also act as official witnesses (bridesmaid or best man) at a Catholic marriage, and Catholics may serve in the same capacity at a marriage which is properly celebrated between separated brethren *(Ecumenical Directory,* May 14, 1967, n. 58).

Mixed Marriage

A "mixed marriage" is one between a Catholic and a non-Catholic. To receive the dispensation to marry a non-Catholic, the Catholic party must make the following affirmation: "I reaffirm my faith in Jesus Christ and, with God's help, intend to continue living that faith in the Catholic Church. I promise to do all in my power to share the faith I have received with our children by having them baptized and reared as Catholics" *(Statement of the United States Catholic Bishops,* January 1, 1971). This promise can be made orally or in writing by the Catholic party. The other party must be informed of the fact and content of this promise.

"Pauline Privilege"

The "Pauline Privilege" is an historical elaboration of 1 Corinthians 7:10-16, where Paul states that, in the case of the marriage of two unbaptized, one of whom later becomes a Christian without the consent of the other, the convert is no longer bound to remain with the non-Christian. "God has called you to live in peace" (v. 15). This principle was used frequently during the missionary expansion of the Church from the sixteenth through the nineteenth centuries and is still employed today.

"Petrine Privilege"

The "Petrine Privilege" is also known as the "Privilege of the Faith." It is not found in the Code of Canon Law but developed as a pastoral practice in the United States after the promulgation of the Code of Canon Law in 1918. The "Petrine Privilege" allows the pope to dissolve a marriage between a Christian and a non-

Christian which, by the very nature of the bond, was not sacramental in the first place (no marriage can be sacramental unless both parties are Christians). There has to be a good reason for such papal action: One of the parties to the first marriage (presumably severed in divorce) wishes to marry a Catholic in a second ceremony, or the non-Christian party wants to become a Catholic and remarry.

Annulment

The Catholic Church does not grant divorces, only annulments. An annulment is an official declaration that a real marriage never existed in the first instance. The traditional grounds for nullity so carefully listed in the 1918 Code of Canon Law have now been broadened to include a whole range of character disorders and deficiencies. Reasons for annulling a marriage now include: lack of discretion (the parties did not really understand what they were committing themselves to), lack of partnership in conjugal life, lack of conjugal love, psychopathic personality, schizophrenia, affective immaturity, psychic incompetence, sociopathic personality, "moral impotence," lack of interpersonal communication.

Pastoral Care of the Divorced and Remarried

The Marriage Tribunal (or court) of a diocese or of the Holy See is referred to as the "external forum." Its proceedings are public. Decisions are rendered in the open. However, it is not always possible to find adequate public reasons justifying an annulment decree. In some such difficult cases, pastoral care commits us to considering carefully and compassionately those who are in stable and responsible second marriages. When a public annulment process is impossible, a Catholic who, after prayerful consultation, has decided to remarry or to remain in the present second marriage may, according to some theological opinion and pastoral practice, be readmitted to the Church's sacramental life, assuming that no grave scandal is involved. (For more on conscience, see chapter 25.)

Ecumenical Reflections

There is agreement between the Catholic Church, on the one hand, and the Orthodox and Anglican churches, on the other, regarding the sacramentality of marriage. The *Orthodox-Roman Catholic* "Agreed Statement on the Sanctity of Marriage" (*Origins* 8/28, December 28, 1978, pp. 446–447) notes that "marriage [is] the fundamental relationship in which a man and woman, by total sharing with each other, seek their own growth in holiness and that of their children, and thus show forth the presence on earth of God's kingdom" (I, par. 2). Although marriage involves a permanent commitment, the statement acknowledges that the Orthodox Church, "out of consideration of the human realities, permits divorce . . . and tolerates remarriages in order to avoid further human tragedies" (II, par. 2).

An *Anglican-Roman Catholic* Commission on the Theology of Marriage and Its Application to Mixed Marriages concluded that there is "no fundamental difference of doctrine between the two Churches, as regards what marriage of its nature is or the ends which it is ordained to serve" (*Final Report*, June 27, 1975, Washington, D.C.: United States Catholic Conference, 1976, p. 20). The report refers favorably to the teaching of Vatican II on the covenantal character of marriage, and to marriage's relationship to the convenantal union of Christ and the Church.

Agreement regarding the sacramental reality of matrimony, however, has not been reached with the churches of the Lutheran and Reformed (Calvinist) traditions. After five years of discussion, Catholic, Lutheran, and Reformed members of an international study commission issued a report in which they insist that they have come "decisively closer" to a common understanding of marriage, but that they could not agree on the sacramentality of marriage or on its indissolubility. (See "An Ecumenical Approach to Marriage," *Origins* 7/31, January 19, 1978, pp. 481, 483–496.)

The Church and Matrimony

When seen as a covenantal rather than contractual bond, Christian marriage is a sacrament of the union between Christ and Church (Ephesians 5:22–32). The sacrament of Matrimony is also a decisive moment when the Church reveals itself as the bride of Christ, as the sign that God is irrevocably committed to the human community in and through Christ. The new community signified and effected by marriage is also a sign of what the Church is, a community of love. The Church comes into being at various levels of Christian fellowship. The family has sometimes been spoken of as "the Church in miniature." Even if that term lacks ecclesiological precision, it does express what the Church discloses in this sacrament, namely, the proclamation that God wills us all to be one in Christ and in his Spirit, and that God is communicated in grace to make that unity possible.

HOLY ORDER
Terminology

This is perhaps the most difficult sacrament of all to treat. It is exceedingly complicated in its origin and in the development of terminology. Tertullian chose the word *ordo* ("order") to apply to the clergy as a whole, probably under the influence of Psalm 109:4 and Hebrews 5–7, which refer to the priesthood "according to the order of Melchisedech." This "order" was composed of various grades of ministers. The bishop, a modern term derived from the Latinization of *episcopos* ("overseer"), was commonly called *sacerdos* ("priest"). The priest was called *presbyter*. The deacon was usually called *minister* ("servant"). In the course of history, the corporate or collegial sense of *ordo* gradually evaporated, only to be rediscovered at Vatican II. Because of these extreme variations in terminology, one must interpret ancient texts with great care, not reading back into them some medieval or modern understanding of the words.

History

Old Testament

As is explained in the Epistle to the Hebrews, Jesus' priesthood must be understood in light of the Old Testament. The patriarchs, as heads of families or tribal groups, performed priestly functions, such as offering sacrifice (Genesis 22:2; 31:54). Eventually, a specific office of priesthood evolved and a priestly professionalism developed, especially in the tribe of Levi (thus, the levitical priesthood). This professionalism involved certain skills and training. It also required sanctity (Leviticus 19:2; 21:8). Deuteronomy 33:8-10 suggests three basic priestly functions: the discernment of God's will through the casting of sacred lots (1 Samuel 14:41-42), teaching (Deuteronomy 33:10), and sacrifice and cultic offering (Deuteronomy 33:10). The priest, therefore, was an intermediary between God and humankind.

New Testament

As noted in chapter 17, the New Testament does not provide an organizational blueprint for the Church. On the contrary, it is practically impossible to say more than that there is some organizational structure in the various New Testament churches, that these are influenced by the political, social, and cultural character of the communities in which these churches existed, and that each organizational or ministerial component was for the sake of the mission of the Church—i.e., for service and not for domination.

Varieties of Ministries and/or Offices: There are *the Twelve* (Matthew 10:2-4; Mark 3:16-19; Luke 6:13-16; Acts of the Aspostles 1:13), called "the Eleven" during the interval between the death of Judas and the election of Matthias (Matthew 28:16; Mark 16:14; Luke 24:9,33; Acts of the Apostles 1:26). The election of Matthias seemed important in order to maintain an apparent symbolic link with the twelve tribes of Israel, which the Twelve will judge (Matthew 19:28; Luke 22:30). All of the Twelve were *apostles* (literally, "those sent forth"), but not all apostles were members of the Twelve—e.g., Paul. (Hereafter, the word apostle is capitalized only when it refers to the Twelve.) And there were other ministries besides those of the Twelve and the other apostles. There were also prophets and teachers, whose authority was very much like that of the Apostles (1 Corinthians 12:28; Acts of the Apostles 13:1; 15:32, Ephesians 2:20; 3:5; 4:11). There were, in addition, wonder-workers, healers, helpers, administrators, speakers in tongues, evangelists, shepherds, elders, deacons, and overseers. The elders (*presbyteroi*), deacons (*diakonoi*), and overseers (*episcopoi*) are of particular interest here because their offices came eventually to be regarded by the Catholic Church as constituting the threefold division of the one sacrament of Holy Order: diaconate, presbyterate, and episcopate—deacon, priest, and bishop. No Christian, however, is ever specifically identified as a priest, probably because early Christians regarded the Jewish priesthood as valid and never thought of a priesthood of their own. They expected, after all, that the Jews would all eventually join the new movement.

Deacons seem to have had their origin in the designation of "the Seven" (Acts of the Apostles 6:1–6) to "wait on tables"—e.g., to distribute food among the widows and to assist the Twelve in other material ways. The *elders* were adult males of a town, city, or tribe, who constituted the community's governing body. In Acts of the Apostles the elders are associated with the Apostles in decisions, especially the council of Jerusalem (15:22). The relationship between elders and *overseers* is more difficult to determine. Sometimes the offices seem interchangeable (Titus 1:5–9); at other times the elders are in charge (1 Timothy 5:17). Some have suggested that the two offices were, in fact, the same; others regard the overseers as the executive board of the elders, a view which is more probable because it is more in harmony with the practices of other social units in which elders appear. In any case, there is no sign that a one single bishop is in charge of a local church.

The elders also became a more select group. They were "established" in each town by election (Titus 1:5), and there was a ritual conferral of office, probably by the imposition of hands (Acts of the Apostles 14:23; 1 Timothy 5:22). Bishops are established by the Holy Spirit (Acts of the Apostles 20:28), whose will is manifested by the assembly of the entire Church. The bishops/elders have care of the Church (1 Timothy 3:4), manage the Church (5:17), are God's stewards (1 Corinthians 4:1), instruct in sound doctrine (Titus 1:7–9), and feed the flock (Acts of the Apostles 20:28; 1 Peter 5:2).

Thus, the bishop/elder, or presbyter/bishop, took up where the Pauline apostles left off. They were responsible for the continued care of churches founded by these apostles. Whereas the apostles, including the Twelve, were ministers "on the move," the presbyter-bishops were ministers in residence. The apostles were charismatic and non-insitutionalized ministers; the presbyter-bishops had to be people who could manage a household well (1 Timothy 3:4–5) and who could organize, stabilize, and combat dangerous innovation (Titus 1:9). They were not to be recent converts, nor married more than once (1 Timothy 3:2,6). They were also to manifest pastoral skills (Acts of the Apostles 20:28–29; 1 Peter 5:2–4).

It is only when we go outside (although not chronologically beyond) the New Testament literature that we find evidence for the so-called *monarchical episcopate*, i.e., a local church presided over by one bishop. The primary source is Ignatius of Antioch (d. 108), and specifically his letters to the *Smyrnaeans* 8:1; 9:1), the *Ephesians* (5:1,3), the *Trallians* (2:1), and the *Magnesians* (4:1; 7:1). Such respect as Ignatius recommended for bishops served as a weapon against disunity and heresy. But we must keep certain qualifications in mind: (1) The local churches over which the bishop presided were not dioceses in the modern sense of the term. They were nothing more than one-parish towns. (2) We have no evidence that the monarchical episcopal structure was universal in the Church at this time. Indeed in Paul's day, some churches had presbyter-bishops (e.g., Philippi) and some did not (e.g., Corinth). (3) On the contrary, in the mid-second century, when *The Shepherd of Hermas* was written, the Roman church still seems to have been ruled by a presbyterate, and Ignatius makes no mention of a bishop in his letter to the *Romans*. (4) Presbyters also served as overseers (bishops) of churches (1 Peter 5:1-3). (5) Neither the presbyter-bishops nor the monarchical bishops can be considered "successors of the Apostles" in the sense that all were duly appointed and ordained by an Apostle, i.e., one of the Twelve.

The Emergence of Christian Priesthood: So long as Christians understood themselves as the renewed, not the new, Israel, they had no idea of replacing the Jewish priesthood with one of their own. The Acts of the Apostles reports that while they broke bread in their homes, the Jerusalem Christians also kept up their daily attendance at the Temple (2:46). Even Paul, who insisted that Gentile Christians were not bound by the Law, still went to the Temple for offerings as late as the year 58 (Acts of the Apostles 21:26).

Not until the early Christians concluded that they were indeed part of a radically new movement distinct from Judaism was there a basis for the development of a separate Christian priesthood. Other events accentuated this process: the increasing numbers of Gentile converts, the shift of leadership away from the Jerusalem church and to the churches of Rome, Antioch, Ephesus, and Alexandria, the destruction of the Temple, and, finally, Judaism's own sectarian tendencies in the post-destruction period. Concomitantly, there was a growing recognition of the sacrificial character of the Eucharist, which called for a priesthood of sacrifice distinct from the Jewish priesthood. This awareness appeared in Christian writings about the end of the first century or the beginning of the second, especially in the *Didache*, in the writings of Clement of Rome (d. 100), and in the *Apostolic Tradition* of Hippolytus of Rome (d. ca. 236).

This historical record requires some modification of the traditional Catholic notion that Jesus directly and explicitly instituted the Catholic priesthood at the Last Supper. As noted in the previous chapter, Jesus' institution of the sacraments is implied and/or included in his proclamation of the Kingdom of God, in his gathering of disciples, and in the special significance he accorded the Last Supper which he ate with his disciples. (The Eucharist, to be sure, was *explicitly* instituted by Jesus at the Last Supper.) The priesthood as we have come to know it represents a fusion of different roles and ministries which are to be found in the New Testament churches. It is not even clear, for example, that anyone in particular was commissioned to preside over the Eucharist in the beginning. Paul never mentions that he presided. In fact, he seems to have been little involved in the administration of sacraments (1 Corinthians 1:14–15). There is no explicit mention that any of the Apostles presided over the Eucharist. Indeed, there is no compelling evidence that they presided when they were present, or that a chain of ordination from Apostle to bishop to priest was required for presiding. Someone must have presided, of course, and those who did so presided with the approval of the community.

We simply do not know how a certain individual came to preside and whether it came to be a permanent or regular function for that person. As we have already seen, there was a remarkable diversity of structure and form in the New Testament churches. The most that can be said is that those who presided did so with the consent of the local church and that this consent was tantamount, but not always equivalent, to ordination.

As the Church grew larger and became more complex in its organizational structure, the element of selection and consent came to be regularized. Presiding eventually became the exclusive privilege of bishops and presbyters. The *Didache* may have been written just at the turning point when the system was placed into effect. There is mention there, for example, of wandering prophets who are not forbidden to hold Eucharist (10:7), and there is an instruction for bishops and deacons to render to the community the ministry (liturgy) of the prophets. By the year 96 Clement's *Epistle to the Corinthians* speaks of the sin of ejecting from office "men who have offered the sacrificial gifts of the episcopate worthily" (44:4). Fifteen years later, Ignatius of Antioch makes it clear that the practice of episcopal and presbyteral presiding is well established (*Smyrnaeans* 8:1). Thus, by the turn of the century or soon thereafter, two roles that were probably once separated are joined together: the role of the presbyter-bishop and the role of the presiding minister of the Eucharist. Significantly, not until the year 1208 is there an official declaration that priestly ordination is necessary to celebrate the Eucharist (Innocent III, *Profession of Faith Prescribed to the Waldensians*), and then, more solemnly, by the Council of Florence (1439) and the Council of Trent (1563).

Third Through Fifth Centuries

The *Apostolic Tradition* of Hippolytus sketches a picture of the third-century Church. The bishop is the *sacerdos*, elected by the people, but he receives the imposition of hands from another bishop. The presbyter, or priest, is ordained by the bishop, with other priests joining in. The deacon is ordained by the bishop alone because the deacon is ordained to the service of the bishop. Significantly, the rite of consecration of a bishop is clearly inspired by the New Testament, while the ordination of the priest is inspired by the Old Testament. This anomaly tends to confirm what was suggested above about the probable origins of the Christian priesthood. At first the Church had no intention of having a priesthood of its own, distinct from the Jewish priesthood. But when the concept of Christian priesthood took hold, the Church understandably drew upon the Old Testament for models, standards, and inspiration.

Early in the fourth century the Church was "blessed" (or "cursed") with the Edict of Constantine, which showered upon the clergy many civil privileges and dispensations. The influence of the Old Testament's notion of priesthood had much to do with this new bestowal of temporal favor.

As the local churches grew, parishes were created outside the major Christian centers, and the presbyters were given pastoral care over them. The Council of Chalcedon (451) would later decree that a priest be ordained for a particular church. The first signs of emphasis on the fundamental equality of bishops and presbyters developed in the fourth century, not only within unorthodox circles, e.g., Arianism, but even within orthodox groups, e.g., John Chrysostom (d. 407) and the *Canons of Hippolytus*. The authors who exercised a decisive influence in this matter on the Middle Ages were Jerome (d. 420) and Ambrosiaster, the unknown author of a series of commentaries on the Pauline epistles. Both stressed the equivalence of the bishop's and the presbyter's power to celebrate the Eucharist and forgive sins.

Sixth Through Twelfth Centuries

With the Germanization of Christianity in the early Middle Ages, the understanding and exercise of priesthood took another turn. Priestly and royal power were fused. Priests themselves were caught up into the feudal system and were ordained not only for the celebration of the Eucharist and the administration of sacraments, but also for certain tax-collecting chores. Their loyalty was to the feudal lords who selected them, not to the bishop. In the Frankish churches new rites of ordination were added. The bishop was anointed with holy chrism, the crozier (staff) and ring were given, and then he was enthroned. The priest was ordained with an anointing of the hands, the giving of bread and wine, and a second laying on of hands in view of the absolution of sins. These developments reflected Germanic customs which attached great importance to the transmission of the emblems of power, a "princely" power for bishops and a cultic power for priests. Toward the end of the tenth century this liturgy was merged with the Roman tradition in the *Romano-Germanic Pontifical* of Mainz. Priesthood became even more of a caste-like existence within the Church with the imposition of *celibacy* in the twelfth century as a universal requirement for priests of the Latin rite.

The Reformation

The increasing alienation of the clergy from the rest of the Church provoked a reaction. The Reformers insisted that there exists in the Church no ministerial power received through the sacrament of Holy Order. There is only a priesthood of all believers. All specialized ministry is delegated by the community. Furthermore, since the Eucharist is not a sacrifice (Calvary cannot, and need not, be repeated), there is no need for a cultic priesthood in the Church. The Council of Trent rejected these views, declaring that priesthood is conferred through one of the seven sacraments, that the Mass is a true sacrifice, and that there is a true hierarchy in the Church consisting of bishops, priests, and deacons and that these ministers do not depend on the call of the community for their authority and powers (*Doctrine on the Sacrament of Order*, Session XXIII, 1563).

The Counter-Reformation to Vatican II

Under the impact of *Trent*, the Catholic Church launched a reform of the clergy. Seminaries for the education and training of future priests were established, and greater emphasis was placed on priestly spirituality. The reform of priestly formation and spirituality was supported by such figures as Charles Borromeo (d. 1584) and Francis de Sales (d. 1622), and by the new religious orders. But the spirituality was still individualistic, and the notion of priesthood on which it was based was still cultic and sacramental. Under the impact of the anticlericalist wave of the *French Revolution* in the eighteenth century, the Church launched yet another spiritual renewal, this time sparked by principles enunciated earlier by Vincent de Paul (d. 1660), Jean-Jacques Olier (d. 1657), Pierre de Bérulle (d. 1629), and others. Under the impact of post-Enlightenment *modernity* (see chapter 3), the Catholic priesthood began losing much of its "mystique" as a spiritually elite form of Christian existence. Young Catholic men concluded that there were other ways of living the Gospel and working for the Kingdom of God. A drastic decline in vocations followed, and large numbers of priests resigned from the active ministry. Many of those priests who did resign complained about the misuse of authority by bishops and other Church leaders, and others protested against the continued imposition of obligatory celibacy.

Vatican II

With its stress on the Church as the whole People of God, the Second Vatican Council acknowledged that all the baptized participate in some way in the one priesthood of Christ (*Dogmatic Constitution on the Church*, n. 11). Although the priesthood of ordination and the priesthood of Baptism differ "in essence and not only in degree," they are nonetheless related to this one priesthood of Christ. The ministerial priesthood of ordination consists of three degrees or orders: episcopate, presbyterate, and diaconate (nn. 20-29). Each order is truly sacramental.

Taken as a body (*ordo*), bishops are the successors to the college of the Apostles in teaching authority and pastoral rule (n. 22). United with their head, the bishop of Rome, the bishops constitute a college and are the subjects of "supreme and full power over the universal Church." The union of bishops among themselves and with the bishop of Rome symbolizes the communion of churches which constitutes the whole Body of Christ (n. 23).

The presbyterate is a specific participation in the priesthood of the episcopate (n. 28). Priests are united with their bishop in priestly dignity. They are collaborators with the bishop and constitute a college with him.

The diaconate is also a sacramental degree of Holy Order (n. 29). The council recommends the restoration of the permanent diaconate (as distinguished from reception of the diaconate as the next-to-last step on the way to priesthood).

Since the priesthood of Christ includes prophetic and shepherding as well as "priestly" or cultic functions, the ordained priesthood of the Church embraces more than sacramental and liturgical responsibilities (*Decree on the Ministry and Life of Priests*, nn. 2–6).

The New Rites of Ordination

The rite of episcopal ordination is now modified to include the consecratory prayer from the *Apostolic Tradition* of Hippolytus of Rome, in order to bring out the apostolic succession of bishops and their various duties and functions beyond the purely cultic. The collegial character of the episcopate is also emphasized. In presbyteral ordination the collaborative relationship between the priest and the bishop is more clearly drawn. Significantly, the Old Testament flavor is preserved in the consecratory prayer. Only minor changes have been made in the rite of ordination to the diaconate to take into account recent prescriptions concerning the diaconate as a proper and permanent grade of the hierarchy in the Latin Church and also for the sake of clarifying and simplifying the ceremony.

Ecumenical Developments

Several of the ecumenical consultations have addressed themselves to the question of ordained ministry: Lutheran-Catholic,

Anglican-Roman Catholic, United Methodist-Roman Catholic, Orthodox-Roman Catholic, and Presbyterian-Reformed-Roman Catholic. The *Lutheran-Catholic* consultation issued an important statement, "Eucharist and Ministry," in 1970 (*Lutherans and Catholics in Dialogue*, vol. 4, Washington, D.C.: United States Catholic Conference, 1970, pp. 7-33). It distinguishes between the general ministry (lower case) of the whole People of God and the ordained Ministry (upper case), which is a particular form of service within and for the sake of the Church in its mission to the world. It is a ministry of proclaiming the Gospel, celebrating the sacraments, caring for the faithful, witnessing, and serving. It stands *with* the People of God under Christ, but also speaks in Christ's name *to* his People. The Catholic participants in this dialogue noted a "gratifying degree of agreement" with the Lutherans "as to the essentials of the sacred Ministry." Specifically, they found that the Lutherans hold that the Ministry is of divine institution, that it includes both preaching of the word and administration of the sacraments, and that there is a distinction between it and the general ministry of all believers. The Catholic parties to the Lutheran-Catholic Consultation concluded that they "see no persuasive reason to deny the possibility of the Roman Catholic church recognizing the validity of this (Lutheran) Ministry," and they urged the Catholic authorities to do so.

Similar agreement was recorded by the *Anglican-Roman Catholic* consultation. In its twelve-year report of December, 1977, the dialogue noted only a continuing difference or emphasis on the ministry of *episcope* (literally "oversight"). For Roman Catholics, this ministry is centered in the bishop of Rome; for Anglicans it is less centralized. But certain pastoral developments in the Catholic Church have brought the two churches closer together even on this matter. Collegiality and coresponsibility are now the order of the day: international synods of bishops, national episcopal conferences, national advisory boards, diocesan pastoral councils, parish council, priests' senates. And the ministry of the bishop of Rome is increasingly perceived and exercised as one of service. (*Origins* 7/30, January 12, 1978, pp. 465, 467-473.)

The *Methodist-Roman Catholic* statement, *Holiness and Spirituality of the Ordained Ministry* (Washington, D.C.: United

States Catholic Conference, 1976) is theologically less substantive than the preceding agreements, but it does report consensus on the traditional and contemporary responsibilities of the ordained ministry: preaching the Gospel, presiding at eucharistic worship, exercising pastoral care, e.g., and now the promotion of peace and reconciliation, participation in the struggle for social justice, e.g.

The *Orthodox-Roman Catholic* joint statement of July 1976 on the pastoral office of "Bishops and Presbyters" lists several points of agreement: Ordained ministry is a commissioning by the Holy Spirit to build up the Church; the offices of bishop and presbyter are different realizations of the sacrament of Order; bishops exercise authority over a whole community, and presbyters share in that authority under the bishop; ordination is required for both offices because they are "an essential element of the sacramental reality of the church"; the pastoral officer is distinct but not separated from the rest of the community; on the other hand, he is not dependent on the community for the exercise of his service, since he receives the special bestowal of the Spirit in ordination (*Origins*, 6/9, August 12, 1976, pp. 142-143).

The *Presbyterian-Reformed-Roman Catholic* consultation offers a more congregational approach to the ordained ministry. It stresses, first, the call of all Christians to ministry, for the building up of the Church. Within this general ministry there are ministers who are "called and ordained to represent Christ to the community and the community before Christ. Through the proclamation of the Gospel and the celebration of the sacraments this ministry has endeavored to unite and order the Church for the ministry of the whole people of God." Its function is to see to it that "the Word of God is proclaimed, the sacraments celebrated, individuals led to Christian maturity, and the Christian community built up" (*The Unity We Seek*, New York: Paulist Press, 1977, pp. 11-13).

What emerges from these assorted consensus statements is a measure of convergence at the following points: (1) There is a general ministry to which all baptized Christians are called. (2) Within that general ministry and in its service there are specialized ministries. (3) The ordained ministry at the local level exists to see to it that the Gospel is proclaimed and the sacraments celebrated. Beyond this there is the abiding demand for pastoral care, spiritual direction, and service to other human needs. (4) The ordained minister speaks not only on behalf of or in the name of the community to God, but also on behalf of and in the name of Christ to the community as well. (5) The ordained minister is not called to a different kind of holiness from the rest of the Church but *is* called to "exemplify" the call to servanthood to which all are in fact called. (6) Bishops have a special role in the Church beyond that of the local pastor, in that bishops serve to unify and coordinate the Christian mission and ministries of a community of churches (diocese). This ministry is one of overseeing (*episcope*), and is always exercised as a service, never for domination. Its mode is always collegial, not monarchical. (7) Finally, in the Roman Catholic tradition there is the special place of the bishop of Rome in the service of the unity and mission of the Church universal.

Contemporary Catholic Theology

To the extent that a debate continues on the nature (essence) of the ordained ministry of bishop and presbyter, the discussion centers on two questions: (1) What is the relationship between the two ministries? (2) What makes either or both of these ministries distinctive within the network of ecclesial ministries?

Regarding the first question, a presbyteral tendency is still pressed by some (e.g., Hans Küng and Edward Schillebeeckx), in spite of Vatican II's strongly "episcopal" doctrine. These theologians ask whether the distinction between episcopacy and presbyterate is of divine institution, and whether the episcopacy as it has developed has any real basis at all in the New Testament.

Regarding the second question, answers vary according to one's operative model of the Church. More traditional approaches (e.g., Avery Dulles) continue to insist on the distinctively cultic and sacramental responsibilities of the ordained bishop and priest as that which sets them apart from other ministers in the Church. Others (e.g., Karl Rahner) underline the priest's call to proclaim the Gospel by word and witness. Still other theologians (e.g., Yves Congar, Hans Küng, Walter Kasper, Edward Schillebeeckx) stress

the leadership role of the bishop and priest. It is this latter understanding which is perhaps most comprehensive and is most readily
integrated with the ecclesiology of Vatican II. Given this perspective, Holy Order is literally a sacrament directed to the *order* of
the Church, "that all according to their proper roles may cooperate in this common undertaking with one heart" (*Dogmatic Constitution on the Church*, n. 30).

The Church and Holy Order

The Church is a sacrament. That means it must be and act as a
sacrament. Among the principal ways in which the Church
manifests itself as a sacrament and acts according to its sacramental nature is the celebration of the sacraments themselves. But the
celebration of the sacraments requires those who will see to it that
the sacraments are celebrated, that everything is ordered to the
benefit of the whole Church and to its upbuilding (2 Corinthians
4:14; 1 Corinthians 14:5). Through the exercise of this sacramental ministry of Holy Order the whole sacramental reality of the
Church is expressed: The good news of the Kingdom of God is
proclaimed, the Eucharist is celebrated, the death and resurrection of Christ are made real and effective for individuals in Baptism, sins are forgiven, the sick are ministered to and healed,
human love is sanctified, the Holy Spirit is poured forth, and the
mediating, priestly work of Christ is continued.

SUMMARY

1.   In addition to the sacraments of *initiation* (Baptism-Confirmation and Eucharist) there are the sacraments of *healing* (Penance and
Anointing of the Sick) and the sacraments of *vocation* and *commitment*
(Matrimony and Holy Order). The former are for the sake of those whose
bond with the Church has been weakened or severed by sin and/or by
serious illness; the latter are for the sake of the Church itself, so that it
will continue to be built up and, at the same time, be faithful to its
mission to proclaim the Gospel in word, in sacrament, in witness, and in
service.

2.   The *forgiveness of sins*, often linked with the healing of the sick,
was an abiding feature of Jesus' own ministry and later of the preaching

and ministry of the Apostles. This is not to say that we can determine a precise moment or event at which Jesus instituted the sacrament of Penance. This sacrament, like the others, issues from the creation of the Church itself which is, in turn, the result of Jesus's proclamation of the Kingdom of God, his gathering of disciples, and his celebration of the Last Supper with his disciples.

3. In the *earliest centuries* of the Church's history, Penance was administered no more than once after Baptism, and then only for the gravest public sins—e.g., apostasy, murder, adultery. There was no private confession of sins to a priest. The bishop was the minister of the sacrament.

4. The character of Penance changed under the influence of the *Irish monks*, who encouraged the practice of private penance for the laity, even for relatively minor offenses. The relationship between sins and penances became very complicated, requiring the publication of special books to help the confessor decide which penance to impose for which sins.

5. By the *Middle Ages* the sacrament of Penance has four separate components: satisfaction (the doing of a penance), confession, contrition, and absolution by a priest. *Trent* made these definitive, over against the opposition to the Reformers. It taught that all grave sins had to be confessed to a priest in kind and number. The priest acted as a judge. The confessional was his tribunal.

6. *Vatican II* mandated a change in the rite of Penance to bring out its *ecclesial* (as opposed to purely private) dimension as an act of *reconciliation*, and to stress the role of the priest as *healer* rather than as judge.

7. Through this sacrament of Penance the Church reveals itself not only as a reconciler of sinners, but also as a community always in need of reconciliation.

8. Apart from James 5:14 there is no mention of Anointing as a sacred rite in the New Testament. Although the text does not "prove" the institution of the sacrament of the *Anointing of the Sick*, it does indicate that such a practice existed in the early Church.

9. The first documentary evidence we have of the administration of this sacrament in the post-biblical period is provided in a letter of Pope Innocent I (d. 417). From the beginning it was not regarded as *the last sacrament*. That function was served by *Viaticum*, one's last Communion. With the Romanization of the Church under Charlemagne, the sacrament of Anointing became "Extreme Unction" and, as such, the sacrament of the dying.

10. Its sacramentality was taught by the Councils of *Florence* and *Trent*. *Vatican II* restored the primitive emphasis on the anointing of the *sick* rather than on the last anointing of the dying. The last sacrament is Viaticum, not the Anointing.

11. The Church discloses itself in this sacrament of Anointing as a *healing community* always on the way to the Kingdom of God and always itself in need of healing. It is a Church which recognizes that salvation is of the whole person, body and soul, and not just of the soul.

12. *Matrimony* is rooted in the Old Testament notions of *creation* and *covenant*. The ambivalence of the New Testament regarding marriage (i.e., that it is at once holy and to be avoided, if possible) may be explained by its sense of the imminence of the Kingdom of God. In later New Testament writings (Ephesians) this sense of the imminence of the Kingdom has waned, and so marriage is linked with the union of Christ and the Church.

13. The ambivalence carries through much of the Church's history. The negative attitude of *Augustine* toward marriage and sexuality is well known, but neither he nor the other Fathers of the Church denied the basic sanctity of marriage. Its sacramentality was affirmed by the Councils of *Florence* and *Trent*.

14. *Vatican II* introduced a whole new perspective on marriage: (1) It is a covenant, not a contract; (2) mutual love is not "secondary" to the begetting of children; (3) mutual love is, in fact, what is sanctified by the sacrament; (4) its sacramentality is not automatic; it requires faith; (5) the consummation of marriage encompasses more than a single biological act; and (6) the sacrament incorporates one more fully into the mystery of the Church. These points are reflected in the new *Rite of Marriage*.

15. The Catholic Church has always taught that marriage is *indissoluble* (permanent) and *monogamous* (one husband, one wife). On the other hand, it has always tolerated certain modifications of this principle through *dispensations* (similar to the Eastern Orthodox application of the principle of *economy*) designed to remove the unintended harshness of the law.

16. Church law requires that Catholics marry before a priest or deacon and two witnesses (*canonical form*). Since Vatican II, however, marriage can, with permission, be performed in a Protestant church before a Protestant minister, and non-Catholic Christians may be permitted to act as witnesses at Catholic marriages, and Catholics at non-Catholic Christian marriages.

17.   A *mixed marriage* is one between a Catholic and a non-Catholic; it requires both a dispensation and a promise by the Catholic party to do all in his or her power to share the Catholic faith with any children of the union.

18.   The *Pauline Privilege* permits a second marriage to one who converts to Christianity when the first partner does not. The *Petrine Privilege* allows the pope to dissolve a marriage between a Christian and a non-Christain when the Christian wishes to marry another Christian or when the non-Christian wishes to become a Catholic and remarry.

19.   An *annulment* is an official declaration that a marriage was invalid from the beginning—e.g., because of the immaturity of the couple. When an official declaration is impossible, some theological opinion and pastoral practice allow Catholics in a second marriage to be readmitted to the Church's sacramental life, assuming no grave scandal is present.

20.   There is fundamental agreement between Catholics and Orthodox, on the one hand, and Catholics and Anglicans, on the other, on the *sacramentality* of marriage. Similar agreement has not yet been reached between Catholics and Protestants of the Lutheran and Reformed traditions.

21.   Through the sacrament of Matrimony the Church reveals itself as the bride of Christ and the sign of God's love for us in Christ. The Church is also shown as a community of love.

22.   The sacrament of *Holy Order* presents a very complicated history. There are, by present theological and doctrinal standards, three grades of this sacrament: diaconate, presbyterate, and espicopate. The *diaconate* is linked with the call of "the Seven" to assist the Apostles in material chores; the *presbyterate* is rooted in the priesthood of the Old Testament and in the system of elders by which towns and communities were governed; and the *episcopate* emerges from the presbyterate, probably as the executive committee of the council of elders and eventually as the office of pastoral leadership over a particular church.

23.   The New Testament does not present an organizational blueprint for the Church. "The Twelve" are not exactly coextensive with "the apostles" (Paul was an apostle, but not one of the Twelve). There were many ministers and officers in the various churches of the New Testament. No clear-cut distinction or job description can be determined. The apostles, however, were missionaries on the move, and the presbyters and presbyter-bishops were ministers in residence, serving the churches established in many instances by the apostles. Evidence for the development of a monarchical espicopate in the early Church is to be

found in the letters of *Ignatius of Antioch*. But this model of governance was not universal.

24. The notion of a *Christian priesthood* does not emerge early because the Jerusalem Church still regarded the Jewish priesthood as valid. Not until certain events occurred (e.g., destruction of the Temple, large influx of Gentiles into the Church) did the concept of a distinctively Christian priesthood emerge, particularly as the Church's consciousness of the sacrificial nature of the Lord's Supper was heightened.

25. But there was still no clear principle governing the *celebration of the Eucharist* in churches of the New Testament period. We cannot say that it was restricted to the Apostles or to ordained priests, although eventually it came to that around the turn of the first Christian century.

26. After the monarchical episcopate was established, the presbyterate was regarded as a *college of priests* in union with the bishop. With the need for parishes outside the Christian centers, the notion of collegiality began to decline. The feudal system, which made the priest more dependent on the nobility than on the bishops, further accentuated this decline. Priests were now ordained principally for the Mass and the sacraments, and with the imposition of obligatory celibacy the priesthood became increasingly a caste within the Church.

27. The issue of the priesthood of all believers and the priesthood of the ordained was joined at the *Reformation*, with the Council of *Trent* insisting on the latter. *Vatican II* restored the understanding of the Church as the whole People of God and stressed the participation of the laity in the priesthood of Christ, without prejudice to the special priesthood of the ordained. Emphasis was placed on the role of bishops in the Church and on their collegial union, one with another and with the bishop of Rome, as a symbol of the collegial nature of the Church itself. The corporate or collegial nature of the presbyterate was also emphasized once again, and the permanent diaconate was restored.

28. *Ecumenical consensus* has been reached on the following points, with varying degrees of agreement: (1) There is a general ministry to which all the baptized are called; (2) specialized ministries serve this general ministry; (3) the ordained Ministry exists to see to it that the Gospel is proclaimed, the sacraments celebrated, pastoral care exercised, the needy attended to, etc.; (4) the ordained Minister speaks both *on behalf of* the community and in the name of Christ *to* the community; (5) the ordained Minister is called to "exemplify" the universal call to servanthood; (6) bishops have a special role in the Church, of unifying and coordinating the mission and ministries of a community of churches, or diocese. It is a Ministry of "overseeing" (*episcope*); and (7) in the

Roman Catholic tradition, the bishop of Rome exercises this function for the Church universal.

29.   Contemporary Catholic theology continues to debate the relationship between the episcopate and the presbyterate, and the distinctive purpose of both ministries over against other ministries in the Church. These questions remain open.

30.   Holy Order is a sacrament which attends to the *order* of the Church. It insures that the Church will, in fact, act sacramentally: proclaiming the Gospel in word, in sacrament, in witness, and in service.

SUGGESTED READINGS

Brown, Raymond. *Priest and Bishop: Biblical Reflections.* New York: Paulist Press, 1970.

Cooke, Bernard. *Ministry to Word and Sacraments: History and Theology.* Philadelphia: Fortress Press, 1976.

Dyer, George, ed. "The Pastoral Guide to Canon Law." *Chicago Studies* 15/3 (Fall 1976).

Fransen, Piet. "Orders and Ordination." *Encyclopedia of Theology: The Concise Sacramentum Mundi.* New York: Seabury Press, 1975, pp. 1122-1148.

Neunheuser, Burkhard. *Penance and Anointing of the Sick.* London: Burns Oates, 1964.

Poschmann, Bernard. *Penance and the Anointing of the Sick.* New York: Herder & Herder, 1964.

Rahner, Karl. "Penance." *Encyclopedia of Theology: The Concise Sacramentum Mundi.* New York: Seabury Press, 1975, pp. 1187-1204.

·XXIII·

SPECIAL QUESTIONS IN ECCLESIOLOGY

This chapter addresses five "special questions" in contemporary ecclesiology: *authority, papacy, ministry, women in the Church*, and *intercommunion*. Insofar as authority is rooted in the will of God, authority is the one overarching question; the other four are component parts of the authority issue. How is authority to be exercised, for what purpose, and by whom? How much common consent to authority is necessary before we have a community that can celebrate the sacrament of unity together?

Each of these topics remains a matter of some theological and pastoral controversy today. Accordingly, the presentations and conclusions of this chapter are more tentative than usual. They are principally designed to introduce the reader to the problem, familiarize him or her with the major terms of the discussion, and show the connection of each question with the mystery of the Church.

AUTHORITY
General Philosophical and Theological Considerations

"Authority" is not an easy concept to define. It is perhaps most often identified with legitimate power, and yet philosophers are quick to point out that authority and power are not the same thing. A mugger with knife in hand has power over his victim, but no authority. On the other hand, authority does have something to do with influencing the thinking and behavior of people.

The word is derived from the Latin, *auctor* ("author"). It may be *de iure* or *de facto* authority. Authority is *de iure* (i.e., by right or by law) when it is attached to, or supported by the power of, an office. A policeman has *de iure* authority. Authority is *de facto* (in fact, i.e., the way it really is) when it is actually obeyed and, therefore, achieves its intended effect. A political columnist who influences governmental policy has *de facto* authority. It is not only possible but ideal that those who legitimately hold and exercise *de iure* authority should also possess *de facto* authority. Thus, the policeman who enforces the law should also be perceived as a law-abiding citizen himself and therefore worthy of one's respect as well as one's obedience. Finally, the word *authority* is also applied to inanimate objects—e.g., books (especially the Bible), institutions, codes of law, symbols. But if such authority exists, it resides in the person or persons who stand(s) behind these objects.

Ultimately, all authority is rooted in God, who is the *Author* of all that is. "Let everyone obey the authorities that are over him, for there is no authority except from God, and all authority that exists is established by God" (Romans 13:1).

Biblical Notions

Old Testament

God is the Author, or source, of all creation. Our own authority over nature comes from God (Genesis 1:28), as does the authority of husbands over wives (3:16) and of parents over children (Leviticus 19:3). Even as society becomes more complex, the same principle obtains. It is God who confers on Hazael the government of Damascus (1 Kings 19:15; 2 Kings 8:9-13), and on Nebuchadnezzar the government of the entire Orient (Jeremiah 27:6).

But the authority entrusted by God is never absolute. The law regulates the exercise of authority by listing the rights of slaves (Exodus 21:1-6,26-27; Deuteronomy 15:12-18; Sirach 33:30). Even the father's authority over his children must look to their good education (Proverbs 23:13-14; Sirach 7:23-24; 30:1). Those holding political power must take care not to deify themselves and thereby blaspheme against the God who alone is absolute Author of all life (Daniel 11:36; 7:3-8,19-25). Such pretensions will meet with destruction 7:11-12,26).

This is true also of authority entrusted to religious leaders, such as Moses, the prophets, and the priests (Exodus 19:6), and of the ancients who assist Moses (Exodus 18:21-26; Numbers 11:24-25). All who hold authority exercise it in the name of God. Conflicts are inevitable—e.g., Saul with Samuel (1 Samuel 13:7-15; 15), Ahab with Elijah (1 Kings 21:17-24), and many kings with their prophets. Religious authority can be abused. The power of the Israelite royalty ends in the tragedy of exile. After the exile, Israel is more openly accepting of God's authority. It is from God that Cyrus and his successors have received the empire (Isaiah 45:1-6). But there is also a new attitude toward *de iure* authority—an attitude which appeals to divine vengeance and, in the end, to revolt when the pagan nation turns persecutor (Judith; 1 Maccabees 2:15-28).

New Testament

Authority *(exousia)* is ascribed also to Jesus (John 17:2; 5:27; Revelation 12:10). He preaches with authority (Mark 1:22 and parallels). He has the power to forgive sins (Matthew 9:6-8; Mark 2:5-10). He is lord of the sabbath (Mark 2:23-28 and parallels). He casts out demons and works cures (Mark 1:27; Matthew 12:27-28; Luke 11:19-20). He interprets the law, as the rabbis did, but with definite authority (Matthew 7:28-29). In Matthew he is depicted as speaking in his own name, unlike the teachers of old: "But I say to you. . ." (Matthew 5:21-48). Indeed, so "authoritative" is Jesus' manner that he is specifically confronted with the question "On what authority are you doing these things? Who has given you the power to do them?" (Mark 11:28). The New Testament, therefore, sees the authority of Jesus as something central to his ministry. Here was "something greater than the temple" (Matthew 12:6), greater than Jonah and Solomon (Matthew 12:41-42), and different from the power of "this world" (John 18:36).

After his death and resurrection, the authority of Jesus is perceived anew. He is declared risen and enthroned at the right hand of God (Acts of the Apostles 2:34-36). He is the Lord (Philippians 2:9-11), the son of God "with power" (Romans 1:4). To him "all authority, in heaven and on earth" is given (Matthew 28:18). All creation is subject to him (Philippians 2:10), and he will sit upon God's judgment seat (2 Corinthians 5:10) to judge the living and the dead (Acts of the Apostles 10:42). Past, present, and future are under the authority of Christ, in whom all God's promises are affirmed (2 Corinthians 1:20).

On the other hand, Jesus exercises his authority in the manner of a servant (Mark 10:45; Luke 22:27). It is precisely because he did not cling to divinity that he became Lord of all (Philippians 2:5-11). And so he charges his disciples to follow his example: "Earthly kings lord it over their people.... Yet it cannot be that way with you. Let the greater among you be as the junior, the leader as the servant [*diakonos*]" (Luke 22:25-26; John 13:14-15). His kingdom, after all, is not of this world (John 18:36). Therefore, his disciples are not to be engaged in any struggles for power or preferment among themselves (Matthew 20:20-28; Mark 10:35-45).

The absolute power which Jesus claims in Matthew 28:18 is not transferred to his disciples. Not even Peter receives absolute authority. In Acts of the Apostles 1-12, where his leadership is most clearly portrayed, decisions are made by "the Twelve" or "the apostles" or "the church," and not by Peter. His action in Acts of the Apostles 10 is reviewed by "the party of the circumcision" (11:1-18). His devious behavior at Antioch elicits an open rebuke from Paul (Galatians 2:11-14). Nor are the apostles the sole participants in Jesus' authority. There are also prophets, teachers, wonder-workers, evangelists, presbyters, and others (1 Corinthians 12:28; Ephesians 4:11). Paul himself is criticized by some of the Corinthians harshly and unjustly. He responds to the criticisms with warmth, and never suggests that he is above criticism because of his status.

The Spirit is, in fact, given to the whole Church and not exclusively to the leaders of the Church (1 Corinthians 12:1-28; Romans 12:3-8). There is a diversity of gifts and charisms, and all must work together as one for the good of the whole. The power which Christian authority has is grounded in the Holy Spirit, and the Holy Spirit is available to all. Indeed, no one can even profess that Jesus is Lord except in the Holy Spirit (1 Corinthians 12:3). Therefore, authority in the Church is always of a unique kind, not simply another form of standard social or political authority. It is a power existing within the Body of Christ, not just within another human organization. Authority as a function of the Body of Christ is a new concept of authority, just as the Body of Christ is a new concept of society. Authority is an operation of the Holy Spirit, but it is only one operation.

And what specifically of *teaching authority*? "Teacher" was a common category, which applied even to the Scribes. Teaching involved commentary on the Sacred Scriptures (i.e., the Old Testament), but the texts were accommodated to whatever point a teacher wanted to make. Jesus himself was a teacher, and was so regarded. He was preoccupied with proclaiming the reign of God, but his teaching filled out his preaching and explained the nature of the Kingdom and its demands. The people were amazed by Jesus' teaching because, unlike the Scribes, he taught with authority.

On the other hand, the entire New Testament conceives the Gospel as a *way of life*. Only in Matthew are the Apostles *commissioned* to teach, which helps explain why interpreters refer to Matthew as the most Jewish of the Gospels. The Apostles did teach, however. The object of their teaching was Christ (Acts of the Apostles 5:42), the word of the Lord (15:35), the word of God 18:11). In Colossians the object is the person and the mission of Christ; in 2 Thessalonians it is the Second Coming of Christ. When teaching is enumerated among the gifts, it is listed after revelation, knowledge, and prophecy (1 Corinthians 14:6).

At Antioch there were prophets and teachers (Acts of the Apostles 13:1). Teachers are listed with other officers of the Church (Romans 12:7; 1 Corinthians 12:28; and Ephesians 4:11). Their function seemed to have been to explain the person and mission of Jesus Christ and the demands of discipleship in light of the Old Testament. The teachers were not an elite group, like the Scribes, nor was teaching limited to certain persons. As the Church grew and its organizational structure became more complex, concerns were expressed about deviations and unsound teaching (1 Timothy 1:3-7; 6:2-5; 2 Timothy 4:3-4; Titus 1:9-14; 3:9). The sure foundation of sound doctrine is the Old Testament (1 Timothy 4:11-16; 2 Timothy 3:14-17).

But in the New Testament, teaching was simply not one of the primary functions of the Church. That distinction belonged to the proclamation of the Gospel, the announcement of the good news of the Kingdom of God. Teaching was an important subsidiary function. It was the explanation of the Gospel; it was not the Gospel itself. The teaching was not the word which saves. Just as proclamation and teaching are not the same, neither are faith and doctrine. Teaching interprets faith; it is not itself faith. (See our discussion of teaching authority in chapter 2.)

Post-biblical Developments

Second and Third Centuries

The insistence upon authority is strong in Ignatius of Antioch and Cyprian. They, and others at this time, link its religious and spiritual significance with its juridical status, i.e., its status as authority of presiding over a community and regulating its life. Ignatius' assertions, in fact, are so vigorous in this regard that Protestant critics formerly doubted the authenticity of his letters, so outrageously "Catholic" were they. By being subject to their bishop, he wrote, the Magnesians or the Trallians are subject to God or to Jesus Christ (*Magnesians* III,1-2; *Trallians* II,1). For Cyprian, "The bishop is in the Church, and the Church in the bishop."

But the Church is always the whole community, and not just the hierarchy. "I have made it a rule, " Cyprian writes elsewhere, "ever since the beginning of my episcopate, to make no decision merely on the strength of my own personal opinion without consulting you (the priests and the deacons) and without the approbation of the people" (*Letters* 14:4). In fact, the whole Church community, laity especially, took part in the election of bishops and the choice of ministers. Even though the early Church already possessed a firm canonical structure, it also wanted to be ready for any movement prompted by the Holy Spirit. And so the intervention of the laity was welcomed as a matter of principle. But the Church also regarded the bishop as possessed of the gifts of the Spirit in a preeminent way. *It was because of the presence of these gifts that one was chosen a bishop in the first place.*

Fourth to Eleventh Centuries

With the *Edict of Constantine* (313) the situation changed markedly. Bishops and presbyters were now invested with civil authority. Monasticism developed, as we pointed out in chapter 18, partly in reaction to this new worldly favor. In monasticism it was possible for a charismatic or spiritual authority to continue to exist, and monastic leaders came to enjoy a kind of independent authority in the Church over against the ordinary hierarchical authority. This was especially true in the East. From the beginning of the eighth century, and as a result of the Monothelite controversy and the iconoclast crisis during which the monks became the defenders of orthodoxy, there was a real transfer of spiritual direction and of the exercise of ecclesiastical authority from the hierarchical priesthood to the monks. It was clear that they were truly men of God. A similar, though less pronounced, development occurred in the West, where saints and abbots developed their own spheres of influence.

This is not to say that there was a fundamental opposition between monastic and hierarchical authority at that time. Many of the bishops were, or had been, monks, or at least men trained in monasteries—e.g., Basil, John Chrysostom, Augustine, Martin, Patrick, Isidore of Seville, Gregory the Great. From St. Augustine of Canterbury's time (d. 604 or 605) until the twelfth century, all archbishops of Canterbury were monks. The connection between the episcopal ministry and the monastic ideal was also evident in the oldest sections of the Latin ritual of ordination, which state the duties, not the powers, of bishops—e.g., assiduous study of Sacred Scripture, prayer, fasting, hospitality, almsgiving, listening, edification of the people by word and through the liturgy. The bishop was to represent the moral ideal of authority, for *genuine authority is moral authority.*

The Church was perceived as more than a juridical organization with rules, regulations, and officials to administer them. It was more fundamentally a body of men and women praying, fasting, doing penance, asking for grace, engaging in spiritual combat to become more like Christ. It was important, therefore, that the bishop and indeed the pope be themselves credible examples of Christian existence. *"Vobis sum episcopus, vobiscum Christianus* ("For you I am a bishop; with you I am a Christian"), St. Augustine of Hippo wrote (*Sermon* 340:1). It is out of this same period (fourth and fifth centuries) that the celebrated formula emerged: *Qui praefuturus est omnibus, ab omnibus eligatur* ("He who would be the head of all should be chosen by all"). The formula is that of Pope Celestine I (d. 432), and it occurs again in the councils of Orleans (549) and Paris (557) and in the *Decretals of Gratian* (d. 1140).

The Middle Ages

The reform of the Church begun by Pope Leo IX (d. 1054) and continued by Gregory VII (d. 1081) represents a turning-point in the history of authority. The reform was aimed not only at the renewal of the Church but also at its liberation from the control of lay princes and other political figures. To do this, Gregory claimed for the Church the completely autonomous and sovereign system of rights proper to a self-contained, spiritual society, and an authority which covered not only the whole Church but kings and their kingdoms as well. To support his argument Gregory ordered the Church's scholars and jurists to comb the archives and uncover every scrap of precedent for his view. Canon law was born, and the foundation was laid for the kind of exaggerated papal claims to be made by Innocent III (d. 1216) and Boniface VIII (d. 1303).

Even the title *Vicar of Christ*, bestowed on the pope, was transformed from an essentially *sacramental* image (Christ and the saints are working through this servant) to a largely *juridical* one (the pope possesses powers given him by Christ). And so a *legalism* was introduced, and it radically changed the originally spiritual notion that obedience to God's representative is obedience to God. The presence of grace in the representative was no longer crucial.

Episcopal authority was no longer *moral* authority but *jurisdiction*, and it was bestowed even before the sacrament was conferred. The bestowal of grace was secondary. And so the idea developed that a priest "governs" his parish, bishops "govern" their dioceses and "judge" in all matters, and the pope rules as a "sovereign"—indeed, is the "Sovereign Pontiff."

A counter-movement developed. Charges were now hurled at the Church's leaders, especially from the spiritual movements of the twelfth century, and later from Franciscanism and from the Hussite movement. Each was saying in effect that the Church, and the pope in particular, had obscured the Gospel with pomp, that it was becoming more the Church of Constantine than of the Apostles. "All this, as well as the claims to prestige and riches, goes back to Constantine, not to Peter," St. Bernard (d. 1153) wrote to Pope Eugenius III (d. 1153).

The new juridicism notwithstanding, Catholic theology preserved many elements of the ancient ecclesiology, at least until the death of the two greatest doctors of the thirteenth century, Thomas and Bonaventure. In Thomas, for example, the idea of the Church as the congregation of the faithful is still very much alive. Authority is not merely juridical. It is linked with spiritual gifts and with the achievement of the perfection of Christian charity. Matthew 16:19 is interpreted as referring principally to Peter's confession of faith. The theology of the new law as formulated in the *Summa Theologica* I-II, q. 106, is completely evangelical. It is a law of love and service, not of fear and slavishness.

But unfortunately this was not the spirit of the Church at large. As Yves Congar has acknowledged, "It is a fact that the authority of prelates of every degree was never insisted on so much as in the fourteenth and fifteenth centuries. The thunderclap of 31 October 1517 [the day Luther posted this ninety-five theses against indulgences on the door of the church at Wittenberg] was only the first of a violent storm" (in *Problems of Authority*, p. 143).

The Council of Trent to the Twentieth Century

The Reformation questioned authority not only in its corrupted forms but in principle. In reaction the Council of Trent (1545-

1547, 1551-1552, 1562-1563) insisted even more strongly on the authority of the hierarchy, so much so that the ecclesiology which developed after Trent was more akin to a *hierarchology* or a treatise on public law. The pope was now regarded as a "universal bishop." Each Catholic was directly under the pope and subservient to him, even more than to the individual Catholic's own bishop. The shift of all significant power to Rome occurred at an accelerated pace. Ecclesiastical authority became increasingly centralized. And people were asked to obey because of the status and office of the legislator, not because he and his decrees were obviously prompted by the Spirit. The definition of papal primacy at Vatican I was the culmination of this development.

This understanding of authority prevailed until the Second Vatican Council. Pope Pius XII's *Humani Generis* (1950), for example, insisted that even papal encyclicals, although they do not engage the fullness of the pope's teaching authority, demand both external and internal assent. "And when the Roman Pontiffs carefully pronounce on some subject which has hitherto been controverted, it must be clear to everybody that, in the mind and intention of the Pontiffs concerned, this subject can no longer be regarded as a matter of free debate among theologians."

Vatican II

Although the Second Vatican Council continued to teach that the pope and the bishops exercise supreme authority over the Church, it says that this authority is always to be exercised as a service and in a collegial manner. Furthermore, it is to be used only for the edification ("building up") of their flocks (*Dogmatic Constitution on the Church*, n. 27). Pastors, too, are not intended to shoulder alone the whole saving mission of the Church. They must collaborate with their brothers and sisters, including the laity, that all might work together as one for the good of the whole (n. 30). The principle of authority-as-service is reaffirmed in other conciliar documents as well: in the *Decree on the Bishops' Pastoral Office in the Church*, the *Decree on the Ministry and Life of Priests*, and the *Decree on the Appropriate Renewal of the Religious Life*. (See chapter 19.)

Ecumenical Developments

Recent ecumenical statements on the question of authority have come from the Anglican-Roman Catholic International Commission and the Lutheran-Catholic Dialogue in the United States. The Anglican-Roman Catholic document is entitled "An Agreed Statement on Authority in the Church" and is also known as *The Venice Statement* (Washington, D.C.: United States Catholic Conference, 1977). The authority with which it is concerned is the authority of Christ, which is activated by the Holy Spirit to create community with God and with all persons. The model is definitely not political, sociological, or structural, but rather one of *koinonia*, i.e., fellowship of loving service in the truth of Christ. Whatever authority the Church possesses is always and only for the sake of promoting *community*.

There are three types of authority that persons in the Church exercise: of holiness, of the gifts of the Spirit, and of sacramental ordination (the authority of *episcope*, "oversight"). Since there is more to the Church than single local communities, this third type of authority may be exercised at diocesan, regional, and international levels. "Primacy fulfills its purpose by helping the churches to listen to one another, to grow in love and unity, and to strive together towards the fullness of Christian life and witness; it respects and promotes Christian freedom and spontaneity; it does not seek uniformity where diversity is legitimate, or centralize administration to the detriment of local churches" (n. 21, p. 13). Of interest is the response to the *Venice Statement* by the Anglican-Roman Catholic Consultation in the U.S.A., which criticized their international counterparts for concentrating too much on the authority of the pope and bishops and too little on the authority of the whole Church, laity and clergy alike. (See "Authority in the Church: Vital Ecumenical Issue," *Origins* 7/30, January 12, 1978, pp. 474-476.)

The Lutheran-Catholic Dialogue touched upon the question of the teaching authority of the Church in connection with its study of papal infallibility. All Christian authority is rooted in Christ and the Gospel, which is a word of power from God (Romans 1:16). It is proclaimed by various witnesses who share in the authority of Christ. (We shall return to this important consultation in our consideration of the papacy below.)

The Church and Authority

All authority has its origin in God, who alone is the Author of all life. God's authority is at once creative and unitive. Jesus Christ's mission was to re-create and reunite what had been wounded by sin. He proclaimed the good news that the power (authority) of re-creation and reunion was about to be released anew in the Holy Spirit and that it would eventually bring all things together at the end in the Kingdom of God.

The Church shares in the authority of Christ and in the power of the Holy Spirit. Its authority is for the same purpose: to proclaim the Gospel of the Kingdom of God and to manifest and release the power of the Holy Spirit to re-create and reunite the whole human community. The Church is itself the sacrament of community. Whatever authority exists within the Church, as distinct from the general authority to proclaim the Gospel, is for the sake of building and sustaining the reality of community, that Christians themselves might taste the firstfruits of the perfect Kingdom and that others outside the Church might be given reason to hope in it at all.

Because the Church is the whole People of God, authority resides in the community as a whole, although it is exercised in various ways, by various persons, for the good of the whole. Wherever and whenever authority is exercised, it is exercised in the manner of Jesus, who was among us as one who serves (Mark 10:45). Authority that is detached from holiness is not real Christian authority. Authority which seeks to coerce places itself above the grace of the Holy Spirit, and so is not real Christian authority either.

The Church comes into being through the free response of individuals to the call of God in Jesus Christ by the grace of the Holy Spirit. Authority can be exercised only in a way that respects the freedom of the act of faith and the voluntary character of membership in the Church (see again Vatican II's *Declaration on Religious Freedom*, and our discussion of it in chapter 19).

PAPACY

The papacy is a matter of central importance in the Catholic tradition. Belief in the Petrine ministry has always distinguished Roman Catholicism from all of the other great Christian traditions. The two principal doctrines pertaining to the Petrine office concern the primacy of the pope over the whole Church and the gift of infallibility which he enjoys when he solemnly speaks as head of the Church on matters of faith and morals. Consideration of both these doctrinal issues follows. The reader who wishes to press beyond the schematic presentations of this section of the chapter is advised to consult the more detailed material in the following volumes: *Papal Primacy and The Universal Church, Lutherans and Catholics in Dialogue V*, Paul Empie and T. Austin Murphy, eds. (Minneapolis: Augsburg Publishing House, 1974); *Peter in the New Testament*, Raymond E. Brown, Karl P. Donfried, John Reumann, eds. (Minneapolis: Augsburg Publishing House, 1973); and "Teaching Authority and Infallibility in the Church," *Theological Studies* 40 (March 1979), 113-166.

Papal Primacy

The Issue

The Church is the sacrament of the unity which God wills for all humankind in Christ and through the Holy Spirit. But the fact is that the Church is divided. There are Catholic Christians and Lutheran Christians and Presbyterian Christians and Pentecostal Christians, and so forth. Ironically, a particular ministry within the Catholic Church which exists precisely for the purpose of symbolizing and helping to realize the unity of the whole Church is also a great obstacle to that unity. Recent ecumenical discussions of the papacy, therefore, are of highest importance.

Separated Christians already embrace and accept realities which serve the unity of the Church as a whole: Baptism, the Sacred Scriptures, liturgies, creeds, confessions of faith, ecumenical councils. The Lutheran-Catholic Dialogue relates these various means of unifying the Church to the "Petrine function," i.e., a particular form of Ministry exercised by a person, officeholder, or local church with reference to the Church as a whole. This Petrine function "serves to promote or preserve the oneness of the church by symbolizing unity, and by facilitating communication, mutual assistance or correction, and collaboration in the church's mission" (*Papal Primacy*, n. 4, p. 12). The function is called Petrine because that is the kind of role the apostle Peter fulfilled among Jesus' original disciples. Among the companions of Jesus, Peter is given the greatest prominence in the New Testament accounts of the Church's origins. He is spoken of in relation to the founding of the Church (Matthew 16:18), strengthening the brethren (Luke 22:32), and feeding the sheep of Christ (John 21:15-17). He is a prominent figure in some of the Pauline letters, in the Acts of the Apostles, and in two of the so-called Catholic Epistles (1 and 2 Peter)—all of which suggests that he was associated with a wide-ranging ministry. The subsequent history of the Church portrayed him as a pastor of the universal Church. Indeed, ". . . the single most notable representative of this (Petrine) Ministry toward the church universal. . . has been the bishop of Rome" (n. 5, p. 12).

But at least three areas of controversy have marked the discussion of the ministry of the bishop of Rome: historical, theological, and canonical. Catholics and other Christians have differed about the meaning and implications of Peter's role in the New Testament Church. *Historically*, Catholics have insisted that it was a function of leadership conferred by Jesus himself and that it has been passed down through the centuries, while non-Catholic Christians have tended to minimize the significance of Peter in the New Testament and have clearly rejected the notion of a succession in pastoral authority from Peter to the bishops of Rome. *Theologically*, Catholics have argued that the papacy is of divine law, i.e., that it exists by the will of Christ, while non-Catholic Christians have insisted that it is of human origin only. *Canonically*, Catholics have looked upon the legal power of the pope as supreme, full, ordinary, and immediate (Vatican I), i.e., not subject to any higher human jurisdiction, while other Christians have viewed such claims as leading to intolerable tyranny.

History

New Testament: Peter was a figure of central importance among the disciples of the Lord. He was the first called, served as spokesman for the other Apostles, and was probably the first to whom the Lord appeared after the resurrection. Nevertheless, the terms *primacy* and *jurisdiction* are probably best avoided when describing Peter's role in the New Testament. They are post-biblical, indeed canonical, terms.

As we noted in chapter 17, the Church of the New Testament is both the church in and of a particular place (e.g., Corinth, Antioch, Jerusalem) and the Church universal (the Body of Christ, as in Ephesians). Although it is not unmistakably clear how Peter relates to the Church universal, it *is* sufficiently clear that he *does* relate to the Church universal in certain significant ways. He is listed first among the Twelve (Mark 3:16-19; Matthew 10:1-4; Luke 6:12-16) and is frequently their spokesman (Mark 8:29; Matthew 18:21; Luke 12:41; John 6:67-69); he is the first apostolic witness of the risen Jesus (1 Corinthians 15:5; Luke 24:34); he is prominent in the original Jerusalem community and is well known to many other churches (Acts of the Apostles 1:15-26; 2:14-40; 3:1-26; 4:8; 5:1-11,29; 8:18-25; 9:32-43; 10:5; 12:17; 1 Peter 2:11; 5:13). His activities after the council of Jerusalem are not reported, but there is increasing agreement that Peter did go to Rome and was martyred there. Whether he actually served the church of Rome as bishop cannot be known through evidence at hand. And from the New Testament record *alone*, we have no basis for positing a line of succession from Peter through subsequent bishops of Rome.

For the Catholic tradition, the classic primacy texts are: Matthew 16:13-19; Luke 22:31-32; John 21:15-19. The fact that Jesus' naming of Peter as the rock occurs in different contexts in the three Gospels does raise a question about the original setting of the incident. We cannot be sure whether this naming occurred during Jesus' ministry or after the resurrection, with subsequent "retrojection" into the accounts of Jesus' earthly ministry. As for the conferral of the power of the *keys*, this suggests an imposing measure of authority, given the symbolism of the keys. And yet special authority *over others* is not clearly attested. Rather, in the Acts of the Apostles Peter is presented as consulting with the

Apostles and even being sent by them (8:14). He and John act almost as a team (3:1-11; 4:1-22; 8:14).

On the other hand, there is a discernible "trajectory" of images relating to Peter and his ministry. He is portrayed as the fisherman (Luke 5:10; John 21:1-14), as the shepherd of the sheep of Christ (John 21:15-17), as an elder who addresses other elders (1 Peter 5:1), as proclaimer of faith in Jesus the Son of God (Matthew 16:16-17), as receiver of a special revelation (Acts of the Apostles 1:9-16), as one who can correct others for doctrinal misunderstanding (2 Peter 3:15-16), and as the rock on which the Church is to be built (Matthew 16:18).

The question, therefore, to be posed on the basis of an investigation of the New Testament is whether the subsequent, post-biblical development of the Petrine office is, in fact, consistent with the thrust of the New Testament. The Catholic Church says "Yes." Some other Christian churches are beginning to say "Perhaps."

Second Century to Middle Ages: The trajectory of biblical images of Peter did continue in the life of the early Church, and those images were enriched by additional ones: missionary preacher, great visionary, destroyer of heretics, receiver of the new law, gatekeeper of heaven, helmsman of the ship of the Church, co-teacher and co-martyr with Paul. At the same time, the early Church was in the process of accommodating itself to the culture of the Graeco-Roman world, particularly the patterns of organization and administration prevailing in areas of its missionary activity. The Church adopted the organizational grid of the Roman Empire: localities, dioceses, provinces. It also identified its own center with the empire's, Rome. Moreover, there was attached to this city the tradition that Peter had founded the church there and that he and Paul were buried there.

In the controversy with Gnosticism, defenders of orthodoxy appealed to the faith of episcopal sees founded by the Apostles, and especially to the faith of the Roman church which was so closely associated with Peter and Paul alike. During the first five centuries the church of Rome gradually assumed preeminence among the churches. It intervened in the life of distant churches, took sides in theological controversies, was consulted by other bishops on doctrinal and moral questions, and sent delegates to distant councils. The church of Rome came to be regarded as a kind of final or supreme court of appeal as well as focus of unity for the world-wide communion of churches. The correlation between Peter and the bishop of Rome became fully explicit in the term of Pope Leo I (d. 461), who insisted that Peter continues to speak to the whole Church through the bishop of Rome. It was also Leo who decisively intervened in the great Christological controversies and whose letter to Flavian of Constantinople in 449 provided the basis for the definitive formulation of faith two years later at the Council of Chalcedon (see chapter 13).

The Middle Ages: In order to protect the Church at large and the papacy in particular against continuing encroachments by lay powers, Gregory VII and Innocent III, relying on such documents as the *False Decretals* of Pseudo-Isidore (ca. 847-852) claimed monarchical status for their office, in accordance with contemporary secular models of government. Boniface VIII carried the claim even further, insisting on absolute power over the whole world, temporal as well as religious. In the high Middle Ages such prominent theologians as Thomas and Bonaventure stressed the powers of the Roman see, and over against both Conciliarism and Protestantism Scholastic theologians and canonists reaffirmed the monarchical structure of ecclesiastical government. This view received official endorsement in the Council of Florence's *Decree of Union for the Greek and Latin Churches* (1439) in terms very much like those of Vatican I in the nineteenth century.

Post-Tridentine Developments to the Twentieth Century: The inclination of the official theologians and canonists to continue to assert papal prerogatives was accentuated by the rise of nationalism (e.g., Gallicanism), the intellectual challenges of the Enlightenment, and the new liberalism of the nineteenth century. Vatican I (1869-1870) was the culmination of this development. In its *Dogmatic Constitution on the Church of Christ (Pastor Aeternus,* "Eternal Pastor"), the council declared that "the primacy of jurisdiction over the whole Church was immediately and directly promised to and conferred upon the blessed apostle Peter by Christ the Lord." The primacy is passed on to whoever "succeeds

Peter in this Chair, according to the institution of Christ Himself. . . ." This power is full and supreme over the whole Church
not only in matters that pertain to faith and morals but also in
matters that pertain to the discipline and government of the
Church throughout the whole world. This power is ordinary and
immediate over each and every church and over each and every
shepherd and faithful. Vatican I's teaching was reiterated by Pope
Leo XIII in his encyclical *Satis Cognitum* (1896), in the Holy
Office's decree *Lamentabili* under Pius X (1907), in Pius XII's
Mystici Corporis (1943), in the Holy Office's letter to Cardinal
Cushing on the Leonard Feeney case (1949), and in Pius XII's
Humani Generis (1950).

Vatican II: With the Second Vatican Council the papacy is
viewed in increasingly collegial terms. The pope exercises
supreme authority over the Church, but the bishops also share in
that authority. To be sure, the supreme authority vested in the
college of bishops cannot be exercised without the consent of the
pope. "This college, insofar as it is composed of many, expresses
the variety and universality of the People of God, but insofar as it
is assembled under one head, it expresses the unity of the flock of
Christ" (*Dogmatic Constitution on the Church*, n. 22). The pope
still has "full, supreme, and universal power over the Church,"
but the bishops are no longer perceived as simply the pope's vicars
or delegates. They receive from the Lord "the mission to teach all
nations and to preach the gospel to every creature" (n. 24). They
govern their diocese not as "vicars of the Roman Pontiff, for they
exercise an authority which is proper to them. . ." (n. 27).

Finally, whatever authority the pope and the bishops enjoy, it
is always to be exercised through the faithful preaching of the
Gospel, the administration of the sacraments, and loving service.
They collaborate thereby in the work of the Holy Spirit, which is
the work of unity: in the confession of faith, in the comon celebration of divine worship, and in the fraternal harmony of the family
of God (*Decree on Ecumenism*, n. 2). Their teaching authority,
too, is subordinate to a higher principle. "This teaching office is
not above the word of God, but serves it. . ." (*Dogmatic Constitution on Divine Revelation*, n. 10).

The Church and Papal Primacy

The Church is at once local and universal. The Body of Christ truly exists in particular locales (*Dogmatic Constitution on the Church*, n. 26) and is also the Church universal. It is indeed a communion of churches. Insofar as the Church is a *communion* of churches, the papal office serves the unity of the Church as "the perpetual and visible source of and foundation of the unity of the bishops and of the multitude of the faithful" (n. 23). The pope's primacy is a primacy of service, in service of unity. Insofar as the Church is a communion of *churches*, the papal office must respect the legitimate diversity of these churches (n. 23), a collegial mode of decision-making (n. 23), and the time-honored Catholic social principle of subsidiarity, which holds that nothing is to be done by a higher group, agency, or level of authority that can be done better or as well by a lower group, agency, or level of authority.

The Church, whether local or universal, is the People of God. The Spirit is given to all. All share in principle in the total mission of the Church: prophetic, priestly, and kingly. The hierarchy, including the pope, exists to serve the rest of the Church in the exercise of that Spirit-rooted mission. The primacy is precisely for that purpose.

Papal Infallibility

The Issue

Infallibility literally means "immunity from error." In theological terms it is a charism of the Holy Spirit which protects the Church from error when it solemnly defines a matter of faith or morals. It is a *negative* gift; i.e., it guarantees that such and such a teaching is *not* wrong. Infallibility does not insure that a particular teaching is an *adequate* expression of a truth of faith or morals or even an *appropriate* formulation of that truth. *Papal* infallibility is a dimension of the *Church's* infallibility, not vice versa. The pope's infallibility is the same infallibility as that "with which the divine Redeemer willed His Church to be endowed" (*Dogmatic Constitution on the Church*, n. 25).

Papal infallibility is conceptually distinct from papal primacy. There is no reason in principle why the pope would have to possess the charism of infallibility in order to function as the chief shepherd of the Church. Conversely, infallibility could in principle be vested in persons who do not hold the supreme office in the Church. In other words, primacy of itself does not require infallibility, nor does infallibility necessarily presume primacy. The Catholic tradition, however, does insist on the correlation of the two terms: *primacy* and *infallibility*. They do, *in fact*, require one another.

Papal infallibility is related to several larger questions: the authority of the Gospel and of the Church, the indefectibility of the Church, and the certitude of Christian faith. Between the First Vatican Council, which defined papal infallibility, and the Second Vatican Council, which placed it in its wider context, the issue of papal infallibility was often discussed in very narrow terms. In the popular mind and even in some of the theology textbooks it was thought that all papal statements were somehow protected by infallibility. Consequently, the faithful Catholic had to receive all papal pronouncements "as if" they were infallible. Encyclicals were sometimes interpreted as infallibly conveying true doctrine even when they did not meet the specific conditions laid down by Vatican I for infallible definitions. Pope Pius XII's *Humani Generis* (1950) may have unintentionally given some currency to this view by stressing the definitive character of papal teaching even in encyclicals. But this has not been the exclusive tendency of the conservative wing of the Church alone. Hans Küng's *Infallible? An Inquiry* (New York: Doubleday, 1971) argued that the birth control encyclical *Humanae Vitae* (1968) was infallible by traditional standards, but then he attacked the dogma of infallibility because the encyclical's teaching on birth control was, for Küng, obviously wrong (p. 71).

The issue of infallibility is also affected by a new understanding of authority abroad in the world because of a variety of factors, some of which were discussed in chapters 3 and 6. Simply stated, the modern world is a world of pluralism, diversity, and the necessity of choice. Sociologist Peter Berger, for example, describes modern consciousness as living under the impact of this need to make our own choices (the word *heresy* is derived from a Greek word meaning "a choice"). He calls this modern phenomenon *The Heretical Imperative* (New York: Doubleday, 1979). We are no longer governed by fate, he argues, nor do we defer automatically to higher authority.

What possible meaning can the claim of immunity from error have in such a world and in light of modern experience? Does it make sense any longer for the Church to press the point that it and its official representatives (the pope, an ecumenical council, the body of bishops in union with the pope) are, in fact, guaranteed this charism of immunity from error when solemnly teaching about the faith and its moral demands? These are the kinds of questions which theologians have to address, even as they remain essentially faithful to the definitive teaching of the Church.

History

New Testament: The basis for our modern concept of infallibility is linked with such New Testament concepts as the authority of Jesus in proclaiming the Kingdom of God, the transmission of that authority in some measure to the Apostles, the authority of the Gospel itself, the authority of various witnesses to the Gospel ("He who hears you hears me"—Luke 10:16), the concern for sound doctrine, especially in the Pastoral Epistles, and the conviction that the Spirit has been given to the Church as a guide to all truth (John 16:13). This is not to suggest, of course, that our modern concept of infallibility appears precisely as such in the New Testament.

Post-biblical Developments: A complete history of the development of the notion of infallibility has yet to be written, even though important special studies are now available (e.g., Brian Tierney, *Origins of Papal Infallibility*, Leiden: Brill, 1972). What is clear is that the concern for the faithful transmission of the Gospel did not diminish after the New Testament period. In the late second-century struggle against Gnosticism, the Fathers of the Church linked the reliable handing on of the apostolic teaching with the faith of the episcopal sees founded by the Apostles themselves. By the middle of the third century, special importance was being accorded the faith of the church of Rome, which by tradition was regarded as having been founded by Peter himself. Some Roman emperors included the faith of the bishop of Rome in the official norm of orthodoxy, and the biblical image of the Church "without spot or wrinkle" (Ephesians 5:27) began to be applied to the church of Rome. Rome became *the* apostolic see. According to the *Formula of Pope Hormisdas* (d. 523), written in the year 515, "the catholic religion has always been preserved immaculate" in Rome. This conviction persisted into the Middle Ages and found expression in such influential documents as the Pseudo-Isidorian Decretals, in statements by various popes and theologians, and in assorted collections of canon law.

But this post-biblical development was neither unilateral nor unequivocal. There were challenges to such claims both in the East and the West. Eastern Christians regarded Rome as only one of several apostolic sees to which protection of the faith had been entrusted. But the faithfulness of such Popes as Liberius (d. 366), Vigilius (d. 555), and Honorius (d. 638) was questioned. Certain Western metropolitans (archbishops) even in the early Middle Ages were sometimes wont to contradict papal decisions. Prophetic voices were raised from the eleventh century on—almost five hundred years before the Protestant Reformation—against the style and practice of the papal ministry. Moreover, it was readily admitted by some theologians and canonists that individual popes in the past had been in error on specific points of doctrine, and canon law itself has always reckoned with the possibility that the pope could deviate from the faith (see Brian Tierney, *Foundations of Conciliar Theory*, Cambridge: Cambridge University Press, 1955, pp. 57-67).

Nonetheless, the formula "Rome has never erred" survived, and in the course of time it came to be understood as meaning that Rome "cannot" err. Roman bishops from the fourth century on regarded their confirmation of conciliar actions as an indispensable sign of authoritative teaching, even though their own doctrinal decisions needed to be accepted by secular authorities, councils, and fellow bishops in order to be enforced. But with the growing practice of making appeals to Rome, the bishop of Rome came to be regarded as the court of final appeal, the last word. The legal maxim "The first see is judged by no one" appeared initially in the sixth century and was later interpreted to mean that the pope's teaching authority is supreme. This was restated in the era of the Gregorian Reform, and Thomas Aquinas would describe the pope as one whose judgments in matters of faith must be followed because he represents the universal Church which "cannot err" (*Quodlibet* IX, q. 7, a. 16).

According to Brian Tierney's study (to which reference was made above), the term *infallibility* was first applied to the pope's teaching authority by a fourteenth-century theologian, Guido Terreni (d. 1344). Use of the word was occasioned by a controversy over poverty in the Franciscan order during the late thirteenth and early fourteenth centuries. Advocates of a rigorist position employed "infallibility" to defend the binding authority of statements by earlier popes against the decisions of their successors. Under the impact of the Reformation, the concept of infallibility quickly gained wider theological currency, especially among such Counter Reformation theologians as Robert Bellarmine (d. 1621), Francis Suarez (d. 1617), and Thomas Stapleton (d. 1598). It was appealed to in the condemnations of Jansenism and Gallicanism in the seventeenth and eighteenth centuries and received solemn approbation in the dogma of Vatican I in 1870. The teaching was reaffirmed by Vatican II, but was placed in the larger setting of the infallibility of the whole Church and the collegiality of bishops with the pope.

Ecumenical Convergences

The Lutheran-Catholic Dialogue of 1978 noted, among others, the following points of convergence: (1) The Bible is normative for all of the Church's proclamation and teaching. (2) The apostolic tradition in which the Word of God is transmitted is interpreted with the assistance of creeds, liturgies, confessions, doctrines, structural forms of government, and patterns of devotion and service. (3) The Holy Spirit remains with the Church until the end of time and will not allow it to deviate fundamentally from the truth of the Gospel, from its mission, or from its life of faith (= *indefectibility*). (4) The Church expresses its faith and fulfills its mission especially in the ministry of word and sacrament, supervised and coordinated by specific ministries and structures, including the ministry of bishops and the bishop of Rome.

(5) Their ministries include overseeing the Church's proclamation and, when necessary, the reformulation of doctrine in fidelity to Sacred Scripture. (6) Harmony between the teaching of these ministers and the acceptance of that teaching by the faithful constitutes a sign of the fidelity of that teaching to the Gospel. (7) No doctrinal definition, however, adequately expresses the truth of the Gospel, given the inevitable cultural and historical limitations of language and concepts.

The two sides agreed that the differences which still exist between them are perhaps more verbal than substantive. Catholics are now more attentive to the abuses of papal authority and are committed to the principle that the Church is the whole People of God, subject always to the Word of God in Sacred Scripture. Lutherans are now more conscious of the intent of the dogma of infallibility, namely, to preserve the Church in fidelity to the Gospel. Thus, ". . . in the new context, each side finds itself compelled to recognize that the other seeks to be faithful to the gospel" (n. 42).

Theological Clarifications

1. Vatican I placed certain conditions on the infallibility of the pope. He is infallible only when he is in the act of defining a doctrine of faith or morals, speaking as head of the Church (*ex cathedra*, "from the chair"), with the clear intention of binding the whole Church.

2. Infallibility is not a personal prerogative of the pope. He is infallible only when he is in the act of defining a dogma of faith. It can be said, without exaggeration, that a pope who never defined a dogma of faith was never infallible. That would apply to such recent popes as John XXIII, Paul VI, and John Paul I.

3. To say that the definitions of the pope are "irreformable by themselves (*ex sese*) and not by reason of the agreement of the Church (*non autem ex consensu ecclesiae*)" does not mean that the pope is above the Church. That phrase was added to the council's definition in order to exclude the tendency of some Gallicans and Conciliarists to regard approval by the bishops as necessary in order to give infallibility to any papal definition. Thus, the term

consensus at Vatican I is to be understood in the juridical sense of official approval and not in the more general sense of agreement or acceptance by the Church as a whole, which, according to Bishop Vincenz Gasser (d. 1879), the definition's author and official interpreter, can never be lacking.

4.   A similar difficulty arises with the notion of "irreformability." It does not mean that infallible teachings are immune from change. On the contrary, as formulations written in human language, they are always historically conditioned and therefore subject to revision. According to *Mysterium Ecclesiae* (Congregation for the Doctrine of the Faith, 1973), doctrinal definitions are affected by the limited context of human knowledge in the situation in which they are framed, by the specific concerns that motivated the definitions, by the changeable conceptions (or thought categories) of a given epoch, and by "the expressive power of the language used at a certain point of time."

5.   If there is any reasonable doubt about the Church's or the pope's intention to engage the charism of infallibility, then the definition in question is not to be regarded as infallible. "Nothing is to be understood as dogmatically declared or defined unless this is clearly manifested" (*Code of Canon Law*, can. 1323, #3).

6.   Infallibility does not apply to non-infallible statements—a truism, to be sure. Although the *Dogmatic Constitution on the Church* (n. 25) restates and carries forward Pope Pius XII's teaching in *Humani Generis*, i.e., that Catholics owe "religious allegiance of the will and intellect" even to non-infallible teachings of the pope, it is significant that the council did not reassert the doctrine of *Humani Generis* forbidding further public discussion of matters settled by the pope, even though this doctrine appeared in the preliminary draft of November 10, 1962.

7.   Vatican II also made it clear that the infallibility of the pope and bishops must always be related to the faith of the whole Church, that there must always be close, collegial cooperation between pope and bishops in the process of definition, that the assent of the Church can never be wanting to an authentic definition, that the Church is always a pilgrim Church, subject to sin and weakness, that there is a hierarchy of truths in the Christian

deposit of faith, and that the doctrine of Vatican II on papal infallibility is not itself the last word on the subject.

The Church and Infallibility

The Church is concerned with the truth of the Gospel, not for its speculative but for its *saving* value. The truth is to be put into action, just as Jesus practiced as well as proclaimed the Kingdom of God. Infallibility is of significance to the Church insofar as the Church is called to proclaim the Gospel faithfully and to be a sign of that Gospel through its unity of both life and faith. Insofar as infallibility attends to the fidelity of the proclamation and the unity of the Church which proclaims the Kingdom of God, it is and will always remain a matter of much theological and pastoral importance. Disengaged from exaggerations of papal authority and placed in the wider context of collegiality and the nature of the Church as the People of God, the dogma of infallibility is much less an ecumenical problem than it once was. The Lutheran-Catholic statement on the subject makes that reasonably clear.

MINISTRY
The Problem

From the time of the Council of Trent, and largely in reaction to Protestantism's stress on the "priesthood of all believers," the Catholic Church has tended to restrict the notion of ministry to the ordained (bishops, priests, and deacons) and to those steps taken in preparation for ordination (lector, acolyte, exorcist). Today the opposite extreme has shown itself: Everyone is regarded as called to ministry by Baptism.

The first extreme is outdated by reason of the Church's return to a fuller understanding of the Body of Christ as including the whole People of God, with a variety of ministries necessary for the fulfillment of its mission. The second extreme, not yet fully challenged, tends to confuse mission with ministry and neglects the particularity of ministry in the New Testament itself.

Ecumenical consultations (e.g., Lutheran-Catholic Dialogue) often make a distinction between ministry (lower case), which does apply to the whole Church as a general call to service, and Ministry (upper case), which applies to particular offices and persons in the Church who are specifically charged with the responsibility of seeing to it that the Gospel is proclaimed, the sacraments celebrated, and witness and service carried out.

History

New Testament

The word *ministry* means "service." Jesus himself gave an example of service (Mark 10:45). The apostolate itself is seen as a ministry (Acts of the Apostles 1:17,25). The call of Paul to the apostolate (Romans 1:1) is also a call to a ministry (1 Timothy 1:12; 2 Corinthians 4:1), which Paul tries to fulfill worthily (Acts of the Apostles 20:24). He understands himself as a minister of God (2 Corinthians 6:3-4) and of Christ (11:23), in the service of the Spirit (3:6-9), of reconciliation (5:18) of the Gospel (Colossians 1:23; Ephesians 3:7), and of the Church (Colossians 1:25).

But the word *diakonia* ("service") is applied beyond the apostolate. It refers also to certain material services necessary to the community, such as serving at table (Acts of the Apostles 6:1-4) and the collection for the poor at Jerusalem (11:29; 12:25; Romans 15:31; 1 Corinthians 16:15; 2 Corinthians 8:4; 9:1,12-13). A ministry is entrusted to Archippus (Colossians 4:17) and to Timothy (2 Timothy 4:5), and the title "minister" is given to Apollos as to Paul (1 Corinthians 3:5), to Timothy (1 Thessalonians 3:2; 1 Timothy 4:6), to Tychichus (Colossians 4:7; Ephesians 6:21), and to Epaphras (Colossians 1:7). There was, in fact, a diversity of ministries (1 Corinthians 12:5) and a diversity of charisms in view of the work of ministry (Ephesians 4:12). Every ministry was to be used under the influence of the Holy Spirit (Romans 12:7) as a mandate received from God (1 Peter 4:11). (See the discussion of the sacrament of Holy Order in the preceding chapter, and of the New Testament structure of the Church in chapter 17.)

Post-biblical Developments

No completely satisfactory history of the development of ministry and of ministries yet exists. One may consult Bernard Cooke's *Ministry to Word and Sacraments: History and Theology* (Philadelphia: Fortress Press, 1976) or Yves Congar's *Lay People in the Church* (Westminster, Md.: Newman Press, 1965). The problem with each is that the historical material is not integrally presented. Both divide ministry by reason of function and then provide a good outline of the development of each function in the history of the Church. For Cooke the functions are: formation of community, proclamation of God's word, service to the People of God, ministering to God's judgment, and the celebration of the sacraments. For Congar, the divisions are based on the threefold mission of Jesus and the Church: prophetic, priestly, and kingly.

What emerges from both these studies is the recognition, already noted in the preceding chapters, of (1) a broad diversity of ministries in the history of the Church, as well as of (2) a relatively wide diversity of modes in which various ministries have been exercised. Thus, as Congar has pointed out, lay persons have "heard confessions" (pp. 217-219), and in more recent decades have been mandated explicitly by the hierarchy to participate in various ministries of the Church (Catholic Action).

Vatican II explicitly acknowledged that Christ instituted in the Church "a variety of ministries for the good of the whole body" (*Dogmatic Constitution on the Church*, n. 18; see also *Decree on Ecumenism*, n. 2), among which are liturgical ministries of servers, lectors, commentators, choir (*Constitution on the Sacred Liturgy*, n. 29), and that of catechists (*Decree on the Church's Missionary Activity,* n. 17). Pope Paul VI's apostolic letter *Ministeria Quaedam* (1972) set aside the Council of Trent's notion that all ministries below priesthood are simply steps toward the priesthood, and restored lay ministries to the Latin Church, to be conferred not by ordination but by installation. The apostolic letter established two lay ministries, those of lector and acolyte, and left open the possibility of the creation of others.

Ecumenical Discussions

Although several of the ecumenical consultations have addressed themselves to the question of ordained ministry, especially of bishops and presbyters (priests), none has as yet dealt with the specific question of non-ordained ministries, except in relation to the general ministry of the whole Church. It is not that these consultations have excluded the possibility of formal but non-ordained ministries over and above the general ministry of all baptized. They have just not raised the question of these ministries. The Lutheran-Catholic Dialogue, for example, does acknowledge the existence of such ministries (citing 1 Corinthians 12, Romans 12, and Ephesians 4), but its own study was deliberately limited to valid Ministry in relation to the Eucharist. Even the Presbyterian-Reformed-Roman Catholic Consultation, which has a broadly inclusive understanding of ministry, does not attend directly to the existence of formal, non-ordained ministries.

Theological Clarifications: Ten Theses

1. There is a variety of ministries within the Church, and several possible combinations of each. Thus, one who is called to preside may or may not also be called to teach. There is no set or inflexible pattern established by the New Testament or by theological principle.

2. Each ministry within the Church is a function of the mission of the whole Church.

3. The mission of the whole Church is, in turn, a function of the mission of Jesus Christ: proclamation of the Kingdom in word, in worship, in witness, and in service.

4. Every Christian is called to ministry in the wide sense (Mark 10:45) as an empowerment to serve others, but not every Christian is called to ministry in a strict or formal sense, i.e., as a service designated by the Church to assist in the fulfillment of its mission.

5. The lay apostolate—and all the ministries it encompasses—is not simply a participation in the ministry of the hierarchy, but rather is "a participation in the saving mission of the

Church itself," commissioned by the Lord himself in Baptism and Confirmation (*Dogmatic Constitution on the Church*, n. 33).

6.   The various ministries of social service are true ministries because the services they provide are part of the essential mission of the whole Church (*Pastoral Constitution on the Church in the Modern World*, n. 43; *Justice in the World*, n. 6, Third International Synod of Bishops).

7.   The ordained ministries of presbyter and bishop exist not to suppress the other ministries, but to integrate and coordinate them (*Dogmatic Constitution on the Church*, n. 30; *Decree on the Bishops' Pastoral Office in the Church*, n. 17).

8.   Ordination, therefore, is directed toward the *order* of the Church, indeed the Church's *holy* order. Ordination establishes a new real relationship between the ordained and the community, a relationship that is once-and-for-all, i.e., non-repeatable (which is the meaning of sacramental "character").

9.   Ordination introduces one to a ministry of pastoral leadership within given Christian communities or, in the case of the diaconate, to a ministry of pastoral assistantship. This is not to say that leadership is not exercised by other ministers (e.g., Director of Religious Education), but only that the responsibility for orchestrating all the other ministries falls upon the ordained ministry of presbyter and bishop.

10.   Every ministry is a form of Church life serving the essential function of the Church. Form follows function. The freedom to abolish old forms (e.g., obligatory celibacy), to create new forms, and to modify existing forms of ministry is essential in order to facilitate the function of the community within which the particular ministry exists.

The Necessity of Ordination

There is no evidence in the New Testament that ordination was required even for presiding over the Eucharist. There *is* evidence in the history of the Church that non-ordained Christians heard confessions, and it is the common teaching of the Church today that the ministers of the sacrament of Matrimony are the two parties to the marriage, not the priest. From history, therefore, it is clear that ritual ordination was not always required for the administration of the sacraments. However, ordination is a public act concerned with *order*, as the name implies, whereby a Christian is designated and empowered to perform particular ministries for the sake of the life and mission of the Church.

Therefore, not every baptized Christian is empowered to celebrate any sacrament under any circumstances he or she may choose. The celebration of certain sacraments is reserved to those who have been set apart by the Church for training and formation, and who have been subsequently approved for ministry.

The sacraments are not simply acts by which grace is conferred, nor are they acts of private devotion. The sacrament of Penance, for example, reconciles a sinner to the Church. To reconcile someone to the Church requires a person who can act truly in the name of the Church and as its representative. That assumes some prior designation and/or authorization. Similarly, the sacrament of the Eucharist is the supreme moment at which the Church manifests and realizes itself as Church. The one who presides over the assembly *at worship* should be the one who presides over the assembly *apart from worship*, or at least one designated to act in the president's stead. The same principle applies to all the other sacraments, with the exception, as stated, of Matrimony. But even there, a representative of the community normally witnesses to the sanctification of the union since that union participates so directly in the mystery of the Church itself.

The sense of disillusionment which prompts some non-ordained Christians to arrogate to themselves the role of an official representative of the community should lead them, and the rest of the Church, to reform the structures which are the source of the disillusionment (e.g., the exclusion of certain qualified Christians from priesthood on the basis of sex or marital status alone). Short-cut strategies often exacerbate rather than improve a defective pastoral situation. The order and unity of the Church can be compromised, and the community is denied its right to test the qualifications of its members for various ministries and to call only those whom it wishes to authorize for ministry.

The Church and Ministry

Ministry is a service publicly or at least explicitly designated by the Church to assist in the fulfillment of its mission. Ministry is not the same as mission; it exists for the sake of mission, as means to end. As such, ministry in this formal sense requires some "call" from the Church, since every ministry is a service to the Church. But "Church" here means more than the Vatican or even the bishop of a diocese. "Church" means any recognizable, integral Christian community (diocese, parish, or other formal grouping) which fulfills the criteria outlined in chapter 20. The public or explicit designation need not be liturgical or ritual (it could be the offering and the signing of a contract after appropriate interviews), although that might be preferable in most cases (e.g., the installation of the Director of Religious Education).

WOMEN IN THE CHURCH
The Issue

"In accordance with the venerable tradition of the Church" (*Ministeria Quaedam*, n. 7), women are excluded from ministries in the Catholic Church today, even from the newly reconstituted lay ministries of acolyte and lector. On the other hand, the recovery of an understanding of the Church as the whole People of God, men and women alike, has led many to question that traditional policy. This ecclesiological development is parallel with an even broader development outside the Church, i.e., a growing recognition of the equality of men and women and of the innumerable ways in which that equality has been denied and thwarted in society. Thus, there is pressure on the Catholic Church from outside, but more intensely from inside, to revise its canon law and pastoral practice, and to admit qualified women to ministry at every level. This is particularly true of the United States.

History

New Testament

We have evidence of at least two ministries exercised by women in the New Testament: *widows* and *deaconesses*. The prestige and functional roles of the female minister, however, seemed to have varied from area to area. Women ministers who gave service within the community are described as early as the year 58 in reference to Phoebe in Romans 16:1. In the context of a discussion of the qualifications of various ministers, 1 Timothy 3:11 notes that "the women, similarly, should be serious, not slanderous gossips. They should be temperate and entirely trustworthy." The widowhood, on the other hand, seems to have been confined throughout its existence to those who were in fact widows. "To be on the church's roll of widows," 1 Timothy declares, "a widow should be not less than sixty years of age. She must have been married only once. Her good character will be attested to by her good deeds" (5:9–10).

Post-biblical Developments

The earliest description of the duties of deaconesses is given in the *Didascalia Apostolorum* (*The Teachings of the Apostles*), written as a kind of rulebook for a community in Syria in the early third century. Deaconesses are to be sent to minister to other women, to anoint them in Baptism, to instruct them, to visit the sick, and to minister to those in need. A deaconess was ordained by the laying on of hands in the presence of the presbyters, deacons, and other deaconesses. The same Syrian document presents widows as respected intercessors who pray over the sick and lay hands on them. As with all women, including the deaconesses, they were not to teach. The details of the position of widows are not so important as the fact that they eventually developed into a class of senior women within the Church, analogous to the presbyters. They were sometimes linked together with bishops, presbyters, and deacons as "ecclesiastical dignitaries" (Origen, *Homily on Luke 17*), and at other times considered as part of the clergy

(Tertullian, *On Monogamy* 11:1,4; 12:1). The fifth-century *Testament of Our Lord*, written also in Syria, provides an ordination prayer and specifies that there should be thirteen widows who sit in front during the celebration of the Eucharist immediately behind the presbyters, on the left side of the bishop. Widows at this time frequently performed the functions of the deaconess, assisting at the Baptism of women. They led prayer services and generally exercised leadership over women members of a community.

The growth of the Church's membership and its spread from the cities and towns to smaller towns and villages during the latter part of the third and early fourth centuries brought about rapid organizational changes, as we have noted in the previous chapter. Presbyters were now regularly delegated to preside over the Eucharist in place of the bishop and soon were established as permanent pastors in the outlying congregations. The deacon, who was originally an assistant to the bishop, either moved up with the bishop in the larger diocesan structure or stayed behind in a local community as assistant to the presbyter. In both instances the importance of the diaconate was lessened. The deacon's administrative duties were gradually taken over by the presbyters, and deacons in parishes lost prestige.

Meanwhile, the political situation outside the Church exerted additional pressure that led to further organizational change. The loosely knit structure of the first three centuries was not adequate in the face of the manipulation of the Church by the imperial power. Greater centralization seemed required, and the Church simply took over the organizational forms already available in the political realm. Diocesan bishops became like city magistrates. Bishops of provincial capitals were metropolitans, with authority over other bishops in their province. They were the counterparts of the provincial governors. The new ecclesial structure became more and more vertical. Lower offices were now regarded as probationary stepping-stones to higher offices. The line between clergy and laity developed, popular election of bishops disappeared, women were forbidden to go to the altar, and eventually lay men as well were excluded from the sanctuary. The office of deaconess was ordered suppressed by the councils of Epaon (517) and Orleans (533) in the West, but it survived for a longer time in the East, although women were absorbed into the monastic life rather than designated for pastoral ministry.

1960 to the Present

Without prejudice to the fact that women have exercised positions of leadership and influence in the history of the Church (see, for example, *Women of Spirit: Female Leadership in the Jewish and Christian Traditions*, Rosemary Ruether and Eleanor McLaughlin, eds., New York: Simon and Shuster, 1979), it has not been until the thoroughly contemporary phenomenon of the women's liberation movement that a new awareness of the place of women in the Church began to emerge. That movement, we cannot forget, began only in the early 1960s, and in many parts of the world has not yet begun. Its impact was already evident in the remarkable encyclical letter of Pope John XXIII, *Pacem in Terris* (1963), which notes that "women are becoming ever more conscious of their human dignity" and are demanding rights "befitting a human person both in domestic and in public life." He called this development one of three "distinctive characteristics" of the present day.

The Second Vatican Council's *Pastoral Constitution on the Church in the Modern World* recognized the "new social relationships between men and women" (n. 8) and noted that women are demanding equality with men in law and in fact (n. 9). Pope Paul VI's birth-control encyclical *Humanae Vitae* made the same observation (n. 2). In 1971 he issued a "Call to Action" (*Octagesima Adveniens*) in which he referred to the struggle to end discrimination against women in many countries (n. 13). Later that same year *Justice in the World*, of the Third International Synod of Bishops, urged that "women should have their own share of responsibility and participation in the community life of society and likewise of the Church."

In 1972 Pope Paul VI issued an apostolic letter, as we noted above, in which he explicitly excluded women even from the new lay ministries of lector and acolyte (*Ministeria Quaedam*), but in 1976 the Pontifical Biblical Commission reported that it could find no support for the exclusion of women from the ordained priesthood on the basis of the biblical evidence alone. "The Bible does not contain a ready answer to the question of the role of women in the Church or in society" ("Can Women Be Priests?" *Origins* 6/6, July 1, 1976, pp. 92-96). This latter document is of major importance, and merits separate study. The reader should also consult the "Consensus Statement from the Symposium on Women and Church Law," sponsored by the Canon Law Society of America, and published in *Sexism and Church Law*, James Coriden, ed. (New York: Paulist Press, 1977, pp. 150-160).

The Ordination of Women

Arguments in Favor

Positive arguments are advanced by committees of learned societies (e.g., Canon Law Society of America, Catholic Theological Society of America), national associations (e.g., Leadership Conference of Women Religious), various ecumenical consultations (e.g., Presbyterian-Reformed-Roman Catholic Consultation, "Women in the Church," in *Journal of Ecumenical Studies* 9, 1972, pp. 235-241), and the works of individual theologians. Some of these arguments are:

1. The exclusion of women from priesthood violates human dignity and the baptismal mandate to participate in the mission of the Church according to one's qualifications, opportunities, and vocation.

2. Women have in fact served as deaconesses in the early Church.

3. There is nothing in Sacred Scripture which positively excludes the ordination of women.

4. Arguments against the ordination of women are deficient:

    a. To say the tradition of the Church is against it assumes that we are already in the adulthood of the Church. But if the Church is still alive in the year 20,000, the latter part of the twentieth century will look like the "early Church" to those in the two-hundred-first century.

b.   Women are equal to men in human dignity and before God. The exclusion of women on the basis of sex assumes a radical inferiority of women and, therefore, a basic incapacity, if not unworthiness, to act on behalf of the Church in the presence of God.

c.   Jesus, in fact, called no one to *ordained priesthood* (as distinguished from discipleship and the apostolate).

Arguments Against

Negative arguments are expressed in such Vatican documents as the 1976 *Declaration on the Question of the Admission of Women to the Ministerial Priesthood* from the Sacred Congregation for the Doctrine of the Faith, the statement of the United States bishops, *Theological Reflections on the Ordination of Women* (1972), certain ecumenical consultations (e.g., Catholic-Orthodox, "Bishops and Presbyters," *Origins* 6/9, August 12, 1976, pp. 142-143), and the works of individual theologians.

1.   The constant tradition of the Church is opposed to ordination of women to priesthood.

2.   Jesus did not call women, not even his mother, to priesthood.

3.   The ordained priest must act in the name of Christ, and, therefore, must be able to represent him physically as well as spiritually. The Orthodox refer to this as "iconic" representation.

4.   No one has a right to ordination.

5.   It is not clear that the women who were called deaconesses in the New Testament were ordained or whether their ordination was sacramental.

(For a fuller discussion of these and similar arguments, both for and against, see the *Research Report: Women in Church and Society*, New York: Catholic Theological Society of America, 1978.)

The Church and Women

Whatever position one takes on the ordination question, recognition of the full Christian and human equality of women with men is essential if the Church is to be perceived, and to function, as the whole People of God. The Church must always be faithful to the example of Jesus Christ, whose sacrament it is. In striking contrast to the contemporary usages of the Jewish world, Jesus surrounded himself with women who followed him and served him (Luke 8:2-3; 10:38-42). It was the women who were charged with announcing the resurrection "to the apostles and to Peter" (Mark 16:7).

The whole purpose of creation and of redemption is the unity of all in God, and the Church is called to be a sign and instrument of the unity of God and humankind, and of the unity of humankind itself (*Dogmatic Constitution on the Church*, n. 1). Therefore, the missionary responsibility of the Church is to attest to the full human and Christian dignity of women not only by word but also by example. The sacramental principle, always central to Catholicism, is here again of utmost importance.

INTERCOMMUNION
The Issue

The mystery of the Church and the mystery of the Eucharist are intimately connected. The Eucharist is the sign as well as the principal instrument of the Church's unity in Christ. Insofar as it is a *sign* of unity, it ought not to be celebrated in common by those who are, in fact, separated from one another. Insofar as the Eucharist is an *instrument* of unity, it can be a means of bringing about the unity which eludes those who find themselves separated.

The term *intercommunion* (also known as *communicatio in sacris*, "communication in sacred realities") refers to this full eucharistic sharing between and among separated Christians. It describes the reception of Holy Communion by a single separated Christian in a church other than his or her own, or it refers to the future possibility of full church-to-church reciprocity in the celebration and reception of the Eucharist. The former is already occurring: Protestants, Anglicans, and Orthodox in fact receive Communion at Catholic Eucharists and vice versa. The latter has not occurred: There has been no public declaration by the Catholic Church, accepted by another church, that full eucharistic sharing between the two churches is now fully operative.

Intercommunion does, of course, occur within the Body of Christ but outside the Catholic Church. Thus, various Protestant churches have the policy that all baptized Christians are welcome to receive Communion at their Lord's Supper service.

The question of intercommunion arises only because there has been some form of *excommunication*, not in the juridical sense of a penalty imposed for some crime (e.g., laying violent hands on the pope), but in the larger ecclesiological sense of declaring another individual or community as unacceptable table companions at the Lord's Supper.

It is not clear what finally determines the possibility of eucharistic sharing. Some churches—e.g., Catholic, Anglican, Orthodox, and to a lesser extent Lutheran—already agree in principle on most, if not practically all, major matters of faith, including even the Real Presence of Christ and the sacrificial nature of the Eucharist. What, then, are the other obstacles to unity which keep these churches from formal intercommunion?

It would seem that, while common faith is a necessary condition for intercommunion, something is required beyond common faith, namely, a recognition that the other party or community really is a member of one's Christian family and should permanently be welcome to enjoy table fellowship with us. There is a mystery of reconciliation here which has its secular analogue in the reconciliation of friends or of relatives who have fallen out of favor with one another. Only time and some generous and gracious gestures can heal the wounds. A precipitous or prematurely arranged "reconciliation" can do more harm than good. Such an occasion can be painful, or at least awkward and uncomfortable, for both sides. The same situation apparently obtains in the Body of Christ today.

On the other hand, what of the case—frequently attested to—where members of the same church find themselves more sharply at odds with one another in the interpretation and practice of Christian faith than they are with members of other churches? Why is it that they can celebrate the Eucharist together, in spite of their internal divisions, when separated Christians with much closer bonds of faith cannot celebrate together? Once again, the family analogue may be appropriate. Even when there are serious conflicts within a home, people still sit down together at table. They may dislike the company very much indeed, but the other is still "my brother" or "my sister" or "my son" or "my daughter" or "my husband" or "my wife." And the same principle would apply to the extended family of relatives: aunts, uncles, cousins, grandchildren.

If "blood is thicker than water" in these secular examples, then perhaps a "sense of community" is "thicker" than theological and doctrinal agreement in the ecclesiastical realm.

Vatican II

If it were not for the ecumenical movement of the twentieth century, so strongly encouraged by Pope John XXIII and promoted by the Second Vatican Council, the question of intercommunion would be entirely moot. As the Catholic Church's vision of "the Church" expanded beyond the one suggested in Counter-Reformation ecclesiology and in Pope Pius XII's *Humani Generis* (the Body of Christ and the Roman Catholic Church are "one and the same"), there developed a growing awareness that other communities were also part of the Church and could themselves be called churches (*Decree on Ecumenism*, n. 3). The *Dogmatic Constitution on the Church* declared that the Church "subsists in" the Catholic Church (n. 8), not that the Church *is* the Catholic Church. On the other hand, the Catholic Church retains a certain normative status in relation to the other churches.

The possibility of intercommunion was no longer unthinkable: "As for common worship (*communicatio in sacris*), however, it may not be regarded as a means to be used indiscriminately for the restoration of unity among Christians. Such worship depends chiefly on two principles: it should signify the unity of the Church; it should provide a sharing in the means of grace. The fact that it should signify unity generally rules out common worship. Yet the gaining of a needed grace sometimes commends it" (*Decree on Ecumenism*, n. 8).

Post-Vatican II Directives

Implementation of this extraordinary principle was left to the Secretariat for Promoting Christian Unity. This Vatican congregation issued an *Ecumenical Directory* in 1967 and released a special instruction on intercommunion in 1972. The conditions under which intercommunion are allowed by these two documents are these: (1) Admission to the Eucharist is confined to particular cases of those Christians who have a faith in the sacrament in conformity with that of the Catholic Church. (2) Such Christians must experience a serious spiritual need for the eucharistic sustenance. (3) They must be unable for a prolonged period to have recourse to a minister of their own community. (4) They must ask for the sacrament of their own accord. (5) They must have proper dispositions and lead lives worthy of a Christian.

Even if these conditions are fulfilled, "It will be a pastoral responsibility to see that the admission of these other Christians to communion does not endanger or disturb the faith of Catholics." These "rules" do not apply to Orthodox Christians, who, "though separated from us, have true sacraments, above all, because of apostolic succession, the priesthood and the eucharist, which unite them to us by close ties, so that the risk of obscuring the relation between eucharistic communion and ecclesial communion is somewhat reduced."

The Church and Intercommunion

The Church is most fully and most visibly itself at the Eucharist. The fact that there are Christian churches which do not, and feel they cannot, celebrate the Eucharist together reflects the correlative fact that the Body of Christ is divided, in spite of the fundamental unity of faith in the Lordship of Jesus, the common celebration of the sacrament of Baptism, the general commitment to the Gospel of love and reconciliation, and the common hope for the coming of God's Kingdom. To attempt a quick solution to the problem of separate Eucharists is to fail to understand the root causes of ecclesial disunity. Correspondingly, only in discovering the solution to the intercommunion problem can the churches come to the heart of the mystery of unity in Christ. For that reason, this issue remains as important an issue as the Church faces in our time.

SUMMARY

1.   This chapter addresses itself to five special questions: authority, papacy, ministry, women in the Church, and intercommunion. Insofar as authority is rooted in the will of God, authority is the one overarching question, and the other four are component parts of it.

2.   *Authority,* from the Latin word *auctor* ("author"), has to do with the capacity to influence the thinking and/or behavior of people. It is closely related to *power,* but not identical with it. Authority may be associated with an office (*de iure* authority) or with certain intrinsic qualities which evoke respect and which lead to persuasion (*de facto* authority). God is the ultimate authority, or Author, of all that is.

3.   In the *Old Testament* authority is exercised by human agents, but it is never absolute. In the *New Testament,* Jesus provides the model for its exercise. He is one who serves. He uses his power to forgive sins, to heal, and thereby to proclaim the Kingdom of God. He shares his authority with his disciples, but again it is never absolute, nor is its exercise limited to the Apostles. Authority in the New Testament is unique because it is a work of the *Holy Spirit.*

4.   *Teaching* authority, while important, is always secondary to the proclamation and practice of the Kingdom. Teaching explains the Gospel; it is not itself the Gospel. Teaching interprets faith; it is not itself the faith.

5.   In the *second and third centuries* authority is identified with those who preside over the Christian churches, especially the bishops and presbyters. But the Spirit is perceived to have been given to the whole community, although in a special way to *bishops.* Only those in whom the gifts of the Spirit were discernible were elected bishops in the first place.

6.   In subsequent centuries *(fourth to eleventh)* authority becomes confused with *political* authority, especially in the aftermath of the Edict of Constantine. Monasticism grows in reaction to the exercise of worldly authority. The only genuine authority, in the monastic view, is *moral authority.* Most of the great bishops of this era are men trained in monasteries, or are themselves former monks.

7.   With the Gregorian Reform (*eleventh century*), in response to lay encroachments against the Church, the papacy claims *monarchical* authority. Papal authority is thoroughly juridicized and exaggerated,

especially under Innocent III and Boniface VIII. This provokes a counter-reaction among certain spiritual groups, e.g., Franciscans.

8.   Against the excesses of the Reformation, the Council of Trent *(sixteenth century)* insists even more strongly on the hierarchical authority of the Church. The pope becomes the Church's "universal bishop," the "Sovereign Pontiff." Authority is centralized in Rome. People are asked to obey because of the power of the office, not because of the obvious promptings of the Spirit in the officeholder.

9.   This trend culminates in the definition of papal primacy at Vatican I *(nineteenth century)* and is carried forward in the encyclicals of Pope Pius XII *(twentieth century).*

10.   Vatican II *(1962-1965)* stresses the notion of authority as *service* and insists that it must be exercised always in a *collegial* mode. Ecumenical consultations also insist on its rootedness in Christ and on its presence throughout the whole Church, exercised in different ways according to different ministerial responsibilities.

11.   *In summary,* authority in the Church exists to serve the mission of the Church, which is to proclaim, celebrate, witness to, and facilitate unity. Ecclesiastical authority is always in the service of a community which is essentially a voluntary society, where the grace of the Spirit, not coercion, is the rule.

12.   The *papacy* is an exercise of the *Petrine function,* i.e., a particular form of ministry exercised by a person, officeholder, or local church with reference to the Church as a whole. *Peter* himself seemed to fulfill something of this kind of ministry toward the universal Church, although Protestants have objected to the various forms in which this ministry has been exercised in the subsequent history of the Catholic Church.

13.   The *New Testament* does not call Peter the first pope. On the other hand, he exercises a unique role in the early Church. No single text "proves" this. Rather, there is a pattern or *trajectory of images* (e.g., fisherman, shepherd) which suggest that the post-biblical development is indeed consistent with the thrust of the New Testament.

14.   The bishop of Rome becomes increasingly important in the *early centuries* of the Church in resolving serious doctrinal controversies. He sends delegates to councils and is appealed to as a court of last resort. The correlation between Peter and the bishop of Rome becomes fully explicit in Leo I (d. 461).

15.   *Primacy* becomes an increasingly juridical concept under the impact of the threats posed by the encroachment of lay political power,

Conciliarism, Protestantism, nationalism, the Enlightenment, and nine-teenth-century liberalism. The doctrine of papal primacy, as formulated by Vatican I, reflects the Church's reaction to all these movements.

16. Vatican II restores a collegial understanding of papal primacy. Supreme authority is vested in the pope and the bishops, forming together a single college. The authority is always fundamentally spiritual, i.e., for the faithful preaching of the Gospel, the administration of the sacraments, and loving service.

17. The Church is at once local and universal. It is a communion of churches. The papacy exists to serve the *unity* of that communion of churches, but it must always respect the *legitimate diversity* of those churches, *collegiality* in decision-making, and the principle of *subsidiarity,* not appropriating to itself decisions which are better reached at lower levels.

18. *Papal infallibility* means literally "immunity from error." It is concerned with the faithful transmission of the Gospel, the indefectibility of the Church, and the certitude of faith.

19. The concept of infallibility does not appear in the *New Testament,* although the concern for sound doctrine does. There was, however, a growing conviction in the *early centuries* of the Church that Rome, and the bishop of Rome in particular, was a reliable touchstone of orthodoxy. And yet popes were conceded to have erred in matters of faith.

20. The term "infallibility" was first applied to papal teaching authority during the course of a *fourteenth-century* dispute about Franciscan poverty. One side appealed to papal views, defending their binding authority, even against the decisions of later popes. The concept was taken up and accentuated by the Counter-Reformation theologians, in the controversy with Jansenism and Gallicanism, and then made the subject of a dogmatic definition at Vatican I. This definition was reaffirmed at Vatican II but was placed in the larger context of the infallibility of the whole Church and the collegiality of bishops with the pope.

21. *Vatican I* taught that the pope is infallible only when he is in the act of defining a doctrine of faith and morals, as head of the universal Church, with the clear intention of binding the whole Church. His teachings are not subject to some subsequent vote on the part of the bishops, as the Gallicans had insisted. On the other hand, those teachings are subject to the same process of revision and improvement that all human formulations require.

22.   *Vatican II* insisted that papal infallibility must always be related to the faith of the whole Church, whose assent can never be lacking.

23.   Infallibility is of significance to the Church insofar as the Church is called to proclaim the Gospel faithfully and to be a sign of that Gospel through its unity of both life and of faith.

24.   The question of *ministry* is distorted at two extremes: One side restricts it to the ordained; the other side opens it to everyone, without regard for a call from the Church.

25.   In the *New Testament* ministry means service. There is a diversity of ministries, and this diversity continues through the history of the Church. Vatican II acknowledged this, and Pope Paul VI recognized it in reinstating two permanent ministries of lector and acolyte open by "installation" (not ordination) to lay men. Ecumenical discussions have focused on the general ministry of the whole Church, on the one hand, and the ordained ministry of the presbyter and bishop, on the other. They have not attended thus far to the place of formal but non-ordained ministries in the Church.

26.   Ministry is always for the sake of mission. In principle, ministry is open to all. By ministry is meant *a service which is publicly or explicitly designated by the Church to assist in the fulfillment of its mission.*

27.   *Ordained* ministry is for the sake of the *order* of the Church, that everyone might work together as one for the good of the whole. The Church must retain the right to designate ministers and to determine qualifications in order to insure that its mission is effectively and competently carried out.

28.   *Women* are presently excluded from all formal ministries in the Catholic Church. In the *New Testament* and in the first five or six centuries of the Church's history, however, women served as *deaconesses* and as *widows* (the latter was also a special office, not simply a civil fact).

29.   With the growth of the Church, an increase in its organizational complexity, and its adoption of political and societal models from contemporary Graeco-Roman life, the so-called lower ministries were absorbed upwards, becoming steppingstones to higher ecclesiastical office. Deaconesses were suppressed in the sixth century, and the office of widow disappeared.

30.   The women's liberation movement in the 1960s encouraged a new attitude toward the place of women in the Church. This positive

change was reflected in Pope John XXIII's encyclical *Pacem in Terris* and was reinforced by Vatican II's *Gaudium et spes*. Nonetheless, resistance to women in formal ministries continues, and Pope Paul VI's *Ministeria Quaedam* opens the ministries of lector and acolyte to men only.

31. Those who *favor* ordination of women to the priesthood point to the injustice of the present exclusion based on sex alone, the tradition of deaconesses in the early Church, and the absence of any evidence against it in the New Testament.

32. Those who *oppose* ordination of women point to the constant tradition of the Church, Jesus' own example, and the necessity of the priest's physical as well as spiritual resemblance to Christ.

33. Whatever position one takes on this issue, the Church is called to be a sign and instrument of unity. It must attest to the full human and Christian dignity of women, therefore, not only by word but also by example.

34. *Intercommunion* is an important ecclesiological issue because of the intimate connection between the mystery of the Church and the mystery of the Eucharist. Intercommunion refers to full eucharistic sharing between and/or among separated Christians. It is also known as *communicatio in sacris* ("communication in sacred realities").

35. If it were not for the ecumenical movement and Vatican II, intercommunion would be a moot question. It is an issue because the Catholic Church now recognizes that "the Church" includes non-Catholic churches also. It has also recovered the Thomistic principle that the Eucharist is not only a sign of unity but also a cause of unity.

36. Intercommunion since Vatican II is permitted on a restricted basis. The non-Catholic Christian must share Catholic eucharistic faith, have a serious spiritual need, be unable to have recourse to his or her own minister, must ask for the Eucharist, and must display the proper dispositions. These restrictions do not apply to Orthodox Christians.

37. Since some separated churches already acknowledge profound and extensive theological and doctrinal agreement with the Catholic Church on major matters of faith, why is it that Catholics do not officially celebrate the Eucharist with them? Is something more required, i.e., a sense of community, a readiness to accept the other as part of one's own Christian family? Only in discovering the solution to the intercommunion problem can the churches come to the heart of the mystery of unity in Christ.

SUGGESTED READINGS

Brown, Raymond, *et al. Peter in the New Testament.* Minneapolis: Augsburg Publishing House, 1973.

Butler, Sara, ed. *Research Report: Women in Church and Society.* New York: Catholic Theological Society of America, 1978.

Congar, Yves. *Lay People in the Church.* Rev. ed. Westminster, Md.: Newman Press, 1965.

Cooke, Bernard. *Ministry to Word and Sacraments: History and Theology.* Philadelphia: Fortress Press, 1976.

Coriden, James, ed. *Sexism and Church Law: Equal Rights and Affirmative Action.* New York: Paulist Press, 1977.

Dyer, George, ed. "The Magisterium, the Theologian and the Educator." *Chicago Studies* 17 (1978).

Empie, Paul C., *et al,* eds. *Papal Primacy and the Universal Church: Lutherans and Catholics in Dialogue V.* Minneapolis: Augsburg Publishing House, 1974.

Kirvan, John, ed. *The Infallibility Debate.* New York: Paulist Press, 1971.

McKenzie, John L. *Authority in the Church.* New York: Sheed & Ward, 1966.

Todd, John M., ed. *Problems of Authority.* Baltimore: Helicon Press, 1962.

· XXIV ·

MARY AND THE CHURCH

THE PLACE OF MARIOLOGY

No theological presentation of Catholicism can claim to be at once comprehensive and complete if it leaves out the Blessed Virgin Mary. Mariology is not an exclusively Catholic concern, to be sure, but it is a theological preoccupation that is more characteristic of Catholicism than of any other Christian tradition.

One is faced immediately with the question, "Where do the Marian doctrines and dogmas fit in?" Medieval theology always located Mariology within Christology. For Thomas Aquinas, Mariology became an appendix to Christology. Beginning in the seventeenth century a gap opened between Mariology and the rest of theology. By the end of the nineteenth century the treatise on Mary had acquired its own definite position in systematic theology, situated immediately after the consideration of the incarnation and the redemption. (For a full history of this development, see Hilda Graef, *Mary: A History of Doctrine and Devotion*, 2 vols., 1963.)

One of the more exciting debates at the Second Vatican Council was centered on the placement of the schema on the Blessed Virgin. Would it be an independent document, stressing Mary's unique relationship with Christ, or would it be considered part of the *Dogmatic Constitution on the Church?* By a margin of just four votes the council decided to follow the latter course, but it did so in the spirit of compromise. *Lumen gentium* incorporates Mary into the mystery of the Church, but insists also on her relation with Christ the Redeemer. Although some Mariologists still insist that "the best place for mariology is between the treatise on the redemption and the theological or dogmatic treatise on the Church" (Cyril Vollert, *A Theology of Mary,* p. 47), we are following Vatican II's course here. Mary is seen as a type of the Church, as its mother, as a model of faith, as a sign of the Church's hope in the coming of God's Kingdom, and as the preeminent member of the communion of saints.

HISTORY
New Testament

What follows here is dependent on the most recent ecumenical investigation of the place of Mary in the New Testament *(Mary in the New Testament,* Raymond E. Brown, *et al.,* eds., 1978).

The only reference to Mary in the *Pauline* writings is in Galatians 4:4: "God sent forth his Son born of a woman. . . ." The theological interest of that statement is Christological, pointing to the true humanity of Jesus. The designation "born of a woman" is found in the Old Testament, at Qumran, and in non-Pauline New Testament passages simply as the designation of a human being. There is no other meaning of it in Paul that one can find. Nor is there any other Pauline text referring to Jesus' origin which assigns any unusual part to Mary in Jesus' birth.

The Infancy Narrative of *Matthew* says little about Mary apart from the virginal conception (see our discussion of the virginal conception in chapter 15). In the Gospel of *Luke,* however, the evangelist's estimation of Mary is found principally in his Infancy Narrative. She is hailed by Gabriel as one favored by God (1:28,30); her response shows her to be an obedient handmaid of the Lord (1:38); Elizabeth calls her "the mother of my Lord" (1:43) and declares her blessed because of what God has done for Mary (1:42) and because of Mary's faith "that the Lord's words to her would be fulfilled" (1:45). In her own canticle, the *Magnificat,* Mary acknowledges that "God who is mighty has done great things for me" (1:49). Luke, therefore, depicts Mary as the spokeswoman and representative of the *anawim,* the poor of Israel. She is a faithful hearer of the word, obedient to it and to the God who utters it.

On the other hand, Luke mentions Mary only once in the *Acts of the Apostles* (1:14). It is after the ascension of Jesus into heaven that the disciples return to Jerusalem, go to the upstairs room, and devote themselves to constant prayer. "There were some women in their company, and Mary the mother of Jesus, and his brothers." Although it is not possible to establish the time when Mary's own belief in her Son's messianic significance began, or even the cause of it, it is clear that she shared the faith in Jesus of the earliest Christian community (see chapter 12). She was from the first a member of the post-Easter community.

We find a strikingly negative portrait of Mary in the Gospel of *Mark* (3:20-35). It is just after Jesus' selection of the Twelve (3:13-19). He is in a house with them and a great crowd gathers outside. His own family concludes that "He is out of his mind" (3:21). When his mother and his brothers arrive, they send word for him to come out. Jesus is given the message. "Who are my mother and my brothers?" he asks. Then he looks at his disciples gathered in the circle: "These are my mother and my brothers. Whoever does the will of God is brother and sister and mother to me" (3:33-35). The negative view is strengthened in 6:4, which reports Jesus' return to his home in Nazareth and the skeptical reaction of his neighbors, friends, and relatives. Jesus complains: "No prophet is without honor except in his native place, among his own kindred, and in his own house."

The Matthaen and Lucan parallels to Mark 3:20-35 (Matthew 12:24-50; Luke 8:19-21) present a different picture. Both drop the harsh introduction in Mark 3:20-21. Luke goes further and eliminates Jesus' question, "Who are my mother and my brothers?" Neither Gospel excludes Mary from the "eschatological family" of Jesus. In Luke especially she is the obedient handmaid of the Lord from the beginning. Later in 11:27-28 Jesus responds to a woman who declares his mother blessed by saying that those are blessed who hear the word of God and keep it. In light of Luke's positive description of Mary in 8:19-21, it is likely that Jesus is emphasizing here that Mary's chief blessedness lies in her being one who obediently hears the word of God rather than in being his biological mother. Consistent with this interpretation, Luke's version of the rejection of Jesus at Nazareth speaks only of a prophet's being unacceptable in his own country (4:24). There is no reference to "his own kindred," as in Mark. Matthew, on the other hand, retains the phrase "in his own house."

Thus, in the *Synoptic* depiction of Mary during Jesus' ministry there is a development from the negative estimation of Mark to the positive one of Luke, with Matthew representing the middle ground.

In the Gospel of *John,* Jesus dissociates himself from his mother because she does not realize that the work which the Father has given him takes precedence over the claims and interests of his natural family (2:4). But Mary's misunderstanding does not rank her among the unbelievers, as in the case of Jesus' brothers (7:5). Thus, the Cana story places Mary in a less negative light than in Mark, but because of her still imperfect faith at Cana she is not the equal to the believing and obedient Mary of Luke's Gospel. More important than the Cana story in John is the account of the crucifixion and of Mary's place at the foot of the cross. In giving the "beloved disciple" (John) to Mary as her son, and Mary to the disciple as his mother (19:25-27), Jesus brought into existence a new community of believing disciples, the same "eschatological family" which appears in the Synoptics. The brothers of Jesus have no part in this family. They are unbelievers. But Mary is now associated with that Johannine Christianity which differs in some respects from the Christianity derived from the witness of Peter and the rest of the Twelve. In John's own symbolic treatment of Jesus' mother, an opening is made for the process of further Marian symbolizing within the Church.

The Book of *Revelation,* chapter 12, tells of "a woman clothed with the sun, with the moon under her feet, and on her head a crown of twelve stars" (v. 1) who gives birth to a son who is "destined to shepherd all the nations" (v. 5). A huge dragon appears in hopes of devouring the child. When he fails in that, he pursues the woman. But he fails there, too, and goes off "to make war on the rest of her offspring, on those who kept God's commandments and give witness to Jesus" (v. 17). Pious commentaries notwithstanding, the "woman" here is not Mary. The primary reference is to the People of God, both Israel, which brings forth the Messiah, and the Church, which relives the experience of

Israel and brings forth other children in the image of Christ. A *secondary* reference to Mary remains possible but uncertain. What is more certain is that the author's symbol of the woman who is the mother of the Messiah might well lend itself to Marian interpretation once Marian interest developed in the later Christian community. Eventually, when the Book of Revelation was placed in the same canon of Scripture with the Gospel of Luke and the Gospel of John, the various images of the virgin, the woman at the cross, and the woman who gave birth to the Messiah would reinforce each other.

Before we leave the New Testament, some more explicit mention should be made of Mary's *virginity*. Attention was given this topic in chapter 15, and the reader should review that material in connection with the present discussion. What we noted in that chapter, and repeat here, is that the New Testament provides evidence only of a *belief* in the *ante partum* ("before birth") virginity of Mary, i.e., in the *virginal conception* of Jesus. The New Testament says nothing at all about Mary's virginity *in partu* ("in the act of giving birth"), i.e., that Jesus was born miraculously, without the normal biological disruptions, nor about her virginity *post partum* ("after birth"), i.e., that she had no normal sexual relationships after the birth of Jesus. On the contrary, the New Testament speaks of the brothers and sisters of Jesus. This does not constitute an insuperable barrier to the belief that Mary remained a virgin after the birth of Jesus, but neither is there any convincing argument from the New Testament against the literal meaning of the words *brother* and *sister* when they are used of Jesus' relatives.

Second Century

The literature of the second century is an important link between the emerging canon of the New Testament writings and the broader life-situation of the Church of the Fathers. We do not find here a fully developed interest in Mary. When she appears at all, it is on the margin of more central Christological discussions. The source material, too, is limited. Even in the literature that we do have, Marian references are extremely rare before the year 150 and are difficult to interpret in works written between 150 and 200.

The texts come from two principal groups of writings: the *apocrypha* (non-biblical gospels, epistles, apocalypses) and the *patristic writings.* The former are so called because they were not accorded canonical authority (i.e., they were not included in the canon of Sacred Scripture) and/or were rejected as products of heretical or dissident groups. Among these, the most important source for Marian material is the *Protevangelium of James* (its oldest title was *Birth of Mary: Revelation of James*). It was probably composed around the year 150 or so. The author posed as James, the brother of Jesus. It contains much detail about the early family life of Mary, her birth, her betrothal to Joseph, the annunciation, the birth of Jesus, the coming of the Magi, etc. Despite its condemnation in official documents, it dominated the development of the Marian legend for centuries. Neither in this document nor in any of the other material is there any clear evidence of a reliable historical tradition about Mary unrelated to what was said of her in the canonical Gospels. Some of the literature, in fact, is frankly Docetic. Thus, the Synoptic passage about Jesus' true family (Mark 3:31-35) is taken in this literature as a denial of his humanity.

The picture is the same when we look at the patristic writings. Most do not even mention Mary. The principal exceptions are Ignatius of Antioch, Justin, and Irenaeus. Ignatius gives an early witness to the belief in Jesus' virginal conception (*Smyrnaeans* 1:1; *Ephesians* 7:2; 18:2; 19:1). Justin's interest in Mary serves a Christological and soteriological purpose. Jesus' birth from a virgin is proof of his messiahship and a sign of a new time (see his *Apology*, especially 32:9-35:1). Justin also draws a parallel between the virgin Eve and the virgin Mary. Eve believed and obeyed the serpent; Mary believed and obeyed the angel. Thus, Eve became the mother of sin through her disobedience, and Mary became the mother of the one who destroyed the works of the serpent through her obedience. Irenaeus, finally, spells out the basis of this Eve-Mary typology by showing its parallel to Paul's Adam-Christ typology (*Adversus Haereses* III, 21:10). Mary is the new Eve, the mother of the new humanity in whom God made a new beginning.

These last two witneses, Justin and Irenaeus, in combination with the *Protevangelium of James*, accelerated the growth of Marian symbolism by the end of the second century. The Mary-Eve parallelism continued in the writings of the Syrian poet Ephrem (d. 373), the Cappodocian Gregory of Nyssa (d. 394), and the Latin Father, Ambrose (d. 397).

The Marian theme with which the second century literature was mainly concerned is the *virginal conception*. The majority of references are affirmative, but there is also a significant amount of dissent. There is, however, no second-century evidence of belief in Mary's remaining a virgin after the birth of Jesus (*post partum*), apart from the implications of the *Protevangelium*. The later development coincided with a newly positive assessment of virginity. The evidence for belief in Mary's virginity during the birth of Jesus (*in partu*), while slight, is more abundant than for belief in her perpetual virginity. Indeed, we do not know the exact origin of the belief in Mary's perpetual virginity. We do know that the idea was actively resisted in the early Church by such writers as Tertullian, lest the Church yield ground to the Docetists and the Gnostics. The tradition of the miraculous birth, on the other hand, clearly originated in the second century. But it created a paradoxical situation for the Church. On the one hand, the Church wanted to uphold the reality of Jesus' birth over against the Docetists and the Gnostics (both of whom denied the humanity of Christ), but the Church fostered at the same time the glorification of the Virgin Mary for ascetical reasons, which allowed an interpretation of the birth in terms of her inviolate virginity and thus introduced a new danger of docetic trends. And that very danger explains again Tertullian's resistance to the *in partu* and *post partum* notions.

Third Century to the Middle Ages

Mary's perpetual virginity, however, came to be almost universally accepted from the third century on. By now consecrated virgins had been established as a special state in the Church, and Mary was presented to them as their model. Both Latin and Greek

Fathers saw in her the model of all virtues, in fact. The outstanding exception was John Chrysostom (d. 407) who, as if in anticipation of modern biblical scholarship, acknowledged the negative flavor of Mark's estimation of Mary, and in his *Homilies on St. John's Gospel*, declared that "she did not cease to think little of (Jesus)...but herself she thought everywhere worthy of the first place, because she was his mother." At Cana, Mary told Jesus there was no more wine only because "she wanted to confer a favor on the others, and render herself more illustrious through her Son." Even at the annunciation she was at fault. The angel had to calm her down lest she kill herself in despair over the news that she was to have a son. Never before had a Christian preacher spoken in such derogatory terms of Mary, and never again for a thousand years would such be heard again.

It was the Nestorian controversy which indirectly promoted Mariology in the fifth century. The Nestorians had so emphasized the distinction of the two natures in Christ, and the integrity of the human nature in particular, that they concluded to two persons as well. The crisis broke out when Nestorius publicly denied to Mary the title "Mother of God" (*theotokos*). According to him, she was only the mother of Christ (*Christotokos*), to whom the Person of the Word of God had united himself. We have already summarized the events surrounding the Council of Ephesus (431) in chapter 13. The council ruled against the Nestorian position and in favor of the term *theotokos*. Mary is indeed the "Mother of God" for there is only one Person in Jesus Christ, not two, and that Person is the very Word of God. The definition, one must remember, was not a Marian definition, but a Christological one. It was intended to safeguard not the motherhood of Mary but the true unity of Christ in one divine Person.

The decision at Ephesus gave a major impetus to Marian devotion. Popular interest in the apocryphal writings increased, especially in the *Protevangelium of James*. It is the source of the belief in her virginity *in partu* (during childbirth), and of the story of her presentation in the Temple (which, in turn, is the source of the liturgical feast of the Presentation). St. Jerome (d. 420), the pioneer Scripture scholar, would have none of this "delirious nonsense." But it caught on nonetheless and was mentioned by the

Council of the Lateran (649) as it formulated its opposition to Monothelitism (one will in Christ).

Before the Council of Ephesus there had been one liturgical feast of Mary, the feast of the Purification, and that was celebrated only in certain parts of the Eastern Church. But after Ephesus the feasts began to multiply. From the beginning of the sixth century various churches celebrated Mary's bodily assumption into heaven. The belief originated not from biblical evidence nor even patristic testimony, but as the conclusion of a so-called argument from convenience or fittingness. It was "fitting" that Jesus should have rescued his mother from the corruption of the flesh, and so he "must have" taken her bodily into heaven. By the middle of the seventh century four separate Marian feasts were observed in Rome: the Annunciation, the Purification, the Assumption, and the Nativity of Mary. At the end of this century the feast of the Conception of Mary began in the East, but it remained unknown in the West until the eleventh century. Andrew of Crete (d. 740) wrote a hymn to Mary, calling her "alone wholly without stain." To Western ears this meant conceived without sin (the Immaculate Conception), but to Eastern ears, which had a different understanding of Original Sin, it meant only freedom from mortality and general human weakness.

Faith in Mary's power of intercession with God received a strong push from the growing belief in her assumption. Germanus (d. 733), patriarch of Constantinople, popularized the view that she had a maternal influence over God, that she could turn away God's anger and vengeance. She is our mediatrix with God. Thus, by the beginning of the eighth century, Mary's intercession and her importance for salvation had become well-established truths, especially in the East, both through popular literature and through preaching. The main contribution of the West at this time, as worked out by Ambrose and Augustine, was the close association of Mary with the Church. But compared with Eastern doctrine and devotion, the West's approach was sober and restrained. It was not yet in touch with the East's Theophilus legend which would so profoundly influence Mariology in the Middle Ages.

The Middle Ages

The idea that Mary appeases the wrath of God, the stern Judge, had been expressed by Germanus in the eighth century. It became one of the most popular themes of medieval Marian piety and devotion. Her power to save us was proclaimed even more dramatically by the story of Theophilus, which was translated into Latin by Paul the Deacon (d. ca. 799), a monk of Monte Cassino who had spent four years at the court of Charlemagne. Paul's version familiarized Western Christians with the story of the man who, like Dr. Faustus, gives his soul to the devil in order to get a desired post. Afterwards he repents and asks Mary to obtain forgiveness for his terrible sin. She does, and the devil is forced to yield control. Mary is seen in the West now, as in the East, as the redemptrix of captives, as refuge of sinners, as mediatrix between God and humankind. The legend was reproduced even by serious theologians and made the subject of a play in which Christ is portrayed as a menacing Judge whose heart is softened only by the pleas of his mother. She also became known as "Star of the Sea" who guides us safely into heaven's port, and as the "Mother of Mercy."

By now theology in the West had become increasingly divorced from the Bible. A rational, deductive kind of argumentation prevailed. One form, to which we referred above, was known as the argument from convenience. Its structure was simple: God (or Christ) *could* do something; it was *fitting* that he should; therefore, he *did* it. *Potuit, decuit, fecit.* This principle would play a large role in the development of medieval Mariology.

One of the most influential of all medieval theologians on the development of Mariology was *Bernard of Clairvaux* (d. 1153). His sermons "In Praise of the Virgin Mary" were as influential as the legend of Theophilus in confirming the medieval Christian in his or her childlike trust in the all-powerful help of Mary. He influenced not only popular devotion but theology as well. It was Bernard's view that Mary had an intimate role in the redemption. She was the aqueduct that leads the waters of divine grace down to earth. God willed us to have "everything through Mary," a saying that became a principle of Mariology, to be repeated again and again by popes, theologians, and spiritual writers down to Pope Pius XII in the middle of the twentieth century.

Bernard did not deny that Christ was the one true Mediator, but felt that men and women might be afraid of him because he is also their God and their Judge. Hence we need "a mediator with that Mediator, and there is no one more efficacious than Mary." If Bernard used the image of the aqueduct, others used the image of the neck. Mary is the neck which joins the Head with the rest of the Body of Christ, which is the Church.

Despite his intense devotion to Mary, Bernard was a strong opponent of the doctrine of the Immaculate Conception, and his whole Order followed his lead. Anselm of Canterbury also opposed the belief as well as the feast. When the feast began making headway in the West, Bernard addressed himself vehemently to the issue. He called the belief a "superstition." It was enough, he insisted, that Mary was sanctified in the womb and remained sinless throughout her life. The doctrine was opposed, because of Bernard and Peter Lombard's *Sentences*, until the beginning of the fourteenth century, at which time two English Franciscans opened a wedge in the opposition: William of Ware (d. early 1300s) and Duns Scotus (d. 1308).

William insisted that he would rather err in giving the Blessed Virgin too much than too little. To that end he employed the medieval formula: *potuit, decuit, fecit.* He also repeated the legend current in England that St. Bernard appeared to a lay brother soon after death in a radiant white garment, on which there was one small stain: his error in the matter of the Immaculate Conception. Scotus' argument was more sophisticated. Christ, he said, was primarily a Redeemer. He came to redeem us not only from actual sin, but from Original Sin. As our most perfect Redeemer, it is to be expected that he would have exercised his power to overcome even Original Sin at least once; and so it was, in the case of his mother. Scotus' approach effectively silenced those who sought to protect the universality of the redemption, and who objected that the Immaculate Conception would leave Mary without any indebtedness to Christ. On the contrary, she owed him more than any other creature because he preserved her alone from sin. The chief opponents were the Dominicans, who followed the lead of their greatest doctor, Thomas Aquinas.

Thomas based his opposition to the Immaculate Conception on the grounds that it would detract from the universality of Christ's redemptive work. Mary was sanctified in the womb and, as such, was the greatest of all the saints of history. Furthermore, her dignity is in some sense infinite because the infinite God took flesh from her. On the other hand, Thomas confined her mediating role to the fact that she gave birth to Christ, the author of grace. He had nothing to say about her connection with the redemptive work on the cross. Bonaventure, contemporary and friend of Thomas, similarly opposed the doctrine, quoting from Bernard. But Bonaventure also ascribed to her some role in the redemptive act of the cross, when she consented to the sacrifice of her Son and paid the price of her compassion. This view led eventually to belief in Mary as Co-Redemptrix of the human race, even though Bonaventure himself insisted on the uniqueness of Christ's redemptive act. One of his sermons, which became widely popular, suggested that Christ reserved to himself the realm of justice while ceding to his mother the realm of mercy.

With this growing reliance on Mary's protection, devotional forms continued to proliferate. "The Little Office of Our Lady" was recommended for use by the laity. The "Hail Mary" became one of the basic prayers to be learned by all the faithful, along with the Lord's Prayer and the Apostles' Creed. Saturday was dedicated to Mary, as Sunday was to Christ. Marian antiphons were composed between the eleventh and twelfth centuries: *Alma Redemptoris Mater* ("Sweet Mother of the Redeemer"), *Ave Regina Caelorum* ("Hail, Queen of Heaven"), *Regina Caeli* ("Queen of Heaven"), and *Salve Regina* ("Hail, [Holy] Queen"). Marian litanies also originated at this time, one of which (the Litany of Loreto) had as many as seventy-three invocations. By the early twelfth century the rosary was in general use. It began as a substitute for the Psalter (a book of one hundred and fifty psalms). The Hail Marys were divided into three groups of fifty and were called *rosarium* after Mary's title *"rosa mystica"* ("mystical rose"). They were eventually counted on beads which had come into use about this time for counting the "Our Fathers" given as a penance. The beginnings of the *Angelus* also appeared: the recitation of Hail Marys and prayers to Mary three times a day, at the ringing of the Angelus bells. The devotion became especially popular when the danger of Turkish invasion in the latter part of the fifteenth century led people to have recourse to the protection of the Blessed Mother.

Marian visions and special revelations, although reported from the earliest centuries, now increased and became more elaborate. St. Bridget of Sweden (d. 1373) claimed that Mary herself confirmed the doctrine of the Immaculate Conception in a private apparition to her. Images of Mary were thought to have miraculous powers, and in the fourteenth century the Holy House of Loreto was believed to have been transported through the air from Nazareth. It became one of the most popular places of pilgrimage. The *Divine Comedy* of Dante Alighieri (d. 1321) sums up the Mariology of the Middle Ages by depicting her as having influence throughout the entire universe: earth, purgatory, heaven, and even hell.

The Reformation to the Mid-Nineteenth Century

All of the great Reformers were brought up as Catholics and shared some measure of contemporary Catholic spirituality—especially Luther, who pointed to Mary as an example of faith and of the goodness of God. But we should ask neither her nor any of the saints for anything. Everything comes from the hand of God alone. The others, Calvin and Zwingli in particular, retained even less of contemporary Catholic spirituality, but they, too, attested to the purity of Mary. They objected, however, to the tendency to ascribe qualities to her which apply only to God—e.g., "our life, our sweetness, and our hope." At first, some of the Marian feasts were retained by the Protestants, but in due course they disappeared from their liturgical calendars.

Defense of Marian devotion and of her important role in our redemption was mounted by the Council of Trent and by various Counter-Reformation theologians: Peter Canisius (d. 1597), Francis Suarez (d. 1617), Robert Bellarmine (d. 1621).

Marian spirituality took another turn with the appearance of the French School: Cardinal de Bérulle (d. 1629), Jean-Jacques Olier (d. 1657), Jean Eudes (d. 1680), and Louis Grignion de Monfort (d. 1716). The last figure had the most enduring influence, having initiated the so-called "true devotion" to the Blessed Virgin, requiring absolute surrender to Mary as mystics had surrendered themselves to Christ. This, he argued, was the only effective way to Christ. If we presented ourselves directly to him, he would see our self-love, but to present ourselves through Mary is to get by his weak side.

With the rise of rationalism in the eighteenth century, Catholic theology assumed a more skeptical posture—e.g., in the works of Cardinal Lambertini, the future Pope Benedict XIV (d. 1758), who laid down rules for the treatment of miracles and mystical phenomena. Benedict protected L.A. Muratori (d. 1750), who had written a treatise on *Moderation in Matters of Religion*, in which he opposed the so-called "bloody vow" to defend the doctrine of the Immaculate Conception even to the shedding of blood. Muratori also attacked other exaggerations of Marian piety—e.g., that Mary could give orders in heaven. In the second half of the eighteenth century, under the impact of the Enlightenment, mild skepticism turned to strong opposition, and the liturgy was stripped of most Marian feasts. Theologians were no longer interested in Mariology, and popular devotions were confined now to Italy, Spain, and a few other places untouched by the general European currents of thought.

In Italy Marian devotion was kept alive through the work of the Redemptorists, and especially of St. Alphonsus Liguori (d. 1787), whose book *The Glories of Mary* defended two beliefs: the Immaculate Conception and Mary's universal mediation of grace. He repeated the medieval idea that Christ is the king of justice, while Mary is the mother of mercy. She alone knows how to appease an angry God by her prayers. Alphonsus supported his teaching by a large number of quotations from medieval authors, including the revelations of St. Bridget. He also reproduced, without critical comment, a wealth of legends and miracles. His book was warmly received in southern Europe and in France, and it remained popular throughout the nineteenth century.

From the Dogma of the Immaculate Conception (1854) to the Dogma of the Assumption (1950)

The dogma of the Immaculate Conception holds that Mary, the Mother of Jesus, was free from Original Sin from the very moment of her conception. The Immaculate Conception of Mary is often confused with the virginal conception of Jesus. The former was described as a "pious doctrine" by the Council of Basle in its thirty-sixth session (1439), but by that time the council was no longer in communion with the pope and, therefore, its decrees were not regarded as binding. Ten years later, however, all members of the University of Paris were required to take an oath to defend it, and other universities followed suit. In 1476 the feast of the Immaculate Conception was approved by Pope Sixtus IV (d. 1484), and the Council of Trent in the next century explicitly excluded Mary from its decree on the universality of Original Sin (*Decree on Original Sin*, Session V, 1546). In 1661 Pope Alexander VII (d. 1667) forbade any attacks on the doctrine, so that even the Dominicans, who had originally opposed it, began to change sides, taking pains to establish that perhaps St. Thomas had not really been opposed to it in the first place.

Interest in the doctrine waned until early in the nineteenth century when on December 17, 1830, St. Catherine Labouré (d. 1876) claimed to have had a vision of the Immaculate Conception, standing on a globe, rays of light emanating from her hands spread out towards the earth. The vision was surrounded by an oval frame on which appeared the words: "O Mary, conceived without sin, pray for us who have recourse to thee." A voice commanded Catherine to have a medal struck depicting the vision. The medal was named "miraculous" because miracles were attributed to it, and it stimulated renewed interest in the doctrine and in demands for its definition.

Pope Gregory XVI (d. 1846) did not accede to these demands, in deference to objections of liberal Catholics in Europe, especially in Germany, France, and England. The situation changed with the succession of Pope Pius IX (d. 1878) to the chair of Peter. He immediately initiated proceedings leading to a definition.

There was a consultation with some six hundred and three bishops, fifty-six of whom, including the archbishop of Paris, opposed the definition. In a papal bull of December 8, 1854, entitled *Ineffabilis Deus* ("Ineffable God"), Pius IX solemnly decreed that "the most Blessed Virgin Mary was, from the first moment of her conception, by the singular grace and privilege of almighty God and in view of the merits of Christ Jesus the Savior of the human race, preserved immune from all stain of original sin, [that this] is revealed by God and, therefore, firmly and constantly to be believed by all the faithful." Thus, the dogma followed the line taken by Duns Scotus, overcoming the difficulty posed by Thomas Aquinas that the Immaculate Conception would infringe upon the universality of Christ's redemptive work.

The dogma was positively received by most Catholics, but it created a storm of protest from Protestants and Orthodox alike. Protestants rejected the view that Mary was unlike the rest of the human race, and the Orthodox dissented from the dogma's underlying notion of Original Sin. For the Orthodox, sin is human infirmity with which every person is afflicted.

The appearance to Catherine Labouré was only one of many attributed to Mary. In 1846 she was reported to have been seen by a young boy and a young girl at La Salette in the French Alps. She appeared sitting on a stone, her face in her hands, weeping over the sins of desecration of Sunday and of blasphemy. After much controversy the apparition was approved, a shrine was erected in 1852, and a missionary congregation, the Missionaries of La Salette, was founded. In 1858 another well-known series of appearances occurred near Lourdes, in France, to Bernadette Soubirous, a simple girl of fourteen. She was ordered by the Blessed Mother to drink from a previously invisible fountain which sprang up as Bernadette scratched the ground. After much consternation and debate, officials asked Bernadette to seek the lady's name. "I am the Immaculate Conception" was the reply. An increasing number of pilgrims came to the site, which was officially recognized in 1862. By the turn of the century a large church had been built and the place became, and remains, a center of devotional interest, with many physical cures attributed to the spring water.

Still another famous apparition was reported in Fatima, a small Portuguese town, in 1917. Again there were small children involved: a ten-year-old girl and two of her younger cousins, all tending sheep at the time. The apparition revealed herself as "the Lady of the Rosary" and urged everyone to pray for peace. A shrine was built and in 1931 permission was given for devotion to Our Lady of Fatima. Other major Marian shrines are located at Guadalupe in Mexico, Knock in Ireland, Czestochowa in Poland, and Montserrat in Spain.

Although various popes since Pius IX mentioned Mary in their official pronouncements, no pope did more to emphasize the importance of Marian devotion than Pope Pius XII (d. 1958), who was particularly devoted to Our Lady of Fatima. He consecrated the entire world to the Immaculate Heart of Mary in 1942, and on the occasion spoke in Portuguese as if to underline the connection between this act of consecration and the events at Fatima. His major contribution, however, was the definition of yet another Marian dogma, that of the bodily assumption of Mary into heaven. It was her "crowning glory . . . to be preserved from the corruption of the tomb," he wrote in his Apostolic Constitution *Munificentissimus Deus* (1950), "and, like her Son before her, to conquer death and to be raised body and soul to the glory of heaven, to shine refulgent as Queen at the right hand of her Son, the immortal King of ages."

There were, of course, many in the Catholic Church who questioned the opportuneness of such a definition. It seemed to them unnecessarily provocative at a time when ecumenical relations among the churches were just gaining strength. On the other hand, it was argued that the human race had just witnessed two world wars and the horrors of concentration camps, and that this was an appropriate moment to reaffirm the dignity of the human body and to rekindle faith in the resurrection of the body. Many, therefore, welcomed the definition.

The terms of the definition, however, are open to legitimate difference of interpretation. It is not clear whether the pope intended to teach that Mary died at all, and nothing is said about the manner or time of her assumption. Protestant reaction was negative, but this time the Orthodox were more positive, since this was a doctrine they also had held for centuries.

Three years later Pope Pius XII declared a Marian year (December 8, 1953—December 8, 1954) in honor of the centenary of the dogma of the Immaculate Conception. He urged frequent sermons on Mary and encouraged visits to her shrines, especially Lourdes. Marian congresses were held, and many books and articles were published. At the end of the year the pope established yet another Marian feast, her Queenship, on May 31, at which time the consecration of the world to the Immaculate Heart of Mary was to be renewed.

Vatican II

An entire chapter (chapter 8) is devoted to "The Role of the Blessed Virgin Mary, Mother of God, in the Mystery of Christ and the Church" in the Second Vatican Council's *Dogmatic Constitution on the Church*. The Preface notes that Mary, who is "acknowledged and honored as being truly the Mother of God and Mother of the Redeemer" and who "surpasses all other creatures," at the same time "belongs to the offspring of Adam [and] is one with all human beings in their need for salvation" (n. 53). She is also the Mother of the Church since, according to St. Augustine, "she cooperated out of love so that there might be born in the Church the faithful, who are members of Christ their Head." Accordingly, she is "a preeminent and altogether singular member of the Church, and . . . the Church's model and excellent exemplar, in faith and charity. Taught by the Holy Spirit, the Catholic Church honors her with filial affection and piety as a most beloved mother" (n. 53). The council comes very close here to calling Mary "Mother of the Church," but it was left to Pope Paul VI to do so explicitly in his closing speech at the end of the third session, November 21, 1964.

The rest of the eighth chapter is divided into three parts: Mary's role in the economy of salvation, her relationship with the Church, and Marian devotions. Her cooperation in the work of salvation is foreshadowed in the Old Testament (n. 55) and is rooted fundamentally in her assent to become the Mother of God

(n. 56). Throughout this section, however, the council consistently follows the most benign interpretation of her role in Jesus' ministry. Thus, the harshness of Mark 3:31-35 is passed over, and the document simply reads: "He declared blessed (cf. Mark 3:35 and parallels; Luke 11:27-28) those who heard and kept the Word of God, as she was faithfully doing (cf. Luke 2:19,51)" (n. 57).

Mary's role continues in the life of the Church, but without any obscuring or diminution of the "unique mediation of Christ" (n. 60). None of the titles given to her, e.g., Advocate, Auxiliatrix, Adjutrix, Mediatrix, adds to, nor subtracts from, "the dignity and efficacy of Christ the one Mediator" (n. 62). On the other hand, the unique mediation of Christ "does not exclude but rather gives rise among creatures to manifold cooperation which is but a sharing in this unique source. The Church does not hesitate to profess this subordinate role of Mary" (n. 62).

With St. Ambrose the council affirms that Mary is a model of the Church "in the matter of faith, charity, and perfect union with Christ" (n. 63). The Church, too, acts as a mother by accepting God's word in faith and by bringing forth children by Baptism to a new and everlasting life. The Church is also a virgin "who keeps whole and pure the fidelity she has pledged to her Spouse" (n. 64). Although Mary has already reached perfection, the Church continues on pilgrimage (n. 65).

From the most ancient times Mary has been revered as the "God-bearer" (*Deipara*), and this is the foundation of the special devotion, or cult, that is directed toward her. But this cult differs "essentially" from the cult of adoration which is offered to the incarnate Word, as well as to the Father and the Holy Spirit. Thus, although the Church has endorsed many forms of Marian piety, the Church always insisted that they be "within the limits of sound and orthodox doctrine. These forms have varied according to the circumstances of time and place and have reflected the diversity of native characteristics and temperament among the faithful" (n. 66). Furthermore, theologians and preachers should "carefully and equally avoid the falsity of exaggeration on the one hand, and the excess of narrow-mindedness on the other....Let them painstakingly guard against any word or deed which could lead separated brethren or anyone else into error regarding the true doctrine of the Church. Let the faithful remember moreover that true devotion consists neither in fruitless and passing emotion, nor in a certain vain credulity" (n. 67).

How explain the discrepancy between the Marian maximalism of nineteenth- and twentieth-century devotional life and papal teachings, on the one hand, and the relatively restrained and balanced Mariology of the Second Vatican Council on the other? The answer is the same here as in chapter 19. Before Vatican II there was more than a single theological current, i.e., the "approved theology" of the manuals. While the "approved authors" continued to speak of the Church as a hierarchical society organized according to a papal-monarchical norm, other theologians, such as Congar, de Lubac, and Rahner, spoke of the Church as the People of God and the sacrament of Christ. It was this latter current that entered the conciliar mainstream, not the textbook theology.

The same was the case with Mariology. The "approved authors," assiduously and not a little uncritically, had followed the lead given by Popes Pius IX and Pius XII; other theologians, however, reworked the soil of history, transcended the culturally conditioned devotionalism of the medieval and post-medieval periods, and returned to the sources, i.e., the Bible and especially the Fathers of the Church.

This "return to the sources" began even in the nineteenth century with Cardinal John Henry Newman (d. 1890) and the German theologian Matthias Scheeben (d. 1888), both of whom captured the patristic spirit and made symbolism of the divine motherhood and of Eve the focal points of their reflections. Newman, however, was the more restrained of the two, rejecting suggestions that Mary somehow shares in the redemptive work of the cross or is the sole refuge of sinners. Scheeben, on the other hand, spoke of Mary as being also the bride of Christ, a mediatrix, a co-offerer of the sacrifice of the cross, and the spiritual mother of humankind. By the 1950s and early 1960s, just before the opening of Vatican II, other influential Catholic theologians had turned their attention to Mary, placing the Marian doctrines in the wider context of the mystery of salvation in Christ and the mystery of the

Church, just as the council would do: René Laurentin, Otto Sem-melroth, Karl Rahner, Edward Schillebeeckx, and Yves Congar. This was true also of Cardinal Leo-Jozef Suenens, one of the most important figures at Vatican II (see his *Mary the Mother of God*, 1959).

THE MARIAN DOGMAS
The Immaculate Conception

How one finally understands and explains the dogma of the Immaculate Conception will depend in very large measure on how one understands and explains the doctrine of Original Sin (see chapter 5). If Original Sin means being conceived and born with a "black spot" on the soul, or being conceived and born without grace, then the dogma of the Immaculate Conception means that Mary alone was born in the state of grace. That interpretation assumes, in turn, that "sanctifying grace" is not given for the first time until Baptism or until an unbaptized human being has an opportunity to make a free act of obedience to the will of God (under the impact, or course, of "actual grace").

If, on the other hand, one understands Original Sin as the *sinful condition* in which every human being is born, then we have to propose a different explanation for the Immaculate Conception. It is not that Mary alone was conceived and born in grace, but that, in view of her role in the redemption, God bestowed upon her an unsurpassable degree of grace from the beginning. This is not to be understood in any quantitative sense. Grace is divine life. To be in the "state of grace" is to be in union with God: God in us, and we in God. By reason of Mary's unique call to be the Mother of the incarnate Word, she was from the very beginning of her existence united with God in the most intimate of ways. And this union was, in turn, grounded in the yet-to-be-accomplished redemptive work of the Son she was to bear.

This does not mean that Mary was exempt also from the "consequences" of Original Sin: sickness, suffering, even death. These, too, are part of the human condition, and they are part of the mystery of sin. We do not know why we are subject to physical deterioration; we only know *that* we are. Paul attributed this condition to sin, just as those before him in the Old Testament consistently linked sin and human suffering. But we no longer accept that connection, nor are we required to do so by the doctrine of the Church. Suffering is a part of the human condition, but we do not know why. Sin is also part of the human condition, and we do not know ultimately why either. We *do* know that we freely sin in individual instances, and that this is a reflection of the sinful situation in which we are all born.

The dogma of the Immaculate Conception teaches that Mary was exempt in a unique and exceptional way from the normal and the usual impact of sin, or, more positively, that she was given a greater degree of grace (i.e., God was more intensely present to her than to others) in view of her role as the "God-bearer." So profound is her union with God in grace, in anticipation of her maternal function and in virtue of the redemptive grace of Christ, that she alone remains faithful to God's will throughout her entire life. *She is truly redeemed, but in an exceptional and unique manner.* The Immaculate Conception shows that God can be, and is, utterly gracious toward us, not by reason of our merits but by reason of divine love and mercy.

The Assumption

The dogma of the Assumption complements the dogma of the Immaculate Conception in the same way that the resurrection of Christ complements his crucifixion and life of sacrificial service to others. Just as the Immaculate Conception was not merely a personal privilege conferred upon Mary but a reality bestowed in view of her role in the economy of salvation, so the Assumption is not merely a personal privilege unrelated to the wider mission of her life. Her union with God in Christ was unique from the beginning. Her call to final union with God in Christ, in the totality of her human existence (body and soul), was also unique in the end. The dogma of the Assumption asserts something about human existence in asserting something about Mary: that human existence is bodily existence, and that we are destined for glory not only in the realm of the spiritual but in the realm of the material as well.

In the midst of the anguish and distress of this generation, the Church, so readily accused of being political
and attached to earthly power, of liking to install herself
far too positively in this world, of being insufficiently
eschatological, raises her head and by proclaiming this
doctrine of the faith, gazes towards the only hope in
which she really trusts, the future of God, who is so far
advanced with his Kingdom, that he has already begun
to be wholly present. The Church looks on high and
greets in Mary her own type and model, her own future
in the resurrection of the body.

(Karl Rahner, *Mary Mother of the Lord*, pp. 91-92.)

Binding Force

In defining the dogma of the Immaculate Conception, Pope Pius
IX warned all those who might be tempted to reject his teaching:
"If, therefore, any persons shall dare to think—which God forbid—otherwise than has been defined by us, let them clearly know
that they stand condemned by their own judgment, that they have
made shipwreck of their faith and fallen from the unity of the
Church." Pope Pius XII issued a similarly severe warning in
connection with the definition of the dogma of the Assumption:
"Wherefore, if anyone—which God forbid—should willfully dare
to deny or call in doubt what has been defined by us, let him know
that he certainly has abandoned the divine and catholic faith."

What is to be said, finally, of the binding force of these
dogmas of faith? (1) Is it possible to deny them and at the same time
remain in the Church? (2) Is it possible to deny them and remain in
the *Catholic* Church?

Concerning the first, Catholics do not hold that membership
in Christ's Church is restricted to persons who formally and
explicitly accept these two Marian dogmas. There is "an order or
'hierarchy' of truths, since they vary in their relationship to the
foundation of the Christian faith" (*Decree on Ecumenism*, n. 11).
No one could reasonably hold that the dogmas of the Immaculate
Conception and the Assumption are so central to Christian faith
that the faith itself would disintegrate without either or both.

Such would be the case, on the other hand, if one were to deny the divinity of Jesus Christ or the redemptive value of his life, death, and resurrection.

Furthermore, the Second Vatican Council permitted limited eucharistic sharing between Catholics and Orthodox, even though the Orthodox do not accept both of these dogmas (*Decree on Eastern Catholic Churches*, nn. 26-29). The presumption must be that, in spite of differences on these two dogmas, the unity of Christian faith that *is* present between Catholics and Orthodox is sufficient for eucharistic sharing. The same kind of reasoning could conceivably be extended to the cases of other Christian communities, such as the Anglicans and the Lutherans.

Concerning the second question (Is membership in the *Catholic* Church contingent upon acceptance of these dogmas?), the problem arises because each of these two dogmatic definitions is accompanied by an anathema or its equivalent. According to canon law, an anathema involves an excommunication (Code of Canon Law, c. 2257, #2), but that consequence follows only when the rejection of the dogma is culpable, obstinate, and externally manifested.

What of those Catholics who wish to belong to the Catholic Church, who confess the Lordship of Jesus, who assemble for the Eucharist in faith, who accept the Word of God, and who bear witness to the Gospel in their love of and service to their neighbor? Should the questioning or even denial of these dogmas be regarded today as presumptive evidence of a lapse from Christian faith, or even from Catholic faith? It could be that in their questioning or denial of these dogmas, some Catholics are reacting not against the Word of God to which these dogmas propose to bear witness, but against the inadequacy, incompleteness, limited expressive power, and historically-conditioned character of these definitions. If such Catholics are otherwise faithful to their Catholic heritage and to the practice of their Catholic faith, would it not be possible to presume the opposite—namely, that they are sincere in their questioning and even denial of these dogmas (i.e., not culpable or obstinate) and that their rejection implies no correlative rejection of the major truths of faith with which these dogmas are related, e.g., the redemptive significance of Christ's life, death, and resurrection; our hope in the resurrection of the body; the power of God's grace to overcome completely the impact of sin?

It is possible, of course, that a Catholic's rejection of either or both of these Marian dogmas would be a sign that one has separated himself or herself from the Catholic tradition and faith, and therefore from communion with the Catholic Church, just as Popes Pius IX and Pius XII warned. A person might, for example, reject these definitions precisely because they are papal actions. That person might believe that the Petrine office has no necessary place in the life and mission of the Church for the benefit of the Church universal. A person might also reject any place for Mary in the Christian dispensation and the Catholic tradition. Such views would effectively disengage one from the Catholic tradition and the community which embodies it. This is not to say, on the other hand, that a faithful and committed Catholic could not question the *process* by which these dogmas were formulated.

MARIAN DEVOTIONS: THEOLOGICAL CRITERIA

There are *two extremes* to be avoided in one's attitude toward devotion to Mary. *First*, there is a temptation to so exaggerate the *divine* role in salvation that the value and importance of *human cooperation* is lost (see the discussion of nature and grace in chapter 5). In this view, human cooperation plays no role at all in our salvation. Therefore, no fellow creature, Mary included, is ever worthy of veneration, because such attention inevitably detracts from the glory owed to God alone and to Jesus Christ in whom and through whom God acted on our behalf for the forgiveness of sins. The consequence of this first extreme is Marian *minimalism*, or "mariophobia."

The *second* temptation is to exaggerate the *human* role in salvation at the expense of the divine and correspondingly to deemphasize the effectiveness of the *mediating work of Christ*, who is perceived as more divine than human. And if he is more divine than human, he is not so much our bridge to God as he is the God from whom we have been alienated by sin. We need access, therefore, not only to the Father but the Son as well. According to this view, we need other ways of reaching God, and these ways must be adapted to our own limited human condition. Consequently, we turn to our fellow human beings who have already won the crown of glory and who have obviously "done something right" in the sight of God. But Mary alone, among the entire "class" assembled by God, achieved a "straight-A record" and earned the enthusiastic favor of her divine Master. It is through the saints, but especially through Mary, the greatest of saints, that we can hope to reach Christ and ultimately reach the Father of our salvation. There is no limit to the help she can give us, nor is there any limit to the veneration we can show her in virtue of her standing before God. The consequence of this second extreme is Marian *maximalism*, or "mariocentricism."

Marian minimalism in effect denies (or at least narrowly applies) the principle of secondary or *instrumental causality*, i.e., that God works through finite agents to achieve infinite ends. It also denies (or narrowly applies) the principle of *sacramentality*, i.e., that God is present to us, is disclosed, and works on our behalf in and through visible, material realities: persons, events, nature, objects, the cosmos. (It is not always clear if the Marian minimalist understands that the humanity of Jesus Christ is also an instrumental cause and sacrament of salvation.) And it denies, finally, that the Church is a *communion of saints*, i.e., that our relationship with God and with Christ is both vertical and horizontal, and that our relationship is always *mediated*. "God vividly manifests to humankind his presence and his face. He speaks to us in them, and gives us a sign of his Kingdom, to which we are powerfully drawn, surrounded as we are by so many witnesses (cf. Hebrews 12:1), and having such an argument for the truth of the gospel" (*Dogmatic Constitution on the Church*, n. 50). Nor is it only by reason of the example the saints give us that we cherish their memory and render them our devotion. "We do so still more in order that the union of the whole Church may be strengthened.... For just as Christian communion among wayfarers brings us closer to Christ, so our companionship with the saints joins us to Christ.... For by its very nature every genuine testimony of love which we show to those in heaven tends toward and terminates in Christ, who is the 'crown of all saints' " (n. 50). According to the council, that union of all faithful Christians, living and dead, is expressed and celebrated in a particularly effective manner in the sacred liturgy and especially in the Eucharist.

Marian maximalism in effect exaggerates the secondary or *instrumental causality* of Mary and the other saints and demeans the instrumental causality of the humanity of Christ. It also misunderstands the *sacramental principle.* Sacramentality means that God works *in* and *through* some visible, material reality. It is always the inner transforming presence of God that ultimately counts, and not the sign and instrument of that presence. Therefore, it is not because Mary and the saints have the power of influence with God that they are objects of veneration and devotion. Rather it is because the grace of God has triumphed *in them.* They have been transformed by, and have become effective images of, Christ (*Dogmatic Constitution on the Church,* n. 50). It is Christ's, not Mary's, achievement that we celebrate. Finally, Marian maximalism misunderstands the nature of the *communion of saints.* The Church is not just an institution of salvation, with Mary and the saints as "successful graduates" who have some measure of influence with "the administration." It is not comparable to a filling station, where automobiles replenish their supply of fuel. The Church is the People of God, the Body of Christ, and the Temple of the Holy Spirit. It is, first and foremost, a *community (communio, koinonia)*, but not just any community. It is a community of those who have been transformed by Christ and the Holy Spirit and who have explicitly and thankfully acknowledged the source of that transformation. Since transformation is a process, to be completed when the Kingdom of God is fully realized at the end of history, our bond in Christ and the Spirit is not broken by death. Mary is the preeminent member of this communion of saints. Our link with her is an expression of our link with the whole Church. It is a bond, however, not just of advocates and supplicants, but of brothers and sisters in the Lord, the very Body of Christ on the way to achieving "the fullness of God" (Ephesians 3:19).

Between these two extremes of Marian minimalism and Marian maximalism there is wide spectrum of legitimate devotional options. One should be careful not to categorize pejoratively those forms of spirituality with which one is not personally comfortable or from which one feels culturally alienated. The following *theological criteria* might be helpful in evaluating various expressions of Marian devotion:

1.   Devotion to Mary, and to all of the saints, is ultimately devotion to Christ, whose grace has triumphed in Mary and the saints.

2.   Jesus Christ in his humanity and divinity alike is the one Mediator between God and humankind. In him we are forgiven our sins, for he is full of mercy and compassion toward us.

3.   On the other hand, just as God worked through the instrumentality of Jesus' humanity for our salvation, so divine grace is symbolized and mediated through other visible, material, bodily realities, including those fellow creatures who have shown themselves striking examples of the transforming power of this grace.

4.   Since God saves us not just as individuals but as members of a people, we are joined one with another in a community of saints, i.e., of "holy ones" sharing in the holiness (the life) of God. "Be holy, for I, the Lord, your God, am holy" (Leviticus 19:2).

5.   Mary is, by reason of her faith and obedience to the Word of God, a model of the Church and is its preeminent member. She is a disciple *par excellence*.

6.   Insofar as Mary is truly the mother of Jesus Christ, she can be called the "God-bearer." Again, she is a model for the Church in that the Church, too, is a "reality imbued with the hidden presence of God" (Pope Paul VI). Just as the hidden presence of God is the basis of all that we believe about the Church in faith, so it is also the basis of all that we believe about Mary in faith.

7.   And yet just as the Church is not itself the Kingdom of God, even though the Church can be called "the initial budding forth" of the Kingdom (*Dogmatic Constitution on the Church*, n. 5), so Mary is not herself the mediator or the redeemer, even though she is the mother of Jesus and bears the incarnate Word within her.

8.   On the contrary, Mary is, before all else, one of the redeemed. Exemption from Original Sin does not mean that she

was herself in no need of the redemptive work of Christ. She was full of grace from the beginning precisely because of the redemptive work of Christ on her behalf.

9. It is less important *that* one affirms or denies some Marian belief than *why* one affirms it or denies it. Thus, on a relative scale at least, one is actually more "orthodox" in *denying* the Immaculate Conception because it might detract from the universality of the redemption (as Thomas Aquinas feared) than in affirming the Immaculate Conception on the grounds that Mary's closeness to God made the redemptive work of Christ unnecessary in her own unique case.

10. Apparitions, visions, and other unusual occurrences attributed directly or indirectly to Mary may or may not be believed. None of them can ever be regarded as essential to Christian faith, whether they are approved by the official Church or not. If these phenomena do have any final authority, they are authoritative only for those who directly and immediately experience them. No one but the recipient(s) can be bound in conscience by whatever is communicated.

11. In any case, the "contents" (messages, directives, etc.) of such events can never be placed on par with the Gospel itself, neither in terms of their authority nor in terms of the attention they elicit and/or demand. Those "contents," in turn, must always be measured against the totality of the Christian faith and must not contradict or contravene any essential component of that faith.

THE CHURCH AND MARY

"Neither the Gospel nor past Christian tradition have been able to separate Mary and the Church," the Protestant monk and theologian of Taizé, Max Thurian, has written. "To speak of Mary is to speak of the Church. The two are united in one fundamental vocation—maternity"(*Mary, Mother of the Lord, Figure of the Church,* p. 9).

There is, of course, more to the relationship between Mary and the Church than maternity, although that is certainly foundational. The Church is a mother in several senses. It brings forth new creatures in Christ out of the womb of the baptismal font. It nourishes the Christian family at the table of the Eucharist. It is the source of encouragement, of forgiveness, of order, of healing, of love. Each of these maternal activites is linked with one or another of the Church's seven sacraments.

Mary, too, is the mother of all Christians insofar as she is first of all the mother of Jesus Christ. She gives birth to Jesus and so makes it possible for Jesus to give birth to us anew in the Holy Spirit. As a model, or type, or figure, or image of the Church, Mary is preeminently a person of faith, of hope, of love, of obedience to the Word of God.

She is conceived without sin and in the fullness of grace, as the Church was. She is a faithful and undefiled virgin, as the Church is called to be. She is redeemed by Christ, as the Church is. She is the sign of God's presence among us, as the Church is. She is transformed and renewed by the presence of God within her, as the Church is. She shared fully in the resurrection of Christ, body and soul, as the Church is destined to share in it. And she intercedes for us before the throne of God, as the Church does.

Devotion to Mary is a characteristically Catholic phenomenon in that it expresses three fundamental principles of Catholic theology and practice: the principle of *mediation*, the principle of *sacramentality*, and the principle of *communion*.

Just as we say that the world is "mediated by meaning" (Bernard J. F. Lonergan), so the universe of grace is a mediated reality: mediated principally by Christ, and secondarily by the Church and other signs and instruments of salvation beyond the the Church. The Catholic understands the role of Mary in salvation and accepts it because the Catholic already understands and accepts the principle of mediation as applied in the incarnation and in the life and mission of the Church (a point made so effectively by Yves Congar in his *Christ, Our Lady, and the Church*, 1957).

The Catholic also understands that the invisible, spiritual God is present and available to us through the visible and the material, and that these, in turn, are made holy by reason of that divine presence. The Catholic therefore, readily engages in the veneration of Mary, not because Mary is confused with some ancient goddess or supercreature or rival of the Lord himself, but because Mary is herself a symbol or image of God. It is the God who is present within her and who fills her whole being that the Catholic grasps in the act of venerating yet another "sacrament" of the divine.

Finally, the Catholic perceives the Church as itself a communion of saints in its visible as well as its invisible dimensions. It is an institutionalized, structured reality in which and through which the grace of the Holy Spirit is disclosed, celebrated, and released for the renewal and reconciliation of the whole world. Our relationship with God and with Christ is not only bilateral but multilateral, which is to say communal. The Church *as* Church enters directly into that saving relationship with God and with Christ. It is not simply the place where one hears the Word of God and testifies to his or her faith in the Word. The Church is itself the very Body of Christ. To be *in* the church is to be *in* Christ and one *with* Christ. It is to share his "meaning" of reality and the "meanings" of those others who belong to his Body. So, too, devotion to Mary is consequent upon the fact that we are united with her, as with one another, in and with Christ. She is the preeminent member of the community of saints by reason of her unique relationship with Christ, but she is a member nonetheless, and the most exalted one at that. Our unity with her is an expression of our unity in and with Christ.

"In Mary," Otto Semmelroth writes, "the Church affirms her own holy, co-redemptive and redeemed essence. . . . Thus, the veneration of Mary is the Church's testimony to herself. . . . (to her) own essence and to her task of imparting salvation" (*Mary, Archetype of the Church*, p. 174).

CONCLUDING REFLECTIONS

It was noted at the beginning of this chapter that some theologians still prefer to locate the theology of Mary between the theology of the redemption and the theology of the Church. Without suggesting that such an arrangement is theologically erroneous, the plan we have followed in this book presents Mary less as a collaborator of Christ *above* the Church than as the preeminent member of the *redeemed* community itself. As such, she is not so much a source of grace and power as she is an image, a model, a figure, or a type of the Church and of Christian existence. She provides, therefore, an important bridge between ecclesiology, on the one side, and Christian existence (ethics and spirituality), on the other. And that is precisely how and why our discussion of Mariology fits in here.

SUMMARY

1.   *Mariology*, the theological study of the person and role of Mary, began in the Middle Ages as an appendix to Christology. By the end of the nineteenth century it had acquired a separate theological position immediately after the Incarnation and the Redemption and before the mystery of the Church. This book, however, follows the lead of the Second Vatican Council and places Mariology within the discussion of the Church. Mary is the type, model, mother, and preeminent member of the Church.

2.   There is relatively little about Mary in the *New Testament*, and what does appear is not unequivocally positive. *Mark's* portrait is remarkably negative: Mary does not understand Jesus' ministry and even tries to interfere with it (3:20-35). *Matthew* and *Luke* tone down the harshness of Mark, and Luke in particular presents her as the obedient handmaid of the Lord from the beginning (see the Infancy Narratives) and as the spokeswoman for the poor of Israel. *John* also reports that Mary's faith was still imperfect during Jesus' public ministry (the Cana story), but at the foot of the cross she is clearly included by her Son in the eschatological family.

3.   The New Testament says nothing about Mary's virginity *in partu* (i.e., nothing about a miraculous birth), nor does it say she was a virgin *post partum* (after the birth of Jesus). On the contrary, it speaks of brothers and sisters of Jesus. It is an open question, on the basis of the New Testament evidence alone, whether or not these references are to actual brothers and sisters or to cousins.

4.   *Second century* literature on Mary is thin. Among the *apocrypha* (non-canonical writings) the most important was the *Protevangelium of James*, for centuries the source of many legends about Mary and the life of the Holy Family. Among the *patristic writings* (most of which do not even mention Mary), the main sources are *Ignatius of Antioch*, *Justin*, and *Irenaeus*, who witness to the virginal conception of Jesus and

who first develop the Eve-Mary parallel which would influence Christian thought thereafter.

5.   Discussions of Mary's *perpetual virginity* were complicated by the fact that, on the one hand, the Gnostics and Docetists denied the humanity of Jesus, and, on the other, by the fact that virginity was being emphasized within the Church at this time for ascetical reasons, and Mary presented a persuasive model for Christian women. Mary's virginity *post partum* came to be almost universally accepted from the third century on. John Chrysostom was an outstanding exception.

6.   *Nestorianism*, with its insistence on the dual personality of Jesus, *indirectly* fostered Mariological interest by provoking the *Council of Ephesus* (431) into defining that Mary is truly the Mother of God (*theotokos*) and not only the mother of Christ. The definition was directly a Christological one, not Mariological.

7.   Following Ephesus, Marian devotion increased. The apocryphal literature became popular again. *Liturgical feasts* were multiplied: the Annunciation, the Purification, the Assumption, and the Nativity of Mary (by the mid-seventh century all four were being observed in Rome). The feast of the Conception of Mary had its origin in the East at the end of the seventh century but was unknown in the West until the eleventh century.

8.   From the eighth century on, faith in Mary's *intercessory power* received a strong push from growing belief in her assumption, especially in the East.

9.   As popular Eastern legends (e.g., the story of Theophilus, who "sells" his soul to the devil only to have it saved by Mary) were translated and circulated in the West, and as theology in the West became increasingly divorced from the Bible and the Fathers, Mariology took a turn toward some measure of exaggeration. The principle of fittingness or convenience became important: If God *could* do something and it seemed *fitting* that it should be done, then God *must have* done it (*potuit, decuit, fecit*).

10.   One of the most influential Mariologists was *Bernard of Clairvaux*, who stressed Mary's role in the channeling of saving grace ("everything through Mary"). He did not deny that Christ was the one Mediator, but pointed out that he is also our God and Judge. Mary provides the component of mercy.

11.   Two centuries later controversy developed on the *Immaculate Conception*. Aquinas and others argued that such a doctrine would contradict the universality of redemption; Scotus replied that Mary, too, was redeemed, but that she was alone preserved from Original Sin in view of

her relationship with Christ and as a sign of Christ's power over Original Sin as well as over actual sins.

12. As appreciation of Christ's co-humanity with us diminished, Mary's own mediating role was accentuated. Marian prayers, hymns, devotions, feasts, and reports of apparitions proliferated between the eleventh and fourteenth centuries.

13. The *Reformers* resisted the underlying assumptions of much of this Marian devotion. God alone is "our life, our sweetness, and our hope," they insisted. Over against the Protestants, the *Council of Trent* and various Counter-Reformation theologians defended Marian devotion and Mary's role in our redemption.

14. *Marian spirituality* continued to develop new forms in the seventeenth and eighteenth centuries, especially the French School ("True Devotion": absolute surrender to Mary in order to get by Christ's "weak" side). But the rise of *rationalism* and the coming of the *Enlightenment* tempered this spirituality, at least in northern Europe. Marian interest was kept alive where these intellectual movements had no impact—e.g., in the eighteenth century works of Alphonsus Ligouri, which incorporated many legends.

15. Concern for the doctrine of the *Immaculate Conception* was rejuvenated in 1830 with a reported apparition of Mary to Catherine Labouré. In 1854 Pope Pius IX solemnly defined the Immaculate Conception as a *dogma of faith*, endorsing the approach taken by Scotus against Thomas.

16. Other reported visions and apparitions (e.g., Lourdes, Fatima) along with various expressions of papal support for Marian devotions between 1854 and 1950 led to a second Marian definition, this time of the *Assumption*. A Marian year was declared in 1954.

17. But there were *other theological currents* in process between the mid-nineteenth and mid-twentieth centuries. *Cardinal Newman* and *Matthias Scheeben* restored the patristic emphases on the symbolism of the divine maternity and of Eve as focal points for Mariology. Modern theologians such as Otto Semmelroth, Yves Congar, Karl Rahner, placed the Marian doctrines in a wider historical and ecclesiological context.

18. This more restrained and more biblically and patristically grounded approach entered the mainstream of the *Second Vatican Council*, which emphasized Mary's role in the economy of salvation, her relationship with the Church, and the subordination of all Marian devotions to the unique mediation of Christ. The council also acknowledged that devotions are shaped by circumstances of time, place, temperament, and culture, and warned against exaggerations and excesses.

19.   Our understanding of the dogma of the *Immaculate Conception* depends on our understanding of *Original Sin.* If grace is *not* given to all from the beginning, then Mary's Immaculate Conception means that she alone possessed grace from the moment of her conception. If grace *is* given to all from the beginning, then her Immaculate Conception means that she received the fullest degree of it, i.e., that her union with God was as intimate as any creature's could be in virtue of her role as the mother of the Lord. It does not mean, on the other hand, that Mary was also exempted from the "consequences" of our sinful condition: sickness, suffering, and even death. *She is truly redeemed, but in an exceptional and unique manner.*

20.   The dogma of the *Assumption* complements the Immaculate Conception. The intimate union with God from the beginning of her existence is fulfilled at the end of her earthly life. The dogma attests to the fact our human existence is bodily existence, too, and that we are destined for glory in the totality of that existence.

21.   These two dogmas are not so central or essential to the integrity of Christian faith that one cannot be in the Body of Christ without accepting them. Indeed, Vatican II encouraged limited eucharistic sharing with the Orthodox in spite of differences on these two dogmas. The council also acknowledged that there is a hierarchy of truths.

22.   *Catholics who question or deny these dogmas* are not necessarily excluded from the Catholic Church. Such denial must be culpable, obstinate, and externally manifested. Those who do reject the dogmas may often be rejecting certain interpretations of them. Also, we must look at the whole orientation and pattern of a Catholic's life and thought. Is he or she also rejecting correlative doctrines (e.g., resurrection of the body, the redemptive significance of the life, death, and resurrection of Christ) or the very idea of the Petrine ministry, or any place at all for Mary in the Catholic tradition? On the other hand, is the person faithful to the Eucharist, the sacraments, the Word of God, and the call to love of neighbor?

23.   Two extremes are to be avoided in Marian devotion: a *minimalism* which withholds any and all veneration from Mary, and a *maximalism* which assumes there are practically no limits to such veneration.

24.   *Marian minimalism* denies (or narrowly applies) the principle of *instrumental causality,* i.e., that God works through finite, secondary causes, including even the humanity of Christ. Marian minimalism also denies (or narrowly applies) the principle of *sacramentality,* i.e., that God is really present in the instrumental cause and does not simply use the instrument without transforming it from within. Finally, Marian

minimalism denies that the Church is a *communion of saints*, i.e., that our relationship with God is always *mediated*, and mediated through the community of faith and holiness of which Mary is the preeminent member.

25.   *Marian maximalism* exaggerates the principle of *instrumental causality* in the case of Mary and deemphasizes it in the case of Christ. It also misunderstands the *sacramental* principle, i.e., that what the sign signifies is more important than the sign. Mary is important, therefore, not for herself but for the presence of God working in and through her. Finally, Marian maximalism misunderstands the nature of the *communion of saints*. Our bond with Mary and the saints is not simply one of supplicants to advocates. We are all brothers and sisters in the Lord on the way to the Kingdom of God.

26.   *Criteria* for evaluating Marian devotions include the following: (1) Is Christ at the center? (2) Is he always a merciful and compassionate Christ? (3) Is there room for human cooperation with Christ? (4) Is there a sense of the Church as a communion of saints? (5) Is Mary's discipleship highlighted? (6) Is her sacramentality ("God-bearer") properly emphasized, and is it linked with the sacramentality of the Church? (7) Is Mary's role always properly subordinate to Christ's in the work of redemption? (8) Is it clear that she, too, is one of the redeemed? (9) If there are denials *or* affirmations of dogma, are the *reasons* orthodox? (10) The fact of apparitions is always an open question; no one is bound to accept them in faith except those to whom they are originally given. Who has received them? (11) The *content* of apparitions is always to be measured against the totality of Christian faith. Is the content consistent with that faith?

27.   The relationship of *Mary and the Church* is *multilateral*. Both have *maternal* roles in the economy of salvation: the Church through the sacraments, and Mary through her giving birth to Christ. Both the Church and Mary are also filled with grace and redeemed by Christ, are signs of God's presence, are transformed and renewed by that presence, share in the resurrection, and intercede for all humankind before God.

28.   *Devotion to Mary* is a characteristically Catholic phenomonen in that it expresses *three fundamental principles of Catholic theology and practice*: (1) The principle of *mediation* affirms that grace is a mediated reality, first through Christ and secondarily through the Church and other human instruments, including Mary. (2) The principle of *sacramentality* affirms that the invisible and the spiritual God is present through the visible and the material, and that these are, in turn, made holy by that presence. This includes Mary, in whom God is very specially

present. (3) The principle of *communion* affirms that the saving encounter with God occurs not only personally and individually but corporately and ecclesially. To be in the Church, i.e., to be in communion with other Christians, is to be in and with Christ. Mary is the preeminent member of this communion of saints. Our unity with her is an expression of our unity in and with Christ.

29. Since Mary is one of the redeemed and a model of the Church and of Christian discipleship, Mariology provides a *bridge* between our understanding of the redeemed community, the Church, and the nature and dimensions of the redeemed life, i.e., Christian existence.

SUGGESTED READINGS

Brown, Raymond E., et al, eds. *Mary in the New Testament: A Collaborative Assessment by Protestant and Roman Catholic Scholars.* Philadelphia: Fortress Press, and New York: Paulist Press, 1978.

Congar, Yves. *Christ, Our Lady, and the Church.* Westminster, Md.: Newman Press, 1957.

Graef, Hilda. *Mary: A History of Doctrine and Devotion.* 2 vols. New York: Sheed & Ward, 1963.

Greeley, Andrew. *The Mary Myth: On the Femininity of God.* New York: Seabury Press, 1977.

Laurentin, René. *The Question of Mary.* New York: Holt, Rinehart & Winston, 1965.

Rahner, Karl. *Mary, Mother of the Lord: Theological Meditations.* New York: Herder & Herder, 1963.

Ruether, Rosemary, *Mary—The Feminine Face of the Church.* Philadelphia: Westminster Press, 1977.

Schillebeeckx, Edward. *Mary, Mother of the Redemption.* New York: Sheed & Ward, 1964.

Semmelroth, Otto. *Mary, Archetype of the Church.* New York: Sheed & Ward, 1963.

Suenens, Léon Joseph. *Mary the Mother of God.* New York: Hawthorn Books, 1959.

Thurian, Max. *Mary, Mother of the Lord, Figure of the Church.* London: Faith Press, 1963.

Vollert, Cyril. *A Theology of Mary.* New York: Herder & Herder, 1965.

PART FIVE

CHRISTIAN EXISTENCE: ETHICAL AND SPIRITUAL DIMENSIONS

CHRISTIAN EXISTENCE: ETHICAL AND SPIRITUAL DIMENSIONS

INTRODUCTION

Christian faith expresses itself through love (Galatians 5:6). Indeed, such faith does not really exist unless there is a commitment to the Gospel of Jesus Christ. This commitment is initially made, shaped and sustained within a community of faith, which is the Church.

We come in this last section of the book to the question of *Christian existence* in its ethical and spiritual dimensions. What does it mean to be a Christian: a disciple of Jesus Christ and a member of his Body, the Church? What kinds of decisions are consistent with the preaching of Jesus and the faith of the Church? What kinds of behavior advance the Kingdom of God? What styles of life distinguish the Christian from other human beings? What sort of hope does the Christian have that makes the Christian's vision of history different from the vision of others?

We began this book with the *question of ourselves* (Part I). Who are we? What does it mean to be human? How are we shaped by the world in which we live, and how do we, in turn, shape and direct its history?

The question of human existence led us next to the *question of God* (Part II). God is the answer we give to the question of meaning and purpose. The triune God—the God who calls us into being, who identifies with our human condition, who sustains us in our lives—is the God of Christian faith.

The God of Christian faith, more specifically still, is the God of Jesus Christ. Christ is both the Word of God addressed to us, and the way through which we gain access to God in return. And so we raised the *question of Jesus Christ* as the concrete, personal, and historical embodiment of what it really means to be human (Part III).

If Christ mediates the presence of God, so the Church mediates for us the presence of Christ. It is the communal and institutional expression, or sacrament, of Christ and of the Kingdom of God which he proclaimed and practiced. And so we moved from the question of Christ to the *question of the Church* (Part IV).

We raise here in Part V the *question of Christian existence* because we look for some experiential verification of the meaning we embrace in Christ and celebrate in the Church. Do his message and ministry, his life and death, really make sense? Is the way of Christ also the way to resurrection and new life? What does it mean to be converted to the Gospel, individually and as part of the total Christian movement known as the Church?

In chapter 25, therefore, we ask how Jesus understood the shape and substance of Christian discipleship? To what extent was his message in continuity with the faith of Israel, and to what extent was it a departure? How was the call to discipleship understood after the resurrection: within the New Testament churches, in the earliest centuries of the Church through the Middle Ages, and into the twentieth century?

In the light of this long and complex historical development, can we identify any distinguishing marks which set apart the moral vision of Christians in general and of Catholics in particular? Who is the Christian, according to this moral tradition? What kind of person is the Christian called to become? How does one become a Christian? What virtues and what sort of character does the authentic Christian display (chapter 26)?

How are the principles of Christian and Catholic moral theology applicable to specific dilemmas and conflict situations? For example, what is the Christian, and particularly the Catholic, to think of contraception, homosexuality, the use of military power, and the intervention of the state in social and economic matters (chapter 27)?

Beyond the requirements, obligations, and just demands of Christian existence, what sort of style or spirit should characterize the Christian's life, and the Church's? How does one establish a relationship with God, with Christ, with the Holy Spirit; and, once established, how is that relationship cultivated and sustained? Indeed, how does one even know that the relationship exists and/or that it is sound (chapter 28)?

If we are convinced in faith that human existence has meaning, that God is the ground of all reality, that Jesus Christ is the embodiment of God's love for the world, that the Church is the Body of Christ and the Temple of his reconciling Spirit, and that we are empowered by that same Holy Spirit to live according to the vocation to which we have been called (Ephesians 4:1), what do we hope for in the end? Is it a hope for ourselves alone? For the whole of humankind? For the whole of the world? For the whole of the created order? Is it a fragile hope, or a firm hope? Is the way to the Kingdom of God smooth and unimpeded, or is it marked by risk and sacrifice and even death? Can we even now enjoy the firstfruits of the final banquet (chapter 29)?

The Kingdom of God, on which not only Part V but the entire book is focused, is both the beginning and the end of Christian theology. The initial experience of God's renewing and reconciling presence, which *is* the Kingdom of God, evokes our theological quest for understanding and excites the hope that one day our union with God and with one another will be realized to its fullest, when God will be "all in all" (1 Corinthians 15:28).

·XXV·

CHRISTIAN EXISTENCE: AN HISTORICAL PERSPECTIVE

MORAL THEOLOGY/CHRISTIAN ETHICS

Moral Theology

The standard distinction between "dogmatic" and "moral" theology has been drawn on the basis of a perceived difference between *theory* and *practice*. In dogmatic theology we specify what we must believe; in moral theology we determine what we are required to *do* (or *not* do) because of those beliefs. And the traditional catechisms would thereafter introduce the sacraments as those God-given "aids" to correct belief and moral action.

These distinctions, however, are based on a faulty understanding of the theory-practice relationship. The two are in reality not separate but are united in the one notion of *praxis*. *Praxis* means more than "practice" alone. It is practice-plus-reflection, and it is reflection-in-practice. Truth is not only to be thought but also done, and the doing of truth is a condition of grasping it. "But he who acts in truth comes into the light, to make clear that his deeds are done in God" (John 3:21). Similarly, Paul insists that "faith...expresses itself through love" (Galatians 5:6). Indeed, faith cannot exist, and does not exist, without commitment to the implementation of the Gospel. Systematic theology, therefore, must embrace both dogmatic (or doctrinal) *and* moral theology. This is how Thomas Aquinas understood their relationship in his *Summa Theologica*. The two disciplines were not formally separated until after the Council of Trent, as we shall see below.

On the other hand, reflection and practice do not collapse completely into one another. Although an *integral* understanding of the Gospel is not possible without a commitment to, and practice of, the Gospel, most people will always find themselves far short of the ideal. The relationship between theory and practice in the integrating notion of *praxis* is a *dialectical* relationship, not one of *identity*. It is possible, in other words, for a person to be a sincere believer in the Gospel of Jesus Christ and yet not fully practice what he or she believes and preaches. There is a psychological complexity to faith which is not touched by sociology or economics alone. Some of the Latin American liberation theologians might not do complete justice to the reality of faith when they suggest that faith is impossible and non-existent without works. Indeed, the Council of Trent took pains to assert the opposite: "If anyone says that with the loss of grace through sin faith is also always lost, or that the faith which remains is not true faith, granted that it is not a living faith; or that the man who has faith without charity is not a Christian, *anathema sit*" (*Decree on Justification*, canon 28, Session VI, 1547). For a *living* faith, there must be an expression of love. But faith itself can exist, at least for a time, without love. Thus, although systematic theology embraces both dogmatic (or doctrinal) and moral theology, the two are not the same, no more than faith and action are the same.

Christian Ethics

The other common term to describe and encompass the theological reflections contained in these next three chapters is *Christian ethics*. Just as the term *moral theology* raises the question of the relationship between faith and action *within* the field of Christian reflection and discourse, so the term *Christian ethics* raises the question of the relationship between *Christian* reflection on human action and *philosophical* reflections on human action, without reference to the Christian tradition. This is another way of putting the question: "Is there a distinctively Christian ethics?"

The question moves us back once again to the discussion of human existence in Part I of the book (especially chapter 5). *How one understands the relationship between Christian ethics and philosophical ethics will reflect how one understands the relationship between grace and nature.* If one accepts the premise, as we have, that all reality is radically graced, that from the very beginning God is present to all that is, then the concept of "pure nature" is only a logical construct, an abstraction. It is possible that God could have created a world without grace, but in fact God did not do so. Thus, although one can make a distinction *in the mind* between grace and nature, the two are *in fact* inseparable. The order of nature (creation) is defined by its relationship to the order of grace (redemption). There is no reality which exists, has ever existed, or ever will exist except in view of the incarnation of the Word.

The Catholic tradition has always insisted that the grace of God is given to us, not to make up for something lacking to us as human persons, but as a free gift that elevates us to a new and unmerited level of existence. Hypothetically, we could have had a purely natural end, but historically we have only a supernatural end. Thus, if grace supposes nature, nature in its own way supposes grace, insofar as the grace of Christ orients our actual human existence to the only end it really has, i.e., the Kingdom of God. Indeed, we should always remember that the very concept of "nature" arises not from the Bible but from subsequent theological reflection on the New Testament's proclamation of "the grace of God through Christ." We infer that we are creatures of God by reflecting on who we have become through Christ.

Human existence is always graced existence. This means, too, that the whole created order is oriented to the glory of God (Romans 8:19-23). The history of the world is, at the same time, the history of salvation. It means also that authentic human progress in the struggle for justice, peace, freedom, etc., is part of the movement of, and toward, the Kingdom of God. It means, too, that human freedom and human action are never to be conceived totally apart from grace, because grace is always modifying and qualifying human freedom and action.

Given this Catholic understanding of the relationship between grace and nature, the question is not so much "Is there a distinctively Christian ethics?" as "Is there a purely philosophical ethics?" "The basic and ultimate thrust of Christian life," Karl Rahner writes, "consists not so much in the fact that a Christian is a special instance of mankind in general, but rather in the fact that a Christian is simply man as he is . . . . From this perspective we could characterize Christian life precisely as a life of freedom," i.e., a life of openness to everything without exception, to absolute truth, to absolute love, to God. "But a Christian believes that there is a path to freedom which lies in going through [the] imprisonment" of ordinary human existence, namely, through the *facticity* of our existence: that we were born without being asked, will die without being asked, and are particular persons without being asked. We do not seize this freedom by force, "but rather it is given to us by God insofar as he gives himself to us throughout all of the imprisonments of our existence" (*Foundations of Christian Faith*, New York: Seabury Press, 1978, pp. 402-403).

It is not adequate, therefore, to suggest that Christian ethics differs from philosophical ethics only insofar as Christian ethics proceeds from reason and revelation, while philosophical ethics proceeds from reason alone. Revelation does not happen where reason gives out, nor is reason completely unaffected by revelation, i.e., by the active presence of God in human experience, in human history, and, therefore, in human consciousness. A similar, although not identical, position is sketched out by Protestant theologian James Gustafson in his *Can Ethics Be Christian?* (see especially pp. 169-179).

It would be preferable to say, in the end, that Christian ethics proceeds from a *conscious* sense of responsibility to the Gospel of Jesus Christ and to the community of faith (Church) which has arisen in response to this Gospel. Thus understood, "Christian ethics is the intellectual discipline that renders an account of this experience [of God in Jesus Christ] and that draws the normative inferences from it for the conduct of the Christian community and its members. The practical import is to aid the community and its members in discerning what God is enabling and requiring them to be and to do" (Gustafson, *Can Ethics Be Christian?*, p. 179).

THE MORAL MESSAGE OF THE OLD TESTAMENT

Faithful *praxis* (practice-plus-reflection, and reflection-in-practice) is linked in ancient Israel with the *Law, (Tôrāh* = "instruction"), and that, in turn, with the *Covenant*. Although scholars do not completely agree, most seem to hold that the Israelites learned and developed their legal traditions from their more sophisticated Canaanite neighbors, after entering the Promised Land. It is also widely assumed that the *Covenant Code* (Exodus 20:22–23:33) belongs to the oldest part of Israelite history because it contains the greatest number of parallels to the pagan laws. Whether this is true, we cannot finally determine here. It is sufficient to note that the Code was inserted into the book of Exodus as part of the terms of the covenant of Sinai (where the Ten Commandments were promulgated). Consequently, the Covenant Code (or Code of the Covenant) is attributed to Moses and given the supreme authority which Israel attributed to all its laws.

Most of the Old Testament laws which have parallels in the ancient Near Eastern law collections are formulated in case form (the common way of teaching law even today); e.g., "If a man strikes his father they shall cut off his hand" (Hammurabi Laws, 195), and "When a man gives money or any article to another for safekeeping and it is stolen from the latter's house, the thief, if caught, must make twofold restitution. If the thief is not caught, the owner of the house shall be brought to God, to swear that he himself did not lay hands on his neighbor's property" (Exodus 22:6-7). In the beginning, of course, such laws were unwritten. When a judge was puzzled about the law, he did not consult the law books but sought the help of a higher official in the capital (Deuteronomy 17:8-11).

Other codes of Israelite law were the "Yahwist ritual decalogue" dealing with the prohibition of images, festivals, and offerings (Exodus 34:17-27), the Deuteronomic Code (Deuteronomy 12-26), which prohibits the worship of gods other than Yahweh, the Holiness Code (Leviticus 17-26), which regulates such matters as diet, worship, hygiene, marriage, and sexual morality, the Priestly Code (scattered throughout the Pentateuch, the first five books of the Old Testament), whose cultic-ritual prescriptions often refer only to priests, and, finally, the Decalogue, or Ten Commandments (Exodus 20:2-17; Deuteronomy 5:6-21).

That ten words (*Dābār* = "word") or commandments were given by God to Moses on Mount Sinai is an accepted part of ancient Hebrew tradition (Exodus 34:28; Deuteronomy 4:13;

10:4). But the enumeration of these ten commandments has taken at least three different forms in subsequent centuries. The best seems to be the one proposed by Philo (d. ca. 50), Josephus (d.ca. 100), the Greek Fathers, and the modern Greek church: (1) Prohibition of false or foreign gods. (2) Prohibition of images. (3) Prohibition of the vain use of the divine name. (4) Keeping holy the Sabbath. (5) Honoring one's father and mother. (6) Prohibition of murder. (7) Prohibition of adultery. (8) Prohibition of theft. (9) Prohibition of false witness against one's neighbor. (10) Prohibition against coveting a neighbor's house, wife, slaves, or possessions.

The first four commandments state one's duties toward God (parents, the source of life, are representative of God), and the last six refer to duties toward other human beings.

The enumeration followed in the modern Latin church, with roots in Origen (d. ca. 254), Clement of Alexandria (d. ca. 215), and Augustine (d. 430), is as follows: (1) Prohibition of false gods *and* images. (2) Vain use of divine name. (3) Sabbath. (4) Parents. (5) Murder. (6) Adultery. (7) Theft. (8) False witness. (9) Coveting of neighbor's wife. (10) Coveting of neighbor's goods. Modern Jews put the introduction, "I am the Lord your God . . .," as (1) and then collapse (9) and (10) into (10). Everything else follows the same order as the Latin form.

One must keep in mind, however, that not even in Jesus' time had the Decalogue acquired the set form and importance as a charter of morality that it would acquire in later Christianity. The separate commandments are mentioned in the New Testament, but never as ten. When Jesus himself was asked by the young man how he could become perfect, Jesus cited some of the ten, but not in the usual order nor completely (Matthew 9:18-19; Mark 10:19; Luke 18:20).

Although the Ten Commandments bear some resemblance to other sources—e.g., the Code of Hammurabi—, they are unique in the sense that they are regarded as the revealed will of God. Other Near Eastern collections were based on the conviction that the gods had authorized their formulation, but the laws themselves were the work of human hands alone. The conception of law as a sacred *covenant* obligation is indeed peculiar to Israel. It is important also to note that *the Decalogue was not intended as the ultimate norm of all morality.* On the contrary, it barely touches upon individual moral obligations. Its consistent focus is *the needs of the whole community*, and it prohibits those actions which might injure the community. What was important was the survival of the People of God. *Thus, the Ten Commandments were not so much an ethical document as a religious document, i.e., a testimony to the unbreakable bond between God and Israel.*

The Covenant, of course, is a basic and constant motif in the whole of the Old Testament. It is the motive for observing the Law (Deuteronomy 4:23), for Yahweh's punishments (Leviticus 26:15, 25), for Yahweh's coming to Israel's aid in times of distress (Leviticus 26:9), for Yahweh's mercy and forgiveness (Leviticus 26:42), and for the permanence both of Yahweh's mercy and of Israel's status as Yahweh's own people (Leviticus 26:45; Psalm 111:9; Isaiah 54:10; 59:21; 61:8; Jeremiah 32:40; Ezekiel 34:25; 37:26). It is never a bilateral contract between equals, but an agreement between a greater and a lesser party. The greater imposes its will upon the lesser, but the contract is also an act of grace and magnanimity. But it is more than a mere contract. It establishes an artificial blood kinship between the parties that is second only to the bond of blood. The word used to signify covenant affection and loyalty (*hesed*) is also used to signify the affection and loyalty of kinsmen. The Covenant has its initial historical grounding in the covenant with *Abraham* (Genesis 15-17), but it was the covenant with *Moses* on Sinai that established Israel definitively as God's people (Exodus 19:1-8). The latter is summed up in the formula: "I will be your God and you shall be my people" (Jeremiah 7:23; see also 11:4; 24:7; Ezekiel 11:20; 14:11; Hosea 2:25).

The ancient Israelites had come to believe that a God who asked for righteousness and justice would also supply the means of instructing the people in the divine ways. Who in ancient Israel was competent to *interpret* the Covenant? Jeremiah 18:18 refers to three groups of leaders: the *priests*, who are the source of "instruction" (the root meaning of the word for Law, *Torāh*); the *prophets*, who convey the word of God; and *wise persons*, who offer counsel.

These three classes of leaders were not mutually opposed to one another, nor indeed to the Law itself. On the contrary, Ezekiel was himself both prophet and priest, and the prophets were within the tradition of the Law. Nor was the teaching authority (*magisterium*) vested in any one group, not even in the priests.

THE MORAL MESSAGE OF JESUS
The Kingdom (Reign) of God

Although the idea of the Covenant is the axis around which the history of ancient Israel revolves, and although there was some expectation of a new covenant among the prophets (Jeremiah 31:31-34; Ezekiel 36:26-28), it was not central to the preaching of Jesus. As we have already noted in chapter 12, the *Kingdom* (or *reign*) *of God* was at the core of Jesus' proclamation and ministry, as it was, and must remain, at the heart of the Church's total mission (chapters 17 and 20). All else flows from that, including our understanding of Christian existence.

The whole of Jesus' preaching is summed up by Mark: "This is the time of fulfillment. The reign of God is at hand. Reform your lives and believe in the gospel " (1:15). Thus, his preaching is at once a proclamation and a warning, i.e., an announcement of a divine act and a demand for a response from men and women. Moral existence is always a response to a divine call. Nowhere in Jesus' preaching, nor in the New Testament at large, do we find an ethical system as such. On the other hand, neither do we find an existence devoid of obligation nor a faith divorced from action.

What Jesus announced was not only a renewal of the Covenant with the people of Israel. His message was even more comprehensive than that. It would embrace the whole world. Jesus returned to his home town of Nazareth to begin his preaching in the synagogue with these words from Isaiah (61:1-2): "The spirit of the Lord is upon me; therefore he has anointed me. He has sent me to bring glad tidings to the poor, to proclaim liberty to the captives, recovery of sight to the blind and release to prisoners, to announce a year of favor from the Lord" (Luke 4:18-19). Then he said, "Today this Scripture passage is fulfilled in your hearing." So obvious was his meaning that his fellow townspeople were filled with indignation and expelled him from Nazareth, attempting even to hurl him over the edge of a hill.

As we noted in chapter 12, Jesus' preaching of the reign of God was often couched in parables in which he often inverted his listeners' whole world view. Thus, the parable of the Good Samaritan (Luke 10:30-37) is not simply an example of neighborliness. If that is all Jesus wanted to communicate, he would have made the Samaritan the injured party and the Israelite the one who comes along to aid him. As it is, no Jew would ever have expected hospitality from a Samaritan (see Luke 9:52-56). Thus, the parable challenges the listener to conceive the inconceivable: The Samaritan is "good." The listener is thereby required to reexamine his or her most basic attitudes and values. The parable is no longer merely instruction; it is proclamation itself.

For Jesus nothing is more precious than the Kingdom of God (see chapter 20), i.e., the healing and renewing power and presence of God on our behalf. "Seek out his kingship over you, and the rest will follow in turn" (Luke 12:31). Like a person who finds a hidden treasure in a field, or a merchant who discovers a precious pearl, everyone must be prepared to give up everything else in order to possess the Kingdom (Matthew 13:44-46). But it is promised only to those with a certain outlook and way of life (see the Beatitudes in Matthew 5:3-12). One can inherit the Kingdom through love of one's neighbor (Matthew 5:38-48), and yet one must also accept it as a child (Mark 10:15). Jesus assured the Scribe who grasped the meaning of the chief of the commandments (love of God and love of neighbor), "You are not far from the reign of God" (12:34). He also insisted to his disciples that their commitment to the Kingdom would make strong demands upon them (Mark 10:1; Luke 9:57-62; Matthew 19:12).

The Call to Conversion and Repentance

Jesus' fundamental though not ultimate demand was that they should *repent*. The Greek word *metanoia* suggests a "change of mind." To the Semite it suggested someone's turning away from his or her former consciousness, now recognized as wrong, and striking out in a completely new direction. Therefore, *metanoia*, or conversion and repentance, is not just sorrow for sin but a fundamental reorientation of one's whole life. Jesus demanded that his listeners not only repent but also believe the Gospel of forgiveness that he preached (Mark 2:10,17). He drove home his point with various parables, especially those in Luke 15 and the parable of the Prodigal Son in particular. Jesus was so committed to the forgiveness of sins in the name of God that he made himself the friend of outcasts—e.g., publicans and sinners (Matthew 11:19)—and did not avoid their company (Mark 2:16). He rejoiced over their conversion (Luke 15:7-10; Matthew 18:13).

The antithesis of a repentant attitude is an attitude of self-righteousness and presumption. Jesus repudiates the proud Phari-see (Luke 18:10-14), the elder brother who resents his father's benevolent reaction to the prodigal son's return (Luke 15:25-30), and the discontented laborers in the vineyard (Matthew 20:1-15). To those who set themselves proudly above others, Jesus declared that publicans and harlots would enter the Kingdom before they would (Matthew 21:31-32). He condemned them for trying to shut the doors of the Kingdom (Matthew 23:13). All of us, he warned, are unprofitable servants (Luke 17:10), ever in God's debt (Matthew 6:12). God will exalt the humble and bring down the proud (Luke 14:11; 18:14). Each must pray that God forgives his or her trespasses. And whoever is without sin should cast the first stone (John 8:7). Repentance, therefore, remains a major requirement of Christian existence. The early Church would continue this message: "You must reform and be baptized ..." (Acts of the Apostles 2:38).

The Demand for Faith

Jesus also demanded *faith*, which is the positive side of conversion (Mark 1:15). He says to the woman afflicted with a hemorrhage for a dozen years and who is cured by touching his clothing, "Daughter, it is your faith that has cured you" (Mark 5:34). From there he went to the official's house where the man's daughter was reported as being already dead. Jesus disregarded the report and said to the official, "Fear is useless. What is needed is trust" (5:36). It was the faith of the lame man's friends which called forth from Jesus the forgiveness of his sins and physical healing (2:5). Faith is central to the narrative of the cured boy (9:14-29). Jesus sighed over this unbelieving generation (9:19) and reminded the boy's father that all things are possible to him who believes (9:23). The great faith of the Syro-Phoenician woman moved Jesus to heal her daughter (7:30), and he drew attention to the faith of the pagan centurion who believed that a mere word from Jesus would heal his sick servant (Matthew 8:10; Luke 7:9). On the other hand, where Jesus encountered an obstinate lack of faith, he was not able to manifest the signs of salvation (Mark 6:5). (See chapter 2 for our fuller discussion of faith.)

The Call to Discipleship

Jesus also gathered disciples around him, a point that is not unrelated to the question of Jesus' intentions regarding the "founding" of the Church (see chapter 17). He encouraged people to leave home, take up their cross, and become his disciples (Luke 14:26-27). He advised the rich young man to sell all that he had, give the money to the poor, and then come follow him (Mark 10:21). To become his disciples meant leaving everything else behind (Luke 5:11; 9:58; 14:26; Mark 2:14). But this was consistent with the traditional Jewish notion of discipleship. *What was not traditional was his sending of disciples to act in his name* (Matthew 10). "Let the dead bury their dead," he chastized the man who wanted to bury his father first. "Come away and proclaim the kingdom of God" (Luke 9:59-60). To do so was to share in Jesus' own destiny. "Where I am, there will my servant be" (John 12:26). There would be an identification of the disciple with the suffering of the master (Mark 8:34-35), but also a participation in his triumph (Luke 22:28-30). *The call to discipleship is a call to the imitation of Christ* (John 13:15).

The Law

It was not Jesus' purpose simply to set aside the Law of the Old Testament. He was in the synagogue on the Sabbath (Mark 1:21; 6:2), went on pilgrimage during the festivals (Luke 2:41-52; John

2:13; 5:1; 7:14; 10:22; 12:12; Mark 11:1-11), taught in the syna-
gogues and in the Temple (e.g., Mark 1:39; 14:49; John 6:59; 7:14;
8:20). He celebrated the paschal feast in the traditional way with
his disciples (Mark 14:12-16; Luke 22:14-23), wore the prescribed
tassels on his cloak (Mark 6:56; Luke 8:44), sent lepers to show
themselves to the priests in accordance with the Law (Mark 1:44;
Luke 17:14). He insisted that he had come not to destroy the Law
but to fulfill it (Matthew 5:17).

On the other hand, Jesus also found himself at odds with
Jewish teachers of the Law. He insisted that the Sabbath was
made for men and women, not men and women for the Sabbath
(Mark 2:27). He defended his disciples when they had neglected to
perform the ritual hand-washing (Mark 7:1-23; Matthew 15:1-20).
He argued that the tradition to which the teachers appealed was a
merely human institution (Mark 7:8), and he gave a concrete
example of what he meant (7:9-13): They neglected the duty of
supporting parents (the fourth commandment of the Decalogue)
because they permitted so-called *korban* oaths, even to the detriment of their parents' rights. These oaths expressed a son's intention to give money to the Temple, and the money, in turn, was no
longer part of the support given to one's parents, even if later on
the son decided not to give it to the Temple. *More fundamentally,
Jesus attacked the traditional notion that every part of the Law was
of equal importance and that the external observance is what finally
counted.* For Jesus it is the inner disposition that determines an
act's moral value (7:14-23).

But he did not ignore the external action itself (Luke 6:43-
45). The final parable of the Sermon on the Mount, the house built
on a rock (Matthew 7:24-27), is a call not only to listen to Jesus'
words but to put them into action. "Treat others the way you
would have them treat you: this sums up the law and the prophets"
(7:12). And this must really be done, in deed and not only in word.
"None of those who cry out, 'Lord, Lord,' will enter the kingdom
of God but the only the one who does the will of my Father in
heaven" (7:21). The same insistence on the connection between
word and action is given in his indictment of the Scribes and
Pharisees (23:1-36). He attacks them for straining at gnats and
swallowing camels and for neglecting the weightier matters of the

law: justice, mercy, and good faith (23:23). He is especially intoler-
ant of their hypocrisy (23:4,28). To return to the notion of *praxis*
to which we referred at the beginning of this chapter: Jesus not
only proclaimed the Kingdom of God; he practiced it, and he
expected the same of others. God's will must be *done*.

The austere demands of Jesus are not to be explained away
simply on the basis of his expectation of the coming of the Kingdom, but they are to be interpreted always in light of the coming
Kingdom. Thus, it is clearly hyperbolic to say, as Jesus did, that it
is easier for a camel to pass through the eye of a needle than for a
rich man to enter into the Kingdom (Mark 10:25). The disciples
expressed alarm: "Then who can be saved?" Jesus answered, "For
man it is impossible but not for God. With God all things are
possible" (10:27). But as severe as his ethical teaching may have
been, his readiness to forgive was even stronger. Thus, a repentant
Peter is singled out as the shepherd of the sheep despite his denial
of Christ (Luke 22:32; John 21:15-17). Admonition and mercy are
found together.

The Commandment of Love

*All of Jesus' moral teaching is concentrated in the one command-
ment of love: the love of God and the love of neighbor* (Mark 12:28-
34; Matthew 22:34-40; Luke 10:25-28). On them all the Law and
the prophets depend (Matthew 22:40). Apart from the great commandment, Jesus did not speak explicitly about loving God. He did
say that we should not offer sacrifice to God unless and until we
have been reconciled with our brother (Matthew 5:23-24) and that
we cannot ask forgiveness for our sins unless we are also ready to
forgive those who sin against us (6:12). But it would be wrong to
equate love for God entirely with love for neighbor. Religious
acts, such as prayer, also belong to the love of God (Matthew 6:1-
15; 7:7-11; Mark 14:38). On the other hand, "religious" access to
God through prayer cannot finally be divorced from the principal
sacramental encounter with God in one's neighbor. The great
picture of the Last Judgment in the parable of the Sheep and the
Goats (Matthew 25:31-46) offers one of the classic illustrations of
this principle.

According to John, Jesus gave himself as an example of unselfish love for others. He humbled himself to wash the feet of the disciples (13:4-15). He insisted that he was in their midst as one who serves (Luke 22:27), who gives his life as a ransom for many (Mark 10:45), and who thereby leaves a new commandment: "Love one another. Such as my love has been for you, so must your love be for each other. This is how all will know you for my disciples: your love for one another" (John 13:34-35). But such love is not to be reserved for one's friends. The disciple of Jesus is also commanded to love the enemy (Luke 6:27-28), to renounce revenge (6:29). We are to avoid judging and condemning others (6:37) and to be careful not to dwell on the speck in our brother's eye while missing the plank in our own (6:41-42). All of this is summed up in Paul's classic hymn to love: "There are in the end three things that last: faith, hope, and love, and the greatest of these is love" (1 Corinthians 13).

Discipleship in the World

Jesus did not come to change the political order, but neither was he indifferent to it. What he preached was bound to affect the consciousness and behavior of those who heard and assimilated his words. The values he proclaimed would surely transform the world of those who shared them. But to make of him primarily a political figure is to put more into the New Testament than is there.

Jesus declared that he was sent to call sinners (Mark 2:17), to save the lost (Luke 19:10), to give his life for many (Mark 10:45). His kingdom was not of this world, he assured Pilate (John 18:36-37). He fled from the desire of his Galilean supporters to make him a political messianic king and national liberator (John 6:14-15). He rejected Peter's plea that he relinquish the path of suffering and death, just as he repelled the temptations of Satan to worldly power (Matthew 16:22-23). He maintained no contacts with the Zealot party. But all of this does not mean that Jesus' moral teaching had no bearing on political life.

He sent his disciples into the world (Matthew 10:16) and prayed, not that the Father would take his disciples out of the world, but that he would keep them safe in the world (John 17:15). He criticized contemporary institutions (Matthew 10). He saw what is dangerous and corrupting in political power as well as in riches: "You know how among the Gentiles those who seem to exercise authority lord it over them; their great ones make their importance felt. It cannot be like that with you" (Mark 10:42-43). When asked if he thought his fellow Jews should pay the tax to Caesar (Mark 12:13-37), he said they should, but he gave this answer only after asking about the image on the coin and pointing out to his interrogators that they already recognized Caesar's political authority over them by using his coinage. And then he added: "Give to Caesar what is Caesar's, but give to God what is God's" (12:17). Always it is the Kingdom which is supreme.

Jesus, of course, was a carpenter's son, and he himself labored for a time as a carpenter (Mark 6:3). His parables reflect his sense of identification with the poor and the workers: on the farm (Mark 4:3-8), in the vineyard (Matthew 20:1-15), on the sea (Matthew 13:47-50), in the home (Matthew 13:33; Luke 12:37-39; 17:7-10). But others also appear in his parables, without his passing judgment on their occupations or professions: e.g., merchants, traders, builders, soldiers, kings, judges, physicians, stewards. He did not attack the notion of private property, nor did he demand a redistribution of worldly goods. "The poor you will always have with you," he declared (Mark 14:7). Although he directed his severest warnings against the rich (Luke 6:24), he accepted hospitality from them (Luke 7:36; 10:38-42; 14:1, John 11:1-3; 12:1-3) and support from women of property (Luke 8:3). He certainly did not intend to exclude from the Kingdom such wealthy men as Nicodemus, Joseph of Arimathea, Zacchaeus the rich publican, and others like them (Luke 19:1-10).

The theme of wealth and property has an important place in the Gospel of Luke, so much so that some scholars have suggested that Luke deliberately intensified Jesus' sayings against the rich and riches. This may have been the case here and there (e.g., 5:11,28; 9:3; 10:4), but not as a general rule. As early as the Infancy Narrative Jesus' earthly origin is characterized as poverty-stricken (1:52-53; 2:7,24). The motif is sounded again in various discourses and parables (12:15-21; 14:12-14,33; 16). In Luke's version of the

Beatitudes, Jesus first blesses the poor, for the reign of God is theirs (6:20)—not just the "poor" in the sense of the "poor in spirit" or the "just," but the economically poor. In the parable of the Rich Man and Lazarus (16:19-31), Lazarus, too, is literally poor. On the other hand, it is not poverty that entitles one to entrance into the Kingdom, but fidelity to the will of God (Matthew 7:21). In comparing the presentation of the Beatitudes in Matthew (5:3-12) and Luke (6:20-26), however, it is clear that Matthew emphasizes the religious and moral attitude of those who are called blessed and to whom the Kingdom of God is promised, whereas Luke stresses their social and economic position. Luke makes the same kind of modification in the parables of the Unfaithful Steward (16:1-7) and of the Rich Fool (12:16-20) and also in Jesus' attack on the Pharisees because of their greed (20:47).

Why do we find such a spirit in Luke? The evangelist had close contacts with certain circles in the original Jerusalem community who were literally poor and may have called themselves "the poor" in the religious sense (see Romans 15:26; Galatians 2:10). He praises the practice of sharing goods within the community of the first Christians (Acts of the Apostles 2:44-45; 4:32; 5:1-11). This contact undoubtedly shaped his own personal theology and piety.

What is of major, if not of revolutionary, significance in all of this is the assertion that *the poor have any place at all in the divine scheme of things*. Not only Luke but Matthew, too, removes the curse on poverty. Poverty is not by any means an obstacle to the Kingdom, as some apparently thought. Although other New Testament writings pay little attention to the poor and to poverty (it must have been discussed intensely in the Hellenistic communities for which Luke wrote), *the Christian movement itself was unique in the Roman world as one springing from the poor and lower classes.*

Marriage and the Family

The linchpin of Jesus' attitude toward marriage and the family was his concern for the *dignity of women*, which went far beyond contemporary Jewish attitudes and customs. He spoke with a Samaritan woman at Jacob's Well, though it was frowned upon for a man and a rabbi to do so (John 4:27). He allowed himself to be touched by the woman with the hemorrhage, even though this made him ritually unclean (Mark 5:27-34). He broke the Sabbath to cure a "daughter of Abraham" (Luke 13:10-17). He healed an unusually large number of women—e.g., Peter's mother-in-law (Mark 1:29-31), Jairus' daughter (Mark 5:21-43), the daughter of the Syro-Phoenician woman (Mark 7:24-30), and Mary Magdalene (Luke 8:2). He praised the widow for contributing her mite to the Temple treasury (Mark 12:41-44) and defended Mary of Bethany for anointing his head and feet (Mark 14:3-8; John 12:1-8). He accepted women among his followers and received help from them (Luke 8:2-3). When he visited the family at Bethany, he wished both sisters to hear what he had to say (Luke 10:38). The risen Lord appeared to Mary Magdalene, who brought the good news of the resurrection to the other disciples (John 20:11-18).

Of special importance was Jesus' insistence that marriage is permanent. Women are not to be cast aside at will, as was the custom. He spoke strongly against adultery and divorce (Mark 10:2-12; Matthew 19:3-9). His injunction "Let no man separate what God has joined" is a clear allusion to Genesis, where women and men are assigned equal dignity, coming as they do from the same creative hand of God. (For a fuller consideration of the so-called "exceptive clause," see Rudolf Schnackenburg, *The Moral Teaching of the New Testament*, pp. 136-141. This has to do with Jesus' apparent willingness to allow divorce in the case of "lewd conduct.")

Jesus' high regard for family life is confirmed by the scene which immediately followed the discussion with the Pharisees on divorce. People brought their children to him to have him touch them, and his disciples began to scold them for it. Jesus became indignant and said, "Let the children come to me. . . . It is to just such as these that the kingdom of God belongs" (Mark 10:13-16). He also emphasized the fourth commandment, "Honor your father and your mother," in his reply to the rich young man (10:19). On the other hand, he spoke almost disdainfully of his family when they came to take him home (3:31-35), and he corrected a woman who blessed his mother (Luke 11:27). His mother, too, must have felt rejected at the marriage feast at Cana when she suggested he might produce more wine (John 2:4). So, too, he seemed to belittle blood ties in his command to his disciples regarding their own families (Luke 9:60; 14:26), and he predicted dissensions within homes on his account (Matthew 10:34-36; Luke 12:51-53; Mark 13:12). What emerges from these assorted sayings is the principle that when Jesus gathers his eschatological family around him, blood ties are of less importance than fidelity to the will of God and readiness for the Kingdom.

Reward and Punishment

The principal motive for living according to the Gospel is, of course, the Kingdom of God and its blessings (Matthew 5:3-11). But Jesus also speaks of both rewards and punishments, and they serve perhaps as secondary motives for Christian fidelity. The standard of measurement is often our attitude to the neighbor (25:31-46). On the other hand, Jesus explicitly warns against those who perform certain actions simply to gain a reward (6:2,5,16). The reward he promises is always the future Kingdom or one of its blessings, such as eternal life (Mark 10:30). The parable of the Laborers in the Vineyard (Matthew 20:1-16) is especially important because it shows that God's criteria and ours are not the same. What finally governs the divine judgment is God's own mercy. Thus, those who come to work in the vineyard at a late hour are rewarded on the same basis as those who come at the first hour. So, too, those who bury their talents are singled out for particular condemnation (25:30). The principle is: "When much has been given a man, much will be required of him. More will be asked of a man to whom more has been entrusted" (Luke 12:48).

In the end, we are called to imitate Jesus (Mark 10:45), to follow his example (John 13:15), to love one another as he has loved us (13:14). This is his first and greatest commandment.

THE MORAL MESSAGE OF THE
CHURCH OF THE NEW TESTAMENT

The reader is referred again to chapter 17 for an outline of the Church in the New Testament. It is a community radically shaped by its expectation of the coming of God's Kingdom and by the conviction that the firstfruits of the Kingdom had already been given in the Holy Spirit (2 Corinthians 1:22; 5:5; Ephesians 1:14). It is the Spirit who is the driving force of Christian existence (Romans 8:12-17; Galatians 5:16-26), which begins at Baptism (Romans 6:4; 1 Corinthians 6:11). The Christian no longer lives according to the flesh but according to the Spirit. The Christian is a "new creature" in Christ (2 Corinthians 5:17).

There is an awareness, too, of being a new community in the Spirit, the new People of God. Christian existence, therefore, is corporate existence. We are called to a life of brotherly and sisterly love. We are all one in Christ, whether Jew or Greek, slave or free, male or female (Galatians 3:28). We are one body, the Body of Christ (1 Corinthians 12:13,27). The ethical significance of this is drawn out in Romans 12:4-8 and Colossians 3:11-17. We are to be clothed with mercy, kindness, humility, meekness, patience. We are to bear with one another and to forgive as the Lord has forgiven us. We are to put on love, which binds the rest and makes them perfect. Christ's peace must reign in our hearts. We are to be grateful people and to do everything in the name of the Lord Jesus. In short, we are "to live a life worthy of the calling [we] have received" (Ephesians 4:1).

As for the Law, it is summed up and fulfilled in this one saying: "You shall love your neighbor as yourself" (Galatians 5:14). The Gospel is a new Law, a perfect law of freedom (James 1:25), the law of love (2:8). Jesus himself is the new Law (John 1:17). "His commandment is this: we are to believe in the name of his Son, Jesus Christ, and are to love one another as he has commanded us" (1 John 3:23). If we do love one another, "God dwells in us, and his love is brought to perfection in us" (4:12). On the other hand, "If anyone says, 'My love is fixed on God,' yet hates his brother, he is a liar. One who has no love for the brother he has seen cannot love the God he has not seen" (4:20). In any case, "perfect love casts out all fear" (4:18).

(For a more complete discussion of the moral teaching of the New Testament Church, see Schnackenburg, pp. 168-388.)

SECOND THROUGH SIXTH CENTURIES

The Church has no moral systems as such until the sixteenth century. Of major concern to the early Church was the threat posed by pagan society and culture. There were prohibitions against pagan worship and the fashioning of idols by Christian craftsmen. Also discussed were the proper Christian attitude toward the theatre, military service, martyrdom, flight from persecution, virginity, prayer. Ignatius of Antioch (d. ca.107) italicized the Pauline and Johannine teaching that Christian existence is life in and with Christ. The Christian is a temple of God and a bearer of Christ (Ephesians 9:1). The Eucharist is the source and center of the Christian life.

Clement of Alexandria (d. ca. 215) made perhaps the first attempt at some modest systematization of moral theology. He strove to point out the connection between the positive values in pagan philosophy and those of the Gospel. Genuine Christian life is imitation of God in Christ. Christ is always our teacher. He is the *Logos*-made-flesh. Against the Gnostic hostility toward marriage, Clement defended the married state as a way of salvation. But he also refused to disparage virginity. What counts in the end is the good of the community of love and the things of the Lord (*Stromata*, III, 12).

Clement's successor in the catechetical school at Alexandria was Origen (d. ca. 254), who was less open to the world than his predecessor but perhaps more realistic. He focused on the imitation of God in the contemplative as well as the active life, and reflected on free will, sin, virtues, and the restoration of all things in God. Ambrose (d. 397) provides the first case-approach to moral theology, laying down the various duties of his priests. He insists on the superiority of the Christian moral ideal over pagan philosophies.

One of the earliest to set Christian moral discourse in the context of sacramental initiation was Cyril of Jerusalem (d. 386). His moral instruction, in keeping with Eastern practice, was drawn principally from the liturgical texts. Christian existence is sacramental existence.

The first great figure in Christian moral theology, however, is Ambrose's disciple, Augustine (d. 430), who attended to such fundamental problems as the relationship of grace and freedom, faith and works, faith and love, original sin and the restoration of grace, grace and the law, natural law and revealed law, and divine love and the natural appetites. Christian morality is the way and means to eternal union with God. Morality, in turn, requires obedience to the divine law of love, but not merely through external observance. The moral disposition of the heart is decisive. And so we find a strongly psychological orientation in Augustine's writings (e.g., his own *Confessions*) which makes him a kind of forerunner of modern thought. But in spite of his obvious genius and the major contributions he has made to Christian theology, all the "returns" are not yet in on the quality of his impact upon the Church. Was he "one of the greatest, if not the very greatest, moral theologian of all time," as Bernard Häring suggested, or was he too much the rigorist, too much the Manichaean, too much the nay-sayer about such fundamental human questions as sexuality?

SEVENTH THROUGH TWELFTH CENTURIES

This is a significant period in the history of moral theology because, as we noted in chapters 18 and 22, it was the period of the Germanization and legalization of Christianity. In particular, moral theology became attached to the specific needs of confessors. The sacrament of Penance, once reserved for public sins, had become more widely used by the sixth century under the influence of the Celtic monks. Appropriate penances had to be determined for particular sins. A new genre of theological literature developed, the so-called penitential books (*libri poenitentiales*), to assist the generally uneducated clergy.

These works did not focus on the ideals of Christian existence but only on varieties of sins. They led to the belief that Christian life is essentially one of avoiding sin; the mere avoidance of sin, in turn, led some to conclude to their own moral righteousness. Absolution was not perceived as an act of forgiveness and mercy, but of judgment. And emphasis was placed increasingly on the nature of the individual moral act, apart from the larger context of one's whole existence. Thus, for example, a basically good person could "go to Hell" if he deliberately missed Mass on a given Sunday and then died before having a chance to recite a "perfect act of contrition" or "get to confession."

THIRTEENTH CENTURY

By now a new institution had come upon the scene in the West: the university. It was to change the character and course of moral theology. Systematization became the rule rather than the exception. There was a push to organize and to integrate, to produce *summae*, or syntheses, of theology. The two great figures were Bonaventure (d. 1274) and Thomas Aquinas (d. 1274).

For Bonaventure, and the Franciscan school generally (e.g., Alexander of Hales, d. 1245), the will, not the intellect, was the primary faculty. The intellect was but the tool of the will, which was the instrument of decision. The purpose of theology is to "make us holy." Thomas Aquinas, on the other hand, stressed the intellectual side of human existence. What Bonaventure played down, i.e., contemplation of the true, Thomas emphasized. Theology is for the sake of understanding. Therefore, there could be no separation of doctrinal from moral theology, because there is no separation of truth from behavior. Thomas' entire moral outlook is based on our relation to creation and the last end, on the fact that we are made in the image and likeness of God, and on the humanity of Christ as our way to God (see the prologues to the second and third parts of the *Summa Theologica*). The foundation for his whole theology is God, the Creator, and Christ, the Redeemer. We shall achieve beatitude or union with God through participation in God's own knowledge and love through the grace of Christ. Indeed, this grace is the heart of the new Law, i.e., "the grace of the Holy Spirit, which is given to those who believe in Christ" (I-II, q. 106, a. 1). The virtues, or God-given "powers" to do what is right and to avoid what is evil, are also explicitly treated: the theological virtues of faith, hope, and love, and the cardinal virtues of prudence, fortitude, temperance, and justice. Aquinas' moral teaching, therefore, centered not upon us and the rewards we seek, but upon God as the source of both created and eternal life. (The reader should not neglect to scan the table of contents of I-II and II-II of the *Summa Theologica* in order to appreciate the comprehensiveness and detailed character of Thomas' reflections on the Christian moral life. Much of the material in the next chapter of this book is rooted precisely in Thomas' vision.)

FOURTEENTH AND FIFTEENTH CENTURIES

Where Thomas had emphasized *habits*, i.e., basic attitudes, the Nominalists who followed him, e.g., William of Ockham (d. 1359), emphasized *individual acts*. Secondly, they defined "the good" as that which conforms with the will of the individual. And so a thoroughly individualistic ethic emerges, one which underlines the unique situation of every person in the face of a moral decision. If society feels threatened by this individualism, it has one recourse: the exercise of power. Individual moral agents can be "collected together" and given some shape and direction by the imposition of law, which demands conformity. Thus, the Nominalist approach generates first an ethical individualism and then an ethical legalism.

This was also a time of extraordinary economic expansion and complexification. Medieval feudalism was yielding to the new middle-class commerce. Such activities as the buying and selling of goods and the making of contracts were commonplace. One could no longer rely on relatively simple principles of charity. It became necessary to state precisely the demands of justice, which has to do with rights and duties. The other virtues, such as faith and love, became secondary to justice. A moral minimalism developed ("What am I absolutely required to do, as a bare moral minimum?").

It was against this state of affairs that Martin Luther (d. 1546) would react so vehemently. "The situation emphasized justice, and Luther was convinced that no one is just. The situation focused on minimums, and Luther felt driven to perfection. The situation cherished good works, and Luther placed his trust in faith" (Timothy O'Connell, *Principles for a Catholic Morality*, p. 16).

This was also the period of the great medieval penitential books, in the tradition of the Irish penitential books of the early Middle Ages. They were not textbooks. They were more akin to reference books, such as a dictionary, presenting basic information on a wide range of topics arranged alphabetically. The most important was that of St. Antonine (d. 1459), which presents a sweeping picture of the moral life of the fifteenth century. It exercised profound influence on subsequent works.

SIXTEENTH CENTURY

Although the first commentary on the *Summa* of Thomas Aquinas had been produced by Henry of Gorkum (d. 1431) in the fifteenth century, it was not until the beginning of the sixteenth century that the *Summa* was used as a textbook in the schools, thereby replacing Peter Lombard's *Book of Sentences*. This Thomistic revival had a pronounced impact on moral theology because Thomas, unlike Peter Lombard, had a relatively complete and well-integrated treatment of moral questions, especially of the virtues (*Summa* I-II and II-II). Conrad Koellin (d. 1536), a German Dominican, published the first complete commentary on the first part of the second part of the *Summa* (I-II), and there followed another major commentary by Thomas de Vio, Cardinal Cajetan (d. 1534), in Italy. The Thomistic revival also took hold in Spain at the school of Salamanca through the teachings and writings of Francis of Vitoria (d. 1546), Melchior Cano (d. 1560), Dominic Soto (d. 1560), Dominic Banez (d. 1604)—all Dominicans, like Thomas Aquinas himself.

Concurrent with this Thomistic revival was the Catholic Church's broader struggle with Protestantism. This effort was focused in the work of the Council of Trent. Its *Decree on Justification* (Session VI, 1547) stressed the freedom of the person to assent to, and cooperate with, grace and thus to dispose himself or herself for justification. Free will was not destroyed by Original Sin. Furthermore, the council also took care to specify the nature and number of the seven sacraments and placed special emphasis on the necessary elements in the sacrament of Penance: contrition, confession, absolution, and satisfaction. Trent also established the Catholic seminary system for the education and training of priests. For the first time in its history, the Church decided that the preparation of its clergy for their ministry should occur apart from the normal world, that future priests should be given precise instruction on what they are to preach and teach, and that they should be impressed with the need for institutional loyalty and obedience. Since priests are also ministers of sacraments, they must know exactly the conditions under which those sacraments can validly and licitly be received.

The Society of Jesus (the Jesuits) was the center of this educational enterprise throughout the sixteenth and seventeenth centuries. Their *ratio studiorum* (order of studies) dictated that those professors who were charged with lecturing on the *Summa* of St. Thomas should limit their courses to the more basic principles of moral teaching. Some professors of moral doctrine, however, were assigned to deal with "cases of conscience" in order to determine the correct solution of problems. As a result, an independent and self-contained field of moral theology emerged. Always the concern was to discover if, in fact, a penitent had sinned. All the necessary sources, including canon law, were incorporated into these moral texts to aid in the solution of each problem. Indeed, some topics such as Matrimony and Penance were treated exclusively from a canonical point of view. The first comprehensive manual of moral theology, whose basic form was followed until the Second Vatican Council, was the *Institutiones Morales*, by John Azor (d. 1603). General principles are followed in order by the commandments of God and the Church, the sacraments, censures, indulgences, and the particular obligations of the various states of life.

SEVENTEENTH AND EIGHTEENTH CENTURIES

Moral theology (or theological reflection on Christian existence) was by now a separate division of theology, no longer flowing from doctrinal theology nor from the classic sources of doctrinal theology, i.e., Scripture and the Fathers. Moralists were expected primarily to answer the question "What morally may I do?" Two extremes developed. On the far right, the *Jansenists* rejected every kind of casuistry (i.e., deciding morality on a case-by-case basis), insisting instead that the strictest standards must always be followed. We are radically corrupted by Original Sin, they argued. Only grace can overcome that corruption, and that grace is given to few. When it *is* given, however, it is irresistible. Jansenism was condemned in 1653 by Pope Innocent X's (d. 1655) Constitution *Cum Occasione*. There was also *Quietism*, which excluded all moral effort from the spiritual life. This was condemned by Pope Innocent XI (d. 1689) in his Constitution *Caelestis Pastor* in 1687. At the far left were the *laxists*, who were devoted exclusively to casuistry and who solved literally thousands of cases, usually in favor of liberty.

These debates led to the growth of a variety of moral systems, one of which was known as "probabilism." This was a method of solving difficult moral cases by allowing the Christian to follow the more lenient opinion, even if it was held by only one reputable theologian. Variations on "probabilism" developed: *Equiprobabilism* required that the two conflicting opinions should have equal support among the experts; *probabiliorism* required that the more lenient opinion should also be the majority opinion.

The principal moderating force at this time was Alphonsus Liguori (d. 1787). He was regarded as a prudent and balanced theologian, one whose opinions could be relied upon. In an age when extreme views were the order of the day, Alphonsus injected a measure of reason and restraint into moral discourse. His methodological approach to moral theology also had a strong impact on subsequent theologies. He always identified and summarized all the opinions on a particular question, then tried to fashion a position somewhere in between the extremes. He counseled against rigorism, i.e., against imposing more on the penitent than was required by the law or by the Gospel, and against laxism, i.e., against disregarding the clear requirements of either law or Gospel, or both.

NINETEENTH TO MID-TWENTIETH CENTURY
General Developments in Moral Theology

A reaction set in at the German University of Tübingen with the work of Johann Michael Sailer (d. 1832), bishop of Ratisbon, and Johann Baptist von Hirscher (d. 1865). Both attempted a reformulation of moral theology disengaged from its customary casuisty and legalism and reconnected with doctrinal theology. Both were also influenced by the renewal of biblical studies, and hence understandably called for a return to the central New Testament notions of conversion and discipleship. In his *Christian Moral Teaching as Realization of the Kingdom of God* (1834), Von Hirscher focused especially on the Kingdom of God as the basis of Christian morality. But neither theologian was without weaknesses. Their understanding of Scripture was often uncritical, and they displayed too little appreciation of the work of the Scholastics.

Contemporaneous and subsequent events impeded a smooth shift in theological gears, however. Pope Pius IX's *Syllabus of Errors* (1864), the First Vatican Council (1869-1870), and a general atmosphere of suspicion and hostility between German and Italian scholars slowed the process. But the Tübingen theologians kept at it: Magnus Jocham (d. 1893), who focused on the theology of grace and the sacraments; Bernard Fuchs (d. 1854), who emphasized the Mystical Body as the context for rebirth in God and growth in grace; Martin Deutinger (d. 1864), who developed a personalism of love based on the idea of human freedom and the capacity to love God; Karl Werner (d. 1888), who put Christ at the center and held up sacrifice as the moral ideal; and Francis Xavier Linsenmann (d. 1898), who also emphasized the Pauline theme of the freedom of the children of God over against the law. There were at the same time, however, other theologians in Germany who continued the more casuistic approach: Francis Friedhoff

(d. 1865), John the Evangelist Pruner (d. 1907), and Francis Schindler (d. 1922).

But the more integrated, biblically and patristically grounded theology carried the greater authority into the twentieth century, particularly in the works of Joseph Mausbach (d. 1931), Otto Schilling (d. 1956), Fritz Tillmann (d. 1953), and Theodore Steinbuechel (d. 1949). For them the law of love, the ethos of the Sermon on the Mount, is the heart and soul of moral theology. When two other German theologians, Joseph Fuchs and Bernard Häring, assumed teaching positions at the Gregorian University and the Alphonsianum in Rome respectively, a wider dissemination of this evolving German theology was assured. Its effects can be seen outside of Europe in the writings of Charles Curran, one of Häring's first American students. Another major influence on recent Catholic moral thought was Gerard Gilleman, whose *The Primacy of Charity in Moral Theology* (Westminster, Md.: Newman Press, 1959) along with Häring's *The Law of Christ*, 3 vols. (Westminster, Md.: Newman Press, 1961-1966), were among the most widely read books in Catholic seminaries in the years just before and during Vatican II.

But even into the 1950s, this broadly based development on the Continent notwithstanding, moral theology in the United States, for example, remained oriented toward the preparation of confessors. The emphasis was on the individual act to determine whether or not it fell into the category of sin, and, if so, whether it was mortal, or venial. Stress was still placed on obedience to law: divine law, natural law, human law. The "good" is what is commanded by law. Therefore, conformity with law is the fulfillment of the good. Analysis of moral action still tended to abstract from the concrete circumstances and situation of the moral actor. The manuals in use in the United States and other countries were based on an understanding of an essentially unchanging human nature. This was the so-called *classicist* approach. Classicist moral theology was largely unbiblical, unsacramental, and unintegrated with the great doctrinal themes of Christ, grace, the Holy Spirit, and the Church understood as the Body of Christ and the People of God. It should be noted, however, that the classicist approach always enjoyed the favor of official teaching before the council, particularly in the various moral pronouncements issued during the pontificate of Pope Pius XII—e.g., the Instruction of the Holy Office on "Situation Ethics" (1956).

That official situation changed with Vatican II. In its *Decree on Priestly Formation* the council urged the renewal of moral theology: "Its scientific exposition should be more thoroughly nourished by scriptural teaching. It should show the nobility of the Christian vocation of the faithful, and their obligation to bring forth fruit in charity for the life of the world" (n. 16). In general, moral theology should be "renewed by livelier contact with the mystery of Christ and the history of salvation." Elsewhere in its two major constitutions, one on the Church and the other on the Church in the modern world, the council proposes an ideal of Christian existence which goes well beyond the observance of law and of juridical norms. Every member of the Church is part of the People of God, and insofar as the whole Church is called to be the sacrament of Christ, the whole Church is also called to holiness (*Dogmatic Constitution on the Church*, n. 40). This consists in the following of Christ (n. 41), which leads to the perfection of love (n. 42). This is at once a love of God and a love of neighbor. These two kinds of love cannot be separated (*Pastoral Constitution on the Church in the Modern World*, n. 24). But the most significant aspect of the council's moral teaching is its advancement of the Church's social doctrine, to which we now turn our attention.

Development of Catholic Social Doctrine

Catholic social doctrine is to be distinguished from the social implications of the Gospel. Catholic social doctrine is a clearly discernible body of official teachings on the social order, in its economic and political dimensions. It is concerned with the dignity of the human person as created in the image of God, with human rights and duties which protect and enhance this dignity, with the radically social nature of human existence, with the nature of society and of the state, with the relationship between society and state (balancing the principle of subsidiarity and the principle of socialization), and with voluntary associations, e.g., labor unions, which serve as a buffer and a bridge between state and society.

Catholic social doctrine as such did not exist before the end of the nineteenth century, which is not to say that the Catholic Church expressed no official interest in, or concern for, the world outside the sanctuary until Pope Leo XIII's encyclical, *Rerum Novarum*, "On the Condition of the Working Man," in 1891. But not until Leo XIII did the Catholic Church begin to articulate in a consciously *systematic* manner a theology of *social justice* and all that this implies. (A fuller discussion of social justice will be presented in the next chapter.) This is not to say that this theology of social justice was well *integrated* with the rest of theology, and particularly with ecclesiology. It was not. Little attention, in fact, was paid in the social teachings of Leo XIII, Pius XI, and Pius XII to forging a clear link between the social ministry of the Church and the nature and mission of the Church. This link was not forged until Vatican II.

Catholic social doctrine is not a blueprint for the reform of the world. It is rather a broad theological and philosophical framework of social analysis. Thus far it has been developed in three stages:

Stage one consists of the Church's response to the problems posed by the *Industrial Revolution*. The key texts are Leo XIII's *Rerum Novarum* (1891) and Pius XI's *Quadragesimo Anno*, "Reconstructing the Social Order" (1931). The principal issues are the role of government in society and in the economy, the right of laborers to organize, the principle of a just wage, and a Christian critique of both capitalism and socialism.

Stage two emerges during the Second World War and continues to the present (overlapping with a third stage). It is the *internationalization* of Catholic social doctrine, confronting the growing material interdependence of the world and seeking to provide a moral framework for the political, economic, and strategic issues facing the human community. The key texts are those of Pope Pius XII (his Pentecost Message of 1941 and his Christmas Addresses of 1939-1957), John XXIII (*Mater et Magistra*, "Christianity and Social Progress," 1961, and *Pacem in Terris*, "Peace on Earth," 1963), Paul VI (*Populorum Progressio*, "The Progress of

Peoples," 1967), the Second Vatican Council's *Pastoral Constitution on the Church in the Modern World* (*Gaudium et spes*, 1965), and the Third International Synod of Bishops' *Justice in the World* (*Iustitia in mundo*, 1971). The principal issues are the political and juridical organization of the international community, the demands of international social justice in determining the rules and relationships of international economic policy, and the moral issues regarding warfare in a nuclear age.

Stage three is represented by Pope Paul VI's apostolic letter *Octagesima Adveniens* ("The Eightieth Year," 1971), reaffirmed to some extent in his apostolic exhortation *Evangelii Nuntiandi* ("On Evangelization in the Modern World," 1975), and Pope John Paul II's *Redemptor Hominis* ("Redeemer of Humankind," 1979). The keynote is sounded in *Octagesima Adveniens* as it addresses "new social questions." It examines the issues faced in an acute way by post-industrial societies, which have been so transformed by *technology* and its effects, especially in the area of communications and mobility (see our discussion in chapter 3). On the other hand, the papal letter returns to the theme of how post-industrial and developing societies are related internationally. The document focuses on the forms of organization which compete for primacy in society and on the intellectual currents which seek to legitimate other kinds of social and political orders. This broader political approach is carried forward in Pope John Paul II's encyclical, which speaks of our alienation from the products and byproducts of technology—e.g., environmental pollution and destruction, the arms race, the widening gap between rich and poor, increasingly sophisticated methods of torture and oppression, wasteful attitudes and practices, inflation, and modern methods of warfare. What is essential today is the right of citizens to share in the "political life of the community" in service of the common good, whether national or international, and in service of the human person, whose dignity in Christ is the foundation and linchpin of the whole social and political order. "Thus the principle of human rights is of profound concern to the area of social justice and is the measure by which it can be tested in the life of political bodies" (section 17, par. 7).

The Second Vatican Council, although still very much a part of stage two, prepared the way for the expansion of Catholic social doctrine to include the political dimension as well. Among the fundamental principles the council stresses, especially in its *Pastoral Constitution on the Church in the Modern World*, are the dignity of the human person created in the image of God (n. 12), the dignity of the moral conscience (n. 16), the excellence of freedom (n. 17), the social nature of human existence and of our destiny (n. 24), the interdependence of person and society (n. 26), the need to promote the common good for the sake of human dignity (n. 26), respect for persons (n. 27), their fundamental equality as the basis of social justice (n. 29), the value of all human activities because of the redemption (n. 34), the rightful autonomy of temporal realities (n. 36), and the missionary responsibility of the Church to attend to this constellation of values and principles (the document as a whole, especially nn. 40-45). The same insistence on human freedom is sounded in the council's *Declaration on Religious Freedom*, a freedom that belongs not only to individuals but to groups (n. 4) and that is always subject to the common good (n. 7).

The social mission of the Church is even more explicitly articulated in the synodal document *Justice in the World*: "Action on behalf of justice and participation in the transformation of the world fully appear to us as a constitutive dimension of the preaching of the Gospel, or, in other words, of the Church's mission for the redemption of the human race and its liberation from every oppressive situation" (Introduction, par. 6). And later the same declaration applies the principle to the Church itself, for "anyone who ventures to speak to people about justice must first be just in their eyes" (III, par. 2). The Church, which is the sacrament of Christ, is called upon by missionary mandate to practice what it preaches about justice and rights.

CATHOLIC MORAL THEOLOGY:
FROM CLASSICISM TO HISTORICAL
CONSCIOUSNESS

How explain the movement from pre-Vatican II to post-Vatican II moral theology? At the risk of oversimplifying, it is principally the effect of *a fundamental shift in methodology*: from classicism to historical consciousness.

Classicism conceives the moral life of the Christian as that which conforms to certain pre-existing norms: divine law, natural law, ecclesiastical law. Its emphasis, therefore, is always on law, authority, *magisterium*, precedent. Therefore, it is deductive rather than inductive in its approach, and it deals with moral issues in the abstract, i.e., according to universal norms rather than in light of particular or even peculiar circumstances and situations. Classicism is *teleological*; i.e., it emphasizes the end (*telos*), or purpose, of human existence as if one can find in the nature or essence of humanity a blueprint for growth and development. Classicism is also *deontological*; i.e., it emphasizes duty and obligation (*deontos*) in relation to law.

The *advantages* of classicism are its clarity, its simplicity, and its assurance of certitude regarding what is good and evil in relation to the will of God. Its *disadvantages* are its authoritarianism (the Church has most, if not all, of the answers), its dogmatism (and those answers are final and binding), its anti-intellectualism (authoritative norms, not theological or philosophical speculation, are the principal guides to Christian fidelity), and indeed its restriction of teaching authority to the pope and bishops, while making little distinction among the various levels of even *their* authoritative pronouncements (e.g., ecumenical councils, synods of bishops, papal encyclicals, papal letters, decrees of a Vatican congregation).

Historical consciousness, on the other hand, conceives the moral life of the Christian as one of personal responsibility within changing historical conditions. Indeed, the norms themselves reflect the historical situation in which they were first formulated and subsequently interpreted. The emphasis, then, is on "the subject," as historical and social (see chapters 4 and 5). Therefore, an historically conscious methodology is more inductive than deductive, and it deals with moral issues in the concrete and in terms of the particularities of the historical moment. It emphasizes the empirical, the evolutionary, the changeable. According to Vatican II, "...the human race has passed from a rather static concept of reality to a more dynamic, evolutionary one" (*Pastoral Constitution on the Church in the Modern World*, n. 5). A moral theology founded on an historically conscious methodology stresses personal responsibility: to God, to oneself, to the Church, and to the wider human community. It does not completely reject teleology. On the contrary, it understands history as moving toward the Kingdom of God. But it does not assume some inexorable, predetermined process or plan that is readily knowable in light of reason (natural law) and faith (divine law and ecclesiastical law). Neither does it reject the place of norms and obligations, as in the deontological approach. But those norms and obligations never adequately embody or capture the values which they purport to express. The values (e.g., the dignity of human life) may be absolute, but the norms to realize them (e.g., no killing) are relative to the historical situation.

The *advantages* of historical consciousness are its respect for the dignity of the person, for human freedom and responsibility, and its understanding of the moral life as something always unfinished and in process. Its *disadvantages* are its tendencies toward subjectivism ("I am my own law"), relativism ("Nothing is finally binding upon me"), and anti-nomianism ("Laws of every kind are completely irrelevant").

Properly understood, these two methodologies are not necessarily antithetical. A balanced moral theology cannot prescind from principles, precedent, and ultimate purpose, and so it must to that extent be deductive, deontological, and teleological. But it must always attend to the person and the situation, and so it must also be inductive and historical. It is not a question, however, of preserving fifty percent of classicism and adding fifty percent of historical consciousness. The relationship is not so much one of equality as of dialectical tension. That is to say, there are values in the classicist approach which an historical–consciousness approach cannot neglect: the concern for clarity, precision, order, consistency, objectivity, and respect for the classic sources of Christian faith, i.e., Sacred Scripture, the writing of the Fathers and great theologians, and the official teachings of the Church.

On the other hand, there *is* perhaps one irreconcilable difference between the two approaches. The classicist assumes that one can know and express absolute truth in ways that are essentially unaffected by the normal limitations of our human condition. Classicism neglects the basic Thomistic principle that "whatever is received is received according to the mode [situation] of the receiver" (*Summa Theologica*, I, q. 79, a. 6) and is generally indifferent to the major findings of anthropology, psychology, sociology, and especially the sociology of knowledge (see, for example, Peter Berger and Thomas Luckmann, *The Social Construction of Reality*, New York: Doubleday, 1966). Because the classicist rejects in principle the assertion that the perception of all truth is historically conditioned, the classicist takes the sources of Christian faith (Scripture, doctrines, etc.) at "face value," i.e., as if the language and concepts found in the original documents have exactly the same meaning for their authors as they do for those of us reading those documents today. Two recent official pronouncements of the Catholic Church explicitly transcend the classicist approach: the Pontifical Biblical Commission's *Instruction on the Historical Truth of the Gospels* (1964), and the Congregation for the Doctrine of the Faith's *Mysterium Ecclesiae* (1973). Excerpts from both of these documents are provided in the Appendix.

ECUMENICAL SITUATION

The growing theological consensus noted earlier on the mystery of the Church and the celebration of the sacraments is not duplicated here in the area of moral theology or Christian ethics. None of the ecumenical dialogues, for example, has addressed itself to a major moral issue in the sustained way in which they have faced such questions as the place and function of the ordained ministry, papal primacy and infallibility, the nature of the Eucharist, or the mission of the Church. The ecumenical exchange has been wider and more intensive among the doctrinal or dogmatic theologians than it has been among the moral theologians of the various Christian denominations and traditions. Exceptions on the Catholic side include Charles Curran (see his *Politics, Medicine, and Christian Ethics: A Dialogue with Paul Ramsey*, Philadelphia: Fortress Press, 1973), Franz Böckle (see his *Law and Conscience*, New York: Sheed & Ward, 1966), and Joseph Fuchs (see his *Natural Law: A Theological Investigation*, New York: Sheed & Ward, 1965), and on the Protestant side, James Gustafson (see his *Protestant and Roman Catholic Ethics*, Chicago: University of Chicago Press, 1978) and Paul Ramsey (see his *Who Speaks for the Church?*, Nashville: Abingdon Press, 1966). If we are to take Gustafson's view as reliable, the fault in this case may be more on the Protestant than on the Catholic side.

Protestants (e.g., see Roger Mehl, *Catholic Ethics and Protestant Ethics*, Philadelphia: Westminster Press, 1971) often fail to appreciate the origins of Catholic moral theology or the major changes which have occurred in it since Vatican II alone. Catholic moral theology came into being as a distinct discipline in order to assist the confessor in his sacramental functions. Seldom in Protestantism has such a juridical role existed, and so Protestant ethics has usually been more diffuse and ambiguous. Furthermore, Catholics have always stressed the mediating role of the Church and of certain ministers within the Church. Thus, Catholic moral theology has been attentive to norms and principles formulated and authoritatively taught by the hierarchy, whereas Protestant ethics has developed in a much freer atmosphere, without any supreme court of appeal and without required loyalty to specific moral teachings.

A major difference between the two approaches has to do with the place of Sacred Scripture in moral reasoning. The Reformation principle *sola scriptura* ("Scripture alone") became deeply embedded in the Protestant tradition, so much so that a wide variety of Protestant ethicists—from the liberal, social Gospel left to the conservative, fundamentalist right—grounded their ethics entirely in Scripture. According to Gustafson, " . . . when the centrality of the natural moral law in Catholic moral theology is set in contrast to the centrality of Scripture in Protestant ethics, a historic divergence of great proportions is made clear" (*Protestant and Roman Catholic Ethics*, p. 21).

If Catholic and Protestant moral theologies are coming closer together, it is because of revision of traditional assumptions on both sides. Thus, Catholics have a more nuanced understanding of natural law and ecclesiastical authority, whereas Protestants have a more critical perception of Scripture and a greater sense of tradition. Gustafson draws a comparison on the basis of certain polarities in moral theology: being and becoming, structure and process, order and dynamics, continuity and change, determination and freedom, nature and history, nature and grace, law and Gospel. Catholic moral theologians are paying increasing attention to the second set of terms, while Protestants are focusing more intently on the first set. Another way of putting it: Catholics have moved toward an historically conscious methodology without yielding the abiding values of the classicist approach, and Protestants have moved toward embracing some of those enduring values of classicism without abandoning the best in the method of historical consciousness.

SUMMARY

1. Just as faith and action are united in the one notion of *praxis* (practice-plus-reflection, and reflection-in-practice), so dogmatic and moral theology are united in one systematic theology. On the other hand, they are not simply the same. For a living faith, there must be an expression of love, but faith itself is not the same as love and can exist, at least for a time, without love. So, too, it is possible to distinguish between what we believe and what we are called to be and to do.

2. *Christian* ethics does not differ from *philosophical* ethics simply on the basis that the former proceeds from revelation as well as reason while the latter proceeds from reason alone. Insofar as all reality is graced, the question is not so much whether there is a distinctively Christian ethics as whether there is a purely philosophical ethics, completely untouched by the order of grace.

3. *Christian ethics* may be *defined* as the intellectual discipline that renders an account of the experience of God in Jesus Christ and that draws the normative inferences from it for the conduct of the Christian community and its members. It seeks to aid the Church and its members to discern what God is enabling and requiring them to be and to do.

4. Faithful *praxis* is linked in ancient Israel with the *Law* and that, in turn, with the *Covenant*. The most solemn expression of the Law

was the *Decalogue*, or Ten Commandments. The Ten Commandments are unique in the sense that they are regarded as the revealed will of God and as a manifestation of the bond that exists between God and the people of Israel. The Decalogue was not the ultimate norm of all morality but was concerned primarily with the community and its survival. It was not so much an ethical document as a covenantal one.

5. The *Ten* Commandments are not recognized *as such* in the New Testament, not even by Jesus. And they had not yet become a charter of morality.

6. The *Covenant* was always the principal motive for obeying the Law in the Old Testament. Its heart and soul is *hesed*, the affection and loyalty which bound the two unequal partners (God and Israel) together. The Covenant is summed up in the formula: "I will be your God and you shall be my people" (Jeremiah 7:23).

7. *Interpretation* of the Covenant was not left to any one group, but was given by the *priests*, the *prophets*, and the *wise persons* alike.

8. The moral message of *Jesus* was centered on the Kingdom of God. His preaching of the Kingdom was both a *proclamation* of good news and a warning and call to *repentance*. Moral existence is always a response to a divine call. We find no ethical system as such in the New Testament, and certainly not in Jesus' teaching.

9. That is not to say that Jesus made no specific *moral demands*. He repudiated self-righteousness and presumption. He demanded faith in himself. He required heavy sacrifices from his disciples: e.g., leaving home, selling their possessions. He set himself at odds with certain aspects of the law, attacking those who equated observance of the law with moral probity. He commanded us to love one another, even our enemies. He gave an example of this love in his own life and death.

10. Jesus was concerned with *the world*, but he did not come to change the political order directly. What he preached was bound to affect the consciousness and behavior of those who accepted his word, but he explicitly rejected every effort to make of himself a *political* figure.

11. Jesus had a special regard for *the poor*, with whom he could identify from his own background and experience, and he warned against the temptations of wealth and power. This is especially evident in the Gospel of Luke. What is revolutionary about Jesus' teaching was that the poor should have any place at all in the divine scheme of things. Poverty is not an obstacle to the Kingdom. On the contrary.

12. Jesus' teaching on *marriage* and the *family* was founded on his concern for the *dignity of women*, far beyond the concern shown in contemporary Jewish attitudes and customs. He was in the company of

women, healed women, and included them among his followers. He insisted on the permanence of marriage, lest women be regarded as mere objects to be set aside at will.

13.   Jesus was not silent about *rewards and punishments*, but he criticized those who acted morally only for the sake of rewards, and he also reminded his listeners that God's standards, dictated by divine mercy, are not our standards. Those who come into the vineyard at the eleventh hour can also be saved.

14.   The *early Church's* moral teaching was shaped by the same focal concern for the coming Kingdom of God. Our movement toward the Kingdom is initiated in Baptism and with the outpouring of the Holy Spirit. We have become a new creation, the Body of Christ. Christian existence is existence in *community*. The Law is summed up in the call to love one another.

15.   Formal *post-biblical reflection* on the nature and demands of Christian existence was influenced by the threat of paganism. Thus, moral questions were concerned with false worship and the use of pagan images. The imitation of God in Christ was an early theme of Christian moral theology—e.g., Clement of Alexandria and Origen.

16.   The first great figure in moral theology was *Augustine*, who attended to such questions as the relationship between grace and freedom, grace and law. He emphasized always the disposition of the heart. On the other hand, there is a negative tone to much of Augustine's work, especially on matters of sexuality, that has had a less happy influence on subsequent moral theology.

17.   Moral theology took a significant turn in the *sixth century*, when, under the influence of the Celtic monks, the sacrament of Penance was administered more widely. The fact that a generally uneducated clergy needed to determine appropriate penances for a broad variety of sins brought about the *penitential books*, which were the forerunners of the post-medieval manuals of moral theology.

18.   Christian moral life was now perceived primarily as a matter of *avoiding sin*. Absolution was less an act of mercy and forgiveness than an act of *judgment*.

19.   With the emergence of *universities* in the high Middle Ages (thirteenth century), attention to moral questions became more systematic: in Bonaventure and especially in *Thomas Aquinas*. However, moral theology was still not separate from theology as a whole. Thomas argued that we must be concerned with the way we act because we are made in the image and likeness of God, we are destined for eternal union with

God, and we have been redeemed by Christ. Thomas' moral teaching, therefore, was framed by the doctrines of creation and redemption.

20. *Nominalism* reintroduced an *individualistic* ethic and an ethical *legalism*. Since each moral act is utterly isolated from all others, the only force that can bring some measure of harmony into human behavior is law.

21. This was also the period of extraordinary *economic* expansion and complexification. Moral theology became preoccupied with such problems as contracts and the buying and selling of goods. A moral *minimalism* resulted, as people asked simply what they were absolutely required to do to avoid sin. It was against this situation that *Martin Luther* reacted.

22. In counter-reaction to Luther and the Protestant Reformation, the *Council of Trent* established a *Catholic seminary system*. This created for the first time in the Church's history a formal need for *textbooks* or manuals to prepare priests for the sacramental ministry, especially the ministry of Penance. The moral theology textbooks were born out of this period (sixteenth century), and moral questions were now treated entirely separately from the broader dogmatic and biblical ones.

23. Extreme approaches to moral theology quickly developed: *Jansenism* followed a rigorist path (the strictest course was always the preferred course), and *laxists* followed a permissive path (when in doubt, follow the easier course). *Probabilism* agreed with the laxist approach if the easier course were approved by at least one reputable theologian. *Equiprobabilism* demanded that the strength of the two positions (the one strict, the other liberal) should be roughly equivalent. *Probabiliorism* demanded that the lenient view be in fact the stronger (i.e., more probable) view as well.

24. The principal moderating force at this time was *Alphonsus Ligouri*, who initiated the practice of identifying and summarizing all opinions and then offering his own prudent view, somewhere near the center.

25. A reaction to the legalism and isolated character of moral theology developed in the *nineteenth century* in Germany, and especially at the University of Tübingen. Moral theology was gradually reconnected with the Bible and with such New Testament themes as conversion, discipleship, and the love commandment. The more traditional (i.e., classicist) approach continued in many countries, including the United States, and in Rome's official teachings, until the work being done in Germany began making a wider impact on the Catholic world.

26.   The *Second Vatican Council* called for a renewal of moral theology, stressing its biblical roots, the idea of Christian vocation, the primacy of charity, the mystery of Christ, and the history of salvation.

27.   Meanwhile, *Catholic social doctrine*, i.e., the body of official teachings on the social order, began to take shape during the pontificate of *Leo XII*. The Church's social teachings have been formulated in *three stages*: (1) the response to the *Industrial Revolution* (emphasis on labor unions, just wage, e.g.); (2) the response to the growing *internationalization* of life (emphasis on peace and international social justice); and (3) the response to *new social questions* posed by *technology* (arms race, development and liberation of Third World, environmental pollution, e.g.).

28.   Catholic social doctrine is focused on the following themes: (1) the *dignity of the human person* as created in the image of God; (2) human *rights* and *duties* which protect and enhance that dignity; (3) the radically *social* nature of human existence; (4) the responsibility of the individual to *society* and vice versa; (5) the responsibility of the *state* to society, and vice versa; and (6) the place of *voluntary associations* as bridges and buffers between society and the state.

29.   The broader *social dimensions* of Christian moral existence are especially emphasized in Vatican II's *Pastoral Constitution on the Church in the Modern World* and are reaffirmed strongly in the Third International Synod of Bishops' *Justice in the World*. The latter document teaches that the struggle for justice and liberation is part of the essential *mission of the Church* and that this struggle must occur within as well as outside the Church.

30.   *Catholic moral theology today* is incorporating some of the insights of an historically conscious methodology while preserving many of classicism's abiding values. *Classicism* stresses conformity with extrinsic norms based on unchanging truth; *historical consciousness* stresses the subjective responsibility of the person, with attention to the wider community and to the process of history. Properly conceived, the two approaches are somewhat complementary. A balanced moral theology cannot prescind from principles, precedent, and ultimate purpose, and so it must, to that extent, be deductive, deontological, and teleological. But it must also attend to the person and the situation, and so it must also be inductive and historical.

31.   In the end, however, classicism rejects the principle that every perception and formulation of truth is historically conditioned. Therein lies the fundamental *opposition* between classicism and historical consciousness.

32. There is less *ecumenical* progress in the realm of Christian ethics or moral theology than on some of the large ecclesiological questions to which we referred in Part IV of the book. Although there are continued differences about natural law and about specific answers given to specific moral problems (e.g., abortion, birth control), a major difference between Catholic and Protestant ethics has been in their respective *uses of Sacred Scripture* as a norm of moral reflection.

33. Ecumenical convergence is in process as Protestants appropriate some of the enduring values in the classicist approach and as Catholics move more confidently into historical consciousness.

SUGGESTED READINGS

Gustafson, James M. *Can Ethics Be Christian?* Chicago: University of Chicago Press, 1975.

——————. *Protestant and Roman Catholic Ethics : Prospects for Rapprochement.* Chicago: University of Chicago Press, 1978.

Häring, Bernard. "Historical Survey of Moral Theology." *The Law of Christ.* Vol. 1, Westminster, Md.: Newman Press, 1965, pp. 3-33.

O'Connell, Timothy E. *Principles for a Catholic Morality.* New York: Seabury Press, 1978.

Regan, George M. *New Trends in Moral Theology: A Survey of Fundamental Moral Themes.* New York: Newman Press, 1971.

Schnackenburg, Rudolf. *The Moral Teaching of the New Testament.* New York: Herder & Herder, 1971.

·XXVI·

CHRISTIAN EXISTENCE: PRINCIPLES AND PROCESS

This is an exceedingly ambitious chapter, since it attempts a comprehensive statement of Catholic moral theology. The material is organized around three fundamental questions: (1) *Who is the Christian?* (2) *What kind of person is the Christian called to become?* (3) *How does one become a Christian?* The focus is the theological principles which permeate and shape the Catholic tradition's answers to each of these questions.

The formulation, interpretation, and application of those principles, however, are always historically conditioned. Christian existence itself is always historical existence. One not only *is* a Christian; one is constantly *becoming* a Christian. Conversion to the Gospel is both an act and a process. Accordingly, Christian existence moves between the polarities of principle and process, of being and becoming, of essence and existence, of the universal and the particular, of conviction and risk, of substance and form. But these are not mutually opposed; the one requires and includes the other. Thus, the universal is that which particulars have in common and which gives them meaning. The universal, in turn, is nothing apart from particulars.

So, too, with the polarity of principle and process. Principles do not appear full-blown apart from experience. They are attempts at coming to terms with the multiplicity and ambiguity of experience. Principles are formulations which try to bring a measure of consistency and coherence to human experience, to find common threads which hold that experience together. But their formulation always presupposes experience itself. Once formulated, those principles also have a critical impact on our subsequent evaluation of experience. We reconsider our estimation of past and present experiences, and we revise our anticipation of future experiences in light of these principles. In other words, principles are at once *products* of experience and *shapers* of experience. For that reason, moral theology cannot follow the method of classicism alone (which may underestimate the impact of process on principles) nor the method of historical consciousness alone (which may attend too little to the impact of principles on process). Catholic moral theology is concerned with principles and process alike.

WHO IS THE CHRISTIAN?

The answer to this question can be formulated in only a cumulative fashion. Thus, the Christian is *a radically social human person in whom God is present in grace but who is, at the same time, prone to act against the divine presence.* Thus far we have described any and every human being. The Christian is, first, a human being. But the Christian is a particular kind of human being, not in the sense that a Christian has a different biological or psychic structure, but in the sense that a Christian has moved to *a different level of human consciousness.* The Christian is one who *believes in Jesus Christ, and whose whole life is shaped by that belief.* The process by which the Christian moves to that new level of consciousness is *conversion.*

Since we have already addressed ourselves at some length to the question of human existence in chapters 4 and 5, we shall not repeat that discussion here. We shall focus instead on those elements of our cumulative definition of the Christian to which specific attention has not yet been given in this book, namely, the questions of *sin* and *conversion.*

Sin

Biblical Notions

A first understanding of the word *sin* in the Bible is "to miss the mark." To sin is to fail to achieve one's goal or to fail to measure up to one's highest standards. In the *Old Testament,* with its emphasis on the Covenant, sin is *infidelity to the covenantal relationship* between God and ourselves. It is our failure to live up to the terms of the agreement. It is a missing of the mark. Sin is also a form of idolatry. It is a substituting of human concerns and interests for God's sovereign will (Exodus 32:1-6; Deuteronomy 9:7-21). We sin against the God whom we do not see by violating the rights of our neighbor whom we do see (Leviticus 19:9-18; Isaiah 1:23-25). Rejection of the neighbor is rejection of God (Ezekiel 18:3-32).

The same relationships are present in the *New Testament.* Love of God and love of neighbor are inextricably linked (Matthew 22:34-40; Mark 12:28-31; Luke 10:25-37). It is striking that where the word for sin appears in the *Synoptics,* it almost always is used in connection with the *forgiveness of sins.* Jesus himself associates with sinners and calls them to repentance (Matthew 9:10,13; 11:19; Luke 7:34; 15:1-2; 19:7). For Jesus sin comes only from the heart, and only insofar as it does is the human person defiled (Matthew 15:18-19; Mark 7:20-22). But the sinner need only ask for forgiveness (Luke 18:13-14). There is joy in heaven over the sinner's return (Luke 15:7,10).

The malice of sin is more explicit in John: It is lawlessness (1 John 3:4), wrongdoing (5:17), lust and pride (2:16), darkness (3:9-11). But Jesus is also the conqueror of sin (John 8:46; 1 John 3:5). He is the lamb who takes away the sin of the world (John 1:29). The fullest theology of sin in the New Testament appears in the writings of Paul, and in the first part of the Epistle to the Romans in particular. It is not observance of the Law which brings us victory over sin, he writes. The Law only makes us aware of our sin. In Christ we die to sin. Our old sinful self is crucified with him "so that the sinful body might be destroyed and we might be slaves to sin no longer" (Romans 6:6). Therefore, we are now all "alive for God in Christ Jesus" (6:11). But if we are indeed new creatures in Christ, freed of sin, we must act in accordance with our status. And yet we do in fact sin. We act against who we are and against the God who is within us: "What happens is that I do, not the good I will to do, but the evil I do not intend" (7:19). Our inner selves want to follow the way of the spirit, but our outer selves are still pulled by the flesh. The Spirit has already been given to us as "first fruits" of the new creation, of the redemption of our bodies (8:23). The Spirit helps us in our weakness and makes intercession for us (8:26). "If God is for us, who can be against us?" (8:31). Therefore, Paul is not conceding here the inevitability of sin, only the permanent state of conflict which characterizes human existence: conflict between the spirit and the flesh. We need not be defeated. We can achieve victory in Christ. His Spirit has taken possession of us.

Freedom and Responsibility

The spirit-flesh conflict raises the larger theological question of freedom and responsibility. It is important to note, first, what freedom is *not*. It is not a faculty alongside other faculties (e.g., intellect, will) by which a person decides to do this or that. Freedom enters into the very definition of what it means to be human. To be free is to be present to oneself, to be in possession of oneself, to be conscious of oneself as a distinct, responsible being. Freedom does not so much allow us to *do something* as to *be someone*.

Such freedom, however, is not absolute. Only God is absolutely free, i.e., fully and perfecting self-possessive and responsible. Human freedom is *limited* from without and from within. *From without* our self-possession is qualified by our situatedness in history. Since the world is "mediated by meaning" (Lonergan), our very self-understanding and, therefore, our very freedom are shaped by the meanings which are mediated through our experience (e.g., what our parents tell us we are, what our friends and relatives and neighbors tell us, what society tells us, how our institutions, including the Church, define us, what our economic and social status discloses to us). Our freedom is also limited from without by various natural and physical realities and events—i.e., by the sheer facticity of worldly existence. *From u ..ain* our freedom is qualified by the fact that we can never be fully present to ourselves. There is a psychic universe, a portion of which Freud and others have only recently discovered, which remains hidden from our consciousness and yet influences profoundly our awareness, our vision, and our sense of personal responsibility.

Freedom, therefore, is *the relatively limited capacity to decide who we shall be.* It is not something that is active only from time to time, such as at the moment of a choice or decision. Freedom is permanently operative. It governs our whole being all the time. Such freedom is not an immediate datum of our experience. We cannot see it or readily identify it by testing. Nor is freedom (to use Karl Rahner's analogy) like a knife which always remains the same in its capacity for cutting, and in cutting always remains the same knife. Freedom is not simply an instrument for meeting specific needs of choice. It is that fundamental capacity for making a final and irrevocable choice to *be* someone, to be a particular kind of human being. In that sense, freedom is the capacity for the eternal, for God. It is that which allows us to orient ourselves beyond ourselves, to recognize who we are ultimately and to shape our entire life (not just this or that individual act) according to that new self-consciousness of who we are in the presence of God.

And this is precisely what contemporary Catholic moral theologians such as Joseph Fuchs and others mean by the *"fundamental option."* In being truly converted to the Kingdom of God, everything we do assumes its direction, purpose, and meaning in light of the Kingdom, i.e., in light of God's will. This does not rule out the possibility, indeed the probability, that we shall occasionally act against this fundamental choice for God. But only a fundamental reversal of that choice (what the traditional textbooks called *aversio a Deo,* a "turning away from God") is sufficient to cancel out the original decision to understand oneself in relation to God and to orient one's whole life in view of that new self-understanding. In other words, no single act by itself is sufficient to merit eternal punishment in hell unless that act is of sufficient depth and magnitude to constitute a fundamental repeal of the conversion experience. Only a *mortal sin,* Thomas Aquinas wrote, truly deserves the name "sin" (*Summa Theologica* I-II,

q. 88, a. 1). So rare an occurrence should that be in the case of one who is sincerely oriented to God that for the first several centuries the Church expected its members to have recourse to the sacrament of Reconciliation no more than once in their entire lifetimes, if that often! (See chapter 22 on the sacrament of Penance.)

Freedom, then, is a *transcendental* capacity (see chapters 4 and 5 on Transcendental Thomism's understanding of human existence). It is a capacity which allows a person to go beyond himself or herself, to become something other than he or she is, and not simply to do this or avoid that. But because it *is* a transcendental capacity, we can never be directly conscious of it. We acknowledged earlier (in chapter 5) that it is impossible for us to answer completely the question "Who are we?" because we are at one and the same time the questioner and the one questioned. Only God has a view of human existence which is objective and comprehensive. Indeed, as soon as we begin reflecting on our freedom we are already exercising it. We experience ourselves as free, but there is no scientific way of verifying our freedom as we verify, for example, the existence of the lungs or the kidneys. We argue to freedom not only on the basis of our experience, which in any case can be distorted by external and internal forces, but on the basis of the implications of its denial. *If we are not free, we are not responsible. And if we are not responsible, human existence is reduced to mechanical existence.* Without freedom and responsibility there is no love, no faith, no hope, no trust, no compassion, no friendship, no justice. Everything is calculated, predetermined, subject only to accident and/or *mis*calculation.

In summary, in our original, transcendental experience of ourselves as *subjects*, i.e., as distinct, conscious, interrelating, free persons, we know who we are. But we can never objectify with absolute certainty what we know. We know more of ourselves than we can say. No statement, no formulation can ever capture fully what we experience of ourselves as selves, no more than we can adequately report to another the beauty of a symphony, the powerful impact of a speaker, or the horror of an accident. We are at once present to ourselves and distant from ourselves. We are *present* to ourselves in that we are who we are and that we alone are directly conscious of who we are. But we are also *distant* from ourselves in that even our self-knowledge is impaired by factors and forces outside and inside ourselves.

The Capacity for Sin

Freedom is the capacity to say either "Yes" or "No" to God, i.e., to see ourselves either as having ultimate worth because we are alive by a principle which transcends us, or, on the other hand, to see ourselves as merely a constellation and network of biological responses and of psychological and sociological conditioning. Evidence (not overwhelming proof) of our capacity to say "Yes" to God appears in various acts of heroism and of extraordinary generosity where self-interest is clearly subordinated to the interests of others. One need only reflect on the obscenity of Auschwitz and Buchenwald to find similar evidence of our radical capacity to say "No" to God.

On the other hand, we can never point to a particular moment or act in our lives and say that precisely here and not somewhere else we made a fundamental and irrevocable choice for or against God. Whether our lives are oriented toward God or away from God can be judged only on the basis of the totality of our lives, not on the basis of a totaling up virtuous acts and sinful acts and then figuring the difference. Nor are we saying that the possibility of a "No" to God is about the same as that of a "Yes." *Although the Church has always taught that we have the capacity to reject God fundamentally (mortal sin), it has never taught that there are, in fact, persons in hell.* Insofar as Sacred Scripture describes the miseries of eternal punishment, it presents them as possibilities of human life and as instructions about the absolute seriousness of our moral decisions.

Furthermore, *we can never be certain that we have finally and fully said "No" to God, even in an act which appears on the surface to be of such a kind.* We cannot say with certitude to what extent outside and inside forces manipulated us, because that is never obvious to superficial examination. "We can never know with ultimate certainty whether we are sinners. But although it can be suppressed, we do know with ultimate certainty that we really *can* be sinners, even when our bourgeois everyday life and our own reflexive manipulation of our motives appear to give us very good grades" (Karl Rahner, *Foundations of Christian Faith*, p. 104).

What is to be said, finally, of *God's sovereignty*? If we have the capacity to say a final and definitive "No" to God, does not that limit God's power over us? It is God who created us as free beings and who willed and established our freedom. Subjectivity, therefore, must exist without limiting the sovereignty of God. If that seems too simple, consider the alternatives: (a) we are not free, and, therefore, not really human; or (b) God is essentially limited, and, therefore, not really God.

Mortal, Serious, and Venial Sin

As we reflect on our own lives and on the lives of others (the latter is usually the easier task), we recognize that those lives are marked by ambiguity and inconsistency. No one is perfectly good all the time, nor absolutely evil all the time. There is good and bad in everyone, it would appear. This indicates, first, that our fundamental option does not insure uniformity of behavior. It also indicates, secondly, that there are forces which impede our intended course of action. Why this should be so, we can never say. *That* this is so, we know all too well. This condition derives from what we know as *Original Sin*.

Venial sin is a human act which is not fully human, i.e., not fully consistent with our fundamental orientation toward God. In venial sin there is a genuine decision to do this or that *action*, but there is no decision to become this or that sort of *person*. In venial sin a person chooses to do a particular deed, but he or she also wants even more deeply to be the kind of person who stands opposed to the deed. In every venial sin, therefore, there is a contradiction between the act and the person doing the act.

Venial sin admits of *degrees* of seriousness. Some actions are objectively more serious violations of the Gospel than others. Some sinful motives are more clearly defined than others. Some circumstances make an attitude or a deed more serious than others. *Serious sin*, therefore, is even more inconsistent with the Gospel than is venial sin. But serious sin is not the same as mortal sin. Missing Mass on Sunday is an example of a serious sin.

Mortal sin is an act which fully engages the person. The person chooses not only the act but also the kind of person he or she wants to be or become in and through the act. An older view in moral theology assumed that the commission of every objectively serious act involved or engaged the fundamental option; in other words, it held that every *serious sin* is a *mortal* sin. That is, if (1) an act was seriously sinful, and (2) a person knew it was seriously sinful, and (3) freely consented to it nonetheless, it was a mortal sin.

The insights of both psychology and sociology compel us to revise that assumption. If these actions were always mortally sinful under these three conditions, and if those who committed them had frequent recourse to the sacrament of Penance throughout their lives, then we are left with the conclusion that many people are constantly changing their very self-definition. Is it conceivable that a person could define himself or herself as someone oriented toward God, then repudiate that definition one Sunday morning by deciding against attending Mass in order to watch a sports event, and then reassert that definition in Confession a few hours or a few days later? To suggest this, some moral theologians are saying, is to undermine our very dignity and to cheapen us as persons.

But is this approach really so much opposed even to traditional (i.e., medieval and post-Tridentine) moral theology? Even that theology insisted that every moral act has to be evaluated in terms of *object, end,* and *circumstances.* First, you have to see if, in fact, it is the kind of act that might engage a person's fundamental relationship with God—e.g., murder. Secondly, you have to attend to the purpose, intention, or motive of the agent; e.g., Did X shoot Y in order to protect the life of Z? Thirdly, you have to consider all of the cirsumtances; e.g., Was the killer acting under hypnosis, or had he or she just suffered a traumatic experience? By bringing together the act, the motive, and the circumstances, the traditional theology also brought together subjective and objective morality.

On the other hand, this *three-source theory* may also have confused the two realms of objective and subjective morality. When asked which of the three sources was the most important, some moralists would answer, "The first, the deed itself." But sin is always in the *will*. The primary determinant of morality must be the *motive*, not the act itself. Indeed, some would say that motive is the *only* determinant insofar as morality is not a matter of deeds but of persons acting as persons. To be moral is to be true to oneself, to be seeking always to *be* the one who responds to the call of God and to *act* in ways consistent with that vocation. To be immoral is to refuse to *be* that kind of person, and therefore to refuse to act in ways consistent with that being.

While it is true that some traditional moralists exaggerated the objective morality of the act, traditional moral theology in general has never divorced the act from the other two subjective factors in the three-source principle. Thus, even though the stealing of a loaf of bread might be a "small matter" (*parvitas materiae*), it could become a grave matter (*gravitas materiae*) if the person one stole it from was at the point of starvation. Accordingly, the three traditional questions we might put to ourselves regarding the morality of particular acts still have value: (1) How serious was the act I performed or failed to perform? (2) What was my motive, as far as I can reasonably determine? (3) What were the circumstances surrounding my decision to do what I did, and how did those circumstances affect my decision?

Capital Sins

Some sins are so deeply rooted in our fallen human nature that they are the source of other, related lapses. These are known as the seven capital sins: pride, covetousness, lust, anger, gluttony, envy, and sloth. They are discussed again below, in connection with the moral virtues. Thus, anger and sloth are sins against the cardinal virtue of fortitude, lust and gluttony against the cardinal virtue of temperance, and so forth. (See Henry Fairlee, *The Seven Deadly Sins Today*, Washington, D.C.: New Republic Books, 1978.)

Conversion

A Christian is not only a radically social human person in whom God is present in grace and who is, at the same time, prone to acting against the divine presence. A Christian is also a person who has moved to a different level of human consciousness. The Christian is one who believes in Jesus Christ and whose whole life is shaped by that belief. The process by which the human person moves to that level of consciousness is called *conversion*. More precisely, it is *Christian* conversion, since conversion to God is an invitation and a possibility for every human being.

In the previous chapter we focused on the element of conversion in the preaching of Jesus (Mark 1:15) and of the early Church (Acts of the Apostles 2:38). It was a call to repentance and belief, to a change of mind, or consciousness, and to a new mode of behavior in keeping with that change of mind. The New Testament, therefore, says that we are to live according to the demands of the Kingdom of God. We are to make God the center and source of our being. We are to allow ourselves to be transformed by the redemptive, healing presence of God and then to allow God to continue to work through us to redeem and heal others and the whole world, enemies as well as friends, the outcasts as well as the respectable, the poor as well as the rich, sinners as well as the righteous.

This, of course, is a broader and more profound understanding of conversion than was traditionally proposed since the Council of Trent, with its necessary emphasis on the intellectual and objective character of faith. To be converted was to accept divine revelation as authoritatively presented by the Church. A "convert" was a non-Catholic who had become a Catholic. The determining feature of conversion, therefore, was ecclesiological, not Christological or anthropological. It had to do, primarily, that is, with one's new relationship to the Catholic Church rather than with one's new self-understanding in relationship to God and/or to Jesus Christ.

To use Bernard Lonergan's terms (*Method in Theology*, New York: Herder & Herder, 1972), conversion means shifting horizons. For Lonergan, an *horizon* is that which circumscribes or sets limits to a person's interests and knowledge. Beyond our horizons are matters which we neither know nor care about. Some horizons are relative, others are basic. *Relative horizons* are those which depend on, or are relative to, our psychological, educational, sociological, and cultural development. *Basic horizons* are those which relate to three transcendental conversions: intellectual, moral, and religious. A *conversion* is a radical transformation from which follows on all levels of life an interlocking series of changes and developments. What had once gone unnoticed becomes present and vivid. What had once been of no concern is now of the highest importance. According to Lonergan, there is a change in oneself (intellectual conversion), in one's relations with others (moral conversion), and in one's relation to God (religious conversion). Conversion, then, is the transformation of the individual and his or her world. One's direction is altered, one's eyes are opened, and one perceives the world in a new way. Indeed, one perceives a new world.

In *intellectual conversion* there is a turning away from what seems to be to what is, from one's own limited world as defined by one's own psychologically, sociologically, and culturally conditioned desires, fears, and achievements to a world that is consistent with the intelligent, the true, the good, and even the holy. Intellectual conversion is more than a change of positions or of style. It is a fundamental alteration of a person's basic stance toward reality.

Moral conversion involves a shift from the level of thought (experience, understanding, judgment) to the level of action (decision). It is the recognition of oneself as a free and responsible subject. The morally converted person is able to make decisions for action that are based not on personal satisfaction but on value, not on what gives pleasure but on what is truly good and worthwhile. Falling in love is a prime example of moral conversion. One's emotions, decisions, and actions are all shaped and directed anew. The love literally takes over the person.

Religious conversion is a total being-in-love with God: heart, soul, mind and strength. It occurs through the coming of the Holy Spirit, and it is manifested in the love of one's neighbor, who is the sacrament of God. One should not think, however, that religious conversion comes last, after intellectual and moral conversion. On the contrary, the sequence is usually in reverse. First, there is God's gift of love. The inner grace of God discloses values and prompts action to realize those values. Among the values discerned by love's eye is the value of believing the truths articulated and taught by the community of faith. Full religious transformation should include intellectual and moral conversion, but these two kinds of conversion are neither prerequisites nor inevitable results of religious conversion. Furthermore, every conversion is only a beginning. It is both act and process, once-and-for-all and ongoing.

The *final test* of religious conversion is whether or not it leads to and is continually manifested in *love for the neighbor*. "One who has no love for the brother he has seen cannot love the God he has not seen. The commandment we have from him is this: whoever loves God must also love his brother" (1 John 4:20-21).

WHAT KIND OF PERSON IS THE CHRISTIAN CALLED TO BECOME?
Character

The Christian convert is called to become a person of *character*— i.e., with the capacity for self-determination. A person of character is one who takes responsibility for his or her actions. Those actions are not determined simply by rules or principles but by an intelligent and sometimes courageous response to a concrete situation and challenge. An ethics of character, such as proposed in recent years by Protestant ethicist Stanley Hauerwas, focuses our attention more on the person performing an act than on the acts performed by the person. The person does not set out to acquire and cultivate moral goodness. The actions a person performs not only shape a particular situation; they also *form* the person who does them. In other words, doing the act which the situation calls for will take care of shaping us into morally good persons.

Protestant ethics has accorded too little attention to the moral character of persons, perhaps because of Protestantism's traditional denial that the actual shape of a person's life has any efficacy in the attainment of the person's righteousness. Catholic ethics, on he other hand, has stressed the concept of character, especially in treatises on the theological and moral virtues. And insofar as moral theology is emphasizing today the dimension of freedom and responsibility, the concept of "character ethics" is being even more widely considered and developed in Catholic circles.

Emphasis on character, however, should not tempt us to deny the significance of the passive aspects of human existence. Much that we are is the result of what happens to us, as we noted in the previous section of this chapter. Thus, psychological, physiological, and environmental factors are not to be discounted in character formation. However, we must insist at the same time that these passive aspects of our existence enter into character formation only to the extent that we intentionally permit them to. Thus, it is our character which gives orientation and direction to our lives. Indeed, there is an old principle: "Plant an act, reap a habit; plant a habit, reap a virtue; plant a virtue, reap a character; plant a character, reap a destiny." *Habits* are regular patterns of activity. *Virtues* are good habits (and vices are bad habits). *Character* emerges from the network of virtues (or vices). Our final *destiny* depends upon the character we build in response to grace.

Character can never be finished once and for all. Good or bad habits can be reversed or broken. A pattern of habits can be modified or uprooted. Sometimes this occurs gradually; at other times it may happen through a single decisive act (as in a profound conversion experience, or in mortal sin). By definition, we are open always to change as we respond to new elements in our lives. Our moral future is created cumulatively out of our present and our past. That moral future is fashioned not by a resolution to obey certain moral rules but by a resolution to become a certain kind of person.

Since character is so closely linked with personality, and since personality is always unique, rooted as it is in self-consciousness and self-determination, there is no one type of character which is normative for everyone. There are different styles of life, even within the Christian community. Through our beliefs, intentions, and actions we acquire a particular moral history befitting our nature as self-determining persons. (See Stanley Hauerwas, *Character and the Christian Life: A Study in Theological Ethics*, San Antonio: Trinity University, 1975.)

Virtue

A virtue is a *power* (*virtus*), in the literal sense of the word. It is the power (ability, skill, facility) to accomplish moral good, and especially to do it joyfully and perseveringly even against inner and outer obstacles and at the cost of sacrifice. (When that power is turned to evil, it is called a *vice*.) Virtues are powers rooted in the presence of God, in grace. They prompt us to act in such a way as to exclude extreme forms of action. Thus, the saying: *In medio stat virtus* ("In the middle stands virtue"). For example, a person may "hope" so strongly in his eventual salvation that he begins to take it for granted. He sins by *presumption*. On the other hand, someone else may be so despondent about her chances for salvation that she "hopes" too little, and falls into *despair*. The *virtue of hope* stands in the middle of these two extremes: It is confidence in the mercy and love of God, but it also accepts responsibility for cooperating with the saving grace that has been bestowed upon us both at birth and in the sacraments. Christ, of course, is the model of all virtue. Christian moral existence, as we noted in the previous chapter, is based on the *imitation of Christ* (John 13:15).

Theology has traditionally distinguished between *natural* and *supernatural* virtues. But in light of our present understanding of the relationship between nature and grace (see chapter 5), this hard and fast distinction seems no longer appropriate. Supernatural virtues are not something added to natural virtues. On the other hand, the distinction does remind us that virtue is rooted in the human, not divorced from it. Another distinction is between *acquired* and *infused* virtues. Seen from the point of view of its source and rootedness, a virtue is "infused" by God. A final distinction—one that we shall employ in this chapter—is between *theological* and *moral* virtues. The former (faith, hope, and charity) have to do immediately with our relationship with God (thus, they are called *theo*logical; *theos* = God). The latter (prudence, justice, temperance, fortitude) have to do immediately with our relationships with one another.

The notion of virtue is not without its parallels in contemporary psychology. Erik Erikson, for example, sees the virtues as representing the strengths of the *ego* over against the animal instincts of the *id* and the imposing claims of the *superego*. "Ego strength" is equivalent to virtue. The *id* and the *superego* can rob the person of his or her freedom. In the one case, the person becomes the slave of passions, and in the other, the slave of "higher authorities." It is at the level of the *ego* that a person takes responsibility for his or her life, keeping the animal drives under some measure of control and maintaining a healthy attitude toward the pressures of an overweening conscience. (See William Meissner, *Foundations for a Psychology of Grace*, New York: Paulist Press, 1966, pp. 153-163.) Similar parallels can be drawn from the writings of Abraham Maslow (d. 1970), especially in his notion of "self-actualization" as an unceasing trend toward unity and toward the integration of energy within the person. For example, the self-actualized person has an increased self-acceptance, acceptance of others, increased autonomy, less hostility, less need for honors and prestige. A person who has achieved these characteristics in the course of personal growth has established a life-pattern very similar to that of the traditional "virtuous person, or person of character." (See *Toward a Psychology of Being*, Princeton, N.J.: Van Nostrand, 1968, and *Motivation and Personality*, New York: Harper & Row, 1970, 2nd. ed.)

The Theological Virtues

Faith

We have already addressed ourselves to certain important aspects of the question of faith in chapters 2, 6, and 7. In chapter 2 we described faith as the foundation of theology, belief, and moral action. In chapter 6 we outlined the present crisis of faith and the challenge to belief. In chapter 7 we placed the problem of faith in the larger context of the theology of revelation. Here we shall only touch again upon some of the points in chapter 2 insofar as they directly relate to the shape and character of Christian existence.

Avery Dulles makes a useful schematization of faith as a theological virtue ("The Meaning of Faith Considered in Relationship to Justice," *The Faith That Does Justice*, John C. Haughey, ed., New York: Paulist Press, 1977, pp. 10-46). Faith can be understood as *conviction*, as *trust*, and as *commitment*. The first is an *intellectualist* approach; the second, a *fiducial* approach; the third, a *performative* approach. In the classical tradition, Catholics have tended to emphasize the first, Protestants the second; today both increasingly support the third.

Faith As Conviction: The so-called "intellectualist" approach takes two forms. The *illuminist* school (Augustine, Thomas Aquinas, *et al.*) understands faith as an inner light or as the beginning of wisdom. Its modern exponents—e.g., Bernard Lonergan—regard faith as "the knowledge that is born of religious love," as the "eye of religious love." This is a view of faith, however, which does not regularly foster an intense human concern. Its primary focus is on the relationship between the individual and God in a contemplative union that could unwittingly encourage a spirit of indifference to the needs of others. Pressed too far, the illuminist notion of faith produces a split between faith and daily life.

The "body of doctrine" school, on the other hand, sees faith as a firm assent of the mind to what the Church authoritatively teaches in the name of God. It tends to equate faith with belief, to think of it as an act of intellectual submission and obedience. Although faith is always expressed in some form, its expressions are always historically conditioned. Furthermore, faith is not the acceptance of someone else's point of view on reality but is one's own interpretation of reality. The "body of doctrines" school also focuses the believer's attention so strongly on what there is to believe that he or she tends to ignore the moral (social, political, economic as well as personal and interpersonal) implications of accepting the Gospel in faith.

Faith as Trust: This is usually called the "fiducial" approach. It underlines the elements of personal trust and stresses the personal relationship of the believer with God. God is less the revealer than the savior. This concept of faith is, of course, solidly biblical (as we saw in chapter 2). It was also the emphasis of the Protestant Reformers. The problem with it is the ease with which it can overlook the importance of human initiative and undermine the sense of human responsibility for the future of the world. Everything is left in the hands of God, who will save us in spite of our iniquity. Although the justified person will perform good works and evil works alike, the deeds themselves do not bring about salvation. Faith alone saves.

Ernst Troeltsch (d. 1923), the Protestant Church historian, pointed out how the Lutheran doctrine of justification entails a lack of real interest in social reform (*The Social Teaching of the Christian Churches*, vol. 2, New York: Harper Torchbook, 1960, p. 540). The Protestant ethicist Reinhold Niebuhr (d. 1971) made a similar criticism of Luther's doctrine of the two kingdoms in his *The Nature and Destiny of Man* (New York: Scribner's, 1964, vol. 2, p. 195). If everything depends upon the grace of God and nothing finally depends on human effort, Christian commitment to social justice and peace is of no ultimate interest to the Kingdom of God.

Faith As Commitment: This is the so-called "performative" approach. Faith can never be a matter of disembodied words. It must be incarnate in *praxis* (faith-in-action). Faith is a transforming acceptance of the Word, which challenges us through the cries of the poor and oppressed. Only in liberating *praxis* can we give to the Word the "warm welcome" that constitutes faith. Faith is not a passive waiting upon God's decision to act; rather, it seizes the initiative and reshapes the world by its God-given power. Faith, therefore, is not a passive virture. It does not protect us from the world; it remakes the world. It is active engagement in the service of the Kingdom of God. This is the understanding especially dominant in Latin American liberation theology today, and it has a stronger biblical basis than many have heretofore acknowledged. Thus, "Whoever does what is true comes to the light" (John 3:21). The Gospel is the power of God revealing God's justice and leading to salvation (Romans 1:16-17). Faith works through love (Galatians 5:6). Our faith overcomes the world (1 John 5:4). But neither is this "performative" view a sufficient understanding of faith.

Faith As Synthesis of Conviction, Trust, and Commitment: Each one of these approaches says something that is enduringly true about the virtue of faith. First, faith inevitably seeks understanding, and the understanding achieved is expressed theologically and sometimes doctrinally, as the "intellectualist" approach insists. Faith, therefore, has content; there are truths to be grasped and become convinced of. Faith is also an inner disposition, an illumination of consciousness by which we see and comprehend reality in a wholly new light. Secondly, faith is acceptance of the Word of God. It is trust in God's power to bestow new life, as the "fiducial" approach argues. Finally, faith is an act of self-surrender, demanding total commitment to the Kingdom of God, as the "performative" approach emphasizes. But that Kingdom is not an other-worldly reality alone. It is also a Kingdom of justice and peace here and now. God is present in history, calling us to collaboration in the coming of the Kingdom. To define faith only as conviction or only as trust is to undermine that principle which is so central to Catholicism: the principle of sacramentality. For it is in and through the neighbor whom we see that we respond to the God whom we do not see.

Faith Development: The recognition that faith is not only an act but also a process is not so revolutionary as it may first appear. Faith has always been understood as a virtue, and virtues are in the category of *habits*. Faith, then, can never be merely a once-and-for-all decision; it is an habitual disposition of the mind and heart toward God (in the case of religious faith in general) and toward Jesus Christ (in the case of Christian faith). Recent developments in the cognate disciplines of social and educational psychology have prompted even deeper probings into the processive or ongoing aspect of faith. Specifically the work of Erik Erikson, Jean Piaget, and Lawrence Kohlberg, on the psychological and secular educational side, have been influencing the work of Methodist theologian James Fowler and the many influenced by him, on the theological and religious educational side. What is characteristic of all of these authors is the conviction that human persons grow and develop morally in *stages*.

Thus, Erikson notes a person's advance through early infancy (with its sense of basic trust), later infancy (sense of autonomy), early childhood (sense of initiative), later childhood (sense of industry), adolescence (sense of personal identity), young adulthood (sense of intimacy), older adulthood (sense of concern for guiding the next generation), and twilight of life (sense of ego integrity in the face of possible ultimate despair). Erikson's stages are easily adaptable to the process of Christian faith. The faith commitment can be viewed sequentially or developmentally as: trust in the Church as mother; a sense of personal autonomy in which self-expression and self-control are balanced; a sense of personal initiative, with the aggressive potential of self-growth balanced by the regulating force of authority; entrance into the give-and-take situation of life, and movement from the private society of the family into the larger, more demanding society of other persons; the experience of a certain disintegration catalyzed by doubt and the struggle for reintegration; interpersonal commitment calling for sacrifice; concern for others who are to follow in the next generation(s); and a heightened eschatological sense of reality. (See *Childhood and Society*, New York: W. W. Norton & Company, 1963, 2nd rev. ed., chapter 7, pp. 247-274.)

For Kohlberg, moral maturity does not consist simply in internalizing rules and norms but in developing one's ability to integrate one's conception of social interaction. Moral development is achieved by the stimulation of the natural development of the individual child's own moral judgment and capacities. This occurs either through discussing moral dilemmas which involve a conflict of interests between persons or through establishing "just communities" which offer many opportunities for engaging in social communication and interaction.

According to Kohlberg, an individual moves through the following stages of moral development: (1) Good is done or evil avoided on a reward-or-punishment basis. (2) Good is done or evil avoided as a result of self-centered use of other people. (3) Good is done or evil avoided as a result of a desire for peer approval. (4) Good is done or evil avoided as a result of devotion to a fixed order established by law, authority, and obligation. (5) Good is done or evil avoided as a result of a sense of equity and mutual obligation arising in a democratic view of the social order. (6) Good is done or evil avoided as a result of conscientious decisions made in the light of values which have been internalized. (See his "Stage and Sequence: The Cognitive-Developmental Approach to Socialization," in *Handbook of Socialization Theory and Research*, David Goslin, ed., Chicago: Rand McNally, 1969.)

James Fowler applies the Kohlberg schema of *moral* development to the development of *faith*:

1. *Intuitive-protective faith.* The imitative, fantasy-filled phase in which the child can be powerfully and permanently influenced by the examples, moods, actions, and language of the visible faith of primal adults.

2. *Mythic-literal faith.* The person begins to take on for himself or herself the stories and beliefs and observances which symbolize belonging to his or her community. Beliefs are appropriated with literal interpretation, as are moral rules and attitudes.

3. *Synthetic-conventional faith.* The person's experience of the world goes beyond the family and primary social groups. Coherence and meaning are certified by either the authority of properly designated persons in each group or by the authority of consensus among "those who count."

4. *Individuating-reflexive faith.* The person begins to take seriously the burden of responsibility for his or her own commitments, life-style, beliefs, and attitudes. This stage develops under the tutelage of ideologically powerful religions or of charismatic leadership. It both brings and requires a qualitatively new and different kind of self-awareness and responsibility for one's choices and rejections.

5. *Paradoxical-consolidative faith.* The person recognizes the integrity and truth in positions other than his or her own. He or she affirms and lives out his or her own commitments and beliefs in such a way as to honor that which is true in the lives of others without denying the truth of his or her own. This kind of faith requires a regard for those who are different and who oppose one's own position.

6. *Universalizing faith.* The person dwells in the world as a transforming presence, but is not of the world. He or she discovers that in being-for-others one is being most truly oneself. (See his *Life Maps: Conversations on the Journey of Faith*, with Sam Keen, Waco, Texas: Word Books, 1978.)

The National Catechetical Directory for Catholics of the United States, *Sharing the Light of Faith* (Washington, D.C.: United States Catholic Conference, 1979), basically accepts this developmental approach to faith and moral development. The life of faith is related to human development, and so passes through stages or levels. Furthermore, different people possess aspects of faith to different degrees. It is the task of catechesis to help at each stage of human development and to lead the person ultimately to full identification with Jesus (par. 174, p. 100). The Directory warns, however, against making any one scientific theory normative. There are different schools of psychology and sociology which do not agree in all respects, nor are all developmental theories of equal merit. Catechists should not assume that any one school or theory has all the answers. Furthermore, these scientific disciplines supply nothing of the doctrinal or moral content of catechetical programs (par. 175, pp. 100-101). The Directory seems finally to adopt, or perhaps *adapt*, Erikson's framework: infancy and early childhood (birth to age 5), childhood (ages 6-10), pre-adolescence and puberty (ages 10-13), adolescence (14–17), early adulthood (ages 18-35), middle adulthood, and later adulthood. There are specific recommendations for catechesis at every stage of development (see pp. 102-113).

With regard to the Kohlberg-Fowler approach to moral and faith development, so popular in recent years among Catholic religious educators, criticisms have centered on the following points: (1) Kohlberg's assumption that morality is a matter of *rational* perception; (2) Kohlberg's focus on *justice alone*, which does not touch upon the human quest for intimacy, community, and friendship, nor on the other moral virtues (prudence, temperance, fortitude); (3) Fowler's distinctly and almost exclusively Tillichian notion of faith as a fundamental *attitude*, and his corresponding deemphasis of faith's *content* (*fides quae creditur*, i.e., that which is believed, faith as "conviction") and its broader *social and political dimension* ("transformative" faith); and (4) the tendency of this approach's adherents to "type-cast" their fellow Christians as if these stages were evaluative rather than descriptive and particular rather than general.

Hope

The virtue of hope received little attention from the classical theologians. Even Thomas Aquinas devoted only a few sections to it in his *Summa Theologica* (II-II, qq. 17-22). Where hope was discussed, it was viewed in an individualistic manner, i.e., as *my* hope for *my* salvation. It was understood as the elevation of the will, made possible by grace, by which we expect eternal life and the means to attain it, ever confident of the omnipotent aid of God. We sin against hope by despair (anticipated failure) and by presumption (anticipated success).

Since the mid-1960s, under the impact of such books as Protestant theologian Jürgen Moltmann's *Theology of Hope* (New York: Harper & Row, 1967), the virtue of hope has assumed a different meaning. *It is that virtue by which we take responsibility for the future, not simply our individual future but the future of the world.* Hope is oriented toward the Kingdom of God, not as heaven alone but as the renewal and re-creation of the whole world. God is not above us but ahead of us, summoning us to cocreate the future. The future holds the primacy. Indeed, in one sense all theology is eschatology. It is *hope* seeking understanding (*spes quaerens intellectum*), and not simply *faith* seeking understanding (*fides quaerens intellectum*), as Augustine, Anselm, Aquinas and others insisted. Revelation is not information about another world but promise about this one. Christian existence is life within the horizon of *expectation*: expectation of the Kingdom of God. The *resurrection* of Jesus Christ is the firstfruits of the Kingdom; it is God's "down payment" on the promise. Our future is the future of the risen Christ.

These same themes, also found in such contemporary Protestant theologians as Wolfhart Pannenberg and Carl Braaten (see chapter 20), were taken over into Catholic theology by Johannes Metz in particular. Our understanding of the world, he insisted, is oriented toward the future. We are not so much contemplative as productive. We are called to build a new world (and not only to interpret it), to engage in "political theology," a theology which constantly critiques the "city" (*polis*) according to the standards of the Kingdom of God. Renunciation of the world is not escape from earthly responsibilities. It is simply the refusal to accept anything in the world as absolute, as identical already with the Kingdom. Nothing is as yet the Kingdom. Everything, therefore, is subject to criticism, including even the Church. The Church, after all, is not the "non-world" but that segment of the world which acknowledges the Lordship of Jesus and lives in light of that confession of faith. It is a community of hope, i.e., a community which lives always for the other, in love of neighbor (*Theology of the World*, New York: Herder & Herder, 1969, pp. 107-140). A similar, although not identical, approach has been fashioned by Latin American liberation theology, but its emphasis remains on the virtue of faith as *praxis* rather than on the virtue of hope.

Karl Rahner reminds us that death relativizes all of our grand designs. It italicizes the hardness and the darkness of human existence. Only in God do we have hope. It is hope that makes us free. Yet it is not, to paraphrase Dietrich Bonhoeffer, a "cheap hope." What we hope for we cannot present in advance, and what we enjoy here and now is not what we ultimately hope for. Hence the Christian will always be regarded as a utopian by the absolute pessimists (those who see no life beyond death and see *this* life as absurd) and also by the absolute optimists (those who find this life completely meaningful and worthwhile without any reference at all to a life beyond death). The Christian "is not a person who grasps for something tangible so that he can enjoy it until death comes, nor is he a person who takes the darkness of the world so seriously that he can no longer venture to believe in the eternal light beyond it" (*Foundations of Christian Faith*, p. 405).

Christian existence, of course, is always historical existence. We experience joy at one moment and tears at another. We experience the grandeur and the vitality of human life, and also taste illusions, disappointment, death. "But to be able to open oneself to the reality of life freely and unsystematically, and to do this without absolutizing either earthly life or death, this can be done only by someone who believes and hopes that the totality of the life which we can experience is encompassed by the holy mystery of eternal love" (p. 405).

This new emphasis on the virtue of hope and on the future has had a significant impact on Catholic moral theology. It helps us to see that ethical norms and obligations are always open-ended, imperfect, incomplete, never finished until the Kingdom comes in all its fullness. It helps us see, too, that humankind is itself in process and in development toward a reality beyond itself: ahead and not above. It helps broaden the scope of moral vision because we hope not only in our own salvation but in the salvation of others and of the whole world. And, finally, it underlines the critical function of all moral reflection, analysis, pronouncement, and action within and by the Church, for hope measures everything against the standard of the coming Kingdom.

We have already seen in chapter 19 how and to what extent the Second Vatican Council also embraced this wider understanding of hope. Hope does not diminish the importance of our duties in this life but rather gives them special urgency (*Pastoral Constitution on the Church in the Modern World*, n. 21). Indeed, it is precisely in our recognition of Christ in our brothers and sisters and in our love of Christ in word and deed alike that we give witness to the truth and share with others the mystery of God's love. "As a consequence, men throughout the world will be aroused to a lively hope—the gift of the Holy Spirit—that they will finally be caught up in peace and utter happiness in that fatherland radiant with the splendor of the Lord" (n. 93). Christian existence, therefore, is existence *in* hope, but also existence which seeks to *give* hope to others.

Charity/Love

We saw in the previous chapter that all of Jesus' moral teachings and those of the early Church have been concentrated in the one commandment of love: love of God and love of neighbor (Mark 12:28-34; Matthew 22:34-40; Luke 10:25-37; Galatians 5:14; 1 John 3:23; 1 Corinthians 13). "There are in the end three things that last: faith, hope and love, and the greatest of these is love" (1 Corinthians 13:13). It should be obvious by now that these three virtues are distinct but not separate. Love is a lived faith and a lived hope. The one virtue without the other two is radically incomplete, dead.

First, what does the word *love* mean? In English there is only the one word; in Greek there are four. *Epithemia* is desire, with the connotation of lust. This is sexual love. (All love is, of course, sexual, but not all sexual action is loving.) *Eros* is the drive toward union with others which brings self-fulfillment. *Philia* is affectionate love such as that among brothers, sisters, and friends. *Agape* is total dedication and devotion to the welfare of the other, regardless of sacrifice and personal cost. Many experiences of authentic love by human beings will entail a proportionate blending of these four elements.

Christian love consists in an intimate participation in the life of God who *is* Love (1 John 4:8,16). It is a gift from God that is mediated by Christ and activated by the Spirit. It calls us to share in the paschal mystery by which Christ handed himself over to death and therefore was raised from the dead and exalted by the Father (Philippians 2:5-11). Christian love is rooted in the whole life, death, and resurrection of Christ. He is its model through his life of service (Mark 10:45), through his complete self-giving on the cross, and through his passing over to the Father. Christian love is the same self-giving, even to the point of crucifixion. "There is no greater love than this: to lay down one's life for one's friends" (John 15:13).

Modern psychologists (Erich Fromm, Rollo May, *et al.*) insist that a person's capacity to love depends on his or her *personal maturity*. Love requires self-knowledge, effort, conviction, courage, generosity, respect, a sense of responsibility, sensitivity, patience, and a fundamental acceptance of oneself with all of one's strengths and limitations. Thus, modern psychology often agrees with the basic Christian principle that we are called to love our neighbor as we love ourselves (Mark 12:31). If, however, an individual has not resolved the inevitable crises of human development, he or she may not attain sufficient human maturity for Christian love. The child starts out by being attached to his or her mother as the "ground of being." The child feels helpless and needs the all-enveloping love of a mother. The child then turns to the father as a guiding principle for thought and action. The child is motivated by the need to acquire the father's praise and avoid his displeasure. At full maturity, the child frees himself or herself from the person of both father and mother as protecting and commanding powers. The adult becomes "his or her own father and mother." Love of God passes through similar stages: love of God in helpless attachment; love of God in obedient attachment; and love of God as personal incorporation of the principles of love and justice into oneself.

If we are really to love as Christ intends, we have to overcome our own narcissism. We must strive for objectivity in every situation and become sensitive to the situations where objectivity eludes us. We must see the difference between our picture of another and the other's behavior, on the one hand, and, on the other hand, the way the other really is, apart from our own interests, needs, fears, and hang-ups. Christian loving also means readiness to take risks, to accept pain and disappointment. It means using one's human powers productively. Loving demands a state of intensity and commitment. Christian love cannot coexist with indifference. Indeed, the opposite of love is not hate but *apathy*, a lack of concern, a suspension of commitment (literally, *apathy* means to be "without pain").

Love is also closely related to the *will*. Will without love becomes manipulation; love without will becomes sentimentality. We are afraid, in the latter case, that if we choose one person rather than another, we will lose something, and we are too insecure to take that chance. And so we hold back, remaining cool and aloof. But the same fear of commitment can be expressed in a flurry of seemingly interpersonal activity, especially of a sexual kind. Sensuality then smothers sensitivity. Sex becomes an instrument to express one's anxieties, about death in particular. We try to prove to ourselves that we are still young and can "perform."

If love is the soul of Christian existence, it must be at the heart of every other Christian virtue. Thus, for example, *justice* without love is legalism; *faith* without love is ideology; *hope* without love is self-centeredness; *forgiveness* without love is self-abasement; *fortitude* without love is recklessness; *generosity* without love is extravagance; *care* without love is mere duty; *fidelity* without love is servitude. Every virtue is an expression of love. No virtue is really a virtue unless it is permeated, or informed, by love (1 Corinthians 13).

"Every benefit which the People of God during its earthly pilgrimage can offer to the human family stems from the fact that the Church is 'the universal sacrament of salvation,' simultaneously manifesting and exercising the mystery of God's love for man" (Vatican II, *Pastoral Constitution on the Church in the Modern World*, n. 45). It is the cross of Christ which is "the sign of God's all-embracing love and...the fountain from which every grace flows" (*Declaration on the Relationship of the Church to Non-Christian Religions*, n. 4).

The Virtue of Religion

The virtue of religion, or worship, is the ritualization of the experience of faith, hope, and charity. (See chapters 8, 21, and 22.) This virtue was traditionally (i.e., in medieval theology) treated as part of the virtue of justice inasmuch as it entails giving to God what is due to God. But we already noted in the preceding chapter how the new economics of the Middle Ages shaped, if not somewhat distorted, Catholic moral theology. Justice was understood almost entirely in contractual terms, and so, too, was the relationship between God and us.

The virtue of religion is neither exclusively a theological virtue (oriented toward God) nor exclusively a moral virtue (oriented toward our relationships with others). The religious person integrates both: Worship demands love of neighbor, and commitment to one's neighbor is directed to the glory of God (1 Corinthians 11:17-22; Matthew 5:23-24). If the human person is merely economic or political, then worship is a waste of time. If, however, we are transcendent subjects, open to the Spirit of God, then worship puts us in touch with, and expresses, that relationship with the Transcendent.

The virtue of religion is intimately related to the whole moral life of the Christian. In the words of Vatican II, the exercise of religion "consists before all else in those internal, voluntary, and free acts whereby man sets the course of his life directly toward God" (*Declaration on Religious Freedom*, n. 3).

Religion, of course, is subject to distortion and corruption. *Idolatry* is the worship of something less than the Absolute—e.g., money, personal gain, political power. We can make an idol even of the Church or of institutional elements within the Church.

Superstition absolutizes something finite and invests it with saving power in itself—e.g., astrology, wearing amulets to ward off evil spirits. Christians can be superstitious when they assume that the performance of a particular practice in some numbered sequence will of itself insure salvation. *Hypocrisy* in religious matters is an attempt to use religion to advance one's own position in life. It is a manipulative abuse of religion. Hypocrisy is always a temptation for those who exercise religious authority or who derive any material benefits whatever from their status in the Church. *Legalism* is a religious attitude that makes observance the end of religion. Obedience to law is the ultimate sign of religious faith and the principal means to holiness. Legalism is usually based on a false understanding of God as an exacting lawgiver, a stern taskmaster, a vindictive superior. *Self-delusion*, or triumphalism, is a misinterpretation of divine election. We assume that we are God's favored ones, that we have privileged status in the world, that we are better than the rest of humankind. It is a form of deafness and blindness. We do not see the games of power and domination at work, nor do we appreciate how alienating these games are to those outside the Church. (See Gregory Baum, *Religion and Alienation: A Theological Reading of Sociology*, New York: Paulist Press, 1975.)

The Moral, or Cardinal, Virtues

Prudence

This is the first of the *cardinal* virtues, i.e., those virtues which are the "hinges" (the literal meaning of the Latin *cardo*) of other virtues. Prudence is essentially the ability to *discern*. It is *not* simply an attitude of caution, restraint, timidity, or conservatism. Rather, the prudent person is one who can make decisions. *Prudence formulates and imposes the correct dictates of reason upon the human person (recta ratio agibilium*, Thomas Aquinas). Prudence does not answer the question: "What is the best way in principle to do the right thing?" Rather: "What is the best way for me, in this situation, to do the right thing?" The prudent person, therefore, must investigate the situation and take counsel from others. A judgment must be formulated in light of this inquiry and advice. And a decision must be made. The prudent person, therefore, is in the moral order what a creative artist is in the intellectual and aesthetic orders. The novelist, for example, is constantly faced with the problem of deciding what to write and how to write it.

Prudence presupposes the following qualities: knowledge of moral principles, experience *and* the ability to profit by it, ability to learn from others, ability to make rational inferences, a certain inventiveness or creativity, vision or foresight, ability to see and weigh circumstances, an ability to anticipate obstacles and plan to surmount them, and finally an ability to decide in light of all the preceding.

The virtue of prudence is closely allied with the *discernment of spirits* and with *spiritual direction*. To be a Christian is to live in communion with the Spirit of God. It is to be open to that Spirit and receptive to the specific promptings of the Spirit. But the promptings of the Spirit are never unequivocally and unmistakably clear. If "no one has ever seen God" (John 1:18), neither has anyone seen the Spirit. One *infers* the Spirit's presence from what we do see and experience. This *discernment* is at once individual and corporate. Community discernment both derives from and leads to individual discernment. Community discernment presupposes prayer, but it also requires community discussion, the free exchange of opinions in a climate of truthfulness and mutual respect.

It is never easy to discern the Spirit. First, the Spirit itself is invisible and transcendent. Secondly, we are prone to rationalize in our own favor—i.e., to highlight those elements which support our predisposition toward one or another course of action and to ignore those elements which work against that predisposition. Thirdly, many issues are complicated and do not admit ready solutions.

Although we can never be absolutely certain that we are indeed responding to the Spirit, there are certain *negative criteria* by which obviously false responses can be exposed: (1) If the discernment process does not issue forth in the classic "fruits" of the Spirit—love, joy, peace, patient endurance, kindness, generosity, faith, mildness, and chastity (Galatians 5:22-23)—it is not "of the

Spirit." (2) If the discernment process leads to doctrinal or moral positions which are clearly inconsistent with the doctrinal tradition of the Church and/or with recognized norms of biblical and theological scholarship, it is not "of the Spirit." (3) If the discernment process intensifies the isolation and even spiritual eccentricities of those involved in it rather than enhancing the life of the whole Body of Christ (Ephesians 4:15-16), it is not "of the Spirit." (4) If the discernment process ignores pertinent information, rejects the counsel of others who have knowledge and experience in the matter at hand, and formulates its judgments by imposition rather than by corporate reflection, it is not "of the Spirit."

Justice

Insofar as the virtue of justice is rooted in Sacred Scripture, it is linked with the idea of *righteousness* (Hebrew, *sedeq,* and Greek, *dikaiosynē*). It is intimately connected with the Covenant, i.e., with the obligations of the Israelite to the community of Israel. A person is righteous insofar as he or she is conformed and faithful to the Covenant. God, too, is righteous insofar as God saves. Yahweh is our righteousness, our salvation (Jeremiah 23:5). Paul developed the Old Testament notion of righteousness in a thoroughly Christian sense. The righteous is "right" with God. He or she is saved and vindicated. A new life has been given because of this vindication. Christian righteousness, therefore, is the state of vindication and deliverance achieved through the death of Christ (2 Corinthians 5:21; Romans 5:16). The Kingdom of God is "justice, peace, and the joy that is given by the Holy Spirit" (Romans 14:17). Accordingly, perfect and complete righteousness is still an object of hope to be achieved beyond history (Galatians 5:5). Christian righteousness requires that the Christian himself or herself live in a way that is consistent with the death and resurrection of Christ and with the new life in the Spirit that flow from Christ's saving work. This righteousness cannot be achieved by the observance of the Law. It is a free gift of God which reaches its fullness in the Kingdom (Romans 3:30; 1 Corinthians 6:11).

Justice is derived from the Latin word *ius,* which means "right." Justice is concerned with *rights* and with *duties* which correspond to those rights. My duty to respect your bodily integrity flows from your right to life in all its fullness. A right, therefore, is a power that we have to do things which are necessary for achieving the end or purpose for which we are destined as rational and free persons. A right is a person's moral claim upon other persons or society in general to the means of reaching an end that is his or hers, and that he or she is responsible for reaching. In that sense, rights flow from duties. This is the so-called *natural right theory*. Others insist that no one has any rights that are not rooted in positive law—that positive law is the source and origin of all human rights. This is the *theory of legal positivism*. Still others propose that all rights are based upon the social good and are subservient to it. One has only those rights which are necessary to advance the common good. This is the *theory of social good*.

Among the principal human rights, as enumerated, for example, in Pope John XXIII's *Pacem in Terris* (1963) are: the right to life and a worthy manner of living; the right to respect for one's person regardless of sex, race, religion, or national origin; the right to freedom in the pursuit of truth and in its expression and communication; the right to be informed truthfully about matters of concern; the right to a basic education; the right to worship God freely; the right to choose one's state in life; the right to gainful employment, to decent working conditions, to a proper compensation, to private property, to organize; the right of meeting and association; the right to freedom of movement (emigration and immigration); the right to participate in public affairs and to contribute to the common good (see pars. 11-45).

There is, however, a *hierarchy* of rights in terms of their relationship to the last end. Rights are also *limited* by the existence of others' rights. When rights are in *conflict*, the virtue of prudence also comes into play. The following criteria apply: (1) Rights to spiritual goods take precedence over rights to purely temporal goods (e.g., the right to live in dignity over another's right to a profit on an investment); and (2) common goods take precedence over individual goods (e.g., the right of the state to exact taxes to pay for social needs over the right to keep what one earns).

It has been said that justice would not be possible unless we were, in fact, separate from one another. Justice regulates relationships between strangers. Where there is perfect love and communion, the question of rights and duties becomes moot. They are completely fulfilled. Justice, therefore, mediates between the otherness which arises from our exteriority and the oneness which arises from our interiority.

But even if unselfish love among all persons were achieved, the virtue of *social justice* would still be required. In the larger community, beyond the small family units or the bonds of love and friendship, there is "a dynamic interpenetration of all those fundamental human rights upon which the aspirations of individuals and nations are based" (*Justice in the World*, Third International Synod of Bishops, 1971). Persons develop fully only in a societal context, since by definition we are fundamentally and radically social. The quality of life in society, the justice of its mode of organization, the orientation of its structures and systems (e.g., political, legal, economic, social, educational, religious) will either enhance or retard the full human development of the person.

Social sin is a situation in which the very organization of some level of society systematically functions to the detriment of groups or individuals in the society. The sinfulness consists in the way social relationships are contrived or allowed to exist. Sometimes people of good will administer those systems. They are caught up in them. Although they may bear no personal guilt, the *situation* is sinful nonetheless. Accordingly, the virtue of justice is engaged even in those situations where there is no discernible culpability on the part of any particular individuals or in the relationships of particular individuals within a given system. The *otherness* from which the demands of justice flow is intrinsic to the human condition itself, apart from the measure of love that exists between or among human beings.

As the Protestant social ethicist Reinhold Niebuhr argued, it is not enough to present Christian ethics as a love ethic. Given the sinful condition of the world, it is impossible to envisage a society of pure love. Christian ethics must come to terms with the reality of inevitable conflicts and with the demands for their harmonization, often on the basis of arrangements that are far from the Christian idea of disinterested love. Christian realism tells us that nations, races, classes, and other groups do not love one another. Nevertheless, their mutual survival demands that they respect their obligations to others. Interests must be balanced and claims recognized. To conceive of a world of love without the imperfect harmonies established by justice is to create an illusion. A simple Christian moralism, Niebuhr insisted, will counsel men and women to be simply unselfish. A profound Christian faith must encourage them to create systems of justice which will save society from its own selfishness. Indeed, if that portion of society that benefits from social inequality attempts to counsel only love, forgiveness, and patience to the discontented and disenfranchised instead of working for justice, it will convict itself of hypocrisy. (See, for example, *Moral Man and Immoral Society*, New York: Scribner's, 1932.)

A correct understanding of social justice demands, furthermore, a correct understanding of the distinction beteen society and the state. *Society* is constituted by the total network of social, political, economic, cultural, and religious relationships which are necessary for full human development. The *state* is the center of coercive power in society. It is the civil authority by which the purposes of society are procured and preserved. The distinction between society and the state is presumed in John XXIII's *Pacem in Terris* and in the Second Vatican Council's *Declaration on Religious Freedom.*

The extent to which the state should intervene in the life of its citizens is attended to in the *principle of subsidiarity*, first enunciated by Pope Pius XI in *Quadragesimo Anno* (1931). This principle seeks to establish and maintain a balance between individual initiative and governmental assistance and direction. The principle holds that the presumption is always in favor of individual or small-group action over against governmental intervention. The state should intervene only when lesser bodies cannot fulfill a given task required by the common good. In broader terms, the principle of subsidiarity means that nothing should be done at a higher level that can be done as well or better at a lower level.

This principle has to be balanced off, however, by the *process of socialization*, first referred to by John XXIII in *Mater et Magistra* (1961) as "the growing interdependence of citizens in society giving rise to various patterns of group life and activity and in many instances to social institutions established on a juridical basis" (par. 59). Thus, given the increased complexity of modern economic and political life, more intervention is required, without prejudice to the principle of subsidiarity. The two—subsidiarity and socialization—must be kept in creative tension.

The virtue of justice, therefore, is divided as follows: *commutative justice*, which relates to contractual obligations between individuals involving a strict right and the obligation of restitution (e.g., one person lends another person a sum of money; the second person is obliged in conscience to return that money according to the agreement); *distributive justice*, which relates to the obligation of a government toward its citizens, by which the government regulates the burdens and benefits of societal life (e.g., a government is to tax its citizens fairly and to distribute those tax monies according to need); *legal justice*, which relates to the citizen's obligation toward the government or toward society in general (e.g., the citizen must pay his or her fair share of the taxes); and *social justice*, which relates to the obligation of all parties to apply the Gospel to the structures, systems, and institutions of society which are the framework in which all human relationships take place (e.g., an individual and/or groups must take an active interest in necessary social reform).

These four kinds of justice are interrelated and mutually limiting. All four are attempts to express the demands of Christian love (*agape*). All four have to do with rights and duties. Such a notion of justice does not provide immediate answers to the complex problems of social existence, but it does provide *principles of discernment and specific guides for judgment*. If the movement of history is toward the Kingdom of God—a Kingdom of "justice, love, and peace" (*Pastoral Constitution on the Church in the Modern World*, n. 39)—the pursuit of justice is itself part of this movement. If we are called in the meantime to participate in the death and resurrection of Christ, justice helps us to specify the terms and demands of that participation. Conversely, efforts toward the fulfillment of human needs, the protection of human rights, and the realization of structures of genuine mutuality are consequences of faith in the saving power of Christ's death and resurrection.

Temperance

One very important dimension of our being human is rooted in what the traditional theology called the "concupiscible appetites," i.e., our desire to achieve the good through food, drink, or sex. The virtue which enables us to achieve some *balance* in these areas while still living in a state of legitimate self-interest is *temperance*. It is a virtue which has attracted the attention of philosophers from the earliest centuries. The ancient Greeks viewed it as a way of insuring "good hygiene." Plato regarded these sensuous cravings as "an ugly brute of a horse" which had to be curbed by the "charioteer" which is the human mind. The Stoics, too, looked upon these appetites as having to be brought under the complete control of reason.

The early Church Fathers saw the virtue as part of the "grace-full" life, as a way of participating in the death and resurrection of Chirst. Death to self leads to greater life in the Spirit. Thomas Aquinas insisted, however, that the virtue is not the *repression* of the desire for sensual pleasure but rather its *tempering* in the service of human growth. Temperance, therefore, is positive, not negative. It is a virtue which humanizes the pleasures of food, drink, and sex. Aquinas referred to three "subjective parts" or divisions of the virtue: *abstinence*, which humanizes our desires for food and other pleasure-producing elements such as tobacco and drugs; *sobriety*, which humanizes our desires for intoxicating drink; and *chastity*, which humanizes our desires for sexual pleasure in accordance with our state in life. Each of these appetites, when properly satisfied, contributes to the preservation of the individual and of the human species. Intemperance makes them ends in themselves.

Moderation of the sensual appetitites through the virtue of temperance is closely allied with Christian *asceticism*. The word *askesis* itself means "exercise." Asceticism is concerned with those exercises which help us regulate the conflict between the spirit and the flesh. It involves a painful struggle, self-denial, and renunciation. The medieval and post-medieval notion of asceticism was not unmixed with rationalism, Stoicism, and Pelagianism—all emphasizing the innate power of the human person to live according to a certain pattern *without grace*. This traditional concept of asceticism was also often founded on a dualistic understanding of human existence, as if the bodily aspects of the human person were unholy, even sinful. Indeed, the traditional moral theology textbooks referred to certain organs of the body as *partes inhonestae* ("dishonorable parts").

In light not only of modern psychology but also of contemporary theology, we understand asceticism as the free and faithful acceptance of one's self, of one's painful limitations, weaknesses, inadequacies, of one's sorrows, disappointments, and frustrations, and, finally, of death itself. One is ascetical in not trying to escape the facticity of human existence by immersing oneself in, or distracting oneself by, purely material pleasures. There is nothing wrong with food, drink, or sexual expression. On the contrary. But they can become crutches or escapes from one's human and Christian responsibilities. At the very least, their misuse is symptomatic of a fundamental disorder. Thus, those who are excessively heavy do not simply have healthier appetites than others. Those who are frequently intoxicated to the point where they cannot function are not simply people who like the taste of liquor. Those who move from one sexual liaison to another with commitment to none are not simply people with uncontainable, overflowing love.

The Christian must pattern his or her life on that of Christ, who did not flee suffering and death but who became obedient even unto death (Mark 10:45; Philippians 2:5-11). Christian asceticism is an asceticism of the cross, a readiness to face death in the service of others and ultimately in the service of the Kingdom of God. Asceticism is an affirmation of the cross as the path to resurrection. The ascetic is one who is patient (literally, "suffering"), prepared for the coming of the Lord, ever vigilant, looking toward the Kingdom. It is life on pilgrimage.

How can one tell if his or her asceticism is genuinely Christian or if it is distorted? *First*, is it an expression of self-acceptance, or of self-loathing? Does one deny oneself because self-denial frees one for greater service to others and makes one a more effective sign of Christ to the world, or does one regard the appetities in question as base and unworthy of a Christian? *Secondly*, is the asceticism oriented to dedicated Christian service, or is it finally a way of avoiding commitment, especially the commitment implied in interpersonal intimacy? *Thirdly*, is the ascetic freer to love, more creative, or is the ascetic an isolated figure, closed-minded, difficult to be with?

Fortitude

Whereas temperance balances our concupiscible appetites, *fortitude* moderates our *irascible* appetites. It strengthens them against the passion of *fear*, on the one hand, and on the other restrains their immoderate tendencies toward *audacity* and *rashness*. Fortitude enables a person to face serious challenges, even death, with some measure of calm. It gives the strength to endure suffering for a just cause. It is *the virtue of courage, by which one overcomes an instinctive fear in order to pursue the good.* Fortitude, therefore, has an active and a passive side. Its active side has to do with taking bold action for the sake of the Kingdom of God; its passive side has to do with enduring some pain, suffering, or even death for the sake of the Kingdom. But not even endurance is merely passive. Martin Luther King, Jr. (d. 1968) always insisted that non-violent resistance was still *resistance*, requiring much courage and commitment.

Biblically, courage and strength are linked (2 Samuel 10:12; Deuteronomy 31:7). The prophets were evidently courageous figures. But every form of true courage and every manifestation of real strength is rooted in God (1 Samuel 17:37; Psalms 27:14; 31:25). In the New Testament this *andreia*, or courage, is commended to us by Paul (1 Corinthians 16:13; 2 Corinthians 5:6-7; 10:1-2) and by the Lord himself (Matthew 9:2; 14:27; John 16:33). The early Church looked to Jesus as the model of courage (Hebrews 12:2). Indeed, the whole eleventh chapter of the Epistle to the Hebrews is a tribute to Christian faith and courage. The martyrs followed in Jesus' path—e.g., Stephen (Act of the Apostles 7) and others (Revelation 7:14).

Prudence and justice precede fortitude. Only the prudent person can be truly courageous. Fortitude presupposes a correct evaluation of a situation and must always be in the service of justice. Fortitude marks a path between the extremes of temerity (rashness) and timidity. Without fortitude, growth is impossible. Nietzsche once said that whatever does not destroy us makes us stronger. We can grow in and through adversity. We can be ennobled by suffering—not that we ever seek it or embrace it for its own sake. Fortitude, then, is our affirmative answer to the inevitable shocks of human existence. It is the ability to dare and to endure.

Without fortitude we suffer *frustration*. We become restless and tense, aggressive and destructive against the perceived sources of our frustration, apathetic and sullen, prone to fantasy and escapism, rigid and locked into comfortable routines, or simply regressive, returning to familiar modes of behavior characteristic of an earlier stage of development.

There are various *defense mechanisms* against frustration. Rationalization assigns logical reasons or plausible excuses for the consequences of frustration (e.g., a person insists that his or her excessive weight is a matter of metabolism). Projection assigns one's own undesirable qualities in exaggerated measure to other people (e.g., a conniving person accuses others of always plotting for their own benefit). Reaction-formation conceals a certain emotion from oneself by giving strong expression to its opposite (e.g., an angry, embittered person smiles frequently or goes to great lengths to be courteous to those who are the objects of his or her anger). Dissociation takes the form either of compulsively physical movements (e.g., twitches) or excessive theorizing that prevents action (e.g., an anxious administrator holds frequent committee meetings but comes to no practical decisions). Repression is the total denial of what frustrates us (e.g., the celibate religious never mentions sex). Substitution generates other activities in place of those which lead to frustration (e.g., the classical "cold shower" in the face of sexual temptations). Compensation is one form of substitution. It is an effort to make up for one deficiency by cultivating a different activity that gives some measure of pleasure and satisfaction (e.g., the shy person takes to painting).

Finally, the virtue of fortitude is missing in a person who is always fearful of displeasing others, who remains silent in the face of injustice, who shuns conflict at all costs, who avoids "rocking the boat," and who, therefore, does whatever he or she thinks is "expected."

Works of Mercy

One of the classic problems in theology has been the reconciliation of divine justice and divine mercy. Justice gives to another what the other deserves by right (*suum cuique*, to each his own); mercy gives to another more than the other deserves. Thomas Aquinas argued that when God shows mercy, divine justice is not defeated. By transcending the exact demands of justice and turning a sinner into a just person, God displays the fullness of justice (*Summa Theologica*, I, q. 21, a. 3), and so mercy enables God to be just to the person whom God has made just. All human mercy is founded in, and evoked by, the mercy of God, and all Christian mercy is rooted in the example of Christ himself (Acts of the Apostles 10:38; John 13:15). Human mercy, however, does not give of its own but of what God has bestowed (Romans 11:30-32; Ephesians 2:4). We see the distress of others as our own distress. Mercy is an act which testifies to our solidarity in sin and our common need for redemption and healing.

It is not ritual that the Lord desires, but love, which is the soul of mercy (Hosea 6:6; Hebrews 10:5-8). "This, rather, is the fasting that I wish: releasing those bound unjustly, untying the thongs of the yoke; setting free the oppressed, breaking every yoke; sharing your bread with the hungry, sheltering the oppressed and the homeless; clothing the naked when you see them, and not turning your back on your own. Then your light shall break forth like the dawn, and your wound shall quickly be healed..." (Isaiah 58:6-8). In the parable of the Sheep and the Goats (Matthew 25:31-46) the Lord proclaims that we will be judged by our response to the hungry, the thirsty, the stranger, the naked, the prisoner. "I assure you, as often as you did it for one of my least brothers, you did it for me" (25:40).

These works of mercy traditionally have been divided into *corporal* works (concerned with needs of the body) and *spiritual* works (concerned with needs of the soul). Such a dichotomy is no longer appropriate in light of our understanding of the integrity of the human person as at once bodily and spiritual, but the listings provide a useful reminder of the kind of life that the Christian is called to lead. Thus, the *corporal works of mercy* are: feeding the hungry, giving drink to the thirsty, clothing the naked, sheltering the homeless, visiting the sick, ransoming the captive, and burying the dead (the last was added out of respect for the sanctity of the body as a temple of the Holy Spirit; see 1 Corinthians 3:16). The *spiritual works of mercy* are: instructing the ignorant, counseling the doubtful, admonishing the sinner, bearing wrongs patiently, forgiving offenses, comforting the afflicted, and praying for the living and the dead.

Although most of these works have to do with a Christian's obligations to other individuals in need, they also have broader social and political implications today and are to be linked in many cases with the overriding demands of *social justice*. But the dimension of mercy reminds the Christian that his or her obligations go beyond even those required by social justice.

HOW DOES ONE BECOME A CHRISTIAN?

One becomes a Christian, as we have already noted, by being converted to Jesus Christ and his Gospel of the Kingdom of God, and by being initiated into the community through which the encounter with Christ and the Kingdom is mediated (see chapter 21 on the sacraments of initiation). One thereby opens himself or herself to the grace of the Holy Spirit so that God might dwell within oneself as the triune principle of faith, hope, and charity, as well as of prudence, justice, temperance, and fortitude. A Christian is a person whose whole life is ruled by the commandment of love. The Christian's commitment to love is rooted in faith and

activated by hope. The Christian, in turn, intelligently, responsibly, and courageously fulfills the Gospel in his or her interpersonal and institutional relationships, and in the manner and style
of his or her own life. Everything is oriented to the glory of God.

But it is one thing to sketch this profile of the committed
Christian. It is entirely another matter to say precisely *how* the
individual Christian determines what the Gospel demands in this
particular situation, in these special circumstances, given these
conflicting claims. This raises the broad moral question of the
interrelationship between *values* and *norms*; and these, in turn,
rest on some prior understanding of what it means to be human
and how the enduringly human qualifies and shapes our moral
vision and decisions. This is the thorny question of *natural law*.

Values and Norms

Values are of two kinds: premoral and moral. *Premoral values* are
those concrete good things that ought to be done, to the extent
possible. They have to do with the real world of such things as life
and death, knowledge and ignorance, health and sickness, friendship and alienation, beauty and ugliness, wealth and poverty.
Insofar as anything exists, it has value. It participates in *being*. If it
is antithetical to human growth, however, it is a *disvalue*. The
attainment of premoral values may or may not contribute to one's
moral growth. Thus, one might preserve the value of life in a
prison camp by killing a fellow prisoner in one's own
place—clearly a disvalue.

Moral values, on the other hand, are those which are essential
to proper human living. They are not merely things that we
should attend to (as premoral values are), but are things we must
possess if we are to be fully human. Thus, one need not be physically attractive to be fully human, but one must be loving. Moral
values include such virtues as honesty, justice, chastity, fortitude,
temperance. They are not only a matter of *doing* just deeds or
courageous acts, but of *being* just and courageous.

Norms are also of two kinds: material and formal. *Material
norms* tell us what we should *do*. They point out premoral values
which we are to pursue, or premoral evils which we are to avoid.

Some examples of material norms are: Do not kill. Do not take what belongs to another. Tell the truth. Pay your debts.

Material norms are not absolute. There are times when I may have to withhold the truth or even kill. Thus, although material norms are concrete, informational, and instructive, they are also debatable, often tentative, and open to exceptions. These norms do not provide final answers to specific problems. They point to values and illuminate situations. They provide the moral agent with at least some of the factors that must be taken into account in reaching a final judgment.

Formal norms point to moral values which must be pursued. They indicate attitudes which we should acquire. They tell us the "form" our conduct should take. They indicate what is the right thing *to be*. Formal norms do not tell us to "do what is good" but to "do what is right." They are vague and almost totally without specific content. They proclaim goals rather than tactics, strategies, or policies. Examples of formal norms are: Be honest. Respect life. Do not murder. Do not steal.

Formal norms challenge us to be responsible, to be faithful Christians. They remind us of what it means to accept the Gospel of Jesus Christ, particularly in those moments and situations where we may be tempted to act against that Gospel. *Only formal norms are absolute, universal, and exceptionless.* Thus, it is not always wrong to kill (a *material* norm), but it *is* always wrong to commit murder (a *formal* norm). The same contrast could be made between taking what belongs to another (material) and stealing (formal), or between telling the truth (material) and being honest (formal).

As human persons and as Christians, we are called to be moral. We must know what we should *be* (formal norms tell us this) and what we should *do* (material norms tell us this). Formal norms point to moral values, i.e., to those things which the moral person must *be*. Material norms point to premoral values, i.e., to those things which the moral person must *do* in the here and now if he or she is to maximize the good and minimize the evil. To be moral, therefore, it is not enough to be sincere (adhering to material norms); one must also be correct and right (adhering to formal norms as well).

Material norms give us information and direction; formal norms give us motivation and encouragement. Both kinds of norms exist because moral theology goes on at two levels simultaneously. Moral theology not only helps us to determine what we must *do* if we are to live faithfully to Christ, but also the kind of person we should *be* if we are to be perceived by God, by others, and by ourselves as faithful Christians.

In the final accounting, there is no authoritative guidebook by which Christians can determine in almost every conceivable circumstance what is consistent with the Gospel and what is not. The Christian lives in a world of premoral and moral values and of material and formal norms which express those values. But those norms have to be applied in each case, and no case is exactly like another. The challenge of moral education, therefore, is not the teaching of moral rules but the development of Christian character. The rudder of that course toward authentic character is the virtue of *prudence*. It is, as we said above, the ability to *discern*, the capacity to make wise and responsible decisions and to act on them.

Natural Law

Values and norms are rooted ultimately in God and penultimately in *natural law*. The reader should not expect here a substantial historical and philosophical analysis of natural law. On the contrary. It is enough for our limited purposes to note the fundamental difference in outlook between the so-called Greek and Roman versions of natural law, a difference which pervades the history of the question.

In its most general sense, natural law means the whole order of things which, by the will of God, defines us as human persons and contributes to human development. For the *Greeks*, this law is entirely apart from us. Reality is a given. We must simply conform ourselves to it. We find ourselves in a world that is unchanging. If we wish to survive and to prosper, we have to come to terms with reality as it is, and accept it for what it is. The *Romans*, on the other hand, were activists—shakers and movers, so to speak. Where the Greeks emphasized the adjective "natural," the

Romans emphasized the noun "law." Where the Greeks tended to be fatalistic and therefore not inventive, the Romans tended to be innovative. Where the Greeks tended to focus on the essential and the static, the Romans tended to emphasize the empirical and the changeable. Through common sense and intelligence, said the Romans, we are challenged to grapple with life, to solve its riddles and to control its fits and starts.

These so-called alternatives are, of course, only a matter of emphasis. We are, in fact, both time-bound and creative. There is a facticity to our existence, and there is also a wide range of options for human freedom and responsibility. But the emphasis one selects is significant. Thus, we can understand natural law as the obligation, perceived by reason, to conform to nature, or as the obligation, built into nature, to use reason in moral judgment. The first emphasis reflects the *classicist* mentality; the second reflects the *historically conscious* mentality (see chapter 25). Why and how the classicist understanding of natural law lost its hold within the Church has been discussed in different contexts throughout this book (see, for example, chapters 3, 4, 5, and 25). It has to do in large part with the intellectual revolution provoked by the Enlightenment, the work of Darwin, Marx, and Freud, various contemporary developments in psychology, anthropology, history, and the sociology of knowledge, not to mention the extraordinary advances in communications and transportation which have exposed the pluralistic character of human experience and expression.

This is not to say, on the other hand, that the human condition has been completely *relativized* by history, that no dimension of continuity, no abiding elements, remain. Recent works of Piaget, Erikson, Kohlberg, Claude Lévi-Strauss, and others (to whom reference was made earlier in this chapter) suggest that, even apart from the Catholic theological community, there is some scientific readiness to affirm the structured character of human existence. There are patterns of behavior and of growth which suggest intrinsic, enduring qualities in the human constitution. Human persons are not infinitely malleable and programmable. There was, and remains, stiff resistance across the board to the deterministic theories of B. F. Skinner. Although most Catholic moral theologians have moved beyond the rigid, classicist notion of natural law, which is so thoroughly grounded in the Greek over against the Roman concept of the law, Catholic moral theology nonetheless retains and employs some fundamental notion of natural law; but that notion is much closer to the ancient Roman than to the ancient Greek approach. That movement or shift from the Greek to the Roman emphasis is suggested in that oft-cited line from the Second Vatican Council's *Pastoral Constitution on the Church in the Modern World*: "Thus, the human race has passed from a rather static concept of reality to a more dynamic, evolutionary one" (n. 5).

The question is, How much *continuity* is there within the dynamic, evolutionary process? Those who oppose any concept of a natural law deny any underlying continuity. Those who accept at least an historically conditioned notion of natural law affirm some measure of continuity amidst change and development. Those who insist on the classicist idea of natural law regard the process as irrelevant in any case. We shall be returning in the next chapter to a more detailed comparison of the second and third views—namely, the historically conscious and the classicist understandings of natural law as they relate to the discussion of birth control and the encyclical *Humanae Vitae*.

A second question arises: How much continuity is there between the *natural* law and the *supernatural* law of the Gospel? This raises again the discussion in chapters 4 and 5 regarding the interrelationship of nature and grace. Since there is no actual, historically real state of pure nature (all reality is graced, fallen and redeemed), there is no purely natural law, in the sense that some moral obligations are known in the light of reason alone. Human reason or, more broadly, human consciousness, is already elevated by grace. We exist only within a redeemed order. The difference between natural law and the supernatural law of the Gospel, therefore, is not a difference between a law that can be known by reason, on the one hand, and a law that can be known only by revelation, on the other hand. Both "laws" are rooted in the one source and are grasped within the same redeemed order, whether the persons doing the "grasping" are Christians or not.

It is in this context that the official teaching of the Church must be read on the existence and knowability of the natural law. Thus, Pope John XXIII's *Pacem in Terris* declares that "the Creator of the world has imprinted in man's heart an order which his conscience reveals to him and strongly enjoins him to obey...." A citation from Romans 2:15 is included. And Vatican II's *Pastoral Constitution on the Church in the Modern World*, without using the term *natural law*, formulates the basis of a true Christian humanism: "Hence, the norm of human activity is this: that in accord with the divine plan and will, it should harmonize with the genuine good of the human race, and allow men as individuals and as members of society to pursue their total vocation and fulfill it" (n. 35). (See the discussion of faith and theology in chapter 2, of revelation in chapter 7, and of the relationship of Christian and philosophical ethics in chapter 25.)

There are moral theologians, finally, who suggest that the term *natural law* is so ambiguous that it would be better to abandon it altogether. But this need not, and should not, lead also to an abandonment of two principal values which the natural law theory has traditionally upheld—namely, the existence of a source of ethical wisdom and knowledge which the Christian shares with all humankind, and the fact that morality cannot be merely the subjective whim of an individual or group of individuals.

Three alternative approaches have been advanced in recent years: the personalist, the relational and communitarian, and the transcendental. All three work within an historically conscious method.

The *personalist* approach sees the moral act in terms of the person performing the act rather than in terms of the physical structure of the act itself. The *relational and communitarian* approach emphasizes the self as existing within a universal community to which the self is *responsible*. One has to consider the moral act in relationship to that larger community and in terms of the act's impact upon it (see, for example, H. Richard Niebuhr, *The Responsible Self*, New York: Harper & Row, 1963). The *transcendental* approach attends to the structures of the human knowing process itself. Truth, including moral truth, exists not in the mind's grasp of reality itself but in the meaning the mind gives to reality. Our meanings can change in such basic realities as community, family, or the state. This is not to say that there is nothing objective "out there" upon which we impose our meanings. The transcendental approach rejects both naive realism and idealism (see Bernard Lonergan, *Collection*, New York: Herder & Herder, 1967, pp. 221–239).

Karl Rahner speaks of a "moral instinct of faith," i.e., a universal knowledge of right and wrong belief. According to Rahner, on the basis of this instinct we make judgments and moral decisions. It is a synthesizing kind of reasoning, formed by the unity of a prudential judgment and a unique moral situation. It is the kind of knowledge that is engaged in the choice of a career or a marriage partner. One cannot simply list the objective factors and criteria to establish the preference of this occupation or this person over others. The decision takes into account a whole range of elements, but it includes a synthesizing component which transcends any one element or even the sum total of the decision's parts.

There are, according to Rahner, "terrible consequences" to ignoring the universal moral instinct of faith and reason. We can look at a moral problem—e.g., the production of a cheap napalm bomb or other instruments of biochemical warfare—and dissect it to the point where its original and obvious moral horror becomes blurred or submerged in casuistry. "Even the Council was not able unequivocally to overcome this kind of mentality, which paralyzes any action which could be said to be clearly Christian" (see "The Faith Instinct," in *A Rahner Reader*, Gerald A. McCool, ed., New York: The Seabury Press, 1975, pp. 270-277).

Conscience

What Conscience Is Not

Conscience is not a *feeling*, whether good or bad. It is not to be equated, therefore, with the *superego*, our psychic policeman. The fact that we feel that something is right or wrong or that we feel very guilty about some action does not mean that our conscience is telling us something. Someone who is trying to lose ten pounds in time for the summer swimming season may feel terribly "guilty" about having broken his or her diet one day. But that does not make it a matter of conscience. Another person knows that it is not a mortal sin to miss Mass when one is sick but wishes to "confess the sin" anyway because he or she does not "feel right" about it. A third person feels "guilty" about going on his scheduled vacation before finishing a project in the office. In themselves such feelings are morally neutral. They indicate nothing at all about the moral character of the actions in question. They have nothing to do with conscience. Similar examples could be drawn from the other side of the line. For example, the fact that many people do not feel guilty about discrimination based on race or sex does not make such discrimination right. Here again, feelings are not indicative of moral rectitude or deficiency.

Secondly, although conscience involves judgment, conscience itself is not *judgment*. The judgment of an action's moral rightness or wrongness is part of the process of forming one's conscience, but it is not an act of conscience itself. It is an act of judgment, of moral reasoning. Thus, one examines all the facts and all the arguments that one can about a particular moral problem. There are reflection, discussion, and analysis. There is also disagreement. Opinions are in conflict. One still is not sure whether something is right or wrong. But even if one were sure, conscience as such has not yet been engaged.

What Conscience Is

Only when one *decides* to do this or that, or not to do this or that, is one acting out of conscience. Conscience is the *radical experience of ourselves as moral agents. Christian* conscience is the radical experience of ourselves as *new creatures in Christ, enlivened by the Holy Spirit.* But since we never know ourselves completely (self-knowledge is something one works at; it is not ready-made), decisions of conscience are necessarily incomplete and partial. And because our own circumstances are always historically, socially, and culturally defined, decisions of conscience are necessarily fallible and subject to correction and change. (See the section on Faith Development earlier in this chapter, noting its correlation with Moral Development.)

Conscience in Sacred Scripture

There is no Hebrew word for conscience in the Old Testament. The Greek word *syneidesis* occurs only once, in Wisdom 17:11. The closest word to it is *heart*. "Oh, that today you would hear his voice: 'Harden not your hearts . . .' " (Psalm 95:7–8). God is spoken of frequently as probing the heart (Jeremiah 11:20; 17:10; Proverbs 21:2; Psalm 26:2). The "pangs of conscience" are described in Genesis 3. Job insists: " . . . my heart does not reproach me for any of my days" (Job 27:6). Fidelity to conscience is a central theme in the whole book of Job, as it is in the call of the prophets to fidelity to the Covenant and to the Law (Ezekiel 11:14–21; Jeremiah 31:31–34).

Although there are references to the inner disposition of the person in the Gospels (Luke 11:33; 14:28-32; 16:8; Matthew 5:8,28; 6:21–22; Mark 7:21), the word for conscience is absent. The word occurs twenty-five times in the Pauline writings, including Hebrews, three times in 1 Peter, and twice in the Acts of the Apostles, both times uttered by Paul. For him conscience is the fundamental awareness of the difference between moral good and evil. The law is written in our hearts (Romans 2:15). Paul appeals to his own clear conscience (2 Corinthians 1:12; Romans 9:1; Acts of the Apostles 23:1, 24:16). Conscience is a principle of freedom (1 Corinthians 10:29), but such freedom is conditioned by our obligations to our neighbor (10:23). We must commend ourselves to every person's conscience before God (2 Corinthians 4:2; 5:11). Conscience itself can be weak and even erroneous (1 Corinthians 8:10–12), but obedience to such a conscience can still lead to salvation (8:11). Love proceeds from a pure heart and a good conscience and genuine faith (1 Timothy 1:5). The sacrificial ritual of the Law cannot purify the conscience (Hebrews 9:9; 10:2), but Christ purifies the conscience (10:22). Those who finally reject a good conscience can make a shipwreck of their faith (1 Timothy 1:19).

Post-biblical Reflections

In spite of individual references to conscience in the writings of some of the Fathers of the Church—e.g., Tertullian, Origen, Chrysostom, and Augustine—we find no systematic treatment of it until the Middle Ages. The occasion was a dispute over the meaning of a text of St. Jerome, the *Commentary on Ezekiel*, which distinguished between the terms *synderesis* and *syneidesis*. Bonaventure and the Franciscans explained the distinction in one way; Thomas Aquinas and the Dominicans explained it in another way. The Thomistic explanation would influence Catholic moral theology for the next several centuries. Aquinas distinguished between conscience as a permanent natural habit (*synderesis*) and conscience as an act of moral judgment (*syneidesis*). The process of moral judgment is essentially rational. The human will affirms and carries out what is affirmed by right reason. It would seem, however, that the whole distinction was based on an error. In preparing the first Latin text of the Bible, Jerome was working from a Greek manuscript that was not entirely legible. Recent scholarship concludes that Jerome was wrong in finding two different Greek words for conscience. We may still make a distinction, as Bonaventure and Thomas did, between conscience as a habit and as an act of moral judgment but that distinction cannot be attributed to the Bible.

The tradition is summed up at Vatican II in its *Pastoral Constitution on the Church in the Modern World*. Conscience is what summons us to love good and avoid evil, to do this and shun that. "To obey it is the very dignity of man; according to it he will be judged. Conscience is the most secret core and sanctuary of a man. There he is alone with God, whose voice echoes in his depths." But conscience is no infallible guide. It frequently errs from invincible ignorance (i.e., an ignorance for which we are not morally responsible). We Christians search for truth and for the genuine solution of problems in collaboration with others and in fidelity to our consciences (n. 16).

A Contemporary View

Timothy O'Connell suggests that we abandon the language of *synderesis* and *syneidesis* and speak instead of three different levels of meaning of the word *conscience*. At the first and most general level, conscience is a fundamental sense of value and of personal responsibility. The human capacity for self-direction and self-determination implies a human responsibility for right direction and correct determination. Human beings may disagree about what in particular is right or wrong, but there is a general awareness that there *is* a difference between right and wrong. In this meaning of the word, conscience belongs to the whole human community and is part of the definition of what it means to be human. In our experience of ourselves as subjects, as human persons, we have an innate sense of the difference between good and evil.

O'Connell suggests a second level of conscience, which is more exactly an *act* of conscience and not conscience itself. This is the judgment that something is morally good or bad. This judgment is subject to error. There are differences of opinion. Thus, some believe that gambling in itself is evil; others insist that it is morally neutral at worst. When individuals try to make up their minds about what they should do, they have to have as much information about their available options as they can get. Accordingly, they will consult their own experience, their parents, their friends, their colleagues, the findings of various scientific disciplines such as psychology. If they are Christians, they will also consult the opinions of theologians and the testimony of Sacred Scripture. And if they are Catholics, they will also pay attention to the official teachings of the Church. This is known as the process of conscience-formation.

A third level, according to O'Connell, is reached with the decision itself. "I may be wrong, but I am convinced that I should do this." This is the final norm by which a person's act must be guided. It is not that it guarantees correctness of judgment, but only that it allows us to be true to ourselves. And we are judged finally by God on the basis of what is in our hearts, not on what we actually did or did not do. "Everyone, of course, must ultimately follow his conscience; this means he must do right as he sees the right with desire and effort to find and do what is right" (Bernard

Häring, *The Law of Christ*, vol. 1, Westminster, Md.: Newman Press, 1961, p. 151). So strongly rooted is this principle of the primacy of conscience over both external act and external authority that Thomas Aquinas himself argued that "anyone upon whom the ecclesiastical authority, in ignorance of true facts, imposes a demand that offends against his clear conscience, should perish in excommunication rather than violate his conscience" (*IV Sentences*, dist. 38, a. 4). This principle is now taken for granted in Catholic theology, even though the opposite would have been thought to be the case a few decades ago.

The Right and Duty to Follow One's Conscience

The Second Vatican Council's *Declaration on Religious Freedom* declares that we are bound to follow our conscience faithfully in all our activity, and that no one is "to be forced to act in a manner contrary to his conscience. Nor, on the other hand, is he to be restrained from acting in accordance with his conscience, especially in matters religious" (n. 3). This principle applies as well to children (see *Declaration on Christian Education*, n. 1). But what do we do in situations where others oppose our conscientious decision? What do we do if we sincerely believe that another's conscientious act will be harmful to the public good?

There are some traditional guidelines: (1) A person should not be prevented from following even an erroneous conscience, unless the action is seriously injurious to himself/herself or to others. Thus, a person should be prevented from committing suicide, if possible, or from killing his family as an act of "reparation" for his sins. (2) No one may morally coerce or persuade another to act against his or her conscience. Thus, the government cannot force someone to engage in military service if the person is convinced in conscience that all forms of physical combat are gravely sinful (*Pastoral Constitution on the Church in the Modern World*, n. 79). This principle does not prohibit someone, however, from trying to reason with others in order to make them change their judgment about a particular moral action.

Conscience and Church Authority

Having noted the inviolable character of conscience and an individual's right to follow conscience, even when it is erroneous, we move finally to the question of the authority of the Church. Are members of the Church bound to obey all official moral teachings of the Church and to assume, almost as a matter of course, that their consciences are necessarily erroneous and not to be followed if they are in conflict with the Church's moral pronouncements? The following principles must be taken into account:

1. It is taken for granted that the Church's moral teaching is normally a source for positive illumination for the Christian in forming his or her conscience. If, however, after appropriate study, reflection, and prayer, a person is convinced that his or her conscience is correct, in spite of a conflict with the moral teachings of the Church, the person not only may but *must* follow the dictates of conscience rather than the teachings of the Church.

2. The Church has never explicitly claimed to speak infallibly on a moral question, so there is probably no question as yet of a conflict between an individual's fallible decision in conscience and a teaching of the Church which is immune from error.

3. No teaching of the Church can hope to account for every moral situation and circumstance. Every teaching still has to be applied in particular cases. One is not necessarily repudiating the values affirmed in the teaching if one decides that the teaching does not bind or apply in this instance.

4. The teachings themselves are historically conditioned. What may have been perceived as morally wrong in one set of circumstances—e.g., charging interest on a loan in the Middle Ages—would be regarded as morally justifiable in another situation—e.g., charging interest on a loan today, in the context of modern commercial life.

On the other hand:

5. No individual or group of individuals can hope to identify and grasp moral truth by relying entirely on their own resources. We all need assistance. We all rely on the moral vision of others as well as our own. The Church, as the Temple of the Holy Spirit, is a major resource of such moral direction and leadership.

It is the product of centuries of experience, crossing cultural, national, and continental lines.

Positively, a Catholic gives prior attention and respect to official teachings, but must also take account of other sources of moral reflection and counsel—e.g., one's associates, the findings of scientific disciplines, the Bible, the writings of theologians. Thus, the *Declaration on Religious Freedom* of the Second Vatican Council asserts: "In the formation of their consciences, the Christian faithful ought carefully to attend to the sacred and certain doctrine of the Church. The Church is, by the will of Christ, the teacher of truth. It is her duty to give utterance to, and authoritatively to teach, that truth which is Christ himself, and also to declare and confirm by her authority those principles of the moral order which have their origin in human nature itself" (n. 14). One is not a Catholic who deliberately and systematically excludes all references to official Church teachings in making moral decisions.

SUMMARY

1.   This chapter raises *three fundamental questions*: (1) Who is the Christian? (2) What kind of person is the Christian called to become? (3) How does one become a Christian? The focus is on the theological principles which permeate and shape the Catholic tradition's answers to each of these questions.

2.   Principles and process are always in a dialectical relationship to one another. *Principles* are formulations which try to come to terms with the process of human experience, and the *process* itself is guided and critiqued by such principles. Principles, therefore, are basic truths which are at once products and shapers of experience. Thus, Catholic moral theology must be concerned with both: principles and process alike.

Who is the Christian?

3.   The Christian is a radically social human person in whom God is present in grace but who is, at the same time, prone to acting against the divine presence. Beyond that, *the Christian is a person who has moved to a different level of human consciousness, i.e., is one who believes in Jesus Christ and whose whole life is shaped by that belief.* The process by which the Christian moves to that new level of consciousness and existence is called *conversion*.

4. The Christian's proneness to act against the divine presence is the tendency to *sin*. There is no single word for "sin" in the *Old Testament*. The closest, *hamartia*, means, in its verb form, "to miss the mark." Sin is infidelity to the *convenantal* relationship with God. In the *New Testament*, and especially in *Paul*, sin is acting against who we are and against the God who is within us. It is at the root of the conflict between the spirit and the flesh. We achieve victory in Christ.

5. Sin presupposes *freedom* and *responsibility*. To be free means to be in possession of oneself, to be conscious of oneself as a responsible being. Freedom is *limited* from without by our historical existence and from within by the fact that we are never fully present to ourselves. Ultimately, freedom is our capacity for God. In freedom we reach beyond ourselves to become something other than we are.

6. This basic orientation toward God is called the *fundamental option*, the state of being converted to the Kingdom of God. Only an equally fundamental reversal of that choice for God is sufficient to cancel out the original act of conversion. Such a reversal is a rare occurrence for one who is sincerely oriented toward God.

7. The Church has always taught that we have the fundamental capacity to reject God (mortal sin), but it has never taught that there are, in fact, human persons in hell. Indeed, because of the forces which limit our freedom, we can never be certain that we have finally and fully said "No" to God, even in an act which appears to involve such a rejection.

8. The situation that makes sin possible is called *Original Sin*. *Venial sin* is a human act which is not fully consistent with our fundamental option for God. There is some contradiction between what we do and the kind of person we are or want to become. *Serious sin* is more inconsistent with our fundamental option than is venial sin, but not so inconsistent as is mortal sin. *Mortal sin* is an act which fully engages the person. The person not only chooses the act but also chooses to be the kind of person who would perform such an act.

9. Although the traditional *three-source theory* is not without criticism today, its threefold norm to judge the morality of a human act is still of some value: (1) How serious was the act I performed or failed to perform (the *object*)? (2) What was my motive, as far as I can reasonably determine (the *end*)? (3) What were the circumstances surrounding my decision to do what I did, and how did those circumstances affect my decision (the *circumstances*)?

10. Some sins are so deeply rooted in our fallen human nature that they are the sources of other lapses. These are the *seven capital sins*: pride, covetousness, lust, anger, gluttony, envy, and sloth.

11. The process by which we reject sin and turn to God is called *conversion*. It is a determination to live according to the demands of the Kingdom of God. This is a fuller understanding of conversion than was common in the decades before Vatican II, when a "convert" was simply one who became a Catholic.

12. Conversion means shifting horizons, i.e., shifting those ranges of vision which set limits to our interests and knowledge. We perceive the world in a new way. *Intellectual conversion* is a fundamental change of a person's basic view of reality. *Moral conversion* is a fundamental change of a person's basic motive for making decisions. *Religious conversion* is a fundamental change of a person's basic orientation: away from self and toward God. It is a total being-in-love with God and is manifested in the love of one's neighbor, who is the sacrament of God. Love of the neighbor is the final test of religious conversion (1 John 4:20–21).

What kind of person is the Christian called to become?

13. The Christian is called to become a person of *character*, i.e., a person who takes responsibility for his or her actions, and not one who simply follows "the rules." It is our character which gives direction and shape to our lives. There is an old adage: "Plant an act, reap a habit; plant a habit, reap a virtue; plant a virtue, reap a character; plant a character, reap a destiny."

14. *Character is never finished once and for all.* Good or bad habits (virtues and vices) can be reversed or broken. Usually this happens gradually; sometimes it occurs in a decisive experience (e.g., conversion or mortal sin). Since character is so closely linked with personality and since personality is always unique, *there is no single type of character which is normative for everyone.* There are different styles of Christian life and different moral histories.

15. A *virtue* is a power, rooted in grace, to realize moral good, and especially to do it joyfully and perseveringly even against inner and outer obstacles and at the cost of sacrifice. The opposite of a virtue is a *vice*.

16. In modern psychology, virtue is equivalent to "ego strength." It is the ability to keep the *id*, or base animal passions, under control, and to make decisions without the interference of the *superego*, or overweening conscience. It is the capacity for self-actualization.

17. *Theological virtues* are those which have to do immediately with our relationship with God: faith, hope, and charity. *Moral virtues* are those which have to do with our relationship with one another: prudence, justice, temperance, and fortitude.

18. The first of the theological virtues is *faith*. Faith is *conviction*, *trust*, and *commitment*. It believes something or someone or sees reality in a new way (the *intellectualist* approach). It trusts in the mercy of God (the *fiducial* approach). And it moves a person to action on behalf of others (the *performative* approach).

19. Such faith is always in process. It develops in *stages*, just as persons develop in stages of self-understanding and moral perception (see Erikson, Kohlberg, *et al.*). According to James Fowler, Christian faith moves through six stages: (1) imitative and fantasy-filled, under the influence of parents and other primal adults; (2) literal understanding of stories and beliefs; (3) acceptance of what is proposed by "those who count"; (4) acceptance of personal responsibility for one's beliefs and attitudes; (5) recognition of, and respect for, legitimate diversity of faith-perspectives; and (6) being-for-others.

20. *Hope* is that virtue by which we take responsibility for the future, both of ourselves and of the world. It is oriented, therefore, toward the Kingdom of God. Hope measures everything against the future Kingdom, and so it is a virtue which has a prophetic edge. The so-called *theology of hope* movement of the middle and late 1960s brought renewed attention to this virtue and especially to its prophetic dimension.

21. *Charity* is that virtue by which we participate in the life of God who *is* love (1 John 4:8,16). It is lived faith and lived hope. It is love of God and love of neighbor, i.e., the total dedication and devotion to the welfare of the other, regardless of sacrifice and personal cost. This love is rooted in the crucifixion.

22. Love is possible only for those who are personally mature, i.e., who can accept themselves and others for who and what they are. Its opposite is not hate but *apathy*, a suspension of commitment, a lack of concern. Love is the soul of all other Christian virtues.

23. The virtue of *religion*, or worship, directs us to ritualize our experience of faith, hope, and charity. It is a virtue which bridges the gap between the theological and the moral virtues. Worship is oriented at once to the glory of God and the service of one's neighbor. It is opposed by the sins of idolatry, superstition, hypocrisy, legalism, and self-delusion, or triumphalism.

24. The *cardinal*, or *moral*, virtues are those on which other virtues "hinge." *Prudence* is the ability to discern. It answers the question "What is the best way for me, in this situation, to do the right thing?" It involves inquiry, taking counsel, judgment, and making a decision. It is

closely allied with the discernment of spirits, which also can be a corporate enterprise.

25. *Discernment* is clearly misguided if it does not issue forth in the fruits of the Spirit: love, joy, peace, etc.; if it leads to doctrinal or moral positions which are clearly at odds with the tradition of the Church and/or with contemporary scholarship; if it intensifies isolation and even eccentricities; and if it ignores information, rejects the counsel of others, and imposes its decisions by force.

26. The virtue of *justice* is concerned with rights and with the duties which correspond to those rights. It is linked with the biblical notion of *righteousness*, i.e., salvation which is given through fidelity to the Covenant (Old Testament) or through the death of Christ (New Testament).

27. A *right* is a power to do things necessary for achieving the end or purpose for which we are destined as rational and free persons. In that sense, rights flow from duties. Rights can be in conflict. And there is also a hierarchy of rights.

28. Since we are radically social and since human growth occurs in a societal context, justice is concerned with our social relationships at various levels: individual(s) to individual(s) (*commutative* justice), government to individual(s) (*distributive* justice), individual(s) to government (*legal* justice), and individual(s) to society at large (*social* justice).

29. Love of itself is never sufficient for societal life. There are systems and structures, claims and conflicts, which have to be attended to with deliberation and care. Christian moralism must be replaced by *Christian realism* (Reinhold Niebuhr).

30. A correct understanding of social justice requires a correct understanding of the distinction between society and the state. *Society* is the total network of social, political, economic, cultural, and religious relationships which are necessary for full human development. The *state* is the center of coercive power in society. It is the civil authority by which the purposes of society are procured and preserved.

31. The *principle of subsidiarity* means that nothing should be done at a higher level that can be done as well or better at a lower level. Thus, the state should intervene only when lesser bodies cannot fulfill a given task required by the common good.

32. The *process of socialization* refers to the growing interdependence of humankind and of nations. As modern economic and political life becomes more complex, more intervention is required. The principle of subsidiarity, therefore, is balanced off by the process of socialization. The two must be kept in creative tension.

33. The four kinds of justice—commutative, distributive, legal, and social—are interrelated and mutually limiting. All four are attempts to express the demands of Christian love. They do not provide immediate answers to complex problems of social existence, but rather they are *principles of discernment and specific guides for judgment.* The fulfillment of the virtue of justice is part of the world's movement toward the Kingdom, which is the final realization of justice.

34. *Temperance* is the virtue which enables us to achieve some balance in the exercise of our concupiscible appetites: desire for food, drink, sex. It humanizes, not represses, these pleasures. The virtue is closely allied with Christian *asceticism,* which is concerned with those "exercises"which help us regulate the conflict between the spirit and the flesh. It involves painful struggle, self-denial, and renunciation. It is the acceptance of one's facticity and the historical limitations of one's existence. Patterned on the cross, asceticism is obedience even to the point of death and leads to the service of others.

35. *Fortitude* is the virtue of courage by which one overcomes an instinctive fear in order to pursue the good. It brings balance to our irascible appetites: fear and rashness. It has an active and passive side: taking bold action for the Kingdom of God, and enduring pain, suffering, and even death for the sake of the Kindgom.

36. The Christian is also called to a life of *mercy.* Mercy, unlike justice, gives to another more than the other deserves. All human mercy participates in the mercy of God, by which we are saved. The works of mercy apply to the needs of the body (corporal works) and to the needs of the soul (spiritual works). The *corporal works of mercy* are: feeding the hungry, giving drink to the thirsty, clothing the naked, sheltering the homeless, visiting the sick, ransoming the captive, and burying the dead. The *spiritual works of mercy* are: instructing the ignorant, counseling the doubtful, admonishing the sinner, bearing wrongs patiently, forgiving offenses, comforting the afflicted, and praying for the living and the dead. Mercy reminds us that our obligations go beyond even the demands of social justice.

How does one become a Christian?

37. One becomes a Christian by being converted to Jesus Christ and his Gospel of the Kingdom of God, and by being initiated into the Church.

38. How the individual Christian determines what the Gospel demands raises the question of values and norms. *Premoral values* are those concrete good things that ought to be done, to the extent possible

(e.g., the achievement of good health). *Moral values* are those good things which are essential to proper human living (e.g., justice). *Material norms* point out the premoral values we are to pursue (e.g., Do not kill). *Formal norms* point to moral values which must be pursued (e.g., Do not murder). Only formal norms are absolute, universal, and exceptionless. Thus murder is always wrong; killing is not.

39.   Material norms tell us what we should *do*; formal norms tell us who we should *be*. Material norms give us information and direction; formal norms give us motivation and encouragement.

40.   The Christian lives in a world of premoral and moral values and of material and formal norms which express those values. Norms have to be applied in each case, and no case is exactly like another. The challenge of *Christian moral education* is not the teaching of moral rules but the development of Christian character. The rudder of the Christian life is always prudence.

41.   Values and norms are rooted ultimately in God and penultimately in *natural law*, i.e., in the whole order of things which, by the will of God, defines us as human persons and contributes to human development. For the Greeks, natural law was the "given" of reality; for the *Romans*, it was something to be discovered and reshaped through common sense and intelligence. The first emphasis reflects the *classicist* mentality; the second, the *historically conscious* mentality.

42.   The *natural-law theory* has traditionally upheld two principal values: the existence of a source of ethical wisdom and knowledge which the Christian shares with all humankind, and the fact that morality cannot be merely the subjective whim of an individual or group of individuals.

43.   Traditional (classicist) understandings of natural law have been complemented by *three newer approaches*: the personalist, the relational and communitarian, and the transcendental. The first attends to the *person* doing the act; the second attends to the *context* in which the act is done and its *social repercussions*; the third attends to the *knowing process* of the subject who does the act.

44.   With regard to the third approach, Karl Rahner speaks of a *"moral instinct of faith"* by which every person knows the difference between right and wrong and which allows us to synthesize all the factors in a given situation and come to a decision which transcends any one factor or the sum total of these factors.

45.   *Conscience* is not feeling or judgment. It is the radical experience of ourselves as moral agents. We make decisions in terms of our self-understanding. We act insofar as we perceive ourselves to be a

particular kind of person. Decisions of conscience are always fallible because we never know ourselves fully and because, furthermore, we are historically situated.

46. In *the Bible* conscience is closely identified with "the heart" (Old Testament) and with the fundamental awareness of the difference between moral good and evil (Paul). It is a principle of freedom (1 Corinthians 10:29).

47. According to *Vatican II*, conscience is what summons us to love good and avoid evil. It is the most secret core and sanctuary of a person. Because conscience can err, all human beings, including Christians, must always search for truth in collaboration with others.

48. Conscience is the final norm of moral action. It must be properly formed, but once a decision in conscience is made, erroneously or not, it cannot yield even to the directives of the Church. We are judged finally by God on the basis of what is in our hearts, not our fidelity to rules. A person can be prevented from following a clearly erroneous conscience only when serious injury to oneself or to others will surely follow.

49. The Church has never explicitly claimed to speak infallibly on a moral question, nor do the non-infallible moral teachings of the Church solve every moral situation and circumstance. The teachings are themselves historically conditioned. On the other hand, the Church does speak from some measure of historical perspective and with collective wisdom and experience. A Catholic will always give prior attention and respect to pertinent moral teachings of the Church before reaching a decision.

SUGGESTED READINGS

Böckle, Franz. *Law and Conscience.* New York: Sheed & Ward, 1966.

Curran, Charles E. *A New Look at Christian Morality.* Notre Dame, Ind.: Fides Publishers, 1968.

——————. *Themes in Fundamental Moral Theology.* Notre Dame, Ind.: University of Notre Dame Press, 1977.

Fuchs, Josef. *Human Values and Christian Morality.* Dublin: Gill and Macmillan, 1970.

Gustafson, James. *Christ and the Moral Life.* New York: Harper & Row, 1968.

Hauerwas, Stanley. *Vision and Virtue: Essays in Christian Ethical Reflection.* Notre Dame, Ind.: Fides Publishers, 1974.

McCormick, Richard A. "Notes on Moral Theology," which appear annually in *Theological Studies.*

McDonagh, Enda. *Gift and Call.* St. Meinrad, Ind.: Abbey Press, 1975.

O'Connell, Timothy E. *Principles for a Catholic Morality.* New York: Seabury Press, 1978.

Pieper, Josef. *The Four Cardinal Virtues.* New York: Harcourt, Brace, & World, 1965.

Rahner, Karl. "On the Question of a Formal Existential Ethics." *Theological Investigations.* Vol. 2, Baltimore: Helicon Press, 1963, pp. 217-234.

Regan, George M. *New Trends in Moral Theology: A Survey of Fundamental Moral Themes.* New York: Newman Press, 1971.

·XXVII·

CHRISTIAN EXISTENCE:
SPECIAL QUESTIONS

This chapter seeks to clarify the meaning of the principles described and explained in the preceding chapter by showing how such principles are variously employed and applied to certain contemporary moral questions. There is no attempt here to raise, or even identify, all of the major ethical questions of our day, with the hope of offering the reader guidance toward the solution of such questions. This is clearly beyond the scope of this book. The reader will not find, for example, any explicit discussion of abortion. Catholic theologians do not generally differ among themselves on its morality anyway. On the other hand, some issues must be treated specifically if the material in the two preceding chapters is not to be reduced to moral generalities.

Four questions are addressed in this chapter, two having to do with *interpersonal ethics* and two having to do with *social ethics*. This is not to say that interpersonal ethics have nothing to do with social ethics or vice versa, but only that the immediate focus of such questions is on the one side rather than the other. Indeed, the adjectives themselves are misleading. *Interpersonal* and *social* are not really opposed. One might also call the first *individual* ethics and the second *societal* ethics. But the terms are less important than the issues themselves.

The two issues of an interpersonal character treated here are *birth control* and *homosexuality*. The two issues of a social, and indeed political, character are *warfare* and the *intervention of the state* in the economic order, specifically in the area of health care.

Our emphasis will always be on method, not solutions. This chapter engages in analysis, not advocacy. Comparisons are drawn, but positions are not fixed.

Section One: Interpersonal Ethics

BIRTH CONTROL
An Overview

There are two sides to this question in Catholic moral theology. Neither side, however, rejects birth control totally and absolutely. The traditional, or conservative, position acknowledges, for example, that a married couple may deliberately employ the rhythm method by which sexual union is restricted to those days when the woman is biologically incapable of conceiving a child. That is clearly a form of birth control. What is really at issue here, therefore, is not birth control in this generic sense, but *contraception,* i.e., the intentional placing of a material obstacle to the conception of a child: e.g., a contraceptive pill, an intrauterine device, contraceptive foam, a condom.

One side argues that contraception by such artificial means is always wrong. The other side argues that contraception may be not only legitimate under certain circumstances but even mandatory. This side speaks in terms of "responsible parenthood." The two sides differ on three major counts: (1) their respective understandings of natural law, (2) their respective understandings of the binding force of official Church teachings; and (3) their respective understandings of the development of doctrine.

The argument was joined in 1968 with the publication of Pope Paul VI's encyclical *Humanae Vitae* ("Of Human Life"). The pope had before him the majority and minority reports of a special papal commission established by his predecessor Pope John XXIII and continued in existence by himself. The majority proposed a change in the Catholic Church's traditional teaching by which contraception was condemned; the minority urged the pope to hold fast to that teaching, and raised the question of the impact of a change of view on the credibility of the papal magisterium. Pope Paul VI decided in favor of the minority view, and the rest is history. Theologians and even some episcopal conferences voiced opposition to the encyclical or at least took positions that were less than enthusiastic in their support. Surveys in the United States indicate that the overwhelming majority (more than 80%) of Catholics of child-bearing ages do not, in fact, observe the encyclical's teaching.

Official Teaching Prior to Humanae Vitae

Pope Pius XI (d. 1939), in his encyclical *Casti Connubii* (1930), declared: "Since the conjugal act is destined primarily by nature for the begetting of children, those who in exercising it deliberately frustrate its natural power and purpose sin against nature and commit a deed which is shameful and intrinsically vicious .... any use whatsoever of matrimony exercised in such a way that the act is deliberately frustrated in its natural power to generate life is an offense against the law of God and of nature and those who indulge in such are branded with the guilt of grave sin ...."

Pope Pius XII (d. 1958) in his *Allocution to Midwives* (1951), reaffirmed this teaching: "Our predecessor ... solemnly restated the basic law of the conjugal act and conjugal relations: every attempt on the part of the married couple during the conjugal act ... to deprive it of its inherent power and to hinder the procreation of new life is immoral: no indication or need can change an action that is intrinsically immoral into an action that is moral and lawful. This prescription holds good today just as much as it did yesterday. It will hold tomorrow and always, for it is not a mere precept of human right but the expression of a natural and divine law."

On June 23, 1964, Pope Paul VI (d. 1978), after much discussion at the Second Vatican Council, promised a thorough review of the subject in the light of new knowledge but asked that the traditional teaching be observed in the meantime. He also reserved to himself the final decision on the matter. After much debate within the drafting committee, the council's *Pastoral Constitution on the Church in the Modern World* formulated its view in 1965 in this way: "Therefore, when there is question of harmonizing conjugal love with the responsible transmission of life, the moral aspect of any procedure does not depend solely on sincere intentions or on an evaluation of motives. It must be determined by objective standards. These, based on the nature of the human person and his acts, preserve the full sense of mutual self-giving and human procreation in the context of true love. Such a goal cannot be achieved unless the virtue of conjugal chastity is sincerely practiced. Relying on these principles, sons of the Church may not undertake methods of regulating procreation which are found blameworthy by the teaching authority of the Church in its unfolding of the divine law" (n. 51).

On October 29, 1966, Pope Paul VI stated that the official magisterium was in a state of "reflection" on the issue but not in a state of "doubt." In July of 1968 the matter was officially settled with the publication of the encyclical *Humanae Vitae*.

Arguments in Support of the Traditional Teaching

The *first argument* given in the minority report of the Papal Commission for the Study of Population, the Family, and Birth (1966) is the "constant and perennial" teaching of the Church. The authors (John Ford, S.J., of the United States, Jan Visser, C.SS.R., of the Netherlands, Marcelino Zalba, S.J., of Rome, and Stanley de Lestapis, S.J., of France) cite those sources already referred to in the previous section of this chapter as well as several other assorted addresses of Pope Pius XII, the encyclical *Mater et Magistra* (1961) of Pope John XXIII, statements of various bishops, and the consistent answers given by the Holy See to questions on the subject from around the Catholic world.

"If the Church could err (on this issue), the authority of the ordinary magisterium in moral matters would be thrown into question. The faithful could not put their trust in the magisterium's presentation of moral teaching, especially in sexual matters." The question is not whether this teaching on birth control is "infallible" (i.e., immune from error) according to the traditional criteria of infallibility. "For if this doctrine is not substantially true, the magisterium itself will seem to be empty and useless in any moral matter." The assumption here seems to be that if the Church, or any comparable moral agency, can be found to be in error on this important matter, its judgment on *all* matters is automatically suspect.

The *second major argument* in favor of the traditional teaching is based on an analysis of the conjugal act itself. The minority theologians acknowledge, in what is perhaps the most remarkable statement in their entire report, that "if we could bring forward arguments which are clear and cogent based on reason alone, it would not be necessary for our commission to exist, nor would the present state of affairs exist in the Church as it is." What the conservative theologians bring forward, therefore, is suggestions of a line of argument based on natural law, but not of such a character that it can equal the argument from authority in either clarity or force. Thus, " . . . the Fathers, theologians, and the Church herself have always taught that certain acts and the generative processes are in some way specially inviolable precisely because they are generative. This inviolability is always attributed to the act and to the process, which are biological; not inasmuch as they are biological, but inasmuch as they are human, namely inasmuch as they are the object of *human acts* and are destined by their nature to the good of the human species." Contraception is evil, the minority report maintains, because it changes an act which is naturally oriented to procreation into an act which is oriented to the mutual benefit of the spouses.

But the minority report returns immediately to its first argument. The case does not depend finally on the strength of philosophical or even theological points. "It depends on the nature of human life and human sexuality, *as understood theologically by the Church*" (my italics). Indeed, in such a matter we "need the help of the teaching Church, explained and applied under the leadership of the magisterium, so that (we) can with certitude and security embrace the way, the truth, and the life."

Arguments Against the Official Teaching

According to the majority opinion, the argument in favor of the traditional teaching based on authority fails to recognize the *evolutionary* character of that teaching. The early Fathers of the Church held that the use of sex in marriage was justified *only* for procreation. Later it was admitted that a sterile woman might marry and enjoy full conjugal relations. Eventually intercourse during the so-called safe period was approved. The next step would be to admit that the procreative value of the conjugal act is not bound up with every individual act of intercourse. Moreover, the official Church has changed its teachings in other matters—e.g., religious liberty and usury. One need only compare the teachings of Pope Pius IX and even of Leo XIII with Vatican II's *Declaration on Religious Freedom* (see chapters 19 and 25).

Catholic legal and ethical scholar John Noonan has argued that the condemnation of usury, or lending money at interest, was far more authoritative in terms of the biblical, patristic, conciliar, and theological sources adduced in support of the condemnation than was the condemnation of contraception (see his *Contraception: A History of Its Treatment by the Catholic Theologians and Canonists,* Cambridge: Harvard University Press, 1965). And yet the teaching on usury changed because certain theologians in the sixteenth century concluded that economic conditions had changed, making the old condemnations obsolete, and that the experience of lay Christians had to be listened to. Thus, Navarrus (d. 1586), a professor at Salamanca in Spain and author of a *Manual for Confessors,* argued that an "infinite number of decent Christians" were engaged in exchange-banking, and he objected to any analysis which would "damn the whole world." Three papal bulls promulgated over a seventeen-year period (1569-1586) had unequivocally denounced and condemned usury. In a similarly short space of time, thirty years, the bulls were deprived of force to influence anyone's behavior. Theologians refused to support the teachings, and the laity continued about their business as if the teachings did not exist (see John Noonan, "The Amendment of Papal Teaching by Theologians," in *Contraception: Authority and*

Dissent, Charles E. Curran, ed., New York: Herder & Herder, 1969, pp. 41-75).

Furthermore, a change in the traditional teaching would not necessarily undermine the moral teaching authority of the Church. According to the majority theologians on the birth control commission (Josef Fuchs, S.J., of Rome, Philippe Delhaye of Belgium, and Raymond Sigmond of Rome), "such a change is to be seen rather as a step toward a more mature comprehension of the whole doctrine of the Church. For doubt and reconsideration are quite reasonable when proper reasons for doubt and reconsideration occur with regard to some specific question. This is part and parcel of the accepted teaching of fundamental theology."

This majority view also rejects the natural-law theory of those who support the traditional teaching. It is a concept of nature as something so mysterious and sacred, they maintain, that any human intervention tends to destroy rather than perfect this very nature. Because of this mentality many advances in medical science were prohibited for a time, and the same was true of other areas of scientific experimentation. The dignity of the human person consists in this: "that God wished man to share in his dominion . . . . In the course of his life man must attain his perfection in difficult and adverse conditions, he must accept the consequences of his responsibility, etc. Therefore, the dominion of God is exercised through man, who can use nature for his own perfection according to the dictates of right reason." It follows that we must use our skill to "intervene in the biological processes of nature so that (we) can achieve the ends of the institution of matrimony in the conditions of actual life, (rather) than (to) abandon (ourselves) to chance."

Indeed, the majority report argues, the conjugal act itself must be viewed not as an isolated reality but in the larger context of human love, family life, education, etc. (the *principle of totality).* Sexuality is not ordered only to procreation. Sacred Scripture says not only "Increase and multiply," but also "They shall be two in one flesh," and it shows the partner as another helpful self. "In some cases intercourse can be required as a manifestation of self-giving love, directed to the good of the other person or of the community, while at the same time a new life cannot be received.

This is neither egocentricity nor hedonism but a legitimate communication of persons through gestures proper to beings composed of body and soul with sexual powers."

Vatican II insisted that the decision to have children must take into account the welfare of the spouses and of their children, the material and spiritual conditions of the times, their state in life, the interests of the family group, of society, and of the Church. "The parents themselves should ultimately make this judgment in the sight of God" *(Pastoral Constitution on the Church in the Modern World,* n. 50). And Paul VI, in his encyclical *Populorum Progressio* (1967), acknowledged that "the population explosion adds to the difficulties of development .... Parents themselves must decide how many children to have. Parents themselves must consider their responsibilities before God and before each other, before their present children and before the community. Parents themselves must follow their consciences, formed by the law of God" (par. 37).

The final report of the Papal Birth Control Commission (June, 1966) followed this same line of argument, appealing to the *Pastoral Constitution on the Church in the Modern World.* The regulation of conception now appears "necessary for many couples who wish to achieve a responsible, open and reasonable parenthood in today's circumstances." The morality of sexual acts between married people "does not depend upon the direct fecundity of each and every particular act .... In a word, the morality of sexual actions is thus to be judged by the true exigencies of the nature of human sexuality, whose meaning is maintained and promoted especially by conjugal chastity ...." On the other hand, the final report condemns what it calls a truly "contraceptive" mentality which egotistically and irrationally opposes all fruitfulness in marriage. But the "true opposition is not to be sought between some material conformity to the physiological processes of nature and some artificial intervention. For it is natural to man to use his skill in order to put under human control what is given by physical nature. The opposition is really to be sought between one way of acting which is contraceptive and opposed to a prudent and generous fruitfulness, and another way which is in an ordered relationship to responsible fruitfulness and which has a concern for education and all the essential human and Christian values."

With regard to the contraceptive method to be used, the report of the Papal Birth Control Commission suggested four criteria: (1) it must be consistent with the humanity of the persons and with the love the conjugal act is intended to express; (2) it must be effective; (3) it must exclude as many negative factors as possible—e.g., threats to health or hygiene; and (4) it must inevitably depend on what happens to be available in a certain region at a certain time for a certain couple, and this may depend on the economic situation. In any event, "condemnation of a couple to a long and often heroic abstinence as the means to regulate conception cannot be founded on the truth."

Humanae Vitae

The central teaching of Pope Paul VI's encyclical on the regulation of births is contained in its eleventh paragraph: " . . . the Church calling men back to the observance of the norms of the natural law, as interpreted by constant doctrine, teaches that each and every marriage act must remain open to the transmission of life." The foundation for that teaching is a particular understanding of natural law as it applies to the conjugal act, namely, that there is an "inseparable connection, willed by God and unable to be broken by man on his own initiative, between the two meanings of the conjugal act: the unitive meaning and the procreative meaning" (n. 12). It is "unitive" in that it brings husband and wife together, and it is "procreative" in that it "capacitates them for the generation of new lives." The *principle of totality,* according to which contraception could be considered morally legitimate in the context of the totality of a fruitful married life, is declared erroneous (n. 14).

The encyclical's particular understanding of natural law clearly emerges in its defense of the rhythm method, or the restriction of marital relations to sterile periods of the month. In this case, the couple makes "legitimate use of a natural disposition; in the [other case], they impede the development of natural processes" (n. 16). The encyclical, therefore, rests its argument on the physiological structure of the act, while some contemporary theologians insist that the basic criterion for the meaning of human actions is the total person and not some isolated aspect of the person.

Indeed, even theologians who accept in principle an inseparable connection between the procreative and unitive elements of sexuality regard the explanation given in the encyclical as too strongly biological. Vatican II allowed for a wider basis for evaluating the morality of such a human act, namely, "the full sense of mutual self-giving and human procreation in the context of true love" *(Pastoral Constitution on the Church in the Modern World,* n. 51).

The encyclical also argues against contraception on the grounds that it leads to certain negative consequences: conjugal infidelity, a general lowering of morality, easy corruption of youth, loss of respect for women (n. 17).

Reaction to Humanae Vitae

The negative reaction of many theologians, ethicists and non-ethicists alike, was vigorous and widespread. These can be sampled in such books as *Contraception: Authority and Dissent* (cited above), *Human Sexuality: New Directions in American Catholic Thought: A Study Commissioned by the Catholic Theological Society of America* (New York: Paulist Press, 1977), pp. 114-128, and Joseph Komonchak's *"Humanae Vitae* and Its Reception: Ecclesiological Reflections," *Theological Studies* 39/2 (June 1978), pp. 221-257. A pro-encyclical view is presented in the same issue of *Theological Studies* by John C. Ford (one of the authors of the Papal Birth Control Commission's minority report) and Germain Grisez, "Contraception and the Infallibility of the Ordinary Magisterium," pp. 258-312.

Bishops' conferences around the world accepted the encyclical as authoritative teaching. However, some of these conferences drew attention, for example, to the primacy of conscience, the need to be understanding and forgiving, and the judgment that Catholics who sincerely cannot follow the encyclical's teaching are not thereby separated from the love of God. Such themes were sounded by the bishops of Belgium, Germany, the Netherlands, France, Canada, and the Scandinavian countries. Catholics who cannot follow the encyclical's teaching "should not consider that because of this they are separated from God's love" (Belgian bishops). "Pastors must respect the responsible decisions of conscience made by the faithful" (German bishops). Although Catholics must show "respect to the authority and pronouncements of the pope," there are "many factors which determine one's personal conscience regarding marriage rules, for examples mutual love, the relations in a family, and social circumstances" (Dutch bishops). Contraception is always a disorder, "but this disorder is not always culpable." Thus, "when one faces a choice of duties, where one cannot avoid an evil whatever be the decision taken, traditional wisdom requires that one seek before God to find which is the greater duty. The spouses will decide after joint reflection" (French bishops). "No one, including the Church can absolve anyone from the obligation to follow his conscience . . . If someone for weighty and well-considered reasons cannot become convinced by the argumentation of the encyclical, it has always been conceded that he is allowed to have a different view from that presented in a non-infallible statement of the Church. No one should be considered a bad Catholic because he is of such a dissenting opinion" (Scandinavian bishops). All of these themes recur in the statement of the Canadian bishops: Such couples "may be safely assured that whoever honestly chooses that course which seems right to him does so in good conscience."

A similar, although more conservative, approach was taken by the Sacred Congregation for the Clergy (April 26, 1971) over the signature of its prefect, Cardinal John Wright (d. 1979), in response to a dispute between certain priests of the archdiocese of Washington, D.C., and their archbishop, Cardinal Patrick O'Boyle. Without equivocating on the clear meaning of *Humanae Vitae,* the Congregation acknowledged that "conscience is inviolable and no man is to be forced to act in a manner contrary to his conscience, as the moral tradition of the Church attests." Thus, in pastoral practice priests must not be too quick to assume either complete innocence or moral guilt in the persons they counsel. One must recognize persons who are "honestly trying to lead a good Christian life." There must be confidence "in the mercy of God and the forgiving power of Christ ...."

Declaration on Certain Questions Concerning Sexual Ethics

On December 29, 1975, the Congregation for the Doctrine of the Faith issued a declaration on sexual ethics which reaffirms the teaching of *Humanae Vitae* as well as that encyclical's particular understanding of natural law. But the declaration fixed its attention primarily on three particular issues: premarital sexual intercourse, homosexuality, and masturbation. It is particularly skeptical about the arguments of contemporary Catholic moral theologians regarding the difficulty of committing a real mortal sin, i.e., an act that involves the rejection of one's fundamental option toward God (n. 10). It is true, the Congregation acknowledged, that sins of the sexual order more frequently than other sins may lack full and free consent of the will, but "it in no way follows that one can hold the view that in the sexual field mortal sins are not committed" (n. 10).

Christian Values Underlying This Issue

In making moral decisions on this issue, there are certain undoubted principles which Catholics have to take into account:

1.   The goodness of procreation, as an expression of mutual love and for the welfare of the human community at large.

2.   The sanctity of human life.

3.   The personal dignity and welfare of the spouses, their children, and their potential children.

4.   The inviolability of conscience.

5.   The responsibility to act on an informed conscience.

6.   The right and responsibility of the Church to teach on matters pertaining to morality. Clearly, the teaching of the Church involves that of pope and bishops, but other qualified teachers have a contribution to make as well.

7. The duty of Catholics to take such teaching seriously into account in the process of forming their consciences.

HOMOSEXUALITY
The Biblical Data

Wherever homosexuality is mentioned in the Bible it is condemned. It is a crime worthy of death (Leviticus 18:22; 20:13), a sin "against nature" (Romans 1:27), which excludes one from the Kingdom of God (1 Corinthians 6:9-10). God is said to have visited a terrible punishment upon Sodom for this sin (Genesis 19:1-29). One must remember, however, that various forms of sexual intercourse, including homosexuality, were considered a necessary part of worship by contemporary pagan groups. The severity of the Old Testament's judgment against homosexuality must be seen in that context. The Israelite would be imitating pagan cultic practices and would thereby defile himself (Leviticus 18:3,20,24,30). The worship of Yahweh was to be unconditionally exclusive. No trace of pagan influence was to be countenanced. Such would be idolatrous and an abomination (e.g., Leviticus 18:26,29-30; Deuteronomy 12:31; 13:14; 17:4; 18:9; 2 Kings 16:3; 21:2,11; 2 Chronicles 33:2; Ezekiel 5:9,11). In a world where worship permeated every aspect of life, anything suggestive of pagan cultic practice—e.g., the fertility rites of the Canaanites—would be for the Israelite tantamount to infidelity to Yahweh.

Even after the danger of ritual intercourse had passed, the prohibition against homosexual activity was retained just as various dietary prescriptions had been maintained. The Talmud extended the prohibition, but not the death penalty, to women as well. The Levitical teaching, of course, had considerable influence on the Church, affecting Paul's estimation of the sexual practices of first-century Greeks. The Genesis story of Sodom and Gomorrah (Genesis 19) was even more influential on Christian thought. The Fathers of the Church would automatically assume that the sin for which Sodom was punished was the homosexual practice of sodomy. A parallel story speaks of the wickedness of the people of Gibeah (Judges 19:22-30) who seize a concubine and abuse her "all night until the following dawn, when they let her go." What is common to the two stories—the one involving the male visitors of Sodom and the other, the female concubine of Gibeah—is rape. If sexuality is involved in the condemnations of both towns, it is less important than the issues of hospitality and justice. Indeed, there is no uniform tradition regarding Sodom's offense: for Isaiah it was injustice (1:10; 3:9); for Jeremiah, adultery, lying, and unrepentance (23:14); for Ezekiel, pride, gluttony, too much comfort, indifference to the poor and needy (16:49); for the Wisdom literature, folly, insolence, and inhospitality (Wisdom 10:8; 19:14; Sirach 16:8). Jesus refers to Sodom but makes no mention of its specific sin (Matthew 10:14-15; 11:23-24; Luke 10:12; 17:29). Not until late in the New Testament is an explicit link made between Sodom and sexuality (Jude 6-7; 2 Peter 2:4,6-10).

Sodom was to become for the early Christians a symbol of the depravity of Greek society. This, in turn, provides some background for the isolated references made to homosexual practices in the New Testament. Jesus says nothing about it. The Epistles mention it three times: in two instances as an item on a list of vices prevalent in first-century Rome (1 Corinthians 6:9-10; 1 Timothy 1:9-10), and in another, extended reference (Romans 1:18,22-28) to those who deliberately choose homosexual over heterosexual relations. There was, of course, no distinction between deliberate perversion and indeliberate homosexual orientation rooted in a particular personality with a particular psychological history and constitution.

Post-biblical Tradition

The Fathers of the Church were consistent in their denunciation of homosexuality: Augustine, John Chrysostom, *et al*. The sixth-century Code of Justinian added to pre-Christian laws protecting minors from homosexual violation the prohibition of all sodomistic practices under penalty of death by fire. This legal document had influence on both ecclesiastical and civil laws even into the Middle Ages, and perhaps indirectly into our own time in the West.

Thomas Aquinas treated homosexual acts in connection with sins against temperance, specifically lust, and listed sodomy along with masturbation and bestiality as "unnatural vices" *(Summa Theologica* II-II, q. 154). Catholic moral theology, until very recently, made no discernible changes in Aquinas' approach. Although there were very few references to the sin in the Church's official teachings, the manuals regularly numbered homosexual acts alongside masturbation and bestiality as against nature and always gravely sinful. The appeal to Scripture is to the Sodom story.

Contemporary Authoritative Statements

Thus, from the time of Paul, through Thomas Aquinas, down to the Vatican's *Declaration on Sexual Ethics* of 1975, the Catholic tradition has consistently judged all homosexual acts as at once unnatural and gravely sinful. The argument is based on the principle of finality which, according to the Vatican document, "states that the use of the sexual function has its true meaning and moral rectitude only in true marriage." The Declaration does not go into further detail regarding the norms of sexual life within marriage, but these norms are clearly taught in the encyclical letters *Casti Connubii* and *Humanae Vitae.* The Vatican document does make a distinction "between homosexuals whose tendency comes from a false education, from a lack of sexual development, from habit, from bad example, or from other similar causes, and is transitory or at least not incurable; and homosexuals who are definitively such because of some kind of innate instinct or a pathological constitution judged to be incurable." This second category of homosexuals "must certainly be treated with understanding and sustained in the hope of overcoming their personal difficulties and their inability to fit into society." But there is no basis for morally justifying their actions. "For according to the objective moral order, homosexual relations are acts which lack an essential and indispensable finality.... homosexual acts are intrinsically disordered and can in no case be approved of."

Three Approaches

Notwithstanding the clear and unequivocal teaching of the hierarchical magisterium on this important moral issue, new questions are arising in light of new developments and scientific research in medicine, psychiatry, and psychology. In attempting to uphold the basic tradition and to respond to the contemporary findings, theologians have reacted in different ways to the question at hand. For purposes of illustration, I list and summarize three theological approaches here: (1) that homosexual acts are always sinful in themselves; (2) that they are neutral; and (3) that they are essentially imperfect, neither always wrong nor an ideal.

Homosexual Acts Are Always Sinful in Themselves

This position follows the approach of Thomas Aquinas. The order of nature requires that a male should join with a female so that procreation will occur and the human species will continue in existence. Sexual union between persons of the same sex is "unnatural" because procreation is impossible, whereas the act itself is ordered for that purpose alone. A leading defender of this view is Catholic theologian John F. Harvey, O.S.F.S. Harvey argues that, while a homosexual is not responsible for his condition, he or she *is* responsible for controlling actions which spring from that condition. Homosexuals, like all other unmarried people, are called to avoid sexual indulgence (see "Homosexuality," *New Catholic Encyclopedia,* New York: McGraw Hill, 1967, VII, pp. 117-119; and "Contemporary Theological Views," in *Counseling the Homosexual,* John R. Cavanaugh, ed., Huntington, Ind.: Our Sunday Visitor Press, 1977, pp. 235-237).

This is also the teaching of the official magisterium. Thus, the *Declaration on Sexual Ethics* from the Sacred Congregation for the Doctrine of the Faith insists that "homosexual acts are intrinsically disordered and can in no case be approved of" (n. 8). And the National Conference of Catholic Bishops of the United States adopted the same approach in its *Principles to Guide Confessors in Questions of Homosexuality* (Washington, D.C.: N.C.C.B., 1973): genital sexual expression may take place only in marriage; each such act must be open in principle to procreation and must as well be an expression of mutual love between a husband and a wife. Because homosexual acts cannot possibly fulfill these principles, they are "a grave transgression of the goals of human sexuality and of human personality, and are consequently contrary to the will of God" (p. 3). Given the factor of compulsion, the confessor must avoid "both harshness and permissiveness . . . . But, generally, [the homosexual] is responsible for his actions, and the worst thing that a confessor can say is that the homosexual is not responsible for his actions" (pp. 8-9). Overt homosexuals are not to be encouraged to receive the Eucharist (pp. 14-15).

Homosexual Acts Are Morally Neutral

This position argues that the morality of the sexual act depends upon the quality of the relationship. The moral determination does not rest on whether the act is heterosexual or homosexual, but rather on the quality of the relationship of the persons. Accordingly, "It is the task of homosexuals to acknowledge themselves as such before God, accept their sexual inclination as their calling, and explore the meaning of this inclination for the Christian life" (Gregory Baum, "Catholic Homosexuals," *Commonweal* 99, February 15, 1974, p. 481). This view in effect denies not only the consistent tradition of Sacred Scripture and the Church but also the majority of all the data from the human sciences which point to the fact that human sexuality has its proper meaning in terms of the love union of male and female. Furthermore, stable homosexual relationships tend to be the exception rather than the rule. "It would seem," some Catholic theologians have argued against this "neutral" view, "that the elements of mutual love, fidelity, and caring need more detailed and specific explanation if this approach is to provide a suitable pastoral norm for counseling homosexuals" *(Human Sexuality,* p. 206). Indeed, freedom is not the only aspect involved in many human relationships—e.g., student-teacher, employer-employee, citizen-government. "Man, human existence, and human relationships can never be merely neutral" (Charles E. Curran, "Dialogue with the Homophile Movement: The Morality of Homosexuality," *Catholic Moral Theology in Dialogue,* Notre Dame, Ind.: Fides Publishers, 1972, p. 209).

Homosexual Acts Are Essentially Imperfect

A third position has been described by one of its principal advocates, Catholic moral theologian Charles E. Curran, of The Catholic University of America, as a mediating one (*op. cit.*, p. 209). It is also called a "theology of compromise." It recognizes that homosexual acts are wrong but also acknowledges that for some people homosexual behavior might not fall under under the total condemnation proposed in the first of these three approaches. The view is somewhat different from that proposed by John J. McNeill, S.J., in his *The Church and the Homosexual* (Kansas City, Mo.: Sheed, Andrews, and McMeel, 1976). McNeill argues that homosexual acts are the lesser of two evils: giving expression to one's sexuality with a person of the same sex, or having no opportunity at all for giving expression to one's sexuality.

Curran's theory of compromise is based on the premise that in the "presence of sin . . . at times one might not be able to do what would be done if there were no sin present . . . . the particular action in one sense is not objectively wrong because in the presence of sin it remains the only viable alternative for the individual. However, in another sense the action is wrong and manifests the power of sin. If possible, man must try to overcome sin, but the Christian knows that the struggle against sin is never totally successful in this world" (*op. cit.*, pp. 216-217; see also his *A New Look at Christian Morality,* Notre Dame, Ind.: Fides Publishers, 1968, pp. 169-173 and 232-233).

Applying this theory of compromise to the issue of homosexuality, Curran asserts two propositions: (1) that "for an irreversible or constitutional homosexual, homosexual acts in the context of a loving relationship striving for permanency can be and are morally good;" and (2) "the ideal meaning of human sexual relationships is in terms of male and female" (see "Moral Theology, Psychiatry, and Homosexuality," *Bulletin of the National Guild of Catholic Psychiatrists,* vol. 24, 1978, pp. 24-25). Thus, the homosexual acts of an irreversible homosexual "in the context of a loving union tending to permanency are objectively good; but at the same time the ideal and normative human meanings of sexuality are in terms of male and female" (p. 26). On the other hand, Curran does not want to appeal to "the presence of sin in the world" to justify every single action, although some of the Fathers of the Church did make such an appeal to justify slavery. It is necessary rather to "consider all the values involved and on the basis of proportionate reason to decide whether or not something is objectively good" (p. 30; see also *Transition and Tradition in Moral Theology,* Notre Dame, Ind.: University of Notre Dame Press, 1979, pp. 59-80).

Curran's mediating theory of compromise is criticized from both sides: from those who follow the traditional natural law approach and from those who resist the argument that heterosexuality is the ideal (see *Human Sexuality,* p. 204).

Christian Values Underlying This Issue

In making moral decisions on this issue, there are certain undoubted principles which Catholics have to take into account.

1. The goodness of procreation, as an expression of mutual love and for the welfare of the human community at large.

2. The personal dignity of every human being, regardless of his or her sexual orientation, and the existence of natural and civil rights which flow from that dignity.

3. The need of every person for love, friendship, even intimacy, although not necessarily of a genitally sexual nature.

4. The inviolability of conscience.

5. The responsibility to act on an informed conscience.

6. The existence of many internal and external impediments to full human freedom.

7. The right and responsibility of the Church to teach on matters pertaining to morality. Clearly, the teaching of the Church involves that of pope and bishops, but other qualified teachers have a contribution to make as well.

8. The duty of Catholics to take such teaching seriously into account in the process of forming their consciences.

Section Two: Social Ethics

WARFARE
Biblical Data

The wars of Israel were the wars of Yahweh (Exodus 17:16; Numbers 21:14; 1 Samuel 25:28). The war against Amalek was the execution of the anger of Yahweh (1 Samuel 28:18). Yahweh was considered present in the war camp (Deuteronomy 23:15). Yahweh is called a warrior (Exodus 15:3; Psalm 24:8) who fights on behalf of Israel (Exodus 14:14; Deuteronomy 1:30; 32:41; Joshua 10:14,42; 23:10; 24:12; Judges 5:23), sending panic into the enemy (Exodus 23:27-28). Yahweh delivers the enemy into the hands of Israel (Joshua 2:24; 6:2,16; Judges 3:28; 1 Samuel 23:4; I Kings 20:28). It is Yahweh, not the strength of arms or numbers, who insures the victory (Judges 7:2-22; 1 Samuel 14:6; 17:45,47). It is Yahweh who leads the armies of Israel (Judges 4:14; Deuteronomy 20:4; 2 Samuel 5:24) and who gives the victory (Exodus 15:14-16; 23:27-28). The enemies of Israel are the enemies of Yahweh (Judges 5:23,31). The priestly ideal of a sacred war is set forth in Numbers 31, and the law of war in Deuteronomy 20 is another earlier rationalization of war. In this regard, the Israelites simply reflected the thought patterns and mentality of their times.

On the other hand, there are several instances where the *prophets* explicitly denounced war. War is a judgment of Yahweh upon Israel (Isaiah 5:25-30; Jeremiah 5:15; Amos 5:27; 6:14). It is through faith, not military means, that Israel is destined to survive (Isaiah 2:1-5; 30:15-17; 31:1-3; 22:8-11; Jeremiah 21:3-10; 27; 34:1-5; 38:2-4; Hosea 8:14; 10:13-14; 14:4; Amos 2:14-16).

Jesus and the disciples have no developed theology of warfare. The New Testament community was hardly in a position, as the Israelites had been, of determining policies affecting military expeditions against other nations. Jesus did warn that "those who use the sword are sooner or later destroyed by it" (Matthew 26:52).

Beyond that, however, the idea of warfare only appears in *metaphors* which describe the Christian life or illustrate the proclamation of the Gospel (Matthew 22:7; Luke 11:17; 14:31-32).

Paul mentions military service to explain the apostolate (1 Corinthians 9:7). The apostle should fight the good fight (1 Timothy 1:18) as a good soldier of Jesus Christ (2 Timothy 2:3-4). The warfare of the Christian is waged against the powers of evil (Ephesians 6:12).

Both Old and New Testaments speak of the final judgment in terms of warfare. The messianic king is a victorious warrior (Psalms 2; 110:5-7). Ezekiel 38-39 describes the attack and defeat of Gog, king of Magog, Meshech, and Tubal. In the New Testament the imagery of an apocalyptic war appears only in Revelation 12:7, the war between the angels led by Michael and the dragon, and in Revelation 20:9, where the dragon's forces are annihilated by God's power.

Post-biblical Developments

Augustine regarded war as both the product of sin and a remedy for it. In a world corrupted by sin, the use of force by public authorities is a legitimate means of avenging evil. Public order must be preserved. On the other hand, Augustine did not approve killing in self-defense. He separated individual morality, which must be dictated by the Gospel mandate of loving one's enemies and turning the other cheek (Matthew 5:39), from social morality, which is for the sake of the common good.

Thomas Aquinas carried forward the Augustinian position but was more specific about the criteria for the just war: (1) The cause must be just; (2) it must be undertaken by legitimate authority; and (3) the intention must be right.

These three basic categories would eventually be expanded into a complex set of criteria and principles. The first set of tests to determine a *just war* are: legitimate authority, just cause, last resort, need for a declaration of war, reasonable hope of success, proportionality between the evil produced by the war and the evil hoped to be avoided or the good hoped to be achieved, and right intention. The second set of principles are: the immunity of noncombatants from direct attack, and proportionality of tactics and of means to end (see James R. Childress, "Just-War Theories," *Theological Studies,* vol. 39, 1978, pp. 427-445).

Since the taking of human life was so obviously opposed to the ideals of the Gospel, warfare remained a serious moral problem for Christians. It could be justified only by an appeal to the common good. *The purpose of the just-war theory, therefore, was not to rationalize violence but to limit its scope and methods.* Thomas' own ambivalence about defending the use of force surfaces in his discussion of the right of self-defense. Whereas Augustine had prohibited it, Aquinas accepted it on the basis of the *principle of the double effect* (two effects follow, one good and one evil, from an essentially good or at least neutral act; if the evil effect is unintended and not a direct result of the act, and if the good effect is proportionate to the evil effect, the act itself is legitimate). Thus, public authorities could directly will the taking of life, but private persons could intend only the deterring of aggression, not the aggressor's death *(Summa Theologica* II-II, q. 64, a. 7; see also F. H. Russell, *The Just War in the Middle Ages,* London: Cambridge University Press, 1977, pp. 16-39, on Augustine, and pp. 60-199, on Aquinas).

The Spanish Scholastics Vitoria (d. 1546) and Suarez (d. 1617) brought the just-war theory to yet another stage of development. By their time the problem of warfare was substantially modified by two changes: the emergence of the nation-state as a new center of secular authority, challenging both the idea of a wider Christian commonwealth and the binding power of any universal moral authority higher than the state, and, secondly, the disintegrative impact of the Reformation on the Christian community. The emphasis in the just-war theory shifted from Aquinas' stress on the just *cause* to the question of *means.* It was acknowledged that both sides might sincerely hold their cause to be just, but they must attend nonetheless to the ways in which they wage war against the other. Indeed, in revising the content of the just-cause category and in enhancing the importance of judgments about the means of warfare, the Spanish Scholastics and also the Protestant theologian Hugo Grotius (d. 1645) provided the foundation for the secular science of international law (see L. B. Walters, *Five Classic Just-War Theories: A Study in the Thought of Thomas Aquinas, Vitoria, Suarez, Gentili and Grotius,* unpublished Ph. D. dissertation, New Haven: Yale University, 1971).

Between the seventeenth and twentieth centuries the only significant change in the just war theory is to be found in the writings of Taparelli d'Azeglio (d. 1862). His efforts to reflect on the international community as a subject of moral law provided the conceptual foundation for some of the major themes in twentieth-century papal teaching, especially that of Pope Pius XII (see, for example, the Christmas Addresses of 1941, 1951, 1952, and 1953 in *Major Addresses of Pius XII,* vol. 2, Vincent Yzermans, ed., St. Paul, Minn.: The North Central Publishing Co., 1961).

Modern Developments

Pope Pius XII (d. 1958) acknowledged that force could be used as an instrument of justice in the international order. However, the destructive capacity of modern warfare had already increased so drastically by his pontificate that he reduced the legitimate causes of war from three (self-defense, avenging an evil, and restoring violated rights) to one, i.e., the defense of one's own nation or that of another against unjust attack. At the same time, the pope rejected pacifism (Christmas Message, 1956).

By the time Pope John XXIII was elected to the papacy in 1958, the just-war doctrine was firmly in place. But development continued, this time in a discernibly pacifist direction. In Pope John XXIII's encyclical *Pacem in Terris* (1963) we find a strong criticism of the arms race and of the balance of terror on which it rests. He called for structural reform of the international political and legal system to deal with this dangerous problem. Significantly, there is no explicit endorsement in this encyclical of the right of self-defense for peoples and for states, although this was the one argument retained by Pius XII. "Therefore, in this age of ours, which prides itself on its atomic power, it is irrational to think that war is a proper way to obtain justice for violated rights" (a text cited by Vatican II's *Pastoral Constitution on the Church in the Modern World,* n. 80).

Is *Pacem in Terris* advocating a pacifist view here? James Douglass thought so *(The Nonviolent Cross: A Theology of Revolution and Peace,* New York: Macmillan, 1966, p. 84). Others, like Protestant ethicist Paul Ramsey contend the opposite *(The Just*

War: Force and Political Responsibility, New York: Scribner's, 1968, p. 78). Later official documents of the Catholic Church, however, continue to assert the right of legitimate defense for states and yet make no attempt to reform, correct, or reinterpret *Pacem in Terris.* Nonetheless, it *is* clear that the encyclical heralded a new approach to warfare in Catholic thought.

An explicit endorsement of a pacifist position occurs for the first time in Catholic teaching in Vatican II's *Pastoral Constitution on the Church in the Modern World.* "The horror and perversity of war are immensely magnified by the multiplication of scientific weapons. . . . (Such) considerations compel us to undertake an evaluation of war with an entirely new attitude" (n. 80). The new attitude generates an acceptance of a philosophy of nonviolence and support for conscientious objection. The council insists that it "cannot fail to praise those who renounce the use of violence in the vindication of their rights and who resort to methods of defense which are otherwise available to weaker parties too, provided that this can be done without injury to the rights and duties of others or of the community itself" (n. 78). *Gaudium et spes* rejects the policy of blind obedience. Conscience must remain supreme. "Moreover, it seems right that laws make humane provisions for the case of those who for reasons of conscience refuse to bear arms, provided however, that they accept some other form of service to the human community" (n. 79).

In the years after the council, Pope Paul VI encouraged this same line of emphasis. He visited the United Nations in 1965 to appeal for the end of all wars and established January 1 as a Day of Peace each year. Protestant theologian John Yoder classified Pope Paul's U. N. speech as an example of "cosmopolitan pacificism" *(Nevertheless: The Varieties of Religious Pacificism,* Scottsdale, Ariz.: Herald Press, 1971). Social ethicists like J. Bryan Hehir, Associate Secretary for International Justice and Peace, United States Catholic Conference, argue that the total content of recent Catholic teaching does not support such a judgment. The Catholic Church has not moved from a just-war ethic to a pacifist position. The reality is more complex. There has been change in the normative doctrine on war, but there is also *continuity.*

The central theme which ties contemporary Catholic teaching to earlier just-war teaching is the repeated assertion of the *right of states to self-defense*. Given the world situation as it is, devoid of any effective international authority, " . . . governments cannot be denied the right to legitimate defense once every means of peaceful settlement has been exhausted" *(Gaudium et spes,* n. 79). But this right is not absolute and unrestricted regarding means. Certain forms of force, even in self-defense, may be prohibited. Everything is to be governed by two principles: the *principle of proportionality* (the evil produced by the means of self-defense should not be greater than the evil produced by the aggression) and the *rule of noncombatant immunity.*

Thus, the arms race is condemned in *Pacem in Terris,* in *Gaudium et spes,* and in various statements of the Holy See on disarmament (see *The Holy See and Disarmament,* Vatican City: Tipografia Poliglotta Vaticana, 1976). It is "an utterly treacherous trap for humanity, and one which injures the poor to an intolerable degree" *(Gaudium et spes,* n. 81). The very same theme is sounded in Pope John Paul II's first encyclical, *Redemptor Hominis* (1979) and later the same year in his address to the thirty-fourth General Assembly of the United Nations Organization.

On the other hand, Vatican II does not demand *unilateral* disarmament. Disarmament must proceed "at an equal pace according to agreement, and backed up by authentic and workable safeguards" *(Gaudium et spes,* n. 82). There is a measured political realism in the teaching even in the face of a situation that can only be described as urgent and fraught with the greatest danger. There is a blending here of prophetic vision and political wisdom.

Contemporary Moral Options

In light of these recent developments in official Catholic teaching, it seems correct to suggest that there are two moral options available to Catholics today: the *just-war ethic* and some form of *pacifism*. Within the context of these two broadly stated positions, other specific positions in Catholic moral thought and teaching include: a condemnation of total war *(Gaudium et spes,* n. 80), a condemnation of acts of war aimed indiscriminately against civilians, an indictment of the arms race as a waste of needed funds, and an affirmation that those who do serve in the military may make a genuine contribution to the establishment of peace (n. 79).

There are a number of general moral perceptions and principles which the just-war and pacifist positions have in *common:* the sacredness of life, the seriousness of taking a human life, and the morally restricted nature of any war. The *difference* between the two positions is obvious: The pacifist holds that no conflict of values, even the defense of innocent life, can ever legitimate the use of violent force; the just-war advocate begins with the pacifist presumption but acknowledges the possibility of the presumption's yielding to circumstances which justify a rule-governed use of force shaped by many different moral criteria.

The *difference* is further manifested in their respective approaches to *conscientious objection.* The pacifist option demands *universal* conscientious objection; the just-war option allows also *selective* conscientious objection. For the pacifist, selective conscientious objection is not an option, since it implies that some uses of force are legitimate. During the Vietnam war, the Catholic bishops of the United States voiced their support for both universal conscientious objection and selective conscientious objection *(The Catholic Conscientious Objector,* October 12, 1969; *Declaration on Conscientious Objection and Selective Conscientious Objection,* October 21, 1971). The question is whether or not the two positions are compatible within one and the same community of faith.

But what of the just-war theory itself? Can it still be held in a nuclear age? Jewish political theorist Michael Walzer, of Harvard University, argues that it cannot. "Nuclear weapons explode the theory of just-war. They are the first of mankind's technological innovations that are simply not encompassable within the familiar moral world" *(Just and Unjust Wars: A Moral Argument with Historical Illustrations,* New York: Basic Books, 1977, p. 282). But Catholic theology and official teaching would seem to contradict that assumption. Catholics have, in fact, used the just-war theory to assess the morality of nuclear weapons, and there is a development of Catholic teaching from the time when Pope Pius XII first confronted the question in 1954 to the strongly worded statement of the Second Vatican Council in 1965: "Any act of war aimed indiscriminately at the destruction of entire cities or of extensive areas along with their population is a crime against God and man himself. It merits unequivocal and unhesitating condemnation" *(Gaudium et spes,* n. 80).

The special moral problem, however, is not with the *use* of nuclear weapons but with the *threat* of use in a *policy of deterrence.* Nuclear pacifists are divided on the morality of the deterrence policy. Pius XII did not have to face that problem, and Vatican II gave an imprecise response to it: "Whatever be the case with this method of deterrence, men should be convinced that the arms race in which so many countries are engaged is not a safe way to preserve a steady peace" (n. 81). It is not that the council or moral theologians find the deterrence policy acceptable. Rather, there are no better alternatives to it which are at once morally acceptable and politically viable.

What are the problems in the present deterrence system? First, there is the implicit intention to use the nuclear weapons if necessary. But their use would be immoral. On the other hand, the very threat of their use may in fact be preventing their use (see *Gaudium et spes,* n. 81). "If the intention to retaliate and the actual use of nuclear weapons both violate the ethics of war, is there a lesser evil in a threat which remains unfulfilled?" J. Bryan Hehir asks.

And what effect is there upon the adversary if it seems that the other side does not really intend to act? Would that show of weakness provoke the adversary into action? A radical move like unilateral disarmament may have the opposite intended effect. Rather than cooling off the nuclear atmosphere and making nuclear war less likely, it could conceivably increase the likelihood of a nuclear strike from the other side or put the adversary in the position of a blackmailer.

Three moral positions, not exclusively within the Catholic tradition, have emerged on this difficult issue. The *first,* adopted by the United States Catholic bishops in 1976, condemns not only the use of nuclear weapons but also the policy of deterrence because of the intent to use: "Not only is it wrong to attack civilian populations, but it is also wrong to threaten to attack them as part of a strategy of deterrence" *(To Live in Christ Jesus: A Pastoral Reflection on the Moral Life,* Washington, D.C.: U. S.

Catholic Conference, 1976, p. 34). Surprisingly, the statement is more uncompromising about deterrence than it is about use. A *second* position argues that some uses of nuclear weapons are legitimate, and that, therefore, a policy of deterrence is similarly justifiable (Paul Ramsey, *op. cit.*, chapters 13-15). A *third* position prohibits use but tolerates deterrence (J. Bryan Hehir, "The New Nuclear Debate: Political and Ethical Considerations," in *The New Nuclear Debate,* R. A. Gessert and J. B. Hehir, eds., New York: CRIA Special Studies, 1976, pp. 35-76). "We threaten evil," Walzer writes, "in order not to do it, and the doing of it would be so terrible that the threat seems in comparison to be morally defensible" *(op. cit.* p. 274).

If this whole discussion about nuclear strategy illustrates anything about Catholic moral theology and official Catholic moral teaching, it is their conscious effort to mix moral vision with political realism. There is, on the one hand, a clear condemnation of the whole business of nuclear strategy, but there are also concessions to the complexity of the issues. So much so, in fact, that a final judgment on what the Catholic position really is remains an open question. What *is* clear is that two different theological methods are at work: one (the pacifist) which allows for no exceptions on life-and-death issues such as war, capital punishment, abortion, euthanasia; the other (the just-war approach) which emphasizes the principle of proportionality (see Richard A. McCormick and Paul Ramsey, *Doing Evil to Achieve Good,* Chicago: Loyola University Press, 1978, chapter 1, "Ambiguity in Moral Choice," by McCormick).

Christian Values Underlying This Issue

Whatever position one adopts regarding the morality of warfare, there are certain values and principles which Catholics and other Christians, and indeed other persons of good will on various sides of the argument, have to take into account:

1. The sacredness of all human life.
2. The utter gravity of taking another human life.
3. The inherent moral limits on every use of force.

4. The right and responsibility of the Church to articulate a moral vision on matters of social and even international morality. Clearly, the teaching of the Church involves that of pope and bishops, but other qualified teachers have a contribution to make as well.

5. The responsibility of the Church to articulate such a moral vision in a manner that is at the same time politically realistic, or attentive to political realities, such as Pope John Paul II provides in his 1979 United Nations address on peace, human rights, and social justice.

6. The duty of Catholics to take such teaching seriously into account in the process not only of forming their consciences but of expressing their views in the political order (e.g., by voting, communication with political leaders, public statements designed to influence public opinion).

INTERVENTION OF THE STATE
IN THE ECONOMIC ORDER
Elements of the Issue

This issue illustrates again the thrust of Catholic teaching on questions of social justice, and indeed shows the nature of the Church as a community of moral discourse. It is "a gathering of people with the explicit intention to survey and critically discuss their personal and social responsibilities in the light of moral convictions about which there is some consensus and to which there is some loyalty" (James Gustafson, *The Church as Moral Decision-Maker,* Philadelphia: Pilgrim Press, 1970, p. 84). The Church does not pretend, and should not be expected, to have precise answers to complex social and political questions. Rather it attempts only to elaborate a framework of values, principles, and responsibilities within which a discussion of such issues can be carried on, the formation of a Christian conscience can be promoted, and decisions fundamentally consistent with the Christian tradition can be made.

The question of the right and duty of the state to intervene in the economic order highlights the relationship between two important elements of Catholic social doctrine: the *principle of subsidiarity* and the *process of socialization.* The *principle of subsidiarity,* according to which nothing is to be done at a higher level which can be done as well or better at a lower level, places the burden of proof for intervention always on the higher body, principally the state. This is a conservative principle; it leans against state intervention. The *socialization process* reminds us of our growing interdependence and the benefits that can be produced when there is planned interventionist action on the part of the state. It is not just that a lower group cannot do something as well or better than the state, but that there are simply too many groups, institutions, structures, and political factors for any one group or level apart from the state to meet a problem common to all of these diverse social elements. To the extent that socialization can also be considered a principle, it is a liberal principle; it encourages state intervention.

These two principles are to be understood as dialectically related, in creative tension. "The thrust of subsidiarity is to preserve a sphere of freedom, while recognizing the need for a certain degree of centralization and control. The counterthrust of socialization is to highlight the need for coordination and direction of complex social systems if they are to benefit the citizens for whom they exist" (J. Bryan Hehir, "Church and State: Basic Concepts for Analysis," *Origins* 8/24, November 30, 1978, p. 381). In deciding for or against state intervention, and also regarding the degree and type of intervention, both values have to be taken into account.

Recent Catholic Teaching

The *principle of subsidiarity* was first formally articulated by Pope Pius XI in his encyclical *Quadragesimo Anno* (1931): "It is a fundamental principle of social philosophy, fixed and unchangeable, that one should not withdraw from individuals and commit to the community what they can accomplish by their own enterprise and industry. So, too, it is an injustice and at the same time a grave evil and a disturbance of right order, to transfer to the larger and higher collectivity functions which can be performed and provided for by lesser and subordinate bodies" (cited also by Pope John XXIII's *Mater et Magistra,* 1961, par. 53). Although this is a conservative principle, it does not justify a laissez-faire approach by which the state allows the economic order to run by its own power and according to its own designs. The encyclical *Quadragesimo Anno* clearly placed the Church on the side of those arguing that economic activity should be regulated for the sake of the common good.

Pope Pius XII and Pope John XXIII carried this principle of subsidiarity forward to meet the growing complexity of the economic order. Although Pius XII's contributions never took the form of an encyclical letter, they were nevertheless incorporated into the explicit social teachings of John XXIII. Pius XII is cited in thirty-four of the seventy-three footnotes in John XXIII's *Pacem in Terris*. In *Mater et Magistra* John XXIII moved the discussion of state intervention to a new level of clarity and development. First, he reasserted the validity of the principle of subsidiarity as a norm of social policy. Secondly, he called attention to the substantially changed social and political context in which that principle has to function today. And, thirdly, he introduced the notion of socialization as a complement to that of subsidiarity.

John XXIII argued that the role of the state in society had to be understood in light of three contemporary elements: (1) the impact of technological change, (2) the rise of the welfare state, and (3) the growing aspirations of people to participate in the political process (pars. 46-50). From the confluence of these three elements, John XXIII proposed his notion of socialization (par. 59). This process, he argued, is at once the result and cause of increasing state intervention in the socio-economic order. The need to intervene follows from such basic needs as health care, education, housing. Such intervention has both positive and negative effects. On balance, John XXIII finds the benefits outweighing the liabilities.

Also at the heart of Catholic social doctrine and centrally related to the policy judgment the state has to make about intervention is the teaching on *rights and duties*. The clearest statement of which rights are necessary to preserve the human dignity of each person in society is found in John XXIII's *Pacem in Terris* (pars. 8-35). The concept of *right* implies a *moral claim* by a person to some good of the physical or spiritual order which is necessary for proper human development and dignity. When such a right is established, a correlative duty is also established to recognize the right and to see to it that it is fulfilled either through private action or through governmental action. It is one of government's principal responsibilities to balance rights and duties of members and groups within society. The state must recognize and reinforce those rights which protect the individual or groups from undue intrusion by public authority. It must also determine when and in what way the state can be used to promote the socio-economic rights of people, especially those in need and/or the politically weak. *Pacem in Terris* refers specifically to those rights: " . . . the right to life, to bodily integrity, and to the means which are necessary and suitable for proper development of life; these are primarily food, clothing, shelter, rest, medical care, and finally the necessary social services. Therefore a human being also has the right to security in case of sickness, inability to work, widowhood, old age, unemployment or in any other case in which he is deprived of the means of subsistence through no fault of his own" (par. 11).

Pope Paul VI brought Catholic social doctrine yet another step beyond John XXIII when, in *Octagesima Adveniens* (1971), he emphasized the responsibility of the political sector in the task of assuring justice for people in society. The ultimate decision in the social and economic field, both national and international, rests with political power (par. 46). The document does not provide solutions to complex policy questions, but it locates the ultimate arena where such questions are decided, and it thereby calls attention to the role of the state as the final agency of justice if other means fail to provide minimum economic justice for people. Thus, state intervention in some cases may be not only legitimate but even imperative.

Finally, in his address to the Thirty-fourth General Assembly of the United Nations Organization (October 1979), Pope John Paul II argued that "it is a question of the highest importance that in internal social life, as well as in international life, *all human beings* in every nation and country *should be able to enjoy effectively their full rights under any political regime or system*" (n. 19).

Health Care

In a country like the United States of America it is agreed that health care, recognized as a right by *Pacem in Terris,* is not evenly distributed throughout the society. In some parts of the nation there are inadequate facilities and too few trained medical personnel. Many citizens have no insurance policies. Only half the population has any major medical coverage. A prolonged or catastrophic illness can bring immediate financial ruination to a middle-class family. Meanwhile, ordinary health care costs continue to rise dramatically.

Ethically the question of health care is a question of *distributive justice.* How are limited resources to be shared with those with a right to them? How much should the state invest in health care over against, for example, education, food, clothing, defense, transportation, or the environment? Who shall receive the necessary life-giving resources when only a limited number are available and when those who do not receive the resources will probably die? Answers have varied. Significantly, very few Catholic moral theologians have even begun to address themselves to such an issue.

1. Protestant situation ethicist Joseph Fletcher recommends a *utilitarian* approach. We must strive to bring about the greatest good for the greatest number ("Ethics and Health Care: Computers and Distributive Justice," in *Ethics and Health Policy,* Robert M. Veath and Roy Bransom, eds., Cambridge, Mass.: Ballinger Publishing Co., 1976, pp. 99-109). His approach has been criticized for giving too little importance to the rights of the individual and for neglecting the principle of fairness by concentrating only on the total amount of health care produced.

2. Others advocate a theory based on the *contribution to society* the sick person is making or is likely to make (Nicholas Rescher, "The Allocation of Exotic Medical Lifesaving Therapy," *Ethics,* vol. 79, 1969, p. 178).

3. Still others insist on the *equal dignity* of all human beings and resist the tendency to assign more value, dignity, and importance to some lives than to others. To protect this dignity, a third approach proposes a random selection procedure: first come, first

served (James Childress, "Who Shall Live When Not All Can Live?" *Soundings,* vol. 43, 1970, pp. 339-355; Paul Ramsey, *The Patient as Person,* New Haven: Yale University Press, 1970, pp. 239-275).

4. An extremely *individualistic* position has been taken by Robert Sade, who denies that anyone has a right to health care. It is neither a right nor a privilege, but a service. The doctor has the right to sell his service as he sees fit, and the state has no business interfering ("Medical Care as a Right: A Refutation," *New England Journal of Medicine,* vol. 285, December 2, 1971, pp. 1288-1292).

5. A fifth approach is rooted in John Rawls' notion of *justice as fairness (A Theory of Justice,* Cambridge: Harvard University Press, 1971). Whatever is done in this particular situation for this particular sick person should be done in all similar situations. Such a theory, according to its proponents, is most compatible with the goal of equal access to health care for all. This is the approach of Protestant ethicists Gene Outka and Robert Veath (Outka, "Social Justice and Equal Access to Health Care," *The Journal of Religious Ethics,* vol. 2, 1974, pp. 11-32; Veath, "What is 'Just' Health Care Delivery?" in Veath and Branson, *Ethics and Health Policy,* pp. 127-153).

6. A sixth approach is taken by Catholic moral theologian Charles E. Curran, who rejects the fifth as too individualistic. Society does not exist simply as the total aggregate of individuals who live in it, nor does the state exist simply to insure the good of individuals. A correct understanding of society and the state within society is essential if we are to construct a responsible answer to the question of the distribution of health-care resources. Both society and state are concerned with the common good, and since the human person is radically social, the common good can never be simply the sum total of individual goods. It is the complex of spiritual, social, and material conditions needed in society for the person to achieve integral human dignity. What is at issue here is *distributive justice.* How do society in general and the state in particular insure the distribution of those goods which are necessary for the achievement of human dignity?

Curran argues that all individual rights are based on the dignity of human life. Society and the state exist to help the individual achieve true fulfillment. Although health care is not the most fundamental of human needs, it is of great significance for the proper and full functioning of a person's life. The basic formulation is straightforward: "A person has the right to that minimum which is necessary for living a decent human life" (*Transition and Tradition in Moral Theology*, Notre Dame, Ind.: University of Notre Dame Press, 1979, chapter 6, "The Right to Health Care and Distributive Justice," pp. 139-170).

In addition to the dignity and fundamental need of the human person, the right to health care is also rooted in the principle that creation exists primarily to serve the needs of all. We are not the ultimate source of the goods we have, but rather the stewards of what has been given to all of us by a gracious God.

Distributive justice, however, does not even begin to answer all the related questions; it only underlines their relevance and importance. What shall be emphasized: preventive medicine, or crisis medicine? Should the government spend large amounts of money on such exotic lifesaving devices as kidney machines which benefit so few? What role should the state take in regulating the training of doctors and other medical personnel? How should a program of national health insurance be paid for? "Ethics and the ethician are not able to supply answers for all the concrete problems facing our society. Questions such as medical care ultimately must be decided by prudential choices in the political realm. However, the principles of distributive justice can well serve as the basis for making political decisions about the provision of health care which are both just and feasible" (Curran *op. cit.*, p. 167).

Christian Values Underlying the Issue

Whatever position one adopts on the general question of state intervention in the economic order or on the particular question of health care, there are certain values and principles which Catholics and other Christians, and indeed other persons of good will on various sides of the argument, have to take into account:

1.   The dignity of every human person.

2.   The fundamental human right to health care.

3.   The correlation of rights and duties.

4.   The radically social nature of the human person.

5.   The subordination of rights and duties to the common good.

6.   Human stewardship, not absolute ownership, of created goods.

7.   The right and obligation of the state to intervene on behalf of human dignity.

8.   The obligation of the state to respect freedom and local initiative (the principle of subsidiarity).

9.   The importance of both the principle of subsidiarity and the principle of socialization, and of their being held together in creative tension in the formulation of public policy.

10.   The right and responsibility of the Church to articulate a moral vision on matters of social and economic policy. Clearly, the teaching of the Church involves that of pope and bishops, but other qualified teachers have a contribution to make as well.

11.   The responsibility of the Church to articulate such a moral vision not as a series of detailed answers to complex questions but as a framework of values and principles within which responsible Christian action can be decided upon and taken.

12.   The duty of Catholics to take such teaching and such a moral framework seriously into account in the process not only of forming their consciences but of expressing their views in the socio-economic and political orders.

SUMMARY

1.   This chapter addresses itself to four separate moral issues: *birth control, homosexuality, warfare,* and *state intervention in the economic order.* The first two issues concern *interpersonal,* or *individual, ethics*; the second two, *social,* or *societal, ethics.*

2.   *Birth control,* or the conscious regulation of births, is not totally and absolutely rejected by Catholic theology and doctrine. The rhythm method, for example, is an accepted way of avoiding pregnancy. What is at issue, therefore, is *contraception* by artificial means—e.g., pill,

IUD, foam, condom. The argument between the two opposing sides in the Catholic Church was joined in 1968 with the publication of *Humanae Vitae*, the papal encyclical which rejected artificial contraception of every kind.

3. The *traditional view*, consistently taught and reaffirmed by such recent encyclicals as *Casti Connubii* (1930) and by various papal statements of Pope Pius XII, rested its case on two principal arguments. The primary argument was drawn from authority and from the consequences a change in the traditional teaching might have on the credibility of the official magisterium; a second argument was based on a structural analysis of the conjugal act itself, i.e., as biologically, and therefore naturally, oriented toward procreation.

4. The argument *against* the traditional teaching emphasized the evolutionary character of the Church's traditional teaching on sexual morality; the fact that the Church had clearly reversed itself on the question of usury; an understanding of natural law requiring the human person to employ reason to shape and control the so-called natural order of things, including the process of procreation; the principle of totality, according to which the conjugal act is to be viewed in relation to such values as human love, family life, education.

5. The Papal Commission for the Study of Population, the Family, and Birth submitted its final report in June 1966 and recommended a change in the traditional teaching, while at the same time condemning what it called a "contraceptive mentality" which egotistically and irrationally opposes all fruitfulness in marriage. The Commission insisted, too, that any method of birth control must be consistent with human dignity, be effective, and be safe.

6. *Humanae Vitae* rejected the Papal Commission's report and reaffirmed the traditional teaching: "Each and every marriage act must remain open to the transmission of life." Unlike the minority report of the Papal Commission, however, the encyclical rested its case more heavily on the purpose of the conjugal act than on the question of authority and its credibility. It also expressed concern for the consequences of contraception—e.g., conjugal infidelity, corruption of youth.

7. The reaction to *Humanae Vitae* was diverse: all the way from unequivocal acceptance to outright rejection. Many other positions fell somewhere in between—e.g., various statements from national bodies of bishops which emphasized the primacy of conscience and the mercy and forgiveness of God. The Vatican carried forward its traditional teaching on sexual ethics in a declaration on the same subject in 1975.

8. There are certain *Christian values* underlying this issue of birth control which must always be taken into account: (1) the goodness of procreation, as an expression of mutual love and for the welfare of the human community at large; (2) the sanctity of human life; (3) the personal dignity and welfare of the spouses, their children, and their potential children; (4) the inviolability of conscience; (5) the responsibility to act on an informed conscience; (6) the right and responsibility of the Church to teach on such matters; (7) the duty of Catholics to take such teaching seriously into account.

9. Wherever *homosexuality* is mentioned in the *Bible* it is condemned. One reason for the severity of judgment against homosexuality was its connection with pagan fertility rites and other cultic practices. The Genesis story of Sodom and Gomorrah was most influential on the Fathers of the Church. Sodom became the symbol of the depravity of Greek society.

10. The *Catholic tradition* has consistently judged all homosexual acts as at once unnatural and gravely sinful. The most recent text is the Vatican's *Declaration on Sexual Ethics* (1975).

11. There are three principal moral approaches to the question today: (1) Homosexual acts are *always sinful* in themselves because they are unnatural, i.e., not open to procreation; (2) homosexual acts are morally *neutral*; i.e., their morality depends on the quality of the relationship; and (3) homosexual acts are *essentially imperfect*; i.e., homosexual behavior is wrong as a general rule, but it is not wrong for those who have no realistic alternative (an irreversible or constitutional homosexual). This last view is also known as a theory of "compromise" in view of the presence of sin in the world.

12. There are certain *Christian values* underlying this issue of homosexuality which must always be taken into account: (1) the goodness of procreation, as an expression of mutual love and for the welfare of the human community at large; (2) the personal dignity of every human being; (3) the need of every person for love, friendship, even intimacy, although not necessarily of a genitally sexual nature; (4) the inviolability of conscience; (5) the responsibility to act on an informed conscience; (6) the existence of many internal and external impediments to full human freedom; (7) the right and responsibility of the Church to teach on matters of this sort; (8) the duty of the Catholic to take such teaching seriously into account.

13. *Warfare* is not automatically condemned in the Bible. In the *Old Testament*, Israel's wars are Yahweh's wars, and Yahweh is himself a warrior. On the other hand, the *prophets* denounced war as a judgment of

Yahweh upon Israel. It is through faith, not war, that Israel is destined to survive. *Jesus and the disciples* had no developed theology of warfare. Jesus spoke only of those who lived by the sword as dying by the sword, and *Paul* spoke in terms of spiritual combat. The final judgment is described in the imagery of warfare.

14.   *Augustine* saw war as both the product of sin and a remedy for it. Public order must be preserved at all costs, even if it means going to war. *Aquinas* listed three criteria for a *just war*: (1) just cause; (2) legitimate authority; and (3) right intention. This was not to rationalize warfare but to limit its scope and methods.

15.   *Later development* of the just-war theory added the following criteria: (1) last resort; (2) formal declaration of war; (3) reasonable hope of success; (4) proportion between the good accomplished or evil avoided and the evil caused by the war itself; (5) immunity of non-combatants from direct attack; and (6) proportionality of tactics and means to end.

16.   In the sixteenth century the *Spanish Scholastics* shifted the focus from just cause to just *means*. Both sides might be sincere about their cause; therefore, both must be attentive to the means employed. A wider *international* dimension was added in the nineteenth century by *Taparelli d'Azeglio.*

17.   *Pope Pius XII* carried d'Azeglio's insight forward in his notion of force as a possible instrument of justice in the international order. Because of the increased destructive capacity of modern weapons, the pope reduced the legitimate causes of war to one: self-defense or the defense of another nation unjustly attacked. He rejected pacifism.

18.   *Pope John XXIII* moved the just war teaching in a pacifist direction. There is strong criticism of the arms race and the balance of terror it creates. War in a nuclear age is "irrational."

19.   *Vatican II* notes that the multiplication of scientific weapons forces us to look at war with "an entirely new attitude." It praises conscientious objectors and condemns a policy of blind obedience. It also denounces the arms race as a "treacherous trap." Granting the right of states to self-defense, everything is to be governed, nevertheless, by the principle of proportionality and by the rule of noncombatant immunity. *Pope Paul VI* and *Pope John Paul II* continued this emphasis, blending prophetic vision and political wisdom.

20.   In light of these recent doctrinal developments, there are two legitimate *moral options* in Catholicism today: the *just-war ethic* and some form of *pacifism.* They hold *in common* the sacredness of human life, the seriousness of taking of human life, and the morally restricted nature of any war. They *differ* in that the pacifist holds that force is never

justified, whereas the just-war advocate acknowledges that circumstances may require the use of force.

21.   The just-war ethic, however, is further challenged by the *threat* of use of nuclear weapons in the *policy of deterrence*. If the *use* of nuclear weapons is immoral, so, too, is their *stockpiling* even for deterrence (U.S. Catholic bishops, 1976). Others argue that the stockpiling is legitimate, even with the intention to use, if it prevents a greater evil, i.e., the use of nuclear weapons by the other side (Paul Ramsey). Still others prohibit the use of nuclear weapons, but tolerate deterrence (Michael Walzer, J. Bryan Hehir).

22.   There are certain *Christian values* underlying this issue of *warfare* which must always be taken into account: (1) the sacredness of all human life; (2) the utter gravity of taking another human life; (3) the inherent moral limits on every use of force; (4) the right and responsibility of the Church to articulate a moral vision of such matters of social and even international morality; (5) the responsibility of the Church to articulate a moral vision in a politically realistic manner; and (6) the duty of Catholics to take such teaching seriously into account in the formation of conscience and in political action.

23.   The question of the right and duty of the *state to intervene in the economic order* for the sake of the common good is answered in terms of the relationship between the principles of *subsidiarity* and of *socialization*. The former discourages intervention; the latter encourages it. The former is attentive to the rights of individuals and groups within society; the latter is attentive to the interdependent character of all individuals and groups in society.

24.   The principle of *subsidiarity* was first formulated by *Pope Pius XI* in *Quadragesimo Anno* (1931); the principle of *socialization* was alluded to in *John XXIII's* encyclical *Mater et Magistra* (1961) and defined more precisely in *Pacem in Terris* (1963).

25.   *Subsidiarity* holds that "one should not withdraw from individuals and commit to the community what they can accomplish by their own enterprise and industry. So, too, it is an injustice and at the same time a grave evil and a disturbance of right order, to transfer to the larger and higher collectivity functions which can be performed and provided for by lesser and subordinate bodies" (Pius XI).

26.   *Socialization* refers to "the growing interdependence of men in society, giving rise to various patterns of group life and activity and in many instances to social institutions established on a juridical basis" (John XXIII).

27.   Besides the principles of subsidiarity and socialization, Catholic teaching on *rights and duties* is also at the heart of the Church's social doctrine. The clearest statement of human rights is found in *Pacem in Terris* (pars. 8-35). *Rights* are *moral claims* to some physical or spiritual good necessary for human development and dignity. A right creates a correlative *duty* on the part of the state to recognize and reinforce it, and to balance it off with other moral claims in conflict with one another. Pope Paul VI in *Octagesima Adveniens* emphasized the *political* character of such responsibility. In his 1979 United Nations address, Pope John Paul II made a similar argument.

28.   *Health care* is one issue of this sort. Should the state intervene to insure health care for all? If so, under what circumstances and according to what conditions? Approaches vary from utilitarian (the greatest good for the greatest number), contributive (health care for the worthier members of society), random selection (first come, first served), individualistic (no right at all; health care is a service), egalitarian (similar cases should be treated similarly), to an argument based on distributive justice: "A person has the right to that minimum which is necessary for living a decent human life. Society has an obligation to provide that which is necessary for a decent human life" (Charles Curran). That minimum includes quality health care.

29.   Ethics and ethicians, however, cannot even begin to answer such questions in any detail. These issues require prudential choices in the political realm. Ethicists can identify the values and principles—e.g., of distributive justice—as a basis for making political decisions.

30.   There are certain *Christian values* underlying this issue of *state intervention in the economic order* which must always be taken into account: (1) the dignity of every human person; (2) health care as a fundamental human right; (3) the correlation of rights and duties; (4) the radically social nature of the human person; (5) the subordination of rights and duties to the common good; (6) the stewardship, not absolute ownership, of created goods; (7) the right and/or obligation of the state to intervene on behalf of human dignity; (8) the principle of subsidiarity; (9) the dialectical relationship between subsidiarity and socialization; (10) the right and responsibility of the Church to articulate a moral vision on such issues; (11) the responsibility of the Church to formulate its vision not as specific answers but as a framework of values and principles for Christian action; (12) the duty of the Catholic to take such teaching and such a moral framework into serious account.

SUGGESTED READINGS

Calvez, Jean Yves. *The Social Thought of John XXIII.* Chicago: H. Regnery, 1965.

Curran, Charles E. *Contemporary Problems in Moral Theology.* Notre Dame, Ind.: Fides Publishers, 1970.

——————. *Transition and Tradition in Moral Theology.* Notre Dame, Ind.: University of Notre Dame Press, 1979.

Dedek, John. *Contemporary Medical Ethics.* New York: Sheed & Ward, 1975.

Gustafson, James. *The Church As Moral Decision-Maker.* Philadelphia: Pilgrim Press, 1970.

Haughey, John C., ed. *The Faith That Does Justice: Examining the Christian Sources for Social Change,* New York: Paulist Press, 1977.

Hollenbach, David. *Claims in Conflict.* New York: Paulist Press, 1979.

Kosnik, Anthony, *et al. Human Sexuality: New Directions in American Catholic Thought.* New York: Paulist Press, 1976.

Macquarrie, John. *Three Issues in Ethics.* New York: Harper & Row, 1970.

McCormick, Richard A. *Ambiguity in Moral Choice.* Milwaukee: Marquette University, 1973.

Murray, John Courtney. "The Issue of Church and State at Vatican II." *Theological Studies* 27 (1966), 580-606.

Reich, Warren T., ed. *Encyclopedia of Bioethics,* 4 vols. New York: Free Press, 1978.

·XXVIII·

CHRISTIAN SPIRITUALITY

THE MEANING AND PLACE OF "SPIRITUALITY"

The previous three chapters were concerned with principles of Christian existence and their application to Christian behavior. They were exercises in moral theology or Christian ethics. This chapter addresses itself not so much to the substance, or the "just demands," of Christian existence as to its style, or "spirit." "Those who live according to the flesh," Paul wrote, "are intent on the things of the flesh, those who live according to the spirit, on those of the spirit" (Romans 8:5).

To live according to the spirit is to enjoy "life and peace." The Spirit of God dwells in such a one as the principle of life (8:6,8,11). *Spirituality*, therefore, has to do with *our way of being religious*. We are not only alive by a principle which transcends us (see chapter 5 on nature and grace); we are consciously aware of, in touch with, and motivated by, that principle of life.

To be "spiritual" means to know, and to live according to the knowledge, that there is more to life than meets the eye. To be "spiritual" means, beyond that, to know, and to live according to the knowledge, that God is present to us in grace as the principle of personal, interpersonal, social and even cosmic transformation. To be "open to the Spirit" is to accept explicitly who we are and who we are called always to become, and to direct our lives accordingly.

Since God is not present to Christians alone, spirituality is not exclusively Christian. What, then, is *Christian* spirituality? It is *the cultivation of a style of life consistent with the presence of the Spirit of the Risen Christ within us and with our status as members of the Body of Christ.* Christian spirituality has to do with *our way of being Christian,* in response to the call of God, issued through Jesus Christ in the power of the Holy Spirit. Christian spirituality, therefore, is *trinitarian, Christological, ecclesiological,* and *pneumatalogical.* It is rooted in the life of the triune God, focused on Jesus Christ, situated in the Church, and ever responsive to the Holy Spirit.

It is also visionary, sacramental, relational, and transformational. Christian spirituality is *visionary* in that it involves a new way of seeing reality and of seeing through things to their spiritual core, of "thus interpreting spiritual things in spiritual terms" (1 Corinthians 2:13). In that sense, Christian spiritual vision is always *sacramental.* Every created reality is imbued, to one degree or another, with the hidden presence of God. Christian spirituality is also *relational.* Neither Christian life nor human life itself is ever isolated existence. We are, by definition, social beings. To be human is to live in community. To be Christian is also to live in community, i.e., the Church. To be spiritually Christian is to live always in relation with others: with our brothers and sisters in the Body of Christ and in the human community at large. Christian spirituality demands sensitivity to the presence, the needs, and the gifts of others. Finally, Christian spirituality is *transformational.* The spiritual Christian is consciously in touch with the presence of the Spirit as the power which heals, reconciles, renews, gives life, bestows peace, sustains hope, brings joy, and creates unity. Christian spirituality requires that the Spirit be allowed to work so that through the instrumentality of the individual and of the Church the transformation of the world into the Kingdom of God might continue to occur.

HISTORY OF CHRISTIAN SPIRITUALITY
Biblical Origins

Although *Christian* spirituality as such did not begin to take shape until Jesus' proclamation of the Kingdom of God and the gathering of the first disciples around him, its foundations were already laid in the *covenantal relationship* between Yahweh and Israel.

The Israelites were convinced of the nearness and even the presence of their God, as the Psalms clearly indicate. Jesus, too, proclaimed that the Father had drawn near to us in a dramatically and definitively new way. The Kingdom of God is "at hand" (Mark 1:15). Jesus suggests that he has a unique relationship with the Father (Matthew 11:25-27). The power of God breaks through in Jesus' words (Mark 4:14; Luke 12:32) and in his healing works (Luke 11:20; Matthew 12:28). To be "in Christ" is to be a "new creation" (2 Corinthians 5:17). It is to be brought to life with Christ "when we were dead in sin" (Ephesians 2:5). It is to have God living in us because God lives in Christ (John 17:23). The love of God for Christ lives in us, because Christ lives in us (17:26).

It is through the death and resurrection of Jesus that we are liberated from sin and for new life (Romans 6:3-11). Jesus was raised from the dead "so that we might bear fruit for God" (7:4). Indeed, the Spirit cannot be given until the resurrection and glorification of Jesus (John 7:39; 16:7), and the first thing the Lord does when he appears to the disciples afterwards is to breathe the Holy Spirit upon them (20:19-23). Our very bodies are given life through the Spirit which now possesses us (Romans 8:11). And the Father will raise us just as Jesus was raised (2 Corinthians 4:14). Christian life and spirituality is knowing that truth, having hope in what we know, and living according to that hope so that our life would not make sense if it were not for such a hope. It is life in possession of "the light of life" (John 8:12).

The Patristic Period:
Second Through Seventh Centuries

If the Kingdom of God was at the center of Jesus' preaching and ministry, it was also necessarily at the center of Christian spirituality from the beginning. But the time of the Kingdom's coming was never clear—not even, it seems, to Jesus himself (see chapter 12). The Thessalonians, for example, thought the Second Coming of the Lord to be so imminent that many of them stopped their normal labors and began waiting in idleness for the end (2 Thessalonians 3:6-15). When it became obvious to all that the *Parousia* was not about to occur and that a considerable span of history would intervene, Christians increasingly perceived their situation as life "between the times": between the initial coming of Christ on earth and the Second Coming at the end. Everything henceforth would be conditioned by this expectation of the Kingdom, but it would no longer divert the Christian community from its earthly mission. On the contrary, the expectation of the Kingdom would add a note of urgency to the Church's call to proclaim the Gospel in word, in sacrament, in witness, and in service.

If spirituality has to do essentially with our union with God in Christ through the Holy Spirit, *martyrdom* provided in the earliest centuries of the Church an ideal, perhaps even infallible, means to such union. Martyrdom's importance was rooted in its close connection with Christ's own death and resurrection. To be martyred (literally, to become a "witness") was to experience ahead of schedule the final eschatological event.

After the persecutions had ended, Christians wondered if the complete union with God in Christ offered by martyrdom was accessible in any other way. Origen (d. ca. 254) suggested that a life of complete self-sacrifice was a kind of unbloody martyrdom, and Clement of Alexandria (d. ca. 215) noted that every death is a true martyrdom provided one approaches it with the proper dispositions.

The first "spiritual" heresy in the Church was Gnosticism, which looked upon matter as evil. Salvation comes only in the rejection of the material world for the world of the spirit. Irenaeus (d. 200) led the counterattack, insisting on the incarnation as a principle of recapitulation of all things, material and spiritual, in Christ. But the Gnostic stress on knowledge, so characteristic of contemporary Greek philosophy, penetrated even orthodox Christian theology and spirituality. The emphasis, however, was much less esoteric and more fully oriented to Christian life. Thus, for Clement of Alexandria, the summit of Christian consciousness is the knowledge of the God of love by loving as God loves. This assimilation to God occurred through *apatheia*, i.e., the domination through grace of everything opposed to Christian love (*agape*). Such a state was itself a kind of anticipation of eternal life. The Gnostic influence was even stronger in Origen, who taught that the soul must struggle to uproot itself from the world in which it is buried by selfish desires. The struggle is won by imitation of Christ and a sharing in his life. The approach carried over into Origen's notion of prayer. For him, the prayer of silence was the ideal since it characterized the state of union with God and liberation from the body.

Monasticism, which developed first as flight from persecution and later as rejection of the Constantinian embrace of the Church in 312, introduced a new expression of spirituality that, for centuries, would mistakenly be regarded as the very norm of Christian life for all. Under the leadership of Anthony of Egypt (d. 356) and others, individual Christians went into the desert to confront the devil and to come to terms with all the dark forces that war against the spirit. Some forms of asceticism were severe. In Syria, for example, various hermits used iron chains to punish themselves; others exposed themselves heedlessly to the elements. Gradually the hermits were joined by others, and a transition was made from the solitary form of monastic existence (anchoritism) to a modified community existence (cenobitism). Almost from the beginning, therefore, monastic life was looked upon as a continuation of apostolic life: perseverance together in prayer, in the community of goods, and in the breaking of the bread (Acts of the Apostles 2:42). The practice of consecrating virgins also developed at this time as yet another way of achieving fuller union with Christ.

Two or three generations passed before a spiritual theology emerged from the new monastic movement. According to Pseudo-Dionysius (d. ca. 500)—probably a Syrian monk who identified himself with Dionysius the Areopagite, mentioned in Acts of the Apostles 17:34—the soul finds union with God only in going beyond itself, by rejecting all particular knowledge and allowing itself to be absorbed totally in the knowledge of God, whose intra-Trinitarian life of love overflows in a stream of self-communicating goodness in creation. Thus, the spiritual life is divided into three stages: purification (*the purgative way*), meditation on the word of God (*the illuminative way*), and union with God (*the unitive way*).

Augustine (d. 430) was himself dependent upon this monastic spirituality as developed and practiced in the East. But he subtly revised it in a more psychological and critical direction. Spiritual discernment does not bring us knowledge of God in Christ so much as *self-knowledge* in the light of Christ, the interior teacher of wisdom. On the other hand, it was also Augustine who wrote in the *City of God* that "no man must be so committed to contemplation as, in his contemplation, to give no thought to his neighbor's needs, nor so absorbed in action as to dispense with the contemplation of God" (Book XIX, chapter 19). It was John Cassian (d. 435), however, who translated the purer form of Eastern monasticism to the West. The monk is not to seek anything beyond the Kingdom of God, and only purity of heart will open the mystery of the Kingdom to him. Christian life is one of constant prayer wholly inspired by the Gospel.

Another key contemporary spiritual leader and writer was Pope Gregory the Great (d. 604), an adept popularizer of doctrine and an influential author on matters of faith and piety. His works are the first major sources of material on the lives of the saints, including Benedict (d. 550), whom he admired and whose rule he observed. One of Gregory's books, *Regula Pastoralis* ("Pastoral Norms"), had almost as much impact on the Church well into the Middle Ages as did Augustine's *City of God*. It was a practical treatise on the spirituality and ministerial skills required of bishops and of all who have the care of souls. The social disruptions created by the so-called barbarian invasions disclosed the fragile character of much of the Christianization that had occurred thus far. Gregory's simple, straightforward style was particularly appealing because reassuring, and the monastic type of life which his work advocated and celebrated proved to be one of the mainstays of the Church and of society generally for the next several centuries.

The Middle Ages:
Eighth Through Fourteenth Centuries

From the time of Gregory the Great until the middle of the eighth century, monks generally maintained a high ascetical ideal and gave an example of Christian life for all: laity, clergy, and bishops alike. Under the new Germanic influence, however, a certain externalism inserted itself into Christian spirituality: devotions to the cross, relics, and tombs of the saints; various forms of penances; the encouragement of confession of sins, etc. But Carolingian piety was also marked by a deep reverence for the Bible and a love of the liturgy—both abiding preoccupations of Christian monks.

By the tenth and eleventh centuries various monasteries began to develop loose federations, which gave rise to congregations of monasteries and eventually to religious orders. The monastic ideal was spread ever more widely throughout the Christian world. Austerity characterized penitential practice even among the laity. Long pilgrimages and self-flagellation were common means of making reparation for sin or for curbing one's unruly appetites. Contemplative prayer, too, was presented as the standard which all Christians should meet. John of Fécamp (d. 1079), one of the most widely read spiritual writers of the time, recommended quiet, meditative reading to induce unimpeded and undistracted thoughts about God.

The new Cistercian Order, founded in 1098, accentuated the *mystical* element in Christian spirituality. Its principal proponents, Bernard of Clairvaux (d. 1153) and William of St. Thierry (d. 1148), regarded the soul as being the image of God because of the gift of free will. But sin marred that image. Only by contemplating the Word of God and conforming oneself to it can the individual soul be restored to its intended perfection, for Christ is the interior Lover who pursues and embraces the soul in a union of intimate love. The stress on contemplation over dialectics (i.e., critical theology) continued into the twelfth century in the Parisian monastery of St. Victor, whose members, known as the *Victorines*, included some of the best-known writers of the period: Hugh of St. Victor (d. 1141), Richard of St. Victor (d. 1173), and others. Richard's work would later be simplified by the English Augustinian Walter Hilton (d. 1396) and Hilton's, in turn, carried forward by Julian of Norwich (d. 1442), an anchoress who lived outside the walls of St. Julian's Church in Norwich, England.

But there also appeared at this time another, more idealistic spiritual movement urging radical poverty and an end to all formalism and legalism. Accordingly, by the end of the thirteenth century many lay persons were criticizing the existing social conditions as well as the lives of the clergy and hierarchy. Extreme forms of this new purist tendency were to be found in Waldensianism and Albigensianism. But there were also more mainstream attempts to confront the same abuses and pastoral problems. The rise of the mendicant orders—Franciscans and Dominicans—brought a more realistic, but no less serious, approach to poverty and service. Dominic (d. 1221) provided his new Order of Preachers with an ideal that combined the best of monasticism with the best of the apostolic life. One of his spiritual sons, Thomas Aquinas (d. 1274), would produce an oft-cited formula on the interrelationship between the two: neither contemplation alone nor action alone is the highest form of Christian life, but contemplation in action (a concept not far removed from the modern notion of *praxis*). Francis of Assisi (d. 1226), on the other hand, stressed imitation of the life of Christ in all its simplicity and poverty. God is reflected in the sun, the moon, and stars, and indeed in all of the things of creation. As with the Dominicans, it took another great theologian to systematize, and thereby give wider circulation to, Francis' basic insight. Bonaventure (d. 1274), who saw the whole of creation as a mirror reflecting the power, wisdom, and goodness of God, identified three elements in the Franciscan way of life: (1) following Christ through the evangelical counsels, especially poverty (the other counsels are chastity and obedience); (2) laboring for the salvation of souls by preaching and hearing confessions; and (3) contemplation.

At the beginning of the fourteenth century a new current of spirituality took root in the Rhineland, the Low Countries, and England. A century earlier the works of Pseudo-Dionysius had been translated and made the subject of an extended commentary. Because the author was commonly associated in people's minds with the Areopagite mentioned in Acts of the Apostles 17:34, his newly translated writings were accorded a quasi-apostolic authority throughout the Middle Ages. They had particular influence on Meister Eckhart (d. 1327), John Tauler (d. 1361), and Henry Suso (d. 1366), three German Dominican mystics, and on Jan von Ruysbroeck (d. 1381), a Flemish canon regular of St. Augustine. Their common concern was the soul's union with God, which reached its zenith in contemplation. Such union is impossible, however, apart from complete abandonment of, and detachment from, all creatures and worldly realities. This orientation was most pronounced in *The Cloud of Unknowing*, composed by an anonymous English author. The same stress on the interior life was to be found in Hildegard (d. 1179) and Hedwig (d. 1243), and it is to be found again today in the "centering prayer" approach (see the discussion of *The Cloud of Unknowing* below, under the treatment of post-Vatican II spirituality).

Other spiritual writers, firmly committed to a life of prayer and penance, saw more clearly the pastoral implications and effects of their contemplative life. Catherine of Siena (d. 1380) was exceedingly concerned with the reform of the Church but insisted that her prayers and penances did more for the Church than her public acts did. The same concern for ecclesiastical renewal in the Low Countries stimulated the formation of a lay group, the Brethren of the Common Life, founded by Gerard Groote (d. 1384). The movement's spirituality was known as the *Devotio Moderna*. Its one great product, written probably by Groote or by Thomas à Kempis (d. 1471), was *The Imitation of Christ*, which asserted, among other things, that "it is better to feel compunction than to be able to define it."

This lack of intellectual and theological substance in such popular piety, however, brought with it many serious problems: superstition (e.g., the belief that one could be saved from blindness by gazing on the Communion host), ignorance of the Bible, fascination with reports of visions, exaggeration of the value of relics, emotionalism, inordinate fears of the after-life and of God's judgment, and devotional excesses unrelated to the central mysteries of Christian faith.

The Post-Medieval Period: Renaissance, Reformation, Counter-Reformation

Although Protestantism rejected contemporary medieval spirituality's emotionalism, superstition, and inordinate reverence for such material objects as relics, it did not at the same time reject its *individualism*. Martin Luther (d. 1546) stressed the uniqueness of the Christian believer's relationship with God and the realm of personal conscience (*sola fides*, "faith alone"). His recourse to the Word of God in Sacred Scripture (*sola Scriptura*, "Scripture alone") only underlined his concern for finding a direct approach to Christ, one in which the individual is illumined by the interior witness of the Holy Spirit (*sola gratia*, "grace alone"). Although it was not always obvious in the midst of medieval excesses, it *is* a matter of Catholic principle that the believer's relationship with God is a *mediated* relationship; mediated not only, nor even primarily, through the biblical Word, but in and through the community of faith in which that Word is proclaimed. "Thus Protestantism tends to produce a spirituality which springs entirely from the co-presence and mutual relationship between the Person of God revealed in the Christ of the Gospels and the individual person of the believer. But, for Catholicism, there is no fully authentic Christian spirituality without the realization of an equal co-presence of our fellow-believers with Christ and ourselves, the Church" (Louis Bouyer, *Introduction to Spirituality*, New York: Desclée Co., 1961, p. 11; see also his *Orthodox Spirituality and Protestant and Anglican Spirituality*, London: Burns & Oates, 1969).

Although various Christian humanists were sympathetic toward the contemporary emphasis on mysticism, they were strongly committed to the general restoration of Christian life itself, so much corrupted then by the worst of the Renaissance spirit. Love for classical antiquity and an optimistic view of human nature were characteristic of this so-called devout humanism, and the spiritual writings of Erasmus (d. 1536) are representative of it.

The same emphasis on the unity of prayer and action is found in one of the classics of Christian spirituality, the *Spiritual Exercises* of Ignatius Loyola (d. 1556). Ignatian spirituality was marked by dialectical parallels: between the medieval concepts of *contemplation* and *action*, on the one hand, and between *flight from the world* and *acceptance of the world*, on the other. Contemplation is adherence to the God who transcends this world. Action is the fulfillment of one's duty within the world, consistent with one's own individuality. Hence the Ignatian formula which originated with the first circle of his followers: *"in actione contemplativus"* (contemplative in action). Ignatius' affirmation of the world, therefore, is not a naive optimism. It springs rather from a true grasp of the cross: at once a judgment upon sin and a proclamation of our liberation from it. On the other hand, his profoundly positive evaluation of the contingencies of history puts him at the head of a whole new spiritual tradition—so much so, in fact, that Karl Rahner is convinced that the Holy Spirit raised up in Ignatius an original, creative reinterpretation of the Christian life.

"Work as if everything depended upon you, but pray as if everything depended upon God," another well-known Ignatian formula has it. Although this is not the exact wording, it is close enough to the sense of the original, which says, in effect, that we should trust in God in such a way that we never forget to cooperate with God, and yet at the same time we should cooperate with God in such a way as to remain always aware that it is God alone who is at work. We are always at a *distance*, therefore, from God and even from our own deeds. We are at a distance *from God*, who is never revealed except in works carried out with the cooperation of secondary causes (i.e., free human beings); and we are at a distance *from our deeds*, which must never be taken as something of final value in themselves. The Christian must look to Christ, in whom alone the divine-human interaction is fully realized, and seek to imitate him. This is the core of Ignatian spirituality. (For the original Ignatian text in Latin and a brief commentary on it, see Hugo Rahner, *Ignatius the Theologian,* New York: Herder & Herder, 1968, pp. 25-27; see also Karl Rahner, *The Dynamic Element in the Church*, London: Burns & Oates, 1964, pp. 84-170.)

But the mystical way continued to flourish, especially in *Spain*. For Teresa of Avila (d. 1582) prayer consisted essentially in an exchange of love with God. From our side, proof of our love for God is manifested in the practice of the virtues, leaving to God the communication of grace whenever and however God wishes (see her *Autobiography*, New York: Doubleday-Image, 1960; and *The Way of Perfection*, New York: Doubleday-Image, 1964). John of the Cross (d. 1591), one of Teresa's companions in her work of reform within the Carmelite Order, is regarded by many as the greatest of the mystical writers (see his *Collected Works,* Washington, D.C.: Institute of Carmelite Studies Publications, 1964). His writings were at once poetic and speculative, drawing not only upon personal spiritual experience but upon Sacred Scripture and the classical authors as well. They detail the processes of spiritual purification, through trials and temptations and through deliberate detachment from external things, and they try to explain the life of union with God—a union brought about through the prayer of infused contemplation.

Although Spanish spirituality became increasingly theoretical and scientific after John of the Cross, *Italian* spirituality was more practical. Reform of the Church, renewal of the interior life, and the improvement of priestly ministry were matters of immediate interest. These priorities are reflected in the works of Philip Neri (d. 1595), Charles Borromeo (d. 1584), and Catherine of Genoa (d. 1510).

In *France* developments in spirituality were exceedingly complicated by the theological controversies surrounding the whole issue of nature and grace. Some argued that human nature was so powerless that we can do absolutely nothing to advance our salvation *(Quietism)*. Others insisted on the evil of the flesh and of all human desires and pleasures, urging a life of total abnegation, self-denial, and even repression *(Jansenism)*. Against the Quietists, Jacques Bossuet (d. 1704) taught that abandonment of the soul to God should actually induce the soul to apply itself more deliberately to its religious exercises and to other Christian duties. Against the Jansenists, Francis de Sales (d. 1622) sought to bring Christian piety out of the monasteries and the convents into the world of the average lay person by showing the connection between Christian life and everyday occupations, and by emphasizing the joy of Christian existence (see his *Introduction to the Devout Life*, New York: Doubleday-Image, 1972). A similar orientation appears in Italy in the writings of Alphonsus Liguori (d. 1787). The spirit of the French school of spirituality, shorn of its heretical excesses, is perhaps best expressed by Jean Jacques Olier (d. 1657), founder of the Sulpicians: "Christianity consists in these three points...to look upon Jesus, to unite oneself to Jesus, and to act in Jesus. The first leads us to respect and to religion; the second to union and to identification with Him; the third, to an activity no longer solitary, but joined to the virtue of Jesus Christ, which we have drawn upon ourselves by prayer. The first is called adoration; the second, communion; the third, cooperation" (cited by E. A. Walsh, "Spirituality, French School of, *New Catholic Encyclopedia,* vol. 13, New York: McGraw-Hill, 1967, p. 605).

Nineteenth Century

The nineteenth century provides a bridge between medieval and modern spirituality. Individualism and even regimented piety (e.g., institutionalized devotions to the Sacred Heart, the Blessed Virgin, the Sacred Wounds, the Eucharist) continued, and reactionary theological ideas were still encouraged, and sometimes endorsed, by magisterial interventions of a highly conservative nature (e.g., *Syllabus of Errors,* 1864). But the forces of renewal were also at work: the renewal of theology, of liturgy, of historical studies, and of social ministry. And so, too, were the forces of innovation: e.g., scientific and technological advances, developments in psychology and sociology. Together these forces of renewal and innovation would have a profound impact on Christian spirituality in the twentieth century.

Perhaps nowhere else was this incipient renewal of Christian spirituality more evident than in *England* and particularly in the Oxford Movement, whose driving force was John Henry Newman (d. 1890). His spiritual orientation was primarily interior, a life lived in intimate union with God under the guidance of the Holy Spirit. But it was also a Christocentric spirituality, stressing the incarnation as the basis for an active Christian life in the world. As in Ignatius, therefore, there was a blending of the contemplative and the practical. Newman, however, was not to exert very much influence as a spiritual writer. More influential was Frederick William Faber (d. 1863), who drew his own inspiration from the Italian and French style of spiritual writing, especially that of Alphonsus Liguori and Cardinal Bérulle (d. 1629). Faber, too, was Christocentric (one of his works was entitled *All for Jesus*), but he was also highly emotional and florid. On the other hand, his emphasis on the psychology of the individual, openness to all people, even non-Catholics and non-Christians, and frequency of reception of the sacraments, all anticipated by a century certain developments that would characterize modern Catholic spirituality.

Twentieth Century

1900-1950

Catholic spiritual writings during the first half of the twentieth century reflected the ambivalent character of Catholic theology itself. On the one hand, traditional scholastic theology was firmly in place in seminaries, in college religion courses, in catechisms, in sermons, and especially in official magisterial pronouncements. The manuals of spiritual or ascetical theology were of the same sort—e.g., Adolfe Tanquerey's *The Spiritual Life* and Reginald Garrigou-Lagrange's *The Three Ages of the Interior Life*. On the other hand, the liturgical movement, spurred by the renewal of historical and biblical studies, guided spirituality in a more Christocentric direction through the writings of such Benedictines as Abbot Columba Marmion (d. 1923) of Belgium, and, in a very different way, in the life and works of Charles de Foucauld (d. 1916).

Tanquerey (d. 1932), by his own account, showed "a certain preference for the spirituality of the French School of the seventeenth century" (*The Spiritual Life*, New York: Desclée, 1930, pp. vii-viii). He was himself a Sulpician priest, a community of priests founded by Olier, one of the leaders of seventeenth-century French spirituality. Certain elements of Tanquerey's system also remarkably anticipate some of the major theological and pastoral developments of the period of Vatican II: (1) the grounding of spirituality in Sacred Scripture and doctrine; (2) an understanding of human existence as spirituality's starting point; (3) the mystery of the Trinity as its primary theological context; (4) the centrality of Jesus Christ and of our union with Christ in the Church, his Mystical Body; and (5) the call of the whole Church, including the laity, to a life of Christian perfection. On the other hand, Tanquerey's use of biblical and doctrinal sources reflects the limitations of scholastic methodology; the human person is conceived as lacking something originally intended by God (which is the more traditional notion of Original Sin and of the relationship between nature and grace); and human existence is portrayed as a process of struggle between higher faculties (especially the intellect) and the lower appetites (including "a lust for freedom and independence"). It is this theological anthropology, or theology of what it means to be human, that appears most inconsistent with the main lines of Catholic theology and of Catholic spirituality today, as we shall see below.

Garrigou-Lagrange (d. 1964), a Dominican professor at the Angelicum University in Rome for many years, presents an even more individualistic approach to the spiritual life than Tanquerey. That life consists of intimate conversation with God, achieved through a threefold process: passing through the purgative, illuminative, and unitive ways successively. Again, the primary emphasis is on the necessity of detaching ourselves from those lower appetites which drag us down and keep us from full union with God. The "one thing necessary" to every human life is the salvation of one's soul. All are called to sanctity, or a life in union with God. Every sin and imperfection will eventually have to be effaced by punishment after death if the soul is to enjoy the eternal vision of God. Having removed the obstacles and purged the senses, the soul moves to a second stage of Christian existence, in which the soul is progressively illumined by the gifts of the Holy Spirit and finds it increasingly easy to contemplate the mystery of God. Finally, there is entrance into a state of perfect mystical union with God in which the theological and moral virtues are practiced to a heroic degree (*The Three Ages of the Interior Life*, 2 vols., St. Louis: B. Herder Book Co. 1947-1948).

The same individualistic emphasis is carried forward in Dietrich von Hildebrand's *Transformation in Christ* (St. Paul, Minn.: Helicon Press, 1948), which describes Christian spirituality in terms of surrender, detachment from self, subordination and abnegation of self, a submerging of oneself in the adoration of God, and always in an I/Thou relationship. Von Hildebrand, formerly a professor of philosophy at Fordham University, rejected various contemporary pastoral developments which underlined the importance of community. He characterized the liturgical movement, for example, as anti-personalist (p. 394). "Our abandonment of self is an indispensable condition of the full unfolding in us of supernatural life" (p. 400). In its highest form, "being possessed" is a state of mystic ecstasy wherein "the mind tends to be aware of nothing besides God" (p. 401). But such an experience of God gives us a clearer perception of all creaturely reality. We see things as they really are in the sight of God (p. 402).

A much less individualistic, more liturgically-oriented, more fully Christocentric and more anthropologically positive approach was taken by Abbot Marmion. It is the last characteristic that is the most significant. Although both Tanquerey and Garrigou-Lagrange assert the importance of the redemptive work of Jesus Christ, they also continue to speak of human existence as if the redemption is, for all practical purposes, a juridical event (i.e., God now "declares" us just) that has not really transformed and renewed the whole human person. The Holy Spirit is given to us in Baptism and Confirmation, filling us with peace and filial confidence in God, Marmion insisted. The Spirit makes us understand that we have everything in Jesus Christ, who is not only holy in himself but has been given to us to be *our* holiness (*Union with God*, Raymond Thibault, ed., St. Louis: B. Herder Book Co., 1934, p. 40).

For Marmion, the Lord is not our distant judge but the source of love, affection, and sympathy, for he is truly human himself. It is above all in the Eucharist that Christ's action in the soul becomes effective and fruitful for us. We are similarly impelled to the love of one another, for we have become one in Christ. This is what *Com-munion* implies and requires, for "to give oneself to Jesus Christ is to give oneself to others for love of Him, or rather to give oneself to Him in the person of our neighbour" (pp. 164-165). "We are neither spirits nor ghosts," he insists, "but human beings" (p. 166). Therefore, we are to love God humanly, that is with all our heart, soul, strength, and mind, and to love our neighbor in the same way. (See also his *Christ the Life of the Soul*, St. Louis: B. Herder Book Co., 1925.)

Another departure from the spirituality of the scholastic manuals of the early twentieth century was taken by Charles de Foucauld (d. 1916), founder of the Little Brothers of the Sacred Heart of Jesus. Foucauld was in the tradition of French rather than Benedictine spirituality, and so his focus on Jesus was less liturgical and less socially oriented than Marmion's. To be a Christian is to follow Jesus in the way of poverty and humility. To take the lowest place among humankind is to be close to Jesus. Foucauld left the Trappist life to establish a small community whose purpose would be to live as nearly as possible the way Jesus lived, following to the letter all the evangelical counsels, possessing nothing, giving to whoever asks (see his *Spiritual Autobiography*, Jean-Francois Six, ed., New York: P. J. Kenedy, 1964). The great Catholic philosopher Jacques Maritain (d. 1973) spent his own last days living in community with the Little Brothers of Charles de Foucauld (see his *The Peasant of the Garonne*, New York: Holt, Rinehart and Winston, 1968).

1950 Through Vatican II (1965)

The turn to a spirituality oriented to the world did not begin in the twentieth century, but the understanding of human existence as *historical* existence *is* a modern development. No Christian spiritual writer contributed more substantially to that new emphasis than Teilhard de Chardin (d. 1955). The more intensely he came to know and experience the world, the closer God was to him. The entire universe is one "divine milieu" (see *The Divine Milieu*, New York: Harper & Brothers, 1960; originally published in French in 1957). We attain an experience of God not, as the traditional ascetical manualists argued, primarily through purgation, contemplation, and mystical union, or a kind of "meditation with closed eyes." Rather we encounter God by turning toward the things of the earth in love and reverence. The natural delight we take in life and in all that exists is the first dawn of divine illumination. The great mystery of Christianity is not that God appears *(epiphany)* but that God shines through the universe *(diaphany)*. Our prayer, therefore, is not that we might see God "as He is in Himself" but that we might see God in all things.

Here again we have an echo of the basic Ignatian vision. It is not merely coincidental that Teilhard himself was a member of Ignatius' company, the Society of Jesus. And yet there is also a trace of Franciscan spirituality in his sense of the presence of God in the physical universe and in his sense of the activating energy of Christ, as the Omega of evolution, across the entire cosmos.

Teilhard's insistence that spirituality is not for the religiously professed alone (priests, nuns, brothers, monks) notwithstanding, monks continued to exercise profound influence on Catholic spirituality in the years immediately preceding the Second Vatican Council. For Dom Hubert Van Zeller spiritual life is a life in search of truth. But the search for truth is not distinct from the quest for love, for the object of both is God, who is at once Truth and Love. Apart from God there is no end to our search, and Christ is the embodiment of God's truth and love.

For the Christian, therefore, the purpose of life is union with Christ, and the Christian's aim is always to live to the fullest possible extent the life outlined in the Gospel. This is no distant ideal proposed only to saints and mystics, but to every baptized person. All are called to a life based on the Christian love ethic, in the individual and the social orders alike. But our search is a prolonged one, involving progressive discovery. We experience frustration and loneliness on the way. "We look for Christ in darkness, and in darkness He reveals Himself. We flounder in unsatisfied longing, and in our floundering we discover love. We think we have lost faith and hope, when in our seeming faithlessness and hopelessness we discover true faith and hope. . . . We discover that the only thing in life which is worth doing is to search. The man in the Gospel who went digging for his buried treasure had already found it" (*The Inner Search*, New York: Sheed & Ward, 1957, pp. 7,9).

The change from a negative to an increasingly positive attitude toward the world is also apparent within the corpus of writings by the Trappist monk Thomas Merton (d. 1968). There is a discernible shift from his perception of the world as wicked in his *The Seven Storey Mountain* (New York: Harcourt, Brace, 1948) to *Conjectures of a Guilty Bystander* (New York: Doubleday, 1966), where he reports how, on a downtown corner in Louisville, Kentucky, he was suddenly overwhelmed with the realization that he loved all those people and that human beings cannot be alien to one another even though they are total strangers. The whole illusion of a separate holy existence is a dream, he insisted.

In his *Life and Holiness* (New York: Doubleday-Image, 1964) he declares that "a Christianity that despises [the] fundamental needs of man is not truly worthy of the name.... There is no genuine holiness without this dimension of human and social concern" (p. 100). Spiritual perfection is available not to those with superhuman powers but to those who, though weak and defective in themselves, trust perfectly in the love of God, who abandon themselves with confident joy to the apparent madness of the cross (p. 119). Perfection means "simple fidelity" to the will of God in every circumstance of our ordinary life. To be a saint means to be oneself, to be what God intended one to be. We are, in fact, called to share with God "the work of *creating* the truth of our identity" (*New Seeds of Contemplation*, New York: New Directions Books, 1961, p. 32; the same point is central to contemporary Catholic moral theology, as we saw in chapter 26).

"Finding God," therefore, "means much more than just abandoning all things that are not God, and emptying oneself of images and desires" (p. 39). Rather, "God discovers Himself in us." To find God, one must find himself or herself. But one cannot find oneself in isolation from the rest of humankind. We must give ourselves to others in the purity of selfless love. "For it is precisely in the recovery of our union with our brothers in Christ that we discover God and know Him, for then His life begins to penetrate our souls and His love possesses our faculties and we are able to find out Who He is from the experience of His mercy, liberating us from the prison of self-concern" (p. 78).

One of the few theologians who attempted a systematic description and definition of Catholic spirituality in the years immediately preceding Vatican II was the French Oratorian Louis Bouyer, perhaps best known for his book *The Spirit and Forms of Protestantism* (Westminster, Md.: Newman Press, 1956). Bouyer acknowledged that spirituality is available to, and practiced by, non-Christians as well as Christians, Protestants as well as

Catholics. Spirituality is engaged wherever there is a personal relationship with God. *Christian* spirituality is engaged where that personal relationship is grounded in God's self-revelation in Jesus Christ. *Catholic* spirituality is more deliberately ecclesial. The Word-made-flesh is proclaimed and encountered in the Church. It is not only the content of the Word that one finds in the Church, but the Word itself.

"It is, therefore, into the Church, the true body of Christ, that we must be incorporated in order to participate in the Spirit of Christ, and, as a consequence, to receive His words, not as a mere dead letter, but as words which remain always living, always uttered by the very Word of God" (*Introduction to Spirituality*, p. 13). Catholic spirituality, for Bouyer, is "Christian spirituality in its fullness" (p. 14). We are called to love as God loves. The Church, which is built up around Christ, is "an extension, an opening out to all mankind of the society of the divine Persons, the Trinity of the *agape*" (p. 17).

Few pre-conciliar formulae provide as clear an introduction to post-Vatican II spirituality, however, as the title of Josef Goldbrunner's essay "Holiness Is Wholeness" (*Holiness Is Wholeness and Other Essays*, Notre Dame, Ind.: University of Notre Dame Press, 1964; originally published in 1955). God, the All-Holy, he argues, is whole. There is "no blemish of disease . . . , no poison of death. . . . The more we seek the perfection that makes man like God, that makes him holy, the more we should become healthy in body and soul, for holiness is health" (p. 1). This is not to say that the way to God is free of suffering and even death. "Only a slow advance in the spiritual life gives the body time to adapt itself, to expel, as it were, the poison of death which it has come to absorb" (p. 2). But there are also many "illegitimate illnesses" which have come to be associated with the spiritual life: sufferings and risks to health that are embraced for their own sake, assaults upon the laws of nature, and the like. The modern Christian should be ready to tread the way of the cross that leads to holiness, but he or she must rebel when "holiness appears in a guise contrary to nature" (p. 3).

Dualism is to be rejected: There is no warring between soul and body as if the two were separate components, the one higher and the other lower and base. The incarnation teaches us that there is a wholeness to human life, which comprehends the bodily as well as the spiritual. But there is more to it even than that. There is as well the universe of the unconscious with which each must get in touch. To live a spiritually healthy life one must find one's own truth; i.e., ". . . one must consciously come to terms with the irrational forces within oneself, incorporating them into the total life of the soul but never allowing them a perfectly free rein" (p. 14). Not every soul is the same. Each has "a certain measure of energy." If the religious life claims a great deal of energy, it must inevitably be subtracted from other spheres of the spirit. It is clear, therefore, that there are limits to our conscious striving for union with God.

Insofar as we *do* manage to continue the lifelong process of conversion, we are empowered by the divine energies known as the three theological virtues: faith, hope, and charity. *Faith* is the ability to think with Christ, to enter into mental communion with him. Fear calls forth the desire for security, but faith demands trust which liberates from fear. *Hope* gives all life a future dimension. All life is waiting, but we are even now "fed with the energies of the coming age" (p. 28). The virtue of hope frees us for the process of maturing, for a growing into the full stature of Christ. It also gives the spirit elasticity and a kind of eternal youthfulness. *Charity*, finally, is a participation in the divine love in which human love can alone find redemption and healing. "In love for man and love for God the yearning heart watches out for the other who can liberate it from the confinement of the single person, break through the wall of isolation, and fill it with the gift of communion" (p. 31).

It was the French philosopher-poet Charles Péguy (d. 1914) who exposed the self-deception of those who believe that the way to God is the way of repression of all desires for intimacy and interpersonal warmth. "Because they love no one," he wrote, "they imagine they love God." This is not to say, of course, that the spiritual life is without paradox. How is one to be wholly worldly and wholly devoted to God? "Through the cross of Christ, holiness and health become one" (Goldbrunner, p. 34).

The Second Vatican Council laid to rest, once and for all, the assumption that spirituality is for priests and religious alone. The fifth chapter of its keynote *Dogmatic Constitution on the Church (Lumen gentium)* is entitled "The Call of the Whole Church to Holiness." The Lord addressed all of his disciples, regardless of their situation, when he said: "You therefore are to be perfect, even as your heavenly Father is perfect" (Matthew 5:48). We are already holy by reason of the Spirit's indwelling within us. Christian spirituality is a matter of living in accordance with who we have become in the Spirit, of manifesting the fruits of the Spirit's presence: mercy, kindness, humility, meekness, patience (Colossians 3:12; Galatians 5:22; Romans 6:22). "Thus it is evident to everyone," the council declares, "that all the faithful of Christ of whatever rank or status are called to the fullness of the Christian life and to the perfection of charity" (n. 40).

The next sentence is almost as significant: "By this holiness a more human way of life is promoted even in this earthly society." Holiness, therefore, is not only for everyone; it also comprehends far more than the individual soul's relationship with God. Furthermore, there is no single mode or style of spirituality for Christians. Each must adapt the call to perfection to his or her own situation. What will always be common to all is love of God and of neighbor. "For charity, as the bond of perfection and the fulfillment of the law (cf. Colossians 3:14; Romans 13:10), rules over all the means of attaining holiness, gives life to them, and makes them work. Hence it is the love of God and of neighbor which points out the true disciple of Christ" (n. 42).

Elsewhere the council reaffirms or elaborates upon these basic principles of Christian spirituality. The call to holiness is a call issued to laity as well as to clergy and religious. The spiritual life of all Christians will be rooted in the mysteries of creation and redemption, in the presence of the Holy Spirit, and in the mission of Christ and the Church (*Decree on the Apostolate of the Laity*, n. 29; see also n. 4). The Christian enters upon the spiritual life in response to the Word of God (*Dogmatic Constitution on Divine Revelation*, n. 21), and the Word of God, in turn, is proclaimed and celebrated in the liturgy of the Church, which is the "summit" and the "fountain" of the whole Christian life. "From the liturgy, therefore, and especially from the Eucharist, as from a fountain, grace is channeled into us; and the sanctification of men in Christ and the glorification of God, to which all other activities of the Church are directed as toward their goal, are most powerfully achieved" (n. 10). And what the council teaches about Catholic spirituality applies to the whole Body of Christ, for there can be "no ecumenism worthy of the name without a change of heart. . . . Let all Christ's faithful remember that the more purely they strive to live according to the gospel, the more they are fostering and even practicing Christian unity. For they can achieve depth and ease in strengthening mutual brotherhood to the degree that they enjoy profound communion with the Father, the Word, and the Spirit" (*Decree on Ecumenism*, n. 7). The council insists that this is "the soul of the whole ecumenical movement, and can rightly be called 'spiritual ecumenism'."

Post-Vatican II (1965-   )

The post-conciliar period has been marked by a full-scale liturgical renewal (vernacular Mass, revised sacramental rites, active participation), by a stronger sense of the ecumenical breadth of the Church, by a more pronounced concern for social justice and the liberating mission of the Church, by a deepening reverence for Sacred Scripture, and by an increased striving for a personal experience of the Holy Spirit. All of these developments—which are outgrowths of movements already at work in the nineteenth century and actively promoted in the pre-Vatican II period—shape contemporary Christian spirituality. Their by-products include the Charismatic Renewal, the Cursillo movement, Marriage Encounter, directed (one-on-one) retreats according to the original Ignatian mode, weekend youth retreats, the resurgence of contemplative prayer, as at the Jesuit Center for Religious Development in Cambridge, Massachusetts, as well as the renewal and reform of religious congregations.

Individual spiritual writers, of course, continue to influence the style of Christian life. Dom Aelred Graham moves beyond the traditional ecumenical boundaries between Catholic and Protestant into the wider dialogue between East and West, in his *Contemplative Christianity: An Approach to the Realities of Religion* (New York: Seabury Press, 1974). What East and West have in common is the conviction that there are three paths to God: the path of self-forgetting adoration, expressed in both private worship and in the Church's liturgy; the path of selfless service of others, which finds expression in compassionate activity for the benefit both of the individual and of society as a whole; and the path of truth-realizing experience, through contemplative meditation (p. 65). Not all three paths have to be traveled. We will be inclined to one or another by temperament. But any one of these paths, selflessly pursued, can lead to union with God. They are not mutually exclusive, and each can be abused. The first can degenerate into mindless piety or an obsessive, even superstitious, preoccupation with rites and ceremonies. The second can be impractical and unrealistic. The third can become an "ego trip" with little regard for the needs of other people. In the end, the spiritual quest is a risk, but a risk that has to be taken in faith. And faith ultimately is "an awareness beyond sense-perception that the power behind the universe is not neutral, but gracious and beneficent, the unshakable confidence that 'all shall be well and all manner of thing shall be well' " (p. 68).

To be spiritual is to have achieved "God-realization," i.e., "to be in a state of awareness such that God is consciously *real*" (p. 74). It means seeing God everywhere and in everything and everyone. Christian spirituality therefore, is incarnational. It welcomes what is fully human, including the physical, the down-to-earth, the concrete. Any yet it is not simply materialistic. There is more to reality than meets the eye. God is present to the world as the power of love which is to be shared with others. The insight is not exclusively Catholic, although one certainly finds it in the Catholic tradition—e.g., in Ignatius, Teilhard de Chardin, Karl Rahner, and many others. It is not even exclusively Christian, although one finds it in such Protestant writers as Dietrich Bonhoeffer. One also finds this insight outside of Christianity—e.g., in Mahayana Buddhism's "man for others" embodied in the Bodhhisattva ideal, succinctly formulated by Shantideva:

"Whoever wishes quickly to rescue himself and another, should practice the supreme mystery: the exchanging of himself and the other" (cited by Graham, p. 94).

Some other post-Vatican II spiritual writings fall to one or another side of Dom Aelred's comprehensive approach. *To the right* are the works of Adrian van Kaam, of Duquesne University in Pittsburgh, Pennsylvania, who carries forward many narrow, pre-conciliar methodological assumptions about the nature of theology, revelation, doctrine, and Sacred Scripture, for example, while at the same time acknowledging, more than Garrigou-Lagrange, Tanquerey, and others, the close relationship between personality development and spirituality (see his *In Search of Spiritual Identity*, Denville, N.J.: Dimension Books, 1975).

And the anonymously produced *Cloud of Unknowing* is a principal guide for the "centering prayer" movement. The term is inspired by Thomas Merton, who stressed in his earlier writings that the only way to come into contact with the living God is to go to one's center and from that point to pass into God. It is a spirituality of *interiority*, of going deeply into oneself in order to get in touch with the divine reality present there. As soon as we become aware of any thoughts, we must disavow them and return to God again. In the spirit of the *Cloud of Unknowing*, everything is to be abandoned except God. Far from removing us from others, this prayer should make us more conscious of our oneness with them. One spiritual writer in this tradition, Jesuit theologian Thomas Clarke, is more insistent upon this than some others appear to be. "The quality and intensity of contemplation is in direct, not in inverse, proportion to the quality and intensity of our action on behalf of justice and peace, and vice versa" ("Finding Grace at the Center," in *Finding Grace at the Center*, Thomas Keating, *et al.*, Still River, Mass.: St. Bede Publications, 1978, p. 59).

Another individually-oriented spirituality, but with a Russian flavoring, is offered by Catherine de Hueck Doherty, foundress of Madonna House in Ontario, Canada. Her approach is developed in a trilogy: *Poustinia* ("Desert"), *Sobornost* ("Unity"), and *Strannik* ("Pilgrimage") (Notre Dame, Ind.: Ave Maria Press, 1975, 1977, and 1978 respectively). We were created to be *one* with

God in paradise. That unity was restored by the incarnation. Christ himself is the total pilgrim, on his way from the bosom of his Father to the hearts of men and women. He invites us to pilgrimage with him, to know God as Adam and Eve once knew God. One goes out to the desert to contemplate the unity God offers us in Christ. Meanwhile, our pilgrimage continues until we meet God again at the Second Coming (see *Strannik: The Call to Pilgrimage for Western Man*, pp. 9-16). Recent biblical, theological, and pastoral developments do not materially enter into the shaping of these works.

To the left are more activist-oriented types, such as Episcopalian Malcolm Boyd's *Are You Running With Me, Jesus?* (New York: Holt, Rinehart and Winston, 1965). Similarly emphatic about the secular and prophetic character of Christian spirituality but perhaps more theologically sober is Johannes Metz, in his *Followers of Christ: Perspectives on the Religious Life* (New York: Paulist Press, 1978). He argues that religious congregations are called in a special way to be a shock force in the Church, giving witness not only to the world but to the Church itself of how the Gospel is to be lived in an uncompromising fashion. Metz's reflections on the evangelical counsels, however, have applicability beyond the concerns of religious orders. *Poverty*, he suggests, is "a protest against the tyranny of having, of possessing and of pure self-assertion. It impels those practising it into practical solidarity with those poor whose poverty is not a matter of virtue but is their condition of life and the situation exacted of them by society" (p. 49). *Celibacy* is "the expression of an uncompromising concentration of longing for the day of the Lord, a concentration that is not afraid of any temptation of loneliness. . . . It impels towards solidarity with those unmarried people whose celibacy (that is to say, loneliness; that is to say, not having anyone) is not a virtue but their social destiny, and towards those who are shut up in lack of expectation and in resignation" (p. 60). *Obedience*, finally, is "the radical and uncalculated surrender of one's life to God the Father who raises up and liberates. It impels one to stand close to those for whom obedience is not a matter of virtue but the sign of oppression and of being placed in tutelage, and to do this in a practical way" (p. 67). For Metz, then, there is a growing proportion between the mystical and the political aspects of Christian discipleship, with the balance apparently tilted in the political direction. It is also a life that is increasingly eschatological, i.e., governed by the expectation of the imminent coming of the Kingdom of God. Since the Lord is close at hand, there is no time for postponement. We must serve the least of the brethren now (p. 79).

Closer again to the middle are the writings of Catholic pastoral theologian Henri Nouwen. Christian spirituality, he suggests, moves through three polarities. The first polarity deals with our relationship to ourselves: the polarity between loneliness and solitude. The second is at the root of our relationship to others: the polarity between hostility and hospitality. And the third, and most important, has to do with our relationship with God: the polarity between illusion and prayer. To live a spiritual life "means first of all to come to the awareness of the inner polarities between which we are held in tension" *(Reaching Out: The Three Movements of the Spiritual Life,* New York: Doubleday, 1975, p. 12). To be Christian we do not have to deny our loneliness, our hostilities, and our illusions. We have to have the courage to allow them to come to our full attention, to understand them, to confess them, and then to convert them into solitude, hospitality, and prayer.

Appealing also to a popular, non-specialist audience is Dominican Matthew Fox, Director of the Institute in Creation-Centered Spirituality at Mundelein College, Chicago, Illinois. The titles of his trilogy of spiritual books tend to veer somewhat from the conventional: *On Becoming a Musical Mystical Bear: Spirituality American Style* (New York: Paulist Press, 1972); *Whee! We, wee All the Way Home: A Guide to the New Sensual Spirituality* (Wilmington, N.C.: Consortium Books, 1976); and *A Spirituality Named Compassion and the Healing of the Global Village, Humpty Dumpty and Us* (Minneapolis: Winston Press, 1979). The first book concentrates on the meaning of the word *prayer* and its relationship to the personal and the psychological (i.e., prayer as "mysticism") as well as to the social (i.e., prayer as "prophecy"). There is a necessary dialectic between the mystical and the prophetic. The second book deals with the recovery of what Fox calls a non-elitist understanding of spiritual experience, especially the experience of ecstasy. Such a spirituality leads, he argues, to a re-examination of the role of body and body politic, of pleasure and the sharing of pleasures that make up the spiritual journey. The third book moves from passion to compassion, which he defines as "a passionate way of living born of an awareness of the interconnectedness of all creatures by reason of their common Creator" (p. 34). Fox draws explicitly from Meister Eckhart, who insisted: "You may call God love; you may call God goodness; but the best name for God is Compassion."

The Humpty Dumpty image reminds us that the egg of our world is cracked. It is the price we have paid for our aggressive, materialistic mode of life. Humpty Dumpty teaches us that the primary issue in spirituality is not redemption of the soul but redemption of the world. We are in the world, and the world is in us. To heal one is to heal the other. The world is only a projection of our inner selves. "It is because we worship upness inside that we build skyscrapers outside. It is because we prefer aggression to gentleness inside that we invest so mightily in armaments and so punily in artists on the outside. Humpty teaches us how the inside is the outside and the outside is the inside. For better or for worse . . . until death do us part" (p. 268).

A quest for balance is evident in the writings of Cardinal Leo Suenens of Belgium, whose *A New Pentecost?* (New York: Seabury Press, 1974) emphasizes both the charismatic and institutional elements of Christian community and the individual and social dimensions of Christian existence. To be spiritual is to be always ready to expect the unexpected from God, for God is even now creating anew. We are not prisoners of determinism or of sociological prognostications. The Holy Spirit is at work in the Church and in the rest of the world, even when unrecognized and unnamed. To those who welcome the Spirit there is liberty, joy, and trust. The Spirit has raised up prophets and saints who, in times of darkness, have discovered "a spring of grace and shed beams of light on our path" (p. xiii). John XXIII and Vatican II were such surprises. Who would dare to say, therefore, that the love and imagination of God are exhausted? "To hope is not to dream, but to turn dreams into reality. Happy are those who dream dreams and are ready to pay the price to make them come true." Pentecost continues.

MYSTICISM

Mysticism is the experiencing of God. It is not confined to the Church. *Christian* mysticism roots the experience of God in Jesus Christ, an experience brought about by the Holy Spirit. All spirituality, and certainly all Christian spirituality, therefore, is oriented toward the experience of God. Individualistic spiritualities assume that we can experience God only to the extent that we *exclude* experiencing everyone else and everything else. Activist liberationist spiritualities assume that we experience God *only* in the other and in the social and political movements of history. Balanced spiritualities insist on a connection between the two: the experience of God as the presence *within,* and the experience of God as the presence *in others* and in the "signs of the times."

Historically, the use of the word *mystical* to describe a special religious experience is peculiar to Christianity. And even at that its use developed only gradually. It was first employed to designate the deepest meaning of Sacred Scripture, a meaning accessible only to faith. For Clement of Alexandria and for Origen, it was equivalent to the Pauline notion of "mystery"—namely, Jesus Christ crucified (1 Corinthians 2:2). The mystery, hidden for ages but now revealed to the saints, is "Christ in you" (Colossians 1:26-27). Christ, in whom are hidden all the treasures of wisdom and knowledge, is the divine mystery (2:2-3).

The term *mystical* next came to be identified with the sacraments—i.e., outward signs of invisible grace. Christ, of course, is the great sacrament, or mystery. With Gregory of Nyssa and Pseudo-Dionysius the word is given another meaning which it retains in Christian spirituality: the fullness of the new life, the divine life communicated in the crucified and risen Christ. Mysticism, therefore, is not something reserved for the few. It is a call to the many. Everyone is invited to intimate union with God, to the experience of God as the principle of one's life and as the meaning and guide of all that is.

To express it another way, mysticism is simply the experience of grace. It occurs within the framework of one's normal, everyday life and within the experience of faith. Therefore, it is correct to say that mystical experience is not specifically different from the ordinary life of grace that is open to everyone. To argue the contrary view would be tantamount to Gnosticism, that earliest of heresies, which supposed that salvation is through knowledge *(gnosis)* and that such saving knowledge is available only to an elite.

Mysticism, furthermore, is not identical with parapsychological phenomena. This is not to suggest, on the other hand, that the experience of God does not have degrees of intensity. Those experiences of the highest intensity available to human consciousness may indeed have an "unnatural" or at least "unusual" character to them. These special, or "peak," experiences do not happen every day, nor frequently within a single lifetime. Many, in fact, would insist that, in spite of their openness to such experiences and the sincerity of their faith, they have never once had such an experience. But to say that one has not ever had a "peak" or exceedingly intense experience of God is not to say that one has not had a *mystical* experience. For a mystical experience is any experience of God, of whatever degree of intensity. Indeed, the adjective *mystical* before the words *experience of God* is perhaps as redundant as the adjective *mystical* before the words *Body of Christ,* when applied to the Church. For the same reason, "mystical theology" is not really distinct from "Christian theology" as such. If the mystic is said to have great difficulty expressing his or her experience of God, so, too, does every theologian. In fact, the process by which we attempt to articulate our experience of God is precisely what we mean by *theology* (see chapter 2).

GLOSSOLALIA: SPEAKING IN TONGUES

The New Testament refers several times to "speaking in tongues" (Mark 16:17; Acts of the Apostles 2:4-11; 10:46; 19:6; 1 Corinthians 14). It is a speech which is unintelligible to the listeners, except in Acts of the Apostles 2:4-11. It is the work of the Holy Spirit, given particularly at Baptism (Acts of the Apostles 10:46;

19:6), and it becomes so routine a part of the life of some churches that the gift has to be regulated (1 Corinthians 14). Furthermore, it is addressed to God, not to "men" (14:2), and it edifies the speaker rather than those who hear the speaker (14:4). Accordingly, what is spoken "in tongues" must be interpreted (14:5-19,27).

It should be noted that one of the effects of religious ecstasy in contemporary Hellenistic and Oriental circles was the utterance of unintelligible speech. The appearance of unintelligible "tongues" in some of the early Christian communities, therefore, may have provided a bridge between the Hellenistic-Oriental world and the emerging world of Christian faith. As the cultural context changed, the gift of tongues gradually disappeared.

Paul, of course, acknowledged that this gift, even in its period of frequent use, was the least important in the hierarchy of gifts (1 Corinthians 12:1-11). It was only occasionally mentioned in subsequent centuries, entering the modern period via small marginal Protestant groups known as Pentecostals. Just after Vatican II, interest in and expression of the gift of tongues surfaced with vigor even in Catholicism. The phenomenon developed in connection with the emergence of the Catholic Charismatic Renewal, whose origin is usually placed at Duquesne University in Pittsburgh, Pennsylvania, in 1967, from where it spread quickly to the University of Michigan at Ann Arbor and the University of Notre Dame in Indiana.

Seen in its most positive light, the gift of tongues is a form of nondiscursive prayer, not unlike the protracted "A" sound at the end of the chanted "Alleluia" or the spontaneous but unstructured communications of a child who has not yet learned to speak. Others have compared it to the gift of tears, i.e., a religious experience by which a person is moved to a profound sense of sorrow for sin, repentance, adoration, or gratitude before God. Such tears are no different from any others, but their religious significance goes far beyond the merely physical. So, too, does that of the gift of tongues.

"In psychological terms, we could say that it is the voice of the subconscious rising to God, finding a manner of praying which is analagous to other expressions of our subconscious in dreams, laughter, tears, painting, or dance," Cardinal Suenens observes. "This prayer within the depths of our being heals at a profound yet often perceptible level hidden psychological wounds that impede the full development of our interior life" *(A New Pentecost?,* p. 103).

On the other hand, the common approach of the great mystics has been to ignore such phenomena, even if they are God-given (John of the Cross, *The Ascent of Mount Carmel,* Part II, chapter 8). One should preserve, in any case, the Pauline principle that in the worship assembly no one should speak in tongues unless an interpreter can explain the meaning to the community, for every gift is, in the final accounting, always for the sake of the Church and ultimately for the sake of the Kingdom of God (1 Corinthians 14:28).

DISCERNMENT AND SPIRITUAL DIRECTION

It is one thing to say, as Ignatius did, that we must see God in all things, but it is quite another matter confidently to affirm that we have, in fact, grasped the reality of God and accurately discerned the divine will for us in these particular circumstances. No one, after all, has ever seen God (John 1:18; 1 Timothy 6:16). One infers the presence and will of God from what one does see and experience.

But our seeing and our experiencing are never isolated acts. We see and experience as part of larger communities: a family, a religious congregation, a parish, an association, a political unit, a business corporation, and so forth. Furthermore, even these larger groups, in which and through which we live our individual lives, are themselves part of a much wider process of social, economic, and political events and of history itself.

Knowledge, in other words, is always conditioned. It is conditioned by who we are (e.g., our age, sex, race, ethnic roots, gifts, native abilities, religious affiliation, economic status), who are our closest relatives, friends, and associates, our occupation, our citizenship, the social, economic, and political events that shape our time, and so forth.

Accordingly, discernment of the presence and will of God is always complex and difficult, especially in a post-Enlightenment age which is at once critical not only of authority (as the first Enlightenment was) but also of the capacity of reason itself (as the second Enlightenment was). There is more to knowing, in other words, than reasoning alone. We are moved not only by external events but also by the dark and utterly mysterious world of the unconscious. To what extent do our emotions, our imagination, and the other affective faculties of human consciousness determine the judgments we make about the will of God for us, for others, for the world, and for history itself? To transcend the limitations of one's own vision and to begin to see reality against a wider horizon ("as God sees reality") is to experience *conversion* (see chapter 26).

As we noted already in connection with the discussion of the virtue of *prudence* (chapter 26), although we can never be absolutely certain that we are indeed responding to the promptings of the Holy Spirit, there are at least certain *negative criteria* by which obviously false responses can be exposed: (1) If the discernment process does not produce the classic "fruits" of the Spirit: love, joy, peace, patience, kindness, generosity, faith, chastity, etc. (Galatians 5:22-23), the discernment process is not "of the Spirit." (2) If the discernment process leads to theological positions which are inconsistent with the Catholic tradition, it is not "of the Spirit" (see the next section of this chapter for a listing of the principal theological criteria). (3) If the discernment process intensifies the isolation and even the spiritual eccentricities of those involved in it rather than enhancing their life and the life of the whole Church (Ephesians 4:15-16), it is not "of the Spirit." (4) If the discernment process ignores pertinent information (even of a social, economic, or political character), if it rejects the counsel of others who have knowledge and experience in the matter at hand (even if they are not members of the Church or even people of religious faith), and if it formulates its judgments by imposition rather than by corporate reflection and with respect for diversity of viewpoints, then it is clearly not "of the Spirit."

The spiritual director is one who assists and guides the discernment process in others. But the "decision" is always made by the individuals themselves, not by the director. The director all the while is guided by the same theological principles which must guide the one who is striving to discern God's will and to enter more deeply into a relationship with God. Indeed, the spiritual director is himself or herself in the same situation, striving to know God's will and to determine the best way to fulfill it now, in these circumstances.

SPIRITUALITY AND SPIRITUALITIES: THEOLOGICAL CRITERIA

We return to the Thomistic philosophical principle: "Whatever is received is received according to the mode of the receiver." Although God is one, the experience of God is individually, socially, historically, even economically conditioned. Thus, there is one God, but there are many religions. There is one Body of Christ but many churches. There is one faith and yet many theologies. And there is one Spirit and yet many spiritualities.

Indeed, as Paul reminded us, "There are different gifts but the same Spirit; there are different ministries but the same Lord; there are different works but the same God who accomplishes all of them in everyone. To each person the manifestation of the Spirit is given for the common good .... But it is one and the same Spirit who produces all these gifts, distributing them to each as he wills" (1 Corinthians 12:4-7,11). According to Thomas Aquinas, the "first cause of this diversity is to be sought on the part of God, who disposes his gifts of grace variously in order that the beauty and perfection of the Church may result from these various degrees" (*Summa Theologica,* I-II, q. 112, a. 4).

But to say that there are inevitably many spiritualities is not to say that all spiritualities are equally good or equally deficient, no more than one could say that all religions, or all theologies, or even all churches are of equal value and are equally faithful expressions of the divine reality. On what basis can one evaluate the worth of spiritualities? What *theological criteria,* consistent with the Catholic tradition, can one apply to the variety of spiritualities?

1.   We are neither purely bodily creatures nor purely spiritual; nor are we primarily bodily or primarily spiritual. *We are body-spirits* (for this and the next four principles, see chapter 5). Accordingly, no Christian spirituality can be predicated on a *dualistic* understanding of human existence, as if the flesh (considered separately from the soul) were always at war with the spirit (considered separately from the flesh). The spirit-flesh opposition in Paul is between the *whole person* as oriented toward the Kingdom of God, and the *whole person* as oriented away from God in the pursuit of selfish interests.

2.   *We are radically social beings.* Accordingly, no Christian spirituality can attend exclusively nor in an exaggerated fashion to the individual's personal relationship with God, as if other persons and the wider created order did not enter intrinsically into that relationship.

3.   *We are individual human persons.* Accordingly, no Christian spirituality can allow the individual to be absorbed into some impersonal collective, as if the experience of God is only corporate or horizontal, never individual or vertical.

4.   *We are also subjects,* i.e., distinct centers of consciousness and freedom. Accordingly, there is no single way of experiencing God or of expressing the experience of God. No Christian spirituality can impose itself as the *only* spirituality for *all*.

5.   *We are graced.* The presence of God enters into the very definition of what it means to be human. The doctrines of creation and of redemption make it impossible for a Christian to reject the material, the fleshly, the bodily, the natural, the tangible, the visible, the concrete (see also chapter 7). Accordingly, no Christian spirituality can counsel a repression of the human nor dismiss whole components of human existence as if they were somehow dishonorable and bestial (e.g., the passions, or so-called "lower appetites").

6.   To be graced is to be alive by a principle that transcends us—namely, the presence of God. For the Christian, *God is always triune* (see chapters 9 and 10). Accordingly, Christian spirituality is trinitarian spirituality. We are created, called, and sustained by the Father; re-created in the Son and given new access to the

Father through the Son; and renewed and empowered to live a fully human life by the Holy Spirit.

7.   Since the triune God is present everywhere, *all reality has a sacramental, or mysterious, character*. The invisible is embodied in, and mediated by, the visible (see chapters 7 and 10). Accordingly, the horizon of Christian spirituality will be as wide as the created order itself. It will be as worldly as it is personal; i.e., it will strive always to see God in all things.

8.   *Human existence and Christian existence alike are destined for, and therefore oriented toward, the Kingdom of God*. But the Kingdom is a kingdom of justice and peace as well as of holiness and grace (see chapters 20 and 26, and also chapter 29). Accordingly, Christian spirituality will always be sensitive to the demands of justice, of peace, of human rights, and will never be closed off from, or indifferent to, the needs and the cries of the poor and the oppressed.

9.   *We are also sinners* (see chapters 5, 12, 22, 25, and 26). Accordingly, there can be no authentic Christian spirituality apart from the cross. It is a spirituality always marked by sacrifice, by denial of selfish interests, even by contradictions. It will be attentive to the impact of Original Sin: to pride, to apathy, to temerity, to lust, to hypocrisy, to sloth, to envy (see chapters 5, 9, and especially 26).

10.   *We are ecclesial persons*. Christian faith is given, received, nourished, sustained, and brought to fulfillment in the context of the Church (see chapters 17, 20, and 21). Accordingly, there is no authentic Christian spirituality that is not at the same time ecclesial spirituality, rooted not only in the primitive, foundational proclamation of the Word in and through Sacred Scripture, but also in the Word's constant re-proclamation and celebration in the Church's liturgy and across the whole range of its sacramental and para-sacramental life (see chapters 2, 7, 21, and 22).

11.   As ecclesial persons, members of the Body of Christ, *we are called to Christian existence, to the practice of the virtues*. Accordingly, Christian spirituality will be an expression of faith, hope, and charity, and of prudence, justice, temperance, and fortitude (see chapter 26). The center will always be charity.

12. *The call to Christian holiness is a universal call (Dogmatic Constitution on the Church,* chapter 5). There is no "higher" spirituality for the ordained and the religiously professed than for the laity. Accordingly, Christian spirituality will never be hierarchical or elitist. There will always be different spiritualities, but the differences will not necessarily imply superiority or inferiority in relation to one another, nor on the basis of ecclesiastical "states of life."

SUMMARY

1. *Spirituality* has to do with one's style of life, with one's way of experiencing God and of shaping one's life on the basis of that experience. It is our way of being religious. Since God is available in principle to everyone, spirituality is not exclusively Christian.

2. *Christian spirituality* is the cultivation of a style of life consistent with the presence of the Spirit of the Risen Christ within us and with our status as members of the Body of Christ. It is *visionary* (is a way of interpreting reality in "spiritual terms"), *sacramental* (sees God in all things), *relational* (is open to the presence and call of God in other people), and *transformational* (is always in touch with and open to the Spirit of reconciliation, renewal, healing).

3. The *foundations* of Christian spirituality were already laid in the *covenantal relationship* between Yahweh and Israel in the Old Testament. *Jesus,* however, proclaimed the nearness of God in a dramatically new way in his preaching of the Kingdom of God. Through his death and resurrection, the Spirit of God comes to dwell within us anew, as the source of light, wisdom, hope, peace.

4. Christian spirituality from the beginning, therefore, is shaped by the Church's *expectation of the coming of the Kingdom of God;* this adds a note of urgency to its mission of proclamation in word, in sacrament, in witness, and in service.

5. In the time of the persecutions *martyrdom* was regarded as the ideal way of achieving union with God. Thereafter, even "natural death" was perceived as a kind of unbloody martyrdom.

6. The first division over Christian spirituality occurs with *Gnosticism* and its variants. Matter is evil, according to this heresy. Therefore, the Christian is to disengage from all material reality to seek the true knowledge *(gnosis)* which alone brings salvation. Over against this

view was Irenaeus' doctrine of *recapitulation:* All reality has been redeemed by Christ in the incarnation.

7. *Monasticism* developed first as a flight from persecution and then as a protest against the newly privileged status of the Church under Constantine. Emphasis was placed on ascetical practices, some of which were severe. It began as a solitary form of existence (anchoritism) and later developed a communal form (cenobitism): common prayers, common goods, and common worship. The *consecration of virgins* was also introduced at this time.

8. A Christian *spiritual theology* developed only gradually from the new monastic movement: *Pseudo-Dionysius* insisted that the soul finds God only in going beyond itself, being absorbed totally in the knowledge of God, whose goodness is overflowing; *Augustine* focused on the principle of self-knowledge in the light of Christ, the interior teacher of wisdom; for *John Cassian,* Christian life is one of constant prayer. The monastic style of spirituality was given wider currency among the laity through the popular writings of *Pope Gregory the Great.*

9. Under *Germanic influence,* Christian spirituality became more externalized: devotions, relics, pilgrimages, penances, confession of sins, etc. The influence of the monasteries continued to grow, especially when, in the tenth and eleventh centuries, federations of monasteries were established and the monastic ideal was spread even more widely throughout the Christian world.

10. Emphasis on *contemplation,* as immediate experience of God without theological reflection, was proposed by the new Cistercian Order, especially by *Bernard of Clairvaux* and *William of St. Thierry,* and by members of the Parisian monastery of St. Victor (the "Victorines": *Hugh, Richard, et al.).*

11. With the decline of social life and of Christian morals even in the Church, various lay movements developed, urging radical poverty and an end to all formalism and legalism. Waldensianism and Albigensianism were extreme forms. The rise of the *mendicant orders*—Franciscans and Dominicans—had a more sustained effect in these areas. The Dominicans (e.g., Aquinas) emphasized the link between contemplation and the apostolate, while the Franciscans (e.g., Bonaventure) emphasized the link between God and creation and our call to live simply and poorly.

12. But the stress on contemplation continued with the increasing popularity of Pseudo-Dionysius, whose works were newly translated in the thirteenth century. Christian spirituality was described in terms of the soul's union with God through abandonment of, and detachment

from, all creatures and worldly realities: *Meister Eckhart, John Tauler, Henry Suso, Ruysbroeck, The Cloud of Unknowing* (anonymous). A more extreme form of this anti-intellectual and individualistic spirituality is to be found in the *Imitation of Christ,* edited, perhaps also written, by Thomas à Kempis.

13. Although *Protestantism* rejected the excesses of medieval spirituality (superstitions and near idolatries), it did not reject its individualism. For Protestantism, access to God is direct and unmediated, guided by the interior illumination of the Holy Spirit.

14. A reaction to contemplative excesses in Catholic spirituality was mounted by such Christian humanists as *Erasmus* and by such Christian activists as *Ignatius Loyola.* They insisted on the fundamental connection between prayer and the apostolate.

15. Mysticism continued to flourish, however, especially in *Spain: Teresa of Avila* and *John of the Cross. Italian* spirituality was more practical, oriented toward the renewal of priestly life: *Philip Neri, Charles Borromeo,* and *Catherine of Genoa. French* spirituality was the most complicated of all because of Jansenism and Quietism: the one stressing the corruption of the flesh, the other stressing the powerlessness of the human person to do anything at all toward salvation. On the other side were ranged *Bossuet, Francis de Sales,* and *Jean Jacques Olier*—all emphasizing in different ways the importance of one's worldly duties, the joy of Christian existence, and the goodness of Jesus.

16. The *nineteenth century* is the bridge between medieval and modern Christian spirituality. Individualism and regimented piety continue (e.g., new devotions) but the forces of renewal are already at work: in theology, liturgy, historical studies, and the social apostolate, as well as in the world of science and technology.

17. The ambivalence of the nineteenth century carried over into the first half of the twentieth. On the one hand, there were spiritualities based largely on scholastic presuppositions *(Tanquerey, Garrigou-Lagrange)* and underlining the individualistic aspect of Christian existence; on the other hand, a broader, Christocentric piety was being developed by such writers as *Abbot Marmion.*

18. With an *historical* understanding of human existence increasingly shaping Catholic theology around the middle of the twentieth century, spiritualities begin to emerge which are more world-centered *(Teilhard de Chardin)*, neighbor-oriented *(Hubert Van Zeller)*, justice-concerned *(Thomas Merton)*, and person-integrating *(Josef Goldbrunner)*, without prejudice at all to the traditional contemplative elements.

19. The *Second Vatican Council* taught that holiness is for every-one and that it comprehends more than the soul's individual relationship with God. Spirituality is shaped by one's situation in life. It is rooted in the mysteries of creation and redemption, in the presence of the Holy Spirit, and in the mission of Christ and the Church. The liturgy is its summit and fountain.

20. *Post-Vatican II* spirituality has been marked by a full-scale liturgical renewal, ecumenism, a more pronounced commitment to liber-ation and social justice, a deepening reverence for Sacred Scripture, and an increased striving for a personal experience of the Holy Spirit. These developments have, in turn, produced such movements as the Catholic Charismatic Renewal, the Cursillo movement, Marriage Encounter, directed retreats, weekend youth retreats, and the reform and renewal of religious congregations.

21. Individual spiritual writers reflect this new ecumenical out-look, attempting to bridge the gap even between East and West *(Aelred Graham).* Others continue to see the spiritual challenge as bridging the gaps within the human person, e.g., between loneliness and solitude *(Henri Nouwen),* between the newly integrated person and the world itself *(Matthew Fox),* and between the charismatic and institutional dimensions of Christian life *(Cardinal Suenens).* A continuing emphasis on interiority and individuality continues (the "centering prayer" approach), along with increased stress on the political aspect of spiritual-ity *(Johannes Metz,* and liberation theology).

22. All Christian spirituality is oriented toward experiencing God in Christ and the Holy Spirit, which is to say that all Christian spiritual-ity is also *"mystical."* The term was first applied to the deepest meaning of Sacred Scripture—i.e., to Christ as the source of all wisdom and knowledge. Then it came to be identified with the sacraments, with Christ perceived as the great sacrament, or mystery. Later, in the writ-ings of Gregory of Nyssa and Pseudo-Dionysius, it refers to the fullness of our new life in Christ: union with God in Christ and the Spirit. In other words, *mysticism is the experience of grace*—i.e., of God's presence within us and throughout the whole of creation. Hence mysticism is not for the few but for all. There are, to be sure, degrees of the experience of God.

23. *Speaking in tongues* (usually unintelligible to the listener) is a gift of the Holy Spirit, according to the New Testament. It is a form of ecstatic prayer, not without parallels in then-contemporary Hellenistic and Oriental circles. The gift was subject to abuse and had to be regu-lated. Like all gifts, it must be for the good of the community.

24. *Discernment* is an exercise of the virtue of prudence. To perceive the presence of God and to discern the divine will are complex and difficult because no one has ever seen God (John 1:18; 1 Timothy 6:16). The process is also complicated by the fact that knowledge itself is historically conditioned and that there is a universe of the unconscious as well as the conscious.

25. There are some *negative criteria* by which false discernment can be exposed. It is not "of the Spirit": (1) if it does not issue forth in the fruits of the Holy Spirit (love, joy, peace, etc.); (2) if it leads to theological positions inconsistent with the Catholic tradition; (3) if it intensifies the isolation and even the spiritual eccentricities of the discerner and does not enhance the life of the Church; and (4) if it ignores pertinent information, the counsel of others, or if it imposes its judgments without corporate reflection or respect for diversity of viewpoints.

26. The *spiritual director* assists and guides the discernment process in others, following the same criteria. The discerner, however, must make his or her own decision and take responsibility for it. The spiritual director, too, is always a discerner.

27. Although there is only one Spirit, there are many gifts of the Spirit. Furthermore, the Spirit is manifested and received in different ways by different people. Accordingly, there are *many different spiritualities,* even within the Church itself. But not all are equally consistent with the Catholic tradition.

28. Some *theological criteria* for determining such consistency are:

(1) We are body-spirits. Christian spirituality cannot be dualistic.

(2) We are social beings. Christianity spirituality cannot be individualistic.

(3) We are individual human persons. Christian spirituality cannot absorb the individual into an impersonal collective.

(4) We are subjects, i.e., distinct centers of consciousness and freedom. There is no one Christian spirituality for everyone.

(5) We are graced. Christian spirituality cannot reject the human nor deny the goodness of the passions.

(6) God is triune. Christian spirituality must be rooted in the life of the whole Trinity: not the Father alone, not the Son alone, not the Holy Spirit alone.

(7) The triune God is present to all reality. The horizon of Christian spirituality will therefore be as wide as the created order itself.

(8)   Everything is destined for, and oriented toward, the Kingdom of God, a kingdom of justice and peace as well as of holiness and grace. Christian spirituality will be marked by a sense of expectation and readiness and by a commitment to justice, peace, and human rights.

(9)   We are sinners. Christian spirituality is a spirituality of the cross: of sacrifice, of denial of selfish interests, of contradiction.

(10)   We are ecclesial persons. Christian spirituality will be at once communal, biblical, and liturgical.

(11)   We are called to the practice of the virtues. Christian spirituality will be an expression of faith, hope and charity, and of prudence, justice, temperance, and fortitude.

(12)   All are called to holiness. Christian spirituality is never hierarchical or elitist, nor of concern only to the ordained and religiously professed.

SUGGESTED READINGS

General Works:

Bouyer, Louis. *Introduction to Spirituality*. New York: Desclée, 1961.
——————— , et al. *A History of Christian Spirituality*. 4 vols. New York: Desclée, 1963.
Dalrymple, John. *Theology and Spirituality*. Cork, Ireland: Mercier Press, 1970.
Rahner, Karl. *The Dynamic Element in the Church*. London: Burns & Oates, 1964.

Ecumenical Spirituality:

Aumann, Jordan, *et. al. Christian Spirituality East and West*, Chicago: Priory Press, 1968. (Catholic, Orthodox, and Evangelical)
Bonhoeffer, Dietrich. *The Cost of Discipleship*. New York: Macmillan, 1959. (Lutheran)
Cox, Harvey. *Turning East: The Promise and Peril of the New Orientalism*. New York: Simon and Schuster, 1977. (Baptist)
Lewis, C. S. *Surprised by Joy: The Shape of My Early Life*. New York: Harcourt, Brace, Janovich, 1973. (Anglican)
Lossky, Vladimir. *The Mystical Theology of the Eastern Church*. London: James Clarke, 1957. (Orthodox)

Thurian, Max. *Modern Man and Spiritual Life.* New York: Association
 Press, 1963. (Reformed)

Journals and Series:

Chicago Studies 15 (1976). "A Spiritual Life Handbook."
Cross Currents 24 (1974). "Word Out of Silence: A Symposium on World
 Spiritualities." John-David Robinson, ed.
Spiritual Life
The Way
The Classics of Western Spirituality. New York: Paulist Press, 1978—.

·XXIX·

CHRISTIAN/HUMAN DESTINY: THE KINGDOM OF GOD

THE MEANING AND PLACE OF ESCHATOLOGY

Catholics share faith in the Lordship of Jesus with all other Christians, faith in the reality of God with all other religious persons and communities, and humanity with all other human beings. All of us inhabit the same earth and are cocreators with God of the same history, even if we "name" God differently or not at all. *Christian destiny* is not distinct from *human destiny*, therefore, nor is either distinct from the *destiny of the world* itself or of its *history*. There is one beginning and one end of all created reality: God.

Eschatology is that area of theology which is directly concerned with the "study of the last thing(s)". The "last thing" is God, or, more precisely, the final manifestation of the reconciling, renewing, and unifying love of God. The "last things" are various moments or stages in the final manifestation process: death, particular judgment, heaven, hell, purgatory, Second Coming of Christ, resurrection of the body, general judgment, consummation of all things in the perfection of the Kingdom of God.

So comprehensive is eschatology's scope that some theologians have argued that all theology begins and ends with eschatology (Jürgen Moltmann, *Theology of Hope*, New York: Harper & Row, 1967, p. 16). At the very least, eschatology provides a wider context for the discussion of every other theological question, for eschatology is about the Kingdom (or "reign") of God, i.e., *the redemptive presence of God actualized through the power of God's reconciling Spirit.* All theology is literally the "study of God." But theology does not reflect on the reality of God as some passive Being or abstract Idea. The God of Christian faith and, therefore, of Christian theology is a God of love (1 John 4:7-21). Love is, by its very nature, active and incarnate. Love is always directed toward the other. Love wishes the other well. Love seeks union with the other. Love heals, renews, reconciles, unites. Love generates peace, joy, kindness, contentment, and all the other fruits of the Holy Spirit, who is the God-of-love in action (Galatians 5:22-23).

But "the other" is not only another individual. "The other" is also *collective*: e.g., family, friends, associates, fellow Christians, the needy. And human existence is always *historical existence*, i.e., existence that is conditioned by social, economic, and political events, by institutions and structures, and by the facticity of life (e.g., we are born at a certain time, of certain parents, of a certain sex, of a certain race, in a certain country). To say, therefore, that God is love and that God loves us means that God loves us as "the other," not only in our individuality but also in our common humanity. Indeed, God loves us in our world and in our history. And because God loves us, God is *active* on our behalf: first in creation, then in redemption, and finally in the consummation of all things in Jesus Christ, by the power of the Holy Spirit. That active love is also an *incarnate* love. God becomes present to us, again not only as individuals but in our total humanity, in our world, and in our history. God is the active, incarnate power of love by which we, our brothers and sisters, our world, and our history are healed, renewed, and brought to the fullness of perfection. And this is precisely what the Kingdom of God is all about.

To reflect on the meaning of the Kingdom of God is to "do eschatology." But to do eschatology is to do what is central to theology: It is to explore the reality of the active, incarnate, redeeming, loving God as that God is known and accepted in faith. Eschatology, however, is not simply coextensive with all of theology, which addresses the total mystery of God. Eschatology centers its attention on that aspect of God by which God is the destiny and consummation of all reality.

This is not to say that eschatology is concerned only with the *future*. On the contrary, the future is being realized even now, in the *present*, and has begun to be realized already in the *past*. We are already redeemed in grace, in faith, in hope, in love (John 5:24; 12:31; 16:8). The Spirit has already been given (Philippians 1:19; Romans 8:23). Our resurrection has already taken place in the Spirit (John 5:25,28). Our *death*, therefore, is, or should be, a participation in the redemptive death of Jesus Christ, which has already taken place. Our *judgment* will be the visible manifestation of the judgment of acquittal already rendered in Jesus Christ (e.g., John 12:31-32; Romans 8:3; Galatians 3:13). The final, *general judgment* will only make clear what is already true— namely, that history is the work of God, that its center is Jesus Christ, and that its moving force is the Holy Spirit. This is, at the same time, the *consummation of all things*, the disclosure of God's acceptance of the world in the incarnation. The Second Coming of Christ (*Parousia*) is simply the final stage of the one coming of Christ (Matthew 12:40). Christ's *return* is really the *arrival* of all things at their final destination in Christ. It is the revelation of God's love for the world (Matthew 24:36; 25:31-46; 1 Thessalonians 5:2; 2 Thessalonians 2:1-8; Revelation 20:11-15; 22:12,20).

The *anticipation* of these final events occurs not only in faith, in hope, and in the active love of one another in charity, but also sacramentally in the *Eucharist*, where we eat and drink of the Lord's body and blood "until he comes" (1 Corinthians 11:26), and in the *Church* itself, which is the eschatological community, the Temple of the Holy Spirit, the carrier even now of the divine glory (Ephesians 5:27).

The movement of history toward its consummation in the Kingdom of God is believed not only because it is *promised* but also because it is *demanded* by graced human nature itself. We are *intentional* beings (see chapters 4 and 5); i.e., we give purpose and direction to our lives. We are constitutionally restless in our quest for truth and in our search for love. Only God, who is the fullness of truth and love itself, can finally satisfy that radical human longing. To say there is no God is to say there is no possibility of ultimate human fulfillment, for the fullness of truth and love obviously transcends our unaided human capacities. There are questions that science can never answer, and problems that science can never solve: What is true justice? How can we create real community? What does it mean to be fully human? Why is there such evil in the world? Why is there such goodness in the world? Why is there being rather than nothing? Where is it all heading? What is the deepest meaning of life?

This "intentionality" is there from the beginning, implanted through God's original self-communication in grace prior even to our free decision to accept or reject it. This is what Rahner has called the "supernatural existential." We are called to accept God's self-communication by responding in faith and love, or we can reject it by sin. The Kingdom of God is the consummation *of* history itself and not just a reward for good deeds *in* history. God completes salvation history by completing history itself. Consequently, there is no such thing as a *purely natural end* for the world or for non-religious people, and a *supernatural end* for the Church and for all who truly believe in God and seek to do the divine will. "For the 'essence' or 'nature' of man is that of a purposeful free being, whose 'nature' it is to be open without limit to the free disposition of God.... And the finality of man is not mechanical, organic, or static, but must be seen from the outset in terms of a dialogal relationship between divine and human freedom.... For the self-communication of God (grace), in spite of being supernatural, is the very 'heart' of man" (Karl Rahner, "Order, IV. End of Man," *The Concise Sacramentum Mundi*, pp. 1119-1120).

Through the mediation of humanity, therefore, the world itself has "intentionality," purpose, direction, conscious freedom. In a word, because of humanity the world itself *has* a history and *is* history. This history has already entered its eschatological phase through the incarnation, the cross and resurrection of Jesus Christ, and the outpouring of the Holy Spirit. The outcome of this history is already decided by Christ, even though that outcome is still hidden and can be grasped only in faith, in hope, and in love. That "outcome" is the finally realized *Kingdom of God*, i.e., *the full and perfect manifestation of the redemptive presence of God through which all things are transformed in the name of Jesus Christ and by the power of the Holy Spirit.*

This is not to say, on the other hand, that history's movement toward the Kingdom of God is smooth and unimpeded. There are powers at work in the world which are hostile to God (e.g., Ezekiel 38-39; Daniel 2:20-45; 7:7-8; Psalm 2) and which are directed immediately against Christ (Revelation 12:1-5) and the Church (12:17), growing in intensity as the end draws near. All of these evil forces are focused in the one known as *Satan* (the Hebrew word *sātān* means "adversary," and it was translated into Greek as *diabolos*, the word which passed into various European languages). He is regarded as the prince of the angels who fell away from God before the creation of the world and who were thrust out of heaven. He becomes in the New Testament the evil one (Matthew 13:19), the enemy (Luke 10:19), the ruler of this world (John 12:31), the father of lies (John 8:44), the evil force behind the passion of Jesus (Luke 22:3,31; John 13:27).

But the passion is also the source of victory over Satan (1 Corinthians 2:8; John 12:31; Acts of the Apostles 12:7-11), who is himself destined to be cast finally into hell (Revelation 20:8,10). (See chapter 9.)

The Church's broadened understanding of the interrelationship between the power of God's love in Christ and the forces of evil personified in Satan is effectively captured in the renewed Rite of Christian Initiation of Adults:

Father of eternal life,

you are a God, not of the dead, but of the living:

you sent your Son to proclaim the good news of life,

to rescue men from the kingdom of death

and to lead them to resurrection.

Free these chosen people

from the power of the evil spirit who brings death.

May they receive new life from Christ

and bear witness to his resurrection.

We ask this through Christ our Lord. Amen.

(*The Rites of the Catholic Church*, New York: Pueblo Publishing Co., 1976, p. 82.)

THE KINGDOM OF GOD:
THE DESTINY OF CREATION AND HUMANITY
Old Testament

Although Jesus repeatedly referred to the Kingdom of God in his preaching—indeed he began his whole ministry with the announcement that the Kingdom of God was at hand (Mark 1:15)—he never once paused to define it. Nor did any of his hearers ever interrupt him to ask him to define it. Jesus used the term with the apparent assurance that his listeners knew what he meant. And they did. The Kingdom of God was an integral part of contemporary Jewish vocabulary. It was something they all understood and longed for. As we already noted (in chapter 12) and shall note again in the next section (on the preaching of Jesus), the notion of the Kingdom received a radically new interpretation from Jesus, but the interpretation did not break the line of continuity reaching far back into the history of Israel and the pages of the Old Testament.

Although the precise *origins* of the term *Kingdom of God* cannot be determined, it developed sometime during the period of the wandering in the desert. The earliest source we come across is the ancient canticle of the sea, sung by Moses and the children of Israel after their crossing of the Red Sea and the destruction of the Egyptians (Exodus 15:11-13,18). And this was "no idea picked up along the way by cultural borrowing, nor was it the creation of the monarchy and its institutions, nor yet the outgrowth of the frustration of national ambition, however much all these factors may have colored it. On the contrary, it is linked with Israel's whole notion of herself as the chosen people of God, and this in turn was woven into the texture of her faith from the beginning" (John Bright, *The Kingdom of God: The Biblical Concept and Its Meaning for the Church*, New York: Abingdon Press, 1953, p. 19).

Subsequent references to the provident and protecting Lordship of Yahweh show that Israel experienced the kingship of Yahweh in the historical action of God. But that kingship was also beyond history. On the one hand, David becomes aware that his own kingdom was instituted by God and established by God's grace forever (2 Samuel 7:12-16). On the other hand, Gideon, the judge, can declare: "I will not rule over you, nor shall my son rule over you. The Lord must rule over you" (Judges 8:23). Furthermore, the Kingdom is at once localized and universal. Thus, God is said to be in royal residence in the ark of the covenant (Exodus 25:8; 40:34-38; Numbers 14:10), but Yahweh's throne is also in heaven itself, and "All the earth is filled with his glory" (Isaiah 6:3). Yahweh's rule, therefore, is not over Israel alone, but over all people (Amos 9:7; Jeremiah 10:7,10-12; Psalm 22:29-30; Isaiah 44:24-28; 45:1-6). Indeed, the whole of creation, and not merely the Gentiles, is destined to share in the Kingdom of God's peace (Hosea 2:20; Isaiah 35:1-10). Everything will be brought together at the end in a divine banquet (Isaiah 25:6-8).

The *liturgical life* of Israel disclosed yet another dialectical aspect of the Kingdom: It is at once present and future. God even now reigns over and guides the people of Israel, all nations, and the whole created order. But in times of severe affliction Yahweh's rule is perceived to be withdrawn temporarily, and Israel prays in hope that one day Yahweh will powerfully restore the Kingdom and destroy Israel's oppressors. Thus, after the fall of the monarchy the so-called royal Psalms (2, 18, 20, 21, 72, 101, 110, 132, 144:1-11) are "spiritualized," and the king is now identified with the messianic king who is to come.

This hope in a future liberation is particularly emphasized in the *prophetic literature*. All peoples will drink of the cup of God's wrath (Jeremiah 25:15-29). Yahweh will deliver the wicked to the sword (25:30-38). The godless armies will be annihilated (Ezekiel 39:1-7), and all nations will see the glory of God and the divine judgment (39:21). A similarly cosmic vision is sketched by Isaiah (24-27) and in Daniel (2 and 7). Jerusalem is identified as the focal point of God's new reign over Israel (Micah 4:7), and the return of the Israelites shall be like a second Exodus (7:14-15). It is to the mountain of God (Zion) in Jerusalem that all nations will stream (Micah 4:1-4; Isaiah 2:2-4), and the glory of God will be manifested there (Jeremiah 16:19; Isaiah 56:7; 60; 66:19-21; Zechariah 2:14-17; 8:20-22; 14:16).

This universal kingship will bear fruit in a whole new moral order where the will of God is operative. As a result, peace will be achieved among the peoples of the earth (Isaiah 2:4; Zechariah

9:9-10) through the Messiah who is the prince of peace, and God will be revealed again as a shepherd (Isaiah 40:11), but a kingly one (43:15; 44:6). The Lord comes, not to punish and to judge, but to bring peace, goodness, and salvation: "How beautiful upon the mountains are the feet of him who brings glad tidings, announcing peace, bearing good news, announcing salvation, and saying to Zion, 'Your God is King!' " (52:7). Jesus begins his own ministry in the same spirit (Mark 1:14; compare also Isaiah 61:1 with Luke 4:18 and Matthew 11:5). And so it is *Deutero-Isaiah* (or Second Isaiah, chapters 40-55) which most directly anticipates Jesus' own conception of the Kingdom.

In *later Judaism*, however, a more nationalistic orientation develops, and this, too, persists into the New Testament and creates a problem for Jesus. The two sons of Zebedee, for example, vie for the first places in the messianic kingdom of Jesus (Mark 10:37), and Peter himself tries to deter the Lord from the way of suffering (8:32). In direct contrast to this nationalistic eschatology which focused on Palestine and the earthly Jerusalem, *apocalyptic* (from the Hebrew *gālāh* and the Greek *apocalypsis*, meaning "revelation") literature directed its vision rather to the heavenly Jerusalem and to paradise as the abode of the elect and the blessed. The book of Daniel provides the original pattern for this literature. The heavenly origin and character of the Kingdom emerges clearly in the vision of the four beasts and the one who is like the Son of Man, who appears in the clouds of heaven after judgment is rendered on the beasts (7:9-12). The whole scene takes place in heaven. "However we interpret the 'Son of man', he is in no sense an earthly savior who wages war in God's name and exercises justice. He is a heavenly and pre-existent being" (Rudolf Schnackenburg, *God's Rule and Kingdom*, p. 65).

The apocalypses, therefore, place the strongest possible emphasis on God's sovereign action and final intervention without any cooperation at all on our part. They sometimes think they can determine the moment of the divine intervention and recognize the signs that will precede it. Accordingly, they divide the history of the world into periods, on the lines of the four world empires (Daniel 2:37-45), or according to weeks of years and jubilees, seven times seven, or after the seventy shepherds of the people, etc. They inquire how much of the course of world history has already elapsed and then work out the conclusion. And, finally, they look for signs and portents such as earthquakes, plagues, confusion, fighting, the fall of rulers and princes (Daniel 12:1). They dwell upon the fantastic and the fearsome and boast of special apocalyptic knowledge, concealed from the common person. There appear a spirit of revenge and a perverted joy in the annihilation of the wicked. However noble the apocalyptic conception of the Kingdom, much of this literature is marred by pettiness, narowness, and self-righteousness. It is also characterized by an individualism that weakens the community's commitment to the abiding struggle for justice and peace and the transformation of all creation.

The Preaching of Jesus

What caught Jesus' contemporaries by surprise was his proclamation that the Kingdom of God was close at hand (Mark 1:15). Thus, he called for conversion and repentance (Luke 10:13-15; Matthew 11:20-24; Luke 13:1-5; 19:41-44) and underlined the importance of watching and being ready for the Kingdom (Luke 12:35-40; Matthew 25:1-13). In the final accounting, however, the Kingdom comes from divine power and grace (Mark 4:26-29). God gives it (Luke 12:32) or assigns it (22:29-30). It is especially for sinners (Mark 2:16-17; Luke 7:34 = Matthew 11:19; Luke 15:7,10,24,32;18:10-14;19:7; Matthew 21:31). The scandal aroused by Jesus' associating with publicans and prostitutes (Mark 2:15-17; Luke 7:34,36-50;19:7) showed how unexpected his proclamation and interpretation of the Kingdom had been. Jesus emphasizes always the mercy of God (Matthew 18:23-35), and, unlike the prophets, he presupposes in his call for repentance that God's redemptive activity on our behalf has already begun (Mark 1:15). In the beatitudes in the Sermon on the Mount, he insists that God shows special favor toward the poor, the oppressed, the despised, the persecuted (Matthew 5:1-12). In fact, entrance into the Kingdom will be determined in large measure by our response to the neighbor in need (Matthew 25:31-46).

Jesus also excluded a political interpretation of the Kingdom; not that the values of the Kingdom have no political consequences, but that its coming is not dependent upon any one political order. He did not accept the widespread Jewish hope for a political kingdom, nor did he cooperate with the Zealots in their own activities against Roman rule. Why else did he conceal the messianic character of his work, as is evident especially in Mark's Gospel? Indeed, he reminds the Sadducees that after the resurrection from the dead there will be no marrying in heaven (Mark 12:24-25).

But Jesus also excluded an elitist understanding of the Kingdom. He carried his ministry to the whole of Israel, just and sinners alike, even the outcasts and the despised. He leaves the separation of the good from the bad to the final judgment (Matthew 13:24-30,47-50) and tolerates failures even within his own circle of followers (Mark 14:27,30; Luke 22:31-34). The doors to the Kingdom are open to all, including those from East and West. Some of the children of the Kingdom will be found unworthy and will be cast out into the exterior darkness (Matthew 8:11-23; Luke 13:24-28). What will be decisive is not membership in Israel but the fulfillment of the call to conversion (Matthew 21:43; Mark 12:1-9). To be converted is to seek first the Kingdom of God (Matthew 6:25-33). The Kingdom will come when the will of God is done (6:9-13).

Doing the will of God involves discipleship (Luke 9:57-60 = Matthew 8:19-22; Luke 9:61-62; Mark 10:21; Mark 9:38 = Luke 9:49), which makes absolute demands upon each disciple (Luke 14:33). He calls for a renunciation of earthly goods when these become an obstacle to entry into the Kingdom (Mark 10:24-27). He takes under his influence those who have made themselves eunuchs for the Kingdom (Matthew 19:12) but does not impose celibacy on all.

Jesus' works give substance to his preaching. His healings and exorcisms are signs that the Kingdom has drawn near in him: "But if it is by the finger of God that I cast out devils, then the reign of God is upon you" (Luke 11:20). When the disciples of John the Baptist come out into the desert to inquire whether or not Jesus is the Messiah, he tells them to go back to John and report what they themselves have seen and heard: ". . . the blind recover their sight, cripples walk, lepers are cured, the deaf hear, dead men are raised to life, and the poor have the good news preached to them" (Matthew 11:4-5). Although Jesus had a unique relationship to God (Matthew 11:25-27), it is not his Kingdom but the Father's (Luke 12:32; 22:29-30), who alone knows the hour of its final coming (Matthew 24:36). In the meantime, we can pray for it (Matthew 6:10; Luke 11:2). But because it *is* the Father's work and because the manifestation of the Father's love cannot be understood in this world's terms, Jesus made no attempt to describe the Kingdom, much less define it, except in parables (Mark 4:33-34). (See chapter 12.)

Early Christianity

With the death and resurrection of Jesus there is a remarkable shift from the proclamation of the Kingdom of God to the proclamation of the Lordship of Jesus (Romans 10:9; 1 John 5:1; John 20:31). The historical details of this transition are probably lost to us forever. But this is not to say that the early Church corrupted the original message of Jesus. On the contrary, the Kingdom of God was still at the core of the primitive proclamation (Acts of the Apostles 1:3; 13:16-41; 28:23,31). Furthermore, insofar as Jesus identified himself so closely with his message that he can be regarded as the very incarnation of the Kingdom of God, the early Church's proclamation of Jesus as the Christ represents no fundamental departure from Jesus' own preaching. Jesus' Gospel about the Kingdom of God thereby became the Church's Gospel about Jesus, the Christ of God.

The early Church recognized not only that the Kingdom of God had broken into history in a new and definitive way in Jesus Christ but also that it continued to grow and develop in the course of post-resurrection history. This is particularly characteristic of the *Lucan* writings (the third Gospel and the Acts of the Apostles). We are living now between-the-times: between the decisive inbreaking of the Kingdom in Jesus Christ and the fulfillment of the Kingdom at the Second Coming of Christ when history is brought to perfection.

Paul speaks only rarely of the Kingdom of God (1 Corinthians 6:10; 15:50; Galatians 5:21). It is realized in the Lordship of Christ (1 Corinthians 15:24; Colossians 1:13) and is present to the faithful (Colossians 3:1-4) in the Church (1:18,24). The exalted Christ continues to exercise his sovereignty over the world through the Church (Ephesians 1:21-23; 3:10; 4:8-10), and that Lordship will be brought to completion at the Second Coming, when God will be all in all (1 Corinthians 15:24-28). Christ's rule, therefore, extends beyond the Church.

Except for one text (John 3:5) the term "Kingdom of God" does not occur in the *Johannine* writings. At times there are glimpses into the future: resurrection of the body, judgment, and eternal life (5:28-29; 12:25). History is the battlefield where the powers of Satan war against the reign of God in Christ (Revelation 11:15; 20:4).

The *early Church*, consequently, is always conscious that the Kingdom of God under Christ is still on the way, and that the Church itself is a pilgrim people, strangers and sojourners in this world (1 Peter). Christ's rule is hidden now, but it will be manifested fully in the end, when the Kingdom of God will be realized in all its perfection. And nowhere is the orientation of the Church toward the Kingdom more explicitly revealed than in its Eucharist, which anticipates the eating and drinking at the Lord's table in the Kingdom (Luke 22:30).

Christian Theology: Before the Twentieth Century

Early patristic theology was influenced by the notion of the Lordship of Jesus and the imminence of his Second Coming (e.g., Ignatius of Antioch, *Letter to the Ephesians*, 11). There were also some apocalyptic elements—e.g., the notion of the thousand-year reign in Justin's *Trypho* (80-81) and Tertullian's *Against Marcion* (3, 24). The reign of God in Clement of Alexandria and in Origen tends to be spiritualized. Prayer for the coming of the Kingdom is a petition for wisdom and knowledge (Origen, *On Prayer*, 13). This strongly interiorized concept of the Kingdom prevailed in the East, especially under the philosophical influence of neo-Platonism. Eusebius of Caesarea (d. ca. 340), however, offered a kind of political theology of the Kingdom by referring to the earthly Roman empire, with its enforcement of peace, as the image of the Kingdom.

In the West, the Church became increasingly identified with the Kingdom of God. This is especially evident in *Augustine*: "It follows that the Church even now is the kingdom of Christ and the kingdom of heaven" (*City of God*, book XX, chapter 9). Even more significant is Augustine's notion of the two cities: the city of God and the earthly city. It would seem that the city of God is closely connected, if not simply identified, with the Kingdom of God. The city of God, he says, is "on pilgrimage in this world, and it is by regeneration that it is brought to another world, whose children neither generate nor are generated" (XV, 20). In any case, Augustine introduces a distinction here which probably laid the foundation for Martin Luther's distinctive doctrine of the two kingdoms; and this, in turn, was at the root of so much of the indifference to social and political questions within Christianity between the Reformation and the nineteenth century. The Kingdom of God is God's work alone. We can do absolutely nothing to bring it about. The kingdom of humankind, on the other hand, is destined to pass away without a trace. Therefore, what point is there in striving to alter the face of this earth, since it will not survive? Only God's work will endure.

For Augustine the earthly city is created by self-love and with contempt for God, whereas the city of God, or heavenly city, is created by the love of God and has contempt for self. The earthly city glories in itself; the heavenly city glories in the Lord. The earthly city lusts for domination; the heavenly city seeks to serve others. The earthly city operates according to human standards; the heavenly city fulfills the will of God. The earthly city is destined for eternal punishment; the heavenly city is destined to reign with God for all eternity. The earthly city is begotten from Cain; the heavenly city, from Abel. The earthly city is born of nature, like Ishmael; the heavenly city is born of promise, like Isaac. And the earthly city is divided against itself; the heavenly city enjoys eternal and perfect peace (*City of God*, XIV, 28—XV, 1-5).

This is not to say that the parallels are always clear and consistent. Thus, Augustine sometimes writes of the earthly city as if it had two aspects itself: one good and one evil: "One part of the earthly city has been made into an image of the Heavenly City, by symbolizing something other than itself, namely that other City; and for that reason it is a servant. For it was established not for its own sake but in order to symbolize another City . . ." (XV, 2). The evil part, in turn, is divided against itself as were Remus and Romulus, ". . . for this is how Rome was founded, when Remus, as Roman history witnesses, was slain by his brother Romulus. The difference from the primal crime was that both brothers were citizens of the earthly city" (XV, 5).

An even more pronounced identification of the Kingdom of God and the Church is found in the succeeding centuries in such writings as those of Pope Gregory the Great, who interpreted Luke 9:27 ("I assure you, there are some standing here who will not taste death until they see the reign of God") to apply to the Church, which is opposed to the "power and glory" of the world.

Once the Franks came to power in the West, this ecclesiastical interpretation of the Kingdom of God was fully *politicized*. Charlemagne was the new David who had taken over the reins of royal lordship in the Church, allowing the pope the role of Moses at prayer (see his *Letter to Leo III*), while remaining himself the sovereign who shared in the reign of Christ and of God. This same notion was one of the inspirations of the Crusades and was used to justify the investiture of bishops by kings.

Apocalyptic notions were then added to the political. The kingdom of the Franks along with that of the Romans was regarded as the "third kingdom" mentioned in the seventh chapter of Daniel, following the kingdoms of the Greeks and the Persians. Thus, the world awaited a last ruler to restore the empire to its glory and lay down his crown in Jerusalem, before the coming of the Antichrist. The most direct opposition to this imperial notion of the Kingdom of God was formulated by Pope Boniface VIII's bull, *Unam Sanctam* (1303), in which he declared that the pope alone has supreme authority over the whole world.

Joachim of Fiore (d. 1202) was the principal source of yet another interpretation of the Kingdom in the medieval period. He divided history into three great periods: (1) the age of the Father (the time of the Old Testament when the human community lived under the Law); (2) the age of the Son (the time of the New Testament and for forty-two generations of about thirty years each, or until the year 1260, during which the human community lived under grace); and (3) the age of the Spirit, in which there would be new religious orders leading to the conversion of the world and the establishment of a spiritual church. Some carried Joachim's vision to extremes—e.g., the Spiritual Franciscans, who saw Francis of Assisi as the "angel with the sign of the living God" ushering in the age of the Spirit, and the Fraticelli, who regarded themselves as the new order of spiritual men foretold by Joachim. This view of the Kingdom persisted well into the Middle Ages and would influence some of the Protestant sects at the margin of the Reformation movement—e.g., Bohemian Brethren and the Anabaptists.

Dominican *mysticism*—e.g., Meister Eckhart, Tauler, Suso—saw the Kingdom of God as "God himself with all his riches" in the depths of the soul, but this notion coexisted with the more ecclesiastical and political interpretations put forth by Martin Bucer (d. 1551), Tommaso Campanella (d. 1639), and Thomas More (d. 1535) in his *Utopia* (1516).

Luther's doctrine of the two kingdoms rejected both the sectarian interpretations as well as the grand theocratic understanding of the Kingdom as proposed by some Catholics. God's reign is essentially invisible and spiritual. The law is the affair of the secular powers. The Church is concerned only with the preaching of the Gospel. Salvation is through faith, not works. The two kingdoms "must be sharply distinguished," he wrote ("Secular Authority: To What Extent It Should Be Obeyed," in *Martin Luther: Selections From His Writings*, John Dillenberger, ed., New York: Doubleday Anchor, 1961, p. 371). The one kingdom produces piety; the other brings about external peace and prevents evil deeds. Each needs the other. Without piety, there is only hypocrisy. Without law, however, evil is given free reign. (For an understanding of Protestant thought on this question as it developed in the United States from its beginnings, see H. Richard

Niebuhr, *The Kingdom of God in America*, New York: Harper & Row, 1937.)

By the eighteenth century, and particularly under the impact of the *Enlightenment*, the Kingdom of God was once again perceived not only as an earthly reality but even as the product of human initiative and effort. It comes about through the establishment of human society according to moral principles. Immanuel Kant defined the Kingdom as an "ethical commonwealth" (*Religion Within the Limits of Pure Reason Alone*). Other philosophical interpretations were placed upon it. Hegel, for example, saw it as the final manifestation of the spirit in which it becomes fully conscious of itself. It is the completion and perfection of history. The same evolutionary and historical understanding shaped the thinking of Karl Marx and then, in the twentieth century, of the Marxist philosopher Ernst Bloch (d. 1977) who inspired much of the "theology of hope" movement in Europe in the 1960s. The future now becomes decisive. *Praxis* replaces reflection, or theory. We are called to participate in the struggle to bring the future kingdom into the present, to narrow the gap between justice and injustice, freedom and oppression. But in none of these views is the sovereignty of God the "incalculable and impenetrable irruption of grace in love" (Peter Hünermann, "Reign of God," *The Concise Sacramentum Mundi*, p. 1356). The Kingdom of God becomes equivalently the kingdom of humankind. It was against this Liberal (i.e., anti-transcendental) interpretation that modern biblical scholarship reacted, as we shall see in the next section (on twentieth-century biblical theology).

At the same time, other interpretations of the Kingdom of God from within the churches adhered to a less historical, more *"spiritual"* line. Thus, for Blaise Pascal (d. 1662) the Kingdom was the order of charity which takes us out of ourselves, and the realm where we experience the forgiveness of sins and the friendship of God. With the rise of the Tübingen School in Germany (see chapter 25), the Kingdom of God becomes "the idea of Christianity which contains and produces all others" (e.g., J. S. Drey, *Introduction to the Study of Theology*). J. B. Hirscher took it to be the "basic idea" for Christian moral theology. Entrance is gained by conversion, and the Kingdom itself is the rule of God in every realm of life.

Twentiety-Century Biblical Theology

Futurist Eschatology: The Kingdom as Future

There is a sense in which it can be said that modern New Testament scholarship begins with the debate about the eschatological question. Over against the dominant nineteenth-century Liberal Protestant view that the Kingdom of God is an earthly reality produced by human hands (Albrecht Ritschl, d. 1889), New Testament exegetes like Albert Schweitzer (d. 1965) and Johannes Weiss (d. 1914) argued that the disciples were to pray for the coming of the Kingdom but that neither they nor we could do anything to establish it. Not even Jesus could do that. When the Kingdom comes, God will destroy this old order which is ruled and spoiled by the devil and will create a completely new world (see Johannes Weiss, *Jesus' Proclamation of the Kingdom of God*, Philadelphia: Fortress Press, 1971; originally published in 1892). A more recent expression of this school of thought, known as *futurist (or consequent, consistent, or thorough-going) eschatology*, is offered by Martin Werner. The irruption of the Kingdom, he argues, signified for Jesus the end of the present natural world. The Kingdom, therefore, was in no sense a present reality. It is always in the future, but imminent (*The Formation of Christian Dogma*, Boston: Beacon Press, 1965).

Realized Eschatology: The Kingdom As Past

Selecting a different set of New Testament passages, the British scholar Charles H. Dodd (d. 1973) argued that "in the earliest tradition Jesus was understood to have proclaimed that the Kingdom of God, the hope of many generations, had at last come. It is not merely imminent; it is here. . . . The *eschaton* has moved from the future to the present, from the sphere of expectation into that of realized experience" (*The Parables of the Kingdom*, London: Collins/Fontana, 1963, pp. 40-41; originally published in 1935). For Dodd, however, the challenge of the Kingdom is a challenge for individuals and for the immediate situation, for "Jesus passed directly from the immediate situation to the eternal order lying beyond all history" (p. 154). History moves by crisis, not by evolution. The Church proclaims the Gospel of the Kingdom that each might experience the "hour of decision" that Jesus brought (p. 152). The school of "realized eschatology" assumes, therefore, that "history in the individual life is of the same stuff as history at large; that is, it is significant in so far as it serves to bring men face to face with God in his Kingdom, power and glory." (See also Joachim Jeremias, *The Parables of Jesus*, New York: Charles Scribner's Sons, 1955.)

Existentialist Eschatology: The Kingdom As Present

For Rudolf Bultmann (d. 1976) the Kingdom of God is a new mode of existential existence, for ". . . the question of God and the question of myself are identical" (*Jesus Christ and Mythology*, London: SCM Press, 1958, p. 53). The living God encounters us here and now in the Word, i.e., in the preaching instituted by Jesus Christ. "The idea of the omnipresent and almighty God becomes real in my personal existence only by His Word spoken here and now" (p. 79). The decisive significance of Jesus Christ is that he—in his person, his coming, his passion, and his glorification—is the eschatological event. That event happens here and now in the preaching of the Word regardless of whether this Word is accepted or rejected (p. 81). "It is only in the light of the proclaimed word that what has happened or is happening here or there assumes the character of God's action for the believer" (p. 85). Our relation to the world remains paradoxical. It is our world, but it is really God's. We must live as if it is not ours at all.

This highly existential, present-oriented, and anti-political understanding of the Kingdom is even more explicitly developed in *Jesus and the Word* (London: Collins/Fontana, 1958; originally published in 1934). The Kingdom of God is "no ideal social order" (p. 78). Jesus paid no apparent attention to the social and economic conditions of his time. *"No programme for world-reformation is derived from the will of God"* (p. 79). Instead, every person stands under the judgment of God at this moment. The decision is against the world and for God. Every claim of one's own is to be silenced. "The *real* future stands before man in decision, not the false future over which he already has control, but the future which will give him a character which he does not yet have" (p. 96).

Salvation-History Eschatology: The Kingdom As Past, Present, and Future

Directly opposed to Bultmann's existentialist interpretation is Oscar Cullmann's notion of salvation history. The Kingdom of God has its beginning at creation, reaches its zenith or midpoint in Jesus Christ, and will be brought to completion at the *Parousia*, or Second Coming. We live now "between-the-times," i.e., between the first and second comings of Christ. This is also "church-time." The mission of the Church is to recall what God has already accomplished in Christ, to focus the attention of the world on the events to come, and to make possible, here and now, a meeting with the Lord through the preaching of the Word and the celebration of the sacraments. What finally distinguishes Christian faith, therefore, from other views of reality is the Christian's conviction that history itself is salvific and that it moves with purpose and direction. Everything leads up to, and flows from, the central Christ-event (see *Christ and Time*, Philadelphia: Westminster Press, 1947).

In a later work he acknowledged the bitter dispute with Bultmann evoked by *Christ and Time*. Cullmann insists in his *Salvation in History* (New York: Harper & Row, 1967) that he agrees with Bultmann that the call to decision is essential to the New Testament faith. Where they disagree, he insists, is over Bultmann's exclusion of salvation history as if it were simply opposed to Christian existence as portrayed in the New Testament. Rather, we find both elements there: the call to decision and salvation history. "By our decision in faith we align ourselves with this very special history, salvation history...comprehending past, present, and future..." (p. 21).

Other contemporary biblical scholars who recognize the threefold temporal dimension of the Kingdom include Rudolf

Schnackenburg (*God's Rule and Kingdom*, 1963), Werner G. Küm-
mel (*Promise and Fulfillment: The Eschatological Message of
Jesus*, London: SCM Press, 1956), and Norman Perrin (*Jesus and
the Language of the Kingdom*, Philadelphia: Fortress Press, 1976).

Twentieth-Century Systematic Theology

Catholic Theologians

Karl Rahner: The Kingdom of God and the Church are not one
and the same. The Church is the sacrament of the Kingdom in the
"eschatological phase of sacred history which began with Christ,
the phase which brings about the kingdom of God" ("Church and
World," *The Concise Sacramentum Mundi*, p. 239). The Kingdom
will not be definitively present until history ends with the Second
Coming of Christ and the last judgment. On the other hand, the
Kingdom is not something totally in the future. It is already
coming to be in the history of the world, wherever obedience to
God occurs in grace as the acceptance of God's self-communication. But this does not take place solely in the Church nor solely in
the personal inwardness of conscience, but in the concrete fulfillment of an earthly task, of active love of others, even of collective
love of others.

All of this follows from basic Catholic principles: (1) that
grace and justification are to be found also outside the Church;
(2) that there is an inseparable unity between material and formal
morality, between action and intention; and (3) that there is a
fundamental unity between love of God and love of neighbor.
This Kingdom is manifested in the "unity, activity, fraternity,
etc., of the *world*" (p. 240).

Is the Kingdom the work of God, or the product of human
effort? Rahner argues that this question can be answered only
dialectically, i.e., by holding in balance two apparently opposed
principles: (1) the Kingdom of God will come about at the end of
history as an action of God; and (2) human history enters somehow
into that endpoint. Thus, human history has ultimate validity, and
yet it will undergo radical transformation. These two propositions
remain unresolved and so must remain dialectically related in

order to keep the future open (God will give the Kingdom when God wills) and to allow the present to keep its basic importance (human effort somehow enters into God's final act). What is permanent in history is the concrete work of love.

Why can it be said that history enters into God's own fullness? "Because the Word of God has himself both made and endured history" ("Christianity and the new earth," *Theology Digest*, 15, Winter 1967, p. 281). Rahner's notion of the Kingdom, therefore, is rooted in the basic Catholic principle of sacramentality, centered in the incarnation.

Edward Schillebeeckx: Schillebeeckx notes that one of the first changes effected by the Second Vatican Council was its abandoning of the earlier tendency to identify the Church too easily with the Kingdom of God. The council also acknowledged the presence of saving grace outside the Church. For Schillebeeckx the Church and the world are on the way to the Kingdom, but are not yet the Kingdom. The powers of the Kingdom, however, are already actively present in the Church and in the world at large. It is, in fact, our common hope in the radically new and final Kingdom that stimulates us never to rest satisfied with what has already been achieved in this world. Historically, we can never say that *this* is the promised future. The Gospel message calls us always to overcome the limitations of the present. It contains a permanent criticism of the present: institutions, structures, mentalities. It urges constant improvement. "Eschatological hope makes the commitment to the temporal order *radical* and by the same token declares any already existing temporal order to be only relative. Thus the Christian's social and political commitment, rooted in his care for mankind, is the hermeneutic of what in Revelation the Kingdom of God's promise implies" (*God the Future of Man*, New York: Sheed & Ward, 1968, p. 161).

For Schillebeeckx, the Kingdom of God is "the divine power itself in its saving activity within our history, but at the same time the final, eschatological state of affairs that brings to an end the evil world, dominated by the forces of calamity and woe, and initiates the new world in which God 'appears to full advantage'; 'your kingdom come' (Matthew 6:10)" (*Jesus: An Experiment in*

Christology, New York: Seabury Press, 1979, p. 141). Thus, present and future are essentially interrelated.

God's Lordship is God's mode of being God. God is shown as a loving and caring God who is mindful of humanity (Titus 3:4). The Kingdom of God is our well-being. To surrender to the Lordship of God is to love the other, to work for the other's well-being. "Man's caring for his fellow-men is the visible form and aspect in which the coming of God's kingdom is manifested; it is the way God's Lordship takes" (p. 153). In its fullness, therefore, Jesus' message of the Kingdom is that we must love one another as God loves us, and he (Jesus) discloses this in and through his own mode of conduct, i.e., his *praxis* of the Kingdom. Jesus brings the message that God says "No" to the continuing course of human suffering, to all forms of hunger and poverty, and that the purpose of life and history is "peace, laughter, total satisfaction: the 'final good' of salvation and happiness.... Showing mercy is, despite everything, the deepest purpose that God intends to fulfill in history" (p. 177).

Jesus is the sacrament of God's universal love for us. He is "God translated" for us. Jesus shows us a "most human God" (*Deus humanissimus*). "The cause of God as the cause of man is personified in the very person of Jesus Christ.... He is the firstborn and 'the leader' of a new mankind in that he has lived out proleptically in his own experience, the praxis of the kingdom of God and because that praxis has been endorsed by God" (p. 670).

Hans Küng: In the light of modern exegesis, Küng asserts, it is impossible to speak of the Church as the Kingdom of God on earth, nor does the Church build up the Kingdom. The Kingdom is *God's* Kingdom. "Man's part is the way of readiness and openness, obedience and watchfulness, faith and repentance" (*The Church*, New York: Sheed & Ward, 1968, p. 92). The Church is the work of humanity; the Kingdom is the work of God. It is not the Church but the Kingdom which is the goal of creation. To belong to the Church is no guarantee of entrance into the Kingdom. The Church is the anticipatory sign of the Kingdom. The Church moves always toward the Kingdom as its goal. It does not bring the Kingdom; it announces it. God alone brings about the Kingdom; the Church is devoted entirely to its service.

Thus, the Kingdom is not merely God's continuing rule, existing from the moment of creation, but is that which is promised for the future. It is not a religio-political theocracy or democracy, but the immediate, unrestricted rule of God over the world, to be awaited without recourse to violence. It is not for an elite but is the glad tidings of God's infinite goodness and unconditional grace, particularly for the abandoned and the destitute. It is not constructed by human effort but is an act of God. It will, therefore, be a Kingdom of "absolute righteousness, of unsurpassable freedom, of dauntless love, of universal reconciliation, of everlasting peace" (*On Being a Christian*, New York: Doubleday, 1976, p. 215). Just as a false interiorizing of the Kingdom once had to be avoided, so a false secularizing of the Kingdom now is to be avoided. In language close to Bultmann's, Küng insists that our situation is critical. We are "pressed to make a final decision, to accept the offer to commit [ourselves] *to the reality of God*, which is ahead....It is a decision in which everything is at stake: an either-or, for or against God" (p. 225).

Walter Kasper: A similar approach is taken by Walter Kasper. The Kingdom of God is "totally and exclusively God's doing. It cannot be earned by religious or moral effort, imposed by political struggle, or projected in calculation. We cannot plan for it, organize it, make it or build it, we cannot invent or imagine it. It is given (Matthew 21:43, Luke 12:32), 'appointed' (Luke 22:29). We can only inherit it (Matthew 25:34)" (*Jesus the Christ*, New York: Paulist Press, 1976, p. 81). This is not to say that we can do nothing at all in relation to the Kingdom. We are not condemned to Quietism or pure passivity. "What is demanded of us is repentance and faith (Mark 1:15 and parallels)." It means ceasing to rely on one's own capabilities, admitting human powerlessness. It means expecting nothing from oneself and everything from God.

With an explicitly Hegelian flavor, Kasper insists that God's divinity consists in God's self-giving, or God's entering into the other without losing "himself." Indeed,"...he is himself precisely when he enters into that which is other than himself. It is by surrendering himself that he shows his divinity. Concealment is therefore the way in which God's glory is revealed in the world" (p. 83). Jesus' message announces that the "ultimate source and meaning of all reality is now becoming a reality in a new and final form. The final decision about the meaning of reality is now being made. With the entry of the Kingdom of God the world enters into salvation."

Johannes Metz: If Küng and Kasper emphasize the role of God in the coming of the Kingdom, Johannes Metz stresses the role of human effort in the political realm.

Christian theology veered too far in an existentialist, personalist, indeed *privatized* direction under the influence of Rudolf Bultmann, Metz argues. The future dimension was all but lost, and so, too, the critical function of theology. "Modern man" no longer experiences the world as an imposed fate, but rather as raw material which has to be shaped and directed into something greater. Christian faith is guided by hope, a "crucified hope for the world." Such a hope is "an initiative for the passionate innovating and changing of the world toward the Kingdom of God" (*Theology of the World*, New York: Herder & Herder, 1969, p. 93). The Church exists within that world as that part of the world which calls the world in question when it takes itself with ultimate seriousness. "The eschatological City of God is *now* coming into existence, for our hopeful approach *builds* this city. We are workers building this future, and not just interpreters of this future. . . . The Christian is a 'co-worker' in bringing the promised universal era of peace and justice. The orthodoxy of a Christian's faith must constantly *make itself* true in the 'orthopraxy' of his actions orientated toward the final future, because the promised *truth* is a truth which must be *made* (see John 3:21ff.)" (pp. 94-95).

Metz rejects, therefore, an eschatology like Bultmann's which focuses on the "making present" of the Kingdom in the moment of personal decision, and also the eschatology of Weiss, Werner, and others, which makes life in this world a time of waiting until God brings about the Kingdom. Metz's eschatology is the basis of a *political theology*, a theology of the emerging social and political order. Political theology, therefore, is "a positive attempt to formulate the eschatological message under the conditions of our present society" (p. 107). It is theology which attends always to the relation between theory and practice, between understanding the faith and social practice.

Gustavo Gutierrez: A similarly strong emphasis on the social and political dimension of the Kingdom is given in Latin American liberation theology. Gustavo Gutierrez warns against a spiritualizing of the reality of the Kingdom. It is "inevitably historical, temporal, earthly, social, and material" (*A Theology of Liberation*, Maryknoll, N.Y.: Orbis Books, 1973, p. 167). The prophets announced a kingdom of peace, but peace presupposes justice. It presupposes the defense of the rights of the poor, punishment of the oppressors, liberation from oppression. The struggle for justice *is* the struggle for the Kingdom of God (p. 168). On the other hand, the Kingdom of God "must not be confused with the establishment of a just society" (p. 231).

The proclamation of the Kingdom, Gutierrez writes, opens up new horizons and leads us to see unsuspected dimensions and to pursue unexplored paths. Only within a commitment to liberation and in solidarity with the oppressed can we understand the meaning of the Kingdom and the implications of the Gospel message (p. 269). The alleviation of poverty and oppression is not identical with the Kingdom, but poverty and oppression are certainly incompatible with the Kingdom of love and justice (p. 295).

And this was the vision of Jesus as well. Misery and social injustice reveal a "sinful situation," a disintegration of community. By freeing us from sin, Jesus attacks the roots of an unjust social order. "Far from showing no interest in...liberation, Jesus rather placed it on a deeper level, with far reaching consequences" (p. 231). Jesus' announcement of the Kingdom is subversive because it heralds the end of domination of human beings over human beings. In preaching the universal love of the Father, Jesus inevitably preached against all injustice, privilege, oppression, and narrow nationalism (p. 232).

Protestant Theologians

Paul Tillich (d. 1965):   The entire fifth part of Tillich's *Systematic Theology* is devoted to the Kingdom of God and its relation to history. For Tillich, the Kingdom is the answer to the ambiguities of history. It has both an inner-historical and transhistorical side. "As inner-historical, it participates in the dynamics of history; as transhistorical, it answers the questions implied in the ambiguities of the dynamics of history" (*Systematic Theology*, vol. III, Chicago: University of Chicago Press, 1963, p. 357).

The first connotation of the Kingdom symbol is *political*, in that it is a manifestation of the power of God. The second characteristic is *social*, since there is no holiness without justice. The third element is *personal*, in that the Kingdom gives eternal meaning to the individual person. And the fourth characteristic is its *universality*, in that it is the fulfillment of all life and not only of human life.

The appearance of Jesus as the Christ is the historical event in which history becomes aware of itself and of its meaning. This is the central manifestation of the Kingdom (pp. 368-369). The churches represent the Kingdom of God but are not themselves identical with it (pp. 376-377). As for individuals, ". . . one cannot reach the transcendent Kingdom of God without participating in the struggle of the inner-historical Kingdom of God" (p. 392). The Kingdom is already present. We stand now in the face of the eternal. But we do so looking ahead toward the end of history and the end of all that is temporal in the eternal (p. 396).

Jürgen Moltmann: The Kingdom of God is a symbol for the "comprehensive Christian horizon of life" (*The Church in the Power of the Spirit*, New York: Harper & Row, 1977, p. 134). It requires conversion to the God of the future, and it brings liberation from the godless and inhuman relationships of this world. The Kingdom of God, therefore, is the "eschatological fulfillment of the liberating lordship of God in history" (p. 190). It is both the actual rule of God in the world and the universal goal of that divine rule. It is thus at once present and future. As present, it is relevant to our earthly concerns. As future, it cannot be identified with anything in history. It draws us into history and beyond history.

Through his own mission and resurrection Jesus has brought the Kingdom into history. It has become the power of the future which determines the present. We can already live in the light of the "new era" in the circumstances of the "old" one. "Since the eschatological becomes historical in this way, the historical also becomes eschatological" (p. 192). Moltmann calls this "messianic mediation." The Lordship of Christ points beyond itself to the Kingdom of God.

The presence of the Holy Spirit puts the new creation into force. Past, present, and future are brought together: "Just as the messianic era stands under the token of the 'not yet', so it also stands under the sign of 'no longer' and therefore under the sign of 'already'.... The dreams of hope lead to the pains of love" (p. 193). The Kingdom of God is the goal of history in the midst of history (p. 196).

The Church in the Power of the Spirit, in effect, broadens the horizon of Moltmann's earlier, and better known, *Theology of Hope* (New York: Harper & Row, 1967, pp. 325-338). Since the Kingdom has not yet come, everything is to be called into question which already identifies itself with the Kingdom. The Church is called to engage in the historic transformation of life into the Kingdom of righteousness, peace, freedom, and humanity. Its mission is shaped by its expectation of the coming Kingdom. To disclose to the world "the horizon of the future of the crucified Christ is the task of the Christian Church" (p. 338).

Wolfhart Pannenberg: Pannenberg defines the Kindgom of God variously as "that perfect society of men which is to be realized in history by God himself," as "the utterly concrete reality of justice and love," and as "the destiny of present society" (*Theology and the Kingdom of God*, Philadelphia: Westminster Press, 1969, pp. 76, 79, and 84). It is the rule, or sovereignty, of God; its principal effect is unity among humankind. That is why Jesus explained the will of God by the commandment of love. But it is not a purely interpersonal love. There is no dualism of religion and society, of love and justice. "Subjective behavior is related always to social institutions.... Obviously, then, the Kingdom of God is pointedly political" (pp. 79-80). Our present world, with its wars, injustices, and brutalities, demonstrates the gap between itself and the Kingdom of God. God's Kingdom has not yet come in all its fullness. No present form of life or society is ultimate. But this situation need not lead to political paralysis. "The future of the Kingdom releases a dynamic in the present that again and again kindles the vision of man and gives meaning to his fervent quest for the political forms of justice and love" (p. 80).

Harvey Cox: Much less emphatic about the *coming* character of the Kingdom and much more insistent on its this-wordly, socio-political dimension is Harvey Cox's *The Secular City* (New York: Macmillan, 1965). Close to the tradition of the Social Gospel Movement, which tended to identify the Kingdom with social and political reform (see Walter Rauschenbusch, *A Theology for the Social Gospel*, New York: Abingdon Press, 1945, pp. 131-145), Cox refers to the Kingdom as "the fullest possible disclosure of the partnerhsip of God and man in history" (p. 112). It is present in history, offering us "an objectively new social situation" and providing us an "occasion within which we are summoned to discard the old and take up something different" (p. 113).

Cox identifies himself thereby with those Protestant sectarians who have worked for the transformation of society: the Anabaptists, Congregationalists, Quakers, and others. "The mainline Reformers," he argues, "never developed a viable theology for social change, one of the most nagging needs of the modern church" (*The Secular City Debate*, Daniel Callahan, ed., New York: Macmillan, 1967, p. 193). Cox agrees, however, that the sectarians sometimes identified the marks of the Kingdom too quickly. Theologians like Reinhold Niebuhr were right in criticizing this tendency. But we may have gone too far in the opposite direction. "In guarding the Kingdom of God from ideological perversion, we rendered it politically irrelevant" (p. 194).

Reinhold Niebuhr (d. 1971):   It was Reinhold Niebuhr more than any other Protestant theologian who challenged both the Liberal equation of Kingdom and "secular city" and the progressive view of history upon which the equation was often based. It is not that history is static or that we have no tasks and obligations within it. Niebuhr insists, however, that grace is related to nature partly as fulfillment and partly as negation. "If the contradiction between 'nature' and 'grace' is not recognized, and the continued power of 'nature' in the realm of 'grace' is not conceded, new sins are brought into history by the pretension that sin has been progressively eliminated" (*The Nature and Destiny of Man*, vol. 2, New York; Charles Scribner's Sons, 1943, pp. 245-246).

"Nature" here represents "the historical possibilities of justice," and "grace" represents the "ideal possibility of perfect love. . . .[in] the complete obedience of all wills to the will of God" (p. 246). Thus, the relation between historical justice and the love of the Kingdom of God is dialectical. "Love is both the fulfillment and the negation of all achievements of justice in history. Or expressed from the opposite standpoint, the achievements of justice in history may rise in indeterminate degrees to find their fulfillment in a more perfect love and brotherhood; but each new level of fulfillment also contains elements which stand in contradiction to perfect love." We are bound to bring about justice in indeterminate degrees, but we can never achieve the perfection of justice within history. "Sanctification in the realm of social relations demands recognition of the impossibility of perfect sanctification" (p. 247).

The Kingdom, or sovereignty, of God, therefore, has the same two relations as eternity has to time. "It is on the one hand the authority of the source of life over all life at any moment. It is on the other hand a sovereignty which is finally vindicated in 'the end' " (p. 300, n. 1). History after Christ is an 'interim between the disclosure of its true meaning and the fulfillment of that meaning. . . .Sin is overcome in principle but not in fact. Love must continue to be suffering love rather than triumphant love. The distinction," he argues, "becomes a basic category of interpreting history in all profound versions of the Christian faith. . ." (p. 49).

The spirit of Niebuhr influenced even such activist Christians as Martin Luther King, Jr., who acknowledged that Niebuhr helped him to "recognize the complexity of man's social involvement and the glaring reality of collective evil" as well as "the illusions of a superficial optimism concerning human nature and the dangers of false idealism" (*Stride Toward Freedom*, New York: Harper & Row, 1958, p. 81).

Anglican Theologians

John A. T. Robinson: The former bishop of Woolwich in South London is best known for his controversial *Honest to God* (1963). In an earlier and must less heralded piece in *The Historic Episcopate in the Fullness of the Church* (Kenneth M. Carey, ed., London: Dacre Press, 1960), Robinson argued that the Kingdom of God is "the controlling category of biblical theology for both Old and New Testaments" (p. 15). The whole constitution of the universe has been transformed through Christ, although the transformation still remains to be acknowledged and fulfilled in obedience. To see all reality, including the Church, always in subordination to the Kingdom is to view everything as situated between the two great moments of Christ's sovereignty over the world: the finished work of Calvary and the Second Coming in glory.

Eschatology, therefore, is not just the teaching about the "last things" but rather the teaching about the relation of all things to the "last things," or about the finality of things. The Christian lives not *at* the end of time but rather *from* the end and *in* the end. Everything is seen from an eschatological perspective, and every moment is, in turn, an eschatological moment. "What the Christian faith provides is not a blue-print for the future of man....Its assurance rests in the fact that the whole of life is *response*, that the initiative—whether in the Beginning or the End—does not lie with us. It speaks of an evocation, a trust, an endurance, by which, in freedom, men find themselves impelled and drawn on. It points to those whose whole way of life betokens a 'beyond' that will not let them rest..." (*In the End God*, New York: Harper & Row, 1968, p. 139).

John Macquarrie: The Kingdom of God is "the full manifestation of the holiness of Being" (*Principles of Christian Theology*, New York: Charles Scribner's Sons, 1977, 2nd. ed., p. 369). It will issue forth in "a commonwealth of free beings, united in Being and with each other through love...." The Kingdom, although not to be identified with the Church, is already present in history. Macquarrie rejects both the extremes of a Liberalism which exaggerates human effort in the coming of the Kingdom, and of an apocalypticism which makes the Kingdom totally otherworldly. But his concern is directed perhaps more strongly against the former: "It is God who is the author of the kingdom, and it is his grace that is realizing it, albeit with the free cooperation of human beings. And while the eschatological interpretation may seem to become otherworldly in placing the kingdom beyond history, it is only being realistic. It is utopian and foolish to suppose that the kingdom could be realized on earth, though on the other hand it is not foolish to strive toward its increasing realization..." (p. 370). He returns to this point: "The eschatological consummation of the kingdom of God is a mystery to be realized by the movement of Being, not by creaturely striving, even if this makes an indispensable contribution. We delude ourselves if we think that some ideal state of affairs is attainable on earth, or that the main business of Christianity is to establish a super welfare state" (p. 519).

Norman Pittenger: Norman Pittenger is, as we have noted in chapter 14, a theologian of the process school of thought. God works in the world, Pittenger argues against the traditional eschatology, by providing "initial aims" for each occasion or event or occurrence or "entity." God's "power" is persuasion. God is present to history as a "lure" (Whitehead's term), not as a coercive force. For the Christian, Christ is the disclosure of what God is up to in the world. Talk about the "last things" is not talk about something that will happen only in the future, after death; rather, it is talk about us as we now live, in this world and with this world's responsibilities as well as its privileges.

Our purpose in life is to be the personalized instruments of cosmic Love. Everything we are and do has to be understood in light of that purpose. Thus, death reminds us that we are mortal and have only a relatively short time to contribute to humankind. Judgment means that we are what our decisions have made us. They cannot be undone. Heaven is the sheer joy of relationship with God and with one another. Hell is the absence of God. It is always and only a possibility—a possibility of rejecting God in freedom. But God's action surrounds us with love, and we respond in love. "The Lord came from God precisely in order to love, in order to be the humanly visible instrument of the divine charity. Christian theology...is nothing other than the explication and application of what that statement *means*" (*"The Last Things" in a Process Perspective,* London: Epworth Press, 1970, p. 105).

Orthodox Theology

John Meyendorff: The Kingdom of God is not one of the major categories of Orthodox theology (see the index of John

Meyendorff's *Byzantine Theology: Historical Trends and Doctrinal Themes*, New York: Fordham University Press, 1974). Where it is mentioned, it is linked always with the Holy Spirit, which is its "content" (p. 169). The prayer "Thy Kingdom come" is understood as "May Thy Holy Spirit come upon us and cleanse us." The Byzantine liturgical tradition addresses the Holy Spirit as "Heavenly King." The Spirit is the firstfruits of the eschatological transfiguration of creation. If salvation is understood essentially in terms of *participation* in, and *communion* with, the deified humanity of the incarnate Logos, it is the Spirit who makes this possible (p. 171). On the other hand, nowhere except in the *sacraments* can we achieve the "truly liberating divine life. . . . The Kingdom to come is already realized in the sacraments, but each individual Christian is called to grow into it, by exercising his own efforts and by using his own God-given freedom with the cooperation of the Spirit" (p. 176). But those efforts are not of a political or even ethical nature. They are part of the process toward "perfection" and "holiness."

Eschatology, however, qualifies the whole of Orthodox theology (p. 218). Everything is viewed in relation to the end, to our destiny in God. But that future reality is also a present experience, accessible in Christ through the gifts of the Spirit. Orthodox eschatology is a realized eschatology. The movement of humankind towards its goal is a mystical movement, not an historical movement (p. 219). We are moving "from glory to glory," i.e., to the moment when we will be restored to our original stature, which has been corrupted by sin and death. This will be the resurrection of the flesh.

Significantly, the last things (Second Coming, cosmic transfiguration, resurrection, and judgment) "are not subjects of detailed speculation by Byzantine theologians; yet they stand at the very center of Byzantine liturgical experience" (p. 220).

Official Teachings of the Church

Nowhere has the Kingdom of God been defined by the official magisterium, nor has any official position been taken regarding the precise relationship between the divine and the human, the transcendental and the immanent, the spiritual and the political in the Kingdom of God. One has to infer a doctrinal position from the explicit teachings on grace, Original Sin, and Jesus Christ (see chapters 4, 5, and 13).

Second Vatican Council

The most explicit conciliar declaration on the meaning of the Kingdom was given by the Second Vatican Council (1965) in its *Pastoral Constitution on the Church in the Modern World*. It describes the Kingdom variously as "the consummation of the earth and of humanity," "a new dwelling place and a new earth where justice will abide, and whose blessedness will answer and surpass all the longings for peace which spring up in the human heart," a "new age," and as a reality "of truth and life, of holiness and grace, of justice, love, and peace" (n. 39). That Kingdom is already growing on this earth, but it is present only in mystery, i.e., sacramentally.

What are some of the signs of God's growing rule? The nurturing on earth of the values of "human dignity, brotherhood and freedom, and indeed all the good fruits of our nature and enterprise," which we shall find again at the end, "but freed of stain, burnished and transfigured."

To what extent is human effort incorporated into, or necessary for, the Kingdom of God? Although the Kingdom will be given in the end by God, ". . . the expectation of a new earth must not weaken but rather stimulate our concern for cultivating this one. For here grows the body of a new human family, a body which even now is able to give some kind of foreshadowing of the new age." Accordingly, "Earthly progress must be carefully distinguished from the growth of Christ's kingdom. Nevertheless, to the extent that the former can contribute to the better ordering of human society, it is of vital concern to the Kingdom of God."

This same Kingdom was at the center of Jesus' own proclamation, and he revealed it to humankind in his word, his works, and his presence (*Dogmatic Constitution on the Church*, n. 5). Although the council describes the Church as the "initial budding forth" of the Kingdom, the Church nonetheless must strain toward the consummation of the Kingdom at history's end. The whole of human history meanwhile is moving toward the same final goal, which it will reach "in the Holy City, whose light shall be the glory of God, when the nations will walk in his light" (*Declaration on the Relationship of the Church to Non-Christian Religions*, n. 1). Human solidarity and all human activity will attain their final destiny therein (*Pastoral Constitution*, nn. 32, 39). For Christ is both the beginning and the end of all creation (n. 45). And so the "final stage of time has already come upon us (see 1 Corinthians 10:11). The renewal of the world is irrevocably determined and, in some real manner, it is anticipated in the present era..." (*Dogmatic Constitution on the Church*, n. 48).

Pope Paul VI, *Evangelii Nuntiandi*

This Apostolic Exhortation, *On Evangelization in the Modern World* (1975), acknowledges at the outset that the whole mission of Jesus is summed up in his own declaration that he was sent to proclaim the good news of the Kingdom of God (Luke 4:43), and in a particular way to the poor (Luke 4:18; Isaiah 61:1). Jesus' evangelizing activities, however, were not restricted to verbal proclamation. Christ also proclaimed the Kingdom by "innumerable signs...: the sick are cured, water is changed into wine, bread is multiplied, the dead come back to life. And among these signs there is the one to which he attached great importance: the humble and the poor are evangelized..." (n. 12). Evangelization,therefore, consists also of "liberation from everything that oppresses man but...is above all liberation from sin and the Evil One..." (n. 9). However closely linked it is with human liberation, the Kingdom of God is not simply identical with it (n. 35). Some notions of liberation are, in fact, incompatible with the Gospel, and the Kingdom itself will not come about even through proper expressions of liberation, well-being, and human development alone.

This Kingdom, of course, is available to every human being "as grace and mercy," and yet each individual gains entrance "through a total interior renewal which the Gospel calls *metanoia*; it is radical conversion, a profound change of mind and heart" (n. 10; see also n. 36). The Church itself comes into being as a community gathered in Jesus' name "in order to seek together the Kingdom, build it up and live it" (n. 13). This means that the Church's call to evangelization, i.e., to the proclamation of the good news of the Kingdom of God, is directed to its total mission. It is a proclamation in word, in sacrament, in witness, and in service.

THE LAST THINGS: THE DESTINY OF INDIVIDUALS

The Destiny of Each Individual: Death and Judgment

Death

Old Testament: Because of the ancient Hebrew concept of the human person as an *animated body* rather than as an incarnated spirit, death was perceived as a state in which the spirit had departed from the body. The deceased continued to exist in *Sheol* (the underworld, or the abode of the dead), but completely shorn of their human powers (Psalms 6:6; 30:10; 88:11; 115:17; Isaiah 38:11,18). Ideally, death comes in the fullnes of age to a person of undiminished powers (Genesis 25:8; Job 21:23-24; 29:18-20). Such a one dies easily and quickly and goes immediately down to *Sheol* (Job 21:13). Death is the natural end of the human person (2 Samuel 14:14), but it is the consequence of sin (Genesis 2-3). On occasion, there is an expression of hope that death is not terminal. In Psalm 16:10 the poet rejoices that Yahweh will not abandon him to *Sheol* ("the nether world") nor permit him to "undergo corruption." In Psalm 49:16 the poet is assured that God will redeem him from *Sheol*. Psalm 73:23-28 is even clearer. If Yahweh's promises and loving kindness are everlasting, then there must be some way in which the faithful Israelite will experience them. Only gradually, however, did this subordinate line of thought emerge as a more dominant force in the Israelite theology of death. Thus, there is no trace of a clear belief in the resurrection of the dead before the second century B.C., in Daniel (12:2).

New Testament: The New Testament is explicit and unequivocal about the origin of death: It is the consequence of sin and a punishment for it (Romans 5:12-14). Likewise in 1 Corinthians 15:22, Paul asserts that we all die in Adam, but rise to life in Christ. Indeed, Jesus overcame death by his own death (15:25-26). He has deprived death of its power (2 Timothy 1:10), rendering the devil, the lord of death, impotent (Hebrews 2:14). Death no longer has power over Christ (Romans 6:9), and so he rules over the living and the dead (14:9). The Christian experiences Jesus' victory over death by sharing in his death (6:2-11). To die with Christ is to live with him (6:8). We overcome death by being baptized into Christ (6:4) and by partaking of the Eucharist (John 6:50-51).

On the other hand, death is at once final and unique. There is no question of *reincarnation*: "... those who might wish to cross from here to you cannot do so, nor can anyone cross from your side to us" (Luke 16:26; see also John 9:4; 2 Corinthians 5:10; Galatians 6:10).

Official Teachings of the Church: At first the Church's eschatological vision centered on the Second Coming of Christ and the entrance of the whole Church into the final Kingdom. The individual received much less attention. The Middle Ages brought about a shift from the communal to the individual. Theologians focused on the moment of death as the key point at which individual destiny was to be decided.

Church documents on the subject of death and the afterlife are comparatively few in number. Since they belong for the most part to the Middle Ages, they also reflect an individual rather than a communal or ecclesial perspective. They deal primarily with the beatific vision and the resurrection of the individual body (as we shall see below). Not until the Second Vatican Council is there once again a fuller, more comprehensive statement on the reality of death and its universal significance.

Council of Trent (1546): Adam's sin not only involved a loss of holiness and justice but also brought death with it as a punishment. This punishment was applied not only to Adam but to all of his offspring. The council cites Romans 5:12 (*Decree on Original Sin,* Session V).

Second Vatican Council (1965): "It is in the face of death that the riddle of human existence becomes most acute. . . .All the endeavors of technology, though useful in the extreme, cannot calm his [the individual's] anxiety" (*Pastoral Constitution on the Church in the Modern World*, n. 18). Only faith can overcome this anxiety. We have been "created by God for a blissful purpose beyond the reach of earthly misery." We are all called to an "endless sharing of a divine life beyond all corruption," and this was won for us by the death and resurrection of Christ. "Through Christ and in Christ, the riddles of sorrow and death grow meaningful. Apart from his gospel, they overwhelm us" (n. 22).

Congregation for the Doctrine of the Faith, "Letter on Certain Questions Concerning Eschatology" (May 1979): This document reaffirms the Church's traditional belief in the resurrection of the dead, the resurrection of the whole person, survival of the human self after death, the meaningfulness of prayers for the dead, the Second Coming and general judgment, the assumption of the Blessed Virgin Mary, and heaven, hell, and purgatory. The document also warns, however, against "arbitrary imaginative representations" of life after death and calls such excesses "a major cause of the difficulties that Christian faith often encounters." At the same time, the document encourages continued theological exploration of these issues.

Theological Reflections: All romantic, idealized versions of human life are brought low by the reality of death. More than anything else, death forces us to acknowledge the radical finitude of our existence. But this is not to say that death nullifies everything, rendering all life absurd and meaningless. On the contrary, death projects an ambiguous character. In spite of the certainty of death, we go on living with a deeply rooted conviction that life does make sense, or at least can make sense. Death itself can be an affirmative, even courageous act. An individual's life—not to say a nation's or a world's—can assume extraordinary significance by the manner in which death is faced. A person dies that another might live, as in the case of Maximilian Kolbe (d. 1941), the Polish priest who went to his death at Auschwitz to spare the life of a family man marked out for execution by the Nazis. The circumstances of a person's death, too, can be understood as in some way redeeming the blameworthy actions of his or her life, as in the case of Sydney Carton in Charles Dickens' *A Tale of Two Cities.*

Although theologians such as Karl Rahner and Ladislas Boros and scientists such as Elisabeth Kubler-Ross have attempted in recent years to illuminate the darkness surrounding this perennial mystery of death (see E. Kubler-Ross, *On Death and Dying*, New York: Macmillan, 1969; K. Rahner, *On the Theology of Death*, New York: Herder & Herder, 1961; and L. Boros, *The Mystery of Death*, New York: Herder & Herder, 1965), perhaps no one has substantially improved upon the fundamental insights of the existentialist philosopher Martin Heidegger (d. 1976). Death is the horizon that closes off the future. All human possibilities are seen in the context of death, because it brings into existence a responsibility and a seriousness that it could scarcely have had otherwise. Death, therefore, not only destroys; it brings some degree of unity and coherence and purpose into one's life. We shape and direct our lives with the certainty of future death in mind. We do not have unlimited time at our disposal. We have a certain amount of time, and everything has to be arranged in relation to that "deadline." Moreover, death exposes the superficiality and triviality of much of what we count as important and to which we dedicate so much of our resources and energies. In the face of death, things get put into perspective (see *Being and Time*, New York: Harper & Row, 1962, pp. 279-311).

For the Christian, of course, the death of Jesus is the model and norm of every human death. He accepted death in freedom. He could have escaped but did not. Moreover, only in death was he able to accomplish what he had proclaimed in life. In dying he made possible the release of the Holy Spirit as the firstfruits of the final Kingdom. Only in death did he reveal to others the ultimate seriousness of the claims of God. His whole existence was oriented toward his death, for he knew that a final conflict between the powers of this world and the Word of God was inevitable, and that this conflict would be played out in the conflict between the contemporary religious establishment and himself (see chapter 12). Such a death brought a wholeness (integrity) to his life, and so it can to ours.

Judgment

Old Testament: Judgment is both *defense* and *vindication* of Israel by Yahweh (Isaiah 1:27; 30:18) and also *punishment* (Ezekiel 5:7-15; 7:3-27; 16:38; 11:10; 24:13-14). Yahweh is also judge of the whole world (Psalms 7:8; 9:9-10; 96:13; 110:6; Genesis 18:25; 1 Samuel 2:10). The idea of the judgment of all nations is characteristic of apocalyptic literature (Joel 4:9-12; Daniel 7:9-11).

New Testament: In the Synoptics, judgment is often condemnation of sinners (e.g., Matthew 5:22; 23:33; Luke 12:58). In Paul such judgment is not only in the future (Romans 2:1-3,16; 3:5-6) but also in the past (Romans 5:16,18) and in the present (1 Corinthians 11:29,32). In any event, the judgment of God is unsearchable (Romans 11:33). In John the judgment is always in the present (3:18; 5:24; 12:31; 16:11). Hebrews looks to the resurrection of the dead and eternal judgment (6:2). It will not go well with those who were unfaithful (10:27; 13:4). Those who break the law, according to James, will be judged mercilessly (2:12-13), and so, too, will unfaithful teachers (3:1). On the other hand, we should be careful not to judge others (4:12; see also Matthew 7:1; Luke 6:37). God will judge the living and the dead (1 Peter 4:5), and that process will begin with the Church (4:17). In 2 Peter and Jude the judgment has an apocalyptic tone, comparable to the judgment of Sodom and Gomorrah (2 Peter 2:6,9; 3:7). This is even more explicit in Revelation, where judgment is the downfall of a world power (17:1—19:2). All will be judged in the end (11:18; 10:12-13).

Biblical belief, therefore, is that the judgment of God is final, that it is outside and beyond history, and that it is *the act by which evil is overcome once and for all*. On the other hand, the judgment also occurs even now in our acceptance or rejection of Christ and the Gospel (Matthew 25:31-46). In faith and hope the future judgment and salvation are already a reality (John 5:24; 12:31; 16:8). The Spirit is already given (Philippians 1:19; Romans 8:23), and the resurrection has already taken place (John 5:25,28; 2 Timothy 2:18).

Official Teachings of the Church: The *fact* of the final judgment is attested to throughout the history of the Church: In the *Apostles' Creed* ("... he shall come again to judge the living and the dead");

the *Nicene Creed* (325) ("He ascended to the heavens and shall come again to judge the living and the dead"); the *Nicene-Constantinopolitan Creed* (381) from the Council of Constantinople ("He shall come again in glory to judge the living and the dead..."); the so-called *Athanasian Creed* (end of the fifth century) ("...He shall come to judge the living and the dead"); the *Fourth Lateran Council* (1215), which added the words: "and to render to each one according to his works, to the reprobate as well as to the elect"; the *Second Council of Lyons* (1274), which said essentially the same thing as Lateran IV; the Constitution *Benedictus Deus* (1336) of Pope Benedict XII (d. 1342); and the *Council of Florence* (1439). The *Second Vatican Council* simply presumes this line of teaching (see the *Pastoral Constitution on the Church in the Modern World*, nn. 17 and 45).

Theological Reflections: One must distinguish always between the general judgment and the particular judgment. The *general judgment* applies to the consummation of the whole world and of history itself. It is connected with the Second Coming, or *Parousia*, of Christ. Because is affects all it is called the "general" judgment. Because it is the act which terminates history it is also called the "last" judgment. Everything in the first part of this chapter, on the Kingdom of God, is applicable to this general or last judgement.

The *particular judgment*, which is also the subject of the preceding biblical texts and of the official teachings of the Church, underscores the uniqueness and particularity of every human person before God. We are not simply part of some larger, impersonal collective reality. Just as it is erroneous to exaggerate the destiny of the individual and to forget the cosmic and communal destiny which is the Kingdom of God, so it is wrong to deny the hope that burns in each individual heart that his or her own life has final meaning and purpose. Correspondingly, we are to be judged not simply on the basis of our community's activity but on the basis of our own as well.

If everything were to return to a kind of undifferentiated unity, then creation itself would have been pointless in the first place. What we look forward to in the end is a community of free and responsible persons united in love. But such a community is impossible unless the persons within it are preserved in some kind of individual identity. It is hardly "good news" to hear that we are worth something on this earth while we are still alive but that we are not worth anything thereafter, for eternity.

The Destiny of the Faithful:
Beatific Vision, Purgatory, Resurrection of the Body

Beatific Vision/Heaven/Eternal Life

New Testament: The vision of God after death, known as the *beatific vision*, is rarely referred to in the New Testament and not at all in the Old Testament. The Old Testament's belief in the invisibility of God generally persists into the New Testament (1 John 3:6; 4:12,20; John 1:18: 1 Timothy 1:17; 6:16). The promise of the vision of God, however, is found in Matthew 5:8: "Blest are the single-hearted for they shall see God." Given the background of Jewish thought, it is remarkable that the promise is uttered without any refinement or explanation. The vision of God which is promised to the peacemakers is the fruit of love in 1 Corinthians 13:12. Paul contrasts the vision of God after death with the dim view seen in a mirror. He chooses the expression "face to face," which echoes the traditions of Moses; a veil concealed the glory of God reflected in the face of Moses. Paul insists that the Christian will behold the glory of the Lord without such a veil (2 Corinthians 3:12-18). In 1 John 3:2 we are assured that we shall see God and that the vision will transform us into God's likeness.

Such a vision inaugurates us into a new life, "eternal life." God gives eternal life to those who are faithful (Romans 2:7; 6:23). It comes through faith (1 Timothy 1:16; John 3:15,36; 20:31) and is assured by hope (Titus 1:2; 3:7). It becomes a present reality by Baptism (Romans 6:4). Jesus has the words of eternal life (John 6:68). His followers retain eternal life by loving one another (12:50). Thus, death is never final (6:39,44,54). Those who partake of the Son will have eternal life (1 John 5:11-12). It consists of the knowledge of the one true God and of Jesus, whom God has sent (John 17:3).

Official Teachings of the Church: The principal texts are the Constitution *Benedictus Deus* (1336) of Pope Benedict XII and the Council of Florence's *Decree for the Greeks* (1439). Both insist that the souls of the faithful, provided they are in no need of purification, will immediately see "the divine essence with an intuitive vision and even face to face, without the mediation of any creature by way of object of vision; rather the divine essence immediately manifests itself to them, plainly, clearly and openly, and in this vision they enjoy the divine essence" (*Benedictus Deus*). Such faithful will "see clearly God, one and three, as God is, though some more perfectly than others, according to the diversity of merits" (Council of Florence). It is made possible by the *lumen gloriae* ("light of glory"). The traditional teaching is reaffirmed by Pope Pius XII (d. 1958) in his encyclical *Mystici Corporis* (1943), by Pope Paul VI (d. 1978) in his *Credo of the People of God* (1968), and by the Congregation for the Doctrine of the Faith, "Letter on Certain Questions Concerning Eschatology" (May 1979).

Theological Reflections: The beatific vision is *the full union of the human person with God.* It is that toward which every person strives. It is that which transcends the person on this earth and draws the person beyond himself or herself to become something other than he or she is at present. It is the goal of every human inquiry, search, and gesture toward the other. It is the completion of all that we are as human beings. "Our hearts are restless," Augustine cried out to God, "until they rest in Thee."

We thereby become fully like God. No trace of selfishness remains. We are fully open to the other. We cling to nothing of our own. We pour out our own being as God poured out the divine Being in Christ. This is why the early Church believed that the martyrs went directly to heaven without purification. The martyrs completely transcended selfish being and attained a likeness to Christ, and so to God. Heaven for them is not a reward for being good. Rather, ". . . it is the reward of having been delivered from any seeking for rewards" (John Macquarrie, *Principles of Christian Theology*, p. 366). The only reward for such self-giving love is an increased capacity for it. Heaven, therefore, is neither mythological nor simply the satisfaction of all egocentric human longings. It is the goal of human existence as such.

Purgatory

Biblical Foundations: There is, for all practical purposes, no biblical basis for the doctrine of purgatory. This is not to say that there is no basis at all for the doctrine, but only that there is no clear *biblical* basis for it. On the other hand, there is no contradictory evidence in either Old or New Testaments. The classic text is 2 Maccabees 12:38-46: ". . . for if he were not expecting the fallen to rise again, it would have been useless and foolish to pray for them in death. . . . Thus he made atonement for the dead that they might be freed from this sin" (12:44,46). The New Testament was insistent on the fact that the Kingdom of God had already come in Jesus Christ, and the Christian's attention was drawn to the immediate and imminent consummation and to the decision required of everyone in the face of the Kingdom's drawing near. The real testing of faith and its works is expected in the "fire" of the last judgment, not in the particular judgment (1 Corinthians 3:12-15). It is clear that notions of *Sheol* are still operative (Luke 16:19-31).

History of the Doctrine: In the *patristic period*, Justin and Tertullian shared this Lucan perspective and taught that the dead are waiting "in the grave" for the consummation. Origen argued that everyone will be saved but that there is a particular purification for each individual. The purification occurs, however, at the moment of judgment and not as some intermediate state between the particular judgment and the final passage into the sight of God. The Origenist belief in universal salvation (*apokatastasis*) was condemned by the provincial council of Constantinople in 543, a judgment approved by all the Eastern patriarchs and confirmed by Pope Vigilius (d. 555).

Augustine emphasized that all the just, not only the martyrs, enter immediately into heaven. But gradually the fire of judgment referred to in 1 Corinthians 3:12-15 becomes after Augustine the purgatorial fire and appears as an intermediate realm after death. The very fact of not yet being totally with God constitutes a punishment, according to Pope Gregory the Great.

The Western theology of the *Middle Ages* emphasized the penal and expiatory character of purgatory. The Christian East, however, rejected this highly juridical approach and stressed instead the more mystical nature of purgatory, as a process of maturation and spiritual growth. The Orientals also denied that the beatific vision was available to anyone, including the just, before the general resurrection and the final judgment. The traditional doctrine is enunciated by the Second Council of Lyons (1274), Benedict XII's *Benedictus Deus* (1336), and especially in the Council of Florence's *Decree for the Greeks* (1439), which tried to strike a careful balance between the Western concept of satisfaction and expiation and the Eastern emphasis on purification. Out of consideration for the Orientals, the council deliberately omitted all reference to fire (which the Orientals considered an echo of Origen's notion that all are saved by the one purifying fire) and avoided any language that would lead to a concept of purgatory as a place.

The *Reformation*, however, called into question what, until now, no one had questioned, either in the East or the West—namely, the appropriateness of prayers for the dead. From 1530 onwards, Luther and Melanchton joined Calvin and Zwingli in rejecting this doctrine, consistently with their teaching that salvation is by grace alone. In reply the Council of Trent defined the existence of purgatory, insisted that the souls detained there are helped by acts of intercession of the faithful, and especially by the sacrifice of the Mass. On the other hand, the council explicitly warned against any dwelling upon "the more difficult and subtle questions which do not make for edification and, for the most part, are not conducive to an increase of piety." These should not be included in popular sermons to uneducated people. Likewise, doubtful theological views should not be given wide circulation, and whatever belongs to the realm of "curiosity or superstition" or smacks of "dishonorable gain" should be forbidden as "scandalous and injurious to the faithful" (*Decree on Purgatory*, Session XXV, 1563).

The doctrine is reaffirmed in Pope Paul VI's *Credo of the People of God* (1968) and by the Congregation for the Doctrine of the Faith's "Letter on Certain Questions Concerning Eschatology" (1979) and is assumed by the Second Vatican Council's *Dogmatic Constitution on the Church*, n. 51.

Theological Reflections: Purgatory is best understood as *a process by which we are purged of our residual selfishness so that we can really become one with the God who is totally oriented to others, i.e., the self-giving God.* It is also part of that larger process by which we are called out of nothingness into existence, from existence to selfhood, or responsible human existence, from responsible human existence to Christian existence, and from Christian existence to full and final incorporation into God. The kind of suffering associated with purgatory, therefore, is not suffering inflicted upon us from the outside as a punishment for sin, but *the intrinsic pain that we all feel when we are asked to surrender our ego-centered self so that the God-centered loving self may take its place.* It is part of the process by which we are called to die and rise with Christ.

A Note on Indulgences: From the earliest days the Church imposed penances upon those who had sinned after Baptism (see chapter 22). It was not enough to be sorry for one's sins; that only removed the *guilt* of sin. One also had to pay the *penalty* of sin. Since sin always involves some violation of the Church which is called to be a holy community and the sacrament of Christ's presence in the world, the Church is also involved in the process by which the sinner is reconciled to God. Not only did the Church decide when the penitent was ready to be restored to communion, but the Church also prayed with the penitent as he or she pursued the path of repentance. At times, the Church drew upon its own spiritual treasury of grace and merit to cancel out some (partial indulgence) or all (plenary indulgence) of the punishment still due to an individual's sin.

The first actual indulgences appeared in France in the eleventh century. They were at once a remission of some penance and a remission of the temporal punishment due to sin. Even into the thirteenth century, however, indulgences were regarded as concessions to the imperfect, which more faithful Christians should not claim. (They are not to be confused with redemptions and commutations, which came out of the Germanic period. These applied only to imposed penances and not to punishment due to sin.) At first, some theologians contested the bishop's right to grant indulgences, but as the actual practice became more widespread, theological opposition diminished.

On the other hand, the practice itself changed. Where previously the Church only *prayed for* the remission of temporal punishment due to sin and had excused a canonical penance on that account, now the Church definitively declared that such temporal punishment was canceled on the basis of the Church's control over the treasury of grace and merit. By the middle of the thirteenth century, the granting of indulgences became increasingly divorced from the sacrament of Penance, and more and more an act of the pope. The number of indulgences multiplied, and the need for doing some penitential work declined. Any reasonable cause was now regarded as sufficient grounds for granting an indulgence (Aquinas, *Summa Theologica*, Supplement, q. 25, a. 2).

Plenary indulgences, i.e., the remission of all temporal punishment due to sin, had come into prominence during the Crusades in the eleventh century when the crusaders were promised complete remission of punishment in return for their military service (Pope Urban II, d. 1099). Indulgences for the dead began to be granted from the middle of the fifteenth century. Their connection with almsgiving was established as early as the eleventh century. In the later Middle Ages, however, they became a convenient source of income for the Church and, as such, were multiplied to scandalous proportions. Simony (i.e., buying and selling spiritual goods) was not unknown. Some preached indulgences in a theologically unsound and exaggerated way. The Council of Trent condemned such practices in its *Decree on Indulgences* (1563), but perhaps too late, since those very abuses were among the proximate causes of the Reformation.

The most recent and fullest official exposition of the meaning of indulgences is contained in Pope Paul VI's Apostolic Constitution *Indulgentiarum Doctrina* (1967). The pope linked the doctrine of indulgences with the doctrine of the Communion of Saints. The Church on earth is united with the Church in heaven and in purgatory. The "treasury of the Church" is not "akin to a hoard of material wealth accumulated over the centuries" but is the "infinite and inexhaustible value which the expiation and merits of Christ have in the sight of God . . . ." An indulgence, he declares, is "the remission in the sight of God of the temporal punishment due to sins which have already been blotted out as far as guilt is concerned." They are either plenary or partial, and they can be applied to the dead. Henceforth, however, partial indulgences will be described without reference to numbers of days and years. (The medieval approach had been to specify the precise amount of time subtracted from one's purgatorial "sentence".) It is, of course, always required that an individual be truly contrite, be a member of the Church in good standing, perform the work attached to the indulgence, and at least have the general intention of gaining the indulgence.

The doctrine of indulgences is best understood in the context of the whole mystery of Christian existence. We are all members of the Body of Christ. As such, we are beneficiaries of Christ's saving work on our behalf. Death is not the end of life, nor, therefore, is it the end of our relationships with our loved ones or with our brothers and sisters in the Church. Our obligations of concern and mutual assistance do not lapse with their death. Accordingly, decline of interest in indulgences is inconsistent with Catholic principles if that decline reflects a growing indifference to the Communion of Saints and/or to our abiding spiritual responsibility toward our dead relatives and friends. On the other hand, a calculating, egocentric approach to Christian destiny, where an individual is concerned primarily with the accumulation of spiritual "credits," is so antithetical to sound theological and doctrinal principles that the disappearance of that sort of interest in indulgences can only be welcomed.

Resurrection of the Body

Old Testament: The Hebrew concept of the human person as an animated body made it impossible for any idea of the afterlife to arise which did not involve a restoration of life to the body. This came, as we have already seen, very late in the Old Testament (Daniel 12:2; 2 Maccabees 7:9,11,23; 14:46). Isaiah 26:19 mentions the resurrection of the dead, but it may refer, as Ezekiel 37:1-14 does, to the restoration of Israel. By the time of the New Testament, resurrection was affirmed by the Pharisees but not by the Sadducees (Matthew 22:23; Mark 12:18; Luke 20:27; Acts of the Apostles 23:8).

New Testament: In his discussion with Sadducees (Mark 12:16-27), Jesus refutes their denial of the resurrection by an appeal to the Torah and above all to the power of God. But he also corrects the Pharisees' doctrine that the resurrection meant a return to the conditions of earthly life (12:25). In the Synoptics no mention is made of the resurrection of the sinner, although it might be implied in what is said about God's judgment upon every person at the end. The reward granted in the resurrection of the just (Luke 14:14) reflects a Jewish rather than a Christian approach.

A resurrection to life is mentioned in John 5:28-29 (see also 6:39-40; 11:25-26) in terms very close to Daniel 12:2, and the same conception is contained in 2 Corinthians 5:10 (see also 1 Corinthians 15:19; Philippians 3:21). Hebrews 6:2 counts it among the basic doctrines of Christian faith. The Book of Revelation alone speaks of a double resurrection, the second being the general resurrection of all the dead at the last judgment (20:11-15); the first is reserved to the martyrs who will then rule with Christ for one thousand years (20:4-6).

Most of the references to the resurrection in the New Testament, however, are references not to the resurrection of the body after death but to the Christian's *present* resurrection with Christ by being baptized into his death and rising with him unto new life (e.g., Romans 6:4-11). Other texts look to the *future* (e.g., 2 Corinthians 4:14; Philippians 3:11; John 11:25; 6:39-44,54; 1 Corinthians 15), but they are not explicit about the *bodily* character of this resurrection.

In fact, whenever the New Testament speaks about the resurrection, it speaks of the resurrection of the dead, never of the resurrection of the body, which is not found until Clement of Rome and Justin's *Dialogue* (80,5). Resurrection of the body, in the sense of resurrection of the flesh (*sarx*), would not have been consistent with Paul's distinction between *sarx* and *soma* ("body"). The latter embraces the whole person, whereas the former is something weak, perishable, and even sinful. The body (*sarx*) cannot rise, because "flesh and blood cannot inherit the kingdom of God; no more can corruption inherit incorruption" (1 Corinthians 15:50).

Some Protestant scholars like Oscar Cullmann have interpreted such texts to mean that death does not consist in the soul's being separated from the body and continuing to live on its own in some intermediate state, awaiting the resurrection of the body, but rather that death is the destruction of the whole person. Only at the general resurrection will there be a completely new creation. We live on between death and resurrection in the mind of God alone. Such a position has to reconcile itself with such texts as Philippians 1:21; 2 Corinthians 5:6-8; Luke 23:42-43; and Revelation 6:9; 20:4.

Official Teachings of the Church: The resurrection of the body is attested to in the *Apostles' Creed* ("I believe in... the resurrection of the body..."); the *Nicene-Constantinopolitan Creed* (381); the so-called *Athanasian Creed* (late fifth century); the Fourth Lateran Council (1215); the Second Council of Lyons (1274); and in the Constitution *Benedictus Deus* of Pope Benedict XII (1336). Usually the belief was simply included with other essential elements of Christian faith. Sometimes, however, the doctrine was deliberately and specifically formulated over against a heretical tendency to deny the radical goodness of the body, as in Lateran IV's rejection of Catharism, Albigensianism, and the Manichaeism upon which they were based. More recently, the belief is reaffirmed by the Second Vatican Council in its *Dogmatic Constitution on the Church* (n. 51) and in its *Pastoral Constitution on the Church in the Modern World* (n. 39), and also by the aforementioned Vatican "Letter on Certain Questions Concerning Eschatology" (1979).

Theological Reflections: We must reassert here what has already been presented in chapter 5—namely, that the human person is not simply an embodied spirit, in the sense that the body is base, inhuman, and without intrinsic worth. "Holiness is wholeness" (Goldbrunner) because the human person is bodily as well as spiritual, or, in biblical terms, is an animated body (*soma*). Our hope is not simply the salvation of our soul but the salvation of our whole being. Our immortality is not something required by philosophical speculation (namely, because the soul is spiritual, it is indestructible) but is grounded on God's promise of eternal life and the conferral of new life in the resurrection of Jesus Christ himself. And not life for part of us, i.e., the soul, but for all that we are, i.e., animated body.

Nor is our resurrection at the end the resurrection only of so many individuals. Our bodiliness also is the natural basis of our solidarity with others and through them with God. We are human insofar as we are oriented toward others. And our orientation toward others is made possible and necessary by our bodiliness. The doctrine of the resurrection of the *body* is a foundation for the doctrine of the Communion of Saints. Thus, life after death is also communal life. And thus, too, the resurrection of the body cannot be achieved until the consummation of history itself.

The Destiny of the Unfaithful: Hell

Old Testament

The word *hell* is not used in the Old Testament. Its counterpart is *Gehenna*, which is an abbreviation of "valley of the son of Hinnon." Gehenna was an actual place on the boundary between the tribes of Judah and Benjamin; it was regarded as unholy because it was the site of a shrine where human sacrifices were offered (2 Kings 23:10; 2 Chronicles 28:3; 33:6; Jeremiah 7:31; 19:2-5; 32:35). It was considered, therefore, to be the place where the dead bodies of those who rebelled against Yahweh would lie (Isaiah 66:24). The term is frequently used in extrabiblical Jewish writings and applies there to a fiery abyss, a place of darkness, chains, etc.

New Testament

Gehenna is mentioned seven times in Matthew, three times in Mark, once in Luke, and once in James. It is a place of unquenchable fire (Mark 9:43; Matthew 5:22; 18:9; James 3:6), a pit into which people are cast (Matthew 5:29-30; 18:9; Mark 9:45,47; Luke 12:5). The wicked are destroyed there (Matthew 10:28). The place is described, although not named, elsewhere (e.g., Matthew 3:10,12; 7:19; Luke 3:9,17). It is the final destination of the wicked (Revelation 19:20; 20:9-15; 21:8). It is a place of weeping and gnashing of teeth (Matthew 8:12; 13:42,50; 22:13; 24:51; 25:30), where the worm does not die (Mark 9:48); it is shrouded in darkness (Matthew 8:12; 22:13; 25:30).

Elsewhere in the New Testament the language is less concrete. Paul speaks of a day of wrath (Romans 2:5) and of death as the wages of sin (6:23). Sinners will have no share in the Kingdom of God (1 Corinthians 6:10; Galatians 5:19-21). The enemies of the cross of Christ are doomed to destruction, and so are all the impious (Philippians 3:19; 2 Thessalonians 1:9). It is a terrible and fearful thing to fall into the hands of the living God (Hebrews 10:26-31).

Official Teachings of the Church

The existence of hell as a condition of eternal punishment for sin is attested to in the *Athanasian Creed* (end of fifth century); the Fourth Lateran Council (1215), which speaks of "perpetual punishment with the devil"; the Second Council of Lyons (1274), which taught that not only those who die in mortal sin but also those who die with Original Sin only "go down immediately to hell, to be punished however with different punishments"—a teaching which differed from an earlier letter of Pope Innocent III to Humbert, the Archbishop of Arles, in 1201, in which the pope made a distinction between those who commit mortal sin and merit the "torture of hell" and those who are not yet baptized and suffer instead the "loss of the beatific vision" (see the discussion of limbo below); and in Benedict XII's Constitution *Benedictus Deus* (1336). Significantly, hell is not mentioned in the Second Vatican Council nor even in Pope Paul VI's otherwise very complete *Credo of the People of God* (1968). There *is* reference to "eternal punishment for the sinner" in the Congregation for the Doctrine of the Faith's "Letter on Certain Questions Concerning Eschatology" (1979).

Theological Reflections

The word *hell* is derived from the German *hel* ("realm of the dead"). The New Testament really assumes rather than affirms its existence when it simply takes over the notions and imagery of later Judaism. What the New Testament says about hell is to be interpreted according to the same principles which govern our interpretation of apocalyptic literature. Apocalypticism is too individualistic, too much oriented to worlds beyond this one, too elitist or Gnostic in its approach to revelation and salvation, and too fascinated with the esoteric and the ominous. Hence what the New Testament says about hell is not to be taken literally, nor is it to be taken as a balanced theological statement of the case.

When Jesus used this imagery, he did so not to describe a particular place but to dramatize the urgency of his proclamation of the Kingdom and the seriousness of our decisions for or against the Kingdom. The stakes are as high as they can be. Our personal integrity and destiny are at issue. To turn our backs on God is to be finally and fully alienated and estranged from God. It is to choose inauthentic existence. It is to reject community with God and with others. It is to opt for isolation and separation.

Neither Jesus, nor the Church after him, ever stated that persons actually go to hell or are there now. He—as does the Church—restricts himself to the *possibility*. *If* somone really and deliberately rejected God, *this* is what he or she would be choosing instead of God: a totally isolated existence. Even in this sense, hell is not the product of divine vindictiveness. Rather, *it is God's yielding to our freedom.* To reject God is to reject life in community. Conversely, it is to choose life in isolation. Hell is absolute isolation. The radical sinner *chooses* that. God does not impose it as a punishment.

Some have argued that if an individual really chooses hell, i.e., a totally isolated existence, that individual is choosing self-annihilation, for one cannot even exist that way. To reject God completely and absolutely is to reject Being itself. It is to opt for non-being, for nothingness. Hell, in this conception, is not a place or a state but simply the condition of non-being.

Jesus' own "descent into hell," to which the Apostles' Creed attests, is the underworld (*Sheol*) rather than the place of fire. By dying Jesus entered the company of those who had died before him and thereby shared with them what he had achieved. The words "he descended into hell," therefore, mean simply that he died and that he remained dead, at least for a short time.

A Note on Demonology: In the *Old Testament*, belief in demons was generally excluded by the severe prohibitions against magic in Hebrew law. This is not to say that Israel knew no superstition at all. There is evidence of it here and there (1 Samuel 28:13; Psalm 106:37; Isaiah 13:21; 34:14). The situation changes, however, in the intertestamental and early New Testament periods. The belief in evil forces that was prevalent in Mesopotamian culture was assimilated almost whole, without change. The apocryphal literature traces the origin of demons to the fallen angels, the sons of God who married the daughters of men (Genesis 6:1-4).

The mention of demons is less frequent in the *New Testament* than in later Judaism. The victims of heathen sacrifices are offered to demons (1 Corinthians 10:20-21). Deceiving spirits are behind false teachings (1 Timothy 4:1). The spirits of demons perform wonders (Revelation 16:14), and the ruins of Babylon are haunted by demons (18:2). The demons are called the angels of Satan, for whom eternal fire is prepared (Matthew 25:41). They are the "principalities" who separate Christians from the love of God (Romans 8:38), but they are disarmed by the crucifixion of Christ (Colossians 2:15). There are, of course, many other references to diabolical possession and to exorcisms (Matthew 8:16; Mark 1:34; Luke 7:21; Acts of the Apostles 5:16).

Demons do not occupy a significant place in the *official teachings of the Church*. The Council of Braga (561), in Portugal, rejected the teachings of Priscillian (d. 385), founder of a Manichaean sect in Spain. The council denied the radical dualism of matter and spirit. All that exists is from God and is under the authority and power of God. Thus, even the devil was created by God and was in the beginning a good angel. The existence of demons is simply presupposed by the provincial council of Constantinople (543) and by the *Decree on Original Sin* of the Council of Trent (1546).

The Church has taught, therefore, that there is evil in the world which transcends the particular evil that human beings do (see chapter 9). But no clear theology of demons emerged until the Middle Ages, when it appeared as part of the discussions of creation. Insofar as a theology of demons has any relevance today, it is more appropriately an element of the theology of sin. Demonology is "an expression of the personal basis of our guilt and mortality which is not within our power to control or reach by any human action in history. It is also an expression of the fact that, as a human situation, evil in the world has a certain depth which is not simply attributable to man and the history which is subject to his autonomous control, but is something that can only be overcome by God's eschatological act in Christ in fulfillment of his promise" (Karl Rahner, "Demonology," *The Concise Sacramentum Mundi*, p. 334).

Beyond that, who really knows, or can know?

The Destiny of the Unbaptized: Limbo

The word *limbo* is derived from the Latin *limbus* ("border"). It is the *state or place*, according to some, *reserved for the dead who deserved neither the beatific vision nor eternal punishment*. The *limbus patrum* ("limbo of the fathers"), containing the pre-Christian just who had to await the opening of heaven by Christ (Luke 16:22; 1 Peter 3:18-22), was distinguished from the *limbus puerorum*, containing unbaptized infants and children, who, therefore, remained in Original Sin without ever incurring any actual sins.

Over against the Pelagians, Augustine (d. 430) had argued that such children were condemned to real, though diminished, pains of hell. Anselm of Canterbury (d. 1109) and the Scholastics after him held to the Augustinian belief that such individuals were forever excluded from eternal happiness, but they allowed them a place of natural happiness, i.e., limbo. The belief was maintained throughout the Middle Ages and into the twentieth century. With the Second Vatican Council and the theological climate it reflected and sanctioned, however, the idea of limbo has seemed less and less tenable in light of the universality of grace from the very beginning of each person's existence (the "supernatural existential").

The Catholic Church continues to endorse, indeed mandate, the practice of immediately baptizing infants in danger of death. There is no indication in the new rites of Baptism, however, that the practice is based on a belief in limbo. Rather, the texts speak of the Church's desire to associate the child with the death and resurrection of Christ, to become a member of Christ's Church, and to share in the glory of the Kingdom of God.

The issue is, therefore, linked with the questions of grace (see chapter 5), of the necessity of the Church for salvation (see chapter 20), and infant Baptism (see chapter 21). Insofar as membership in the Church is not necessary for the salvation of each individual, and insofar as grace is present to each person from the beginning of existence, the Baptism of a dying infant is not of absolute necessity. Insofar as membership in the Church is a call from God without regard for age, talent, or longevity, and insofar as the Church has a wider dimension beyond death in the Communion of Saints, the Baptism of a dying infant may be a matter of pastoral urgency. In neither instance, however, is belief in limbo a necessary component of the problem.

THE COMMUNION OF SAINTS

The article on the "communion of saints" was first found in the Apostles' Creed at the end of the fifth century and was used much earlier in the East, through not as a part of the creed. It was understood as our participation in the blessings of salvation and in the fellowship of God's holy people. Although this community of salvation encompassed the whole Church, the term *communion of saints* only gradually came to apply principally to the communion between the heavenly Church and the earthly Church. More recently still, the term has come to apply only to the exchange of graces and blessings between individuals here on earth and the saints in heaven and the souls in purgatory (the Church militant, triumphant, and suffering). Its fundamental biblical and theological meaning, however, remains locked in the noun *communion* (*koinonia*). The Church is, first and foremost, a communion, a fellowship called by the Father, in Christ, through the power of the Spirit (Hebrews 2:14-17; Romans 5:8-10; 8:3,32-35; John 1:14; and especially 2 Corinthians 13:13).

The doctrine is explicitly affirmed in the Second Vatican Council's *Dogmatic Constitution on the Church* (and reaffirmed in Pope Paul VI's *Credo of the People of God*): "For all who belong to Christ, having his Spirit, form one Church and cleave together in him (see Ephesians 4:16). Therefore the union of the pilgrims with the brethren who have gone to sleep in the peace of Christ is not in the least interrupted." Those in heaven, because of their close union with Christ, "establish the whole Church more firmly in holiness, lend nobility to the worship which the Church offers on earth to God, and in many ways contribute to its great upbuilding (see 1 Corinthians 12:12-27)" (n. 49). Such persons intercede for those of us on earth and place their merits at our disposal.

Because of this sense of union linking all Christians, both living and dead, the Church has "from the first ages . . . cultivated with great piety the memory of the dead," through the offering of prayers on their behalf (n. 50). The Church has also always venerated the saints, especially the Blessed Mother, and has sought their aid. "For when we look at the lives of those who have faithfully followed Christ, we are inspired with a new reason for seeking the city which is to come (Hebrews 13:14; 11:10). . . . In the lives of those who shared in our humanity and yet were transformed into especially successful images of Christ (see 2 Corinthians 3:18), God vividly manifests to humankind the divine presence and face. God speaks to us in them, and gives us a sign of the kingdom, to which we are powerfully drawn, surrounded as we are by so many witnesses (see Hebrews 12:1)" (n. 50).

The council's vision is eschatologically wide-ranging. When Christ appears at the end and the glorious resurrection of the dead occurs, ". . . the splendor of God will brighten the heavenly city and the Lamb will be the lamp thereof (see Revelation 21:24)" (n. 51). At that supreme moment, the charity of the whole Church will be manifested in adoration of God and of the Lamb who was slain, and all will proclaim with one voice: "To the One seated on the throne, and to the Lamb, be praise and honor, glory and might, forever and ever!" (Revelation 5:13).

Herein, cosmic eschatology and individual eschatology converge. Our hope in the Kingdom of God for all humankind and for all the world and its history is at once our hope in our own personal entrance into that Kingdom, that we might share with others and with the whole cosmos the fruits of the saving work which the Father has accomplished in Jesus Christ, by the power of the Holy Spirit.

SUMMARY

1.   *Christian destiny* is not distinct from human destiny, nor is either distinct from the destiny of the world and of its history: *the Kingdom of God.*

2.   *Eschatology* is that area of theology which is directly concerned with the "study of the last thing(s)," i.e., the Kingdom of God (the "last thing") and death, particular judgment, heaven, hell, purgatory, Second Coming of Christ, resurrection of the body, general judgment, and the consummation of all things in the Kingdom (the "last things").

3.   The *Kingdom of God* is the redemptive presence of God actualized through the power of God's reconciling Spirit.

4.   Since the Kingdom is not only in the *future*, eschatology is concerned also with the *present* and the *past*. The final events are grounded in the redemptive work of Jesus Christ and are anticipated even now in faith, hope, charity, in the sacraments, and in the Church itself, the carrier of the divine glory.

5.   Our movement toward the Kingdom is believed not only because it is *promised* but also because it seems to be *demanded* by graced human nature itself. Otherwise, there is no basis at all for our endless quest for truth and love (the meaning of "intentionality"), nor is there any real possibility of ultimate human fulfillment.

6.   Through the mediation of humanity, the world itself also has "intentionality," i.e., purpose, direction, conscious freedom. In other words, *the world has a history* and *is* history. The outcome is already decided in Christ, but there are powers at work which impede the movement of history toward the Kingdom of God. These evil forces are focused in the one known as *Satan*. They have decisively been overcome by the passion of Christ.

7.   The *Kingdom of God*, the destiny of creation and humanity, was a reality woven into the texture of Israel's faith from the beginning. It referred to the provident and protective kingship of God over the chosen people. It was a kingship that was at once *in* history and *beyond* history, *local* (e.g., in the ark of the covenant) and *universal*, over *Israel* and over *all* people and all *creation*, in the *present* and in the *future*.

8.   The *fruit* of the Kingdom is a whole *new moral order* of peace, justice, and mercy. This is the vision of *Deutero-Isaiah* (61:1), which Jesus made his own (Luke 4:18).

9.   *Later Judaism* gave the Kingdom a more *nationalistic* orientation, a conception with which Jesus had to contend. But there was also an *apocalyptic* notion (Daniel) which saw the Kingdom as the heavenly Jerusalem and saw paradise as the abode of the elect. The emphasis was

always on God's action, and attention was focused constantly on the signs and portents of the coming Kingdom.

10.   Jesus startled his listeners not because he proclaimed the Kingdom of God but because he proclaimed it as *near at hand* (Mark 1:15). He called, therefore, for conversion and repentance and for watchfulness.

11.   He emphasized, too, the *mercy of God*: that the Kingdom was for sinners and outcasts, the poor and the despised. Entrance into the Kingdom will be determined by our response to the neighbor in need.

12.   Although there were political implications to the proclamation, Jesus excluded a *political* interpretation of the Kingdom. He was not a Zealot, nor did he cooperate with the Zealots. And he discouraged people from calling him the Messiah because of the political and nationalistic overtones of the term.

13.   Jesus' preaching of the Kingdom was underscored by his *praxis*: healings, exorcisms, eating with outcasts, etc.

14.   Where Jesus proclaimed the Kingdom, the *early Church* proclaimed Jesus as the personification of the Kingdom. We are living between-the-times, i.e., between the first and second comings of Christ (Luke); Christ is destined to rule over all creation, even beyond the Church (Paul); in the meantime we are pilgrims, still on the way to the Kingdom (1 Peter); the final Kingdom is anticipated in the Eucharist (Luke 22:30).

15.   *Early patristic theology* (Ignatius of Antioch, Justin, Tertullian, Origen, *et al.*) emphasized the Lordship of Jesus, the imminence of the Kingdom, and its interior, or spiritual, character. *Western theology*, however, increasingly identified the Kingdom with the *Church* (Augustine, Gregory the Great), and Christian political leaders even identified it with the Holy Roman Empire (Charlemagne). This notion would be vigorously rejected by Pope Boniface VIII in 1303. Emphasis on God's action, even to the detriment of human collaboration, was strong in Augustine (the two cities).

16.   Coinciding with the Augustinian and Gregorian tendency to equate the Kingdom and the visible, institutional Church was another medieval tendency to identify the Kingdom with a *spiritual* sectarian Church (Joachim of Fiore).

17.   Other *medieval notions* of the Kingdom included those of the Dominican *mystics* (Eckhart, Tauler, Suso), who saw the Kingdom as God in the depths of the soul, and of *Luther*, who rejected both the sectarian and the theocratic understandings of the Kingdom, insisting instead on the sharp distinction between the kingdom of humankind and the Kingdom of God.

18. With the *Enlightenment* of the eighteenth century, the Kingdom was once again perceived not only as an earthly reality but as the product of human initiative and effort. It is an ethical commonweal (Kant), the completion of history (Hegel), the classless society (Marx). But other, more spiritual interpretations continued in the Church (Pascal), and the symbol "Kingdom of God" became the central idea of Christianity in the *Tübingen School* in Germany in the nineteenth century.

19. Modern New Testament scholarship begins as a reaction against the more Liberal Protestant views of the Kingdom (Ritschl). The sequence of biblical theologies of the Kingdom follows:

    a. *Futurist eschatology* (Schweitzer, Weiss, Werner): The Kingdom is in the *future*; it is God's act alone; when it comes, history as we know it will end; the Kingdom is now imminent.

    b. *Realized eschatology* (C. H. Dodd): The Kingdom is already realized in the *past*; the "hour of decision" has to be experienced anew by each individual.

    c. *Existentialist eschatology* (Bultmann): The Kingdom is present; we are called to decide for or against God, to choose authentic or inauthentic existence.

    d. *Salvation-history eschatology* (Cullmann and Catholic biblical theology generally): The Kingdom is *past, present, and future*; it proceeds in linear fashion through history, from the moment of creation, through the central Christ-event, to the Second Coming of Christ. Between the first and second coming of Christ is the time of the Church.

20. Twentieth-century *Catholic systematic theology* insists that the Church and Kingdom of God are not the same, that the Kingdom is the product of divine initiative and human collaboration alike, and that this follows from the universality of grace, the incarnation, and the fundamental unity of the love of God and the love of neighbor (*Karl Rahner*). A stronger emphasis on the human and prophetic side of the Kingdom is given by *Edward Schillebeeckx* (the Kingdom of God is our "well-being"), and a correspondingly stronger emphasis on divine initiative is given by *Hans Küng*, who worries as much about a false secularizing of the Kingdom as we once worried about a false interiorizing of it. *Walter Kasper* makes a similar point. *Johannes Metz*, on the other hand, stresses, like Schillebeeckx, the role of human effort in the political realm and speaks even of a "political theology" which formulates the eschatological message under the conditions of our present society. Finally, *Gustavo*

Gutierrez and Latin American liberation theology carry the point even further, insisting that the struggle for justice and for liberation *is* the struggle for the Kingdom of God.

21. *Protestant systematic theology* sees the Kingdom of God as the "answer to the ambiguities of history," at once present and future, cosmic, social, and individual (*Tillich*), the "eschatological fulfillment of the liberating lordship of God in history" (*Moltmann*), "the utterly concrete reality of justice and love" (*Pannenberg*), and the renewed "secular city" *(Cox)*. A more traditional, neo-Reformation warning comes from *Reinhold Niebuhr*, who notes that the relationship between historical justice and the love of the Kingdom of God is a dialectical one, as is the relationship nature and grace. We are bound to realize justice as far as we can, but we can never forget that God alone can bring about the Kingdom in all its fullness beyond history.

22. *Anglican theology* emphasizes the supremacy of the Kingdom of God as a theological category (*J. A. T. Robinson*), warns at the same time against identifying it with social or political achievements (*Macquarrie*), and insists on its evolutionary character as a processive unfolding of the cosmic Love that is God (*Pittenger*).

23. *Orthodox theology (Meyendorff)* sees everything in terms of the destiny of humankind and the world, but it speaks more of the Holy Spirit than of the Kingdom of God. In fact, the Spirit is the Kingdom's "content." The Kingdom is realized already in a mystical rather than a social or political way, especially in the sacraments.

24. The Catholic Church has never officially defined the meaning of the Kingdom of God. One has to infer a doctrinal position from explicit teachings on grace, Original Sin, and Jesus Christ. The *Second Vatican Council's Pastoral Constitution on the Church in the Modern World* speaks of it as "the consummation of the earth and of humanity," signified in the present by the realization of human dignity, brotherhood, and freedom. Pope Paul VI's *Evangelii Nuntiandi* links, but does not completely identify, the Kingdom with "liberation from everything that oppresses man but which is above all liberation from sin and the Evil One." It is the center of the Church's proclamation, as it was of Jesus'.

25. The *last things* pertain to the destiny of *individuals* as well as the whole of humanity and the world. *The destiny of each individual* includes *death* and *judgment*.

26. *Death* was perceived in the *Old Testament* as a state in which the spirit had departed from the body to dwell in *Sheol*, the underground or abode of the dead. For the *New Testament* we overcome death by sharing in Christ's victory over it. The *post-biblical Church* at first

emphasized the Second Coming and the destiny of the Church, but in the Middle Ages there was a shift to the death of individuals and to life after death for the individual. Vatican II restored the fuller, more comprehensive view.

27.   Death forces us to confront the *radical finitude* of our existence, but it also gives our lives *shape and direction*. It can be an affirmative act, providing significance to our lives (as in a hero's death). The death of Jesus is our model. Only in death did he reveal the ultimate seriousness of the claims of God's Kingdom.

28.   *Judgment* is both vindication and punishment in the *Old Testament*. For the *New Testament* the judgment of God occurs even now in our acceptance or rejection of Christ and the Gospel and in the giving of the Spirit. But it is also to take place outside and beyond history, and it will be the act by which evil is finally overcome. The *fact* of judgment is consistently taught by the official Church.

29.   We must distinguish between the *general judgment*, as the consummation of the whole world, and the *particular judgment*, as the fulfillment of the individual's personal life.

30.   The *destiny of the faithful* includes the *beatific vision* (heaven, eternal life), *purgatory*, and the *resurrection of the body*.

31.   The *beatific vision* (heaven, eternal life) is not a part of the *Old Testament*, in which God is always invisible, veiled. The *New Testament* speaks of seeing God without a veil, "face to face" (Paul). We are already tasting eternal life in Christ (John). The reality of the beatific vision is affirmed by *Benedictus Deus* of Pope Benedict XII (1336) and the *Council of Florence* (1439).

32.   The beatific vision is the *full union* of the human person with God, and so with one another in God. It is not a reward for being good, but the *fulfillment* of who we are and who we have been called to become.

33.   *Purgatory* is without clear *biblical* foundation. On the other hand, there is no contradictory evidence in the Bible. The classic text is 2 Maccabees 12:38-46. *Origen's* notion of the universal salvation *(apokatastasis)* was condemned by the provincial council of Constantinople (543). *Augustine* insisted that the just enter heaven immediately. Only gradually, by the time of the Middle Ages, did the idea of a penal and expiatory state develop in the West. The *East* did not reject purgatory, only its juridical character. Rather, purgatory is a process of maturation and spiritual growth after death. The Western and Eastern traditions were blended in the Council of Florence's *Decree for the Greeks* (1439). The *Reformers* rejected purgatory on the principle that

grace alone saves. Prayers for the dead are useless. The *Council of Trent* defined its existence and defended prayers for the dead, especially the Mass. But it also warned against superstition and other spiritual excesses.

34.   Purgatory is best understood as a *process* by which we are purged of our residual selfishness so that we can really become one with the God who is totally oriented to others.

35.   *Indulgences* are the remission of punishment still due to sins which, however, have already been forgiven. If the indulgences remit all punishment, they are *plenary*. Otherwise, they are *partial*. At first they were linked with the sacrament of Penance, but gradually, in the Middle Ages, became an act of the pope. They were applied to the dead, beginning in the fifteenth century. In the later Middle Ages they became a convenient source of income. Abuses followed, and so, too, did the Protestant Reformation.

36.   The doctrine of indulgences at best reflects a proper understanding of the *Communion of Saints*. At worst, it reflects a selfish, calculating approach to Christian destiny.

37.   In the *Bible* the *resurrection of the body* is always the resurrection of the whole person *(soma)* and not of the flesh alone *(sarx)*, since the Bible knew no sharp distinction between body and soul. The New Testament speaks rather of the resurrection of the *dead*. Our resurrection has already begun by our Baptism into Christ's death and resurrection (Paul). The official Church taught the resurrection of the body against those who denied the goodness of the body; see especially *Lateran IV, Lyons II,* and *Benedictus Deus* of Pope Benedict XII. It is also an integral part of the traditional *creeds* of the Church.

38.   The doctrine of the resurrection of the body testifies to the importance of our *bodiliness* as the basis of our *solidarity* with one another, and through others with God. Our hope, therefore, is not simply in the salvation of our soul but in the salvation of our whole being.

39.   The *destiny of the unfaithful* is *hell.*

40.   In the *Old Testament* it is called *Gehenna*. In later Judaism it is understood as a fiery abyss, a place of darkness and chains. This carries over in the *New Testament*. When *Jesus* used such imagery, he did so not to describe a place but to dramatize the urgency of his proclamation of the Kingdom and the seriousness of our decision for or against God. *Paul* is less concrete, speaking instead of a day of wrath and death as the wages of sin. Hell is attested to in the Athanasian Creed, Lateran IV, Lyons II, and *Benedictus Deus* of Pope Benedict XII. Significantly, it is not mentioned in Vatican II or Pope Paul VI's *Credo of the People of God.*

41.   The Church has never defined that anyone is actually *in* hell, only that it exists as a *possibility* for those who totally and deliberately reject God. Hell is not a punishment by God, but it is God's yielding to our freedom to reject the Kingdom.

42.   What of the "occupants" of hell, i.e., the *demons*? Demonology was prevalent in Mesopotamian culture, but the *Old Testament* generally rejected it because of Israel's severe prohibitions against magic. Later Judaism, however, tended to assimilate such beliefs. There are some few references to demons in the *New Testament*. Demons do not occupy a significant place in the official teachings of the Church, except where the Church wanted to insist that whatever exists, including evil spirits, exists by the creative act of God and is under the authority of God (Council of Braga, 561).

43.   Demonology is to be linked with our understanding of *Original Sin*. There is evil in the world which is not simply attributable to our free choice, and it can only be overcome by God's final act in Christ.

44.   The *destiny of the unbaptized* is *limbo* (literally, "border").

45.   There is the limbo of the *pre-Christian just*, and the limbo of *unbaptized infants* and young children. The belief was maintained throughout the Middle Ages and into the twentieth century. Although the Catholic Church continues to endorse and even mandate the Baptism of infants who are in danger of death, the idea of limbo seems less tenable in light of the universality of grace from the very beginning of each person's existence.

46.   Cosmic and individual eschatology converge in the doctrine of the *Communion of Saints*. First found in the Apostles' Creed at the end of the fifth century, it meant from the beginning our participation in the blessings of salvation and in the fellowship of God's holy people. In turn, it became identified with the union of earthly and heavenly Churches, and then with the exchange of spiritual benefits between individuals on earth and individuals in heaven and purgatory.

47.   The doctrine is explicitly affirmed and elaborated upon in the *Second Vatican Council's Dogmatic Constitution on the Church*, where it is described as the foundation of our union with one another in Christ, of our veneration of the saints, and of our hope in the final Kingdom. Our communion with one another in Christ will be brought to fulfillment at the Second Coming and the resurrection of the dead.

SUGGESTED READINGS

Bright, John. *The Kingdom of God: The Biblical Concept and Its Meaning for the Church*. Nashville: Abingdon Press, 1953.

Fortman, Edmund J. *Everlasting Life After Death*. New York: Alba House, 1976.

Guardini, Romano. *The Last Things*. New York: Pantheon Books, 1954.

Pannenberg, Wolfhart. *Theology and the Kingdom of God*. Philadelphia: Westminster Press, 1969.

Papin, Joseph, ed. *The Eschaton: A Community of Love*. Villanova, Pa.: Villanova University Press, 1971.

Schnackenburg, Rudolf. *God's Rule and Kingdom*. London: Nelson, 1963.

Simpson, Michael. *The Theology of Death and Eternal Life*. Notre Dame, Ind.: Fides Publishers, 1971.

CONCLUSION

· XXX ·

CATHOLICISM: A SYNTHESIS

CATHOLICISM IN CONTEXT

Catholicism is not a reality that stands by itself. The word *Catholic* is a qualification of *Christian*, and *Christian* is a qualification of *religious*, and *religious* is a qualification of *human*. Thus, the Catholic Church is a community of persons (the *human*) which believes in the reality of God and shapes its life according to that belief (the *religious*). The Church's belief in, and response to, the reality of God is focused in its fundamental attitude toward Jesus Christ. For the Catholic, as for every *Christian*, the old order has passed away and we are a "new creation" in Christ, for God has "reconciled us to himself through Christ" (2 Corinthians 5:17,19).

If Catholicism is to be described, much less defined, it must be described (and defined) according to a method which respects, and takes into account, each of these constitutive relationships: the human, the religious, and the Christian. And that, in fact, is how we have proceeded throughout this book.

Following some introductory probings into the present crisis in which Catholicism finds itself (chapter 1) and some explorations into the meaning and interrelationships of faith, theology, and belief (chapter 2), we moved in *Part I* to the question of *human existence*. To be a Catholic is, before all else, to be human. Catholicism is an understanding and affirmation of human existence before it is a corporate conviction about the pope, or the seven sacraments, or even about Jesus Christ.

But Catholicism is also more than a corporate understanding and affirmation of what it means to be human. To put it another way: Catholicism answers the question of meaning in terms of ultimacy. With Dietrich Bonhoeffer, Catholicism affirms that there is more to life than meets the eye, that there is "a beyond in our midst." With Paul Tillich, Catholicism affirms that there is a ground of all being which is Being itself. With Thomas Aquinas, Catholicism affirms that all reality is rooted in the creative, loving power of that which is most real (*ens realissimum*). Catholicism answers the question of meaning in terms of the reality of God. In a word, Catholicism is a *religious* perspective, and not simply a philosophical or an anthropological one. And so in *Part II* we raised the issues of belief and unbelief, of revelation, of religion and the plurality of religions, and of the triune *God*.

But Catholicism is not some undifferentiated religious view. Indeed, religion *as such* does not exist. There are particular religion*s*. They share a belief in the Transcendent, but they "name" and "interpret" the Transcendent differently, and they shape their response to the Transcendent (worship, moral behavior, institutional expressions) in accord with those names and interpretations. For the Christian, the ultimate dimension of human experience is a triune God: a God who creates and sustains us, a God who draws near to us and identifies with our historical condition, and a God who empowers us to live according to the vocation to which we have been called. More specifically, the God of Christians is the God of Jesus Christ. In *Part III*, therefore, the book developed the thesis that Catholicism is a *Christian* religious perspective, and not a generically religious one.

Christianity itself, however, is not some undifferentiated Christian reality. Christian faith *as such* is an abstraction. It is always a mediated faith, in terms of its origin, its forms of expression, and its exercise. *Part IV* examined the context in which Christian faith is mediated in the community of faith, *the Church*. But the Church is itself composed of churches. The Church universal is a communion of local churches, and the Body of Christ is composed of denominations (for want of a better term). Thus, the noun *Church* is always modified: the Catholic Church, the Methodist Church, the Orthodox Church, the Lutheran Church, and so forth. Moreover, even these modifiers are themselves modified: the Lutheran Church, Missouri Synod; the Lutheran Church in America; the American Lutheran Church, and so forth. The Body of Christ "subsists in" the Catholic Church (Second Vatican Council, *Dogmatic Constitution on the Church*, n. 8), but it is not coextensive with it. There are other churches which have "a right to be honored by the title Christian." Their members are "incorporated into Christ" through Baptism, and they are "properly regarded" as brothers and sisters "in the Lord" by the Catholic Church (*Decree on Ecumenism*, n. 3).

We moved, therefore, in *Part V* to the ecclesial dimension of *Christian existence* and to its *moral* vision and commitments, its *spiritual* resources, and its *hopes* for the future, in light of which its whole understanding of human existence, of God, of Jesus Christ, and of itself is fashioned, refined, and deepened.

THE QUESTION OF CATHOLICISM'S DISTINCTIVENESS

To what extent, however, is the *ecclesial experience* of Jesus Christ *distinctively Catholic*? To what extent are the *moral vision and commitments distinctively Catholic*? To what extent are the *hopes* in the coming Kingdom of God *distinctively Catholic*?

If Catholicism is distinguishable within the Body of Christ from Protestantism, Anglicanism, and Eastern Orthodoxy, it must be on the basis of some belief(s) or characteristic(s) which Catholicism alone possesses. One belief that is obviously distinctive is Catholicism's commitment to the Petrine office, the papacy. At this point in the history of the Church, the Catholic Church alone affirms that the Petrine ministry is an integral institutional element in the Body of Christ, and that without the papal office the Church universal lacks something essential to its wholeness. It is the one issue which still finally divides the Catholic from all other Christian churches and traditions, notwithstanding various other differences regarding liturgy, spirituality, theology, polity, and doctrinal formulations. When all else is stripped away, the official Catholic position on the Petrine ministry and office is different from every other official and/or representative position of every other formal Christian Church. This is not to suggest that it must always be so, however, and therein lies the difficulty in linking Catholic distinctiveness with the papacy alone.

The Lutheran-Roman Catholic consultation in the United States, for example, has achieved a remarkable measure of consensus already on the question of papal primacy (see chapter 23), giving promise of even greater breakthroughs. It is conceivable, in other words, that Catholicism's affirmations about the Petrine ministry will, at some later date, no longer be Catholicism's affirmations alone. They may be shared by Lutherans, Anglicans, the Orthodox, Presbyterians, Methodists, and others. Will all of Christianity at that point be identified simply with Catholicism? Will Lutheranism, Calvinism, Anglicanism, and Orthodox Christianity fade from the scene once and for all? Will there, then, be one theology, one spirituality, one liturgy, one canon law, one vehicle of doctrinal formulation? If so, it would be the first time in the entire history of the Church, not excluding the New Testament period itself (see, for example, Raymond E. Brown's *The Community of the Beloved Disciple*, New York: Paulist Press, 1979; see also chapters 17 and 18 of this book).

A more fruitful, and more theologically and historically naunced, approach to the question of Catholic distinctiveness would seem to lie in the direction of identifying and describing various *characteristics* of Catholicism, each of which (apart from the commitment to the papacy) Catholicism shares with one or another Christian church or tradition. But how can one distinguish Catholicism from other theological, doctrinal, spiritual, liturgical, and institutional expressions of Christianity on the basis of characteristics which Catholicism presumably *shares* with one or another Christian church? It is true: There is no one characteristic, apart from the Petrine doctrine, which sets the Catholic Church apart from *all other* churches. On the other hand, a case can be made that nowhere else except in the Catholic Church are *all* of Catholicism's characteristics present in the precise *configuration* in which they are found within Catholicism.

The point is crucial to the central thesis of this chapter. An example may help to illustrate it. The flag of the United States of America has individual characteristics which it shares with the flags of other nations of the world. (1) It is *tri-colored*. But so, too, are the flags of Australia, Belgium, Botswana, Colombia, the United Kingdom, France, Ireland, Italy, the Federal Republic of

Germany. (2) Its three colors are *red, white, and blue.* But so, too, are the flags of Burma, Cuba, Czechoslovakia, France, the Netherlands, Panama, the United Kingdom, New Zealand, Yugoslavia. (3) It has *stars* in its basic design. But so, too, do the flags of Australia, the People's Republic of China, Honduras, Venezuela.

Despite these common characteristics, no flag in the entire community of nations is identical with the flag of the United States, a reasonably close similarity to the flag of the African nation of Liberia notwithstanding. What is *distinctive* about the United States' flag is not any one of its several *characteristics* but the precise *configuration* of those characteristics. So, too, with the Catholic Church in relation to all of the other churches and traditions within the Body of Christ.

GENERAL CHARACTERISTICS OF CATHOLICISM

As its very name suggests, Catholicism is characterized by a *radical openness to all truth and to every value.* It is *comprehensive* and *all-embracing* toward the totality of Christian experience and tradition, in all the theological, doctrinal, spiritual, liturgical, canonical, institutional, and social richness and diversity of that experience and tradition. Catholicism is not a post-biblical phenomenon. It does not emerge from some historical moment and from particular historical (i.e., national, cultural, political) circumstances which are removed in time from Jesus' proclamation of the Kingdom, his gathering of disciples, and the formation of the Church in the period encompassed by the New Testament. Catholicism does not begin as a distinctive expression of Christian faith in the sixteenth century, nor are its basic lines already fixed by the fourteenth. It is not itself a sect or a schismatic entity, although sectarianism and schism are not unknown to it. Nor is it inextricably linked with the culture of a particular nation or region of the world. Catholicism is, in principle, as Asian as it is European, as Slavic as it is Latin, as Mexican or Nigerian as it is Irish or Polish.

There is no list of "Catholic Fathers" (or Catholic "Mothers," for that matter) which does not include the great theological and spiritual writers of the period *before* as well as after the division of East and West and the divisions within the West. Gregory of Nyssa is as much a Catholic Father as is Augustine or Thomas Aquinas.

Nor are there *schools of theology* which Catholicism excludes, variations in their inherent strengths and weaknesses notwithstanding. Catholicism continues to read Ignatius of Antioch and Clement of Alexandria, Athanasius and Cyril of Jerusalem, Gregory of Nazianzen and Augustine, Anselm of Canterbury and Bernard of Clairvaux, Abelard and Hugh of St. Victor, Thomas Aquinas and Bonaventure, Robert Bellarmine and Johann Adam Möhler, Karl Rahner and Charles Journet, not to mention John and Luke (see chapters 2, 9, 13, 18, and 25).

Nor are there *spiritualities* which Catholicism excludes, their variations again notwithstanding. Catholicism is open to *The Cloud of Unknowing* and the *Introduction to the Devout Life*, to the way of Francis of Assisi and of Bernard of Clairvaux, to Ignatius Loyola and John of the Cross, to Marmion and Merton (see chapter 28).

Nor are there *doctrinal* streams and mighty rivers that Catholicism closes off. Catholics are guided by Nicea as by Vatican I, by Chalcedon as by Lateran IV, by Trent as by Vatican II. They read Gregory the Great as well as Paul VI, Clement of Rome as well as Leo XIII, Pius XII as well as John XXIII.

Catholicism is characterized, therefore, by a *both/and* rather than an *either/or* approach. It is not nature *or* grace, but graced nature; not reason *or* faith, but reason illumined by faith; not law *or* Gospel, but law inspired by the Gospel; not Scripture *or* tradition, but normative tradition within Scripture; not faith *or* works, but faith issuing in works and works as expressions of faith; not authority *or* freedom, but authority in the service of freedom; not the past *versus* the present, but the present in continuity with the past; not stability *or* change, but change in fidelity to stable principle, and principle fashioned and refined in response to change; not unity *or* diversity, but unity in diversity, and diversity which prevents uniformity, the antithesis of unity.

There have been many moments in the history of the Catholic Church when these delicate balances were disrupted, often through events beyond anyone's control and at other times through narrow-mindedness, blindness, stubbornness, and malice. But the Church is at once holy and sinful, not in the sense that sin exists *alongside* grace, but in the sense that even graced existence is ambiguous, fragile, and subject to disintegration. The record is always mixed. The Kingdom of God is neither coextensive with the Church nor totally divorced from the Church (see chapter 20).

One person looks at a glass and sees that it is half empty; another looks at the same glass and declares it half full. One person looks at the story of the Church and sees only the Church's complicity in the feudal system, the Crusades, the pretentious claims of Innocent III and Boniface VIII, its blindness to the gathering storm clouds of the Reformation, its insensitivities to the East, its arid Scholasticism of the post-Reformation period, its handling of the Galileo affair, its declaration of war against modernity in the nineteenth century, its suppressions of theological freedom under Pope Pius X, its diplomatic hesitancies in the face of Nazism.

Another looks at the same Church and notes the extraordinary, and finally inexplicable, manner in which it drew unity out of seeming chaos in the Christological controversies of the fourth and fifth centuries. Still another marvels at how the Church can be the Church of both John and Paul, of Luke and Timothy, of the martyrs and apologists, of Gregory of Nyssa and Augustine of Hippo, of Gregory the Great and Anselm of Canterbury, of Francis of Assisi and Thomas Aquinas, of monasticism as a protest against political and social privilege and later as the carrier of Western civilization, of heroic reformers like Catherine of Siena, of contemporary saints like John XXIII or Dorothy Day (see chapters 18 and 28).

But perhaps more than anything or anyone else, one must marvel at the Church of *Vatican II*: a *pluralistic* Church open to pluralism, a *modern* Church open to modernity, an *ecumenical* Church open to the whole wide world (the literal meaning of *ecumenical*), a *living* Church open to new life and to the change it brings and requires, a *catholic* Church open in principle to all truth and to every value (see chapter 19.)

For Lutheran Church historian Martin Marty, of the University of Chicago, "Catholicism is a family of apostolic churches, rich in regional, national, ethnic diversity; it is a faith that teaches me that because you have a *core* or center, you can make room for a variety of apparently competitive and interactive elements" ("Something Real and Lumpy," *U.S. Catholic*, vol. 44, May 1979, p. 24).

Like the flag of the United States of America, there are colors here that others share; there are patterns here that others display; there are symbols here that others use. But no other church or tradition within the Body of Christ puts them all together in quite this way. It is in their special configuration that the distinctiveness of Catholicism is disclosed and expressed. It is expressed in its systematic theology, in its body of doctrines, in its liturgical life, especially its Eucharist, in its variety of spiritualities, in its religious congregations and lay apostolates, in its social teachings and commitments to justice, peace, and human rights, in its exercise of collegiality, and in its Petrine ministry.

THE PHILOSOPHICAL FOCUS OF CATHOLICISM: CHRISTIAN REALISM

Catholicism is not bound to any one school of theology, although there is something distinctively Catholic in the way the pluralism of theologies is integrated, systematized, and applied within the Catholic tradition. If the Catholic Church is not linked exclusively to a particular theology, much less is it linked to a particular philosophy: existentialist, process, phenomenological, even Thomistic. And yet there is a distinctively Catholic way of integrating the pluralism of philosophies underlying its various theological and doctrinal orientations. For want of a better term, that distinctively Catholic philosophical focus is "Christian realism," as outlined, for example, by Bernard J.F. Lonergan (see his "The Origins of Christian Realism" in *A Second Collection*, William Ryan and Bernard Tyrrell, eds., Philadelphia: Westminster Press, 1974, pp. 239-261).

Lonergan reminds us that infants, in contrast to adults, do not speak. They live, therefore, in a world of immediacy: of sights and sounds, of tastes and smells, of touching and feeling, of pleasure and pain. But as infants learn to speak, they gradually move into a larger world, a world mediated by meaning. That world includes the past and the future as well as the present, the possible and the probable as well as the actual, rights and duties as well as the facts.

The criteria of reality in the infant's world of immediacy are given in immediate experience. They are simply the occurrence of seeing, hearing, tasting, smelling, touching, pleasure and pain. But the criteria of reality in the world mediated by meaning are far more complex. They include immediate experience but also go beyond it.

"For the world mediated by meaning is not just given," Lonergan insists. "Over and above what is given there is the universe that is intended by questions, that is organized by intelligence, that is described by language, that is enriched by tradition. It is an enormous world far beyond the comprehension of the nursery. But it is also an insecure world, for besides fact there is fiction, besides truth there is error, besides science there is myth, besides honesty there is deceit" (p. 241).

Now this insecurity and ambiguity does not really bother too many people. But it does trouble philosophers and those whose sciences, like theology, depend in some significant measure on correct philosophical presuppositions. Philosophical answers to the question of reality differ. First, there is *naive realism*, which insists that knowing is simply a matter of taking a good look; objectivity is a matter of seeing what is there to be seen; reality is whatever is given in immediate experience. The offspring of naive realism is *empiricism*. The empiricist takes naive realism seriously. The only reality that counts is the reality that one can determine by quantitative measurement. Empiricism, in turn, begets its philosophical opposite, *critical idealism* (Kant), in which the categories of understanding of themselves are empty and refer to objects only insofar as the categories are applied to the data of the senses. This is the world of *phenomena*. We cannot know things in themselves, the *noumena*.

"Insofar as Christianity is a reality, it is involved in the problems of realism," Lonergan suggests. First, Christianity itself is mediated by meaning. "It is mediated by meaning in its communicative function inasmuch as it is preached. It is mediated by meaning in its cognitive function inasmuch as it is believed. It is mediated by meaning in its constitutive function inasmuch as it is a way of life that is lived. It is mediated by meaning in its effective function inasmuch as its precepts are put into practice" (p. 244).

But there is ambiguity within the Christian's world, as there is in human life itself. For the Christian world is not *exclusively* a world mediated by meaning. There is also the immediacy of God's grace creating the new creature in Christ by the power of the Holy Spirit. The grace of God is not produced by the preacher, nor is it the result of believing the Gospel, nor does it come as a reward for good works. Grace is present to the individual person, as we have seen (chapter 5), from the very beginning of the person's existence. Grace enters into the definition of what it means to be human.

Thus, the real is not only what I can see and touch, as naive realism suggests. Nor is the real just an idea in the mind, as idealism insists. The real is what I judge to be real. The reality of the world mediated by meaning is known not by experience alone, nor by ideas alone, but by judgments and beliefs.

It is this commitment to *critical* realism that has moved the Catholic Church, first at Nicea (325) and again and again in its official teachings, to deliberate, to issue decrees, to condemn, to explain, to defend, to make distinctions, to use technical terms, to engage in the most acute rational reflection. Indeed, it is this commitment to critical realism that is at the foundation of the medieval effort toward systematization and of our own contemporary systematic enterprises as well.

What does all this mean? It means that the Catholic tradition philosophically rejects both naive realism and idealism as adequate bases for Catholicism's theological vision. One contemporary form of naive realism is *biblicism.* For the biblicist, the meaning of the Word of God is obvious. "Just take a look," the biblicist seems to say. "The requirements of Christian existence are clear. The answers are readily available in the pages of Sacred Scripture." *Moralism* is another contemporary form of naive realism. "Just consult your gut feelings, or use your common sense," the moralist insists. "Of course, violence is against the Gospel of Jesus Christ." Or: "Of course, violence can be justified to counteract oppressive violence." But moralism provides no arguments, no warrants, no reasons. It is assumed that the convictions are self-evidently true and their intrinsic power compelling.

Idealism, on the other hand, makes of Christianity a system of principles and ideas, but without clear or meaningful connection with the pastoral situation or the human condition at large. One need not worry about the effectiveness of preaching and teaching, for example, if one is convinced that the ideas to be preached and taught are plainly, even though not infallibly, true. One need not engage in time-consuming and ultimately diverting moral speculation about what it is one must do in such-and-such a conflict-situation when there is a clear statement of moral principle already "on the books." The contemporary forms of idealism are *dogmatism* and *legalism.* Dogmatism assumes that salvation is linked primarily to "right belief" and that the rightness of beliefs is clear and almost self-evident. Legalism assumes that salvation is linked primarily to "right practice," i.e., of obedience to Church laws. There is never any serious doubt about what the law demands, so specific and so detailed is it.

Critical realism, or what Lonergan calls Christian realism, insists that experience itself is not enough. One can "take a look," but one cannot be sure that what one sees corresponds entirely to what is real. "Appearances can be deceiving," the old saying has it. Christian realism also rejects the notion that clear and distinct ideas (doctrines, dogmas, canonical directives) are equivalent to the real itself. Ideas are never formulated except in relation to other ideas, to events, to one's associates, to the problems and resources at hand, to the historical circumstances, to social, economic, and political conditions, to one's own background, age, sex, nationality, occupation, income level, social status, and the like. Just as Christian realism rejects biblicism and moralism in favor of a critical and systematic approach to reality, so Christian realism rejects dogmatism and legalism in favor of a critical and systematic approach to reality, an approach that goes beyond what seems to be there and that takes historicity into account in the use and interpretation of ideas and principles.

This critical realism carries over into everything the Church does. Thus, the Church's moral vision and its approach to the demands of Christian existence are qualified always by its confidence in the power of grace and by its readiness to expect and understand the weaknesses and failures rooted in Original Sin. And so Catholicism is a moral universe of laws but also of dispensations, of rules but also of exceptions, of respect for authority but also for freedom of conscience, of high ideals but also of minimal requirements, of penalties but also of indulgences, of censures and excommunications but also of absolution and of reconciliation.

THE THEOLOGICAL FOCI OF CATHOLICISM: SACRAMENTALITY, MEDIATION, COMMUNION

No theological principle or focus is more characteristic of Catholicism or more central to its identity than the principle of *sacramentality*. The Catholic vision sees God in and through all things: other people, communities, movements, events, places, objects, the world at large, the whole cosmos. The visible, the tangible, the finite, the historical—all these are actual or potential carriers of the divine presence. Indeed, it is only in and through these material realities that we can even encounter the invisible God. The great sacrament of our encounter with God and of God's encounter with us is Jesus Christ. The Church, in turn, is the sacrament of our encounter with Christ and of Christ's with us, and the sacraments, in turn, are the signs and instruments by which that ecclesial encounter with Christ is expressed, celebrated, and made effective for the glory of God and the salvation of men and women.

A corollary of the principle of sacramentality is the principle of *mediation*. A sacrament not only signifies; it also causes what it signifies. Thus, created realities not only contain, reflect, or embody the presence of God. They make that presence effective for those who avail themselves of these realities. Just as we noted in the previous section that the world is mediated by meaning, so the universe of grace is a mediated reality: mediated principally by Christ, and secondarily by the Church and by other signs and instruments of salvation outside and beyond the Church.

Catholicism rejects naive realism, which hold to the immediacy of the experience of God as the normal or exclusive kind of

encounter with the divine presence. Catholicism also rejects idealism, which holds that the encounter with God occurs solely in the
inwardness of conscience and the inner recesses of consciousness.
Catholicism holds, on the contrary, that the encounter with God
is a mediated experience but a *real* experience, rooted in the
historical and affirmed as real by the critical and systematic judgment that God is truly present and active here or there, in this
event or that, in this person or that, in this object or that.

Finally, Catholicism affirms the principle of *communion*: that
our way to God and God's way to us is not only a mediated way
but a communal way. And even when the divine-human encounter
is most personal and individual, it is still communal in that the
encounter is made possible by the mediation of the community.
Thus, there is *not* simply an individual personal relationship with
God or Jesus Christ that is established and sustained by meditative
reflection on Sacred Scripture, for the Bible itself is the Church's
book and is the testimony of the Church's original faith. The
mystic (even in the narrow sense of the word) relies on language,
ideas, concepts, presuppositions when he or she enters into, or
reflects upon, an intimate, contemplative relationship with God.
We are radically social beings; our use of language is clear evidence of that. There is no relationship with God, however intense,
profound, and unique, that dispenses entirely with the communal
context of *every* human relationship with God.

And this is why, for Catholicism, the mystery of the Church
has so significant a place in theology, doctrine, pastoral practice,
moral vision and commitment, and devotion. Catholics have
always emphasized the place of the Church as both the *sacrament*
of Christ, *mediating* salvation through sacraments, ministries, and
other institutional elements and forms, and as the *Communion of
Saints*, the preview or foretaste, as it were, of the perfect communion to which the whole of humankind is destined in the final
Kingdom of God.

And so it is with the *mystery of the Church* that we come at
last to the point at which the distinctively Catholic understanding
and practice of Christian faith most clearly emerges. For here we
find the convergence of those principles which have always been
so characteristic of Catholicism: sacramentality, mediation, and

communion—principles grasped and interpreted according to the mode of critical realism rather than of naive realism or idealism.

These principles, at once philosophical and theological, have shaped, and continue to shape, Catholicism's Christology, ecclesiology, sacramentology, canon law, spirituality, Mariology, theological anthropology, moral theology, liturgy, social doctrine, and the whole realm of art and aesthetics. The last item is a particular case in point. In contrast, Protestantism, as a religion of the word, has had a "mixed" record when it comes to the arts. It has been "uneasy about objectification of the divine drama in images which might themselves draw the devotion of the supplicant from the invisible God beyond the gods. It has often and maybe even usually been uneasy about unrestricted bodily attention, and has rather consistently feared the ecstasy of the dance through most of the years of its history" (Martin Marty, *Protestantism*, p. 228; for a broader view of Catholicism's aesthetical impact, see Kenneth Clark's *Civilisation*, pp. 167-192).

Baptist theologian Langdon Gilkey saw many of the same characteristics when he probed the reality of Catholicism in search of its distinctive identity. First, he concluded, there is Catholicism's "sense of reality, importance, and 'weight' of tradition and history in the formation of this people and so of her religious truths, religious experience, and human wisdom."

Secondly, there is, "especially to a Protestant, a remarkable sense of humanity and grace in the communal life of Catholics. . . . Consequently the love of life, the appreciation of the body and the senses, of joy and celebration, the tolerance of the sinner, these natural, worldly and 'human' virtues are far more clearly and universally embodied in Catholics and in Catholic life than in Protestants and in Protestantism."

Thirdly, there is Catholicism's "continuing experience, unequalled in other forms of Western Christianity, of the presence of God and of grace mediated through symbols to the entire course of ordinary human life." For Gilkey, a symbol points to and communicates the reality of God which lies beyond it. A symbol can be viewed and appropriated "as *relative*, as a 'symbol' and not God, without sacrificing this relation to the *absoluteness* that makes it a vehicle of the sacred." The experience of the symbol can unite "sensual, aesthetic, and intellectual experience more readily than the experiences of proclamation or of an ecstatic spiritual presence." The Catholic principle of symbol or sacramentality, according to Gilkey, "may provide the best entrance into a new synthesis of the Christian tradition with the vitalities as well as the relativities of contemporary existence."

Finally, there has been "throughout Catholic history a drive toward rationality, the insistence that the divine mystery manifest in tradition and sacramental presence be insofar as possible penetrated, defended, and explicated by the most acute rational reflection" (*Catholicism Confronts Modernity: A Protestant View*, pp. 17-18, 20-22).

A CONCLUDING WORD

It is not a question here in this chapter, or indeed in this book, of arguing that the Catholic Church and the Catholic tradition are necessarily superior to all of the other churches and traditions on this point or that, but that there is within Catholicism a configuration of values which enjoy a normative character in discerning the Christian tradition as a whole.

These values include Catholicism's sense of *sacramentality* (God is present everywhere, the invisible in the visible, within us and within the whole created order); its principle of *mediation* (the divine is available to us as a transforming, healing, renewing power through the ordinary things of life: persons, communities, events, places, institutions, natural objects, etc.); its sense of *communion*, or of peoplehood (we are radically social and so, too, is our relationship with God and God's with us); its drive toward *rationality* and its *critical realism* (reality is neither self-evident nor confined to the realm of ideas); its corresponding respect for *history*, for *tradition*, and for *continuity* (we are products of our past as well as shapers of our present and our future); its conviction that we can have as radical a notion of *sin* as we like so long as our understanding and appreciation of *grace* is even more radical; its high regard for *authority* and *order* as well as for *conscience* and *freedom*; indeed its *fundamental openness to all truth and to every value*—in a word, its *catholicity*.

SUMMARY

1. Catholicism is not a reality that stands by itself. The word *Catholic* is a qualification of *Christian*, and *Christian* is a qualification of *religious*, and *religious* is a qualification of *human*.

2. The larger *context* of Catholicism has dictated the structure of this book: the meaning of human existence (Part I), the experience of God as the ground of human existence (Part II), the experience of Jesus Christ as the focal point of our experience of God (Part III), the experience of Church as the sacrament of Christ (Part IV), and the moral vision and hopes evoked by such meanings and experiences (Part V).

3. The Catholic Church alone affirms that the *Petrine ministry*, or papacy, is an integral institutional element in the Body of Christ, and that without the papal office the universal Church lacks something essential to its wholeness. It is the one issue which finally divides the Catholic from all other Christians. But this may not always be so, as the Lutheran-Roman Catholic consultation in the U.S.A. suggests.

4. The *distinctiveness* of Catholicism, therefore, lies not simply in its affirmation of the Petrine office but in the unique *configuration of characteristics* which Catholicism possesses and manifests as a Church and as a tradition within the Body of Christ and Christianity at large.

5. *In general*, Catholicism is characterized by a *radical openness to all truth and to every value*. Catholicism does not emerge from a particular time after the foundational period of the New Testament, nor is it tied to a particular nation or culture. It endorses no one school of theology or spirituality and no single interpretation of doctrine.

6. Catholicism is characterized by a *both/and* rather than an either/or approach to nature and grace, reason and faith, law and Gospel, Scripture and tradition, faith and works, authority and freedom, past and present, stability and change, unity and diversity.

7. The *historical record* of Catholicism is mixed: There are, e.g., the triumphalism and even the decadence of the medieval papacy and the simplicity and sanctity of Francis of Assisi, the condemnatory spirit of Pius IX and the openness of John XXIII.

8. Nowhere is the *catholicity* of the Church more evident, however, than at *Vatican II*: A Church at once *pluralistic* and open to pluralism, *modern* and open to modernity, *ecumenical* and open to the

whole wide world, *alive* and open to new life, and *catholic* and open in principle to all truth and every value.

9.   Catholicism is not alone in possessing or manifesting such characteristics, no more than the flag of the United States of America is the only tri-colored flag in the world, or the only one using red, white, and blue, or the only one with stars in its design. But that flag is unique in the configuration of those characteristics. There is no other flag exactly like it. So, too, with Catholicism.

10.   *Specifically*, Catholicism's *philosophical focus* is *critical*, or *Christian, realism*. It sees the world as mediated by meaning. Thus, it sees neither a world of immediate experience alone (naive realism, empiricism) nor a world of ideas alone (idealism).

11.   Christian realism insists that experience ("taking a look") is not enough, as biblicism and moralism suppose, and that reality is not to be identified simply with clear and distinct ideas (doctrines, dogmas, canonical directives), as dogmatism and legalism suppose. It maintains that "appearances can be deceiving," on the one hand, and that ideas are always historically conditioned, on the other.

12.   This critical realism carries over into everything the Church does. In the realm of moral demands, for example, Catholicism is a religion of laws but also of dispensations, of censures but also of absolutions.

13.   The *theological foci* of Catholicism include the principles of *sacramentality, mediation*, and *communion*.

14.   The principle of *sacramentality* means that God is present and operative in and through the visible, the concrete, the tangible, the finite, the historical: persons, communities, places, events, natural objects, the whole created order. The great sacrament of encounter with God is *Christ*, and the *Church*, in turn, is the sacrament of encounter with Christ, and the *sacraments*, in turn, are the signs and instruments by which that ecclesial encounter with Christ is expressed, celebrated, and made effective for all.

15.   The principle of *mediation* is a corollary of the principle of sacramentality. God uses signs and instruments to communicate grace—i.e., to become present to the whole of creation. Catholicism rejects naive realism, which holds to the immediacy of the experience of God as the normal or exclusive kind of encounter with God, and also idealism, which holds that the encounter with God occurs solely in the inwardness of conscience and consciousness.

16.   The principle of *communion* means that our way to God and God's way to us is mediated through community: the human community

at large and the Church in particular. Communion is both the way and the goal. The *Communion of Saints* is the preview or foretaste of the perfect communion to which the whole of humankind is destined in the final Kingdom of God.

17.   These principles, philosophical and theological alike, have shaped, and continue to shape, the total reality that is Catholicism: e.g., theology, liturgy, spirituality, structures, art.

18.   By way of contrast, for example *Protestantism*, a religion mainly of the word, has had a "mixed" record when it comes to the arts, the celebration of the bodily, and bodily expression.

19.   *Langdon Gilkey* identifies the following as characteristic of Catholicism: its sense of tradition and history, its sense of peoplehood and community, its sense of symbol and sacrament, and its drive toward rationality and rational reflection.

20.   It was not the purpose of this chapter or of this book to establish the superiority of Catholicism but to identify its *distinctiveness* by calling attention to the *configuration of values* which one finds nowhere else in the Body of Christ or in Christianity at large: sacramentality, mediation, communion, rationality, continuity, the triumph of grace over sin, the regard for authority and order as well as conscience and freedom, and its fundamental openness to all truth and to every value. In a word, its *catholicity.*

SUGGESTED READINGS

Clark, Kenneth. *Civilisation*, New York: Harper & Row, 1969.

Delaney, John J., ed. *Why Catholic?* New York: Doubleday, 1979.

Gilkey, Langdon. *Catholicism Confronts Modernity: A Protestant View.* New York: Seabury Press, 1975.

Lossky, Vladimir. *The Mystical Theology of the Eastern Church.* London: Clarke, 1957.

Marty, Martin E. *Protestantism.* New York: Holt, Rinehart and Winston, 1972.

APPENDIX

The Creed of the Council of Constantinople (381) (The council of Constantinople was convened to reaffirm the faith of the council of Nicea, of 325. Though not itself promulgated by the council of Constantinople, this creed soon acquired greater authority than even the Nicene Creed. Since the seventh century it has been known as the *Nicene-Constantinopolitan Creed.*)

> We believe in one God,
>> the Father, the Almighty,
>> maker of heaven and earth,
>> of all that is seen and unseen.
>
> We believe in one Lord, Jesus Christ,
>> the only Son of God,
>> eternally begotten of the Father,
>> God from God, Light from Light,
>> true God from true God,
>> begotten, not made, one in Being with the Father.
>> Through him all things were made.
>> For us men and for our salvation
>>> he came down from heaven:
>> by the power of the Holy Spirit
>> he was born of the Virgin Mary, and became man.
>
> For our sake he was crucified under Pontius Pilate;
>> he suffered, died, and was buried.
>> On the third day he rose again
>>> in fulfillment of the Scriptures;
>> he ascended into heaven
>>> and is seated at the right hand of the Father.
>
> He will come again in glory to judge the living and the dead,
>> and his kingdom will have no end.
>
> We believe in the Holy Spirit, the Lord, the giver of life,
>> who proceeds from the Father and the Son.
>> With the Father and the Son he is worshiped and
>>> glorified.
>> He has spoken through the Prophets.
>> We believe in one holy catholic and apostolic Church.
>> We acknowledge one baptism for the forgiveness of sins.
>> We look for the resurrection of the dead,
>>> and the life of the world to come. Amen.

• • •

Instruction on the Historical Truth of the Gospels, Pontifical Biblical Commission, April 21, 1964. (Excerpt. Full text in the *Catholic Biblical Quarterly,* vol. 26, July 1964, pp. 305-312.)

1. The Catholic exegete, under the guidance of the Church, must turn to account all the resources for the understanding of the sacred text which have been put at his disposal by previous interpreters, especially the holy Fathers and Doctors of the Church, whose labors it is for him to take up and to carry on. In order to bring out with fullest clarity the enduring truth and authority of the Gospels he must, whilst carefully observing the rules of rational and of Catholic hermeneutics, make skillful use of the new aids to exegesis, especially those which the historical method, taken in its widest sense, has provided; that method, namely, which minutely investigates sources, determining their nature and bearing, and availing itself of the findings of textual criticism, literary criticism, and linguistic studies. The interpreter must be alert to the reminder given him by Pope Pius XII of happy memory when he charged him "to make judicious inquiry as to how far the form of expression or the type of literature adopted by the sacred writer may help towards the true and genuine interpretation, and to remain convinced that this part of his task cannot be neglected without great detriment to Catholic exegesis."[5] In this reminder Pius XII of happy memory is laying down a general rule of hermeneutics, one by whose help the books both of the Old Testament and of the New are to be explained, since the sacred writers when composing them followed the way of thinking and of writing current amongst their contemporaries. In a word, the exegete must make use of every means which will help him to reach a deeper understanding of the character of the gospel testimony, of the religious life of the first churches, and of the significance and force of the apostolic tradition.

In appropriate cases the interpreter is free to seek out what sound elements there are in "the Method of Form-history," and these he can duly make use of to gain a fuller understanding of the Gospels. He must be circumspect in doing so, however, because the method in question is often found alloyed with principles of a philosophical or theological nature which are quite inadmissible, and which not infrequently vitiate both the method itself and the conclusions arrived at regarding literary questions. For certain exponents of this method, led astray by rationalistic prejudices, refuse to admit that there exists a supernatural order, or that a personal God intervenes in the world by revelation properly so called, or that miracles and prophecies are possible and have actually occurred. There are others who have as their starting-point a wrong notion of faith, taking it that faith is indifferent to historical truth, and is indeed incompatible with it. Others practically deny *a priori* the historical value and character of the documents of revelation. Others finally there are who on the one hand underestimate the authority which the Apostles had as witnesses of Christ, and the office and influence which they wielded in the primitive community, whilst on the other hand they overestimate the creative capacity of the community itself. All these aberrations are not only opposed to Catholic doctrine, but are also devoid of any scientific foundation, and are foreign to the genuine principles of the historical method.

2. In order to determine correctly the trustworthiness of what is transmitted in the Gospels, the interpreter must take careful note of the three stages of tradition by which the teaching and the life of Jesus have come down to us.

Christ our Lord attached to Himself certain chosen disciples[6] who had followed Him from the beginning,[7] who had seen His works and had heard His words, and thus were qualified to become witnesses of His life and teaching.[8] Our Lord, when expounding His teaching by word of mouth, observed the methods of reasoning and of exposition which were in common use at the time; in this way He accommodated Himself to the mentality of His hearers, and ensured that His teachings would be deeply impressed on their minds and would be easily retained in memory by His disciples. These latter grasped correctly the idea that the miracles and other events of the life of Jesus were things purposely performed or arranged by Him in such a way that men would thereby be led to believe in Christ and to accept by faith the doctrine of salvation.

The Apostles, bearing testimony to Jesus,[9] proclaimed first and foremost the death and resurrection of the Lord, faithfully recounting His life and words[10] and, as regards the manner of their preaching, taking into account the circumstances of their hearers.[11] After Jesus had risen from the dead, and when His divinity was clearly perceived,[12] the faith of the disciples, far from blotting out the remembrance of the events that had happened, rather consolidated it, since their faith was based on what Jesus had done and taught.[13] Nor was Jesus transformed into a "mythical" personage, and His teaching distorted, by reason of the worship which the disciples now paid Him, revering Him as Lord and Son of God. Yet it need not be denied that the Apostles, when handing on to their hearers the things which in actual fact the Lord had said and done, did so in the light of that fuller understanding which they enjoyed as a result of being schooled by the glorious things accomplished in Christ,[14] and of being illumined by the Spirit of Truth.[15] Thus it came about that, just as Jesus Himself after His resurrection had "interpreted to them"[16] both the words of the Old Testament and the words which He Himself had spoken,[17] so now they in their turn interpreted His words and deeds according to the needs of their hearers. "Devoting (themselves) to the ministry of the word,"[18] they made use, as they preached, of such various forms of speech as were adapted to their own purposes and to the mentality of their hearers; for it was "to Greek and barbarian, to learned and simple,"[19] that they had a duty to discharge.[20] These varied ways of speaking which the heralds of Christ made use of in proclaiming Him must be distinguished one from the other and carefully appraised: catecheses, narratives, testimonies, hymns, doxologies, prayers and any other such literary forms as were customarily employed in Sacred Scripture and by people of that time.

The sacred authors, for the benefit of the churches, took this earliest body of instruction, which had been handed on orally at first and then in writing—for many soon set their hands to "drawing up a narrative"[21] of matters concerning the Lord Jesus—and set it down in the four Gospels. In doing this each of them followed a method suitable to the special purpose which he had in view. They selected certain things out of the many which had been handed on; some they synthesized, some they explained with an eye to the situation of the churches, painstakingly using every means of bringing home to their readers the solid truth of the things in which they had been instructed.[22] For, out of the material which they had received, the sacred authors selected especially those items which were adapted to the varied circumstances of the faithful as well as to the end which they themselves wished to attain; these they recounted in a manner consonant with those circumstances and with that end. And since the meaning of a statement depends, amongst other things, on the place which it has in a given sequence, the Evangelists, in handing on the words or the deeds of our Savior, explained them for the advantage of their readers by respectively setting them, one Evangelist in one context, another in another. For this reason the exegete must ask himself what the Evangelist intended by recounting a saying or a fact in a certain way, or by placing it in a certain context. For the truth of the narrative is not affected in the slightest by the fact that the Evangelists report the sayings or the doings of our Lord in a different order,[23] and that they use different words to express what He said, not keeping to the very letter, but nevertheless preserving the sense.[24] For, as St. Augustine says: "Where it is a question only of those matters whose order in the narrative may be indifferently this or that without in any way taking from the truth and authority of the Gospel, it is probable enough that each Evangelist believed he should narrate them in that same order in which God was pleased to suggest them to his recollection. The Holy Spirit distributes His gifts to each one according as He wills;[25] therefore, too, for the sake of those Books which were to be set so high at the very summit of authority, He undoubtedly guided and controlled the minds of the holy writers in their recollection of what they were to write; but as to why, in doing so, He should have permitted them, one to follow this order in his narrative, another to follow that—that is a question whose answer may possibly be found with God's help, if one seeks it out with reverent care."[26]

Unless the exegete, then, pays attention to all those factors which have a bearing on the origin and the composition of the Gospels, and makes due use of the acceptable findings of modern research, he will fail in his duty of ascertaining what the intentions of the sacred writers were, and what it is that they have actually said. The results of recent study have made it clear that the teachings and the life of Jesus were not simply recounted for the mere purpose of being kept in remembrance, but were "preached" in such a way as to furnish the Church with the foundation on which to build up faith and morals. It follows that the interpreter who subjects the testimony of the Evangelists to persevering scrutiny will be in a position to shed further light on the enduring theological value of the Gospels, and to throw into clearest relief the vital importance of the Church's interpretation.

[5] *Divino afflante Spiritu; EB* 560.
[6] Cf. *Mc.* 3,14; *Lc.* 6,13.
[7] Cf. *Lc.* 1,2; *Act.* 1,21-22.
[8] Cf. *Lc.* 24,48; *Jn.* 15,27; *Act.* 1,8; 10,39; 13,31.
[9] Cf. *Lc.* 24, 44-48; *Act.* 2,32; 3,15; 5,30-32.
[10] Cf. *Act.* 10,36-41.
[11] Cf. *Act.* 13,16-41 with *Act.* 17,22-31.
[12] *Act.* 2,36; *Jn.* 20,28.
[13] *Act* 2,22; 10,37-39.
[14] *Jn.* 2,22; 12,16; 11,51-52; cf. 14,26; 16,12-13; 7,39.
[15] Cf. *Jn.* 14,26; 16,13.
[16] *Lc.* 24,27.
[17] Cf. *Lc.* 24,44-45; *Act.* 1,3.
[18] *Act.* 6,4.
[19] *Rom.* 1,14.
[20] *1 Cor.* 9,19-23.
[21] Cf. *Lc.* 1,1.
[22] Cf. *Lc.* 1,4.
[23] Cf. St. John Chrys., *In Mat. Hom.* I,3; *PG* 57,16,17.
[24] Cf. St August., *De consensu Evang.* 2,12,28; *PL* 34, 1090-1091.
[25] *I Cor.* 12,11.
[26] *De consensu Evang.,* 2, 21, 51 s.; *PL* 34,1102.

Declaration in Defense of the Catholic Doctrine on the Church Against Certain Errors of the Present Day (Mysterium Ecclesiae), Congregation for the Doctrine of the Faith, June 24, 1973. (Excerpt. Full text in *Origins: NC Documentary Service,* vol. 3, July 19, 1973, pp. 97,99,100.)

The transmission of divine Revelation by the Church encounters difficulties of various kinds. These arise from the fact that the hidden mysteries of God 'by their nature so far transcend the human intellect that even if they are revealed to us and accepted by faith, they remain concealed by the veil of faith itself and are as it were wrapped in darkness'. Difficulties arise also from the historical condition that affects the expression of Revelation.

With regard to this historical condition, it must first be observed that the meaning of the pronouncements of faith depend partly upon the expressive power of the language used at a certain point in time and in particular circumstances. Moreover, it sometimes happens that some dogmatic truth is first expressed incompletely (but not falsely), and at a later date, when considered in a broader context of faith or human knowledge, it receives a fuller and more perfect expression. In addition, when the Church makes new pronouncements she intends to confirm or clarify what is in some way contained in Sacred Scripture or in previous expressions of Tradition; but at the same time she usually has the intention of solving certain questions or removing certain errors. All these things have to be taken into account in order that these pronouncements may be properly interpreted. Finally, even though the truths which the Church intends to teach through her dogmatic formulas are distinct from the changeable conceptions of a given epoch and can be expressed without them, nevertheless it can sometimes happen that these truths may be enunciated by the Sacred Magisterium in terms that bear traces of such conceptions.

In view of the above, it must be stated that the dogmatic formulas of the Church's Magisterium were from the very beginning suitable for communicating revealed truth, and that as they are they remain for ever suitable for communicating this truth to those who interpret them correctly. It does not however follow that every one of these formulas has always been or will always be so to the same extent. For this reason theologians seek to define exactly the intention of teaching proper to the various formulas, and in carrying out this work they are of considerable assistance to the living Magisterium of the Church, to which they remain subordinated. For this reason also it oftens happens that ancient dogmatic formulas and others closely connected with them remain living and fruitful in the habitual usage of the Church, but with suitable expository and explanatory additions that maintain and clarify their original meaning. In addition, it has sometimes happened that in this habitual usage of the Church certain of these formulas gave way to new expressions which, proposed and approved by the Sacred Magisterium, presented more clearly or more completely the same meaning.

As for the meaning of dogmatic formulas, this remains ever true and constant in the Church, even when it is expressed with greater clarity or [is] more developed. The faithful therefore must shun the opinion, first, that dogmatic formulas (or some category of them) cannot signify truth in a determinate way, but can only offer changeable approximations to it, which to a certain extent distort or alter it; secondly, that these formulas signify the truth only in an indeterminate way, this truth being like a goal that is constantly being sought by means of such approximations. Those who hold such an opinion do not avoid dogmatic relativism and they corrupt the concept of the Church's infallibility relative to the truth to be taught or held in a determinate way.

•••

"A Courageous Worldwide Theology," an address by Karl Rahner, S.J., at John Carroll University, Cleveland, Ohio, April 6, 1979, on the occasion of receiving an honorary degree marking his seventy-fifth birthday. (Excerpt. Full text in *National Jesuit News,* vol. 8, June 1979, p. 10.)

It is my preference that both the tribute and my thanks be directed toward the contemporary theology in its entirety—that theology shaped in the last 30 years and recognized somewhat officially by the Second Vatican Council.

Of course, I have in mind an orthodox Catholic theology. That goes without saying. A theology which would not be obedient and docile under the word of God as it is proclaimed in the Church would not be Catholic theology. But I am envisaging a Catholic theology that is courageous and does not shun relative and restricted conflicts with Church authorities. I am thinking of a theology which can no longer be uniform in a neoscholastic approach.

I call that time of uniformity the "Pius epoch," but that era of the Popes who bore the name "Pius" has after all come to an end. I envisage a theology which is in dialogue with its time and lives courageously with it and in it.

This is all the more possible because it is characteristic of this time to be at a critical distance from itself, something *God makes possible*. It is a special grace to this age to be able now to have a critical distance from ourselves given us from the Cross of Christ.

From this more critical distance, I envisage a theology which in the Church at large must be the theology of a worldwide Church. That means a theology which does not only recite its own medieval history, but one that can listen to the wisdom of the East, to the longing for freedom in Latin America, and also to the sound of African drums.

I envisage a systematic theology that is an inner unity and what Trinitarian theologians call *perichoresis* (literally a dancing around together) of fundamental and dogmatic theology. I envisage a theology that enables human beings of our time to have a real grasp on the message of freedom and redemption, a theology that courageously abandons external stanchions of seemingly self-evident truths and things, something which does not stem necessarily from what is Christian, but rather from the changing historical situation structured by its intellectual and social elements.

I envisage a theology that does not only move along the numbers in our familiar friend "Denzinger" interpreting old ecclesiastical pronouncements, but a theology which breaks new ground for *new* pronouncements of the Church.

It would be a theology which takes seriously the hierarchy of truths, a theology which lives by the ecumenical hope that baptized Christians should be able to communicate in that which they all live in their faith. Such a communication should be possible without losing sight of the multiplicity of charisms of life and thought.

I envisage a theology which comprehends itself as an interpretation of the reality which through grace is present in every human being; a reality which is not only given to man by external indoctrination.

It would be a theology through which this reality would find itself, and which would not pride itself upon its clear concepts but would force them to open over and over again into the incomprehensibility of God himself. Such a theology would not secretly seek to understand itself as *the* theoretical underpinning of a life of middle-class ethics supervised by God.

One could continue in this vein for long. But my purpose is not to degrade the old theology, whose grateful children we are and remain. It has been rather to hint from afar that our time calls also us theologians sleeping under the broom tree of orthodoxy like Elijah in old days: *Surge, grandis tibi restat via*—Arise, a long journey lies ahead of you.

HOW TO USE THIS BOOK

This book is usable as both a textbook and a reference work. The material is organized in such a way that it can be assimilated in self-contained, coherent units presented in a logical sequence of instruction.

Each chapter begins with a statement and explanation of the problem under discussion. An effort is made to locate the topic in relation to others. The history of the discussion is then reviewed, with constant attention to biblical foundations, major theological points of view, and the official teachings of the Church. Current positions are summarized, and, where appropriate, criteria are offered by which the reader can reach his or her own responsible judgment on the matter at hand. The perspective is at once Catholic and ecumenical.

Detailed summaries follow each chapter. These are, in a sense, the author's own underlinings of the text. The reader will never be in serious doubt about what the author was attempting to say, even if his efforts toward clarification were not always successful within the chapter itself. The summaries might also profitably be consulted *before* reading the chapter, as a useful preview.

A brief listing of books and articles is appended to each chapter for the reader who wishes to pursue the topic in greater breadth and depth. Discussion questions for each chapter are to be found near the end of the book. They are suggested, not for the sake of review but for the sake of helping the user to carry the theological principles forward, to test their applicability in the pastoral or human situation in which the user finds himself or herself.

Each chapter can be read as an independent essay or unit. Some may choose, for example, to begin reading the book at the end, at chapter 30, since that chapter summarizes and synthesizes the whole book. Others may follow whatever sequence is consistent with their own interests and educational needs. Still others may find one or another chapter helpful for a particular project or for updating in a single area.

The glossary of terms will enable the reader to refresh his or her memory about some technical expression without searching through the index for various references to it in the text itself. The glossary should be of special value to those who will be reading individual chapters apart from their given sequence.

The book should be usable for the following courses:

1. A one- or two-semester course on Catholicism in general.

2. Single-semester courses on (a) the meaning of human existence, (b) the reality of God, (c) Jesus Christ, (d) the Church, or (e) Christian ethics.

3. Shorter courses, especially at the parish level, on more limited topics—e.g., the sacraments.

It should also be useful background for courses in biblical theology, liturgy, spirituality, church history, and the history of Christian thought, and for all theological courses presented from a perspective other than Catholic.

If the book is used for a general course on *Catholicism*, it can be adapted in the following ways:

For a *two-semester* course, chapters 1-16 would be covered in the first half of the course, and chapters 17-30 in the second half. For a *one-semester* course, the entire book should be read by the student and presupposed for the classroom lectures and discussions, but the teacher should attend particularly to chapters 2, 5, 7, 9, 10, 12, 13, 15, 17, 18, 19, 20, 21, 22, 23, 24, 25, 26, 28, 29, and 30. The following chapters might usefully be combined: 9 and 10, 13 and 15, 18 and 19, 20 and 23, 21 and 22.

For a one-semester course on the theology of *human existence*, the following sequence is recommended: chapters 2, *3, 4, 5*, 6, 7, 8, 11, 12, 25, 26, 28, and 29.

For a one-semester course on the reality of *God*: chapters 2, 5, *6, 7, 8, 9, 10*, 12, 13, and 29.

For a one-semester course on *Jesus Christ*: chapters 2, 5, 6, 7, 8, 9, 10, *11, 12*, 25 (third section, The Moral Message of Jesus), *13, 14, 15, 16*, 17, and 29.

For a one-semester course on the *Church*: chapters 2, 3, 5, 6, 8, 12, *17, 18, 19, 20, 21, 22, 23, 24*, 29, and 30.

For a one-semester course on *Christian ethics*: chapters 2, 3, 4, 5, 12, 17, *25, 26, 27, 28*, and *29*.

But this book is not for use only in colleges, universities, and seminaries. Parish programs which do not follow the semester structure or which have fewer weeks available to them for presentations and discussion can also use this book for courses. For example, a course on *the sacraments* could be based on chapters 20, *21, 22*, 23, 28, and 30. A course on *the Church today:* chapters 1, 17, 18, *19*, and *20*. A course on *Christian discipleship:* chapters *25, 26*, 27, and *28*. A course on *revelation and faith:* chapters 2, *6*, and 7. A course on *Christianity and other religions:* chapters 8, 19, and 20.

These same parish programs could also employ the book for mini-courses—e.g., on *faith, theology, and belief* (chapter 2; see also chapter 23), *Mary* (chapter 24; see also chapter 15), or *Christian spirituality* (chapter 28; see also chapter 25). Individual religious educators will undoubtedly find many more uses for the book than the author himself can envision.

Although the book tries to be as complete as it is comprehensive, so that the reader is not required constantly to be consulting other books and articles in order to fill out the presentation, there are certain basic reference tools to which the serious reader should have access. They are listed in the Preface. The religious educator may also want to consult Thomas H. Groome's *Christian Religious Education: Sharing Our Story and Vision* (New York: Harper & Row, 1980).

DISCUSSION QUESTIONS

I Catholicism in Crisis (3)

1. Does the present crisis of Catholicism have anything in common with previous crises in the Church? If so, what are the similarities? To what extent, if at all, is the present crisis without precedent?

2. From your own personal observation and experience, which factors (social, cultural, philosophical, theological, etc.) have the most to do with the present crisis?

3. To the extent that the present crisis can be resolved within our own lifetimes, what remedies would you suggest? What changes in the life of the Church would you recommend? Why? What changes, now contemplated by some, would you be least likely to support? Why?

4. Why is it always so difficult to maintain a balance between fidelity to tradition and openness to change? What happens when you emphasize tradition too much? Give examples. What happens when you emphasize the need to keep up with the times, even when that need seems to conflict with certain traditional values or positions? Give examples. Which tendency do you think is stronger in the Church today? Give examples. Why do you think this is so?

5. To what extent are our opinions about the Church and its mission conditioned by our deeper convictions about the meaning of human existence, of God, and of Jesus Christ? Go back to some of the examples you just gave. Indicate how these differences on Church matters do, in fact, reflect deeper differences about our understanding of human existence, of God, and of Jesus Christ.

II Faith, Theology, and Belief (23)

1. If you think that reason, evidence, and argument play little or no part in the process of *Christian* faith, how do you explain the faith of so many exceedingly insightful, intelligent, and logical people? If you think, on the other hand, that the evidence for *Christian* faith is fairly clear and convincing, how do you explain (a) its lack of persuasive force for other insightful, intelligent, and logical people who choose to remain outside the Church and (b) the continued alienation of insightful, intelligent, and logical people from the Church of their Baptism?

2. Apply these same questions now to *Catholic* faith. Why do so many extraordinarily gifted people remain Catholics? Why are other gifted people still outside the Catholic Church (first, non-Christians, and, secondly, Protestants, Anglicans, and Orthodox)? Why are many gifted Catholics leaving the Church today?

3. Outline an essay, chapter, or full-length book entitled "Why I Am a Catholic."

4. Which makes you more uneasy: the critical reflections of biblical scholars and theologians, or the confident testimonies of faith of the charismatics and evangelicals? Why? If neither pleases you, what other approach to faith do you prefer?

5. Is it possible to have faith without belonging to a particular religion? Explain. Is it possible to have Christian or Catholic faith without belonging to the Church? Explain.

6. Although the question will be raised more formally in chapter 7, what is your present working definition of the word *revelation*? How does it relate to your understanding of the phrase *the word of God*? To what extent is the Bible an expression of revelation of the official teachings of the Church? How do you recognize revelation when you encounter it?

7. How would you have defined *theology* before reading this chapter? How does that definition differ from the one provided here? Were there certain assumptions in your own definition about the relation of theology to faith, to the Bible, and to doctrine? To what extent would you be prepared to revise those assumptions now?

8. How much theology should the average Catholic know? How much theology beyond that should a Christian educator know? a priest? Do you think your standards are being met? Explain.

9. Apart from this book, have you ever read a work of professional theology? Which theologians have you found most helpful? To what extent is their approach similar to this book's? To what extent is it different? What do you make of the similarities and differences?

10. What *is* a theologian? Does the Church really need theologians?

11. If you regard the Bible as no more inspired or authoritative than, let us say, *The Prophet* by Khalil Gibran, how do you reconcile your view with the constant conviction of the Church to the contrary? If you do regard the Bible as inspired, how did you reach this conclusion?

12. Do you think fundamentalism in the interpretation of the Bible is still a problem in the Church today? Among which groups and/or on which issues?

13. How have you previously understood the relationship between Scripture and Tradition? Have you changed your understanding in the light of this chapter? Why do you think this distinction has been such an important ecumenical issue?

14. Can you think of any traditions (small *t*) which some Catholics confuse with Tradition (capital *T*)? To what effect? Can you think of any elements of Tradition which are taken too lightly, as if they were a matter only of tradition? To what effect?

15. Do you agree that the distinction between a doctrine and dogma is not often easy to determine? If not, give some examples of each. Check the opinion of others in your group.

16. What was your understanding of the term *magisterium* before reading this chapter? Did your view make too much or too little of the teaching authority? Why do you think so? Which view of *magisterium* (1. the whole Church; 2. the hierarchy and the theologians; or 3. the hierarchy alone) do you think is most common in the Catholic Church today? To what effect? Which view is most common among religious educators? among priests? among bishops? What effects do these views have on the life of the Church?

17. Do you agree that dissent against an official teaching of the Church is appropriate under certain circumstances? If not, why not? Apply the criteria suggested in this chapter to some recent official teaching, e.g., the papal encyclical on birth control, *Humanae Vitae* (1968). Would you add to, or subtract from, the list of criteria offered in this chapter? Why?

18. How effectively does the liturgy as presently structured convey the substance of faith to the Church? Can you think of anything in liturgy (whether prayer formulae, rituals, distribution of roles, or other elements) that reflects an unsatisfactory understanding of faith? If you had the chance to change anything in today's liturgy, what would you change, and why?

19. Apply the same kinds of questions to Christian education. Do our catechisms, textbooks, and religious education programs reflect good theology, or defective theology? Explain. If you had a chance to change anything in the field of Christian education today, what would it be, and why?

20. Which point or points in this chapter do you think need the most emphasis in the Catholic Church today? Why? Would your answer differ in any way if the question pertained to other Christian churches as well? If so, how?

III   The Human Condition Today   (83)

1. How do you explain the fact that, within a century or so, the Catholic Church officially condemned and then officially welcomed, if not fully endorsed, the modernization of the world?

2. Which items would you add to those given in this chapter as representative of important changes in the modern world?

3. Which of the changes do you regard as most important and far-reaching in their effects? Which seem least significant? Why?

4. If you are convinced that some of the changes introduced into modern life are evil in themselves and not just in their by-products, which

changes are they, and what, if anything, could the Church have done to prevent them?

5. Which changes do you think have been the most positive and beneficial to humankind? To what extent are they consistent or inconsistent with Christian faith?

6. Do you have a general impression of the so-called secular theology movement of the 1960s (Bonhoeffer, Robinson, Cox, *et al.*)? If so, is it a positive or a negative impression, and why?

7. Do you think that the growth of a new Christian spirituality, partially in reaction to this secular theology, was a generally positive, or a generally negative, development? Why?

8. If dialogue and the experience of human interdependence are characteristic of modern life, to what extent is the Church embodying those characteristics in its own structures and institutions and missionary work, and to what extent is it resisting or ignoring them?

IV   Understandings of Human Existence   (101)

1. Which do you think poses the greater threat to human existence today: the trend in the direction of greater freedom (leading in some cases to extreme permissiveness and license), or the trend in the direction of greater controls over human behavior (whether through behavior modification, advertising, censorship, or other forms of political coercion)?

2. Before reading this chapter, did you have any knowledge or opinion about Charles Darwin and his biological discoveries? Do you think his views are as inimical to Christian faith as they were first perceived to be? Why, or why not?

3. Answer the same question with reference to Sigmund Freud.

4. And the same with reference to Karl Marx.

5. To what extent are the views of Darwin, Freud, and Marx still influential in our common human struggle to deal with the question "Who are we?" What positive impact do you think such views can have, and have had?

6. Select your own sampling of current novels and explore the notion of human existence presented in them. Do you think modern literary trends are in the direction of a transcendental, or spiritually-oriented, understanding of the human person, or in the direction of a materialistic understanding? Why do you think this is so? In what ways are novels a reflection of contemporary consciousness?

7. Of the various philosophical approaches to the meaning of human existence, which one comes closest to your own? Is your own view inconsistent, however, with some of the others? If so, why? If not, how do some of the other philosophical approaches fit in with your own?

8. Answer the same set of questions with reference to contemporary theological approaches.

9. With reference especially to Rahner's position, does it make sense to you that statements about God are also statements about human existence? Can you think of any exceptions? Can you think of some excellent examples where such a correlation does, in fact, occur?

10. In general, do you think that the official teachings of the Church are consistent with, or at odds with, other major approaches to the meaning of human existence? To what extent are the teachings consistent? To what extent are they at odds? Are you surprised by the differences? How do you explain them?

V   Toward a Theology of Human Existence (141)

1. What is your present understanding of the nature and mission of the Church? How does that understanding reflect your deeper understanding of human existence, and specifically your understanding of nature, grace, and Original Sin?

2. Answer the same question with reference to your understanding of the person and work of Jesus Christ.

3. List some traditional Catholic devotional practices which you, or at least your parents, have experienced over the years (e.g., giving up candy and films for Lent, making novenas, reciting prayers as a penance following Confession), or which you have seen other members of the Church, especially priests and sisters, practice in their own lives (e.g., celibacy, periods of silence, the wearing of special dress). How do such practices reflect an understanding of human existence, again with specific reference to nature, grace, and the Original Sin? Do actual or recommended changes in such practices necessarily imply a compromise with the world or a weakening of standards? If so, why? If not, why not?

4. Grace supposes nature, and nature supposes grace. Are these two principles ignored or violated today: in the Church? in society at large? Explain.

5. Which do you think is the greater danger today: an exaggerated emphasis on human powers (Pelagianism), or an exaggerated emphasis on human limitation, even depravity (Manichaeism, classical Protestantism)? Are you persuaded that the Catholic theological and doctrinal traditions provide a sound middle course? If not, why not? What is your own position, in that case? How have you overcome the problems you discerned in the Catholic position?

6. Does the notion of a "supernatural existential" and of a *potentia obedientialis* make sense to you? If not, is it because these are difficult philosophical concepts, or is it because they are unpersuasive concepts in themselves? What would you offer in their place?

7. If our knowledge of God, or at least our quest for God, is not *a priori* (i.e., if it is not present in us even before we have a chance to think about it and be explicitly aware of it), how do you explain the persistence of some fundamental belief in God among people across the whole spectrum of intellectual, ethnic, racial, cultural, and chronological differences?

8. Can the dignity of the human person be grounded in anything less than a theological anthropology, such as we presented here in this chapter? If so, what would the alternative be?

9. How did you explain Original Sin before reading this chapter? To what extent, if any, has your understanding changed? What questions remain in your mind? How would you at least begin to answer them?

10. How does the reality of Original Sin affect our own personal struggle for psychic integrity and health? How does it affect our struggle for social justice and human rights? Does it make any difference, on either level, whether one believes in Original Sin at all? If not, why not? And in that case how do you explain or come to terms with the evil and imperfection that you find in yourself and in society at large?

VI   Belief and Unbelief Today (183)

1. Do you know anybody who says he or she does *not* believe in God? Have you ever discussed the matter? What reasons, if any, do such persons have for their unbelief? What kinds of responses have you made to them until now? In the light of your reading of this book thus far and the discussions provoked by the book, how, if at all, would you modify your responses today?

2. What arguments would you offer to someone who asked for an explanation and perhaps also a defense of your own belief in God?

3. What other reasons, besides the ones suggested in this chapter, do you think people have for rejecting or ignoring God? How do you deal with those reasons?

4. Do you agree with the Second Vatican Council that it is not enough to communicate our beliefs more effectively, but that we must chiefly live up to what we believe and teach? Why do you think that, for many people, example *is* more important than forcefulness of argument?

5. Do you think that education necessarily undermines belief in God? If so, how do you explain the faith of so many intellectually gifted and educationally sophisticated people? If not, how do you explain the data presented by the sociologists and historians?

6. What do you think of Robert Bellah's notion of "civil religion"? What other examples of it can you propose? What are the dangers of "civil religion"? What are its strengths?

7. Which of the contemporary theologians' views do you find most convincing? If you find none of them convincing, what troubles you about their arguments? What alternative do you suggest? If you have no alternative, what does your failure to provide one imply about the possibility of an intelligent faith? If you do agree with their basic methodology, what other depth experiences, or signals of transcendence, or whatever else, can you think of?

8. How important is the Second Vatican Council's teaching on the problem of atheism or unbelief? Do you think most Catholics appreciate its importance? Explain.

9. Does the admission that neither belief nor unbelief can be proved beyond all reasonable doubt make sense to you, or does it shake your faith? Why?

10. If you were once inclined to the so-called textbook position that unbelievers are morally culpable for their unbelief, are you now happier with the contemporary view, or would you rather see the earlier view retained? Why?

VII Revelation (201)

1. What was your own working definition of *revelation* before reading this chapter? How would you revise that definition now, if at all? Why?

2. What do you make of all the accounts in the Old Testament where individuals are depicted as if they actually saw God and spoke with God? If you thought that God was once actually visible to people and conversed with them, what answer did you give to the inevitable question "Why did God suddenly stop making appearances?"

3. If you had been alive at the time of Christ, do you think it would have been easier, or harder, to believe him to be the Son of God? Why?

4. In your own past understanding of the meaning of revelation, have you tended to emphasize the objective more than the subjective, or the intellectual more than the personal? Can you appreciate the concerns of the Catholic semi-Rationalists and Modernists on the left and the Catholic Fideists on the right? What can you say in their defense? Why would you not follow their views totally?

5. Which of the present-day theologians do you find most helpful in articulating a theology of revelation? Why?

6. Given the reasons for not trying to construct a complete theology of revelation in this chapter alone, would you have nonetheless added any other elements to the discussion besides creation, history, prophecy, and mystery? Which elements, and why?

7. What were your views on prophecy before reading this chapter? Has there been any change in those views? Explain.

8. Do you understand the assertion that the principle of sacramentality is one of the distinguishing characteristics of Catholic theology and of the Catholic tradition generally? Explain it in your own words, giving your own examples. Do you agree with the assertion? If not, why not? Which principles, if any, are more characteristic or even distinctive of Catholic theology?

9. In what sense is it true to say that revelation has been closed? In what sense is it true to say that revelation is a continuing reality? What do you make of the possibility of private revelation? Are there any private revelations you find credible? Why? Are there any you find particularly unpalatable? Why? What are your criteria for judging, one way or the other?

10. Do you still have any difficulty with the assertion that revelation is available in principle to all, even outside the communities of the Old and New Testaments? If so, why?

VIII   Religion and Its Varieties   (245)

1. Did you ever catch yourself saying, "She (He) is a very religious person"? What did you mean by "religious"? How would you now distinguish a religious person from a non-religious person?

2. Assuming you do not think that religious persons are always better people (more sincere, more just, more compassionate, e.g.) than non-religious people, how do you explain the fact that non-religious people can achieve such a level of humane living? Do you think they are motivated at all by faith?

3. Have you ever spoken to a non-Christian about his or her religion? What have you found most attractive about his or her religion? Least attractive? Why? Do you think you individually, and the Church collectively, really have anything substantial to learn from non-Christian religions? If so, what specifically? If not, how do you explain the teaching of Vatican II?

4. Are the five characteristics of religion given in this chapter verified in your own experience? Explain.

5. What do you make of the balance between the charismatic and institutional elements of Catholicism today? Do you think the one dominates the other? If so, to what effect? Give examples.

6. Are you generally comfortable with people who criticize the Church? If not, why not? If so, which people do you think are genuinely prophetic in the Church today? Is there any evidence that the Church has changed for the better because of them? Be specific.

7. Have you ever met persons who use the argument that they have no need for religion, that they have a personal relationship with

God wherever they happen to be? How have you answered them in the past? How would you answer them today?

8. Most Christians know relatively little about non-Christian religions. In the light of the brief review offered in this chapter, were you more surprised by the similarities, or by the differences, between Christianity and the non-Christian religions? Explain.

9. Do you think a comparative study of religions is more likely to lead to doubts about the special place of Christianity, or to a firmer conviction of its truth? Explain.

10. Which of the non-Christian religions, other than Judaism, seems most attractive to you? Why? Are those elements consistent with your own Christian faith? If so, how can they be incorporated better into your own expression of that faith?

11. In the final analysis, how do you assess the salvific value of the non-Christian religions? Do you think all people of good will are "anonymous Christians," or do you think some other religions have validity in themselves?

12. What is your own attitude toward Jews? To what extent has it been theologically accurate and fair? To what extent has it been inaccurate and unfair? How do you explain the antagonism toward Jews? Do you think the Church can do more than it is doing to improve Jewish-Christian relations? Be specific.

13. Were you surprised by the summary of official Church teachings on the non-Christian religions? If surprised, what did you expect? Why? If not surprised, do you think that the Church has now gone about as far as it can on the matter? Why?

IX   The Christian Understanding of God   (283)

1. Have you ever had to explain to anyone the apparent discrepancy between your belief in one God and your belief in the Trinity? How did you proceed? How would you proceed now? What's the difference?

2. Are you satisfied that the distinctively Christian understanding of God is our belief in the incarnation and in the Trinity? If more than that, what? If less than that, why?

3. Do you really understand and appreciate the significance of the Council of Nicea and of the course of theological discussion thereafter? Many Christians today are satisfied to "explain" their faith in biblical terms alone. In view of the actual history of the early Church, why was it not possible to remain within the limits of biblical language to answer the kinds of questions being raised about the reality of God?

4. Is there anything at all in the history outlined in this chapter which surprises you, either in the teaching of certain theologians or in the official teachings of a council or a pope? If so, what and why? What

contribution do you think the twentieth-century Church has made to our understanding of God?

5. How have you explained divine Providence in the past? Would you modify anything now?

6. Do you believe in miracles: the miracles of Jesus, first of all, and then other, more modern miracles (Lourdes cures, for example)? Is your attitude toward miracles challenged in any way by the principles summarized in this chapter?

7. How do you explain the mystery of evil? If it is difficult to reconcile evil with a merciful God, is it easy to explain heroic charity if there is no God? What would (or do) you say to console a parent whose young son or daughter has just been killed in an auto accident? How, if at all, would your comment be different if the child had been murdered? had taken his or her own life? had died of cancer?

8. Do you think of God as "a person"? Do you see the problem with that? Can you think of ways in which the "personality" of God has been exaggerated by religious people? Can you think of ways in which the God of our faith has been diminished because some people refuse to attribute any form of "personality" to God?

9. Do you agree that our language about God is a matter of great importance? Do you think, in other words, that constant references to God as "he" distort our understanding not only of God but of human existence, specifically of the relationship between women and men? On the other hand, do you believe we should completely eliminate all reference to the Fatherhood of God? What pastoral solution would most fully respect the principle of human equality and the content of our biblical, liturgical, and doctrinal traditions?

10. Why do you pray? How do you pray? Is your prayer consistent with the theology outlined in this chapter? If not, what theology is implied in the way you pray and in your intentions at prayer?

X   The Trinity (343)

1. What has been your own theological and spiritual stance with regard to the mystery and doctrine of the Trinity? Has it really been fundamental and central to your thinking about your faith and to its practice? If the doctrine of the Trinity were declared null and void by the Church tomorrow, would it really make any difference to you? If so, why? If not, why not?

2. Do you think other religions are poorer for not having a trinitarian understanding of God? Why? Why not?

3. If you were writing this book, where would you have placed the doctrine of the Trinity? Why?

4. Are you surprised to learn that the doctrine of the Trinity is *not* "foreshadowed" in the Old Testament? Does the doctrine's absence from the Old Testament make any difference one way or the other?

5. Did you expect that this doctrine would be unequivocally presented and taught in the New Testament? How do you account for the apparent discrepancy between the New Testament formulations and those of the ecumenical councils of the Church?

6. If you were preparing a class lecture on the Trinity, how would you present it: (a) to a group of Catholic adults, of reasonably good educational background; (b) to a group of high school students; (c) to grammar school students (pick the grade); (d) to children preparing for First Holy Communion; or (e) to a group of Jewish adults?

7. How much emphasis would you give in these lectures to the material this chapter has drawn from (a) the Bible; (b) the Greek Fathers of the Church; (c) the Latin Fathers of the Church; (d) the major ecumenical councils; (e) theologians; (f) other sources? Why?

8. Outline a sermon for Trinity Sunday.

XI   Christ and Contemporary Culture   (373)

1. Do you agree that people, even within the Church, have different notions of Jesus Christ? How many different ideas about Christ are you aware of among your friends, in your parish, school, or elsewhere? Which ideas seem to predominate? Why do you think so? What practical effect, if any, do these ideas about Christ have on the life of the Church?

2. Take each of the five popular notions of Christ—as teacher, judge, holy man, liberator, and brother—and indicate the major strength and the major weakness of each emphasis. Which notion(s) do you identify most closely with? Why?

3. How do you explain the sudden surge of interest in Jesus during the early part of the 1970s (*Jesus Christ Superstar, Godspell,* the "Jesus People," and so on)? Where does all that enthusiasm stand now? To the extent there has been a change, how do you explain the change?

4. Do you think young people take Christ seriously today? If so, what is their principal understanding of Christ? If not, why not? What practical suggestions would you urge upon the Church to help it do a better job of reaching young people? What, if any, are the Church's major failings in this regard at present?

5. Can you think of other images of Christ besides the ones mentioned in this chapter? Can you add to the Christ-and-culture list as well?

6. If you passed a car bearing the bumper sticker "Honk If You Love Jesus," would you honk your horn? If so, why? If not, why not? If you had to design a bumper sticker of your own, what wording would you use to get your own message across concerning Christ?

7. Outline a ten-minute homily you would like to hear on "Why Jesus Christ Makes a Difference."

XII   The Christ of the New Testament (391)

1. Before reading this chapter, what was your own understanding of the historical character of the New Testament? Did you regard the gospels as biographies of Jesus? If not, to what do you attribute your more nuanced understanding?

2. Which of the following approaches is most nearly like your own with regard to the connection between the early Church's understanding of Jesus and Jesus' own self-evaluation: non-scholarly conservatism, non-scholarly liberalism, scholarly liberalism, Bultmannian existentialism, or moderate conservatism? Have you changed your views in recent years? since studying this chapter? How would you characterize the views of most of your friends and acquaintances? What about the evangelical Christians, those who make frequent use of television and radio to preach Jesus Christ?

3. Outline a one-hour classroom session designed to explain the Jesus of the New Testament to: (a) an adult education group; (b) a public high-school group; (c) a parish junior high-school group.

4. Do the same as in #3, but this time concentrate on the resurrection alone.

5. Is there anything in this chapter regarding the resurrection that especially surprised (or even disturbed) you? Explain.

6. If the bones of Jesus were discovered, what implications would that have for Christian faith?

7. Summarize the way in which Good Friday and Easter Sunday have traditionally been linked. Over against that approach, outline a Good Friday homily which explains the contemporary understanding of the connection between the crucifixion and the resurrection.

8. What has been your understanding of the purpose of Jesus' death? Are you troubled by the explanation of vicarious atonement suggested in this chapter, or reassured? Why?

9. Do you usually think of Jesus as a Jew? If not, why not? Do you think your view is the usual view of other Catholics or of other Christians? If not, why not?

10. Why is it important that we understand correctly how the Jews at the time of Jesus were involved in his being handed over to the Romans for judgment? Do you think our understanding has anything to do with our attitude to Jews today?

11. If you had been asked before reading this book—and certainly before reading this chapter—what was at the heart of Jesus' whole message, how would you have answered the question? How would you

answer it now? If your present answer is different, indicate some of its practical implications for Christian faith.

12. Jesus proclaimed the Kingdom of God throughout his ministry. Yet after he died and rose, the Church proclaimed *him*. Did that represent a turning away from Jesus' priorities? If so, how do you explain it? If not, how do you reconcile the two?

13. What place does the Kingdom of God occupy in the Church's preaching and teaching today? Does it make a difference one way or the other? Explain.

XIII The Christ of the Fathers, the Councils, and Medieval Theology (439)

1. Some have suggested that the post-biblical developments in Christology described in this chapter were fundamentally a mistake. They suggest that the Church allowed a "Hellenization of dogma" which diverted Christian faith from the straightforward, concrete, earthy simplicity of the New Testament and made it instead a matter of complicated philosophical speculation. Without denying the complicated character of this post-biblical theology, how do you answer this complaint?

2. In every heresy there is a measure of truth. In fact, the word *heresy* means literally "a choice." The heretic is one who "chooses" a particular aspect of the truth but fails to see it in its larger context. The heretic confuses a portion of the truth with the whole truth. Given this understanding of heresy, identify and, as far as possible, sympathetically explain whatever *truth* you see in Arianism, Nestorianism, and Monophysitism.

3. Which do you think had been most in danger of being undermined in the early centuries of the Church: the divinity of Christ, or his humanity? What about the situation in the Church today? Explain.

4. Does this historical survey make it any easier to understand why we cannot simply quote texts from one ecumenical council or another in order to "prove" a particular theological argument? If so, why? If not, why not?

5. Are you surprised by the political dimension of some of these Christological conflicts? In the spirit of Question #2, can you see why that political aspect was an inevitable part of the historical picture? Can you think of any modern examples where political factors have an impact on doctrinal and theological positions?

6. In your opinion, why did doctrinal development stop in the seventh century with the Third Council of Constantinople? If you were

the pope today and were urged to call another Christological council, how would you respond?

7. Do you think Anselm's theory of satisfaction is still influential? If so, what spiritual effects does it have?

8. Put yourself in Anselm's shoes. If you were asked "Why did God become man?" what would you say? And how would you answer "Why did the God-man have to die?"

9. Do you think it really makes much difference if theology focuses more on Christ as he is *in himself* than on Christ as he is *for us*? How about the other way around?

10. In your own catechetical and/or theological education, was the resurrection presented as an integral part of Christ's redemptive work, or was it seen principally as a reward for Christ and a proof of his divinity? Again, what difference does it make one way or the other in the life of the Church and in your own spiritual life?

XIV   The Christ of Twentieth-Century Theology (469)

1. If you asked a random sample of churchgoers "What was the heart of Jesus' preaching and teaching?" what kind of answer(s) would you expect to receive? Why do you think so? How would you yourself answer the question?

2. Which of the modern Christologies do you find most attractive, at least on the surface? Why? Which are you least attracted to? Why?

3. Our understanding of the Church will always reflect our prior understanding of Jesus Christ. What understanding of the mission of the Church would logically follow from each of the various Christologies summarized in this chapter?

4. Take up a copy of an older textbook in Catholic theology (pre-1950, if possible) and point out the differences between its Christology and the Christology which has been developing over the last two or three decades. What are the older text's strengths and weaknesses? Have we carried forward the strengths? Have we successfully transcended the weaknesses?

5. What is the operative Christology of the so-called evangelical, or pentecostal, or charismatic Christians? In what ways is it consistent with the principles outlined in this chapter and in the two previous chapters? In what ways is charismatic Christology inattentive to these Christological principles?

6. Do you think it is possible to develop an understanding of Jesus Christ that is simply unorthodox, i.e., inconsistent with even the widest meaning of Christian tradition? Give examples of heretical Christologies on the extreme left and extreme right. Do you see any of them as temptations for Christians today?

7. Outline a thirty-minute talk, "Do We Need Jesus?", for an audience of reasonably well-read adult Christians.

8. Outline a sermon for each feast: (a) Christmas, (b) Good Friday, and (c) Easter.

9. How would you answer a person who says, "I don't care whether Jesus was divine or not, whether he rose from the dead or not, or anything like that. What matters for me is that Jesus is a symbol of what it means to be human, and by following his example I, too, can be fully human"?

10. How would you answer a person who says, "I don't like all this talk about liberation and politics in reference to Our Lord. He wasn't a political person. He was the Son of God, interested not in changing the world but in saving our souls"?

XV Special Questions in Christology (513)

1. Before reading this chapter, what was your general understanding of the virginal conception of Jesus? Did you think it an important truth of Christian faith? If so, why? If not, why not? Do you think it is possible to deny the historicity of the virginal conception without necessarily denying its theological meaning? Explain.

2. What did you understand about the sinlessness of Jesus before doing this chapter? Do you find the distinction between *impeccantia* and *impeccabilitas* important and helpful—namely, that Jesus did not sin, but that that does not mean he was absolutely incapable of sinning? If you are convinced also of his impeccability, how do you make your case? How does your explanation avoid Monothelitism, or even Monophysitism?

3. Were you surprised to learn that some scholars and theologians are ready to concede that Jesus was ignorant about certain things, and even occasionally was in error? How did you understand the knowledge of Jesus before reading this chapter? Do you see how Jesus' freedom as a human being would have been compromised if he knew precisely what the future had in store for him? If not, why not?

4. Do you find helpful the distinction between Jesus' precise knowledge about himself as the unique Son of God and his fundamental conviction about his unique role in preaching, practicing, and personifying the Kingdom of God in the world? If there were evidence that he lacked such conviction, do you think this would make any difference for our understanding of Jesus?

5. Did you ever raise in your own mind the question of Jesus' sexuality? If not, why not? If so, how did you answer your own questions? Have you ever heard others raise this question? How did they approach it? How do religious people (not just priests, sisters, and brothers) usually deal with this question? Explain your answer.

6. Does it shake your faith at all to contemplate the possibility that Jesus may have had sexual desires? What if it were historically verified that Jesus was married? Would that undermine his message and the Church's faith in him as the unique Son of God? If not, why not? If so, why?

7. Are you generally satisfied with the way sexuality has been discussed and taught by the Church—for example, in the Church's art, spirituality, catechisms, sermons, retreats, and counseling sessions? If not, why not? If so, how do you explain the fact that so many people have complained about the effect of the Church's attitude on their own psychic health?

8. Do you have any problems with the criteria given at the end of the chapter? Which criteria would you delete or change? Why? Which criteria would you add? Why? If you are against the whole idea of having any criteria at all, why?

9. Assuming you believe that we have to have some objective criteria for Christian faith, which criteria do you think are most frequently violated? Why do you think so? To what effect are they violated?

10. Do you agree that one can be *too* "orthodox"? How? To what effect?

XVI   The Christ of the Liturgy (547)

1. The ancient axiom "The rule of prayer is the rule of belief" brings out the intimate connection between convictions and their ritual or dramatic expression. What we "act out" we believe, and what we believe we "act out." What happens when we do not believe what we "act out"? What happens when we do not "act out" what we believe? Give examples drawn from political and cultural life as well as from religious life.

2. Do you remember how the sacrament of Baptism was administered in a parish before the Second Vatican Council? If not, ask someone who does remember. To what extent does the new baptismal rite reflect a different understanding of the mystery of Jesus Christ? In your reflections do not neglect the connection with the restored rites of Holy Week in which baptismal imagery occupies a central place, particularly in the Easter Vigil service.

3. Confirmation supposedly has to do with the Holy Spirit. Where does Jesus Christ fit into this sacrament? For that matter, where does Jesus Christ fit in with the Holy Spirit in Christian life, mission, and spirituality?

4. In the liturgical reforms mandated by Vatican II and approved by Pope Paul VI, the celebrant is allowed considerable freedom in adapting prayers to the circumstances of a given assembly or occasion. Sketch

out some petitions for a penitential rite at the beginning of Mass that do not repeat what is already "on the books" but which reflect some important aspects of contemporary Christology.

5. Some people complain that the ancient creeds do not "speak to" the modern mind, especially to the young. If you were asked to produce a so-called "modern creed" for use at Mass, how would you do the section on Jesus Christ?

6. Compose a modern Preface in the light of contemporary Christology.

7. Compose some memorial acclamations which differ from what is now given but which are faithful to the central principles of Christology we have been outlining thus far.

8. Suggest some different Christological introductions to the Lord's Prayer.

9. Do you remember how the sacrament of Penance was administered before the revision of the rite of Reconciliation? In what ways does the new rite reflect a different understanding of the mystery of Christ?

10. If you were administering the sacrament of Penance to someone, how would you express the connection between the mystery of Jesus Christ and the reality of sin? Distinguish among the following cases: (a) an adult who has seriously harmed another's reputation by betraying a confidence; (b) an adult who was instrumental in firing another because of race or sex; (c) a young adult who damaged property and then saw another accused and punished for the crime; (d) a priest, sister, or brother who violated celibacy.

11. Focusing on the mystery of Jesus Christ, outline an instruction you would give to a couple preparing for marriage.

12. You are the ordaining bishop at the ordination of twelve deacons. Outline your instruction to them at the beginning of the ceremony, stressing always the mystery of Christ. Do the same for the ordination of a group to the priesthood.

13. You have just been ordained a bishop and have an opportunity for a brief homily following the ceremony. How would you incorporate the mystery of Jesus Christ into your remarks?

14. As minister of the sacrament of the Anointing of the Sick, what words of comfort would you give to the recipient? to the family? In each case, the mystery of Jesus Christ must somehow be central.

XVII   The Church of the New Testament (569)

1. Which of the various interpretations of the connection between Jesus' evaluation of the Church and the Church's self-understanding is, or was, closest to your own? Does this summary of the New Testament data strengthen your understanding, or weaken it?

2. Which view do you think is most commonly held today by the average Catholic churchgoer? by the average Catholic bishop or pastor? To what effect?

3. In the past, even some Catholic *theologians* would contend that if the text "You are Peter..." did not report history as it happened, the Catholic Church would lose all support for its claims and its faith. How would you answer if someone were to make the same argument today?

4. The relationship between local Church and universal Church is important, but it is sometimes misunderstood. Give examples of instances where the universality of the Church has been exaggerated at the expense of its local character, and examples of instances where its local character has been stressed to the point of neglecting its universality. Do you think the relationship between the two is properly understood and operative in the Catholic Church today?

5. On the basis of the New Testament, how would you answer someone who says, "I don't need a Church. My faith is in the person of Jesus"?

6. Outline a homily on "Pentecost: The Birthday of the Church."

7. In the New Testament, the Church assumed a different charac-ter and structure as it took root in different communities (Jewish, Helle-nistic, or combinations of the two). Can you think of anything comparable in the Church of the twentieth century? What does this adaptation say about the need for unity rather than uniformity?

8. The experience of the Church of Corinth shows that the gifts of the Spirit can be abused, can be a source of division rather than unity. Do you see that as a possibility even today? How would you determine when the Spirit is really at work and not at work in the Church?

9. Are the common elements (summarized in #14 of the Summary) still the common elements present in all of the local churches today? If not, which are missing? Why? To what effect? Are there additional common elements? If so, which are they?

10. Do you think the balance between the Church of glory and the Church of the cross is always maintained? If not, give examples.

11. Outline a Holy Thursday homily on "The Eucharist and the Kingdom of God."

12. Why do you think there was such opposition to extending the mission of the Church to the Gentiles? Can you think of comparable examples drawn from present-day Church life? To what extent does the Church's solution in the Acts of the Apostles provide a model for our own time?

13. Are you surprised to learn that there is no uniform order or structure in the New Testament Church? Did you expect that every Church would have a bishop, priests, and deacons, and that each Church,

in turn, would be clearly subject to a pope? What do you make of the difference between the New Testament situation and the assumptions of many Catholics, past and present, about the structures of the Church?

14. Take the same set of questions from the other end. Are you surprised that the New Testament Church had as much structure as it did? Did you expect to find nothing at all, or very little, in the way of authority and offices? What do you make of the difference?

15. All offices and ministries are for the sake of service, not domination. Do you think that that New Testament ideal has been adhered to in today's Church? Explain.

16. In your view, how important was Peter to the early Church? Are you surprised that there is as much about him in the New Testament as there is? Or are you surprised that there is less about him than you thought? Comment on the difference between your expectations and what the texts themselves disclose.

17. The term *People of God* has been used frequently since the Second Vatican Council. How, if at all, does its popular usage compare with its meaning in the Bible?

18. Do you think the image of the Body of Christ makes much difference? Is it just a metaphor? If not, what practical effect should that doctrine have on our life as Christians and on the activity of the Church today?

19. Answer the same questions in relation to the image of the Temple of the Holy Spirit.

XVIII   The Church in History   (605)

1. Why was the decision to exempt Gentile Christians from circumcision so significant? Can you think of any modern practices, customs, or laws the exemption from which would be comparable to the exemption from circumcision? How far, in other words, can *aggiornamento*, or updating, go without destroying the substance of Christianity?

2. Would the abolition of obligatory celibacy for priests of the Latin rite be comparable to the exemption from circumcision? What about the ordination of women to the priesthood?

3. Does it necessarily follow that when the Church is persecuted it must be doing something right? Does it necessarily follow that the Church will always be a more committed Church when under persecution? Discuss these questions in relation to the history of the Church and of conditions in Eastern Europe today.

4. Do you think the Edict of Constantine was, in the long run, a positive factor in the subsequent history of the Church, or a negative one?

5. What was your initial understanding of the origins of monasticism? Are you surprised by monasticism's varied history? What is your

impression of it today? Do you think it is important to the life of the Church?

6. What was your initial understanding of the so-called barbarian invasions? Are you surprised by the influence these new Christians had upon the development of spirituality and ecclesiastical authority? What does this say about both in terms of the "will of God" or the "plan of Christ"?

7. Do you think very many Catholics appreciate the significance of the vicissitudes of the papacy—e.g., its dark age (tenth and eleventh centuries) when under the control of the Roman nobility, its political and financial dealings in the high Middle Ages, the Great Western Schism, the corruption of the papacy during the Renaissance? Given the lessons of history, what is there in the papacy as we know it today that could be changed or even abolished without abandoning the substance of the Petrine ministry?

8. The Gregorian Reform of the twelfth century was not an unmixed blessing. Some evils were rooted out, but the papacy itself accrued too much power to itself. Does this say anything about the nature of reform? Does it say anything about where reform should be initiated, and by whom?

9. In the light of history, discuss the significance of Pope John Paul I's decision not to be crowned with the papal tiara, a decision which broke a nine-hundred-year tradition.

10. Notice how many heresies have to do with moral "purity": Montanism and Donatism in the early centuries, and Albigensianism and Jansenism in the later Middle Ages. Why, in your opinion, has this anti-natural tendency always had such a favorable response in the Church? Do you see any evidence of it today? If so, what are its theological presuppositions?

11. Have you ever discussed the East-West Schism with an Eastern Orthodox Christian? For what reasons does the division continue today?

12. Do you think Marsilius of Padua and other conciliarists would have been pleased with the Second Vatican Council? Do you see any differences between the medieval discussion and our own regarding ecclesiastical authority?

13. You have been asked to deliver a fifteen-minute sermon in a Lutheran church on Reformation Sunday. What do you say in your sermon?

14. You are a panelist in an ecumenical discussion on the Reformation. The moderator turns to you and asks, "When all is said and done, does a Catholic look upon the Reformation as a completely unjustifiable revolt, an unfortunate occurrence, or something legitimate in the history of the Church?" How do you answer?

15. One of the two practical reforms undertaken by the Catholic Church at the Council of Trent was the Index of Forbidden Books and the establishment of seminaries for the training of future priests. In the light of history, were these constructive responses, or negative ones?

16. Why, in your opinion, is the Enlightenment such an important event in the history of the Church, not to say of Western civilization? Give examples of the Enlightenment's continuing influence on the Church today. Give examples of pre-Enlightenment thinking in the Church.

17. Catholicism first grappled with the problem of modernity in the nineteenth century. How do you think it did overall? To what effect(s) in the twentieth century?

18. Have you ever heard anyone speak about Modernism apart from this book? How has it been explained? Are you aware of the effects of the anti-Modernist atmosphere in the Catholic Church during the first several decades of this century? If so, give examples.

19. In view of the recent history of the Church, was the Second Vatican Council a leap into the future, or the product of some organic development? Explain.

20. In general, do you think Christians (and Catholics in particular) know much, little, or no Church history? Comment on the implications of your answer.

XIX   The Church of the Second Vatican Council   (657)

1. Were you old enough to be aware of the Second Vatican Council when it was in session? What impressions did you have at the time? How have those impressions changed over the years? Has this chapter prompted any change in your attitude toward the council?

2. If you were too young to take much notice of Vatican II when it was in session, what were you first told about it? Do those "first reports" match your present understanding? If not, how do they differ?

3. Were you aware of the two currents of theology in existence *before* Vatican II? If not, how did you think Vatican II happened? Were you under the impression it was a natural evolution, or a break with the immediate past? Do you still see any evidence of these two currents of theology in the Church today?

4. What did you know about Pope John XXIII before reading this chapter? Do you remember him while he was alive? What were your impressions then, and now? If you do not personally remember him, what were you first told about him? How does that information compare with your present appreciation? Compare him with other popes you are familiar with, either in early history, in the recent past, or in the present.

5. How would you change the lists in this chapter, if at all? Would you move any of the "major" documents to the "minor" list, and vice versa? Why?

6. Outline a single one-hour presentation on "The Meaning and Importance of the Second Vatican Council" for (a) an adult education group, (b) a high-school group, or (c) an ecumenical group.

7. Outline a semester course on the council for (a) high school (upper or lower level; take your pick), or (b) an adult study group.

8. From your knowledge of the council documents, would you add or subtract any principles on the list of ten principles in the last section of the chapter? Give reasons.

XX The Church Today: Its Nature and Mission (691)

1. Are there any postconciliar Catholic or Protestant ecclesiologies which you have found particularly helpful but which are not among the list given in this chapter? If so, which are they, and describe their perspective insofar as it differs from what is summarized here.

2. Do you think the post-Vatican II ecclesiology, as summarized in this chapter, is reflected in (a) homilies, (b) religious education programs, (c) official statements from your local bishop, (d) university, college, and seminary courses, (e) catechisms and other textbooks, (f) church laws and regulations, (g) the thinking of your fellow parishioners and/or students, (h) the thinking of your closest friends? Do you think there are discrepancies between the post-Vatican II ecclesiology and any or all of these categories? If so, what are some of these discrepancies?

3. Which of the post-Vatican II ecclesiological developments do you think most significant in the long run, and why? Which would you have been least likely to predict ten years ago? Which emphases do you still find missing in contemporary ecclesiology?

4. Which of the three models, or perspectives, is dominant in (a) your parish, (b) your school, (c) your religious education program, (d) your community (religious or geographical), (e) your home and among your closest friends, (f) the rules and regulations of the Church? If all three are integrated at each of these levels, how do you explain that? If they are not integrated, how do you explain *that*? How can any imbalance best be corrected?

5. Do you have a definition of the Church that differs from the one in this book? If so, how does it differ?

6. Would you add to, or subtract from, the list of criteria by which we can determine when a group of people becomes a church? Give reasons.

7. Would you add to, or subtract from, the threefold mission of the Church? Give reasons.

8. Suggest some ways in which the Church could be more effective than it is in the mission of (a) proclamation (give special attention to teaching, preaching, worship, and prophecy), (b) signification (give special attention to life-styles and institutional changes), and (c) service (indicate problems in the world, the nation, your area, or your parish which the Church could help solve).

9. Would you add to, or subtract from, the list of criteria given for the intervention of the Church in the political arena? Give reasons.

10. How would you answer someone who insists that the age of the Church is over, that it belongs to another era?

11. How would you answer someone who insists that unless people profess faith in the Lordship of Jesus and are reborn in the Holy Spirit, they cannot be saved?

12. Do you think all Christian churches are pretty much alike, no better or no worse than the others? Explain.

13. Outline a thirty-minute presentation to a local Protestant parish (pick the denomination) on the subject "Why I Am a Roman Catholic." If you are *not* a Catholic, outline a thirty-minute presentation to a local Catholic parish on the subject "Why I Am Not a Catholic."

14. Do you think the word *Catholic* applies only to members of the Roman Catholic Church? Do you know some non-Roman Catholics who are Catholic in spirit? Explain. Do you know some Roman Catholics who are *not* Catholic in spirit? Explain.

XXI The Sacraments of Initiation: Baptism, Confirmation, and Eucharist (731)

1. Can you think of any "secular sacraments," i.e., ways in which people apart from the Church express their relationship with God through the things of this world? Do you think the Church's seven sacraments have any "secular" equivalents? In other words, are there "secular" forms of initiation, of expressing fellowship with one another, of reconciliation, of healing, and so on?

2. Do you think there is a balance today in our understanding of sacraments as both signs of faith and causes of grace? If not, where do you find an imbalance? Why do you think it exists? What can be done about it?

3. Do you think most people recognize the liturgical dimension of every sacrament—that every sacrament is an act of worship? How would you explain that dimension to someone who does not understand it?

4. Do you know of anyone today who believes in limbo? If so, how would you go about sorting out for that person such issues as the universality of grace, the relationship between nature and grace, and the "necessity" of the sacraments for salvation?

5. Did you have any understanding at all of the meaning of the sacramental character before reading this chapter? If so, how did it compare with the perspective offered here? Do you think the theology of the character has any pertinence today? If so, outline a brief talk to an adult education group on "Sacramental Character and the Mission of the Church."

6. What do you think about the case (referred to in this chapter) of the Jewish nurse who baptizes the dying person?

7. Do you think the validity of a sacrament should depend on the holiness and faith of the minister? Do you think the holiness and faith of the minister have anything at all to do with a sacrament's effectiveness?

8. Have you ever had the experience (referred to by Vatican II) whereby "the very act of celebrating" a sacrament actually produced the proper disposition in your heart and mind? Has the opposite ever happened to you, where a poorly celebrated sacrament actually undermined a good disposition?

9. Outline a homily you would like to give at the Baptism of one or several infants.

10. Did you think that each of the seven sacraments was directly, immediately, and explicitly instituted by Christ? If not, how did you link the sacraments with Christ? How would you explain this question of "institution by Christ" to someone who thinks that Christ did indeed arrange for each rite?

11. Is there a catechumenate program in your parish? Do you see the point in restoring the catechumenate today? If not, why not? If so, how can a good catechumenate program affect the life of the whole parish?

12. What do you think of the notion of "baptism of desire"? Do you have a better way of explaining the problem?

13. Have you been to a Confirmation recently? What did the bishop say during his homily? What do you think is the common understanding of your friends and/or fellow parishioners regarding Confirmation? Do you think most are aware of the historical development of the separate rite of Confirmation? Were you aware of it? Suppose you were the bishop. What points would you make in a Confirmation sermon?

14. Do you remember much of the traditional Latin Mass? Compare it with the present Eucharist in the light of the historical development. Do you think the liturgical changes mandated by Vatican II are an improvement, a regression, or of no consequence one way or the other?

What do you think are the most significant changes in the celebration of the Eucharist?

15. If you were appointed a member of a special Vatican commission to reform the eucharistic liturgy even further, what changes, if any, would you recommend?

16. Are you familiar with the various ecumenical statements to which this chapter refers? Do you think most Catholics (and perhaps most Protestants, too) think the differences between Catholics and Protestants on the Eucharist are about what they were at the time of the Reformation? What can be done about that gap in understanding, if it exists?

17. Outline a 30-45 minute talk on "A Catholic Understanding of the Eucharist" to (a) a group of Protestant high-school students and (b) a Protestant adult study-group. If you are not a Catholic, do the same: "A [Presbyterian, Lutheran, etc.] Understanding of the Lord's Supper" to comparable Catholic groups.

XXII   The Sacraments of Healing, Vocation, and Commitment (775)

1. If you have "received" and/or administered the sacrament of Penance in both the "old way" (confession in a darkened confessional box) and the "new way" (face-to-face exchange in a reconciliation room, with Scripture readings and varied penances), compare them in the light of the principles outlined in this chapter. Do you think the Church should return to the ancient practice of once-in-a-lifetime Penance? Why? How else would the forgiveness of sins be carried out if the sacrament of Penance were not regularly available as it is today?

2. Outline a brief homily on the occasion of a communal Reconciliation service.

3. Have you ever been anointed, or seen anyone anointed, in the "old way" and/or according to the new rite? If so, how did either or both act(s) of celebration reflect the historical facts and theological principles outlined in this chapter?

4. What would you say to a person who expressed fear of receiving the sacrament of the Anointing of the Sick?

5. Can you think of situations where it might be more appropriate for someone who is not a priest to administer this sacrament? Even under the present law of the Catholic Church (restricting its administration to a priest), what can a lay person or religious or deacon do that would communicate much of the grace of this sacrament?

6. Do you think the recent emphasis on healings in certain Christian circles is consistent with the New Testament concern for healing

and the forgiveness of sins? Do you think many people still regard sickness as a punishment for sin? To what effect?

7. Before reading this chapter, did you realize how significant the teaching of Vatican II was on the sacrament of Matrimony? Do you find the council's broadened perspective reflected in (a) your own attitude, (b) the attitude of your friends, (c) the attitude of priests, or (d) the attitude of society at large? How do those attitudes differ from Vatican II, if at all?

8. Do you think the Catholic Church is still too strict about divorce and remarriage? If so, why? Do you think the Church has become too permissive about remarriage? If so, why? If you were giving advice to an engaged couple and you heard one or both of them say, "Oh, well, if it doesn't work out, we can try again with someone else," what response would you make?

9. Outline a homily on the occasion of a marriage between (a) two Catholics, (b) a Catholic and a Protestant, and (c) a Catholic and a non-Christian.

10. Outline a pastoral letter entitled "Marriage: The Call to Fidelity."

11. What is your reaction to the complexity of the New Testament record on the sacrament of Holy Order? Does the biblical evidence tend to undermine your faith in the authority of bishops and priests?

12. On the basis of the various historical details presented in this chapter, would you agree with the following hypothesis: In the case of extreme pastoral emergency, any baptized member of the Church could in principle validly celebrate any of the seven sacraments. If so, why? If not, why not?

13. Apart from present laws limiting priesthood in the Latin rite to celibate males, would you like to serve the Church as a priest? Why? Why not? A bishop? Why? Why not?

14. You have been asked to write a 500-word article for the diocesan newspaper for its special vocations issue, "What a Vocation Means to Me." Outline the article.

15. Are you surprised by the extent of ecumenical agreement on the question of Ministry? What implications does such agreement have in the life of the Catholic Church and the other Christian churches? Do you see any evidence of the impact of these ecumenical agreements on the actual life of those churches today? Comment on the situation.

16. Where do you stand on the debate that continues among Catholic theologians regarding the episcopate and the presbyterate? Do you think it can be said that, in a very real sense, every presbyter is a bishop? If not, why not? If so, would you distinguish between presbyters who

actually oversee a particular church, and presbyters who are engaged in non-pastoral work?

17. In connection with the last question, what do you think finally differentiates a bishop and a priest from the rest of the Church? What is special about their ministry—"special" in the sense that no one else in the Church is responsible for it or is authorized to do it?

XXIII   Special Questions in Ecclesiology (817)

1. Can you think of examples in society at large where *de iure*, or official, authority is exercised without *de facto*, or persuasive, authority? Answer the question from the other side also; i.e., where is *de facto* authority exercised without benefit of office (*de iure*)? Apply the same analysis now to the churches, and to the Catholic Church in particular.

2. Give an example of ecclesiastical authority which is exercised today in a manner consistent with the model of Jesus and the principles of the New Testament. Give an example of the opposite.

3. Is teaching authority exaggerated in the Church today, or is it insufficiently emphasized? Give examples.

4. Briefly outline essays on the following topics: "The Church As Teacher," "The Bishop As Teacher," "The Religious Educator As Teacher," and "The Parent As Teacher."

5. In the early Church, bishops were assumed to have special gifts of the Holy Spirit, and they were selected bishops for that reason. What qualities would you look for in a prospective bishop if this ancient principle were to be adhered to?

6. Do you think *moral* authority is sufficiently effective for governing the Church, or do you think that some measure of juridical authority is also necessary? Do you think juridical authority without moral authority can be effective? Give reasons.

7. Given the history of the development of papal authority, do you think it necessary that the pope reserve to himself all important decisions, e.g., the appointment of bishops, the approval of the ordination of women, the elimination of obligatory celibacy for priests of the Latin rite?

8. If you were writing a history of the Catholic Church or a textbook such as this, would you include a list of the popes? Why? Why not? If you did include such a list, would you entitle it "A List of *Popes*," or "A List of *Supreme Pontiffs*," or "A List of the *Bishops of Rome*," or would you give it some other title? Give reasons.

9. On the basis of the historical evidence (including the New Testament), do you think it possible for a Catholic to dismiss the Petrine ministry as essentially unimportant to the life and mission of the Church?

If so, why? If not, why do you think so many Catholics today do discount the significance of the bishop of Rome?

10. Outline two thirty-minute talks, one to a Catholic adult education group and the other to a Protestant (name the denomination) adult group, entitled "Why the Church Needs a Pope." If you cannot accept the thesis, outline the opposite one: "Why the Church Can Get Along Without a Pope."

11. Is papal infallibility a problem for you? Do you find it acceptable, or not? Why? Do you think it an important issue? Why?

12. Repeat the exercise in #10 above, changing only the titles: "Infallibility: Updating the Concept," or "Infallibility: An Outdated Concept."

13. Among the various elements of Vatican I's definition of papal infallibility, which do you think is (are) least understood? To what effect?

14. What was your own operative definition of ministry before reading this chapter? Would you change it in light of the chapter? Why? Why not? Do you agree that the two sides which the chapter describes as "extreme" are, in fact, extreme? Give reasons. Which extreme would more gravely undermine the mission of the Church? Why?

15. Comment on the following assertion: "Ordination just creates a caste-system in the Church. We should eliminate it and rely instead on the call of the Spirit. Each Christian should be free to test and to exercise his or her vocation."

16. Were you surprised that women were so much (or so little) involved in the life of the early Church? Explain your reaction.

17. What do you think of the arguments for and against the ordination of women to the priesthood? Which side would most of your friends be on, and why? What about the majority of your fellow parishioners? Do you think the Catholic Church will ever ordain women? Why? Why not?

18. Have you ever received Communion in a liturgical service of another Christian church? Have you ever encouraged a member of another Christian church to receive Communion in your own church? If your answer to either or both question(s) is affirmative, comment on your reasons and your reactions after the event.

19. Do you think the present guidelines of the Secretariat for Promoting Christian Unity are too strict? too permissive? Why?

20. If you were presiding over a Eucharist at which intercommunion was officially allowed, what biblical texts would you select for the liturgy and what basic orientation would you give your homily?

XXIV Mary and the Church (865)

1. If you were writing a catechism or a textbook or organizing a curriculum for a religious education program, where would you place the treatment of Mary? Why?

2. Are you surprised by the New Testament data on Mary? Did you expect more, or less, about her? Were you aware of the diversity of attitudes toward Mary—e.g., those of Mark and Luke? If not, why do you think this was never mentioned in sermons, in catechism classes, and so on? Does the Marcan material distress you, or does it actually enhance your appreciation of Mary?

3. Have you ever heard any of the ancient legends about Mary and the Holy Family? What were some of them? Did you ever believe in them? Do you think people still do? Do you think it makes any difference if they do?

4. Forget for the moment what you think you "must believe as a Catholic" and consider the following question: Does it really make any difference, *in principle*, whether Mary was a virgin before, during, and/or after the birth of Jesus?

5. *In fact*, there is a doctrinal tradition about the virginity of Mary. If you were giving an instruction to a potential Catholic (or a convert to any Christian church of your choice), how would you answer this question: "I'd really like to become a Catholic (or whatever denomination), but do I have to believe in the virginity of Mary?"

6. Do you pray *to* Mary? Why do you do it? If not, why not?

7. Review the material on Original Sin in chapter 5. Can you reconcile the Immaculate Conception with it? Explain.

8. What do you make of the reported apparitions of Mary at places such as Lourdes and Fatima? Do you believe in them? If so, do they make any difference in your life? Do they enhance your understanding of Christian faith? If you do not believe in them, why not?

9. Suppose that neither of the two Marian dogmas, the Immaculate Conception and the Assumption, had yet been defined. Suppose further that you are the pope. Pressure is being placed on you to make both of these beliefs matters of faith. What would you do? Explain.

10. Do you have any difficulty accepting either or both of these dogmas? Why? Why not?

11. Secure a copy, or copies, of some Marian devotional literature and analyze it theologically, in light of the teachings of the Second Vatican Council. Is it consistent, or inconsistent, with Vatican II?

12. In your parish and/or within the circle of your own friends and colleagues, is there a stronger tendency toward minimalism, or toward maximalism, in Marian devotion? Explain.

13. Keeping in mind the criteria suggested in this chapter, compose a Marian prayer for use in a special service of readings, prayers, hymns, and homily in Mary's honor.

14. Examine samples of paintings and statues depicting Mary. Evaluate them in terms of their theological "content."

15. It is the Week of Prayer for Christian Unity and you have been asked to give a thirty-minute presentation to an ecumenical group, including a fairly wide assortment of Christians, on "Mary and the Church." Outline the talk.

16. What do you think of the suggestion that devotion to Mary is important to highlight the femininity of God? What role, if any, has Marian devotion played in the way the Church has understood and depicted women? Do you think Mary has anything at all to "say" to the feminist movement today, whether positive or negative?

17. Again, forget for the moment what you think a Catholic "is supposed to believe" about Mary. Do you think Mary is important to Christian faith and practice? If so, why? If not, why not?

XXV Christian Existence: An Historical Perspective (909)

1. From your own experience and/or observations, has the traditional separation of doctrinal from moral theology had any negative effects on the thinking and behavior of Catholics or of other Christians? Where the separation has been overcome, do you notice any improvements?

2. How does the discussion about the specificity of *Christian* ethics in this chapter relate to our previous discussions about religious pluralism in chapter 8 and the necessity of the Church in chapter 20? In other words, "Do you have to be Christian to be moral? If not, why be Christian?"

3. When some complain today that the Church does not put enough emphasis on the Ten Commandments, are they concerned about the loss of a sense of our covenantal relationship with God, or are they regarding the Decalogue principally as a charter of Christian morality? In any case, how would you respond to this complaint?

4. Are you surprised that there was no single teaching authority in the Old Testament? Is this consistent, or inconsistent, with what we saw about teaching authority in the New Testament? How important do you think teaching authority is in relation to the actual observance of God's will? If very important, what room do you leave for personal responsibility? If unimportant, what role, if any, do extrinsic or objective norms have in moral decision-making?

5. Compare or contrast the development of Catholic moral theology from the second century to the present with the priorities of Jesus' own moral vision and teaching.

6. Without neglecting the discussion of Jesus' outlook as presented in chapters 12 and 17, what do you make of Jesus' interest in the political order? Was he a political revolutionary? a moderate? a conservative? Was he simply indifferent to politics? Are the developments in Catholic social doctrine over the last century consistent with the answer you've given?

7. What do you make of the connection between Christian faith and poverty? For example, is it always better to be poor than to be rich? Does God speak primarily through the poor? Does God speak at all through those who are not poor? If the Church is called to live according to the spirit of poverty, what does that mean?

8. Was Jesus a feminist? What difference does it make one way or the other?

9. There has been a strongly anti-sexual bias in Catholic moral theology from time to time. Do you know of Catholics who have left the Church because of this bias? Do you know of other Catholics who are upset because the Church seems too permissive these days about matters of sexual morality? What is your own impression of the present state of Catholic moral teaching on this question: too negative about sexuality, too liberal, or just about right?

10. Were you aware, before reading this chapter, of how much the needs of priest-confessors dictated the growth and development of Catholic moral theology? Can you recall evidence of that connection in your own religious education? Are you satisfied that textbooks on morality are no longer primarily oriented to the sacrament of Penance?

11. Moral minimalism ("How much can I get away with?") developed at least partly because of moral theology's preoccupation with economics. Is there a danger today that some might be emphasizing the economic side of Christian morality too much? too little? Explain.

12. Do you think most Catholics, not to say most Christians and most human beings, understand and appreciate the main lines of Catholic social doctrine? Outline a 30- to 45-minute talk on "Catholic Social Doctrine: Yesterday and Today," for an ecumenical group of adults.

13. In general, do you think the Church (Catholic or other) has become too much interested in social, economic, and political issues today, or is it not interested enough? How would you answer those who complain that the Church is losing its spiritual and religious significance, that its principal task is somehow to link time and eternity?

14. The distinction between classicism and historical consciousness is a crucial one. How would you explain it to a group of high-school students who are convinced that anything is "moral" so long as "it

doesn't hurt anyone"? How would you explain it to a group of middle-aged Catholics who learned their moral theology at a time when the dos and don'ts were clear-cut?

15. If you are a Catholic, have you ever read anything written by a Protestant moral theologian? What did you make of it? What seems to you to be the main difference between Catholic and Protestant approaches to moral questions? If you are not a Catholic, have you ever read anything by a Catholic moral theologian? In light of the material you read, how do you understand the difference between Catholic and Protestant (or Anglican and Orthodox) approaches to moral issues? If you have not read anything outside your own tradition, do you think it important that you do sometime soon? Explain.

XXVI Christian Existence: Principles and Process (951)

1. When some Catholics and other Christians complain that nowadays we do not seem to be paying sufficient attention to sin, what do you think they mean? How would you respond to their concern?

2. Give concrete examples of how human freedom can be limited or impaired in moral judgment, decision-making, and action.

3. How frequently do you think mortal sins are committed? Explain your answer with examples and cases. How about venial sins?

4. Do you think the traditional three-source theory is still useful in analyzing a moral act: attending to the act itself, the motive, and the circumstances? Explain your answer with examples and cases.

5. Do you think all, most, many, some, a few, or no Christians have truly been converted to Christ and the Kingdom of God? Explain. In that connection, what do you make of the recent emphasis of some evangelical Christians on the need to be "reborn" in Christ?

6. Assuming that Christian moral education is really character formation rather than the teaching of moral rules to be obeyed, outline a curriculum of moral education for a Catholic high school.

7. Do you think modern psychology is a help, or a hindrance, to understanding what it means to be a Christian today? Explain in some detail.

8. Outline a 30- to 45-minute presentation on the interrelationship of faith, hope, and charity to (a) an adult education group, (b) a high-school group, (c) a group of religious women, and (d) a group of priests and/or ministers.

9. To the extent that you are familiar with the literature beyond the summary given in this chapter, what do you make of the stages of faith development as proposed by James Fowler and others?

10. What was your understanding of the virtue of prudence before reading this chapter? What do you think is the general understanding of

prudence in the Church? Outline a pastoral letter entitled "Prudence and Moral Responsibility."

11. Have you heard much about "discernment"? If not, skip to the next question. If so, what do you make of recent interest in it? Do you think it is a positive, or a negative, development in the Church? Explain.

12. Give examples of how the four kinds of justice (commutative, distributive, legal, and social) can be fulfilled and violated.

13. If you were asked to draft the pope's next encyclical on justice, how would you outline it?

14. Does the principle of subsidiarity apply to such cases as the ordination of women, obligatory celibacy for priests, standards of seminary education and religious formation, the election of bishops? Is the principle violated in the Church today? in society at large? Explain.

15. You have been asked to give a retreat conference on "Christian Asceticism: Is It Outmoded?" Outline your presentation.

16. Are there particular people you admire for their courage? Who are they, and what evidence of courage do you see in them? To what extent was Jesus courageous?

17. Outline an essay entitled "The Four Cardinal Virtues: Pillars of the Christian Life."

18. Do you think the institutionalization of charity today has diminished the need or the opportunity for works of mercy? How can the works of mercy be carried out in highly technological societies that have strong central governments? Could you add to the list of corporal and spiritual works of mercy?

19. Do you find the distinction between values and norms helpful, or not? Explain. If you find it helpful, how would you explain it to a group of junior high-school or high-school students? If you prefer another approach, what is it?

20. Could you make moral decisions without reference to the natural law? Do you think everyone has some moral instinct of faith? Explain.

21. In light of this chapter, what meaning does the principle "Let your conscience be your guide" have?

22. How far would you allow someone else to go in the name of his or her conscience if you were convinced the intended action was immoral? It is important that you indicate the principles which would govern your decision in each case that follows. Case #1: You are the parent of a son or daughter who wants to live with another person without benefit of marriage. Case #2: Your husband (or wife) insists on having an abortion. Case #3: Your superior in the U.S. State Department wants to send a memo to the president urging the bombing of civilian targets. Case #4: You are a bishop, and a religious educator in your

diocese is teaching that abortion is a woman's right and is her decision alone.

23. Do you think that Pope Paul VI's teaching on birth control (*Humanae Vitae*, 1968) should, or should not, be followed? Is there a position somewhere in between? Give reasons.

24. What happens if a Catholic finds himself or herself constantly at odds with official moral teachings of the Church? Does it make any difference how many or of what kind those teachings are? Are you surprised that the Church has never officially defined a moral doctrine? Would you like the Church to do so? Which one(s)? How would the teaching(s) be worded?

25. Can you think of moral cases which are not covered, in whole or in large part, by the principles provided in this chapter? Which moral principles would apply to them?

26. A publisher has just asked you for an outline of a book tentatively entitled *Christian Morality Today*. He or she wants it to be useful as a textbook, either in high school, in college, or in an adult education program. What would your Table of Contents look like? Why would you organize the material that way? Why would you select those issues?

XXVII   Christian Existence: Special Questions (1015)

1. Reflecting on this chapter, would you have selected some other moral issues as representative of interpersonal ethics and of social ethics? Which would you have chosen? Which of the four issues in this chapter would you have replaced if you were limited to four? Explain each decision.

2. Can you think of any other arguments in favor of the traditional teaching against contraception? Can you think of any additional arguments against the traditional teaching? Do you think *Humanae Vitae*'s case looks stronger, or weaker, in light of developments since 1968?

3. Why do you think the overwhelming majority of Catholics of childbearing age do not follow the moral directives of *Humanae Vitae*? What is your own view, and would you follow it? Do you think Catholics who do not follow the teaching of *Humanae Vitae* are unworthy Catholics?

4. Were you aware of the official teachings of the Catholic Church against usury? Do you see any parallel with the teachings on contraception? Explain.

5. Read *Humanae Vitae*. List the principles and points with which you agree and disagree. Even if you oppose its central teaching, do you find that there is much in the encyclical that needs to be emphasized? If you accept its central teaching, do you find any significant weaknesses in

the document, i.e., places where the argument could have been improved or points that could have been clarified?

6. Are you surprised by the reaction of various national bishops' conferences to the encyclical? If you were a bishop and were asked to draft a statement on birth control for your national bishops' conference (*"Humanae Vitae* Today"), what would you say in your statement?

7. Can you think of any additional values at stake in this birth control issue besides those listed in this chapter?

8. Which position regarding the morality of homosexuality do you most readily identify with: always sinful, neutral, or essentially imperfect? Do you prefer a fourth position? How do you reconcile your position (if it is not the first one) with the biblical record and the teaching of the Catholic Church? How do you reconcile your position (if it *is* the first one) with recent developments in psychology and even in moral theology?

9. Do you think homosexuality is an appropriate topic for this chapter? Do you think it provides a good exercise in moral analysis to face such a controversial issue head-on? If not, why not?

10. Can you think of any additional values at stake in this issue of homosexuality besides those listed in this chapter?

11. What do you make of the Old Testament's attitude toward warfare? How about Jesus' apparent indifference to the question?

12. In general, do you think the just-war theory was a positive development in moral theology, or another instance of a highly rationalized veiling of the gospel? Do you see any other uses of the just-war ethic—e.g., to justify the intervention of the state or even of the Church in major areas of social, economic, or political conflict?

13. Are you surprised, or not, by the recent development toward a pacifist option in Catholic moral theology? Do you think a Christian *may* be a pacifist? *must* be a pacifist? may *never* be a pacifist?

14. Where do you stand on the policy of nuclear deterrence? Give reasons.

15. Can you add any values to those listed in this chapter regarding the morality of warfare?

16. Do you think Catholics, or Christians generally, take either the principle of subsidiarity or the process of socialization into account when making up their political minds? Do you think Catholic social doctrine makes any significant difference to Catholic and/or Christian political opinions and behavior? If so, why do you think so? If not, why not?

17. Select an economic issue like health care and analyze it according to the moral principles and values given at the end of this chapter.

18. Would you add any other values and principles to that final list? Explain.

XXVIII   Christian Spirituality (1057)

1. What was your understanding of "spirituality" before reading this chapter? Has your understanding changed at all? If so, how? If not, why not?

2. Have you ever referred to another person or persons as "very spiritual"? What did you mean by that? What do you look for in such a person's character and behavior? Do you think that many people who have been regarded as "unspiritual" were really more "spiritual" than their detractors thought? If so, give some examples.

3. A basic tension between a positive and negative attitude toward the human, the physical, the fleshly, has characterized much of the history of Christian spirituality. Were those attitudes more positive than negative during your childhood? early adulthood? present experience?

4. Based on your own experience and/or reading, indicate what you think is the best spiritual development or emphasis in the Church today? Which development or emphasis are you least enthusiastic about? Why?

5. Why do you think people enter monasteries today? How do their reasons compare with the reasons for the original establishment of the monastic life? Do you think there is a place for the monastic life today? Explain.

6. Do you think Christian spirituality is still too much influenced by the concerns of monks, priests, and religious? If so, give examples. What points would you like to see incorporated into and emphasized in a genuinely "lay" spirituality?

7. How important to Christian spirituality are popular devotions (e.g., Sacred Heart, Blessed Mother)? Do you have any such devotional interests in your own life? If so, why are they important to you? If not, why do you think they are so unimportant to your Christian life?

8. Have you ever had a contemplative experience of God? If so, describe it. How did you know it was truly an experience of God? If not, do you think your Christian life is missing something essential?

9. Have you read any of the masters of Christian spirituality—e.g., Teresa of Avila, John of the Cross, Bernard of Clairvaux, Ignatius Loyola, Francis de Sales, Meister Eckhart? If so, who has influenced your spirituality, and to what extent? If you have not read any of the major spiritual writers of the past, why not? Do you think it is important to do so? If so, why? If not, why not?

10. Which twentieth-century spiritual writers have most influenced your own spirituality, either directly (through your own reading and reflection) or indirectly (through the homilies and teachings of your priests, sisters, and catechists)?

11. Do you read any contemporary spiritual books? If so, which ones, why, and to what effect? If not, why not?

12. Do you think the basic principles of the Second Vatican Council regarding the spiritual life have been assimilated into the Catholic Church today? Indicate where they have and where they have not.

13. Have you had any contact with some of the modern movements mentioned in this chapter—e.g., Marriage Encounter, Cursillo, Charismatic Renewal, retreats? If so, what has been your reaction? If not, do you at least know of people who have been involved with these movements? What impression do these people make on you?

14. Outline a thirty-minute talk for an adult education group entitled "Taking the Mystery Out of Mysticism."

15. When you hear Church officials and others saying that we need a renewal of spirituality today, what do you think they really mean? What would you mean if you made the same kind of statement? Would you make such a statement? If not, why not?

16. Have you ever spoken in tongues? Do you know anyone who has? Do you think the gift is important? Explain.

17. Do you have trouble discerning the will of God? If so, why? If not, why not? Are the negative criteria given in this chapter helpful? Would you add any others?

18. Do you have a spiritual director? If not, why not? Have you ever had a spiritual director? What was your experience with spiritual direction? If you were asked to be a spiritual director for the following, what would you emphasize in your first meeting with (him/her/them): a 40-year-old pastor of a run-down urban parish; a 75-year-old widow with several children and grandchildren but living alone; a convent of nuns ranging from ages 35 to 80, with most in the 45-60 bracket; a high-school class (pick your grade); a group of Catholic lawyers?

19. Can you think of any additional theological criteria by which to judge the consistency of spiritualities with the Catholic, or indeed the Christian, tradition?

XXIX Christian/Human Destiny: The Kingdom of God (1101)

1. What is your own experience and/or impressions of the way eschatology is presented in sermons, catechisms, religious education, and even formal theology courses and programs today? Is the emphasis more on the destiny of all humankind and all creation, or on the individual? Is there any future dimension at all? Is it only future-oriented?

2. The themes of the last Sunday of the liturgical year and the first Sunday of Advent are eschatological. Look over the Scripture readings

for those two Sundays and prepare, or at least outline, a 10- to 15-minute homily on "Christian Expectation and Hope."

3. On what basis do you believe in individual and/or cosmic fulfillment after death? God's promises in Christ? an analysis of human intentionality? something else? a combination of these? Do you know of people who do not believe in the coming of the Kingdom in any sense? If so, how do such persons make sense of life? On what basis, if any, do they have hope?

4. Do you have trouble reconciling the conviction that the outcome of history is already decided in Christ with the conviction that evil forces are still at work and failures can occur?

5. Given the variety of views and emphases in contemporary Judaism regarding the Kingdom, was it surprising that Jesus should have attracted some attention by his proclamation of the Kingdom? What would he have to do today if he were to make a similarly profound impact and impression? Is the Church doing that? Is anyone?

6. Why have there been such different views of the Kingdom of God in the history of the Church: e.g., Kingdom = Church, Kingdom = God in the depths of the soul, Kingdom = social justice?

7. Which of the various biblical theologies of the Kingdom of God appeals to you most, and why? Do you see value in each? Explain.

8. Are there elements of the Kingdom which you believe are not sufficiently attended to in contemporary Catholic theology, or in Protestant, Anglican, and Orthodox theology? What are they? Are there elements in this contemporary theology which disturb you? Which, and why?

9. What do you think of Vatican II's understanding of the Kingdom?

10. Do you think it important, or not, to deal with questions of individual destiny, as we do in the latter part of this chapter?

11. Although you would adapt your remarks to specific situations, what themes would you consistently sound in a funeral homily?

12. A young man or woman has just been killed in an auto accident. What do you say to the parents? Would your words or gestures be any different if the young person had died after a long illness?

13. A Catholic complains to you that the Church does not emphasize God's judgment any more. What response would you give?

14. How can we "see" God "face to face" if God is spirit? What do you say to a child who asks, "What is heaven like?" What do you say to a skeptical friend who asks, "Do you still believe in that heaven stuff?"

15. Had you assumed that the doctrine of purgatory was "out"? Does anyone you know talk about it at all? What do you make of the

present attitude toward purgatory? Do you believe in it? Explain your answer.

16. Do you think indulgences are better left behind as part of the Church's unwanted medieval baggage? Or do you think there is something salvageable and enduringly important about indulgences? Explain.

17. Do you have in your mind a picture of the resurrection of the body? How do you think others imagine it? Do you think it would make any difference if we dropped reference to it from the creeds?

18. What do you believe about hell? Is it a place? If so, what is it like? Do you think anyone is there? Is it a state? If so, what do you mean by that? Is it nothing at all? If so, why has the Church taught about it so long?

19. Do you believe in demons, or evil spirits? Apparently, many of our contemporaries do, to judge by films, television shows, books, and radio dramas. How do you explain this fascination with the world of evil spirits?

20. Some students have just returned from viewing one of these films, and they ask you what the Church teaches about the existence of demons and evil spirits. What do you say?

21. Do you believe in limbo? Do you know anyone who does? Do you think, on the whole, the doctrine of limbo has been helpful, or unhelpful, to parents who have lost a child at birth or in infancy (before Baptism)?

22. Do you believe in the Communion of Saints? If not, why not? If so, what difference does that belief make in your understanding and practice of Christian faith?

23. If you had been writing this chapter, would you have organized it any differently? Why? Would you have added any other topics? Which, and why? Would you have deleted any topics? Which, and why?

XXX   Catholicism: A Synthesis (1169)

1. What element(s), apart from the papacy, did you once think distinguished Catholicism from every other Christian church and tradition? What is your estimate of that (those) distinguishing characteristic(s) now?

2. Can you think of any other characteristics, not specifically mentioned in this chapter, which might usefully be included in a comprehensive description of Catholicism?

3. Do you think the distinctiveness of Catholicism—its openness in principle to all truth and to every value, for example—is reflected in (a) the sermons you hear, (b) the official pronouncements you receive from the pope and bishops of the Church, (c) the catechisms and textbooks you read, or (d) the attitudes of your children, parents, relatives,

and friends? If not, wherein lies the discrepancy, and what needs to be emphasized to close the gap?

4. List some prominent former Catholics. From what you know of their lives, careers, writings, and public statements, what prompted most of them to leave the Church? What do you think of their reasons? Can you think of any reasons or circumstances which could induce you to leave the Catholic Church? If you are not a Catholic, what reasons or circumstances might prompt you to consider becoming a Catholic?

5. A project: Visit various churches (Protestant, Anglican, Orthodox, Catholic) and note how, if at all, the distinctiveness of their respective traditions is reflected in architecture, sculpture, paintings, images, music, prayer books, and the like.

6. If you are a Catholic, outline a chapter of a book (much like *Why Catholic?*, mentioned in Suggested Readings) in which you indicate your reasons for being and remaining a Catholic. If you are not a Catholic but were asked to contribute a chapter to such a book, what would you say in appreciation of Catholicism? What constructive criticisms would you offer?

GLOSSARY

(The purpose of this glossary is *not* to provide new information or greater precision. Each term has already been explained, and in most cases defined, in the text itself. The reader should consult the Index of Subjects for such references. The glossary is provided instead as a convenience to the reader, as a quick memory-refresher and time-saver.)

ADOPTIONISM General term for views which look upon Jesus Christ as the purely human, "adopted" son of God.

AGNOSTICISM The suspension of belief regarding the reality of God.

ALEXANDRIA, SCHOOL OF Theological and catechetical center in Egypt, from the end of the second century, which emphasized the divinity of Christ. (Principal representatives: Clement, Origen.)

ANATHEMA An official condemnation by the Church of a doctrinal or moral position.

ANNULMENT An official declaration by the Church that a presumed marriage never really existed in the first place—e.g., because the couple was psychologically incapable of making a permanent commitment.

ANTHROPOLOGY, THEOLOGICAL The meaning of human existence in light of God, Christ, redemption, etc.

ANTICHRIST The embodiment of all historical forces hostile to God.

ANTINOMIANISM An attitude which rejects any and every law as the basis of Christian conduct.

ANTIOCH, SCHOOL OF Theological and catechetical center in Syria, from the end of the second century, which emphasized the humanity of Jesus. (Principal representatives: Arius, Theodore of Mopsuestia, John Chrysostom.)

APOCALYPTICISM A comprehensive name for a style of thought and writing associated with the later period of the Old Testament (e.g., Daniel), the period between the two Testaments, and the New Testament itself. Emphasis is on visions, signs, and predictions of future events brought about entirely by divine power, beyond history.

APOKATASTASIS The belief, associated especially with Origen, that every human being will eventually be saved.

APOLOGETICS. That part of theology which tries to show the reasonableness of Christian faith.

APOSTLE A missionary or messenger of the Church in the New Testament period. The term is not coextensive with *the Twelve* (see below).

APOSTOLIC SUCCESSION In the wider sense, the process by which the whole Church continues, and is faithful to, the word, the witness, and the service of the Apostles. In the stricter sense, the legitimation of the bishops' office and authority by their valid derivation from the Apostles.

ARIANISM The heresy, condemned by the council of Nicea (325), which made the Son of God the highest of creatures, greater than we but less than God.

ASCETICISM Exercises undertaken to live the Gospel more faithfully, especially in light of the cross of Christ and the sacrificial nature of his whole life.

ASSUMPTION Dogma defined in 1950 by Pope Pius XII that the body of the Blessed Virgin Mary was taken directly to heaven after her life on earth had ended.

ATHEISM The denial of the reality of God.

ATONEMENT The act of healing the breach between God and humankind opened by sin. Usually associated with the crucifixion of Christ.

AUTHENTICITY OF CHURCH TEACHINGS A quality of teachings which have authority because they are issued by persons holding a canonically recognized teaching office in the Church.

AUTHENTICITY OF SACRED SCRIPTURE A quality of the various books of the Bible by which they are recognized to have been produced by the individuals or communities with whom the Church associates these writings.

BAIANISM Unorthodox sixteenth-century view which held that after Original Sin everything we do is sinful. We have no real freedom of choice.

BAPTISM OF DESIRE The process by which individuals are said to merit eternal life because of their good will, even though, through no fault of their own, they have not been baptized with water.

BASILEIA The Greek word for "Kingdom (of God)."

BEATIFIC VISION Our final union with God in heaven.

BELIEF Any expression of faith. Not all beliefs are *doctrines* or *dogmas* (see below).

CANON A list which seves as a "measure" or standard.

CANON LAW The code of Church laws promulgated in 1918. More generally, any official code, or listing, of Church laws.

CANON OF SCRIPTURE The official list of inspired books of the Bible, solemnly defined by the Council of Trent (1546).

CANONICAL FORM The requirement of the Catholic Church that every Catholic be married in the presence of a priest and two witnesses, unless specifically dispensed.

CASUISTRY An approach to the solution of moral problems which reduces theology to canon law, i.e., to a solver of "cases" ("Is it sinful? If so, how seriously?").

CATECHESIS The process of "echoing" the Gospel, of introducing young people or adult converts to the main elements of the Christian faith.

CATECHISM A handbook for catechesis. Usually in question-and-answer form.

CATECHUMEN One who is undergoing catechesis.

CATECHUMENATE The formal stage of preparation for entrance into the Church.

CHALCEDON The city in Asia Minor where in 451 the fourth ecumenical council was held in which it was defined that Jesus Christ is true God and true man, and that his divine and human natures are united in one divine person, without confusion, change, division, or separation.

CHARACTER, MORAL That which gives orientation, direction, and shape to our lives. The cluster of virtues which make a person what he or she is.

CHARACTER, SACRAMENTAL The permanent effect of three sacraments: Baptism, Confirmation, and Holy Order. (Hence, these sacraments are never conferred more than once.)

CHARISM A gift of the Holy Spirit—e.g., wisdom.

CHARISMATIC One who manifests and is attentive to the gifts of the Holy Spirit.

CHRISTOCENTRISM Seeing all reality, and therefore all of theology, in light of Jesus Christ.

CHRISTOLOGY The theological study of Jesus Christ: natures, person, ministry, consciousness, etc. Christology "from above" starts with the Word of God (*Logos*) in heaven and views Jesus as the Word who has come down to earth for our salvation (John and Paul). Christology "from below" starts with the Jesus of history and shows how his earthly life is significant for our salvation (the Synoptics).

CHRISTOMONISM Seeing all reality, and doing all theology, only in light of Jesus Christ, so that there is no revelation or salvation apart from Christ and apart from explicit faith in him.

CIRCUMINCESSION The presence, or indwelling, of the three divine Persons in one another. The Son and the Holy Spirit are present in the Father, and the Father in the Son and the Holy Spirit. The Father and the Son are present in the Holy Spirit, and the Holy Spirit in the Father and the Son. And so forth. Known also as *perichoresis*.

CLASSICISM The philosophical world view which holds that reality (truth) is essentially static, unchanging, and unaffected by history. Such truth can readily be captured in propositions or statements whose meaning is fixed and clear from century to century.

COGNITIVE Pertaining to knowledge. A theological approach is said to be "cognitive" if it emphasizes knowledge, the intellect, principles rather than emotions, imagination, the will, the subject, the situation, and circumstances.

COLLEGIALITY The principle that the Church is a community (college) of local churches which together make up the Church universal. In practice, collegiality introduces a mode of decision-making in the Church which emphasizes coresponsibility not only between the pope and the bishops but also among all communities and groups within the Body of Christ.

COMMUNICATIO IDIOMATUM The "communication of properties" between the divine and human natures of Jesus Christ because both natures are united in one divine Person, without confusion. The properties of both natures can and must be applied to, or predicated of, the one divine person; e.g., "The Word of God was crucified."

COMMUNICATIO IN SACRIS Literally, "communication in sacred things." It refers to Catholic and non-Catholic Christians sharing in the Eucharist by receiving Holy Communion in one or another's liturgy.

COMMUNION OF SAINTS The whole community of believers in Christ, living and dead. Those on earth are called the *Church Militant*. Those in purgatory are the *Church Suffering*. Those in heaven are the *Church Triumphant*.

CONCILIARISM The medieval movement which viewed an ecumenical council as superior in authority to the pope.

CONCUPISCENCE Natural "desires," impulses, or instincts of the human person which move the person toward something morally good or morally evil even before he or she has begun any moral reflection about it.

CONSCIENCE The experience of ourselves as moral agents, as persons responsible for our actions. Decisions are made in light of who we think we are and are called to become.

CONSERVATISM, BIBLICAL The tendency to take the accounts of Sacred Scripture at face value— e.g., Jesus really understood himself to be the Messiah and the Son of God right from the beginning of his life and ministry.

CONSERVATISM, THEOLOGICAL The tendency to adhere to the literal meaning of the official teachings of the Church and to emphasize their decisive authority in matters under discussion among theologians.

CONSUBSTANTIATION The Reformation view that the bread and wine remain along with the body and blood of Christ after the eucharistic consecration ("This is my body.... This is my blood...."). It is distinguished from *transubstantiation* (see below).

CONTEMPLATION Conscious attention to the presence of God in the depths of oneself, in others, and in the world. A form of prayer.

CONTEMPLATIVE Generally, one whose life is governed by the spirit and practice of contemplation. Specifically, a member of a monastic community.

CONVENIENCE, ARGUMENT FROM A method of reaching theological conclusions not on the basis of sources (Bible, doctrines, etc.) but on the basis of the seeming appropriateness of a particular conclusion. The usual form of such an argument is: It is fitting that God should have done so; God had the power to do so; therefore, God must have done so. Especially applicable to *Mariology* (see below).

CONVERSION The fundamental change of heart (*metanoia*) by which a person accepts Jesus as the Christ and orients his or her whole life around Christ and the Kingdom of God which he proclaimed.

COREDEMPTRIX A title sometimes given to the Blessed Virgin Mary to emphasize her cooperative role in the redemption of the human race by Christ.

COUNCIL An official church assembly. It is *ecumenical*, or *general*, if it draws representatives from the "whole wide world." It is *regional* if it draws representatives from various dioceses in a particular region of the world or of a particular nation. It is *local* if it involves only a particular diocese, or local church.

COUNTER-REFORMATION The Catholic response to the Protestant Reformation of the sixteenth century. At the center was the *Council of Trent* and its reform of doctrine, liturgy, and law.

COVENANT The bond, contract, or "testament" between God and Israel in the Old Testament, established with Noah, Abraham, Moses, and David, and between God and the whole human community in the New Testament, established by the blood of Christ.

COVENANTAL Pertaining to the close bond of love and friendship between God and ourselves.

CREED An official profession of faith, usually promulgated by a council of the Church and used in the Church's liturgy.

CRITICISM, FORM A method of biblical study employed to uncover the second layer of tradition in the composition of the Gospels, namely, the oral proclamation of the Apostles and the disciples (catechesis, narratives, hymns, prayers, etc.).

CRITICISM, HISTORICAL A method of biblical study employed to uncover the first layer of tradition in the composition of the Gospels, namely, the original words and deeds of Jesus. It asks, "How can we know the historical Jesus?"

CRITICISM, REDACTION A method of biblical study employed to uncover the third layer of tradition in the composition of the Gospels, namely, the writings themselves. It tries to identify the dominant ideas which governed the final editing of the texts as we have them today.

DECALOGUE The Ten Commandments.

DEISM A view of God which looks upon God as a divine "watchmaker." Once the world has been created, God no longer takes an active part in its course. Rejected by Vatican I (1869).

DEMYTHOLOGIZATION A method of New Testament interpretation originated by Rudolf Bultmann. It seeks to get back to the original message of Jesus by stripping away all irrelevant stories (myths) about Jesus' divine powers and his comings and goings between heaven and earth.

DEONTOLOGICAL Pertaining to a way of doing moral theology which emphasizes duty and obligation (*deontos*) in relation to law.

DEPOSIT OF FAITH The "content" of Christian faith given by Christ and the Apostles and preserved as a treasury by the Church ever since.

DESCENT INTO HELL The item in the Apostles' Creed which refers to the time between the crucifixion and the resurrection when Jesus was "among the dead." It does not refer to hell as a state of eternal punishment for sin, but rather to *Sheol* (see below).

DIACONATE The ministry of, and state of being, a deacon of the Church, i.e., an ordained assistant to the bishop or the *presbyter* (see below).

DIALECTICAL Pertaining to a way of understanding reality by noting and keeping in balance seemingly opposite values—e.g., God is wholly Other, but God is also one with us in Christ; the Bible is the Word of God, but it is also the product of human effort; we are sinners, but we are also graced and redeemed.

DISCERNMENT The process, associated with the virtue of prudence, by which we try to decide what God wills us to do in these particular circumstances and for the future.

DISCIPLE A follower of Christ. One who literally "learns from" Christ. All Apostles were disciples, but not all disciples were *Apostles* (see above).

DISPENSATION An action of the official Church by which an individual or individuals are exempted from an ecclesiastical law, temporarily or permanently.

DOCETIC Pertaining to a theological attitude which tends to deny the reality of the material and the bodily in creation, redemption, and salvation.

DOCETISM A view which held that Christ only "seemed" to have a human body.

DOCTRINE An official teaching of the Church.

DOCTRINE, DEVELOPMENT OF The process by which official teachings are revised in accordance with changes in historical circumstances and understanding.

DOGMA A doctrine which is promulgated with the highest authority and solemnity. Its denial is a *heresy* (see below). Every dogma is a doctrine, but not every doctrine is a dogma.

DOGMATIC THEOLOGY Systematic reflection on the Christian faith as that faith has been articulated by the official Church.

DONATISM A North African movement of the fourth century which held that Baptism had to be administered a second time to those who had left the Church and then returned. Opposed strongly by Augustine.

DOUBLE EFFECT, PRINCIPLE OF The principle which holds that an evil effect can be permitted so long as it is not directly intended, is not the means of achieving a good effect, and is not out of proportion to the good effect.

DUALISM The general theological view that all reality is composed of, and arises from, two distinct, absolutely independent, antagonistic, and co-equal principles: Good and Evil.

ECCLESIAL Pertaining to the Church as a mystery, i.e., as the Body of Christ and the Temple of the Holy Spirit, as distinguished from *ecclesiastical*, which pertains to the Church as an institution.

ECCLESIOLOGY The theological study of the Church.

ECUMENICAL Pertaining to a theological attitude which is attentive to the experience and critical reflections of other churches and traditions.

ECUMENISM The movement which seeks to achieve unity of Christians within the Church and ultimately of all humankind throughout the "whole wide world" (the literal meaning of the word).

ENCYCLICAL A letter written by the pope and "circulated" throughout the whole Church and even the whole world beyond the Church.

ENLIGHTENMENT The eighteenth-century philosophical movement which exalted freedom of inquiry and freedom in decision-making. A *post-Enlightenment* mentality criticizes the Enlightenment for its "uncritical" celebration of reason and its failure to attend to the imagination and the larger social context of our ideas.

EPHESUS A city in Asia Minor where the third ecumenical council was held in 431. It condemned *Nestorianism* (see below) and held that Mary is truly the Mother of God (*theotokos*).

EPISCOPACY The highest level of the sacrament of Holy Order. Those who are ordained to the episcopacy are called "bishops." The word is derived from *episkopos*, meaning "overseer."

EPISCOPATE The body of bishops.

ESCHATOLOGICAL Pertaining to a theological attitude which sees all reality in light of the coming Kingdom of God.

ESCHATOLOGY Literally, "the study of the last things." That area of theology which focuses on the Kingdom of God, judgment,

heaven, hell, purgatory, the resurrection of the body, and the Second Coming of Christ.

EUCHARIST Literally, a "thanksgiving." The common name for the Mass, or Lord's Supper.

EVANGELICAL Pertaining to the Gospel and to a theological approach which emphasizes the preaching of Jesus and the biblical expression of that preaching.

EVANGELIZATION The proclamation of the Gospel.

EX OPERE OPERANTIS "From the work of the worker." A phrase explaining how a *sacramental* (see below) achieves its effect: not only by the prayer of the Church but also, and necessarily, by the faith and disposition of the recipient and minister.

EX OPERE OPERATO "From the work done." A phrase explaining how a sacrament achieves its effect: not because of the faith of the recipient and/or the worthiness of the minister but because of the power of Christ who acts within and through it.

EXCOMMUNICATION The expulsion of an individual from the Church, more particularly from the Eucharist.

EXEGESIS The scientific interpretation of the texts of Sacred Scripture.

EXISTENTIALIST THEOLOGY An approach to theology which emphasizes the value of the individual person, the primacy of conscience, and the importance of freedom and authenticity in decision-making.

EXPIATION See *atonement*.

EXTRA ECCLESIAM NULLA SALUS "Outside the Church no salvation." The belief that unless one is somehow related to the Church, that person cannot be saved. The meaning of the formula has been disputed. Father Leonard Feeney, S.J., of Boston, was condemned by the Vatican in 1949 for an extreme interpretation of the principle.

EXTREME UNCTION The former name for the sacrament of the Anointing of the Sick.

FAITH Personal knowledge of God. Christian faith is personal knowledge of God as disclosed in Jesus Christ.

FAITH DEVELOPMENT The process by which faith advances progressively through various stages of human growth—e.g., from an adolescent's desire to win approval to a mature adult's commitment to values apart from self-interest.

FATHERS OF THE CHURCH Writers of Christian antiquity who had a major impact on the doctrinal tradition of the Church. The period of the Fathers is said to have ended by the mid-eighth century.

FIDEISM The nineteenth-century view that faith has no rational content at all. Conviction is rooted in the heart, not the mind.

FIDES FIDUCIALIS Luther's notion of faith as "trust." This view was rejected by the Council of Trent (1547) because it seemed to deny any objective content to faith.

FILIOQUE Literally, "and from the Son." This word was added to the Creed of Nicea-Constantinople at the end of the seventh century, contending that the Holy Spirit proceeds from the Father and the Son as from a single principle. It was opposed by the Greek Church, which preferred the term *"per Filium"* to emphasize the primacy of God the Father in the work of salvation.

FLORENCE An ecumenical council, held in this Italian city in 1439, which not only tried to heal the East-West schism but also defined the seven sacraments.

FUNDAMENTAL OPTION The radical orientation of one's whole life toward or away from God. Akin to conversion. Our destiny is determined by this fundamental "choice" and not by individual acts, unless those acts are such that our basic relationship with God is fully engaged.

FUNDAMENTAL THEOLOGY That area of theology which deals with the most basic introductory questions: e.g., revelation, faith, authority, the ways of knowing God, the nature and task of theology itself.

GALLICANISM A form of national *conciliarism* (see above) peculiar to France (Gaul), and implicitly rejected by the First Vatican Council (1869-1870).

GAUDIUM ET SPES Vatican II's *Pastoral Constitution on the Church in the Modern World.*

GNOSTIC Pertaining to a theological attitude which exaggerates the role of knowledge (*gnosis*) in salvation and which insists that such saving knowledge is available to only a select few.

GNOSTICISM The earliest of Christian heresies, first refuted in the Fourth Gospel. Besides stressing the role of saving knowledge, it also denied the goodness of creation and of the material order.

GOSPEL The "good news" proclaimed by Jesus Christ and thereafter by the Apostles and the Church. The Gospel is interpreted and recorded in the four Gospels of Matthew, Mark, Luke, and John.

GRACE The presence of God.

GRACE, ACTUAL The presence of God given as a power to guide particular human actions.

GRACE, CREATED The presence of God in particular persons, manifested in virtues, in gifts of the Holy Spirit, etc.

GRACE, SANCTIFYING The abiding presence of God in the human person.

GRACE, UNCREATED God. The uncreated Word of God in Jesus Christ. The Holy Spirit.

HEILSGESCHICHTE See *salvation history.*

HELLENISM Theological and philosophical movements dictated and shaped by Greek culture, where the emphasis is on the realm of ideas and universal principles rather than on the world of the concrete and the changeable.

HELLENIZATION OF DOGMA The progressive introduction of Greek categories in the formulation and interpretation of the Christian faith. They are often distinguished from biblical categories of faith.

HERESY Literally, a "choice." It is the denial of a *dogma* (see above).

HERMENEUTICS The science of interpretation; the body of principles which governs the interpretation of any statement or text.

HIERARCHICAL Pertaining to a theological mentality which emphasizes the role of ecclesiastical officers in the life and teaching of the Church.

HIERARCHY Literally, "rule by priests." It is the body of ordained ministers in the Church: pope, bishops, priests, and deacons.

HISTORICAL CONSCIOUSNESS A theological and philosophical mentality which is attentive to the impact of history on human thought and action and which, therefore, takes into account the concrete and the changeable. Distinguished from *classicism* (see above).

HISTORICITY That fundamental human condition by which we are set in time and shaped by the movement of history.

HISTORY The movement of the world toward the final Kingdom of God under the impact of God's grace and the shaping influence of human freedom.

HOMOIOUSIOS Literally, "of a *similar* substance." This term was proposed by Eusebius of Caesarea, who thought it was closer to the teaching of Sacred Scripture, namely, that the Son is *like* the Father. It is simply a different emphasis and approach and is not regarded as unorthodox if correctly understood.

HOMOOUSIOS Literally, "of the *same* substance." Used in the teaching of the early Christological councils, especially Nicea (325), to affirm that the Father and the

Logos (see below) are of the same substance, or nature. Therefore, Jesus is truly divine.

HORIZON A philosophical term meaning the range, or context, of one's view of reality and, therefore, the spectrum of questions one is prepared to ask about human existence, the world, meaning, etc.

HUMANAE VITAE The 1968 encyclical of Pope Paul VI in which he condemned as immoral all artificial means of regulating births.

HUMANIZATION The process by which the world and its history, through heightened consciousness and freedom, become progressively truer to their vocation and closer to their final destiny in the Kingdom of God.

HYLOMORPHISM A medieval Scholastic notion which regarded all reality as composed of matter and form. The notion was applied to the theology of the Eucharist, grace, the human person, and the sacraments in general; e.g., the *matter* of a sacrament is what is used (water in Baptism), the *form* of a sacrament is the words and gestures (pouring the water and saying the baptismal formula); or, the body is the *matter* of the human person, the soul is the *form*.

HYPOSTATIC UNION The word *hypostasis* refers to the person of the *Logos* (see below). The hypostatic union is the permanent union of divine and human natures in the one divine Person of the Word in Jesus Christ (see *Chalcedon* above).

ICONOCLASM Literally, "the destroying of images." The negative attitude toward images (*icons*) and their veneration. An iconoclastic controversy raged in the East during the eighth and ninth centuries.

IDEALISM The philosophical attitude which identifies reality with ideas. It is distinguished from *realism* (see below).

IDOLATRY The worship of idols. The term applies to any tendency to equate something finite with the infinite (God).

IMMACULATE CONCEPTION The dogma defined by Pope Pius IX in 1854 which holds that the Blessed Virgin Mary was free from sin from the very first moment of her existence. This is not to be confused with the *virgin birth* (see below).

IMPECCABILITAS The attribute of Jesus Christ by which he is incapable of sinning.

IMPECCANTIA The sinlessness of Jesus. Even if Jesus Christ were capable of sinning, in fact he did not sin.

INCARNATION The process by which the Word of God became flesh. (See also *hypostatic union*.)

INDIFFERENTISM A theological attitude which holds that one religion is as good, or as bad, as another.

INDISSOLUBILITY The quality of permanence (literally "unbreakability") which applies to marriage.

INDULGENCE The partial or full remission of the penalties still due to sins which have already been forgiven.

INERRANCY The immunity of Sacred Scripture from fundamental error about God and the things of God.

INFALLIBILITY Literally, "immunity from error." The charism by which the Church is protected from fundamental error in matters of faith and morals. It can be exercised by the pope and by an ecumenical council.

INFRALAPSARIAN Pertaining to the period of history after the "fall" of Adam.

INITIATION, CHRISTIAN The total liturgical and catechetical process of becoming a Christian through Baptism, Confirmation, and Eucharist.

INITIUM FIDEI Literally, the "beginning of faith." The grace of God is necessary for the whole process of faith, from beginning to end. There is no point at which the movement of, and toward, faith is possible without the impulse of divine grace.

INSPIRATION, BIBLICAL The guidance of the Holy Spirit in the writing of Sacred Scripture. More generally, inspiration refers to the guidance of the Holy Spirit over the whole Church.

INTEGRALISM A theological attitude, prevalent especially in France in the nineteenth and twentieth centuries, which insists that everything must become formally and explicitly Christian before it is good. Literally, nothing is "whole" (integral) unless and until it is brought within the orbit of the Church.

INTENTIONALITY A philosophical and theological term which refers to the purposive character of human decision-making and behavior.

INTERCOMMUNION See *communicatio in sacris* (above).

INTERNAL FORUM The realm of conscience and/or of the sacrament of Penance. A decision reached in the "internal forum" is known only to God, the individual, and the confessor or spiritual director.

IURE DIVINO Literally, "by divine law." The term refers to institutions (e.g., sacraments) which are said to exist by the explicit will of God, as articulated by Christ and/or the Church. Hence, they are not subject to abolition or substantial tampering by the Church or other human agents.

JANSENISM A seventeenth- and eighteenth-century movement in Europe, especially France, which stressed moral austerity, the evil of the human body and of human desires, and an elitist notion of salvation (Jesus died for a few).

JANSENISTIC Pertaining to a moral attitude which displays a negative appreciation of the bodily and a fear of the sexual. It passed from France to Ireland and then to the United States of America in the late nineteenth and early twentieth centuries.

JESUS OF HISTORY/CHRIST OF FAITH Refers to the distinction between Jesus as he actually was (and whom we can never fully know on the basis of historical evidence) and Jesus as he was understood and interpreted by the Church after the resurrection (namely, as the Christ).

JOHANNINE Pertaining to the writings of the New Testament attributed to John, the Evangelist and the "beloved disciple," or at least to those influenced by him. These are the Fourth Gospel, the three epistles, and the Book of Revelation. They present a high Christology ("from above") and emphasize the law of love and the work of the Spirit.

JURIDICAL Pertaining to a theological attitude which stresses the importance of law in the formation and exercise of Christian life.

JUSTIFICATION The event by which God, acting in Jesus Christ, makes us holy (just) in the divine sight. The immediate effect of justification is *sanctification* (see below). The ultimate effect is *salvation* (see below). The foundation of justification is the *redemption* (see below).

KENOSIS A biblical term (Philippians 2:5-11) which refers to the "self-emptying" of Christ. He did not cling to his divinity but became obedient even unto death.

KERYGMA The "message" of the Gospel. That which was originally proclaimed.

KERYGMATIC THEOLOGY A theology which adheres closely to the literal meaning and emphasis of the biblical message (see also *evangelical*).

KINGDOM OF GOD The reign, or rule, of God. It is the presence of God in the heart, in groups, in the world at large, renewing and reconciling all things. It is both a process ("reign of God") and the reality towards which the process is moving ("Kingdom of God").

KOINONIA Community, or fellowship, produced by the Holy Spirit.

LAST THINGS Death, judgment, heaven, hell, purgatory, Second Coming of Christ, resurrection of the body, and the fulfillment of the Kingdom of God.

LAW In the Old Testament: the Ten Commandments, the Torah, and other norms of conduct, founded in the *Covenant* (see above). In the New Testament: the law of the Gospel, fulfilled in the commandment of love of God and love of neighbor.

LAXISM A moral attitude which tries to find ways of getting around Christian obligations and which always resolves the doubt in favor of exemption, even when good reasons are not present.

LEGALISM A moral attitude which identifies morality with the literal observance of laws, even if the spirit of the law requires something more or different.

LEX ORANDI, LEX CREDENDI "The law of praying is the law of believing." Christian belief is expressed in Christian worship. Christian worship is, in turn, a norm of faith.

LIBERALISM, BIBLICAL The tendency to reduce the content of the Bible to its most natural meaning; e.g., Jesus had no idea that he was the Messiah or the Son of God.

LIBERALISM, THEOLOGICAL The tendency to place a rational or humanistic interpretation on all dogmas and doctrines so that they are devoid of supernatural content. The word is sometimes used in Catholic circles to describe those who assume a critical attitude toward the teaching authority of the Church or toward traditional doctrines of the faith.

LIBERATION THEOLOGY A type of theology which emphasizes the motif of liberation in both Old and New Testaments and which reinterprets all doctrines in terms of that motif. Forms of liberation theology include: Latin American, black, and feminist.

LITURGY The official public worship of the Church, especially the Eucharist and the sacraments.

LOGOS The Word of God, the Second Person of the Trinity, who became flesh in the *incarnation* (see above).

LUMEN GENTIUM Vatican II's *Dogmatic Constitution on the Church.*

LUMEN GLORIAE "The light of glory." That power by which we are enabled to "see God face to face" in heaven. (See also *beatific vision.*)

MACEDONIANISM A fourth-century heresy which denied the divinity of the Holy Spirit. It was condemned by the Council of Constantinople (381).

MAGISTERIUM The teaching authority of the Church, which belongs to some by reason of office (pope and bishops). Others contribute to the teaching mission by scholarly competence (e.g. theologians).

MANICHAEISM A blend of *dualism* and *Gnosticism* (see above for both terms), which began in the mid-third century and did not finally die out until the fourteenth.

MARIOLOGY The theological study of the Blessed Virgin Mary in terms of her role in the Church and in our redemption.

MARTYR Literally, a "witness." One who is put to death because of his or her faith in Jesus Christ.

MASS The Eucharist, or Lord's Supper.

MATER ET MAGISTRA The 1961 encyclical of Pope John XXIII on social justice.

MEDIATION The theological principle that God is available to us and acts upon us through secondary causes: persons, places, events, things, nature, history.

MEDIEVAL Pertaining to the period known as the Middle Ages, the beginning of which some place as early as the seventh century and the end as late as the sixteenth. The high Middle Ages are the twelfth and thirteenth centuries, which are sometimes mistakenly identified with the origins of Catholicism itself.

MERIT Spiritual "credit" earned with God for having performed some good action.

METANOIA See *conversion.*

METHOD A regular and recurrent pattern of operations. A fundamental way of doing theology. Thus, an historical method treats every question from the point of view of its development from its origins to the present time.

MINISTRY Literally, a "service." Any service publicly designated by the Church to assist in the fulfillment of its mission.

MIRACLE An unusual event by which God makes a special impact on history. A special manifestation of the presence and power of God.

MISSION OF THE CHURCH That for which the Church has been "sent"; i.e., its purpose: to proclaim the Gospel in word, in sacrament, in witness, and in service.

MIXED MARRIAGE A marriage between a Catholic and one who is not a Catholic.

MODALISM A general theological approach to the Trinity which sees the three Persons as three different modes of the one God's operations (creation, incarnation, and sanctification).

MODERNISM An early-twentieth-century movement in Catholicism condemned by Pope Pius X because it seemed to deny the permanence of dogmas and tended to reduce all doctrines to their rational or humanistic components. (See also *liberalism, theological.*)

MODERNITY A frame of mind induced by technology, and especially by the innovations effected by advances in communications and transportation. The modern mentality is characterized by its stress on the necessity of making choices from among a relatively large number of possibilities and, therefore, of consulting as wide a spectrum of views as possible. (See also *pluralism.*)

MONASTICISM A style of Christian life, begun in the third century as a flight to the desert to avoid persecution and later to protest the newly privileged status of the Church; it emphasizes life-in-community, common prayer, silence, and contemplation.

MONOGENISM The view that the whole human race is descended from a single couple, Adam and Eve. It is distinguished from *polygenism.*

MONOPHYSITISM The teaching, condemned by the Council of Chalcedon (451), that the human nature of Christ was totally absorbed by the divine nature. As an expression of the *Alexandrian School* (see above), it emphasized the divinity of Christ.

MONOTHEISM The belief in one God. It is distinguished from *polytheism.*

MONOTHELITISM The view, rejected by the Third Council of Constantinople (681), that there is only one will in Christ, the divine will. This is also known as *Monenergism.*

MONTANISM A second-century charismatic belief which stressed the imminent end of the world and imposed an austere morality in preparation for the event. Tertullian was its best-known adherent.

MORAL THEOLOGY That branch of theology which attends to the individual and social implications of the Gospel, and which draws normative inferences for the conduct of the Church and its individual members.

MORTAL SIN So fundamental a rejection of the Gospel and/or the will of God that it merits eternal punishment. Thus, the adjective "mortal."

MYSTERIUM ECCLESIAE The 1973 declaration of the Congregation for the Doctrine of the Faith on infallibility and on the development of doctrine. The document is especially significant because it acknowledges the historicity of doctrinal and dogmatic statements.

MYSTERY A reality imbued with the hidden presence of God. The term is most akin to the word *sacrament.* It also refers to the plan of God for our salvation, as worked out historically in Christ.

MYSTICISM A human's experience of God. Christian mysticism is the experiencing of God in Jesus Christ in light of the Holy Spirit.

NATURAL LAW The whole order of reality which, by the will of God, defines us as human persons and contributes to human development. For the Greeks, it was a "given" of reality; for the Romans, it was something to be discovered and reshaped through common sense and intelligence.

NATURE The human condition apart from grace, but with the radical capacity to receive grace. ("Pure" nature, i.e., without the capacity for grace, does not exist.)

NEO-ORTHODOXY The early-twentieth-century movement within Protestantism (especially Karl Barth) which sought to return to the basic principles of Reformation theology: the primacy of the Word of God, e.g.

NEOPLATONISM The final stage of ancient Greek philosophy which strongly influenced certain Christian thinkers, especially Origen and Augustine. It stressed the reality of God as *Logos*, of finite beings as participants in the *Logos*, and as always in movement back to their source in God. Negatively, it tended to underestimate the goodness of the material order and the importance of the individual person.

NESTORIANISM The teaching, condemned by the Council of Ephesus (431), that posited two separate persons in Jesus Christ, the one human and the other divine. Therefore, Mary was the mother of the human Jesus only. As an expression of the *Antioch School* of theology (see above), it emphasized the humanity of Christ.

NICEA The city in Asia Minor where in 325 the first ecumenical council was held to condemn *Arianism* (see above).

NOMINALISM A medieval philosophical view which denied the reality of universal principles. Emphasis was always on the individual person, situation, or term, and on its uniqueness.

ORDAINED MINISTRY A *ministry* (see above) conferred by the imposition of hands: diaconate, presbyterate (priesthood), and the episcopate.

ORDINATION A sacramental act, usually involving a laying on of hands by a bishop, through which an individual is admitted to the diaconate, the presbyterate (priesthood), or the episcopate.

ORIGENISM A tendency in Eastern theology of the third through fifth centuries which emphasized the necessity and eternity of the world and of souls and which looked upon matter as a consequence of sin.

ORIGINAL JUSTICE The state in which the first human beings were thought to have existed before Original Sin.

ORIGINAL SIN The state in which all human beings are now born. It is a situation or condition in which the possibility of sin becomes instead a probability because grace is not at our disposal in the manner and to the degree that God intended.

ORTHODOXY Literally, "right praise." Consistency with the faith of the Church as embodied in Sacred Scripture, the Fathers, official teachings, and the liturgy.

PACEM IN TERRIS The 1963 encyclical of Pope John XXIII on social justice and international development.

PARABLE A story which makes a theological point through the use of metaphors.

PAROUSIA The Second Coming of Christ at the end of history.

PARTHENOGENESIS See *virgin birth*.

PASTORAL Pertaining to the actual life of the Church, especially at the parish and diocesan levels.

PATRISTIC Pertaining to the *Fathers of the Church* (see above).

PAULINE Pertaining to the writings of the New Testament attributed to Paul. They are known as Epistles, or letters: Romans, 1 and 2 Corinthians, Galatians, etc.

PAULINE PRIVILEGE Based on 1 Corinthians 7:10-16, the principle which allows a convert to the Church to remarry if his or her unbaptized spouse does not also become a Christian.

PELAGIAN Pertaining to a theological attitude which exaggerates the role of human effort in moral life.

PELAGIANISM A heresy with roots in the fifth century which declared that salvation is possible through human effort alone, without grace.

PENTATEUCH The first five books of the Old Testament: Genesis, Exodus, Leviticus, Numbers, and Deuteronomy. Also known as the *Torah*, or the *Law* (see above).

PERICHORESIS See *circumincession*.

PERSON An existing being with the capacity for consciousness and freedom. In the Trinity, the word "person" is used analogically; i.e., Father, Son, and Holy Spirit are "like" human persons, but there are not three separate Gods, only different relationships within the Godhead and different ways in which the one God acts outside the Godhead itself. (See also *subject*.)

PERSONALISM A theological and philosophical view which stresses the importance of the individual human being, or person, in reaching moral decisions.

PETRINE MINISTRY, OFFICE The service rendered the Church by the pope. The papacy. Both ministry and office attend to the universal Church's need for unity in life and mission.

PETRINE PRIVILEGE Also known as the "Privilege of the Faith." It allows the pope to dissolve a marriage between a Christian and a non-Christian when the Christian wishes to marry another Christian or the non-Christian wishes to become a Catholic and remarry.

PHENOMENOLOGY A philosophical and theological view which begins with, and emphasizes, observable realities (phenomena) rather than general principles.

PHILOSOPHY The branch of knowledge concerned with the ultimate meaning of reality, but it does not assume responsibility (as *theology* does) for articulating that meaning in terms of particular religious traditions. Closely related to, and sometimes indistinguishable from, theology itself.

PIETISM A seventeenth- and eighteenth-century movement within

German Lutheranism which stressed the interior life, the experience of conversion, and personal devotion to Jesus.

PIETISTIC Pertaining to a spiritual or moral attitude which stresses personal devotion at the expense of sound biblical, theological, and doctrinal principles.

PLURALISM The inevitable variety of human experiences and of expressions. The "discovery" of pluralism is a modern phenomenon brought about especially by advances in communications and in transportation.

PNEUMA The Greek word for "spirit." It refers to the spiritual principle in human existence, opposed to the flesh (*sarx*).

PNEUMATOLOGICAL Pertaining to the Holy Spirit.

POLITICAL THEOLOGY A type of theology which stresses the relationship between Christian faith and the socio-political order or, more generally, between theory and practice.

POLYTHEISM Belief in many gods.

POSITIVISM A philosophical and theological view which not only begins with observable realities, as does the *phenomenological* approach (see *phenomenology* above), but insists that reality consists *only* of the concrete, the visible, and the particular. In theology it leads to reflection on God not in terms of the totality of reality but in terms of the understanding of God as given in certain sources— e.g., the Bible, the teachings of the Church.

POTENTIA OBEDIENTIALIS The fundamental human capacity for grace.

PRAXIS Reflective action. Reflection which is the fruit of one's concrete experience and situation. Action which is the expression of such reflection. Not identical, therefore, simply with "practice." A central term in *liberation theology* (see above).

PREDESTINATION The eternal decree of God regarding the destination, or final goal, of all reality and especially of humankind.

PREDESTINATIONISM The Calvinist doctrine that God decides, independently of a person's exercise of freedom and manifestation of good will, who will be saved and who will be damned. The latter decree is also known as *antecedent negative reprobation*.

PRESBYTER A priest of the second "order"—i.e., less than a bishop but more than a deacon. A priest.

PRESBYTERATE The body of priests.

PRIMACY The authority which the pope has over the whole Church.

PROBABILISM The moral principle which holds that one can safely follow a theological opinion if it is proposed by someone having sufficient theological authority and standing. *Equiprobabilism* requires that the more lenient opinion be at least as strong as the stricter opinion. *Probabiliorism* requires that the more lenient opinion be stronger than the stricter opinion.

PROCESS THEOLOGY A type of theology which emphasizes the movement, dynamism, changeability, and relativity of God, of history, and of all reality. Closely linked on the Catholic side with the writings of Teilhard de Chardin; on the Protestant side, with Alfred North Whitehead.

PROPHECY Literally, a "speaking on behalf (of God)." More specifically, the proclamation of a word and the doing of a deed on behalf of the Kingdom of God.

PROTOLOGY The "study of the first things" (creation, Original Justice, Original Sin).

PROVIDENCE God's abiding guidance of the whole created order toward the final Kingdom.

PURGATORY The state of purification and/or maturation which one may need to enter after death and before the *beatific vision* (see above).

QUIETISM A seventeenth-century movement in France which held that we can do nothing at all for our salvation and that the way of Christian spirituality is a way of inwardness, of resignation, and of complete passivity.

RATIONALISM The philosophical view which holds that nothing can be accepted as true unless it can be proved by reason alone.

RATIONALISTIC Pertaining to a philosophical and theological approach which exaggerates the powers of human reason to know truth and even God to the point where revelation is denied.

REALISM A philosophical view which emphasizes the objectivity of things, apart from the person thinking about them. *Naive* realism assumes that things are exactly what they seem to be ("Just take a look"). *Critical* realism insists that all reality is "mediated by meaning"—i.e., the real is what we

judge to be true, on the basis of our experience.

REAL PRESENCE The sacramental presence of Christ in the Eucharist.

REDEMPTION The act by which we are literally "bought back" into the grace of God by the work of Jesus Christ. See also *soteriology*.

REIGN OF GOD The more active, or dynamic, expression for the Kingdom of God (see above). It is the Kingdom as it is now in process.

RELIC An object regarded as worthy of veneration because of its connection with a saint—e.g., a piece of bone.

RELIGION The external, social, institutionalized expression of our faith in God.

RELIGIOUS Pertaining to an attitude of seeing all reality in light of the presence and action of God, and of responding to God's presence and action with reverence, gratitude, and appropriate moral behavior.

RELIGIOUS CONGREGATION, ORDER An organized group of Christians who have taken vows to live in community and to observe the evangelical counsels of poverty, chastity, and obedience.

RELIGIOUS EDUCATION That field which comes into existence at the point of intersection between theology and education. It is concerned with interpreting and directing human experience in light of the conviction that God is present to that experience, that Jesus Christ is the sacrament of God's presence in the world, and that the Church is the primary place where the presence of God in

Christ is acknowledged, celebrated, and lived out.

RES ET SACRAMENTUM Literally, "the reality and the sign." In sacramental theology, it refers to the lasting effect of a sacrament—e.g., the Real Presence of Christ in the Eucharist.

RES TANTUM Literally, "the reality alone." In sacramental theology, it refers to the immediate effect of a sacrament, namely, grace.

REVELATION God's self-disclosure (literally, "unveiling") to humankind through creation, events, persons, and especially Jesus Christ.

REVIVISCENCE The revival of grace from a *character* sacrament (see above) received in *mortal sin* (see above). If a person receives a character sacrament in the state of mortal sin, the grace of that sacrament is not given. But that grace "revives" and is applied to the individual as soon as contrition blots out the sin.

RIGHT A power that we have to do things which are necessary for achieving the end or purpose for which we are destined as rational and free persons.

RIGHTEOUSNESS The state of being just in the sight of God.

SABELLIANISM A third- and fourth-century heresy which held that God is three only in relation to the world. There is no trinity of Persons *within* the godhead. A form of *Modalism* (see above).

SACRAMENT In general, any visible sign of God's invisible presence. Specifically, a sign through which the Church manifests its faith and communicates the saving reality (grace) of God which is present in the Church and in the signs themselves. In Catholic doctrine there are Baptism, Confirmation, Eucharist, Penance, Marriage, Holy Order, and the Anointing of the Sick.

SACRAMENTAL A grace-bearing sign which does not so fully express the nature of the Church and which, according to Catholic doctrine, does not carry the guarantee of grace associated with the seven sacraments—e.g., holy water, the palm branches used on Palm Sunday, a crucifix.

SACRAMENTALITY, PRINCIPLE OF The fundamentally Catholic notion that all reality is potentially and in fact the bearer of God's presence and the instrument of divine action on our behalf. Closely related to the principle of *mediation* (see above).

SACRAMENTUM TANTUM Literally, "the sign alone." In sacramental theology, it is a rite or sacred action—e.g., the pouring of the water and the recitation of the formula "I baptize you...."

SALVATION From the Latin word *salus*, meaning "health." It is the goal and end-product of creation, the incarnation, the redemption, conversion, justification, and sanctification. To be saved is to be fully and permanently united with God and with one another in God.

SALVATION-HISTORY History perceived as the arena in which God progressively brings humankind toward the Kingdom. Salvation-history begins with creation, ends with the Second Coming of Christ, and has its midpoint in Jesus Christ. Such a view of history is associated with Luke in the New Testament and with Oscar Cullmann in modern theology.

SANCTIFICATION The state of holiness by reason of the presence of God within oneself. It is not to be confused with *justification* (see above), which is the act or process by which we are made holy, or just, in God's sight.

SANCTIFYING GRACE See *grace*.

SARX The Greek word for "flesh." It is the body apart from the spirit, and even opposed to it.

SATAN Literally, "the evil one." The personification of evil. The one in whom all evil is focused.

SCHISM A breach of Church unity which occurs when a whole group or community separates itself from the rest of the Body of Christ. In Catholic theology, this happens when communion with the pope is broken.

SCHOLASTIC Pertaining to a general approach to the doing of theology which derives its style from the medieval "schools." Such theology is deductive, abstract, doctrinal, and *classicist* (see above).

SCHOLASTICISM A theological and philosophical movement in the Middle Ages attached to certain "schools" (thus, the term "scholastic") and emphasizing the interpretation of texts, especially of other theologians and philosophers rather than of the Bible and the Fathers of the Church.

SEMI-PELAGIANISM The heresy, condemned by the Second Council of Orange (527), which held that the beginning of faith (*initium fidei*) is made independently of God's grace but that thereafter the

grace of God is necessary for salvation.

SENSUS FIDELIUM Literally, "the sense of the faithful." It is one of the norms of theological truth, namely, the actual belief of Christians down through the centuries.

SHEOL The Old Testament name for the "underworld" inhabited by all the dead. Not to be confused with hell, which is a state of eternal alienation from God because of sin.

SIMONY The buying and selling of spiritual goods.

SIMUL JUSTUS ET PECCATOR Literally, "at the same time just and sinner." A formula made famous by Martin Luther to make the point that even though we have been declared just by God because of Christ, we are still as corrupt as ever inside. Catholic doctrine insists that *justification* leads to *sanctification* (see above).

SIN Any deliberate infidelity to the will of God. It can be individual or social. The condition that makes sin possible, not to say probable, is *Original Sin* (see above). Sins which reverse our *fundamental option* (see above) for God, are *mortal sins*. Sins which reflect poorly on our commitment to God but which do not reverse our course toward God are *serious sins*. Less serious sins are *venial sins*. Below those in gravity are *imperfections*.

SOCIAL DOCTRINE The body of official teachings, developed since Pope Leo XIII in 1891, which identify the implications of the Gospel in matters pertaining to social justice, peace, and human rights.

SOCIALIZATION A process by which nations and humankind in general are becoming increasingly interdependent. Emphasized by Pope John XXIII's social encyclicals, *Mater et Magistra* (1961) and *Pacem in Terris* (1963).

SOLA FIDE Literally, "by faith alone." The Protestant principle that we are saved by faith alone, not by good works. Catholic doctrine insists that faith must issue in good works and that good works are saving insofar as they are expressions of faith.

SOLA GRATIA Literally, "by grace alone." The Protestant principle that we are saved by grace alone, i.e., by God's action and not at all by our own. Catholic doctrine insists that God requires our free cooperation although it is God alone who makes that cooperation possible.

SOLA SCRIPTURA Literally, "by Scripture alone." The Protestant principle that the Word of God is given to us in the Bible alone and not in the official teachings of the Church. Catholic doctrine insists that the Bible itself is the Church's book—i.e., that the authority of the Church has determined which books are inspired and, therefore, *canonical* (see above). Furthermore, all official teachings are subject to the authority of the Word of God as contained in the Bible.

SOMA The Greek word for "body." But in contradistinction to *sarx* (see above), *soma* stands for the whole person: flesh and spirit together.

SOTERIOLOGY Literally, "the study of salvation." It is that area of theology which focuses on the passion, death, resurrection, and exaltation of Christ insofar as they bring about our salvation.

SPIRITUAL Pertaining to an attitude and style which reflect an attentiveness to the presence and action of God within us and in the world around us.

SPIRITUALITY Our way of being *religious* (see above). *Christian* spirituality is the cultivation of a style of life consistent with the presence of the Spirit of the Risen Christ within us and with our status as members of the Body of Christ.

SUBJECT The human *person* (see above) insofar as the person is conscious, interrelates with others, and freely determines who and what he or she will become.

SUBJECTIVE Pertaining to a philosophical and theological attitude which emphasizes the values of individual consciousness and freedom.

SUBORDINATIONISM A second- and third-century heresy which held that the Son and the Holy Spirit are less than the Father because they proceed from the Father. Therefore, the Son and the Spirit are not fully divine.

SUBSIDIARITY A principle in Catholic social doctrine which holds that nothing should be done by a higher agency which can be done as well, or better, by a lower agency.

SUMMA THEOLOGICA The major work of systematic theology done by Thomas Aquinas.

SUPERNATURAL Pertaining to that which exceeds the power and capacity of human nature apart from the grace of God.

"SUPERNATURAL EXISTENTIAL" A term used by Karl Rahner, meaning our radical capacity for God. It is the permanent modification of the human person, in the depths of one's being, by which the person is transformed from within and oriented toward God. It is not grace itself, but God's offer of grace.

SYMBOL A sign which embodies what it signifies. Close to the meaning of *sacrament* (see above). Therefore, it is not an arbitrary sign, but a sign that is intimately connected with what it signifies.

SYNOD An official assembly of the Church at the international, national, regional, provincial, or diocesan level.

SYNOPTICS The first three Gospels, Matthew, Mark, and Luke, so called because when they are read side by side (synoptically), certain parallels in structure and content readily emerge.

SYSTEMATIC THEOLOGY That theology which tries to see the Christian tradition as a whole, by understanding the whole in terms of the interrelationships among all its parts, and each part in terms of its relationships to other parts and to the whole.

TELEOLOGICAL Pertaining to a way of doing moral theology which emphasizes the end (*telos*), or purpose, of human existence.

THEOLOGY The ordered effort to bring our experience of God to the level of intelligent expression. It is "faith seeking understanding" (Anselm).

THEOTOKOS Literally, "the Bearer of God." The title given to Mary at the Council of Ephesus (431), which taught that there is one divine person in Jesus Christ, not two as the Nestorians argued. Therefore, Mary is truly the "Mother of God" and not only the mother of the human Jesus.

THOMISM An approach to theology derived from Thomas Aquinas. It is based on *critical realism* (see above under *realism*) and follows a strongly *systematic* method (see above). It is not to be confused with *Scholasticism* (see above).

TRADITION Both the process of "handing on" the faith and that which has been handed on. Tradition (upper-case) includes Scripture, the essential doctrines of the Church, the major writings and teachings of the Fathers, the liturgical life of the Church, and the living and lived faith of the whole Church down through the centuries. Tradition (upper-case) is not to be confused with tradition (lower-case), which includes customs, institutions, practices which are simply usual ways of thinking about, and giving expression to, the Christian faith.

TRADITIONALISM The nineteenth-century opinion, rejected by Vatican I, that reason can know nothing at all about religious truth because such knowledge comes only through the revelation that has been "handed down" to us. As a modern term, it refers to the attitude of those Catholics who are opposed to the reforms of Vatican II and who wish the Church would return to its traditional pre-Vatican II ways.

TRANSCENDENTAL Pertaining to that which is above and beyond the ordinary, the concrete, the tangible—i.e., to God.

TRANSCENDENTAL THOMISM That twentieth-century approach to theology which is rooted in the principle that God is already present to life as a principle that renders all life open to becoming something more than it is already.

TRANSUBSTANTIATION The official Catholic teaching, given by the Council of Trent, that the substance of the bread and the wine are changed into the substance of Christ's body and blood at the Eucharist, so that nothing of the bread and wine remains except what is accidental—e.g., taste, shape, weight. This teaching is distinguished from *consubstantiation* (see above).

TRENT The Italian city in which the nineteenth ecumenical council was held from 1545 to 1563, and hence the council itself. This council was the Catholic Church's principal response to the Protestant Reformation. It defined the canon of Sacred Scripture, Original Sin, grace, justification, the seven sacraments, etc. Trent was the primary influence on Catholic life until the pontificate of John XXIII (1958-1963).

TRINITARIAN Pertaining to a theological emphasis which views all doctrines in light of the creative activity of the Father, the redemptive work of the Son, and the reconciling action of the Holy Spirit.

TRINITY, ECONOMIC The reality of the Trinity insofar as the triune God is active and manifested in the world and its history: the Father as creator, the Son as redeemer, the Spirit as reconciler. Refers, therefore, to the exterior activity of the Trinity in history.

TRINITY, IMMANENT The reality of the Trinity insofar as the three Persons are different not in terms of their different work on our behalf but in terms of their different relationships, one to another; e.g., the Father is unbegotten, the Son is begotten. Refers, therefore, to the inner life of the Trinity.

TRITHEISM Belief in three gods. An exaggeration of the doctrine of the Trinity.

TWELVE, THE The twelve men directly called by Jesus to carry his message of the Kingdom of God to the world. All of the Twelve were apostles, but not all apostles were among the original Twelve.

TYPE A person in whom the qualities of a greater or later reality are somehow "typified" or anticipated—e.g., Mary as a "type" of the Church, and Moses as a "type" of Christ.

ULTRAMONTANISM Literally, "beyond the mountains" (the Alps). It is a form of rigid *traditionalism* (see above) developed in France, distrustful of theological reflection, and excessively loyal to the Holy See "beyond the mountains."

VATICAN The territory politically operated and controlled by the papacy, and the site of the twentieth (1869-1870) and twenty-first (1962-1965) ecumenical councils. *Vatican I* addressed itself to the questions of reason and faith, on the one hand, and papal primacy and papal infallibility, on the other. *Vatican II* opened the Church to more of its own members, to other Christians, and to the whole world.

VENIAL SIN A less serious infidelity to the will of God, sufficient to diminish one's Christian character (see *character, moral*) but not to reverse one's fundamental orientation toward God.

VIATICUM Literally, "on the way with you." The last sacrament, i.e., the final reception of Holy Communion before death.

VIRGIN BIRTH The belief that Jesus became a human being without the cooperation of a human father. This is not to be confused with the *Immaculate Conception* (see above).

VIRGINAL CONCEPTION The belief that Jesus was conceived in the womb of Mary without the cooperation of a human father.

VIRGINITY OF MARY The belief that Mary was a virgin throughout her life, including the time when she conceived and brought forth Jesus, her Son.

VIRTUE The power to realize moral good and to do it joyfully and with perseverance in spite of obstacles. *Theological* virtues are those which have been *infused* by God: faith, hope, and charity. The *moral* virtues—prudence, justice, temperance, and fortitude—are those which have to be *acquired* through cooperation with God's grace and which, in turn, are the linchpins (*cardinal* virtues) of other, lesser virtues.

VOLUNTARISM A theological and philosophical view which exaggerates the place and function of the human will in the attainment of truth as well as moral good. It is the opposite of *rationalism*.

VULGATE The name given since the thirteenth century to the Latin translation of the Bible done by St. Jerome.

WORLD The totality of created reality. Insofar as the world is shaped and directed by human consciousness and human freedom under the grace of God, the world is identical with *history* (see above).

YAHWEH The Old Testament name for God.

INDEX OF PERSONAL NAMES

INDEX OF SUBJECTS

This index should be used in conjunction with the Table of Contents, Index of Personal Names, and Glossary.

Quakers, 383, 1128
Quietism, 934, 1068, 1123
Qumran Community. *See* Essenes

Racism, 3, 276, 678
Radical theology, 60, 317
Rationalism, 43, 217, 233, 291
Real Presence, 738-9, 759-60, 764-5,
    766
Reality and meaning, 131-2, 1178
Realized eschatology, 1117-18, 1132
Reason: and revelation, 217, 912;
    and grace, 996
Rebaptism, 751
Recapitulation, theory of, 146
Reception of doctrine, 71, 668-9
Reconciliation. *See* Penance
Redaction criticism, 395
Redemption: universality of, 165; and
    the resurrection, 410; as ransom,
    421-2; legalistic notion of, 447,
    1072; Anselm on, 461-2; social
    implications of, 541
Redemption (penitential), 779
Redemptor Hominis, 137, 706,
    939, 1039
Redemptorists, 878
Reformation, the: 10, 631-4, 1175;
    and grace, 157; causes of, 631-3;
    and priesthood, 805
Reformers, the: on faith, 42, 967-8;
    on Original Sin, 164; on
    revelation, 215; on God, 308-9;
    on Penance, 780; on marriage,
    790-1; and Mary, 877; and
    spirituality, 1065-6; and
    purgatory, 1144. *See also*
    Protestantism
Regula Pastoralis, 1062
Reign of God. *See* Kingdom of God
Reincarnation, 1136
Relativism, 942
Relics, 1063, 1065
Religion: etymology, 245; definitions
    of, 247-8, 250; Aquinas on, 249;
    and justice, 249-50;
    characteristics of, 251-4; as
    institutional, 253-4, 255; types

of, 256-7; virtue of religion,
    978-9
Religious education, 26, 29-30, 747
Religious experience, 190
Religious liberty, 274, 275, 276, 686,
    1020
Religious life, 682
Religious orders, 1063, 1082
"Remnant of Israel," 264
Renaissance, the, 631
Rerum Novarum, 643, 673, 706, 938
Res et sacramentum, 738, 739
Res tantum, 738, 739-40
Restitution, 985
Resurrection: 405-17, 480; and the
    kerygma, 404; and apologetics,
    405; and the Holy Spirit, 410;
    and the redemption, 410, 470,
    540-1; historicity of, 411;
    appearances, 412, 414-16;
    bodiliness of, 412-13; and
    women, 416; as revelation, 416;
    and the empty tomb, 416-17;
    and the crucifixion, 417-18, 423;
    in Scholastic theology, 465;
    Bultmann on, 495
Resurrection of the body, 142, 144,
    145, 1147-50
Revelation: defined, 234; and
    prophecy, 203; and creation,
    206, 224-8; content of, 206-7,
    213; etymology, 207; as private,
    208, 238-9; and the Beatific
    Vision, 211, 213, 216-17;
    Irenaeus on, 211; Augustine on,
    212; as divine illumination, 212,
    213-14; and inspiration, 212-13;
    Aquinas on, 213-14; as
    propositional, 213; signs of, 213;
    as knowledge, 214, 221; sources
    of, 214; and nature, 216, 225;
    necessity of, 217; and reason,
    217, 912; universality of, 217,
    236; and history, 221, 228-30,
    235, 473; and *praxis*, 221-2; as
    Christian, 223, 686; and Jesus
    Christ, 223, 235; and prophecy,
    230-2; theology of, 234-7; as
    process, 235; the closing of,

ABOUT THE AUTHOR

Richard P. McBrien, a priest of the Archdiocese of Hartford, has authored twelve books on theology. He is the Crowley-O'Brien-Walter professor of theology and chairman of the department of theology at the University of Notre Dame. Until mid 1980 he was professor of theology at Boston College and director of its Institute of Religious Education and Pastoral Ministry. He is past president of the Catholic Theological Society of America, and in 1976 he received the Society's John Courtney Murray Award "for distinguished achievement in theology." Father McBrien received a 1980 Christopher Award for *Catholicism*, and in 1981 *Catholicism* received the Annual Book Award from the College Theology Society.

Richard McBrien has taught and lectured at many colleges and universities throughout the nation—among them, Harvard University, Yale University, Cornell University, Purdue University, the University of Wisconsin, Andover Newton Theological School, and the Weston School of Theology in Cambridge, Massachusetts. He has published many articles and reviews in professional and popular journals, and his syndicated weekly theology column won awards in 1974, 1975, and 1978 from the Catholic Press Association as the best column in its field.

Father McBrien has served in several projects for the Canon Law Society of America and has been a member of the board of directors and vice-president as well as president of the Catholic Theological Society of America.

His ecumenical activities have included the chairmanship of the
int Graduate Program of Boston College and Andover Newton Theo-
'cal School, two terms as a trustee of the Boston Theological Institute
'argest ecumenical consortium in the United States), and the chair-
ip of the Catholic Theological Society of America's special com-
o evaluate the bilateral consultations.

v will recognize Father McBrien as an on-air commentator on
'ents for CBS television.